THE OXFORD ENCYCLOPEDIA OF

ARCHAEOLOGY IN THE NEAR EAST

THE OXFORD ENCYCLOPEDIA OF ARCHAEOLOGY IN THE NEAR EAST

PREPARED UNDER THE AUSPICES OF THE
AMERICAN SCHOOLS OF ORIENTAL RESEARCH

Eric M. Meyers
EDITOR IN CHIEF

VOLUME 3

New York Oxford
OXFORD UNIVERSITY PRESS
1997

Oxford University Press

Oxford New York
Athens Auckland Bangkok Bogotá
Bombay Buenos Aires Calcutta Cape Town
Dar es Salaam Delhi Florence Hong Kong Istanbul
Karachi Kuala Lumpur Madras Madrid Melbourne
Mexico City Nairobi Paris Singapore
Taipei Tokyo Toronto

and associated companies in
Berlin Ibadan

Published by Oxford University Press, Inc.,
198 Madison Avenue, New York, New York 10016

Library of Congress Cataloging-in-Publication Data
The Oxford encyclopedia of archaeology in the Near East / prepared
under the auspices of the American Schools of Oriental Research;
Eric M. Meyers, editor in chief.
p. cm.
Includes bibliographical references (p.) and index.
1. Middle East—Antiquities—Encyclopedias. 2. Africa, North—Antiquities—
Encyclopedias. I. Meyers, Eric M. II. American Schools of Oriental Research.
DS56.09 1996 96-17152 939'.4—dc20 CIP

ISBN 0-19-506512-3 (set)
ISBN 0-19-511217-2 (vol. 3)

Many photographs and line drawings used herein were supplied by contributors to the work. Others were drawn from the archives of the American Schools of Oriental Research, from commercial photographic archives, and from the holdings of major museums and cultural institutions. The publisher has made every effort to ascertain that necessary permissions to reprint materials have been secured. Sources of all photographs and line drawings are given in the captions to illustrations.

Printing (last digit): 9 8 7 6 5 4 3 2 1

Printed in the United States of America on acid-free paper

ABBREVIATIONS AND SYMBOLS

ACOR	American Center of Oriental Research
AD	*anno Domini,* in the year of the (our) Lord
AH	*anno Hegirae,* in the year of the Hijrah
AIA	Archaeological Institute of America
AIAR	(W. F.) Albright Institute of Archaeological Research
AJA	*American Journal of Archaeology*
Akk.	Akkadian
Am.	*Amos*
ANEP	J. B. Pritchard, ed., *Ancient Near East in Pictures*
ANET	J. B. Pritchard, ed., *Ancient Near Eastern Texts*
AOS	American Oriental Society
APES	American Palestine Exploration Society
Ar.	Arabic
ʿArakh.	*ʿArakhin*
Aram.	Aramaic
ASOR	American Schools of Oriental Research
Assyr.	Assyrian
A.Z.	*ʿAvodah Zarah*
b.	born
B.A.	Bachelor of Arts
Bab.	Babylonian
BASOR	*Bulletin of the American Schools of Oriental Research*
B.B.	*Bava' Batra'*
BC	before Christ
BCE	before the common era
Bekh.	*Bekhorot*
Ber.	*Berakhot*
Bik.	*Bikkurim*
BP	before the present
BSAE	British School of Archaeology in Egypt
BSAI	British School of Archaeology in Iraq
BSAJ	British School of Archaeology in Jerusalem
B.T.	Babylonian Talmud
c.	*circa,* about, approximately
CAARI	Cyprus American Archaeological Research Institute
CAD	computer-aided design/drafting
CAORC	Council of American Overseas Research Centers
CE	of the common era
cf.	*confer,* compare
chap., chaps.	chapter, chapters
1 Chr.	*1 Chronicles*
2 Chr.	*2 Chronicles*
CIG	*Corpus Inscriptionum Graecarum*
CIS	Corpus Inscriptionum Semiticarum
cm	centimeters
CNRS	Centre National de la Recherche Scientifique
col., cols.	column, columns
Col.	*Colossians*
1 Cor.	*1 Corinthians*
2 Cor.	*2 Corinthians*
CTA	A. Herdner, *Corpus des tablettes en cunéiformes alphabétiques*
cu	cubic
d.	died
DAI	Deutsches Archäologisches Institut
diss.	dissertation
Dn.	*Daniel*
DOG	Deutche Orient-Gesellschaft
D.Sc.	Doctor of Science
Dt.	*Deuteronomy*
EB	Early Bronze
Eccl.	*Ecclesiastes*
ed., eds.	editor, editors; edition
ED	Early Dynastic
EEF	Egyptian Exploration Fund
e.g.	*exempli gratia,* for example
Egyp.	Egyptian
Elam.	Elamite
En.	*Enoch*
Eng.	English
enl.	enlarged
esp.	especially
et al.	*et alii,* and others
etc.	*et cetera,* and so forth
Eth.	Ethiopic
et seq.	*et sequens,* and the following
Ex.	*Exodus*
exp.	expanded
Ez.	*Ezekiel*
Ezr.	*Ezra*
fasc.	fascicle
fem.	feminine
ff.	and following
fig.	figure
fl.	*floruit,* flourished
ft.	feet
frag., frags.	fragment, fragments
gal., gals.	gallon, gallons
Geog.	Ptolemy, *Geographica*
Ger.	German
GIS	Geographic Information Systems
Gk.	Greek
Gn.	*Genesis*
ha	hectares
Heb.	Hebrew
Hg.	*Haggai*
Hist.	Herodotus, *History*
Hitt.	Hittite
Hos.	*Hosea*
Hur.	Hurrian
IAA	Israel Antiquities Authority
ibid.	*ibidem,* in the same place (as the one immediately preceding)
IDA(M)	Israel Department of Antiquities (and Museums)
i.e.	*id est,* that is

IEJ	*Israel Exploration Journal*
IES	Israel Exploration Society
IFAPO	Institut Français d'Archéologie du Proche-Orient
Is.	*Isaiah*
IsMEO	Istituto Italiano per il Medio ed Estremo Oriente
Jb.	*Job*
Jer.	*Jeremiah*
Jgs.	*Judges*
Jn.	*John*
Jon.	*Jonah*
Jos.	*Joshua*
JPOS	*Journal of the Palestine Oriental Society*
JRA	*Journal of Roman Archaeology*
J.T.	Jerusalem Talmud
KAI	H. Donner and W. Röllig, *Kanaanäische und aramäische Inschriften*
Kel.	*Kelim*
Ket.	*Ketubbot*
kg	kilogram
1 Kgs.	*1 Kings*
2 Kgs.	*2 Kings*
km	kilometers
KTU	M. Dietrich and O. Lorentz, *Die keilalphabetischen Texte aus Ugarit*
l	liter
l., ll.	line, lines
Lat.	Latin
lb.	pounds
LB	Late Bronze
lit.	literally
Lk.	*Luke*
LM	Late Minoan
Lv.	*Leviticus*
m	meters
M.A.	Master of Arts
masc.	masculine
Mal.	*Malachi*
MB	Middle Bronze
Mc.	*Maccabees*
M.Div.	Master of Divinity
Meg.	*Megillah*
mi.	miles
Mk.	*Mark*
mm	millimeter
mod.	modern
Mt.	Mount
Mt.	*Matthew*
n.	note
NAA	Neutron Activation Analysis
Nat. Hist.	Pliny, *Naturalis Historia* (Natural History)
n.b.	*nota bene*, note well
n.d.	no date
Nm.	*Numbers*
no., nos.	number, numbers
n.p.	no place
n.s.	new series
O.P.	Ordo Praedicatorum, Order of Preachers (Dominicans)
p., pp.	page, pages
para.	paragraph
PEF	Palestine Exploration Fund
Pers.	Persian
Ph.D.	Philosophiae Doctor, Doctor of Philosophy
Phil.	*Philippians*
pl.	plate; plural
PN	Pottery Neolithic
ppm	parts per million
PPN	Pre-Pottery Neolithic
Prv.	*Proverbs*
Ps.	*Psalms*
pt., pts.	part, parts
1 Pt.	*1 Peter*
2 Pt.	*2 Peter*
r.	reigned, ruled
RCEA	*Répertoire chronologique d'epigraphie arabe*
Rev.	*Revelations*
rev.	revised
Ru.	*Ruth*
SBF	Studium Biblicum Franciscanum
SBL	Society of Biblical Literature
SEG	*Supplementum Epigraphicum Graecum*
ser.	series
sg.	singular
Sg.	*Song of Songs*
Shab.	*Shabbath*
S.J.	Societas Jesu, Society of Jesus (Jesuits)
1 Sm.	*1 Samuel*
2 Sm.	*2 Samuel*
sq	square
St., Sts.	Saint, Saints
Sum.	Sumerian
supp.	supplement
Syr.	Syriac
Taʿan.	*Taʿanit*
Th.D.	Theologicae Doctor, Doctor of Theology
Ti.	*Titus*
Tk.	Turkish
1 Tm.	*1 Timothy*
2 Tm.	*2 Timothy*
trans.	translated by
Ugar.	Ugaritic
v.	verse
viz.	*videlicet*, namely
vol., vols.	volume, volumes
vs.	versus
Yad.	*Yadayim*
ZDPV	*Zeitschrift des Deutschen Palästina-Vereins*
Zec.	*Zechariah*
*	hypothetical; in bibliographic citations, English language pages in Hebrew journals
?	uncertain; possibly; perhaps
°	degrees
′	minutes; feet
″	seconds; inches
+	plus
−	minus
±	plus or minus
=	equals; is equivalent to
×	by
→	yields

H

CONTINUED

HAZOR, site located in the Upper Galilee, 15 km (9 mi.) north of the Sea of Galilee (map reference 2032 × 2691). The site is comprised of two distinct parts: the tell (or upper city), approximately 18 acres in area, and a vast rectangular plateau (the lower city), to its north, measuring some 200 acres. It was first identified by J. L. Porter in 1875 as Tell el-Qedaḥ (also Tell Waqqas), based on geographic references to Hazor in the Bible and in the works of Josephus. The name Hazor is mentioned in a clay tablet from the Old Babylonian period found at the site in the 1970s.

Excavations. Trial soundings were first made at Hazor by John Garstang in 1928. Large-scale excavations were conducted by the James A. de Rothschild Expedition between 1955 and 1958 and again in 1968, under the direction of Yigael Yadin, on behalf of the Hebrew University of Jerusalem, the Palestine Jewish Colonization Association (PICA), and the Anglo Israel Exploration Society. A small-scale trial excavation took place at the southeastern foot of the mound in 1987, under the direction of Amnon Ben-Tor. Large-scale excavations directed by Ben-Tor, the Hazor Excavations in Memory of Yigael Yadin, were resumed in the upper city in 1990. This current project is a joint venture of the Hebrew University; Complutense University, Madrid; and the Israel Exploration Society, in cooperation with Ambassador University, Texas.

History. The earliest reference to Hazor, as *hdwizi,* appears in the Egyptian Execration texts of the late twelfth–early thirteenth dynasties (nineteenth–eighteenth centuries BCE). It is in the Mari archives of the eighteenth century BCE that Hazor emerges as a major city. At least fourteen Mari documents refer to the city (as *Ha-su-ra, Ha-sura-yu,* or *Ha-su-ra-a*), the only one in Israel to be mentioned in that archive. Hazor's role as one of the major commercial centers in the Fertile Crescent, together with such city-states as Yamḫad and Qatna, is evident. The name of the king of Hazor, Ibni-Adad, appears several times in the documents.

Another group of documents mentioning Hazor (as *Ha-su-ri*) and its king, Abdi-Tirshi, is the Amarna letters of the mid-fourteenth century BCE. It also is included, as *ḥḏr,* in the lists of conquered towns in Canaan compiled by the pharaohs of the New Kingdom, such as those of Thutmosis III, Amenophis II, and Seti I. The latest Egyptian reference to Hazor is in Papyrus Anastasi I, ascribed to Rameses II.

Hazor is mentioned several times in the Hebrew Bible in connection with the conquest and settlement accounts, first in *Joshua* 11:10–13 and then in *Judges* 4–5. The apparent contradiction between these two sources with regard to the process of conquest of Canaan by the Israelites in general, and to the history of Hazor during that time in particular, has been one of the most controversial subjects in the study of the history of ancient Israel as well as in the understanding of the books of *Joshua* and *Judges*. In *1 Kings* 9:15, Hazor is mentioned, along with Megiddo and Gezer, as one of three cities Solomon rebuilt. The last reference to Hazor in the Bible. *2 Kings* 15:29, describes the conquest of Hazor and most of the northern kingdom of Israel by Tiglath-Pileser III of Assyria.

The latest reference to Hazor in connection with historical event—the battle between the Hasmonean Jonathan and the Syrian Demetrius in 147 BCE, on the Plain of Hazor—is made in *1 Maccabees* 11:67. It is last mentioned in Josephus (*Antiq.* 5.199).

Excavation Results. Excavation has revealed that there is a difference in the history of occupation for the lower and upper cities. For this reason, the strata encountered in the upper city, where six areas were opened (A, AB, B, G, L, and M) were designated by Roman numerals, while those in the lower city, where seven areas were opened (C, D, E, F, H, K, and 210), were designated by Arabic numbers.

Hazor was first settled in the Early Bronze Age, but only in the upper city. The lower city was not occupied until the second millennium BCE. For most of the second millennium the upper and lower cities existed side by side as one city. Toward the end of the Late Bronze Age, both the upper and lower cities were violently destroyed. Following that destruction, occupation was confined once again to the upper city, until Hazor was finally deserted in the second century BCE.

Early Bronze Age (strata XXI–XIX). Remains datable to the Early Bronze period have been encountered only in deep soundings in areas A and L. Because of this limited exposure, the extent of the EB settlement is not yet known, and the date of its establishment is yet to be determined.

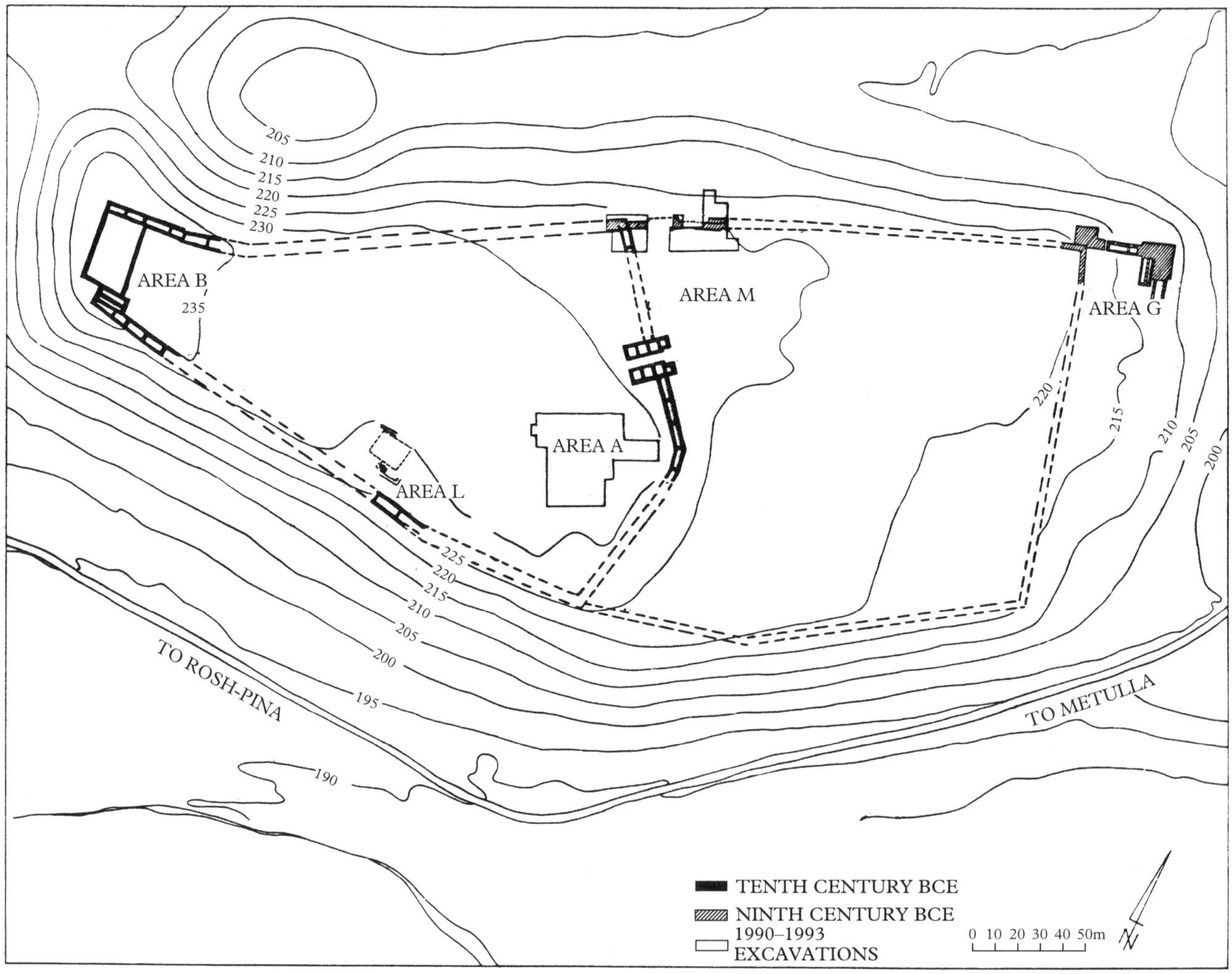

HAZOR. *Plan of the ancient city and excavation areas.* (Courtesy A. Ben-Tor)

The earliest sherds clearly connected with architectural remains date to EB II, and it is to that phase that Yadin ascribes Hazor's earliest occupation. A fine assemblage of Khirbet Kerak ware indicates a settlement in EB III. In general, the ceramic repertoire of these early strata shows a close affinity with Syria. Noteworthy are several cylinder seal impressions on storage jars, of types well known from other EB sites in the north of the country.

Middle Bronze I (stratum XVIII). The transitional phase between the Early and Middle Bronze Ages is represented at Hazor by a handful of sherds found exclusively in the upper city. Most of these belong to the black-slipped and reserve-slipped wares of the Orontes valley, demonstrating again the site's close relationship with Syria.

Middle Bronze Age II (upper city: strata pre-XVII, XVII, XVI, and post-XVI; lower city: 4, 3). The question of the date of the first settlement and that of the construction of the first fortifications in the lower city are of the center of a wide scholarly debate. Hazor's floruit as the most important city in southern Canaan is assigned by Yadin to the MB II–III, when the lower city was first settled (strata 4 and XVII), and when both the upper and lower cities were first encircled by impressive defensive systems. According to Yadin this "greater Hazor," founded sometime in the mid-eighteenth century BCE is the city mentioned repeatedly in the Mari archive. In the preceding phase, the MB I (stratum pre-XVII), Hazor was a rather insignificant site, confined only to the upper tell, consisting of a few buildings and several tombs. A tomb containing a large assemblage of complete clay vessels, discovered in area L in 1971, seemed to Yadin to confirm this view. The entrance to the burial cave must have been located under the (as yet undiscovered) line of the city's fortifications, so it must have preceded their construction. Because the vessels were attributed typologically to the transitional MB IIA-B phase and dated by Yadin to the mid-eighteenth century, the construction of the fortifications must have occurred later—early in the MB IIB, in the second half of the eighteenth century. Other scholars differ with regard to such points as the date of the first occupation in the lower city, the date of construction of the fortifications, and the absolute dates to be assigned to the different phases of the Middle Bronze Age.

The most important monuments dating to that period are the huge earthen rampart and moat defending the western and, to a lesser extent, the northern flanks of the lower city; the city gates (one in area K and one in area P); the first in a series of temples (in area H); and the corner of a huge building, probably a palace (in area A). The earthen rampart is some 90 m wide and 15 m high. Similar examples known from such sites as Carchemish, Qatna, and Ebla, in Syria; from Dan, in Israel; and from other sites. The gates are of the "Syrian" direct-axis type, with three pairs of pilasters flanking the entrance. Similar gates are known again from such sites as Carchemish, Qatna, Ebla, and Alalakh in Syria, and Tel Dan, Beth-Shemesh, Yavneh-Yam, and elsewhere in Palestine. The area H temple, built in stratum 3, consists of an entrance hall flanked by two small rooms and a main room with a rectangular niche in the wall opposite the entrance. It is similar in plan to the temple in stratum VII at Alalakh. The same is true of the corner of the palace in area A: both stratum VII and the stratum IV palaces at Alalakh have a staircase located in the corner of the building, just as at Hazor. The use of finely cut orthostats, such as those incorporated into the walls of the area H temple and in the area A temple and palace, is another indication of the strong influences that reached Hazor from the north. The close connections between Hazor and the Syro-Mesopotamian cultural sphere, evidenced in the Mari documents, are also clearly reflected in a few cuneiform documents discovered at Hazor. These include a clay liver model for divination and a fragment of a bilingual Sumero-Akkadian text discovered by the Yadin expedition; the legal document discovered on the surface in the 1970s (see above); and an economic text and fragment of a royal letter discovered by the present excavation team.

Transitional Middle Bronze II–Late Bronze I (stratum post-XVI). The end of the prosperous MB city was catastrophic: a thick layer of ash separates its remains from those of the first Late Bronze Age city. A transitional phase was encountered only in areas A and B of the upper city, termed post-XVI by the Yadin expedition. It consists of several graves unrelated to any architectural remains.

Late Bronze Age (upper city: strata XV–XIII; lower city: strata 2–1A). No major change in population accompanied the destruction separating the Middle from the Late Bronze Age settlements at Hazor. The material culture, including the major architectural monuments (the earthen rampart, the city gates, the area H temple), shows a marked degree of continuity. A more profound change occurred at the end of the first LB stratum (XV; 2), dated to LB IB. In the next stratum, LB IIA (Yadin's LB II; stratum XIV of the upper city and 1B of the lower city), an open cultic area succeeded the stratum XV longroom temple in area A; a temple was founded in area C; an open High Place was founded in area F; and a major change took place in the plan of the area H temple. The city's defenses underwent minor changes, but the layout of the domestic buildings differs completely from that of the previous stratum. Stratum XIV (and 1B) was violently destroyed, perhaps by the end of the fourteenth century BCE, by Seti I, while, according to Yadin, Mycenaean IIIA was still in use. The last LB stratum at Hazor (XIII; 1A), dated to LB IIB (Yadin's LB III), shows a marked decline. Imported pottery, such as Mycenaean and Cypriot wares, is found in much smaller quantities than in the previous strata, and there is even some doubt about whether the city's fortifications were still in use.

Among the most significant finds attributable to LB Hazor are the various temples and the cultic and artistic objects connected with them. Noteworthy from the Stelae Temple in area C are several small stelae; a stela decorated in relief bearing the emblem of the moon god, Sin; a small orthostat of a crouching lion; a small basalt statue of a decapitated deity (or king) whose head was found nearby: a silver-plated bronze cult standard; and a pottery mask. Another important building is the Orthostat Temple in area H. Its plan in stratum 2 more or less follows that in stratum 3. In strata 1B and 1A, however, its plan is tripartite—including an entrance hall, a middle hall, and a rear hall (the temple's Holy of Holies)—an arrangement similar in concept to that in the Solomonic Temple in Jerusalem. The temple's walls are lined with smoothly cut basalt orthostats, which, together with its plan, are clearly reminiscent of the stratum IV temple at Alalakh. Important finds from this temple are a lion orthostat, a basalt statue of a decapitated king (or deity?), and offering and libation tables. The palace at LB Hazor is probably located in area A, on the acropolis. The Yadin expedition uncovered a corner of this impressive building in the mid-1950s. The current expedition is continuing the investigation of this building. Several orthostat-lined walls, two enormous column bases, and two steps uncovered so far probably belong to its entrance.

The last LB city at Hazor was violently destroyed. A level consisting of fallen mud brick, debris, ash, and burnt wood (in some places more than 1 m thick) was encountered almost everywhere in both the upper and lower city. It is the best indication of Hazor's catastrophic end. In areas C and H there is evidence of the deliberate mutilation and desecration of cult objects. Yadin fixed the date of that destruction in the last quarter of the thirteenth century BCE and tended to attribute it to the conquering Israelites, as described in *Joshua* 11:10. The current excavation encountered that same destruction layer in area A. The date of the

HAZOR. *Cultic stela.* From the Canaanite temple, area C. (Courtesy A. Ben-Tor)

destruction Yadin proposed, as well as its cause, should, for the time being, be left open.

Iron Age I (strata XII–XI). Meager remains of a settlement clearly postdating the destruction of LB Hazor have been discovered in various places on the acropolis. The remains consist mainly of stone-lined storage pits, close to thirty of which were encountered in areas A and B; cooking installations; and what appear to be foundations of huts and tents. The pottery associated with these remains is characteristic of Iron IA. In area B, a second level containing that same pottery was discerned. The most important feature of this stratum, XI, is the so called high place, consisting of several walls, remnants of pavements, stone pillars (some of which may have had cultic significance), two broken incense stands, and what is most probably a foundation deposit, a jar containing metal votive objects, the most important of which is a bronze figurine of a seated male deity. Yadin believed that the remnants of strata XII–XI belonged to an Israelite settlement in the twelfth–eleventh centuries BCE.

Iron Age II–III (strata X–IV). Stratigraphically, the following phases were established in the Iron II–III: X (Solomonic), with minor changes in IX, ending in a destruction attributed to the Aramean king Ben-Hadad I; VIII, with minor changes in VII (Omride dynasty), ending in a destruction attributed to the Aramean king Hazael; VI, destroyed by an earthquake in the mid-eighth century BCE; V, restoration and then final destruction by the Assyrians in 732 BCE; and IV, a minor phase of later Israelite squatters in the ruined city.

The most important monuments belonging to strata X–IX are the six-chambered city gate and casemate walls. Built in the tenth century BCE, Yadin ascribed them to Solomon, believing that, as at Megiddo and Gezer, they represent the defenses Solomon undertook (*1 Kgs.* 9:15). During that time only the western half of the acropolis was settled. The most prosperous period in the history of Israelite Hazor was the ninth century BCE. Under King Ahab the city expanded eastward, and the entire acropolis was encircled by a solid 3-meter-thick defensive wall. A water system, to ensure the water supply to the city in times of siege, was cut to groundwater level (area M). It is one of the most impressive engineering works so far found in Israel. A citadel was built on the western tip of the city (area B), and huge storage facilities were constructed (area A). In the second half of the eighth century BCE (stratum V), in the face of the growing

HAZOR. *Reconstructed entranceway to the citadel.* Ninth century BCE. (Courtesy Israel Museum, Jerusalem)

threat posed by the Assyrian Empire, Hazor's fortifications were strengthened and a watchtower was constructed in area B. Even these improved defensive works could not withstand the might of Assyria, which conquered and destroyed Hazor in 732 BCE.

Later periods (strata III–I). The stratum III settlement is confined to the western edge of the upper city. The Assyrians constructed a citadel in area B, and remnants of an Assyrian palace, contemporary with the stratum III citadel, were encountered within the bounds of nearby Kibbutz Ayyelet ha-Shaḥar.

Stratum II dates to the Persian period. Meager building remains and pits were encountered throughout the upper city. The most important remains are the restored and partially altered citadel in area B and a cemetery in area A. Imported Attic ware and a silver coin fix the date of stratum II to the fourth century BCE.

Stratum I is mainly the final phase of restoration of the area B citadel, which dates to the third-second centuries BCE.

[See also Alalakh; Mari Texts; *and the biography of* Yadin.]

BIBLIOGRAPHY

Ben-Tor, Amnon, ed. *Hazor III–IV: An Account of the Third and Fourth Seasons of Excavation, 1957–1958.* Jerusalem, 1989.

Ben-Tor, Amnon. "The Hazor Tablet: Foreword." *Israel Exploration Journal* 42 (1992): 18–20, 254–260.

Ben-Tor, Amnon, and M. T. Rubiato. "Tel Hatsor. El gran montículo mágico de la Alta Galilea." *Arqueologia* 148 (1993): 22–33.

Cole, Dan P. "How Water Tunnels Worked." *Biblical Archaeology Review* 6.2 (1980): 8–29.

Geva, Shulamit. *Hazor, Israel: An Urban Community of the Eighth Century B.C.E.* British Archaeological Reports, International Series, no. 543. Oxford, 1989.

Hallo, William W., and Hayim Tadmor. "A Lawsuit from Hazor." *Israel Exploration Journal* 27 (1977): 1–11.

Malamat, Abraham. "Silver, Gold, and Precious Stones from Hazor in a New Mari Document." *Biblical Archaeologist* 46 (1983): 169–174.

Malamat, Abraham. *Mari and the Early Israelite Experience.* Oxford, 1989. See pages 55–69.

Reich, Ronny. "The Persian Building Ayyelet ha-Shahar: The Assyrian Palace at Hazor?" *Israel Exploration Journal* 25 (1975): 233–237.

Shaffer, Aaron, and Wayne Horowitz. "An Administrative Tablet from Hazor: A Preliminary Edition." *Israel Exploration Journal* 42 (1992): 21–33, 165–167.

Tufnell, Olga. "Hazor, Samaria, and Lachish." *Palestine Exploration Quarterly* 91 (1959): 90–105.

Yadin, Yigael et al., *Hazor: An Account of the Excavations, 1955–1958.* 4 vols. in 3. Jerusalem, 1958–1961.

Yadin, Yigael. *Hazor: The Head of All Those Kingdoms.* London, 1972.

Yadin, Yigael. *Hazor: The Rediscovery of a Great Citadel of the Bible.* New York, 1975.

Yadin, Yigael. "The Transition from a Semi-Nomadic to a Sedentary Society in the Twelfth Century B.C.E." In *Symposia Celebrating the Seventy-Fifth Anniversary of the Founding of the American Schools of Oriental Research, 1900–1975,* edited by Frank Moore Cross, pp. 57–68. Cambridge, Mass., 1979.

AMNON BEN-TOR

HEALTH. *See* Medicine.

HEBREW BIBLE. *See* Biblical Literature, *article on* Hebrew Scriptures.

HEBREW LANGUAGE AND LITERATURE.

The Hebrew language, or more accurately Biblical Hebrew, in the main the language of the Hebrew Bible is also called Early Hebrew, in contradistinction to the language's later stages (Rabbinic, Medieval, and Modern). It belongs, with, for example, Moabite and Phoenician, to the Canaanite family of Northwest Semitic languages (to which Ugaritic and Aramaic also belong). [*See* Phoenician-Punic; Ugaritic; Aramaic.]

Biblical Hebrew. As a Semitic language, consonants in Biblical Hebrew almost exclusively constitute its roots, while its vowels modify them, through the formation of verbal and nominal themes. As a West Semitic language, its suffix conjugation (e.g., *kāṯaḇtī,* "I wrote") has become a veritable verbal form denoting the past, rather than a state (as in East Semitic). By not expanding the use of broken plurals and of the conative verbal theme *fāʿala,* as have the Southwest Semitic tongues (e.g., Arabic, Ethiopic); and by shifting *w* in initial position to *y,* Hebrew pertains to the Northwest Semitic languages. [*See* Arabic; Ethiopic.] By exhibiting for example, the consonantal shifts *ā* > *ō*, *ḏ* > *z*, *ṯ* > *š*, *ḏ/ẓ* > *ṣ* and showing the vowels *i-i,* rather than *a-a,* in the active derived verbal themes; and by forming many participles from the stem of the suffix conjugation (*qām, zāqēn, nišmār*) and themes like *rōmēm,* "he exalted," rather than **riyyēm,* in the hollow and geminate verbs, it belongs to the Canaanite family (although the last two features occur in Ugaritic as well).

Sources. Biblical Hebrew is mainly known from the predominantly Hebrew parts of the Bible (only *Dn.* 2:4–7:28, *Ezr.* 4:8–6:18, further *Jer.* 10:11, and two words in *Gn.* 31:47 are in Aramaic). It is transmitted in a consonantal script of which the characters are historically Aramaic, adopted for the (also consonantal) Old Hebrew alphabet following the destruction of the First Temple. Inscriptions written during the period of the First Temple were in the Old Hebrew script and, during the Second Temple period, in Old Hebrew and Aramaic characters alternatively. Because they are written in a consonantal script, little precise information regarding the vocalization of the language can be elicited from inscriptions. Ancient transcriptions are also of uncertain value for determining vocalisms because of the pitfalls connected with transcription from one language to another. Nevertheless, they serve as an important corrective for the biblical material, transcriptions because they include vowel markings, and inscriptions because they provide new pho-

Latin (English)	Original name	Graphic Picture	Earliest known forms	South Semitic (Sabaean)	Modern Ethiopic	Northwest Semitic (Early Hebrew)	Phoenician	Aramaic (Modern Hebrew)	Arabic
A	'alf	ox-head		𐩱	አ	𐤀	𐤀	א	ا
B	bēt	house	□	𐩨	በ	𐤁	𐤁	ב	ب
C,G	gaml	throw-stick		𐩴	ገ	𐤂	𐤂	ג	ج
D	dāg	fish		𐩵	ደ	𐤃	𐤃	ד	د
E	hē	man calling		𐩠	ሀ	𐤄	𐤄	ה	ه
U, V, W	waw	mace		𐩥	ወ	𐤅	𐤅	ו	و
Z	zēn	?	X ∓	𐩸	ዘ	𐤆	𐤆	ז	ز
H	ḥēt	fence		𐩢	ሐ	𐤇	𐤇	ח	ح
I, J, Y	yad	hand w/closed fist		𐩺	የ	𐤉	𐤉	י	ي
K	kapp	palm		𐩫	ከ	𐤊	𐤊	כ	ك
L	lamd	ox-goad (whip)		𐩡	ለ	𐤋	𐤋	ל	ل
M	maym	water (waves)		𐩣	መ	𐤌	𐤌	מ	م
N	naḥāš	snake		𐩬	ነ	𐤍	𐤍	נ	ن
O	ʻayin	eye		𐩲	ዐ	𐤏	𐤏	ע	ع
F, P	pēh	mouth/corner		𐩰	ፈ	𐤐	𐤐	פ	ف
Q	qu(p-)	?	8	𐩤	ቀ	𐤒	𐤒	ק	ق
R	ra'š	head		𐩧	ረ	𐤓	𐤓	ר	ر
S, X	ṯann	composite bow		𐩪	ሠ ሰ	𐤔	𐤔	ס ש	س
T	taw	cross-marker	+	X	ተ	+ X	𐤕	ת	ت

HEBREW LANGUAGE AND LITERATURE. *The Semitic background of the Roman alphabet.* The letters *tet* and *ṣade* are excluded since they have no counterparts in the Roman alphabet.

netic and morphological material. Moreover, inscriptions provide additions to the limited vocabulary of Biblical Hebrew.

The transcriptions are, to a great extent, limited to the transliteration of proper nouns—for example, into Akkadian and Greek (as in the Septuagint [third century BCE onward]) or Latin (as by St. Jerome [342–420 CE]). Yet, Greek transcriptions are not restricted to proper nouns because Origen (185–254 CE) transliterated the Hebrew Bible into Greek letters and a few fragments of the transliteration of *Psalms* are preserved. [*See* Akkadian; Greek; Latin.]

The most important Old Hebrew inscriptions from the biblical period are the Gezer Calendar (c. tenth century BCE); the Kuntilet ʿAjrud votive inscriptions (from the site on the Sinai border; late ninth century BCE); ostraca from Samaria (from the eighth [?] century BCE); the Murabbaʿat palimpsest (*Mur.* 17), the oldest Hebrew papyrus (eighth–seventh centuries BCE); the Siloam tunnel inscription (c. 700 BCE); the Meṣad Ḥashavyahu ostraca; two small silver amulets found in Jerusalem in the Hinnom Valley, one of which contains the Priestly blessing also known from *Numbers* 6:24–26 (seventh century BCE); the Arad and Lachish letters (sixth century BCE); as well as a large number of inscribed seals. [*See* Gezer Calendar; Kuntillet ʿAjrud; Samaria Ostraca; Murabbaʿat; Siloam Tunnel Inscription; Jerusalem; Meṣad Ḥashavyahu Texts; Arad Inscriptions; Lachish Inscriptions; Seals.]

The biblical text itself is not easy to evaluate. It is made up of three distinct historical strata. In order of their antiquity and their importance, they are the consonantal text, the use of consonants as reading indicators (*matres lectionis*, "mothers of reading"; Heb., *ʿimmôt qěrî'â*), and the system of diacritical marks for vowels and cantillation. The twenty-two letters of the Hebrew alphabet were originally purely consonantal. Some were polyphonic—*šin*/*śin*—and distinguished even in modern traditional pronunciation as *š*/*s*, except according to the Samaritan tradition, and also presumably *ʿayn*/*ġayn* and *ḥet*/*ḫet*, respectively. This implies that the Hebrew speakers took over the alphabet from a dialect in which these consonants coincided, preferring to use these letters polyphonically, rather than invent new letters for the consonants not represented. A more original form of the alphabet, as reflected in Ugaritic, contained twenty-seven letters. (The Ugaritic alphabet also included three additional letters, added secondarily at the end of the alphabet.) The existence of twenty-nine consonantal phonemes is usually posited for Proto-Semitic. It stands to reason (and is also proved by deviating translations of the Septuagint) that the earliest stage of the biblical text was written in a purely consonantal script and that the use of *matres lectiones* came about through changes in pronunciation and subsequently through analogical usages and intentional reform. These *matres lectionis*—namely *waw*/*yod* marking *o* and *u*/*e* and *i* (originally *ō* and *ū*/*ē* and *ī*), respectively, and *heh* in word final only and *'alef* only in words in which it had been used as a consonant—were increasingly utilized by the scribes of the Bible, yet they were a rather restricted aid for enabling the exact reading of the holy text. [*See* Writing and Writing Systems; Scribes and Scribal Techniques.]

It was for that reason that vowel and cantillation marks were introduced. This occurred at a rather late period (between 600 CE, the date of the final redaction of the Talmud, in which they are not yet mentioned, and the beginning of the tenth century, from which time dated manuscripts are known). The marks are, however, based on a much older tradition. The only vocalization and cantillation system used today by the Jewish community is the so-called Tiberian system. It is the most elaborate system and the only one completely preserved. Accordingly, it serves as the main basis for linguistic investigation. In principle, however, the other vocalization (and cantillation) systems are equally important: the Babylonian one (in which *a* and *æ* are not distinguished) and the so-called Palestinian system (a subsystem of which corresponds to modern Sephardi pronunciation used in academic teaching and in modern Israeli speech). The Tiberian vocalization differs from both the Babylonian and Palestinian by the shift of *u* to *å*, thus coinciding with *å* < *ā*. The Samaritan tradition is quite different.

Layers. Despite the multilayered character of the linguistic tradition, Biblical Hebrew though stretching over many hundred of years and stemming from different parts of ancient Palestine, reflects a surprisingly uniform language. This is the result of its being a standardized literary language, presumably emerging from Judea (Judah) in general and Jerusalem in particular, on the one hand, and to the later changes the that text (especially its vocalization) underwent, on the other. Nevertheless, a distinction must be made between poetry and prose, and then between early and classical poetry and between classical and late prose, without going into details and differentiating between various types of prose (e.g., historical, legal). Thus, poetry in general uses the longer (original) forms of the prepositions *'*^{æ}*le*, "to"; *ʿ*^{a}*le*, "on"; and *ʿ*^{a}*de*, "until"; it restricts the use of the definite article, the relative pronoun, and the definite direct object marker; it sometimes adds the endings *-i*/*o* to nouns in construct (*-i* in other cases as well); it utilizes the pronoun *-mo*, "their/them"; and it uses construct forms preceding prepositional phrases. Early poetry has preserved the short prefix conjugation to mark the past (even when not following the "conversive" *waw*). For Late Biblical Hebrew, see below.

Phonetics. The Hebrew alphabet's twenty-two letters originally marked only consonants—*'b g d h w z ḥ ṭ y k l m n s ʿ p ṣ q r š*/*ś t*. The adduced order of the letters is very old, reflected not only by internal evidence (i.e., by biblical acrostic), but also by the Ugaritic alphabet. The penultimate letter remained polyphonic, yet the lateral *ś* disappeared in pronunciation. It was replaced by *s*, identical with the fifteenth letter, so that the alphabet reflects the pronunciation of twenty-two letters only. Historically, however, it exhibits twenty-three phonemes (though in biblical orthography *ś* and *s* sometimes are interchanged). On the other hand, the letters *b*, *g*, *d*, *k*, *p*, *t* have allophones, for after vowels they are pronounced as spirants—*ḇ*, *ḡ*, *ḏ*, *ḵ*, *p̄*, *ṯ*. Yet, the automatic shift of these plosives (which are regularly marked in the Tiberian system by an internal point, the so-called *dageš lene*) to spirants (which are, in accurate manuscripts, marked by a superposed line, the so-called *raphe*) has been preserved in word-initial position only; elsewhere the spirant allophones are on the point of becoming phonemes (cf. *låqaḥat*, "you took" [fem. sg.], as against *lāqaḥaṯ*, "to take"; cf. also the very same word with alternating plosive and spirant pronunciation: *qorbān*, "offering," as a rule with b; but see *Ez.* 40:43, *qorḇān*, with *ḇ*).

The realization of the phonemic status of noninitial *b*, *g*, *d*, *k*, *p*, *t* is of utmost importance also for understanding the biblical vowel system: because the plosive/spirant pronunciation does not necessarily depend on being preceded by zero vowel or by *ə* respectively, *ə* must not be analyzed as a phoneme (see below). Between short vowels, *h* tends to disappear, as does *aleph* in certain positions, especially in syllable final; *n* preceding a consonant is almost invariably totally assimilated to it. The doubling of final consonants is given up (**gabb* > *gaḇ;* only final *tt* tends to be preserved, as *'att*, "you" [fem. sg.]). This may also occur in a medial position preceding a consonant (*tåsoḇnå*, "they will turn" [fem.]), even when the originally following *ə* has only later become *zero* (as **wayyəhī* > *wayhī*, "and it was"). Final consonant clusters tend to be opened by an auxiliary vowel, usually *æ*, which, however, as a rule, does not acquire phonemic status. At a later phase, laryngeals/pharyngeals—', *h*, *ḥ*, ʿ—became weakened. Therefore, not only did they (and *r*) lose their ability to be doubled, they also often trigger the insertion of ultrashort vowels (^{a}, ^{æ}, ^{å}) when they are in word-medial position immediately followed by a consonant. These vowels also regularly replace *ə* after laryngeals/pharyngeals, which also tend to change *i*/*u* to *a* (*i* also to *æ*).

As to vowels, the Tiberian vowel system, with the exception of ultrashort vowels (^{a}, ^{æ}, ^{å}), denotes only quality, rather than quantity. That is proven, inter alia, by the use of the same vowel sign to mark *å* both when it developed from long *ā* and short *u*. It also tends to mark allophones, not only, as mentioned above, *b*, *g*, *d*, *k*, *p*, *t*, whether plosive or spirant, in word-initial position, and auxiliary vowels opening a final consonantal cluster, but also when it is inserted automatically as a vocalic glide before final *h*, *ḥ*, ʿ after vowels other than *a*/*å* (the so-called furtive *pataḥ*). It marks both the absence of a vowel and *ə* (according to Tiberian tradition, often pronounced ᵃ) by the same sign (*šwa*). Because the spirantization of *b*, *g*, *d*, *k*, *p*, *t* does not necessarily depend on a preceding vowel, including *ə*, and because *ə* often shifts to zero and vice versa, no phonemic status should be accorded to the opposition *ə*:zero.

Historically, the Hebrew vowels derive from the Semitic triads—short *a:i:u*, long *ā:ī:ū*. Whereas the number of the Semitic consonantal phonemes has been reduced in Hebrew, that of the vowels has increased. The original short vowels are preserved in closed, unstressed syllables. However, *a* is often "attenuated" to *i* (a rather late feature, in which the various vocalization systems differ), and *u* tends to shift to *å*, except when followed by a doubled consonant; *a* is also preserved in stressed closed syllables of verbs, as well as in nouns originally terminating in a doubled consonant, and in construct. Otherwise, *a* shifts to *å*, *i* to *e*, *u* to *o*. In stressed closed syllables, *i* tends to shift to *a* (sometimes also to *æ*)—the so-called Philippi's law, which occurred much later than generally assumed. In pretonic open syllables, *a* (and sometimes also *i*) shifts to *å* (and *e*, respectively; *i*, however in this position is often elided). Sometimes the consonant following the pretonic syllable is doubled, especially after *u*, and quite often this doubling spreads to the whole paradigm. Short open syllables two or four syllables before the stress are reduced. Long *ī* and *ū* are preserved (without length), whereas *ā* was originally kept in unstressed syllables, shifting to *o* in stressed ones (this distribution has, however, largely been altered by analogy). When unstressed, the diphthongs *aw*/*ay* were monophthongized to *o*/*e*, respectively—yet preserved, for example, preceding double *w*/*y*. In closed syllables bearing the main stress, they were split into two syllables, as **mawt* > *må:wæṯ*, "death"; **bayt* > *ba:yiṯ*, "house."

Stress. Because the cantillation marks in the Tiberian system are, as a rule, on the stressed syllable, the Tiberian stress system is known with certainty. Synchronically, stress, as a rule, falls on the ultima, not rarely on the penult. A stage of general penult stress can be reconstructed historically because words stressed in pause on their ultima are generally forms that have elided final vowels; those stressed on their penult in pause, however, have preserved their final syllables. Adding the vowels elided to the words stressed on their ultima even in pause results in the great majority of Hebrew vocabulary stressed on the penult. In pause, the penult stress of words that did not elide their final vowel, was as a rule, preserved because the penult, even when originally short, was lengthened in pause. Long vowels, as a rule, preserved their penult stress (e.g., **kātā:bū*, "they wrote," with penult lengthening of the first syllable, according to the Tiberian system, in which no long vowels existed, *kåṯå:ḇu*). In context, however, the penult was often short, which caused the stress to move to the ultima. Because pretonic lengthening preceded the shift from penult to ultima, the first syllable of the context form **kāta:bū*, "they wrote," was preserved, being long. Pretonic lengthening had already ceased operating, however, and therefore the open short unstressed penult, now losing the stress, was reduced to *ə*: **kātəbū:* and, according to the Tiberian system, *kåṯəḇu:*

This theory of general stress is of special importance for the proper understanding of Biblical morphology. Without this theory, chaos obtains; it enables discovering regularity almost everywhere, although it was often blurred by analogy. Thus, for example, the "conversive" *and* preceding the (generally short) prefix conjugation has the form *wa*, and the following consonant is doubled. Because, according to the theory of general penult stress, many forms of the short prefix conjugation, which consisted of two syllables only, were stressed on their first syllable, the *a* of *wa* was preserved by pretonic doubling.

Pronouns. In Hebrew in particular and in Semitic tongues in general, triradical consonantal structure prevails, and the main meaning is carried by the radicals. Vowels only add shades to it. Interjection and pronouns, because of their emotional character (which, to be sure, is to a large extent blurred in pronouns), deviate from this structure. Moreover, pronouns allow word composition, a feature alien to Semitic linguistic structure (with the exception of negations): for example, see *hallåzæ*, "this," compounded of the demonstrative *ha* (which serves as the definite article as well) + the emphatic element *lå* + the demonstrative *zæ*.

Although a substantive to which an attributive demonstrative is attached is automatically definite, it nevertheless is always also formally defined. When this is done by the definite article, it is attached to the demonstrative as well: *ballay:ıå hahu*, "in that night"; yet, the more archaic form *ballay:ıå hu*, in which the definite article is attached to the substantive only, is also attested.

The personal pronouns have basically two forms: the "nominatival" ones, serving as subject and predicate, are separate words. The "genitival" (denoting possession and governed by substantives and prepositions) and accusatival forms (denoting direct object and governed by [transitive] verbs) are enclitic and suffixed to the preceding governing word. The genitival and accusatival suffixes are identical, except for the first-person singular, "mine," being stressed *-i*, "me" unstressed *-ni*. Most of these suffixes are preceded by "connecting" vowels, stemming from the short final vowels in which the preceding words are terminated; the absence of these vowels is the result of secondary development. It is only after the third-person feminine singular of the suffix conjugation, which originally terminated in a consonant (the suffix *-aṯ*), that the pronominal suffixes join the governing word directly, without a connecting vowel.

Tense system. The Hebrew tense system, beside the imperative (in the second person only, in a form closely related to the short prefix conjugation), consists of four finite forms: the simple suffix and the conversive suffix conjugation, the simple prefix and the conversive (as a rule short) prefix conjugation. The prefix conversive forms are preceded by *wa*, "and." It is a moot question whether the verbal forms originally denoted aspects or time. In classical biblical prose, at any rate, these forms seem to mark time: the difference between the simple suffix and the conversive (as a rule short) prefix conjugation, both referring to the past, and between the simple prefix and the conversive suffix conjugation, both referring to the future/present, respectively, depends on the syntactical environment only. As a rule, whenever the use of *w*, "and," is possible, the "converted" forms are applied, in accordance with the demanded time; otherwise, the simple forms are used. This tense system, exhibiting two pairs of forms identical in meaning and differing in the syntactical environment only in which they occur, is quite unlooked-for. It was, to a great extent, therefore that Hans Bauer considered Biblical Hebrew to be a *Mischsprache*, a "mixed language."

It is, however, with Gotthelt Bergsträsser (1918–1929, vol. 2, p. 3, n. 1), very difficult to imagine that two systems should be absorbed in their entirety into one language. Accordingly, it stands to reason that originally the simple suffix conjugation denoted state, as it does in Akkadian, whereas the past was marked by the short prefix conjugation (which in Akkadian and Arabic, as in Hebrew, combines the meanings of past and jussive). As a designation of the past, the short prefix conjugation was then superseded by the suffix conjugation. It was only preserved (except in archaic poetry) in this usage in the closed syntagma preceded by *wa*. Accordingly, from the historical point of view, this *wa* is not conversive but rather preservative. The "converted" suffix conjugation is, it seems, secondary. It is formed by the analogy of *wa* + prefix conjugation, perhaps also because wishes could be denoted by the past tense verbal form as well. In poetry, however, the use of tenses is quite free, presumably because of an intentional archaism as well as a pseudoarchaism.

Besides the indicative, the prefix conjugation also denotes mood—some sort of volitive action: in the first person, the "cohortative," a lengthened form (by the suffix *-å*), is utilized, whereas in the second and third persons, a short form, the "jussive," is used. This jussive is basically identical with the short converted prefix conjugation after *wa*. It later differs from it in that the converted form often preserves the original penult stress.

Verbal themes. It is in verbs that consonantal triliterality has evolved most completely. Although historical traces of biliteral roots can be discovered, synchronically the Hebrew verb has to be analyzed as triradical—no doubt a late development, the result of analogy. The impact of far-reaching analogy can also be felt in the very restricted number of verbal themes, as against a plethora of nominal themes. There are seven main verbal themes, all but one of which are named after the form of the third-person masculine singular of the suffix conjugation: the basic theme, without any affixation or doubling, called *qal*, "light"—that is, "light" as regards addition, without any addition; *nifʿal*, formed with prefixed *n*, originally only reflexive, later, after the original passive of the *qal* had fallen into desuetude, also passive. From the passive of the *qal*, the *puʿal*, only some vestiges have been preserved. Even fewer have been preserved from its (reflexive-reciprocal) *t*-form (*hiṯpåʿal*) and the *t*-form of *hifʿil*, the *hiṯafʿal*. Both the causative *hifʿil* and the doubled middle radical (intensive-factitive) *piʿʿel* have (internal) passive forms, *hofʿal (hufʿal)*/*puʿʿal*, respectively. The latter also has a (reflexive-reciprocal) *t*-form, the *hiṯpaʿʿel*. Accordingly, with the exclusion of *nifʿal*, the well-balanced system shown in table 1 can be reconstructed.

Among the nonfinite forms, the Hebrew verbal system possesses a participle (in the basic theme also a passive participle) that has both nominal and verbal rection. There are two "infinitives": The so-called infinitive construct has the usual infinitive functions (but also that of a gerund); it is, as a rule, preceded, even when not used in a final sense, by the preposition *lə*, "to," which may, however, when the infinitive clause does not have a final sense, be missing. The so-called infinitive absolute (so-called because it does not stand in construct and is not governed by prepositions) is a peculiar blend between verbal noun and verbal interjection. It is often used, in addition to its rare infinitive functions, for example, to emphasize the verbal action, as a rule preceding the main verb. It also serves as a modal adverb, presumably an archaic feature, because in Akkadian and Ugaritic it terminates in the adverbial ending *-u*. Finally, it may substitute for any finite verbal form, though the replacement of the imperative is particularly well attested.

In the suffix conjugation of the basic theme fientive *fåʿal* tends to supersede stative *fåʿel* and *fåʿol*. The original patterns of the prefix conjugation of the basic theme were fientive *yafʿil* (which has been absorbed by *hifʿil*), *yafʿul*, and stative *yifʿal*. Yet, only vestiges of these patterns have been preserved, as *yaḥ*^{a}*loš*, "he weakens," as against *yæḥ*^{æ}*laš*, "he is weak"; *yaqum*, "he rises," as against *yeḇoš*, "he is ashamed"; *yåsoḇ*, "he turns," as against *yeqal*, "he is

TABLE 1. *Verbal Themes*. Obsolete forms are marked by an asterisk.

	Basic Theme	Double Theme	Causative Theme
	qal	piʿel	hifʿil
Internal passive	*puʿal	puʿʿal	ho/ufʿal
ṯ-form (reflexive-reciprocal)	*hiṯpåʿal	hiṯpaʿʿal	*hiṯafʿel

light." In *pi"el* the *e* of the suffix conjugation is mainly preserved in the third-person singular masculine in pause. In context, as well as in the other persons (except in the third-person singular feminine), the *e*, through Philippi's law, shifts to *a*.

Nouns. Both triliteralism and the development of themes are less conspicuous in nouns than in verbs. There exists a set of biradical substantives with a fixed vowel. By their meanings they demonstrate that they belong to the oldest stratum of the language and are, even synchronically, best analyzed as biradical. Substantives are used in different states: in the absolute state (when standing alone), in construct (when closely attached to a following noun, the *nomen rectum,* historically a genitive, denoting relation of possession, etc.) and in the pronominal state (when attached to a genitival pronominal suffix). Two genders exist, the masculine, as a rule with zero ending, and the feminine, with *-å* (spelled *-h* in construct and pronominal state *-at*) and *-t* ending.

Numerals. The cardinal numbers 3–10 reflect the very surprising common Semitic feature that, in opposition to the other noun classes, those with a zero ending modify feminine nouns; those with an *-å* ending (in construct *-[a]t̲*) modify masculine ones. They precede or follow the counted noun in the absolute state, but they may precede it in construct—historically an archaic feature. This is the rule with definite nouns, as well as with nouns often counted, as *yom,* "day." The "ten" in numbers 11–19 is *ʿåśår* for masculine, *ʿæśre* for feminine, spelled *ʿśrh.* The ordinal numbers have special forms only for the digits and ten built, as a rule, according to the theme *pəʿili.* The exceptions are *šišši,* "sixth," built secondarily off of *šeš,* "six," and perhaps *šeni,* "second," "first" is *rišon,* derived from *roš,* "head," a relatively late form, as is customary in Semitic languages. The older usage of the cardinal number 1 appears in *Genesis* 1:5, *yomʿæḥad̲,* "one day" = the first day."

Clause formation. It is in the domain of clause formation that Biblical Hebrew has best preserved the ancient Semitic character. In contradistinction to Arabic, it has not relinquished free sentence structure in favor of systemization. Yet, although it has lost, like Aramaic, case and mood endings, it has not been affected by a similar syntactic formlessness. The boundary lines between main and subordinate clauses, however, as well as between the coordination of sentences and subordination, is sometimes blurred. Thus, the main clause, when it follows the subordinate clauses, may be introduced by *wə,* "and." In classical prose, main clauses, as a rule, open with a verb preceded by the conversive *wa.* Sentences describing background tend to open with the subject and may even be nominal. Yet, because the sentence following the background sentence may open again with *wa* + verb, either when it continues the background sentence or resumes the main action, it is often difficult to understand the exact sentence structure. Moreover, if the verbal clause does not open with the finite verb or with the subject (i.e., it begins with an object or an adverbial), the finite verb has to precede the subject (i.e., the obligatory word order is object/adverbial + finite verb + subject). An example in *Genesis* 1:1–3, *bərešit̲ bårå' ʾᵉlohim 'et̲ haššåma:yim wə'et̲ hå'å:ræṣ wəhå'å:ræṣ håyt̲å t̲o:hu wåb̲o:hu . . . , wayyo:mær ʾᵉlohim:* "in the beginning God created the heaven and the earth [main action, opening with an adverbial], the earth being without form and void . . . [nominal clause serving as background], and God said [again main action; yet theoretically, it could have continued the background clause as well]. Quite frequently *wə* introduces the main clause in phrases like *wayhi ki . . . , wə,* "and it happened when . . . , then . . . ." After a jussive or an imperative, for example, the prefix conjugation following *wə,* by attraction to the preceding volitive, is transferred into the volitive mood (i.e., the long prefix conjugation in the first, the short one in the second and third persons—the so-called indirect volitive). This expresses consecutive or final action (e.g., *Gn.* 27:4, *håb̲i:'å li wə'ok̲e:lå,* "bring me in order that I eat"; *Dt.* 32:7, *šə'al 'ab̲ik̲å wəyaggedk̲å,* "ask your father that he may tell you").

Circumstantial clauses resemble main clauses even more. Usually, they follow the main clause, connected by *wə* or asyndetically (e.g., *Gn.* 18:1, *wayyerå 'ælåw . . . wəhu yošeb̲,* "and He appeared unto him . . . while he was sitting"). When circumstantial clauses precede the main clause, it is the main clause that is connected by *wə,* and it is only the internal structure of the circumstantial clause (the subject preceding the verb, nominal clause, etc.) that differentiates it from the main clause; *Genesis* 38:25–26, reflects a quite intricate sentence structure: *hi muṣet̲ wəhi šålḥå . . . wat-to:mær . . . wayakker,* "and while she was being brought forth [preceding circumstantial clause], and she had already sent [background clause, the subject preceding the finite verb] . . . and had said [continuation of the background clause, yet theoretically it could denote the main action as well], . . . and he acknowledged [main action]"). The number of subordinating conjunctions is relatively small. The main relative pronoun is *ʾᵃšær.* In Hebrew, relative clauses differ in their structure from, for example, English ones, being much more independent. In their full form, pronominal suffixes, governed by a preposition/verb, refer back to the antecedent. In English it is the relative pronoun that is governed by the preposition/verb (e.g., *ʾᵃšær . . . bo* = "in which"). ʾᵃšær is also used to introduce substantive clauses. The main conjunction for introducing substantive clauses is *ki,* which has a variety of functions, including emphasizing particle and causal and temporal conjunction. Important particles are the conditional *'im,* hypothetical *lu,* and presentative *hinne,* "behold"; the latter is often followed by a participle marking the future, whereas *wəhinne,* literally "and behold," is often dependent on verbs of "seeing." It marks what has been seen, as in *Genesis* 30:6: *wayyar(') 'ot̲åm wəhinnåm zoʿᵃp̄im,* "and he saw that they were vexed."

Vocabulary. The vocabulary of the Bible (and even moreso of Hebrew inscriptions), is restricted; its language is also somewhat one-sided: it deals with religion, morals, and emotion, being the tongue of prophets, legislators, and poets. Small wonder that many semantic fields are poorly represented and that the number of hapax legomena is relatively high. Biblical vocabulary is especially influenced by Aramaic, whose impact increases in the book's later portions. Aramaic has also served as the intermediary for several Akkadian loanwords.

Second Temple Period. The destruction of the First Temple (587 BCE and the Babylonian Exile marked a new stage in the development of Hebrew culture and language. The returning exiles brought with them the Aramaic language and culture. The books of the Bible had been written during the First Temple period by people whose spoken language, for all their differences, did not differ from the literary tongue more than any other spoken language differs from its literary layer. With the return of the exiles a very much different dialect prevailed in everyday speech that was more and more influenced by Aramaic. This dialect had existed in the First Temple period (reflecting an only marginal Aramaic influence), but people speaking it were, as a rule, cut off from the literary tongue. In the Second Temple period, however, people speaking this dialect were among the authors of literary works written in Late Biblical Hebrew, which, accordingly, reflected genuine diglossia. It was only later that the rabbis adopted this spoken dialect as a literary language and utilized so-called Rabbinic Hebrew, which became the second classical Hebrew tongue, after Biblical Hebrew.

The biblical books composed during this period—such as *Chronicles, Ezra and Nehemiah, Esther, Ecclesiastes,* and *Daniel*—are, for all their differences, written in Late Biblical Hebrew. Besides utilizing *matres lectionis* more frequently, the language prefers, inter alia, *ʾᵃni,* "I," to *ʾånoḵi* and tends to mark the direct object by *lə*, presumably through the impact of Aramaic. The latter might also have caused the reduction of the use of converted forms, and the increased use of noun patterns like *malḵūṯ,* "kingdom," instead of the classical *mamlāḵā.*

The apocryphal books are also written in Late Biblical Hebrew. Fragments of them have been discovered in Hebrew in *Jubilees,* the *Testaments of the Twelve Patriarchs,* and *Ben Sira.* The Hebrew parts of the latter, a book belonging to the Wisdom literature and composed in about 180 BCE, were first discovered in the Cairo Genizah (the storeroom of the Ben-Ezra Synagogue in Cairo in which worn Hebrew books and documents were kept) and later in the excavations on Masada. The Dead Sea Scrolls, the manuscripts found at Qumran, near the northern edge of the Dead Sea), and in its vicinity, were, except for biblical texts, composed by Jewish sectarians. Their historical importance lies in the light they shed on the two centuries following the Hasmonean uprising, a period decisive for the history of monotheistic religions. [*See* Dead Sea Scrolls; Qumran; Masada; Hasmoneans.] These scrolls are written in another variety of Late Biblical Hebrew, dubbed Qumran Hebrew. It utilizes, inter alia, pronoun doublets (forms with and without final *heh*), *bəlō(ʾ)/ləlō(ʾ)* with finite verbs, and predicatively used infinitives. Yet, although the language of the scroll *Miqṣat maʿaśe ha-Torah* from Qumran Cave 4 grammatically resembles Biblical Hebrew more than Rabbinic Hebrew, it is closer to the latter in its use of *še,* "that," and in its vocabulary, perhaps because of its halakhic character. Nothing certain can be said so far about the *Copper Scroll,* which reflects affinities with Rabbinic Hebrew as well. [*See* Copper Scroll.]

Rabbinic Hebrew is to be divided into two main periods: tannaitic and Amoraitic. In the Tannaitic era (in the first two centuries CE.), Hebrew was still a spoken language, though rivaled by Aramaic and even by Greek. The tannaim composed all their works in Rabbinic Hebrew: the large collections dealing with law (halakha)—the Mishnah, the Tosefta, and the Baraitot (halakhic traditions not accepted into the Mishnah and Tosefta)—and the early Midrashim, which comprise both halakhic and homiletic (haggadic) exegesis. No early manuscripts written in Rabbinic Hebrew survive. The earliest specimen in a somewhat different species of Rabbinic Hebrew are the Bar Kokhba letters, some of which were written in Aramaic and even in Greek (c. 135 CE), found mainly in Naḥal Ḥever and Wadi Murabbaʿat in the Judean Desert. [*See* Bar Kokhba Revolt; Judean Desert Caves.]

Later manuscripts were decisively influenced by Biblical Hebrew, so that the reconstruction of genuine Rabbinic Hebrew is somewhat precarious. The latter clearly differs from the former not only in vocabulary (partly the result of the Aramaic influence), but in grammatical structure as well. Converted verbal forms disappeared, as did the infinitive absolute. The infinitive construct coalesced with *lə* preceding it and in the basic verbal theme was restructured according to the prefix tense. In final position, the opposition of *m:n* was neutralized. The past is marked by the suffix tense, while the present and, as a rule, the future, are marked by the participle. The prefix tense is, to a great extent, used as a sort of subjunctive. The lengthened, and as a rule also shortened, forms of the prefix tense are no longer extant. The attributive use of the demonstrative pronoun is archaic when compared with Biblical Hebrew because it is not pleonastically determined by the definite article (Rabbinic Hebrew's *bayiṯ ze,* "this house," as against Biblical Hebrew's *hab-bayiṯ haz-ze*). The number of subordinate clauses is much higher than in Biblical Hebrew, and most are built with the conjunction *še.*

It was in the wake of the collapse of the Bar Kokhba Revolt in 135 CE that Hebrew ceased to be a living language and was used for cultural (religious) purposes only—though it often flourished as a literary tongue. It was not spoken again until the end of the nineteenth century in Israel (Palestine). Because Biblical and Rabbinic Hebrew, despite the differences between them, continued to serve as cultural unifiers—Bible and Mishnah being the two main pillars of Judaism—once Hebrew ceased being spoken, various mixtures of Biblical and Rabbinic Hebrew were utilized in every historical period. Each of these dialects was influenced by the spoken non-Hebrew vernacular wherever Jews lived. In the Hebrew of later periods, significant archaizing tendencies can also be detected. Amoraitic Rabbinic Hebrew (c. 200–500 CE), attested in the later Midrashim, as well as in the primary source of Jewish law, the Palestinian and Babylonian Talmuds (compiled in the first half of the fourth and the second half of the fifth centuries, respectively), already reflects the mixture of the two, although Rabbinic Hebrew is its main component. It is decisively influenced by the vernacular—Aramaic—in which a great part of the Talmuds and the late Midrashim are written.

Similar mixtures of Biblical and Rabbinic Hebrew and the vernacular are reflected in the medieval varieties of literary Hebrew. Thus, Spanish Hebrew poetry, in the main, imitates Biblical Hebrew, yet it is not entirely devoid of elements belonging to Rabbinic Hebrew; moreover it is also influenced by the vernacular—Arabic.

Modern Hebrew. The revival of Hebrew as a living language in Modern (Israeli) Hebrew is the only case in the history of languages in which a dead language (i.e., one used only for literary purposes) again became a spoken tongue. The coincidence of three factors at the beginning of the twentieth century in Palestine (later the State of Israel) made the revival possible. Many of the Jews in Palestine had emerged from traditional Jewish society, which taught its members the Hebrew language as a part of Jewish culture, thus imparting to them a working knowledge of the language. Because these Jews used various vernaculars, Hebrew was their only common language. Many of the Jews in Palestine additionally were influenced by the zeitgeist of nationalism, which pleaded for the use of the national language in every domain. This provided the members of the Zionist movement with the motivation to revive Hebrew. It was through the Hebrew Language Committee (later the Academy of the Hebrew Language) that missing words, especially technical terms, were created. The morphology of Modern Hebrew is in the main identical with that of Biblical Hebrew. Yet, from doublets forms were chosen that occur in Rabbinic Hebrew as well. Its sentence formation is much closer to Rabbinic Hebrew, but it is also influenced by Standard Average European, in which the number of subordinate clauses is also much higher than in Biblical Hebrew. Standard Average European has also considerably influenced Modern Hebrew phraseology.

[*See also* Biblical Literature, *article on* Hebrew Scriptures.]

BIBLIOGRAPHY

Bauer, Hans. "Die Tempora im Semitischen." *Beiträge zur Assyrologie* 8.1 (1912): 1ff.

Bauer, Hans, and Pontus Leander. *Historische Grammatik der hebräischen Sprache des Alten Testaments* (1922). Hildesheim, 1962. Linguistically sound approach, but sometimes impaired by an excessive desire for innovation; includes phonetics and morphology only.

Ben-Ḥayyim, Zeev. *The Literary and Oral Tradition of Hebrew and Aramaic amongst the Samaritans,* vol. 5, *Grammar of the Pentateuch* (in Hebrew). Jerusalem, 1977. Authoritative grammar of Hebrew according to the Samaritan tradition, including phonetics and morphology.

Bergsträsser, Gotthelf. *Hebräische Grammatik.* 2 vols. Leipzig, 1918–1929. Although a torso, containing only phonetics and the morphology of the verb, and somewhat dated, it is still the best Hebrew grammar.

Bergsträsser, Gotthelf. *Introduction to the Semitic Languages* (1928). Translated by Peter T. Daniels. Winona Lake, Ind., 1983. Masterly, though somewhat antiquated, introduction to Semitic linguistics that also contains a superb description of Biblical Hebrew.

Blau, Joshua. *A Grammar of Biblical Hebrew.* 2d ed. Wiesbaden, 1993. Short grammar expatiating on problems referred to in this entry.

Brown, Francis, et al. *A Hebrew and English Lexikon of the Old Testament.* Corr. ed. Oxford, 1952. Superb, though somewhat obsolete, dictionary of the Bible that can only be compared with Buhl's dictionary (see below).

Buhl, Frants. *W. Gesenius' hebräisches und aramäisches Handwörterbuch über das Alte Testament.* 17th ed. Leipzig, 1921. Superb, though somewhat outdated, dictionary of the Bible, comparable to Brown's (above).

Cohen, Harold R. *Biblical Hapax Legomena in the Light of Akkadian and Ugaritic.* Missoula, 1978. The most reliable treatise on hapax legomena.

Davidson, A. B. *Hebrew Syntax.* 3d ed. Edinburgh, 1924. Clear, sound work.

Driver, Samuel R. *An Introduction to the Literature of the Old Testament* (1891). New York, 1963. Still one of the best introductions to the Bible, with superb linguistic analysis.

Driver, Samuel R. *A Treatise on the Use of the Tenses in Hebrew and Some Other Syntactical Questions.* 3d ed. Oxford, 1892. Even if one disagrees with the author's conception of the Hebrew tenses, it is possible to profit greatly from this masterful collection of material and clear exposition.

Elliger, Karl, and Wilhelm Rudolph. *Biblia Hebraica Stuttgartensia.* Stuttgart, 1968–. The best-known Western edition of the Bible; its apparatus criticus should be used cautiously.

Joüon, Paul, and Takamitsu Muraoka. *A Grammar of Biblical Hebrew.* Rome, 1991. The most up-to-date, comprehensive grammar.

Kautzsch, Emil. *Gesenius' Hebrew Grammar.* Translated by Arthur E. Cowley. 2d ed. Oxford, 1910. Though obsolete and often linguistically unsound, the collection of material is of great importance.

Köhler, Ludwig. *Hebräisches und Aramäisches Lexikon zum Alten Testament.* 3d ed., revised by Walter Baumgartner et al. Leiden, 1967–. The most up-to-date dictionary of the Bible, although not up to the standard of Brown's and Buhl's dictionaries (see above).

Kutscher, Eduard Y. *A History of the Hebrew Language.* Jerusalem, 1982. Unfinished original account by one of the foremost Hebrew linguists.

Sáenz-Badillos, Angel. *A History of the Hebrew Language.* Cambridge, 1993. Well-balanced history of the Hebrew language.

Waltke, Bruce K., and Michael O'Connor. *An Introduction to Biblical Hebrew Syntax.* Winona Lake, Ind., 1990. Up-to-date treatment, with a good bibliography; the conclusions should be used cautiously.

JOSHUA BLAU

HEBREW UNION COLLEGE (Jerusalem). *See* Nelson Glueck School of Biblical Archaeology.

HEBRON (Ar., El-Khalil), site situated some 30 km (18 mi.) south of Jerusalem (31°30′ N, 35° E). Twenty-five springs in the area, along with two ancient pools, provided an adequate water supply in antiquity for the inhabitants, their flocks, and their fields. The ancient city is mentioned more than sixty times in the Hebrew Bible, from *Genesis* to *Nehemiah,* as well as in the Pseudepigraphy. Traditionally built "seven years before Zoan in Egypt," the city was undoubtedly a Canaanite cultic place, made important by the "Oak of Mamre," under which Abraham is said to have pitched his tent, "built an altar to the Lord," entertained divine messengers, and pleaded for the innocents of Sodom. Much later, the spies of Moses beheld the richness of Hebron's vineyards. After the Hebrew tribes occupied the land, Hebron was "given" as an inheritance to Caleb and became a city of Judah, a place of refuge, and a Levitical sinecure (*Jgs.* 1:20; *1 Chr.* 6:57).

In the days of King David, the city achieved its greatest renown. At the death of Saul, David settled there and was subsequently anointed king of Judah. Joab's murder of Abner precipitated the fall of the unstable house of Saul in the north, and the elders of Israel came to Hebron to proclaim David king over all the land (*2 Sm.* 5:3). Jerusalem became the new capital of the United Monarchy (*2 Sm.* 5:7), but it was to Hebron that Absalom, David's son, went to attempt the usurpation of his father's throne (*2 Sm.* 15:10–11). Josephus (*Antiq.* 8.2.1) assigns Solomon's vision to Hebron, but in the Hebrew Bible it is mentioned again only in the lists of Rehoboam's fortified cities (*2 Chr.* 11:10).

Extrabiblical evidence may indicate that Hebron was an early Canaanite royal, as well as cultic, city, and some scholars have seen it as a possible Hyksos city during the Middle Bronze Age. [*See* Hyksos.] The Amarna letters include a possible reference to a local prince named Shuwardata, who may have ruled there; the Medinet Habu list of Rameses III may also contain a possible reference to the site. [*See* Amarna Tablets.] Stamped jar handles from the eighth century BCE suggest that the city functioned then as a royal pottery works of some sort. Wares bearing the name of the city are found throughout the borders of ancient Palestine.

No Assyrian or Neo-Babylonian records note the existence of the site, but its lush fields could hardly have escaped the notice of either set of conquerors. After the fall of Jerusalem, Edomites (Idumeans) occupied the area but were dislodged later by Judas Maccabaeus, who took the city and pulled down its fortifications in about 164 BCE. Herod the Great refurbished the city as part of his extensive building operations and enclosed the Cave of Machpelah, as his characteristic masonry there still proclaims. During the First Jewish Revolt, Shimʿon bar Giora captured the city (in 68 CE), but the Roman general Cerealis recaptured and destroyed it. The emperor Hadrian later had a road built and established a market of some prominence nearby. [*See* First Jewish Revolt.] In the seventh century, the prophet Muhammad gave Hebron to the Tamin ed-Dari tribe and its families.

During the Latin Kingdom the site was known as the Castle of St. Abraham and was a major link in the fortress cities guarding the kingdom. In 1100 the city became the fief of Gerhard of Avennes, but it was under Baldwin I that the city achieved its military strength. It was also in this later period that the city's glass factories were revived, which continue to the present time. In 1167 Rainald became the Latin bishop of Hebron, further elevating the city's position. With the fall of the Latin Kingdom, the city reverted to Islamic control and soon became an important Muslim religious site.

The modern Arabic name, *El-Khalil* ("the friend"), harkens back to the Abrahamic saga ("the friend" = Abraham—*2 Chr.* 20:7, in which Abraham is called the "friend" of God; the site is also called variously Hebron and Kiriath-Arba in the biblical text). The designation *Kiriath-Arba,* after Arba, father of the giantlike Anakim (*Jos.* 14:13, 15:13, 34, 20:7, 21:11; *Gn.* 23:2, 35:27; *Jgs.* 1:10) led Jewish writers, followed by Jerome, to curious etymological gymnastics. The Hebrew word *'arbaʿ* ("four") was taken to mean *the* "four"—Abraham, Isaac, Jacob, and Adam. During the Middle Ages, Hebron was also known as Castellum Aframia, Karicarba, and Arbothe. Charles Clermont-Ganneau also identified the site with the Roman Diocletianopolis. [*See the biography of Clermont-Ganneau.*]

Modern archaeological investigation of the site began in 1964, after a preliminary survey of the area in 1963 by the American Expedition to Hebron, led by Philip C. Hammond. Two further seasons were conducted by the same expedition, in 1965 and 1966. The American expedition concentrated on the observed ancient ruins located on Jebel er-Rumeide, across the valley from the modern city. Excavation produced material remains from the Chalcolithic, Early Bronze, Middle Bronze, Late Bronze, Iron, Hellenistic, Byzantine, and Islamic periods. Most significant was the identification of the city's original MB wall, which dates to the first half of the eighteenth century BCE and the mapping of its perimeters. Chalcolithic, EB, MB ("Hyksos"), and Byzantine burials were recovered, as well as ceramic and other cultural materials from those periods and extending into the Early Islamic period. Excavations were renewed at the site from 1983 to 1986 by Avi Ofer and Tel Aviv University. Major finds from those excavations included a fragment of cuneiform tablet written in sixteenth–seventeenth-century BCE East Akkadian and jar handles bearing the royal *lmlk* stamp.

BIBLIOGRAPHY

Anbar, Moshe, and Nadav Na'aman. "An Account Tablet of Sheep from Ancient Hebron." *Tel Aviv* 13–14 (1987): 3–12.
Hammond, Philip C. "David's First City: The Excavation of Biblical Hebron, 1964." *Princeton Seminary Bulletin* 58.2 (1965): 19–28.
Hammond, Philip C. "Ancient Hebron, the City of David." *Natural History* 75.5 (1966): 42–49.
Hammond, Philip C. "Hebron." *Revue Biblique* 73 (1966): 566–569.
Hammond, Philip C. "Hebron, cité de Juda et première capitale de David." *Bible et Terre Saint* 80 (1966): 6–8.
Hammond, Philip C. "The American Expedition to Hebron." *Explorers Journal* 45.4 (1967): 232–244.

PHILIP C. HAMMOND

HEINRICH, ERNST (1899–1984), scholar of ancient Near Eastern architecture and professor of architectural history and Bauaufnahme (the recording of buildings) at the Technical University of Berlin (1951–1965). Heinrich's scholarship embraces the prehistoric periods in the Near East through classical antiquity to nineteenth-century urban development in Berlin and its reconstruction after World War II.

The son of an elementary school principal, Heinrich pursued a degree in architecture, became an assistant professor of architectural history, and later oversaw the preservation of historic monuments in Potsdam and Trier. As a government architect, he met Ernst Walter Andrae, who entrusted him with the final publication of the 1902–1903 German excavations at Fara (1931). [*See* Fara.] Heinrich gained practical experience as architect on the German excavations at Uruk-Warka (1930–1938), which generated numerous publications (1932, 1934–1939). [*See* Uruk-Warka.] He is noted best for his then exemplary excavation and publication of several temples and cult precincts at Eanna and area or square (plan quadrant) K XVII, which includes the first high temple (White Temple) on the Anu ziggurat. Together with Adam Falkenstein, he conducted the first survey of the region surrounding Warka (1938, p. 31ff.). The results of his deep sounding at Eanna (1932, p. 6ff.) are still central to the chronology of the prehistoric and early historical periods in Mesopotamia. His later fieldwork included Tell Fakhariyah, Munbaqa, and Habuba Kabira in North Syria. [*See* Fakhariyah, Tell; Habuba Kabira.]

Heinrich's lifetime research on ancient Near Eastern architecture was crowned by a series of articles and monographs that concentrate on Mesopotamia. A general overview (1975) and an article on domestic architecture (1972–1975) were followed by three volumes devoted to the development of temples and temple precincts (1982) and palace architecture (1984).

Heinrich was a consultant at the German Archaeological Institute beginning in 1942. He later served as a board member of the Koldewey Society and the German Oriental Society (Deutsche Orient-Gesellschaft), where he succeeded Andrae as president. Heinrich received the Order of the Federal Republic of Germany in 1974.

[*See also* Deutsche Orient-Gesellschaft; *and the biographies of Andrae and Koldewey.*]

BIBLIOGRAPHY

For appreciations of Heinrich's life and work, see Barthel Hrouda in *Mitteilungen der Deutschen Orient-Gesellschaft* 116 (1984): 7–9, and Ursula Seidl in *Archiv für Orientforschung* 31 (1984): 234–235. For a complete list of Heinrich's publications up to 1974, see Gisela Siegenthaler, "Bibliographie von Ernst Heinrich," *Archäologische Mitteilungen aus Iran* 7 (1974): 9–14. A list of selected publications by Heinrich follows.

Fara: Ergebnisse der Ausgrabungen der Deutschen Orientgesellschaft in Fara und Abu Hatab. Edited by Walter Andrae. Berlin, 1931. Final report of the German excavations conducted in 1902–1903, providing detailed information on the architecture and traceable small finds (Jemdet Nasr to Isin-Larsa period). Information on their context is included in Harriet P. Martin, *Fara: A Reconstruction of the Ancient Mesopotamian City of Shuruppak* (Birmingham, 1988), where corrections are made to Heinrich's original publication (Appendix I), which is reproduced on microfiche.
Vierter Vorläufiger Bericht über die von der Notgemeinschaft der Deutschen Wissenschaft in Uruk unternommenen Ausgrabungen. Berlin, 1932. See "Die Schichten und ihre Bauten" (pp. 6–24).
Schilf und Lehm: Ein Beitrag zur Baugeschichte der Sumerer. Studien zur Bauforschung, no. 6. Berlin, 1934a.
Fünfter Vorläufiger Bericht über die von der Notgemeinschaft der Deutschen Wissenschaft in Uruk unternommenen Ausgrabungen. Berlin, 1934b. See "Arbeiten in Eanna, im Stadtgebiet und im Südbau" (pp. 5–38).
Sechster Vorläufiger Bericht über die von der Deutschen Forschungsgemeinschaft in Uruk-Warka unternommenen Ausgrabungen. Berlin, 1935.
Kleinfunde aus den archaischen Tempelschichten in Uruk-Warka. Berlin, 1936.
Achter Vorläufiger Bericht über die von der Deutschen Forschungsgemeinschaft in Uruk-Warka unternommenen Ausgrabungen. Berlin, 1937. See "Die Grabungen im Planquadrat K XVII" (pp. 27–55).
Neunter Vorläufiger Bericht über die von der Deutschen Forschungsgemeinschaft in Uruk-Warka unternommenen Ausgrabungen. Berlin, 1938. See "Grabungen im Gebiet des Anu-Antum-Tempels" (pp. 19–30), and "Forschungen in der Umgebung von Warka" (with A. Falkenstein, pp. 31–38). For the dating, see Heinrich 1982 (pp. 35–39).
Zehnter Vorläufiger Bericht über die von der Deutschen Forschungsgemeinschaft in Uruk-Warka unternommenen Ausgrabungen. Berlin, 1939. See "Grabungen im Gebiet des Anu-Antum-Tempels" (pp. 21–33). For the dating, see Heinrich 1982 (pp. 35–39).
"Haus." In *Reallexikon der Assyriologie und Vorderasiatichen Archäologie,* vol. 4, pp. 176–220. Berlin, 1972. Reference article on house forms from the Mesolithic to Neo-Babylonian periods in Palestine, Syria, Anatolia, Iran, and Soviet Armenia.
"Sumerisch-akkadische Architektur" and "Architektur von der alt- bis zur spätbabylonischen Zeit." In *Der Alte Orient,* edited by Winfried Orthmann, pp. 131–158, 241–287. Propyläen Kunstgeschichte, vol. 14. Berlin, 1975.
Die Tempel und Heiligtümer im alten Mesopotamien. Denkmäler Antiker Architektur, 14. Berlin, 1982. Typological and morphological investigation of temples and temple precincts from the Late Uruk to the Seleucid periods, with a useful update on dating.
Die Paläste im alten Mesopotamien. Denkmäler Antiker Architektur, 15. Berlin, 1984. Survey of palace architecture from the Uruk to Neo-Babylonian periods.

DIANA L. STEIN

HELIOPOLIS, ancient Egyptian center of astronomy and theology, located northeast of modern Cairo (30°05′ N, 31°20′ E). The site is largely covered by the modern settlements of Mataria and Tell Hisn. Unlike most ancient Egyptian sites, it is situated not on the Nile but inland some 20 km (12.5 mi.) east of the river, to which it was connected by an ancient canal beginning at the southern edge of modern Cairo.

The ancient Egyptian name of the city was *jwnw* ("pillar"). A cuneiform transcription gives the pronunciation *a-na,* which is also preserved in the biblical Hebrew *'ōn* (Gen. 41:45). The name Heliopolis ("city of the sun") occurs in classical sources from Herodotus (c. 450 BCE) onward, reflecting the city's association with solar theology.

Most of what is known about Heliopolis comes from textual sources rather than from archaeology. By the time of the Old Kingdom (beginning c. 2650 BCE) it was already established as a center of astronomy, aptly characterized by the title of its high priest, "chief of observers." The city also had a reputation for learning and theological speculation, which it retained until classical times (Strabo reports visiting schools of Plato and Eudoxos there). Much of this activity was centered on the role of the sun in the creation and maintenance of the world in the persons of the gods Atum and Re-Harakhti. Heliopolitan theology was summarized in the concept of the Ennead, a group of nine gods embodying both the creative source and the chief operational forces of the universe. By the beginning of the Old Kingdom this system had already been largely formulated into a coherent philosophy, and it continued to dominate Egyptian thought for the next three thousand years.

Despite the intellectual prominence of Heliopolis, very little is known about the city itself. Its chief feature was a temple devoted to Atum and Re-Harakhti, the precise location and shape of which is uncertain. The only standing monument visible today is a large obelisk, which is still in situ, dedicated by Senwosret (Sesostris) I (twelfth dynasty, c. 1970 BCE). Earlier structures include a fragmentary shrine of King Djoser (third dynasty, c. 2650) and part of an obelisk of the sixth-dynasty pharaoh Teti (c. 2300), as well as several tombs of high priests from the Old Kingdom. A stela of Thutmosis III (eighteenth dynasty, c. 1433) commemorates his erection of an enclosure wall around the solar temple. Excavations have also revealed extensive Ramesside construction (nineteenth–twentieth dynasties, c. 1290–1100), comprising several temples and a cemetery for the Mnevis bulls (incarnations of the sun god).

Donation lists from the time of Rameses III (twentieth dynasty, c. 1190) indicate that the temples of Heliopolis were second only to those of Amun at Thebes. After the Ramesside period, however, the fortunes of Heliopolis began to decline. Later building activity is represented primarily by a few Saite tombs (twenty-sixth dynasty, c. 650). The city was largely destroyed during the Persian invasion of 525, though enough of its structures and reputation remained to attract tourists such as Herodotus and Strabo. In the first century CE most of its statuary and obelisks were removed to Alexandria and Rome, and its remaining structures served as a quarry for the building of medieval Cairo. Apart from the standing obelisk of Senwosret I, the ancient site is commemorated today only in the name "Heliopolis," designating northeast Cairo.

BIBLIOGRAPHY

Helck, Wolfgang. "Zur Topographie von Heliopolis." *Zeitschrift für Ägyptische Sprache und Altertumskunde* 82 (1957): 109–116. Discussion of the site's geography based on textual sources and earlier excavations.

Kákosy, László. "Heliopolis." In *Lexikon der Ägyptologie,* vol. 2, pp. 1111–1113. Wiesbaden, 1977. Recent summary, intended as a basic reference for Egyptologists.

Kees, Hermann. *Ancient Egypt: A Cultural Topography.* Translated by Ian F. D. Morrow. London, 1961. Includes the most accessible summary of the history, archaeology, and significance of the site (see pp. 147–179).

Petrie, W. M. Flinders. *Heliopolis, Kafr Ammar, and Shurafa.* Publications of the Egyptian Research Account and the British School of Archaeology in Egypt, vol. 24. London, 1915. Report of the only archaeological excavation of the site so far published in detail.

Porter, Bertha, and Rosalind Moss. *Topographical Bibliography of Ancient Egyptian Hieroglyphic Texts: Reliefs and Paintings,* vol. 4, *Lower and Middle Egypt.* Oxford, 1934. Includes a list of all monuments from the site known at the time of publication, with summary bibliography (see pp. 59–65).

James P. Allen

HERMON, MOUNT (Heb., Har-Ḥermon), one of the highest peaks in the southern Anti-Lebanon range, rising some 5,146 m (8,300 ft.) above sea level. To the west and southwest is a magnificent panorama across southern Lebanon and northern Israel; to the northwest, a view to well beyond Damascus; and to the south a view of the whole of the Upper Jordan Valley. The upper peaks are covered with snow much of the year, making Mt. Hermon a notable landmark. The lower slopes are thick with oak, pine, and fruit trees of various kinds. The prominence, natural beauty, and fertility of Mt. Hermon are often praised in the Hebrew Bible, as well as by classical authors.

The name, not known from ancient Near Eastern sources outside the Bible, derives from the common Semitic *ḥrm,* which in Hebrew and Arabic denotes something that is "taboo," that is, set apart or consecrated, as for instance a sacred place.

In the Hebrew Bible, in addition to references to its beauty and sanctity, Mt. Hermon is often referred to as a prominent natural boundary or as marking the northern borders of the territory claimed by Israel east of the Jordan River. The Bible alludes to other names, such as Senir, which occurs in Assyrian texts; or Sirion, which is attested in the Egyptian Execration texts and at Ugarit. Both names occur in Talmudic texts, and Josephus (*Antiq.* 5.3.1) uses the name Mt. Lebanon. Later Arabic names are Jebel esh-Sheikh, "mountain of the sheikh"; and Jebel eth-Thalj, "mountain of snow."

The cultic associations of Mt. Hermon are easily understood in light of its majesty and the frequent association of ancient Near Eastern deities with mountains. The Hebrew Bible alludes to shrines there to Baal-Gad and Baal-Hermon, as well perhaps as to the Israelite deity (cf. *Jos.* 11:17; *1 Chr.* 5:23; *Ps.* 89:12). More than twenty temples and sanctuaries have been located around Mt. Hermon, including a large Roman temple on the highest peak, known as Qaṣr esh-Shabib, with a large enclosure wall and a Greek inscription to the "Greatest and Holiest God."

BIBLIOGRAPHY

Aharoni, Yohanan. *The Land of the Bible: A Historical Geography.* Philadelphia, 1967.

Arav, Rami. "Hermon, Mount." In *The Anchor Bible Dictionary,* vol. 3, pp. 158–160. New York, 1992.

Dar, Shimʿon. "The Temples of Mount Hermon and Its Environs." In *Abstracts of a Conference on Greece and Rome in Eretz Israel* (in Hebrew). Haifa, 1985.

WILLIAM G. DEVER

HERODIAN JERICHO, site located in the Jordan Valley (31°80′ N, 35°30′ E; map reference 192 × 142), northwest of the Dead Sea, about 2 km (1 mi.) northwest of the modern oasis of Jericho (Ar., er-Riḥa) and to the east of the mountains of Judah. The Jericho valley was probably first developed in the days of Alexander Jannaeus (103–76 BCE). Jericho itself flourished during the first century BCE as a garden city and royal estate. The Hasmoneans were the first to build aqueducts in the western Jordan Valley, where the availability of water and land, as well as the mild climate, enabled the development of agriculture. Date palm and balsam cultivation, spurred the city's economic growth. It was for these reasons that first the Hasmoneans and later King Herod built winter palaces here.

History of Excavation. The site was discovered by Edward Robinson in 1838. Charles Warren excavated in 1868 at two of the mounds; A. Nöldeke, Carl Watzinger, and Ernst Sellin conducted excavations in 1909 and 1911. In 1950, a joint expedition of the American Schools of Oriental research and the Pittsburgh-Xenia Theological Seminary, directed by James L. Kelso and D. C. Baramki, conducted an extensive excavation at the two mounds, and on the other side of Wadi Qelt. In 1951, James Pritchard directed the excavation on behalf of the American Schools. He discovered buildings on the southern mound and the structure he identified as the "Gymnasium." During the years 1973–1983 excavations were carried out by the Hebrew University, Jerusalem, under the direction of Ehud Netzer.

Hasmonean Palace Complex. Built at the outlet of Wadi Qelt, on a hill overlooking the Jericho valley, the Hasmonean palace complex included a 50- × 50-m building surrounded by a moat, recently excavated, on three sides. This building was later covered by an artificial mound constructed by Herod. The palace probably had a central open court. In its southeast part, a hall decorated with stucco and frescoes was found in the excavations. Its walls are preserved to a height of 7 m, indicating that the palace was two stories high. Two small swimming pools were probably surrounded by a peristyle-shaped building also decorated with frescoes and mosaic floors. The drowning of Aristobolos III, as described by Josephus in *Antiquities* 15.53, may have occurred in one of these pools. The Hasmoneans also erected a splendid building, a pavilion similar to a Doric temple. It may have been destroyed by an earthquake, as only its foundations, columns, and architrave survive. This leisure complex had a magnificent view of the valley and Wadi Qelt. At a later period, it was extended to the south. Two "twin" palace complexes were found by Ehud Netzer, dating to the reign of Queen Alexandra (Shlomzion, 76–67 BCE). Each has a central open court surrounded by rooms, a hall, a bathhouse, and a *miqveh* ("ritual bath"). The palaces were decorated with frescoes. Each had an adjacent court with a small swimming pool. Other buildings, houses, installations, and *miqveh* complexes were built around the palaces, perhaps used by priests for purification rites. The Hasmonean palace complex was likely still standing at the outset of Herod's reign. [*See* Ritual Baths.]

Herodian Winter Palace I ("Gymnasium"). Winter Palace I, identified by Pritchard as the Gymnasium, was used for residential and ceremonial purposes. It is dated to the early years of Herod's reign, following his defeat of Mattathias Antigonus (c. 35–30 BCE). The Herodian palace, a splendid villa, was built south of Wadi Qelt. It was rectangular in plan, with a central peristyle court, a triclinium, a peristyle hall, a bathhouse, and a pair of pools that may have been ritual baths.

Winter Palace II. In 31 BCE an earthquake destroyed the Hasmonean palace complex. Herod rebuilt and extended it to include several wings. The south wing, a small building, was erected on an artificial platform above the buried Hasmonean palace. It was probably Herod's private villa. The two pools from the Hasmonean complex were retained and combined into one large swimming pool; another smaller pool was surrounded by gardens, as evidenced by archaeological finds such as flower pots and water installations. Gardens were also planted over the remains of the destroyed Hasmonean twin palaces. The eastern wing of this palace was constructed on two levels. On the upper level a peristyle court was surrounded by rooms on three sides and had a hall decorated with frescoes. The lower level consisted of two swimming pools from the Hasmonean palace inside a peristyle court. Attached to these was a bathhouse. This wing seems to have been devoted to recreation.

Winter Palace III. Herod built his enlarged palace on both sides of Wadi Qelt. It consisted of a northern wing on the north bank of the wadi, a sunken garden, a large pool, and an artificial mound with a building on the south bank. The north wing contained two triclinia and one large hall with three rows of columns open to the south to Wadi Qelt. Included in the north wing was a five-room bathhouse. This wing also possessed two peristyle courts, the western one of which had a wide semicircular apse. Several other rooms and an entrance were included in the north wing, which probably was used for leisure activities. The sunken garden had an impressive facade with a semicircular structure at its center. On both sides of this structure were twenty-four rows of niches. Two colonnades were located at either end. The orientation of the large pool west of the sunken garden differed from that of all the other structures, probably because it is parallel to the natural slope. It was used for swimming and water games. The south mound had a rectangular interior and round exterior. A bridge connected the mound with the garden.

Hippodrome Complex. The hippodrome and theater complex near Jericho was unique in the Greco-Roman world. It was uncovered at Tel el-Samarat, 600 m south of ancient Jericho. The hippodrome's rectangular course is evident, but no trace remains of its spina. The spectators presumably sat in the theaterlike structure at the northern end of the course. This structure has survived nearly intact, lacking only its benches, steps, and passages. It is built on an artificial platform. Its excavator, Ehud Netzer (1980), asserts that this hippodrome complex was used for Olympic games that could be viewed from the theaterlike structure. A building is attached to the rear of the theater, interpreted by Netzer (1992) as a guesthouse or a gymnasium.

Cemetery. The cemetery at Jericho in the Second Temple period was located outside the town, on the hills flanking the Jordan Valley. A large necropolis, with approximately fifty tombs, containing both primary burials in wooden coffins and secondary collected bone burials in ossuaries, was excavated by Rachel Hachlili on behalf of the Israel Department of Antiquities; approximately seventy-five robbed tombs were surveyed. The Jericho cemetery consists of loculi tombs only, which are hewn into the hillsides, each loculus serving as a family tomb but with provision for individual burials.

Burial Types. Two distinctly different types of loculi tomb burials, primary and secondary, were discovered during the excavations in the Jericho cemetery. They can be classified typologically, chronologically, and stratigraphically into primary burials in wooden coffins (type 1) and secondary burials of collected bones that were either placed in individual ossuaries (type 2a) or piled in heaps (type 2b).

Type 1. Primary burial in wooden coffins is the earliest type of burial in the Jericho cemetery. The coffins were placed in the rock-cut loculi tombs, each loculus usually holding one wooden coffin. The deceased were evidently brought to the cemetery inside their coffins. The coffin, once inside the tomb, its lid securely in place, was deposited in the loculus; only when all the loculi were filled would additional coffins be placed on the benches or in the pit.

Coffins took the form of a wood chest (several kinds of wood were used) with a post at each corner and a gabled roof. They were constructed by means of mortising. One well-preserved example has a hinged lid. Iron nails and knobs found with the coffins were probably used for decoration or structural support. The coffins were decorated with painted red and black geometric patterns and designs.

Manner of burial. All the bodies were extended, face upward, in the coffin, usually with the head to one side and the hands close to the side of the body. Most of the coffins contained one individual. There are, however, several instances in which one or two bodies were added to a coffin that already contained an individual.

The orientation of the bodies in the *kokh* and tomb does not seem to be significant, as the heads are pointed in various directions. The discovery of several coins inside skulls may indicate that coins were traditionally placed on the mouth of the deceased. It should be noted that the wooden coffins in Jericho were used for primary burials only and never as containers for secondary burials.

Grave goods. In most of the coffin tombs, grave goods consisting of both personal possessions and objects of daily use were found with the deceased. The articles were usually placed near the head or the feet and were found mostly with women and children.

Type 2. Secondary burial in ossuaries was initially practiced only in Jerusalem but later spread to other parts of Palestine. It is clear from the finds and stratigraphy of the ossuary burials at Jericho that they postdate coffin burials. Ossuaries were hewn from one large block of limestone, usually in the shape of a small rectangular box resting on four low legs. A stone lid—flat, slightly curved, or gabled—was placed on top. The ossuaries were often decorated and many had inscriptions recording names and family relations (Hachlili, 1978, 1979b). [*See* Ossuary.]

Manner of burial. The ossuaries were placed in the loculi or on the benches. Often, two ossuaries would be stacked one above the other or placed next to each other. The bones were placed inside the ossuary in a traditional order. Usually, the bones of a single individual were placed in the ossuary, but there are several examples of more than one individual interred.

Grave goods. No personal objects were found inside the ossuaries. However, objects identical to those used in daily life were found in the Jericho ossuary burials: unguentaria and other glass vessels, bowls, and "Herodian" lamps and cooking pots dated to the first century CE. They were usually placed close to the ossuaries or in the pit. [*See* Grave Goods.]

Burial Dating. The dates for the appearance of these burial customs are still the subject of debate. Nevertheless, the Jericho cemetery can provide a chronology for the two types of burials: primary burials in coffins can be dated from the mid-first century BCE to about 10 CE; secondary burials in ossuaries followed immediately, and are dated to about 10–68 CE. These dates are based on the coins found in the tombs, the ossuary inscriptions of Agrippina and others, the comparative stratigraphy of the tombs, as well as the pottery. L. Y. Rahmani (1986) dates the practice of secondary burials in ossuaries in Jerusalem to 30/20 BCE–70 CE, a practice that continued sporadically until about 135 CE or until the third century.

[*See also* Baths; Burial Techniques; *and* Hasmoneans. *For the site in earlier periods, see* Jericho.]

BIBLIOGRAPHY

Hachlili, Rachel. "A Jerusalem Family in Jericho." *Bulletin of the American Schools of Oriental Research,* no. 230 (1978): 45–56.

Hachlili, Rachel. "čient Burial Customs Preserved in Jericho Hills." *Biblical Archaeology Review* 5 (1979a): 28–35.

Hachlili, Rachel. "The Goliath Family in Jericho: Funerary Inscriptions from a First Century A.D. Jewish Monumental Tomb." *Bulletin of the American Schools of Oriental Research,* no. 235 (1979b): 31–66.

Hachlili, Rachel, and Patricia Smith. "The Genealogy of the Goliath Family." *Bulletin of the American Schools of Oriental Research,* no. 235 (1979c): 67–70.

Hachlili, Rachel. "A Second Temple Period Jewish Necropolis in Jericho." *Biblical Archaeologist* 42 (1980): 235–240.

Hachlili, Rachel. "The Nefes: The Jericho Column-Pyramid." *Palestine Exploration Quarterly* 113 (1981): 33–38.

Hachlili, Rachel, and Ann Killebrew. "Jewish Funerary Customs during the Second Temple Period, in the Light of the Excavations at the Jericho Necropolis." *Palestine Exploration Quarterly* 115 (1983): 109–132.

Hachlili, Rachel, and Ann Killibrew. "The Saga of the Goliath Family as Revealed in Their Newly Discovered 2,000-Year-Old Tomb." *Biblical Archaeology Review* 9 (1983): 44–53.

Hachlili, Rachel, and Ann Killibrew. "Was the Coin-on-Eye Custom a Jewish Burial Practice in the Second Temple Period?" *Biblical Archaeologist* 46 (1983): 147–153.

Hachlili, Rachel. "Jewish Funerary Wall-Painting of the First Century A.D." *Palestine Exploration Quarterly* 117 (1985): 112–127.

Hachlili, Rachel. "Jericho: The Second Temple Period Jewish Cemetery at Jericho." In *The New Encyclopedia of Archaeological Excavations in the Holy Land,* vol. 2, pp. 693–695. Jerusalem and New York, 1993.

Kelso, James L., and D. C. Baramki. *Excavations at New Testament Jericho and Khirbet en-Nitla.* Annual of the American Schools of Oriental Research, 29–30. New Haven, 1955.

Netzer, Ehud. "The Hasmonean and Herodian Winter Palaces at Jericho." *Israel Exploration Journal* 25 (1975): 89–100.

Netzer, Ehud. "The Winter Palaces of the Judean Kings at Jericho at the End of the Second Temple Period." *Bulletin of the American Schools of Oriental Research,* no. 228 (1977): 1–13.

Netzer, Ehud. "The Hippodrome That Herod Built at Jericho" (in Hebrew). *Qadmoniot* 13 (1980): 104–107.

Netzer, Ehud. "The Winter Palaces and the King's Estate in Jericho" (in Hebrew). *Jericho* (Kardom Series) 28–30 (1983): 95–112.

Netzer, Ehud. "Jericho, Tulul Abu el-'Alaiq." In *The New Encyclopedia of Archaeological Excavations in the Holy Land,* vol. 2, pp. 682–692. Jerusalem and New York, 1993.

Pritchard, James B. *The Excavation at Herodian Jericho, 1951.* Annual of the American Schools of Oriental Research, 32–33. New Haven, 1958.

Rahmani, L. Y. "Ancient Jerusalem's Funerary Customs and Tombs." *Biblical Archaeologist* 44 (1981): 171–177, 229–235; 45 (1982): 43–53, 109–119.

Rahmani, L. Y. "Some Remarks on R. Hachlili and A. Killibrew's 'Jewish Funerary Customs.'" *Palestine Exploration Quarterly* 118 (1986): 96–100.

RACHEL HACHLILI

HERODIUM (Gk., Herodion; Ar., Jebel Fureidis), a securely identified site (map reference 1729 × 1193) 5 km (3 mi.) southeast of Bethlehem and 12 km (7.2 mi.) south of Jerusalem. The site's Arabic name evidently derived from *Herodis* (i.e., "Herod's mountain"), the site's designation during the period of the Second Jewish Revolt against Rome (see below). Herod the Great constructed Herodium at some time between 24 and 15 BCE on a conical mountain whose shape Josephus compared to a woman's breast (*Antiq.* 15.324). According to Josephus, Herodium was intended to serve as a fortress, as the capital of a toparchy, and as a memorial to Herod (*Antiq.* 15.324; *War* 1.419, 3.55). Josephus also describes the procession of Herod's funeral and his burial at Herodium (*War* 1.670–673; *Antiq.* 17.196–199). During the First Jewish Revolt against Rome (67–70 CE), Herodium was occupied by Jewish rebels, one of the last three strongholds to fall to the Romans after the destruction of Jerusalem (*War* 4.518–520, 7.163). [*See* First Jewish Revolt.] Texts found in Wadi Murabbaʿat that were written during the revolt led in 132–135 by Shimʿon (Simeon) Bar Kokhba indicate that he used Herodium as a headquarters. [*See* Murabbaʿat; Bar Kokhba Revolt.]

Between the seventeenth and nineteenth centuries CE, Herodium was visited by a number of explorers, including Richard Pococke (1743), Edward Robinson (1838), Félicien de Saulcy (1863), Conrad Schick (1879), and Claude R. Conder and Horatio H. Kitchener (1881). From 1962 to 1967 Virgilio C. Corbo of the Studium Biblicum Franciscanum excavated on the top of the mountain. In 1967 and 1970 Gideon Foerster conducted conservation and restoration work on behalf of the Israel National Parks Authority. Between 1970 and 1987 Ehud Netzer of the Hebrew University of Jerusalem excavated the lower part of Herodium. [*See the biographies of Robinson, Saulcy, Schick, Conder, Kitchener, and Corbo.*]

The site of Herodium consists of a palace-fortress on the

top of the mountain and a Lower City. The palace-fortress is located inside the summit of an artificial mountain created by pouring vast quantities of earth and stone fill around the outside of a double circular wall (the diameter of the outer wall is 62 m). A round tower (18 m in diameter) was set into the double wall on the east. Three semicircular towers projected from the wall at the three other cardinal points. The double wall and towers, constructed on a series of vaults, rose several stories in height, with their tops originally protruding above the earth and stone fill. Herod's palace-fortress was built inside the double circular wall, as if set into the mouth of a volcano. A stepped, vaulted passage was cut through the fill from the base of the mountain to an entrance on the northeast side at the summit.

The circular area at the top of the mountain is divided into two symmetrical halves. The eastern half was occupied by a peristyle garden flanked by exedrae. The palatial rooms, including dwellings, service rooms, a triclinium, and a bathhouse, occupied the western half. During the period of the First Revolt, the triclinium was converted into a synagogue. In the Byzantine period (fifth–seventh centuries CE) a small monastic community occupied the summit (Foerster, 1993, pp. 619–621).

The buildings in the Lower City, or Lower Herodium, have the same axial orientation as those of the mountain and apparently were constructed as part of the same overall plan (Netzer, 1993, p. 622). A large (46 × 70 × 3 m deep) pool with a circular pavilion in the center dominated the Lower City. The pool was surrounded by a garden with porticoes along the sides. To the southeast of the pool complex was a long, narrow racecourse or track (350 × 30 m), with a large palace just above it to the north. The racecourse is too narrow to have served as a hippodrome. An elaborate structure described by Ehud Netzer, its excavator, as a "monumental building" faces directly onto the western edge of the racecourse (Netzer, 1981, pp. 35–45). It consisted of a single rectangular hall of ashlar masonry, whose bottom part was cut into the bedrock. The interior of the hall is surrounded by niches with half-columns set on pedestals between them. The thickness of the side walls indicates that there was a vaulted ceiling and perhaps also a monumental roof. Netzer considered, but rejected, the possibility that the monumental building was Herod's mausoleum; however, he believes that the latter may have been located in the vicinity and that the racecourse may have been used for Herod's funeral procession. Netzer has also noted the similarity between the interior of the monumental building and the triclinium of the Roman Soldier Tomb at Petra (Netzer, 1981, pp. 43–45; p. 135, n. 70). Post-Herodian remains at Lower Herodium include a network of tunnels (mostly at the northeastern edge of the mountain) that served as hiding places during the Bar Kokhba Revolt and three churches from the Byzantine period.

BIBLIOGRAPHY

Corbo, Virgilio. *Herodion,* vol. 1, *Gli edifici della reggia-fortezza.* Jerusalem, 1989. The Italian expedition's excavations on top of the mountain.

Foerster, Gideon. "Herodium." In *The New Encyclopedia of Archaeological Excavations in the Holy Land,* vol. 2, pp. 618–621. Jerusalem and New York, 1993. Excellent, up-to-date account of the archaeological excavations and remains on top of the mountain.

Netzer, Ehud. *Herodium: An Archaeological Guide.* Jerusalem, 1978. Slender paperback guidebook to the site.

Netzer, Ehud. *Greater Herodium.* Qedem, vol. 13. Jerusalem, 1981. The author's excavations at Lower Herodium, 1972–1978.

Netzer, Ehud. "Lower Herodium." In *The New Encyclopedia of Archaeological Excavations in the Holy Land,* vol. 2, pp. 621–626. Jerusalem and New York, 1993. Excellent, up-to-date account of the archaeological excavations and remains of Lower Herodium.

JODI MAGNESS

ḤESBAN (biblical Heshbon), Transjordanian mound rising 895 m above sea level that guards the northern edge of the rolling Madaba plains, where a southern tributary of Wadi Ḥesban begins to descend sharply toward the Jordan River, about 4 km (15 mi.) to the west (map reference 1344 × 2267). The tell is about 56 km (35 mi.) east of Jerusalem, 19 km (12 mi.) southwest of Amman, 6 km (4 mi.) northeast of Mt. Nebo, and 180 m higher than ʿAin Ḥesban, the perennial spring with which it is associated.

Werner Vyhmeister (1968) has traced Ḥesban in the work of Early Arab historians, followed by its mention in travel accounts of nineteenth- and twentieth-century Western explorers such as Ulrich Seetzen (1806), John S. Buckingham (1816), Charles L. Irby and James Mangles (1816–1817), and Edward Robinson (1838). The first archaeologists to explore the site include John Garstang (1931), Nelson Glueck (1933), and Bernhard Anderson (1963); all assumed it to be biblical Heshbon.

From 1973 to 1976, a regional survey of most of the territory within a 10-km (6 mi.) radius of Tell Ḥesban was conducted by Andrews University (Berrien Springs, Michigan). It heightened interest in the hinterland correlates of changes observed on the tell. The ruins and pottery discovered by the survey as it crisscrossed the tell's hinterland provided opportunities for comparisons between what was happening both on the tell and nearby (LaBianca, 1986, 1990).

There are altogether thirty-eight biblical references to Heshbon; its earliest history appears in *Numbers* 21:21–25 (cf. *Dt.* 2:16–37; *Jdt.* 5:15), where it is referred to as the city of the Sihon king of the Amorites. *Numbers* 21:26–31 claims that at least the southern half of Sihon's kingdom, the geographic tableland known in the Hebrew Bible as the Mishor (*Nm.* 21:30; cf. *Dt.* 2:36), had been Moabite, but that Sihon had earlier wrested it from Moabite control. Israel's claim that though Moabite territory was forbidden to them, the Mishor was an exception because it had been Amorite during the conquest is again made in *Judges* 11:12–28. The tribes of Reuben and Gad requested the territory of Sihon's kingdom for their tribal allotment (*Nm.* 32:1–5), but it was actually Reuben that built Heshbon and other nearby towns (*Nm.* 32:37), whose names were changed, according to the difficult and cryptic verse 38. *Joshua* 13:15–23 confirms the allotment of Heshbon to Reuben, though verses 24–28 indicate that it was contiguous to Gad's allotment. When Heshbon became a Levitical city it was considered a city of Gad (*Jos.* 21:34–40). *Song of Songs* 7:4 (Masoretic Text 5) says, "Your eyes are like [with the versions] pools in Heshbon, by the gate [pl. in Septuagint and Vulgate] of Bath-rabbim." Heshbon figures in both extant recensions of a prophetic oracle against Moab (*Isa.* 15:4, 16:8f; *Jer.* 48:2, 34f). By that time it may have been a steep tell, for fugitives stop in its shadow (*Jer.* 48:45). In *Jeremiah* 49:3, Heshbon appears again in an oracle against the Ammonites (it may have changed hands again). Heshbon's final biblical mention is in *Nehemiah* 9:22, where it is included in a historical allusion to the Israelite conquest.

In the postbiblical literary sources (collected by Vyhmeister, 1968), Heshbon is commonly called Esbus (though there are many variant spellings). Josephus says that in the second century BCE Tyre of the Tobiads was located "between Arabia and Judea, beyond Jordan, not far from the country of Heshbon" (*Antiq.* 12.4.11.233). Further on he lists Heshbon among the cities (perhaps the capital) of Moabitis (*Antiq.* 13.15.4.397) and among the Jewish possessions in Moab during the reign of Alexander Jannaeus (103–76/75 BCE) (*Antiq.* 13.15.4.397). Esbus is next mentioned in the late first century BCE, when Josephus includes Esbonitis among several fortresses and fortified cities that King Herod built to strengthen his kingdom (*Antiq.* 15.8.5.294). During the rule of Herod's son, Antipas (4 BCE–39 CE), his territory of Peraea was on the south "bounded by the land of Moab, on the east by Arabia, Heshbonitis, Philadelphia, and Gerasa" (*War* 3.3.3.47). Then, at the beginning of the First Jewish Revolt against Rome (66 CE) the Jews sacked Esbonitis (*War* 2.18.1.458). [*See* First Jewish Revolt.] When the Roman province of Arabia Petrea was created in 106 CE, Esbus was certainly part of it—at least it appears there in Ptolemy's *Geography* (5.17), which reflects political conditions in about 130–160.

Though Late Bronze Age sherds have been identified, six seasons of archaeological excavation at Tell Ḥesban between 1968 and 1978 failed to uncover any architectural or soil remains antedating about 1200 BCE. This poses a problem for locating biblical Sihon's Amorite capital (see above). [*See* Amorites.] Amorite Heshbon may not have been found either because it is elsewhere on the site (unlikely) or because its (seminomadic) impermanent nature left no trace to be discovered (more likely). More extreme options are to consider the biblical account unhistorical or at least anachronistic (now favored by such Hebrew Bible scholars as J. M. Miller and John Van Seters) or to seek the Amorite capital at another location—Jalul (S. H. Horn). Most at least identify Tell Ḥesban with Greco-Roman Esbus, based on coin and milestone evidence coupled with Ptolemy's geographic specifications (see above) and those in Eusebius's *Onomasticon* (84:1–6). Acceptance of Frank M. Cross's reading of (Ammonite) ostracon A.3 found at the site in 1978 would support such an identification for Iron Age Ḥeshbon as well (Cross, 1986). The preferred transliteration of the Arabic name for the tell is now Ḥisban, identified with biblical Heshbon (Heb., *hesbon;* Septuagint, Esebon).

The expedition from Andrews University is responsible for the first five of the six seasons of excavation at the site (1968–1976). Baptist Bible College in Clark Summit, Pennsylvania, continued the excavation of a Byzantine church in 1978. The university team has reconstructed nineteen superimposed strata from the excavated remains, which cover a period from about 1200 BCE to 1500 CE.

The Iron Age remains (c. 1200–500 BCE) are very fragmentary as a result of periodic removals of earlier strata on top of the hill by later builders; nevertheless, evidence for at least four strata remains. Stratum 19 (twelfth–eleventh centuries BCE) probably represents a small, unfortified village with an agrarian-pastoral economy. In its earliest phase, its most notable installation was a trench (15 m long and 3.6 m deep) crudely carved out of bedrock on the tell's southern shelf. There is no real clue as to its purpose, but suggestions include a moat for defense, storage, cultic activity, subterranean habitation, and a water channel (if not a narrow reservoir itself). In its later phase, this installation was filled in with soil and both the cobbled floor of a room and a "filler" wall 2.5 m wide were built into it. An egg-shaped cistern may also be associated with this phase, which produced so many loom weights they may represent a cottage industry. [*See* Cisterns.] Stratum 18 (tenth century) left no in situ remains; however, its typologically later pottery was found in deep dump layers outside the contemporary settlement on the western slope (it may have been a continuation of the stratum 19 village).

Stratum 17 (ninth–eighth centuries) is also represented by sloping debris layers dumped to the west, but it is better known for what may be the initial construction on the tell's southern shelf of a reservoir of almost 2 million l, 15 m to a side (its thrice-plastered eastern wall supplemented bedrock cut by a header-stretcher retaining wall) and 6 m deep. Though several channels carved out of the adjoining bedrock tunneled rainwater to the reservoir, its capacity appears to exceed the normal amount of winter rain that would fall in the catchment area; it may be that the extra water was transported up to the reservoir from below the mound. If so, this stratum may be what is left of King Mesha's attempt to fortify his northern border with Israel. (Might this be the pool referred to in *Sg.* 7:4?) Stratum 16 (seventh–sixth centuries) was the best-preserved Iron Age stratum; its remains indicate a general prosperity and continued growth, probably clustered around a fort. A few scattered domestic units came to light on the western slope, and the reservoir continued in use—perhaps as part of a way station or supply depot on the King's Highway. It was probably controlled by the Ammonites, to judge from the pottery and several ostraca found in the reservoir fill. The ostraca have added to what is presently known of the Ammonite dialect and script. Stratum 16 may have come to a violent end, considering the great quantity of ash in the debris scraped from the abandoned town into the reservoir by rebuilders (Maccabeans?) in the second century BCE.

After about a three-hundred-year absence of settled remains at the site, Tell Ḥesban was again occupied in the Late Hellenistic period. The remains from the Hellenistic and Roman periods (c. 200 BCE–365 CE) comprise at least five strata. Stratum 15 (c. 200–63 BCE) consisted primarily of a rectangular military fort at the site's summit, probably surrounded by the dwellings of dependents that were often associated with bell-shaped subterranean silos. [*See* Granaries and Silos.] In Stratum 14 (c. 63 BCE–130 CE) Esbus came under the control of Herod the Great, probably as a border fort against the Nabateans. [*See* Nabateans.] There is abundant evidence for extensive underground dwellings on the mound and characteristic Herodian-period family tombs in the cemetery (two such tombs were sealed with rolling stones). [*See* Tombs; Burial Techniques.] The stratum 14 town was destroyed by an earthquake, so that stratum 13 (130–c. 193 CE) contained much new building. A new inn with an enclosed courtyard south of the fort testifies to the increased traffic past the road junction (Via Nova Trajana and Esbus/Livias) at which Roman Esbus was located. In stratum 12 (c. 193–284 CE), the inn was partially rebuilt and saw considerable use. On the acropolis, earlier masonry was incorporated into what has been interpreted as a small temple—perhaps the one depicted on the Elagabalus coin minted for Esbus, a very fine example of which was found at the site in 1973. Access to the temple from the south was via a ramp. Stratum 11 (c. 284–365 CE) continued to demonstrate a modest level of prosperity. A porch was added to the temple and a double colonnade was built to the east of it. The inn south of the acropolis platform was demolished, and a wide monumental stairway replaced the earlier earthen ramp. The stratum came to an abrupt end with the severe earthquake of 365. Apart from the earthquake, the transition from the Roman to the Byzantine period was a gradual one. The Roman cemetery continued to be used.

At least six strata encompass the Byzantine and Early Arab remains (365–c. 1000). Two basilica-style churches were built during this period, though at the end of the period the site was apparently abandoned. [*See* Basilicas.] Although it was a village of no particular significance during the early periods of Islamic rule, after a gap in its sedentary occupation Ḥesban flourished again immediately after the Crusades. It even replaced Amman as the capital of the Belqa region of central Transjordan. [*See* Amman.] Its remains comprise at least three strata (c. 1200–1456) that were relatively well preserved compared to earlier remains. The tell was apparently deserted in the fifteenth century, but in the late nineteenth century there was a gradual return to limited occupation in the Ottoman and modern periods.

[*See also* Ammon; *and the biographies of Garstang, Glueck, and Robinson.*]

BIBLIOGRAPHY

Boraas, Roger S., and S. H. Horn. *Heshbon 1968: The First Campaign at Tell Ḥesbân, a Preliminary Report.* Andrews University Monographs, vol. 2. Berrien Springs, Mich., 1969.

Boraas, Roger S., and S. H. Horn. *Heshbon 1971: The Second Campaign at Tell Ḥesbân, a Preliminary Report.* Andrews University Monographs, vol. 6. Berrien Springs, Mich., 1973.

Boraas, Roger S., and S. H. Horn. *Heshbon 1973: The Third Campaign at Tell Ḥesbân, a Preliminary Report.* Andrews University Monographs, vol. 8. Berrien Springs, Mich., 1975.

Boraas, Roger S., and Lawrence T. Geraty. *Heshbon 1974: The Fourth Campaign at Tell Ḥesbân, a Preliminary Report.* Andrews University Monographs, vol. 9. Berrien Springs, Mich., 1976.

Boraas, Roger S., and Lawrence T. Geraty. *Heshbon 1976: The Fifth Campaign at Tell Ḥesbân, a Preliminary Report.* Andrews University Monographs, vol. 10. Berrien Springs, Mich., 1978.

Boraas, Roger S., and Lawrence T. Geraty. "The Long Life of Tell Ḥesbân, Jordan." *Archaeology* 32 (1979): 10–20.

Bullard, Reuben G. "Geological Study of the Heshbon Area." *Andrews University Seminary Studies* 10 (1972): 129–141.

Cross, Frank Moore. "An Unpublished Ammonite Ostracon from Hesban." In *The Archaeology of Jordan and Other Studies Presented to Siegfried H. Horn,* edited by Lawrence T. Geraty and Larry G. Herr, pp. 475–489. Berrien Springs, Mich., 1986.

Geraty, Lawrence T., and Leona Glidden Running, eds. *Hesban,* vol. 3, *Historical Foundations: Studies of Literary References to Heshbon and Vicinity.* Berrien Springs, Mich., 1989.

Geraty, Lawrence T., and David Merling. *Hesban after Twenty-Five Years.* Berrien Springs, Mich., 1994. Reviews the results of the excavations of the Heshbon expedition a quarter-century after its first field season; full bibliography.

Horn, S. H. "The 1968 Heshbon Expedition." *Biblical Archaeologist* 32 (1969): 26–41.

Horn, S. H. "Heshbon." In *Encyclopedia of Archaeological Excavations in the Holy Land,* vol. 2, pp. 510–514. Englewood Cliffs, N.J., 1975–.

Ibach, Robert D., Jr. *Hesban,* vol. 5, *Archaeological Survey of the Hesban Region.* Berrien Springs, Mich., 1987.

LaBianca, Øystein S., and Larry Lacelle, eds. *Hesban,* vol. 2, *Environmental Foundations: Studies of Climatical, Geological, Hydrological, and Phytological Conditions in Hesban and Vicinity.* Berrien Springs, Mich., 1986.

LaBianca, Øystein S. *Hesban,* vol. 1, *Sedentarization and Nomadization: Food System Cycles at Hesban and Vicinity in Transjordan.* Berrien Springs, Mich., 1990.

Lugenbeal, Edward N., and James A. Sauer. "Seventh-Sixth Century B.C. Pottery from Area B at Heshbon." *Andrews University Seminary Studies* 10 (1972): 21–69.

Mitchel, Larry A. *Hesban,* vol. 7, *Hellenistic and Roman Strata.* Berrien Springs, Mich., 1992.

Sauer, James A. *Heshbon Pottery 1971: A Preliminary Report on the Pottery from the 1971 Excavations at Tell Ḥesbân.* Andrews University Monographs, vol. 7. Berrien Springs, Mich., 1973.

Sauer, James A. "Area B." *Andrews University Seminary Studies* 12 (1974): 35–71.
Terian, Abraham. "Coins from the 1968 Excavations at Heshbon." *Andrews University Seminary Studies* 9 (1971): 147–160.
Vyhmeister, Werner. "The History of Heshbon from Literary Sources." *Andrews University Seminary Studies* 6 (1968): 158–177.

LAWRENCE T. GERATY

ḤESI, TELL EL-, site located on Israel's southeastern coastal plain (31°32′ N, 34°43′ E; map reference 124 × 106) 23 km (14 mi.) from the Mediterranean coast, near the borders of the Shephelah and the Negev. Situated on a cluster of sand dunes on the south bank of Naḥal Shiqmah (Wadi Ḥesi), the site consists of a 25-acre terrace with a 4-acre mound at its northeast corner. Ḥesi was occupied almost continuously from the Chalcolithic through the Hellenistic period (c. 4300–200 BCE), with a gap in occupation during the Middle Bronze Age.

The ancient identity of Ḥesi is unknown. In 1878, Claude Conder identified Ḥesi with ancient Lachish. This seemed to be supported by the discovery there in 1891 of an Amarna tablet mentioning Lachish. In 1924, William Foxwell Albright suggested that Ḥesi was not Lachish but Eglon, a Canaanite city-state conquered by the Israelites. Excavations in the 1930s at Tell ed-Duweir, however, revealed that site to be Lachish. Biblical Eglon was located in the foothills of the Shephelah, so Ḥesi, situated several kilometers west of the Shephelah, is not likely to be Eglon.

Two major excavations have taken place at Ḥesi, the first by the British Palestine Exploration Fund from 1890 to 1892. The first season's work was directed by Sir Flinders Petrie. It was at Ḥesi that Petrie first applied the principles of stratigraphic excavation and ceramic chronology that have become the essentials of modern archaeological method. Because the site's summit was under cultivation, Petrie probed into the sides of the mound and into the terrace. He was able to identify three major periods of occupation: Amorite (c. 1700 BCE), Phoenician (1350–850 BCE), and Jewish (to 450 BCE). His Amorite period can now be equated with the Early Bronze Age, the Phoenician with the Late Bronze and Iron ages, and the Jewish with the Persian and Hellenistic periods. [*See the biography of Petrie.*]

The 1891 and 1892 excavations were directed by an American, Frederick Jones Bliss. He removed the entire northeast quadrant of the mound in search of the horizontal exposure of architecture. Bliss enumerated eleven layers of architectural features and grouped them into eight "cities" that he correlated with Petrie's chronology. [*See the biography of Bliss.*]

The second excavation, the Joint Archaeological Expedition, was affiliated with the American Schools of Oriental Research and carried out eight seasons of fieldwork between 1970 and 1983. Both the mound and the terrace were found to be covered by a modern bedouin cemetery. A trench along the south slope of the mound revealed occupation from the Chalcolithic through the Hellenistic period, with a gap in the Middle Bronze Age. Excavation along the southern perimeter of the terrace revealed an Early Bronze Age occupation. Surface survey also revealed unstratified Roman period sherds and, on the east bank of the Wadi Ḥesi, remains of the Paleolithic period.

Major finds date to the Early Bronze, Iron II, and Persian periods. The Early Bronze Age city, occupying the full 25 acres of the terrace, was surrounded by a mud-brick city wall about 7 m wide, supported at the southeast corner by a crushed limestone glacis. Inside the city wall were remains of domestic and industrial activities. During the ninth century BCE, the site was confined to the mound, which was surrounded by a casemate, or double wall, system. A platform 7 m high elevated the summit to provide better defense, and a large courtyard building filled the area. These structures parallel contemporary constructions at Lachish, and at this time Ḥesi probably served as a military outpost to protect the southwestern border of Judah. A military function continued into the Persian period, when once again a large platform prepared the summit for the construction of a small citadel, which probably served as a depot and storehouse for the Persian military.

BIBLIOGRAPHY

Bennett, William J., Jr., and Jeffrey A. Blakely. *The Joint Archaeological Expedition to Tell el-Hesi*, vol. 3, *The Persian Period (Stratum V)*. Winona Lake, Ind., 1989. Final publication of finds from the Persian period and their interpretation.
Bliss, Frederick Jones. *A Mound of Many Cities, or, Tell el Hesy Excavated.* London, 1894. First publication of a Palestinian excavation to show large-scale architectural remains in stratigraphic context.
Dahlberg, Bruce T., and Kevin G. O'Connell, eds. *The Joint Archaeological Expedition to Tell el-Hesi*, vol. 4, *The Site and the Expedition.* Cambridge, Mass., 1989. Essays on the site, its environment, and the methdology of the Joint Expedition, and a summary of results of the first four seasons.
Petrie, W. M. Flinders. *Tell el Hesy (Lachish).* London, 1891. First publication of a Palestinian excavation to present architecture and pottery in a sequential manner and to correlate pottery and artifacts with stratigraphy.
Toombs, Lawrence E. *The Joint Archaeological Expedition to Tell el-Hesi*, vol. 2, *Modern Military Trenching and Muslim Cemetery in Field I, Strata I–II.* Cambridge, Mass., 1985. Thorough treatment of the most recent strata at the site, in particular, several hundred burials from a bedouin cemetery of the seventeenth century CE.
Toombs, Lawrence E. "The Joint Archaeological Expedition to Tell el-Hesi and the Results of the Earlier Excavations." *Palestine Exploration Quarterly* 122 (July–December 1990): 101–113. Correlation of the results of the Joint Expedition with those of Petrie and Bliss.

VALERIE M. FARGO

HIEROGLYPHS. Used since the Ptolemaic period (323–30 BCE) the term *hieroglyphs* is the Greek counterpart (*hieroglyphika grammata* "sacred incised letters") of the Egyptian expression *mdw.w-nṯr* "god's words" to indicate the basic writing system of the ancient Egyptian language. Because of the formal similarities with Egyptian hieroglyphs, the term has also been applied less appropriately since the nineteenth century to the writing system of Luwian, an Anatolian language related to, but not identical with, cuneiform Hittite (hence the misleading definition "Hittite hieroglyphs"). Luwian was spoken and written during the Late Bronze and Iron Ages (c. 1500–700 BCE) in southern and southwestern Anatolia and northern Syria.

Egyptian Hieroglyphs. A variable set of graphemes, Egyptian hieroglyphs range from about 1,000 in the Old Kingdom (third millennium) to approximately 750 in the classical language (early second millennium) to many thousands during the Ptolemaic and Roman rule in Egypt (third century BCE–second century CE). Hieroglyphic signs are pictograms (picture signs) that represent living beings and objects, such as gods or categories of people, animals, parts of the human or animal body, plants, astronomical entities, buildings, furniture, and vessels.

This pictographic system represents a combination of phonological and ideographic principles. A written word usually consists of a sequence of uniconsonantal, biconsonantal, or triconsonantal signs called *phonograms,* which convey a substantial portion of its phonological structure: normally all the consonants, occasionally also the semivocalic phonemes (sound units), vowels remaining for the most part unexpressed. This sequence of phonograms is usually followed by a *semagram,* called *determinative* by Egyptologists, which specifies iconically the semantic sphere of the word. For example, a sitting man 𓀀 expresses the lexical sphere of man, mankind; a sitting man touching his mouth 𓀁 denotes the realms of eating, feeling, thinking, sensing; a scribe's equipment 𓏞 indicates the semantic realm of writing; the stylized map of a settlement 𓊖 identifies the word as a toponym. Although some words of common use (such as pronouns, prepositions, a few lexical items such as *rn* "name" or *ḏd* "to say") are written only phonologically, that is, with the combination of consonantal signs indicating <r> + <n> or <ḏ> + <d> respectively, many items of the basic vocabulary of Egyptian are expressed only by semagrams, which directly represent, evoke through rebuses, or metonymically symbolize their own semantic reference. These are called *logograms* (often improperly termed *ideograms* by Egyptologists): for example, the hieroglyph representing the enclosure of a house (𓉐) means "house" (phonologically **pār*), or the sign representing a human head (𓁶) means "head" (phonologically **tap*). In order to distinguish the logographic ("HOUSE" = /pār/ = "house") from the purely phonological use of the same sign ("HOUSE" = /p (+ optional vowel) + r/, independent of the lexical sphere of the word in which it appears), logographic uses are often marked by a vertical stroke following the sign.

TABLE 1. *Egyptian Monoconsonantal Signs*

Sign	Transliteration	Object Depicted
𓄿	*ꜣ*	Egyptian vulture
𓇋	*j*	flowering reed
(1) 𓇌, (2) 𓏭	*y*	(1) two reed-flowers (2) oblique strokes
𓂝	*ʿ*	forearm
𓅱	*w*	quail chick
𓃀	*b*	foot
𓊪	*p*	stool
𓆑	*f*	horned viper
𓅓	*m*	owl
𓈖	*n*	water
𓂋	*r*	mouth
𓉔	*h*	reed shelter in fields
𓎛	*ḥ*	wick of twisted flax
𓐍	*ḫ*	placenta(?)
𓄡	*ẖ*	animal's belly with teats
(1) 𓊃, (2) 𓋴	*s*	(1) bolt (2) folded cloth
𓈙	*š*	pool
𓈎	*q*	hill-slope
𓎡	*k*	basket with handle
𓎼	*g*	stand for jar
𓏏	*t*	loaf
𓍿	*ṯ*	tethering rope
𓂧	*d*	hand
𓆓	*ḏ*	snake

Egyptian writing also displays a set of twenty-four "alphabetic," that is, uniconsonantal signs. Although these covered almost completely the inventory of consonantal and semiconsonantal phonemes of the Egyptian language (the only exception being the phoneme /*l*/, for which an autonomous sign appears only in Demotic), this set of signs never developed into a genuine alphabet, but always remained embedded in the original complex system of word signs and sound signs. This situation shows that the development of the alphabetic writing is not, as often assumed, the result of a predictable evolution from a nonalphabetic system, but rather that there is a very different "philosophy of writing" underlying the two graphic models. With the final breakthrough of the Hellenistic cultural Koine and eventually the emergence of Christianity in Egypt (second–third century CE), when a changed cultural and religious setting suggested the adoption of an alphabetic system, the hieroglyphic system was completely superseded by the Coptic writing, an alphabet written from left to right and derived from that of Greek, with the addition of six or seven Demotic signs for the indication of phonemes absent from Greek: ϣ = /š/, ϥ = /f/, ϧ (in some dialects ⳉ) = /χ/, ϩ = /h/, ϫ = /c/, ϭ = /kʲ/, ϯ= /ti/.

Table 1 shows the set of Egyptian "alphabetic" signs (from Gardiner, 1957, p. 27).

Some examples of biliteral and triliteral signs are as follows:

jr	*bꜣ*	*ḥꜣ*
wr	*wʿ*	*ḫʿ*
nfr	*ʿnḫ*	*ḥtp*

The signs below illustrate semagrams, used either as determinatives (i.e., following a sequence of phonograms) or as logograms (i.e., indicating both the phonological structure and the semantic value of the word they represent or evoke).

man, person	star	*pr* house
woman	fire, heat, cook	*jrt* eye
people	air, wind, sail	

Alan H. Gardiner (1957, p. 25) provides a very accessible specimen of how the Egyptian hieroglyphic system worked (figure 1). Numbers indicate the sequence of the individual signs. Phonograms are indicated in *italic,* logograms in SMALL CAPITALS, and semagrams also in SMALL CAPITALS and "quotation marks"; Supplements necessary to complete the grammatical structure of the corresponding words are added in parentheses.

Unlike most other systems of pictographic origin, such as Mesopotamian cuneiform or Chinese ideograms, Egyptian hieroglyphs kept their original iconic structure throughout their entire history without progressively developing stylized forms. Quite on the contrary, the increasing consciousness of the symbolic potential inherent in the relation between the signs used to write words and the semantic meaning of the words themselves led to the development of new, previously unknown phonological associations and also of so-called cryptographic solutions in Ptolemaic Egyptian. For example, the two signs and were used in the classical system only to indicate the phonemes /m/ (or the sequence /g [+vowel] + s/) and /f/ respectively; in Ptolemaic Egyptian, they are creatively combined to represent the two verbs *ʿq* "to enter" (with the *f*-snake "entering" the *m*-sign) and *prj* "to exit" (with the snake "coming out" of the sign):

ʿq "to enter" *prj* "to exit"

On the one hand, this evolution threatened the accessibility of the system and eventually favored its purely aesthetic, rather than linguistic use; on the other hand, it expanded the meaning of the individual hieroglyphs and made the system more perfect as a pictorial-linguistic form. It is exactly this radical change in the nature of the writing system in the Greco-Roman periods that is at the origin of the view held in the Western world since Late Antiquity until the emergence of modern Egyptology (and still surviving to the present day in some aspects of popular culture) of the "symbolic," rather than functional character of the hieroglyphic writing. One needs only to think of the decorative use of Egyptian hieroglyphs during the Renaissance and the Neoclassical period in Europe.

The hieroglyphic system was used mainly for monumental purposes, more rarely (in a cursive form) for religious texts in the Middle and the New Kingdoms (c. 2000–1070). During their history, however, hieroglyphs developed two cursive varieties: Hieratic (2600–third century CE), which represents a direct rendering in the scribes handwriting (with ligatures and diacritic signs) of a sequence of hieroglyphic signs; and Demotic (seventh century BCE–fifth century CE), which radically modifies the writing conventions by introducing a shorthandlike simplification of hieratic sign-groups. (For samples of Hieratic and Demotic writing followed by their hieroglyphic transcription, see Gardiner, 1957, pl. 2.)

The basic orientation of the Egyptian writing system—and the only one used in the cursive varieties—is from right to left, with signs facing the right; in epigraphic, that is, monumental texts, this order may be inverted for reasons of symmetry or artistic composition. In the monumental text of the Middle Kingdom (King Sesostris I, c. 1971–1928) shown in

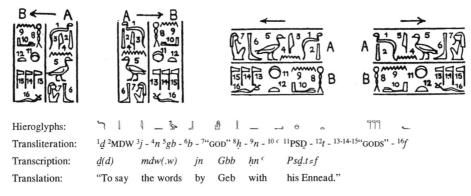

Hieroglyphs:	
Transliteration:	[1]*ḏ* [2]MDW [3]*j* - [4]*n* [5]*gb* - [6]*b* - [7]"GOD" [8]*ḥ* - [9]*n* - [10]*ʿ* [11]PSḎ - [12]*t* - [13-14-15]"GODS" - [16]*f*
Transcription:	*ḏ(d)* *mdw(.w)* *jn* *Gbb* *ḥnʿ* *Psḏ.t=f*
Translation:	"To say the words by Geb with his Ennead."

HIEROGLYPHS. Figure 1. *Example of hieroglyphic writing.* The same sentence is shown in four different arrangements, the arrows showing the direction in which the sentence is to be read. Note that the human and animal figures face toward the beginning of the text. (Griffith Institute, Ashmolean Museum, Oxford)

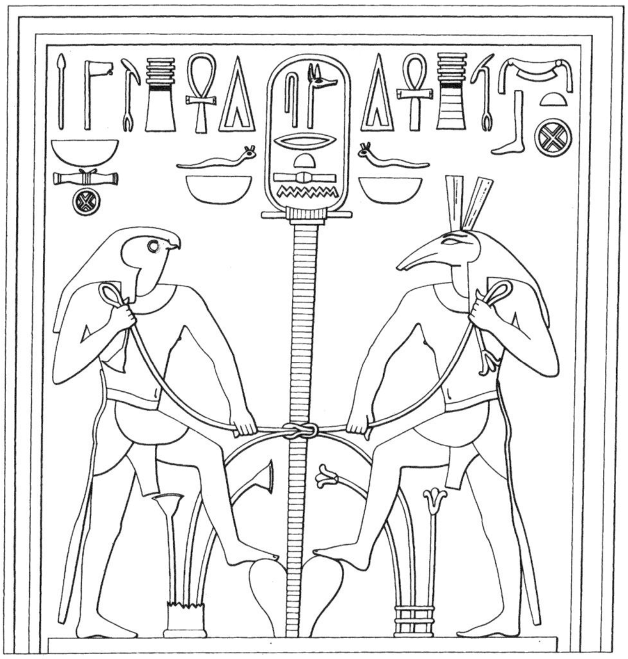

HIEROGLYPHS. Figure 2. *Monumental text from King Sesostris I.* Middle Kingdom. (After B. J. Kemp. *Ancient Egypt: Anatomy of a Civilization,* London-New York, 1989, p. 28)

figure 2, the hieroglyphic sign in the middle, pictographically representing a lung with windpipe, phonologically a triconsonantal sequence /z + m + 3/, semantically a verb with the meaning "to unite," is being tied together with papyrus and lotus, the heraldic plants of Upper and Lower Egypt, by the two gods Horus and Seth. The cartouche in the center encircles the king's name *z(j)-n(j) wsrt*. The inscription on the left side is read from right to left and refers to the god Horus *nṯr ʿ3 nb msn dj.f ʿnḫ ḏd w3s nb* "the great god, lord of Mesen, may he give every life, stability, and power," whereas the one on the right side is read from left to right and refers to the god Seth *nbwt(j) dj.f ʿnḫ ḏd w3s nb* "the Ombite, may he give every life, stability and power" (from B. J. Kemp, *Ancient Egypt: Anatomy of a Civilization,* London and New York, 1989, p. 28). Beginning with the Middle Kingdom Egyptian developed a particular use of hieroglyphic sign-groups to express words of foreign languages, mostly of northwest Semitic origin. This procedure, commonly known as "syllabic orthography," allowed the rendering of sequences of Semitic syllables (consonants and vowels) by combining Egyptian signs in a conventional groups. More specifically, Egyptian weak consonants (such as *'aleph*) semiconsonantal signs (such as *yod* and *waw*) were used to express vowels, in a procedure similar to the *matres lectionis* in Northwest Semitic. Although the general trends of Egyptian syllabic orthography are well understood, disagreements remain as concerns the exact vocalic values to be attributed to specific sign-groups.

The most decisive contribution to the decipherment of the hieroglyphs was achieved around 1822–1824 by the French Orientalist Jean-François Champollion. On the basis of the writing of Greek royal names in the so-called Rosetta Stone, a trilingual (hieroglyphic, Demotic, and Greek) document from the Ptolemaic period discovered in 1799 in the Egyptian town of Rosetta (in Arabic, al-Rashid) during Napoleon's expedition to Egypt, Champollion was able to establish the nature of the system. He thereby broke away from the traditional symbolic approach that had prevailed in the West since the knowledge of this writing was lost during the first centuries CE. [*See the biography of Champollion.*]

Hittite Hieroglyphs. Between 1500 and 700 BCE, Luwian, an Indo-European language of the Anatolian group related to Hittite, was written in a logographic script, traditionally called *hieroglyphic* because of its formal resemblance to the Egyptian writing system. During the first part of this timespan, that is, between 1500 and 1200, hieroglyphic Luwian was sporadically used in the Hittite Empire, especially on seals. From 1200 to 700, it was the language of monumental inscriptions in all the Neo-Hittite kingdoms in southeast Anatolia and northern Syria.

The structure of Luwian hieroglyphs is completely different from the Egyptian counterpart, to which it probably bears no historical connections. Rather, its ancestors have to be sought within the Aegean world and the Cretan Linear A writing. The Luwian hieroglyphic system is a syllabary consisting of pictorial signs, which, unlike Egyptian hieroglyphs, from their earlier to their later stages show a progressive loss of their original iconic content (see figure 3) to become stylized signs mostly indicating a syllable consisting of a sequence "consonant + vowel" or, in very rare cases, a sequence of phonemes derived through rebus writing from the original pictorial value of the sign. The direction of writ-

a b

HIEROGLYPHS. Figure 3. *Specimens of (a) earlier and (b) later Luwian hieroglyphic writing.* (After Gelb, 1963, pp. 82–64)

ing changes from line to line. Although monuments with Hittite hieroglyphs were known since 1870, their decipherment was significantly favored by the discovery in 1947 of the Phoenician-Luwian bilingual inscription from Karatepe in Cilicia, dating from the eighth century. [*See* Karatepe Phoenician Inscriptions.]

[*See also* Egyptian; *and* Luwians.]

BIBLIOGRAPHY

Gardiner, Alan H. *Egyptian Grammar: Being an Introduction to the Study of Hieroglyphs.* 3d ed. Oxford, 1957. Still the basic handbook for the study of the Egyptian language and writing system.

Gelb, Ignace J. *A Study of Writing.* 2d ed. Chicago and London, 1963. The most authoritative, though idiosyncratic, work on the origin and development of writing systems throughout the world.

Hawkins, J. D., et al. *Hittite Hieroglyphs and Luwian: New Evidence for the Connection.* Nachrichten der Akademie der Wissenschaften in Göttingen, Philologische-Historische Klasse, no. 6. Göttingen, 1974.

The Hieroglyphics of Horapollo. Translated and introduced by George Boas. Bollingen Series, 23. New York, 1950. An ancient compendium of bogus hieroglyphs with fantastic explanations that led to the symbolic interpretation. The introduction is a superb and succinct summary.

Hoch, James E. *Semitic Words in Egyptian Texts of the New Kingdom and Third Intermediate Period.* Princeton, 1994. Monumental analysis of the evidence for the writing of foreign words in Egyptian, with particular attention devoted to syllabic orthography.

Iverson, Erik. *The Myth of Egypt and Its Hieroglyphs in European Tradition.* Copenhagen, 1961. Study of the symbolic interpretation of hieroglyphs from late antiquity through the nineteenth century and their impact on European civilization.

Lacau, Pierre. *Sur le système hiéroglyphique.* Cairo, 1954. Typological study of the nature and structure of the Egyptian writing system.

Laroche, Emmanuel. *Les hiéroglyphes hittites,* part 1, *L'écriture.* Paris, 1960. The first complete study of Luwian hieroglyphic inscriptions.

Meriggi, Piero. *Manuale di eteogeroglifico.* 3 vols. Incunabula Graeca, vols. 13–15. Rome, 1966–1975. Thorough handbook for the study of Luwian hieroglyphs.

Valeurs phonétiques des signes hiéroglyphiques d'époque gréco-romaine. 3 vols. Montpellier, 1988–1990. The product of many years of research by an international team, this work is the necessary companion for the reading of the complex hieroglyphic signs of the Greco-Roman period.

Antonio Loprieno

HILPRECHT, HERMANN VOLLRAT (1859–1925)

HILPRECHT, HERMANN VOLLRAT (1859–1925), Assyriologist. Born in Hohenerxleben in Anhalt, Germany, Hilprecht was professor of Assyrian (1886–1902) and later Clark Research Professor of Assyriology (1902–1911) at the University of Pennsylvania. He was a member of the first expedition to Nippur (1888–1889) and scientific director of the fourth expedition (1889–1900), there. Hilprecht is perhaps best known as a major figure in American Assyriology in the nineteenth century, having set high standards for the publication of cuneiform texts. He apparently laid out plans for the publication of the results of the Babylonian expedition in four series—a total of twenty volumes. Hilprecht was general editor of series A (cuneiform texts), which he inaugurated by publishing *Old Babylonian Inscriptions Chiefly from Nippur* in 1893.

In 1905–1908, Hilprecht was embroiled in a bitter dispute with John P. Peters that eventually involved not only everyone connected with the Nippur excavations, but a good number of scholars in the discipline. Peters sparked the dispute when he alleged that Hilprecht had exaggerated his claims to having found a temple library during the fourth campaign of excavations in 1900 and had misrepresented purchased tablets as excavated artifacts and falsified the findspots of others. There was also the question of who owned certain artifacts the Ottoman sultan had given to Hilprecht.

In 1893, while in Constantinople working on the Nippur finds, Hilprecht was asked to reorganize the Imperial Ottoman Museum. In recognition of his efforts, over a period of many years, the sultan presented him with a large number of tablets and other artifacts excavated at Nippur or purchased while the expedition was in Mesopotamia. Hilprecht maintained that the artifacts were his personal property but gave the bulk to the museum. He did, however, keep some very important pieces. His critics argued that the sultan's "gift" was a legal fiction and suggested that the finds really belonged to the University of Pennsylvania Museum (the excavations' sponsoring institution).

The university's trustees appointed a committee to act as a court of inquiry in the so-called Peters-Hilprecht controversy. In its report, the committee found the charges unsustainable and untrue, but the controversy did not end. A subsequent controversy arising over Hilprecht's publication of a Sumerian cuneiform tablet fragment that he claimed confirmed the biblical Flood story eventually led to his resignation in 1911.

Hilprecht maintained a residence in Jena, from 1899 to 1905. His first wife, Ida Haufe, died there in 1902. In 1903 he married Sallie Crozer Robinson, a Philadelphia socialite. Following his resignation from the University of Pennsylvania, Hilprecht went to Germany, where he remained during World War I. He returned to the United States after the war. He died in Philadelphia, leaving most of the antiquities and small finds from the Nippur excavations to the University of Jena. He ceded a nearly complete *kudurru* and two copper goats' heads, acquired at Abu Ḥabbah (Fara), to the University of Pennsylvania Museum as the Sallie Crozer Hilprecht Collection.

[*See also* Babylon; Nippur; *and the biography of Peters.*]

BIBLIOGRAPHY

For biographical details, see George A. Barton's article in *Dictionary of American Biography,* vol. 9, pp. 58–59 (New York, 1932), as well as the obituaries published in the *Philadelphia Public Ledger* and the *New York Times,* 20 March 1925; *Journal of Biblical Literature* 45 (1926): iii–iv; and *Zeitschrift für Assyriologie* 36 (1925): 309–310. For Hilprecht's bibliography, see Rykle Borger, *Handbuch der Keilschriftliteratur,* vol. 1, pp. 190–194 (Berlin, 1967), and Ferdinand Hestermann, "Die Bibliographie Hilprechts über Nippur," *Wissenschaftliche Zeitschrift der Friedrich-Schiller-Universität Jena* 4 (1954–1955): 35–47. For further reading, see the following:

Hilprecht, Hermann V. *Die Ausgrabungen der Universität von Pennsylvania im Bel-Tempel zu Nippur*. Leipzig, 1903.

Hilprecht, Hermann V. *Explorations in Bible Lands during the Nineteenth Century*. Philadelphia, 1903. See pages 289–568.

Hilprecht, Hermann V. *The So-Called Peters-Hilprecht Controversy*. Philadelphia, 1908.

Hilprecht, Hermann V. *The Earliest Version of the Babylonian Deluge Story and the Temple Library of Nippur*. Philadelphia, 1910. For the reaction covered even in the public press, see, for example, the *Philadelphia Press*, 6 June 1910.

Oelsner, Joachim. "Zur Geschichte der Frau Professor Hilprecht-Sammlung Vorderasiatischer Altertümer im Eigentum der Friedrich-Schiller-Universität Jena." In *Zur Geschichte der klassischen Archäologie Jena-Krakow*, edited by Ernst Kluwe and Joachim Sliwa, pp. 46–53. Jena, 1985. See, for example, the newspaper account of Hilprecht's will in the *Philadelphia Record*, 6 April 1925.

Ritterband, Paul, and Harold Wechsler. "A Message to Lushtamar: The Hilprecht Controversy and Semitic Scholarship in America." *History of Higher Education Annual* 1 (1981): 5–41.

RICHARD L. ZETTLER

ḤIMYAR, region located in the southern highlands of modern Yemen. In antiquity Ḥimyar was the land of the Homeritae (Homerites), or Hameroi, of classical authors. The last and largest of the indigenous South Arabian kingdoms, it may have been founded in 115 BCE, the approximate starting point for the Ḥimyarite dating system. Otherwise, the earliest firmly datable references to Ḥimyar are found in classical sources. Aelius Gallus observed in 24 BCE, via Pliny (*Nat. Hist.* 6.32.161), that the Homeritae were the area's most numerous tribe. During the mid-first century CE, the author of the *Periplus of the Erythrean Sea* (23) mentioned Charibael, king of the Homerites and Sabaites, reigning at Ẓafar, who was in diplomatic contact with Rome. The kingdom lasted until shortly before the arrival of Islam. The language of the Ḥimyarites is known primarily from highly formalized monumental and dedicatory inscriptions that employed standard South Arabic based on the Sabaean dialect and used the consonantal South Arabic alphabet of twenty-nine characters.

By the beginning of the common era the older South Arabian kingdoms (Maʿin, Saba'/Sheba, Qataban, and Ḥadhramaut) were in decline, and population and political power were shifting to the highlands. The highlands required new agricultural techniques that emphasized terracing and using local rainfall runoff. New kingdoms arose, among the earliest and foremost of which was Ḥimyar, with its capital at Ẓafar. [*See* Sheba; Qataban; Ḥadhramaut; Ẓafar.]

The next two and a half centuries were marked by a complex rivalry between the kings of Ḥimyar and other highland dynasties, a process only sketchily documented by surviving inscriptions. The Ḥimyarites at times managed to take and hold the ancient Sabaean capital of Marib, a principal prize in these contests, while on other occasions Ẓafar itself was overrun and occupied. By the early fourth century CE, the Ḥimyarites had largely defeated their highland rivals, the older eastern kingdoms were extinct, and Ḥimyarite control extended from Ḥadhramaut to Najran and included bedouin tribes from the adjacent deserts. [*See* Marib; Najran.]

Inscriptions and other historical sources for Ḥimyar are sparse for the fourth and fifth centuries, consisting primarily of a few dedicatory inscriptions mentioning building projects and occasional military campaigns. The reign of Abu-Karib Asad, a particularly long-lived king of the late fourth and early fifth centuries, may have marked the apogee of Ḥimyar. Later Arab traditions credit him with conquests as far afield as India and China. Late Ḥimyar is usually characterized as increasingly feudal, though there is little evidence for its social and governmental organization.

Behind-the-scenes serious sectarian rivalries must have been developing. South Arabia's indigenous religion had primarily been astral, with ʿAthtar, a male god associated with the planet Venus, worshipped under various epithets in the Ḥimyarite heartland. By the mid-fourth century, however, paganism was in decline. When the missionary ambassador Theophilus Indus, sent by the emperor Constantius II, arrived in about 350, he found Jews already present at the Ḥimyarite court. He reportedly converted the king to Christianity and built churches at Ẓafar and Aden. Dedicatory inscriptions referring to pagan deities disappeared shortly thereafter, to be replaced with monotheistic formulae that might be Christian, Jewish, or of an indigenous monotheism. The royal house ultimately converted to Judaism. [*See* Aden.]

Systematic excavation is needed to detail cultural developments in South Arabia during the Ḥimyarite period. Material from Ẓafar, Marib, al-Huqqa, Sanʿa, and objects in the National Museum in Sanʿa demonstrate that the region was in close contact with the cosmopolitan world of the Mediterranean basin and the Near East in the early centuries of the common era. The museum's collection displays a rich variety of fluted columns, acanthus capitals, and reliefs with vine scrolls, winged Victories, griffins, sphinxes, and various other motifs of the orientalized Hellenism of Late Antiquity. [*See* Sanʿa.]

By the early sixth century, Christian and Jewish rivalries had led to open conflict, marked by occasional Ethiopian intervention on behalf of Ḥimyarite Christians, perhaps at Byzantine instigation. The details are lurid though sketchy. The king, Yusuf Asar Yathar, the *dhu nuwas* ("lord of curls") of later traditions, determined to purge his kingdom of Christians, massacring Christian communities at Ẓafar and Najran. These events brought on a massive Ethiopian invasion that resulted in the defeat and death of Yusuf and the installation of an Ethiopian viceroy named Abraha. [*See* Ethiopia.] The Ethiopians were later expelled with the aid of Sasanian Persia. When emissaries of the Prophet Muhammad came to South Arabia in 628, they found a Persian governor in San'a. He adopted the new faith. Yemen, as the region would thereafter be known, was the first area outside the Hijaz to submit to Islam.

[*See also* Yemen.]

BIBLIOGRAPHY

Beeston, A. F. L. "The Religions of Pre-Islamic Yemen." In *L'Arabie du Sud: Histoire et civilisation,* vol. 1, *Le peuple yéménite et ses racines,* by Joseph Chelhod et al., pp. 259–269. Islam d'Hier et d'Aujourd'hui, vol. 21. Paris, 1984.

Casson, Lionel, ed. and trans. *The "Periplus Maris Erythraei": Text with Introduction, Translation, and Commentary.* Princeton, 1989.

Corpus des inscriptions et antiquités sud-arabes, vol. 2, *Bibliographie générale systematique.* Louvain, 1977. Excellent bibliography for pre-Islamic South Arabia through 1975.

Müller, W. W. "Survey of the History of the Arabian Peninsula from the First Century A.D. to the Rise of Islam." In *Studies in the History of Arabia,* vol. 2, *Pre-Islamic Arabia,* pp. 125–131. Riyadh, 1984.

Shahīd, Irfan. *The Martyrs of Najrân: New Documents.* Subsidia Hagiographica, no. 49. Brussels, 1971.

Wissmann, Hermann von. "Ḥimyar, Ancient History." *Le Muséon* 77 (1964): 429–497.

RAYMOND D. TINDEL

HIPPOS. *See* Decapolis.

HISTORICAL ARCHAEOLOGY. In contrast to prehistoric archaeology, which deals with periods when there were no written records, historical archaeology is both the archaeology of historical periods and a methodology in which archaeological materials are discussed in the context of a theoretical framework determined by the study of written documents. In the latter sense, historical archaeology is to be contrasted not with prehistoric archaeology but with, for example, anthropological archaeology. In anthropological archaeology, anthropological theory rather than historical studies provides the matrix within which both excavated archaeological materials and historical documents are understood.

Much Near Eastern archaeology was traditionally "historical," in the second of the two ways described above. This was the result of a keen and persistent interest in exploring archaeology's potential to shed new light on the study of the Bible and other ancient texts. Even where there were no explicit points of contact between materials recovered from an excavation and written records, the excavated materials were frequently interpreted within categories defined by the study of historical documents. Elsewhere, however, other methods of interpretation are the norm. For instance, archaeology in the Americas (New World archaeology) is notable for its study of cultures that achieved a high level of complexity but for the most part without leaving written records.

The invention of alphabetic writing in the Near East, and the creation of the Bible and the many other pieces of literature that are central to Western civilization, account for the fact that archaeologists working in the Near East have very often been critical students of the ancient literature as well as archaeologists. This has made for a lively and critical intersection of textual and archaeological studies.

However, some attempts to use archaeological information to shed new light on historical or textual problems have met with a surprising lack of success. For example, when brought to bear on the historical problem of settlement narratives in *Joshua* and *Judges,* the archaeological data apparently conflict irreconcilably with the textual evidence at major points. The relationship between textual evidence on the one hand and artifactual data on the other turned out to be more problematic than many had hoped.

Written Records and Excavated Material. In the early 1960s many archaeologists, especially those specializing in American, or New World, archaeology but also including European scholars, began to advocate a split between archaeology and historical studies. The conceptual framework of historical studies, they felt, simply did not fit the materials they were trying to interpret. One of their concerns was the very different nature of excavated materials and of written documents. For one thing, most written documents handed down from ancient times were produced, transmitted, and preserved by a relatively narrow spectrum of society, a literary elite, reflecting its biases and interests. Archaeological evidence, being essentially refuse, is more democratic in its origins.

Another concern was dating. Historical documents contain a mixture of evidence: some of this evidence no doubt dates to the time of the subject matter, but some dates to the time of writing, which could be much later, especially where there is an oral tradition behind the written texts. Information can also be inferred from a corpus of historical documents because only a tiny minority of documents has been passed down. Much has been lost, but what has been preserved also bears the stamp of selective community interests that chose to preserve some documents and not others.

A deeper concern shared by those scholars was the absence of a meaningful theoretical context within which to interpret their excavated finds. Their data, if properly approached, could be used to articulate models of ancient cultures that addressed political and economic dimensions of human activity. However, the conceptual vocabulary available to them from historical studies was geared to the written word and historical epochs, not to material artifacts and stratigraphic phases. Generations of historians had created and refined theories about various aspects of human history, but those theories were based on evidence fundamentally different from the kind of data archaeologists study. Many archaeologists began to believe that they had to replace historical models with theoretical models based on archaeological data and the conceptual associations native to those data.

Related to this theoretical concern was a practical concern about the destruction of evidence. Once excavated, the archaeological site in its original form is lost. The materials chosen for preservation and the observations recorded are limited by the excavator's interests and training and by the field and laboratory technology available. Subsequent archaeologists, with other interests or training, or better tools, can never go back to an excavated site to study it in its pristine state. It is the essentially destructive character of the discipline that exacerbated the need for a theoretical framework to guide excavation activity.

Text-Assisted Archaeology. If modern archaeology is understood as a discipline in its own right, then historical archaeology is to be thought of as archaeology in which textual data are available for further study and analysis. The primary source of data for archaeologists, whether they deal with historic or prehistoric periods, is excavated artifacts, their spatial relationship both locally and regionally, and the physical environment in which they are found. Artifacts include both manufactured items and naturally occurring ones, such as shells or other remains of human foods, that have been used or acted on by humans. These data form the basis of a theoretical framework within which questions can be posed. To the extent that information contained in written documents can be determined to derive from a human group that also produced excavatable artifacts, the documentary information may be thought of as an "intellectual artifact" of that group. As such, it contributes along with the other data, to an understanding of the group. Other features of this kind of archaeology follow here.

Material-cultural framework. One virtue of historical archaeology as formerly understood was that, superficially at least, it provided a chronological framework within which it was easy to orient a discussion of excavated materials. However, this historical framework has already largely been displaced in scholarly archaeological discussions by the ceramic chronology of the region in which the excavations take place. Decades of careful stratigraphic excavation have established sequences of pottery types from the initial appearance of ceramic technology in the Neolithic period through medieval times. The ubiquitousness of potsherds makes it possible to establish relationships among the finds associated with them—not only within sites but also between sites. Using strict stratigraphic controls on the materials they excavate, modern archaeologists are in the process of establishing a material-cultural-analytical framework that is independent of historical documents.

Systems approach. Establishing a chronological framework largely independent of historical documents allows the development of a series of archaeological "pictures" of ancient times that complement the "story" told by historical documents. In general, the archaeological pictures will show more about the everyday life of people of all ranks than say anything particular about the great events or individuals usually featured in the historical record. These pictures derive from analysis of the people and of their physical environment. Archaeologists see humans, their cultural institutions, and their physical environment as interacting parts of a systemic whole. This "ecological" focus helps balance the urban and elite emphases of written records with an understanding of the rural environment that was the economic backbone of preindustrial societies.

Explanations for cultural change. In general, explanations for cultural change that were based on interpretations of historical documents saw change as driven by events. In contrast, consonant with an approach to understanding human experience in terms of systems, archaeological explanations for change focus on adaptation. Human institutions and behavioral patterns adapt in response to ecological factors (gradual desalinization of soils or variations in the extremity of topography in a region), internal systemic factors (evolution of social institutions and technologies), and interactions with other human groups across regions and over time. Furthermore, these factors interact with one another in unexpected ways to produce further change: when systems change, gradually or very suddenly, the explanation is sought in the complex interactions of a range of factors, some internal, some environmental.

Looking to the Future. Archaeology is well along the way toward becoming a scientific discipline with an agenda independent of, though still in communication with, historical studies per se. It will contribute to what is understood of the human experience in its ecological context in ways that, in many respects, have little to do with insights gained from the traditional kinds of study of historical documents. Archaeologists are developing increasingly sophisticated models of human society that include political, economic, and religious dimensions. In doing so, the value of artifact-based models will increase as objective and independent sources of information that can be more meaningfully integrated with text-based models of human societies.

[*See also* Biblical Archaeology.]

BIBLIOGRAPHY

Adams, Robert McC. *Heartland of Cities.* Chicago, 1981. Pioneering work in regional surveying, analysis of human societies as adapting systems in an environmental context, and intersection of textual studies with archaeological findings (for the historical periods).

Albright, William Foxwell. "The Impact of Archaeology on Biblical Research." In *New Directions in Biblical Archaeology,* edited by David

Noel Freedman and Jonas C. Greenfield, pp. 1–16. Garden City, N.Y., 1969.
Binford, Lewis R. "Archaeological Systematics and the Study of Culture Process." *American Antiquity* 29 (1965): 203–210. Binford was the leading American advocate of archaeology as a scientific discipline based on theory formulation, hypothesis generation, and hypothesis testing.
Clarke, David L. *Analytical Archaeology*. 2d ed. New York, 1978. The first chapter contains one of the strongest arguments for archaeology as a discipline distinct from traditional historical studies.
Flannery, Kent V. "Culture History v. Cultural Process: A Debate in American Anthropology." *Scientific American* 217.2 (1967): 119–122. Concise review of the debate on why human societies as studied by archaeologists change as they do.
Flannery, Kent V. "The Cultural Evolution of Civilizations." *Annual Review of Ecology and Systematics* 3 (1972): 399–426. Landmark depiction of human societies as adapting systems.
Gottwald, Norman K. *The Tribes of Yahweh: A Sociology of the Religion of Liberated Israel, 1250–1050 B.C.E.* Maryknoll, N.Y., 1979. Provocative and pioneering use of sociological theory as a consistent framework within which to interpret both textual and artifactual data.
Kohl, Philip L. "Materialist Approaches in Prehistory." *Annual Review of Anthropology* 10 (1981): 89–118. Concise review of the theoretical underpinnings of studies of artifactual data.
Peebles, Christopher S., and Susan M. Kus. "Some Archaeological Correlates of Ranked Societies." *American Antiquity* 42 (1977): 421–448. Frequently cited example of using theory (the "Fried-Service" model of ranked societies) to generate hypotheses testable through excavation.
Renfrew, Colin, and Paul Bahn. *Archaeology: Theories, Methods, and Practice.* New York, 1991. Thorough and very readable overview of modern archaeology worldwide.

David W. Jamieson-Drake

HISTORICAL GEOGRAPHY. Multidisciplinary in nature, historical geography is a comprehensive examination of a region's ecosystems, cultures, and artifactual remains. It depends on teams of scholars and bodies of data compiled and analyzed to determine the factors in settlement patterns, the environmental impact of human activity, and the cultural developments that grow out of natural resources, trade routes, and diffusion patterns.

For example, the manner in which the ancient cultures of Mesopotamia and Egypt developed was based in large part on the activities, both beneficial and devastating, of their river systems and on the presence or absence of natural barriers to invaders. Thus, cyclic invasions by new peoples characterize Mesopotamia throughout its history because it lacked the desert and sea barriers that effectively protected Egypt. The divergence in the cultures of these two cradles of civilization can also be traced to the regularity of the Nile River's flow and flooding and to the intermittent, catastrophic flooding of the Tigris-Euphrates river valley.

More specifically, historical geography has been an important approach in the analysis of the cities of the Mesopotamian alluvial plain. Examination of that region's basic topography suggests that the growth, and often the physical survival, of cities was based on their ability to channel watercourses into irrigation systems, to keep those canals free of the heavy load of river sediment, and to respond to the increasing salinization of farm land. [*See* Irrigation.] Trade and warfare also followed river systems, contributing to shifts in political control. For instance, cuneiform texts from the Old Babylonian period (1800–1700 BCE) describe revenues derived from river tolls and cities captured by troops traveling down the river.

History of the Field. The historical geography of the ancient Near East has been a topic of interest since Christian pilgrims visited the region and noted its sites, rivers, and major landmarks in their diaries. The Byzantine (sixth century CE) Madaba map provides clues to the routes these pilgrims followed and the sites of major religious centers. [*See* Madaba.] With the advent of the nineteenth century, perhaps heralded by Napoleon's scientific expedition to Egypt (1798–1799), travel and the need for accurate maps and site reports once again became of great importance. Among the most helpful of the travel accounts produced during this period are those of the American explorer Edward Robinson (1838, 1853). [*See the biography of Robinson.*] His maps and compilation of geographic data laid the foundation for modern historical and scientific geography, the practical aspects of map making and information gathering, and later, more systematic surveys, such as that produced for the Palestine Exploration Fund/Society (1870–1876), the efforts of Nelson Glueck (*Explorations in Eastern Palestine*) from 1935 to 1949, and a recent survey of Jordanian sites (J. M. Miller et al., *Archaeological Survey of the Kerak Plateau,* 1991.) [*See* Palestine Exploration Fund; *and the biography of Glueck.*]

The enterprises of historical geography in the Near East from the nineteenth century to the present have included the identification of biblical sites through survey, excavation, and the examination of modern Arab place names. Among the pioneers in this effort was George Adam Smith, whose *Historical Geography of the Holy Land* (1894) is still a valuable primary source for modern scholars. [*See the biography of Smith.*] W. F. Albright and G. Ernest Wright also contributed to the discipline through their philological studies of Arab place-name traditions, their development of modern field-school techniques for analyzing artifactual remains, and their regional approach to ceramic chronology. [*See the biographies of Albright and Wright.*]

Among the first truly scientific treatments of the geography of the regions of the Near East was that of Denis Baly (*Geography of the Bible,* 1957), which served as a model of data collection for climate, topography, and geology. Also of importance were the efforts of Yohanan Aharoni (*The Land of the Bible,* 1979) and Michael Avi-Yonah (*The Holy Land,* 1966). They not only gathered a wealth of data, but also trained a generation of scholars in the tools of historical geography and created a model for scientific atlases of the Near East: *The Macmillan Bible Atlas* (3d ed., 1992).

The legacy of these and many other scholars has been the expansion of what is understood of the geographic features of the lands of the Near East. This, in turn, has markedly increased interest in the relationship between the environment and human activity that shaped the cultural development of the peoples in the region.

Approaches to Historical Geography. It is tempting to take a deterministic attitude regarding historical geography. Environmental conditions can too easily be cited as the primary or even sole factor in cultural development. Certainly the basic character of any geographic location will affect the nature of culture and the directions it takes. However, it is short-sighted to assume that humans will not place their own peculiar mark on an area. Factors other than environment influence cultural forms.

The study of historical geography in the Near East is complex because of the region's numerous ecosystems: deserts, savannahs, steppes, wetlands, marshes, and swamps. The topography includes floodplains, plateau regions, hill country, and mountainous areas. The availability of water and arable farmland have been the prime elements in the establishment of permanent human settlements. This does not discount the pastoral nomadic groups that have ranged over it, but their cultural mark is less visible than that made by village and urban dwellers. [*See* Pastoral Nomadism.]

Because of the wide range of topographic features, it seems best to take, as the ancients did, a regional approach to the problems of Near Eastern historical geography. They understood that the interaction between an area and its adjacent regions was responsible for the initiation of all types of economic activity (agriculture, pastoralism, industry). [*See* Agriculture.] The ancients thought beyond their immediate, local concerns, establishing communication and economic links. [*See* Roads; Seafaring; Transportation.]

Just as pastoralists had to know the physical characteristics of the areas in which they grazed their herds, the leaders of ancient city states needed to obtain information that would allow them to target effectively particular locales to be exploited through trade and military conquest. In this way, and at the speed allowed by the terrain and the determination of the exploiters, cultural diffusion occurred and new ways of dealing with environmental conditions were introduced. The many Mesopotamian royal annals that describe a king's "march to the sea" and the Gilgamesh epic, in which the hero conquers the monster Humbaba and captures the resources of the cedar forest, demonstrate how widespread this determination was. A multidisciplinary approach involving many subdisciplines is necessary to study this process and these phenomena.

Topographic analysis. Fieldwork, mapping, and aerial photography are necessary in analyzing the natural resources of any geographic area. [*See* Photography.] A topographic analysis can point to the origin of settlements, the opportunities for economic exploitation, and the likelihood of contact with other regions. Analysis also utilizes records of important natural resources—minerals, timber, arable land, and water. The availability of water, in terms of average annual rainfall, water-table levels and accessibility, as well as streams, lakes, and rivers, must be traced. Fossil sources, such as the dry riverbeds in the Sinai and Negev deserts and on the southern Arabian Peninsula, enable researchers to speculate on the possible demographics in prehistory and in antiquity in regions often no longer inhabited.

Contiguous regional analysis. No locale in the Near East is so isolated that it has been without outside influences. Thus, the historical geographer must treat each area both specifically and as part of a region. In so doing, ancient routes of travel (on land and sea) must be traced with an eye to locating commercial centers and areas of intense agricultural and industrial activity. Additionally, the movements of empires as they absorb wide areas must be taken into account, especially in regard to cultural diffusion—such as the introduction of new architectural styles and technologies (e.g., the use of iron).

Disparate regional analysis. Comparative studies can be made between settlement patterns in the Near East and in other parts of the world. For instance, it is informative to compare Near Eastern architectural styles, strategies for dealing with dry farming, and the harnessing of water for power and irrigation purposes with those in Greece or Italy. These noncontiguous regions had an impact on the material culture of the Near East in the Hellenistic period, but studies comparing settlement strategies can be useful even when areas have not directly or historically, influenced one another. One example is the comparison that can be made between the transhumant pastorals of Spain (as described by F. Braudel, *The Mediterranean and the Mediterranean World in the Age of Philip II,* New York, 1972) and those of the ancient Near East.

Cartographic analysis. With the introduction of satellite imagery, Geographic Information System (GIS) databases, and computer programming and modeling, a truly regional approach to historical geography is possible. These tools allow for a finer analysis of the interrelationship of natural resources and human settlement patterns than was previously possible. Using mathematical models and infrared photography, the extent of topographic change that has occurred over time can be determined, thereby facilitating the identification of ancient sites. [*See* Computer Mapping; Computer Recording, Analysis, and Interpretation.]

Settlement and demographic analysis. Once a settlement area has been identified, the researcher can use the region's basic geographic features (terrain, natural defenses, water sources) to estimate the size of the population and the extent of the land used for cultivation, mining, or grazing in antiquity. [*See* Paleoenvironmental Reconstruction.] The remains of architectural forms can also be examined, keeping in mind that building styles might have been influenced by aesthetic or functional concerns. For instance, specific forms of Roman architecture (baths and theaters) are identifiable in vastly different geographic settings (from Damascus to sites in England and France) but generally exhibit regional variation. [*See* Baths; Theaters.] Climatic or topographic factors are often the basis for design and construction, but the use of structures for religious or political purposes may also dictate size and the inclusion of forms with a symbolic rather than practical origin.

Sociocultural analysis. Ingenuity and resourcefulness were often the key to the success of a settlement, especially in an environmentally marginal area. Irrigation techniques and the terracing of hillsides to provide additional farmland are reflections of local inventions based on geographic features. In addition, the degree of borrowed cultural ideas (clothing styles, religious practices, architectural styles) and the appearance and variety of trade goods may also testify to the economic ties with other regions and/or the political control extended over wide areas by ancient empires. The creation of social mechanisms to help shape behavior and cultural expression (hospitality customs, taboos, marriage customs) can often be found in written or artifactual evidence.

Diachronic and synchronic analysis. Effective geographic research is not possible unless it is a dual approach that attempts to determine the interaction of human activities within defined periods of time and between periods. Multigenerational projects, such as the temple complexes at Karnak in Egypt, as well as the revival of cultural ideas in later eras make for useful comparisons.

Onomastic analysis. Beginning with the early fourth-century Christian historian and theologian Eusebius, onomostics, as a subdiscipline of historical geography, has involved the attempt to establish a link between site names and the archaeological evidence uncovered in excavations. In Israel, for example, many ancient Hebrew names, such as *Beth-Shemesh,* were preserved in their Arabic and/or modern names—in this case, as ʿAin Shems. Sometimes a text excavated at a site helps with identification, as has been the case at Gezer, Lachish, and Dan. [*See* Gezer; Lachish; Dan.] However, because many city names, such as *Migdal* (Heb., "tower") or *Hazor* (Heb., "enclosure"), can apply to several sites, the name cannot always be utilized as a sole identifying factor. The danger of a site identification becoming prematurely "canonized" through scholarly consensus can distort subsequent research.

Archival research. In addition to relics and artifacts, ancient economic and administrative (government) records may contain crop-yield figures, tax rolls, census data, military conscriptment figures, construction projects, and climactic and geological information (see the mention of the earthquake in *Am.* 1:1), which are invaluable in helping to date or describe particular cultural periods.

Archaeological fieldwork. No geographic analysis is complete without the excavation and analysis of material culture: architecture (domestic and monumental), sacred sites (e.g., temples, sacred groves, high places), agricultural and pastoral installations (e.g., sheepfolds and camp sites), and industrial sites (mines, factories, refineries). These remains of former activity can be used to provide a broad picture of regional and local cultural expression. While specialization is necessary, given the huge amount of information in any one field, it is necessary for the geographer either to work with archaeologists or conduct his or her own surveys and excavations. [*See* Survey, Archaeological.]

Using a variety of disciplines to examine and analyze the historical geography of any area or time period, the researcher must then become familiar with the region to be studied and establish a plan of action. The broad perspective of a multidisciplinary, regional approach helps avoid distortions that can arise if an area is regarded as unique. It also makes tracing cultural and economic development through time much more reliable. Spatial as well as physical approaches to the diverse aspects of settlement locales and types will also give a fuller picture of ecological and cultural interrelationships.

BIBLIOGRAPHY

Aharoni, Yohanan. *The Land of the Bible: A Historical Geography.* Translated and edited by Anson F. Rainey. 2d ed. Philadelphia, 1979.

Albright, William Foxwell. *The Archaeology of Palestine.* Harmondsworth, 1949.

Avi-Yonah, Michael. *The Holy Land from the Persian to the Arab Conquests, 536 B.C.–A.D. 640: A Historical Geography.* Grand Rapids, Mich., 1966.

Avi-Yonah, Michael. *Gazetteer of Roman Palestine.* Qedem, vol. 5. Jerusalem, 1976.

Baly, Denis. *Geographical Companion to the Bible.* New York, 1963.

Baly, Denis. *The Geography of the Bible.* Rev. ed. New York, 1974.

Ben-Arieh, Yehoshua. *The Rediscovery of the Holy Land in the Nineteenth Century.* Jerusalem, 1979.

Carter, Charles E. "The Province of Yehud in the Post-Exilic Period: Soundings in Site Distribution and Demography." In *Second Temple Studies 2: Temple and Community in the Persian Period,* edited by Tamara C. Eskenazi and Kent H. Richards, pp. 106–145. Sheffield, 1994.

Eusebius. *Das Onomastikon der biblischen Ortsnamen.* Edited by Erich Klostermann. Leipzig, 1904.

Finkelstein, Israel. *The Archaeology of the Period of Settlement and Judges* (in Hebrew). Tel Aviv, 1986.

Glueck, Nelson. *Explorations in Eastern Palestine.* 4 vols. Annual of the American Schools of Oriental Research, 14, 15, 18/19, 25/28. New Haven, 1934–1951.

Glueck, Nelson. *The Other Side of the Jordan* (1940). Rev. ed. Cambridge, Mass., 1970.

Har-El, Menashe. *The Sinai Journeys.* Rev. ed. Los Angeles, 1983.

Kallai, Zecharia. *Historical Geography of the Bible.* Leiden, 1986.

Rowton, M. B. "The Role of the Watercourses in the Growth of Mesopotamian Civilization." In *Lišān mīṯḫurti: Festschrift Wolfram*

Freiherr von Soden, edited by Wolfgang Röllig, pp. 307–316. Alter Orient und Altes Testament, vol. 1. Berlin, 1969.

Rubin, Rehav. "Historical Geography of Eretz-Israel: Survey of the Ancient Period." In *The Land That Became Israel: Studies in Historical Geography,* edited by Ruth Kark, pp. 23–36. New Haven, 1990.

Smith, George Adam. *Historical Geography of the Holy Land.* London, 1896.

VICTOR H. MATTHEWS

HISTORIOGRAPHY. [*This entry provides a consideration of major historiographers and chronographers, including such factors as how they wrote history and what data was available to them. It is chronologically divided into two articles:* Historiography of the Hellenistic and Roman Periods *and* Historiography of the Byzantine and Islamic Periods.]

Historiography of the Hellenistic and Roman Periods

Starting with Ephorus of Cyme (405–330 BCE), and Theopompus (b. 378 BCE), Greek historians emancipated themselves from the kind of monographic writing done by Thucydides, Androtion, and Philochorus. The greatest historian of the third century BCE in the Greek West was Timaeus of Tauromenium (355–260 BCE), who wrote thirty-eight books on the history of Greece and Italy down to 264 BCE (the beginning of the First Punic War), of which we have only fragments preserved through later historians.

In the second century BCE, Polybius wrote a universal history of the inhabited world. His main theme was the phenomenon of Roman expansion in the Mediterranean. Polybius wrote a pragmatic history—a history from which, he believed, people would learn lessons in the future. His is a rationalistic writing of history that stresses cause and effect in the historical process. Polybius believed that only universal histories should be written, and that there is a certain force (Gk., *tyche*) directing the destinies of peoples. Polybius had an enormous influence on later historiography (from *2 Macc.* through Josephus to Zosimus), and his twelfth book, in which he analyzes the methods of writing history, is required reading for every historian. His history in forty books covers the period 222–146 BCE.

His successor in Greece was Posidonius of Apamea (first century BCE), who wrote a history in Greek that continues from where Polybius ends (146 BCE), through the first century BCE. Unfortunately, only fragments are preserved. However, because many later historians used Posidonius extensively, we know what his work was like.

Alongside these great historians who wrote world histories, there were, in the Greek West (including Magna Graecia), historians who composed local histories, some of which may be considered "tragic" histories. For instance, at the beginning of the third century BCE, Duris of Samos wrote a Samian chronicle (probably two volumes) alongside his *Histories* (in twenty-three volumes), and a history of Agathocles; in that same century, Phylarcus wrote a history of the world, parts of which dealt with Sparta. We also know of local histories that can be considered more as mythography, such as the *Aetoliaca, Thessaliaca,* and *Messeniaca.*

In the final three centuries of the last millennium BCE, we find, in the Hellenistic East, historians of Alexander the Great and his successors. Among those writing were Nearchus of Crete, Aristobulus, Ptolemy I, Hieronymus of Cardia, and, later, those, who created the "vulgate" of Alexander's history—people like Callisthenes. There were also many historians who in Greek wrote local histories of certain peoples *(ethnē),* such as Dius, Menander of Ephesus, and Laetus (all Phoenician histories); Manetho and Hecataeus of Abdera (Egyptian histories); Megasthenes (history of India); Apollodorus (Parthian history); and Eupolemus the son of John (Israelite history). Most of these histories are concerned with the nations' mythological and remote past. In the second century BCE, a Jew wrote a history (in Hebrew) of the Maccabean revolt and its aftermath (*1 Macc.*), and somewhat later a Jew in the Diaspora, Jason of Cyrene, wrote a history of the Maccabees in five volumes. This history was epitomized and is the form in which we have it now (*2 Macc.*). Even a world history was written in the first century BCE by Nicolaus of Damascus, a pagan who was friend and adviser to Herod the Great. This history is only partially preserved through later historians, however. There is no history of the ancient Near East available that includes a general, comprehensive report of the region in the Hellenistic period.

During that period (third–first century BCE) Italy also produced important historians, some of whose writings are only known through citations in the annalistic tradition and through fragments in works composed in the Greek West. These historians include Philinus of Acragas (a pro-Carthaginian who wrote about the First Punic War) and, in the third century BCE, Fabius Pictor, who composed in Greek a history of Rome from its foundation through the Second Punic War. In the Greek language there were also the histories of Cincius Alimentus, Postumius Albinus, and Gaius Acilius. In 123 BCE, the *annales maximi* were published in Rome, and they marked an important stage in the formation of the annalistic historiogaphic tradition in that city. Gnaeus Gellius, Valerius Antias, and Claudius Quadrigarius followed this line, which Livy and Tacitus pursued later. In about 100 BCE, Rome became an important center for various forms and styles of historiography. Rutilius Rufus and Aemilius Scaurus wrote autobiographies, and Sulla left his *hypomnemata* ("memoirs"), all of which are now lost. At about the same time, Nepos (100–25 BCE) wrote biographies in Latin, while Caesar wrote the *De Bello Gallico* and the *De Bello Civili.* Sallustius (86–35 BCE) composed several works of importance in Latin. His *War of Juqurtha* is considered a fine specimen of the historiography of this age. It was at that time that Cicero was defining what Roman historiography should be.

At the end of the first century BCE, during the principate of Augustus, a number of great historians were active, only a few of whom can be mentioned here: Dionysius of Halicarnassus, whose *Roman Antiquities* began appearing in 7 BCE, wrote, in Greek, a history of Rome from its beginnings to the First Punic War. Only the first ten books survive; they are very important for those interested in the recycling of history during the early principate. Livy (59 BCE–17 CE) wrote his vast book *Ab Urbe Condita Libri* in 142 books, of which only parts survive. Livy wrote in Latin, in line with the annalistic tradition (proceeding according to years). He is one of our most important sources for the Hellenistic Near East because he mainly used Polybius's work for Eastern matters. Thus, in books 21–45 we are given considerable information about the third and second centuries in the East, information that would otherwise have been lost with much of Polybius's work. Somewhat earlier (60–30 BCE), under Caesar and Augustus, Diodorus Siculus wrote the *Bibliotheke,* a universal history from the creation through his own time (54 BCE), in forty books. This history attempted to combine the mythologies and histories of the whole universe in a single book. Diodorus's work (in Greek) is important inasmuch as he used a great many sources, most of which are no longer available to us (such as Ctesias, Hecataeus of Abdera, Dionysius Scytobrachion, Matris of Thebes, Posidonius, and Hieronymus of Cardia). Yet, like most historians of antiquity, he does not always say when he uses which source.

During the Augustan era, Pompeius Trogus wrote the *Historiae Philippicae,* an important and comprehensive history in forty-four books that is now lost. L. Cornelius, Vibius Maximus, and others followed suit, but their works are no longer available. We know about the nature of Trogus's work from Justinus, who used it extensively in the third century CE while writing his epitome. In the Augustan era, one of the greatest geographers of antiquity composed a *Geography;* this was Strabo of Amaseia, who wrote in Greek, describing the various regions of the empire and beyond. His geography is an indispensible source for historians because of the rich historical information he included. Strabo had access to many sources, most of which are not available to us today (such as Erathosthenes and Posidonius).

In the first century CE, Curtius Rufus wrote a history of Alexander the Great in Latin, and Valerius Maximus wrote a history (preserved only in two later epitomes). Velleius Paterculus wrote his *Historiae Romanae* during this time, an important source, particularly for the reigns of Augustus and Tiberius. In the middle of the century, Pliny the Elder wrote some important, now lost, works of history (*Bella Germaniae* and *A fine Aufidi Bassi,* for example). The end of the first century CE and the beginning of the second witnessed two great Latin historians, Suetonius and Tacitus. Suetonius wrote biographies of the emperors from Julius Caesar to Domitian, and Tacitus wrote some of the most significant works dealing with the history of the first century CE, the *Annals* and the *Histories.*

At the same time, there was impressive historiographic activity in the ancient Near East concerning the events in Palestine. We know that Justus of Tiberias probably wrote a history of the Jews from Moses to Agrippa II. Of the extant works, the most important are the histories of Josephus. He wrote his *Jewish War* (seven books) in the seventies of the first century CE; later, in the nineties, while in Rome, he completed his *Antiquities* (twenty books), the *Contra Apionem* (two books), and the *Vita* (his autobiography). Josephus was a prolific historian whose books, because they are preserved, are a unique phenomenon in ancient historiography. Although he deals mainly with Jewish history, he preserves much information about the surrounding world. At the time, the evangelists were writing the histories of Jesus and his followers in Greek. Their compositions appear in the historiographic part of the New Testament (*Matthew* through *John,* and the *Book of Acts,* written by Luke).

Between 50 and 120 CE, in Greece, there lived one of the greatest intellectuals of the period, Plutarch. In addition to his philosophical works, he wrote biographies of past heroes, Greek and Roman. He is one of our main sources for the zeitgeist in Greece in the first century CE. Plutarch wrote moralizing biographies in Greek, such as those of Solon, Tiberius Gracchus, and T. Q. Flamininus.

In the second and third centuries CE, Appian and Cassius Dio composed their important histories. The beginnings of Christian "historiography" are to be found in the writings of Clement of Alexandria.

In the second century CE, while Lucian of Samosata was writing a book called *How to Write History* (on the historians of the Parthian War), Arrian was a student of the philosopher Epictetus, which influenced his various books. His famous work, the *Anabasis,* a history of Alexander the Great, was based in particular on the histories of Alexander by Ptolemy I (king of Egypt), Aristobulus, and the Vulgate. He also wrote a *Parthica* (now lost), as well as a history of Alexander the Great's successors, based on Hieronymus of Cardia. Only fragments are preserved of the latter work. Arrian also wrote an *Indica,* taken mainly from Megasthenes and Nearchus. Appian of Alexandria wrote his *Romaika* under Antoninus Pius; it describes Roman conquests arranged according to the regions of the Roman Empire. The work, written in Greek, is dependent on some imperial annalistic tradition but also relies extensively on older historians, such as Polybius, Sallust, Livy, and Nicolaus of Damascus.

Early in the third century CE, Herodian wrote biographies of the emperors Marcus Aurelius through Gordian III (180–238 CE). Dio Cassius, another great historian, wrote some important works in the first quarter of the third century, including his Roman history from the beginning to 229 CE. Only parts of this history (written in Greek) are preserved; other parts were epitomized in the Byzantine era by Xiphilinus and Zonaras. Dio Cassius's history is based on the republican annalistic tradition (Livy or his sources) and the imperial annalistic tradition, as well as on his own experiences as a politician—he was governor of Cilicia and Dalmatia as well as a praetor and *consul suffectus*). In the third century, Sextus Julius Africanus wrote his *Chronographies* in five books, attempting a synchronization of Jewish, Christian, and pagan histories from the creation to 221 CE. This work was an important source for Eusebius's *Chronicle*.

Eusebius wrote his *Ecclesiastical History* at the end of the third century and the beginning of the fourth century. It is the first church history combining biblical and pagan history alongside much else. Eusebius's history (in ten volumes) focuses on the history of the church, its apostolic succession, and its victory over heresies, Judaism, and paganism up to Eusebius's own time. Somewhat later in that century, Ammianus Marcelinus, in Latin, wrote his thirty-one books on the history of the years 96–378 CE (the extant narrative begins with the year 353). In that century we also find the epitomators, who made summaries of history, historians such as Eutropius, Justin, and Aurelius Victor.

BIBLIOGRAPHY

Aune, David E. *The New Testament in Its Literary Environment*. Philadelphia, 1987.

Fornara, Charles W. *The Nature of History in Ancient Greece and Rome*. Berkeley, 1983.

Meister, Klaus. *Die griechische Geschichtsschreibung*. Stuttgart, 1990.

Momigliano, Arnaldo. *Studies in Historiography*. London, 1966.

Villalba i Varneda, Pere. *The Historical Method of Flavius Josephus*. Leiden, 1986.

DORON MENDELS

Historiography of the Byzantine and Islamic Periods

Byzantine and Islamic historiography describe overlapping but not identical parts of the world, chronological spans, and dating systems. Several forms of Byzantine histories exist, whereas early Islamic historiography tended to be religious and legal in inspiration. The structures and stylistic rules for Byzantine secular history (Lat., *historia*) imitate pre-Byzantine—that is, classical Greek—historical models for history and rhetoric. This borrowing included style and vocabulary, or those of Greek historical writing within the Roman Empire—not those from Latin classical or medieval historiography or Islamic historiography. Although Byzantine historiography exhibited versatility and adaptability, it had no great innovators. Audiences tended to be well-educated elites, probably from the imperial and ecclesiastical administration, who were able to read and appreciate histories as literature in a venerable tradition. Some historians were mere compilers.

Byzantine secular historians often strove to produce new narratives of approximately contemporary events or reigns. Although their objective was the truth, many failed to give attention to sophisticated or profound historical explanation; to be precise in their use of numbers and geography; to consider chronology, rather than concentrate on individuals, moral issues, and teaching truths; and to identify or engage in source criticism or exercise critical judgment, as had the best earlier Greek historians. The critical acumen of a Procopius or a Niketas Choniates was exceptional. Political and military subjects prevail, together with an emphasis on rulers and elites, not on economic and social subjects. Encomiastic historiography existed because honest criticism and self-criticism were difficult to include in an unveiled fashion if it involved criticism or embarrassment of a reigning dynasty or dominant groups. Gradually, traditional conservative forms of history adjusted, by the end of the sixth and the beginning of the seventh centuries, to include Christian subject matter, frameworks of interpretation and explanation, and terminology, even though this process of adjustment took place long after the conversion of the vast majority to Christianity. Waning interest in topographic and geographic details contributed to a shrinking of horizons, which often became Constantinopleocentric. Many tended to relate foreign peoples to the schema and typing of earlier historical models and *topoi* (literary commonplaces). Among the best historians are Procopius, Michael Psellos, Michael Attaleiates, and Niketas Choniates. One distinguished, although admittedly biased (in favor of her father, Emperor Alexius I), woman historian is Anna Comnena (Komnenos).

Ecclesiastical historians restricted their subject matter in a broad sense to the history of the church and its doctrinal controversies, from the perspective of the established (i.e., usually Nicene and Chalcedonian) orthodoxies, churches, and related imperial and local topics of a political and dynastic kind. They normally selected and interpreted events to demonstrate their conjunction with established religious creeds and hierarchies and seldom investigated ethnic, social, or economic dimensions. Their audience was primarily, but not exclusively, ecclesiastical.

Another historical form is the universal or world chronicle (Gk., *chronikon, chronographia*), an annalistic narration commencing with the creation of the world and terminating with the chronicler's lifetime. Chroniclers were not necessarily monks. Chronicles often are more precise about dates and local events than secular histories and may provide insight into ordinary language and concerns. Some later narrative histories are entitled chronicles. Saints' lives preserved another highly selective part of the past, especially for the edification of monastic audiences.

Controversy surrounds the fate of Byzantine historiography in the course of the seventh century. This break in classicizing historical writing after the 630s may be the result of a contraction in the numbers of the literary elite who could serve as a sophisticated audience: education and funding had collapsed and there was a lack of great victories to celebrate. A difficult subject for the Byzantine historians was the explanation of the Islamic conquest of the Holy Land, Egypt, Syria, and North Africa; hence, they usually tended to avoid it. Local provincial schools of historiography did not survive the end of antiquity. Historical writing reappeared in the late eighth century and persisted, in a more or less continuous sequence of narrative histories, to the fifteenth.

Islamic historiography developed from pre-Islamic oral history traditions, both of *akhbār* (plural, or *khabar,* singular), that is, a piece of information or reports or accounts about events) and early Islamic ones (of *ḥadīth,* "conversation or narrative," especially of the prophetic tradition, on religious doctrine and juridical subjects). *Ta'rīkh* originally meant assigning a date; hence, it first designated chronological narratives, but it came to mean any account of the past—that is, a history. Criticism of the *isnād,* or "tradition of transmission of authorities," developed into an elaborate form; however, the authenticity of apparently impressive *isnād* can neither be assumed nor easily ascertained. Materials ascribed to particular collectors of traditions do not display ideological uniformity or any homogeneous historical view. Islamic historians had their own criteria for ascertaining the creditworthiness of traditions, according to the reliability of the transmitter; this was not in itself wholly dissimilar from early criticism within Hellenic historiography, but it was not explicitly used by Byzantine historians.

The form, structure, and norms of Islamic historiography, which also started and reached its culmination later, differed from the Byzantine, as did their genesis. Arabic historical writing sifted and transmitted oral traditions concerning the genealogies and the prophet Muhammad. Early scholarly-religious histories often reflected a schema of the Islamic religious community. They were usually composed by those trained in Islamic jurisprudence who sought to make doctrinally correct statements reflecting the outlook of the mosque and religious school *(madrasah).*

Another form of later Islamic historiography, the court history, sought to glorify a ruler, or his dynasty, or to make and prove general statements about wisdom in statecraft. To an extent this genre drew on earlier Persian and even occasionally on Byzantine and Christian Oriental (especially Syriac) historical traditions, but in a limited fashion, and especially for models of writing court histories of reigns and dynasties. Collections of biographies (including scholarly, religious, tribal, and local ones), organized by classes *(ṭabaqāt),* are other important historiographic form.

Yet, for some subjects, such as the Islamic conquests, Byzantine and Islamic traditions are not completely divergent. At some early date, and to an extent that still cannot be fully determined, Oriental Christian chroniclers and historians preserved and transmitted information about the Islamic conquest that reappears in different forms in both Byzantine and Islamic historiography. The Islamic conquest's exposition may be confused by contamination with later issues such as land taxation and legal titles. Probably exaggerated was the nineteenth- and early twentieth-century critique of Islamic historians as divided into schools with competing self-serving interpretations and traditions (e.g., Syrian and Iraqi), with its excessive dependence on traditions of biblical scholarship and criticism. Islamic historians' critical sense also differed from that of the Byzantine historians, for unlike that of the Byzantines, it involved, as in the case of tradition about their religion, the criticism of the chain of transmission of traditions.

The process of recording, compiling, and editing Muslim historiography; collecting narratives; and selecting the most creditworthy flowered in the eighth and ninth centuries and matured by the late ninth and tenth centuries. Investigation of this process has not yet achieved a modern scholarly consensus. Presumably, independent traditions often possess common elements. Modern scholars disagree whether the entire corpus of early traditions should be rejected as hopelessly corrupt and fabricated, or whether there is an underlying truth behind some of the traditions—and if so, the proper methodology for achieving a sound critical evaluation. A majority probably agree that something of value survives but disagree concerning techniques for determining that genuine core. Islamic historiography's best specimens include al-Balādhurī (d. 892), al-Ṭabarī (from Tabaristan, d. 1058), al-Yaʿqūbī (d. 897), and other historians after the beginning of the tenth century. However, such later historians as the Egyptian al-Maqrīzī (d. 1447) and the Maghrebi Ibn Khaldūn (d. 1406) are of high quality. Local historians such as the Damascene Ibn ʿAsākir (d. 1176), Ibn al-ʿAdīm (b. Aleppo, d. Cairo, 1262), and al-Azdī (fl. early ninth century in Cairo and Jerusalem) composed another important form of Muslim historiography; the form started in the ninth century but developed more intensively after the eleventh century. Islamic historiography's second major burst of productivity and qualitative creativity in the later medieval era (thirteenth–early fifteenth centuries) culminated in the historical analyses and reflections of Ibn Khaldūn in his introduction to his history.

Archaeological objects and sites are seldom subjects of interest for Byzantine and Islamic historians, and archaeological proofs are not normally used to support Byzantine or Islamic historical reasoning. Archaeology can serve as an important (but not exclusive) control on both Islamic and Byzantine historiography, however. Actual measurements can enable modern researchers to check the veracity of historical reports about architecture, distances, and topography (subject to adjustment for alteration by erosion, and sedimentation during the passage of time). Study of toponymics, terminology, and materials consistent with archaeology and epigraphy can add or diminish the credibility of specific historians' accounts, be they Byzantine or Islamic, for some of these may simply be using *topoi* or literary/rhetorical embellishment. The methodologies and limitations in such investigations are still being developed and require sensitivity.

BIBLIOGRAPHY

Cameron, Averil, and Lawrence I. Conrad, eds. *The Byzantine and Early Islamic Near East,* vol. 1, *Problems in the Literary Source Material.* Princeton, 1992. Important collection of essays on aspects of Byzantine and Islamic historiography.

Corpus fontium historiae byzantinae. Berlin, 1967–. New critical editions and translations of Byzantine historical texts by an international group of scholars.

Donner, Fred McGraw. *The Early Islamic Conquests.* Princeton, 1981. Fundamental discussion of difficulties in interpreting Early Islamic historiography.

Duri, ʿAbd al-ʿAziz. *The Rise of Historical Writing among the Arabs.* Translated by Lawrence I. Conrad. Princeton, 1983. Important essay by a leading Arab historian.

Humphreys, R. Stephen. *Islamic History: A Framework for Inquiry.* Princeton, 1991. The standard introduction to problems of Islamic history and historiography.

Hunger, Herbert. *Die hochsprachliche profane Literatur der Byzantiner,* vol. 1, *Philosophie, Rhetorik, Epistolographie, Geschichtsschreibung, Geographie,* pp. 243–504. Munich, 1978. The basic study of Byzantine high-style literature, including histories.

Kaegi, Walter E. *Byzantium and the Decline of Rome.* Princeton, 1968. Study of fifth-century Byzantine historiography.

Kaegi, Walter E. *Byzantium and the Early Islamic Conquests.* Cambridge, 1992. Interpretation of Byzantine and Islamic historiography on the early conquests.

Karayannopoulos, Ioannes, and Gunter Weiss. *Quellenkunde zur Geschichte von Byzanz, 324–1453.* 2 vols. Wiesbaden, 1982. Reference work on Byzantine historical texts and authors.

Noth, Albrecht, with Lawrence I. Conrad. *The Early Arabic Historical Tradition: A Source-Critical Study.* Translated by Michael Bonner. Studies in Late Antiquity and Early Islam, 3. Princeton, 1994. A basic reinterpretation and critique of Early Islamic historiography.

Rosenthal, Franz. *A History of Muslim Historiography.* 2d ed. Leiden, 1968. Classic study of Islamic history writing.

Sezgin, Fuat. *Geschichte des arabischen Schrifttums,* vol. 1, *Qur'ānwissenschaften,* pp. 50–389. Leiden, 1967. Description of Arabic historical writing to 1000 CE.

WALTER E. KAEGI

HISTORY OF THE FIELD. [*This entry surveys the history of archaeology in the Near East, including a discussion of major figures, discoveries, and excavations, seminal methodological and theoretical developments, and problems of definition, chronology, and comparative chronology. It comprises eleven articles:*

An Overview
Archaeology in Syria
Archaeology in Israel
Archaeology in Jordan
Archaeology in Mesopotamia
Archaeology in Persia
Archaeology in the Anatolian Plateau
Archaeology in Egypt
Archaeology in Cyprus
Archaeology in the Aegean Islands
Archaeology in the Arabian Peninsula

The first article provides the background of archaeological work in the entire Near East; the subsequent articles focus on a specific country or region. For related discussion, see the entries on each region, (e.g., Palestine; Transjordan; Mesopotamia; Anatolia).]

An Overview

Heightened interest in classical antiquity and the ancient Near East was one of the most important by-products of the Renaissance and its successor movement, the Enlightenment. Indeed, so great was the interest in ancient civilization in the sixteenth century that scholars and travelers regularly visited Greece and Italy and the countries that make up the Near East. Collectors of antiques were so numerous they were called *dilettanti*—those who delighted in the arts. In 1732 the Society of Dilettanti was founded in England. Until that time most scholars believed the world was only six thousand or so years old, calculating its origins based on the Hebrew Masoretic Bible (3740 BCE), the Catholic Vulgate Bible (5199 BCE), or simply accepting the Anglican Archbishop Usher's calculation of 4004 BCE. At the dawn of the modern period, in the seventeenth and eighteenth centuries, all of the ancient world was believed to have fit into this chronological scheme. The belief that the world was older than six thousand years was one of the major advances of nineteenth-century scholarship, which came about with the development of prehistoric, scientific archaeology (Trigger, 1989, pp. 73–109).

Late Eighteenth to Mid-Nineteenth Century. It is not surprising that in the late eighteenth century interest in Egyptian and Mesopotamian civilizations sparked a renewal of exploration and antiquarianism in both. With the christianization of the Roman Empire in the fourth century, Egyptian monuments and writing had either been desecrated or banned, though travelers began visiting the country again in the sixteenth century. Their focus, however, was primarily the pyramids and Great Sphinx of Giza, familiar already in ancient classical sources. [*See* Pyramids; Giza.] All of this changed dramatically in 1798, when Napoleon Bonaparte undertook his expedition to conquer Egypt. Because France was at war with Britain at the time, Napoleon no doubt hoped to use Egypt as a land base from which to disrupt British trade with India and the East. In addition to an army of thirty-five thousand, Napoleon took with him 175 savants, also known as donkeys, who constituted a Commission of Arts and Science; the commission included scientists, geographers, cartographers, architects, Orientalists, artists, and historians (Stiebing, 1993, pp. 56–57; Daniel, 1981, p. 64). It was in 1799, in the Corps of Engineers, while preparing for a British attack, that the Rosetta Stone was discovered 64 km (40 mi.) east of Alexandria. [*See* Alexandria.] The surrender of the French forces in 1801 resulted in the Rosetta Stone's transfer to the British Museum. The commission's scientific results, however, were published by the French in twenty-one volumes. The two-volume English summary was published by D. V. Denon as *Travels in Upper and Lower Egypt during the Campaigns of General Bonaparte* (London, 1802). It is a watershed in Near Eastern scholarship. [*See the biography of Denon.*]

Those volumes and the subsequent decipherment of the Rosetta Stone in 1822 by Jean François Champollion demonstrated vividly to Europeans that Near Eastern culture and monuments were as impressive, or even more so, than the remains of classical Greece and Rome. [*See the biography of Champollion.*] In part as a result of the work of the adventurer and Italian explorer Giovanni Belzoni (who succeeded in bringing to the British Museum the colossal granite head of Rameses II from Thebes and who began the excavations at Abu Simbel), Europe soon became enamored of ancient Egyptian art and archaeology. [*See* Abu Simbel.] Despite the development later of a more refined methodology for excavation in Egypt by William Flinders Petrie, who spent virtually his entire career excavating there, the plundering and pillaging of sites continued unabated until 1882 and the establishment of the Egyptian Exploration Fund. [*See the biography of Petrie.*]

Napoleon's invasion of Egypt also extended to Palestine, which had the effect of bringing even more closely into Western consciousness areas that were familiar because they are mentioned in the Bible. In 1801 the English explorer and geographer Edward Daniel Clarke set out to identify the major sites in the Bible. His skeptical views regarding some of the holy sites proved a helpful corrective to most other visitors, who accepted late pilgrim traditions as completely reliable. One of Clarke's students at Cambridge was the Swiss Jean Louis Burckhardt; after learning medicine, Arabic, and other Oriental subjects, Burckhardt moved to Aleppo for three years, during which time he explored Palmyra and copied inscriptions at many Syrian sites. [*See* Aleppo; Palmyra.] Subsequently, in disguise as a Muslim sheikh, he explored Transjordan and Palestine, identifying and describing many of the sites not visited by his mentor, including Petra. [*See* Petra.] Burckhardt went on to Egypt to work at Abu Simbel. He died in Cairo in 1817, and his journals were published posthumously.

The Americans who came after Clarke and Burckhardt followed a much more literal line with respect to the accuracy of the Bible. Chief among them was Edward Robinson, professor of Old Testament at Andover Theological Seminary in Massachusetts, and later at Union Theological Seminary in New York. [*See the biography of Robinson.*] With a young missionary from Beirut, Eli Smith, he set out in 1838 to follow the route of the Exodus from Egypt, following the names and places in the Hebrew Bible and New Testament. Together they identified hundreds of places from the Bible as they made their way through Sinai, Transjordan, Judea (Judah), Samaria, and Galilee, and then back to Beirut. While they literally created the discipline of historical geography, which became the basis for all later fieldwork, they were unable to prove the accuracy of the Bible through their explorations. [*See* Historical Geography.] What they did, however, was to set the tone for later work, much of which was to be done in the twentieth century and was also to focus primarily on biblical sites. The publication of their journey in *Biblical Researches in Palestine, Mount Sinai, and Arabia Petraea,* (London, 1841) brought their pioneering work to the attention of the Christian world and transformed what had once been a field dominated by missionaries into the newly constituted field of biblical archaeology (Silberman, 1982, pp. 42–47).

Just as Napoleon's scientific expedition to Egypt had had an imperialist thrust and character to it, so too did British and subsequent French interest in Mesopotamia. It was in 1808 that Claudius James Rich, a linguist and a British resident of Turkish Arabia, was hired by the British East India Company in Baghdad. All of his free time was spent visiting Mesopotamian ruins and collecting artifacts. His publications on Babylon, Nineveh, and Persepolis, among other places, caught the attention of Western readers. [*See* Baghdad; Babylon; Nineveh; Persepolis.] They were made even more famous by Lord Byron when he recalled them in *Don Juan:*

> Claudius Rich, Esquire, some bricks has got
> And written lately two memoirs upon't.

Rich's personal antiquities collection was subsequently purchased by the British Museum and constituted the first major exhibition of Mesopotamian antiquities in a European museum. So great was the public interest in Rich's memoirs, which appeared posthumously in 1836, that French interest in the region greatly accelerated. As a result, a prominent scholar and antiquarian, Emile Botta, was appointed French consul in Mosul in 1842. [*See the biography of Botta.*] He immediately began excavations at Nineveh in 1842, across the Tigris River from Mosul, and in Khorsabad in 1843. [*See* Tigris; Khorsabad.] These were the first excavations ever in Mesopotamia (Daniel, 1981, pp. 72–75). Botta's work at Khorsabad revealed it to be the city of Sargon II (721–705 BCE), Dur Sharrukin. Botta and his artist, M. E. Flandin, published the results of their work at Nineveh in 1849–1850 in five volumes; in 1846 many of Khorsabad's finest sculptures arrived at the Louvre museum in Paris, where they are still displayed. [*See* Museums and Museology.]

Prior to Rich's explorations and Botta's excavations, a small number of individuals had been involved in the decipherment of cuneiform, paralleling developments that had surrounded the decipherment of Egyptian hieroglyphics. [*See* Cuneiform; Hieroglyphs; Inscriptions.] In 1802 Georg Friedrich Grotefend, using copies of two short cuneiform inscriptions from Persia, announced his translation results to the Göttingen Academy of Sciences—which refused to publish them. Thirty-three years later, in 1835, Henry Creswicke Rawlinson, unmindful of Grotefend's research, duplicated those results when he was stationed some 35 km (22 mi.) from Bisitun in Persia as a cadet in the British East India Company. [*See* Bisitun; *and the biography of Rawlinson.*] By 1837 he had copied and translated half of the Bisitun inscriptions ordered in 516 BCE by Darius I Hystapes (521–485 BCE) and written in Old Persian and Elamite. [*See* Persian; Elamites.] In 1837 and in 1839, he presented his results to the Royal Asiatic Society. All four hundred lines of the inscriptions appeared in translation in the society's journal in 1846–1847 (Stiebing, 1993, pp. 94–95).

At about this time, a lasting friendship between the Frenchman, Botta, and an Englishman by the name of Austen Henry Layard had already been made. [*See the biography of Layard.*] The two had met in 1842 and maintained a close relationship throughout their lives, despite the fact that their respective nations saw their work as competitive. In 1845 Layard began his own excavations at Nimrud, where he discovered the palaces of the Assyrian kings Ashurnasirpal, Esarhaddon, and Shalmaneser III; the most famous of the artifacts Layard shipped to the British Museum included the Black Obelisk of Shalmaneser II and the sculptures of Ashurnasirpal. Layard's work was covered by a reporter for the *Morning Post* in 1847 and made him an instant celebrity. His popular account of his work, *Nineveh and its Remains* (New York, 1849), became Near Eastern archaeology's first bestseller (Daniel, 1981, p. 75). Though Botta and Layard disagreed as to which site was Nineveh—Botta thought Khorsabad was, Layard thought Nimrud was—their combined archaeological work, their extensive publications and popular readership, and the spectacular exhibits at the Louvre and British Museum presented Near Eastern archaeology in new ways to the public and to the scholarly community. What began as a friendly competition between the British and French archaeological missions, however, soon deteriorated into a "frantic scramble" between them, ending temporarily with the outbreak of the Crimean War in 1855 (Stiebing, 1993, pp. 106–109).

Defining Period. With the cessation of excavations at mid-century, the emphasis in Near Eastern scholarship shifted to linguistic study of the enormous array of cuneiform that had reached libraries in the West. One of the immediate results was the discovery of Sumerian. [*See* Sumerian.] Even more dramatic, perhaps, was the discovery by George Adam Smith in 1872 of the story of the Flood among the tablets found at Nineveh. [*See the biography of Smith.*] A missing section of the account led to the reexamination of the debris at Kuyunjik in 1873, where, on the fifth day, Smith discovered the missing seventeen lines of the Mesopotamian story. The expedition was funded and covered by the London *Daily Telegraph.* Given the remarkable similarity to the biblical story of the Flood in *Genesis*, public interest in Near Eastern archaeology was once again drawn to the Bible and the land of the Bible, even as further work in Mesopotamia and Egypt continued to prosper. Interest in the Sumerians inspired the work of the University of Pennsylvania at Nippur in 1888, begun rather unsuccessfully by John Prunnett Peters but culminated more successfully under the direction of Hermann Hilprecht in 1899–1900. [*See* Sumerians; Nippur; *and the biographies of Peters and Hilprecht.*] A similar interest was focused on the Hittites, in part because they were mentioned in the Bible as a great power (*2 Kgs.* 7:6), and in part because Assyrian and Egyptian documents confirmed it. [*See* Hittites; Assyrians.] The culmination of these efforts came in 1906, when the German Assyriologist Hugo Winkler began excavations at Boğazköy and discovered a cache of Hittite cuneiform tablets. [*See* Boğazköy.] This excavation and the decipherment of the tablets and identification of Hittite as an Indo-European language led to the certain knowledge that Boğazköy had been the capital of the Hittite Empire (Stiebing, 1993, pp. 113–114). [*See* Hittite; Indo-European Languages.]

From 1899 to 1917 the German Oriental Society excavated the ruins of Babylon, under the directorship of Robert Koldewey. [*See* Deutsche Orient-Gesellschaft; Babylon; *and the biography of Koldewey.*] Though others had explored and dug at the site, there had been no significant finds of bas-reliefs. Koldewey, who had excavated in Italy, Sicily, Syria, and in the Aegean, was an experienced field person who trained a core of workmen to excavate carefully and slowly. The results were astounding, as he soon uncovered the great city wall of Nebuchadrezzar II (605–562 BCE) and determined that Babylon's circumference was some 18 km (11 mi.), making it the largest city of its time. He also discovered the ziggurat, or stepped tower, on which a Temple of Marduk had once stood approximately 100 m high. [*See* Ziggurat.] Most spectacular, however, was the discovery of the Processional Way leading to the temple, a roadway lined with walls decorated with colorfully glazed bricks and featuring reliefs of bulls, lions, and sacred dragons. Where the Processional Way passed through a monumental gate decorated in glazed blue bricks he located and identified the Ishtar Gate, subsequently completely reconstructed and exhibited at the Pergamon Museum in Berlin—a feat equaling Koldewey's fieldwork.

During the time that such significant progress was being made in Near Eastern archaeology in the broadest sense, more and more interest was being directed to the heartland of that vast region, Syria-Palestine. Contributing to this were the colonial interests of the great powers and their specific interest in the lands of the Bible, which had only recently been explored by the Americans Edward Robinson and Eli Smith. It is significant that Americans first focused on Palestine, and Europeans on Egypt and Mesopotamia. In due course, the scales would balance: in the second half of the nineteenth century, all nationalities would be firmly established in the region, and, by the end of the century, with major societies and institutes to guide them. [*See* Nationalism and Archaeology.] American colonial interest combined with an awareness of the area's biblical heritage inspired the first U.S. naval expedition to investigate the possibility of establishing a trade route in the Holy Land. In particular, the Americans chose to circumnavigate the Dead Sea, explore the biblical cities around it, and sail the Jordan River. William Francis Lynch conducted this mission in 1847–1848, setting sail from the Sea of Galilee in two metal ships, the *Fanny Mason* and *Fanny Skinner*. During the trip down the Jordan River, the expedition mapped its course and described its environment. Thirteen months after they had left the United States they completed their explorations. The results of the work were published in 1849 and 1852 (Silberman, 1982, pp. 51–62; King, 1983, p. 6). The proposal to open a trade route through the Holy Land was never accepted by the U.S. government, while the attendant publicity surrounding the Lynch expedition had the effect of arousing even greater interest in the Holy Land among Americans. Missionaries described their visits to the Holy Land, and even P. T. Barnum sent the director of his American Museum to Palestine to collect antiquities for display (Silberman, 1982, p. 62).

In 1842, just prior to the Lynch expedition, the American Oriental Society had been established to promote the study of Asian and African languages and interest in ancient Mesopotamia in particular. Edward Robinson, the explorer of Palestine and a Semitist, became president in 1846. In 1865 the British established the Palestine Exploration Fund to promote scientific exploration of the Holy Land, sending Charles W. Wilson to oversee the mapping of Jerusalem in 1867. [*See* Palestine Exploration Fund; *and the biography of Wilson*.] In 1872–1878 the British conducted the geographical survey of western Palestine, in which ten thousand sites were mapped; a limited survey of eastern Palestine followed in 1881. It was during this remarkable period of intense interest in the Holy Land that the ill-fated American Palestine Exploration Society was established (1870–1884). [*See* American Palestine Exploration Society.] A forerunner of the American School(s) of Oriental Research (ASOR), the purpose of the society was "the illustration and defense of the Bible" (King, 1983, p. 8). Because the British had concentrated their efforts on explorations west of the Jordan, the Americans focused their efforts on Transjordan. Those early explorations were led by Selah Merrill and published as *East of the Jordan* (London, 1881). [*See the biography of Merrill*.] As a result of lack of funds, internal bickering, and its limited purview, the society was dissolved in 1884. The Germans established their society for the exploration of Palestine (Deutscher Palästina-Verein) in 1877. [*See* Deutscher Palästina-Verein.] It too was modeled after the British society and, like its American predecessor, had a distinctively Lutheran and biblical orientation. In 1890 the French Dominicans established the École Biblique et Archéologique Française in Jerusalem, which resembled the British, German, and defunct American societies. [*See* École Biblique et Archéologique Française.]

It was in such a context that ASOR was established in 1900, its existence called forth by a series of pressures that had been building in America since the beginning of the nineteenth century. The three parent societies that were instrumental in its founding represented the diverse strands of American scholarship affecting Near Eastern scholarship at the time: The American Oriental Society, preoccupied with the linguistic and literary heritage of Mesopotamia; the Archaeological Institute of America, focused on the West and most closely allied to the schools in Rome and Athens; and the Society of Biblical Literature, preeminent in promoting biblical scholarship. [*See* Archaeological Institute of America; Society of Biblical Literature.] Given all that had preceded, the founding of ASOR was inevitable. Given its sponsors, it was clear from the outset that its home in the Near East would be in Jerusalem and that its ties to Transjordan, Mesopotamia, and Egypt would remain in place permanently. America's unique attachment to the Bible and its allied civilizations, therefore, has been the central motivating factor in ASOR's history since its founding (King, 1983, pp. 25–28). [*See* American Schools of Oriental Research.]

The centrality of biblical archaeology as a major stream in Near Eastern archaeology is thus very much a result of the Western preference for the languages, literatures, and cultures that illuminate aspects of its own tradition and culture. To some cultural critics this is the stuff of Orientalism at its worst: "To reconstruct a dead or lost Oriental language meant ultimately to reconstruct a dead or neglected Orient" (Said, 1978, p. 123). To be sure, Western interests in recovering the archaeological heritage of the Near East were tied to imperial, colonial, and Judaeo-Christian goals. Be that as it may, the emergence of a more detached scientific archaeology and advanced philology in more recent generations has only increased what is understood and appreciated of those cultures. What motivated the spiritual forebears of Near Eastern archaeology may no longer exist. However, it is important also to recognize that the founding fathers of a scientific archaeology in the twentieth century had other shortcomings and prejudices beside their commitment to bolster the Bible, just as their nineteenth-century counterparts had.

Twentieth Century. The founding of ASOR in 1900, just ten years after the French school and ten years after Petrie's excavations at Tell el-Ḥesi in Palestine, signaled the beginning of a new era in Near Eastern archaeology, one that witnessed the growth of the overseas national institutes for Near Eastern research and related studies. [*See* Ḥesi, Tell el-.] Petrie's work in Egypt in behalf of the Egypt Exploration Fund prior to his excavations in Palestine had laid the groundwork for ceramic typology, seriation analysis, and comparative dating. Petrie even visited Mycenae to test his dating of his finds at Gurob and Kahun, establishing a synchronism between "proto-Greek" ware and Egypt's twelfth dynasty and identifying some of the foreign pottery from Egypt as Aegean and proto-Greek ware. He published the methods of digging and ceramic typology he developed as *Methods and Aims in Archaeology* (New York, 1904). The principles enunciated in that work resonate well even with today's exacting standards: conservation of monuments, meticulous recording and collecting of data, accurate recording and planning of all monuments and areas of excavation, and timely publication of all results. [*See* Conservation Archaeology; Recording Techniques; Excavation Strategy.] His criteria for analyzing ceramics are still used. His American counterpart in the early part of the twentieth century was George A. Reisner, whose excavations at Samaria were to become a showcase for American methods. [*See* Samaria; *and the biography of Reisner.*]

What has only emerged in recent scholarship, however, is that Petrie's interpretative scheme, by means of which he distinguished between periods of racial domination by groups of abler peoples, was based on contemporary theories of racial superiority. [*See* Eugenics Movement.] In evaluating the reasons for the rise and fall of civilizations, Petrie embraced such views. Building also upon historical ideas of the rise and fall of civilizations, he attributed the decline of certain populations to inbreeding among their subjects. In adopting such a scheme, Petrie was not alone. R. A. S. Macalister, the famed Irish archaeologist who excavated Tel Gezer, also adhered to such an interpretative scheme, claiming that the ancient Semites, Hebrews, Arabs, and other civilizations had absorbed all their most important elements of civilization from neighboring cultures (Bunimovitz, 1995, pp. 60–61). [*See* Gezer; *and the biography of Macalister.*] Looking back again at these old pioneers in field archaeology, it is difficult to dispute the accuracy of cultural critics like Edward Said (1978) who have questioned the motives of many of the first Orientalists committed to imposing Western rubrics of thought, values, and standards of superiority on the region's "primitive cultures."

It is not difficult to see how much improved the situation became when scholars such as William Foxwell Albright, George Ernest Wright, and Nelson Glueck dominated the field of Palestinian/biblical archaeology from about 1920 to 1970, especially in terms of recording and field methods. [*See* Biblical Archaeology; *and the biographies of Albright, Wright, and Glueck.*] Each of these scholars and others—Roland de Vaux, Kathleen M. Kenyon, and Yigael Yadin—introduced numerous refinements of method to the discipline, as well as new insights into long-standing problems and issues. [*See the biographies of Vaux, Kenyon, and Yadin.*] The fact remains, however, that all of them worked within the interpretative framework of biblical history and theology. To be sure, each no doubt gave greater credence to the archaeological data when there was a clash with biblical tradition or history. However, the Bible stood very much at the core of their work, just as it undergirded the quest of their nineteenth-century forbears for synchronicity between the Bible and contemporary scientific explanations of its history and culture. If anything, such a bibliocentrisim contributed to the growing perception that Westerners were more interested in tracing their roots than in exploring the full range of the region's cultures. In so doing it could be argued that the Americans, like the British, French, and Germans before them and alongside them, imposed something of themselves upon the Near East and were also very much in the Orientalist tradition. It must also be said, however, that as much as this might have been a shortcoming, especially in view of the Near East today being overwhelmingly Islamic, it also provided the money, enthusiasm, and determination to advance a complex subject and discipline (Cooper, 1992).

The 1970s inaugurated an era that saw the decline of biblical archaeology and the emergence of a multidisciplinary approach frequently called the New Archaeology. [*See* New Archaeology.] Many individual aspects of this new approach had been anticipated in the earlier research of American and other scholars. Regional studies had been conducted by Glueck in Transjordan, and Robert J. Braidwood had studied the origins of agriculture in Kurdistan in the 1940s. Surface surveys had been conducted by all the national schools in virtually all regions of the Near East. The introduction of new technologies in the 1970s and after, especially, for example, the computer, resistivitors, high-resolution photography, DNA analysis, and neutron activation analysis and all the other items that made digging more efficient, also moved the discipline toward maturation. [*See* Computer Mapping; Computer Recording, Analysis, and Interpretation; Photography; Neutron Activation Analysis; Ethics and Archaeology.] Similarly, the emergence of new subdisciplines, such as gender studies and cultural studies, makes the contemporary archaeologist more sensitive to nomenclature, to the categories assigned to artifacts, and to interpretative strategies for understanding diverse and complex groups of evidence. [*See* Ethnoarchaeology; Ethnobotany; Ethnozoology.] The archaeology of the ancient Near East is at last at home in the richness of the diversity of its cultures and traditions, having advanced beyond the narrower confines of its past.

BIBLIOGRAPHY

Bunimovitz, Shlomo. "How Mute Stones Speak: Interpreting What We Dig Up." *Biblical Archaeology Review* 21.2 (1995): 58–67. Thoughtful

review exposing the interpretive strategies that influenced some of this century's greatest archaeologists.
Cooper, Jerrold S. "From Mosul to Manila: Early Approaches to Funding Ancient Near Eastern Studies Research in the United States." In *Culture and History II,* edited by Ann Gunter, pp. 133–163. Copenhagen, 1992. Insightful review of the circumstances and context influencing the funding of Near Eastern research.
Daniel, Glyn E. *A Short History of Archaeology.* London, 1981. Excellent overview of the place of archaeology in the broader context of the study of the human past.
King, Philip J. *American Archaeology in the Mideast: A History of the American Schools of Oriental Research.* Winona Lake, Ind., 1983. Valuable study of ASOR's history, with important historical information regarding the emergence of European interest in Near Eastern and biblical archaeology.
Said, Edward W. *Orientalism.* New York, 1978. Programmatic essay about Western attitudes toward the "Orient," an area embracing the Islamic Near East.
Silberman, Neil Asher. *Digging for God and Country: Exploration, Archaeology, and the Secret Struggle for the Holy Land, 1799–1917.* New York, 1982. Engaging and authoritative account of early American and European interests in excavating ancient Palestine.
Stiebing, William H. *Uncovering the Past: A History of Archaeology.* New York, 1993. Concise and reliable guide to the history of the discipline, with an especially strong section on the Near East.
Trigger, Bruce G. *A History of Archaeological Thought.* Cambridge, 1989. Definitive treatment of the place of archaeological thought and theory in the history of ideas, from medieval times to the present.

ERIC M. MEYERS

Archaeology in Syria

In the middle of the nineteenth century, when Europeans were beginning to take an active interest in excavating Near Eastern sites, especially ancient ruins dating to the Assyrian period, Henry Austen Layard made brief soundings at a site on the Khabur River in northeastern Syria, Tell Hajajah (Assyrian Shadikanni, called Araban in tenth-century Arabic sources). The imposing ruins of Tell Ḥalaf (ancient Guzana) led Max von Oppenheim to excavate there in 1899, 1911–1914, and 1927–1929. Carchemish, which had been identified by the geographer George Adam Smith in 1876, was excavated by David G. Hogarth and C. Leonard Woolley in 1908–1911 and 1920. In 1902 German excavations were begun at Palmyra (continued in 1917 under Theodor Wiegand); although previous studies had been made there, this was the beginning of research on the city as a whole. In 1860 Ernest Renan made soundings at the coastal sites of Byblos, Tyre, and Sidon and on the island of Arwad for the French Mission to Phoenicia.

The impetus for these excavations was the discovery of original sources related to the Bible and biblical peoples. However, they were also driven by the recovery of the monumental architecture and large-scale reliefs decorating Assyrian and Neo-Hittite palaces. Cuneiform inscriptions written on these reliefs were deciphered by European scholars in the late nineteenth century. A lively interest in Europe for cuneiform texts had begun as early as 1625, when an Italian traveler, Pietro della Valle, brought back the first cuneiform inscriptions. In 1897 the French Assyriologist François Thureau-Dangin published a tablet from the area of Terqa on the Euphrates River; this was the first cuneiform tablet to be published from Syria, although it was not recognized as such at the time.

Between the two wars, large first-millennium BCE sites in northern and eastern Syria continued to interest excavators. In 1928 Thureau-Dangin, Maurice Dunand, and Georges Dossin began excavations at Arslan Tash (Hadatu). Previously, a group of Neo-Assyrian sculptures dating to the reign of Tiglath-Pileser III had been recovered there. Part of the provincial palace and ivories dating to the eighth century were discovered. Tell Ahmar (ancient Til Barsip, also called Kar Shalmaneser) was excavated in three campaigns (1929–1931) by the same team from the Louvre museum. They established that it had been an important city in the state of Bit Adini and that its palace had been decorated with Neo-Hittite sculpture (similar to those previously recorded at Carchemish). Rarely preserved Assyrian wall paintings dated near to the reign of Tiglath-Pileser III were also recovered, as well as a hypogeum dating to the third millennium. [*See* Wall Paintings.] In 1988 Guy Bunnens renewed those excavations. He has excavated two large Assyrian houses containing objects (including ivories) acquired through the city's international contacts.

Before the advent of satellite photos, Antoine Poidebard in 1927 utilized air photos of sites in eastern Syria in his research (Poidebard, 1934). This early use of air photos was followed at the Mari excavations by a photo of the palace when excavation was completed. Kite photos were taken by Robert Anderson at Dipsi Faraj and later at Terqa. Kite or balloon photos are by now standard on many excavations in Syria.

Prehistoric Sites. The surge of excavations at prehistoric Syrian sites has revolutionized what is known of the period's social and economic development. Multidisciplinary approaches to excavation have revealed more about the Paleolithic lithic technology and social interaction from sites with evidence of *Homo erectus* and eventually of *Homo sapiens sapiens.* Prehistoric sites are rich in the area of el-Kowm near Palmyra, particularly at Umm el-Tlel (Jacques Cauvin) and Nadawiyah I (Sultan Muhesen and Jean Marie Le Tensorer). Discoveries that profoundly altered what was known of later prehistory came from excavations on the Middle Euphrates River, where the evidence demonstrated that the establishment of permanent settlements and the transition from hunting and gathering to agriculture and animal domestication were separate stages. Settlement in permanent villages with a high economic and cultural standard developed without similar advances in agriculture and animal domestication. The Late Natufian village at Abu Hureyra 1 (Andrew Moore) engaged in specialized hunting practices (mostly gazelles) and gathered a wide variety of plants (more than 150 species); this specialization presupposed permanancy. At Abu Hureyra 2, settled in about 9000 BCE, agriculture was practiced but wild-plant gathering continued; meat mostly came from wild gazelles. In about 8000 BCE this changed, and most of the population was engaged in cereal production and raising domesticated sheep and goats. [*See* Cereals; Sheep and Goats.] In the second half of the seventh millennium, new ecological zones were exploited, as in the village of Bouqras, in an arid zone along the Middle Euphrates. From there, substantial domestic architecture, in some cases decorated with painted plaster or painted reliefs, and small, but exceptionally fine, human figures and stone vessels were found.

Starting in the 1960s, interest was renewed in excavating Halaf sites, especially in the heartland of the Halaf culture along the Upper Khabur, the Balikh, and the Middle Euphrates Rivers. At Tell Sabi Abyad, in the Balikh, excavations directed by Peter M. M. G. Akkermans have shown that the earliest phases of the Halaf culture developed gradually out of the preceding local Neolithic culture (and not, as previously thought, imported from northern Iraq). During the Ubaid period the intensification of international contacts included North Syria, but thus far few sites from this period have been excavated. An exception is Tell ʿAbr (Hamid Hammade); at Tell Bisnada, east of Latakia, Ubaid material has been found in limited soundings. [*See* Syria, *article on* Prehistoric Syria.]

Coastal and Central Syria. In 1928 a local farmer discovered a tomb in the area of Minet el-Beida that attracted the attention of the French archaeologist Claude F.-A. Schaeffer. In the following year he began excavations at this ancient port and at the nearby site of Ras Shamra, ancient Ugarit. Almost immediately the excavations at Ugarit produced a number of texts, the most startling of which are alphabetic cuneiform texts from the fourteenth–thirteenth centuries BCE. Other texts written in Akkadian, Hittite, and Hurrian attest to the international contacts of this coastal city. The Ugaritic texts are also important because of their relevance to studies in Hebrew Bible. [*See* Ugarit Inscriptions.] A large royal palace with its offices and workshops was excavated in addition to the temples of Baal and Dagan. Work continued at the site, with an interruption during the World War II, under Schaeffer's direction until the mid-1970s; the present French director is Marguerite Yon.

Of major importance for the history of Ugarit and coastal Syria are the recent Syrian-French excavations carried out under Adnan Bounni, Elizabeth Lagarce, and Jacques Lagarce at the site of Ras Ibn Hani, located a short distance from Ugarit, and situated directly on the coast. There, two thirteenth-century BCE residential palaces served as administrative centers; as a result of their ongoing research, a variety of Ugaritic texts—including letters and ritual and administrative texts—have been found. Tell Sukas, the ancient city called Shuksu in the Ugarit texts, had previously been excavated along the coast by P. J. Riis. Excavations at Tell al-Kazel (probably ancient Simira), initiated by Bounni and continuing under Leila Badre, have shed light on one of the most important Late Bronze sites on the coast (probably a New Kingdom Egyptian administrative center and then a major city of the kingdom of Ammuru). [*See* Amorites.] Important late third-millennium remains, also exhibiting Egyptian connections, are now being uncovered at Tell Sianu, in central Syria, by Bounni and Michel al-Maqdissi.

Bounni, the director of excavations in the Directorate General of Antiquities and Museums, is noted as an excavator for his historic work at Palmyra (begun in 1957) in the Valley of the Tombs, the Temple of Nabu, the main street, the agora, the theater, the nymphaea A and B, and the Street of Baʿal Shamin (Bounni, 1982). In addition he has excavated a large number of sites from the third millennium BCE to the Roman period. His colleague, Nassib Saliby, an authority on Palmyrene architecture and prominent Islamic architectural monuments, is excavating at the Damascus citadel and carrying out a number of salvage projects in the city.

Inner Syria has had a long history of archaeological work, starting with the activities of Maurice Pézard at Tell Nebi Mend in 1921. Recent excavations (Peter Parr) have found a Middle Bronze Age city wall and monumental Late Bronze Age buildings. Four seasons of excavations were conducted by Robert du Mesnil du Buisson at Mishrifeh/Qatna from 1926 to 1929. Qatna's MB and LB texts of temple inventories give a king list for the city during a portion of the fifteenth century BCE, before its destruction. He also worked at several sites north of Hama, including Tell Suran, Tell As, and Khan Sheikhun, which gave the first indication of the importance of this area for the third millennium. Excavations at Tell Qarqur are being conducted by the American Schools of Oriental Research (ASOR) under the direction of Rudolph H. Dornemann. The Hama excavations (1932–1939), directed by Harald Ingholt and Riis, established a stratified sequence of pottery that is linked to the sequence in the ʿAmuq region, thus giving a firm ceramic chronology for this area.

The site that has most revolutionized what is known of the importance of northern Syria from the middle of the third to the middle of the second millennium (2400–1600 BCE) is the ancient city of Ebla, modern Tell Mardikh. Excavations began there under Paolo Matthiae in 1964; he specifically set out to test the hypothesis that third-millennium Syria had been a major urban civilization, parallel to contemporary civilizations in Egypt and Mesopotamia. It was only after ten years of excavation that the Ebla archive was discovered, confirming the city's ancient name. [*See* Ebla Texts.] Matthiae is almost single-handedly responsible for third-millennium urban Syria taking its place in the scholarly literature. The archive came from a palace complex that in addition yielded the remains of wood inlays, parts of alabaster and diorite vessels from pharaonic Egypt, gold and lapis objects, and a large amount of unworked lapis. The military campaigns of Sargon and his grandson Naram-Sin destroyed the city. It revived at the beginning of the second millennium BCE, when a large palace and several temples were constructed. The excavation of the royal tombs of the period from 1800 to 1650 BCE exhibit the city's immense wealth and the international contacts of its rulers in both Anatolia and Egypt. The excavations at Ebla transformed what was known of the importance of cities in Syria during the third millennium, highlighting their central role in the era's internationalism, which previously had been understood to have only begun in the Late Bronze Age (Matthiae, 1980).

Matthiae began excavating near Ebla, at the first-millennium site BCE of Tell Afis (ancient Apesh?); that work is now being directed by a member of the Ebla excavation team, Stefanie Mazzoni, who has published ceramics and jar sealings from Ebla (Mazzoni, 1985, 1992). Excavation at Tell Afis has uncovered an uninterrupted sequence of strata bridging the crucial period between the end of the Late Bronze and the beginning of the Iron Age. Recently, substantial Chalcolithic remains were also uncovered.

North of Aleppo, excavations at the site of ʿAin Daraʿ, directed most recently by Ali Abou Assaf and Wahid Khayyata, have identified the city potentially as ancient Kinalua, often mentioned in Neo-Assyrian annals; the excavations have found a *ḫilani*-type palace and a large temple decorated with Neo-Hittite-style orthostats; two stone thresholds were decorated with three large footprints pointing toward the temple interior.

Salvage Projects. With Syrian independence in 1946 and the establishment of the Syrian Directorate General of Antiquities and Museums, the new administration of the cultural inheritance of the country concentrated on decentralizing Syria's museums by building a major museum in Aleppo to supplement the collections in Damascus. Smaller museums were established in Palmyra, Hama, Tartus, Homs, Latakia, ar-Raqqa, and Idlib; most recently a major new museum was constructed in Deir ez-Zor. The department's policy from the beginning has been to encourage foreign excavation—by European, American, and Japanese teams.

A phenomenon that has characterized Syrian archaeology of the last few decades is the prevalence of salvage operations. Starting in the 1960s the construction of large dams on the Euphrates and Khabur Rivers necessitated the rescue of ancient sites. The most important of these is the Tabqa dam, which formed a lake covering an area of 80 × 8 km (50 × 5 mi.) Answering a call issued by the Syrian government through UNESCO, an international team of archaeologists worked between 1967 and 1974 to excavate sites ranging in date from the ninth millennium BCE to the fifteenth century CE (Freedman, 1979). A sense of the opening up of a new archaeological frontier resulted from the expanded information about this region. Revolutionary discoveries were made for the fourth millennium, especially at Tell Kannas (André Finet) and Habuba Kabira (Ernst Heinrich and Eva Strommenger), where a large, important settlement, including niched temples whose architectural plan resembles contemporary Uruk period temples in southern Mesopotamia, were excavated; in addition, the ceramic and glyptic material is very close to the south. At Jebel ʿAruda (H. J. Franken and Sander E. van der Leeuw), similar Uruk IV remains were found. The significance of salt sources near these sites and the connection of the salt-refinement process with beveled-rim bowls was shown in part from the American excavations farther downstream at Qraya. New French excavations at Tell Mashnaqa and Ramadi, near Mari, are extending what is known of the Uruk connection. The revelation of a strong Uruk presence ("colonies") in the Euphrates bend region of Syria has entirely changed the view of fourth-millennium Uruk culture. In addition, it has confirmed the strength of the regional Syrian material culture that reasserted itself immediately after the cessation of the Uruk incursion. Sites with later occupation included Tell Hadidi, with a very well-documented ceramic sequence from the beginning of the third to the middle of the second millennia BCE. Tell Selenkahiyeh, a large third-millennium site, yielded twelve important private houses in the heart of the city that give a picture of its economic organization. At Tell Halawa, Winfried Orthmann uncovered important third-millennium strata, including a temple. Major second-millennium BCE levels were discovered at Meskene where an archive of approximately fifteen hundred cuneiform texts has identified the city as Emar. The excavator, Jean-Claude Margueron, uncovered a number of structures from the fourteenth- and thirteenth-centuries BCE, when this region was under Hittite domination. The structures included two long-room type temples and a governor's palace of the *ḫilani* type, characteristic of the first millennium BCE. Similar temples were also excavated at Tell Mumbaqat and Tell Fray.

Appeals by the Syrian government through UNESCO were also connected with the construction of a dam along the Euphrates near the Syro-Turkish border (the Tishrin dam) and two near Hassekeh, one south of the city and one to the west. South of Hassekeh, excavations concentrated on small sites along the course of the Khabur River. The excavation of one of them, Tell 'Atij, by Michel Fortin (1986–1988, 1992–1993), has illuminated the specialized economic importance of this area in the early third millennium. He was the first to uncover a series of granaries that could store large amounts for later shipment to other areas (e.g., to Tell Brak or areas to the south). Subsequent excavations at nearby Ziyada and Tell Raqa'i revealed similar facilities. [*See* Food Storage.] The excavations at Tell Tuneinir under Michael Fuller found an early church and an

Ayyubid bath. [*See* Baths.] A deep sounding confirmed the site's third-millennium occupation. Northwest of Hassekeh, Tell Kashkashuk III (Antoine Soleiman) had important remains from the mid-third millennium, including what probably is a temple and a tomb with the skeleton of a young woman with more than six thousand beads of various materials, including gold, lapis, and rock crystal. He is also excavating a Neo-Assyrian site (Tell Boueid) with a large administrative building and a number of jar burials. In the Tishrin dam area, the Late Bronze strata of el-Qitar (Thomas L. McClellan) reveal a city organized around upper and lower sections. The city was probably destroyed by a campaign of Thutmosis III. This area was important in the Pre-Pottery Neolithic B period as is being shown by the excavations at Tell Halula (M. Molist) and Ja'det al-Maghara (Danielle Stordeur).

Eastern Syria. The landscape of eastern Syria is dominated by numerous mounds along the Middle Euphrates River, with its main tributaries the Khabur and the Balikh. In the period between the two world wars, partly as a consequence of the discoveries at Ugarit, European archaeologists took a greater interest in excavations in Syria. In 1933 André Parrot began excavating at Tell Hariri, which William Foxwell Albright had proposed identifying with the ancient city of Mari, attested in the Sumerian king lists. The early years of excavation at Mari uncovered the Zimrilim palace, excellently preserved with a vast number of cuneiform texts relating to palace activities, including a diplomatic archive. The archaeological remains both for the third and early part of the second millennium BCE, until the destruction of the city in about 1760 BCE by Hammurabi of Babylon, attest to the importance of this urban center and to Mari's border position between the cities of southern Mesopotamia and the urban centers and fertile countryside of northern and western Syria. There too a large palace dating to the third millennium has been partly excavated along with a major temple dedicated to Ishtar.

The new program of research at Mari, under Margueron's direction, has concentrated on enlarging the area where excavations and soundings have been conducted, in order to study the urban plan. In addition, he has initiated a regional study to understand better the reasons for the placement of the city on this part of the river, as well as its geographic and ecological relationship with the surrounding countryside. This research has concluded that when the city was founded in the early part of the third millennium, a series of canals and an artificial lake were constructed in order to utilize the Euphrates River basin for agriculture. The most important of these canals (120 km long) connected Mari directly with the Khabur River. The width of this canal (11 m) allowed river craft to shorten the trip south and avoid the turbulent intersection of the Khabur with the Euphrates. The city therefore controlled both river traffic and probably also the overland caravan route. This new program of archaeological research, combined with new initiatives connected with the publication of the Mari texts (Jean-Marie Durand), is of profound importance for understanding all of Syria in the Mari period.

The narrowness of the Euphrates River valley in southeastern Syria permits the existence of only one major city at any given time. After the destruction of Mari, Terqa (about 60 km, or 37 mi., north of Mari, near the juncture of the Khabur and the Euphrates) became the major urban center. Excavations at Terqa, conducted by Giorgio Buccellati and Marilyn Kelly-Buccellati between 1976 and 1984, uncovered an administrative building from the Khana period (1760–1600 BCE), a complex of artifacts identified as the "office" of a scribe. From this same period a temple of Ninkarrak contained a hoard of 6,637 beads, including seven contemporary scarabs. In the burnt house of Puzurum, the excavators found a storage room with a number of sealed contracts; in this same house a pantry contained a jar with cloves inside. Before Roman times, cloves had to come from the Melakas (Moluccas, Spice Islands) in Indonesia. In the excavations of Olivier Rouault and Maria Grazia Masetti-Rouault, tablets dating to the Late Khana period and down into the Mitanni period have been discovered. [*See* Mitanni.]

Along the Khabur River south of Hassekeh, the site of Sheikh Ḥamad (ancient Dur Katlimmu) has been excavated since 1978 by Hartmut Kuhne, in collaboration with the Assyriologist Wolfgang Röllig. A Middle Assyrian palace on the highest part of the mound contained five hundred and fifty tablets dating to the reigns of Shalmaneser I and Tukulti-Ninurta I. In the Lower City, a building with a *ḫilani*-type reception area contained an archive of thirty-five tablets written in three languages: Assyrian, Babylonian, and Aramaic. Also in the Lower City (building G), cuneiform tablets dating to the reign of Nebuchadrezzar yielded the first evidence of a Neo-Babylonian presence in Syria. Kuhne's extensive excavations have provided the most complete understanding of the importance of the Assyrian period in eastern Syria. At the site of Tell Hajajah (ancient Shadikanni), excavations were begun by As'ad Mahmoud in 1982, who rediscovered Layard's excavation trenches and uncovered part of the ninth-century BCE governor's palace decorated with relief orthostats and glazed bricks.

To the north, in the Khabur triangle, pioneering excavations were carried out by M. E. L. Mallowan. The site of Chaghar Bazar (1934–1937) was significant in the Halaf period, as was all of the Wadi Darʿa region. The excavations discovered an archive of cuneiform documents from the early second millennium BCE onward. The stratified sequence of pottery from the third and the second millennia BCE, especially the sequence of painted Khabur ware, became the basis on which many of the other sites in the area were later dated. During this same period, Mallowan began excavations at one of the largest sites in eastern Syria, Tell Brak (Mallowan, 1947). Brak was an extensive city as early as the Uruk period; its Eye Temple was built on a southern model with a high terrace and a tripartite plan with an elaborately decorated podium. The "palace" of Naram-Sin can more likely be identified as a royal storehouse that sustained his subsequent military activities in western Syria. Mallowan's example of the rapid publication of his primary excavation data (in *Iraq*) was followed by the present excavators of Brak, David and Joan Oates, who resumed excavations there in 1976. From the Akkadian period they have excavated a large ceremonial complex containing a temple (area SS); in this complex a beautiful statue of a reclining human-headed bull in one of the ritual objects found. Impressive architectural remains from the Mitanni period include a palace and a temple. The Brak excavations are one of the primary benchmarks of archaeology in Syria, with comprehensive stratigraphic and architectural interpretations and an equally secure analysis of the ceramic sequences.

The excavations at Tell Barri (ancient Kakhat), begun in 1980 under the direction of Paolo Emilio Pecorella, have uncovered thirteen periods dating from the Halaf to the thirteenth century CE, with few gaps (Pecorella and Anastasio, 1996). During the Mari and Mitanni eras, Kakhat was the major center for the worship of the storm god, Teššup. Assyrian inscriptions indicate that Tukulti-Ninurta II (890–884 BCE) constructed a palace at Kakhat. The long and very carefully documented Tell Barri ceramic sequence is now a basic tool for ceramic chronology in the Upper Khabur region. Just to the north of Tell Barri, at Tell Hamidiya, Markus Waefler began excavations in 1984 and has explored a palace built on three levels of such massive dimensions that it appears to occupy the whole of the acropolis, making it one of the most imposing buildings of the ancient Near East. This trilevel palace had supporting walls preserved up to 16 m high and 12 m wide and contained a large number of ivories dating to the reign of Shalmaneser III. [*See* Palace.]

The excavations of Shamshi-Adad's city of Shubat-Enlil at Tell Leilan were begun by Harvey Weiss in 1978; on the acropolis they have uncovered a long-room temple whose north and south facades were decorated with elaborate mudbrick relief columns. Soundings in the Lower City found many public buildings dating to the period of Shamshi-Adad and his successors that attest to the vastness of his administrative complex there. Two large buildings, identified as palaces, contained important tablets of the royal archive. During the third-millennium occupation (2600–2200 BCE) the city was called Shekhna; it had a city wall built in two phases around both the acropolis and the Lower City (Akkermans and Weiss, 1987; Akkermans et al., 1991; Parayre and Weiss, 1991). The excavations at Mohammad Diyab (ancient Azamhul), begun in 1987 (by Durand and Dominique Charpin) have recovered second-millennium BCE houses and tombs.

Urkeš/Tell Mozan, a large third-millennium site in the Wadi Dara region has been excavated since 1984 by Giorgio Buccellati and Marilyn Kelly-Buccellati (1984). They have uncovered a mid-third millennium temple (BA). The storehouse (AK) is characterized by a symmetrical plan that includes two small vaults; on a floor in front of one of these vaults more than six hundred Early Akkadian seal impressions were excavated along with cuneiform tablets containing some Hurrian names and words. The inscribed seal impressions have led to the identification of the site with the Hurrian city of Urkeš. In the Khabur area 144 Early Dynastic III tablets have been excavated at Tell Beydar, under the direction of Marc Lebeau (1991).

The Tell Chuera excavations of Anton Moortgat and Ursula Moortgat-Correns that began in 1958 are being continued by Orthmann. These excavations have revealed a large third-millennium urban center located between the Balikh and the Upper Khabur Rivers. A number of temples have been found, including what must have been a large temple placed on top of a significant stone platform (steinbau III) opposite a monumental entrance to the city. Two statues sculpted in the Early Dynastic II style are the northernmost examples of this type of sculpture. A late third-millennium palace (F) and a large Middle Assyrian building have also been excavated. The site is identified as Ḫarbe in the Middle Assyrian period.

In the north Balikh area, the site of Tell Hammam et-Turkman (ancient Zalpa?) was an important regional center with evidence of palaces from both the Middle and Late Bronze Ages. The excavators, Maurits N. van Loon and Diederik J. W. Meijer, have recovered a number of cuneiform tablets and cylinder seals; the seal impressions attest to a high level of administrative organization, including a scribal school. Van Loon has made substantial contributions to Syrian archaeology through his work at Tell Mureybet, Selenkhiye, and Hammam et-Turkman, in addition to training a whole generation of American and European archaeologists.

Tell Biʿa (ancient Tuttul), near the confluence of the Balikh and the Euphrates, has been excavated by Strommenger since 1980; she has uncovered a burnt palace from 2500 BCE containing many wood features, including pilasters. In a palace dated just prior to the reign of Shamshi-Adad I, one level contained a common grave with the remains of eighty skeletons showing evidence of violent death, probably during a battle.

Conclusions. In the early decades of the twentieth century, some exploration of major sites, such as Mari and Ugarit, came about through accidental discoveries. Many tells, however, were selected for excavation as a result of a well-planned research strategy: Ebla, where the research strategy posited a major third-millennium urban area in this part of inner Syria; Tell Hamidiya, where research revolves around the hypothesis that this site is the Mitanni capital of Taidu; the Khabur region, based on the reasoning that major third-

and second-millennium cities should exist there; and the el-Kowm region, east of Palmyra, in the Syrian steppe, where large-scale regional research deriving from specific research interests and research strategy has been undertaken. Salvage operations initiated by dam construction have given impetus to excavations in geographic areas that might otherwise have been overlooked. Research on these sites, especially for the sites connected with the Tabqa dam, often was connected at a second stage with a specific research strategy. In Syria more than seventy Syrian and foreign excavations are being conducted, researching the prehistoric through the Islamic period, from coastal Syria through the Khabur region; nine large survey projects are also being conducted (al-Maqdissi, 1993). For much of this intensive period of the excavation of archaeological sites in Syria during the last thirty years, Najah al-Attar has been the minister of culture. She has been responsible and directly involved in all phases of promoting the cause of archaeology within Syria itself and in bringing the results of this endeavor to the wider international audience. International exhibits of objects excavated in Syria have been bringing Syrian history and culture to a much wider public. Syria has been an area where the recovery of ancient culture through excavations by an international collaboration have resulted in a significantly changed historical picture.

[*See also the biographies of Albright, Dunand, Layard, Mallowan, Moortgat, Parrot, Poidebard, Renan, Schaeffer, Smith, Thureau-Dangin, and Woolley. In addition, many of the sites mentioned are the subject of independent entries.*]

BIBLIOGRAPHY

Excavation reports and textual studies for important sites can be found in the journals *Iraq* (for Chagar Bazar and Brak), *Mari: Annales de Recherches Interdisciplinaires* (for Mari), and *Studi Eblaiti* (for Ebla). The reader may also consult the following:

Akkermans, P. A., and Harvey Weiss. "Tell Leilan, 1987, Operation 3: Preliminary Report on the Lower Town Palace." *Annales Archéologiques Arabes Syriennes* 38 (1989): 1–19.

Akkermans, P. A., et al. "An Administrative Building of the King of Andarig at Shubat Enlil." *Nabu* 4 (1991): 68–70.

Anastasio, Stefano. *The Archaeology of Upper Mesopotamia: An Analytical Bibliography for the Pre-Classical Periods.* Subartu, 1. Brussels, 1995.

Bounni, Adnan. *Le sanctuaire de Nabu.* Damascus, 1982.

Buccellati, Giorgio, and Marilyn Kelly-Buccellati. *Mozan,* vol. 1, *The Soundings of the First Two Seasons.* Bibliotheca Mesopotamica, 20. Malibu, 1988.

Freedman, David Noel, ed. *Archaeological Reports from the Tabqa Dam Project—Euphrates Valley, Syria.* Annual of the American Schools of Oriental Research, 44. Ann Arbor, Mich., 1979.

Mallowan, M.E.L. "Excavations at Brak and Chagar Bazar, Syria." *Iraq* 9 (1947): 1–266.

Maqdissi, Michel al-. "Chroniques des activités archéologiques en Syrie." *Syria* 70 (1993): 443–576.

Matthiae, Paolo. *Ebla: An Empire Rediscovered.* Translated by Christopher Holme. Garden City, N.Y., 1980.

Mazzoni, Stefania. "Frontières céramiques et le Haut Euphrate au Bronze Ancien IV." *Mari: Annales de Recherches Interdisciplinaires* 4 (1985): 561–577.

Mazzoni, Stefania. *Le Impronte su Giara Eblaite e Siriane nel Bronzo Antico.* Materiali e Studi Archeologica di Ebla, 1. Rome, 1992.

Parayre, D., and Harvey Weiss. "Cinq campagnes de fouilles à Tell Leilan: Bilan et perspectives." *Journal des Savants* (1991): 3–26.

Pecorella, Paolo E., and Stefano Anastasio. *The Second Millennium at Tell Barri–Kakhat.* 1996.

Poidebard, Antoine. *La trace de Rome dans le désert de Syrie.* Paris, 1934.

MARILYN KELLY-BUCCELLATI

Archaeology in Israel

Interest in local antiquities was first aroused among the Jewish settlers in the land of Israel, even among members of the Orthodox community, in the nineteenth and early twentieth centuries. A. M. Lunz, a prominent scholar in the nineteenth century, studied the country's historical geography. In 1914, the Jewish Palestine Exploration Society (later known as the Israel Exploration Society) was founded in Jerusalem. [*See* Israel Exploration Society.] It concerned itself with Jewish antiquities, first excavating at Hammath Tiberias (Nahum Slouschz, 1921–1922). The society has, ever since, been central to all archaeological activity in Israel and its journal the focal publication of the status of research on the country's antiquities.

One of the pioneers in archaeological research by Palestinian Jews was Eleazar L. Sukenik, the first professor of archaeology at the fledgling Hebrew University of Jerusalem, where in 1926 he founded the Department of Archaeology and the Museum for Jewish Antiquities. [*See the biography of Sukenik.*] His first important excavation was the synagogue at Beth Alpha (1929). His subsequent excavations included the Jewish burial caves in the vicinity of Jerusalem and, beginning in 1927, several seasons at Tel Gerisa, a multistrata mound of the Bronze and Iron Ages. Sukenik also participated in the expedition to Samaria led by John W. Crowfoot, where he and his assistant, Nahman Avigad, were exposed to British excavation methods. [*See the biographies of Crowfoot and Avigad.*] Another inspiring scholar in that period was Benjamin Mazar (Maisler). Trained as a historian and an Assyriologist, he was influenced by William Foxwell Albright to practice interdisciplinary research that would include history, philology, Bible, historical geography, and archaeology. [*See the biographies of Mazar and Albright.*] Following his excavation of the Jewish necropolis at Beth-Sheʿarim, Mazar joined the faculty of the Hebrew University, where he trained a group of Israeli scholars who were to become prominent in the disciplines of ancient history and archaeology.

Other Jewish archaeologists worked for the Department of Antiquities organized by the British during their mandate in Palestine (1917–1948) or in the Jewish Palestine Exploration Society. Moshe Stekelis laid the foundations for research at the country's prehistoric sites; Emmanuel Ben-Dor and Ruth Amiran conducted ceramics studies; Naphtali Hertz Torzcyner (Tur-Sinai) and others studied paleography and Semitic languages; Shmuel Yeivin and J. Leibovitch studied Egyptology; Mazar studied the ancient Near East; Michael Avi-Yonah, Avigad, and others studied classical art and archaeology; and Leo A. Mayer specialized in Islamic art and archaeology. [*See the biographies of Stekelis, Yeivin, and Avi-Yonah.*]

These Israeli historians and archaeologists combined two traditions: the broad knowledge and pedagogy involving classical and ancient Near East studies brought from European universities and the methodologies of archaeological fieldwork, particularly as applied to the large-scale expeditions, carried out in the country prior to 1948.

1948 to 1967. Following the foundation of the State of Israel, several factors determined the progress of archaeology in Israel: Israeli scholars were excluded from direct contact with their colleagues in other parts of the Near East; the state was encouraging the archaeological investigation of its heritage; and the country was developing rapidly. The newly established and rather small Department of Antiquities, directed by Yeivin, was conducting salvage excavations at many sites. Management of the country's antiquities followed the traditions of the British Mandatory Department of Antiquities. In 1949–1950, Mazar conducted the first systematic excavation at a biblical site, at Tell Qasile near Tel Aviv, under the auspices of the country's then only academic institution, the Hebrew University of Jerusalem. Mazar uncovered remains of a Philistine and Israelite town. Another consequential factor during the first years following independence was the discovery of the Dead Sea Scrolls, some of which Sukenik purchased for the Hebrew University. His son and student, Yigael Yadin, would later purchase additional scrolls. [*See* Dead Sea Scrolls.] The discovery of the scrolls opened new research vistas for philologists, historians, and Bible scholars. A number of Israeli archaeologists, including Sukenik, Avigad, and particularly Yadin, devoted years of study to translating them.

Yadin, a brilliant scholar and an engaging lecturer, gave a major impetus to Israeli archaeology. Following his service as chief of staff of the Israel Defense Forces, he joined the Hebrew University in 1954. [*See the biography of Yadin.*] From 1954 to 1958, and again in 1968, he conducted a large-scale excavation at Tel Hazor, which served as a field school for a generation of Israeli archaeologists and as a crucible for the discipline of biblical archaeology. Most of Israel's preeminent archaeologists in this field were senior members of the Hazor team: Aharoni, Amiran, Trude Dothan and Moshe Dothan, Claire Epstein, and others. An inspiring figure at the time was architect Immanuel Dunayevsky. [*See the biographies of Aharoni and Dunayevsky.*]

The search for the Dead Sea Scrolls in Jordan and the illegal looting of caves in the Israeli part of the Judean Desert prompted Israeli archaeologists to survey caves and conduct salvage excavations in that region. Following Aharoni's pioneering surveys, teams of archaeologists excavated in the desert's deep ravines and cliffs in 1961–1962. Documents and human remains from the time of the Bar Kokhba revolt in 135 CE discovered in this operation by the team led by Yadin have elucidated this period of Jewish history. [*See* Bar Kokhba Revolt.] Exploration in the Judean Desert reached its peak in 1963–1964, with Yadin's large-scale excavations at Masada, which various teams of Israeli archaeologists had previously explored and surveyed. To many in Israel and abroad, Masada had deep historical and emotional significance. Hundreds of volunteers from all over the world participated in its excavation, initiating a practice now common on both Israeli and foreign expeditions working in Israel. For the general public the extensive, well-publicized excavations at Masada became a virtual symbol of Israeli archaeology, as well as a tourist attraction.

During those same years, Aharoni initiated field surveys in the Galilee that demonstrated the significance of this method for studying settlement patterns. The result was a critical new methodology for interpreting historical data and writing history. In 1964, the Association for the Survey of Israel was founded, whose goal was a comprehensive archaeological survey of the country, an endeavor still underway, utilizing a methodology the association developed. [*See* Survey of Israel.]

In the late 1950s and early 1960s a generation of new Israeli archaeologists, most of whom had participated at Hazor, engaged in independent projects of their own. Important achievements were made in the study of the earliest agricultural communities of the Neolithic and Chalcolithic periods (Naḥal Oren cave of the Pre-Pottery Neolithic A period, the exploration of the Chalcolithic period in the Beersheba region, and the discoveries in the Judean Desert of the ʿEin-Gedi temple and Naḥal Mishmar treasure-cave, both revolutionary finds relating to the Chalcolithic period). The Bronze and Iron Ages were studied by Aharoni at Ramat Raḥel and Arad, by Amiran at Early Bronze Age Arad, by Moshe Dothan at Tel Mor and Ashdod, and by Benjamin Mazar at ʿEin-Gedi. Archaeologists interested in the Roman-Byzantine periods directed their efforts to excavating Nabatean and Byzantine cities in the Negev (Avdat, Mamshit [Mampsis], primarily by Avaham Negev), as well as Caesarea (Avi-Yonah and Negev), the synagogue at Hammath Tiberias (Dothan), the town and necropolis of Beth-Sheʿarim (Mazar and Avigad), the Roman theater at Beth-Shean, the Roman limes (Mordechai Gichon), and more.

The sole academic research and teaching institute at the time was the Department of Archaeology of the Hebrew University, later to become the Institute of Archaeology. In 1962, the newly founded Tel Aviv University established an

Institute of Archaeology and Ancient Near East Studies, headed first by Yeivin and subsequently by Aharoni, that soon became a viable center of research and teaching.

1967–1994. In the late 1960s, unprecedented economic opportunities and a new order of international cooperation made possible a flourishing of Israeli archaeological research, during which exploring Jerusalem became the major endeavor of Hebrew University archaeologists. Three main expeditions were conducted: south of the Temple Mount (Mazar, 1968–1978), the Jewish Quarter (Avigad, 1969–1983), and the City of David (Yigal Shiloh, 1978–1984). Additional archaeological projects in Jerusalem included the Valley of Hinnom (Gabriel Barkai); the Jaffa Gate area and the Mamilla area (Magen Broshi, Ronny Reich). The Damascus Gate area; the Third Wall; and the aqueducts. Also explored were the vast necropoli of both the First and Second Temple periods surrounding the city and its agricultural periphery, where numerous farmsteads and agricultural settlements belonging to various periods were studied, mostly in salvage excavations. This comprehensive undertaking in the archaeology of Jerusalem greatly expanded what is known of the city over millennia.

Excavations and surveys were conducted for all periods and subjects. In prehistory, excavations at Tell el-ʿUbeidiya (Stekelis, Ofer Bar-Yosef, and others) revealed the earliest human culture in the ancient Near East. Various phases of the Stone Age were explored at such sites as Hayonim cave in the western Galilee, at Paleolithic sites in the Golan Heights, and at Neolithic sites in the Jordan Valley and in the Sinai Desert. Caves on the Carmel ridge that had been explored during the 1930s were reexcavated, utilizing more sophisticated methods (Kebara cave, el-Wad cave, and others). Prehistoric research in the Negev and Sinai deserts enabled the study of climatic changes and the history of indigenous Epipaleolithic and early Neolithic communities.

The field of biblical archaeology was enriched by wide-scale excavation projects and surveys that generated an ever-growing body of data and new interpretations. The major multistrata tells yielding important remains of the Bronze and Iron Ages, excavated by Israeli expeditions or by joint endeavors of Israeli and foreign archaeologists, are (from north to south): Dan (Avraham Biran), Hazor (Amnon Ben-Tor), Tel Hadar (Moshe Kochavi and Pirhiya Beck), Kabri (Aharon Kempinski and Hans G. Niemeyer); Akko (Dothan), Yoqneʿam, Tel Qiri, and Tel Qashish (Ben-Tor), Jezreel (David Ussishkin and John Woodhead), Beth-Shean (Amihai Mazar), Tel Nami (Michal Artzy), Dor (Ephraim Stern), Tel Michal (Ze'ev Herzog and others), Tell Qasile (Amihai Mazar), Aphek (Kochavi and Beck), Jaffa (Jacob and Haya Kaplan), Tel Gerisa (Herzog and others), Shiloh (Israel Finkelstein), Beth-Shemesh (Shlomo Bunimovitz and Zvi Lederman), Tel Batash (Amihai Mazar and George L. Kelm), Tel Miqne/Ekron (Trude Dothan and Seymour Gitin), Lachish (Ussishkin), Tel Seraʿ and Tel Haror (Eliezer Oren), Deir el-Balaḥ (Trude Dothan), Tel Sheva (Aharoni), Tel ʿIra, (Itzhag Beit-Arieh and Biran), ʿAroʿer (Biran), Tel Masos (Kempinski and Volkman Fritz), and Tel Malḥata (Kochavi, Beit-Arieh, and Bruce Cresson).

In addition, significant data have been collected from excavations at single-period sites, either salvage excavations or as part of regional or subject-oriented projects. Only a few can be mentioned here: the Chalcolithic sites in the Golan Heights (Epstein) and the megalithic monument of Rujm el-Hiri (Kochavi and Yonathan Mizrahi); the Early Bronze I villages at Yiftaḥel, Ḥorvat Ilin, and Palmaḥim (Eliot Braun) and Ḥartuv (Amihai Mazar and Pierre de Miroschedji); the Middle Bronze II Age sites in the vicinity of Jerusalem (Emmanuel Eisenberg, Gershon Edelstein); the Iron Age I sites on Mt. Ebal (Adam Zertal), at ʿIzbet Ṣarṭah (Kochavi and Finkelstein), and at Giloh (Amihai Mazar); the exceptional Iron Age II site of Kuntillet ʿAjrud with its Hebrew inscriptions (Zeev Meshel), the Iron Age II sites along the shores of the Dead Sea (Pessah Bar-Adon), the Iron Age II citadels at Qadesh-Barnea (Rudolph Cohen) and Ḥorvat ʿUza (Beit-Arieh and Cresson), the Edomite temple at Ḥorvat Qitmit (Beit-Arieh) and the Negev highland sites (Cohen). This vast activity was supplemented by a multitude of salvage excavations at cemeteries and small sites carried out by archaeologists from the Israel Antiquities Authority.

Survey work also reached sites located throughout the country. The emergency survey conducted, in 1968 in Judah, Samaria, and the Golan Heights underscored the potential of this methodology. Subsequently, younger scholars, of the "third generation" of Israeli archaeologists (Yehudah Dagan, Finkelstein, Zvi Gal, Mordechai Heimann, Avi Ofer, Zertal), extensively surveyed geographic regions, employing modern methods to analyze their data. These regional studies opened new vistas in terms of the patterns and processes of settlement in various periods, enabling demographic studies and illuminating such central historical issues as the Israelite settlement of the hill country.

Numerous Hellenistic, Roman, Byzantine, Early Islamic, and medieval sites were explored during this period. Currently, the largest archaeological enterprise in Israel is the excavations at Beth-Shean, where Yoram Tsafrir, Gideon Foerster, Gabi Mazor and Rachel Bar Nathan have exposed the entire civic center of the Roman and Byzantine city. Large-scale research at Caesarea, both on land and underwater, has uncovered the harbor built by King Herod and large parts of the surrounding city (Avner Raban, Joseph Patrich, Josef Porath, and Ehud Netzer in collaboration with American scholars); at Sepphoris, American and Israeli expeditions have revealed a well-planned city with a plethora of ornate mosaic floors in elaborate dwellings (Eric Meyers, James Strange, Netzer, Zeev Weiss); in the Golan Heights synagogues have been explored (Dan Urman and Zvi Uri Maʿoz), the Jewish town at Gamla that fell to the Romans in 67 CE has been excavated (Shmaryahu Gutman), the Roman city of Banias has been partially excavated (Maoz, Vassilios Tzaferis); at Shechem, Yitzhak Magen excavated the public buildings of Roman Neapolis, while on Mt. Gerizim, he uncovered the enclosure of the Samaritan temple and parts of the Hellenistic Samaritan city; at Jericho and Herodium, Netzer uncovered elaborately constructed Hasmonean and Herodian palaces; at Mareshah and Beth-Guvrin (Eleutheroplis) Amos Kloner revealed complex underground installations and cisterns, Hellenistic dwellings, and a Roman amphitheater; and work continues in the cities of the Negev (Mareshah, Avdat, Ḥaluṣah, Reḥovot, Shivtah and Neṣṣana). In general, the forts, roads, and aqueducts of all these periods have been investigated, and numerous Byzantine churches, as well as Jewish and Samaritan synagogues, have been excavated throughout the country. This list is partial and by necessity omits the hundreds of salvage excavations and small-scale projects carried out at agricultural farmsteads and installations and in small villages. Desert and underwater archaeologies have defined themselves as distinct disciplines in the course of archaeological activity in Israel. This vast activity has turned Israel into one of the most intensively explored countries in the world.

Institutions. At the time of writing, five universities in Israel have institutes or departments of archaeology for teaching and research. Each has it own organization, approach, and emphasis, yet together they create the academic framework for archaeological exploration in the country. In 1989, the governmental Department of Antiquities, a relatively small division in the Ministry of Education, was transformed into the independent Israel Antiquities Authority (IAA). Headed by Amir Drori (from 1989), the IAA's budget supports an enlarged support network of inspectors, salvage excavation teams, archaeological surveys, conservation and preservation teams for sites and objects, and research and publication systems. Today, the IAA's more than two hundred archaeologists and hundreds of other workers make it an effective government agency. [*See* Israel Antiquities Authority.]

Other archaeological activity is carried out by museums (the Israel Museum and local museums), which sponsor archaeological exhibits and research. The Israel Exploration Society, directed since its inception by Joseph Aviram, is a voluntary body that aids in arranging and financing archaeological research, publishes it, and disseminates it by organizing local and international congresses. The Archaeological Council of Israel, which is elected according to the Antiquities Law of Israel by the Minister of Education is another voluntary public body. The council and its committees advise the director of the IAA on matters of archaeological policy.

Methodology. Archaeological research in Israel emerged from European pedagogic traditions and the fieldwork carried out in the Near East in the 1930s. In the universities, archaeology is taught in the framework of the faculty of humanities, and is closely allied to the fields of history, Bible, ancient Near East studies, classics, and art history. Field-excavation methods are rooted in the sweeping architectural approach of traditional Near Eastern archaeology, in which large architectural complexes are exposed and their stratigraphy is analyzed on the basis of the relationship between building remains and floor levels. The British method of analyzing debris layers in vertical sections developed by Mortimer Wheeler and Kathleen M. Kenyon has guided most Israeli excavators since the early 1960s, although the method was applied as a supplement to refine the architectural approach. [*See the biographies of Wheeler and Kenyon.*] The synthesis between these two approaches has characterized many excavations in Israel in the last decades.

Israeli archaeology has concentrated largely on fieldwork, its interpretation, and publication, complemented by the comparative study of classes of finds. The theoretical aspects of archaeological research never played an important role in local research (except in the field of prehistory) until recently. Israeli archaeologists were, for the most part, detached from the anthropological and social-studies approach that figured in the interpretation of data in western Europe and the United States. Today, new paths for research are being explored in the theoretical realm by some younger scholars who emphasize reconstructing ancient social structures and take an environmental approach to archaeological studies. Subjects such as nomadism and sedentarization, family structure, family and tribal structures, processes of urbanism and rural settlement distributions are being examined, settlement distribution and demography are studied alongside the more traditional emphasis on comparative architecture and art, glyptics, iconography, paleography, numismatics, and the interraction between finds and ancient texts. These subjects have transformed the discipline's scope to one that is panoramic in its research possibilities.

Another important development is the concentration by certain research centers in special subjects. Thus, Haifa University developed its Center for Maritime Studies and underwater archaeology, while Ben Gurion University is a center for desertic studies in the arid zones of the Negev and Sinai.

Publications. Archaeological subjects are published in both Hebrew and English in Israel. The Israel Exploration Society publishes the periodicals *Qadmoniot* (in Hebrew), *Eretz Israel* (in Hebrew with a section in European languages), and the *Israel Exploration Journal* (primarily in English), as well as final excavation reports and occasional collections of essays, congress volumes, and monographs (again, primarily in English). The Israel Antiquities Authority publishes the periodicals *ʿAtiqot* and *Excavations and Surveys in Israel* (the English translation of *Hadashot Arkheologiot,* which includes short reports on all fieldwork carried in Israel). The Institute of Archaeology of the Hebrew University publishes the series *Qedem* (monographs and final reports), and the Institute of Archaeology of Tel Aviv University publishes the periodical *Tel Aviv,* as well as occasional monographs and final reports. Museum publications contribute to this list, as do the papers and books published outside Israel.

Impact on Society. The breadth and intensity of archaeological activity in Israel has kept the public's attention, in particular when it is engaged at sites and in subjects central to Jewish history, such as Jerusalem, Masada, Qumran and the Dead Sea Scrolls, Gamla, and ancient synagogues. Archaeological sites are well preserved, with upkeep the responsibility generally of the National Parks Authority and the IAA, and attract both local and foreign tourists. Archaeological museums exist in almost every city, providing educational activities for schoolchildren and adults. Archaeology is even taught in some Israeli high schools. The eminent role archaeology plays in Israeli society means that the issues that concern the discipline—limiting the antiquities trade, the difficulties created by rapid development and construction in those parts of the country in which there are antiquities, illicit digs, and the frequent demand by Orthodox Jews that ancient tombs and burials not be excavated, a conflict of interest that has often led to ideological clashes—also arouse the public debate. By meeting challenge and controversy, Israeli archaeology has matured and greatly extended the scope of its activities. It is today a rich and varied field of research that is also an integral component of modern life in Israel.

[*See also* Nationalism and Archaeology; Tourism and Archaeology. *In addition, most of the sites mentioned are the subject of independent entries.*]

BIBLIOGRAPHY

Amitai, Janet, ed. *Biblical Archaeology Today: Proceedings of the International Congress on Biblical Archaeology, Jerusalem, April 1984.* Jerusalem, 1985.

Bar-Yosef, Ofer, and Amihai Mazar. "Israeli Archaeology." *World Archaeology* 13 (1982): 310–325.

Ben-Tor, Amnon, ed. *The Archaeology of Ancient Israel.* New Haven, 1992.

Ben-Tor, Amnon. "The Institute of Archaeology of the Hebrew University of Jerusalem." *Biblical Archaeologist* 56 (1993): 121–151.

Biran, Avraham, and Joseph Aviram, eds. *Biblical Archaeology Today, 1990: Proceedings of the Second International Congress on Biblical Archaeology, Jerusalem, June–July 1990.* Jerusalem, 1993.

Broshi, Magen. "Religion, Ideology, and Politics and Their Impact on Palestinian Archaeology." *Israel Museum Journal* 6 (1987): 17–32.

Dever, William G. "Two Approaches to Archaeological Method: The Architectural and the Stratigraphic." *Eretz-Israel* 11 (1973): 1*–8*.

Kempinski, Aharon, and Ronny Reich, eds. *The Architecture of Ancient Israel: From the Prehistoric to the Persian Periods.* Jerusalem, 1992.

Levine, Lee I., ed. *Ancient Synagogues Revealed.* Jerusalem, 1981.

Mazar, Amihai. "Israeli Archaeologists." In *Benchmarks in Time and Culture: An Introduction to Palestinian Archaeology Dedicated to Joseph A. Callaway,* edited by Joel F. Drinkard et al., pp. 109–128. Atlanta, 1988.

Mazar, Amihai. *Archaeology of the Land of the Bible, 10,000–586 B.C.E.* New York, 1990.

Silberman, Neil Asher. *A Prophet from Amongst You: The Life of Yigael Yadin—Soldier, Scholar, and Mythmaker of Modern Israel.* New York, 1993.

Stern, Ephraim, et al., eds. *The New Encyclopedia of Archaeological Excavations in the Holy Land.* 4 vols. Jerusalem and New York, 1993.

Tsafrir, Yoram, ed. *Ancient Churches Revealed.* Jerusalem, 1993.

AMIHAI MAZAR

Archaeology in Jordan

The archaeological exploration of Jordan (Transjordan) is closely connected historically and physically with that of Cisjordan (western Palestine). Jerusalem, being the focal point of Judaism as well as one for Christianity and Islam, is surrounded by concentric circles of historical and religious interest that involve the entire region. Archaeological investigation of the land east of the Jordan River and of its past has emerged slowly but is revealing its distinct identity.

Only a few of the many pilgrims who visited the region in antiquity (e.g., the Bordeaux pilgrim in 333, and the monk Bernard in the late ninth century) extended their journeys beyond the Jordan. Usually, they were content to contemplate the holy sites of Jerusalem, Bethlehem, and Nazareth. Two exceptions from this early period were Paula of Rome (382 CE) and Silvia of Aquitaine (379–388 CE). Between the ninth and the fifteenth centuries, Arab and Persian geographers (e.g., Muqaddasi in 985, Yaqut in 1225, and Nasir-i-Khusrau in 1047) traveled widely in the region, making careful observations. Unfortunately, like the early pilgrims, they were not especially concerned with archaeological ruins.

When the Crusaders gained control of Jerusalem (1099–1187) and portions of Transjordan, it acted as a new impetus for Western travelers to explore the land—a trend that continued even after the Crusaders were routed. In the period after the Crusades, travelers to the Holy Land included Magister Thietmar (1217), who visited Petra without recognizing it as such; Burchard of Mt. Zion (1283), who thought that the site of Kerak (mod. Al Karak) was also the site of Petra and Montreal; and Rabbi Esthori Ben Mose Ha-Parchi, who spent seven years exploring eastern and western Palestine. There are many others, from the methodical Felix Fabri (1480–1483) to the more archaeologically motivated Cotovicus (Kootwyk, 1598–1599), De la Rocque (1688), and Richard Pococke (1738). Even in the reports of these scholars Transjordan was still of only minor interest.

Jordan Rediscovered: 1805–1918. During the period from 1805 to 1918, more and more Westerners traveled through Transjordan, recording relics and turning increasingly to intensive exploration and mapping. Among the most adventurous were the German explorer Ulrich Jasper Seetzen, who visited between 1805 and 1807, and the Swiss explorer Johann Ludwig Burckhardt, who visited between 1810 and 1812. During his extensive travels, Seetzen discovered Jerash/Gerasa and Amman/Philadelphia, while Burckhardt rediscovered Petra, whose location had been forgotten for six centuries (Seetzen had been there but could not identify the site.) [*See* Jerash; Amman; Petra.]

What was known of Transjordan was increased by the recorded observations of the British traveler James Silk Buckingham (in 1816, 1821) and navy officers Charles Leonard Irby and James Mangles (in 1817–1818). Irby and Mangles traveled with explorers William John Bankes and Thomas Legh from south of the Dead Sea to northern Transjordan, eventually discovering the temple and other ruins at ʿIraq el-Amir. [*See* ʿIraq el-Amir.] The travels of Léon de Laborde and Linant (in 1828) included Petra, where they made excellent drawings.

The emphasis on identifying place names and on mapping increased in the mid- and late nineteenth century. An especially extensive survey, with attempts to identify biblical sites from their modern Arabic names, was made by the Americans Edward Robinson and Eli Smith (1838, 1852). Their travels east of the Jordan included brief visits to Petra and Pella. [*See* Pella.]

Holy Land (historical) geography, which is intimately connected to archaeological research, progressed from the broad principles laid down by Robinson to their precise application by the German Titus Tobler, who visited the Holy Land in 1845–1846, 1857, and 1865, and the Frenchman Victor Honoré Guérin, who visited five times between 1852 and 1875. [*See* Historical Geography.] However, it was the Englishmen Claude Regnier Conder and Horatio Herbert Kitchener who carried out a detailed survey of western Palestine (1871–1878) for the PEF to produce maps using a scale of one inch to one mile. Conder attempted the same for eastern Palestine in 1881, but difficulties interposed and the work was left to be completed by Gottlieb Schumacher (see below) during the next twenty years. Work in the northern regions was supplemented by the American Archaeological Expedition to Syria led by Howard Crosby Butler (1899–1900). In 1904 Butler returned, leading a Princeton University team that made detailed observations at the sites of ʿIraq el-Amir and Rabbath-Ammon/Ammon.

Special interest in the Dead Sea area had already been awakened in 1848 by William F. Lynch, whose U.S. expedition traveled from the Sea of Galilee to the Dead Sea by means of two metal boats (Bliss, 1906). He spent three weeks in the Dead Sea region, including a side trip to Kerak. [*See* Kerak.] In 1863 and 1864, Henry Baker Tristram led a British expedition that investigated the regions of the Dead Sea and the Sea of Galilee. Duc de Luynes investigated the Dead Sea in 1864, along with Ammon, Moab, and the ʿArabah, down to the Gulf of ʿAqaba; and geologist Edward Hull, in 1883–1884, further explored the Dead Sea region and the ʿArabah for the PEF. [*See* Ammon; Moab; ʿAqaba.] The discovery of the Moabite stone (Mesha stela) by Anglican minister F. A. Klein in 1868 and the world's focus on the attempts to recover it, led to expectations of more rich discoveries there. [*See* Moabite Stone.] This victory monument was made by Mesha, a ninth-century BCE Moabite king. The stela was broken up by local bedouin who were confused and suspicious over Franco-German rivalry to obtain it, and in fear of intervention by the hated Turkish governor (see Horn, 1986). About two-thirds of the fragments were recovered by French diplomat and amateur archaeologist Charles S. Clermont-Ganneau and Charles Warren of the PEF and these were taken to the Louvre in Paris. There a reconstruction was made with the assistance of a rough paper squeeze. This discovery remains the longest (34 lines) ancient monumental inscription found anywhere in Palestine.

The American Selah Merrill collected considerable data on his expeditions to Jordan from 1870 to 1877, building a notable collection of Palestinian pottery. George L. Robinson (representing McCormack Theological Seminary and the American Schools of Oriental Research) spent considerable time investigating Petra between 1900 and 1928, having rediscovered the Great High Place in 1900 and realized its function. (The first to have recognized the site was an American editor, Edward L. Wilson, in 1882.) Several European scholars explored the Petra tombs and other structures, including Rudolf-Ernst Brünnow and Alfred von Domaszewski, between 1897 and 1898, and Gustaf Dalman several years later. Cooperation from the Turkish governor of Kerak made it possible for Frederick Jones Bliss in 1895 and Domaszewski in 1895, 1897, and 1898 to clarify many details of the Moab plateau, its ancient roads, and its fortifications.

A number of organizations were involved as sponsor or director of programs involving many of the foregoing contributions. Most had their headquarters in Jerusalem and worked primarily in western Palestine: the American Oriental Society, the forerunner of the American Schools of Oriental Research (ASOR); the British Palestine Exploration Fund (PEF), which supported the surveys of Conder and Kitchener (see above); the American Palestine Exploration Society (APES), an even more direct forerunner of ASOR; the Deutscher Palästina-Verein, which sponsored, with the PEF, Schumacher's mapping work; and the École Biblique et Archéologique Française, which sponsored the work of Brünnow and Domaszewski at Petra, in cooperation with Dalman of the Deutsches Evangelisches Institut für Altertumswissenschaft des Heiligen Landes.

Excavations: 1918–1948. Political changes in the region at the close of World War I included the establishment of a British Mandate in Palestine. A Department of Antiquities was formed in 1920 under the leadership of John Garstang that made unauthorized digging illegal and adopted a liberal antiquities ordinance that remains in place today in Jordan with only some modifications. The special needs of the Transjordan region were soon recognized, and a Department of Antiquities was opened in Amman in 1923. At the same time, travel to and work at isolated sites became safer as a result of the establishment of the Arab Legion.

Perhaps of greatest significance for this period was the scientific use made of regional surveys alongside ceramic and other indicators of habitational patterns. The first expedition to use surface sherding was led by William Foxwell Albright in 1924 under the auspices of ASOR and Xenia Theological Seminary. His associates were Melvin Grove Kyle of Xenia, Alexis Mallon of the Pontifical Biblical Institute (PBI) in Jerusalem, and Eliezer Sukenik from ASOR in Jerusalem (King, 1983). The survey involved essentially the southern Ghor (Jordan Rift Valley), Kerak, and a portion of the plateau north of Kerak; it was also the first to discover the Early Bronze Age site of Bab edh-Dhraʿ (Mallon actually made the discovery). [*See* Bab edh-Dhraʿ.] Between 1932 and 1934, German Fritz Frank from Jerusalem surveyed areas south of the Dead Sea.

The most important and influential survey of this period was that by Nelson Glueck (1940, 1946). Between 1933 and 1947, he attempted to survey all of Jordan, with an emphasis on Ammon, Moab, and Edom. [*See* Edom.] This involved mapping, photographing, surveying (with sherding), and some aerial reconnaissance. The scope of this project was so vast that it is today thought to have been superficial in some areas. One of Glueck's conclusions was that the region from the modern capital of Amman to the Gulf of ʿAqaba had essentially been devoid of sedentary habitation during the Middle and Late Bronze Ages. This conclusion has required considerable correction and qualification as a result of subsequent surveys and excavations.

Some of the most important excavations carried out from 1918 to 1948 follow:

Amman. Initial excavations were commenced in 1927 in Amman/Philadelphia by an Italian Archaeological Mission team led by Giacomo Guidi and concluded in the 1930s by Renato Bartoccini. Their discoveries included several tombs and structures on top of the acropolis. Gerald Lankester Harding, director of the Department of Antiquities of Jordan from 1936 to 1956, was responsible for salvage operations in Amman at a time when rapid expansion of the city was leading to many accidental discoveries. In 1944, Harding cleared seven Iron Age tombs that yielded a wide range of pottery vessels and an inscribed ivory seal. [*See* Tombs; Seals.]

Gerasa/Jerash. Between 1925 and 1940 there were almost continuous projects underway to excavate and restore the ruins at Gerasa. Directors included George Horsfield, P. A. Ritchie, and A. G. Buchanan for the Transjordan Department of Antiquities (TDA); John W. Crowfoot for the British School of Archaeology and Yale University; Clarence S. Fisher and Glueck for ASOR; and Harding (TDA). The dramatic nature of the site's Roman and Byzantine structures as they emerged and were progressively reconstructed has made this one of the most impressive archaeological sites in the Near East. [*See* Restoration and Conservation.]

Petra. Some general excavations at Petra were begun by Agnes Conway and George Horsfield in 1929. They uncovered mainly Nabatean artifacts in some tombs and rubbish dumps. [*See* Nabateans.] Albright followed by clearing the Conway high place (an installation with a large sacred rock and surrounding processionway named after its discoverer Agnes Conway) in 1934; he was followed by Margaret Murray, who excavated two tombs in the central valley in 1937 under the auspices of the British School of Archaeology in Egypt. These various discoveries indicated habitation in the valley between about the fourth century BCE and the fourth century CE.

Teleilat el-Ghassul. Alexis Mallon and Robert Koeppel of the PBI in Jerusalem directed excavations at Teleilat el-Ghassul, a distinctive Chalcolithic site north of the Dead Sea, between 1929 and 1938. [*See* Teleilat el-Ghassul.] Following the discovery of the Baluʿ stela by R. G. Head (of the TDA) in 1930, Crowfoot (TDA and PEF) dug briefly at Baluʿ in 1932. [*See* Baluʿ.]

Ader. Albright and Head made exploratory excavations at the site of an ancient temple at Ader in 1933. Habitational clues indicated rather consistent use of the site from the Early Bronze to the Byzantine period.

Mt. Nebo/Khirbet el-Mukhayyat. The dual site of Mt. Nebo and nearby Khirbet el-Mukhayyat were dug by Sylvester J. Saller and Bellarmino Bagatti (for the Studium Biblicum Franciscanum) in an on-going program between 1933 and 1937, with the latter site extended to 1939 and 1948. Among the discoveries were Early Christian churches and a monastery/church complex. [*See* Nebo, Mount; Churches; Monasteries.]

Khirbet et-Tannur/Tell el-Kheleifeh. Glueck excavated two sites in quick succession: a Nabatean temple at Khirbet et-Tannur (1937–1938) and the fortified port/industrial site of Tell el-Kheleifeh (Ezion-Geber?) at the head of the Gulf of ʿAqaba (1938–1940). [*See* Kheleifeh, Tell el-, Tannur, Khirbet et-.]

Stratigraphic Excavations: 1948–1967. Jordan gained its national independence in 1946. Harding remained director of the Department of Antiquities until 1956, when he was succeeded by a series of Jordanian directors, including Awni Dajani, Yacub Quweis, Adnan Hadidi, Ghazi Bisheh, and Safwan Tell.

During this period the Jordanian Department of Antiquities (JDA) was involved in excavations at Qumran, together with the Palestine Archaeological Museum (now the Rockefeller Museum) and the French École Biblique (École Biblique et Archéologique Française). Continuing excavations in the vicinity of Qumran (and with the additional support of ASOR) led to further Dead Sea Scroll discoveries during the 1950s. [*See* Dead Sea Scrolls; Qumran; Copper Scroll.]

A mosaic map of the Holy Land had been discovered on the floor of a sixth century church in Madaba in 1884 and publicized in 1897 by Deacon Cleopas Kikilidis (Koikylides). This map was restored by a German Mission in 1965 under the direction of H. Donner. In 1966 and 1967 Ute Lux of the German Evangelical Institute excavated two additional churches in Madaba. [*See* Madaba.]

A regional survey conducted for the Department of Antiquities from 1952 to 1953 investigated the Jordan Valley and included minor excavations. [*See* Jordan Valley.] The survey was led by James Mellaart and Henri de Contenson. Kathleen Kenyon excavated at Jericho from 1952 to 1958, using stratigraphic techniques that would influence future field methodology on both banks of the Jordan. The following sampling of the excavations conducted on the east bank between 1948 and 1967 illustrates the progress of the discipline in the field.

Dhiban/Dibon. Fred V. Winnett, William L. Reed, A. Douglas Tushingham, and William M. Morton (under ASOR auscpices) uncovered mainly Moabite and Nabatean structures at Dhiban from 1950 to 1956. [*See* Dibon.]

Jordan Valley. In 1953 Henri de Contenson and James Mellaart surveyed various sites in the Jordan Valley for the Department of Antiquities, and made some soundings at places like Tell es-Saʿidiyeh, which James B. Pritchard excavated from 1964 to 1967 for the University of Pennsylvania. [*See* Saʿidiyeh, Tell es-.]

Ghrubba/Gharuba. In 1953 James Mellaart surveyed and did some limited digging at Ghrubba. The site included an ash pit measuring 150 × 5 × 3 m that was thought to have been rapidly filled by successive occupation during a Pottery Neolithic period. It is considered to be one of the earliest indicators of a substantial population in Jordan for this period (see Geraty and Willis, 1986).

Pella. Robert W. Funk and H. Neil Richardson dug two exploratory trenches at Pella in 1958, finding evidence of considerable Iron Age use (in addition to other periods). In 1964 Sami Rashid of the Department of Antiquities cleared eleven tombs there.

Irbid. At Irbid/Arbela, Rafik W. Dajani excavated four LB–Iron Age tombs in 1958–1959. Most of the remains of Arbela lie beneath the modern city of Irbid. [*See* Irbid.]

Deir ʿAlla. H. J. Franken led a Dutch expedition from the University of Leiden to Tell Deir ʿAlla (1960–1964, 1967), where an Aramaic inscription on the plaster walls of a temple gave details of the biblical prophet Balaam (*Nm.* 22–24). [*See* Deir ʿAlla, Tell; Deir ʿAlla Inscriptions.]

Umm Qeis/Gadara. In 1966, Ute Lux (German Evangelical Institute) excavated in the Greco-Roman city of Umm Qeis/Gadara, uncovering a late classical bath with an intricate mosaic floor design. [*See* Umm Qeis; Baths; Mosaics.]

Khirbet Iskander. Peter J. Parr carried out some initial excavations (British School and Ashmolean Museum) at Khirbet Iskander, a Late Chalcolithic–Middle Bronze Age site, in 1955.

Petra. Between 1954 and 1968 teams led by Philip Hammond and Peter J. Parr and G. R. H. Wright worked on many of the main buildings and sites at Petra. This program was carried out by the British School with the Jordanian Department of Antiquities.

Teleilat el-Ghassul. Robert North (Pontifical Biblical Institute) in 1960 and J. Basil Hennessy (British School in Jerusalem) in 1967 continued the excavation work at Teleilat el-Ghassul. The latter attempted to establish a sequence of habitational levels.

ʿIraq el-Amir. In 1961–1962 Paul W. Lapp (ASOR) excavated various features at ʿIraq el-Amir, including the *qaṣr* ("temple"). The impressive ruins and cliff-face caves—the latter with the name *Tobiah* carved in two places—appear to be the family heritage of the successors of "Tobiah the Ammonite" mentioned as an enemy in *Nehemiah* 2:10, 19, and elsewhere.

ʿAroʿer. From 1964 to 1966, Emilio Olávarri (for the Spanish Center in Jerusalem) excavated the fortress site of ʿAroʿer on the north bank of Wadi Mujib (Arnon River). This strategic building guarded the King's Highway from the north bank of Wadi Mujib. It is mentioned eight times in the Hebrew scriptures (e.g., *Jos.* 12:2; *2 Kgs.* 10:33).

Bab edh-Dhraʿ. One of the most dramatic sites excavated was Bab edh-Dhraʿ, by Lapp (1965–1967). He worked for two seasons in the huge cemetery and one in the town itself.

Interdisciplinary Excavations: 1967–1996. After the Six-Day War in 1967, the eastern sector of Jerusalem was no longer a part of Jordan; as a result, new research institutions were established in Amman. This benefited Jordan, which earlier had been only a part of a broader research context headquartered in Jerusalem. In addition to the Department of Antiquities of Jordan and the Department of Archaeology at the University of Jordan, the American Center of Oriental Research in Amman (ACOR) was founded in 1968. The British Institute in Amman soon followed, and, together, these institutions undertook surveys and excavations in various parts of the country, along with the Department of Antiquities, whose directors encouraged and cooperated with international projects. The archaeology of Jordan is seen today as a unique continuum running from prehistoric to modern times. Projects tend to be interdisciplinary in character, often with large teams and broad goals.

"Interdisciplinary" in this context means that a team does not consist only of archaeologists, and is not simply interested in reconstructing buildings or collecting artifacts. The entire team works toward reconstruction of the ancient human environment, life style, and food systems. Such an approach calls for a variety of support teams of specialists. These may include experts in geology who study the site, but who also determine which stone artifacts have been made from imported material. It may include specialists in ecology, botany, and zoology, who gather bones, seeds, and carbon specimens, but are also equipped to collect and examine microscopic paleobotany samples (ancient pollen grains, etc.). Since about 1967 there has been much more awareness of the need for this broader approach to archaeology and most excavations in Jordan have been involved, though in varying degrees.

The Madaba Plains Project. An example of interdisciplinary archaeology, the Madaba Plains Project grew out of the excavations at Tell Ḥesban/Heshbon, which began in 1968. [*See* Madaba; Ḥesban.] The expansion included surveys of the Madaba plain. Leadership passed from Siegfried Horn to Lawrence Thomas Geraty, and by the 1990s, the project incorporated three teams excavating and surveying simultaneously at Tell el-ʿUmeiri (Larry G. Herr), Tell Jalul (Randall Younker), and Tell Jawa (Michele Daviau). [*See* ʿUmeiri, Tell el-.]

Khirbet Iskander. Since 1981, a series of excavations has been sponsored by ASOR, with affiliates Drew University, Upsala College, and Seton Hall University. Directed by Suzanne Richard and Roger Boraas, work focused on clarifying the end of the Early Bronze period at Khirbet Iskander. Excavations have supported the view that agrarian settlement was an alternative to subsistence pastoralism in the closing phase of the Early Bronze age (c. 2350–2000 BCE) in this region.

ʿIraq el-Amir. At ʿIraq el-Amir, the French Institute of Archaeology in the Near East has been working on the reconstruction of the Hellenistic temple in collaboration with JDA. Work commenced in 1976 under the direction of Ernest Will.

Gadara. Work at Umm Qeis/Gadara was continued by Ute Lux directing an Amman branch of the German Evangelical Institute in Jerusalem. The emerging ruins of churches, theater, and city on this spur overlooking the Jordan and Yarmuk valleys and the Sea of Galiliee may eventually be as impressive as any of the other ancient sites in Jordan.

Deir ʿAlla. Franken (1976–1978) and Gerit van der Kooij (since 1979) continued work at Tell Deir ʿAlla, with Moawiyah M. Ibrahim as codirector, representing Yarmouk University and the Department of Antiquities.

Pella. Impressive work has been done at Pella, especially by Hennessey and Anthony Walter McNicholl (Univerity of Sydney, 1979–1991) and Robert Houston Smith (College of Wooster, 1967, 1979–1985) in uncovering churches, a cemetery, and a civic complex.

Edom. Crystal-M. Bennett of the British School of Archaeology in Jerusalem excavated at Tawilan (1968–1970) and at Iron Age II Buṣeirah (1971–1974). In 1979 the British Institute at Amman for Archaeology and History was founded, with Bennett as its first director. As a result, in 1980 another season was carried out at Buṣeirah and in 1982 another at Tawilan. [*See* Tawilan; Buṣeirah.]

Petra. Ongoing excavations at Petra throughout this period included Hammond's excavation of the Temple of the Winged Lions, which he discovered in 1974, and a marble-workers' establishment found in 1981; and Fawzi Zayadine's excavation of a potters' establishment there in 1982. Manfred Lindner of the Nuremberg Prehistoric Society also worked on various projects beginning in 1973. In the 1990s considerable activity and excitement surrounded work on the Winged Lion Temple (Phillip Hammond) and the Southern Temple (Martha Joukowsky of Brown University working with ACOR). A Byzantine church discovered by Kenneth Russell in 1990 has been excavated by Pierre Bikai of ACOR, with funding from USAID and support from JDA and the Ministry of Tourism. A quantity of burnt papyri found within the church needed special treatment to enable preservation and copying. Our knowledge of Petra in the Byzantine period has been considerably enhanced by these latter discoveries.

Bab edh-Dhraʿ, Numeira. Walter Rast and Thomas Schaub (ASOR), who had worked with Lapp at Bab edh-Dhraʿ, continued work at Bab edh-Dhraʿ and commenced work at Numeira, excavating there through the 1970s and 1980s.

Umm el-Jimal. Out on the desert fringe of Jordan, Bert De Vries (of Calvin College under ASOR auspices) surveyed and then excavated at Umm el-Jimal, beginning in 1973, in an ongoing project among the site's basalt ruins. [*See* Umm el-Jimal.]

International Outreach and Publications. As a result of the direct interest of Crown Prince Hassan, Jordan organized a series of international archaeological conferences, the first of which was held in Oxford, England, in 1980. Subsequent conferences were held in Amman, Jordan (1983); Tübingen, Germany (1986); Lyons, France (1989); Irbid, Jordan (1992); and Turin, Italy (1995). The results of the conferences have been published by volume in the series *Studies in the History and Archaeology of Jordan.* An organization known as the Friends of Archaeology sponsors lectures and trips to sites in Jordan and publishes a newsletter, now called *Ancient Jordan.*

In addition to ACOR, which is probably the largest archaeological entity in Jordan, the following international archaeological centers are now located in Jordan: the British Institute at Amman for Archaeology and History (BIAAH);

the Deutsches Evanglisches Institut für Altertumswissenschaft des Heiligen Landes; the Institut Français d'Archéologie du Proche-Orient (IFAPO); the Franciscan Institute on Mount Nebo; and the Italian-Jordanian Institute of Archaeological Sciences.

By 1986, Yarmuk University in Irbid had established an Institute of Archaeology and Anthropology. The institute has sponsored many projects, trained a good number of promising archaeological students, and published a newsletter. Mutah University near Kerak also has established an archaeology program. Notable archaeological museums have been established in Jordan that are constantly being expanded. The largest is on the citadel in Amman, adjacent to the reconstructions being pursued in the Roman temple; the others are at the University of Jordan in Amman, at Yarmouk University in Irbid, and in Madaba.

Future Programs. The number of archaeological projects in Jordan expanded in the 1990s, and the peace and normalized relations between Israel and Jordan promise an increase in substantial international research. At the same time, concerns created by utilization from increased tourism at archaeological sites are being balanced with restoration and conservation. [*See* Tourism and Archaeology.] Excavation and restoration programs are likely to continue into the twenty-first century at the country's three most dramatic sites—Amman, Petra, and Jerash—while other sites are being further developed. The potential number of sites for excavation continues to rise: the Jordanian Antiquities Database and Information System (JADIS), a computerized list of archaeological sites in Jordan, lists 8,680 sites (it is available in book form from the Department of Antiquities and ACOR). In addition, an ongoing project sponsored by the University of Western Australia has begun utilizing aerial photographs taken in 1953 with ground-verification fieldwork to build a more comprehensive list of Jordan's archaeological sites.

[*See also* American Center of Oriental Research; American Palestine Exploration Society; American Schools of Oriental Research; British Institute at Amman for Archaeology and History; British School of Archaeology in Jerusalem; Deutscher Palästina-Verein; Deutsches Evangelisches Institut für Altertumswissenschaft des Heiligen Landes; École Biblique et Archéologique Française; Palestine Exploration Fund; *and the biographies of Albright, Bagatti, Bennett; Bliss, Clermont-Ganneau, Conder, Crowfoot, Dalman, Fisher, Garstang, Glueck, Guérin, Harding, Horsfield, Kenyon, Kitchener, Lapp, Mallon, Robinson, and Saller.*]

BIBLIOGRAPHY

Albright, William Foxwell. *The Archaeology of Palestine.* Rev. ed. Gloucester, Mass., 1971.

Bikai, Pierre, ed. *ACOR, the First Twenty-Five Years: The American Center of Oriental Research, 1968–1993.* Amman, 1993.

Bliss, Frederick Jones. *The Development of Palestine Exploration.* New York, 1906. Comprehensive history for all of Palestine to 1900 by one personally involved.

Dever, William G. "Syro-Palestinian Archaeology 'Comes of Age': The Inaugural Volume of the Hesban Series, A Review Article." *Bulletin of the American Schools of Oriental Research,* nos. 290–291 (May–August 1993): 127–130.

Dornemann, Rudolph H. *The Archaeology of the Transjordan in the Bronze and Iron Ages.* Milwaukee, 1983. Detailed review for these periods.

Geraty, Lawrence T., and Larry G. Herr, eds. *The Archaeology of Jordan and Other Studies Presented to Siegfried H. Horn.* Berrien Springs, Mich., 1986.

Geraty, Lawrence T., and Lloyd A. Willis. "Archaeological Research in Transjordan." In *The Archaeology of Jordan and Other Studies Presented to Siegfried H. Horn,* edited by Lawrence T. Geraty and Larry G. Herr, pp. 3–72, 695–697. Berrien Springs, Mich., 1986. Historical survey and site-by-site descriptions.

Geraty, Lawrence T., and David Merling. *Hesban after Twenty-Five Years.* Berrien Springs, Mich., 1994. Comprehensive view of one site; accessible for nonprofessionals.

Glueck, Nelson. *The Other Side of the Jordan* (1940). Rev. ed. Cambridge, Mass., 1970.

Glueck, Nelson. *The River Jordan.* Philadelphia, 1946.

Hadidi, Adnan. "The Archaeology of Jordan: Achievements and Objectives." In *Studies in the History and Archaeology of Jordan,* vol. 1, edited by Adnan Hadidi, pp. 15–21. Amman, 1982. Helpful overview.

Harding, G. Lankester. *The Antiquities of Jordan.* New York, 1959. Popular survey.

Homès-Fredericq, Denyse, and J. Basil Hennessy, eds. *Archaeology of Jordan,* vol. 1, *Bibliography;* vol. 2.1–2, *Field Reports.* Louvain, 1986–1989.

Horn, Siegfried H.. "Why the Moabite Stone Was Blown to Pieces." *Biblical Archaeology Review* 12 (1986): 50–61.

King, Philip J. *American Archaeology in the Mideast: A History of the American Schools of Oriental Research.* Winona Lake, Ind., 1983. Excellent overview of American contributions.

Miller, J. Maxwell. "Recent Archaeological Developments Relevant to Ancient Moab." In *Studies in the History and Archaeology of Jordan,* vol. 1, edited by Adnan Hadidi, pp. 169–173. Amman, 1982.

Sauer, James A. "Prospects for Archaeology in Jordan and Syria." *Biblical Archaeologist* 45 (1982): 73–84. Useful historical, archaeological, and site survey.

Stern, Ephraim, et al., eds. *The New Encyclopedia of Archaeological Excavations in the Holy Land.* 4 vols. Jerusalem and New York, 1993. Comprehensive and well illustrated.

Vogel, Eleanor K., et al. "Bibliography of Holy Land Sites." *Hebrew Union College Annual* 42 (1971): 1–96; 52 (1981): 1–92; 58 (1987): 1–63.

JAMES A. SAUER and LLOYD A. WILLIS

Archaeology in Mesopotamia

The archaeology of Mesopotamia has followed an eventful path since its origins in the early nineteenth century CE. From an amateur pursuit, enjoyed by adventurers and intellectuals of the age, the study of ancient Mesopotamia has evolved over the decades into a rigorous scientific discipline employing a full range of modern analytical techniques. While these developments have led to a remarkable understanding of many aspects of ancient communities in Mesopotamia, there is still a great deal to learn, and future technical and analytical advances are likely substantially to expand the state of that knowledge.

The birth of Mesopotamian archaeology can be ascribed to the year 1807, when the young Claudius Rich arrived in Baghdad to assume the post of resident of the East India Company. During his nine years in Iraq, at that time the Ottoman Pashalik of Baghdad, Rich carried out a study of the ruins of Babylon, which he described in some detail, and produced accurate accounts of the ruins of Nineveh and Nimrud in northern Mesopotamia. After Rich's death in 1821, his collection of Mesopotamian artifacts was purchased by the British Museum. [*See* Babylon; Nineveh; Nimrud.] These objects, including many clay tablets in cuneiform script and inscribed bricks, formed the first substantial group of ancient Mesopotamian artifacts to arrive in Europe and aroused considerable interest. At about the same time, the first steps in deciphering some elements of the distinctive cuneiform script were being made by European scholars, particularly Georg Grotefend and Henry Creswicke Rawlinson, through their studies of the trilingual Bisitun inscription in Iran. [*See* Cuneiform; Bisitun; *and the biography of Rawlinson.*]

After Rich's death, more than twenty years passed before the first archaeological excavations were begun in Mesopotamia. It was a Frenchman, Paul-Émile Botta, who sank the first trenches into the mound of Kuyunjik, part of ancient Nineveh, in December 1842. Botta's appointment as French consul in Mosul, the modern town adjacent to Nineveh, had been stimulated by the publication of Rich's accounts of Babylon and Nineveh. Not enjoying great success at Kuyunjik, Botta transferred his operations in March 1843 to the site of Khorsabad, 23 km (14 mi.) to the northeast. There Botta immediately made the spectacular discovery of stone sculptures in bas-relief and monolithic human-headed winged bulls and lions belonging to the palace of the Assyrian king Sargon II of the late eighth century BCE. The stones of Assyria had begun to speak for the first time in more than twenty-five hundred years. [*See* Khorsabad; *and the biography of Botta.*]

Botta's discoveries at Khorsabad aroused the interest of an Englishman employed at the British Embassy in Constantinople, Austen Henry Layard. Layard was encouraged by the British ambassador, Stratford Canning, to open excavations on the mound of Nimrud, southeast of Nineveh, in late 1845. Within a short time, Layard had uncovered large stone slabs with cuneiform inscriptions and scenes in bas-relief from two Assyrian palaces of kings resident at Nimrud, ancient Kalḫu. Kalḫu had been the second great Assyrian capital after Aššur, but prior to Nineveh and Khorsabad. [*See* Aššur.] Layard continued work at Nimrud until 1847, during which time he excavated remains of several Assyrian palaces. Large quantities of sculptures and uniquely important artifacts, such as the Black Obelisk of Shalmaneser III, were transported to the British Museum, creating considerable public interest. Following the publication in 1849 of Layard's immensely popular book *Nineveh and Its Remains*, funds were provided for him to return to Mesopotamia for further excavation. While working at Nimrud, Layard conducted excavations at Nineveh, exposing the tremendous stone relief sculptures of the palace of Sennacherib, including scenes showing the siege of Lachish. The site's substantial depths of overlying deposits meant that Layard excavated by the dangerous method of tunneling along buried wall faces. By this means he uncovered a total of almost 3 km (2 mi.) of wall faces with sculpted reliefs.

Apart from the sculptures, another major class of finds was cuneiform texts. In Sennacherib's palace at Nineveh, Layard found a massive collection of inscribed tablets (some twenty-four thousand), belonging to the royal library of Ashurbanipal. Decipherment of these documents was to bring a rich reward to historians of ancient Assyria. At the time, major developments, principally by the English scholars Henry Creswicke Rawlinson and Edward Hincks, were being made in the decipherment of cuneiform script. In 1857 four scholars—Rawlinson, Hincks, William Henry Fox Talbot, and Jules Oppert—independently produced translations of a cuneiform document found at Aššur, thus convincing sceptics of their new-found understanding of the Assyrian script and language.

After Layard's departure from Mesopotamia in 1851, there was an increase in the pace and intensity of excavation throughout Mesopotamia. Standards, however, were low, and fieldwork took the form of small soundings at a large number of sites in the hope of recovering important artifacts to adorn museum collections with a minimum investment of money and labor. In particular, lack of familiarity with the excavation of mud-brick architecture meant that whole buildings were removed without being recorded or even noticed, especially in southern Mesopotamia, or Babylonia, where attention had then shifted. During the 1850s, British excavations were conducted by Rawlinson at Borsippa; by William Kennett Loftus at Warka; and by J. E. Taylor at Ur and Eridu. Loftus, the first to conduct excavations in southern Mesopotamia, also initiated soundings at Senkereh, now known as ancient Larsa, and at Tell Sifr. French archaeologists working at Kish and Babylon were disappointed, like Loftus, in not finding any of the spectacular stone sculptures which had so amply rewarded the first excavators in northern Mesopotamia. For the time being, the lack of immediate returns from Babylonia encouraged a return to the north, to the great cities of Assyria, where the first discoveries had caused such excitement. [*See* Assyrians; Uruk-Warka; Ur; Eridu; *and the biography of Layard.*]

Excavations at Nineveh had been continued by Hormuzd Rassam, once Layard's assistant, and work at Khorsabad, and also at Nineveh, was conducted by Botta's successor, Victor Place, who had traced the plans of all the Assyrian royal buildings on the summit of Khorsabad. At Nineveh, beginning in 1852, Rassam recovered more spectacular wall reliefs, including the famous lion-hunt scenes, and informative tablets from the newly revealed palace of Ashurbanipal. He also explored the mounds at Nimrud and Aššur, among many others in the region. Tragically, many of the objects so hastily removed from the Assyrian cities of Nineveh and Khorsabad were permanently lost in a disaster on the Shatt al-Arab at Qurna in 1855, when three hundred packing cases full of priceless sculptures and other antiquities were sent to the bottom of the river by marauders. The commencement of the Crimean War in the same year put an end to European investigations in Mesopotamia for almost two decades.

In 1873 George Smith led a British Museum expedition back to Nineveh in search of a missing portion of a cuneiform tablet that clearly provided an account of the Flood, now known as part of the Epic of Gilgamesh. Smith's early death in 1876 led the British Museum to reassign Rassam to the task of excavating Nineveh. With Layard's help, Rassam in fact obtained a capacious permit to excavate in all areas of the Ottoman Pashaliks of Baghdad, Aleppo, and Van, which he proceeded to do between 1878 and 1882. In a thoroughly unsatisfactory arrangement, Rassam left gangs of workmen in the charge of local supervisors at widely separated points all over Assyria and Babylonia. As well as reopening excavations at Nineveh and Nimrud, Rassam dug at Balawat to the east of Mosul, where he recovered the great bronze gates of Shalmaneser II, now in the British Museum. In Babylonia, Rassam sank trenches into many mounds, including Babylon, Borsippa, Cutha, and Telloh, yielding results commensurate with his archaeological skills. To the southwest of Baghdad, at Abu Habbah (ancient Sippar and biblical Sepharvaim), Rassam recovered a vast number of tablets from a large Neo-Babylonian religious precinct adjacent to the ziggurat. [*See* Balawat; Sippar; *and the biography of Smith.*]

In the last quarter of the nineteenth century, archaeology in Mesopotamia began to take on something of its modern shape, with long-term excavations at sites and the emergence of scientific interest in Babylonia and Assyria. Ernest de Sarzec, the French vice-consul at Basra in southern Iraq, conducted excavations at Telloh (ancient Girsu of Lagash state) from 1877 to 1881 and 1888 to 1900. [*See* Girsu and Lagash.] These were the first-ever substantial excavations at a Sumerian site, and the objects recovered, especially the diorite statues of rulers of Lagash and the Stela of the Vultures, aroused immense excitement in France, ensuring a long-term commitment to Telloh that lasted until 1933. Study of the thousands of Sumerian tablets from Telloh still provides the basis of much of what is understood of Sumerian society. Nevertheless, de Sarzec's methods were still primitive, particularly in regard to the tracing of the mudbrick walls used in almost all buildings in southern Mesopotamia. Telloh also suffered greatly from illicit excavations during de Sarzec's absences. At the same time as de Sarzec was beginning his excavations at Telloh, the appointment of Hamdi Bey as first director of the Imperial Ottoman Museum in Istanbul saw both an increase in the control exercised by the Ottoman authorities over foreign expeditions in Mesopotamia and the creation of an extremely important museum in Istanbul.

The first American involvement in fieldwork in Mesopotamia came with an expedition in 1884; it was followed by the start, in 1887, of a long-term program of excavations at the southern site of Nippur, a connection that lasted until modern times. The early work was directed by Hermann V. Hilprecht, John P. Peters, and J. H. Haynes, who, after a difficult start, recovered thousands of clay tablets, mainly Sumerian, which, to this day, provide the bulk of what is known concerning Sumerian literary compositions. [*See* American School of Oriental Research in Baghdad; Sumerian; *and the biographies of Hilprecht and Peters.*]

In the dying years of the nineteenth century CE, archaeology in Mesopotamia at last took on its modern form with the first appearance of German scholars in the field. The foundation of the German Oriental Society in 1898 and its excavations at Babylon in March 1899 under the direction of Robert Koldewey mark a genuine development in the discipline. The work was characterized by a concern to investigate the architectural and social context of the Mesopotamian artifacts which had attracted so much attention in Europe. During an intensive program of excavations up to 1913, Koldewey uncovered and recorded in commendable detail a remarkable series of temples, palaces, houses, and other structures of the Neo-Babylonian town of the time of Nebuchadrezzar, including the Ishtar Gate and the Processional Way. During this work, his staff acquired and exercised new skills in tracing and recording mud-brick walls—precious skills soon put to use elsewhere in Mesopotamia. [*See* Deutsche Orient-Gesellshaft; *and the biography of Koldewey.*]

From 1901 to 1903 Koldewey excavated at Borsippa and at the Sumerian city of Fara, ancient Shuruppak. [*See* Fara.] More significantly, from 1903 to 1914 a superb program of excavations at the early Assyrian capital of Aššur was carried out by Walter Andrae, an assistant of Koldewey's at Babylon. As at Babylon, the Germans meticulously recovered a plan of the city and many of its important buildings and residential areas. Of major new importance, however, was their excavation of a deep stratigraphic trench down through the Ishtar temple at Aššur. For the first time in Mesopotamian archaeology, a sequence of buildings was revealed that was securely related through careful stratigraphic observation. Thus, at Babylon and Aššur, German archaeologists set standards in architectural and stratigraphic investigation and observation which formed the basis of Mesopotamian archaeology. [*See the biography of Andrae.*]

During these early years of the twentieth century, archaeologists other than Germans were conducting excavations very much in the old mold. The Sumerian city of Bismaya, (ancient Adab) was rudely treated by the American Edgar James Banks, while French excavations at Kish and British excavations at Nineveh produced little in the way of scientific results. The first surveys of Islamic remains in Mesopotamia were also being conducted by L. Massignon, Conrad Preusser, Ernst Herzfeld, and others. With the outbreak of World War I in 1914, all archaeological work in Mesopotamia came to a halt. [*See* Kish.]

The modern state of Iraq, created after World War I, included virtually all of ancient Mesopotamia within its boundaries. It was fortunate that the antiquities of Iraq found a talented and considerate protector in Gertrude Bell, an official of the British administration who became director of antiquities. Under her guidance, foreign excavations in Iraq were carefully monitored and new laws ensured that much of Iraq's heritage remained in Iraq, largely housed in the uniquely important Iraq Museum, of which she was founder. Not surprisingly, much fieldwork was subsequently conducted by British expeditions, culminating in the foundation in 1932 of the British School of Archaeology in Iraq. Initial soundings at Ur and Eridu were made by R. Campbell Thompson in 1918, while H. R. Hall excavated again at Ur and at nearby Tell al-Ubaid in 1919. [*See* British School of Archaeology in Iraq; Ubaid.]

Those tentative postwar steps set the scene for the arrival of C. Leonard Woolley, whose excavations at Ur from 1922 to 1934 recovered a wealth of material which receives scientific study to this day. Woolley's excavations in all quarters of the city provided a broadly informative picture of life, and death, at Ur during several phases of its occupation. In particular, his excavation of the Sumerian royal cemetery, which yielded the most spectacular objects of gold and other materials, captured the public's imagination to an extent that had been unknown since Layard's day. A deep sounding probed levels of prehistoric occupation, similar to those encountered by Woolley in new work at Tell al-Ubaid in 1923–1924. This work provided the first detailed information concerning the prehistory of southern Mesopotamia. [*See* Ur; and *the biography of Woolley*.]

Elsewhere during the 1920s, a wide range of foreign teams could be found exploring sites in southern Mesopotamia. The French had returned to Telloh, a British-American team worked at Kish and Jemdet Nasr, and an American team at Fara. [*See* Jemdet Nasr.] At the huge site of Warka (biblical Erech), the Germans, from 1928 onward recovered detailed plans of late-fourth-millennium temples, as well as thousands of clay tablets inscribed in the protocuneiform signs now known to represent the earliest form of writing anywhere in the world. A major new development was the arrival in Mesopotamia of teams from the Oriental Institute of the University of Chicago in the late 1920s, initially continuing the work of Botta and Place at Khorsabad and then, in the 1930s, excavating four sites in the Diyala region east of Baghdad. [*See* Diyala.] From these Sumerian sites came a fine series of sculptures. More significantly, however, the excavations at Khafajeh, Tell Asmar, and Tell Agrab provided the basis upon which the Early Dynastic period in Mesopotamia is still understood. [*See* Khafajeh.] In northern Mesopotamia, American work at Tepe Gawra and British work, under Max Mallowan, at Nineveh, Tell Brak, and Arpachiyah, gave remarkable new information on the prehistory and early history of this region. The first traces of Paleolithic occupation in Mesopotamia were recovered in the 1920s by Dorothy Garrod in the Kurdish mountains. [*See* Tepe Gawra; Brak, Tell; *and the biographies of Mallowan and Garrod*.]

Conferences in Baghdad in 1929 and Leiden in 1931 attempted to make some sense of the ever-increasing amount of archaeological information being recovered from the soil of Mesopotamia. The naming of periods in southern Mesopotamian prehistory and early history was agreed upon, giving the sequence Ubaid, Uruk, Jemdet Nasr, and Early Dynastic I–III. Subsequent work in northern and central Mesopotamia established the existence of the Hassuna, Samarra, and Halaf cultures, existing prior to the Ubaid. [*See* Hassuna; Samarra, *article on* Chalcolithic Period; Ḥalaf, Tell.] Of particular significance was Iraqi work with Seton Lloyd during World War II at Tell Uqair and Hassuna, and at Eridu from 1947 to 1949. [*See the biography of Lloyd*.] Iraqi investigations at ʿAqar Quf and Hatra shed new light on the later historic periods. [*See* ʿAqar Quf; Hatra.] The chronological framework established in 1929 and 1931 remains in place, although with many minor modifications.

The 1950s and 1960s saw a resurgence of fieldwork in Iraq, led by a return of the British, under Mallowan and David Oates, to Nimrud and the Americans to Nippur. A new concern with the ancient economy and environment underlay the large-scale American project, led by Robert J. Braidwood, to investigate sites in the Fertile Crescent connected with the origins of agriculture. [*See* Agriculture.] Excavations at Jarmo, in northeastern Iraq, were especially successful in this regard. [*See* Jarmo.] At the same time, excavations by Ralph and Rose Solecki at Shanidar cave demonstrated the existence of Neanderthal communities in northern Mesopotamia. [*See* Shanidar Cave.]

A new development in the late 1970s was the start of rescue archaeology in Iraq, stimulated by programs of dam building and irrigation undertaken by the Iraqi government. Multinational programs of survey, excavation, and research have been conducted in the Hamrin, Haditha, and Eski Mosul regions, yielding extremely detailed results still being studied. [*See* Hamrin Dam Salvage Project; Eski Mosul Dam Salvage Project.] In the late 1980s, a return to research excavation at major Mesopotamian sites, such as Nimrud, Nineveh, Kish, Jemdet Nasr, Hatra, and Seleucia amongst many others, reinforced ideas of the uniquely important archaeological heritage of the modern state of Iraq. [*See* Seleucia on the Tigris.] Spectacular discoveries of Assyrian royal tombs containing magnificent goldwork and other items were made by Iraqi archaeologists working at Nimrud. These modern excavations in Iraq have generally employed the full range of techniques available to archaeology, many borrowed from other disciplines—such as the earth sciences—to enable the recovery of information about many aspects of ancient life. In addition, the renewed study of material excavated earlier in the century has enabled some refinements in the chronology and distribution of the various cultures of Mesopotamia. Foreign excavation in Iraq came to a halt in 1990, although the study of Mesopotamian material continues to be undertaken in universities and museums across the world and publication of previously excavated sites is proceeding. The many unexcavated, or only partially excavated, sites remaining in Iraq ensure that a future return to fieldwork in Mesopotamia would be richly rewarded.

BIBLIOGRAPHY

Andrae, Ernst Walter, and Rainer Michael Boehmer. *Sketches by an Excavator: Walter Andrae im Orient, 1898–1919*. Berlin, 1989. Beautifully produced volume containing many color reproductions of paintings made in Mesopotamia by Andrae, as well as accounts of his archaeological work.

Curtis, John E., ed. *Fifty Years of Mesopotamian Discovery: The Work of the British School of Archaeology in Iraq, 1932–1982*. London, 1982. Amply illustrated account, largely written by the excavators, of work at a wide range of sites.

Lloyd, Seton. *Foundations in the Dust: The Story of Mesopotamian Exploration* (1947). Rev. and enl. ed. London, 1980. Brilliant survey of early exploration in Mesopotamia; articulate, amusing, and vastly informative.

Lloyd, Seton. *The Archaeology of Mesopotamia: From the Old Stone Age to the Persian Conquest*. London, 1978. Masterly summary of a large subject in one well-illustrated volume.

Oates, David, and Joan Oates. *The Rise of Civilization*. Oxford, 1976. Very readable and well-illustrated volume covering all major developments in the prehistory of Mesopotamia.

Oates, Joan. *Babylon*. Rev. ed. London, 1986. Excellent account of the history of one of the most important archaeological sites in Mesopotamia.

Postgate, J. N. *The First Empires*. Oxford, 1977. First-rate account of the early history of Mesopotamia and its discovery; were illustrated.

R. J. MATTHEWS

Archaeology in Persia

From 1800 onward, with the arrival of foreign missions in Persia, an interest in the identification of places mentioned in the Bible and by classical authors (e.g., Shushan and Ecbatana, Pasargadae, and Persepolis, respectively) grew. [*See* Ecbatana; Pasargadae; Persepolis.] In the first half of the nineteenth century, an effort was made to provide written descriptions and hand-drawn illustrations of visible monuments. Systematic excavations were begun later in the century. At the same time, general surveys aimed at the history of ancient Persian art and architecture were prepared (Flandin and Coste, 1843–; Dieulafoy, 1884–1889; Perrot and Chipiez, 1892). This work was followed in 1938–1939 by the six-volume *A Survey of Persian Art* (Pope, 1967). These volumes, and the organization of the International Congress of Iranian Art and Archaeology, did much to promote an interest in Persian art and archaeology in the West.

Achaemenid Archaeology. Work on Persian inscriptions began in 1802 with George F. Grotefend's identification of the inscriptions at Persepolis as belonging to the Achaemenid kings (Hoeck, 1818). Real progress, however, awaited Henry C. Rawlinson's study of the trilingual cuneiform texts of Darius the Great (522–486 BCE) at the site of Bisitun, east of Kermanshah (Rawlinson, 1846–1849). [*See* Bisitun.] This publication initiated the decipherment of Old Persian cuneiform and set the stage for later studies of Bisitun (Cameron, 1951, pp. 47–54) and Persepolis (Kent, 1953). Persepolis, the capital of the Achaemenid kings (521–330 BCE), was first illustrated in watercolor by Robert Kerr Porter in 1821. Such workmanship was superseded in 1872 by Franz Stolze's pioneering photographic records of Persian sites (Stolze, 1882). The new technique further revolutionized field recording with the aerial photographs taken in 1936 by Erich F. Schmidt (1940).

Systematic excavations were begun at Persepolis in 1931 by the Oriental Institute of the University of Chicago, which remained in the field until 1939. The excavations were originally directed by Ernst Herzfeld (1931–1934) and then by Schmidt (1934–1939). After 1939, the work was continued by the Archaeological Service of Iran under André Godard, Mohammad T. Mustafavi, and Ali Sami. From 1968 to 1974, a program of exploration and restoration was undertaken by Giuseppe and Ann B. Tilia from the Istituto Italiano per il Medio ed Estremo Oriente (IsMEO), Rome. [*See* Istituto Italiano per il Medio ed Estremo Oriente.]

The nearby site of Pasargadae, capital of Cyrus the Great (559–530 BCE), also attracted the attention of early travelers such as Robert Ker Porter and Marcel Dieulafoy. Herzfeld visited the site in 1905 and undertook the first excavations there in 1928. Further studies were made in 1955 by Sami. A definitive excavation was carried out between 1961 and 1963 by David Stronach, director of the newly established (1960) British Institute of Persian Studies (Stronach, 1978). [*See* British Institute of Persian Studies.]

A third major Achaemenid site, Ecbatana (modern Hamadan), began to be formally excavated in 1974 by Masoud Azarnoush (Iranian Archaeological Services) although many clandestine finds have been made there previously (Muscarella, 1980, pp. 31–35). [*See* Ecbatana.] Susa, the Achaemenid capital of southwestern Iran, also contains extensive Achaemenid remains. [*See* Susa.] Between 1884 and 1886, Dieulafoy exposed parts of Darius's palace (521–485

BCE) there. The French Mission Archéologique en Iran (MAI), originally called the Délégation Archéologique en Perse, worked at Susa from 1897 to 1978. [*See* Palace.] From 1900 to 1939 the main plan was exposed by Jacques de Morgan and Roland de Mecquenem. In the 1970s, Apadana was resurveyed by Jean Perrot (MAI) using a magnetometer. Perrot revised and completed the city plan. [Perrot, 1977, 1978.] A new palace belonging to Darius across the Chaour River joined a "Persian village" Roman Ghirshman found in the 1950s in the quarter known as the Ville des Artisans (dated to the seventh–fifth centuries BCE) as two important new aspects of Achaemenid Susa. In the 1960s another important Achaemenid site was cleared by Umberto Scerrato for IsMEO (1966) in Sistan at Dahan-i Ghulaiman.

Elamite and Pre-Elamite Archaeology. Between 1850 and 1852, William K. Loftus's excavations at Susa, while serving on a British boundary commission, uncovered the first evidence for the Elamites under extensive Achaemenid remains. [*See* Elamites.] In 1897 de Morgan was made director of France's newly established Délégation en Perse. Subsequent directors were de Mecquenem (1908–1946), Ghirshman (1946–1967), and Perrot (1967–1990), the first prehistorian at the site. From 1900 to 1930 the directors enjoyed a French monopoly on archaeology in Iran.

The excavations at Susa and of the ziggurat in the nearby Elamite city of Chogha Zanbil by Ghirshman from 1951 to 1962 established the outlines of Elamite civilization in southwestern Iran from about 2500 BCE to its destruction by the Assyrians in the seventh century BCE. [*See* Chogha Zanbil; Ziggurat; Assyrians.]

By 1908 the prehistoric sequence, established on the acropolis at Susa by the French mission, and which began in 4000 BCE, was unique in the Near East. It provided the reference point for prehistoric remains in southern Mesopotamia until 1930. During the 1930s this sequence was revised by de Mecquenem's additional cuts into the acropolis and at smaller nearby sites. Under Perrot, a new and detailed stratigraphic excavation was undertaken by Alain Le Brun, augmented by the reexcavation of nearby small sites by Genevieve Dollfus (MAI). This revised sequence (Perrot, 1978) put in developmental order the numerical and textual Proto-Elamite tablets from about 3000 BCE, products of one of the earliest writing systems. [*See* Writing and Writing Systems.]

Prehistory on the Iranian Plateau. Excavations at prehistoric sites were initiated on the Iranian plateau for the first time in the 1930s at Tepe Giyan by Ghirshman and George Contineau (1931–1932, for the Louvre Museum); Tepe Hissar (1931–1932) and Rayy (1934–1936) by Schmidt; and Tureng Tepe by Frederick R. Wulsin (1931–1932), all three for the University of Pennsylvania Museum; and Tepe Sialk by Ghirshman (1933–1934 and 1937 for the Louvre). Sialk became the reference point for the prehistoric plateau until the period of excavation that followed World War II. Hissar and Sialk were the models at the time for the stratigraphic recovery of regional prehistoric sequences.

After the interregnum of World War II, excavations resumed with a new university-trained generation of prehistorians who introduced interdisciplinary specialists and new methods. Computers became available for laboratory analysis (although portable models appeared only after 1980). This influx of new people, methods, and interests greatly enhanced the study of prehistory. Carleton S. Coon (University Museum; 1949, 1951) initiated the first excavations in Paleolithic and Epipaleolithic archaeology. By 1986 it was possible to outline the Stone Age in Iran (Smith, 1986).

Interest in the transition from the Paleolithic to the farming cultures of the following Neolithic period led in 1960 to the Oriental Institute of Chicago's Iranian Prehistoric Project, led by Robert J. Braidwood. Survey work for this project in turn led to the exploration of the Deh Luran Plain beginning in 1961 by Frank Hole and Kent Flannery for the University of Michigan (1969). Subsequent excavations and surveys, espeically by Michigan's Henry Wright, produced a sequence from about 7500 BCE to about 3000 BCE with the help of the first computer analyses (Hole, 1987). These results were further augmented in Susiana by extensive settlement surveys by Robert Adams, Henry Wright, and others interested in problems surrounding the rise of the state in antiquity (Hole, ed., 1987). Following this approach, the use of surveys thereafter became standard in the field.

An interest in stratigraphically based chronology and cultural history led to the University of Pennsylvania Museum's Hasanlu Project, directed by Robert H. Dyson, Jr., from 1959 to 1977. The project was modeled along the lines of Hissar and Sialk but with refined methods of excavation, recording, and analysis that led to a six-thousand-year sequence of material culture. The unexpected discovery of a rich burned ninth-century BCE level focused the work on the Iron Age (Dyson and Voight, eds., 1989).

In 1969, to the north of Hasanlu, the German Archaeological Institute of Tehran (established in 1968) brought its architectural expertise to bear on the study of the kingdom of ancient Urartu. [*See* Hasanlu; Urartu.] Excavations at the site of Bastam by Wolfram Kleiss and extensive surveys carried out for the institute combined, in the 1970s, to provide a detailed outline of the ninth–fifth centuries BCE there. Another important Iron Age excavation was carried out by Stronach (British Institute of Persian Studies) at Nush-i Jan from 1967 to 1975; it was the first site to yield monumental Median architecture (Stronach, 1985). [*See* Medes.]

The Hasanlu Project preceded a number of similar regional projects initiated in the 1960s and 1970s: the Godin Project of the Royal Ontario Museum under T. C. Young, Jr., from 1965 to 1974; the Tepe Yahya Project of Harvard University's Peabody Museum under C. C. Lamberg-Karlovsky from 1967 to 1975); the Italian IsMEO Shahr-i Sokhta Expedition under Maurizio Tosi from 1967 to 1978;

the Baba Jan Expedition of the Institute of Archaeology, London, under Claire Goff from 1967 to 1972; the University of Manchester's Haftavan Project under Charles Burney from 1968 to 1978; the Qazvin Project of the University of Tehran under Ezat O. Negahban since 1970; and the University of Pennsylvania's Malyan Project under William M. Sumner from 1971 to 1978. [*See* Godin Tepe; Tepe Yahya; Malyan.] Each of these projects produced a regional sequence several thousand years long, associated with ceramics, artifacts, architecture, animal bones, and plant remains. Godin Tepe produced an important fortified residence from the Median period and an "enclave" containing tablets and ceramics from the lowland from about 3200 BCE; Tepe Yahya produced a similar concentration of lowland ceramics and blank tablets. The two sites suggest political or economic contacts among the plateau, Mesopotamia, and Elam in about 3000 BCE. The Qazvin Project's excavations at Saqzabad, Gabristan, and Zaghe produced an important sequence of early painted pottery linked to Sialk and Hissar. Baba Jan, in addition to its earlier levels, yielded important Median structures (sixth century BCE), and Shahr-i Sokhta in Sistan provided links to both western Iran and Central Asia in the late fourth and third millennia BCE. Malyan provided Proto-Elamite pictographic tablets (c. 3000 BCE) and Middle Elamite inscribed brick fragments identifying it as ancient Anshan, the upland capital of Elam. Haftavan provided pottery connecting northern Iran to the Caucasus.

Later Historical Periods. The excavation of sites from the Seleucid (330–250 BCE), Parthian (249 BCE–224 CE), and Sasanian (224–650 CE) periods also dates largely to the period after World War II. [*See* Seleucids; Parthians; Sasanians.] Royal cities and temples were the focus of attention for excavations that were carried out generally using traditional methods. Work on the Seleucid period was begun by Ghirshman at Susa in 1947–1948 in the Ville des Artisans and was followed in 1961–1963 by Stronach's discoveries at Pasargadae. Akbar Tadjvidi (Iranian Archaeological Service) worked at Persepolis from 1969 to 1972, and John Hansman and Stronach worked at Shahr-i Qumis from 1968 to 1978.

Only about a dozen sites from the Parthian period have been systematically explored. These have included cemeteries at Kangavar by Seyfollah Kambaksh-Fard (Iranian Archaeological Service) since 1968 and at Ecbatana/Hamadan by Masoud Azarnoush (Iranian Center for Archaeological Research) since 1975; several sites in the Dailaman area of Gilan by Namio Egami and Shinji Fukai (Tokyo University) from 1960 to 1964; ruined temples at Bard-i Nishandeh and Masjid-i Suleiman by Ghirshman from 1964 to 1966 and 1961 to 1971; settlement remains at Susa by Ghirshman from 1946 to 1950; Bisitun by Heinz Luschey (German Archaeological Institute) from 1965 to 1967; Qal'eh Yazdigird by Edward Keall (Royal Ontario Museum) from 1967 to 1978; Nush-i Jan by Stronach from 1967 to 1974; Shahr-i Qumis by Hansman and Stronach from 1968 to 1978; Yahya by Lamberg-Karlovsky from 1967 to 1975; and Kuh-i Khwaja by Giorgio Guillini (Italian Archaeological Mission) in 1964. The minor Parthian remains found at Takht-i Suleiman by H. H. von der Osten and Rudolf Naumann (German Institute) from 1959 to 1978 have made the identification of that site as Parthian Phraaspa now untenable.

Excavations of substantial Sasanian remains began in the 1930s at the sites of Hissar by Schmidt (for the University Museum) from 1931 to 1932; Qasr-i Abu Nasr by Walter Hauser and J. M. Upton (Metropolitan Museum of Art, New York) from 1932 to 1935; Istakhr by Schmidt (for the Oriental Institute, Chicago) from 1934 to 1939; and Bishapur by Ghirshman from 1935 to 1941. A new cycle of systematic work on the Sasanian period began in 1959 at Takht-i Suleiman by von der Osten and Naumann. In 1968, excavations were undertaken by the Iranian Archaeological Service at Kangavar, directed by Kambaksh-Fard, that proved to be the remains of a Sasanian palace rather than a Parthian temple. In the 1970s, excavations were carried out at Sasanian settlements at Tureng Tepe by Jean Deshayes (French Ministry of Foreign Affairs) from 1971 to 1978; Shahr-i Qumis by Hansman and Stronach from 1968 to 1978; Tepe Yahya by Lamberg-Karlovsky from 1967 to 1975; Siraf by David Whitehouse (British Institute of Persian Studies) from 1966 to 1972; Firuzabad/Qal'eh-i Dukhtar by Darrell Huff and Kleiss from 1975 to 1978; and Qal'eh-i Yazdegird by Keall from 1975 to 1978. Smaller excavations were also carried out at such sites as Ivan-i Karkha by Ghirshman in 1950 and at Jundi Shapur by Adams and Hansen in 1963 in the Susa area; Malyan by Sumner in 1974 in Fars; and on Kharg Island in the Persian Gulf by Ghirshman in 1959. The revolution of 1978–1979 ended all ongoing foreign projects in Iran.

[*See also* Persia; *and the biographies of Ghirshman and Rawlinson.*]

BIBLIOGRAPHY

All publications of the excavators mentioned in the text will be found listed and indexed by site and period in Louis Vanden Berghe, *Bibliographie analytique de l'archéologie de l'Iran ancien* (Leiden, 1979), and Louis Vanden Berghe and E. Haerinck, *Bibliographie analytique de l'archéologie de l'Iran ancien: Supplément 1, 1978–1980* and *Supplement 2, 1981–1985* (Leiden, 1981–1987). Reports of excavations and other summaries appear in the following annual publications: Deutschen Archäologischen Institut, *Archäologische Mitteilungen aus Iran* (Tehran, 1968–); *Cahiers de la Délégation Archéologique Française en Iran* (Paris, 1971–); Istituto Italiano per il Medio ed Estremo Oriente (IsMEO), *East and West* (Rome, 1974–); University of Pennsylvania Museum, *Expedition* (Philadelphia, 1959–); British Institute of Persian Studies, *Iran* (London, 1963–); *Iranica Antiqua* (Leiden, 1961–); Oriental Institute, *Journal of Near Eastern Studies* and *Annual Report* (Chicago, 1942–); and *Paléorient* (Paris, 1973–).

Primary Sources

Amiet, Pierre. *Elam.* Auvers-sur-Oise, 1966. Major survey of artifacts from the excavations at Susa now in the Louvre museum.

Amiet, Pierre. *L'âge des échanges inter-iraniens, 3500–1700 avant J.-C.* Paris, 1986. The best current synthesis of recently found materials on the Iranian plateau and their relationship to Mesopotamia and Central Asia.

Basaglia, Piero, et al. *La città bruciata del deserto Salato/The Burnt City and the Salt Desert.* Venice, 1977. Beautifully illustrated bilingual presentation of the results of work at Shahr-i Sokhta by the Italian expedition to Sistan.

Burney, Charles, and David Marshall. *The Peoples of the Hills: Ancient Ararat and Caucasus.* New York, 1972. The only extant survey of the archaeology of all periods of Azerbaijan.

The Cambridge Ancient History, vol. 1.2, *Early History of the Middle East.* Edited by I. E. S. Edwards et al. 3d ed. Cambridge, 1971. Authoritative articles on different periods and aspects of Iranian archaeology and history.

The Cambridge History of Iran, vol. 2, *The Median and Achaemenian Periods.* Edited by Ilya Gershevitch. Cambridge, 1985. Definitive survey of early historic Iran.

Curtis, John E. *Ancient Persia.* London, 1989. Short survey of recent work, with color illustrations.

Curtis, John E., ed. *Early Mesopotamia and Iran: Contact and Conflict, 3500–1600 B.C.* London, 1993. Seminar by specialists on cultural relationships across the Iranian plateau.

Ehrich, Robert W., ed. *Chronologies in Old World Archaeology.* 2 vols. 3d ed. Chicago, 1992. The chapter on Iran by Mary M. Voigt and Robert H. Dyson, Jr. (vol. 1, pp. 122–125; vol. 2, pp. 125–153) gives a systematic summary of regional sequences and an extensive bibliography to 1986, when the text was completed.

Ghirshman, Roman. *The Arts of Ancient Iran.* New York, 1962. Well-illustrated overview of Persian art to the Parthian period.

Ghirshman, Roman. *Persian Art: The Parthian and Sassanian Dynasties, 249 B.C.–A.D. 651.* New York, 1962. Well-illustrated overview of Persian art in later periods.

Herzfeld, Ernst. *Iran in the Ancient East.* London, 1941. Observations and descriptions of problems and artifacts through the Sasanian period, in a dated but still valuable survey.

Hicks, Jim. *The Persians.* New York, 1975. Competent, up-to-date survey by Time-Life Books.

Hole, Frank, et al., eds. *Prehistory and Human Ecology of the Deh Luran Plain: An Early Village Sequence from Khuzistan, Iran.* University of Michigan, Memoirs of the Museum of Anthropology, no. 1. Ann Arbor, 1969. Integrated summary of research by the Deh Luran project.

Hole, Frank, ed. *The Archaeology of Western Iran: Settlement and Society from Prehistory to the Islamic Conquest.* Washington, D.C., 1987.

Matheson, Sylvia A. *Persia: An Archaeological Guide.* 2d ed. London, 1976. Authoritative survey done with the aid of archaeologists and on-site visits, full of useful information.

Perrot, Jean, et al. "Actes de la rencontre internationale de Suse (Iran) du 23 au 28 octobre 1977: La séquence archéologique de Suse et du Sud-Ouest de l'Iran antérieurement à la période Achéménide." *Paléorient* 4 (1978): 131–244. Definitive presentation of the results of the work at Susa done since 1967.

Pittman, Holly. *Art of the Bronze Age: Southeastern Iran, Western Central Asia, and the Indus Valley.* New York, 1984. Brief but useful introduction to new materials contributing to a realignment of thinking about the foreign relations of the Iranian plateau in the Bronze Age.

Porada, Edith. *The Art of Ancient Iran: Pre-Islamic Cultures.* New York, 1965. Excellent survey of Iranian art, with color illustrations, by one of the outstanding scholars of both art and archaeology.

Schmidt, Erich F. *Persepolis.* 3 vols. Oriental Institute Publications, 68–70. Chicago, 1953–1970. Definitive volumes on the excavations at Persepolis.

Specialized Sources

Cameron, George G. "The Old Persian Text of the Behistun Inscription." *Journal of Cuneiform Studies* 5 (1951): 47–54.

Dieulafoy, Marcel. *L'art antique de la Perse: Achéménides, Parthes, Sassanides.* 5 vols. Paris, 1884–1889.

Dyson, Robert H., Jr, and Mary M. Voight, eds. "East of Assyria: The Highland Settlement of Hasanlu." *Expedition* 31 (1989).

Expedition 31.2–3 (1989). Special issue entitled "East of Assyria," edited by Robert H. Dyson and Mary M. Voigt.

Flandin, Eugène, and Pascal Coste. *Voyage en Perse,* vol. 5, *Perse ancienne.* Paris, 1843–.

Hoeck, Karl. *Veteris Mediae et Persiae monumenta.* Göttingen, 1818.

International Congress of Iranian Art and Archaeology. London, 1936–. Ongoing series of conference proceedings.

Kent, Roland G. *Old Persian: Grammar, Texts, Lexicon.* 2d ed. New Haven, 1953.

Muscarella, Oscar White. "Excavated and Unexcavated Achaemenian Art." In *Ancient Persia: The Art of an Empire,* edited by Denise Schmandt-Besserat, pp. 31–35. Malibu, 1980.

Perrot, Georges, and Charles Chipiez. *History of Art in Persia.* London, 1892.

Pope, Arthur Upham, ed. *A Survey of Persian Art* (1938–1939). 13 vols. New York, 1967.

Rawlinson, Henry Creswicke. *The Persian Cuneiform Inscription at Behistun Decyphered and Translated.* 2 vols. Journal of the Royal Asiatic Society, vols. 10–11. London, 1846–1849.

Schmidt, Erich F. *Flights over the Ancient Cities of Iran.* Chicago, 1940.

Smith, Philip E. L. *Palaeolithic Archaeology in Iran.* Philadelphia, 1986.

Stolze, Franz. *Persepolis.* 2 vols. Berlin, 1882.

Stronach, David B. *Pasargadae: A Report on the Excavations Conducted by the British Institute of Persian Studies from 1961 to 1963.* Oxford, 1978.

Stronach, David B. "Tepe Nūsh-i Jān: The Median Settlement." In *The Cambridge History of Iran,* vol. 2, *The Median and Achaemenian Periods,* edited by Ilya Gershevitch, pp. 832–837. Cambridge, 1985.

ROBERT H. DYSON, JR.

Archaeology in the Anatolian Plateau

As early as 1764, the Greco-Roman and Byzantine ruins in Mysia, Ionia, and Caria attracted the attention of the London-based Dilettante Society. In the early nineteenth century, some government-sponsored European institutions began to divert resources for research in eastern Anatolia. In 1827 the French government, interested in the inscribed rock-monuments in Van, commissioned Friedrich E. Schulz, a young German scholar, to investigate the nature and content of those cuneiform inscriptions. He was killed by local bandits two years after starting the project, but not before he copied the inscriptions. Although his work drew the attention of fellow Orientalists in Europe, it was not until the end of the nineteenth century that it was finally realized that the inscriptions were Urartian, not Assyrian, texts. [*See* Cuneiform; Urartu.]

During the nineteenth century, numerous archaeological

discoveries were made on the Anatolian plateau by foreign scholars, among whom the most prominent was the French archaeologist and architect Charles Texier. In 1834 he discovered Boğazköy/Ḫattuša and Yazılıkaya although he was not aware of their Hittite origins. [*See* Boğazköy; Hittites.] In 1936 William J. Hamilton, a British geologist and researcher, discovered Alaca Höyük and a year later Eflatun Pinar. He, too, failed to grasp the true identity and date of these sites. Nevertheless, his book *Researches in Asia Minor, Pontus and Armenia* (London, 1842), three years after the publication of Texier's book *Description de l'Asie Mineure,* inspired other scholars and major European museums. The latter, spurred by the publicity given to dramatic archaeological discoveries, started to organize and finance large expeditions. However, those expeditions were not immediately sent to the central Anatolian plateau, but rather to areas on the periphery of Syro-Mesopotamia where the potential of finding historical monuments seemed greater. Long after having completed three seasons of excavation at Carchemish (1878–1881), the British Museum finally initiated archaeological excavations in eastern Anatolia. [*See* Carchemish.] These were undertaken for them by Hormuzd Rassam at Toprakkale in Van in 1897. Despite his controversial personal motives and unprofessional approach, Heinrich Schliemann's excavations at Troy, begun in 1870, were the first attempt to investigate the previously unknown preclassical civilization of Anatolia. [*See the biography of Schliemann.*]

In the closing years of the nineteenth century, exploration of the Anatolian plateau was undertaken on a large scale by Ernest Chantre, David G. Hogarth, K. Humann, J. G. Anderson, and William M. Ramsay, who published the results of their investigations at short intervals. Discoveries included sites with monumental art and architecture, rock-carved monuments, and the first cuneiform texts from Kültepe and Boğazköy. [*See* Kültepe Texts.] In 1882, Humann, a German archaeologist, inspected the ruins of Boğazköy and Yazılıkaya on behalf of the Preussischen Akademie der Wissenschaften in Berlin, making copies of some of the reliefs at the latter site. Later, in 1890, Humann and his colleague Otto Puchstein published their findings and observations in *Reisen in Kleinasien und Nordsyrien* (Berlin). In 1893–1984, Chantre, a French anthropologist and prehistorian, carried out probes at Boğazköy and discovered the first Hittite tablets. He also made several soundings at Alaca Höyük in areas were Hittite sculptures were visible. His book *Mission en Cappadoce* (Paris, 1898) provided additional encouragement to continue with archaeological research on the Anatolian plateau.

At about that time, it was already suspected that the roots of the North Syrian Late Hittite civilization might well lie on the central Anatolian plateau. Gordion, in the Sakarya valley, was the first scientific excavation project undertaken by Gustav and Alfred Koerte in 1889 on behalf of the Kaiserlich Deutschen Archäologischen Instituts in Berlin. Its purpose, however, was solely to investigate Phrygian remains. [*See* Gordion.] Chantre's discovery of tablets at Boğazköy changed the attitude of European scholars toward the archaeology of the Anatolian plateau. The German Oriental Institute took the initiative and sponsored archaeological excavations at Boğazköy in 1906, under the direction of Hugo Winckler. [*See* Deutsche Orient-Gesellschaft.] After briefly investigating the large temple complex (temple I), Winckler correctly shifted his attention to the palace complex at Büyükkale, where he recovered ten thousand tablets. In the same year he tried to locate the source of the Kültepe tablets, but without success. Winckler collaborated with the Turkish archaeologist Makridi Bey in subsequent campaigns, until 1912. Although World War I put a temporary stop to archaeological fieldwork, the evaluation and interpretation of the linguistic data led to considerable advances in Hittitology. For instance, as early as 1915, the first edition of a Hittite grammar was published by Bedrich Hrozny, and by 1918 a tentative list of Hittite kings had been assembled by emerging Hittitologists.

In 1925 a Czechoslovakian expedition led by Hrozny went to Kültepe, suspected of being the source of Cappadocian tablets being sold by local farmers. He eventually succeeded in collecting more than one thousand tablets from the terrace mound (the *kārum* Kaneš). It was at about this time that the Oriental Institute, founded by John D. Rockefeller at the University of Chicago, began to take an active part in field archaeology. James H. Breasted, its director, organized large-scale excavations in several Near Eastern countries, including Anatolia, in 1926. [*See the biography of Breasted.*] This was in fact the beginning of pioneering work in systematic and stratigraphic excavations on the Anatolian plateau by Hans H. von der Osten and his colleagues. [*See the biography of Osten.*] In his extensive surveys he concentrated mainly on recording mounds, hilltop forts, and ancient roads, with a particular emphasis on preclassical sites. In 1927, after a preliminary survey of archaeological sites in and near the bend in the Halys River (see below), and a tentative sounding at Gavur Kalesi, the Oriental Institute selected Alişar Höyük, 80 km (50 mi.) southeast of Boğazköy, for excavation as the key regional site. The excavators hoped that this site too would reveal rich remains of Hittite settlement and in particular Hittite tablets like those being found at Boğazköy. To their great disappointment, this was not the case. Instead, the site revealed a long and previously unknown pre-Hittite cultural sequence described as Neolithic, Chalcolithic, Copper Age, and Early Bronze Age. This stratified sequence produced one of the cornerstones of a relative pre-Hittite Anatolian chronology and cultural terminology. Furthermore, the excavation and recording methods used by the excavators set the basic standards for archaeological digs in Anatolia.

In the 1930s, numerous foreign and Turkish expeditions

became involved in archaeological research on the Anatolian plateau and its periphery, including the Cilician and ʿAmuq plains. [*See* Cilicia; ʿAmuq.] During the decade between 1931 and 1941, Turkish research institutions became organized, taking a more active part in archaeological research. The establishment of the Turkish Historical Society in 1931 by Kemal Atatürk was the main guiding force behind Turkish archaeological enterprises. Hamit Koşay was the most prominent archaeologist working on the Anatolian plateau, at Ahlatlıbel (1931); Alaca Höyük, initiated by Remzi O. Arik (1935); Pazarlı (1937); Etiyokuşu, with Ṣeuket A. Kansu (1937); and Karaoğlan, with Arik (1937–1941). The main purpose of these excavations was to investigate the pre-Hittite material culture record on the Anatolian plateau. While probing the pre-Hittite levels at Alaca Höyük in 1936, Koşay discovered the much publicized EB "royal tombs", a turning point in Anatolian archaeological research. The typology of the tombs and the technology of the metal finds led to questions of the possible origins of the Hittites and their civilization. [*See the biography of Koşay.*]

There also were small-scale excavations in the outlying parts of the Anatolian plateau, in an attempt to estimate the extent and possible origins of EB culture. The investigations by Tahsin Özgüç and Koşay at Dündartepe, Tekeköy, and Kavak south of Samsun and by Seton Lloyd and Nuri Gökçe at Polatlı produced not only a clearly stratified pottery typology covering most of the Early to Middle Bronze periods, but also regional ceramic repertoires for the Anatolian plateau. [*See the biography of Lloyd.*]

The nature and duration of EB II on the Anatolian plateau, defined at the time as the Copper Age, was initially recorded only at Alişar Höyük. The sophisticated metal objects from the royal tombs at Alaca Höyük made scholars aware that the so-called Copper Age and the following EB III on the Anatolian plateau were more complex and regionally varied than previously thought. The early 1930s saw not only the beginning of numerous new archaeological projects, but also the reactivation of earlier major excavations. In 1931 Kurt Bittel reopened the excavation at Boğazköy. During the eight years prior to the outbreak of World War II, he exposed the remains of many Hittite buildings both in the city itself and at Yazılıkaya. In 1932 the University of Cincinnati developed a long-term plan to reexcavate Troy under the direction of Carl Blegen. Since the conclusion of the architect Wilhelm Dorpfeld's collaboration with Schliemann in 1892, knowledge of preclassical civilization in the eastern Mediterranean had greatly advanced. New discoveries on Crete, Cyprus, and the Greek mainland and in Macedonia and the Cyclades had yielded enough archaeological data to make the establishment of a comparative chronology for the various Aegean cultures possible. [*See* Crete; Cyprus.] For this purpose Trojan analogies were important, but the stratigraphic confusion caused by the earlier excavations made reexamination through controlled excavations mandatory. In reopening the excavation, Carl Blegen's policy was to approach Troy's stratigraphic problems unprejudiced by his predecessors' complicated and often conflicting inferences. While Blegen's excavation was in progress, new information on cultural interaction between the Aegean world and the Anatolian plateau surfaced in Winifred Lamb's excavations at Kusura, near Afyon Karahisar, and at Demircihöyük, west of Eskişehir, excavated by Bittel and Heinz Otto. Among the major field projects carried out between the two world wars, the excavations of L. Delaporte at Arslantepe, near Malatya, in 1932 is the most outstanding. [*See* Arslantepe.] This site, already visited by von der Osten in 1926, revealed a rich collection of Neo-Hittite sculptures unmatched on the Anatolian plateau.

By the outbreak of World War II, Anatolian archaeology had become the subject of systematic study relying on records from stratigraphic excavations. The earlier study pattern, based on chance finds on which the preclassical history of Anatolia had rested, was abandoned. Improvements in excavation techniques made archaeological records more reliable sources of information. During World War II, only Turkish archaeologists were able to advance archaeological research on the Anatolian plateau, largely because Turkey was not involved in the war. The war prevented the German, Italian, French, and British archaeologists from continuing their work since Turkey's neutrality prevented them access. While work was in progress at Alaca Höyük, additional projects were carried out: on the mound of Bitik, excavated by Arik (1941); at Karaz Höyük in Erzurum, excavated by Koşay (1942, 1945); and at Has Höyük, dug by Halet Çambel (1943). In 1941 the provinces of Ankara, Konya, and Eskişehir were partly surveyed by Arik. His survey records, which included descriptions of a number of settlements, were published by Özgüç in 1956. However, despite new excavations, not all problems concerning chronology, ethnicity, continuity, or origins were entirely solved in the early 1940s. For instance, the meaning and origin of Hittite hieroglyphs, which had previously defied all attempts at decipherment, was partially solved at Karatepe beginning in 1945 by a team of archaeologists led by Helmuth Th. Bossert and Çambel and joined later by U. Bahadir Alkim. [*See* Hittite.] Another important Turkish enterprise in the postwar period was organized by the Turkish Historical Society in 1948: to resume excavations at Kültepe under the direction of Tahsin and Nimet Özgüç. This major decision led, in fact, toward exposing one of the most interesting historical chapters in early Anatolian civilization. At about this time, the Koşay and Mahmut Akok's team excavated another pre-Hittite site, at Büyük Güllücek.

Other enterprises included the excavation of Old Smyrna by a joint team headed by Ekrem Akurgal and John Cook (1949–1952); the excavations by the French Institute in Istanbul at the Midas city site (Yazılıkaya) in 1937–1939; and the resumption of excavations at the Phrygian city of Gordion by the University Museum of the University of Pennsylvania (1949).

The 1950s and 1960s opened a new era of intense preclassical archaeological investigation in Anatolia, including extensive field surveys aimed at recording the geographic and chronological distribution of preclassical settlements in different regions. In the 1950s, excavations at Horoztepe by Özgüç and Akok, Mahmatlar by Koşay and Akok, and Kayapinar by Raci Temizer added new dimensions to the regional EB archaeology and relative chronology on the northern half of the Anatolian plateau. One of the major field projects of the 1950s was the survey carried out by Charles Burney (1954–1955) in the northern provinces. While the Boğazköy excavations were reactivated in 1952 by Bittel, Sedat Alp started excavating the large EB–MB mound of Karahöyük near Konya in 1953.

Following his extensive field surveys on the southern Anatolian plateau and in southwestern Anatolia, in 1954 James Mellaart formed a team with Lloyd to excavate Beycesultan, the key Bronze Age site on the southwestern plateau. While this project was in progress, Mellaart initiated the Hacılar excavation project (1957–1960). [*See* Hacılar.] At the time, this was the most important prehistoric project being carried out in Anatolia. In fact, interest in the central Anatolian Neolithic and Chalcolithic period grew particularly strong following the Hacılar excavations. In 1961, while Mellaart initiated a new project at Neolithic Çatal Höyük, David French initiated the excavation of the prehistoric settlement of Can Hasan in Karaman. In 1963, Çayönü Tepesi, with its well-recorded aceramic remains, provided the first clues concerning the question of an incipient farming stage in Anatolia. [*See* Agriculture; Çayönü.]

Not only prehistoric sites, but also major second-millennium BCE sites were investigated in the 1960s. Nimat Özgüç undertook the excavation of Acemhöyük in 1963, trying, among other things, to shed some light on the identity of that MB city. In 1965 Burhan Tezcan investigated Koçumbeli and R. Temizer concentrated on the Hittite settlements at Inandık in 1966 and later at Eskiyapar.

Excavation in the eastern provinces intensified in the late 1950s and early 1960s. Burney's field survey in eastern Anatolia was followed by a growing interest in east Anatolian archaeology. Pulur and Güzelova, key sites of EB east Anatolia were excavated by Koşay and Hermann Vary (1960, 1961). Major Urartian sites were also targeted for exploration: Altin Tepe by Tahsin Özgüç and Çavuştepe (which was begun by A. Erzen in 1959); Patnos by Temizer and Kemal Balkan (1960–1963); Adilcevaz by Emin Bilgiç (1964); and Malatya, resumed by the Italians under Salvatore M. Pugilisi and Piero Meriggi (1961).

In the 1960s, the preclassical sites of western Anatolia, including the area of Iznik in the Marmara region, were investigated by French, who proposed regional pottery sequences for the hinterland east of the Aegean coast (see his articles in *Anatolian Studies* 17 [1967]: 165–178; 19 [1969]: 41–98).

From the late 1960s and early 1970s onward, Anatolian archaeology advanced considerably. Most expeditions adopted the Western multidisciplinary approach to field investigation, using palynological, environmental, ethnographic, and nonartifactual data studies to reconstruct the interaction between environment, subsistence economies, and social organization in ancient communities. The rescue excavations in the Keban in the late 1960s and early 1970s and in the Lower Euphrates River basin in the late 1970s and 1980s gave Anatolian archaeology an unprecedented boost—not only in terms of a dramatic increase in the number of excavations and the volume of finds, but also in the use of newly developed excavation and recording techniques. Beginning in the early 1970s, intensive field surveys in northern Turkey by Jak Yakar and Ali Dinçol and the subsequent excavations at Ikiztepe under the direction of Alkim in Bafra emphasized the cultural links of the Black Sea zone both with the Balkans and inner Anatolia. In the 1970s two major excavations further enriched the archaeological record of Bronze Age Anatolia: Maşat Höyük, excavated by Tahsin Özgüç, proved to be an important source for Hittite archaeology and history, and the environmental studies carried out at Demircihöyük, reexcavated by Manfred Korfmann, illustrated the importance of estimating the carrying capacity of the land surrounding ancient settlements in reconstructing socioeconomic structures. In recent years, Japanese archaeologists have also taken an interest in Anatolian archaeology. The excavations of Tsugio Mikami and Sachihiro Omura at the multiperiod site of Kaman-Kalehöyük and their systematic field surveys at the bend of the Halys River are producing results bearing on the character and distribution of preclassical sites on the Anatolian plateau. Renewed excavation of such major sites as Troy, Gordion, Alişar, Mersin, and Tarsus/Gözlü Kule reflects the new problem-oriented archaeological approach of the present generation of scholars.

[*See also* American Research Institute in Turkey; Anatolia; British Institute of Archaeology at Ankara; Deutsches Archäologisches Institut, Abteilung Istanbul; *and* Institut Français d'Études Anatoliennes d'Istanbul.]

BIBLIOGRAPHY

Akurgal, Ekrem. *Ancient Civilizations and Ruins of Turkey.* 4th ed. Istanbul, 1978.

Alkim, U. Bahadir. *Anatolia I.* Geneva, 1968.

Bittel, Kurt. *Les Hittites.* Paris, 1976.

Gurney, O. R. *The Hittites.* Rev. ed. London, 1990.

Lloyd, Seton. *Early Anatolia.* Baltimore, 1956.

Mellaart, James. "Pre-Classical Remains in Southern Turkey." *Anatolian Studies* 4 (1954): 175–240.

Yakar, Jak. *The Later Prehistory of Anatolia: The Late Chalcolithic and the Early Bronze Age*. British Archaeological Reports, International Series, vol. 268. Oxford, 1985.

JAK YAKAR

Archaeology in Egypt

The history of archaeological work in Egypt may conveniently be divided into five rather arbitrary periods of unequal length, each of very different character. The first phase consists of ancient interest in Egypt's past. The second stage did not transpire until the seventeenth century CE. The third era took place in the nineteenth century. Both the fourth and fifth periods unfolded in the twentieth century.

Phase One: From Antiquity to the Seventeenth Century. More than four thousand years ago, ancient Egyptians themselves excavated parts of their archaeological patrimony. Most of the work was motivated by practical concerns: a pharaoh could show his love of the gods and respect for their priests by restoring temples. He could demonstrate his own legitimacy by preserving the monuments of his ancestors. In the twelfth dynasty, for example, Senwosret (Sesostris) III removed two sarcophagi from beneath the third-dynasty Step Pyramid and placed them in the foundation deposits of his own pyramid complex as a means of demonstrating a historical affinity with Egypt's more ancient kings. In the nineteenth dynasty, Khaemwese, a son of Rameses II, carefully explored necropoleis from Saqqara north to Giza, cleaning and restoring many ancient monuments. He considered his actions to be both pious and historically important. Greeks and Romans, too (Egypt was under their control from 332 BCE to 337 CE), took an antiquarian interest in Egyptian monuments and restored or rebuilt those that played significant roles in their own religious ritual.

These early ventures into Egypt's past were harmless; some even protected the monuments. By the end of the Roman period, however, the treatment of Egyptian antiquities had become much more brutal. Perhaps it was because they no longer had meaning or cultural relevance: by the fifth century CE, the last Egyptian temples had closed, the last priests had died, and knowledge of the Egyptian language had died out. It was also because of two new and jealous religions, Christianity and Islam, which dominated Egypt in turn from the third century CE onward. Egyptian monuments were now seen as threats to man's relationship with the True God, best used only as convenient sources of building material. Local villagers plowed artifacts into the mud, burned papyri as fuel for bread ovens, hacked out pagan images on temple walls, and tore out stone blocks for new construction. The ancient Egyptians had sometimes abandoned or dismantled monuments; the Romans had carted several obelisks back to Rome, but there had not been destruction of this magnitude before.

Such destruction has continued into recent times. European travelers, who had begun visiting Egypt in numbers in the sixteenth century, were not concerned with archaeological preservation. Early pilgrims carried off Christian objects, anxious to acquire relics that would confirm their religious beliefs and offer proof of biblical history. They too destroyed figures that they could no longer understand or that seemed threatening. Medieval travelers picked over ancient sites, collecting mementos of their visit and carving their names on temple walls. Renaissance entrepreneurs dug for mummies that could be shipped to Europe and ground into what many believed were efficacious medicines. In all these instances, the digging was primitive and random, the record-keeping nonexistent, and the destruction of what we today would consider essential information nearly total.

Until the nineteenth century Europeans derived most of their knowledge about ancient Egypt from classical sources (especially Herodotus, Diodorus Siculus, Horapollo, and Pliny the Elder), biblical texts and exegesis, and the often fraudulent writings of travel writers such as John Mandeville (who, in fact, had never visited Egypt). Rarely accurate, these descriptions of Egypt and its monuments conspired to convince European scholars that Egypt was a truly exceptional country whose culture and history followed none of the rules that had governed the rest of human development. For example, both Pliny and Mandeville claimed that Egypt was a country inhabited by one-legged human beings who hopped about cultivated fields so fertile that frogs spontaneously generated in the mud, whose people drank from a Nile so potent it instantly made women pregnant, a people who built temples and pyramids with the direct assistance of God and the angels. Egypt was said to be the site of the garden of Eden, the earthly model of paradise. Surely, Europeans argued, the usual rules could not be applied here. Egypt was a unique country that had appeared suddenly, fully developed, with no predecessors, survived for three thousand years, and disappeared, leaving no obvious descendants.

Gradually, this view was expanded as tales about Egypt assumed an ever greater role in European myth and art. That the ancient Egyptians possessed knowledge far greater than modern humans was a popular opinion. This belief was regularly confirmed by the misinformation published in Europe about the magical powers of Egyptian objects, the potency of Egyptian symbols, and the special relationship between Egypt and the supernatural. For example, Europeans had long believed that the bodies of Christian saints, unlike those of ordinary mortals, were incorruptible. If their corpses were exhumed, it was claimed, they would be as perfectly whole and sweet-smelling as a living person's. How saintly, then, must the ancient Egyptians have been because thousands of perfectly preserved bodies (mummies) were found there every year! The whole population must have sat at the right hand of God!

Phase Two: Seventeenth- and Eighteenth-Century Collecting. By the late seventeenth century, Egyptian artifacts were to be seen throughout Europe. At this time museums were first established, and *cabinets des curiosités* could be found in the homes of the well-to-do. These Egyptian collections exerted a profound influence on Europe's views and on its own decorative arts and architecture. People wanted to possess Egyptian "things," the older, the more mysterious, the better. From the late 1600s onward, European collectors enthusiastically sought after Egyptian *objêts,* and agents happily ran an antiquities trade to satisfy them. In a short time, not only were small amulets, statuettes and mummies being shipped abroad, but even monumental sculptures, obelisks, whole tombs and temple walls. The peculiar features of Egyptian art that these collections displayed—human figures with animal heads, elaborate pieces of golden jewelry, and fascinating but unreadable texts—only confirmed the Egyptians' special status.

Phase Three: Nineteenth-Century Exploration. The distorted European picture of ancient Egypt did not begin to change until early in the nineteenth century. The first step toward a more accurate representation resulted from the Napoleonic expedition of 1798–1802. Bonaparte had brought 175 savants with his army, a committee of artists and scholars, whose task was to prepare as complete a record of the country as possible. The result was the *Description de l'Égypte* (1809–1828), a stunning record of Egypt's archaeological monuments, natural history, and local cultures, published in twenty-one volumes of text, maps, and plates. The *Description*'s elaborate illustrations gave Europeans their first accurate view of the country and its monuments. For almost the first time, Europeans could see the real Egypt, not the fanciful country that earlier sources had described.

In 1799 Napoleon's men found what was later to be called the Rosetta Stone while digging coastal defenses near the Rosetta branch of the Nile. It was immediately recognized as a possible source for the decipherment of Egyptian hieroglyphic script. Although the Rosetta Stone was confiscated by the British (it is now in the British Museum), copies had been made, and, working from them, Jean-François Champollion declared in 1822 that the key to ancient Egyptian had been found. With that announcement, it became possible for the first time in fourteen hundred years to read ancient texts and to learn about Egypt from the ancients themselves. Almost overnight, a vast new source of information was available, and there was a scramble to acquire inscribed materials to study. [*See* French Archaeological Missions; *and the biography of Champollion.*]

This desire for texts, either the originals or copies, led to numerous expeditions to the Nile Valley. Champollion himself visited Egypt in 1828 to copy texts, and a dozen other scholars from throughout Europe came as well. The most important was Richard Lepsius (1810–1884), whose thirteen-volume *Denkmäler aus Aegypten und Aethiopien* (1849–1859) included hundreds of folio plates of ancient texts, relief scenes, and temple plans. Today, Lepsius's work is still a rich source of information for Egyptologists; then, it and the *Description* were the most reliable and comprehensive sources available. So too were the superb watercolors of David Roberts (1796–1864), and the works of Sir John Gardner Wilkinson, whose brilliant three-volume *Manners and Customs of the Ancient Egyptians* (1837) provided descriptions and explanations of nearly every aspect of the ancient culture.

As positive as the contributions made by these descriptive publications may have been, they had unintended negative impact too. Although in the nineteenth century, in other parts of the world, archaeology was rapidly developing new techniques of excavation, dating, and interpretation, in Egypt it was being pushed into the background of scholarship. Egyptologists, most of them philologists by training, considered archaeological data merely footnotes to the story told by the written word. Archaeology's goal, it was argued, should simply be to find more texts. Archaeological context was ignored, and objects were saved only if they were deserving of display in museums. Excavators felt perfectly justified in plowing through sites (not habitation sites, but cemeteries or temples for they were the ones known to contain the treasures), saving only inscribed objects and pieces of aesthetic appeal and tossing the rest into the Nile. Not only would the texts reveal all that one needed to know, scholars claimed, but also there would be more to dig. Egypt was an archaeological cornucopia that could never be exhausted. By the late nineteenth century, dozens of expeditions were at work on sites from the Mediterranean to Aswan. It was an exciting time: excavators plundered tombs, dynamited temples, committed piracy, and shot their competitors in order to assemble great collections. Enactment of antiquities laws (the first in 1835), the founding of the Egyptian Antiquities Service, and the establishment of a national museum (1863) did little to reduce the scale of pillaging.

Phase Four: Early Twentieth-Century Excavation. Indeed, it was not until the beginning of the twentieth century that properly controlled excavations could be seen in Egypt. These rare early projects, in which careful digging was accompanied by proper recording procedures and contextual analyses, were the work of William Matthew Flinders Petrie (1853–1942) and George Andrew Reisner (1867–1942). Petrie's work on artifact typologies, seriation, and sequence dating demonstrated that even without associated texts, archaeological material could provide important information and not just pretty objects. His numerous publications, particularly of predynastic materials, helped set a new standard for the analysis of archaeological data. Similarly, Reisner's meticulous excavations of cemeteries at Giza and at Naga ed-Deir established new chronological guidelines for Early Dynastic and Old Kingdom artifacts. [*See also* Giza; *and the biographies of Petrie and Reisner.*]

Unfortunately, Petrie's and Reisner's emphases and methods were slow to influence other excavators' techniques. What we today would consider "proper" excavations remained the exception. The first half of this century was a time of spectacular archaeological discoveries in Egypt, including the tomb of Tutankhamun (excavated by Howard Carter), the treasures of Illahun and Thebes (the Metropolitan Museum of Art); the Early Dynastic cemeteries at Saqqara (Walter B. Emery); the Giza cemeteries (Reisner and Hermann Junker). Yet, important and well-executed as these projects were, they indicate that Egyptologists still preferred clearing tombs and stone temples to sifting through habitation debris or working with mud brick, still preferred well-preserved sites along the desert edge to the complex remains in the Nile Valley and Delta. The excavations of the necropolis at Tanis (a Delta site dug by Pierre Montet) and the long-term projects at Tell el-Amarna and Deir el-Medineh (both townsites) were among the few exceptions. Thus, there were few attempts in the early twentieth century to work at sites being threatened by new irrigation schemes, growing towns, new roads, or expanding agriculture, and many of these sites simply disappeared. This bias in favor of desert and stone continues to be an increasingly serious problem even today. [*See* Saqqara; Amarna, Tell el-; *and the biographies of Carter and Montet.*]

Phase Five: Modern Analysis. One of the most significant changes in the character of Egyptian archaeology occurred during the Nubian Salvage Campaign in the 1960s. Deeply concerned about the hundreds of sites that would be destroyed by rising Nile waters when the new Aswan High Dam was completed, Egypt and UNESCO issued a joint appeal to archaeologists from around the world to conduct salvage archaeological projects in the area south of Aswan. Although in ancient times this area, which was part of Nubia, did not belong to Egypt politically or culturally, excavations there had traditionally been conducted by Egyptologists (among them, Reisner, Junker, and Emery). Now, dozens of archaeologists, many of them trained in fields very different from Egyptology, came to work. With backgrounds in European prehistory and North American archaeology, they brought with them more rigorous approaches to excavation and analysis than Egyptian archaeology had ever developed. Lithics and ceramics were subjected to detailed study; typologies were created; chronological schemes were expanded and refined; and such disciplines as palynology, botany, zoology, chemistry, and statistics were used to reveal changing patterns of climate, describe minute details of lifestyle, and track changes in culture.

When the Nubian campaign ended, many of these archaeologists turned their attention farther north to Egyptian sites, bringing a whole new approach to Egyptian materials. They took an interest in urban sites. These archaeologists gave emphasis to finds that earlier generations of Egyptological excavators had considered worthless: for example, animal bones, vegetation, stone tools, potsherds, soils, and mud-brick architecture. They were eager to work in areas formerly though to be impossible, in the Delta, the Nile alluvium, and the oases. They gave to archaeological data an interpretive emphasis formerly reserved only for textual evidence. They also asked new questions about subjects as diverse as health and disease, social stratification, the influence of climatic change on agriculture and trade, the development of ceramic technology, and the origins of complex society.

Today, archaeological work in Egypt is increasingly more anthropological rather than object or text oriented. Not surprisingly, many of its practitioners have as much social science in their backgrounds as traditional Egyptology. Karl Butzer, for example, is a geographer and anthropologist who has examined the impact of the environment on Egyptian culture and on the development of irrigation in the Nile Valley. [*See* Environmental Archaeology.] Bruce Trigger is an anthropologist interested in the origins of civilization and its dynamics. Fekri Hassan is a prehistorian with a long-standing interest in the origins of Egyptian society and the theoretical framework for its study. William Y. Adams is a prehistorian by training whose Nubian ceramic studies are benchmarks that have put Nubian chronology on a solid footing. Barry Kemp is an Egyptologist and archaeologist who has studied the dynamics of Egyptian society as revealed by the archaeological record. His work at Tell el-Amarna and his processual approach to dynastic culture have had major impact. The activities of these and other scholars provide examples of archaeological analysis and interpretation as good as any in the world today. Furthermore, excavations—the long-term work at Hierakonpolis; Mark Lehner's studies of the Giza plateau; Robert Wenke's surveys and excavations in the Faiyum and the Delta; Manfred Bietak's superb studies of the site of Tell ed-Dabʿa (ancient Avaris); and those of the Germans and Swiss at Elephantine, to name a few examples—are truly state-of-the-art projects. [*See* Faiyum; Dabʿa, Tell ed-; Elephantine.] No longer is the emphasis on pretty objects or simple description. There is a deep committment to problem-oriented excavations and to the utilization of new techniques and cross-cultural comparisons to extract the maximum amount of information from Egyptian sites.

It has taken several centuries, but Egyptologists today recognize that ancient Egyptian culture is not a unique phenomenon that can only be explained by suspending the rules and invoking the gods. Egyptian culture *is* very special and very impressive. By acknowledging that it *is* the work of humans, however, that it can best be understood by being studied like other civilizations, we have finally come to give ancient Egypt relevance to our own history and to an understanding of human development.

This newfound relevance has come at a critical time. Without carefully planned archaeological work coupled with meticulous conservation and recording, Egypt's cultural patrimony will not survive. Egypt's archaeological sites are being seriously threatened today, from pollution, agriculture, growing population, theft, and other insidious forces. These threats make it even more crucial that we treat Egypt's archaeological remains not as inexhaustible curiosities we once thought they were, but as fragile and finite resources. It would be mankind's loss if they were to vanish. It certainly will be mankind's gain if we can insure that ancient Egyptian monuments will survive for future generations. The modern approaches to Egyptian archaeological sites significantly contribute to this goal.

[*See also* American Research Center in Egypt; British School of Archaeology in Egypt; *and* Institut Français d'Archéologie Orientale.]

BIBLIOGRAPHY

Assmann, Jan, et al., eds. *Problems and Priorities in Egyptian Archaeology.* London, 1987. Series of reports on some of the current archaeological work being conducted in Egypt, especially in the Nile Delta.

Bietak, Manfred. "Avaris and Piramesse: Archaeological Exploration in the Eastern Nile Delta." *Proceedings of the British Academy* 65 (1979): 225–290. Accessible introduction to Bietak's excellent work at an important Delta site. Also published as a separate volume (Oxford, 1981). More recent information on his work there, and on other Egyptian projects, may be found listed and abstracted in the *Annual Egyptological Bibliography* (Leiden, 1947–).

Butzer, Karl W. *Early Hydraulic Civilization in Egypt: A Study in Cultural Ecology.* Chicago, 1976.

Description de l'Égypte. 21 vols. Paris, 1809–1828.

Greener, Leslie. *The Discovery of Egypt.* London, 1966. The most readable account of Egyptology's early history to 1855.

Kemp, Barry J. "In the Shadow of Texts: Archaeology in Egypt." *Archaeological Review from Cambridge* 3 (1984): 19–28.

Lepsius, Richard. *Denkmäler aus Aegypten und Aethiopien.* 13 vols. Berlin, 1849–.

Reeves, C. Nicholas. *After Tut'ankhamun: Research and Excavation in the Royal Necropoleis at Thebes.* London, 1992. Examples of the kind of archaeological work currently being done in the Valley of the Kings.

Trigger, Bruce G. *A History of Archaeological Thought.* Cambridge, 1989. General work with occasional discussion of Egyptian data.

Trigger, Bruce G. *Early Civilizations: Ancient Egypt in Context.* Cairo, 1993. Good example of how current anthropological theory is making use of Egyptian archaeological data.

Weeks, Kent R., ed. *Egyptology and the Social Sciences: Five Studies.* Cairo, 1979. Egyptologists discuss the future needs of Egyptian historical, anthropological, and archaeological studies.

Weeks, Kent R. *An Historical Bibliography of Egyptian Prehistory.* American Research Center in Egypt, Catalog no. 6. Winona Lake, Ind., 1985. Useful source for work done on Paleolithic through Early Dynastic Egyptian sites.

Wilkinson, John Gardner. *Manners and Customs of the Ancient Egyptians.* 3 vols. London, 1837.

KENT R. WEEKS

Archaeology in Cyprus

To the extent that all Near Eastern archaeology has been a reflection of Western preoccupations and interests, the history of archaeology in Cyprus may best be understood in terms of its involvement with Western scholarship. Because for most of this history Western ethnocentric concerns focused on Greece as the birthplace of democracy, Palestine as the home of the Bible, and Egypt and Mesopotamia as the centers of the oldest civilizations, Cyprus remained somewhat of a Cinderella in the wider picture of Near Eastern archaeology. A more significant attitude that shaped this history was the view that Cyprus was neither Oriental nor Greek, but a hybrid unworthy of study by scholars of the "great traditions." This status had and continues to have serious funding implications for archaeological research. Ambivalent western perceptions are manifested in many ways: the only foreign archaeological institute in Cyprus is established under the aegis of the American Schools of *Oriental* Research, the annual report of all discoveries appears in the *Bulletin de Correspondance Hellènique.* The list of paradoxes is endless. Because of the island's particular history, its archaeological development was closely synchronized with its political fortunes. This development may, therefore, be divided into three stages: precolonial, British colonial, and independence.

Precolonial Period, to 1878. In Cyprus, as elsewhere in the Near East, this period is characterized mainly by antiquarians who collected objects from cemeteries. Already in 1576, Poracchi mentions ancient tombs "in which have been found many wonderful things" at Kouklia, Paphos, and Salamis (C. D. Cobham, *Excerpta Cypria: Materials for a History of Cyprus,* Cambridge, 1908, p. 164). By the middle of the nineteenth century, foreign officials on the island vied with each other in amassing collections to enhance their prestige, for general edification and personal profit: the motives were not considered incompatible. Chief amongst these entrepreneurs were Sir Robert Hamilton Lang and the infamous General Luigi Palma di Cesnola. Cesnola's exports of innumerable antiquities helped to found the Metropolitan Museum of Art in New York City. He became its first director. Of Cesnola, D. G. Hogarth wrote in 1888: "It is much to be regretted that his want of all archaeological qualifications, coupled with his desire that that want should not be apparent to the world, has introduced such confusion into his results" (E. Gardner, D. Hogarth, M. James, R. Elsey Smith, "Excavations in Cyprus, 1887–8," *Journal of Hellenic Studies* 9 [1888]: 150). So many sites were rifled and so much exported during this and the start of the next period that it is hard to underestimate its significance for later fieldwork developments. [*See the biographies of di Cesnola and Hogarth.*]

British Colonial Period, 1878–1960. Although the British administration enacted new antiquities laws, engaged antiquarians to excavate, established the Government Collections Museum (1883), and encouraged the foundation of the Cyprus Exploration Fund (1887) which worked on a large scale at major sites, the pervasive collecting mentality was not modified until the 1920s. Only John L. Myres fearlessly criticized the government and attempted to bring order into chaos. [*See the biography of Myres.*] However, Cyprus lacked a Flinders Petrie to apply systematic typological and stratigraphic methods; therefore, fieldwork lagged behind standards of some excavations in Egypt and Palestine. The situation improved when a young Swedish scholar, Einar Gjerstad, came to the island in 1923, published his seminal *Studies on Prehistoric Cyprus* (Uppsala, 1926), and gained funding for an ambulatory excavation program (1927–1931) that was breathtaking in scope. Its aim was no less than the elucidation of the entire cultural history of Cyprus from the Stone Age to the Roman period. To understand this turn of events, it should be remembered that in 1927 the old antiquities law was modified to permit the export of antiquities, thus enabling Gjerstad to obtain funding more easily. His research strategy emphasized two other aspects: the role of Cyprus as intermediary between the Orient and the Occident and its own indigenous civilization. These perceptions formed the *leitmotif* of archaeological activity on the island for much of this century. [*See the biography of Gjerstad.*]

Results of Gjerstad's and his colleagues' excavations have been published in the *Swedish Cyprus Expedition* I–IV (Stockholm, 1934–1972), an indispensable research tool. They demonstrate conscientious achievement. Their discoveries and sites are among the most important in Cyprus. To name but a few of their successes, Gjerstad and his associates revealed the Bronze and Iron Age cemeteries at Lapithos; the spectacular Late Bronze Age tombs at Enkomi; the hilltop palace at Vouni with its elegant *kore* and Persian treasure; the rural shrine at Ayia Irini with two thousand statuettes (some life-size, found undisturbed round its altar), the Archaic sanctuary at Idalion, capital of an Iron Age kingdom, where they found an entire coat of mail; the temple of Heracles-Melqart at Kition, so evocative of the syncretic beliefs of Iron Age Cyprus; and the Roman theatre at Soli.

Because Cyprus lacks tells (mounds), greater emphasis was placed on art history and artifact-based analysis than stratigraphy as the basis for the sequential reconstruction of Cypriot antiquity. Gjerstad, E. Sjöqvist, and others provided meticulous artifact studies in which artistic connoisseurship often passed for theory. Ceramic types established by Max Ohnefalsch-Richter and Myres were refined and put into a chronological sequence. Although modified since then, the Swedes' Bronze and Iron Ages typologies and dates are still commonly used. Their formulations are influential beyond Cyprus since distinctive Cypriot pottery was widely exported, and by crossdates, it provided undue precision for chronological schemes in Palestine and elsewhere.

As in Near Eastern archaeology generally, the Swedes and other archaeologists neglected Gordon Childe's culture concept (V. G. Childe, *The Dawn of European Civilization*, London, 1925) in favor of the traditional Three-Age techno-evolutionary model. In keeping with their views about the arrival of the Greeks on Cyprus by the beginning of the Iron Age, Gjerstad and his colleagues divided the period according to the Greek mainland chronological framework: Cypro-Geometric, Cypro-Archaic, and Cypro-Classical.

During the 1930s three archaeologists rose to prominence and helped to define the archaeology of the island for many years to come. The first was Porphyrios Dikaios, pioneer of Cypriot prehistory, who excavated the key sites of Khirokitia, Sotira, and Erimi, and documented the Neolithic and Chalcolithic periods for the first time. The second was C. F. A. Schaeffer, who in 1934 discovered the city of Enkomi. Because previous excavators were so intent on recovering "Mycenaean" tombs there, they failed to recognize that the tombs were inside the houses of the city. Schaeffer's objective was to obtain Late Bronze Age comparanda for material from his established excavations at Ras Shamra/Ugarit. The third was A. H. S. Megaw, who became director of the newly founded Department of Antiquities in 1936, developed a model organization during his tenure of office until 1960, and investigated classical and later remains such as Kourion and the Forty Columns castle at Paphos. During the 1930s, a long and productive project at Kourion was also initiated by George McFadden. For many years, classical archaeology in Cyprus was synonymous with discoveries by his University Museum, Philadelphia, team. [*See the biographies of Dikaios, Schaeffer, and McFadden.*]

Such was the perceived importance of Enkomi that in 1948 Dikaios was sidetracked from his prehistoric researchers to direct Cypriot excavations there. His painstaking, monumental report of ten-years' work demonstrates the influence of the Swedes, and it can be contrasted with Schaeffer's volumes in which only choice historical problems are treated or the most spectacular finds studied with panache. The subjective retrieval policies and incomplete publication of Schaeffer's Enkomi excavations are a continued source of regret. While Dikaios was engaged at Enkomi in 1957 he also rescued an extraordinary, half-looted tomb in a neighboring Iron Age cemetery, and so discovered the Royal Cemetery of Salamis.

Two quite different events mark the archaeological history of the island during the last decade of British administration. One was the excavation by J. Iliffe and T. Mitford of the Persian siege mound at Palaipaphos, which unexpectedly yielded destroyed statuary, including what is arguably the finest Archaic sculpture from the island, and remarkable details of counter-siegeworks. The other was the creation in 1955 of a Survey Branch under H. W. Catling. This led to the first systematic surveys, the production of invaluable studies by Catling and an accessible reference collection for scholars.

The colonial power, intentionally or otherwise, had sought to deflect the Hellenization of Cypriot archaeology by emphasizing the island's cultural diversity. However, it was not possible to divorce archaeology from the struggles for independence and Enosis. With the founding of the new state in 1960, the issue of the earliest Greek presence on the island, never low on the agenda of earlier, classically trained archaeologists, came to the fore.

Independence, Since 1960. In the first flush of their independence, emerging modern states often produce outstanding figures. Independent Cyprus was fortunate in having first Dikaios (until 1963), then Vassos Karageorghis (until 1989), as directors of the Department of Antiquities. Karageorghis's astute policy of promoting international interest in the role of ancient Cyprus, while pursuing his own very active program of excavations, ensured a balanced yet lively development of the subject. Another stimulating policy, that of withholding licences to excavate until applicants' previous fieldwork was published, a policy now widely emulated, thrust Cypriot discoveries more forcefully into the mainstream of Near Eastern and Mediterranean archaeology.

During the 1960s major excavations were carried out by the French at the city of Salamis; by Karageorghis at its necropolis and at Kition; and by Kyriakos Nicolaou at Nea-Paphos, the Roman capital of Cyprus and a treasure house of mosaics. [*See the biography of Nicolaou.*] The immensely rich royal tombs of Salamis raised issues concerning the late expression of Homeric funerary rites. The role of the early Greeks on the island was being continually redefined, not only by excavations but also by publications such as H. W. Catling's provocatively titled *Cypriot Bronzework in the Mycenaean World* (Oxford, 1964) and conferences like the seminal *The Mycenaeans in the Eastern Mediterranean* (Nicosia, 1972). Although this topic also embraced the larger themes of the Sea Peoples and Philistines, debates paradoxically grew ever narrower as scholars vied to identify the foreign perpetrators of Late Bronze Age destructions. It is only recently that this empirical positivism was questioned and the whole basis of old theories of interpretation was reappraised.

One of the benefits of 1960s New Archaeology was the application of explicit models and a closer association between archaeology, science, and social science. Prehistorians were the first to respond. Dikaios already made use of radiocarbon dates in 1962 to radically revise upward the date of the Khirokitia culture, then regarded as the first evidence for humans on the island. Radiometric evidence from Ayios Epiktitos-Vrysi contradicted the prevailing sequence of "Neolithic I–II" and introduced compelling evidence for strong regional variation on the island. During the 1970s, self-critical concerns began to be voiced about theoretical concepts, research designs, and epistemological goals.

Meanwhile, fieldwork projects multiplied. Some of the more important included the Americans at Idalion, Toumba tou Skourou, Phlamoudhi, and Kourion; the French at Salamis and Cape Andreas; the British at Philia and Ayios Epikititios; the Poles at Paphos; the Germans at Tamassos; the Swiss at Palaipaphos; and, not least, the Cypriots at Kition. The last, in particular, yielded exciting results with the discovery of a Late Bronze Age holy precinct and the largest-known Phoenician temple, both associated with copper-working, anchors, and depictions of ships.

Armed conflict between Greeks and Turks in 1974 led to the cessation of excavations in the archaeologically rich northern part of the island. Major projects nonetheless ensued in the south and continue in the mid-1990s. The French worked at Amathus, at Kition where classical slipways were recently uncovered, and at Khirokitia where Dikaios's famed roadway was reinterpreted as a town wall. The Americans excavated in the Vasilikos Valley, where an urban center associated with the Kalavassos mines provides new impetus to thriving studies on the rise of complex society in Cyprus and its relationship with copper exploitation, and at Aetokremnos, where there is evidence for pre-Khirokitia pygmy-hippopotamus hunters. The British continue to work at Lemba and Kissmenga, where the lengthy Chalcolithic period is finally being investigated, and at the Bronze Age manor at Maroni. Rescue excavations at Kouklia-Skales revolutionized understanding of the eleventh–tenth century BCE "Dark Age." Other projects, like that of the Swedes at Hala Sultan Tekke, the Canadian survey in the west, and those of the Cypriots themselves at a variety of sites, emphasize the intensity of current fieldwork. Equally important was the introduction of influential theories for explanations in archaeology.

These anthropological theories came about as a result of western dissatisfaction with neo-evolutionary approaches. Labeled as processual, structural, postprocessual and other kinds of archaeology, they exhibit the influence of neo-Marxism and emphasize the social context of past changes. This new intellectual climate is fostering innovatory proposals such as the replacement of the traditional period labels and the application of explicit models, like secondary state formation to explain the relationship between the emergence of the Salamis royal tombs and the Phoenicians.

The archaeological policies of independent Cyprus averted the excesses of nationalist archaeology characteristic of new states. As the impact of new directions indicates, however, this decision was at the price of continuing to accept western goals and methodologies for the interpretation of a polyethnic past. Thus, the current geopolitical context of Cyprus remains inseparable from interpretations of its past.

[*See also* Cyprus. *In addition, many of the sites mentioned are the subject of independent entries.*]

BIBLIOGRAPHY

Catling, H. W. *Cypriot Bronzework in the Mycenaean World.* Oxford, 1964. Seminal, well-illustrated analysis of Bronze Age metalwork in Cyprus. Underestimates Levantine influences, and now in need of updating.

Gjerstad, Einar. *Studies on Prehistoric Cyprus.* Uppsala, 1926.

Gjerstad, Einar, et al. *The Swedish Cyprus Expedition: Finds and Results of the Excavations in Cyprus, 1927–1931.* 4 vols. Stockholm, 1934–. Indispensible research tool for all pre-Byzantine periods.

Gjerstad, Einar. *Ages and Days in Cyprus.* Studies in Mediterranean Archaeology, Pocket-book 12. Göteborg, 1980. Candid, firsthand account of the Swedes' mold-breaking investigations in Cyprus. Although no substitute for the *Swedish Cyprus Expedition* volumes, many fieldwork policies and practices are articulated more clearly here.

Goring, Elizabeth. *A Mischievous Pastime: Digging in Cyprus in the Nineteenth Century.* Edinburgh, 1988. Although this survey of nineteenth-century fieldwork appears as an introductory essay to an exhibition catalogue, it is the most valuable and readable account of that period.

Karageorghis, Vassos, ed. *Acts of the International Archaeological Symposium, "The Myceneans in the Eastern Mediterranean."* Nicosia, 1972. Now rather dated, but still highly influential studies.

Karageorghis, Vassos, ed. *Archaeology in Cyprus, 1960–1985.* Nicosia, 1985. Major discoveries and developments from 1935 to 1985, summarized in introductory studies by the outstanding practitioners of the day: Karageorghis, Merrillees, Muhly, Coldstream, and Tatton-Brown. In the absence of a definitive history of archaeology in Cyprus, this provides the best alternative.

Karageorghis, Vassos, ed. *Acts of the International Archaeological Symposium, "Cyprus between the Orient and the Occident."* Nicosia, 1986. Comprehensive, international treatment of a perennial theme in Cypriot archaeology. F. G. Maier's contribution, "Kinyras and Agapenor," is an instructive example of the new movement to reassess traditional frameworks.

Merrillees, R. S. *Introduction to the Bronze Age Archaeology of Cyprus.* Studies in Mediterranean Archaeology, Pocket-book 9. Göteborg, 1978. Thoughtful, outspoken primer for the period that has received a great deal of attention in recent studies in Cypriot archaeology.

Stanley Price, N. "On Terminology and Models in Cypriote Prehistory." In *Studies Presented in Memory of Porphyrios Dikaios,* edited by Vassos Karageorghis et al., pp. 1–11. Nicosia, 1979. Early attempt to show that the Three-Age system conventionally used to order archaeological data might hinder rather than help understand past developments.

EDGAR PELTENBURG

Archaeology in the Aegean Islands

The history of archaeology in the Aegean islands begins in the late nineteenth century. Very little archaeological or scholarly research was carried out in Greece during the centuries of Turkish rule, and work on the islands only began some fifty years after independence was won. The main period of Turkish rule, usually given as 1460–1821, is far more complicated for the islands: Thasos came under Turkish rule in 1455, Lesbos in 1462, Naxos in 1566, and Melos in 1580, but Rhodes was not conquered by the Turks until 1522, Crete did not become part of the Ottoman empire until 1669 and Aigina not until 1718.

The end of Turkish rule on the islands presents an equally complex picture. The islands of the Cyclades became part of Greece in 1832. The Ionian islands, governed as a British protectorate since 1815, were ceded to Greece in 1864. The islands of Ionia, such as Chios and Samos, and those of the North Aegean, including Thasos, Samothrace, Lemnos, and Lesbos, along with the northernmost part of the country including the Chalkidiki, all became part of Greece in 1913 (the latter as a consequence of the successful Balkan wars that Greece and her Balkan allies fought against the Ottomans in 1912–1913). In 1912, however, the islands of the Dodecanese—principally Rhodes, Kalymnos, Karpathos, and Kos—were given to Italy. Italian rule in the Dodecanese lasted until 1947. This variegated pattern in the recent history of the Aegean islands is reflected in the nature of the archaeological work carried out in the islands.

European knowledge of the Aegean islands was minimal prior to the late nineteenth century. The piles of rubble that had once been the Colossos of Rhodes, toppled by the earthquake of 226 BCE, were finally hauled away by the Arabs, in 653 CE and sold to a Jew from Edessa who needed nine hundred camels to transport all the bronze. In 1103 the Anglo-Saxon merchant Saewulf, on his return from pilgrimage to the recently liberated Holy Land, refers to the islands of Scio (Chios), Meteline (for Mytilene, the chief city of Lesbos), and Tenit (Tenedos) before going on to "the very ancient and famous city of Troy . . ." (Easton, 1991). In 1445, Cyriacus of Ancona visited Mykonos and Delos, giving his impression of the colossal statue of Apollo of the Naxians. Not content simply to describe ancient sculpture, Kenelm Digby, in the seventeenth century, carried off pieces of marble sculpture from Delos for the royal collection of Charles I.

Travelers to Crete in the seventeenth century were given a tour of the labyrinth of Daedalos, actually the remains of the stone quarry of Roman Gortyn/Gortyna. A more serious exploration of the Idaean Cave, the legendary birthplace of the god Zeus, had been carried out by Joseph Goedenhuize in 1590 or 1591, who remarked on the large quantity of broken lamps (of Roman date) in the cave. [*See* Lamps.] In the late 1830s, the German traveler Ludwig Ross toured the islands of the Aegean. His observations, published in three volumes (1850–1852) provide an account of the islands in the premodern era that is matched in English only by the work of James Theodore Bent, published in 1885. Bent also excavated some forty Early Cycladic graves on the island of Antiparos in 1884, but this does not represent the beginning of archaeological work in the Cyclades. In 1869 the French geologist F. Fouqué discovered remains of a prehistoric town on the southern coast of the island of Thera (actually that part of the island known as Therasia). The vases found at that time are still in the collection of the French School at Athens. What Fouqué had discovered was the Minoan settlement at Akrotiri, buried by the eruption that took place in about 1600 BCE. It was excavated by Spyridon Marinatos from 1967 until his death in 1974.

In 1811 the Temple of Aphaia on the island of Aigina was "explored," and seventeen pieces of sculpture from it were subsequently sold to Ludwig I, king of Bavaria. The Venus di Milo (a first-century BCE copy of a fourth-century original), now in the Louvre museum, was found in fragments on Melos in 1820 and bought by the French ambassador to Constantinople as a gift for Louis XVIII. In 1854–1855 the Englishman Charles Thomas Newton, looking for more treasure to add to the collections of the British Museum, "excavated" the Temple of Apollo on Kalymnos. In 1863 the French consul Champoiseau discovered the Winged Victory of Samothrace. The statue, actually a Rhodian work of 187 BCE, is one of the treasures of the Louvre. In 1873 and 1875 an Austrian expedition under Alexander Conze worked at the Ptolemaion on Samothrace. In 1873 the French School began work on the island of Delos and these excavations, which are still in progress, can be said to mark the real beginning of official archaeological work on the Aegean islands (although large-scale excavation on Delos only took place between 1902 and 1914).

In 1878 the Archaeological Museum of Herakleion was founded and in that same year Minos Kalokairinos began work at what he called Kephala, a site now known as Knossos. In 1880 the newly established (1879) Archaeological Institute of America sent William J. Stillman to investigate the possibilities of archaeological work at Knossos and Gortyn, an enterprise strengthened by the establishment of the American School of Classical Studies in Athens in 1881. Although troubles between Greeks and Turks on Crete made work impossible, the American School maintained its interest in Crete into the 1890s, employing the Italian scholars Federico Halbherr and Antonio Taramelli in survey work and in the exploration of the Kamares cave, the latter soon to be made famous by Arthur Evans. After an ill-fated attempt to gain permission to excavate at Delphi, the American School finally settled upon the site of Corinth in 1896, which remains the official school excavation to this day.

Halbherr, on the other hand, remained on Crete. In 1884 he discovered the monumental stone inscription known as the Gortyn Law Code (mid-fifth century BCE). This remarkable discovery encouraged the Italians to remain in the vicinity of Gortyn and the plain of the Mesara. In 1885 they began work at the Temple of Pythian Apollo at Gortyn and, intermittently, continued to work in different areas of Gortyn into the 1960s. Halbherr also spent August 1885 excavating rich votive deposits from the Idaean cave (eighth and seventh centuries BCE), especially a series of important but poorly preserved bronze "shields," for which influence (and even provenience) has been sought in lands as far distant as Urartu. [*See* Grave Goods; Urartu.] In 1894 Halbherr began work at Prinias, a site covering a period from about 1300 to 300 BCE. The excavation of Prinias was continued by Luigi Pernier (1906–1908) and, more recently, by Giovanni Rizza (1969–1978). Work at the Idaean cave was reopened by Yiannis Sakellarakis in 1982.

In 1898 Turkish rule over Crete came to an end. An independent Crete was governed as a European protectorate under the leadership of Prince George of Denmark (until 1913, when Crete became part of Greece). In that same year Halbherr founded the Italian Mission to Crete, which, after 1937, became the Italian Archaeological School of Athens. In 1900 the main excavation of the Italian Mission was the Minoan palace at Phaistos. Work at Phaistos, directed by Pernier continued from 1900 to 1909 and then from 1928 to 1932 (Pernier and Banti, 1947). In 1950 the Italians reopened excavations at Phaistos, under the direction of Doro Levi. Levi dug there for seventeen seasons (1950–1966), publishing his results in a series of final excavation reports.

Work at Ayia Triadha, an adjacent site in some way related to Phaistos, began in 1902. The major excavations at Ayia Triadha (1903–1905, 1910–1914), directed by Halbherr and E. Stephani, were finally edited for publication by Luisa Banti in 1977. The famous well-known sarcophagus of Ayia Triadha, now securely dated to the fourteenth century BCE (LM IIIA), was discovered by R. Paribeni in 1903. [*See* Sarcophagus.] The current excavations at Ayia Triadha, under the direction of Vincenza La Rosa, began in 1977. A Pre-Palatial quarter at Ayia Triadha was discovered by chance in 1970 and excavated in 1973 and 1977. A Minoan pottery kiln (at first identified as a copper-smelting furnace) was excavated in 1976 and 1977. In 1959 Doro Levi excavated a remarkable Middle Minoan tholos tomb outside the village of Kamilari, near Phaistos. The Italians also worked on Crete during their period. (Di Vita and La Regina 1984). [*See* Tombs.]

In 1900, the year the Italians began work at Phaistos, Arthur Evans began his excavation of the palace of Minos at Knossos. He dug for six seasons (1900–1905) and published the results of his work in a series of five volumes (four volumes of text plus an index), *The Palace of Minos* (1921–1936), surely the best-known publication in the history of Minoan archaeology. By the time the last volume appeared, written with his half-sister Joan Evans (who also wrote a very informative biography of her brother), Evans was eighty-five years old. In 1905, during the last season of excavation at Knossos, Evans presented a paper at an international congress in Athens outlining the basic chronological framework of Minoan civilization. His basic sequence of Early, Middle, and Late Minoan, with each period having three subdivisions, is still used (MacEnroe, 1995). Carl Blegen, in 1921, used this basic tripartite structure to work out a similar sequence for the Greek mainland, designating the basic periods as Helladic, in place of Minoan. This, too, is still the sequence used.

Evans was really a gifted amateur, with no experience in field archaeology, much like Heinrich Schliemann. As Schliemann had made use of the expertise of Wilhelm Dörpfeld, so Evans employed Duncan Mackenzie. Mackenzie was a skilled field archaeologist who had just spent four years (1896–1899) excavating the site of Phylakopi on the island of Melos (Momigliano, 1995). This was the first major excavation sponsored by the British School of Archaeology at Athens and the first long-range excavation in the Aegean islands. The results of this work were published in 1904. After only a brief season there in 1911, the British returned to Phylakopi in 1974, under the direction of Colin Renfrew. This time fieldwork (1974–1977) was combined with an extensive regional and ecological survey of the island.

After World War II and the German occupation of Crete (during which the Germans conducted some excavations, notably those of Frederich Matz at the site of Monastiraki), the excavation of Knossos was resumed by the British School, under the direction of Sinclair Hood (1951–1961). Hood is best known for his extensive excavations in the vicinity of the Royal Road, which remain unpublished. Since then the British School has excavated in many different areas at the site, under the direction of Peter Warren, Mervyn Popham, J. N. Coldstream, and Colin Macdonald.

Joseph Hazzidakis, director of the Syllogos of the Friends of the Herakleion Museum, and an important figure in the early years of Cretan archaeology, excavated at a complex of three Minoan villas at the site of Tylissos (1909–1913), finding, among other things, three huge bronze cauldrons. [*See* Villa.] These excavations were published by the French School (in their series Études Crétoises) in 1934. In 1915 Hazzidakis discovered the Minoan palace at Mallia. He conducted some exploratory work, in 1915 and 1919, and then turned the site over to the French School. The French opened excavations at Mallia in 1921 and are still there. Work before World War II was directed by Fernand Chapouthier (among others) and, after the war, by Micheline and Henri van Effenterre. Mallia, or Malia as it is known to its present excavators, remains the Minoan palace most appreciated by the modern visitor to Crete (for French work on Crete see Tiré and van Effenterre, 1978).

In 1901 the American scholar Harriet Boyd (later Hawes) began work at Kavousi, in the Bay of Mirabello. She soon shifted to the Minoan town of Gournia, where she remained through 1904. Gournia, excavated on behalf of the American Exploration Society of Philadelphia, an organization affiliated with the University of Pennsylvania, remains the only Minoan town ever excavated. Her final excavation report, published in 1908, was a model for its day and remains an indispensable publication for the study of Minoan archaeology. The new Gournia Project, currently conducting a regional survey, is directed by L. Vance Watrous (1994).

At Gournia, Boyd Hawes was assisted by Richard Berry Seager, who went on to conduct excavations at Vasiliki (1903–1906), Pseira (1906–1907), and Mochlos (1908). On the tiny island of Pseira, Seager excavated more than forty houses and thirty-three graves, but little of this material was ever published. From 1985 to 1991, Pseira was reexcavated, under the direction of Philip Betancourt and Costis Davaras. The first volume on the new Pseira Project appeared in 1995. At Mochlos, Seager found a spectacular series of Early Minoan tombs, with stone bowls and much gold jewelry, but publication was again quite sketchy. In 1989, Jeffrey Soles reopened excavations at Mochlos, working primarily in levels dating to Late Minoan times (Shaw, 1990).

The Greek Archaeological Service has also worked extensively on the island of Crete, especially under the direction of Marinatos (see above), Nikolaos Platon, and Stylianos Alexiou. At the beginning of this century the Greek archaeologist Stephanos Xanthoudides excavated a series of Early and Middle Minoan vaulted tombs on the plain of the Mesara, beginning with Koumasa, in 1904. His final report, published in 1924, raised many problems of chronology and interpretation that may be solved when the related tombs excavated by Alexiou at Lebena (1958–1960), the ancient port of Gortyn, are published. Xanthoudides also excavated a Late Minoan villa at Nirou Khani in 1918–1919. In 1912, Xanthoudides called attention to the importance of the site of Arkhanes. Some work was done at the site by Evans (1922), Marinatos (1935, 1956), and Platon (1948, 1957), but it was only in 1964 that Sakellarakis began large-scale work there. From 1965 to 1972 he excavated five very rich tholos tombs at Phourni and in 1979 discovered a structure identified as a Minoan shrine at Anemospilia, with evidence for human sacrifice.

In 1899–1900, the British School, under the direction of David Hogarth, excavated at the Cave of Psychro, usually identified with the Diktaean cave. Most of the finds from this excavation ended up in the Ashmolean Museum, Oxford, and were eventually published by John Boardman in 1962. In 1901, Hogarth moved to the site of Zakros, on the east coast of Crete, where he excavated a series of Late Minoan houses. It is now known that he came very close to finding the remains of the Late Minoan palace at Zakros that Platon only discovered in 1961 (although it had been known for some time to looters in the district). In 1962, Platon opened excavations at Zakros on behalf of the Greek Archaeological Society. Zakros is thus the fourth great Minoan palace to be excavated, and the results of Platon's work at the site (1961–1980) have been spectacular. Although he did publish a popular book on his excavations (Platon,

1971), the final excavation report will be published by his son, Eleftherios Platon, who, since 1981, has been excavating at the site, including the surrounding caves, houses and tombs.

In recent years large, possibly palatial complexes have been excavated at Khania, in western Crete (by a joint Greek-Swedish team directed by Yannis Tzedakis and Eric Hallager), at Kommos (by an American School team directed by Joseph Shaw), and at Palaikastro (by a British School team directed by J. A. MacGillivray, returning to a site the British School excavated from 1902 to 1906). George Rethemiotakis is also excavating a new Minoan palace site at Galatas, near Herakleion, on behalf of the Greek Archaeological Service. In addition to its Minoan remains Kommos has produced a series of Iron Age Greek temples (tenth century BCE) and even a structure identified as a Phoenician tripartite shrine. [*See* Phoenicians.] From Palaikastro a remarkable ivory and stone figurine has been identified by the excavators as a representation of the young Zeus.

On Naxos the physical anthropologist Klon Stefanos excavated some four hundred Early Cycladic graves in eighteen cemeteries (1903–1905), on behalf of the Greek Archaeological Society. This material was finally published by George Papathanasopoulos in 1963. Serious archaeological work on Naxos began in 1949 with the excavations by Nikolaos Kontoleon at the settlement of Grotta (in the town of Naxos) and the cemetery of Aplomata. In 1985 Kostas Zachos began work at the Zas cave, uncovering evidence for continuous occupation from Neolithic times to an early phase of Early Cycladic.

On Syros, the Greek archaeologist Christos Tsountas excavated, in the 1890s, some six hundred Early Cycladic graves at the cemetery of Chalandriani as well as a fortified Early Cycladic settlement at the site on Kastri. Tsountas published some of this material in two lengthy articles, in 1898 and 1899. The Kastri site was reexcavated by Eva-Marie Bossert in 1962. Another site named Kastri, a Middle and Late Minoan settlement on the island of Kythera, was excavated by the British School, under the direction of George Huxley, from 1963 to 1965. On Kea (also known as Keos), important excavations were conducted by the American School, under the direction of Jack Caskey, who dug, from 1960 to 1974, at the small Final Neolithic site of Kephala and at the large Bronze Age site of Ayia Irini. John Coleman published Kephala in 1977; Ayia Irini is being published in many volumes by multiple authors.

On Delos the prehistoric (Early Cycladic II and IIIA) settlement on Mt. Kythnos was explored in 1916. Beside the prehistoric circular, hut-shaped shelters of the third millennium BCE, the excavators found remains of an Archaic temple dedicated to Zeus Kythnios and Athena Kythnia. Prehistoric Paros (especially the Early Cycladic period) was explored by the German Institute under the direction of Otto Rubensohn, whose report appeared in 1917. Important evidence for understanding the end of the Bronze Age on Paros has come from recent excavations at the site of Koukounaries, conducted by Demetrius Schilardi on behalf of the Greek Archaeological Society. At the site of Skarkos, on the Island of Ios, Marisa Marthari is excavating a very well-preserved Early Cycladic settlement, on behalf of the Greek Archaeological Service. On the island of Saliagos, between Paros and Antiparos, the British School (1964–1965) excavated an important Middle Neolithic settlement, under the direction of John Evans and Renfrew, the first evidence for human occupation in the Cyclades in the Neolithic period.

From 1896 to 1903, the German Institute excavated the ancient Greek city of Thera, under the direction of Hiller von Gärtringen, finding many important Early Greek inscriptions. [*See* Greek; Inscription Sites.] The cemeteries of ancient Thera (Geometric, Archaic, and Classical) were excavated by Nikos Zapheiropoulos who, while ephor of the Cyclades in the 1950s–1970s, built local museums on many of the islands, including the one on Mykonos. Following the death of Marinatos in 1974, Christos Doumas continued work in the Minoan town of Akrotiri, where a great controversy developed over the date of the volcanic eruption that blew apart the island and buried Akrotiri under meters of ash and pumice. Various dates have been proposed, ranging from 1648 to about 1450 BCE; no resolution is in sight.

On Chios, an island noted for its production of mastic (a resin of the lentisk tree used in making a liqueur and in chewing gum) and as the traditional birthplace of Homer, "the blind man of Chios," the most important archaeological work has been that carried out by the British School at Emporio (1951–1955), a site covering the Late Neolithic and the entire Bronze Age, under the direction of Sinclair Hood and John Boardman. In the North Aegean, the most important prehistoric excavations have been those of the Italian School at Poliochni (1931–1936), on the island of Lemnos, directed by Alessandro della Seta, and of the British School at Thermi (1929–1933) on the island of Lesbos, directed by Winifred Lamb. Both are Early Bronze Age sites, covering roughly the period of Troy I–II. The exploration of prehistoric Samothrace began in 1984 with the excavations of Dimitris Matsas at the site of Mikro Vouni. The discovery there of clay sealings of Minoan type added a new chapter to the history of an island known mainly for its Hellenistic Sanctuary of the Great Gods, under investigation by the Institute of Fine Arts, New York University, since 1938. [*See* Seals.] The current excavations at this site are being directed by James McCredie.

In the islands of the Dodecanese the important work in prehistoric or Bronze Age archaeology has been done on Rhodes and Kos, mainly during the period when the islands belonged to Italy. Rhodes, in particular, was published in the periodical *Clara Rhodos* (published from 1928 to 1941). At Trianda on Rhodes, a habitation site under strong Minoan influence, if not an actual Minoan colony, was excavated by G. Monaco from 1935 to 1936. The Mycenaean cemeteries on Rhodes, located at Moschou Vounara and Makria Vounara, near Trianda, were excavated by G. Jacopi from 1924 to 1928. The Italian interpretation of Late Bronze Age Rhodes was revised by Arne Furumark, in a classic article published in 1950. On Kos two large Mycenaean cemeteries, at Langadha and Eleona, were excavated by Luigi Morricone, in 1935 and 1940–1941. On both islands a great deal of recent work has been carried out by members of the Greek Archaeological Service, especially by T. Marketou at Trianda.

Descriptions of the antiquities of Samos go back almost 150 years. The tunneled aqueduct built by Eupalinos for the tyrant Polycrates (Herodotus 3.60) was described by Victor Honoré Guérin in 1856. [*See* Aqueducts.] The earliest map of the island was made by Tournefort in 1777 and the first plan of the city walls was drawn by Bishop Pococke in 1792. For those interested in the Near East, especially the Near East of the first half of the first millennium BCE, the most important excavations are unquestionably those conducted by the German Institute at the Sanctuary of Hera, the Heraion, on the island of Samos. The excavations there (1910–1914, 1925–1939, 1952 to the present), under a number of field directors, but especially Ernst Buschor and then Hans Walter, have uncovered a spectacular array of imported bronze votives. These bronzes, dedicated to the goddess Hera, came from Egypt, Cyprus, Phrygia, North Syria, Assyria, Babylonia, Luristan (or Iran), Urartu, and the Caucasus (Jantzen, 1972). No other Greek sanctuary and no other Greek site has such a quantity of imported Oriental objects. Only Olympia, Delphi, and now the Idaean cave have produced anything remotely comparable.

[*See also* Aegean Islands; Crete; *and the biographies of Evans, Guérin, Hogarth, Mackenzie, and Schliemann.*]

BIBLIOGRAPHY

Barber, R. L. N. *The Cyclades in the Bronze Age.* London, 1987. The only recent survey, but a very traditional work.

Barber, Robin, ed. *Blue Guide to Greece.* 6th ed. London, 1995. Basic information on numerous archaeological sites written principally by people associated with the British School.

Bent, James Theodore. *The Cyclades or Life among the Insular Greeks.* London, 1885.

Boardman, John. *The Cretan Collection in Oxford.* Oxford, 1962.

Boardman, John, and C. E. Vaphopoulou-Richardson, eds. *Chios. A Conference at the Homereion in Chios, 1984.* Oxford, 1986.

Davis, Jack L. "Review of Aegean Prehistory I: The Islands of the Aegean." *American Journal of Archaeology* 96 (1992): 699–756. Superb discussion of recent archaeological work; full bibliography.

Di Vita, Antonio, and Adriano La Regina, eds. *Ancient Crete: A Hundred Years of Italian Archaeology (1884–1984).* Rome, 1984. Published on the occasion of the centennial of Italian work on Crete. The place to begin for all Italian excavations on Crete.

Easton, Donald F. "Troy Before Schliemann." *Studia Troica* 1 (1991): 111–129.

Evans, John D., and Colin Renfrew. *Excavations at Saliagos near Antiparos.* London, 1968.

Furumark, Arne. "The Settlement at Ialysos and Aegean History, c. 1550–1400 B.C." *Opuscula Archaeologica* 6 (1950): 150–271. Basic revision of the Italian work on LB Rhodes.

Jantzen, Ulf. "Samos VIII." *Ägyptische und Orientalische Bronzen aus dem Heraion von Samos.* Bonn, 1972. The Samos bronzes excavated prior to 1965.

Leekley, Dorothy, and Robert Noyes. *Archaeological Excavations in the Greek Islands.* Park Ridge, N.J., 1975. Now dated, but valuable for work done by the Greek Archaeological Service.

MacEnroe, John. "Sir Arthur Evans and Edwardian Archaeology." *Classical Bulletin* 71 (1995): 3–18. Interesting discussion of the ideological background of British archaeology at time Evans worked at Knossos.

Matsas, Dimitris. "Minoan Long-Distance Trade: A View from the Northern Aegean." In *Politeia: Society and State in the Aegean Bronze Age,* edited by Robert Laffineur and Wolf-Dietrich Niemeier, pp. 235–247. Liège, 1995. Discussion of important recent work on Samothrace and in the northern Aegean.

Marangou, Lila, ed. *Cycladic Culture: Naxos in the 3rd Millennium.* Athens, 1990. Catalog of an important exhibition at the Goulandris Museum in Athens, based on excavated material.

Momigliano, Nicoletta. "Duncan Mackenzie: A Cautious Canny Highlander." In *Klados: Essays in Honour of J. N. Coldstream,* edited by Christine Morris, pp. 163–170. London, 1995.

Morricone, Luigi. "Coo: Scavi e Scoperte nel 'Serraglio' e in locala minori (1935–43)." *Annuario della Scuola Archeologica di Atene e delle Missioni Italiane in Oriente* 50–51 (1973): 139–396. The most important publication for LB Kos.

Overbeck, John C. *The Bronze Age Pottery from the Kastro at Paros.* Jonsered, 1989. Publication of the pottery from Rubensohn's excavations.

Pernier, Luigi, and Banti, Luisa, eds. *Guida degli scavi italiani in Creta.* Rome, 1947. Basic account of the early Italian work on Crete.

Platon, Nikolaos. *Zakros, the Discovery of a Lost Palace of Ancient Crete.* New York, 1971.

Ross, Ludwig. *Reisen auf dem griechischen Inseln des ägäischen Meeres.* 3 vols. Stuttgart and Tübingen, 1840–1852.

Shaw, Joseph W. "North American Archaeological Work in Crete, 1880–1990." *Expedition* 32 (1990): 6–14. Historical article, in a special issue of *Expedition* devoted to Crete.

Tiré, Claude, and Henri van Effenterre. *Guide des fouilles françaises en Crète.* 2d ed. Paris, 1978. Basic account of French archaeological work on Crete.

Watrous, L. Vance. "Review of Aegean Prehistory III: Crete from Earliest Prehistory through the Protopalatian Period." *American Journal of Archaeology* 98 (1994): 695–753. Excellent account of recent archaeological work on Crete (to about 1700 BCE); full bibliography.

J. D. MUHLY

Archaeology in the Arabian Peninsula

No history of archaeological research in the Arabian Peninsula can proceed as a smooth, uninterrupted narrative for the reason that explorations and excavations in northwestern Arabia, southwestern Arabia, inner Arabia, and the Gulf region (including Oman) followed separate, if not always unrelated, trajectories. Arabian scholars working in one area may have been aware of developments in other regions, but the scholarly traditions to which they belonged were quite distinct. Thus, because of its proximity to the Holy Land, the Hijaz (northwestern Arabia) always attracted the vast majority of its students from the ranks of Palestinian archaeology. South Arabian scholars, overwhelmingly philologists until the 1950s, had wider interests in Semitic philology but tended to be a highly specialized band until quite recently. (Today, archaeologists with backgrounds in Syrian, Mesopotamian, and Iranian archaeology are on the scene.) Finally, the Gulf region attracted a mixture of scholars whose interests originally lay, for the most part, in the prehistory of Iran, the Indus Valley, Mesopotamia, and, in the case of the Danish expedition (see below), Scandinavia.

Political conditions have directed archaeological developments in many parts of the world, and the Arabian Peninsula is no exception. Many commentators on the history of archaeological research on the Arabian Peninsula have noted that political instability, the xenophobic tenets of Wahhabism, and the belligerence of bedouin tribes hampered the growth and development of archaeology in this region during the nineteenth century to an extent unknown in neighboring areas of western Asia. In this state of affairs, therefore, and given the very life-threatening situations encountered by early explorers, it is striking just how many archaeological observations were made prior to the inception of excavation in 1879. Much of this achievement must be ascribed to a heroic desire to explore a hostile corner of the globe generally regarded as inaccessible to those who valued their life; to record inscriptions in as yet undeciphered tongues; and to join what was, until quite recently, a very exclusive club of intrepid explorers. The history of Arabian exploration has been reviewed on several occasions by scholars such as David G. Hogarth, Fritz Hommel, Detlef Nielsen, and Adolph Grohmann. Only those discoveries of relevance to the archaeology of the peninsula will be discussed here. For the sake of continuity, each major subarea of the Arabian Peninsula will be dealt with in turn.

South Arabia. The German teacher Ulrich Jasper Seetzen became the first Western scholar to copy a South Arabian inscription as a result of his visit to the Ḥimyarite capital Ẓafar in 1810–1811. [*See* Ẓafar.] Other significant texts were copied in 1834–1835 and in 1838 by the British military adventurers James R. Wellsted and Charles J. Cruttenden. In 1843 Thomas Joseph Arnaud, a French pharmacist attached to an Egyptian regiment, became the first European to visit the Sabaean capital Marib and to describe its famous dam, as well as to collect more inscriptions. [*See* Marib.] The French Orientalist Joseph Halévy traveled to Yemen in 1869 on behalf of the Académie des Inscriptions et Belles Lettres, copying almost seven hundred inscriptions and thereby laying the foundations of the systematic study of epigraphic South Arabian. [*See* South Arabian.]

It was the great Austrian scholar Eduard Glaser, however, whose four expeditions to Yemen (1882–1884, 1885–1886, 1887–1888, 1892–1894) were to have the most profound impact on the early course of South Arabian studies. The initial results of Glaser's work were published in the *Corpus Inscriptionum Semiticarum,* but the inscriptions he copied continue to be edited in the Austrian Academy of Science's series Sammlung Eduard Glaser. The last great South Arabian expedition of the nineteenth century was the Vienna Academy's unsuccessful attempt, in 1898, to reach Shabwa, capital of the Ḥadhramaut, under the direction of Carlo Landberg and the Orientalist David Heinrich Müller [See Ḥadhramaut; Shabwa.]

In 1928 the German scholars Carl Rathjens and Hermann von Wissmann, working at the site of al-Huqqa, became the first scholars to undertake archaeological excavations in Yemen. A decade later, in 1937–1938, Gertrude Caton-Thompson worked at Ḥureidha, and R. A. B. Hamilton excavated at Shabwa. [*See* Ḥureidha.] Archaeological activity in Yemen was interrupted by World War II, but in 1950 Wendell Phillips, with the help of such renowned scholars as William Foxwell Albright, led the first of his American Foundation for the Study of Man (AFSM) expeditions to South Arabia, working at a series of important sites including Timnaʿ, the capital of Qataban; Hajar Bin Ḥumeid, a stratified mound in the Wadi Beiḥan; the Sabaean capital Marib, where the Awwam temple was excavated; and Khor Rori, a Ḥadhrami foundation on the coast of Dhofar. In 1968 the American scholar Gus W. Van Beek, a veteran of the Hajar Bin Ḥumeid excavation, surveyed Najran, the northernmost of the great South Arabian cities. [*See* Hajar Bin Ḥumeid; Najran; Qataban; Timnaʿ (Arabia); *and the biographies of Caton-Thompson, Phillips, and Albright.*]

Excavations at Shabwa, capital of the Ḥadhramaut, were begun in 1974 by a French mission led by the late Jacqueline Pirenne and Jean-François Breton; such other scholars as Walter W. Müller of Marburg, Jacques Ryckmans of Louvain, and Christian Robin of Aix-en-Provence universities continued carrying out epigraphic surveys in Yemen during the 1970s and 1980s. The establishment of a station of the German Archaeological Institute at Sanʿa in the 1970s resulted in much new work at Marib and other sites, under the direction of Jürgen Schmidt. In the early 1980s, an important Italian expedition led by Alessandro de Maigret began, for the first time, locating and excavating Bronze Age sites in Yemen; in 1982 the AFSM initiated new work in Wadi al-Jubah, under the direction of James Sauer. [*See* Jubah, Wadi al-.] Meanwhile, a Soviet-Yemeni expedition, working both at Raybun in the Ḥadhramaut and at Qana' on the coast, in the mid- and late 1980s, added considerably to what is known of South Yemen. More recently, a French expedition directed by Serge Cleuziou began investigating the later prehistory of Yemen. [*See* Yemen.]

Eastern Arabia and the Gulf Region. Foreign political advisers and military officers were the first active pursuants of the archaeological record of eastern Arabia and the Gulf. Lewis Pelly, Her Majesty's political resident in the Persian Gulf, described the ruins at Thaj in northeastern Arabia in the diary of his 1865 journey to Riyadh. In 1879 Edward L.

Durand conducted the first archaeological excavations ever undertaken on the Arabian Peninsula at the site of Aali, on the island of Bahrain. In 1899 an unidentified Ottoman official wrote an account of archaeological sites in the Hofuf oasis area of northeastern Arabia, that was published posthumously in 1917. William Henry Irvine Shakespear, the British political officer at Kuwait, visited Thaj in 1911, at which time he copied several Hasaitic inscriptions. Excavations were resumed on Bahrain in 1889 by Mr. and Mrs. Theodore Bent; in 1903 by the Belgian scholar Arnold Jouannin; in 1906 by Francis B. Prideaux; from 1921 to 1926 by Clive Kirkpatrick Daly; and in 1925 by Ernest J. H. Mackay. [*See* Bahrain; Thaj.]

The renowned British Arabist Harry St. John B. Philby collected stone tools in eastern Saudi Arabia, near the border with Qatar, in 1931, just as the British political agent at Kuwait, Harold Richard Patrick Dickson did in the Wadi al-Batin of western Kuwait in 1935. [*See* Kuwait; Qatar.]

In 1933 an agreement was signed by Standard Oil of California and the Saudi Arabian Ministry of Finance that initiated the search for oil in Saudi Arabia. With this act, thousands of Americans gained access to what had formerly been the province of but a few intrepid explorers, and information on archaeological finds began to accumulate. In 1940–1941, in collaboration with Standard Oil, Peter Bruce Cornwall, then a graduate student in history at Harvard University, conducted test excavations at several sites in the Eastern Province of Saudi Arabia. In 1947 Richard LeBaron Bowen, Jr., an engineer working for ARAMCO (Arabian American Oil Company), collected pottery and described ʿAin Jawan, the site of a limestone quarry worked during World War II. This led to an important publication that was long the main point of reference for the late pre-Islamic past of eastern Saudi Arabia.

It was also oil that brought T. Geoffrey Bibby, on behalf of the Iraq Petroleum Corporation, to Bahrain and led to the inception, in 1953, of the Danish expedition to the Arabian Gulf (University of Aarhus), led by the eminent Danish prehistorian Peter Vilhelm Glob. Soon after establishing themselves on Bahrain, the Danish Gulf expedition began working in Qatar (1957), Kuwait (1958), and the Trucial States (1958), all of which had been, archaeologically speaking, terra incognita. In 1968 the Danes conducted a season of survey and excavation in the Eastern Province of Saudi Arabia. In 1972 Abdullah H. Masry, a Saudi Arabian educated at the University of California at Berkeley and at the University of Chicago, began excavations at a number of important Ubaid-related sites in eastern Saudi Arabia. He was followed shortly thereafter by Constance Maria Piesinger at the third-millennium BCE sites of Umm ar-Ramad and Umm an-Nussi. Surveys of the region between Hofuf and the Kuwaiti border were conducted in 1976 and 1977 by American scholars from the University of Chicago and Harvard working for the Saudi Arabian Department of Antiquities. Between 1982 and 1985 excavations were carried out at Thaj and in the Dhahran tomb field.

New excavations on Bahrain were undertaken by several Arab missions in the late 1970s, when it became clear that the construction of the causeway that now links Saudi Arabi and Bahrain was going to destroy thousands of burial mounds. An Australian team led by Anthony McNicoll worked briefly on Bahrain in the early 1980s. The French scholar Monique Kervran resumed excavations at Qalʿat al-Bahrain during the late 1970s since continued by Pierre Lombard. [*See* Qalʿat al-Bahrain.] A British expedition has been excavating the early second millennium BCE settlement of Saar since 1990. Between 1983 and 1990 a French mission to Failaka (in Kuwait), under the direction of Jean-François Salles, carried out extensive excavations at both Bronze Age and Hellenistic sites. [*See* Failaka.]

Northwestern Arabia. Apart from surreptitious visits to Mecca and Medina by the likes of Richard Burton and others, northwestern Arabia was not explored until 1876–1878, when the great English Orientalist Charles M. Doughty visited the southerly Nabatean site of Meda'in Saleh and the earlier Iron Age metropolis of Tayma', where the sixth century BCE Babylonian monarch Nabonidus spent a decade of his reign. [*See* Meda'in Saleh; Tayma'.] The visit yielded an important harvest of Nabatean, Lihyanite, Thamudic, Aramaic, and Minean inscriptions. [*See* Nabatean Inscriptions; Safaitic-Thamudic Inscriptions.] The year 1884 witnessed the important expedition by the Alsatian scholars Julius Euting and Charles Huber to Tayma' and al-ʿUla (Dedan). [*See* Dedan.]

From 1907 to 1910 two French Dominican fathers, Antonin J. Jaussen and Raphael Savignac, conducted extensive surface investigations at Meda'in Saleh, al-ʿUla, Tabuk, and briefly at Tayma'. Between 1908 and 1915 the Austrian Orientalist Alois Musil made a series of journeys through northern Arabia, reaching Hail, al-ʿUla, al-Jawf, and Wadi es-Sirḥan which, although not intended to serve an archaeological purpose, gathered an enormous amount of topographic data scholars working on the archaeology and early history of this area continue to mine.

Thereafter, it was not until 1962 that two Canadian scholars, Fred V. Winnett and William L. Reed, returned to northern Arabia, where they visited most of the important, known sites (e.g., Tayma', al-ʿUla, and Mada'in Saleh), recording dozens of Thamudic, Taymanite, Minean, Dedanite, Liḥyanite, Nabatean, Palmyrene, and Hebrew inscriptions. [*See the biography of Winnett.*] In 1968 the English archaeologist Peter J. Parr led a team that returned to Meda'in Saleh, al-ʿUla, Tayma', and other North Arabian sites of importance but was still not entitled to conduct sondages. During the late 1970s and early 1980s, archaeologists working on behalf of the Saudi Arabian Department of Antiquities conducted surveys and sondages throughout northwestern Arabia, but particularly at Khuraybah and Tayma'.

Oman Peninsula. In the early nineteenth century, the interior of Oman was almost as inaccessible as Yemen. The coasts, however, were visited frequently by the navies and merchant vessels of many European countries, as well as of America. On one such visit in 1844, Henry John Carter, an assistant surgeon aboard the British East India Company's brig *Palinurus,* noted the presence of early traces of copper metallurgy on the island of Masira off the southern coast of Oman. Copper metallurgy was to remain an important area of research in Omani archaeology. The year 1924 saw the establishment of a committee "to report on probable sources of the copper used by the Sumerians" by the British Association for the Advancement of Science. This research project, which lasted until 1936, involved the analysis by the English metallurgist Charles H. Desch of, among other things, copper ore samples from Oman acquired in 1925 by the British geologist G. M. Lees.

Actual excavations in Oman, however, were not initiated until 1958, when Ray Cleveland, a junior colleague on Phillips's AFSM team, conducted brief soundings at Sohar, on the Batinah coast of Oman. [*See* Sohar.] Meanwhile, in the same year, Glob and Bibby were shown a group of burial mounds on the island of Umm an-Nar, in Abu Dhabi, and shortly thereafter in the Buraimi/al-ʿAin area oasis (divided between Abu Dhabi and Oman). It was there that the Danes were to uncover the first traces of the third-millennium Umm an-Nar culture that dominated most of the Oman peninsula.

In 1968 the British archaeologist Beatrice de Cardi, accompanied by Brian Doe, conducted her first survey in the emirate of Ras al-Khaimah, and the Danish archaeologist Karen Frifelt began work at sites such as Hili, Qarn Bint Saud, and Rumeilah. It was the accession of Sultan Qaboos in Oman in 1970 and the formation of the United Arab Emirates (UAE) in 1971, however, that paved the way for the subsequent systematic archaeological exploration of the Oman peninsula. Beginning with the appointment in 1973 of the British scholar Andrew Williamson (d. 1975) as archaeological adviser in Oman, foreign expeditions from Britain, the United States, Italy, France, and Germany have carried out a great deal of work in Oman, investigating a wide range of sites of all periods. For the first time such neglected problem areas as copper metallurgy, oasis agriculture, irrigation, paleopathology, and ceramic technology were addressed, rather than concentrating exclusively on site sequences and chronological questions. In this they were greatly aided for many years by Williamson's successor, Italian archaeologist Paolo M. Costa. [*See* Oman.]

The surveys and sondages carried out by an Iraqi expedition to the UAE in 1973 led to the discovery of many important sites, a number of which were subsequently investigated. Teams from France, Germany, Belgium, Denmark, the United Kingdom, Switzerland, Japan, and Australia have worked at a wide range of sites, including Hili 8, Rumeilah, Shimal, ed-Dur, Bithna, Rafaq, Julfar, and Tell Abraq; the departments of antiquities and museums in al-ʿAin (Abu Dhabi), Ras al-Khaimah, and Sharjah have been particularly active.

Inner Arabia. Apart from several crossings made by Philby, the "Heart of Arabia" remained largely unknown to Western scholars until 1951 when, at the invitation of King Abdul Aziz Ibn Saud, the Belgian scholars Gonzague Ryckmans and Jacques Ryckmans, together with Philippe Lippens and Philby, surveyed the territory between Jiddah, Najran, and Riyadh, recording more than ten thousand rock-cut inscriptions.

In 1972 Abdul Rahman al-Ansary of Riyadh (now King Saud) University initiated excavations at the important central Arabian metropolis of Qaryat al-Fau, which the Philby-Ryckmans-Lippens expedition had visited. [*See* Qaryat al-Fau.] This project, in which a generation of Saudi Arabian archaeologists was trained, continues under al-Ansary's direction. In 1976 Masry, as newly appointed director of antiquities, launched the long-term Comprehensive Survey of the Kingdom of Saudi Arabia. The project ran into the mid-1980s and recorded thousands of archaeological sites scattered throughout the interior of Saudi Arabia. Excavations at al-Rabadah, a caravan stop on the Darb Zubaydah, or Pilgrim Road, between Baghdad and Mecca, began in 1979 under the direction of Sa'ad al-Rashid of King Saud University. [*See* Darb Zubaydah.]

The establishment of Arabian archaeology as a recognized subfield within Near Eastern archaeology is attested to not only by the large number of excavations in the region during the last few decades, but by the number of journals now devoted to it: *Arabian Archaeology & Epigraphy* (Copenhagen), *Atlal* (Riyadh), *Dilmun* (Bahrain), and the *Journal of Oman Studies* (Muscat). In addition, the first academic post in the West devoted exclusively to Arabian archaeology was established at the Institute of Archaeology, University College London, in the late 1980s.

[*See also* Arabian Peninsula.]

BIBLIOGRAPHY

Bibby, Geoffrey. *Looking for Dilmun.* New York, 1969. Popular account of the Danish Gulf expedition, with primary reference to the work carried out on Bahrain and the search for Dilmun.

Hogarth, David G. *The Penetration of Arabia.* London, 1904. Exhaustive history of Arabian exploration from earliest times to the beginning of the twentieth century.

Hommel, Fritz. "Explorations in Arabia." In *Explorations in Bible Lands during the Nineteenth Century,* edited by Hermann V. Hilprecht, pp. 693–752. Philadelphia, 1903. Comprehensive survey of exploration in the Arabian Peninsula from the late eighteenth to the turn of the twentieth century.

Phillips, Wendell. *Qataban and Sheba: Exploring the Ancient Kingdoms on the Biblical Spice Routes of Arabia.* New York, 1955.

Potts, Daniel T. *The Arabian Gulf in Antiquity.* 2 vols. Oxford, 1990. General survey of the archaeology of the Gulf region, with a full discussion of the history of archaeological research in Kuwait, eastern Saudi Arabia, Bahrain, Qatar, the UAE, and Oman.

Winnett, Fred V., and William L. Reed. *Ancient Records from North Arabia.* Toronto, 1970.

D. T. POTTS

HITTITE. The language called Hittite belongs to a family of languages spoken in Asia Minor during the second pre-Christian millennium. These languages, which constituted the old Anatolian branch of the Indo-European family, included Hittite, Luwian, and Palaic. Hittite is by far the best attested of all these languages, represented by thousands of clay tablets inscribed in cuneiform writing stemming from the capital of the great Hittite Empire the city Ḫattuša, whose ruins lie adjacent to the modern Turkish town of Boğazkale. [*See* Boğazköy.] Excavations there have been conducted on behalf of the German Oriental Society and the German Archaeological Institute, almost continuously since 1906, under the direction of Hugo Winckler, Kurt Bittel, and Peter Neve. Well over ten thousand tablets were found in several locations: on the acropolis, in the large temple in the Lower City, in the House-on-the-Slope, and, in recent years, in the smaller temples in the Upper City. Tablets from Ḫattuša include a small number of Old Hittite (c. 1650–1500) and many more from the succeeding Middle Hittite (c. 1500–1380) and New Hittite periods (c. 1380–1180). [*See* Deutsche Orient-Gesellschaft; Deutsches Archäologisches Institut, Abteilung Istanbul.]

Writing System. The Hittites adopted a form of the Sumero-Akkadian cuneiform writing system. The sign forms resemble those in contemporary inscriptions from Syria and Egypt (Alalakh, Ugarit, Amarna). The phonetic values of the signs are also largely the same as in these other areas of western peripheral cuneiform, with the exception of a few values coined on the acrophonic principle: for example, the value *wi* for the GEŠTIN ("wine") sign, whose Hittite equivalent was *wiyanaš*. Hittite cuneiform writing consisted of signs for syllables (e.g., *ba, ug, par*) together with others which represent entire words, represented in transcription by their Sumerian value (e.g., LUGAL "king"). [*See* Cuneiform; Sumerian.]

Phonology. Because Hittite is a dead language, its phonology can be judged today only on the basis of variations in writing. Although the cuneiform writing system was capable of representing the distinction between voiced and voiceless stops, Hittite scribes did not employ this method. The same words were written with *t*- and *d*-containing signs, *g* and *k*, and *b* and *p*. Instead of employing separate signs for voiced and voiceless consonants, wherever the stop in question occurred intervocalically, the voiceless variant was written doubled: a-ap-pa for pronounced /apa/, and *a-pa-a-aš* for /abas/. [*See* Scribes and Scribal Techniques; Writing and Writing Systems.]

Hittite seems to have distinguished at least the following consonants: *b, d, g,* g^{w}, *ḫ, k,* k^{w}, *l, m, n, p, r, š, t,* and *z*. Although the graph *z* may occasionally represent a sibilant distinct from *š*, it usually represents the cluster *t* and *š* (e.g., *aniyaz* for *aniyat-* + nominative case ending *š*).

The vowels are *a, e, i,* and *u*, which can be long or short in quantity. A minimal contrasting triad illustrates three distinct vowels: *ḫarkan,* "destruction"; *ḫarkin,* "white"; and *ḫarkun,* "I held." Next to nothing is known today of the quality of these vowels. Vowel length was often indicated by plene spellings (e.g., *a-pa-a-aš* for /abās/; *a-pu-u-uš* for /abūs/). But because such spellings were sometimes necessary to disambiguate vowel quality in cuneiform writing (e.g., *p*^{é}/*i-e-da-an,* "place," to indicate /pedan/ versus */pidan/), the presence of vowel quantity cannot always be concluded through their presence. Two glides, *y* and *w*, existed.

Nouns, Adjectives, Pronouns, and Numbers. Nouns show two genders, animate (or common) and inanimate (or neuter). There is no formal distinction between masculine and feminine gender. In number, nouns and adjectives distinguish singular and plural, but no dual. Animate and inanimate nouns and adjectives have identical endings in the genitive (sg., *-aš;* pl., *-aš*), dative-locative (sg., *-i;* pl., *-aš*), allative (*-a*), instrumental (*-it*), ablative (*-az*), and vocative (*-e, -i,* or zero). In the nominative and accusative cases, animate and neuter nouns and adjectives employ different case endings (see table 1).

Pronouns can be independent words or clitics. Examples of the former are *uk,* "I"; *ammuk,* "me"; *ammel,* "my"; *zik,* "thou"; *tuk,* "thee"; and *tuel,* "thy." Sample clitics are *-mu,* "me," and *-naš,* "us"; *-ta,* "thou," and *-šmaš* "you (pl.)"; *-še,* "to him/her/it," and the third-person nominative and accusative forms (*-aš,* "he"; *-an,* "him"; *-at,* "it"). Demonstratives are *ka-*, "this," and *apa-*, "that." Relative and interrogative pronouns share the stem k^{w}*i-* "who, which."

Hittite numbers are almost always written with number signs (1-*aš*, 3-*eš*) and share some of the distinctive endings of the pronouns: 2-*el,* "of two." The full forms of only a few are known, such as *teriyaš,* "three," and *meyawaš,* "four." Numerical expressions employing derivational suffixes are 2-*anki,* "twice" (*-anki*) and the ordinal 2-*anna* "second."

Verbs. Verbs show root and thematic stems. Two conjugations exist in the active voice, whose endings differ only in the singular (see table 2). The present plural is formed

TABLE 1. *Animate and Inanimate Nouns and Adjectives*

	Animate	Inanimate
sg. nom.	*-š*	zero or *-n*
sg. acc.	*-n*	zero or *-n*
pl. nom.	*-eš, -uš* (NH)	zero, *-i, -a*
pl. acc.	*-uš, -eš* (NH), *-aš* (NH)	zero, *-i, -a*

TABLE 2. *Verb Conjugations*

	-*mi* conjugation	-*ḫi* conjugation
Pres. 1	-*mi*	-*ḫi*
2	-*ši*	-*ti*
3	-*zi* (<*-*ti*)	-*i*
Pret. 1	-*un*, -*nun*	-*ḫun*
2	-*š*	-*š*
3	-*t*	-*š*

with -*weni*, -*teni*, -*anzi* (from *-*anti*); and the preterite plural is formed with -*wen*, -*ten*, -*er*. There is no difference in meaning between the -*mi* and -*ḫi* conjugations. Verbs can be in either the active or middle voice. A participle (ending in -*ant*-) serves intransitive verbs and as a passive of transitives. Verbal substantives end either in -*war* (gen. -*waš*), or -*atar* (gen. -*annaš*). Infinitives end either in -*wanzi* or -*anna*. Two tenses exist: a present-future and a preterite. The perfect is expressed analytically, by means of the neuter form of the participle with a form of the verbs *ḫar(k)*-, "to have," or *eš*-, "to be."

Negation and Questions. Four words are specialized for negating different modes: *natta*, "not," and *nawi*, "not yet," negate statements; *lē* negates commands; and *nūman* negates wishes or statements about others' wishes. Questions were undoubtedly marked in speech with an intonation pattern and stress. Many interrogative sentences contain question words: *kuiš*, "who?"; *kuwat*, "why?"; *kuwabi*, "where?"; and *maḫḫan*, "how?/when?."

Vocabulary. Hittite vocabulary consists of a core of inherited Indo-European words (*wadar*, "water"; *nebeš*, "sky"; *padaš*, "foot"; *genu*, "knee"; *ed*-, "to eat") enlarged by a significant number of words borrowed from neighboring cultures (*tuppi*, "tabletcharacter."; *šankunniš*, "priest"; *nitri*, "natron"). [*See* Indo-European Languages.]

Literary Genres. The archives of ancient Ḫattuša contained texts in a variety of literary genres: historiographic, administrative, legal, and literary. In addition, tablets on which scribes wrote their training exercises have been recovered.

Historiographic texts. Texts relating events either of the reign of a particular king (royal annals) or of a period of time (prologues to state treaties) or relating the (mis)behavior of a particular civil servant (anecdotal texts from the Old Kingdom) are known as historiographic. No claim is made that they follow the same standards of objectivity and accuracy that might be claimed for modern historiography.

Procedure handbooks. The largest single category of tablets represented in the archives which describe the course of religious ceremonies. More than two hundred compositions describe festivals in the cultic calendar. The archives contained, in addition, many tablets representing around twenty distinct hymns or prayers to be employed in the cult.

Outside the cult proper procedures were often prescribed to invoke deities through magical means. More than one hundred such texts describe private rituals performed to free a client (sometimes specifically the king or queen) from various problems, ranging from a physical illness, sexual impotence, or insomnia to being haunted by the ghost of a deceased relative. In many cases the underlying cause of the ailment is said to be "impurity," which can be removed by manipulating symbolic materials and reciting incantations. A small group of texts is called medical, but its procedures are less physical therapy than ritual manipulation.

A special category of procedural handbook is represented by hippological treatises. The best-known one is authored by a certain Kikkuli, who has a Hurrian background. The Kikkuli manual shows clear traces of having arisen in a society of chariot-drawn warrior-aristocrats with a linguistic and cultural background in the lands to the east of Mesopotamia. These texts describe a daily training regime that extends for more than a year and includes instructions for the feeding, exercise, and stabling of horses. The procedures seem to be aimed at producing horses capable of sustained exertion rather than short bursts of speed, and for chariot drawing rather than horseback riding.

Legal literature. Although the king was the supreme judge and administrator of the law, he was himself subject to its strictures and could, in rare cases, be removed for its violation. Law was defined by the collection of precedent cases known to scholars as the Hittite laws, the earliest manuscripts of which date from the Old Kingdom. Later copies from the New Kingdom show a modernization both of language and of the law itself. In addition to these late copies of the Old Hittite law collection, a New Hittite collection is also attested, whose changes in the law are more substantial. The individual cases are described, using the formulation that had become standard in Mesopotamia centuries earlier: "If a person does such-and-such, he shall pay such-and-such a fine." The penalty clauses are almost all payments of various kinds, with a very small number requiring bodily injury or death. The cases covered involve homicide, bodily injury, damage to or theft of property, prices for livestock, agricultural and artisan products, and obligations to the crown by persons holding land.

The laws deal with marriage, divorce, and sexual crimes; inheritance, contracts, loans, debts, and business are largely untouched. Laws concerned with royal succession were occasionally promulgated by royal edict rather than in the collection of laws. Such edicts include the so-called Political Testament of Ḫattušili I (c. 1650), regarding his choice of Muršili I as his successor; the Telipinu Proclamation (c. 1550), to stabilize royal succession after a period of regicide and anarchy; and the Apology of Ḫattušili III (c. 1250), intended to legitimize his seizure of the throne from his nephew Muršili III.

Unlike the cuneiform tablet archives at other major political centers in the Near East, the archives of ancient Ḫattuša contain no substantial collection of deeds, contracts, wills, and other legal records. There is, however, a small collection of records that could be either minutes of court proceedings or depositions of testimony taken elsewhere but intended to be presented in court. The texts contain testimony offered by various civil servants regarding charges of misconduct against a particular member of their group. The defendant himself also gives testimony. There is no mention of responses made by any judge hearing the case. These documents all date from the second half of the New Hittite period—the last two centuries of the Hittite capital's existence.

Archival or administrative texts. Texts intended to keep records for bureaucratic purposes include censuses, inventories of materials in the palace or temple storerooms, catalogs (or possibly shelf lists) of tablets in the palace library, and records of land grants. Also belonging to this general category are records of questions put to various kinds of oracles regarding formations on the liver of sacrificed animals, observation of the flight of birds, the behavior of sacrificial animals just prior to slaughter, or the movements of snakes observed in a controlled environment.

Scribal training. Some tablets were part of the curriculum for training scribes. The principal genre in this category is the Sumero-Akkadian lexical text. Texts devised in Mesopotamia for training Akkadian-speaking scribes in the use of Sumerian were further annotated in the Hittite capital by the addition of Hittite translations. In some cases there were only two columns: an Akkadian one and a Hittite translation. Most texts, however, included at least Sumerian, Akkadian, and Hittite, and some added a column indicating syllabically the pronunciation of the Sumerian word-signs. Seven of the principal lexical series known from Mesopotamia are well attested: Syllabary A, Diri, Erim-ḫuš, ḪAR-ra = ḫubullu, Izi, and Proto-LÚ. Scribes also practiced by copying Mesopotamian literary compositions, such as the great hymns to the sun god Shamash and the storm god Adad. In fact, Hittite translations of some of these hymns are known. Other Mesopotamian literary works, both copied in their Akkadian form and translated into Hittite, include the Gilgamesh and the Atraḫasis epics. A Canaanite mythological text translated into Hittite concerns the storm god Baal, the elderly god El, and his consort the goddess Asherah.

Native literature. Anatolian narrative literary works included myths about the deities of the old Hattian stratum, and others about the newer wave of Hurrian deities. Among the former are the stories about the battles of the storm god with a great serpent and the stories of retrieving runaway gods whose disappearance brought on famines, droughts, and infertility. Among the latter is the cycle of tales concerning the Hurrian gods Kumarbi and Teššub.

[*See also* Hittites.]

BIBLIOGRAPHY

Carruba, Onofrio, ed. *Per una grammatica ittita: Towards a Hittite Grammar*. Studia Mediterranea, 7. Pavia, 1992. Collection of good articles on the current status of Hittite grammatical studies.

Friedrich, Johannes. *Hethitisches Wörterbuch: Kurzgefasste kritische Sammlung der Deutungen hethitischer Wörter*. Heidelberg, 1952. Accurate and judicious. Although no longer complete, still the best Hittite glossary.

Friedrich, Johannes. *Hethitisches Elementarbuch*, vol. 1, *Kurzgefasste Grammatik*. 2d ed. Heidelberg, 1960. Although only an outline and somewhat dated, still the best grammar of Hittite; the first edition appeared in 1940.

Friedrich, Johannes, and Annelies Kammenhuber. *Hethitisches Wörterbuch*. 3 vols. Rev. ed. Heidelberg, 1975–1991. Revision and enlargement of Friedrich's 1952 volume, which diverges from the views of many Hittitologists, principally in matters of text dating.

Garrett, A. "Hittite Enclitic Subjects and Transitive Verbs." *Journal of Cuneiform Studies* 42 (1990): 227–242. Relates transitivity to ergativity in Hittite and observes the nonoccurrence of enclitic pronominal subjects in transitive clauses.

Güterbock, Hans G., and Harry A. Hoffner, Jr. *The Hittite Dictionary of the Oriental Institute of the University of Chicago*. Chicago, 1989. The first complete Hittite dictionary written in English, with numerous completely edited and translated illustrative examples. Volume L–N was finished in 1989; subsequent volumes will cover P–Z, then A–K.

Held, Warren H., et al. *Beginning Hittite*. Columbus, Ohio, 1987. This first elementary grammar of Hittite written in English is marred by careless philology. See the careful critical review by Gary Beckman in *Journal of the American Oriental Society* 111 (1991): 658–659.

Hoffner, Harry A., Jr. "An English-Hittite Glossary." *Revue Hittite et Asianique* 25 (1967): 7–99. Based upon Friedrich's 1952 volume and therefore incomplete, but no more recent English-Hittite index exists.

Hoffner, Harry A., Jr. "On the Use of Hittite *-za* in Nominal Sentences." *Journal of Near Eastern Studies* 28 (1969): 225–230. Discusses the use of the reflexive particle to mark first- and second-person subjects in New Hittite sentences with the verb *to be* expressed or understood.

Hoffner, Harry A., Jr. "Hittite *mān* and *nūman*." In *Investigationes philologicae et comparativae: Gedenkschrift für Heinz Kronasser*, edited by Erich Neu, pp. 38–45. Wiesbaden, 1982. Important consideration of the expression of wish, which makes an interesting distinction between "speaker wish" and "subject wish"; illustrated with examples. The ideas presented here are now developed in the *mān* and *nūman* articles of the *Hittite Dictionary of the Oriental Institute* (Güterbock and Hoffner above).

Kammenhuber, Annelies. "Hethitisch, Palaisch, Luwisch und Hieroglyphenluwisch." In *Altkleinasiatische Sprachen*, edited by Bertold Spuler, pp. 119–357. Leiden, 1969. Thorough coverage of the secondary literature and quite up to date for its day, although heavy on theory, light on data, and somewhat rigid. Now needs to be supplemented and qualified. Definitely not a pedagogical tool for the language.

Kimball, Sara E. "Hittite Plene Writing." Ph.D. diss., University of Pennsylvania, 1983.

Melchert, H. Craig. *Studies in Hittite Historical Phonology*. Ergänzungshefte zur Zeitschrift für Vergleichende Sprachforschung, no. 32. Göttingen, 1984. Perceptive and clear analysis of the development of the Hittite phonological system.

Melchert, H. Craig. "Hittite Vocalism." In *Per una grammatica ittita: Towards a Hittite Grammar,* edited by Onofrio Carruba, pp. 181–196. Studia Mediterranea, 7. Pavia, 1992.

Melchert, H. Craig. "Historical Phonology of Anatolian." *Journal of Indo-European Studies* 21 (1993): 237–257.

Oetinger, N. "Die hethitischen Verbalstämme." In *Per una grammatica ittita: Towards a Hittite Grammar,* edited by Onofrio Carruba, pp. 213–252. Studia Mediterranea, 7. Pavia, 1992.

Puhvel, Jaan. *Hittite Etymological Dictionary.* 3 vols. Berlin, 1984–1991.

HARRY A. HOFFNER, JR.

HITTITES. Long before the Hittites, about whom we know so much today from excavations in central Turkey, were known, every serious reader of the Bible knew the name. According to the *Book of Genesis* Hittites sold a field and a burial cave to Abraham (*Gn.* 24), the ancestor of the people of Israel. Abraham's grandson Esau displeased his parents by taking Hittite wives from the neighboring peoples of Canaan (*Gn.* 26:34). Hittites are mentioned with other ethnic groups inhabiting the land of Canaan on the eve of the invasion under Joshua (*Jos.* 1:4, 3:10). These people had been at home in southern Palestine for centuries before the time of the Israelite monarchy and show no traces of foreign origin. Their names are linguistically Canaanite. Their customs and way of life were no different from those of other semitic groups in Palestine at that time. If they originated in the north among the stock of the Late Bronze Age Anatolian Hittites, they have lost all trace of their origin. In fact, the genealogical "Table of Nations" in *Genesis* 10 includes their eponymous ancestor, Heth, among the sons of Canaan. All this suggests that the "Hittites" of the earlier parts of the Hebrew Bible were Canaanite aborigines, with no Anatolian roots.

On the other hand, the historical records of the Davidic and post-Davidic period in Israel clearly attest contacts with the "Hittite" kingdoms of northern Syria. The Hittites spoken of here are clearly foreigners. Their Syrian states represent the continuation of the Syrian vassal states of the great Hittite Empire of the Late Bronze Age.

In the final decades of the nineteenth century, large stone blocks inscribed in a previously unknown hieroglyphic script were found built into mosques in Syria. Scholars correctly suspected that these inscriptions were the work of the ancient Hittite kingdoms of Syria. As the search for more of these inscriptions widened into Anatolia, attention was drawn to the remarkable hieroglyphic inscriptions on living rock in the vicinity of the small village of Boğazköy, about 160 km (100 mi.) east of Ankara, in central Turkey.

Boğazköy. Excavations were begun on the large mound in 1906, under the joint directorship of Hugo Winckler and Theodore Makridi. What was found forever changed our concept of the Hittites [*see* Boğazköy]. More than ten thousand clay tablets were concentrated in two places on the large city mound: the first area was the palace administration complex on the acropolis; the second was the large temple library in the Lower City. Excavators found that several of the rooms in which the tablets from the acropolis were found had been libraries. Wooden shelving around the walls allowed the tablets to be systematically arranged. Small clay shelf labels identified the locations of important tablet collections. Several tablets contained what we would today call shelf lists, or catalogs, of the collection.

Most of the tablets were in fragments, having fallen from their shelves in the conflagration that destroyed the city in about 1180 BCE. Some were so badly overheated through direct, sustained contact with burning roof beams, that the clay blistered and became badly disfigured. But many tablets whose fragments were fairly large could be reconstituted by the epigraphers.

The city itself, as revealed by the archaeologists, was large by the standards of its day. The acropolis, on which the king's residential quarters and the palace administration were located, was entered by a gateway at its southwestern corner. At that point, it was connected by a large bridge or viaduct to the Upper City, to the south. This large area accommodated more than thirty temples and temple precincts for the "Thousand Gods" of the Hittite pantheon. Some of the city's most impressive reliefs were found in this area: depictions of the kingdom's major deities and several of its last kings.

Three impressive gateways punctuate the city's southern wall. The easternmost gateway is called the King's Gate because on its inner side stood a large relief depicting a heroic male figure, originally assumed to be a king, but possibly a god. A great festival procession exited the city through this gate and wound its way south and west to the Sphinx Gate at the central point in the southern wall. Farther west is the Lion Gate, so named from the relief of a large lion on the outside, easily observed by processions reentering the city at this point. The centrally located Sphinx Gate is equidistant from the Lion Gate and King's Gate.

To the northwest of the Upper City and directly west of the Acropolis area lies the Lower City. Its most conspicuous monument is the largest temple of ancient Ḫattuša. This temple has a twin cella, indicating that the primary deities worshipped here were the storm god of Hatti and the sun goddess of Arinna. The temple proper was built around a central courtyard. This complex in turn was surrounded, like the smaller temples in the Upper City, by a temenos wall. Southward, across a street from the main temple complex, a large building housed workshops for the temple personnel: priests, musicians, weavers, potters, smiths, carpenters, stonecutters, and others serving the needs of the temple. Huge pottery storage vessels containing grain and other commodities stood in the western rooms of the temple.

A road leading from the city gate in the extreme northwestern corner of the city wound to the northeast for 1.5 km, where it reached the impressive sanctuary of Yazılıkaya, which means "inscribed rock" in Turkish. Here the Hittites had constructed temple buildings to guard access to a pair of natural rock galleries. Carved into the faces of these galleries in low relief are the figures of most of the gods and goddesses. The main chamber shows two processions of deities converging from the left and the right on a central point, where the chief male and female deities face each other. The left-hand procession shows male deities, the right-hand one, female. Across from the central panel on which the processions met stands a rock on which is carved the figure of King Tudḫaliya IV, under whom this sanctuary was finished. The second, smaller chamber contains reliefs depicting this same king in the protective embrace of his patron deity, the god Sharruma, and other reliefs that suggest this second chamber was mortuary in character.

History. The earliest sure evidence for the presence in Anatolia of the Indo-European groups associated with the Hittites is the occurrence of Hittite or Luwian names in the commercial documents from the Old Assyrian Colony Period (c. 1850–1700). It has been surmised that these groups entered Anatolia in about 2300, and that after approximately five hundred years of settled life there, at least three large groups were speaking three distinct languages developed from a common Proto-Anatolian branch of the earlier Proto-Indo-European language family. These distinct languages are today known as Hittite (or Nešite), Luwian, and Palaic. Other ethno-linguistic groups had been in central Anatolia before the arrival of the Indo-Europeans. The best known of these are the Hattians, whose language we call Hattic.

During the Old Assyrian Colony period, there were Hittite groups. The king of one of these, whose name is Anitta, left behind a royal inscription, an Old Hittite copy of which was found at Ḫattuša. The inscription commemorates the stages of his military expansion from control of a small area around the city of Kaneš to control of most of central Anatolia, stretching from Ḫattuša, in the north, to Purušanda, in the south.

Hittite history begins in the Old Kingdom period (c. 1680–1420), with the establishment of a Hittite-speaking group on the site of the city of Ḫattuša. The dynasty founder bears the name *Labarna,* which later becomes a Caesarlike title for Hittite kings. His immediate successor, Ḫattušili I, was the first Hittite king to expand militarily into northern Syria, into an area that included Aleppo and Alalakh.

Ḫattušili's successor, Muršili I, led a spectacular, but short-lived, raid far to the east, where his army sacked the city of Babylon in about 1590 and brought to an end the city's first dynasty. After Muršili's death, a period of internal strife, regicides, and usurpations weakened the state. The area of its effective military control shrank drastically.

Around 1420 a new line of kings, bearing traditional Hittite throne names, but also identified on their seals by Hurrian names, came to power in Ḫattuša. The first of this line bore the name Tudḫaliya. Because a list of Hittite kings identifies a Tudḫaliya in the Old Kingdom, we traditionally call this new king Tudḫaliya II. The new line of kings with a Hurrian background cultivated political connections to the southeast, in Syria.

The fortunes of the new line rose dramatically around 1345, under the rule of a new king, Šuppiluliuma I, who led his armies into Syria and reduced the previously highly successful dynasty of Mitannian kings to the status of vassal kings. Šuppiluliuma I was a contemporary of the Egyptian pharaohs of the Amarna period. In fact, he just missed an opportunity to establish one of his sons on the throne of Egypt. But if Šuppiluliuma failed to gain a foothold in Egypt itself, he did not fail to secure Syria as a Hittite province. Kings of Aleppo, Carchemish, Ugarit, Nuḫašše, and Amurru entered into treaties with the Hittite Empire, making Šuppiluliuma's successors "great kings"—big players in the game of international politics of the ancient Near East. The Kingdom of Ḫatti became a super power. Armed competition, if not open conflict, with Egypt continued from Šuppiluliuma I to Ḫattušili III, when a treaty with Egypt formally ended the period of struggle and conflict. Ḫattušili III visited Egypt, where his daughter was married to the pharaoh Rameses II.

The final century after Ḫattušili III saw the flowering of the capital city with the building of the Upper City area, which shows Egyptian architectural influence so strikingly in the Sphinx Gate. Militarily, a new force was building in the east, Assyria. Ḫattušili's successor, Tudḫaliya IV, the finisher of Yazılıkaya and the Upper City, was much occupied militarily with staving off Assyrian advances. At one point, the central government was so weak that a prince named Kurunta from a parallel line, who was king of the small state of Tarḫuntašša, was able to dethrone Tudḫaliya IV and to leave his own royal seal on documents found in the Upper City. During the reigns of Tudḫaliya IV and his two successors, the Hittites extended their control to a part of the island of Cyprus. Local Cypriot representatives contracted by treaty to render vassal's tribute to the Hittite king.

During the Last Days of Ḫattuša (c. 1205–1180), a complex alignment of enemies, which may have included groups of "Sea Peoples" from the Aegean, finally reduced the capital city to flames. Not all urban centers of the Hittite Empire fell when the capital city Ḫattuša did. Carchemish in the east and Tarḫuntašša in the south survived to carry the tradition of descent from the line of kings from Ḫattuša into the first millennium.

Hittite Royalty. Like other nation states of the ancient Near East, the Hittites were ruled by kings. A once-popular theory, according to which the Old Kingdom kings were chosen by members of a primitive senate, has been abandoned. Hittite kingship from the first was hereditary and dynastic. Royal succession passed from father to son, although the reigning king could designate any son he wished. He was not bound by law to choose the oldest.

The Hittite king controlled all areas of life. As the chief priest, he presided at the principal religious festivals and made offerings to the gods on behalf of his people. As the chief judge and lawgiver, he was responsible for the collection and distribution of the laws in the official corpus and served as the judge in the highest court in the land. Cases of particular gravity or difficulty were referred to this court. In addition, the king was head of the armed forces and as such usually accompanied the troops into the field. Only an aged king would be exempt from traveling on a military campaign. The king conducted all foreign policy, writing letters to the kings and high officials of foreign lands, contracting alliances, arranging marriages that tied his own royal line with the ruling families of other states, and occasionally even visiting other courts in person.

The king's dress conformed to the occasion. He is shown on rock reliefs in two forms of attire. In both he wears earrings and shoes with toes that turn up in a point. His priestly garb consisted of a long robe with sleeves, open in front, a skull cap, and a crook with its curved end pointing downward and to the rear. His military attire was a short, belted tunic, with a short sword or dagger hanging from the belt. He carried a bow over his shoulder and a spear in his hand. His headgear was conical, perhaps a kind of helmet.

The king's person was sacred. It was important to guard him from sources of impurity that might damage his sacred powers. Contact with the general public was therefore restricted. His food and clothing were prepared under strict conditions of purity control. If the king was ever threatened by an evil omen, a procedure known from Assyria was followed: a man was chosen as a royal stand-in until the death predicted by the omen occurred, at which time the true king returned to his post. All that we know about the Hittite ritual of enthronement, such as the anointing of the king with oil, we learned from the Hittite texts describing this substitute king procedure.

Hittite queens were more than sexual partners to their royal husbands. They had real powers of their own. Queens had their own personal royal seals and shared a royal seal with their husbands. Queens seem to have had the right to conduct official correspondence with foreign courts. When the king died, his primary wife remained queen as long as she lived, serving as her son's consort, although she did not become his sexual partner. If her son was young and inexperienced, she often assumed some duties normally reserved for the king, such as making legal decisions or issuing decrees. Queens in the Empire period seem to have had control over many aspects of the religious cult and over vast amounts of resources and temple property. As a result, queens who fell from favor were occasionally accused of misappropriation of temple funds.

Hittite laws distinguish two social classes: free and slave. Slaves were not without independent means, for the laws indicate that a slave could pay a free husband to marry his daughter. However, in addition to these two classes there were foreigners taken captive in battle and used to work crown lands. According to the law code, their rights differed from those of freemen or slaves: they could not sell their fields or their children. While texts mention kings emancipating slaves of the crown, we have no knowledge of the practice at the level of the common citizen. Because census lists of small estates do not indicate the presence of slaves, it is possible that only the very rich owned them.

Economy. The Hittite heartland was the central high plateau of Turkey, where broad valleys and rivers encouraged agriculture. Rainfall is seasonal but ample. Winters are hard with heavy snowfall, and summers are hot and very dry. The rains come in the spring, which is a short but lush season.

According to the Hittite texts, the principal domestic animals were oxen, sheep, goats, horses, mules, asses, pigs, and dogs. Of these, the first three were also used as sacrificial animals. Plowing was done with oxen, never with horses. Horses were used to draw chariots. Mules were used for carrying loads over long distances and were the most expensive of the equids, both because of their sure-footedness and the fact that they do not reproduce. Sheep were exploited for their wool, milk, and meat. The milk of the sheep and goat were also made into cheese. Some wild animals were hunted, principally deer and boars.

The many bird names in the texts attest the richness of the variety of the aviary, although most named birds are unidentified as to type. They include predatory birds, such as the eagle and the buzzard, and water birds, such as ducks. Although there is a generic term for fish, no species names are used.

Specific tree and bush names exist, both coniferous and deciduous. The dense forests of central Anatolia in Hittite times were harvested for timber, which was used for construction and fuel. Aromatic trees were highly prized for the sweet fragrance of their leaves and wood shavings.

Several grain types are known both from textual and archaeological evidence: *Triticum aestivum* (common bread wheat), emmer wheat, and several types of barley. It is not clear if the Hittites knew oats, although the use of a particular type of grain in the feeding of horses suggests that they did. The grains were used to make a large number of different types of named breads, cakes, and pulpy dishes like porridge.

A wide variety of fruits is attested, among them apples, pears, plums, and figs. The grapevine was cultivated for its fruit, which was dried into raisins, and for wine. Nuts are also mentioned, although the type has not been determined. Vegetables are also known from the texts. The appearance of one particularly popular bulbous plant of the onion family was celebrated with an annual religious festival.

Among the crafts and tradesmen were potters, leather workers, weavers, blacksmiths, bakers, beekeepers, carpenters, and physicians. Some crafts would only have been of interest to the wealthy: sculptors, gold- and silversmiths, glassmakers, divination specialists, and scribes. Physicians were not highly skilled; they used folk remedies and charms. Hittite royalty who were seriously ill secured highly trained physicians from Egypt and Mesopotamia.

The widespread notion that Hittite military supremacy was the result of a monopoly of iron production for weaponry is a myth. Although the Hittites could produce limited quantities of iron, but it was not used for weapons.

People who sold or traded their own products in small local markets are not referred to in texts. The "merchants" that are mentioned were grand entrepreneurs operating under royal patronage and engaging in international trade. For this reason, the penalty for killing a merchant was much higher than that for killing an ordinary free man.

Law. The Hittites already possessed a written collection of two hundred laws in the Old Kingdom. Their laws resembled, in form and phraseology, the better-known collections of Mesopotamia and of the Hebrew Bible. All relevant topics of ancient law are covered: homicide, theft, assault and battery, marriage, sexual conduct, land tenure, and taxation. Like some Mesopotamian law collections, a tariff of ideal prices is included.

Hittite treaties with foreign countries show the outlines of what may be called the international law of the era. Treaties with states of equal power and prestige express obligations as reciprocal and those with inferior states as unequal. Concerns of the former are mutual guarantees of dynastic stability against overthrow by insiders or outsiders, mutual defense against foreign attacks, mutual extradition of fugitives, and the stabilization of international boundaries. Concerns of the latter include these as well as the vassal's obligations to pay annual tribute.

Religion. Hittite religion reflects the diversity of ethnic groups comprising the population. Hattians, Hurrians, Luwians, and Hittites—as well as smaller numbers of immigrant Syrians, Palestinians, or Assyrians—worshiped their own deities according to their traditional rites. The totality of the pantheon was called the Thousand Gods. Indeed, the number of attested divine names in the texts approximates one thousand. All but the smallest towns had many temples. Each town had local traditions about the cultic calendar that Hittite regional governors were instructed to honor and preserve.

The official archives in the capital, which are our almost exclusive source of information, are understandably limited in their concerns. Local cults and the domestic cult are almost totally ignored. The official state cult included seasonal festivals, celebrated in the spring and fall, and a monthly festival. The king, queen, or a royal prince represented the royal family at such festivals. There were two types of male priest and one female type. In addition, the religious texts reveal that musicians playing various stringed and percussion instruments accompanied cultic liturgy.

HITTITES. *Stone relief from Yazılıkaya depicting the sword god.* (Courtesy J. S. Jorgensen)

The center of the cult was the serving of the statue of the deity. The image was given food and drink, a change of clothing, and entertainment in the form of music, acrobatics (including sword swallowing), and athletic contests. Prayers were offered for the removal of drought or plague, for the defeat of enemy armies, and for the welfare of the community and its king.

Divination was energetically pursued both at home and on trips. Omens were sought to determine the likely success of all sorts of ventures, from marriages to business to military campaigns. Oracles were questioned to determine the causes for divine anger manifested by catastrophes such as disease, drought, or military defeat. The most popular form of divination was the inspection of the internal organs of a sacrificed sheep, but several other kinds were practiced, including bird omens.

Language and Literature. The Hittite language shows its Indo-European character primarily by its grammatical structure, but also by a minimal stock of primary vocabulary (*padas,* "foot"; *watar,* "water"; *ed-* "to eat"). It represents the earliest attested form of an Indo-European language.

Hittite texts include historical narratives (military annals), legal texts (law code, treaties, land grants, edicts), letters, myths and epics, hymns and prayers to deities, descriptions of religious festivals, prescriptions for the performance of magical rituals, and records of divination.

[*See also* Anatolia, *article on* Ancient Anatolia; Hittite; *and* Luwians.]

BIBLIOGRAPHY

Bittel, Kurt. *Hattusha: The Capital of the Hittites.* New York, 1970. English-language survey, less current than Peter Neve's book, by the director of excavations at Ḫattuša.

Gurney, O. R. *Some Aspects of Hittite Religion.* Schweich Lectures, 1976. Oxford, 1977. Thorough coverage of Hittite religion.

Gurney, O. R. *The Hittites.* Rev. ed. London, 1990. The best general English-language introduction.

Güterbock, Hans G. "Some Aspects of Hittite Festivals." In *Compte rendu de la rencontre Assyriologique internationale,* vol. 17, pp. 175–180. Brussels, 1969.

Güterbock, Hans G. "The Hittite Palace." In *Le palais et la royauté: Archéologie et civilisation; compte rendu de la 19e rencontre Assyriologique internationale,* edited by Paul Garelli, pp. 305–314. Paris, 1974.

Güterbock, Hans G. "The Hittite Temple according to Written Sources." In *Le temple et le cult: Compte rendu de la 20e rencontre Assyriologique internationale,* edited by E. J. van Donzel, pp. 125–132. Leiden, 1975.

Hoffner, Harry A., Jr. "Some Contributions of Hittitology to Old Testament Study." *Tyndale Bulletin* 20 (1969): 27–55.

Hoffner, Harry A., Jr. *Alimenta Hethaeorum.* American Oriental Series, vol. 55. New Haven, 1974. Complete study of Hittite flora, fauna, and food production.

Hoffner, Harry A., Jr. "Histories and Historians of the Ancient Near East: The Hittites." *Orientalia* 49 (1980): 283–332.

Hoffner, Harry A., Jr. "Ancient Views of Prophecy and Fulfillment: Mesopotamia and Asia Minor." *Journal of the Evangelical Theological Society* 30 (1987): 257–265. Short summary of Hittite divination procedures.

Hoffner, Harry A., Jr. "Hittite Religion." In *Religions of Antiquity,* edited by Robert M. Seltzer, pp. 69–79. New York, 1989. Current and accurate general picture.

Hoffner, Harry A., Jr., trans. *Hittite Myths.* Writings from the Ancient World, no. 2. Atlanta, 1990. Collection in English translation.

Hoffner, Harry A., Jr. "The Last Days of Khattusha." In *The Crisis Years: The Twelfth Century B.C., from beyond the Danube to the Tigris,* edited by William A. Ward and Martha Sharp Joukowsky, pp. 46–52. Dubuque, 1992. Contribution to a symposium held at Brown University, May 1990, providing current data on the final phase of Hittite history.

Hoffner, Harry A., Jr. "Ancient Anatolia: Legal and Social Institutions." In *Civilizations of the Ancient Near East,* edited by Jack M. Sasson et al. New York, 1993. Current and comprehensive discussion of Hittite law.

Klengel, Horst. "The Economy of the Hittite Household (É)." *Oikoumene* 5 (1986): 23–31.

Macqueen, James G. *The Hittites and Their Contemporaries in Asia Minor.* Boulder, 1986. Particularly useful for its large number of excellent illustrations.

Neve, Peter. *Hattuša: Stadt der Götter und Tempel; Neue Ausgrabungen in der Hauptstadt der Hethiter.* Mainz am Rhein, 1993. Up-to-date summary of the archaeology of the Hittite capital.

Harry A. Hoffner, Jr.

HOGARTH, DAVID GEORGE (1862–1927), eminent British archaeologist of the Aegean and the ancient Near East. Hogarth's greatest contributions were made in investigations of Anatolia and ancient Hittite civilization and in illuminating relationships between Anatolia and its neighbors. His early career in Greece and the Greek islands included excavations in Cyprus, Melos, and Crete. Hogarth also worked briefly at Asyut in Egypt for the British Museum before turning to Anatolia, the region that was to hold his interest throughout his life. Hogarth proposed that Anatolia was the source of inspiration for early Greek art and religion. As an archaeologist, he is best known as the excavator of the Artemision at Ephesus and as the first excavator of the ancient city at Carchemish.

Hogarth belonged to a generation for which Arabic-language skills qualified a small number of scholars to serve Britain as diplomatic and military intelligence officers. During World War I, he headed the Arab Bureau in Cairo, where he found T. E. Lawrence (the so-called Lawrence of Arabia), his former Oxford protégé, a position in intelligence. Hogarth had also brought Lawrence to Carchemish. [*See the biography of Lawrence.*] After the war, Hogarth returned to Oxford to direct the Ashmolean Museum and to hold numerous public positions. His scholarly interests refocused on Anatolia, and in 1920 he published a seminal work on Hittite seals.

Hogarth published over thirty books and numerous articles. He wrote on Anatolia and the Hittites for the first edition of the *Cambridge Ancient History.* He also wrote travel books, which are captivating and are considered among the best of their genre.

[*See also* Carchemish; *and* Ephesus.]

BIBLIOGRAPHY

Hogarth, David G., ed. *Authority and Archaeology, Sacred and Profane: Essays on the Relation of Monuments to Biblical and Classical Literature.* New York and London, 1899. Includes an introductory essay by Hogarth on the enterprise of archaeology.

Hogarth, David G. *Excavations at Ephesus: The Archaic Artemesia.* London, 1908.

Hogarth, David G. *Carchemish: Report on the Excavations at Djerabis,* vol. 1, *Introductory.* London, 1914.

Hogarth, David G. *Hittite Seals.* Oxford, 1920.

Hogarth, David G. *The Wandering Scholar.* London and New York, 1925. Combines two earlier travel books. Hogarth's vivid and lively descriptions of life on the road and in the field are important resources for the history of Near Eastern archaeology.

Hogarth, David G. *Kings of the Hittites.* Oxford, 1926.

Kaplan, Robert D. *The Arabists: The Romance of an American Elite.* New York, 1993. Traces the history of American and British diplomacy in the Near East, including the roles played by scholars serving as military officers.

Sayce, A. H. "David George Hogarth, 1862–1927." *Proceedings of the British Academy* 13 (1928): 379–383. A colleague's brief tribute to the life and work of Hogarth.

KATHRYN E. SLANSKI

HOMS, site located in central Syria, on the road between Damascus, 162 km (100 mi.) to the south, and Hama, 47 km (29 mi.) to the north (34°42′ N, 36°48′ E). It is situated between two of the oldest archaeological sites in the area: Qadesh (Tell Nebi Mend), about 15 km (9 mi.) to the southwest, and Qatna (Mishrifeh), about 18 km (11 mi.) to the northeast. The plain around Homs is quite flat and fertile and is partially irrigated by water from the al-ʿAsi (Orontes) River, which flows from the south to the northwest of Homs.

The identification of Homs with Emesa does not require discussion as the name did not disappear. The historian Pliny the Elder was the first to mention Emesa. Other Roman historians spelled the name *Emessa*. The Arabic scholar Mahmud Al-Dimashqi (d. AH 259) wrote (*Tabaqat Ahil Homs* ["The Categories of the Inhabitants of Homs"], p. 202) that the old name of Homs was *Souriya*. The Crusaders did not settle in the city, but they named it La Chamelle.

There is insufficient evidence that the city existed before the Roman period. Scholars believe that it was erected by Seleucus Nicator, who gave it the Greek name *Emesa*. During the Seleucid period Arabic tribes were settled in the area all along the Orontes, from Homs to Hama. [*See* Hama.] In 96 BCE an Arab dynasty known as Samsigram rose against the Seleucids and established an independent small kingdom in the city of Homs. The names of ten kings of this dynasty are known who reigned from 96 BCE to 79 CE. When the dynasty disappeared, in 79 CE, Homs was annexed to the Provincia Arabia. The city flourished again, but the turning point in its history occurred with the visit of the Roman general Septimius Severus (193–211), who married Julia Domena, the daughter of the priest of the Temple of the Sun God. After his inauguration in Rome as emperor, Septimius was very friendly to Syria. Caracalla and Elagabalus reigned after him as Syrian emperors when Homs was the capital of Syrian Phoenicia. [*See* Phoenicia.]

The city again flourished in the Byzantine period, when the archbishop converted its Roman temples into churches. In the Islamic period, Homs was a capital of the Agnad province, along with Palestine, Jordan, and Damascus. In the Hamadanite period (944–1019) Homs became the center of the state of Wilayah (Tell el-Wilayah), a position it subsequently retained. The city became the center of a province in modern Syria. During the wars between the Arabs and the Byzantines and between the Umayyads and ʿAbbasids, as well as between the small Arab kingdoms in Syria and Egypt in the ninth–fifteenth centuries, the city suffered the destruction of many historical monuments.

Seleucid Period. There is no archaeological evidence for the Hellenistic period. Several scholars believe that its plan was similar to the contemporary cities of Damascus, Antioch, and Laodicea. Its two main streets, the *decumanus* and *cardo,* may have crossed where the modern city hall is located.

Roman Period. Nothing is preserved of the monuments of the Roman period or the epoch of the Samsigram dynasty. A Greek inscription indicates that King Samsigram erected a mausoleum to the west of the city in 78 BCE. This single monument of the Roman period was destroyed in 1911. A cemetery discovered by peasants in 1936 belongs to this period. It was situated near the mausoleum in Djurt Abu Sabun. The objects the peasants found are now in the National Museum of Damascus. The most important pieces were two helmets. One of them consists of the helmet itself and a mask: the helmet is hollow cast iron with silver decoration; the mask, which represents a human face, is also made of iron and is covered with a layer of silver. The other mask is made of gold. Both date to the first century CE.

According to many written sources there was a Sun Temple at Homs within which a black stone stood that was taken to Rome in 217, during the reign of Emperor Elagabalus. The temple was situated at the site of the present Nuri mosque. It is believed that the city was enclosed by a fortification wall in this period.

Byzantine Period. When Christianity replaced polytheism, a number of churches were built in Homs, such as the Church of St. Helena (326) and the great church in which the head of John was buried. This church was the largest in Syria during the Byzantine period. In addition to these churches there was the Monastery of Mar Maron (451) and the Monastery of Mar Tommy. [*See* Churches; Monasteries.] These monuments were destroyed either by earthquake or enemy attack. Many of them were rebuilt, such as the Orthodox Church of Mar Lian in Bab Dreb and the Syrian Church of al-Arabiʿan (the forty). All of these churches were in the *hay* ("quarter") of Jamal ed-Din.

In 1923, 1940, and 1957, several below-ground Byzantine tombs were discovered by chance—no superstructure marked the site. One of the tombs is a huge cave with a number of small chambers for burials. Its inner walls were plastered and partially decorated with figural and geometric designs; the roof was supported in places by a series of arches and pillars. Among the many objects found were glass, jewelry, and bronze bracelets and earrings.

Islamic Period. Between 636 and 1919 (the Umayyad, ʿAbbasid, Ayyubid, Mamluk, and Ottoman periods) Homs suffered numerous changes of rulers and continuing depredatations. No monuments from the Umayyad and the ʿAbbasid periods are preserved: the existing historical monuments in Homs were restored and indeed rebuilt under several Ayyubid, Mamluk, and Ottoman monarchs. Many old mosques in Homs have been renovated several times.

The most famous is the Khaled ibn al-Walid mosque, which was built at the beginning of twentieth century on the site of a Mamluk mosque with the same name.

The fortification wall and towers were pulled down during the Ottoman period (their remains are visible in the eastern and northern parts of the city). They belonged to the Ayyubid period and were constructed of basalt stones. The city had seven gates, but the remains of only two are preserved: Bab al-Masdud in the west and Bab Tadmur in the northeast. In order to strengthen Homs's defenses, the Ayyubid sultans built a citadel opposite the southwest corner of the city wall on a high (32 m) mound. This citadel resembles many others in Syria, such as the citadels at Aleppo, Hama, and Shazar, which belong to the twelfth–thirteenth centuries.

BIBLIOGRAPHY

Abdul-Hak, Sélim. "The Archaeology of the City Homs" (in Arabic). *Annales Archéologiques Arabes Syriennes* 10 (1960): 5–36.

As'ad, Pater 'Aesa. *The History of Homs* (Part I). New ed. Damascus, 1983.

As'ad, Muner 'Aesa. *The History of Homs* (Part II). Damascus, 1984.

Bounni, Adnan. "Les catacombes d'Émèse (Homs) en Syrie." *Archeologia* 37 (1970): 42–49.

Dussaud, René. *Topographie historique de la Syrie antique et médiévale.* Paris, 1927. See pages 103–115.

Elisséeff, Nikita. "Ḥimṣ." In *Encyclopaedia of Islam,* new ed., vol. 3, pp. 397–402. Leiden, 1960–.

Seyrig, Henri. *Antiquités syriennes.* 6 vols. Paris, 1934–. See volume 6, page 53.

Seyrig, Henri. "Antiquités de la nécropole d'Émèse." *Syria* 29 (1952): 204–250; 30 (1953): 12–24.

ALI ABOU ASSAF

HORSES. *See* Equids.

HORSFIELD, GEORGE (1882–?), British excavator of Petra and the first chief British officer of the Department of Antiquities of Transjordan (1928). Born in the north of England, Horsfield trained as an architect, working first in New York City and then, following World War I, with the British Army in India. In the early 1920s he was one of John Garstang's students at the British School of Archaeology in Jerusalem. In 1924 Garstang gave Horsfield responsibility for the Antiquities of Mandate Transjordan. Much of the work he performed in this role was directed to clearing and restoring the antiquities of Jerash. He began repair and conservation work on the South and North Theaters, Nymphaeum, and the propylaeum of the Temple of Artemis and cleared one of the vaults under the temple's temenos to house the inscriptions he was finding. By 1930 Horsfield's pioneering enterprise was being supplemented by American and British excavations at Jerash. Few published reports of Horsfield's work are available, but his notes survive at the Department of Antiquities in Jordan.

Horsfield's notebooks, later elaborated by G. Lankester Harding, form the basis of the sites and monuments archive of the Department of Antiquities of Jordan. Horsfield recorded entries for most of the major sites in Transjordan and their condition and the periods represented; his text is accompanied by clear photographs.

In 1929 Horsfield undertook the first archaeological excavations at Petra, which he later published in some detail. It was there that he met and worked with Agnes Conway, whom he married in 1932 and who gave her name to that site's Conway Tower. Their publications, which are well illustrated, offer details regarding provenance; those works also include photographs of painted houses that no longer exist and provide a comprehensive account of the topography of Petra and of the finds from their excavations on the city walls and at the high place (Jabal Madbah). They also cleared the Palace Tomb, al-Khazneh, the Urn Tomb, and the Tomb of the Roman Soldier.

Horsfield's work is significant as the first concentrated investigation of two of the major sites in Jordan, Jerash, and Petra. He left careful records, still in use, not only of those sites but also of others he explored.

[*See also* British School of Archaeology in Jerusalem; Jerash; Petra; *and the biographies of Garstang and Harding.*]

BIBLIOGRAPHY

Horsfield, George, and Agnes C. Horsfield. "Sela-Petra, the Rock, of Edom and Nabatene: I. The Topography of Petra. II. Houses." *Quarterly of the Department of Antiquities of Palestine* 7 (1938): 1–42.

Horsfield, George, and Agnes C. Horsfield. "Sela-Petra, the Rock, of Edom and Nabatene: III. Excavations." *Quarterly of the Department of Antiquities of Palestine* 8 (1938): 87–115.

Horsfield, George, and Agnes C. Horsfield. "Sela-Petra, the Rock, of Edom and Nabatene: IV. The Finds." *Quarterly of the Department of Antiquities of Palestine* 9 (1942): 105–204.

Kraeling, Carl H., ed. *Gerasa, City of the Decapolis.* New Haven, 1938.

ALISON MCQUITTY

HOUSE. [*To provide a general typology and morphology of houses, this entry comprises three articles:*

Mesopotamian Houses
Syro-Palestinian Houses
Egyptian Houses

Each article surveys the historical development, forms, and functions of houses in the region specified.]

Mesopotamian Houses

Plans of domestic architecture are sensitive indicators of social organization and household composition because houses form the framework within which people live out their social lives. It is houses that provide the spaces needed for privacy and task differentiation. However, intervening millennia interfere with the ability to read Mesopotamian social structure from architectural remains. Two approaches can be used to bridge this gap. First, where cuneiform documents that pertain to household composition are found within domestic architecture, they can be used to infer the relationship between houses and households. Where such textual sources are absent, ethnographic and ethnoarchaeological studies of modern Near Eastern settlements can sometimes be used as models; however, because most such studies are village studies, they are probably more relevant to the study of the small sites characteristic of the Neolithic period than of the large urban sites that are almost all that has been excavated for the later periods. [*See* Ethnoarchaeology.]

The earliest Mesopotamian houses date to the eighth millennium, and there is a long, complex development of domestic architecture from that time until the rise of the first cities in the fourth millennium. With the establishment of urban centers in Mesopotamia, house forms seem to have stabilized around a limited number of different types, all adhering to the same principle. This does not mean, however, that more variety might not have existed in the nonnucleated village sites, virtually none of which have been excavated.

Neolithic Houses. The earliest Mesopotamian houses are found only in northern Mesopotamia (see Aurenche, 1981). Two sites, Qermez Dere and Nemrik, date to the eighth millennium, when the inhabitants seem to have practiced intensive hunting and plant-food collection but not agriculture; the architecture at the two sites seems quite similar: the houses were round, single-room, subterranean or semisubterranean structures, 4–6 m in diameter, with a bowl-shaped floor thickly coated with plaster, as were the walls, and with access only through the roof. The Qermez Dere houses are characterized by two–four nonfunctional pillars (see figure 1), but the Nemrik houses used four posts to support the roof. In general, the houses at Nemrik and Qermez Dere are reminiscent of the Pre-Pottery Neolithic (PPN) A houses from the Levant (e.g., Jericho), and the material culture and special treatment of skulls at burial also suggest such associations.

Two other sites, dated nearly as early, present a somewhat different picture: Jarmo, located in the western Zagros Mountains and traditionally dated to 6750 BCE, and the more or less contemporary Tell Maghzaliyeh, located very close to Qermez Dere; both demonstrate evidence for a mixed agricultural and hunter-gatherer economy. [*See* Jarmo.] In spite of the closeness in date and location between Qermez Dere and Maghzaliyeh, both their material culture and architecture are quite different.

The architecture at Jarmo and Maghzaliyeh is characterized by multiroomed houses built at ground level, sometimes using quite substantial stone foundations. As such, they depart distinctly from Qermez Dere and Nemrik and seem to represent a break with the more Levantine traditions those

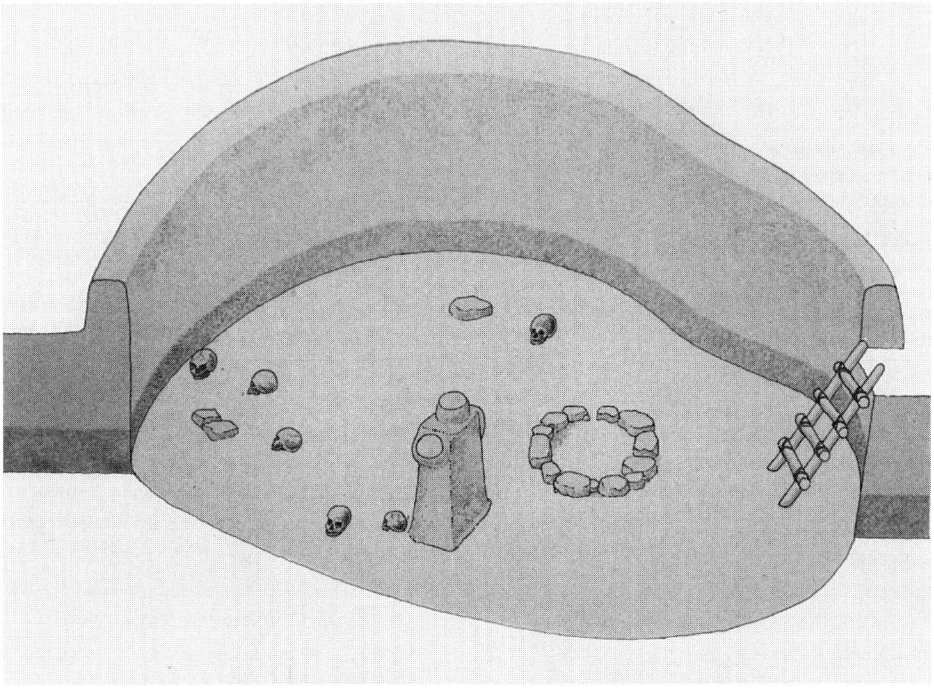

HOUSE: Mesopotamian Houses. Figure 1. *Reconstructed drawing of house interior at Qermez Dere.* (Courtesy Andromeda Oxford, Ltd.)

sites represent, perhaps presaging the development of truly Mesopotamian domestic architecture. At Jarmo, where the house remains are more plentiful, a typical house had an entrance into a main living/sleeping room that in turn led into both a passageway to a rear courtyard and to more living quarters and some small storage areas. Grinding equipment was found in the rear courtyard, where an oven was often built into one of the walls. The probable roofed area of the Jarmo houses was within the upper size limit of the Nemrik and Qermez Dere examples, except that at Jarmo the space was divided into four or more different spaces. Some of the Maghzaliyeh houses may have been larger, with one reported to be 85 sq m in area.

By and large, the somewhat later Hassunan houses are similar to those from Jarmo and Maghzaliyeh in their multiroomed rectilinear construction and lime plastered floors and walls. [*See* Hassuna.] The major difference is that the stone foundations are replaced by large potsherds or matting. Built-in features are typical of these houses: sunken storage vessels, hearths, large ovens, and benches.

Major changes in architecture are seen in the Samarran and Halaf periods that followed: the Halaf is found toward the north and northwest of Mesopotamia and the Samarran farther south. [*See* Ḥalaf, Tell; Samarra, *article on* Chalcolithic Period.] Halaf architecture is typified by the so-called tholos, a round house, usually some 3–4 m in diameter—although structures as large as 7–9 m in diameter have been excavated at Tell Arpachiyah. These houses generally had stone foundations and were, like the earlier Hassunan houses, built of tauf or pressed mud. Most, especially at Yarim II, had only one room, which rose to a domed roof; some, however, especially at Tell Arpachiyah, had a rectangular room added to one side. In some cases internal buttresses, or even partitions, subdivided the large rooms, but round houses are usually single-roomed structures, quite different from the multiroomed houses typical of the preceding Hassunan period.

This is not to say that rectangular architecture did not exist in the Halaf period, it did—not only in the form of the rectangular annexes, but also as stand-alone, multiroomed structures. Rectangular architecture was not, however, dominant at the Halaf sites, although it is typical of the Samarran sites located farther south.

The most important Samarran sites are Chogha Mami and Tell es-Sawwan, both of which exhibit much more nucleated architecture—and buildings whose use of very long mud bricks allowed much more regular construction. At the minimum (more typical of Chogha Mami), the houses were tripartite in organization, with three parallel ranges of rooms. At the maximum (especially at Tell es-Sawwan), they could be much larger and more complex. Although many of these houses were T-shaped, their plans were markedly asymmetrical. The tripartite plan of Samarran houses and their use of buttresses not only continued into the Ubaid period in southern Mesopotamia, but also became key features of later Mesopotamian temples. [*See* Ubaid.]

The discovery of Ubaid 0 remains at Tell el-'Oueili in southern Mesopotamia has made clear the degree of continuity between the Samarran and the earliest Ubaid remains. [*See* 'Oueili, Tell el-.] Thus, now the development of the complex Samarran into the more symmetrical Ubaid houses with their central halls seems unremarkable. The best-preserved Ubaid houses were excavated in the Hamrin area, at Tell Abada and Madhhur (Henrickson and Thuesen, 1989), but similar structures have been found both earlier (at Tell el-'Oueili) and later and farther north (at Tepe Gawra, where many were originally interpreted as temples). [*See* Hamrin Dam Salvage Project; Tepe Gawra.] These houses have a large T-shaped, or cruciform, central room with additional ranges of rooms on each side. On occasion, as in the case of building A at Tell Abada, more than one of these units is combined into a single large building. The large central room with its hearth was at the heart of these houses; the smaller of the side rooms must have served the important role of food storage, while the larger were loci for food preparation, toolmaking, and other such activities.

Two trends can be identified, then, in the evolution of house forms during the Neolithic. One, beginning with the Aceramic Neolithic sites of Jarmo and Maghzaliyeh, sees the development of increasingly complex, multiroomed rectangular architecture—perhaps designed to house extended families—that eventually developed into the tripartite Ubaid house. The second trend is less easy to follow. The circular houses of Qermez Dere and Nemrik can be associated with similar structures found much farther west, and the same may be argued for the later Halaf round houses as well. Certainly both the PPNA and Halaf manifestations suggest cultural continuity between northern Iraq and Syria in ways that do not exist for the Hassunan, Samarran, and Ubaid cultures.

Mesopotamian Urban Housing. There are several basic functional distinctions between the houses built in Neolithic villages and those associated with later Mesopotamian cities. The former generally included considerable amounts of unroofed communal space. In the later urban centers, areas set aside for outdoor activities (because for much of the year it is cooler and pleasanter to be outside, so long as there is shade) had to be incorporated within the houses themselves—either in the form of courtyards or flat roofs. Thus, most, but not all, archaeologists interpret the central spaces within Mesopotamian houses as courtyards, and do not necessarily assume that all stairways lead to a second story because they could also have been designed to provide access to the roof (Veenhof, forthcoming).

Private-house areas are not distributed evenly over time and space. Protoliterate houses have not been excavated in Mesopotamia proper; the only extensive remains are at Habuba Kabira, an Uruk site on the Upper Euphrates River.

[*See* Habuba Kabira.] There, many of the houses resemble their Ubaid predecessors, although the addition of partitions within the large central hall may indicate the development of the courtyard house. By the third millennium, there are good examples of domestic areas that have been recorded in the south at Abu Salabikh, at the various Diyala and Hamrin sites (including the only truly rural settlements), and in the north, at Tell Taya. [*See* Abu Salabikh; Diyala; Taya, Tell.] The largest areas of domestic housing date to the early second millennium BCE at Ur, Nippur, Sippar, and at the small sites of Haradum and Tell Harmal (Woolley and Mallowan, 1976; Stone, 1987). [*See* Ur; Nippur; Sippar.] Associated private documents found in these houses provide additional information about their inhabitants. Farther north, and a little later, is the extensive domestic area at Nuzi, which includes some rural villas. [*See* Nuzi.] For the first millennium BCE, Ur and Babylon have some domestic areas, and there are Neo-Assyrian domestic structures at Nimrud, Khorsabad, and Aššur (Preusser, 1954). [*See* Babylon; Nimrud; Khorsabad; Aššur.]

All of the houses in Mesopotamia's urban centers were built in solid blocks, with neighboring houses sharing party walls. All Mesopotamian houses were built around an enclosed courtyard, which provided light, air, and a shady place to be during the long hot summers. This is not to say that the arrangement of rooms was the same. Houses could have rooms on one, two, three, or four sides of the courtyard, and in some cases had extra banks of rooms added onto one or more sides. The largest houses had more than one court and appear to have been composite structures. It is possible that some of the very smallest structures were commercial establishments; there is also evidence for workshops located in parts of some of the houses. Houses varied greatly in size at each site, and every house area excavated has included both large and small houses, houses using more relatively expensive materials (baked brick in the south, stone in the north), and houses using the bare minimum—an indication that there was little segregation of the population according to wealth or status. Not all of these differences reflected wealth distinctions, however. Where textual data can be brought to bear, it appears that the houses with rooms on all sides may have served extended families, whereas those with rooms on three or fewer sides were occupied only by nuclear families (Stone, 1981).

Most Mesopotamian houses included entrance chambers with the doorways offset, so that the courtyard was not visible from the street. It seems likely that nonfamily members did not generally penetrate beyond the entrance chamber. Where the entrance was directly into the courtyard, the space that was most probably used for living does not connect directly with the courtyard; instead, it is preceded by a subsidiary room that may have served the same function as the entrance chamber.

The smallest houses have only one or two rooms at the back of the courtyard. Where there are two rooms, it seems probable that one was for living space and the other—generally accessible only through the first—for storage. Small houses do not generally have any special-purpose rooms like kitchens or bathrooms, which are most often found only in composite houses or in those with rooms on all sides of the courtyard.

In most instances kitchens are marked by the presence of bread ovens, but on occasion larger stoves with built-in grills have been found. Bread baking might take place either in a room or in a courtyard, but true kitchens with stoves are generally in one corner of the house.

Bathrooms present a more difficult problem. While some bathrooms have been found—especially in the Old Babylonian houses at Ur—they are not common; it is a moot question whether they were merely used for washing or if they represent toilets. One indubitable toilet, virtually identical to those in use today in the Arab world, was found at Ur (Woolley and Mallowan, 1976); in general, however, cess pits, which are archaeologically unmistakable, are rare, and in most instances the ceramic drains beneath these rooms are designed for seepage rather than the disposal of solid waste. At Ur, bathrooms were generally located beneath the stairway; at other sites, while they were always small and tucked away, this association cannot be demonstrated. Baked-brick paving and drains were not only found in these apparently special-purpose rooms, but were encountered frequently in courtyards, and sometimes in other rooms, especially kitchens.

Staircases are far from ubiquitous and are generally quite small, either built into courtyards or tucked into tiny square rooms or into long narrow ones. In the south, where walls tended to be thin and available wood for construction rare, most scholars, but not all, interpret staircases as giving access to the roof. Farther north there is more evidence suggesting the presence of second stories, including textual references from Sippar referring to the lease of second-story property.

In addition to the normal domestic offices, some of the larger houses have evidence of rooms set aside for religious purposes. These were especially common in the second-millennium BCE houses at Ur, where they are found at the back of the house. They can be identified by the presence of altars and niches and may have the tombs of family members beneath them. [*See* Tombs.]

In summary, Mesopotamian cities were characterized by dense blocks of houses that focused on a central court. The larger the house, the more likely it was to have special-purpose rooms like bathrooms, kitchens, and chapels. In all probability the same functions were carried out in the smaller houses, but without the characteristic built-in features.

Although most house remains from the historical period in Mesopotamia come from urban centers, there are some data from smaller sites. For the Early Dynastic period, several small sites, generally not much more than 1 hectare (2.5 acres) in size, were excavated as part of the Hamrin rescue project. At Tells Razuk, Gubba, and Madhhur, the sites were dominated by circular buildings where a series of rooms surround a round, central courtyard; the entire arrangement is generally about 30 m in diameter. Although these sites also include the remains of more rectilinear architecture, they seem to have been dominated by a single round structure. Farther south, on the west mound at Abu Salabikh, an initial rural occupation had rectilinear architecture surrounded by curvilinear compound walls incorporating significant amounts of open space.

For the second millennium BCE, two single-hectare sites have been excavated, Haradum and Tell Harmal (Kempinski-Lecomte, 1992); both seem to be miniature versions of the large cities: densely packed courtyard houses. At the slightly later and more northern city of Nuzi, large rural villas housed some of its most prominent citizens (while those structures were somewhat larger than those in the center of town, they did not differ in plan in any significant ways; see Starr, 1939).

What is not clear from these data is whether they indicate that by the second millennium BCE there was no longer any difference either in organization or in sophistication between large and small settlements (i.e., Tell Harmal and Haradum were as rich in cuneiform tablets as any other Old Babylonian cities); or if only those for which this is the case have been sampled. Certainly there is a suggestion that at least in the Diyala basin in the third millennium there were significant differences between rural settlements and urban centers.

Conclusion. After a lengthy period of experimentation in house forms during the Neolithic, the urban dwellers of Mesopotamia took the Late Neolithic house form as the basis for their religious structures; they developed the courtyard house, which was more suited to the crowded conditions inherent in urban life. Once invented, the courtyard house remained in use in all parts of Mesopotamia for as long as the civilization continued; indeed, it is found in many parts of the Near East to this day. There is some evidence for experimentation in rural architecture in the third millennium, but the limited evidence from the second millennium BCE suggests that by that time the courtyard house dominated the form of both rural and urban dwellings.

[*See also* Mesopotamia; Syria, *article on* Prehistoric Syria; *and* Temples, *article on* Mesopotamian Temples.]

BIBLIOGRAPHY

Aurenche, Olivier. *La maison orientale: L'architecture du Proche Orient ancien des origines au milieu du quatrième millénaire.* 3 vols. Paris, 1981.

Delougaz, Pinhas, et al. *Private Houses and Graves in the Diyala Region.* Oriental Institute Publications, 88. Chicago, 1967.

Gibson, McGuire, ed. *Uch Tepe I.* Chicago and Copenhagen, 1981.

Henrickson, Elizabeth F., and Ingolf Thuesen, eds. *Upon This Foundation: The ʿUbaid Reconsidered.* Carsten Niebuhr Institute of Ancient Near East Studies, 10. Copenhagen, 1989.

Kempinski-Lecomte, Christine, ed. *Haradum I: Une ville nouvelle sur le Moyen-Euphrate.* Paris, 1992.

Preusser, Conrad. *Die Wohnhäuser in Assur.* Ausgrabungen der Deutschen Orient-Gesellschaft in Assur, 4. Berlin, 1954.

Starr, Richard F. S. *Nuzi.* Cambridge, Mass., 1939.

Stone, Elizabeth C. "Texts, Architecture, and Ethnographic Analogy: Patterns of Residence in Old Babylonian Nippur." *Iraq* 43 (1981): 19–33.

Stone, Elizabeth C. *Nippur Neighborhoods.* Studies in Ancient Oriental Civilization, 44. Chicago, 1987.

Veenhof, Klaas R., ed. *Houses and Households in Ancient Mesopotamia.* Istanbul, forthcoming.

Woolley, C. Leonard, and M.E.L. Mallowan. *Ur Excavations,* vol. 7, *The Old Babylonian Period.* London, 1976.

ELIZABETH C. STONE

Syro-Palestinian Houses

This treatment of a large and difficult topic begins with the Early Bronze age, c. 3300 BCE, and ends with the end of Iron II, c. 580 BCE. Earlier materials have been addressed by Edward B. Banning (1996); later materials remain to be analyzed. [*For some discussion of the later periods, see* Syria, *articles on* Syria in the Persian through Roman Periods *and* Syria in the Byzantine Period; *and* Palestine, *articles on* Palestine in the Persian through Roman Periods *and* Palestine in the Byzantine Period.]

Following an introduction to the difficulties of interpreting three dimensional, and probably mostly multi-storied, remains from their (often incomplete) ground plans, we turn to a brief overview of key architectural aspects of archaeo-ethnographically documented peasant households in the modern Middle East. [*See* Ethnoarchaeology.] From this perspective, we develop a working model of a functional peasant's house, as this might be witnessed in Syria-Palestine. Following this, we briefly visit the social anthropology of "round" versus "rectangular" houses, and the possible socio-economic implications of "exotic" or atypical architecture in a Levantine setting, before working our way—hopefully in an empirical, transparent fashion—through key aspects of what can be seen of the history of domestic architecture in Syria-Palestine.

Because archaeologists typically deal with fractional remains, sound models for reconstruction and interpretation are paramount to their work. Houses are the most common architectural form encountered and one of the most neglected, whether in terms of fieldwork, reporting, or interpretation. Despite frequent indications of a second story (e.g., stairways, two distinct levels of cultural deposits within a particular room or building, evidence for second-floor surfacing, lack of suitable living quarters on the ground floor), archaeologists seldom recover more than the ground-floor plan of any building. It thus becomes important to explore other avenues of knowledge to determine, for model building, the spatial and functional requirements or potentials of a "typical house." These will vary depending upon a household's economic pursuits. Traders, weavers, and members of the ruling elite would have different spatial needs, and their needs would differ from those of a farmer or herder. During the Syro-Palestinian Bronze and Iron Ages (c. 3300–580 BCE), most people were farmers. Therefore, most houses should have belonged to farmers, with atypical houses possibly belonging to people with other livelihoods (how this applies to urban settings might be problematic). During these periods, the dominant modes of production were intensive plow-assisted dry farming, horticulture (principally vines and fruit trees), and pastoralism, with each household typically practicing two or three modes of agriculture as a way of managing the risks inherent in the subsistence agriculture of marginal areas (Hopkins, 1985, pp. 245–250; Holladay, 1992a, p. 315; 1995, pp. 386–393). Similar constraints and risks still determine life in traditional farming communities in the region. Near Eastern ethnoarchaeological research has proven to be of great value for modeling "constants" (see, e.g., Watson, 1979; Kramer, 1979, 1982; Hall et al., 1973).

Settled Agriculturalists: Basic House Model. Typically, the architectural requirements of Near Eastern peasants are living space; kitchen space; storage space for household goods and foods; quarters for their donkey(s), cow/ox/bullock(s), and sheep/goat herd; seasonally adjustable storage space for fuel (dung, dung cakes, brush), straw (chaff), fodder, grain and legume reserves (including seed reserves); agricultural implements; young animals; spare beams or posts; and, in olive-oil producing, non-Islamic communities, large wine and oil jars. Courtyards are considered essential, although in tightly packed, fortified villages many of their functions can be taken over by the roof (Jacobs, 1979, p. 179). In such settings, strongly built flat roofs are used for a wide variety of outdoor activities, especially by women and children. Holes through the roof allow for communication between living rooms and rooftop activities. Windows often are extremely primitive, with mere holes (blocked in winter) sometimes sufficing.

Each nuclear family requires its own living room, in which it lives, works, eats, entertains, and sleeps. Larger houses may have more than one living room, the second used for entertaining or for rental, if not required for the extended family. Living rooms are characterized by a central hearth (necessary for winter heating, though supplemental portable braziers are also used). Where there are kitchens, the hearths may be leveled with mud plaster for the summer. Living rooms are often whitewashed and have better flooring than the mud plaster or packed earth that characterizes utility and storerooms. Even in nonurban settings, second-floor living rooms are considered more desirable, as they catch the summer breezes. Where there is a second story, it is invariably used as living room (Kramer, 1982, p. 102). In the restricted space of the fortified Iranian village of Tel-i Num, forty-eight of the fifty-nine compounds (81 percent) were two storied: the lower used for animals, and the upper for humans (Jacobs, 1979, p. 179). In addition to the living room, there is often a second-story utility room for storing light goods (foods and household goods) and, in some areas, a kitchen (Hall et al., 1973, fig. 7).

Stables and storerooms for heavy or bulky storage are invariably found on the ground floor. Grains and legumes may be stored in bins or in above-ground silos, grain pits, sacks, or jars. Storerooms are typically mud plastered, including the floors. High thresholds may serve as (inadequate) barriers to rodents and animals. Wealthy families tend to have relatively more storage space, and absentee landlords may have their own storehouse (and a well set-up agent) in the village for collecting in-kind land rent. From the archaeologist's perspective, such a storehouse—and the prosperous agent's house—should be archaeologically visible (Watson, 1979, pp. 40, 48, 241, fig. 5.29). Stables should be identifiable by their built-in mangers. As opposed to the typically paved Israelite stables, traditional village stable floors are unfinished and covered with decaying fodder and animal waste. Subterranean stables for housing sheep and goats at night and during winter storms, typical in western Iran (e.g., Watson, 1979, pp. 160–161, 204–205, 208), are not found in Syria-Palestine in the periods considered here (unless the cave under the northwest tower at Tell Beit Mirsim is such a stable), and some roofed folding space should be reckoned into any defensible space equation. [*See* Beit Mirsim, Tell.] Two underground stables illustrated for Patty Jo Watson's "Hasanabad," were, respectively, about 64 and 80 sq meters in site (1979, pp. 154, 160).

Exterior surfaces (including courtyards) are uneven, littered, develop damp spots, and may have piles of dirt, rocks, or other materials in corners or elsewhere. Archaeologically, streets and alleyways are generally hardened against the winter rains by potsherds and small stones. "Public areas" and major streets near important structures are generally much better hardened (suggesting governmental behest) than cul-de-sacs, alleyways, and peripheral streets. Because it is eroded by winter rains and summer sun and wind, the mud-and-chaff plaster of roofs and exterior walls is renewed annually. A portion of this annual increment, plus litter and garbage, forms a significant part of street and alleyway buildup, which seems to average between .5 and 1.0 m per century. Some streets, such as those running through gateways or near important buildings, may be cleared out periodically and reestablished at lower levels, particularly during renovations or rebuilding programs.

Kitchens at "Aliabad" had 1-meter-deep ovens, which restricted them to the ground floor (Kramer, 1982, pp. 99–100). Originally whitewashed, they then became progressively sooty. Vertical looms at Aliabad were generally set up in the kitchen. Kitchens are not necessarily synonymous with oven locations, however, because ovens are frequently located outside the house, in a spot sheltered from the wind. Inside the house they may be sited in some sheltered corner of the ground floor, with no trace of hearth. Communities without kitchens, such as Watson's "Hasanabad" (1979), cook (and bake bread on flat metal pans) on the living room hearth. In some communities, a kitchen may be shared with other members of the extended family. Sometimes dependent family (e.g., a widow) will live and entertain in a kitchen, which then will be kept ash free, with suitable floor coverings (Kramer, 1979, p. 104). Archaeologically, such a room might be distinguished by its relative cleanliness. Living rooms and kitchens used for living are not entered through other rooms, aside from entry halls, although rooms used by children may be entered from the main living room.

Ethnographically documented Iranian living rooms averaged from 15 to 18 sq m, possibly depending on whether there is a kitchen. The archaeological data from one-story structures (see table 1) suggest "needs averaging" at 19–22 sq m. In addition, the typical family will have one or two stables (averaging about 12 sq m each), one or two storerooms (about 12 sq m each), an entrance hall, and a kitchen. Carol Kramer's average size for kitchens (18 sq m) includes wall thickness, which makes the data unusable for this discussion. (Kramer, 1982, table 4.2, p. 122). The average size of five illustrated kitchens was 11.5 (sq) m with a standard deviation (SD) of 3.5 sq m (Kramer, 1982, figs. 4.18, 4.6, 4.7, 4.12). A fairly minimal folding space (20–25 sq m) may be arbitrarily assigned for the sheep/goat herd. These and other dimensions, such as room width (averages for three modern villages were 2.8, 2.9, and 3 m) and ceiling height, are fundamental to the suitability of the house and must be considered carefully in interpreting remains. These distributions are positively skewed (there are no stables or storerooms that are 2 sq m or living rooms that are 5 sq m), and most have relatively large standard deviations. In general, it is assumed that free spans of about 4 m or less could have been achieved with generally available timbers (see below). Finally, with respect to the applicability of the full model to every situation, it should suffice to note that, for example, plans specifically developed for warm, dry climates such as the lower Jordan Valley or the Negev desert might differ with respect to roofed nighttime facilities for animals (e.g., in most of the Early Bronze and Middle Bronze I plans illustrated below; see figures 1, 2.c). However, this caveat might not apply when the normative house style was carried over from areas with severe weather conditions such as the Galilee, the central hill country, and most of Syria and Lebanon.

The relevance of the preceding model for interpreting imperfectly preserved, complex domestic structures may be seen in figure 1.a, which shows the foundation plan of a hypothetical one-story house, based on a slightly enlarged version of the Iron II house 1727 at Shechem (Wright, 1965,

TABLE 1. *Comparative sizes of "large" and "small" rooms in representative domestic structures of EB and MB I towns and campsites.* Breaks occurred in the large room sizes at Tel Yarmut and Nabi Salah, Chuera B, Gebel Gunna, and Be'er Resisim. The most economical explanations seem to be first, that living rooms were no longer located on the ground floor in the rectilinear Chuera B structures. That probably holds true for many of the complex Palestinian EB III houses as well (e.g., Tell el-Far'ah [North] and Tel Yarmut), which, characteristically, no longer exhibited features or floor surfaces characteristic of EB II one-story houses (exceptions help prove the rule: e.g., the benches in Tell el-Far'ah [North] room 609, [de Vaux 1961, pl. 34]). Second, that, in contrast to Yiftaḥel and Jawa, the curvilinear Nabi Salaḥ, Gebel Gunna, and Be'er Resisim, structures were no longer designed to "accommodate *families*" (cf. Flannery, 1972, p. 39).

Period: Site (Figure)	Large Rooms (sq m)	Small Rooms (sq m)
Chalcolithic: Meṣar (3.a *solid*)	35	10
EB I: Yiftaḥel (2.a)	34.1	$\bar{x}$ = 5.75 (n = 2)
EB I: Jawa (2.b)	$\bar{x}$ = 22.2 (n = 5)	$\bar{x}$ = 51.1 (n = 5)
EB II: Meṣar (3.a *open*)	22.4	13
EB II: Arad (3.c)	$\bar{x}$ = 19 (n = 8)	$\bar{x}$ = 6.2 (n = 8)
Syrian EB: Chuera A (3.b)	19.6	$\bar{x}$ = 4.2 (n = 4)
EB III: Tell el-Far'ah (North) and Tel Yarmut (3.e)	$\bar{x}$ = 16.5	3.78 (Yarmut, n= 1)
EB II: Nabi Salaḥ (2.c)	$\bar{x}$ = 14.1 (n = 5)	$\bar{x}$ = 7.1 (n = 14)
EB II–III: Gunna 25 100 (2.d)	$\bar{x}$ = 10 (n = 11)	$\bar{x}$ = 1.4 (n = 3)
Syrian EB: Chuera B (3.d)	—	$\bar{x}$ = 6.7 (n = 11)
MB I: Be'er Resisim (2.e)	9.4 to 12.6	—

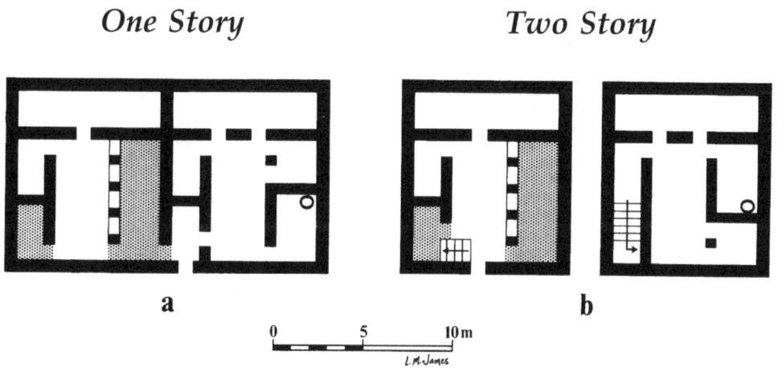

HOUSE: SYRO-PALESTINIAN. Figure 1. *Hypothetical House Plans.* (a) Ground plan when built as a one-story structure; (b) Ground plan of the same house, built as a two-story structure. (Courtesy J. S. Holladay)

pp. 158–163, figs. 76–77; Campbell, 1994). [*See* Shechem.] It is comprised of one stable area (14.6 sq m), a roofed folding area (28.5 sq m), one heavy- and two light-storage rooms (16 sq m, 16 sq m, and 4.5 sq m, respectively), one living room (25.5 sq m) with an entry hall (4.5 sq m), and a kitchen (8.1 sq m). The left hand portion of figure 1.b shows what would be seen in a typical excavation report for exactly the same house built with two stories. Nothing of the family's domestic space is seen, although all of their economic domain is clearly visible. If all of the family's activities were interpreted solely on the evidence of the ground plan (perhaps still the reigning mode), half of the picture would be missed (i.e., righthand portion of figure 1.b).

Round Houses and Rectilinear Houses. Our understanding of the relationships obtaining between house shapes and sizes and settlement patterns and dominant modes of production have been vastly advanced by recent anthropological research (Hunter-Anderson, 1977, building on earlier work by Robbins, 1966; Whiting and Ayres, 1968; Flannery, 1972). Kent V. Flannery summarizes: "rectangular houses . . . are associated . . . with full-time sedentism, large community size, and intensive agriculture . . . [and] round houses [in compounds], . . . [while they may be] associated with permanent settlement, . . . [regularly] are 'designed to house only one, or at most two, persons' . . . [while] the rectangular houses of the village are 'designed to accommodate families.' . . . [Various facilities] are attached to or within rectangular houses [cf. the Arad kitchens, below]. In contrast, the few facilities found in the compounds are separate, round structures located in the open between the huts [cf. the subsidiary structures of the Sinai encampments, below]" (1972, as cited by Hunter-Anderson, 1977, p. 314).

Design Stability and Foreign Traits. Both cuneiform records and ethnographic parallels indicate that house building in Near Eastern societies was a craft profession (Stone, 1981, p. 27, for "municipal housing"; Chicago Assyrian Dictionary, vol. 17, s.v. *Šitimgallu;* Watson, 1979, pp. 121–122, cf. Kramer, 1982, p. 94), although people often did their own construction work (Watson, 1979, p. 121; cf. Kramer, 1982, p. 94). It seems equally clear that various ethnic groups preferred certain architectural configurations. These twin observations go a long way toward explaining similarities, differences, and eccentricities in house form across large cultural areas and through long stretches of time that are punctuated in a variety of instances:

1. *Population relocation, cultural innovation, or stress.* The evolution—or local introduction—of new (or new to the region) house forms, presumably reflects either new arrivals or altered social organization and changing modes of production. Examples include Babylonian insula-style houses at Megiddo strata III–II (see below), Israelite three- and four-room houses in the central hill country in the latter part of the Late Bronze II, and round EB IV/MB I shelters in the central Negev. [*See* Megiddo.]

2. *Cultural dominance or acculturation.* The four-room house spread to the Shephelah, coastal plain, Esdraelon, Negev (and perhaps into Transjordan) the Early Iron II period.

3. *Resident aliens or mercenaries.* Phoenicianlike (?) benches and the rear cult room in the atypical Hazor house 14 (see figure 7.e). [*See* Phoenicians; Hazor.]

4. *(Some) trade diasporas.* The Hittite diaspora (see below; see figures 6.c–f), and Egyptian agents abroad, who also may have functioned as part of a trade diaspora (?). The latter were responsible, possibly under royal patronage, for buildings or such groups of buildings as the Egyptian villas at Tananir, at the Amman Airport, and possibly at Tell Selenkahiye in Syria, (see figure 10.b; Herr, 1983; see figure 10.c). [*See* Hittites; Amman.] In contrast, members of the Old Assyrian Karum Kaneš lived in local Hittite-style houses (see figure 6.a). [*See* Assyrians; Kaneš.]

5. *Symbols of imperial power and legitimacy.* Egyptian officers' houses and egyptianized temples appear at Beth-Shean; an Egyptian temple appears at Lachish (James, 1966, pp. 8–13; James and McGovern, 1993, vol. 1, pp. 4–5, 27–56; Rowe, 1940; Ussishkin, 1978, pp. 10–25); Egyptian residencies appear throughout southern Palestine (Oren, 1984); and Assyrian palace-forts (see, e.g., figure 9.c) appear at Megiddo, Hazor (Yadin et al., 1958, pl. 177), and Beidha(?) (Bennett, 1977, pp. 1–3, figs. 1-A, 2). [*See* Beth-Shean; Lachish; Palace; Beidha.]

Early Bronze Age. For northeastern Jordan, Syria, Palestine, and the Sinai at least five distinct types of houses are found. The first two types and the last are curvilinear structures seemingly associated with particular ethnic groups. The first type is associated with the invasive EB I Esdraelon culture (gray-burnished ware) and was formerly taken, based on inadequate data, to be apsidal. In the light of better analysis and new finds, this type (see table 1) is now seen to have an elongated oval plan (see figure 2a). This example has a central enclosed area of about 35.5 sq m and walled-off end spaces (for storage?) of 4.5 and 7 sq m (total = 11.5 sq m, mean [$\bar{x}$] = 5.75 sq m) (Braun, 1989). At the transi-

Palestine

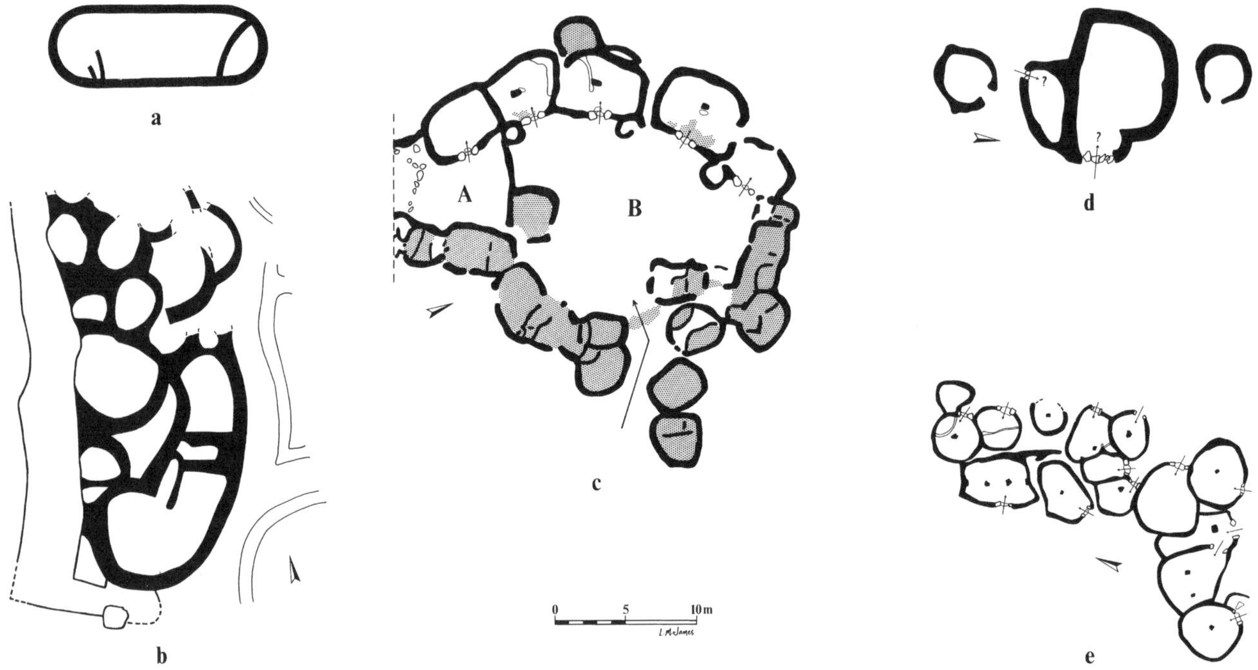

HOUSE: SYRO-PALESTINIAN. Figure 2. *Curvilinear Houses, EB to MB I.* (a) Oval EB I building from Yiftaḥel (after Ben-Tor, 1992); (b) houses and store facilities at EB I Jawa (after Helms, 1981, pp. 123–125); (c) EB II houses and store facilities at Nabi Salaḥ in the southern Sinai (after Beit-Arieh, 1981); (d) EB II or EB III sleeping chambers and enclosure at Gebel Gunna, in the Sinai (Gunna 100), presumably of a local non-sedentary group (after Bar-Yosef et al., 1986); (e) MB I shelters at Be'er Resisim (after Cohen and Dever, 1981). (Courtesy J. S. Holladay)

tional site of Meṣar (see figure 3.a), oval houses appear stratigraphically sandwiched between a rectilinear Chalcolithic house (large room = 34.1 sq m, small room = 10 sq m)—perhaps housing an extended family group and a typical EB II broad-room house (with a kitchen?) similar to those at Arad (see figure 3.c; Dothan, 1959). [*See* Arad, *article on* Early Bronze Age Period.] The larger unit is 22.4 sq m and the smaller about 13 sq m (see table 1). The second type of curvilinear house, at EB I Jawa (Helms, 1981, pp. 123–125, figs. 57–58), is cell-like (see figure 2.b). It was partially dug into the ground, and—according to the excavator—new houses were successively added on to existing semiround houses and smaller facilities in an agglutinative manner. [*See* Jawa.] Spaces between the adjacent expanding clusters—which presumably housed different extended family groups—eventually became streets. Each living room had access, through a small doorway, to a smaller rounded space, perhaps a beehive-shaped silo. [*See* Granaries and Silos.] An average of five large cells yielded a mean living room size of 22.2 sq m (SD = 8.3 sq m), while an average of five small (storage?) cells yielded a mean of 5.1 sq m (SD = 1.7 sq m) (see table 1).

The third example, from EB II Arad, in the Negev, is a strongly typed rectilinear sunken broad-room house (Amiran et al., 1978, pp. 14–17; see figure 3.c). The type is reasonably similar to an EB house near the small anten temple at Tell Chuera (Chuera A, see figure 3.b; table 1), in northeastern Syria (Moortgat and Moortgat-Correns, 1978, plans 2–5). [*See* Chuera, Tell.] Room 53, with alcove 51, totals 20 sq m, which compares well with the mean of 19 sq m from eight houses at Arad (see below). The Arad houses are, however, not like other EB complexes at Tell Chuera (Chuera B, phase 3; cf. figures 3.c–d; table 1). Given the size of the individual cells (about 3.7–11 sq m, $\bar{x}$ = 6.6 sq m, SD = 2.2 sq m, number [n] = 11); see table 1), the plan appears to represent the ground floors of three (?) two-storied buildings—presumably around a family courtyard—with living quarters to be reconstructed upon their second floors (fully realized, in the 15–40 sq m range, with a mean of about 25 sq m). In their respective settings, these fully rectilinear structures, with their incorporated kitchens/oven rooms (see above), may be taken as typical early and quite sophisticated—particularly at Tell Chuera—regional responses to the demands of intensive plow-assisted agriculture within a common larger culture area. [*See* Agriculture.]

As at Chuera, the Arad houses are grouped in what would

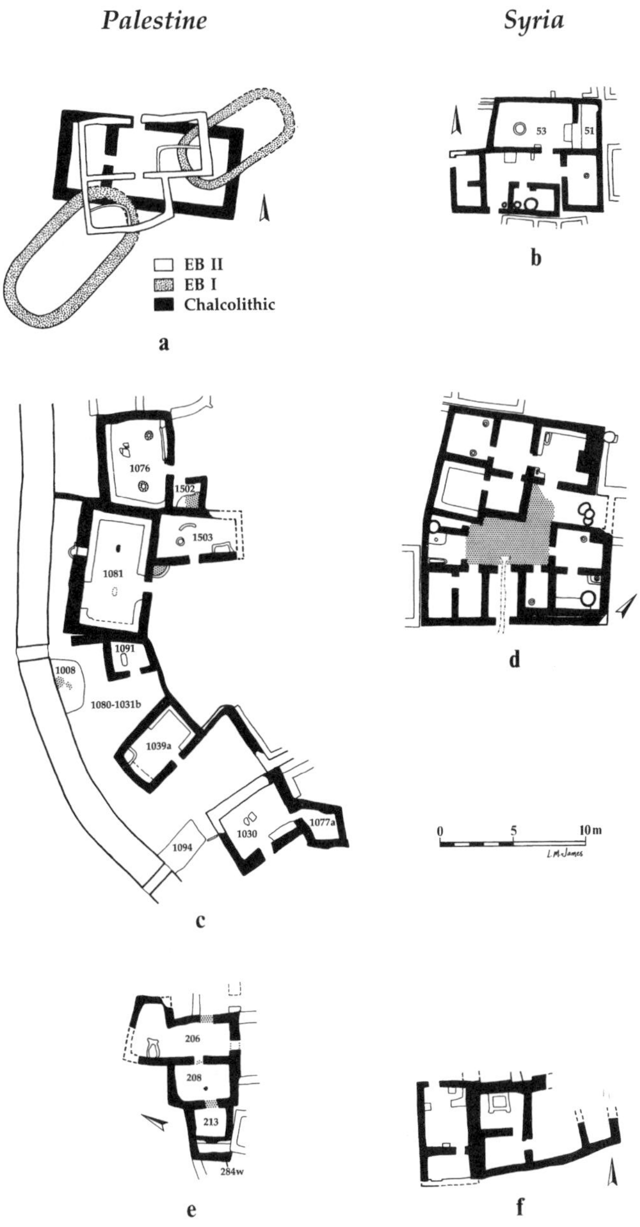

HOUSE: SYRO-PALESTINIAN. Figure 3. *Early Bronze Age rectilinear houses.* (a) Meṣar, oval EB I structures sandwiched between a rectilinear Chalcolithic house and a typical EB II broadroom house (with attached kitchen?) (after Dothan, 1959); (b) an EB house near the "Small Anten-Temple" at Tell Chuera, in northeastern Syria (after Moortgat and Moortgat-Correns, 1978, plans 2–5); (c) EB II complex at Arad, in the Negev, including four living rooms, three kitchens, one storeroom, compound walls, a fortification wall, and two rectangular stone platforms (for silos?) (after Amiran et al., 1978, pl. 178); (d) more common type of EB complex at Tell Chuera (after Moortgat and Moortgat-Correns, 1978; plans 2–5); (e) EB III development at Tel Yarmut of the EB II broadroom house, with forecourt(?), pillared room (with living room over?), subsidiary room, and an additional rear wall (see text) (after Miroschedji, 1988, pl. 9); (f) Late EB houses at Halawa with a longroom with rear chamber on the left, and seemingly part of a courtyard house more typical of the MB II on the right (after Meyer and Orthmann, 1989). (Courtesy J. S. Holladay)

appear to be family compounds, or "farm compounds" (Edward B. Banning, personal communication). At Arad, the individual house is a single living room opening off of an irregularly walled courtyard. The house and wall are built of blocks of soft Eocene chalk, laid without attention to bedding planes; the easily available chert is reserved for use in pyrotechnical installations, such as cooking hearths. Party walls are common. Typically, the living room is furnished with benches around its periphery (see figure 3.c). Some houses also have a platform, silo, clay or mud-brick bins (some holding carbonized grain), a stone mortar embedded in the floor, a plastered floor pit (for accumulating flour?). Some small hearths were planned, but not in every house. Depending on the size of the house, one or more stone column bases may appear along the long axis, deeper houses being more likely to have column bases. There may be more than one step down from the threshold to the floor. The inner walls, benches, and often the floors were surfaced with a "limey clay plaster" (Amiran et al., 1978, p. 16). Smaller rooms (usually at surface level), most of which served as kitchens or kitchen-storerooms, lack these features (at least one, room 1077a, which opened directly into the house, served another function: a storeroom?). Some of these rooms also have mortars embedded in the floors, built-up silos or stone-lined pits, slab-built ash bins, flagstone platforms, or raised stone [chert] hearths (see Arad rooms 1502, 1503). They are usually attached to the house, often directly outside the doorway, but may also be variously arranged around the courtyard. Larger houses may have larger kitchen-storerooms (e.g., room 1503). There are many raised round (sometimes half- or quarter-circles) and rectangular stone platforms (e.g., platform 1008), but not near every house. These are best interpreted as foundations for the collective (mud brick) granaries of extended families. Of the eight houses in area H, stratum II (Amiran et al., 1978, pp. 26–29, pl. 178), the mean width was 5.4 m with an SD of 1.1 m. The mean depth (front to back) was 3.5 m (SD = 0.5 m). Because only house 1039a lacked probable pillar bases (depth = 2.8 m), the mean depth (plus bearing lengths at each end) cannot be taken as a function of the lengths of locally available beams. Living rooms ranged from 12.8 to 30.4 sq m, ($\bar{x}$ = 19 sq m, SD = 6.2 sq m) (see table 1). From the same excavation area, the mean dimensions of the three kitchen-storerooms and one other small room were width $\bar{x}$ = 2.9 m (SD = 1.3 m), depth $\bar{x}$ = 2 m (SD = 3 m); interior areas ranged from 0.3 to 13.1 sq m ($\bar{x}$ = 6.2 sq m, SD = 4.6 sq m) (see table 1). The enclosed open area (area H, loci 1080–1031b) of one walled-in two-house compound is about 90 sq m. A house model confirms initial assumptions that the houses were one story, flat-roofed, and apparently plastered and painted on the outside (Amiran, 1978, p. 52, pl. 66, 115). The roofs were of reeds overlaid with clay (Amiran, 1978, p. 26).

The fourth type but closely related to the foregoing type) was excavated by Itzhak Beit-Arieh (1981) in a number of small EB II settlements in southern Sinai and the Negev highlands that appear, for a variety of reasons, to be encampments of peoples closely affiliated with the Arad culture (see below). In these camps, subcircular to subrectangular stone foundations characterize both houses (living rooms)—mostly pillared, many with benches, and sometimes even with a door socket—and smaller subsidiary structures. The houses are cut into the earth in a fashion similar to the Arad houses, but, as at Arad, most of the subsidiary structures seem to be at surface level (Beit-Arieh, 1981, p. 38, fig. 7). Where structures are not contiguous, short stretches of connector wall fill the gap. The units are strung like beads in a necklace: houses are regularly connected to other houses, with the subsidiary structures (Flannery's "facilities," see above) being "located elsewhere around the courtyard" (Beit-Arieh, 1981, p. 37). The whole forms a roughly circular corral-like encampment, often with a smaller—perhaps one of Beit-Arieh's "pens" (1981, p. 42)—and a larger "enclosure" area. The enclosure has only one (less often two) entrance(s). As published (the drawing is cut off to the left), Nabi Salaḥ, one of the settlements Beit-Arieh excavated, lacks its southernmost subsidiary structures, but is otherwise well preserved and may be taken as typical (see figure 2.c: Beit-Arieh, 1981, pp. 37–38, fig. 8). The interior areas of the five houses (living rooms) range from 9.7 to 18.75 sq m, with a mean of 14.1 sq m (SD = 3.7 sq m), on average 4.9 sq m smaller than the Arad living rooms, but larger than the MB I shelters, and much larger than the sleeping chambers near Gebel Gunna (see table 1).

The fourteen subsidiary structures range from 2 to 11.7 sq m, with $\bar{x}$ being 7.1 sq m (SD = 2.6 sq m), on average a probably insignificant 1.1 sq m larger than the Arad kitchen-storerooms. A larger corral area is about 150 sq m (area B), and a smaller one (area A) is about 27 sq m. On a per living room basis, this equates well with the free compound area in area H at Arad (44.25 sq m vs. 45 sq m), suggesting that one of the primary determining factors for each enclosed space might be the overnight folding area required for the group's donkeys, sheep, and goats. [*See* Sheep and Goats.] The entrance typically has a certain depth, which makes for easy blockage with brush and camel thorn. While it is not impossible that this setting belonged to some family groups, there is a stronger possibility, compatible with the reduced living-room size, relatively low head space, and small doorways, which are (55–60 cm wide × 70 cm high (Beit-Arieh, 1981, p. 34), that these were seasonal encampments. The outer walls are preserved maximally to 1.6 m, and two monolithic central pillars are 1.85 and 2.2 m high, respectively (Beit-Arieh 1981, p. 47). The encampments likely belong to specialized pastoralist resource-gathering groups proceeding from and domiciled at permanent settlements such as Arad (see below). [*See* Pastoral Nomadism.] The resources gathered or traded included copper; semiprecious stones; mother of pearl, other shells, and other Red Sea commodities; and even temper for the stratum III–I cooking pots found, and presumably manufactured, at Arad (Amiran, 1978, p. 50). Six (75 percent) of the eight published EB II pendants from Arad were of mother of pearl, as were 341 (64 percent) of the 531 published beads (Amiran et al., 1978, pls. 68–69).

The fifth type of structure is represented by oval structures near Gebel Gunna (sites 25, 50, and 100), investigated by Ofer Bar-Yosef and others in Sinai (see figure 2.d), which also appear to be EB II (or III?) in date and which the investigators propose may derive from the indigenous population of Sinai (Bar-Yosef et al., 1986, pp. 164–165). In general, these structures take the pattern of subrectangular to oval to subrounded courtyards—distinguished by ashes and quantities of animal dung (?)—with one or two small attached oval sleeping chambers (?). Usually, there were other unattached small, rounded to subrounded sleeping chambers in the vicinity. Even smaller circular installations ($\bar{x}$ = 1.4 sq m, SD = 0.6 sq m, n. = 3) were considered storage facilities (see table 1), sometimes clustered within a larger oval structure (Bar-Yosef et al., 1986, figs. 4–6). The enclosures ranged from about 35 sq m to about 129 sq m ($\bar{x}$ = 62 sq m, SD = 40 sq m), while the sleeping chambers ranged from 5.6 sq m to 16.6 sq m ($\bar{x}$ = 10 sq m, SD = 3.4 sq m, n = 11).

In the later EB II and the ensuing EB III periods, it appears that an additional room or rooms were frequently added to the plan, often secondarily. Houses are not sunken at sites like Tell el-Farʿah(North) and Tel Yarmut and are typically much more closely packed and forced into irregular spaces. [*See* Farʿah, Tell el- (North); Yarmut, Tel.] Often they make up sprawling insulae, although, where details are clearer, the individual houses seem to remain discrete, allowing the inference that the nuclear family was still the basic unit of society. Internal courtyards are recognizable, off of which living rooms may open (e.g., Loud, 1948, fig. 302; Miroschedji, 1988). One variant (EB II, rooms 622–612, 629-623–624, de Vaux, 1961, pl. 34; EB III, rooms 206, 208, 213, Miroschedji, 1988, pl. 9) has a centrally columned room or rooms (rooms 612, 623, and 208 are 24.5 sq m, 17.1 sq m, and 8.4 sq m, respectively; $\bar{x}$ = 16.7 sq m, SD = 8.1 sq m, n = 3; see table 1) directly behind a front broad room or courtyard (see figure 3.e). Room 206 could easily have been roofed over, although it is very shallow and has too many entrances to be considered a living room. While it is possible that these were living rooms, it is more probable that the living room was then on the second story, much as in the later Syrian house models (e.g., figure 5.f), which feature a second story on the rear half to third of the house length—the best dated examples are all Late Bronze (Margueron, 1976, pp. 213–227). At 8.4 sq m, the posited Tel Yarmut second floor seems too small to serve its expected living-room function, unless the rearmost wall, 284, is taken as the expanded house's back wall (making the room about 15 sq m). Presumably, the invasive and ill-published Khirbet Kerak culture brought its own exotic architectural traditions with it, as is evidenced in the great granary at Khirbet Kerak/ Beth-Yeraḥ (Hestrin, 1975, p. 258), but these remain obscure. [*See* Beth-Yeraḥ.]

MB I/EB IV. With the collapse of nucleated occupation in Palestine and much of Syria, caves and, presumably, tents or other impermanent structures became the norm. Beginning early in EB IV and lasting throughout the later EB IV/ MB I (henceforth MB I), in winter encampments scattered across the Negev, small, round stone huts, plastered on the interior and almost certainly on the exterior, with stone-and-plaster roofs, were the norm (see figure 2.e). The roofing was ingenious and suited to the windswept nature of the locale: locally abundant, flat chalk slabs were held together with marly clay plaster and set on a low-pitched frame of locally available tamarisk roofing beams radiating out from one or more central pillars. The pillars were often constructed of more than one stone; composite pillars were held in place by compression from the weight of the roofing stones and plaster (Cohen and Dever, 1981, fig. 7). It seems likely that these utilitarian structures were smaller and rounder simplifications of the curvilinear EB II hut. There was earlier EB II occupation at Be'er Resisim and at nearby site 126 (Cohen and Dever, 1981, pp. 64, 72–73). [*See* Be'er Resisim.] MB I structures at Be'er Resisim were not arranged around large open spaces, but in short ragged rows and clumps. The rows mostly face northeast, east, and southeast (fifteen out of 20 appear in Cohen and Dever, 1979, fig. 6; they are partly illustrated in figure 2.e), and south (four examples), away from the prevailing westerly winds (one example does face west). With diameters between 3 and 4 m (9.4–12.6 sq m), a maximum interior height of about 1.8 m (Cohen and Dever 1981, p. 61, figs. 4–5, 7–8), sloping downward to 1.5 m or less at the exterior walls, and with the only intact doorway being .4 m wide and .55 m high, they were too small and cramped to be more than shepherds' camps or sleeping chambers (Cohen and Dever, 1979, p. 51; Dever, 1985, p. 19). Presumably, the inhabitants were, as in some contemporary pastoralist societies, young boys and older men, rather than family groups (Dever, 1985, p. 21; n. 14 interprets the evidence to reflect polygynous family groupings).

The dimorphic forms of EB II houses, both round and rectilinear, versus the totally opposite characteristics of EB II–III town sites (all rectilinear) and MB I campsites (all curvilinear), may help to understand the early EB IV and MB I. Against the vast majority of round-chambered shaft tombs characteristics of the developed Palestinian MB I, the earliest northern culture's shaft tombs at Megiddo (Dever, 1980, fig. 1) were strictly rectilinear, an architectural statement somewhat more weakly echoed by the same cultural group in the Northern Cemetery at Beth-Shean (Oren, 1973a, n. 13; 1973b, p. 16 [tomb 227], fig. 7; p. 24). At Har Yeroḥam, in the central Negev highlands, a densely built settlement bounded by a relatively inconsequential rectilinear stone fence contained "various workshops—square structures built up against the stone fence . . . and a [lightly built, rectilinear] public building with large rooms. . . . The numerous grindstones and querns, flint scrapers, and sickles found on the site indicate that seasonal agriculture was practiced nearby, probably in the adjacent Yeroḥam basin, which has a high water table. Two animal figurines, unique for this period, one of clay and one of stone, were found near a pottery kiln which still had a Middle Bronze Age I vessel inside it" (Kochavi, 1978, p. 1219). This settlement was succeeded by one with round structures and animal pens. Little can be said for the affinities of the plans, but the sequence should be noted: from early multiroom rectilinear structures with workshops, animal figurines, and agricultural implements, to later round structures with large animal pens. Also, while animal figurines may be rare in MB I contexts, they abound in Chalcolithic, EB, and Iron Age contexts, all periods dominated by sedentarized horticulture and/or intensive agriculture—in each case significantly buffered from risk by the individual ownership of small household flocks.

Late in MB I, a reverse movement can be seen: straggling rectilinear mud-brick buildings with small, irregular rooms and walls only one brick thick reappeared at Jericho (Kenyon, 1970, pp. 153–154, fig. 29), after an extended period in which the site was occupied by people using typical late MB I pottery but who left no visible structures. [*See* Jericho.] Such an oscillation from substantial rectilinear houses (with family and work-group values reflected in the multiple burial tombs of the EB I–III) to easily built round and impermanent habitation (with family and work-group values reflected in the single and, rarely, double-burial MB I shaft tombs) and back to permanent rectilinear architecture (with renewed family vaults in MB II) may reasonably be correlated with an oscillation from sedentary family-based agriculture (EB I–III) to pastoralism (MB I) and back again (MB IIA) to a renewed emphasis upon sedentism, intensive agriculture, and the family (LaBianca, 1990, pp. 33–49). At Jericho, the new movement may involve late "Jerichoan MB I" elements returning to sedentary agriculturalism under the influence of incoming MB IIA agriculturalists.

On the basis of data normally consulted, MB I would seem to represent the last gasp of a long period of curvilinear houses stretching back through the early Beersheba culture to the Pre-Pottery Neolithic. However, farther afield other data are discovered, such as the one-room round, "temporary" structures and the one- to several-room rectilinear "farmhouses" found in the Negev from the Byzantine and Early Islamic periods (Haiman, 1995). There are averages of room sizes for the excavator's two farm groups: the mean for group 1 being 21 sq m (n = 19) and for group 2, 22 sq m (n = 25); the standard deviation cannot be calculated from the data (Haiman, 1995, tables 1, 2). While the notion of independent invention may be posited for each new manifestation of the circular form, following intervals characterized by rectangular houses, it seems better to hypothesize that groups of people using round structures, perhaps often in less durable materials, persisted throughout the prehistoric and historic periods at the margins of "civilized" sedentary societies and served as a reservoir for the various technologies required for survival during periods of societal collapse (Tainter, 1988).

Middle Bronze II: Palestine. Despite restored plans from Tell Beit Mirsim (see figures 4.b, d, g, h) and elite houses at Megiddo (see figures 4.e, f), relatively little was known about housing in the Middle Bronze and Late Bronze Ages prior to Michèle Daviau's pioneering study of domestic activity areas (Davian, 1993). Most Palestinian specialists seem to agree that the standard MB–LB house form is based on a courtyard with single-story rooms on one or two sides. This is not true for two of the three Tell Beit Mirsim examples, however. Largely on the basis of debris analysis, William Foxwell Albright maintained from the start that the palatial mud-brick stratum D house (MB IIC), with its 6-meter-wide courtyard (see figure 4.g), was two storied (Albright, 1938, pp. 35–39). If the second story was confined to just the nearly square western block, in the pattern of the (mostly—or all?—LB) Syrian model houses, that floor would have had an enclosed area of some 42.5 sq m, without its internal walls—enough for a living room, a small kitchen, and an upper storeroom. It seems more plausible that the entire building, without the courtyard, was two-storied (Daviau, 1993, p. 157). The MB IIA stratum G house (see figure 4.b) had a columned room (room 1, probably without a porticoed courtyard) about 37 sq m in area. However, the lack of an entry hall, and the twin facts that the side rooms are all under 12 sq m and all face into room 1, speak against the ground floor being the family's living space. The line of column bases reduces the overall free span of room 1 from 4.5 m to free spans of less than 2.5 m—well under the free-span widths of the three small rooms (2.9, 3.1, and 3.2 m, respectively). The peculiar broken wall line near the northern end of room 1—if not a digging or planning mistake—may be construed as part of the foundation for the staircase. Given the ethnographic data, the small rooms most reasonably can be seen as storerooms (and as an excellent basis for a second story), with the large room serving for daytime work space and overnight and storm shelter for the sheep and goat herd. Having proposed this, it is significant that in the entire body of MB II–LB II housing Daviau reviewed, no formal facilities for housing large animals (horses, donkeys, cows) could be identified (Daviau, 1993, pp. 455–456—except for the LB Tablet Building at Tell Hadidi (see below). [*See* Hadidi, Tell.] A second story, erected only over the smaller rooms, could have had an overall area of some 40 sq m, without the internal walls—more than enough for a living room and kitchen, or even for a living room, small kitchen, and small storeroom, with a means of exiting to the expansive roof over the pillared hall. This is, however, not the only possible reconstruction and is probably less desirable than a full second story.

The pillared stratum E buildings (SE2–12, SE3–13) at Tell Beit Mirsim (see figure 4.d; Albright, 1938, paragraphs 39, 46–47, pls. 50–51) appear to be entirely two-storied (for staircases, see below). Albright, however, cites persuasive evidence for a radical change in plan from stratum E (MB IIB) to stratum D (MB IIC): from a previously wholly roofed structure (figure 4.d) to one only partially roofed—a courtyard building (see figure 4.h). Accepting this interpretation for Tell Beit Mirsim (at Megiddo, this change seems to have happened early in MB IIB; see below), in stratum D a relatively large courtyard bounded by two small rooms to the west and one large room (about 7.14 × 3.33 = 23.8 sq m) to the south are seen for the first time. Given the density of building in this area and the thickness of the walls, it is probable that at least the north end of the eastern house, and perhaps the south end as well, was two-storied. Stairways in both periods seem to be concentrated at the northwest corner of the eastern building: there is a descending staircase in the western house shown on the stratum E plan (see figure 4.d) in S.1D (Albright, 1938, pl. 50). This is a strong argument for the roofed character of this space. The overly thick ascending western "wall" exterior to the building shown in figure 4.h is also probably a staircase (locus 2, on the stratum D plan (Albright, 1938, pl. 51).

At urbanized Jericho, the density and small room size of the MB II (=MB IIB–C) houses (Kenyon, 1960, pp. 187–188, fig. 45) supports Kathleen M. Kenyon's early judgment that the ground floor was given over to the economic domain—whether storage or shops—with the "upper storey rooms . . . as today, provid[ing] the living accommodation" (1960, p. 187). As given, the plans do allow for buildings with 4-× -4–5-meter corner rooms, which may or may not be courtyards, with a double range of rooms on one or two sides (see Daviau's extended analysis in favor of roofed space: 1993, pp. 213–218, and LB II Ugarit, below). Megiddo, area BB, stratum XII (Loud, 1948, fig. 398, N14-O14; see figure 4.f) appears similar to the less-complete Jericho plans. Two houses, each with four rooms on two sides of a larger space, seem fairly secure. Anything else on the plan is problematic, although the pattern seems to repeat itself with variations. The eight small rooms average 1.9 m of free span across their narrow dimension (SD = 0.4 m), and the two larger rooms/courtyards average just a little under 4 m in their narrow dimensions (see LB II Ugaritic below). The largest small rooms in each house are about 5.1 sq m and 7.6 sq m, and the two large rooms/courtyards are about 15 sq m and 20 sq m, respectively. As at Jericho, adequate living rooms and a kitchen could be fitted in, utilizing the space above just the small rooms, without roofing the

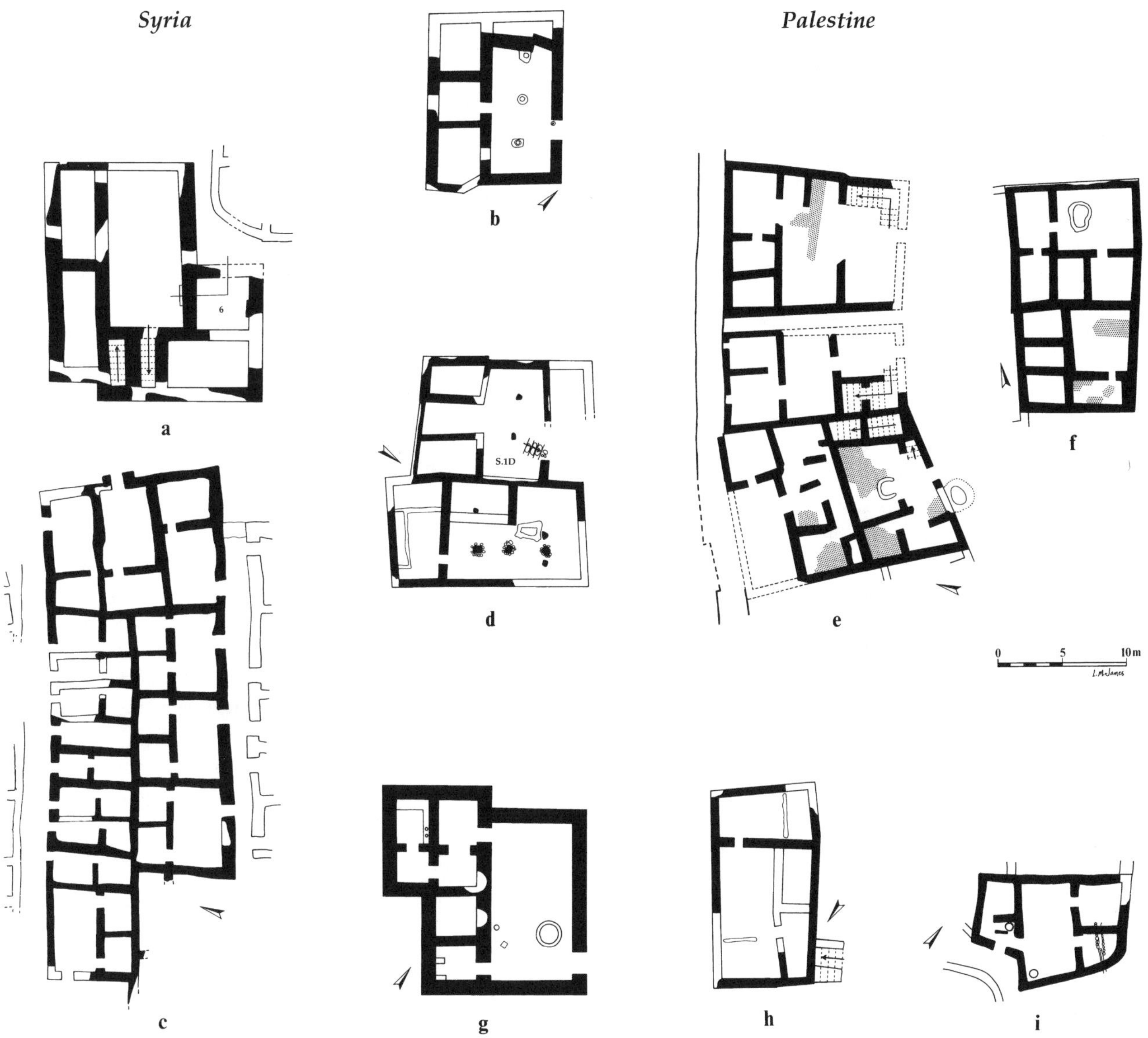

HOUSE: SYRO-PALESTINIAN. Figure 4. *Middle Bronze Age II houses.* (a) Tell Bi'a, courtyard house with rooms on three sides of the courtyard (after Herbordt et al., 1982); (b) Tell Beit Mirsim stratum G, MB IIA house with rooms to one (?) side of a large hall (after Albright, 1938, pl. 56); (c) Halawa, a MB II insula of two and three-room houses of Hittite style (cf. figure 6) (after Meyer and Orthmann, 1989); (d) Tell Beit Mirsim stratum E, MB IIB houses with pillared halls (after Albright, 1938 pl. 50); (e) Megiddo statum XII, MB IIB buildings in area AA (after Loud, 1948, fig. 378b); (f) Megiddo area BB, stratum XII, MB IIB houses with rooms on two adjacent sides of a courtyard (after Loud, 1948, fig. 398); (g) Tell Beit Mirsim stratum D, MB IIC multistoried building with courtyard to one side (after Albright, 1938, pl 55); (h) Tell Beit Mirsim stratum D, MB IIC version of one of the houses in (c) above, with rooms on three sides of a courtyard (after Albright, 1938, pl. 51); (i) Hazor MB IIC house 6205, from Hazor area C, stratum 3 (after Yadin et al., 1960, pl. 207). (Courtesy J. S. Holladay)

larger spaces. A more satisfactory plan would have involved a complete second story.

Aside from the fact that the buildings are a complex insula in style, it is difficult to make much out of the Tell Nagila plans (Amiran and Eitan, 1965, fig. 3; cf. Amiran and Eitan, 1977, p. 895). Because "in some cases a flight of several steps leads down to the house from the street" (Amiran and Eitan, 1977, p. 895) without a mention of drains, fully roofed construction (and a raised threshold) must be argued. The broadest free spans shown are consistently under 4 m. Using the excavators' evaluation, the typical house consisted of "one or two small rooms (averaging 2 by 3 meters), opening onto a courtyard (averaging 3 by 5 meters)" Amiran and Eitan, 1977, p. 895). Pillar bases are mentioned, as are paved floors. One large silo, in its own space, is shown. Because the "rooms" are said to average 6 sq m—small even for storerooms or stables—only the "courtyard" (or the space above it) would have been sufficiently large for anything even approaching the average ethnographically documented living room. Given the compact insula plan, and the evidence for pillars, the buildings were probably two-storied, with the usual low first story, despite the relative thinness of the walls. (See Netzer, 1992, pp. 20–21.) Similar considerations govern any ethnographically aware interpretation of the three large, ill-preserved buildings in area AA, stratum XII (MB IIB) at Megiddo (cf. Ben-Dov, 1992, p. 101, and Loud, 1948, p. 13, fig. 23; see figure 4.e; and see Loud, 1948, fig. 378b), and a same-period building at Beth-Shemesh (Grant and Wright, 1939, p. 28, fig. 2). [*See* Beth-Shemesh.] What does seem common to all these units is that the ground floor, and presumably the second story, was regularly fronted by a large room, with one to three or more smaller rooms arrayed behind it.

MB IIC house 6205 from Hazor, area C, stratum 3 (see figure 4.i) illustrates a variant well attested in LB Syria—although, on this evidence, originating in the Middle Bronze Age (Yadin et al., 1960, pl. 207). The house has rooms on either side of a "courtyard," and the parallelism is complete even to the detail of entering through a small entry room (cf. figure 5.d). The small rooms range from just over 4 to about 9.3 sq m ($\bar{x}$ = 6.5 sq m, SD = 2.4 sq m); the "courtyard" is 28 sq m. Suitable space for a living room can only be attained by positing a two-story plan. If the "courtyard" space were left open (about 4 m of free span), the two resulting spaces would be about 15.5 sq m and 22 sq m, without the internal walls. Considering the problems inherent in having two separate second stories in one house, it seems better to posit a complete second story, with a wooden staircase probably ascending along the northeastern side of the southwest room.

Middle Bronze II: Syria. The many two- and three-roomed houses in MB II stratum 2 at Tell Halawa (see figure 4.c; Meyer and Orthmann, 1989, pp. 20–33), are treated below (see section "Hittite houses"). Other MB II houses are poorly attested in Syria, but the next to the latest MB II building phase on mound E at Tel Bi'a (Herbordt et al. 1982) yielded one example of a strongly built house all of whose walls are more than 1 m wide (see figure 4.a). This is already in the mode of later Syrian houses, albeit of a variant posited for, but not yet attested in LB Syria: the courtyard house with "rooms on three . . . sides" (see below; Herbordt et al., 1982, fig. 8). Entry appears to be through a relatively large room with the usual bent axis and staircase near at hand in what most surely is an open courtyard (free span = 5.5–5.75 m). The shortest free spans for the various rooms are 3.5, 2.6, and 2.6 m. Room 6 would be wider but probably utilizes a wide, slightly off-center pilaster for a compound bearing beam (of costly cedar), which would reduce the resultant north–south free spans to less than 2 m. The respective room sizes are 17.2, 18.4, 21.4, and 15.2 sq m ($\bar{x}$ = 18.1 sq m, SD = 2.6 sq m, on average larger than any other house in the present study).

Late Bronze Age. Despite data from Megiddo, Hazor, and Tell el-ʿAjjul (Daviau, 1993, 219–299) and an apparently unique, for Palestine, LB IIA house at Tel Batash/Timnah (Kelm and Mazar, 1982, figs. 8–10; see figure 5.n), firm conclusions about house form are hard to reach. [*See* ʿAjjul, Tell el-; Batash, Tel.] It will help, therefore, first to examine the extensive data from Syria, which show a broad diversity of forms. Figure 5.a illustrates just one portion of a complex insula from Ras Shamra, ancient Ugarit: three closely intertwined, but functionally separate houses (A–C) (Yon et al., 1987). [*See* Ugarit.] Marguerite Yon comments on the processes that yielded this particular configuration: "The city blocks [insulae] . . . are divided into living units (houses) closely linked with one another and imbricated, so that not one of them alone constitutes an autonomous architectural unit. That is why the interior partitions have changed over the course of the history of each block [insula], according to inheritances and sales: it was sufficient to pierce a hole or board up a doorway to modify the size or the orientation of a house" (Yon, 1992, p. 704). Yon summarizes the organization of the typical house: "In the ground plan, access to the street is from a vestibule whence the interior traffic patterns branch out, horizontally by the doorways and vertically by a staircase, the first flight of which is of stone. One area is reserved for domestic activities, recognizable from culinary utensils (stone, ceramic, bone), another perhaps for the treatment of textiles, and another area for storage, with jars and sunken silos. The living quarters on the next floor up must be reconstructed. Fairly frequently, a separate area, with its own entrance but linked to the rest of the house, housed a family tomb. These private homes abutted industrial establishments [e.g., oil presses, jewelry, or figurine workshops]" (Yon, 1992, p. 705). Their eighteen rooms range from 1.6 to 23.7 sq m, with a mean of 11.2 sq m (SD = 6.3 sq m). The free spans on the narrowest axes range from 1 to 3.6 m ($\bar{x}$ = 2.7 m, SD = .9 m), with nine of them grouped between 3 and 3.6 m. Only the widest free span—a space of 4 × 4.2 m—seems to belong to an open court (piece 1265, see Yon, 1992, pl. I). Given that these are relatively rich households in a region where cedar should have been easily obtained, it is notable that the covered free spans seem to peak in the range of 3.5–3.6 m (four out of the top eight widths). This seems to constitute relatively strong—though not absolute—grounds for ruling out free spans approaching or exceeding 4 m in areas such as ancient Palestine. On the other hand, many large spaces in MB and LB Palestinian houses seem to be governed by a 4-meter standard, suggesting that spans of this length were possible, but not ones of, say, 4.25 m or more.

Two points need emphasizing: in the densely packed, long-lived urban environment, most houses have a functional plan, but not necessarily a fixed architectural form; and LB (and presumably earlier) urban houses are typically multistoried, with no living quarters on their ground floors. The differential deposition of fine objects in the debris of collapse strongly indicates that domestic quarters were on the second (or higher) floors. These insights help to understand not only ill-defined plans from, say, Alalakh, but also from such urban Palestinian sites as Hazor, Megiddo, and Tell el-ʿAjjul. [*See* Alalakh.]

Standard MB–LB house type. In the less urbanized setting of the Middle Euphrates River, a variety of house forms can be distinguished (see esp. Meijer, 1989). [*See* Euphrates.] As already noted, versions of what can be termed standard already appear in the Middle Bronze Age in both Syria and Palestine and will also appear in the Palestinian Iron I and II. Its fullest expression can be seen in the more broadly excavated LB strata of the Middle Euphrates, particularly at the long-standing excavations at Tell Munbaqat (Machule et al., 1992, fig. 14; 1993, fig. 12). The most common variants of this type are characterized by rooms on one side of a large hall (see figure 5.b,c; cf. figure 4.b,g) or rooms on two opposing sides of such a hall (see figure 5.d; cf. figures 4.i, 7.c) A third alternative has rooms along one long side and an adjacent short side (see figure 5.e; cf. figure 4.f). A fourth variety has rooms on three or even four sides (cf. figures 4.a; 7.a, b, d; 8.a, b). In LB, Syrian, the partition walls defining these rooms are simple: they are either straight segments, L-shaped, or T-shaped. Short doorjams, probably associated with bars to lock the exterior door appear at the house entrance, occasionally at the entrance to the central court, and only rarely elsewhere (Watson, 1979, pl. 5.4). As in the Israelite three- and four-room houses, these large areas/courts/halls are almost surely roofed, as the stairs make clear. In smaller, simpler houses, the entrance leads directly into the large hall; in larger, more complex houses, the entrance characteristically lets into a small entry hall that, in turn, leads into the large hall. In enough examples to establish the general pattern, stairways are directly at hand upon entering the larger hall (figures 5:a–c, e, h–j). Examples without stone stairways undoubtedly had wooden stairways (Margueron, 1980, p. 293). It is historically, socially, and economically significant that these buildings have unmistakable descendants in Iron II Philistia and Israel (Holladay, 1995, pp. 382–385).

Palestinian houses. If the Tell Beit Mirsim LB house selected for publication (Albright, 1938, pl. 56, cf. pl. 52) is correctly reconstructed, house forms current in Megiddo stratum XII (MB IIB, cf. figure 4.f) persisted into late LB II Palestine, as they did in Syria (see figure 5.e). This assessment would be in keeping with contemporary scholarly views of the relationship of the Late Bronze to the Middle Bronze Age (cultural continuity, not discontinuity). Some curious materials from Hazor, area C, stratum 1B, reflect a foreign presence and are treated below (see section "Hittite houses"). The plan of area F, stratum 1B, at Hazor resembles a rabbit warren, with entrances at both the northern and southern ends and multiple branching entrances from the south (see figure 5.k; Yadin et al. 1960, pl. 210). In part, different construction may have been conflated into a single-phase plan. At least one, and perhaps two staircases may be posited, but no discrete house emerges without violence to the plans as published. Viewed as a whole, these remains may represent a version of complex multigenerational inheritance and sale parcels on the order of Yon's interpretation of the Ugaritic insula shown in figure 5.a—the whole being ultimately based upon three or four instances of the standard house variant having rooms on three sides.

An incomplete LB II insula house from Ashdod, area B (figure 5.1), not yet fully published (Dothan, 1975, p. 108), bears a surprising resemblance to what was published as a late Iron II house from area D at Ashdod (cf. figures 5.m and 5.1) (Dothan, 1971, plan 8, building 1). [*See* Ashdod.] Given that intrusive (!) Late Iron II materials (mostly burials from locus 1114) form the bulk of the local stratum 3b publication from the building, it seems more than possible that building 1 (and probably buildings 2 and 3 as well) should also be dated to LB II. In area B, building 1 covers an area of about 167 m and may have had two courtyards. Even those were probably covered, the greatest free span being on the order of 3.8 m. Overall, the narrowest dimension ranged from 1.6–3.8 m, averaging 2 m (SD = 0.6 m). Not including the paved entry hall(?), which is 2.5 m wide, or the largest space, the other measurable rooms (n = 7) ranged from 4.8 to 14.9 sq m, averaging 8.2 sq m (SD = 4.5 sq m). The large courtyard(?) 1107 and 1108, without the reconstructed entry hall and stairs, has only 27.2 sq m of free space, while the next largest room (or smaller courtyard), 1156, is only 14.9 sq m (Dothan, 1971, p. 89a). In other words, for a house of this size, the assumed two living

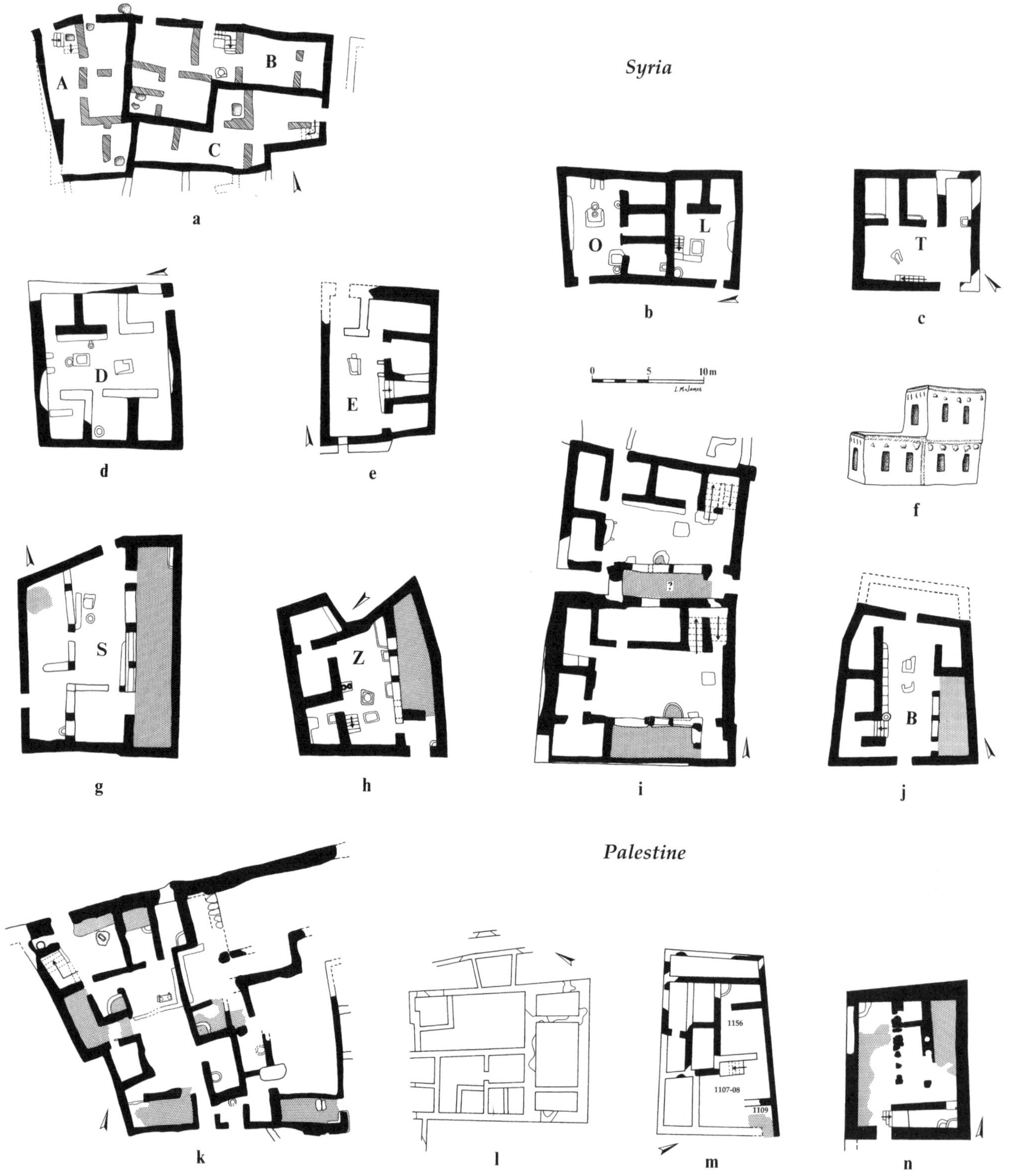
Syria
A
B
C
a
O
L
b
T
c
0 5 10m
D
d
E
e
f
S
g
Z
h
?
i
B
j
Palestine
k
l
1156
1107-08
1109
m
n

rooms will have to be looked for above the ground floor—at least for one, and most probably for both.

Ancestors of the Israelite four-room house? A second major style, derivative of the LB house series, is clearly ancestral to the typical Israelite four-room house. Typologically, spatially, and temporally removed from any known Israelite houses, it seems to have gone largely unrecognized to date. It is a variant on the standard Palestinian/Syrian MB II–LB II type with a center hall and opposing sets of smaller rooms. In the new type, an extra room may be added at the end opposite the entryway and stairs, but, more significantly, one of the long side rooms is converted to a stable through the use of pillars, the flagging or cobbling of floors, and the addition of bench-style mangers (see figures 5.g–i). The hypothetical reconstruction of figure 5.j shows a standard house similar to figure 5.d similarly modified, with a central exterior doorway (as in figure 5.g) and an added shallow broad room at the far end. The latter illustrates the one small step required for full conformity with the later standard Israelite house form. This stabled dwelling is uncommon at Tell Munbaqat, and it probably was equally uncommon at Tell Hadidi. However, its double presence at two separate sites points to its integrity as a distinct type, probably economically, ethnically, or socially determined. Because, contrary to those in the typical Israelite house, all the stables so far discovered are deep enough for horses (i.e., they range from 3.4 to 3.2 m at Tell Hadidi [figure 5.i] to 3.7–4.0 m [figure 5.g] and 3.3–3.6 m [figure 5.h] at Munbaqat). The average depth for thirteen ancient horse stables is 3.18 m [± 0.31]. The houses may be those of *maryanū* (Akk., "charioteers"). [*See* Chariots.] The plan may, however, also suit a trader (housing pack donkeys—although the stalls are much deeper than would be necessary). Generic agriculturalists (housing traction animals) seem ruled out on the grounds that most of the residents of Munbaqat and similar sites probably were agriculturalists and managed without stables in their houses. [*See* Stables.]

◀ HOUSE: SYRO-PALESTINIAN. Figure 5. *Late Bronze Age houses.* (a) Part of a complex insula from Ras Shamra-Ugarit, with three distinct "houses," A-C (after Yon et al., 1987, pl. 1); (b–c) Tell Munbaqat, houses with small rooms on one side of a large roofed hall, cf. the location of the staircase in (c) (after Machule et al., 1993, figs. 12 and 18, houses L, O, and T); (d) Tell Munbaqat, house with rooms on opposite sides of a large hall (after Machule et al., 1993; fig. 18, house D); (e) Tell Munbaqat, house with rooms on two adjacent sides of a large hall (after Machule et al., 1993), fig. 18, house E); (f) Tell ʿAṭchana-Alalakh, model house (after Woolley, 1955, pl. 9b; cf. Margueron, 1976, pp. 213–227); (g–h) Syrian houses incorporating pillared stables with hardened standings (= "Proto-Israelite"?) (after Machule et al., 1992, fig. 14, house S, and 1993, fig. 12, house Z); (i) as (g–h) above, Tell Hadidi, "Tablet Building" and its northern counterpart (after Dornemann, 1981, fig. 2); (j) hypothetical alteration of a LB II house plan from Tell Munbaqat (after Machule et al. 1992, fig. 14, house B), incorporating a pillared, hardened stable area and a transverse "rear room" (top), to illustrate the very slight distance between some LB II houses at Tell Munbaqat and the typical Israelite four-room house; (k) Hazor, LB II, an ill-defined, multi-accessed building complex of area F, stratum 1B (after Yadin et al., 1960, pl. 210), possibly witnessing to long-term multiple hereditary/sale ownership resulting in a "common" first story with various living rooms on the second story (see text); (1) Ashdod insula-type house (after Dothan, 1975, p. 108); (m) Ashdod insula-type house attributed to the late Iron II period, but probably to be dated to the Late Bronze II period (see text; after Dothan, 1971, plan 8, building 1); (n) Tell Batash-Timnah, LB IIA pillared house 341, with hardened standings and probable mangers (cf. (g) above; after Kelm and Mazar, 1982, figs. 8–10). (Courtesy J. S. Holladay)

Building 314 at Tel Batash/Timnah belongs to the late fourteenth century BCE (see figure 5.n), based on finds that include Mycenaean and Base-Ring II wares (Kelm and Mazar, 1982, pp. 9–13, figs. 8–10, 12). It appears to be roughly contemporary with the Syrian buildings listed above and is characterized by standings hardened with flagstones and mangers, partly made of wood, toward the northern end of the eastern aisle at about 2.75 m deep. The depth of the standings is below ancient means for horse stables but is equal to Edwin Gunn's minimal specifications (Gunn, 1935). The pillars were of wood, set on flagstone bases. The upper part of the stairs were also made of wood. The excavators describe center and western aisles as floored with thick lime plaster (Kelm and Mazar, 1982, pp. 9, 11). The semicircular floor-level manger presumably provided for the sheep and goats confined at night. The staircase, immediately before the outer doorway, and the debris from the second-floor collapse mark the second floor as the residence of a wealthy important individual with widespread connections, as evidenced by five cylinder seals of widely diverse origins, including Mitanni and Cyprus, and two Egyptian scarabs. Inclusive of interior walls and the stairway, the lower floor covered 98 sq m, and, with thinner walls, the upper floor would have added up to more than 100 sq m—again inclusive of interior walls and the stairway area. Only two small storerooms were located on the lower floor—seemingly not enough to support an agriculturalist interpretation of the owner's livelihood. In itself, this building, which may well have belonged to a trader or to a *maryanū* warrior (a curated arrowhead and javelin head[s?] as well as bronze mace heads and spearheads were recovered), goes far toward establishing close connections between inland Syria and southern Palestine during the period of Egyptian imperialism in Palestine (Kelm and Mazar, 1982, fig. 1, p. 12). [*See* Weapons and Warfare.] The Tell Munbaqat and Tell Hadidi exemplars (figures 5.g–i), though considerably different, lessen the singularity of this Palestinian example.

Hittite houses. As Jean-Claude Margueron (1980) has shown, the typical LB house form (see figures 6.c, f) at ancient Emar/Meskene, a site on the Middle Euphrates near Munbaqat and Tell Hadidi, is similar to the (local style) houses of the Old Assyrian colony at Kültepe/Kaneš (see figure 6.a) and virtually identical to those (see figure 6.b) from contemporary (fourteenth–thirteenth centuries BCE) Boğazköy (Margueron, 1980, figs. 4 and 5). [*See* Emar; Kaneš; Boğazköy.] It is also, with a two-room variant, the principal house form found at MB II Tell Halawa (Meyer and Orthmann, 1989, pp. 20–33, fig. 6; see figure 4.c). Although it appears at many sites, the highly standardized plan is not that of Emar's immediate neighbors (Meijer, 1989, pp. 227–229). Margueron (1980) concludes that Emar was a Hittite colony but it is probably better understood as an entrepôt of a widespread and well-connected Hittite trade diaspora (Curtin, 1984, esp. pp. 1–14). This is not altogether unexpected, considering the role of the Hittites in the Levant in the late fourteenth–thirteenth centuries BCE (Roaf, 1990, pp. 137–139) and the perduring role of the Middle Euphrates in interarea trade (e.g., Dion, 1995, pp. 70–71). More significantly, it opens up vistas with respect to other Hittite *karum*like settlements (Akk., "community of merchants") in the suburbs of some major Hittite cities (Larsen, 1976; Veenhof, 1972; Eidem, 1991).

Significant with respect to this trade and its international significance are three clay *Räucherbecken* from Tell Halawa (Meyer and Orthmann, 1989, pp. 32–33, fig. 14) and the fifteen caskets and three troughs from Emar (Margueron, 1982), that resemble Late Iron II and Persian-period limestone and pottery cuboidal incense altars from North and South Arabia, Babylonia, Palestine, and Tell el-Maskhuta in the eastern Nile Delta (Stern, 1973). [*See* Altars; Delta; Maskhuta, Tell el-.] Because these altars virtually define the course of the incense trade during the Iron II through Hellenistic periods, it seems highly probable that their MB and LB ceramic parallels stand in the same relationship to the Middle Euphrates trade in South Arabian aromatics during the second millennium BCE.

Following the lead of Margueron (1980, figs. 6a–b, 7, 8), these Hittite settlements would include a large predecessor colony in stratum 2 at MB II Tell Halawa, isolated LB houses at Alalakh (stratum IV) and Hama (stratum G I), an LB II quarter at Hazor (area C, stratum 1A–B; see below), and probably the port of Tell Abu Hawam stratum IV (see figure 6.d, e). [*See* Hama; Abu Hawam, Tell.] To these may

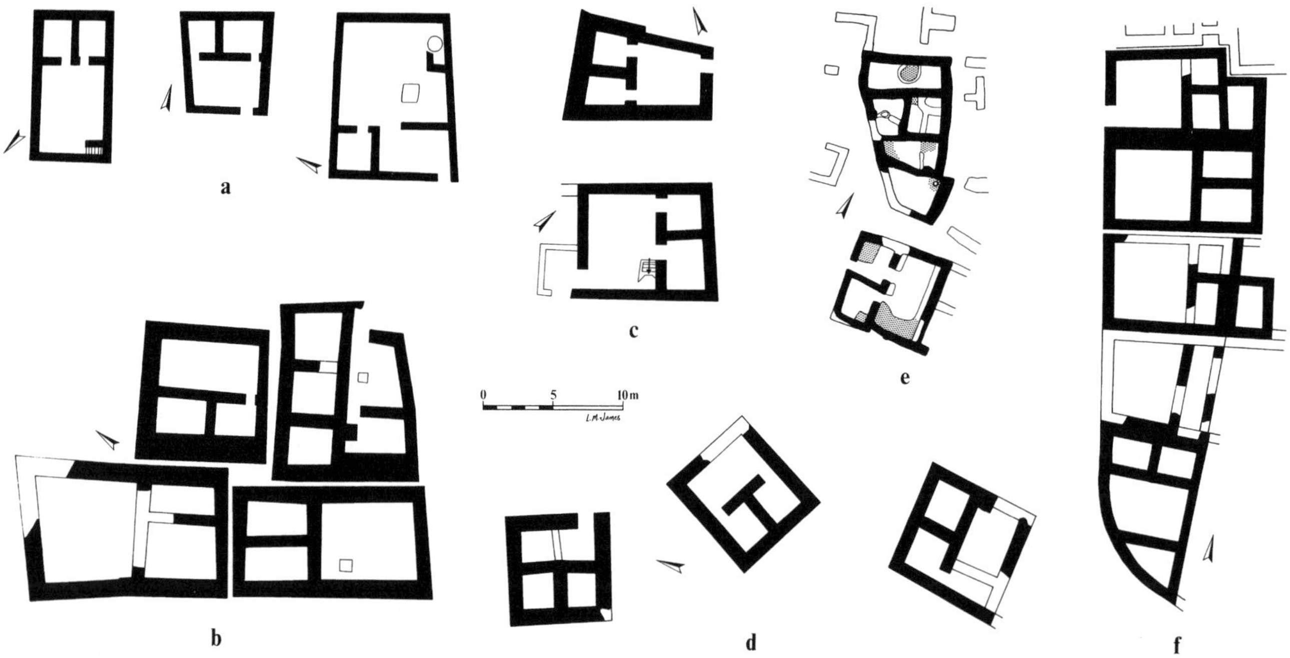

HOUSE: SYRO-PALESTINIAN. Figure 6. *Hittite MB II and LB II houses, with similar Syrian and Palestinian LB II exemplars (see also figure 4.c).* (a) Typically Hittite MB IIA houses from the Old Assyrian *karum Kaneš* at Kültepe (after Margueron, 1980, fig. 5); (b) "deconstructed" LB II Hittite houses from Boğazköy (after Margueron, 1980, fig. 5); (c) LB II houses from Meskene-Emar (after Margueron, 1980, fig. 1); (d) Tell Abu Hawam stratum IV houses (after Margueron, 1980, fig. 8); (e) LB II houses from area C, stratum 1A–B at Hazor (after Yadin et al., 1960 pl. 208, cf. (f) below); (f) a "deconstructed" block of houses from Meskene-Emar (after Margueron, 1980, fig. 2b). (Courtesy J. S. Holladay)

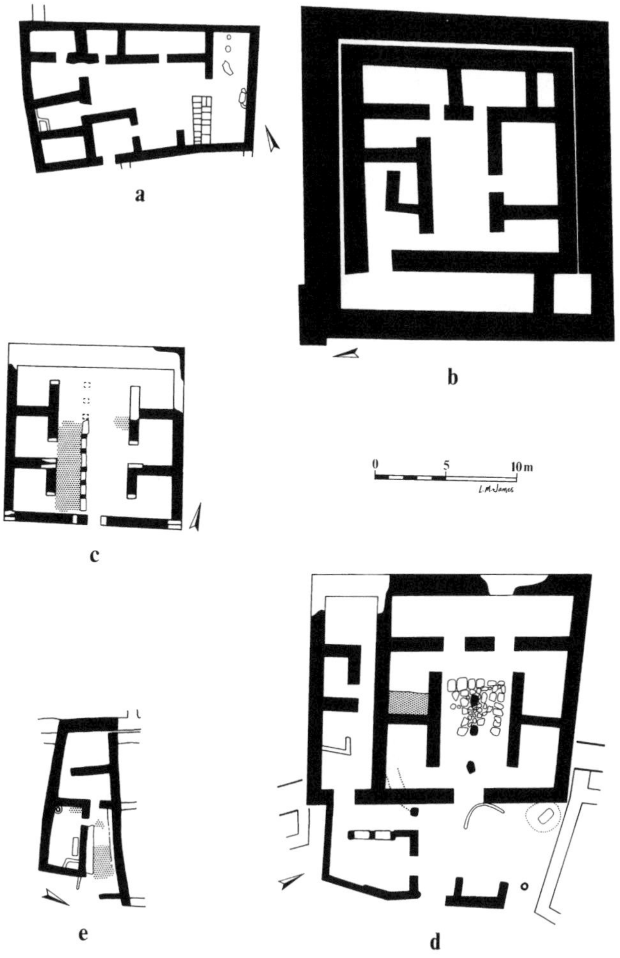

HOUSE: SYRO-PALESTINIAN. Figure 7. *"Canaanite" or "Phoenician" houses with Late Bronze Age antecedents in Iron Age II Israel/Judah.* (a) Tell Masos area H, stratum II house 314 (after Fritz and Wittstock, 1983, pp. 39–43, plan 14); (b) "Phoenician Fort" or fortified trader's residence at Ḥorvat Rosh Zayit (after Gal, 1992); (c) elite residence at Hazor (after Yadin et al., 1960, pl. 204); (d) "Northwest Tower" or governmental residence at Tell Beit Mirsim, from a late component of stratum A (after Albright, 1943, pl. 6); (e) Hazor stratum V, house 14, distinguished by a phoenicianizing cultic assemblage (after Yadin et al., 1960, pl. 203). (Courtesy J. S. Holladay)

be added a possible example from LB Tell Keisan (Niveau 9, squares J11–K11: Briend and Humbert, 1980, pl. 3). It would not be surprising to find a few at Tell ed-Dabʿa/ancient Avaris (cf. Holladay, n.d.; Holladay et al., forthcoming). [*See* Dabʿa, Tell ed-.] A close study of Margueron's lone Hazor exemplar in its surroundings (1980; see figure 6.e) reveals other links with the architecture of Emar (figure 6.f), suggesting that this entire quarter, with its outlandish stele shrine, may be a substantive Hittite *karum,* complete with Hittite architecture and its own shrine.

Egyptian houses. Recognition of Egyptian Amarnalike villas—which can be traced back to the twelfth dynasty—in the Levant must begin with houses 1500 (see figure 10.a) and 1700 at Beth-Shean (James, 1966, pp. 8–13), together with their center-hall predecessors (James and McGovern, 1993, vol. 1, pp. 4–5, 27–56). [*See* Amarna, Tell el-; Villa.] Unquestionably "domestic," they provide the lens through which the Tananir villas (Boling, 1975; see figure 10.b), the Amman Airport Temple (Herr, 1983), and the LB Egyptian governors' residencies (see Daviau, 1993, pp. 403–434) can be reassessed. [*See* Amman Airport Temple.] None betrays any significant body of cult trappings (charred human bones are not proof of cult performances). It seems likely that the anomalous "mansion" (figure 10.c) at Tell Selenkahiye, on the Middle Euphrates, also fits this pattern, rather than that of the nascent *bit-ḫilani.* The mansion is dated to the twenty-second and twenty-first centuries BCE (Meijer, 1989, pp. 226–227), but dates assigned to materials in northern Syria do not necessarily correlate with those in either Egypt, Palestine, or Transjordan.

Iron Age: "Canaanite" and Phoenician Plans. Aside from the early four- and three-room houses known from the central hill country and Galilee, very little is known about Iron I houses. At Tel Qiri, later walls left in place and digging into the spaces between them leaves too much responsibility to the restorer (Ben-Tor et al., 1987, pp. 98–99, photo 44). [*See* Qiri, Tel.] During the Early Iron II period, in addition to large, somewhat unusual versions of typically Israelite houses, at Tel Masos a clearly trade-related version of the standard Syrian LB house (stratum II, area H, house 314) was found (Fritz and Kempinski, 1983; Fritz and Wittstock, in Fritz and Kempinski, 1983, pp. 39–43, plan 14). In this case there are rooms on all four sides (cf. figures 5.e and 7.a). Entrance was through a hall, as in the larger houses at Munbaqat (see above). A similar house (house 96)—probably belonging to a coppersmith—was found in area A, stratum II (Kempinski et al., in Fritz and Kempinski, 1983, pp. 20–21, plans 3, 6). In both cases, the ground floor was given over to storerooms and work areas, probably in addition to providing overnight shelter to domestic animals.

The plan of the Phoenician fort at Ḥorvat Rosh Zayit (Gal, 1992; see figure 7.b), more plausibly a fortified Phoenician trader's residence, is essentially the same as the foregoing example, and, in view of the Phoenician contents of Tel Masos house 314, probably affords a view of a typical tenth-century BCE Phoenician house plan. Somewhat later, three examples of a large version of the standard Syrian LB house with storerooms on two opposing sides of a hall are found in the elite quarter at Hazor, stratum VIII, area B. Two of the houses also included a stable area. The stables' pillars served to support the spanning timbers (cf. figures 4.b, d and 6.c). The respective free spans without the pillars are 4.5 m (house 3100) and 5 m (house 3067/3235); with the pillars, the longest free spans are 2 m and 2.9 m. In the absence of clear evidence, it is best to assume that the buildings were always pillared. While pillars and mangers are not shown in the featureless strata VIII–VI "courtyard" plans, some of the pillars and manger elements in each house are in fact founded below the claimed earlier—and unnaturally constant—floor levels, while others are higher. Over the 130-year-plus life of these buildings, some rebuilding must have occurred. House 3208 lacked the stables and had a free span of about 3.3 m. The much later northwest tower at Tell Beit Mirsim has a similar plan (see figure 7.d), although with a rear room, an added side hall (both features modeled after late four-room houses), and the stable relocated to the house's forecourt. Free spans in the northwest tower's central hall ranged from 4.7–5 m, but a centered line of three large stones probably indicates a row of wooden pillars, reducing the required free spans to less than 2.5 m.

A Phoenician probably lived in house 14 at Hazor in stratum V (figure 7.e)—inferred by the anomalous benches and cult materials found in its innermost room (Yadin et al., 1960, pls. 57:22, 60:10). [*See* Cult.] The plan differs in several respects from that of the preceding wineshops (buildings 14a and 111), so it may contain "Phoenician" elements. In the absence of better information about Phoenician houses of the late eighth century BCE, it is difficult to be certain.

Philistine houses. Two large stratum 5C–A houses (Iron I, c. 1125–1050 BCE) at Gezer may be Philistine (see figures 8.a–b), but they share the common Syro-Palestinian plan of the standard MB–LB house with rooms on three sides (Dever et al., 1986). [*See* Gezer.] During the Late Iron II period, Tel Batash/Timnah presents a plan somewhat like an Israelite three-room house (see figure 8.c). However, the proportions—in particular the depth of the rear rooms—fall outside the ranges seen in Israelite and Judean houses. The plans of two late seventh-century BCE houses from Tel Miqne/Ekron further help to define this uniquely Philistine plan (figure 8.d). [*See* Miqne, Tel.]

Babylonian (?) houses. Following the incorporation of Megiddo into the Assyrian provincial system, a new style of insula housing (figure 9.a), apparently opaque to the sorts of nuclear-family analyses afforded by the local Canaanite, Israelite (Stager 1985; Holladay, 1995, pp. 386–389), Syrian, Hittite, Phoenician, and (some) Philistine house forms, was introduced in strata III–II (Lamon and Shipton, 1939, pp. 62–74). A logical inference might be that these are some form of dwelling place based on social norms involving co-residence, presumably of the extended family—but, by virtue of multiple lines of inheritance and sales or through, perhaps, temple housing projects (in the case of Megiddo, governmental housing projects) or an approximation of modern apartments or "cooperative" residences and condominiums (Yon, 1992, p. 704; Stone, 1987, p. 76). Biblical materials (*2 Kgs.* 17:24), the presence of Babylonian-styled grater bowls (Zertal, 1989), and a direct comparison of plans with Babylonian house plans (figure 9.b) all produce converging lines of evidence pointing to a wholesale replacement of native "Israelite" populations and forms of architecture with Babylonian and Assyrian (figure 9.c) forms. One of the smaller and best-preserved insulae is shown in figure 9.a. Locus 1490 and the large area north of locus 1466 were much larger than any other spaces and must be considered courtyards (roughly 61 and 44 sq m, respectively). Also, ignoring the three smallest areas, the average room size was 17.7 sq m (SD = 6.5 sq m, n = 11), and the average length of the beams required (free span, not including bearing lengths) was 2.53 m (SD = 0.27 m). Given virtually no information about the small finds or features other than bins (mangers), drains, ovens, and paved areas, it is difficult to arrive at useful conclusions about room usage or the need for a second story. There are some plan indications of possible staircases, however, and wall widths throughout appear adequate to the demands of a second story. Given the prevalence of required second stories in other periods and areas, it is reasonable to reconstruct these buildings as largely two-storied as well.

Conclusions. There was considerable uniformity in domestic architecture in antiquity across both Syria and Pal-

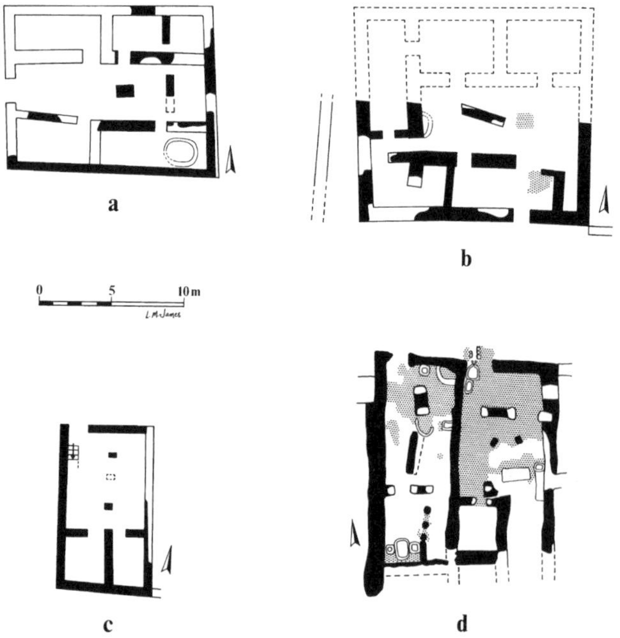

HOUSE: SYRO-PALESTINIAN. Figure 8. *Philistine houses, Iron Age I to II.* (a–b) Two large stratum 5C–A houses (Iron I, c. 1125–1050 BCE) at Gezer (after Dever et al., 1986) adapted from the typical Syro-Palestinian plan of the "standard" MB–LB house with rooms on three sides; (c) Tel Batash/Timnah, late Iron II, strata III–II, house 743, note location of stairway (after Kelm and Mazar, 1982, fig. 27); (d) Miqne-Ekron, two late seventh century BCE buildings, presumably houses with living quarters above and olive presses on the ground floor (after Gitin, 1989, fig. 2.3). (Courtesy J. S. Holladay)

HOUSE: SYRO-PALESTINIAN. Figure 9. *Assyrian and Babylonian buildings in Israel/Judah, Iron Age II.* (a) Megiddo stratum III, small insula house, probably Babylonian, with two courtyards (after Lamon and Shipton, 1939, pp. 62–74, fig. 72); (b) part of a Neo-Babylonian insula from Ur (after Castel, 1992, pl. 4); (c) Megiddo stratum III, Neo-Assyrian palace-fort 1369 (after Lamon and Shipton, 1939, fig. 89). The average free span is 4.2 m (SD = 0.3), that of the throne-room (bottom) is 5.4 m, perhaps nearing the practical limit of unsupported Cedar of Lebanon beams. (Courtesy J. S. Holladay)

estine, where a reasonably large body of data exists, as well as some diversity. The uniformity is particularly evident in the second millennium BCE, which has a great deal to say about shared perceptions and common cultural conventions. Differences exhibited by foreign styles are equally evident. For the first time a network is seen along which a Hittite trade diaspora operated and, later, traces of Phoenicians operative within Israel and Judah. We also are given tantalizing glimpses into the ancestory of Israel's distinctive houses. Given the nature of sites uniformly selected for archaeological investigation (city mounds), it is not surprising that to find the space required for a suitable living room, probably averaging nearer 25 sq m than 20 sq m for most of the second and first millennia BCE, attention must system-

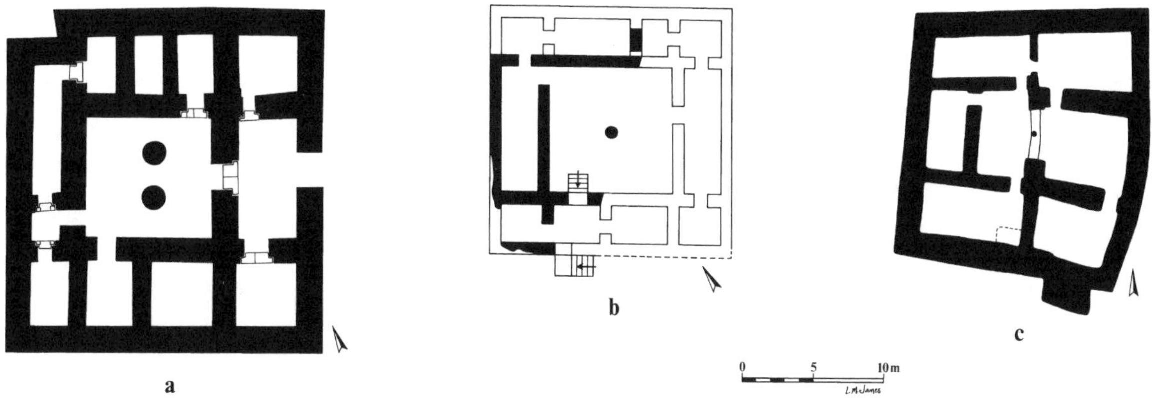

HOUSE: SYRO-PALESTINIAN. Figure 10. *Egyptian or egyptianizing villas, EB to Iron Age I.* (a) Beth-Shean, Iron I, stratum VI house 1500 (after James, 1966 p. 9); (b) Tananir, MB IIC building A (after Boling, 1975, fig. 2); (c) Tell Selenkahiya, late EB "Mansion" (after Meijer, 1977, p. 121) (Courtesy of J. S. Holladay)

atically turn to the now-vanished second story. This points up one of the chief benefits of working out the present model. In effect, we have created a series of hypotheses for testing in future fieldwork. To date we have almost completely ignored the evidence for mud-brick buildings' superstructures. In particular, the practice of systematically shattering collapsed brickwork (originally pieces of floors, walls, ceilings, and roofs, all, one way or another, different in composition and conformation, and all with distinctive faces to their fragments) to powder in the process of "clearing" stone foundations has resulted in the loss of information we can obtain in no other way. Perhaps soon, surely later, all practicing archaeologists will recognize that a clump of mud-bricky material is potentially as informative as a carved stone architectural fragment, and then we will begin patiently to piece together what has been regarded as lost beyond recall. While sufficient information is still lacking with which to reconstruct the domestic structures of Iron Age Syria and Lebanon, within the small territory of Israel, Judah, and the Philistine coast there is considerable diversity, seemingly following ethnic (Philistines, Israelites) and socioeconomic lines (elite housing at Hazor, the northwest tower at Tell Beit Mirsim; the probable Canaanite/Phoenician houses at Tel Masos, Ḥorvat Rosh Zayit, Hazor house 14). This may be a reflection of political boundaries and ethnic/nationalist differentiation on the one hand, and trade, professional expertise, and international commerce on the other. Finally, when we begin to see and understand where people—families—of the distant past ate, slept, and stored their treasures and the work of their hands, we will also begin, however imperfectly, to recognize the bonds of common humanity that link their generations with ours.

[*See also* Four-room House.]

BIBLIOGRAPHY

Albright, William Foxwell, ed. *The Excavation of Tell Beit Mirsim,* vol. 2, *The Bronze Age.* Annual of the American Schools of Oriental Research, 17. New Haven, 1938.

Albright, William Foxwell, ed. *The Excavation of Tell Beit Mirsim,* vol. 3, *The Iron Age.* Annual of the American Schools of Oriental Research, 21–22. New Haven, 1943.

Amiran, Ruth, and Avraham Eitan. "A Canaanite-Hyksos City at Tell el-Nagile." *Archaeology* 18 (1965): 113–123.

Amiran, Ruth, and Avraham Eitan. "Nagila, Tel." In *Encyclopedia of Archaeological Excavations in the Holy Land,* vol. 3, pp. 894–898. Jerusalem, 1977.

Amiran, Ruth, et al. *Early Arad,* vol. 1, *The Chalcolithic Settlement and Early Bronze Age City, First–Fifth Seasons of Excavations, 1962–1966.* Jerusalem, 1978.

Banning, E. B. "Houses, Compounds, and Mansions in the Prehistoric Near East." In *People Who Lived in Big Houses: Archaeological Perspectives on Large Domestic Structures,* edited by Gary Coupland and E. B. Banning, pp. 165–185. Madison, Wis., 1996.

Bar-Yosef, Ofer et al. "*Nawamis* and Habitation Sites near Gebel Gunna, Southern Sinai." *Israel Exploration Journal* 27 (1986): 121–167.

Beit-Arieh, Itzhaq. "A Pattern of Settlement in Southern Sinai and Southern Canaan in the Third Millennium B.C." *Bulletin of the American Schools of Oriental Research,* no. 243 (1981): 31–55.

Ben-Dov, Meir. "Middle and Late Bronze Age Dwellings." In *The Architecture of Ancient Israel: From the Prehistoric to the Persian Periods,* edited by Aharon Kempinski and Ronny Reich, pp. 99–104. Jerusalem, 1992.

Bennett, Crystal-M. "Excavations at Buseirah, Southern Jordan, 1974: Fourth Preliminary Report." *Levant* 9 (1977): 1–10.

Ben-Tor, Amnon, et al. *Tell Qiri, a Village in the Jezreel Valley: Report of the Archaeological Excavations, 1975–1978.* Qedem, vol. 24. Jerusalem, 1987.

Ben-Tor, Amnon. "Early Bronze Age Dwellings and Installations." In *The Architecture of Ancient Israel: From the Prehistoric to the Persian Periods,* edited by Aharon Kempinski and Ronny Reich, pp. 51–67. Jerusalem, 1992.

Boling, Robert G. "Excavations at Tananir, 1968." In *Report on Archaeological Work at Ṣuwwānet, eth-Thanīya, Tananir, and Khirbet Minḥa (Munḥhata),* edited by George M. Landes, pp. 25–85. Missoula, 1975.

Braun, Eliot. "The Problem of the Apsidal House: New Aspects of Early Bronze I Domestic Architecture in Israel, Jordan, and Lebanon." *Palestine Exploration Quarterly* 21 (1989): 1–43.

Briend, Jacques, and Jean-Baptiste Humbert. *Tell Keisan, 1971–1976: Une cité phénicienne en Galilée.* Fribourg and Paris, 1980.

Campbell, Edward F. "Archaeological Reflections on Amos's Target." In *Scripture and Other Artifacts: Essays on the Bible and Archaeology in Honor of Philip J. King,* edited by Michael David Coogan et al., pp. 32–52. Louisville, Ky., 1994.

Castel, Corrine. *Habitat Urbain Néo-Assyrien et Néo-Babylonien de l'espace Bâti . . . à l'espace vécu. Tomb 2.* Paris, 1992.

Cohen, Rudolph, and William G. Dever. "Preliminary Report of the Second Season of the 'Central Negev Highlands Project.'" *Bulletin of the American Schools of Oriental Research,* no. 236 (1979): 41–60.

Cohen, Rudolph, and William G. Dever. "Preliminary Report of the Third and Final Season of the 'Central Negev Highlands Project.'" *Bulletin of the American Schools of Oriental Research,* no. 243 (1981): 57–77.

Curtin, Philip D. *Cross-Cultural Trade in History.* Cambridge, 1984.

Daviau, Paulette M. "Michèle." *Houses and Their Furnishings in Bronze Age Palestine: Domestic Activity Areas and Artefact Distribution in the Middle and Late Bronze Ages.* Sheffield, 1993.

Dever, William G. "New Vistas on the EB IV ('MB I') Horizon in Syria-Palestine." *Bulletin of the American Schools of Oriental Research,* no. 237 (1980): 35–64.

Dever, William G. "Village Planning at Be'er Resisim and Socioeconomic Structure in Early Bronze Age IV Palestine" (in Hebrew). *Eretz-Israel* 18 (1985): 18–28.

Dever, William G., et al. *Gezer IV: The 1969–71 Seasons in Field VI, the "Acropolis."* Jerusalem, 1986.

Dion, P. E. "Les Araméens du Moyen-Euphrate." In *Congress Volume, Paris 1992,* pp. 53–73. Supplements to Vetus Testamentum, 61. Leiden, 1995.

Dornemann, Rudolph H. "The Late Bronze Age Pottery Tradition at Tell Hadidi, Syria." *Bulletin of the American Schools of Oriental Research,* no. 241 (1981): 29–47.

Dothan, Moshe. "Excavations at Meṣer, 1956." *Israel Exploration Journal* 9 (1959): 13–29.

Dothan, Moshe. *Ashdod II–III: The Second and Third Seasons of Excavations, 1963, 1965, Soundings in 1967.* ʿAtiqot, 9. Jerusalem, 1971.

Dothan, Moshe. "Ashdod." In *Encyclopedia of Archaeological Excavations in the Holy Land,* vol. 1, pp. 103–119. Jerusalem, 1975.

Eidem, Jesper. "An Old Assyrian Treaty from Tell Leilan." In *Marchands, diplomates et empereurs,* edited by Dominique Charpin and Francis Joannès, pp. 185–207. Paris, 1991.

Flannery, Kent V. "The Origins of the Village as a Settlement Type in Mesoamerica and the Near East: A Comparative Study." In *Man, Settlement, and Urbanism*, edited by Peter Ucko et al., pp. 21–53. Cambridge, Mass., 1972.

Fritz, Volkmar, and Aharon Kempinski. *Ergebnisse der Ausgrabungen auf der Hirbet el-Msas (Tel Masos), 1972–75*. Wiesbaden, 1983. See "1.1.3. Area H" (pp. 36–44.) and "1.1.1. Area A" (pp. 7–33.).

Gal, Zvi. "Ḥurbat Rosh Zayit and the Early Phoenician Pottery." *Levant* 24 (1992): 173–186.

Gitin, Seymour. "Tel Miqne-Ekron: A Type-Site for the Inner Coastal Plain in the Iron Age II Period." In *Recent Excavations in Israel: Studies in Iron Age Archaeology*, edited by Seymour Gitin and William G. Dever, pp. 23–58. Annual of the American Schools of Oriental Research, 49. Winona Lake, Ind., 1989.

Grant, Elihu, and G. Ernest Wright. *Ain Shems Excavations*. Parts 4–5. Haverford, 1938–1939.

Gunn, Edwin. *Farm Buildings New and Applied*. Surrey, 1935.

Haiman, Mordechai. "Agriculture and Nomad-State Relations in the Negev Desert in the Byzantine and Early Islamic Periods." *Bulletin of the American Schools of Oriental Research*, no. 297 (1995): 29–54.

Hall, G., et al. "Architectural Analysis." In David H. French et al., "Aşvan, 1968–72: An Interim Report." *Anatolian Studies* (1973): 245–269.

Helms, S. W. *Jawa: Lost City of the Black Desert*. London, 1981.

Herbordt, Suzanne, et al. "Ausgrabungen in Tall Bi'a 1981." *Mitteilungen der Deutschen Orient-Gesellschaft zu Berlin* 114 (1982): 79–101.

Herr, Larry G., ed. *The Amman Airport Excavations, 1976*. Annual of the American Schools of Oriental Research, 48. Winona Lake, Ind., 1983.

Hestrin, Ruth. "Beth Yeraḥ." In *Encyclopedia of Archaeological Excavations in the Holy Land*, vol. 1, pp. 253–262. Jerusalem, 1975.

Holladay, John S. "House, Israelite." In *The Anchor Bible Dictionary*, vol. 3, pp. 308–318. New York, 1992a.

Holladay, John S. "Stable, Stables." In *The Anchor Bible Dictionary*, vol. 6, pp. 178–183. New York, 1992b.

Holladay, John S. "The Eastern Nile Delta during the Hyksos and Pre-Hyksos Periods: Towards a Systemic/Socioeconomic Understanding." Unpub. ms., n.d. An introductory study of ancient Near Eastern diasporas, with special reference to Tell ed-Daʿba/Avaris and Tell el-Maskhuta.

Holladay, John S. "The Kingdoms of Israel and Judah: Political and Economic Centralization in the Iron IIA–B (ca. 1000–750 BCE)." In *The Archaeology of Society in the Holy Land*, edited by Thomas E. Levy, pp. 368–398. New York, 1995.

Holladay, John S., et al. *The Wadi Tumilat Project II: Tell el-Maskhuta, the Middle Bronze Age*. Forthcoming.

Hopkins, David C. *The Highlands of Canaan: Agricultural Life in the Early Iron Age*. Sheffield, 1985.

Hunter-Anderson, Rosalind L. "A Theoretical Approach to the Study of House Form." In *For Theory Building in Archaeology*, edited by Lewis R. Binford, pp. 287–315. New York, 1977.

Jacobs, Linda K. "Tell-i Nun: Archaeological Implications of a Village in Transition." In *Ethnoarchaeology: Implications of Ethnography for Archaeology*, edited by Carol Kramer, pp. 175–191. New York, 1979.

James, Francis W. *The Iron Age at Beth Shan: A Study of Levels VI–IV*. Philadelphia, 1966.

James, Francis W., and Patrick E. McGovern. *The Late Bronze Egyptian Garrison at Beth Shan: A Study of Levels VII and VIII*. 2 vols. Philadelphia, 1993.

Kelm, George L., and Amihai Mazar. "Three Seasons of Excavations at Tell Batash—Biblical Timnah." *Bulletin of the American Schools of Oriental Research*, no. 248 (1982): 1–36.

Kenyon, Kathleen M. *Archaeology in the Holy Land*. 3d ed. New York, 1970.

Kochavi, Moshe. "Yeruḥam, Mount." In *Encyclopedia of Archaeological Excavations in the Holy Land*, vol. 4, pp. 1219–1220. Jerusalem, 1978.

Kramer, Carol. "An Archaeological View of a Contemporary Kurdish Village: Domestic Architecture, Household Size, and Wealth." In *Ethnoarchaeology: Implications of Ethnography for Archaeology*, edited by Carol Kramer, pp. 139–163. New York, 1979.

Kramer, Carol. *Village Ethnoarchaeology: Rural Iran in Archaeological Perspective*. New York, 1982.

LaBianca, Øystein S. *Hesban*, vol. 1, *Sedentarization and Nomadization: Food System Cycles at Hesban and Vicinity in Transjordan*. Berrien Springs, Mich., 1990.

Lamon, Robert S., and Geoffrey Shipton. *Megiddo I: Seasons of 1925–34*. Oriental Institute Publications, 42. Chicago, 1939.

Larsen, Mogens T. *The Old Assyrian City-State and Its Colonies*. Copenhagen, 1976.

Loud, Gordon. *Megiddo II: Seasons of 1935–1939*. Oriental Institute Publications, 62. Chicago, 1948.

Machule, Dittmar, et al. "Ausgrabungen in Tall Munbāqa/Ekalte." *Mitteilungen der Deutschen Orient-Gesellschaft zu Berlin* 124 (1992): 11–40; 125 (1993): 69–102.

Margueron, Jean-Claude. "'Maquettes' architecturales de Meskéné-Emar." *Syria* 53 (1976): 193–232.

Margueron, Jean-Claude. "Emar: Un exemple d'implantation hittite en terre syrienne." In *Le Moyen Euphrate, zone de contacts et d'échanges: Acts du colloque de Strasbourg, 10–12 mars 1977*, edited by Jean-Claude Margueron, pp. 287–314. Leiden, 1980.

Margueron, Jean-Claude. "Les coffrets." In *Meskéné-Emar: Dix ans de travaux, 1972–1982*, edited by Dominique Beyer, pp. 95–97. Paris, 1982.

Margueron, Jean-Claude. "Emar, Capital of Aštata in the Fourteenth Century BCE." *Biblical Archaeologist* 58 (1995): 126–138.

Meijer, D. J. W. "The Excavations at Tell Selenkahiye." In *Le Moyen Euphrate, zone de contacts et d'échanges: Acts du colloque de Strasbourg, 10–12 mars 1977*, edited by Jean-Claude Margueron, pp. 117–126. Leiden, 1980.

Meijer, D. J. W. "Ground Plans and Archaeologists: On Similarities and Comparisons." In *To the Euphrates and Beyond*, edited by O. M. C. Haex et al., pp. 221–236. Rotterdam, 1989.

Meyer, Jan-Waalke, and Winfried Orthmann. "Tell Halawa A." In *Halawa 1980 bis 1986*, pp. 11–84. Saarbrücker Beiträge zur Altertumskunde, 52. Bonn, 1989.

Miroschedji, Pierre de, et al. *Yarmouth 1: Rapport sur les trois premières campagnes de fouilles à Tel Yarmouth (Israël), 1980–1982*. Paris, 1988.

Moortgat, Anton, and Ursula Moortgat-Correns. *Tell Chuera in Nordost-Syrien: Vorläufiger Bericht über die achte Grabungskampagne 1976*. Berlin, 1978.

Netzer, Ehud. "Massive Structures: Processes in Construction and Deterioration." In *The Architecture of Ancient Israel: From the Prehistoric to the Persian Periods*, edited by Aharon Kempinski and Ronny Reich, pp. 17–30. Jerusalem, 1992. See pp. 20–21 for the role of intermediate flooring in reinforcing the construction of multistory buildings.

Oren, Eliezer D. "The Early Bronze IV Period in Northern Palestine and Its Cultural and Chronological Setting." *Bulletin of the American Schools of Oriental Research*, no. 210 (1973a): 20–37.

Oren, Eliezer D. *The Northern Cemetery of Beth Shan*. Leiden, 1973b.

Oren, Eliezer D. "'Governors' Residencies' in Canaan under the New Kingdom: A Case Study of Egyptian Administration." *Journal of the Society for the Study of Egyptian Antiquities* 14 (1984): 37–56.

Roaf, Michael. *Cultural Atlas of Mesopotamia and the Ancient Near East*. New York, 1990.

Robbins, Michael C. "House Types and Settlement Patterns: An Application of Ethnology to Archaeological Interpretation." *Minnesota Archaeologist* 28.1 (1966): 3–26.

Rowe, Alan. *The Four Canaanite Temples of Beth-Shan*, vol. 1, *The Temples and Cult Objects*. Philadelphia, 1940.
Stager, Lawrence E. "The Archaeology of the Family in Ancient Israel." *Bulletin of the American Schools of Oriental Research*, no. 260 (1985): 1–35.
Stern, Ephraim. "Limestone Incense Altars." In *Beer-Sheba I: Excavations at Tel Beer-Sheba, 1969–1971 Seasons*, edited by Yohanan Aharoni, pp. 52–53. Tel Aviv, 1973.
Stone, Elizabeth C. "Texts, Architecture, and Ethnographic Analogy: Patterns of Residence in Old Babylonian Nippur." *Iraq* 43 (1981): 19–33.
Stone, Elizabeth C. *Nippur Neighborhoods*. Chicago, 1987.
Tainter, Joseph A. *The Collapse of Complex Societies*. Cambridge, 1988.
Ussishkin, David. "Excavations at Tel Lachish, 1973–1977: Preliminary Report." *Tel Aviv* 5 (1978): 1–97, pls. 1–32.
Vaux, Roland de. "Les fouilles de Tell el-Far'ah: Rapport préliminaire sur les 7e, 8e, 9e campagnes, 1958–1960." *Revue Biblique* 68 (1961): 557–592, pls. 31–46.
Veenhof, Klaas R. *Aspects of Old Assyrian Trade and Its Terminology*. Leiden, 1972.
Watson, Patty Jo. *Archaeological Ethnography in Western Iran*. Tucson, 1979.
Whiting, John W., and Barbara Ayres. "Inferences from the Shapes of Dwellings." In *Settlement Archaeology*, edited by Kwang-chih Chang, pp. 117–133. Palo Alto, Calif., 1968.
Woolley, C. Leonard. *Alalakh: An Account of the Excavations at Tell Atchana in the Hatay, 1937–1949. Oxford*, 1955.
Wright, G. Ernest. *Shechem: The Biography of a Biblical City*. New York, 1965.
Yadin, Yigael, et al. *Hazor I: An Account of the First Season of Excavations, 1955*. Jerusalem, 1958.
Yadin, Yigael, et al. *Hazor II: An Account of the Second Season of Excavations, 1956*. Jerusalem, 1960.
Yon, Marguerite, et al. "L'organisation de l'habitat." In *Ras Shamra–Ougarit 3: Le centre de la ville (38e–44e campagnes)*, edited by Marguerite Yon, pp. 11–128. Paris, 1987.
Yon, Marguerite. "Ugarit: History and Archaeology." In *The Anchor Bible Dictionary*, vol. 6, pp. 695–706. New York, 1992.
Zertal, Adam. "The Wedge-Shaped Decorated Bowl and the Origin of the Samaritans." *Bulletin of the American Schools of Oriental Research*, no. 276 (1989): 77–84.

JOHN S. HOLLADAY, JR.

Egyptian Houses

Conforming to Near Eastern custom, the Egyptian house was traditionally oriented inward, excluding the outer world and thus creating a climatic and social microcosm. The appearance of the exterior of the house was consequently of less concern to the Egyptian than the design of the interior. The furnishing of inner spaces had a greater representational value than the facade of the house, which was normally left undecorated. A minimum of openings (for example, doors and windows) guaranteed the privacy of the inhabitants and protected the microclimate of the house from outside influences. Usually the house was completely enclosed by walls; only a single door or gate provided access to the interior. Entrance areas and corridors with frequent changes of direction often served to isolate farther sections of the house. Rooms were generally organized around central elements, either halls or interior courtyards. Such nuclei may—in the widest sense—be regarded as places of gathering and the setting for communal activities. The number of central elements and their relationship to each other indicate the social status and behavior of the inhabitants. Most rooms of the house were multifunctional; few spaces were exclusively dedicated to a specific defined purpose. The larger and the more architecturally organized a house was, however, the more functionally defined the spaces became. Apart from the various social, functional, and historical factors to be discussed below, the design of houses was influenced by two environmental factors: building materials and climate.

Building Materials. In ancient Egypt, domestic buildings were traditionally made of sun-dried mud brick. More than the conceptual significance of the perishable material, mud bricks were valued for thermodynamic properties that make them well suited to the Egyptian climate. Mud bricks were an economical choice because of the abundance of the raw material and the simple production methods. Stone was employed only for special architectural elements such as door frames and column bases; roofing beams, window frames, and grills, door wings, and column shafts were usually made of wood.

Climate. The orientation and design of Egyptian houses generally incorporated two climatic factors—the sun and the cool north wind. The main rooms of the house were shielded from the direct rays of the sun by means of thick outer walls and the arrangement of the surrounding rooms. Windows and doorways were generally placed in positions that facilitated the circulation of air into the house and between the rooms. The entrance to the private apartments, for example, was usually located to the north in order to allow the cool north wind to enter the house. On the roof above the bedroom, a funnel-shaped wind trap directed the fresh air directly into the bed niche. A portico frequently shaded the doorway from the rays of the sun.

House types varied according to era, social class, and location. The principal distinction was the number of halls in the house. More complex designs were reserved for the palaces of the New Kingdom and the multistory town houses.

Houses without Halls. The simplest houses did not have developed halls; small multifunctional chambers were more or less randomly clustered around open spaces or courts that primarily functioned as service areas. The basic design of these houses reflects simple, undifferentiated living arrangements. Houses of this type have been found at several prehistoric settlement sites including Merimde, Maadi, and Hierakonpolis. The typical farmhouse of the fourth millennium BCE appears to have contained several isolated single room structures—either semisubterranean, oval mud constructions or rectangular wattle-and-daub huts—loosely arranged around yards enclosed by reed fences. In dynastic times, only members of the lowest social groups, such as unskilled laborers who were completely dependent on state institutions for their basic necessities, were sheltered in houses without developed halls. Consequently houses lacking halls may be observed most frequently in orthogonally planned settlements. In Kahun, the pyramid city of Senusert II (twelfth dynasty), for example, more than half of the population was accommodated in standardized houses occupying less than 75 sq m (807 sq. ft.). These houses were composed of small courts surrounded by several chambers. Small oven rooms next to the entrance appear to have been statutory at Kahun. Similar houses with an area of only 30 sq m are also found in the orthogonally planned settlement of the early Middle Kingdom at Tell ed-Dab'a. A special type of house lacking a developed hall is found in the military fortresses of the Middle Kingdom, mainly in Nubia. A broad courtyard, used primarily as a service area, gives access to several adjoining, individual, long chambers. Examples have been found with two (Shalfak, Semna, Uronarti), four (Mirgissa) and five (Qaṣr el-Sagha) chambers. In the New Kingdom, the appearance of increasing luxurious houses leads to the general decline of dwellings without halls.

Single-hall Houses. A hall, the meeting place of the domestic community and a reception area for guests, was a fundamental requirement for economically and socially semi-independent households—that is, families headed by lower-ranking officials, priests, artisans, and other skilled workers employed by state institutions, as well as independent farmers. The hall was the nucleus of the private life of the household and as such served as a status symbol. Access to all other private rooms of the house, usually small, multifunctional chambers was provided by the hall. Large houses inhabited by extended households had several private apartments, each with their own hall as the nucleus of a distinct unit. Apart from the private apartments, houses sometimes contained one or more entrance rooms or corridors, service areas, and various other additional chambers. The design of the house proper, comprising the hall and the

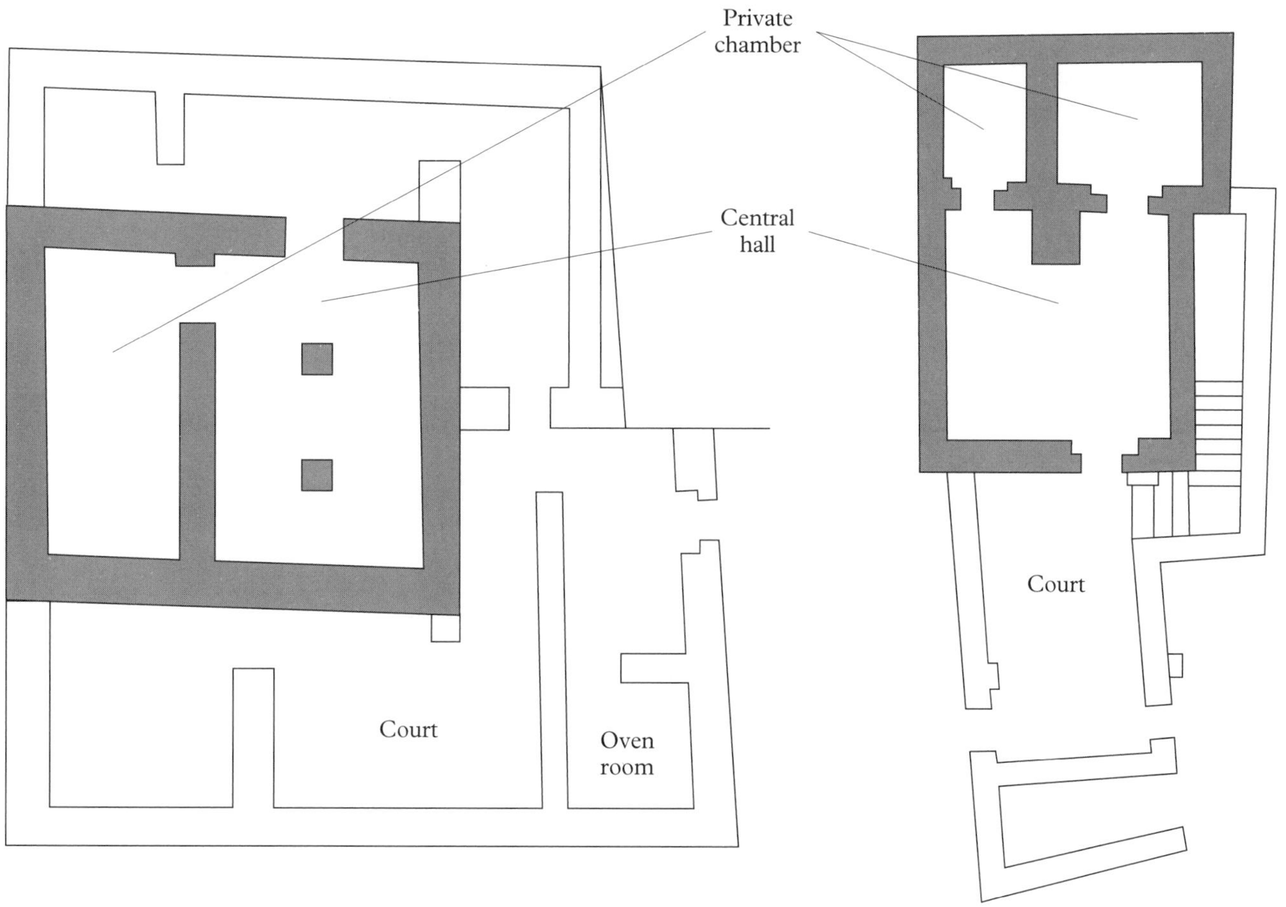

HOUSE: Egyptian Houses. Figure 1. *Single-hall houses at Lisht North.* Left: Middle Kingdom house A 1.3; Right: New Kingdom house B 4.2. (Courtesy F. Arnold)

surrounding private chambers, underwent a gradual development during Egypt's long history.

Single-hall houses of the Old Kingdom. Because the evidence for domestic buildings is particularly scarce in the Old Kingdom, it is not possible to define the characteristics of the single-hall house during this period. In the funerary complex of Queen Khentkaues at Giza, houses have been found with halls distinguished by a niche at one end, an area possibly occupied by the chair of the master of the house. The private chambers surrounded the hall on all sides.

Single-hall houses of the Middle Kingdom. In the Middle Kingdom, the house proper had a characteristic bipartite layout that has become known as the "snail house" (see figure 1a). Typically, the hall was a long or nearly square chamber, sometimes with one or more columns. The walls were frequently painted, the upper portion in yellow, the lower in black, and the area between them in stripes of various colors. A door at one end of the side wall provided access to a single long chamber, a multifunctional private room. Additional smaller private chambers were sometimes accessible from the hall. The "snail house" was usually entered from a courtyard, often partially roofed over, which was almost certainly considered part of the private apartment and was the setting for various private and public activities. In most Middle Kingdom houses, a small oven room was placed next to the entrance of the house. Although this room has been interpreted by some scholars as a household shrine, no confirmation exists.

Single-hall houses of the New Kingdom. In houses of the New Kingdom, well preserved at Amarna and Deir el-Medineh, the hall was generally broad or nearly square (see figure 1b). The walls, if painted, were usually white; a decoration of garlands is sometimes found near the roof. A dais for the chair of the master of the house is frequently built against the back wall of the hall. Emplacements for the evaporation of water during the summer and fireplaces for warmth during the winter were common. The main private chambers were located behind the back wall; other rooms could be situated along the sides of the hall. Additional chambers were frequently located on a second story, accessible by means of a staircase located next to the hall. Small shrines for household gods were sometimes found in the front portion of the house near the entrance.

Multiple-hall Houses. Higher officials of the state including the king not only had larger spatial needs, but also required rooms with more differentiated functions. Halls and private chambers with more specifically defined functions have been distinguished, reflecting the higher social status of the occupants. In Kahun, for example, about 2.5 percent of the population—economically independent officials—inhabited houses with two or more multifunctional halls.

Houses of the Middle Kingdom with two halls. The hall of the bipartite "snail house" was divided into two separate, interconnected rooms, thus creating a tripartite private apartment (see figure 2). The central hall (H), usually the largest element of the tripartite unit, appears to have served as a private hall, the nucleus of the private apartment. The second hall (H2), accessible both from the central (private) hall and through a separate outside entrance, seems to have had a more public function. A dais for the chair of the master of the house and table stands have been found in such halls, indicating that guests were received and banquets held there. In houses of this size, the third element of the tripartite unit, the private chamber, was frequently furnished with a niche in the back wall for the bed of the master, defining the chamber as a bedroom (C1). Additional chambers were usually accessible from the central private hall, some serving primarily as storerooms for private possessions, others designated as bathrooms by their installations (C2).

Houses of the Middle Kingdom with three halls (official residences). Some of the largest domestic buildings found in Egypt (the mansions at Kahun [see figure 2] and the official military residences in the fortresses of Buhen and Mirgissa in Nubia) have a third hall (H3), sometimes con-

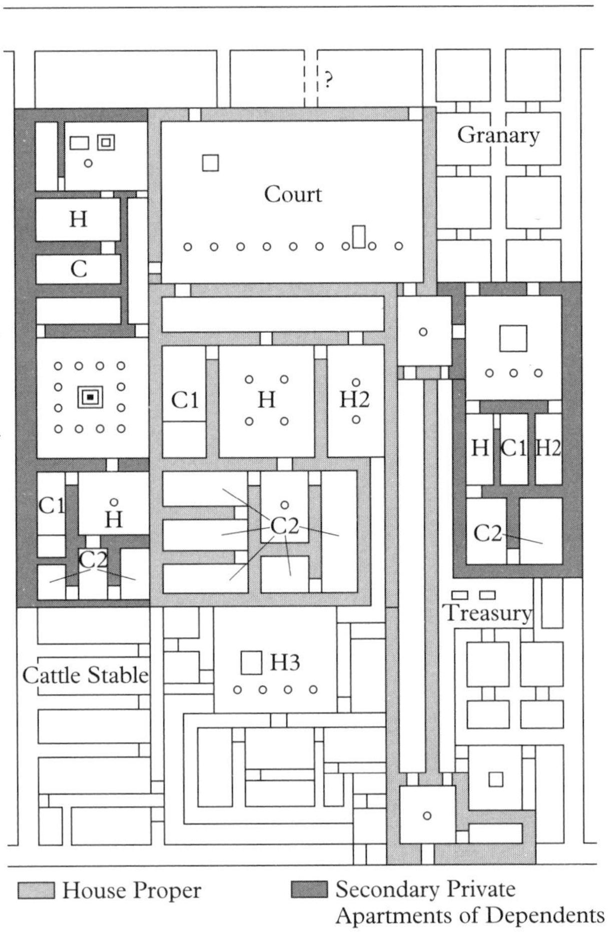

HOUSE: Egyptian Houses. Figure 2. *House of an official at Kahun.* (Courtesy F. Arnold)

structed as a courtyard surrounded by various chambers. The third hall is usually accessible both from the private apartments—either through the second hall or from the front of the court—and directly from the outside of the house, from the street or from service areas. Evidence suggests that the third hall served as an office for the master of the house, where business was transacted and official audiences were held.

Houses of the New Kingdom with two halls (the "Amarna villa"). The functional requirements of the upper class appear to have been different in the New Kingdom (see figure 3). The central hall (H) with its high ceiling car-

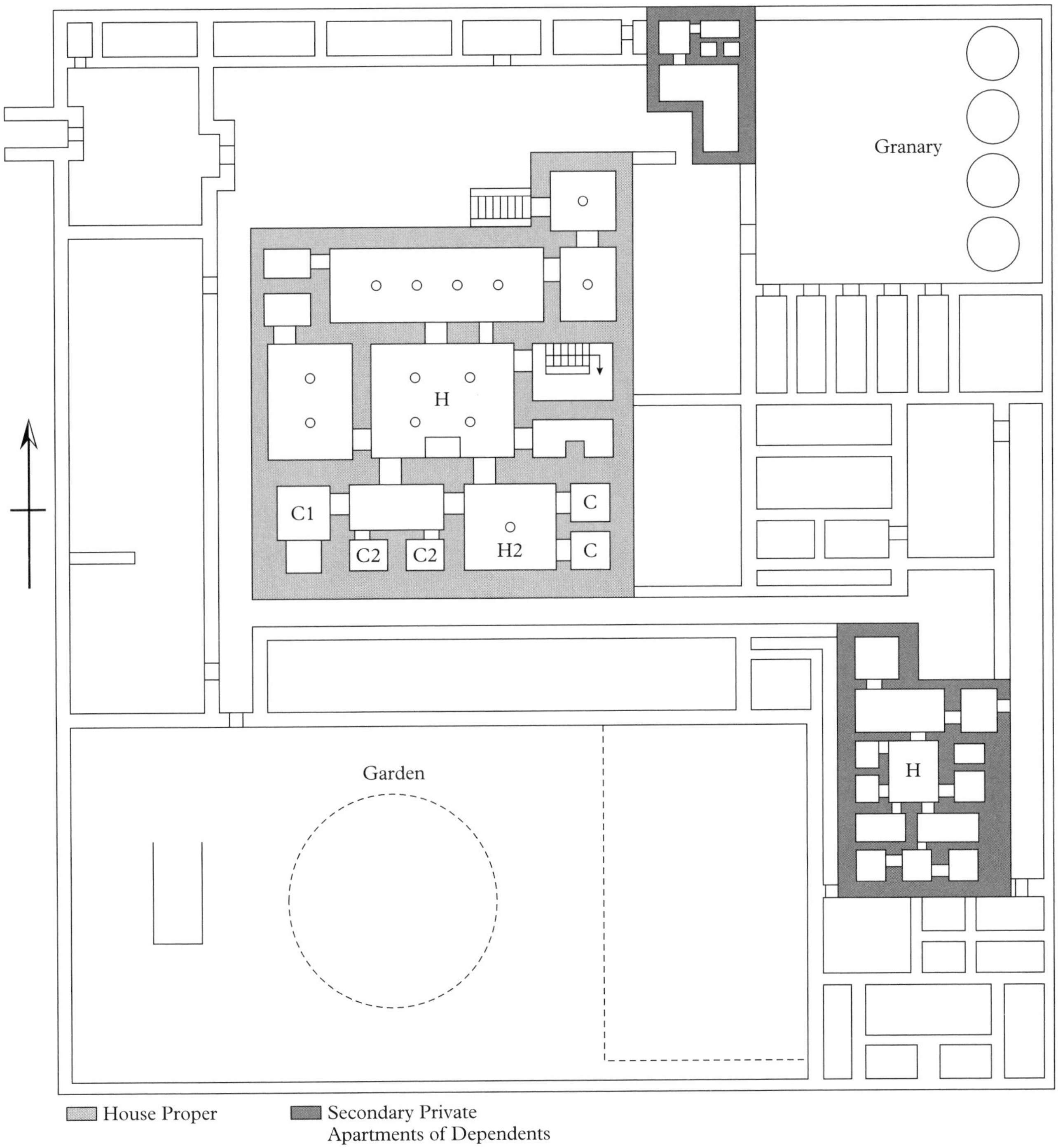

HOUSE: Egyptian Houses. Figure 3. *House of the general Ramose at Amarna* (P 47.19). (Courtesy F. Arnold)

ried by tall wooden columns rose above the rest of the building. The step created by the different ceiling levels was used for the accommodation of windows. A second smaller hall (H2) was added to the private chambers surrounding the main hall (H). Like the central hall, the second hall was usually nearly square in shape, supplied with a column, and often surrounded by small multifunctional chambers. A dais for the chair of the master of the house is found both in the central hall and in the second hall. Although the central hall was used for public functions, the second hall was a more intimate private hall for the household. The second hall was accessible both from the central hall and from the major chambers, but not from the outside. A separate connection between the second hall and the outside has been found only in the king's house at Amarna, the so-called window of appearances. As in the Middle Kingdom, houses with two halls usually have private chambers with specifically defined functions, including a bedroom with a narrow bed niche, a bathroom and storerooms. Bathrooms, separated from the toilet by a screen wall, were equipped with two basins, one for washing and another for drainage. The villa was surrounded by a large court filled with trees and plants; a water shaft was accessible by means of a spiral staircase. The complex included groups of huge, beehive-shaped granaries, stables, workshops, and smaller buildings for family members and servants. A common feature at Amarna was a private open air shrine in a corner of the enclosure.

Representational palaces of the New Kingdom. The representational royal palace forms a distinct category of domestic buildings that were designed to meet special functional requirements; these are known from the mortuary complexes of western Thebes and Memphis as well as from Amarna and Malkata. The palaces were characterized by their axial organization. A large outer hall, corresponding to the central hall of the private house, is distinguished from the more intimate interior hall by a dais for the royal throne. Private chambers, including the royal bedroom and bathroom, were accessible only from the interior hall, not from the central outer hall. None of the palaces of this type served the king in his role as secular ruler of the country; the interior hall was therefore not an office, but a representational audience hall.

Multistory town houses. Clay models of the Middle Kingdom, wall paintings in Theban tombs of the New Kingdom, and stone models of the Ptolemaic period represent houses with three, perhaps even four stories. These structures were apparently town houses that expanded upwards because of the limited building space in crowded cities. As in modern Eastern buildings, the ground floor was used for artisans' installations and the high-roofed upper floors for residential purposes; the servants' quarters faced the street. The roof was surrounded by a parapet wall and served as another cooking and storage area. Higher floors were reached by steep staircases. Few traces of actual buildings have survived from pharaonic times (for example a three-story house at Lisht). However, numerous town houses are exceptionally well preserved in Ptolemaic to Late Roman towns such as Karanis (Kom Aushim), Bacchias (Kom el-Qatl), and Soknopaiou Nesos (Dime), located in the Faiyum, and in Alexandria. Evidence from these settlements establish that four-story houses (including the vaulted cellar rooms) were quite common in cities of Egypt. Such huge, fortresslike buildings required extra thick walls, reinforced by cross beams and corners strengthened by stone masonry. The ten–twelve-meter-high houses occasionally resembled dwelling towers and were equipped with kitchens, toilets, and the necessary drainage systems; the rooms often contained numerous, sometimes decorated wall cabinets. Doors and windows were framed with sophisticated woodwork. The cellars, staircases, and sometimes more important rooms of the main floor were vaulted. Dovecotes and animal pens are also preserved, as well as multiroomed military barracks and huge public granaries.

BIBLIOGRAPHY

Arnold, Felix. "A Study of Egyptian Domestic Buildings." *Varia Aegyptiaca* 5 (1989): 75–93.

Badawy, Alexander. *A History of Egyptian Architecture.* 3 vols. Giza and Berkeley, 1954–1968.

Borchardt, Ludwig, and Herbert Ricke. *Die Wohnhäuser in Tell el-Amarna.* Berlin, 1980.

Ricke, Herbert. *Der Grundriss des Amarna-Wohnhauses.* Ausgrabungen der deutschen Orient-Gesellschaft in Tell el-Amarna, vol. 4. Leipzig, 1932.

Rodziewicz, Mieczyslaw. *Les habitations romaines tardives d'Alexandrie.* Alexandria, 3. Warsaw, 1984.

Roik, Elke. *Das altägyptische Wohnhaus und seine Darstellung im Flachbild.* Frankfurt, 1988.

FELIX ARNOLD

HOUSE CHURCHES. As a movement within Judaism of the Second Temple period, the Christian sect originated with no distinct institutions, including church buildings. Following the death of Jesus, the disciples reportedly continued in Jewish temple piety and table fellowship "from house to house" (*Acts* 2:46, 5:42). There are also references in *Acts* to household conversions (*Acts* 16:15, 34; 18:8) in which the earliest preaching was conducted in the homes of individuals, who offered hospitality to Paul (or others). This basic picture is substantiated by the letters of Paul, the earliest writings of the New Testament (50–60 CE). Paul refers to entire households forming churches (*1 Cor.* 1:16, 16:15), and he regularly addresses greetings in the letters to churches in the house of so-and-so (*1 Cor.* 16:19; *Rom.* 16:5; *Phlm.* 2; *Col.* 4:15). These references suggest that existing households served as a nucleus of organization with cellular communities formed around them. In some of Paul's communities—in large urban centers—it appears that there were several such house-church cells, often identified by the home of the patron. For example, in Corinth there were as many as five or six known groups during the 50s, and Paul seems to address eight distinct cells in Rome in his final salutations of the Roman letter (*Rom.* 16:3–16). The existence of several such cells organized around individual household social ties contributed to diversity in the worship, organization, and social life of early Christian groups.

The extended-household structure typical of the Hellenistic-Roman world included not only immediate family members, but also other relatives, domestic slaves, and a larger coterie of freedmen, hired workers, business associates, and other clients or dependents. The head of the household (Lat., *pater familias*) served as patron and host to the group that met in the home, reflecting similar patterns of patron-client social relations to that of the household structure. Paul regularly stayed in the homes of the house-church patron on his visits, who provided him with financial support (*Rom.* 16:23; *Phlm.* 18–22; *Phil.* 4:10–20). Increasingly in the Roman period, women were able to retain functional control of personal estates and manage their own households *(mater familias)*. A number of Paul's house-church communities were under such patronesses (Nympha, *Col.* 4:15; Chloe, *1 Cor.* 1:11; Lydia, *Acts* 16:14–16; Euodia and/or Syntyche, *Phil.* 4:2). The best example is Phoebe (*Rom.* 16:2), who is clearly called the patroness (Gk., *prostatis*) of a house church at Kenchreai (a port of Corinth) and was Paul's host and supporter. Her wealth and social standing are attested by the fact that she was the one who actually carried Paul's letter to the Christians of Rome; she was sent, at least in part, to pave the way for Paul's arrival among Rome's diverse house churches and to raise financial support for his planned mission to Spain. In other cases, the wife seems to be the predominant member of a couple who hosted the church in their house (cf. Prisca, *Rom.* 16:3). The case of Prisca and Aquila indicates further that some of these individuals had substantial means: they were able to travel and set up house churches in Corinth, Ephesus, and Rome (*Acts* 18:2–4; *1 Cor.* 16:19; *Rom.* 16:3–5).

The most common reference for the place of Christian meetings in the New Testament is simply to houses, but with little or no description of the actual type of edifice or particular area of activity. Other references in Paul's letters suggest that the communal worship met in the dining room of the house and around a common table, where the meal proper served as a focal point for the activities of worship. Other places used for meetings included a domestic "upper room" (*Acts* 20:7) and a commercial hall (Gk., *scholē*) of indeterminate plan (*Acts* 19:9). The apocryphal *Acts of Paul* (late second century) further suggests that Christians in Rome met in large warehouses (Lat., *horrea;* cf. *Passio Pauli* 1). That such private or semiprivate architecture was used by Christian groups is not in itself unique. Many other small or newly arrived religious groups and collegial associations in the fluid and mobile social environment of the Roman Empire regularly adapted houses or other private edifices as places of assembly or cultic activity. All six of the synagogue buildings of the Diaspora (second century BCE–fourth century CE) known from archaeological remains were adapted from existing edifices, and five of the six were originally houses or apartment buildings (Lat., *insulae*). Often, the adaptation of these structures progressed gradually through multiple stages of renovation and remodeling to accommodate specific religious or social functions. The cult of Mithras is similarly predominantly found to have adapted existing edifices for its purposes. Of more than sixty excavated Mithraic sanctuaries (Lat., *mithraea*) from across the Roman Empire, only ten were constructed de novo for the cult; the remainder were found in renovated houses, apartments, shops, warehouses, basement cryptoportici, and the like. This includes all the excavated mithraea in Ostia and Rome, as well as the one at Caesarea Maritima (Israel). [*See* Caesarea.] At Dura-Europos (Roman Syria/Mesopotamia), there are three such adapted houses on the same street: a synagogue, a mithraeum, and a Christian building (see figure 1). [*See* Dura-Europos; Synagogues.]

In archaeological terms, a distinction needs to be made between a house or other edifice that might be used for religious purposes on a casual basis and an edifice actually renovated architecturally to meet specific spatial or iconographic needs. While it is clear that in Paul's day (and through much of the second century) Christians met in the homes of members, it does not appear that significant renovations occurred. These cases are properly termed house churches, and they continued in primarily domestic or other nonreligious functions. Yet, it is not likely that any archaeological evidence can be discerned for them because they lack distinguishing architectural, spatial, or artistic features. Archaeological evidence arises only with physical adaptation of the edifice. While the terminology has been inconsistent, it is preferable to use the term *domus ecclesiae* ("house of the church") to denote renovated Christian edifices on their way to becoming more formal church buildings. This terminology is reflected in some third-century Christian writers, where further expansion and remodeling are indicated. Such edifices are referred to by Eusebius (*Hist. Eccl.* 7.30.19, 8.1.5) in Greek as *oikos ekklesias* (= Lat., *domus ecclesiae*) or *oikos kyriakou* ("house of the Lord").

The earliest and most clearly attested archaeological evidence of a house renovated architecturally into a place of Christian assembly and worship is from Dura-Europos. It was buried substantially intact in 256 CE, when the city was destroyed. It was a typical domestic edifice by local standards, with rooms grouped around a central court. While Christians might have been in Dura earlier, no other direct archaeological evidence exists of their activity or assembly. There is no direct evidence that the Dura building was used as a house church prior to its renovation (in c. 241 CE),

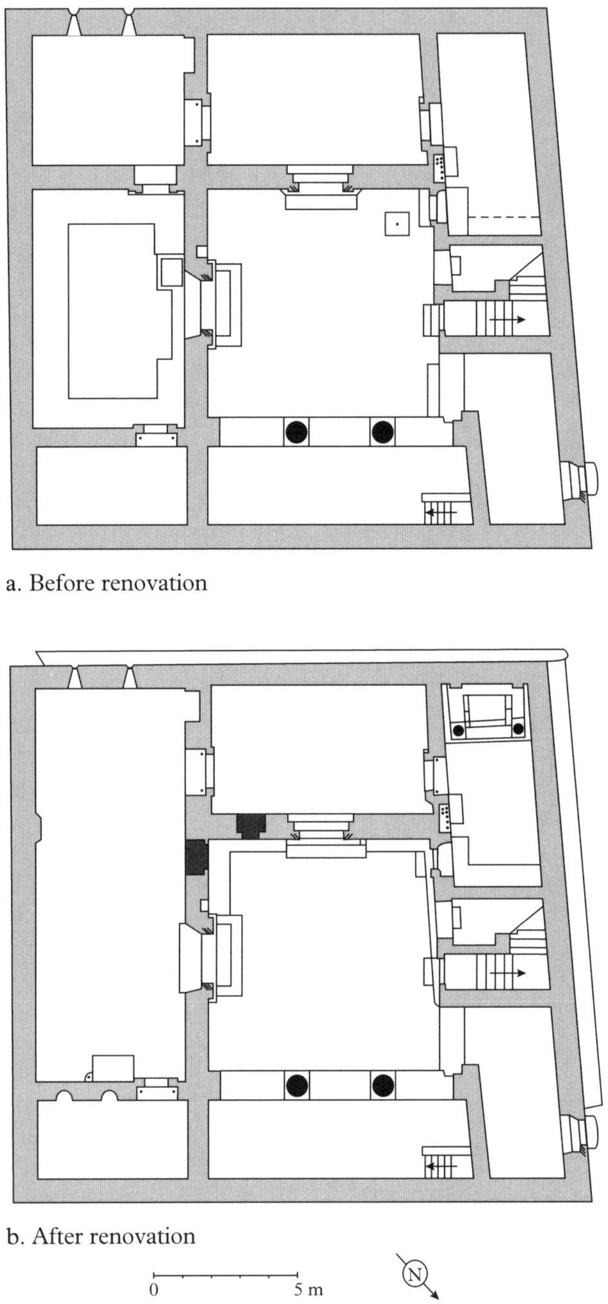

HOUSE CHURCHES. Figure 1. *Reconstruction of the Christian Building at Dura-Europos, before and after it was renovated into a house church.* (After White, 1990, p. 108)

though it is possible. When it was renovated all domestic functions ceased, and the building was given over completely to the spatial needs of religious (or cultic) activities. Even though the building retained its exterior domestic form and plan, it had become a "church building." Such features can be detected archaeologically from the nature of the renovation and other surviving epigraphic and artistic decoration. On the south side of the court, a partition wall was removed in order to open up two rooms to form a rectangular hall for assembly. A small dais was then installed at the east end of the room. A small adjoining room seems to have been used for storage. A single fragmentary inscription preserved from the room likely refers to ecclesiastical personnel. In the northwest corner of the house another room had a small font pool with an arched canopy installed to serve as a baptistery. [*See* Baptisteries.] This room also shows clear Christian usage in its artistic program, which depicts scenes from the life of Jesus on the walls. Other memorial inscriptions from the walls of this room clearly reflect a Christian identity.

Several other sites from across the Roman world provide further archaeological evidence for the adaptation and renovation of existing buildings prior to the implementation of formal basilical church architecture under Constantine (c. 314–319). [*See* Basilicas; Churches.] The evidence suggests that partial adaptation occurred as an intermediate stage, and that subsequent enlargements or rebuilding overlaid earlier phases of the renovation of domestic or private architecture. One site, at the Lullingstone Villa, near Eynsford, England, has only part of the house given over for renovation as a kind of "chapel wing"; the site is important also for its relatively late date (c. 350–410), which shows that the process of gradual adaptation continued well after the empire had become officially Christian and public Christian architecture had begun. The continued renovation and reuse of sites over centuries has often made the archaeological evidence difficult to read. For example, in Rome, a large apartment building with shops on the ground floor and domestic quarters above seems to have been partially renovated for use as a Christian hall in the third century. This basic plan may have continued until the beginning of the fifth century before being fully rebuilt in basilical form; however, some of the earlier structure was preserved in the foundation levels below the basilica, now called the Church of Saints John and Paul (Ss. Giovanni e Paolo). Similarly, the Church of St. Clement (San Clemente) near the Colosseum was originally built in basilical form in about 400, over a large third century hall that may have been used by Christians. In turn, this hall stood over a large warehouse complex dating to the first century that Christian tradition associates with the name of Clement of Rome (d. about 96) and a church ostensibly located on his property. No direct archaeological evidence indicates such usage in the lower layers, even though the adjacent house clearly had a mithraeum installed in a lower level cortile. Similarly, there is no evidence that the so-called House of St. Peter at Capernaum was actually used as a house church, or *domus ecclesiae,* prior to the construction of a quadrilateral enclosure in the fourth century, later rebuilt on an octagonal plan in the fifth and sixth centuries. [*See* Capernaum.] In this case it is better to view the building in the context of the beginning of memorial architecture stimulated by Constantine to commemorate Christian holy sites, rather than its being in direct continuity with the older pattern of house church and *domus ecclesiae*.

Other archaeological evidence suggests that by the mid-third century Christians were beginning to enlarge spaces on a rectangular hall plan, but well before the beginning of formal basilical church architecture. Such buildings may be called *aula ecclesiae*, or "hall churches." At least one case, from Parentium (Roman Istria, modern Parenzo or Porec), shows a private house first renovated as a *domus ecclesiae* (third century) and subsequently renovated to form a large hall (fourth century), before it was converted to the basilical plan (fifth–sixth centuries; now known as the Basilica Eufrasiana). A hall was also installed in a block of private houses in the early fourth century at Umm el-Jimal (in Roman Arabia, modern Jordan). [*See* Umm el-Jimal.] Other examples can be found in the first levels below the Church of San Chrysogono in Rome (c. 310), the double halls below the church at Aquileia (c. 317–319), a small plane hall from Qirk Bize in Syria (c. 320–333), and the first hall below the Octagonal Church of St. Paul at Philippi, Greece (c. 343). Each of these cases was transformed, by subsequent phases of renovation and construction, into more formal or recognizable church architecture (either basilical or octagonal in plan).

BIBLIOGRAPHY

Finney, Paul Corby. "Early Christian Architecture: The Beginnings." *Harvard Theological Review* 81 (1988): 319–339.

Judge, E. A. *The Social Organization of Christian Groups in the First Century*. London, 1960.

Klauck, Hans-Josef. *Hausgemeinde und Hauskirche im frühen Christentum*. Stuttgart, 1981.

Kraeling, Carl H. *The Christian Building*. The Excavations at Dura-Europos, Final Report 8, part 2. New Haven, 1967.

Krautheimer, Richard. *Corpus basilicarum christianarum romae*. 5 vols. Vatican City, 1939–1956.

Krautheimer, Richard *Early Christian and Byzantine Architecture*. 3d ed. Harmondsworth, 1981.

Malherbe, Abraham J. *Social Aspects of Early Christianity*. 2d ed. Philadelphia, 1983.

Meeks, Wayne A. *The First Urban Christians: The Social World of the Apostle Paul*. New Haven, 1983.

Petersen, Joan M. "House Churches in Rome." *Vigiliae Christianae* 23 (1969): 264–272.

White, L. Michael. *Building God's House in the Roman World: Architectural Adaptation among Pagans, Jews, and Christians*. Baltimore, 1990.

White, L. Michael. *The Social Origins of Christian Architecture*, vol. 1, *Architectural Adaptation among Pagans, Jews, and Christians* (reprint of above); vol. 2, *Texts and Monuments of the Christian Domus Ecclesiae in Its Environment*. Minneapolis, 1995.

L. MICHAEL WHITE

ḤUMEIMA (Ar., Ḥumaima, Ḥomeima, Ḥumayma), ancient Auara (Gk.; Lat., Hauara, Hauarra), major Nabatean, Roman, Byzantine, and early Islamic center in the Ḥisma, Jordan's southern desert (29°57′00″ N, 35°20′38″ E). The ruins of the settlement, approximately 10 ha (25 acres) in area, are at an elevation of 955 m above sea level, in sandstone hills between the Jebel Qalkha and Jebel Ḥumeima, 3 km (2 mi.) east of Wadi ʿArabah. Precipitation averages only 80 mm per year. The plain east of the site is watered by runoff from a roughly triangular catchment area of 240 sq km (149 sq. mi.). Petra is 44 km (27 mi.) to the north, the modern settlement of Ma'an 50 km (31 mi.) to the northeast, ʿAqaba (ancient Aila) 55 km (34 mi.) to the south, and Meda'in Saleh (ancient Hegra) 250 km (155 mi.) to the southeast.

Although Alois Musil identified the ruins of Ḥumeima as ancient Ammatha, the Peutinger Table establishes that the site is Auara: it places Havarra 23 Roman miles (36 km, or 22 mi.) north of Praesidio (Khirbet el-Khalde) and 20 Roman miles (30 km, or 19 mi.) south of Zadagatta (Sadaqa), which is Ḥumeima's exact location. According to Ouranios's *Arabika* (F. Jacoby, *Fragmente der griechischen Historiker*, Leiden, 1923–, 675 frag. A.1.b), Auara was founded by the Nabatean king Aretas III (87–62 BCE), in response to an oracle. Nothing is known of the settlement's early history, but an extensive water-supply system was built in the first century BCE to attract settlers, caravans, and a market. A Nabatean north–south road, rebuilt as Trajan's Via Nova, passed through, or very close to, the settlement. The archaeological and literary evidence reveals that Auara flourished in the Late Roman, Byzantine, and Umayyad periods. Ptolemy includes Auara in his list of towns in Arabia Petraea (*Geography* 5.16.4), and Stephanus Byzantinus provides the alternate name Auatha. The *Notitia Dignitatum* (*Oriens* 34.25) records the presence of a unit of *equites sagittarii indigenae* at Hauare (Havarra). At the same time, the Beersheba Edict records that the governor of Palaestina Tertia assessed Auara the second highest sum of any of the settlements in Transjordan. A military camp was built at the north edge of the site in the Late Roman or Early Byzantine period. Auara continued to flourish in the Early Islamic period, and soon after 687/88, ʿAli ibn ʿAbd Allah ibn al-ʿAbbas purchased the town, which became a center for the ʿAbbasid family's revolt against the Umayyad dynasty. Ceramic evidence shows a marked decline in habitation after the mid-eighth century.

The Department of Antiquities of Jordan cleared part of the lower church and one Early Islamic house in the settlement in 1965, but the results were not published. David Graf initiated a survey of the site in 1979 and was later joined by John W. Eadie (1980–1983) and John P. Oleson (1981–1983). In 1986–1987 Oleson surveyed the region around Ḥumeima for structures related to Auara's water-supply system and in 1989 began the excavation of the settlement center.

Soon after Auara was founded, an aqueduct of traditional Nabatean design (a ground-level, roofed conduit of stone gutter blocks) was built to carry water for 26.5 km (16 mi.)—from ʿAin Ghana, ʿAin Jamam, and ʿAin Shara—to an open reservoir at the north end of the site. The habitation center was also served by a pair of large, rectangular, roofed reservoirs fed by runoff water from a catchment to the north of the settlement area. More than fifty ancient rock-cut and built cisterns, several wadi barriers, a dam, and carefully modified runoff fields have been identified in the catchment area north, east, and south of Auara. Rock-cut tombs of Nabatean through Byzantine date occupy the ridges west of the site.

The habitation area of Auara is occupied by heaps of tumbled building blocks from approximately thirty structures, probably domestic, whose plans are clearly visible in aerial photographs. They consist for the most part of square or rectangular complexes of small rooms arranged on two or three sides of a courtyard. Ceramic scatter and the excavation of one of the houses (Oleson Field F102, Oleson et al., 1992, 1993a–b, 1994) indicate that the structures on the surface are Umayyad/ʿAbbasid in date, but that at least some of them are built on earlier walls of the Nabatean and Roman periods. There is a typical Roman *castrum* at the northeast edge of the site, with its own reservoir and located close to the Nabatean reservoir fed by the aqueduct. There is a door in each of the four walls, and twenty-four projecting corner and curtain wall towers. Excavation indicates the fort was built in the later second century and probably abandoned in the fourth century (Oleson et al., 1994).

Four structures had been excavated by 1993: a late Roman bath building probably associated with the fort (Oleson no. 77; Oleson, 1990), a three-apsed Byzantine Church with intramural burials (Oleson Field C101; Oleson et al., 1992, 1993a–b, 1994), a one-apsed Byzantine church with traces of painted plaster and marble architectural elements (Oleson Field C119; Oleson et al., 1994), an Umayyad/early ʿAbbasid house or market complex built on top of a Byzantine church (Oleson Field B100; Oleson et al., 1992, 1993a–b, 1994), and an Umayyad house built on top of a Nabatean or Roman structure adjacent to a Nabatean-type cistern (Oleson Field F102; Oleson et al., 1992, 1993a–b, 1994). A large structure (Oleson Field F103; Oleson et al., 1994) earlier assumed to be a Roman *castellum* (rectangular fortress) or Nabatean caravanserai was identified after excavation in 1993 as the *qaṣr* (fortified house), garden, and mosque reported in historical sources to have been built by the ʿAbbasid family after they purchased the site. One room contained the remains of carved ivory furniture and colourful frescoes with floral motifs, all dating to the mid-eighth century. A substantial Nabatean structure lies beneath the Roman bath, and it seems likely that other early structures are now covered by Byzantine and early Islamic rebuilding or by the deep layer of water-deposited silt in the settlement center.

[*See also* Nabateans.]

BIBLIOGRAPHY

Oleson, John P. "The Humeima Hydraulic Survey: Preliminary Report of the 1989 Season." *Annual of the Department of Antiquities of Jordan* 34 (1990): 285–311. Report on results of excavation of bath building.

Oleson, John P. "Aqueducts, Cisterns, and the Strategy of Water Supply at Nabataean and Roman Auara (Jordan)." In *Future Currents in Aqueduct Studies,* edited by A. Trevor Hodge, pp. 45–62. Leeds, 1991. Discussion of the planning of the water-supply system.

Oleson, John P. "The Water-Supply System of Ancient Auara: Preliminary Results of the Humeima Hydraulic Survey." In *Studies in the History and Archaeology of Jordan,* vol. 4, edited by Ghazi Bisheh, pp. 269–275. Amman, 1992. Results of the survey of the water-supply system around Ḥumeima.

Oleson, John P. "The Humeima Excavation Project: Preliminary Report of the 1991 Season." *Echos du Monde Classique/Classical Views* 11 (1992): 137–169. Preliminary report of excavation in the church and several early Islamic houses.

Oleson, John P., and J. Eadie. "The Water-Supply Systems of Nabataean and Roman Humayma." *Bulletin of the American Schools of Oriental Research,* no. 262 (1986): 49–76. An early report on the water-supply system and history of the settlement.

Oleson, John P., David Graf, and J. Eadie. "Humayma." In *Archaeology of Jordan,* vol. 2, *Field Reports,* edited by Denyse Homès-Fredericq and J. Basil Hennessy, pp. 270–274. Louvain, 1989. Brief summary of the site and its history.

Oleson, John P., K. ʿAmr, R. Schick, R. Foote, and J. Somogyi-Csizmazi. "The Humeima Excavation Project, Jordan: Preliminary Report of the 1992 Season." *Echos du Monde Classique/Classical Views* 12 (1993a): 123–158.

Oleson, John P., K. ʿAmr, R. Schick, R. Foote, and J. Somogyi-Csizmazi. "The Humeima Excavation Project: Preliminary Report of the 1991–1992 Seasons." *Annual of the Department of Antiquities of Jordan* 37 (1993b): 461–502.

Oleson, John P., K. ʿAmr, R. Schick, R. Foote, and J. Somogyi-Csizmazi. "Preliminary Report of the Humeima Excavation Project, 1993." *Echos du Monde Classique/Classical Views* 13 (1994): 141–179.

JOHN PETER OLESON

HUNTING. Little is known about the prehistoric hunter-gatherer of the Near East who created the Natufian and similar cultures. With the development of civilization, people who lived by hunting (Esau) were sometimes represented in a less favorable light than builders of cities (Gilgamesh) or pastoralists (Jacob). The story of David, however, who "slew both the lion and the bear," foreshadows his future greatness (*1 Sm.* 17:36).

The introduction of the horse-drawn chariot into Egypt before the middle of the second millennium enabled kings to display themselves spectacularly in the hunt. Tutankhamen (c. 1348–1339 BCE) is represented on a painted box shooting with bow and arrow as his chariot team gallops in pursuit of game; and the pylons at Medinet Habu show Rameses III (c. 1190–1158 BCE) stepping onto the pole of his chariot in order to transfix a wild bull with a gigantic lance. These representations are not realistic, for in real life a charioteer would have accompanied the king; and the Ramesside reliefs combine the originally separate motifs of the royal chariot and of the Pharaoh striding forward to smite his enemies. Most probably the game—which included lions, antelopes, and ostriches—was shot with the bow from a stationary chariot, which was driven up to it by spearmen and archers. These are shown at Medinet Habu below the king and on a smaller scale. Military training was thus combined with sport.

The royal hunt appears frequently in the palace reliefs of the Assyrian New Kingdom (see figure 1). Ashurnasirpal (885–860 BCE) hunts lions and bulls from a four-horse chariot in which he is accompanied by a driver and weapon bearers. Ashurbanipal (669–627 BCE) hunts with a spear and bow both in a chariot and on horseback. His skill as a mounted archer may reflect the influence of the Scythians, to whose kings the Assyrian royal house had allied itself by marriage. Ashurbanipal also killed lions on foot, and inscriptions accompanying his monuments refer contemptuously to the terror of subject kings compelled to share this royal sport. Lions are sometimes released from traveling cages to be destroyed by the king; and the monuments also show large-scale drives leading to the wholesale slaughter of lions, wild asses, and gazelles, which may be driven into long nets or toward a pit in which the king, holding a bow and arrow, is concealed. Sometimes these hunts are represented as taking place in parks to which the populace, including women, is admitted to witness the royal prowess.

The theme of Assyrian official art is the brutal crushing of the king's enemies; but the major monuments of Achaemenid Persia (c. 550–330 BCE) represent "all the kingdoms of the earth" (*Ezr.* 1:2) as the peaceful subjects of the Great King, who is portrayed on reliefs in Persepolis destroying imaginary monsters, allegories of evil, rather than hunting real animals. Herodotus shows that to hunt on horseback with bow or spear was for the Persian nobility the epitome of manly virtue—and excellent training for leaders of armies whose strength lay in their cavalry. Game parks, or "paradises," are frequently mentioned as a feature of courtly life. Xenophon, in his romance *Cyropaedia,* tells how, as a boy, Cyrus the Great (c. 550–527 BCE) rode after boar, first in his grandfather's park and then in open country. More historical is the account in Xenophon's *Anabasis* of how Cyrus the Younger (fl. 401 BCE) killed a bear that had clawed him down from his horse.

In the provincial art of the Achaemenid Empire, hunting is often represented—notably on the marble sarcophagi created by Greek sculptors for the kings of Sidon and now in the Archaeological Museum at Istanbul. The Satrap sarcophagus portrays the perils of hunting big game on horseback; a less realistic hunt, on the Lycian sarcophagus, allegorises the virtue of a dead prince; and the Alexander sarcophagus may show, from the point of view of an Asiatic

HUNTING. Figure 1. *Relief from the Palace of Ashurnasirpal II in Nimrud, Mesopotamia.* King Ashurnasirpal hunting lions, a lion leaping at the king's chariot. British Museum, London. (Erich Lessing/Art Resource, NY)

ruler, an incident of a historical lion-hunt in which Alexander the Great (336–323 BCE) took part with his generals. Engraved gems often show hunting on horseback or on foot, with bow or spear. The hunters are generally Persian nobles, but Darius I (522–486 BCE) is himself conventionally portrayed on an official seal, in the Assyrian manner, hunting lions from a chariot. The hunt is the symbol of the ruler's personal qualities and of the protection he affords his people.

In Asia Alexander the Great and his generals practiced, on an unprecedented scale, sports that the Macedonian kings had traditionally enjoyed in Europe. Under the successor kings, notably Ptolemy Philadelphus of Egypt (283–247 BCE) and Antiochus IV of Syria (175–164 BCE), big-game hunts and displays of exotic beasts were staged as popular spectacles, comparable to the later *venationes* (hunting shows) in the Roman amphitheater. The Roman conquerors of the Mediterranean basin at first availed themselves of the captured apparatus of the royal hunt, but in general, even under the emperors, Roman hunting (as distinct from collecting beasts for the amphitheater) seems to have been on a scale suitable to the fiction that the emperor was first citizen (princeps). Thus, Hadrian (117–138 CE) hunted a bear in Mysia and lions in Egypt on horseback, in the company of intimate friends.

Marble sarcophagi decorated with hunting scenes, many of them carved in Asia Minor, were used throughout the Roman Empire from the second century CE onward. The hunt as an allegory of virtue is splendidly represented in mosaics of the fifth-sixth centuries CE, notably at Apamea in North Syria and Antioch on the Orontes, where Magnanimity (Megalopsychia) appears personified.

From Sasanian Persia (224–651 CE) come silver-gilt plates, on which kings are shown hunting, usually on horseback, with bow or sword. Rock-cut reliefs at Taq-i Bostan (ascribed to Khusrau II, 591–628 CE) show royal hunts on a gigantic scale. Elephant riders drive wild boar into a swamp where the king, seated in a barge, shoots them with his bow; and herds of driven gazelles are pursued on horseback. Female musicians are in attendance, recalling the story of Bahram Gur (420–438 CE) and the Greek singing girl Azada, which is portrayed on some of the hunting plates.

After the Islamic conquest in the seventh century, hunting retained its interest as a sport and its value in military training.

[*See also* Lions; Mosaics; Pigs; *and* Wall Paintings.]

BIBLIOGRAPHY

Anderson, J. K. *Hunting in the Ancient World.* Berkeley and Los Angeles, 1985. Brief general survey, emphasizing Greece and Rome but including Assyrian and Achaemenid material.

Barnett, Richard D. *Sculptures from the North Palace of Ashurbanipal at Nineveh, 668–627 B.C.* London, 1976. Definitive publication of the most important Assyrian hunting reliefs, with full commentaries.

Boardman, John. *Greek Gems and Finger Rings: Early Bronze Age to Late Classical.* London, 1970. Includes an authoritative chapter on "Greco-Persian" gems of the Achaemenid period and excellent illustrations.

Hamdy, Osman Bey, and Theodore Reinach. *Une nécropole royale à Sidon.* Paris, 1892. Original publication of the Sidon sarcophagi, with magnificent illustrations recording details of color now lost.

Harper, Prudence Oliver. *The Royal Hunter: Art of the Sasanian Empire.* New York, 1978. Splendidly illustrated catalog of an exhibition of Sasanian art, with a useful historical introduction and valuable notes on the separate items.

Levi, Doro. *Antioch Mosaic Pavements.* Princeton, 1947. Full publication of important material, including the "Megalopsychia" mosaic.

Porada, Edith. *The Art of Ancient Iran: Pre-Islamic Cultures.* New York, 1965. Accessible general survey by one of the chief authorities on Near Eastern art.

Smith, William Stevenson. *The Art and Architecture of Ancient Egypt.* Harmondsworth, 1958. Well-illustrated general survey, including pictures of the Egyptian objects mentioned in the text.

J. K. ANDERSON

ḤUREIDHA, site located in Wadi ʿAmd, about 39 km (24 mi.) south–southwest of its junction with the Ḥadhramaut in southern Yemen (15°36′ N, 48°11′ E). Situated in the bed of the wadi, the site has been badly eroded by flash floods that cut through the 4-meter-high tell, stratigraphically isolating the buildings and leaving mounds of debris spread over an area of about 17 acres. Three inscriptions recovered indicate that the name of the ancient town was Maḏabum.

The site was discovered and excavated by the archaeologist Gertrude Caton-Thompson; Elinor Gardner, a geologist; and Freya Stark, a writer, from December 1937 to March 1938. The focus of the excavation was a small, rectangular temple dedicated to the moon god Sin. Although it had been destroyed to floor level, three phases of construction were distinguished: the first consisted of the original temple, and the second and third were limited to repairs and additions to the former. These phases spanned the period from the sixth to the second century BCE. Outside the temple, several shrines with altars were constructed during the third phase, with material reused from the temple. A farmhouse built of mud brick, located near the temple, was also excavated. Two circular cave tombs, which had been dug in the scree slope of the cliff along the west side of the wadi, were also cleared; these yielded the first skeletons of ancient South Arabs.

The small corpus of pottery recovered from these excavations proved that the temple, farmhouse, and tombs belonged to the same period. Dated by other artifacts, especially beads and Achaemenid seals, the pottery provided the beginnings of a chronology for these four centuries. It also served as an independent source for dating inscriptions, which previously could only be assigned dates on the basis of paleography and filiation.

Gardner, at Ḥureidha, was the first to investigate a flash-flood irrigation system in southern Arabia. With a deflection dam to channel run-off water into the primary canal, 16 km (c. 10 mi.) upstream, and a distribution network of secondary canals and tertiary earthen ditches, water was moved quickly and efficiently to already plowed fields downstream and surrounding the town.

Gardner also studied the geology of the region as opportunities occurred, commenting on the geologic history during the Quaternary era. Paleolithic flakes and Levallois-type cores appear everywhere, on the plateau above Wadi ʿAmd and on its terraces, providing the earliest evidence of human occupation of the region.

Ḥureidha is of considerable importance in the archaeology of pre-Islamic southern Arabia because it was the first site excavated by a professional archaeologist. Caton-Thompson's work set a high standard for archaeological methodology by its scope: geological investigations and prehistory, superior research on artifacts, reasoned interpretation, and comprehensive publication.

[*See also the biography of Caton-Thompson.*]

BIBLIOGRAPHY

Caton-Thompson, Gertrude. *The Tombs and Moon Temple of Hureidha (Hadhramaut).* Society of Antiquaries of London Research Committee Report, no. 13. Oxford, 1944. Readable, model excavation report.

GUS W. VAN BEEK

HURRIAN. The Hurrian language is associated with an ethnic group that first appears in areas in the northern and eastern parts of Mesopotamia (i.e., Assyria) in the Ur III period (the last centuries of the second millennium BCE). From Assyria through northern Syria to Ugarit to Ḫattuša (Boğazköy), and in the Amarna archives, the group leaves textual and onomastic evidence of its presence for about one thousand years and then vanishes abruptly. The language is a close relative of, but not a direct ancestor of, Urartian, attested somewhat farther north and east in the first half of the first millennium BCE. It has been suggested, although it is not widely accepted, that Hurrian may be related to the Dagestanian languages spoken today in the northeastern Caucasus. Except for the Dagestanian reference, Hurrian and Urartian constitute a linguistic isolate among the languages of the world.

The corpus of Hurrian texts begins with a single, short "Old Hurrian" monumental inscription of uncertain provenance, probably the upper Khabur or Tigris, in northern Syria or Mesopotamia, at about the end of the Ur III dynasty. The Old Babylonian period yields only a small number of poorly understood fragments from Mari and elsewhere, some of which seem to be incantatory in nature. The bulk of Hurrian texts come from four mid- and late second-millennium sites: Ugarit—bi- and quadrilingual vocabularies (Akkadian, Sumerian, Hurrian, and Ugaritic), literary and religious fragments, and a unique small corpus of musical texts; Boğazköy—a large, and still poorly understood, corpus of ritual texts and religious literature, usually with a Hittite version; Emar (Syria)—a small, still unpublished corpus of lexical, medical, and omen texts; and Amarna (Egypt)—a long, carefully written and perfectly preserved Hurrian letter from the Mitanni ruler Tušratta to Amenhotep III. The latter is the best-understood Hurrian text and the basis for almost all that is known of Hurrian grammar.

With the exception of a few texts (perhaps offering lists) written in the Ugaritic alphabetic script, Hurrian is written in cuneiform. It is possible that the Hurrians formed part of the chain of transmission by which the cuneiform writing system reached the Hittites. By the time of the Tušratta letter, it is clear that the Mitanni chancellery had developed a set of very consistent and systematic orthographic conventions for representing Hurrian in cuneiform. These conventions include systematic use of single and double writing to convey consonantal distinctions that did not exist in the languages—very different from Hurrian—of the Sumerian originators or Akkadian adaptors of the system.

Morphologically, the Hurrian noun and, especially, its verb are typically constructed out of complex chains of suffixes and enclitics. The noun, for example, distinguishes eight possible suffix/enclitic positions after the root, according to the pattern:

0:*ROOT* + 1:*Derivational suffix* + 2:*Possessive* + 3:*Article* + 4:*Plural* + 5:*Case* + 6:*Enclitic Obj* + 7:*Agreement* + 8:*Enclitic Conj/Adv*

An example, from the Mitanni letter (4, l. 39), is *šen+iff+da+lla+an:* "0:brother + 2:my + 5:to (directive case) + 6:them + 8:and"—that is, "and them to my brother." The verbal pattern, which distinguishes thirteen positions, is

0:*Root* + 1:*Derivational suffix* + 2:*Tense* + 3:*Derivational suffix* + 4:*Plural* + 5:*Transitivity* + 6:*Neg-1* + 7:*Subject* + 8:*Neg-2* + 9:*Relative* + 10:*Plural* + 11:*Enclitic Obj* + 12:*Agreement* + 13:*Enclitic Conj/Adv*

An example, again from the Mitanni letter (4, l. 31), is *kad+ož+a+šše+na:* "0:ask + 2:past + 7:third-singular-ergative + 9:relative + 10:plural"—that is, "which (pl.) he has asked."

In syntax, Hurrian belongs to the ergative language type (that is, like Sumerian, it has a special case for subjects of transitive verbs, whereas subjects of intransitive verbs have the same case as objects of transitive verbs). As can be seen from the above formulae, Hurrian makes extensive use of enclitics for pronominal, conjunctival, and adverbial elements.

[*See also* Boğazköy; Emar Texts; Hurrians; Mitanni; Ugarit; *and* Ugaritic.]

BIBLIOGRAPHY

Bush, F. W. "A Grammar of the Hurrian Language." Ph.D. diss., Brandeis University, 1964. Most detailed analysis of the language since Speiser (1941). Available from University Microfilms.

Diakonoff, Igor M., and S. A. Starostin. *Hurro-Urartian as an Eastern Caucasian Language.* Munich, 1986. Best attempt yet to discover a wider affiliation for Hurrian, but it has not found many adherents.

Haas, Volkert, et al., eds. *Corpus der Hurritischen Sprachdenkmäler.* Rome, 1984–. This series will eventually contain editions of the entire corpus of Hurrian texts.

Laroche, Emmanuel. *Glossaire de la langue hourrite.* Revue Hittite et Asianique, vols. 34–35. Paris, 1980. First and only dictionary of Hurrian.

Speiser, Ephraim Avigdor. *Introduction to Hurrian.* Annual of the American Schools of Oriental Research, 20. New Haven, 1941. First and still fundamental Hurrian grammar.

Wilhelm, Gernot. *The Hurrians.* Translated by Jennifer Barnes, with a chapter by Diana L. Stein. Warminster, 1989. Reliable, concise survey of Hurrian history, culture, and literature.

GENE GRAGG

HURRIANS. The term *Hurrian* may be derived from *hur,* a stem denoting war. Although the name appears to be related to the biblical *ḥōrî(m),* it is not. The Hurrians were a people identified by their non-Semitic, non-Indo-European language, Hurrian. Their origin northeast of Mesopotamia, in Caucasia or beyond, is inferred from an indirect link between Hurrian and Urartian, both descendents of a common "root language" (Proto-Hurrian-Urartian) and connected to northeast Caucasian languages. Textual attestations of Hurrian proper names indicate a gradual migration from east of the Tigris River in the late third millennium across northern Mesopotamia to the Mediterranean coast in the late second millennium BCE, although isolated linguistic associations suggest a Hurrian presence in northern Syria and Anatolia as early as 2000 BCE.

Based on records mainly from Mari, Ugarit, Alalakh, Emar, Nuzi, and Kurruḫanni, the Hurrians are divided historically and geographically into two cultural spheres. [*See* Mari Texts; Ugarit; Alalakh Texts; Emar Texts; Nuzi.] The older eastern sphere encompasses the Hurrian heartland, stretching from the region of Lake Van and Lake Urmia in the north to Kirkuk in the south. The later western sphere centers on southeastern Anatolia and North Syria. They each absorbed Sumero-Akkadian traditions and were briefly united under the Mitannian hegemony in the mid-second millennium BCE. Records of their religious and literary heritage were presumably compiled in Waššukanni, the still-undiscovered capital of Mitanni in northern Syria. Records were thence passed on via Kizzuwatna to the Hittite capital, Ḫattuša/Boğazköy where they were found much altered and adapted, mostly in Hittite translation. Based largely on the archives from Ḫattuša, what is known of Hurrian religion, culture, and literature is biased toward the western traditions. [*See* Mitanni; Boğazköy.]

History of Research. The focus of early Hurrian scholarship was on language. Philological research began in the late nineteenth century with studies on the "Mitanni letter" found in the diplomatic archives at Tell el-Amarna, Egypt, in 1887. [*See* Amarna Tablets.] The unknown language of the letter from Tušratta, king of Mitanni, to Amenophis III was first called Mitanni after the sender's country of origin. Its decipherment was aided by contemporary letters in Akkadian containing the same subject matter and style. [*See* Akkadian.] Similarities between words in the Mitanni letter and words marked with the gloss *su(-bir$_4$^{ki})* in Old Akkadian texts led to the designation *Subarian,* after the vague regional name of *Subartu* found in Akkadian and Babylonian records. This term was ultimately replaced by *Hurrian,* following the self-descriptive term used by the Hittites to characterize a related language on tablets from Ḫattuša.

Initial attempts to trace the origin of Hurrian and its speakers were influenced by the Indo-Aryan throne names of second-millennium Mitannian kings and certain gods invoked in their treaties found in Ḫattuša. While this association has long been discredited, the presence of Indo-Aryan proper names, loanwords, and technical terms in Hurrian texts indicates some interaction between the two language groups either before or after they entered the Mesopotamian scene (see below). The proposed equation between Hurrians and Subarians was dismissed on the grounds that textual evidence for the latter antedates references to the former (Gelb, 1944; and for the theory that Subartu represents an imaginary "literary" land, see Michalowski, 1986).

Interest in the Hurrians was rekindled during the 1930s by new discoveries of texts at Nuzi, Ugarit, Alalakh, and Mari. With the publication of texts from Ḫattuša, the basis for philological and historical research was broadened. Prewar analyses of the Hurrian language and grammar, summarized by Ephraim Speiser (1941), have been emended and updated by several scholars. Its characteristics include an ergative sentence structure and the use of suffixes.

The east Hurrian sphere is represented by the fifteenth- and fourteenth-century BCE texts from sites in and around Kirkuk, particularly Nuzi, whose Hurro-Akkadian archives provide key information on the sociolegal institutions, customs, and practices of its predominantly Hurrian population. The publication of these texts, begun in the 1930s and now nearing completion, has given rise to a wide range of studies on these subjects. This material is balanced for the west by the archives from Alalakh and Ugarit. Research into the Hurrian tradition from Ḫattuša is well underway, with the aid of Hittite-Hurrian bilinguals discovered in 1983 and the systematic publication of Hurrian texts.

Material evidence of the Hurrians has long been sought by archaeologists. In keeping with theories of cultural change current in the 1930s and 1940s, the Hurrians were linked with the appearance of novel ceramic types and glyptic styles. Khirbet Kerak ware, Khabur ware, Bichrome ware, Nuzi ware, and Nuzi/Kirkuk/Mitannian glyptic are among many supposed hallmarks of the Hurrians. These have since been discarded on the grounds of their different origin, chronology, or distribution (Barrelet, 1977). Indeed, recent studies have left little hope of ever identifying a distinctive culture of the Hurrians, whose main contribution, after more than a millennium of assimilation, lies in the transmission of traditions they encountered before and during their migration across northern Mesopotamia to Syria and Asia Minor.

History. The earliest (Akkadian period) evidence of the Hurrians is in the form of personal names on a tablet dated to Naram-Sin, tablets from Gasur (later Nuzi), and a marble inscription from Nippur concerning a gift of garments. [*See* Nippur.] According to these, the Hurrians controlled minor states to the north and northeast of Akkade, and they formed a minority of the population at Gasur east of the Tigris, near Kirkuk. [*See* Akkade.] The oldest known Hurrian ruler from this area is Talpuš-atili of Nagar, whose Late Akkadian seal was found at Tell Brak (perhaps ancient Nagar/Nawar or Taide). Atal-šen, king of Urkeš (possibly Tell Mozan) and Nawar, is known from an inscribed bronze foundation tablet that, though dated to the Late Gutian (2090–2048 BCE) or Early Ur III (2047–1940 BCE) period, adopts older Akkadian period curse formulas. [*See* Brak, Tell; Mozan, Tell.]

Repeated campaigns conducted against Hurrian populations during the Ur III period brought large numbers of Hurrian prisoners to Sumer from regions north, northeast, and east of the Tigris, above the Diyala. Toward the end of this period (c. 1970), the northern Tigris region appears to be ruled by the Hurrian Tiš-atal, "man of Ninua" (Nineveh), probably also known as Tiš-atal, *endan* ("ruler" or "god") of Urkeš, who left a foundation inscription—the oldest known Hurrian text adopting the widespread cuneiform syllabary. [*See* Nineveh.] His title suggests that he was deified in the tradition of the Ur III kings, like his namesake, Tiš-atal, king of Karahar (Harhar), and other contemporary Hurrian rulers east of the Tigris.

A letter to the king of Kaneš from Anumhirbi, prince of Mama, may indicate that the region around Maraş was populated by Hurrians in the early eighteenth century BCE. [*See* Kaneš.] Their expansion from the Zagros foothills to the Middle Euphrates River and northern Syria is documented in the late eighteenth–mid-sixteenth century BCE archives of Mari and Alalakh VII; by the seventeenth century BCE they had filtered into Palestine. In the wake of Shamshi-Adad I's death and the disintegration of his empire, numerous Hurrian dynasties sprang up between the Zagros and the Euphrates, and rulers with possible Hurrian names are attested west of the Euphrates at Urshum and Hashshum. While the proposed identification between the Hurrians and the seventeenth-century BCE Hyksos dynasty in the Nile Delta has been refuted, it is possible that the Hyksos infiltration resulted from the expansion of the Hurrians and the gradual collapse of the urban system of Palestine at this time. [*See* Delta; Hyksos.]

This latest Hurrian incursion into northern Mesopotamia following the collapse of the Old Assyrian kingdom was accompanied by the arrival of Indo-Aryan immigrants. Little of those immigrants survives other than a few loanwords—the names of deities and personal names that distinguish the ruling dynasty of Mitanni, a Hurrian kingdom probably already founded in the sixteenth century BCE, although it is first mentioned in an inscription dated to Thutmose I (1494–1482 BCE). At this time, in about 1560 BCE (short chronology), the Hurrians posed a threat and eventually contributed to the downfall of the Old Hittite kingdom, whose frontier had reached the Euphrates. In about 1470 BCE, Parrattarna, king of the Hurrians, extended the borders of Mitanni to the Mediterranean. The archives of Alalakh IV show a dramatic increase in the Hurrian population, which is thought to have also penetrated central and southern Syria. The kingdom of Mitanni (Hurri, Naharina, Ḫanigalbat) reached its zenith under Saustatar, whose realm embraced the entire Hurrian-speaking area from the Zagros to the Mediterranean and Cilicia. [*See* Cilicia.]

Thereafter, during the fourteenth and thirteenth centuries BCE, as the kingdom was reduced to the Upper Khabur basin, the Hurrians of Cilicia and northern Syria fell under Hittite supremacy, while those in northern Mesopotamia were subjugated by the Assyrians, who vied against Kassite Babylonia for control of Arrapḫa east of the Tigris. [*See* Khabur; Kassites.] The Mitannian decline, which began in about 1400 BCE with the defection of Kizzuwatna to the Hittites under Saustatar's successor, Artatama I, was hastened by internal power struggles during the reign of Tušratta, which led to the formation of a rival regime under Aratatama II, an ally of the Hittites and the Assyrians. Following Tušratta's death, sometime between 1340 and 1330 BCE, Mitanni survived as a vassal state first of the Hittite Empire and then of the Assyrian Empire. By the end of Shalmaneser I's reign (1263–1234 BCE), the Assyrians had established direct rule over the former territory of Ḫanigalbat (an Akkadian term for Mitanni first attested in an Old Babylonian text). Thereafter, the title "king of Ḫanigalbat," is connected with two high-ranking Assyrian dignitaries but may have survived as a formality. Sporadic references to Hurrian rulers in the Upper Tigris region continued into the twelfth century BCE, and Hurrian proper names were still attested in the mid-first millennium BCE in the region south of Lake Van. However, the survival of the Hurrian language, which in the fourteenth century BCE had spread at least as far as central Syria, is uncertain.

Religion and Mythology. The impact of the Hurrians and their traditions extended far beyond the shrinking boundaries of Mitanni. This is evident in the Hurrian throne names adopted by Hittite viceroys at Carchemish and by the Hittite veneration of Hurrian deities, notably the weather god, Teššup, whose cult was imported to Kizzuwatna from Ḫalab (Aleppo), probably by Tudḫaliya I, in the late fifteenth century BCE. [*See* Carchemish.] The introduction of west Hurrian cults to Ḫattuša may date back to the Old Hittite period, when Muršili I presumably removed the local deities from the Hurrian towns he besieged following his conquest of Ḫalab. The major influx of Hurrian-Kizzuwatnean rituals and incantations began in the reign of Arnuwanda I and climaxed during the empire period, when the state religion reflects strong Hurrian influence.

Pantheon. Foremost among the oldest Hurrian deities is the weather god, Teššup, whose rise to the head of the pantheon, in the early second millennium BCE, coincided with his identification with Syro-Mesopotamian counterparts of similar standing. His consort/sister in most areas is Šawuška, the goddess of war and sex, who was identified with the Mesopotamian Ishtar and the Syrian Išara. Supreme goddess of Mitanni, she also headed the local pantheons of many eastern towns, where she was worshipped under numerous guises. The most famous of these was Ishtar of Nineveh, whose healing powers were famed as far as Egypt and whose cult survived at least to the reign of Sargon II (721–705 BCE). The grain god Kumarbi—counterpart of Enlil, Dagan, and El—features at the center of several Hurrian myths on divine succession. Among these, the "Song of the Kingship and Heaven," itself influenced by Babylonian prototypes, foreshadows the theogony of Hesiod (700 BCE). The related theme of the Ḫedammu myth and the "Song of Ullikummi," in which Kumarbi challenges his succession by the weather god, is also paralleled in Greek mythology. The dethroned Kumarbi becomes one of the "ancient gods"—a group of underworld deities attested only in Hittite myths, rituals, state treaties, and art—derived from Hurrian theology but who may be pre-Hurrian and pre-Semitic. Their depiction at Yazılıkaya is connected with the cult of the dead king Tudḫaliya IV.

The adoption of Sumero-Akkadian deities goes back to Akkadian times, when Nergal, and probably also Ea, was incorporated into the Hurrian pantheon. Others, such as the moon goddess Ningal, were absorbed later in the second millennium BCE via Syria, where the native cults of Aštabi, Adamma, Išhara, Allani, and Hepat also influenced the west Hurrian tradition. Information on this tradition comes from Hittite-Hurrian bilinguals from Kizzuwatna and from the rock sanctuary at Yazılıkaya, where Hepat, identified with the Hittite sun goddess of Arinna, replaces Šawuška as Teššup's consort in the representation of the Hurrian pantheon based on Kizzuwatnean lines.

Rituals and cult. What little is known of Hurrian ritual and cult comes almost entirely from texts. Their anthropomorphic deities were anointed, clothed, and provided with food and drink. The abundance of composite creatures in the earliest seal impressions from Nuzi suggests that east Hurrian rituals included a demonic component, also apparent in early Middle Assyrian glyptic. [*See* Seals.]

The temple was the main place of worship. The *hamri,* a place of worship associated with the worship of Teššup, is widely attested also in Babylonia. [*See* Babylon.] Nuzi texts mention a sacred grove, and part of the Hittite-Hurrian rock sanctuary at Yazılıkaya may have been used for cathartic rites.

Cathartic rites are central to Hurrian magical practice, based as it is on monistic thought. Rites of homeopathic and contagious magic were accompanied by incantations. The oldest Hurrian incantations from Mari and southern Babylonia date to the Old Babylonian period, but may derive from Ur III period penetrations into Hurrian territories in the north. The practice of extispicy (the examination of entire entrails to receive divine messages) and omen inquiries was adopted entirely from Babylonian traditions.

Settlement Pattern and Social Structure. Apart from slaves exported to southern Mesopotamia, the Hurrians settled the northern Fertile Crescent above the 200-mm isohyet, where animal husbandry and dry farming were possible without irrigation. This situation favored the formation of self-sufficient villages founded partly on kin relationships, implying the inalienability of land. In time, these villages fell under the jurisdiction of numerous Hurrian dynasties, which exacted taxes and military services. The military was headed by an elite known as *rākib narkabti* ("chariot drivers") in the east and *marianni-na* in Syria and Palestine, who were skilled in the use of horse-drawn light war chariots. [*See* Chariots.]

The primary source for Hurrian socioeconomic and legal practices are the mid-second millennium BCE archives at Nuzi. Recent studies have shown, however, that many of these practices, once considered the antecedents of biblical conventions and narratives, are Mesopotamian in origin.

Material Culture and Technology. No trend in monumental or minor art, style, or iconography has the life span and distribution of the Hurrians. Their penchant for assimilation is evident in their art and architecture, which reflect long-established local traditions that vary from one end of the Hurrian-speaking realm to the other. The temple, palace, painted pottery, and cylinder seals of Alalakh IV are marked by Syrian and Aegean influences, while at Nuzi, in the east, Mesopotamian and Elamite traditions predominate. The stylized frontality of certain mid-second-millennium BCE sculptures from Aššur, Alalakh, and Tell Brak was perceived as Hurrian until the recent discovery of precursors in Mesopotamia and Syria. The synthesis of Hurrian and foreign concepts and style is apparent in later reliefs and statues of the Late Hittite Empire period and from minor Neo-Hittite states in southern Anatolia and northern Syria of the first millennium BCE. Foremost among these is the monumental rock relief at Yazılıkaya, which represents the west Hurrian pantheon in local Hittite attire and composition. Both an older rock relief near Imamkulu and a later libation scene from Malatya also focus on the Hittite/Hurrian storm god, Teššup, whose stance and attendants recall scenes on seals of Mitannian date. Certain seals of this period may portray the death of Humbaba, as described in the Sumero-Akkadian Epic of Gilgamesh, of which Hurrian copies have been found. Scenes related to myths introduced by the east Hurrians occur on seal impressions from Nuzi (Ḫedammu myth) and on the ninth-century BCE gold bowl from Hasanlu IV in Iran (Kumarbi epic). [*See* Hasanlu.]

The Hurrians have been linked to a number of trades and technological innovations. The oldest of these is the trade of the copper worker, *ta/ibira,* based on an Old Sumerian term of Hurrian derivation (Wilhelm, 1988). Less compelling is the evidence linking Hurrians with the introduction of the light horse-drawn war chariot, the composite bow, the "Hurrian ram," and scale armor for men and horses, most of which existed well before they were adapted to military use by a military elite. The supposed Hurrian origin of technical terms relating to glass- and glazed-ware production is doubtful. Glassmaking reaches back to the third millennium. [*See* Glass.] The sudden surge in the scale and range of glass objects produced from the fourteenth century BCE onward reflects the economic and political climate during the Amarna period, when palace patronage of specialists crafts is widespread.

[*See also* Hurrian.]

BIBLIOGRAPHY

Language

Speiser, Ephraim Avigdor. *Introduction to Hurrian.* Annual of the American Schools of Oriental Research, 20. New Haven, 1941. Summary of all prewar research on the Hurrian language and grammar; still a basic reference for all subsequent studies.

History

Chiera, Edward, and Ephraim Avigdor Speiser. "A New Factor in the History of the Ancient Near East." *Annual of the American Schools of Oriental Research* 6 (1926): 75–92. Introduction to the Nuzi material, which the authors correctly link with the Hurrian records from Ḫattuša and the "Mitanni letter" from Tell el-Amarna, leading to one of the first discussions on the Hurrians.

Eichler, B. L. "Nuzi and the Bible: A Retrospective." In *DUMU-E$_2$—DUB-BA-A: Studies in Honor of Åke W. Sjöberg,* edited by Hermann Behrens et al., pp. 107–119. Occasional Publications of the Samuel Noah Kramer Fund, 11. Philadelphia, 1989. A critical review of the impact of Nuzi scholarship on biblical studies from the early comparisons between sociolegal customs at Nuzi and those in the Bible to more recent scepticism regarding the Hurrian background of the customs at Nuzi and their relevance for dating and interpreting specific biblical narratives and institutions.

Gelb, Ignace J. *Hurrians and Subarians.* University of Chicago, Oriental Institute, Studies in Ancient Oriental Civilization, no. 22. Chicago, 1944. Classic monograph in which Gelb counters the then-prevalent identification between the Hurrians and Subarians with the thesis that they represent two distinct ethnic groups, the Subarians being older than the Hurrians. Reviewed by Speiser in *Journal of the American Oriental Society* 68 (1948): 1–13, in which he argues that the truth lies somewhere in between.

Matthews, Donald M., and Jesper Eidem. "Tell Brak and Nagar." *Iraq* 55 (1993): 201–207. Recent contribution of textual and glyptic evidence for the oldest known Hurrian king, with suggestions on the locations of Nawar and Nagar.

Michalowski, Piotr. "Mental Maps and Ideology: Reflections on Subartu." In *The Origins of Cities in Dry-Farming Syria and Mesopotamia in the Third Millennium B.C.,* edited by Harvey Weiss, pp. 129–156. Guilford, Conn., 1986. A new look at the study of ancient Near Eastern geography that challenges many existing reconstructions of history. Taking the example of "Subartu," a word whose meaning fluctuates from period to period, the author demonstrates that geographical terminology is dependent on contextual usage. Geographical naming and description is figurative, and references in both literary and so-called history texts cannot be taken at face value.

Na'aman, Nadav. "The Hurrians and the End of the Middle Bronze Age in Palestine." *Levant* 26 (1994): 175–187. The most recent evaluation of Hurrian infiltration into Palestine and its effect on the decline of the Middle Bronze Age urban culture of Canaan and its subsequent conquest by the Egyptians.

Speiser, Ephraim Avigdor. "Ethnic Movements in the Near East in the Second Millennium B.C." *Annual of the American Schools of Oriental Research* 13 (1933): 13–54. Key, but now superseded, article delimiting the proper designation for the Hurrians and determining their relation to the ḫabiru and Hyksos.

Speiser, Ephraim Avigdor. "The Hurrian Participation in the Civilizations of Mesopotamia, Syria, and Palestine." *Cahiers d'Histoire Mondiale* 1 (1953–1954): 311–327. Still relevant objective analysis of the origin, appearance, and contribution of the Hurrians, with an emphasis on the cultural synthesis among the Hurrian, Sumero-Akkadian, and West Semitic traditions in Mesopotamia and in Syria-Palestine.

Wilhelm, Gernot. "Gedanken zur Frühgeschichte der Hurriter und zum hurritisch-urartäischen Sprachvergleich." In *Hurriter und Hurritisch,* edited by Volkert Haas, pp. 43–67. Konstanzer Altorientalische Symposien, vol. 2. Constance, Germany, 1988. The author opts for a later Gutian/Ur III date over the Akkadian date proposed by some scholars for the earliest known Hurrian royal inscription of Atal-šen, based on orthographic discrepancies in its pseudo-Akkadian curse formula. A case is made for the Hurrian derivation of the Sumerian designation for *copper worker,* which introduces a new link between Old Hurrian and Urartian.

Wilhelm, Gernot. *The Hurrians.* Translated by Jennifer Barnes. Warminster, 1989. Introduction to the history and culture of the Hurrians; provides a masterful synthesis of the research to date. Reviewed by M. C. Astour in *Journal of Near Eastern Studies* 53.3 (1994): 225–230.

Material Culture

Barrelet, M.-T. *Méthodologie et critiques,* vol. 1, *Problèmes concernant les Hurrites.* Paris, 1977. Collection of essays concerned with the problems inherent in defining a Hurrian material culture on the basis of available archaeological and linguistic evidence. The conclusions show that it is impossible to relate one category of archaeological material to an ethnic sector of a composite community.

Moorey, P. R. S. "The Hurrians: The Mittani and Technological Innovation." In *Archaeologia Iranica et Orientalis: Miscellanea in honorem Louis Vanden Berghe,* edited by Leon De Meyer and E. Haerinck, pp. 273–286. Ghent, 1989. Critically reviews a supposed innovation accredited to the Hurrians: the introduction of the light horse-drawn war chariot with its associated armory; it concludes that both precede their documented adoption and adaption by the Hurrian military aristocracy.

Stein, Diana L. "Mythologische Inhalte der Nuzi-Glyptik." In *Hurriter und Hurritisch,* edited by Volkert Haas, pp. 173–209. Konstanzer Altorientalische Symposien, vol. 2. Constance, Germany, 1988. Interpretation of mythological imagery in the Nuzi iconography relating, in particular, to Teššup and Ishtar-Šawuška.

DIANA L. STEIN

HYDRAULICS. The absence of artificial waterworks at Stone Age sites discovered so far leads to the assumption that human activity then centered around natural water sources, such as rivers and springs. In some instances permanent dwellings were established near a natural water source, while in others nomads wandered in its environs. The earliest evidence of a built water installation in Israel is from the end of the Stone Age, in the Pottery Neolithic (PN) period. At the site of ʿAtlit, a well, dated to the sixth millennium, was dug to the water table. The earliest concept of a well probably developed when a river ran dry and people began digging to reach the point in the riverbed where access to the retreating water level would be reached. In this manner, the world's first water installation, the well, was invented. The well at ʿAtlit is lined with stone; because the Mediterranean's water level has risen, the well-head is today situated about 10 m below where it was in the sixth millennium (Galili and Nir, 1993).

The second earliest well in Israel was discovered in the Beersheba region and dates to the fourth millennium, to the Chalcolithic period. Irrigation channels from this period exist on the Beersheba plain, which testifies to the use of water for irrigation farming. There are also early signs of water storage at Beersheba and Meṣar. [*See* Beersheba; Irrigation; Cisterns; Reservoirs.]

A concomitant of the appearance of the earliest planned walled cities, from the Early Bronze period on, was a new type of waterwork: a tunnel quarried to reach underground water (Khirbet ez-Zeraqun, Jordan) and a central water installation for collecting runoff water (Arad and Ai in Israel and Jawa in Jordan). [*See* Zeraqun, Khirbet ez-; Arad, *article on* Iron Age Period; Ai; Jawa.] These waterworks formed part of the urban plan. City planners incorporated waterworks within the city wall, to serve them in times of siege. At small, unfortified sites, cisterns were cut into soft, impermeable, chalky rock to store water. In mountainous regions, such as the Samaria hill country, where the inhabitants were familiar with the composition of the rock, natural springs were adapted for use as water sources for the nearby settlements.

The earliest use of partially plastered water cisterns is attested at Hazor from the Middle Bronze Age onward. [*See* Hazor.] In that same period, a brilliant innovation was implemented at several planned, fortified cities: a spring with an abundant yield of water was encompassed within the city walls. The method was employed at Tel Dan, where one of the Dan springs was enclosed within the walls; at Tel Kabri, where the city ramparts encircle ʿEin-Shepaʿ, and at Jericho, where the Elisha Spring is included within the perimeter of the walls. [*See* Dan; Kabri, Tel.] At Qatna, in Syria, too, the city wall encompasses a natural water source. This method signals a return to the Neolithic exploitation of a natural water source, but in a more technically sophisticated manner. At Tel Gerisa, near Tel Aviv, the uppermost section of the waterworks, situated within the city walls, reaches as far down as the water table. [*See* Gerisa, Tel.] It is a round pit, hewn into the half hard limestone (kurkar), with a diameter of 5.5 m. A flight of steps leading to the water is cut into the wall of the pit. Wells that descend vertically to the water table have also been found at Lachish, Tel Nami, and Tel Haror. [*See* Lachish; Nami, Tel; Haror, Tel.] The various types of MB water installations reveal a high level of engineering and technological expertise.

In the Late Bronze Age, the use of similar installations continued while new ones were developed: a well at Beth-Shean; a huge, well-plastered cistern, 150 cu m in volume, at Hazor, beneath the Canaanite palace; and many cisterns at Beth-Shemesh. [*See* Beth-Shean; Beth-Shemesh.] The waterworks at Gezer may also date to this period. [*See* Gezer.] Mycenaean waterworks, designed in this period to provide a regular water supply, are found in the large fortified Mycenaean cities of Mycenae, Tiryns, and Athens.

From the Early Iron Age onward, only a few cisterns and wells are known: at Beersheba, Dor, and Gerisa. [*See* Dor.] It would seem that during this period water was obtained for the most part from natural springs, so that no water installations have been found within the perimeters of settlements. The absence of such installations accords with what is known of the simple way of life of this period, which overlaps with the period of the Israelite settlement. The only known cities in Israel at the time were inhabited by the Sea Peoples, and, indeed, at Dor a well built of hewn stones dating from the eleventh century BCE was discovered.

During the Iron II period, large water installations were constructed at Hazor, Gezer, Megiddo, Gibeon, Jerusalem, Yoqneʿam, Yableam, and elsewhere. [*See* Megiddo; Gibeon; Jerusalem; Yoqneʿam.] Characteristic of these projects is the quarrying of huge pits out of the bedrock on which the city was founded, in order to reach the water table and secure a constant supply of water, even in times of siege. These waterworks are monumental in scope and size: the depth of the shafts at Hazor and Megiddo is 36 m, and the length of the excavated tunnel at Megiddo is about 50 m. [*See* Water Tunnels.] The volume of the tunnel space is that great in order to allow better ventilation (oil lamps were used for lighting, which diminished the air supply). These waterworks fell into disuse at the end of the Iron Age and were buried beneath millions of cubic meters of dirt and rubble.

They were only discovered through archaeological exploration.

In light of these finds, it is reasonable to conclude that every fortified city of this era included a water installation for times of siege. The magnitude of these projects and their appearance at the most important sites in the kingdoms of Judah and Israel testify to a high level of engineering and geological expertise, as well as to the economic and administrative capability of the state bureaucracy. In Jerusalem, at the end of this period, Hezekiah's tunnel was dug, the longest of all Iron Age tunnels, to convey the water of the Gihon Spring into the city. In that period, King Sennacherib of Assyria built the world's longest aqueduct to bring water from a distance of 55 km (34 mi.) to Nineveh, his capital. [*See* Aqueducts; Nineveh.] The use of cisterns also increased then. They have been discovered at many sites, but especially noteworthy are those unearthed at Tell en-Naṣbeh. [*See* Naṣbeh, Tell en-.] At several locations in Phrygia, subterranean water systems have been found that in structure closely resemble those in Israel: a vertical shaft cut into the rock to reach the water table.

From the Persian period, only two wells have been discovered, cut into the limestone on the coastal plain. The first, unearthed in the Tell Qasile excavations, is quadrangular, and the second, excavated at Tel Mikhmoret, is round. [*See* Qasile, Tell.] Some of the cisterns found at Tell en-Naṣbeh also date to this period, which witnessed a decline in the technology of waterworks.

In the Hellenistic period, cisterns continued to be used and the first aqueducts appear at desert sites in Israel that are closely connected to the activities of the Hasmonean kings. Some of those aqueducts were designed to trap and collect water from flash floods; others conveyed water from natural springs. At Jericho, a ceramic pipe was discovered that operated as an inverted siphon (see below) to bring water up to one of the Hasmonean palaces. [*See* Jericho.] The first urban aqueduct was engineered at Akko; it conducted water underground to the city from a distance of about 14 km (9 mi.). [*See* Akko.] In this period there is a marked influence of Greek culture on the development of water installations, especially aqueducts, which increased continually into the Roman period.

The Roman period signals the apex of aqueduct construction. Most cities in the Roman Empire at large, and in the Near East in particular, including desert cities such as Petra and Palmyra, had a system of aqueducts that brought water from afar. [*See* Petra; Palmyra.] Only the southern coastal cities, such as Ashkelon and Lod, lacked aqueducts because there were no natural springs in their vicinity. The city of Antipatris (Aphek), which lies near a water source, had no need of waterworks. In Jerusalem and at Caesarea, the chief cities of Israel in that period, a high level of engineering overcame various topological obstacles (e.g., use of an inverted siphon in Jerusalem, arched aqueduct in Caesarea). [*See* Ashkelon; Aphek; Caesarea.] In many places pools and reservoirs were hewn and constructed. [*See* Pools.] Settlements each had many water cisterns and various irrigation installations. At three locations, inverted siphons were built of stone: Jerusalem, Hippos/Susita (see figure 1), and Beth-Yeraḥ. [*See* Beth-Yeraḥ.]

In the Byzantine period, the existing aqueducts continued to be used and additional ones were built. Elaborate water systems were constructed as a basic element of the foundation of monasteries in the Judean Desert. Every village and settlement had numerous cisterns, as many as one per household. Some aqueduct water was directed into the bathhouses originally built in the Roman period. [*See* Baths.]

During the Early Arab period, the main centers of the Umayyad caliphate were Jericho and Ramla, to which aqueducts were built. [*See* Ramla.] In desert areas, water systems in the form of chains of wells (Ar., *qanat, fugarot*) were developed to irrigate agricultural estates. These can be seen along the Syro-African Rift Valley from Faṣael in the north to ʿEin-ʿEvrona in the south. The end of the Umayyad period witnessed severe crises, both politically with changes

HYDRAULICS. Figure 1. *Holes for cleaning in the stone pipe of the inverted syphon.* Under the pavement of the main street (cardo) at Susita. (Courtesy Tsvika Tsuk)

under the ʿAbbasids and physically with a large earthquake, and water systems fell into disuse, except for the Ramla aqueduct, which continued to be used into the reign of the ʿAbbasid Caliphs.

In the Crusader period considerable use was made of water systems designed to gather runoff into the large cisterns of fortresses. Most noteworthy are those at Belvoir (Kokhav ha-Yarden) and Qalʿat Nimrod.

The use of the lower aqueduct to Jerusalem was renewed in the Mamluk period to convey drinking water to the inhabitants of the city. Several *sabil*s ("drinking troughs"/"fountains") were erected alongside it. In the Ottoman period the same aqueduct was used, but a clay pipe was inserted in it. An impressive aqueduct was built leading to the city of Akko in the days of Gizar Pasha that was later destroyed. A new aqueduct was built by Süleiman in its stead. This aqueduct, borne on arches, operated from 1814 to 1948. As it approached the city it entered an inverted siphon made of interlocking stone rings, which were incorporated into towers *(suterazi)*, to release the water pressure.

At the time of the British Mandate (1917–1948), the Akko aqueduct and a Roman-built aqueduct outside Jerusalem, the Biyyar aqueduct, operated. The latter led water to Solomon's Pools, from which the water was then pumped and conveyed in pipes to Jerusalem. Although this aqueduct has been abandoned, water still flows in it.

BIBLIOGRAPHY

ʿAmit, David, et al., eds. *The Aqueducts of Ancient Palestine* (in Hebrew). Jerusalem, 1989.

Galili, Ehud, and Yaacov Nir. "The Submerged Pre-Pottery Neolithic Water Well of Athlit-Yam, Northern Israel, with Its Paleoenvironmental Implications." *The Holocene* 3 (1993): 268–270.

Garbrecht, Günther. "Hydrologic and Hydraulic Concepts in Antiquity." In *Hydraulics and Hydraulic Research: A Historical Review*, edited by Günther Garbrecht, pp. 1–22. Rotterdam, 1987.

Shiloh, Yigal. "Underground Water Systems in Eretz-Israel in the Iron Age." In *Archaeology and Biblical Interpretation: Essays in Memory of D. Glenn Rose*, edited by Leo G. Perdue et al., pp. 203–244. Atlanta, 1987.

TSVIKA TSUK

Translated from Hebrew by Ilana Goldberg

HYDROLOGY. Water economy in the Syria-Palestine region is subject to the influence of the Mediterranean climate on the one hand, and the desert climate on the other. The rainy season extends from October to May, with most of that rain falling between December and February. During the rest of the year (June–September), the amount of rainfall is negligible. Annual rainfall on the coastal strip is 500–600 mm; in the central hill country 600–800 mm; in the semiarid regions approximately 100–200 mm; and in the desert only 25–100 mm.

Because the region does not have any large rivers whose sources lie outside of it (such as Egypt's Nile River), its primary source of water is precipitation. Rainfall replenishes the water table and sometimes creates powerful streams of runoff water. The region has a great number of natural springs, mostly in the hill country and on the periphery of the coastal region. Most of the springs have a small flow, ranging from 10,000 to 350,000 cu m per year, with a considerable decrease in summer and fall. The few large springs, with flows ranging between several million cubic meters to 250 million cu m, depend on long-term rainfall patterns. Consequently, they yield a consistently strong flow of water through the summer and fall and until the following rainy season. In northern Israel and in the western Levant, such springs are large enough to create rivers. The largest sources, at the foot of Mt. Hermon, feed the tributaries of the Jordan River. The Yarkon River springs are the most important water source for the coastal region (220 million cu m per year).

Throughout history, humans have exploited these water sources in various ways. In the coastal region, most commonly, wells were dug or hewn to reach the water table. In the hill country, inhabitants enjoyed natural springs. In addition, cisterns were hewn to collect runoff. In desert areas, some water was obtained from springs at oases, but mostly from collection in cisterns.

Streams and springs served as the prime water source. Running streams attracted human settlement, especially in the Stone Age period. Material remains of human activity in the biblical period have been discovered along stream and riverbanks. Water that is both clean and of high quality is found in springs, which led humans to establish dwellings as close to their source as possible. In the classical period, aqueducts were built to bring water to cities, invariably from natural springs. Even the city of Tiberias, on Lake Kinneret (Sea of Galilee), obtained water from a source 15 km (9 mi.) away via an aqueduct, rather than from the lake. [*See* Tiberias.]

Wells were a second best water source, providing clean water from an aquifer. In contrast to a natural spring, an artificial well could be located in accordance with a settlement's needs. Its major drawbacks were its great depth; the labor required to dig, hew, and construct it; and the possibility that water would not be found. Wells were used as early as the sixth millennium BCE, as was found in the underwater excavation near ʿAtlit.

Water cisterns were tertiary sources, although in many areas they were the only solution for collecting and storing water. Cisterns first appear in the third or second millennium BCE. To ensure the quality of cistern water, cisterns were cleaned annually, the channels leading water to them were maintained, and the top of the cistern was covered to prevent the growth of algae and to keep out dirt as well as to enable the cistern to be sealed and to prevent people from falling into it. In this way, it was often possible to preserve good drinking water in a cistern from the end of spring until fall. Domestic animals such as dogs and cats were kept away from the house to prevent them from soiling the courtyard or roof where rainwater was collected. In Pergamon, Turkey, city statutes were discovered that warn of strict measures against citizens who do not keep their cisterns clean. [*See* Pergamon.] In addition to cisterns, water was stored in reservoirs of various types: huge underground cisterns and open-air reservoirs such as dams and pools. These were all designed to store runoff or spring water conducted via an aqueduct to an open or closed reservoir. Drinking water did not generally come from open reservoirs because of the possibility of pollution. It was kept in the closed reservoirs and retrieved with pails or conducted into the city either by aqueduct or on beasts of burden.

In the course of time, the region has experienced both wet and dry climatic periods, which have dictated settlement patterns. Because the Chalcolithic period is known to have been wet, settlement proliferated in the Beersheba valley, which had many more water sources then than at present. [*See* Beersheba.] In the hill country, however, the climate was much colder than today, which explains the scarcity of settlement in that region. [*See* Judah.] There seems not to have been considerable climatic change between the Chalcolithic period and the present. As a result, today's hydrological data can serve as a basis for investigating the limitations of water use and seasonal differences with a margin of error of only about 20 percent. Climatic change is not to be confused with years of meager rainfall, when drought presented a threat to the inhabitants of the land, as is mentioned occasionally in the Hebrew Bible (*Jer.* 14). Nevertheless, some researchers have sought to attribute the proliferation of settlement in the Negev both in the Early Bronze Age and in the Roman period to wet periods.

[*See also* Aqueducts; Cisterns; Dams; Hydraulics; Irrigation; Pools; *and* Reservoirs.]

BIBLIOGRAPHY

Garbrecht, Günther. "Hydrologic and Hydraulic Concepts in Antiquity." In *Hydraulics and Hydraulic Research: A Historical Review*, edited by Günther Garbrecht, pp. 1–22. Rotterdam, 1987.

Karmon, Y. *Eretz Israel, Geography of the Land and Its Regions* (in Hebrew). Tel Aviv, 1973. See pages 36–38.

TSVIKA TSUK

Translated from Hebrew by Ilana Goldberg

HYKSOS. In the reign of Ptolemy II (282–246 BCE), the Egyptian priest-historian Manetho used the Greek name *Hyksos* to identify his fifteenth dynasty, an Asiatic line of kings who ruled northern Egypt. The word itself is derived from an Egyptian term, *Ḥḳ3(w) ḫ3swt*, meaning "ruler(s) of foreign countries." On linguistic grounds, a West Semitic background can be inferred for these Asiatics; the archaeological data point to a more southern, Palestinian origin, although a few scholars prefer a Syrian background.

Rise of the Hyksos. Asiatics migrated down into northern Egypt in increasing numbers during the twelfth (1963–1786 BCE) and early thirteenth (c. 1786–1700 BCE) dynasties. Their principal focus of settlement activity appears to have been the eastern Delta. Initially, they lived peacefully alongside the Egyptians; some were even in their employ (e.g., at the town of Kahun in the Faiyum region).

The Asiatic population in the eastern Delta expanded simultaneously with the deterioration of Egypt's central authority in the late Middle Kingdom (mid- to late thirteenth dynasty [c. 1700–1633 BCE]). This development is reflected in an increase in the number of Delta sites containing Levantine materials whose Middle Bronze II character is especially evident in the area east of the ancient Pelusiac branch of the Nile River, in the region of Khatana-Qantir. Commercial relations between Egypt and Palestine were expanding at the same time. Eventually, the Asiatics may well have taken control of parts of the eastern Delta. In 1648 BCE, the Asiatics captured the old administrative capital at Memphis, the event that inaugurates Manetho's fifteenth dynasty. Whether the takeover of Memphis and northern Egypt was quick and violent, as described in the epitomes of Manetho and in some pharaonic documents, or the control the Asiatics assumed was more gradual—taking advantage of Egypt's weakness to fill a power vacuum—remains under discussion. The former explanation seems more likely, however.

Hyksos Period in Egypt. The Turin king list reports a total of six Hyksos kings who ruled for 108 years (c. 1648–1540 BCE). The name of only the last of those rulers, Khamudy, is preserved on the Turin papyrus. There is considerable debate regarding the identification and order of reign of Khamudy's five predecessors. Donald B. Redford (*Egypt, Canaan, and Israel in Ancient Times,* Princeton, 1992) suggests a dynastic sequence starting with Maaibre Sheshi, followed by Merwoerre Yaqobher, Seweserenre Khyan, Yannass, Apophis, and Khamudy. Many other Asiatic royal names are attested on scarabs from the time of the fifteenth dynasty; some may belong to minor Asiatic princes who held a vassal status to the great Hyksos rulers.

Attempts to reconstruct the internal history and governmental organization of the Hyksos remain largely speculative. The adoption of the Egyptian royal titulary by the Hyksos kings, their dating of events to regnal years in the same manner as the Egyptians (e.g., the dating of the Rhind Mathematical Papyrus to regnal year 33 of Apophis), and the frequent use of the Egyptian administrative title *treasurer* by their officials suggest that the Hyksos government at least partially imitated that of the Egyptians. At the same time, however, the apparent Hyksos practice of ruling through local vassals (both Asiatic and Egyptian) reflects a more Near Eastern tradition.

Archaeology of the Hyksos Period. As an archaeological term, *Hyksos* is often employed to refer to the material remains associated with the Asiatics living in Egypt during the Second Intermediate period, especially at their eastern Delta capital. Avaris (a Greek name derived from the Egyptian term *Ḥwt-wʿrt,* "mansion of the desert plateau") was the site of the Hyksos capital; it later became the royal residence of the nineteenth–twentieth-dynasty pharaohs (1295–1069 BCE), at which time it was known as Piramesse. The largest surviving portion of Avaris is at Tell ed-Dabʿa, which the Austrian archaeologist Manfred Bietak has been excavating since 1966. This is the only site in Egypt where uninterrupted Asiatic occupation during the Second Intermediate period can be traced—and the only Hyksos urban center discovered so far in Egypt.

Archaeological evidence of Asiatic activity in Egypt in the Second Intermediate period appears at several other sites east of the former Pelusiac branch of the Nile. These include Ghita, Inshas, Tell Basta, Tell Farasha, Tell el-Maskhuta (situated along the Wadi Tumilat), Tell es-Sahaba, and Tell el-Yahudiyeh. Tell el-Maskhuta has produced a small, seasonal Asiatic village and burials, while a cemetery and perhaps a large defensive enclosure were found at Tell el-Yahudiyeh. Only cemetery materials are attested at the other sites.

The material goods, cultic architecture, and religious practices of the Asiatics in the Delta during the Hyksos period reflect an amalgam of Syro-Palestinian and Egyptian features. This is evident in the burials at Tell ed-Dabʿa and Tell el-Maskhuta. The principal grave type at Tell ed-Dabʿa during most of the Second Intermediate period was the vaulted mud-brick chamber tomb. Donkey sacrifices were found outside some of these tombs. Similar tombs with donkey sacrifices are attested at Tell el-Maskhuta and at Inshas, while tombs with brick vaulting but without donkey burials have been found at Tell el-Yahudiyeh. Vaulted Middle Bronze II–III tombs have also been reported from Tell Basta, Ghita, and Tell es-Sahaba, while the equine burials are paralleled at several sites in southern Palestine.

Funerary offerings in these Delta tombs and in the Wadi Tumilat include scarabs, jewelry, pottery (of both Egyptian and Levantine types), and alabaster vessels. Tombs in the later phases at Tell ed-Dabʿa sometimes contain Cypriot pottery and follow Egyptian rather than Asiatic funerary practices (the Asiatics having become highly Egyptianized in late Hyksos times). No royal burials have been excavated at Tell ed-Dabʿa. A rich collection of funerary offerings, possibly from a Hyksos royal tomb, is said to come from es-Salhiya, located about 10 km (7 mi.) southeast of Tell ed-Dabʿa (though this hoard may in fact come from Tell ed-Dabʿa).

An important, though controversial, source of information for the history and chronology of the fifteenth dynasty consists of scarabs inscribed with royal names and private names and titles. Because so few texts survive from that era, our knowledge of most Hyksos rulers and officials derives from the appearance of their names on scarabs and such related items as cylinder seals and seal impressions. The Hyksos adopted the Egyptian hieroglyphic script for writing their documents and transcribing their personal names. Through typological analysis of Hyksos royal-name scarabs, Egyptologists have been able to arrange many of the Hyksos rulers in a relative sequence and to link a few of the royal names to the bleak historical record. A concentration of royal-name scarabs in southern Palestine suggests a connection between this region and the eastern Delta, although the exact nature of this relationship is in dispute. Finally, numerous scarabs inscribed with the names and/or titles of officials who may have been Hyksos officials (e.g., the treasurer, Har) have been found, but the common practice among the Asiatics of using Egyptian names makes it difficult to distinguish scarabs of Hyksos officials who adopted Egyptian names from scarabs belonging to contemporary Egyptian bureaucrats.

Data on Hyksos fortifications in Egypt are limited. The high water table and the activities of local peasants searching for mud brick and lime to use as fertilizer have combined to remove any traces of a defensive system surrounding most of the mound at Tell ed-Dabʿa; however, a fortification wall has been uncovered at the village of Ezbet Helmi, situated at the western end of the site. (In the debris above a garden adjacent to the wall hundreds of fragments were found of Aegean-style frescoes from the seventeenth–sixteenth centuries BCE.) Large square earthwork enclosures with brick facing and rounded corners have been found at Tell el-Yahudiyeh and Heliopolis. The similarity between these two structures and those constructed in the Levant in the Middle Bronze Age has led many archaeologists to identify the Delta embankments as Hyksos defense systems. Other archaeologists, however, believe that these embankments are retaining walls for Egyptian temple foundations.

Monuments associated with the Hyksos are rare in the Nile valley, and there is no evidence for Asiatic settlements in that area. The southernmost occurrence of inscriptions, mentioning Hyksos rulers is at Gebelein, located just upriver from Thebes, where a granite block naming Khyan and a lintel containing the name of Apophis were found. It is unclear whether the Hyksos ever controlled Egypt that far south, however. Near the end of the seventeenth dynasty, the border between Theban and Hyksos territory was at Cusae (on the west bank of the Nile, just south of el-Amarna), but it is doubtful that the Hyksos continuously occupied the Nile valley that far south. Instead, they probably maintained authority in Middle and Upper Egypt through local vassals such as Teti, son of Pepi (a local Egyptian ruler at Nefrusy, who is mentioned on the Carnarvon Tablet of the late seventeenth dynasty), and through garrisons positioned at strategic points in the valley. In any event, the history of Hyksos expansion and rule in Egypt cannot be traced in any detail.

The Asiatics in the eastern Delta maintained an active commercial relationship with Cyprus, the Levant, and Nubia. International trade was an important factor in the development of their wealth and power. The seventeenth-dynasty Theban ruler Kamose reports on a historical stela erected at Karnak that he seized several hundred ships in the harbor at Avaris. The goods aboard these ships included numerous Asiatic materials and substances: gold, silver, bronze, lapis lazuli, turquoise, oil, incense, fat, honey, and precious woods. Stone and faience vessels, jewelry, amulets, scarabs, and other Egyptian merchandise were exported to the southern Levant in exchange for such raw materials and finished products. Egyptian objects from this period have been found in considerable numbers at Tell el-ʿAjjul, Gezer, Tell el-Farʿah (South), Jericho, Megiddo, and elsewhere in Palestine. The distinctive Tell el-Yahudiyeh ware, produced both in Egypt and the Levant and widely distributed from Nubia in the south to Syria and Cyprus in the north, demonstrates the far-reaching nature of this trade network. The presence of Middle Kingdom statuary in Middle Bronze II–III contexts in Palestine, as well as in a few contemporaneous deposits in the Aegean and Nubia, suggests that some trade in the Hyksos period consisted of items plundered from Egyptian cemeteries belonging to the early second millennium BCE. As for the small number of monuments containing Hyksos royal names found at Knossos, Baghdad, and the Hittite capital of Ḫattuša (modern Boğazköy), efforts to see in these items evidence for a Hyksos "empire" have long since been abandoned by all but a small minority of academics. The absence of archaeological materials of the Second Intermediate period in the northern Sinai indicates that Egyptian-Levantine trade went by sea rather than over land.

End of the Hyksos Period. The first effort to dislodge the Hyksos from the Nile valley appears to have taken place in the reign of the seventeenth-dynasty Theban king Seqenenre Tao, a contemporary of Apophis; wounds consistent with those made by an Asiatic battle axe were found in the skull of his mummy, suggesting that he met his death in battle. Seqenenre's successor, Kamose, was perhaps initially a vassal of the Hyksos, but he continued the war of liberation. According to a pair of stelae he erected at Karnak (the text of the first of which is partially preserved on two stela fragments and a writing board known as the Carnarvon Tablet), Kamose recaptured much of the Nile valley and besieged, though did not take, Avaris itself. He was followed by his younger brother, Ahmose, the first king of the eighteenth dynasty, who captured Memphis, thereby completing the reconquest of the Nile valley.

The autobiographical inscription of one of Ahmose's naval officers reports that the king subsequently besieged and plundered Avaris. Occupation in the latest Hyksos-period stratum at Tell ed-Dabʿa appears to have ended abruptly, and the tombs of this phase were looted. After taking Avaris, Ahmose besieged and plundered Sharuhen. That town probably should be identified with Tell el-ʿAjjul in Gaza (although Tell Abu Hureirah [Tel Harar] has also been proposed as the site of Sharuhen), which has produced a large number of Hyksos royal-name scarabs and considerable gold jewelry. It may have served as a Hyksos stronghold and commercial emporium. Numerous other towns in ancient Palestine were destroyed and/or abandoned in the second half of the sixteenth century BCE. Whether most of this devastation should be attributed to the Egyptian army has yet to be resolved.

[*See also* ʿAjjul, Tell el-; Dabʿa, Tell ed-; Farʿah, Tell el- (South); Maskhuta, Tell el-; *and* Yahudiyeh, Tell el-.]

BIBLIOGRAPHY

Beckerath, Jürgen von. *Untersuchungen zur politischen Geschichte der zweiten Zwischenzeit in Ägypten.* Ägyptologische Forschungen, vol. 23. Glückstadt, 1964. Fundamental reference work for the history and archaeology of the Second Intermediate period.

Bietak, Manfred. "Avaris and Piramesse: Archaeological Exploration in the Eastern Nile Delta." *Proceedings of the British Academy* 65 (1979): 225–290. First major English-language summary of the Austrian excavations at Tell ed-Dabʿa.

Bietak, Manfred. "Canaan and Egypt during the Middle Bronze Age." *Bulletin of the American Schools of Oriental Research,* no. 281 (1991): 27–72. Discussion of Egyptian-Levantine relations during the Middle Bronze Age, focusing on the stratigraphy and chronology of Tell ed-Dabʿa. Utilizes the author's low chronology for the Levantine materials.

Bietak, Manfred. "Minoan Wall-Paintings Unearthed at Ancient Avaris." *Egyptian Archaeology: The Bulletin of the Egypt Exploration Society* 2 (1992): 26–28. Preliminary report, with color photographs, of an important series of Aegean-style frescoes recently discovered at Avaris.

Dever, William G. "Relations between Syria-Palestine and Egypt in the 'Hyksos' Period." In *Palestine in the Bronze and Iron Ages: Papers in Honour of Olga Tufnell,* edited by Jonathan N. Tubb, pp. 69–87. University of London, Institute of Archaeology, Occasional Publication, no. 11. London, 1985. Disputes Bietak's low chronology for the Middle Bronze Age materials found at Tell ed-Dabʿa, proposing instead a middle chronology.

Habachi, Labib. *The Second Stela of Kamose and His Struggle against the Hyksos Ruler and His Capital.* Abhandlungen des Deutschen Archäologischen Instituts Kairo, Ägyptologische Reihe, vol. 8. Glückstadt, 1972. Translation of Kamose's important historical stela found at Karnak, with textual notes and historical interpretation.

Hoffmeier, J. K. "Reconsidering Egypt's Part in the Termination of the Middle Bronze Age in Palestine." *Levant* 21 (1989): 181–193. Argues against the idea that the Egyptians were responsible for the demise of the Middle Bronze II cities in ancient Palestine, based on an analysis of early eighteenth-dynasty Egyptian texts.

Kaplan, Maureen F. *The Origin and Distribution of Tell el Yahudiyeh Ware.* Studies in Mediterranean Archaeology, vol. 62. Göteborg, 1980. Detailed study of the manufacture, geographic distribution, and chronology of Tell el-Yehudiyeh ware.

Redford, Donald B. "[Hyksos] History." In *The Anchor Bible Dictionary,* vol. 3, pp. 341–344. New York, 1992. Brief, up-to-date survey of Hyksos history.

Tufnell, Olga. *Studies on Scarab Seals,* vol. 2, *Scarab Seals and Their Contribution to History in the Early Second Millennium B.C.* Warminster, 1984. Detailed analysis of Middle Kingdom and Second Intermediate period scarabs (including those inscribed with Hyksos royal names), employing a very high chronology.

Van Seters, John. *The Hyksos: A New Investigation.* New Haven, 1966. Comprehensive study of Hyksos history and archaelogy, based on data available through the early 1960s; must be supplemented by more recent publications.

Ward, William A. "Some Personal Names of the Hyksos Period Rulers and Notes on the Epigraphy of Their Scarabs." *Ugarit Forschungen* 8 (1976): 353–365. Study of Hyksos royal names written in Egyptian hieroglyphs. Most names are identified as Semitic, although a few Hurrian names may also be present.

Weinstein, James M. "The Egyptian Empire in Palestine: A Reassessment." *Bulletin of the American Schools of Oriental Research,* no. 241 (1981): 1–28. Includes a historical analysis of Hyksos royal-name scarabs found in ancient Palestine and assigns the destructions and abandonments of Middle Bronze sites in southern and inland Palestine to the Egyptians.

Weinstein, James M. "[Hyksos] Archaeology." In *The Anchor Bible Dictionary,* vol. 3, pp. 344–348. New York, 1992. Short overview of Hyksos archaeology.

JAMES M. WEINSTEIN

I

IDALION, ancient city-kingdom on Cyprus, located at the modern village of Dhali, twelve miles south of Nicosia, (35°7′ N, 33°25′ E). In 1850 the French antiquarian Honoré d'Albert, the Duc de Luynes, purchased a bronze tablet found on the western acropolis of Idalion, and inscribed in Phoenician and Cypro-syllabic scripts. From 1867 through 1875 Luigi Palma di Cesnola dug at the site, claiming to empty fifteen thousand tombs. He uncovered the remains of an edifice on the summit of the east acropolis, the hill known as "Mouti tou Arvili," said to be a temple to the mother goddess, which had already been cleared by previous treasure hunters. The British banker and consul to the Ottoman Empire in Cyprus, R. Hamilton Lang, in 1868 excavated a "temple" to a god (Apollo Amyklos in Greek; Resheph Mikal in Phoenician). In 1883 and 1885 German newspaper correspondent turned antiquarian Max Ohnefalsch-Richter became superintendent of works for replating under the British Mandate. As such, he excavated there and investigated antiquities in Dhali for several years thereafter.

From 1927 to 1931 the Swedish Cyprus Expedition established the modern chronology for the site. On the western acropolis of Idalion, the hill known as "Ambelliri," Einar Gjerstad and his team excavated all of the structures visible on the highest peak. They dated the fortified "settlement and cult place" they believed they found there to the Late Cypriot III period (1200–1050 BCE). The Swedish publication of the supposed Bronze Age levels shows photographs of whole vessels on "floors" (*SCE,* vol. 2, p. 593, figs. 240–241). Because the area is dotted with tombs, the floor from which the bull rhyton and other Bronze Age artifacts were recovered was perhaps a tomb underlying the Iron Age occupation strata. They believed there was pottery, but no architecture, from the subsequent Cypro-Geometric I–II periods (1050–850), but the area was refortified, they felt, in Cypro-Geometric III (850–700). At that time, they reported construction of a new temenos and altar, court, and sanctuary dedicated to the Phoenician goddess Anat (Greek Athena), the complex continuing to around 475 (*SCE,* vol. 2, pp. 516–532). Gjerstad's team also uncovered tombs of the Late Iron Age and Hellenistic period outside the ramparts of the Lower City.

From 1971 to 1980 the Joint American Expedition to Idalion (Lawrence E. Stager and Anita M. Walker, directors) dug and conducted site-catchment analysis, examining the surrounding agricultural, mining, and settlement areas by surface survey and periodic sounding. They found Hellenistic structures on the east acropolis dating from the fourth through the third centuries BCE. In the lower-city domestic precinct below the west acropolis, they found a street with houses dating to the Cypro-Classical period (sixth–fourth century) overlying Archaic pits (c. 700–475). On the west acropolis they found monumental structures including a fortification wall 11 m (36 ft.) thick founded around 500 BCE. Structures in this area, including metalworking, continued into the Hellenistic period. A small Roman bath installation was found at the foot of the east acropolis, and a Neolithic refuse deposit was dug on the banks of the Yialias River to the north.

In the 1990s the Department of Antiquities of Cyprus (Maria Hadjicosti, director) continued excavation of the monumental buildings on the west acropolis. It has demonstrated that the fortified area was destroyed twice, around 450 and abandoned about 300. In the Hellenistic period the only elite structures are on the east acropolis. During their 1995 excavating season the Department of Antiquities located apparent workshop installations dating to the eleventh–eighth centuries BCE in a field below the west acropolis.

American excavations (Pamela Gaber, director) continue in the lower-city domestic areas, extending their dates down through the Hellenistic and early Roman periods. Lang's "temple" was rediscovered on the east acropolis in 1992 (the latest strata are Hellenistic and Roman). It appears to have been an outdoor temenos approximately six acres in extent with structures of various sizes and functions. The city *per se* had ceased to exist by the time Pliny wrote his *Historia Naturalis* in the first century CE. He lists Idalium among the "former cities" (5.129–139). There is evidence of medieval domestic occupation to the north of the Roman houses in the lower city.

The cult of the Magna Mater (Aphrodite to the Greeks; Venus to the Romans) was the basis of the city's fame. Poets, from Theocritos (*Idylls* 15.100–103) through Vergil (*Aeneid* 1.681, 694; 5.760; 10.48–53) to Catullus (36.11–17; 61.16–19; 64.94–96) and others extol the beauties of Idalium, site of the worship of the goddess. The Venus and Adonis myth is sited at Idalion (e.g., Propertius, *Elegies* 2.13.51). (For a full list of ancient citations see Oberhummer, 1914.)

[*See also the biographies of di Cesnola, Gjerstad, and Ohnefalsch-Richter.*]

BIBLIOGRAPHY

Di Cesnola, Luigi P. *Cyprus: Its Ancient Cities, Tombs, and Temples.* London, 1877.

Gaber, Pamela, and M. Morden. "University of Arizona Expedition to Idalion, Cyprus, 1992." *Cahiers du Centre d'Études Chypriotes* 18.2 (1992): 20–26.

Gjerstad, Einar, et al. *The Swedish Cyprus Expedition (SCE).* Vols. 2 and 4.2. Stockholm, 1935–1948.

Hill, George F. *A History of Cyprus,* vol. 1, *To the Conquest by Richard Lion Heart.* London, 1940.

Lang, R. H. "Narrative of Excavations in a Temple at Dali (Idalium) in Cyprus." *Transactions of the Royal Society of Literature* 11 (1878): 30–71.

Oberhummer. "Idalion." In *Paulys Real-Encyclopädie der classischen Altertumswissenschaft,* vol. 11, cols. 867–872. Stuttgart, 1914. Includes a complete list of ancient references.

Ohnefalsch-Richter, Max. *Kypros, the Bible, and Homer.* London, 1893. See pages 5–18.

Pritchard, James B., ed. *Ancient Near Eastern Texts.* Princeton, 1950. See page 291 for the prism inscription of Esarhaddon.

Stager, Lawrence E., et al. *American Expedition to Idalion, Cyprus: First Preliminary Report, Seasons of 1971 and 1972.* Bulletin of the American Schools of Oriental Research, Supplement no. 18. Cambridge, Mass., 1974.

Stager, Lawrence E., and Anita M. Walker, eds. *American Expedition to Idalion, Cyprus, 1973–1980.* Chicago, 1989.

PAMELA GABER

IDEOLOGY AND ARCHAEOLOGY. There is a profound connection between archaeological research and the nonmaterial belief systems of both the ancient cultures and the modern societies in which archaeology is itself supported and pursued. Any discussion of the complex interplay of ideology and archaeological interpretation must take into account the essentially dual nature of the issue: the study of the belief systems of ancient cultures through the "reading" of material artifacts for their symbolic, ritual, or ideological meaning; and the conscious or subconscious imposition of elements of modern belief systems (e.g., perceptions of gender, ethnicity, economics) onto the interpretation of ancient cultures in both scholarly and popular literature.

In most cases, the penetration of modern ideologies into archaeological interpretation is subtle and unwitting. In a few cases, particularly where political or cultural institutions exploit readings of the past as the basis of their legitimacy or power, some scholars may enthusiastically cooperate in the dissemination of ideologically inspired interpretation in public forums. They may also feel constrained in their choice of acceptable research subjects, when funding or professional status is at stake. Such was certainly the case regarding racial theories in ancient Near Eastern history by German scholars during the Nazi era (1933–1945), and by the scholars of many nations who have found themselves entangled in the religious and territorial conflicts of the modern Near East. Yet, whether their ideological basis is subtle or overt, archaeological interpretations, like other scholarly understandings of society and culture, are necessarily formulated in contemporary contexts. As such, they can be seen as modern social behavior and cannot help but embody contemporary ideologies and social ideals.

The seemingly logical assumptions by which an archaeologist connects an excavated destruction level with a historically attested event; how he or she attributes a particular distribution of seeds or ratio of animal bones to the consumption patterns of certain ancient ethnic groups; or how an excavator identifies the function of a certain room or building are all derived from the scholar's most basic perceptions of how the world works. Such perceptions are, however, subject to dramatic transformation. Recent studies of the origin of modern concepts of race, progress, nationalism, labor specialization, gender roles, and even the idea of the autonomous "individual" have shown them to be closely linked to the social dislocations and reorganizations of the industrial age.

Ideologies, as systems of cultural logic—not merely explicit religious or political doctrines—are a natural part of human thought. Thus, it could be argued that archaeologists' interpretations can reveal as much about the societies in which they are members and political actors as about the ancient societies whose cultures they attempt to explain. Artifacts, architecture, and settlement patterns, however well documented and dated, possess meaning only within a culture. They cannot be interpreted without fitting them into a larger conceptual framework. As a result, the problem of reconstructing ancient ideologies is compounded by coming to terms with the outlines of modern ideologies as well.

Because excavated artifacts and preserved archaeological sites can be seen as part of the material world of the society that discovers and studies them, as well as of the society that produced them, they possess—as museum pieces and tourist attractions—a social significance quite distinct from the function for which they were originally designed. A cuneiform tablet, fertility figurine, or offering vessel, for example, would each have quite a different place in the world view of an ancient Near Eastern priest and a late twentieth-century archaeologist. The relationship between material culture and ideology in the Near East should therefore be seen as a complex process of reinterpretation. Any serious study of this process must come to recognize that the intellectual challenge is not to attempt to strip archaeology of its modern ideological perspectives, but to document and analyze the function—and interplay—of both ancient and modern ideologies.

Ideology: A Changing Concept. The definition of ideology itself underwent a radical reformulation after it first appeared in the late eighteenth century. First used by the French social philosopher Destutt de Tracy (1754–1836) to designate the scientific study of human thought and ideational systems, the earliest conception of "ideology" contained within it the Enlightenment belief that human ideas were closely linked to bodily sensations and were thus ultimately part of the material world. The assumption that human belief systems are finite, structured, and closely connected material conditions has always been central to the concept of ideology. As such, it has been opposed by religious conservatives who believe that (at least some) human belief systems cannot be so easily analyzed and dissected, that they are unconnected to social conditions and are essentially expressions of a transcendent spiritual truth. In the course of time, the term *ideology* has taken on additional meanings, contributed by both supporters and detractors of its validity. Thus, some use the term in archaeological contexts to refer to an active study of a material-based belief system, while others use it essentially as a synonym for religion or philosophy, generally denying explicit functional connections to social or economic reality.

The study of antiquity was connected with the concept of ideology from the very beginning. With the eighteenth-century European discovery of the monumental ancient remains and language systems of India and China, the French Encyclopedists attempted to distinguish structural similarities in those ancient societies' grammar and symbolism—similarities that transcended the specifics of regional culture and might reveal the essential character of human thought. The civilizations of ancient Greece, Rome, and Egypt were eventually included in this comparison. The guiding principle was that all human ideas and beliefs could be neatly categorized according to types and arranged in ascending orders of complexity. Like plants and animals, there was a logical structure that could be apprehended by human reason, and that like botany and zoology, ideology should be considered a respectable academic discipline.

Ideology, however, did not long remain a passive intellectual exercise. In the decades following the American and French Revolutions, visionary schemes for social change through the application of Reason arose on both sides of the Atlantic Ocean. The confidence that scholars could identify and delineate human belief systems, and demonstrate their direct connection to material conditions, led some French social philosophers (later derisively called *ideologues*) to see the study of ideology as a springboard for action. Like physiology, biology, and psychology, ideology might serve as an instrument for improving the material world. If human thought could be understood, it might be manipulated to end hatred, greed, jealousy, and aggression among social groups. This visionary social project proved to be a failure. As a result, the term acquired the negative connotation it still possesses.

Bitter conservative criticism of the *ideologues* and their liberal social programs, spearheaded by the outspoken attacks against ideology by the emperor Napoleon, transformed the common meaning of the term to refer to a mistaken, shallow, or deceptive body of beliefs. This more general usage was further refined by Karl Marx in the 1850s. Marx came to see ideology as the ruling ideas and symbolic systems of every society, in which the domination of the ruling class is made to seem natural, inevitable, and uncontestable to everyone. This conception of ideology, in which the social logic of a society is linked in a functional way to the preservation of the power of a small group within that society, went beyond earlier structural understandings to provide a dynamic motive for the creation and overthrow of ideologies.

In the early twentieth century, the group of German philosophers known as the Frankfurt school further developed Marx's conception of ideology in what has come to be called critical theory. The theory asserts that all ideologies are essentially coercive and suggests that the study of belief systems is inherently emancipatory. In trying to uncover what they defined as the conscious and subconscious control systems established by both ancient and modern elites, the Frankfurt school and later critical theorists, such as Louis Althusser and Michel Foucault, established a socially engaged and politically activist dimension to the study of ideology. Although based on historical analysis, its effects were directed to the present and future. In attempting to expose the hidden self-interest that directed every belief system, the critical theorists specifically sought to analyze and deconstruct contemporary capitalist ideology.

Ideology in Near Eastern Archaeology. Through most of the history of Near Eastern archaeology, the concept of ideology has been restricted to that of ancient religion and other nonmaterial belief systems. Although certainly not valid as transcendent truths (they could be described as rather primitive superstitions), they were nonetheless entirely spiritual. Thus, during the early archaeological exploration of Egypt and Mesopotamia, the discovery of temples, tombs, remains of sacrifices, and ritual implements were studied in an attempt to understand the "religions" of ancient Egypt and Mesopotamia as if there were a coherent body of religious beliefs and practices that could be studied in isolation from those societies' technological, economic, military, or governmental practices. In time, progressivist and social evolutionary theories suggested that the religions of the ancient Near East were in a process of transformation, moving ever onward toward a biblical ideal.

In this respect, William Foxwell Albright in Palestine,

James Breasted in Egypt, and Henri Frankfort in Mesopotamia can be seen as originators of an archaeological approach to the nonmaterial belief systems of the ancient Near East. In it the elements of greatest prominence in modern religions—monotheism, standardized rituals and religious architecture, and religious texts and law codes—were interpreted as the primary bearers of ancient ideologies. For Albright, in particular, details of religious practices and cult places recorded in the Bible became the base line for distinguishing their counterparts in the material record. The literalism of this correspondence between material artifact and text, however, prevented many scholars from ever going beyond mere illustration of conventional modern conceptions of the role of prayer, sacred spaces, and ritual sacrifice. [*See the biographies of Albright, Breasted, and Frankfort.*]

Similarly, the early archaeological study of tombs and tomb architecture in Egypt, Syro-Palestine, Anatolia, and Mesopotamia was concerned with the presumed, direct relationship between material forms of tombs and burial with the society's beliefs about the afterlife as recorded in religious texts. [*See* Tombs; Grave Goods.] This was also true of the excavation and study of later forms of religious expression such as the temples, synagogues, and churches of the Roman and Byzantine period. [*See* Synagogues; Churches.] Details of material culture (orientation, special-use chambers, decoration) were also linked to changes in specific religious practices. Few attempts were made by scholars of the late classical periods to go beyond conventional historical definitions of Hellenistic paganism, Judaism, and Christianity, to formulate a cross-cultural functional theory of ideology.

Only in the realm of Near Eastern prehistory, far beyond the chronological limits of direct connection with the historically attested religions of Egypt, Canaan, and Mesopotamia, did archaeologists attempt to link nonmaterial belief systems with stages of social development. Thus, in the discovery of apparent funerary offerings connected with Natufian burials and the excavation of anthropomorphic figurines and plastered skulls beneath the dwelling floors in the Neolithic levels at Çatal Höyük, Jericho, ʿAin Ghazal, Tel Ramad, and Tell Abu Hureyra, archaeologists connected a certain form of religious ideology (i.e., ancestor worship) to the beginnings of sedentary settlement. [*See* Çatal Höyük, Jericho, ʿAin Ghazal.]

With the expansion of material forms of religious expression in the Chalcolithic period at sites like Teleilat el-Ghassul, ʿEin-Gedi, and Tell Ḥalaf; at predynastic sites in Egypt; and at Ubaid and Early Uruk sites in Mesopotamia, the geographic dispersion of decorative motifs and burial customs prompted some scholars to link the spread of religious ideology with population movements or less precisely defined "cultural influence." [*See* Teleilat el-Ghassul; ʿEin-Gedi; Ḥalaf, Tell; Ubaid; Uruk-Warka.] More recently, the differentiation in the size and elaborateness of Chalcolithic burials in the Beersheba valley, when added to the evidence of settlement patterns, has prompted Thomas Levy to characterize the nonmaterial belief system of the period as representing the "chiefdom" stage of social organization (Levy, 1995). Similarly, Early Bronze Age religious specialization has been linked by some scholars to the rise of urbanism. At least in the earliest archaeologically attested periods, religious ideologies have been typologically analyzed, even though their function is seen as basically reflective, not transformative, of the material reality.

While some attempts have been made to utilize structural anthropology to "read" the cultural grammar of ancient Near Eastern societies through symbolic inside/outside, left/right, male/female oppositions expressed in material culture, other recent approaches have studied ideology not as a neutral cultural grammar, but as the calculated misrepresentations of powerful elites. The political significance of exaggeration and even chauvinistic fantasy has long been recognized in studies of the ancient reliefs of Egypt and in the material culture of the Neo-Assyrian Empire. A few studies have attempted to distinguish nonverbal, nongraphic expressions of ideology. In recent examinations of the significance of the impressive encircling ramparts of many Syro-Palestinian cities of the Middle Bronze Age, Shlomo Bunimovitz and Israel Finkelstein have suggested that the defensive significance of these massive structures was less important than the psychological impact they would have had on both local inhabitants and potential foes (Bunimovitz, 1992; Finkelstein, 1992).

Ancient and Modern Ideologies: An Interplay. In all archaeological attempts to reconstruct ancient ideologies—be they of specific cult, transcendent beliefs, systems of cultural logic, or calculated political misrepresentations—scholars run the risk of unwittingly imposing their own ideological or religious values on material remains. To a certain extent, the scholar's understanding of the nature of ideology itself will determine how much danger from this direction he or she perceives. For those scholars who see ideology as explicit, yet highly circumscribed sets of beliefs about religious or political systems, there has long been a reluctance to believe that a fair-minded scholar's modern religious or political beliefs (also tightly circumscribed and therefore presumably separable) would necessarily prevent an "objective" study and assessment of archaeological remains.

It is becoming increasingly clear, however, that role of modern ideologies in the conduct and direction of Near Eastern archaeology is far more fluid and pervasive than traditionally believed. In the nineteenth century, basic theological disputes between Protestant and Catholic scholars in Europe gave rise to the first systematic explorations of Palestine; competing European national interests and imperial expansion into the region served as the background of much of the later nineteenth-century exploration and excavations in Egypt, Mesopotamia, Asia Minor, Cyprus, Palestine, and

Syria. The close connection between archaeology and the post–World War II nationalisms of the region has also been observed in the governmental utilization of archaeological sites as national monuments and, in some cases, shrines. Debates over the ethnicity of ancient groups and their possible genetic relationship to modern Near Eastern peoples have also been motivated in large measure by modern territorial, religious, or political conflicts. [*See* Biblical Archaeology.]

Beyond the influence of explicit belief systems, however, there may be a more pervasive modern belief system that makes the separation of modern ideology from archaeological interpretation virtually impossible. Mark Leone (1982) and Michael Shanks and Christopher Tilley (1987) have argued for the widest possible definition of ideology. They see it as a society's takens-for-granted—that is, not so much an expressed set of governing ideals, but an unexpressed, yet artificial and often self-serving construction of reality. In line with the assertions of critical theory, they see ideology as a system through which the power of elites is maintained: not so much by memorized catechisms or pledges of allegiance, but through the incessant training of all of the society's members about the "natural order of things."

In the field of historical archaeology in North America and Europe, a number of scholars have attempted to delineate the rise of the modern industrial consciousness and its material manifestations through changes in uniformity and regimentation (city planning, landscape alteration, house forms, and interior room arrangement); changes in the role of the individual in society (through the increasing numbers of artifacts linked to the individual for personal hygiene, grooming, and status differentiation); and through conspicuous public use of symbols of order (neoclassical facades, formal gardens, radiating street plans) to counteract the elites' fear of disorder—imagined or real. These elements of modern cultural logic about work, self, reason, and efficiency, they argue, are still potent and affect deeply how modern archaeologists see the cultures of antiquity.

Thus, despite the calls to introduce processual and anthropological approaches in Near Eastern archaeology as a means of making the discipline more objective or "scientific," some critics suggest that this merely represents the imposition of a modern ideology. Indeed, as Thomas Patterson (1995) has noted, the prominence of systems theory, resource exploitation, and measures of labor efficiency in some processualist interpretations of ancient societies merely retrojects the modern ideology of transnational industrial development on the past. [*See* New Archaeology.]

Is an ideology-free archaeology possible? The material world is always mediated through ideological symbols. To a certain extent, the visual and intellectual impact of archaeological finds often provides raw material for the crafting or apparent substantiation of modern ideologies, as well—whether of the conscious, overt types (church history, nationalism, racialism) or more pervasive relations (gender, work, the individual). It might therefore be said that it is impossible to strip archaeological interpretation of its modern ideological components. It is, after all, the cultural logic of modern society—its ideology in the broadest sense—that is precisely the conceptual framework with which scholars make sense of the ancient world.

In this respect, Near Eastern archaeology is, and always has been, a powerful social, religious, and political activity. It is fully involved with the illustration, or, alternatively, the challenge, to modern social, religious, and political ideologies. It is therefore to be hoped, in light of the growing awareness of the role of ideology in both ancient and modern societies, that archaeologists in the Near East will come to recognize the wider ideological implications of their interpretations and recognize the constructive role they can play in the ongoing debates and discussions about the region's present and future, as well as its past.

BIBLIOGRAPHY

Broshi, Magen. "Religion, Ideology, and Politics in Palestinian Archaeology." *Israel Museum Journal* 6 (1987): 17–32.

Bunimovitz, Shlomo. "The Middle Bronze Age Fortifications in Palestine as a Social Phenomenon." *Tel Aviv* 19 (1992): 221–234.

Finkelstein, Israel. "The Middle Bronze Age 'Fortifications': A Reflection of Social Organization and Political Formation." *Tel Aviv* 19 (1992): 201–220.

Glock, Albert E. "Tradition and Change in Two Archaeologies." *American Antiquity* 50 (1985): 464–477.

Handsman, Russell G. "Historical Archaeology and Capitalism." *North American Archaeologist* 4 (1983): 63–79.

Hodder, Ian, ed. *Symbolic and Structural Archaeology.* Cambridge, 1982.

Larsen, Mogens T. "Orientalism and the Ancient Near East." *Culture and History* 2 (1987): 96–115.

Leone, Mark P. "Some Opinions about Recovering Mind." *American Antiquity* 47 (1982): 742–760.

Leone, Mark P., et al. "Toward a Critical Archaeology." *Current Anthropology* 28 (1987): 283–302.

Levy, Thomas E. "Cult, Metallurgy, and Rank Societies." In *The Archaeology of Society in the Holy Land,* edited by Thomas E. Levy, pp. 226–244. London, 1995.

Miller, Daniel, and Christopher Tilly, eds. *Ideology, Power, and Prehistory.* Cambridge, 1984.

Patterson, Thomas C. *Toward a Social History of Archaeology in the United States.* Fort Worth, Tex., 1995.

Pinsky, Valerie, and Alison Wylie, eds. *Critical Traditions in Contemporary Archaeology.* Cambridge, 1989.

Shanks, Michael, and Christopher Tilly. *Re-Constructing Archaeology: Theory and Practice.* Cambridge, 1987.

Trigger, Bruce G. "Alternative Archaeologies: Nationalist, Colonialist, Imperialist." *Man* 19 (1984): 355–370.

NEIL ASHER SILBERMAN

IDUMEANS. The origin of the name *Idumean* (also *Idumaean;* Aram., **'dwmy*) is derived from *Edom* (Heb., *'dwm, 'ĕdôm,* "red"; cf. Heb., *'dmh,* "earth" or "field"). *Edom* refers to the kingdom in southern Transjordan during the Iron Age, but substantial emigration of Edomites westward across the Wadi ʿArabah into the southern Judean hill country began in the late seventh and early sixth centuries BCE (as suggested in *2 Kgs* 24.2 and *Ez.* 35.6 and in Arad inscription no. 24). Finds of Edomite pottery, inscriptions, ostraca, and seals of this period have appeared in the eastern Negev at ʿAroʿer, Ḥorvat ʿUza, Tel Malḥata, and Ḥorvat Qitmit. By the late sixth and fifth centuries BCE, an Edomite presence is attested in the western part of this southern Shephelah region, extending toward the Mediterranean coast, by finds that include a cuboid incense altar from Lachish inscribed in Aramaic. In the fourth century BCE, Aramaic ostraca bearing Edomite and Arab names appear at Arad, Beersheba, and Tell el-Farʿah, presumably the location of Persian garrisons of mercenary troops. The Idumean region constituted the southern frontier for Persia after Egypt became independent (404–343 BCE), explaining why a fortress system was created in the region. Idumea is still called both an eparchy and a satrapy by Diodorus (19.95.2 and 98.1) in the Hellenistic era, suggesting that it was a former administrative district of the Persian Achaemenid Empire.

Hellenistic Period. Under the Ptolemaic kingdom (third century BCE), the area comprised a toparchy, one of the external administrative districts of the Egyptian kingdom. The most important recent discovery from this period is the Aramaic ostraca from Khirbet el-Qom (north of Hebron), the remains of the archive of an Idumean moneylender or "shopkeeper" (Gk., *kapēlos*) that include a Greek-Edomite bilingual ostracon dated to 277 BCE. The Zenon papyri also attest official Ptolemaic journeys in 259 BCE from Gaza on the coast to the Idumean settlements of Mareshah (Marisa, modern Tell Ṣandaḥanna) and Adora (modern Dur, 8 km, or 5 mi., southwest of Hebron) in the Negev (*PCZ* I.59006, ll. 64–66), where slaves were purchased (*PCZ* 59015, verso 16, 29; cf. 4. 59537/4). Within Egypt, third-century BCE papyri mention Idumean mercenary soldiers stationed along the Nile (*P. Tebt.* 815 fr. 5/29; *P. Bat.* 20.18/3 = *SB* 8 9797). The latter text includes an Idumean with the patronym *Apollodotos,* an early occurrence of a theophoric name composed with Apollo. The name is common afterward among the Idumeans, who evidently identified the Greek god with Qos, the chief god of their pantheon. It appears that the Greek god was especially honored at Adora (Josephus, *Apion* 2.9 [112–116]), and at the Sidonian military colony at Marisa/Mareshah founded under Ptolemy II Philadelphus in about 257 BCE. By the second century BCE, with the decline of Greek emigration into Ptolemaic Egypt, Idumeans formed sizable military colonies at Memphis and Hermopolis Magna in the Upper Nile region. The *politeuma* of Idumeans at Memphis included both soldiers and nonmilitary settlers who shared a quarter of the city.

Idumean relations with the Seleucids were also intimate. In 163 BCE, Idumea was administered by the experienced Seleucid general (Gk., *stratēgos*) Gorgias, a member of the "King's Friends," who reorganized the territory and enlarged it, perhaps to include Ashdod. During the Maccabean Revolt, Marisa was a base of operations for the Seleucid regime and the center of the conflict in southern Judea. Idumeans probably constituted auxiliary military forces in the Seleucid army at the time. In 138 BCE, the general Diodotus Trypho, a contestant for the Seleucid throne, marched through Adora toward Jerusalem before his defeat and death. Afterward, Antiochus VII Sidetes regained control of the "numerous cities" of Idumea, including Mareshah and Adora. After Antiochus's death in a Parthian campaign in 129 BCE, John Hyrcanus captured the Idumean cities of Adora and Mareshah and forced the Idumeans to accept circumcision and the Jewish law or be expelled from the land. U. Rappaport connects this action with the influx of Idumeans into Egypt, but there are indications the emigration began earlier. Subsequently, the "judaizing" Idumeans were incorporated into the Hasmonean state but never fully integrated into the Jewish population. As an Idumean, Herod the Great was regarded as a "half-Jew" and inferior to the Jewish aristocracy. His mother was a notable Arab named Cypros, perhaps a Nabatean.

Roman Period. Under Pompey's reorganization of the East, Marisa and Adora were detached from Judea and assigned to the Roman governor of Syria as an annex. Afterward, the Roman proconsul Gabinius partitioned Judea and its Hasmonean-Palestine conquests into five "districts" (Gk., *synodoi*) with separate aristocratic "councils." As a result, Idumea was apparently divided, with Mareshah forming the administrative center for the west and Adora for the east. Both of the capitals were rebuilt by Gabinius. The known native governors of Idumea were all from or related to the Herodian family. Both Herod's grandfather, Antipas I, and father, Antipas II, served as "governors" (Gk., *stratēgoi*) under the Hasmoneans, followed by Herod in the same capacity for Rome. After Herod became the Roman overseer (Gk., *epitropos*) of Judea, both his brother Joseph and son-in-law Kostobar governed Idumea, which Herod still used as his retreat and refuge. After the Parthians destroyed Marisa in 40 BCE, Herod transfered the administrative center for western Idumea several miles north to Beth-Guvrih and moved the center of eastern Idumea from Adora to ʿEin-Gedi. After Herod's death, Augustus charged his son Archelaus with the job of ethnarch for Idumea; from 6 to 41 CE, it was administered by the governors of Syria. Agrippa I briefly inherited the region from 41 to 44 CE, before it reverted again to the Syrian procurators. Josephus's list of the toparchies of Judea includes "Idumea and Engeddi" (*War* 3.3.5 [55]), but Pliny omits them (*Nat. Hist.* 5.14 [70]), probably because they constituted an annex rather than an integral part of the Jewish state. Other designations for the same toparchies appear to be "upper Idumaea" (*War* 4.9.9 [552]) and perhaps "eastern Idumaea."

Military and Social Organization. The Idumeans formed the basic core of Herod's army and were extremely loyal to the dynasty. As a militia, they were well equipped and organized and could be speedily mobilized. Herod once settled more than three thousand Idumeans in Trachonitis to quell the brigandage in the region, which signified their commitment and sturdiness in difficult situations. A sizable number of foreigners were also employed in the Herodian army, including Thracians, Germans, and Gauls. Mordechai Gichon has characterized the rural militia of the Idumeans as a frontier force comparable to the *limitanei,* the soldiers in frontier areas in the Late Roman Empire. This emphasis on a Herodian *limes,* a fortified frontier, and the military nature of the region remains disputed. Marisa appears to have been an important agricultural center. Kostobar, Herod's "governor of all Idumea and Gaza," a descendant of priests of Qos, owned estates in Idumea, as probably did the Herodians and other aristocratic families. The Idumeans last appear in the Jewish Revolt against Rome (66–70) as confederates of the Zealots and in defiance of Rome. During the conflict, Vespasian devastated the region and decimated the population; Jewish partisans later further ravaged the region. Idumea later became part of the province of Judea and was administered by Beth-Guvrin, which incorporated most of the region as part of its extensive *chōra.* The city continued to prosper and was honored in 200 CE by Septimius Severus with the name of Eleutheropolis and issued its own coinage. Mosaic floors from a villa and a Byzantine chapel are now in the Israel Museum, but by this time Idumea as a toponymn and ethnic term had faded from existence.

Language and Material Culture. Edomite texts from Transjordan are mainly concentrated in the capital city at Buseireh and at Tell el-Kheleifeh at ʿAqaba. Within Idumea, they are distributed over a wide area but are still few and laconic. This limited attestation provides only a few distinctive paleographic and grammatical aspects of the language. The script shows a similarity to Moabite, with distinctive forms for *dalet* (probably to avoid confusion with *resh*), *he,* and *mem* (e.g., the Ḥorvat ʿUza ostraca). Specific linguistic features are more difficult to isolate because the corpus mainly shares affinities with Hebrew, Phoenician, Ammonite, and Moabite. The basic means of determining Edomite remains the theophoric names formed with the "Qos" element that appear throughout the Near East from Egypt to Persia (see Maurice Sartre, *Inscriptions Grecque et Latines de la Syrie* 13 [1982]: no. 9003, with a discussion). Identification of Idumean material culture also remains vexed because the architecture and other material remains reflect few, if any, distinctive characteristics. Partially, this is the result of the culture's mixed population, consisting of Sidonians, Arabs, Edomites, and Greeks. The late Iron Age Edomite shrine at Ḥorvat Qitmit and the ruins of the Hellenistic city at Marisa afford rare insights into Idumean culture.

[*See also* Mareshah.]

BIBLIOGRAPHY

Abel, F.-M. "Marisa dans le Papyrus 76 de Zénon et la traite des esclaves en Idumée." *Revue Biblique* 33 (1924): 566–574.

Beit-Arieh, Itzhaq. "The Edomite Shrine at Ḥorvat Qitmit in the Judean Negev: Preliminary Excavation Report." *Tel Aviv* 18.1 (1991): 93–116.

Crawford, Dorothy J. T. "The Idumeans of Memphis and the Ptolemaic *Politeumata.*" In *Atti del XVII Congresso internazionale di papirologia, Napoli, 1983,* pp. 1069–1075. Naples, 1984.

De Geus, C. H. J. "Idumea." *Jaarbericht "Ex Orient Lux"* 26 (1979–1980): 53–74. Excellent basic survey, to be used with more recent studies.

Gichon, Mordechai. "Idumea and the Herodian Limes." *Israel Exploration Journal* 17.1 (1967): 27–42.

Israel, Felice. "Miscellanea Idumea." *Rivista Biblica* 27 (1979): 171–203. Comprehensive study, with the supplement cited below, of the epigraphic and linguistic aspects of Edomite; includes a complete bibliography.

Israel, Felice. "Supplementum Idumeum I." *Rivista Biblica* 35 (1987): 337–356.

Kanael, B. "The Partition of Judea by Gabinius." *Israel Exploration Journal* 7.2 (1957): 98–106.

Kasher, Aryeh. *Jews, Idumeans, and Ancient Arabs.* Texte und Studien zum Antiken Judentum, 18. Tübingen, 1988. The most recent substantial account of the history and relations of Idumea; should be used with caution.

Launey, Marcel. *Recherches sur les armées hellénistiques* (1949–1950). 2 vols. Reprint, Paris, 1987. Basic discussion of the Idumean military colonies in Egypt (vol. 1, pp. 556–559) and the onomasticon (vol. 2, pp. 1235–1241), with a postface by Y. Garlan, P. Gauthier, and C. Orrieux.

Rappaport, U. "Les Iduméens en Égypte." *Revue Philologique* 43 (1969): 73–82.

DAVID F. GRAF

IKTANU, TELL, site located at the edge of the foothills in the southeast Jordan Valley, 12 km (7 mi.) northeast of the Dead Sea, at approximately the −150 m contour below Mediterranean Sea level (31°49′ N, 35°40′ E; map reference 215 × 136). The occupation covers the tops of two natural spurs south of the perennial Wadi Ḥesban. The area receives a low annual rainfall (modern average 164 mm), but the site overlooks alluvial soils responsive to irrigation cultivation as well as to dry farming. It has a strategic position in relation to routes, water, and arable and grazing land.

The history of discovery of the site reflects changing perspectives in archaeology. In the nineteenth century the principal interest in the site was biblical. The first recorded visitor to the site was Selah Merrill, in 1876, for the American Palestine Exploration Society. He described the ruins on the north tell and proposed an identification with one of the Cities of the Plain, specifically Zoar. Claude R. Conder visited the site in 1881 for the Palestine Exploration Fund and rejected the identification. In 1926, William Foxwell Albright, then at the American School of Oriental Research in Jerusalem, proposed an identification with the Gadite settlement at Beth-Ḥaram.

Alexis Mallon, of the Pontifical Biblical Institute in Jerusalem, made the first modern assessment of the site between 1929 and 1934. He published a sketched plan of the ruin of "Beth-Haram" on the north tell and identified the pottery found there. He was the first to describe the remains of a large settlement which lacked defensive walls on the south tell and correctly dated the associated material (Mallon, 1929, pp. 230–232; Mallon et al., 1934, p. 151). Nelson Glueck appears not to have known of Mallon's work when he paid a brief visit to the site in 1943.

A survey and a small excavation concentrated mainly on the south hill were carried out in 1965–1966 by Kay Wright (Prag), for the British School of Archaeology in Jerusalem. The site was included in the East Jordan Valley Survey of Moawiyah Ibrahim, James Sauer, and Khair Yassine of Jordan University, ACOR, and the Jordan Department of Antiquities, respectively, in 1976. Prag returned to the site in 1987, 1989, and 1990 under the auspices of the British Institute at Amman for Archaeology and History. In 1987 and 1990 the project was extended to Tell Ḥammam, 3 km (2 mi.) north on the south side of the Wadi Kafrain. The project, to develop a regional archaeology, includes environmental studies, with analysis of the ancient and modern flora and fauna, investigation of the local vernacular architecture, and ethnographic work.

The current analysis of occupation at Iktanu resulting from the work of this project indicates that it was first occupied in the Early Bronze Age I. The evidence suggests a small settlement supported by a mixed farming regime, in which the principal cereal crop was wheat. The site was then abandoned.

The most extensive occupation of the site was during EB IV. On the south hill a well-planned village of rectangular structures, with courtyards separated by unpaved lanes, was built over an area of 22 hectares (54 acres). A minimum population estimate suggests that 2,000–2,500 people occupied the settlement. They practiced mixed farming, with goat and barley as the dominant food resources, but with cattle, sheep, wheat, legumes, pulses, and tree crops. The food production, storage, and processing systems are very well documented. Though relatively short-lived, the settlement is one of the largest and most important known for the period. Its stratigraphy provides the basis for the current division of EB IV into two or more phases. At least two other large settlements and several small sites also existed in the region. The excavation adds considerably to the evidence recovered from the work of Kathleen M. Kenyon at Jericho, only 20 km (12 mi.) to the west. The village was abandoned as suddenly as it was established.

There is no evidence of Middle Bronze Age sherds or settlement on the site. Some sherds dating to the Late Bronze Age and Iron Age I were found in survey. The excavations on the north tell indicate with certainty that a substantial fort was constructed in Iron II, and possibly earlier. It commanded a strategic view in all directions, was built in brick on a platform supported by stone foundations which extended the hill's natural narrow rocky crest, and had a defended lower enclosure. Its use continued into the Persian period. Scattered sherds of later dates, but no occupation, are attested. The final use of the site, in the late Ottoman to the modern period, was strategic and for burials, a pattern observed on most prominent tells in the region.

[*See also the biographies of Mallon and Merrill.*]

BIBLIOGRAPHY

Mallon, Alexis. "Notes sur quelques sites du Ghôr oriental." *Biblica* 10 (1929): 230–232.

Mallon, Alexis, R. Koeppel, and René Neuville. *Teleilāt Ghassul I. Compte rendu des Fouilles d' l'Institut Biblique Pontifical 1929–1932.* Rome, 1934.

Prag, Kay. "Preliminary Report on the Excavations at Tell Iktanu and Tell al-Hammam, Jordan, 1990." *Levant* 23 (1991): 55–66. The most recent report, containing references to earlier publications, including the works listed above.

Kay Prag

IMPERIAL ARAMAIC. The English counterpart of the German term *Reichsaramäisch,* the term *Imperial Aramaic* was originally applied in 1927 (by its coiner, Joseph Markwart), to the administrative language of the Achaemenid empire and to the Aramaic of the books of *Ezra* and *Daniel.* Although Biblical Aramaic has strong affinities with the standard administrative language of the Persian period, the Aramaic of *Ezra* is not identical with that administrative language. The Aramaic of *Daniel* is even further removed. Thus, the inclusion of Biblical Aramaic immediately attenuates the term.

The ambiguity of the term is deepened by its extension in the other direction to include even earlier Aramaic inscriptions. It is often inferred from the incident (c. 701 BCE) in *2 Kings* 18:26–28 (cf. *Is.* 36:11–13) that Aramaic was normally the language used in the Neo-Assyrian empire for diplomacy and administration—at least in its western sphere of influence. This supposition is confirmed by both iconographic and epigraphic evidence (*KAI* 233; Fales, 1986). Assyrian palace reliefs show an Aramaic scribe with pen and ink exercising official functions alongside an Akkadian scribe with reed stylus and clay tablet (e.g., *ANEP* 367; Driver, 1976, pls. 23, 24). [*See* Palace; Scribes and Scribal Techniques; Writing Materials; Writing and Writing Systems; Akkadians; Tablet.] However, the presumption that the Aramaic sponsored by the Neo-Assyrian empire in the west was in essential continuity with the standard Aramaic sponsored by the Neo-Babylonian and Persian empires several centuries later is too facile. If, thus, the label *Imperial Aramaic* is to be applied to a genuinely linguistic entity, which empire and which texts must be specified. Of course, *Imperial,* or *Official, Aramaic* can be defined in purely chronological terms (e.g., of the period c. 700–200 BCE), following the influential division proposed by Joseph A. Fitzmyer (1979, pp. 60, 61). The problem is that the term together with its historical usage connotes more than mere chronology and is therefore misleading.

It is best to define Imperial, or Official, Aramaic first in its narrow sense as the ideal standard language in which scribes in the Persian period (probably from Darius I to Darius III [522–330 BCE]) would draft official documents. Then the relationship of other texts and periods can be defined in relation to that standard. Official Aramaic in this more restricted sense is strikingly homogeneous in orthography and grammar, which can be reconstructed fairly comprehensively on the basis of three corpora: the Elephantine legal papyri (fifth century BCE) from Egypt; the Arsames correspondence (fifth century BCE) from Egypt; and the Samaria papyri from Wadi ed-Daliyeh (fourth century BCE) in ancient Palestine. [*See* Elephantine; Samaria; Papyrus; Daliyeh, Wadi ed-.] It is this level of homogeneity that had a real functional existence for scribes in the Persian period; it is missed, however, when the term is used in a quasi-chronological sense. A fuller appreciation of this homogeneity allows finer judgments to be formed about the language of texts from a wider period.

Within the Persian period, genre correlates more closely with language than either geographic, temporal, or ethnic provenience. Thus, Official Aramaic applies to legal documents, administrative correspondence, literary (e.g., the Ahiqar narrative, Hor bar Pawenesh) and monumental texts (e.g., the Bisitun inscription). [*See* Bisitun.] On the other hand, the language of private letters, including the Hermopolis papyri, deviates from the standard and represents a complex compromise between the conventions of Official Aramaic and the vernacular of the writers. The relatively few Aramaic texts that fall after the period of Old Aramaic (inscriptions of the ninth and eighth centuries BCE) but before the Persian period—whether in the Neo-Assyrian or Neo-Babylonian sphere—tend to show a transition in grammatical forms toward the Official Aramaic of the Persian period.

The coming of Alexander and the collapse of the Persian empire (330 BCE) form a watershed for the history of Aramaic. The homogeneous standard language was broken up, but then quickly reconsolidated locally into forms of standard literary Aramaic: Nabatean, Palmyrene, Hatran, Old Syriac (in inscriptions from Edessa), and texts in the tradition of Jewish literary Aramaic. [*See* Nabatean Inscriptions; Palmyrene Inscriptions; Hatra Inscriptions; Syriac.] These forms show strong continuity with Official Aramaic but are colored to varying degrees by local vernaculars. The Aramaic of *Ezra* is especially close to Official Aramaic but shows significant modernization of grammar as well as of spelling. The Aramaic of *Daniel* is typologically more advanced and approaches the literary forms of Aramaic exemplified by various texts from Qumran. [*See* Qumran.] The Aramaic of Targums Onkelos and Jonathan, as well as the Bar Kokhba letters and Megillat *Taʿanit* represents the end point of this literary tradition before the emergence of a new literary tradition based on the Jewish Palestinian vernacular. [*See* Bar Kokhba Revolt.]

Unlike the Old Aramaic of the group of inscriptions from the eighth century BCE described by Rainer Degen (1969), Official Aramaic seems to be based on a dialect stock whose origins must be located farther to the east. Whereas the Old Aramaic inscriptions from Syria anticipate (in a few respects) features of the later Aramaic dialects of Jewish Palestinian, Christian Palestinian, and Samaritan Aramaic, a number of features of Official Aramaic are already anticipated by the ninth-century BCE Tell Fakhariyah inscriptions from Sikan on the Khabur River in Syria. [*See* Fakhariyah Aramaic Inscription.] At the other end, the fact that there is no radical break in the literary tradition at Edessa from the literary successor to Official Aramaic throughout the whole period of Classical Syriac may be construed as an argument that the original home of Official Aramaic lies not too far from Edessa. Official Aramaic (in the restricted sense) has several distinctive features in phonology and orthography, morphology, syntax, and its lexicon.

Phonology and Orthography. Official Aramaic exhibits a number of phonological mergers for which there is no evidence in Old Aramaic. The consistent spelling of etymological /ḏ/, /ṯ/, and /ẓ/ with *dalet, taw,* and *tet*—with the regular exception of a more conservative spelling for the demonstatives and relative with *zayin* (*znh, z', zk(y),* and *zy*)—shows that these consonants had merged with /d/, /t/, and /ṭ/. The mergers are to be correlated with the development of the fricative variants of the nonemphatic stops /b, d, g, k, p, t/ (a process that eventually found its way into the reading traditions of Hebrew). Occasional spellings of etymological /ḍ/ (perhaps originally an emphatic fricative lateral) with *ʿayin* shows that it had merged with /ʿ/. Still, the preferred spelling of this consonant is with *qop*, as in Old Aramaic (perhaps for [ɣ]). Etymological /ś/ may have merged with /s/), even though the spelling with sĭn is retained fairly consistently. Also in contradistinction to Old Aramaic, syllable-closing /'/ quiesced, although the scribes consistently maintained the distinction between the determined state [-ā] spelled with a final *'alep* and the phonetically identical absolutive feminine-singular ending on adjectives and participles spelled with *he*. The negative /lā/ is spelled with a final *'alep* and written as a separated word (in contrast to *l-* in Old Aramaic). As in Old Aramaic the diphthongs /ay/ and /aw/ are retained, but they were already contracted in the Hermopolis letters (see above). At the same time, /n/ is not assimilated before a following consonant (regarded as secondary nasalization by many); similarly, /l/ is unassimilated in prefixal and infinitive forms of the root $\sqrt{}$*lqḥ*. Assimilation is consistent in these forms in Old Aramaic (outside of the Tell Fakhariyah bilingual), the Hermopolis letters, and most later Aramaic dialects. The formative element *h-* is consistently retained in word-initial position in particles and in the causative stem; however, it already is changing to '- in the Hermopolis letters and then in many later dialects of Aramaic. Official Aramaic increases the use of medial matres lectionis (for stem syllables), while preferring the defective spelling of the absolutive masculine plural ending in [-īn]. Final unaccented syllables ending in [-ā] tend to be spelled without a final *mater* (e.g., the first-person plural inflectional and pronominal suffix *-nā*, and the second-person masculine-singular independent pronoun *'antā*, spelled *'nt*). On the other hand, a final unaccented *-ī* (as in the third-person masculine-singular suffix *-why* on a plural base (cf. also the second-person feminine-singular forms *'nty, ktbty, -ky*) is now spelled with a final *mater*, in contrast to Old Aramaic (which has *-wh* for the corresponding third-person masculine-singular suffixal form).

Morphology. The internal passive is progressively lost in competition with *-'it-* forms. It is first lost in prefixal verb forms but is retained for a while in the perfect and participle; eventually, it is retained only in the participle of the basic and factitive stems in the later dialects. The formative element serves to mediate object suffixes on the imperfect. Several I-*yod* verbs are treated like I-*nun* in the imperfect and infinitive (as in the later dialects). The infinitive of the basic stem is formed with *mem*-preformative (as at Tell Fakhariyah but not in other Old Aramaic inscriptions), in contrast to derived stems without *mem*-preformative. The *mem*-preformative had already spread to the derived stems in the Hermopolis letters and in the Proverbs of Ahiqar (as in later Syriac and Western Aramaic). The determined masculine-plural ending on masculine-plural nouns is still *-ayyā* (in contrast to later eastern dialects, whose *-ē*, nevertheless, first makes its appearance in the Persian period). The consonantal contrast between masculine and feminine plural pronominal suffixes (*-hm, -km* :: *-hn, -kn*) is maintained in Official Aramaic, whereas the emergence of the later masculine-plural forms (masculine-plural -hōn, -kōn) is attested in private letters from the same period.

Syntax. *l-* serves as a facultative direct-object marker for definite direct objects (especially personal), corresponding to *'yt* in Old Aramaic and *yāṯ* in the later western dialects. The use of *zy* in genitive constructions is increased greatly over the few instances found in Old Aramaic. The new construction of noun + proleptic suffix before *zy* + noun for close genitive relation also begins to appear. The paradigmatic distinction between imperfect and jussive, well established in Old Aramaic and maintained in private letters and to some extent in later dialects, tends to be lost in Official Aramaic (where an occasionally unambiguous jussive form will be used as a jussive but more commonly is replaced in this usage by an imperfect form). In contrast to Old Aramaic, where the participle is used only as a substantive, the participle increasingly becomes part of the verbal system alongside the perfect and imperfect (as already in the Nerab inscriptions). [*See* Nerab Inscriptions.] In addition, the periphrastic use of the participle with a form of the verb *həwā* ("to be") begins in this period and continues in the later dialects. In the Old Aramaic of the ninth and eighth centuries BCE (with the notable exception of the Tell Fakhariyah bilingual), the finite verb seems to be restricted to the first and second position in its clause, with VSO (verb-subject-object), being the most unmarked word order. In Official Aramaic, apparently under the influence of Late Babylonian and Persian, the position of the verb is not so restricted. [*See* Persian.] Especially under Persian influence there is a strong tendency to place the object before the verb.

Lexicon. Among the distinctive elements in the lexicon of Official Aramaic are the new formation *brt-* for "daughter" (only rarely attested before the Persian period) replacing the earlier **bint-*; the preposition *'l* encroaching on *'l*; the quasi-pronoun *mnd 'm* ("something, anything"); the pro-form *tnh* ("here"; in opposition to *tmh*, "there"); an increasing number of Akkadian loanwords; and the presence of Persian loanwords and calques.

[*See also* Aramaic Language and Literature.]

BIBLIOGRAPHY

Degen, Rainer. *Altaramäische Grammatik der Inschriften des 10.-8 Jh. v. Chr.* Wiesbaden, 1969. A positivistic, but useful description of the language of Old Aramaic inscriptions from Syria.

Driver, Godfrey R. *Semitic Writing: From Pictograph to Alphabet.* Schweich Lectures of the British Academy (1944), pls. 23, 24. 3d ed. London, 1976.

Fales, Frederick Mario. *Aramaic Epigraphs on Clay Tablets of the Neo-Assyrian Period.* Rome, 1986.

Fitzmyer, Joseph A. "The Phases of the Aramaic Language." In *A Wandering Aramean: Collected Aramaic Essays*, pp. 57–84. Chico, Calif., 1979.

Greenfield, Jonas C. "Standard Literary Aramaic." In *Actes du premier congrès international de linguistique sémitique et chamito-sémitique, Paris 16–19 juillet 1969*, edited by André Caquot and David Cohen, pp. 280–289. The Hague, 1974. Seminal discussion of the place of Imperial Aramaic among the Aramaic dialects and its literary successor in Jewish tradition.

Greenfield, Jonas. "Aramaic in the Achaemenian Empire." In *Cambridge History of Iran*, vol. 2, *The Median and Achaemenian Periods*, edited by Ilya Gershevitch, pp. 698–713. Cambridge, 1985. A more detailed survey of Imperial Aramaic, including historical background and texts and their linguistic affinities; copious references.

Gropp, Douglas M. "The Language of the Samaria Papyri: A Preliminary Study." *Maarav* 5–6 (1990): 169–187. Analysis of the linguistic features of the Samaria papyri in relation to other Aramaic corpora within the Persian period.

Kaufman, Stephen A. *The Akkadian Influences on Aramaic.* Assyriological Studies 19. Chicago, 1974. Much more than a treatment of loanwords.

Kutscher, Eduard Y. "Aramaic." In *Current Trends in Linguistics*, vol. 6, *Linguistics in South West Asia and North Africa*, edited by Thomas A. Sebeok, pp. 347–412. The Hague and Paris, 1970. A valuable critical survey of literature on the earliest phases of Aramaic (including Imperial Aramaic and Biblical Aramaic).

Porten, Bezalel, and Ada Yardeni. *Textbook of Aramaic Documents from Ancient Egypt*, newly copied, edited, and translated into Hebrew and English. 3 vols. to date Jerusalem, 1986–1993. A preliminary publication of a complete *Corpus of Aramaic Texts of the Persian Period* projected as four volumes: 1. Letters (1986), 2. Contracts (1989), 3. Literature, Accounts, and Lists (1993), and 4. Ostraca.

Pritchard, James B., ed. *The Ancient Near East in Pictures Relating to the Old Testament*, pl. 367. 2d ed. Princeton, 1969.

Whitehead, J. David. "Some Distinctive Features of the Language of the Aramaic Arsames Correspondence." *Journal of Near Eastern Studies* 37 (1978): 119–140.

DOUGLAS M. GROPP

INCENSE. Odoriferous plants of various origins and species growing in various parts of the ancient Near East became important elements in the religious, political, and economic life of the region beginning in the third and second millennia BCE and increased in importance in the first millennium BCE. The sap, wood, bark, roots, and fruit of the plants were used both as incense and as ingredients in perfume and medicine. Trees and shrubs growing in East Africa and South Arabia, such as *Boswellia papyrifera* and *Boswellia sacra,* yielded frankincense; *Commiphora myrra* yielded myrrh. Both of these incense substances were already important trade commodities from the region called Punt in southern Egypt and from South Arabia to cultures in the Fertile Crescent in the second millennium BCE (cf. the reliefs at Deir el-Baḥari in Egypt representing Queen Hatshepsut's expedition to Punt, and Tell el-Amarna letter 269, l. 16). Other incense-producing trees grew in what are today Turkey, Lebanon, Syria, and Iraq. They include *Astragalus gummifera,* which yields gum tragacanth; *Cistus laurifolius,* which yields ladanum; *Commiphora balsamodendron* and *gileadensis,* which yield the balm used in various medicinal ointments; *Liquidambar orientalis,* which yields storax; *Pistacia lentiscus,* which yields mastic; and, finally, *Pinus brutia,* which yields an oleoresin, used by the Sumerians for medical purposes.

Although the use of incense is considered a symbolic expression of a mythic reality in the ancient Near East, there are hardly any traces of etiological myths explaining the origin or beginning of the use of specific incense materials. This is surprising in a world permeated by mythology because myth legitimizes the use of specific materials for specific purposes. The only complete myth of origin of a specific incense material is found in Ovid's *Metamorphoses* (10:298–518). It deals with the origin of myrrh and legitimizes its use in connection with death and funerals. The Hebrew Bible testifies to various uses of incense, but has no myth of origin; it only informs us that God likes the smell of offerings, including or excluding incense (cf. *Gn.* 8:21; *Lv.* 1:9, 2:2). The gods of ancient Assyria-Babylonia also appreciated the fragrance of incense offerings (cf. the Gilgamesh epic, 11:158). Even in Egypt, where so much incense was burned, there is no myth of origin, although there is the Egyptian word for incense, *sntr,* "that which makes divine." In the linguistic metaphors and images connected with incense there are hybrid expressions of exalted feelings that allow for the use of mythological images in connection with incense. For instance, incense is called the Eye of Horus, although it does not play any major role in the myths connected with Horus and Osiris. The term is, therefore, a symbolic expression at best. In the pyramid texts, which describe the funeral and the worship of the dead ruler, it is said of the dead king about to become a god that his "sweat is the sweat of Horus," his "odor is the odor of Horus," referring to the incense fumigation in the cult of the dead king. Incense makes divinity.

Incense and the Human Body. Although there is no myth of origin for the use of incense in the ancient Near East, it can still be maintained that its use is legitimized by myth—by the gods—simply because its use is supposed to be appreciated by the gods. This appreciation has far-reaching consequences for the way it is used. It seems that the earliest use of incense is connected with death, funerals, and the worship of the dead. In Egypt the pyramid texts relate the funeral of the dead king. The mythic idea of the ceremonies associated with the funeral and the cult of the dead king is to make him a god who lives forever. It is for that purpose the incense is being burned. Incense enables the king to obtain the stated purpose because it possesses divine qualities: it purifies from putrefaction and evil odor, it protects against evil, and it bestows upon the king the odor of the divine world, from where incense mythically derives. Incense furthermore facilitates the physical transference of the king to heaven: the smoke forms a staircase from earth to heaven. Incense is able to make the dead live again because death in the ancient Near East was never considered a natural necessity but, rather, a mythic accident.

Incense material was also used in embalming the dead body. It was thought to preserve it and keep it alive. Incense has the same function in the cult of the dead. In the tombs statues representing the dead were erected in inaccessible rooms that the Arabs call serdab, "basement." These rooms have one or two small openings in one of the walls through which the cult of the dead person could take place. The serdab statues were fumigated with incense to assure that the dead stay alive. The same belief can be found behind the Phoenician sarcophagus inscription from Byblos that tells its reader that the dead person lies in myrrh and bdellium.

In the Bible there is only slight evidence of the use of incense at funerals: for example, Joseph's body may have been prepared according to Egyptian standards (*Gn.* 50:26). *2 Chronicles* 16:14 describes the funeral of King Asa. His bier is said to be filled with all kinds of spices prepared by the perfumer's art. Incense may have been among those spices, but Israel did not share the same profound belief in the divinity of afterlife as the Egyptians. Thus, the Israelites used less incense at funerals and in the cult of the dead. The same is true for Assyria-Babylonia; like Israel, it had a more somber view of life after death.

The belief that incense ultimately derives from the gods is also responsible for its use as medicine. Medicinal use is amply testified in Egyptian and Assyro-Babylonian medical texts and in the Bible. *Jeremiah* 8:22 seems to indicate that *ṣŏrî* ("storax"?) could be used to cure diseases and wounds. It is also a mythic idea that incense used as a perfume is able to make an individual divinely beautiful. Perfume is thought to transfer a person to another, more elevated sphere of life (cf. the Egyptian queen Hatshepsut, who perfumes herself in myrrh oil or stacte, a sweet spice used in preparing incense; cf. *Sg.* 5:5).

INCENSE. *Chalcolithic incense burner, c. 3500 BCE.* (Courtesy Pictorial Archive)

Incense in Divine Worship and in Trade. The use of incense in divine worship was widespread throughout the ancient Near East in pre-Christian times. At Medinet Habu, the temple of Rameses III, the priest fumigated the statue of Amun to pave the way for the god who, in the morning, would enter his image. Fumigation with incense meant purification and offering in a single act, an offering intended to attract and soothe the deity at one and the same time. Ashurbanipal gave an excellent reason for using incense in divine worship: he maintained in a prayer that the "gods inhale incense." The Hebrew Bible relates that there were daily incense offerings in the Temple in Jerusalem in front of the Holy of Holies. This so-called *tāmîd* ritual was enacted to purify the room, to attract and please the deity, and to protect the priests in the Temple area.

The ritual use of incense required altars and such incense tools as censers, shovels, and containers, which, in variant forms, have been unearthed at various locations and identified in reliefs and paintings. Among them is the incense burner in the shape of an arm and hand, which is especially characteristic in the reliefs and paintings of Egyptian culture. The horned incense altar belongs to the Canaanites and Hebrews (cf. *Ex.* 30:2), as examples excavated at Megiddo from the tenth–ninth centuries BCE testify. The small South Arabian cubic burner inscribed with the names of incense materials is well known from many sites in South Arabia. One was recently found at Baraqish, in Yemen, in a fourth-century BCE context. The same type of burner has also appeared at Beersheba, Lachish, and elsewhere in Israel in eighth–fifth-century BCE contexts. Incense shovels have been found at Tel Dan in Israel (eighth century BCE) and may be the same type of utensil as the tool described in *Levitcus* 16 as used by the high priest on Yom Kippur in the Temple in Jerusalem. The incense shovel is later depicted in synagogue art. It appears, for example, in the mosaic floor of the synagogue of Severus at Hammath Tiberias (250–300 CE), where it seems to depict a symbol of Jewish worship in the Jerusalem Temple. Numerous ceramic incense shovels of this kind have also been found in the excavations at Sepphoris in Israel. [*See* Dan; Hammath Tiberias; Sepphoris.]

The use of incense created vivid trade relations between South Arabia and the Fertile Crescent (cf. the potsherds with South Arabian inscriptions found in Jerusalem from the seventh to sixth centuries BCE), between Egypt and Syria-Lebanon (cf. *Gn.* 37:25 and many Egyptian literary sources), and between Egypt and Punt. That trade, which included many other commodities, created vast riches and therefore had political consequences: as early as the beginning of the first millennium BCE, the Neo-Assyrians and Babylonians expanded toward the south and west to capture the incense trade. This same trade, in a later period, with the Ptolemies in Egypt and their dominions (cf. the Zenon papyri), became one of the foundations of the kingdoms of Petra and Palmyra. [*See* Petra; Palmyra.]

The New Testament relates that Jesus was buried with myrrh and aloe used as ointments (cf. *Jn.* 19:38–42). In ancient Greece and Rome, fumigations at funerals and in divine worship were common. It seems that the non-Jewish Christians continued the habit of fumigating at funerals but, wanting to distance their liturgy from pagan cults, were reluctant to use incense in divine worship in the first three centuries of the common era. During the fourth century, however, the literary and archaeological evidence suggests that a change took place. In the Syrian church, the Testament of St. Ephraim recommends the use of incense in wor-

INCENSE. *Iron Age II stone incense spoon, c. 800 BCE.* (Courtesy Pictorial Archive)

ship. The Western church also begins to use incense in the fourth century, and Christian censers begin to appear in strata from that time. The idea behind the use of incense in the Christian church is to honor God, to exorcise evil, and to symbolize prayer (cf. *Ps.* 141:2).

The Jews abandoned the use of incense with the destruction of the Jerusalem Temple. Only in the Havdalah ceremony, which marks the end of the holy Sabbath and the beginning of the profane week, do the Jews continue the use of fragrant spices. A benediction was and still is uttered over the box containing the spices, a symbolic act that utilizes the fragrance of the aromatic plants as a device to comfort the Jewish soul saddened by the end of the Sabbath.

[*See also* Burial Techniques; Grave Goods; Medicine.]

BIBLIOGRAPHY

Antonini, Sabina. "Nuovi incensieri iscritti Yemeniti." *Oriens Antiquus* 27 (1988): 133–141.

Atchley, Edward G. C. F. *A History of the Use of Incense in Divine Worship.* London, 1909.

Hepper, F. Nigel. "Trees and Shrubs Yielding Gums and Resins in the Ancient Near East." *Bulletin on Sumerian Agriculture* 3 (1987): 107–114.

Martimort, A.-G., ed. *Handbuch der Liturgiewissenschaft,* vol. 1, pp. 179–180. Freiburg, 1963.

Müller, W. W. "Weihrauch." In *Paulys Realencyclopädie der classischen Altertumswissenschaft,* supp. vol. 15., cols. 699–777. Munich, 1978.

Nielsen, Kjeld. *Incense in Ancient Israel.* Supplements to Vetus Testamentum, vol. 38. Leiden, 1986.

Zwickel, Wolfgang. *Räucherkult und Räuchergeräte.* Orbis Biblicus et Orientalis, 97. Göttingen, 1990.

KJELD NIELSEN

INDO-EUROPEAN LANGUAGES. An extensive linguistic family, the Indo-European (IE) languages are spoken in the western half of Eurasia, stretching from Europe through Central Asia to the Indian subcontinent, across the northern Near East from Anatolia to Iran and Afghanistan, and at one time as far east as western China and Siberia. They are now also the dominant languages in the Americas, Australia, and southern Africa.

The close linguistic relationship of the IE languages is most immediately evident by comparing lexical cognates. The word for *daughter* may serve as an example: among the modern languages, one finds *Tochter* in German, *duktẽ* in Lithuanian, *doč'* in Russian, *thugatéra* in Greek, *dustr* in Armenian, and *dokhtar* in Persian. [*See* Greek; Persian.] The word was *tkācer* in Tocharian, written between the fifth and sixth centuries CE in western China. It is first documented as *duatra* in thirteenth-century BCE Anatolia.

Recognition of the genetic relationship among IE languages began with occasional observations, mainly of lexical similarities between two or three member languages throughout recorded history, but became especially vivid and more comprehensive in the seventeenth and eighteenth centuries. A decisive event was an observation in a speech made by William Jones in 1796, then chief justice in British India, as well as a Persianist and Sanskritist. He postulated that not only Persian and Sanskrit, but also Greek, Latin, Germanic, and Celtic must go back to a common root and must therefore be members of the same family. [*See* Latin.]

The first major breakthroughs in the systematic establishment of the relationships among Indo-European languages were made in the early nineteenth century. This led to the development of linguistic science—that is, the study of language in its comparative, historical, and synchronic aspects, conjoined with the study of cultural history. The methodologies developed by Indo-Europeanists soon began to be applied also to the research of other language families and provided the foundations of general linguistics. Overall, there are eleven well-attested dialect groups, or dialects, that can be distinguished.

The Anatolian languages were first recognized as Indo-European in 1902, and their discovery resulted in a fundamental reassessment of the diachrony and structure of IE. These languages were spoken in large parts of Anatolia and the northern Levant during the second and first millennia BCE. They include Hittite, Palaic, Luwian, Lydian, and Lycian and a few other less well-attested dialects. [*See* Hittite; Luwian.] Best documented in Cuneiform Hittite. [*See* Cuneiform.] Beside personal names and a few Hittite loanwords in Assyrian tablets found in Kaneš/Kültepe in Cappadocia (eastern Turkey), dated to the nineteenth century BCE, it is most abundantly documented on some twenty-five thousand tablets found in the archives of the Hittite capital, Ḫattuša/Boğazköy, now Boğazkale, in central Turkey. [*See* Assyrians; Tablet; Kaneš; Kültepe Texts; Libraries and Archives; Boğazköy.] Its three stages are Old Hittite (c. 1700–1500 BCE), Middle Hittite (c. 1500–1350 BCE), and Neo-Hittite (1350–1200 BCE). Palaic, spoken to the north of the Old Hittite empire, is found in a small number of texts from the same archives.

Luwian was spoken throughout the southern parts of Anatolia. It is documented from about 1400 to 200 BCE in three periods, which also reflect dialect variants: Cuneiform Luwian is found in the archives of the Hittite New Empire (c. 1400–1200). [*See* Hittites.] Eastern Luwian is represented by Hieroglyphic Luwian (formerly called Hieroglyphic Hittite) from the period of the Neo-Hittite states (c. 1200–700 BCE) in northern Syria. Western Luwian is represented by Lycian, documented by some 150 inscriptions (c. 400–200 BCE), and Lydian, with some seventy inscriptions, mostly from the capital city of Sardis in northwestern Turkey, dated to the sixth–fourth centuries BCE. [*See* Sardis.] These were written in eastern and western types of the Greek alphabet, respectively.

The Indo-Iranian, or Aryan, languages consist of three groups: Iranian, Indic (also called Indo-Aryan), and Nuristani. The earliest attestation of these languages is an early form of Indo-Aryan. It is reflected in royal and divine names and technical terms related to horse training and racing in Hurrian texts of the Mitanni period (fifteenth century BCE onward) and found in the Hittite archives. [*See* Hurrian; Mitanni.] Thereafter, Indo-Aryan emerges first in the northwest of the Indian subcontinent. The vast literature begins with the religious texts, the Vedas, whose earliest parts may date to the middle of the second millennium BCE. The classical language, Sanskrit, was codified in a quasi-algebraic code in about 400 BCE by the grammarian Panini in the Panjab and has remained the standard learned language. Middle Indic begins in about the third century BCE, notably Buddhist Pali and the vernaculars, the Prakrits. The modern Indic languages have been attested since the end of the first millennium CE and are spoken in the northern half of the subcontinent, but also in Sri Lanka and the island groups; they include such languages as Kashmiri, Panjabi, Gujarati, Marathi, Nepali, Sinhalese of Sri Lanka, and Hindi/Urdu (in Devanagari/Arabic script, respectively), which is lexically replete with Persian (with the latter's Arabic and Turkish components), and finally Romany, the language of the Gypsies. [*See* Arabic.]

The Iranian languages were once spoken from the southern Ukraine across Central Asia into western China and western Siberia. They are divided, geographically, into a northern (traditionally called eastern) and a southern group and, historically, into old, middle (c. third century BCE–eighth century CE), and modern stages. Speakers of the southern group, notably the Medes and Persians, entered the plateau of Iran during the first centuries of the first millennium BCE. [*See* Medes.] Iranian is first documented in the Old Persian cuneiform inscriptions of the Achaemenids (559–330 BCE). Little is known about the language of the Medes, who preceded the Achaemenids. Linguistically older are the texts in Avestan, probably spoken in northeastern Iran, which include Gathic Avestan, the language of Zarathushtra (c. 1000 BCE), and so-called Younger Avestan texts, some of which may date in part to the middle of the second millennium BCE. Middle Persian is well attested, and to a lesser degree (Middle) Parthian, spoken in northeastern Iran. The old and middle northern Iranian languages include Scythian, once found from the Black Sea to Siberia and best documented in extensive texts in the Saka dialect from Chinese Turkistan (late first millennium CE); Sogdian, in Central Asia, documented in extensive texts (first millennium BCE); Khwarazmian, documented south of the Aral Sea and known mainly from glosses in early medieval Arabic texts; and Bactrian (first millennium CE), known from inscriptions. Today, the southern Iranian languages include such widely spread languages as Persian, spoken in Iran, Afghanistan, and Tajikistan; Kurdish, spoken in eastern Turkey, northern Iraq, and northwestern Iran; and Baluchi, spoken in southeastern Iran, southern Afghanistan, and southwest Pakistan. The modern northern languages are confined to the east and include Yaghnobi in Tajikistan; the so-called Pamir dialects; and, foremost, Pashto in Afghanistan and Pakistan. Ossetic is spoken in the central Caucasus as their sole representative in the west, continuing the language of the Alans.

The Nuristani languages are attested only from modern times and are spoken in a few villages in the mountainous Hindukush area on the borders of Afghanistan, Pakistan, and India; they may have branched off from Early Indo-Aryan, rather than constitute an independent branch of Indo-Iranian.

Greek, also called Hellenic as a language group, is first attested in its most archaic form, called Mycenaean, in the thirteenth century BCE. It was written on more than thirty thousand tablets, in the so-called Minoan B syllabary script, that were found at Knossos on Crete and at Mycenae and Pylos on the Greek mainland and deciphered in 1952. [*See* Crete.] This culture collapsed by the twelfth century BCE. Later epigraphic records of Greek appear from the seventh century BCE. Four main dialect groups are distinguished: Arcadic, Aeolic, Doric, and Ionic, with a complex distribution pattern; they were spoken on the mainland and on the islands and in western Anatolia and in Greek colonies around the Mediterranean and Black Seas. The dialect of the Homeric epics, dated to about 800 BCE, combines both Aeolic and Ionic features. Beginning in the fifth century BCE Attic Greek increasingly overlaid the dialectal diversity in Greece, Anatolia, and elsewhere, and as the koine "common" dialect, gradually replaced it. This happened most significantly after Alexander's conquests in the late third century BCE, which led to the Greco-Bactrian culture in northern Afghanistan, the Gandhara culture in northwest Pakistan (until the seventh century CE), Ptolemaic culture in Egypt, and the hellenization of Anatolia and the Levant (where the New Testament was composed in Hellenistic Greek). [*See* Ptolemies; Biblical Literature, *article on* New Testament.] Medieval Greek was the language of the Byzantine empire (since 330 CE). Modern Greek (since c. 1200 CE) developed out of this koine, which led, by the end of the nineteenth century, to the contest between atticizing *kathareúousa* ("purist") and *dēmotikḗ* ("popular") literary styles, the latter becoming dominant.

Italic languages comprise Latin, spoken originally in the small region of Latium and Rome; Faliscan, in a tiny area north of Latium; Oscan and Umbrian, found over the entire area of central to southern Italy; and Venetian, between the Po River, the Carnic Alps, and Istria. The earliest documents in Latin come from Latium and are dated to the sixth century BCE. Oscan-Umbrian and Venetian documents, mainly tablets and inscriptions, date to the last centuries BCE. By 100 CE at the latest, Latin had erased the other languages and dialects from Sicily to the Alps, with the exception of the southern Greek colonies. Similarly, the expansion of the Roman empire brought about the emergence of the Romance languages, including (beside Italian), Sardinian,

Spanish, Portuguese, French, Rhaeto-Romanian, and Rumanian. [*See* Sardinia.]

The Celtic languages had their widest distribution, across Europe, between the fifth century BCE and the third or fourth century CE. Known from inscriptions beginning in the second century BCE and from glosses, Continental Celtic includes Ibero-Celtic in central Spain, Gaulish in France up to the Low Countries (Belgae), and Italo-Celtic in northern Italy, all of which were erased by the evolving Romance languages by the fourth century CE, while the Celtic of Germany succumbed to Germanic. Celts, called Galatians, moved into Anatolia in the third century BCE and appear to have retained their language amid Phrygians in central Anatolia until the fifth century CE (according to St. Jerome). Celts appear to have reached the British Isles in the fifth century BCE. Insular Celtic is found in two branches. Goidelic, or Gaelic, the old name for Irish, has three branches, Irish, Scottish Gaelic, and the Gaelic of the island of Manx (extinct since the late nineteenth century). The earliest Irish-Gaelic texts were written in the stroke-and-notch ogham alphabet between the fourth and eighth centuries CE, followed in the late seventh century by Old Irish texts in Roman characters. Brittonic, or Brythonic, includes Welsh, which is first known from texts dating to about 800 CE, as well as Cornish (extinct since the late eighteenth century) and Breton, imported to Brittany before 800 CE, both first known from glosses between 800 and 1100 CE.

The Germanic languages originated in southern Scandinavia and initially spread to the coastal areas of the North Sea and the Baltic Ocean from the Netherlands to the Vistula River. They are first mentioned in Roman records in the late second century BCE and are first documented in third-century CE runic script from southern Scandinavia. There is much debate about the early groupings. They include North Germanic in southern Scandinavia; North Sea Germanic, along the North Sea; Rhine-Weser Germanic, along the middle Rhine and Weser Rivers; Elbe Germanic, along the Middle Elbe River; and East Germanic, between the middle Oder and Vistula Rivers. By 250 CE, Elbe Germanic is found in the south at the Danube River and East Germanic in the area of the Carparthian Mountains. Many of these groups began their great tribal migrations toward the end of the fourth century CE, to the west (the Low Countries, England), south into Celtic-speaking areas, and east. The East Germanic Goths appear to have moved to the Vistula area as early as the second century CE. Farther south, they subjected the Iranian-speaking Sarmatians in the southern Ukraine in about the middle of the fourth century. The Gothic Bible translation by Bishop Ulfilas at about that time represents the earliest and most extensive documentation of early Germanic. While the tribal federations of the Visigoths and Ostrogoths migrated farther west to Gaul, Spain, and Italy, Gothic appears to have lasted in the Crimea into the sixteenth century CE. The other Germanic languages (texts in the various dialects are found from about 750 CE onward) are roughly grouped into two divisions: Old Low German (including Saxon and Lower Franconian) and Old High German (represented by the remainder, including Upper Franconian, Alemannic, Bavarian, and Langobardic in northern Italy). The middle period leads to the modern period by about 1400 CE, including such languages as Modern German; English; the languages of the Lower Countries, Scandinavia, Iceland; and Afrikaans in South Africa.

The Slavic, or Slavonic, languages probably originated in the northern Balkans. They are first alluded to in the first two centuries of the common era. Their vast and rapid expansion in all directions began in the fifth century, especially after the disintegration of Hunnic power in the east, and lasted until the tenth century. They expanded into Baltic and Finnic areas (Novgorod, c. ninth century CE) and, farther east, toward the Ural Mountains, reached the Dnjepr River and established the Ukraine "borderland" (Kiev was founded in c. 600 CE). In the west, they expanded into formerly Germanic-speaking territory to the Elbe and Saale Rivers, south into Moravia and Bohemia up to the Austrian Danube valley, farther east to the Great Central European plains into Hungary, to Slovenia, and, from there, together with the Turkish-Iranian Avars, into the Balkans, Serbia, and Croatia. They reached Greece and even the Aegean islands and Crete, and good numbers of Slavic-speaking people settled and were absorbed in northwestern Anatolia. This coherent Slavic-speaking area was split by the reassertion of German in the Austrian Danube valley and of Rumanian and by the incursion of the Finne-Ugric Magyars, or Hungarians, in 896 CE. Written Slavic began with Old Church Slavonic, or Old Bulgarian. It is based on the Macedonian-Bulgarian Slavic dialect of the city and hinterland of Salonika, which the Greek brothers Cyril and Methodius employed for translating Christian texts from Greek, beginning in 863 CE. This church language considerably affected the subsequent developing literary languages, including Russian.

The Baltic languages probably originated in the present Polish-Russian border area and, as suggested by place and river names, once reached as far east as Moscow. Except for the Baltic coastal areas, they were superseded by the expanding Slavic languages beginning in the middle of the first millennium CE. Both Lithuanian and Latvian, or Lettish, are first documented by texts dated to the sixteenth century, while Prussian, spoken in the coastal areas from the Vistula to the Nemen, or Memel, River, is first recorded in the fourteenth century but was absorbed by German by 1700. Baltic is often joined with Slavic into a single dialect group of IE called Balto-Slavic. However, they are so different they must be considered to have originally been separate groups that converged considerably. It is probable that the origins of Slavic are to be partially sought in the Iranian languages of the Ukraine and southern Russia.

In addition to these IE dialects, there are a number of poorly attested examples in the Balkans. These include Dacio-Thracian in Romania and Bulgaria (some twenty-five words are from the fourth or fifth century BCE), which may have survived sporadically into the sixth century CE. Phrygian, spoken in northwest Anatolia, where the capital was Gordion, is documented in two stages: Old Phrygian is found in some twenty-five inscriptions from the eighth to sixth centuries BCE, and New Phrygian is found in some one hundred inscriptions from the first three centuries CE, written in an archaic and common Greek alphabet, respectively. [*See* Gordion; Writing and Writing Systems.]

Armenian, spoken in the southwestern Caucasus mountains, is an original member of the East Balkan group of IE dialects and may have originated in Moesia, the province just south of the lower Danube River separating Dacia from Thracia. [*See* Armenian.] The name is also found as Mysia in northwestern Anatolia and may be reflected in the Muski, who, in cuneiform records, are located on the Upper Euphrates River early in the twelfth century BCE. [*See* Euphrates.] Their self-designation *Hay* (pl., *Hayk*ʿ) may continue the term *Hatti/Hittite*. Armenians would thus be the easternmost reflex of the expansion of the East Balkan group of IE that swept into and through Anatolia in the twelfth century BCE and destroyed the Hittite empire.

Linguistically, Armenian appears to have emerged out of the convergence of the immigrant language with the local Urartean, Hurrian, and Caucasian languages. [*See* Urartu.] It was under heavy Iranian influence from the eighth century BCE through the first half of the first millennium CE, under the Medes, Achaemenids, Parthians, and Sasanians, during which time Armenian lost much of its inherited lexicon. [*See* Parthians; Sasanians.] Old, or Classical, Armenian began to be written in the early fifth century CE in a Greek-based alphabet, with similarities to early Middle-Persian Aramaic-based alphabets invented by Bishop St. Mesrob. [*See* Aramaic Language and Literature.] Western Armenian developed with the Armenian colonization of Cilicia and the establishment of the kingdom of Cilicia (1198–1375 CE). [*See* Cilicia.] The modern period began in the fifteenth century. During the nineteenth century, two main literary variants evolved, a western one in the Armenian colony of Constantinople/Istanbul and an eastern one in Armenia, based on the dialect of Yerevan and the Ararat (cf. ancient Urartu) valley.

Albanian is an isolated IE language on the eastern Adriatic coast, with two main dialects, Gheg in the north and Tosk in the south, the official language since 1950. Albanians are first mentioned by Ptolomy about 150 CE, and have withstood early celtization, then romanization and slavization. The first written records begin only in the late fifteenth century CE with a brief religious text. Linguistically, Albanian appears to have closest affinities with Thracian, about which little is known, rather than with Illyrian, which was once spoken in the western half of the Balkans.

Tocharian is only known since 1908. It is an isolated IE language once spoken in the Tarim Basin in western China. There are two distinct languages, labelled Tocharian A and Tocharian B, or Eastern and Western Tocharian, respectively. Linguistically, Tocharian is strikingly different from the neighboring Iranian languages, and closer to the European dialects of IE, so that it has been suggested that the Tocharians may have migrated east as early as the end of the third millennium BCE prior to the Iranian expansions. The discovery of Tocharian in the far east forced the rethinking of the traditional groupings of the IE dialects, in particular, it proved to be a centum-language with plain velar stops like the European languages where the eastern satem-languages Indo-Iranian and Slavic have developed sibilants (see discussion of velars below).

Finally, it is only recently (1987) that Bangani, a language in the Garhwal district of the Indian Himalayas, has become known. It has proven to have an archaic centum-layer overlaid by Indic; a similar layer was found in Baltic and Slavic areas.

Grammatical Features. The grammar reconstructed for common IE is an abstraction—the result of systemic comparison. The evidence of the attested dialects was retraced to common denominators, from which, in turn, all features can be derived. Before the Anatolian languages became known early in the twentieth century, the reconstruct was essentially the common denominator of Indo-Iranian and Greek, the two best-known and most highly developed systems, so that the other dialects appeared as reductive. This system of the so-called Neogrammarians continues to be held by a few scholars, albeit with substantial adjustments (e.g., Szemerényi, 1990). With the discovery of Anatolian, the question of common IE became a major issue—in particular whether Anatolian and the rest of the IE languages derive from a yet earlier Hittite-IE ancestor called Indo-Hittite, or Anatolian split off from common IE, as is now generally held.

"Common" is generally understood to be the last stage before dispersal and major dialectal differentiation. At the other end is the notion of the earliest stage that can be reconstructed. In effect, staging is essentially based on the degree of complexity in inflection. Accordingly, the earliest stage of IE is assumed to have had no inflection—leading to the stage shared by Anatolian and the remainder of the dialects and to a stage where major groupings have already occurred. Given the known geographic areas of the dialects relative to each other, the diachronic scheme is correlated with approximate location. A prominent model is the so-called space-time model (Meid, 1975). For example, Francisco Adrados (1992) proposes the following diagram:

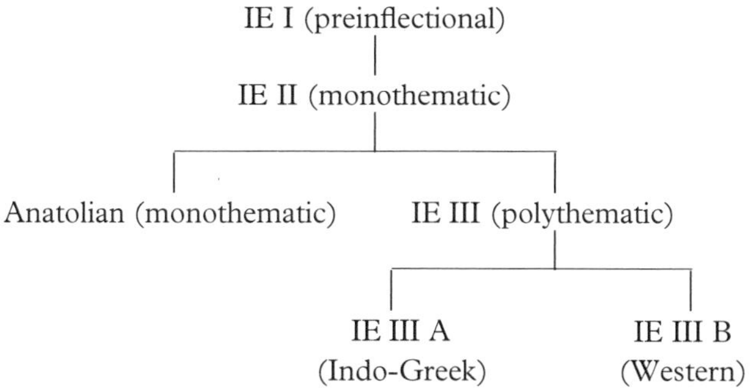

For a summary of the features thought to have characterized the stage common to Anatolian and the other dialects, see Mayrhofer (in _Indogermanische Grammatik_ 1.2, 1986) on phonology and Szemerényi (1990) on morphology.

The focus on phonology and inflection has resulted in the relative neglect of larger syntactic issues, and the syntactic studies that have been done have not attracted general attention. A notable early example is the monumental study by Berthold Delbrück (1871–1888), who established IE as a S O V (subject-object-verb) language. With the renewed attention to linguistic universals and typology, syntactic issues are increasingly the focus in comparative historical reconstruction. The basic systems of nominal and verbal inflections are described below.

Nouns. The nominal inflection in IE is based on stems, which are either the plain root or derived by suffixes. They are grouped morphologically into stem classes: consonantal, diphthongal, resonantal-vocalic _i-_, _u-_ stems, and vocalic "thematic" _o_-stems, which are relatively more recent than the others. For example, _*ped-_, "foot"; _*gwow-_, "cow"; _*pót-i-_, "master"; _*suAn-ú-_, "son"; _*kwékwl-o-_, "wheel, wagon."

The basic gender distinction is that between animate and nonanimate, which is morphologically marked by the formal identity of the nominative and accusative in neuters. This basic gender distinction corresponds to the distinction between genus commune and genus neuter in Anatolian. In the other dialects is found the further distinction between masculine and feminine gender, the latter marked by the long stem endings _*-ā_, _*-ī_, _*-ū_ (_*-eA_, _*-iA_, _*-uA_), and the feminine _*-o_. The origin of this triple distinction remains unclear. It may have originated partially in the pronominal system (but cf. the female kinship terms below). The three diachronic layers are still reflected in such languages as Latin: no distinction in m./f./n. _fēlix_, "frugal, happy" (consonantal stems); binary distinction in m./f. _facilis_, n. _facile_, "easily done"; and triple distinction in m. _bonus_, f. _bona_, n. _bonum_, "good."

The nominal endings distinguish the three numbers—singular, plural, and dual—and inflectional cases, which are grouped as follows: three "grammatical" cases—nominative, accusative, and genitive; four "adverbial" cases—ablative, dative, locative, and instrumental; and the vocative. Morphologically, the cases are most differentiated in the singular and least in the dual. In the singular, genitive = ablative; in the plural, dative = ablative; in the dual, dative = ablative = instrumental and nominative = accusative. In these two numbers, vocative = nominative. Table 1 shows the pattern in the singular of consonantal stems (vocative omitted).

The case endings of the thematic _o_-declension differ to some degree. Thus in the singular the endings are: nom. _*-os_, acc. _*-om_, gen. _*-os-yo_, abl. _*-ōd_, dat. _*-ōi_, loc. _*-ei/oi_, instr. _*-ē/ō_; voc. _*-e_; the neuter has _*-om_ in both nominative and accusative.

This system overlayed an archaic inflectional pattern, the so-called heteroclisis. The latter is marked by the opposition of continuants (_*s_, _*H_, resonants) in the nominative-accusative vs _*-n_ in the genitive. Hittite has preserved some of this inflection, e.g., Hittite nom.-acc./pahur/, gen./pahwen-as/ < _*peAwr_, _*pAwen-_. In the other dialects, either stem was generalized and fitted into the new inflectional patterns. For example, _*-r_ is generalized in English _fire_, but _*n_ in Gothic _fōn_, "fire." A particularly archaic example may be animate _*mar-/*man-u_, "human." The _r_-stem is found in Anatolian-Aryan _mar-ya-nnu_, "charioteer, young nobleman"; Indic _már-ya_, "young man"; Greek _meīrax_, "girl"; Lith. _mar-tì_, "bride, virgin." The _n_-stem is found in Indic _mánu-ṣ_, "man, human"; Russian _mu-ž_ "man"; German _Mann_, _Men-sch_.

While in nouns the basic pattern is nominative-accusative

TABLE 1. _IE case endings_

SING.	Indic	Greek	Latin	Hittite	IE
Nom	s	s	s	s	*s
Acc.	am	a	em	an	*m
Gen.	as	os	is	as	*es/os/s
Abl.	as (at)		(od)	az	= Gen. or*-d
Dat.	e	i	i	i	*ei
Loc.	i	i	e	a	*i/*Ø
Instr.	a	e	e	it	*eH/oH, bhi/mi

TABLE 2. *Basic case forms*

	Indic	Greek	Slavic	Hittite	IE
1s nom.	ahám	egṓ	azu	ug/amug	*eg′ (h)-
acc.	mām	emé	mene	amug	*me-
2s nom.	tvam	su	tu	tsig	*tu
acc.	tvām	se	tebe	tug	*t(w)e-
1p nom.	vayám	hemeīs	mu	wes	*wei/*n̥smés
acc.	nas	heméas	nasu	nas	*nes/*nos
2p nom.	yūyám	humeīs	vy	sumes	*yūs/*usmés
acc.	vas	huméas	vasu	smas	*wes/*wos

vs. genitive, the personal pronouns have the basic binary opposition nominative versus accusative-genitive. The adverbial case endings, which are more archaic than the nominal ones, are added to the latter. Table 2 shows the two basic case forms in the singular and plural of the first and second persons.

Common IE therefore distinguished between three types of declension. If these are considered as a system, they reveal a scale of animacy and an intersecting pattern of morphological, syntactic, and semantic case distinctions that are shown as in Table 3.

Verb system. The typical finite verb form of IE distinguishes the following categories: aspect-mood-person-number-voice-tense, in that order. Within these categories, the following basic distinctions are made: aspect—imperfective versus perfective (i.e., incomplete versus complete action), mood—indicative, subjunctive, optative, and imperative; person and number—first, second, and third person in singular, plural, and dual; voice (also called verbal gender, or diathesis)—active versus mediopassive, or middle (i.e., person as agent versus person affected by action or situation); and tense—present versus past (also called preterit). Anatolian lacks the subjunctive and optative, as well as the dual.

Morphologically, aspect is distinguished in the stem (root, or root + suffix, with ablaut). The other categories are indicated by suffixes and endings. For example, Avestan *bar-a-t-i* ("bears, carries") has the imperfective stem *bar-a-* ("present" stem **bher-* + thematic **-e-*); the mood is indicative (absence of the subjunctive **-e-* or optative **-yeE-*/**-iE-*); the person is third singular **-t*; the voice is active (absence of the mediopassive suffix **-o-*); and the tense is present, which is indicated by **-i*. Finite verbs do not show gender distinctions that correspond to masculine, feminine, and neuter in the nominal inflection. There is no original verbal prefixation. There are various other differentiations, attested as early as Hittite: suffixes and infixes that originally specified incomplete action as to the kind of action (called *aktionsart*), such as intensive, iterative **-s-k'-*, and **-n-* (reflected in pairs such as the Latin *jug-are*, "yoke," and *ju-n-g-ere*, "join").

Comparative reconstruction suggests that, underlying this developed system, is the yet more fundamental distinction between activum and perfectum. These can be described as the marking of agency and action as opposed to a situation, state, and result. This distinction differs from that between the active and mediopassive voice). The perfectum is exemplified by the root **weid-* ("see"), whose perfect has developed into a so-called perfectopresent, "have seen" > "come to know." This is reflected, for example, in Indic *vḗd-a, vḗt-tha, vḗd-a;* Greek *(u)oid-a, (u)ois-tha, (u)oid-e;* Gothic *wait, waist, wait*—all meaning "I know, you know, he/she/it knows." This is comparable to the English *put on* ("activum") versus *wear* ("perfectum").

Indo-European Homeland. The IE homeland has been

TABLE 3. *Basic semantic case distinctions*

SEMANTIC SYNTACTIC MORPHOL.	Agent Subject Nominative	Patient Object Accusative	Other Other Genitive	
Pronoun	*eg′(h)-	*me-	*me-	"I"
Animate	mā̆tēr *wl̥kwo-s	*mātér-m̥ *wl̥kwo-m	*mātr-ós *wl̥kwo-s-yo	"mother" "wolf"
Inanimate (neuter)	*peAwr *yugó-m	*peAwr *yugó-m	*pAwen-s *yugó-s-yo	"fire" "yoke"

located anywhere between western Europe and northern Central Asia, in Anatolia, and in the southern Caucasus region. A consensus is emerging that the formative area was the northern Pontic (Black Sea), from the Dniepr River to the Caspian Sea. The period suggested for the formative phase is the Late Neolithic/Eneolithic (4500–3500 BCE). The common phase may have ended by 2500 BCE. The main lines of the arguments here largely follow James Mallory (1989).

The earliest attestation of IE is Hittite, in approximately 2000 BCE. Also found in Anatolia, by about 1500 BCE, is Indo-Aryan, which is already clearly differentiated from Iranian. Accordingly, even though there are no yardsticks for the rate of linguistic change, the latest date for the breakup of the IE unity could be set by 2500 BCE. (The earliest known IE term may date to about 3000 BCE, if the Sumerian *gigir* and Semitic **gagal* derive from IE **kwé-kwl-o-*, "wagon wheel".)

The lexicon shared by all IE dialects reflects the first revolution and the secondary-products revolution in economy and technology—including the domestication of animals, agriculture, and vehicular technology—and, finally, the innovative coinage of vocabulary (nouns and verbs) to reflect the technology of the equine revolution, which is dated to the early fourth millennium or earlier.

One approach to locating the homeland of IE is to identify its so-called center of gravity. By taking the distribution of the dialects in use by about 100 BCE, when most of the known IE dialects had emerged (the Iberian Peninsula to western China and India) and considering the area of highest variety (Central-Eastern Europe), the center of the belt can be located at between 20 and 30° East—the Pontic region. The region is compatible with the common IE lexical material relating to the physical environment, fauna, and flora. This is supported by observations concerning naming. For example, the referential meanings of IE tree names are best preserved in the Baltic-Slavic regions but are shifted considerably in Greek (Friedrich, 1970). Similarly, the domestication of the horse, which is recognized as a determining factor in the IE expansion, appears to have occurred between the northeastern Pontic-Caspian region and the southern Ural Mountains.

The next line of arguments considers linguistic contacts. There are no known transitional languages between reconstructed IE and other language families. However, contact is clearly evident with the Uralic language family, in particular Finno-Ugric. There are two distinct layers. The younger layer are loans from Indo-Iranian, and specifically Iranian; for example, **pork'-o-* ("pig"), Iranian **parsa,* Finnish *porsas,* ("pork"), and Votyak, *pars;* Iranian *satam* ("one hundred"), Finnish *sata.*

None of the other language families has the same degree of similarities with IE as Uralic, although Semitic continues to be seriously discussed. A large number of Semitic-IE lexical pairs have been suggested, but the systematic sound correspondences are difficult to ascertain. The Semitic laryngeals have been compared with the IE laryngeals, but again there are few convincing correspondences, and the phonological features of the IE laryngeals are quite uncertain.

There may nevertheless be a truly archaic connection between these families. It has been argued that the six language families—Afro-Asiatic (Hamito-Semitic), Kartvelian, Indo-European, Uralic, Altaic, and Dravidian—belong to a single phylum, for which Holger Pedersen (in 1903) coined the term *Nostratic* (from Lat., *nostras,* "one of ours"). Nostratic studies were propelled in the 1960s by Illič-Svityč but have found strong opposition, largely because of the difficulties in indentifying sound rules as exacting as those that are customary in IE studies. Part of the difficulty in evaluating these efforts may be that it is not always realized that Nostratic cognates are established via common Nostratic, not between two families—for example, IE and Kartvelian, directly—and that not all items identified as Nostratic can be expected to be found in IE (see Manaster-Ramer, 1993).

The next step toward identifying the area of common IE combines linguistics with archaeology and correlates the layers of the dialectological configurations of IE with major archaeologically identified cultural layers and patterns of diffusion. Two such major patterns are known. The first is the spread of agriculture from eastern Anatolia into Europe; the second is the much later spread of numerous distinct cultural features from the Pontic-Caspian regions into Europe and into Asia. [*See* Agriculture.]

The spread of agriculture from Anatolia into Europe, called the wave of advance, begins in the Early Neolithic period, about 7000 BCE (Renfrew, 1987). It first reaches Greece and the Balkans and from there spreads into the remainder of western and northern Europe. This wave swings around the northwestern corner of the Pontic region and, from there, farther east, where steppe pastoralism becomes the main feature. This wave is followed by the progress of the secondary-products revolution. Moving east, the wave reached Iran and the Indian subcontinent, as well as Central Asia.

Colin Renfrew (1987) advocates the correlation of this wave with the spread of IE, which would make Anatolia the IE homeland. However, it has become obvious that the pattern of its progress does not agree at all with the internal dialectal structuring of the IE dialects: it would require the move of the original speakers of IE out of Anatolia and the return of such groups as the speakers of the Anatolian languages back into it. The original group would also have to become entirely extinct because the Anatolian languages as well as Armenian are entirely superimposed on non-IE, such as Hattic and Hurrian-Caucasian. Moreover, those languages are typological, and lexically they are completely different from IE—they lack any discernible trace of earlier contact with IE. It has also been noted that an early spread across Europe would have resulted in much greater differentiation of IE than is found in the attested dialects. Equally crucial is that the source area of IE must have known not only vehicular technology, but also the technology of the equine revolution, which excludes seventh-millennium Anatolia. The source of the second differentiation is the Pontic-Caspian region. It fits well both geographically and temporally with the technoeconomy and with the internally reconstructed dialectology and its phases of IE. This conclusion was forcefully drawn in the 1960s by Marija Gimbutas (1965) and has been argued convincingly by Mallory (1989).

Indo-European Kinship Terminology and Social Structure. The kinship terminology of IE is the only cognitive system, beside the decimal system of numbers, that has remained so remarkably intact it can by and large be linguistically reconstructed, at least phonologically (e.g., Szemerényi, 1977; Mayrhofer, in *Indogermanische Grammatik,* 1986); however, its etymology has remained obscure. Delbrück (1889) pioneered the first major survey and study of the topic but rejected much of the speculation of his time, both in terms of etymology and of the societal systems derived from it. The most recent study focuses on etymology, much of which has been subjected to strong criticism (Szemerényi, 1977). There appears to be little agreement, except that the system overall seems to have been patriarchal, patrilineal, and patrilocal. A large number of kinship terms can be reconstructed for common IE. The dialects vary greatly—from Anatolian, with very few, to Slavic, whose inherited linguistic network is virtually intact in a modern setting and should serve as the guideline for reconstructions.

Reconstruction and Reality. In the late twentieth century a renewed and vigorous debate occurred about the emergence of languages, the principles of reconstruction and their underlying assumptions, and the reality of the reconstruct. Most, if not all, of the issues and points appear to be commonsensical and to have already been made during the two hundred years of Indo-European study. However, a new degree of consensus appears to have been reached. First, it is commonly agreed that IE is not the Ursprache of humankind, and that it did not evolve out of naught, but that its nucleus emerged out of non-IE. There is agreement that the development of diversified forms is the result of multiple mergers. Three main models have been isolated. For the initial emergence of IE the model is the creole, which typically develops out of the pidgin, inflectionless amalgam of the languages of a *colluvies gentium* (including cossack-type mercenaries returning from the Near East), into a functioning natural language within one of two generations. However, pidgins and creoles always reflect one major donor language (note Pidgin English), which is still unidentified for earliest IE. Another model is the *Sprachbund,* in which genetically unrelated languages develop not only lexical, but also phonological and grammatical, similarities (according to the wave theory of language diffusion). The third model is that of the koine, in which a dominant dialect erases most others. These three models are not mutually exclusive, nor do they exclude the participation of already diversified dialects anywhere at any stage with others and with non-IE dialects. In each case, one of the dominant speech groups continued IE in the form into which it had changed, which may be incompletely learned IE.

As to the real time it might have taken for the initial consolidation and the subsequent diversifications, there are only guesses. Both Romance and Slavic developments are documented, but they cannot be generalized and projected backward into entirely different conditions. No method yet exists for measuring the rate of linguistic change similar to DNA sequencing. Glottochronology, by calculating the rate of loss of a set of assumed basic lexical items, has not proven convincing.

Recent attempts by archaeologists to correlate archaeological trajectories with the expansion of IE are part of the reason for the epistemological debate in IE studies. There is either common ground or agreement in many respects, including the recognition that genetic-linguistic relationships are not the same as ethnic or as biological relationships. However, linguistic expansion involves the initial move of people, and more people have to find it advantageous to adopt a language—there must be motivation, such as the new technology of rapid transit (the horse, e.g., would have made it cost efficient to move). Beside economic motivation, social mobility is made easier in hierarchically structured societies. The IE social structure must have made it easier for others to adopt that language. What is known of early recorded IE is based on the dialects of dominant elites, whose mobility must have played a major role in the spread of IE. Important information on expansive warrior elites, alliances, peoples, localities, and gods is found in the profuse, but confusing, references in epic and mythology.

It is also agreed, however, that linguistics and archaeology operate with different data within different epistemologies: "Picture and text each require separate specialists in their reconstruction" (Yoffee, 1990). Neither ceramic patterns nor reconstructed rituals or cultures, or their particular assembly, allow for the reconstruction of the language, or languages, that was part of them. Language disappears and can only be reconstructed; artifacts are remains. Language change is not synchronized with cultural change. Locating the emergence of IE in the Pontic-Caspian area assumes that the relative location in time and space of the attested dialects and their immediately preceding stages is sufficiently close to project by triangulation their source backward into the empty linguistic slot. It is here, however, that archaeological data appear to confound linguistic projections, as there does not seem to be a direct link between the Pontic-Caspian cultures to northern central Europe.

Finally, a topic widely debated, but unrelated to the interdisciplinary one, is the ontological status of the linguistic reconstruct, whether identified as common IE, as a preceding stage with less inflection, or as a stage without any inflection. Opinions range from near reality to mere algebraic abstract. A case cited for the former is the verification of the algebraically postulated laryngeals in Hittite. Such discoveries, however, are not seen by many as sufficient for the recognition that any reconstruct by itself is unanchored in time and space. Reconstruction is reductive, ending with a single common source of sound, structure, or lexical item. It cannot recover those that left no traces. The majority opinion seems to hold that while it is possible to identify relative chronologies and tentative areas, it is impossible to reconstruct IE as a natural, synchronically functioning language—which always is an unpredictably mixed one.

BIBLIOGRAPHY

Adrados, Francisco Rodriguez. "The New Image of Indoeuropean: The History of a Revolution." *Indogermanische Forschungen* 94 (1992): 21–44.

American Heritage Dictionary of Indo-European Roots, rev. and edited by Calvert Watkins. Boston, 1985.

Anthony, David W. "The Archaeology of Indo-European Origins." *Journal of Indo-European Studies* 19 (1991): 193–222. Succinct reevaluation, with maps.

Baldi, Philip. *An Introduction to the Indo-European Languages.* Carbondale, Ill., 1993. Handy overview, with minigrammars and sample texts.

Benveniste, Emile. 1935. *Origines de la formations des noms en indoeuropéen.* Paris, 1935. Fundamental study of the origins and structure of the Indo-European root.

Benveniste, Emile. *Indo-European Language and Society.* London, 1969. (A translation of *Les structures élémentaires de la parenté,* Paris, 1967.) Brilliant, most comprehensive analytical-comparative study of Indo-European society; partially controversial.

Brugmann, Karl. Karl. *Grundriss der vergleichenden Grammatik der indogermanischen Sprachen,* 7 vols. 2d ed. Strassburg, 1897–1916. Still the standard documentation of Indo-European phonology and morphology.

Buck, Carl Darling. *A Dictionary of Selected Synonyms in the Principle Indo-European Languages: A Contribution to the History of Ideas.* Chicago, 1949. Unsurpassed and topical.

D'iakonov, Igor M. "On the Original Home of the Speakers of Indo-European." *Journal of Indo-European Studies* 13 (1985): 92–174. Brilliant but sharp criticism of Gamkrelidze and Ivanov's theories of IE-South Caucasian and IE-Semitic relationships.

Delbrück, Berthold. *Syntaktische Forschungen.* 5 vols. Halle, 1871–1888. Pioneering; still the best documentation of the mostly neglected aspects of grammar.

Delbrück, Berthold. *Die indogermanischen Verwandtschaftsnamen. Ein Beitrag zur vergleichenden Alterthumskunde.* Leipzig, 1889. Pioneering and sober evaluation of anthropological and linguistic epistemologies and theories; still the most detailed and best-documented analysis of IE kinship.

Friedrich, Paul. "An Evolutionary Sketch of Russian Kinship." In Viola E. Garfield et al., eds. *Symposium on Language and Culture: Proceedings of the 1962 Annual Spring Meeting of the American Ethnological Society,* edited by Viola E. Garfield et al., pp. 1–36. Seattle, 1963. This and the influential article below are informed by anthropological theory.

Friedrich, Paul. "Proto-Indo-European Kinship." *Ethnology* (Pittsburgh) 5 (1966): 1–36.

Friedrich, Paul. *Proto-Indo-European Trees: The Arboreal System of a Prehistoric People.* Chicago, 1970. Thorough documentation and analysis of terminology; shows the least shift in eastern Europe regarding flora's evidence for the IE homeland.

Friedrich, Paul. *Proto-Indo-European Syntax: The Order of Meaningful Elements.* Butte, Mont., 1974. Pioneering factual reassessment.

Gamkrelidze, Thomas V., and Vjaceslav V. Ivanov. "Sprachtypology und die Rekonstruktion der gemeinindogermanischen Verschlüsse." *Phonetica* 27 (1973): 150–156. Proposing the "glottalic theory" that the system of IE stops developed from a South Caucasian type whose central series were glottalized ejectives.

Gamkrelidze, Thomas V., and Vjaceslav V. Ivanov. *Indo-European and the Indo-Europeans: A Reconstruction and Historical Analysis of a Proto-Language and a Proto-Culture,* edited by Werner Winter. Berlin, 1995. Updated from *Indoevropejskij jazyk i Indoevropejcij* (2 vols.; Tbilisi, 1984). The most comprehensive and insightful recent reevaluation; includes proposal that IE was an "active" language, with separate active and stative classes of verbs and nouns.

Gimbutas, Marija. *Bronze Age Cultures in Central and Eastern Europe.* The Hague, 1965. Pioneering work by an archaeologist to correlate cultural trajectories from the Pontic-Caspian area into Europe.

Gimbutas, Marija. *The Civilization of the Goddess. The World of Old Europe.* San Francisco, 1991. Focus on pre-IE matriarchal, artistic Old Europe.

Indogermanische Grammatik, edited by Jerzy Kurylowicz, (later by) Manfred Mayrhofer, Heidelberg. Cowgill, Warren, *Einleitung,* vol. 1.1 (1986): 11–71; Mayrhofer, Manfred, *Lautlehre,* vol. 1.2 (1986): 75–185; Kurylowicz, Jerzy, *Akzent. Ablaut,* vol. 2 (1968); Watkins, Calvert, *Geschichte der indogermanischen Verbalflexion,* vol. 3 (1983). The up-to-date standard of Indo-European linguistics.

Lehmann, Winfred P. *The Theoretical Bases of Indo-European Linguistics.* London, 1993. Insightful, up-to-date discussion of theory and methodology.

Lehmann, Winfred P. *Residues of Pre-Indo-European Active Structure and their Implications for the Relationships among Dialects.* Innsbruck, 1995.

Levin, Saul. *Semitic and Indo-European: The Principle Etymologies with Observations on Afro-Asiatic.* Amsterdam, 1995. A renewed, cautious, and thorough attempt to establish the linguistic relationship, considering the Nostratic macrophylum of language families.

Lockwood, William B. *A Panorama of Indo-European Languages.* London, 1972. A most readable overview.

Mallory, James. *In Search of the Indo-Europeans.* London, 1989. Factual reassessment of the controversial correlation between archaeology and comparative-historical linguistics for IE.

Manaster-Ramer, Alexis. "On Illič-Svityč's Nostratic Theory." *Studies in Linguistics* 17 (1993): 205–250. Fairest and most insightful critique of establishing the macrophylum of language families called Nostratic.

Mayrhofer, Manfred. *Die Indo-Arier im alten Vorderasien.* Wiesbaden, 1966. Still the best on the subject of the Indo-Iranian linguistic loan component in Anatolian.

Meid, Wolfgang. *Probleme der räumlichen und zeitlichen Gliederung des Indogermanischen.* In Helmut Rix, ed. *Flexion und Wortbildung,* pp. 204–219. Wiesbaden, 1975. Programmatic and influential; suggests a three-dimensional space-time model.

Pokorny, Julius. *Indogermanisches etymologisches Wörterbuch.* 2 vols. Bern, 1951, 1969. The unsurpassed standard dictionary.

Renfrew, Colin. *Archaeology and Language. The Puzzle of Indo-European Origins.* London, 1987. Controversial proposal for the origins of IE in Anatolia.

Schmidt, Johannes. *Die Verwandtschaftsverhältnisse der indogerman-*

ischen Sprachen. Weimar, 1872. Introduced the model of the wave theory to account for the spread of innovations and linguistic filiation.

Schrader, Otto, and A. Nehring. *Reallexikon der indogermanischen Altertumskunde.* 2 vols. Berlin-Leipzig, 1917–1929. Still an indispensible compendium.

Schwink, Frederick W. *Linguistic Typology, Universality and the Realism of Reconstruction.* Washington, 1994. The best-documented assessment of recent theories on IE linguistics and the relative value of linguistic typology.

Skomal, Susan N., and Edgar C. Polomé, eds. *Proto-Indo-European: The Archaeology of a Linguistic Problem.* Washington, 1987. One of the many volumes edited and coedited by Polomé, the editor of the *Journal of Indo-European Studies.*

Szemerényi, Oswald. "Studies in the Kinship Terminology of the Indo-European Languages." *Acta Iranica* 16 (1977): 1–240. A book in article form, this is the most comprehensive, but often idiosyncratic, etymological study of IE kinship terminology and reconstructable social structures.

Szemerényi, Oswald. *Einführung in die vergleichende Sprachwissenschaft.* 4th ed. Darmstadt, 1990. The unsurpassed statement of IE historical-comparative phonology and morphology, with an ample, updated bibliography on linguistic matters (only).

Yoffee, Norman. "Before Babel. A Review Article." *Proceedings of the Prehistoric Society* 56 (1990): 299–313. Insightful and to-the-point assessment of the viability of conjoining linguistics with archaeology; reviews Renfrew, 1987 and Mallory, 1989.

Yoffee, Norman. "Too Many Chiefs? or, Safe Texts for the '90s." In *Archaeological Theory: Who sets the Agenda?,* edited by Norman Yoffee and Andrew Sherratt, pp. 60–78. Cambridge, 1993.

Zimmer, Stefan. *Ursprache, Urvolk und Indogermanisierung.* Innsbruck, 1990. An admonition against the facile correlation of artifact with an abstract linguistic reconstruction.

GERNOT WINDFUHR

INK. *See* Writing Materials.

INSCRIPTIONS. [*To provide a broad survey of the inscriptional material that has been recovered from the Near East, this entry comprises four articles:*

Ancient Inscriptions
Inscriptions of the Classical Period
Inscriptions of the Hellenistic and Roman Periods
Inscriptions of the Islamic Period

Each article treats the material supports on which inscriptions are found; the languages, literary genres, and chronological and geographical distribution of the inscriptions; and the role of inscriptional materials in reconstructing ancient Near Eastern history.]

Ancient Inscriptions

An overview of Near Eastern inscriptions down to the Persian period is, in effect, an account of the origins of modern literate society. It must take into account virtually all extant written documents from the dawn of writing to the rise of Classical Greek civilization. These documents stand alongside noninscriptional artifacts as the two principal types of archaeological data available for reconstructing the history of these periods. The two types of data must be correlated in a history intended to include the political, economic, social, and intellectual aspects of ancient civilization.

The history of decipherment of the various inscriptions discovered constitutes an important part of the history of modern archaeology. During the heroic period of Egyptian and Mesopotamian archaeology (late eighteenth and early nineteenth centuries CE), for example, the decipherment of inscriptions contributed greatly to understanding the place in history both of artifacts and of those who had produced them.

The texts from these early periods are more exclusively archaeological artifacts than are those from later periods. The cultures they represent have not provided a chain of tradition down to the modern era, such as has been preserved in, for example, the Hebrew Bible, the Qur'an, the Syriac Christian corpus, or the principal literary texts from Classical Greece. There is evidence for an ancient chain of tradition for some literary texts (e.g., the Gilgamesh story), and some genres show evolution and accretion over centuries (e.g., Mesopotamian divinatory and lexical texts). The majority of ancient inscriptional material, however, represents primary documents—the documents as they came from the first writer's hand, often intended for one-time use, as in the case of letters and accounts.

For such primary documents to have been preserved, they need to have been written on materials capable of preservation across millennia. This means that, with the exception of Egypt, where the dry climate has preserved papyri back to the earliest stages of writing, most extant documents are inscribed either on stone or on clay tablets. [*See* Papyrus; Tablet.]

Origins of Writing. The prehistory of writing—the steps that led up to the well-attested writing systems of Mesopotamia and Egypt—is a subject of debate, but actual texts are attested by the last quarter of the fourth millennium. The scripts of both civilizations originally had a strong pictographic character, but the Mesopotamian version rapidly developed into a syllabary. Egyptian hieroglyphics retained, at least in formal inscriptions, their pictographic form, even though they became representations of consonantal phonemes (the system was not proto-alphabetic, however, for each sign could represent one, two, or three consonants). [*See* Writing and Writing Systems; Hieroglyphs.] Both systems used certain signs as semantic determinatives (e.g., GIŠ, "wood," in Sumerian, is written before names of objects made of wood). Another pictographic-syllabic system came into use in Anatolia in the late second millennium BCE—the so-called Hittite hieroglyphic system, used to write the Luwian language. [*See* Hittite; Luwians.] The invention of the consonantal alphabet ("abjad") probably did not occur until about the middle of the second millennium BCE, somewhere in the Levantine area; its earliest tokens are the Proto-Sinaitic and Proto-Canaanite inscriptions. [*See* Proto-

Sinaitic; Proto-Canaanite; Alphabet.] The true alphabet, wherein both consonants and vowels are noted, was the contribution of the Greeks after they had borrowed the consonantal alphabet from the West Semites in the early first millennium BCE. [*See* Greek.]

Writing Materials. There were, in the ancient world, three primary systems for recording a text: producing signs by transferring a colored substance onto a relatively flat surface (e.g., ink on papyrus or on an ostracon) by means of a penlike instrument; gouging signs into a soft material (e.g., clay or wax) by means of an instrument with an angular tip; and carving signs into a hard surface (e.g., wood or stone) by means of a chisel-like instrument. [*See* Writing Materials; Ostracon.]

As is still the case, the last system was used for texts with permanent value (e.g., funerary inscriptions), and they were often placed where they would be generally visible (e.g., royal proclamations in Assyrian palaces or on Egyptian obelisks). Few inscriptions in wood are preserved—both because wood was probably used less frequently for this purpose than was stone and because wood is more perishable than stone. Inscriptions on stone are attested from all parts of the Near East, in many of its languages. They range in size from tiny (e.g., seal inscriptions) to gigantic (e.g., Egyptian obelisks). [*See* Seals.] They appear on all types of stone (e.g., semiprecious stones for seal inscriptions, carved limestone or basalt for royal inscriptions) and in various contexts (e.g., in tombs, on architectural elements, and even on cliff faces). [*See* Inscription Sites.]

Though using ink and gouging signs into soft material are also attested everywhere, there was certainly a predilection in Mesopotamia for stone. In Egypt the ready availability of papyrus made it a common surface for writing (texts on papyrus are attested from the Old Kingdom onward). In Mesopotamia the invention of writing is attested as impressions on clay. The system was the primary one used there until the end of classical Mesopotamian civilization. However, with the increased use of Aramaic in the Late Assyrian and Babylonian periods, writing on wax-covered wooden tablets and on parchment became more common. [*See* Aramaic Language and Literature; Parchment.]

It is possible that the relative dearth of documents from the Levant in general (Palestine, Transjordan, Phoenicia, southern Syria) is owing to the extensive use there of papyrus and other soft materials for writing the local languages. In any case, the Ugaritic novelty (a West Semitic language written in cuneiform on clay tablets) has provided a corpus of texts, ranging from the great myths to mundane lists, unparalleled at any other Levantine site. [*See* Ugarit; Cuneiform.]

Languages/Areas. With few exceptions (e.g., Amorite), if the existence of an ancient Near Eastern language is known, inscriptions exist in that language. [*See* Amorites.] The numbers of texts in a given language range from only a few (Hurrian, mainland Phoenician) to thousands or even hundreds of thousands (Akkadian, Egyptian). [*See* Hurrian; Phoenician-Punic; Akkadian; Egyptian.] Because the area is the homeland of the Semites, most inscriptions are in various Semitic languages or, in the case of Egyptian, in a language closer to the origins of Semitic: the Afro-Asiatic (or Hamito-Semitic) group. The Semitic languages attested during these periods are classified geographically as Eastern (Akkadian) and Western (specifically Northwestern: Ugaritic, Phoenician/Hebrew, and Aramaic). [*See* Ugaritic; Hebrew Language and Literature.]

The principal Indo-European languages attested are the various languages of Anatolia (principally Hittite and Luwian) from early in the second millennium BCE—and almost to the end of the period covered here in the case of Luwian. [*See* Indo-European Languages.] The first Indo-Aryan inscriptions are those in Old Persian; there are no native-language inscriptions from the Mitannians or Kassites. [*See* Mitanni; Kassites.]

Mesopotamian writing was invented for a language that was neither Semitic nor Indo-European—that is, Sumerian—and this writing system, as well as Sumerian thought and literature, exercised a major influence on Akkadian throughout its existence. [*See* Sumerian.] Other important non-Semitic languages, attested primarily to the east and to the north of Mesopotamia proper, are Hurrian, Urartian, and Elamite. [*See* Hurrians; Elamites; Urartu.] The latter two languages are written with Mesopotamian cuneiform. Hurrian is poorly attested, but texts have been discovered written in both Mesopotamian cuneiform and Ugaritic alphabetic cuneiform.

Important aspects of the correlation of languages and areas are the related phenomena of bilingualism or multilingualism, of prestige languages, and of linguae francae. Because writing was invented in Mesopotamia to express the Sumerian language, that language remained the principal means of written expression for hundreds of years, even for Semitic speakers. By the Old Akkadian period (c. 2400 BCE), this was, however, principally a graphic phenomenon: the use of Semitic words and phonetic indicators shows that the use of Sumerian could be logographic—that is, that a text written principally or even entirely in Sumerian could be read in the local Semitic language (e.g., Akkadian in Akkad or Eblite at Ebla). [*See* Akkade; Ebla; Ebla Texts.] Learning Sumerian remained an important part of the curriculum of Mesopotamian scribes long after the language had disappeared from daily use. [*See* Scribes and Scribal Techniques.] In any case, the use of Sumerian logograms became a permanent part of Akkadian; in certain genres (e.g., divinatory texts) logograms constituted a major form of the expression. Sumerian logograms were also important in Hittite, so much so that the Hittite form of many words is still unknown, for the word was always written logographically.

From about 2000 BCE until the rise of Aramaic in the Persian Empire, Akkadian (with its usual Sumerian underpinnings) was both the prestige language of Mesopotamia, Anatolia, and Syria/Palestine and the international lingua franca, much like Latin in medieval Europe. As is clear from the Amarna letters, Akkadian was used for the correspondence between the New Kingdom pharaohs and their Levantine client rulers. [*See* Amarna Tablets.] This required, of course, an Egyptian scribal class that was bilingual.

When a lingua franca is used, the command of the language may vary considerably from one area to another—whence the modern Romance languages, to cite the European model. This is clear from the use of Akkadian in the Syro-Palestinian area in the second millennium BCE, where, depending on whether a text was from Mari, Alalakh, Ugarit, or the Phoenician and Palestinian city states, the purity of the language varied considerably. [*See* Mari; Alalakh.]

That Akkadian was not only a practical lingua franca, but also the prestige language representing the prestige culture during this time, is clear from the relatively large numbers of texts representing Mesopotamian culture discovered in the West. This is clearest from Ugarit, where hundreds of lexical texts and a significant number of literary texts have been discovered. The numbers go beyond those expected of simple schools for learning the language; they represent an attempt at mastering Mesopotamian literary culture. Ugaritic scribes also seem to have prided themselves on their ability to manipulate the Akkadian language (Arnaud, 1982). In other instances, genres that seem likely to have originated in Mesopotamia have been thoroughly assimilated into the local language: this is true of "scientific" texts at Ugarit (hippiatric texts, various ominological texts), written in pure Ugaritic with few Akkadianisms.

The extent of bilingualism in a given culture depended on the degree of isolation and self-sufficiency: Egypt constituted one extreme, its geographic isolation often translating into cultural isolation; the Levantine states, which dealt regularly with people from all over the Near East, were at the other extreme. This is best illustrated by Ras Shamra (Ugarit), the Levantine site that has produced the largest number of texts, in eight different languages/scripts. [*See* Ugarit Inscriptions.]

Types of Texts. The mundane will usually hold pride of place in a collection of primary documents for, to varying degrees, such texts reflect everyday activities. In most archaeological text discoveries, literary and explicitly historical texts will be in a very small minority or entirely absent. During the first century of the study of ancient Near Eastern texts, such texts were nevertheless considered the most important, and they received the lion's share of attention. In the last few decades, a reaction has set in to this preponderance of energy expended on a minority production of the elite: more attention is now being paid to documents that permit a broader reconstruction of socioeconomic history.

The content of a group of texts discovered in an archaeological excavation can vary considerably, depending on various factors:

1. The social status of whoever (in antiquity) assembled the collection (i.e., whether the individual(s) was private or royal)
2. Whether the texts constitute an archive, a random assemblage, or even discards
3. If the texts come from an administrative archive, the place in the administration occupied by whomever collected the archive (e.g., many of the texts from Mari represent royal correspondence, whereas almost all the Ebla texts are account tablets)
4. The time period covered (from a few decades in the case of the Ebla archives to centuries in the case of the library of Ashurbanipal)
5. The interests and aptitudes of the collector or collectors (e.g., a high percentage of Ugaritic mythological texts were the work of a single scribe)
6. Whether the texts represent a working archive or scribal training (e.g., "the classics" were part of the scribal curriculum, and in Egypt extracts from these were found written in ink on ostraca)
7. The origin of the archaeological deposit (with an instantaneous destruction more likely to contain a cohesive archive than a stratum, which reflects either continuous habitation or the gradual abandonment of a site)

In addition to these and other definable factors, there is also the simple fortune of discovery: only a fraction of a site is usually excavated and because only a fraction of the available sites have been touched, only a fraction of the potentially available texts, themselves only a fraction of the texts actually produced in antiquity, are known.

To some degree, the material selected for inscription will reflect the genre of the text: precious materials or unwieldy objects (such as large stones) will be used for texts upon which a certain value is placed. On the other hand, everything from account texts to the highest literature will be written with the primary media of the culture (clay tablets in Mesopotamia and Anatolia, papyrus in Egypt). Priorities were different from one culture to another: Egypt is well known for monumental inscriptions, particularly in tombs and temples, whereas these are relatively rare in the rest of the ancient Near East. In this case the iconic value of the hieroglyphic script and the accompanying artistic representations were important: only a very small percentage of the population would have been capable of actually reading the texts in any ancient culture. In Mesopotamia, the cuneiform script lacked the iconic value of hieroglyphs. The linking of text and pictorial representations achieved major importance only relatively late, at the time of the Neo-Assyrian Empire. [*See* Assyrians.]

It is possible to classify ancient Near Eastern texts into a representative list of a number of categories, depending on the criteria chosen:

Administrative texts—accounts of all sorts; legal texts, including treaties

Epistolary texts—letters between individuals
Ritual texts—prescriptions or descriptions of liturgy
Scientific texts—astronomy, mathematics, medicine, lexicography, ominology
Historical texts—royal inscriptions and preambles to legal documents; some annals and, toward the end of the period covered here, chronicles
Belletristic works—myths, legends, and stories, often characterized by poetic composition; however, "poetry" may have been expressed in ancient languages

As with any such categorization, there are overlapping subgenres (e.g., a business letter or one recounting an observation of the stars). This list is meant consciously to exclude the very transitory writing (few graffiti are known from the early periods; school texts can reflect any genre) and historiography (the relatively few historical documents tend to be strongly apologetic; the dates of the nascent historiographic documents in the Hebrew Bible are debated).

Religious texts belong to several literary types, for religion so infused ancient society that it is reflected in several genres (e.g., temple accounts, celestial omens, temple histories, myths). Prose ritual texts, however, constitute a formal type concentrated in the sphere of religion, for no other aspect of life generated sets of prescribed acts couched in writing to the same extent as religious rites. Furthermore, poetry was used almost exclusively in these early periods when topics were treated that touched on the divine.

Administrative texts and letters constitute the backbone of many archives, for they represent the day-to-day and summary aspects of accounting, the legal basis for the ownership or use of various sorts of property, and the communication across space of all sorts of matters relating to households or larger social entities. [*See* Libraries and Archives.] Such texts provide the principal basis for reconstructing ancient societies and economies; having been produced by a literate elite, they do tend to represent the concerns of the upper levels of society, making it difficult to reconstruct a true cross section of society.

Science was, of course, the science of the day, but much of modern science has nonetheless developed from it, particularly mathematics, astronomy, and medicine. Divinatory texts are classified as scientific because they are formally similar to medical texts and were plausibly considered by the ancients to be equivalent in nature: both are characterized by the protasis-apodosis structure ("if such-and-such an omen is observed, such-and-such an event will occur," "if such-and-such a symptom is observed, give such-and-such a remedy"). Most of the explicitly scientific texts are from Mesopotamia, though certain types are attested in Anatolia and in Syria-Palestine. The Egyptians are known to have developed mathematics, geometry, and astronomy, but they left few writings dealing with the topics. The classification of the world, natural and human, was an important part of Mesopotamian science, expressed in lexical terms: long lists of words organized into broad semantic categories, usually based on the Sumerian term and with or without the corresponding Akkadian term. The concept developed into virtual polyglot dictionaries in the West (tablets are attested at Ugarit with columns for Sumerian, Akkadian, Hurrian, and Ugaritic).

It is the belletristic works that have most potently captured the imagination of modern readers, for their combination of elevated expression and metaphysical topics seems to reveal aesthetic and religious aspirations similar to modern sensibilities. Indeed, these texts were first seen as important in comparison with the Hebrew Bible, a document at least partially from this early period and that has endured. The Ugaritic mythological texts have provided a particularly meaningful background to the Bible, while those from Mesopotamia, Anatolia, and Egypt have done so less directly. These texts are now being studied as witnesses to their own cultures and have thus, to some extent, been liberated from a Bible-centered perspective.

Inscriptions and History. The virtual absence of historiographic texts from this early period means that the ancient sources provide only the narrowest of viewpoints on ancient Near Eastern history—and then it often is the personal account of a monarch or a courtier. The modern historian must, therefore, work extensively from the ephemera of the time. Modern historians of the ancient Near East can be characterized broadly as belonging to two categories: archaeologists with few, if any, documents who reconstruct the history of a site on the basis of its material remains, and specialists in texts, who, perforce, work only on areas and periods for which texts are extant. The two types work in cooperation. Anyone working on the long-term history of a region or of a site works of course with both artifactual and textual evidence according to availability. Certain types of data—for example, names and the specifics of many events—are only available from textual sources, whereas many realia are best known from archaeological sources; the correlation between the two types of data is improving as cooperation between archaeologists and text specialists builds a databank.

Because of the importance of ephemera, epistolary documents constitute one of the most important types of text for reconstructing political history, while other administrative documents provide the main basis of economic history. The texts from Old Babylonian Mari illustrate this well: thousands of letters from that site permit the reconstruction of a quite-detailed history of Upper Mesopotamia and of Babylonian interests there; many administrative texts have provided a great number of data on the contemporary economy—at least from the perspective of the royal administration. The Amarna letters, on the other hand, with their disparate origins and without the contribution of administrative texts, contain primarily political data. Only Ugarit has provided texts of both types, both in Akkadian and in the local language, allowing a unique perspective on the organization and international dealings of a royal city-state at the end of the Late Bronze Age.

Intellectual history and the history of religious beliefs and practices are most plausibly pursued where a wealth of documents gives several perspectives on these topics—principally, therefore, in Egypt and Mesopotamia and to a lesser extent in Anatolia and Syria. Considerably more is thus known about the beliefs and practices of New Kingdom Egypt or of Mesopotamia in the eighteenth century BCE than is known about those of the pre-Exilic "Hebrews," simply because most information about Israelite religion comes from a single source, the Hebrew Bible, the precise origins of which are still debated. Indeed, most of the light cast on the Hebrew Bible has been either from nontextual archaeological discoveries or from non-Hebrew texts. (In the Northwest Semitic languages alone, inscriptions in Ugaritic, Phoenician, and Aramaic far outnumber those in Hebrew.) There is nothing ungrateful in this description of the current status of affairs, for great progress has been made since the beginning of modern archaeology. It is nonetheless true that additional written sources from South Canaan must be discovered—preferably in the local languages, though any archive would be welcome—in order for a more precise description of the intellectual and religious history of the peoples of the area to be possible. [*See* Literacy.]

BIBLIOGRAPHY

Arnaud, Daniel. "Une lettre du roi de Tyr au roi d'Ougarit: Milieux d'affaires et de culture en Syrie à la fin de l'âge du Bronze Récent." *Syria* 59 (1982): 101–107. Scribal professionalism and internationalism from the perspective of Ugarit.

The Cambridge Ancient History. Vols. 1–3. 2d and 3d eds. Cambridge, 1970–1991. Written by major specialists, but the first two volumes are already out of date.

Ebeling, Erich, et al., eds. *Reallexikon der Assyriologie*. 7 vols. to date. Berlin, 1932–. Includes articles on important texts and archives.

Foster, Benjamin R. *Before the Muses: An Anthology of Akkadian Literature*. 2 vols. Bethesda, Md., 1993. Up-to-date translation, including texts difficult to find in English or previously untranslated.

Freedman, David Noel, ed. *The Anchor Bible Dictionary*. 6 vols. New York, 1992. Covers all aspects of biblical studies; includes articles on other ancient Near Eastern cultures.

Godart, Louis. *Le pouvoir de l'écrit: Aux pays des premières écritures*. Paris, 1990. Comprehensive and well-illustrated introduction to early writing systems in the Near East and the Mediterranean basin.

Grayson, A. Kirk. "Assyria and Babylonia." *Orientalia* 49 (1980): 140–194. Overview with historical and historiographic textual data.

Gurney, O. R. *The Hittites*. Rev. ed. London, 1990. General introduction to the Indo-European cultures in Anatolia.

Helck, H. Wolfgang, and Eberhard Otto, eds. *Lexikon der Ägyptologie*. 7 vols. Wiesbaden, 1975–1986. Articles on important texts and archives.

Hoffner, Harry A., Jr. "The Hittites." *Orientalia* 49 (1980): 283–332. Overview with historical and historiographic textual data.

Hooker, J. T., ed. *Reading the Past: Ancient Writing from Cuneiform to the Alphabet*. London, 1990. Six articles by eminent specialists covering early writing systems in the Near East and the Mediterranean basin.

Lichtheim, Miriam, comp. *Ancient Egyptian Literature: A Book of Readings*. 3 vols. Berkeley, 1973–1980. Authoritative translations of the most important Egyptian literary texts.

Lichtheim, Miriam. *Ancient Egyptian Autobiographies Chiefly of the Middle Kingdom: A Study and an Anthology*. Orbis Biblicus et Orientalis, 84. Freiburg, 1988.

Littératures anciennes du Proche-Orient. Paris, 1967–. Ongoing series of volumes (fifteen to date), each devoted to a single group of texts, defined generically and/or linguistically.

Matthews, Victor H., and D. C. Benjamin. *Old Testament Parallels: Laws and Stories from the Ancient Near East*. New York, 1991. Very free English translations of major ancient Near Eastern texts arranged as pertinent to the books of the Hebrew Bible.

Oppenheim, A. Leo. *Ancient Mesopotamia: Portrait of a Dead Civilization*. Chicago, 1964. Classic portrait of Mesopotamian civilization by someone who knew the texts as well as anyone in his day.

Pritchard, James B., ed. *Ancient Near Eastern Texts Relating to the Old Testament*. 3d ed. Princeton, 1969. English translations with brief notes; still a standard but becoming out dated.

Texte aus der Umwelt des Alten Testaments. Gütersloh, 1982. Recent translations of ancient Near Eastern texts by multiple authors, arranged in separate fascicles and volumes according to genre and origin. Nearly complete.

Van Seters, John. "The Israelites." *Orientalia* 50 (1981): 137–185. Overview with historical and historiographic textual data.

Wevers, John W. "Preface." *Orientalia* 49 (1980): 137–139. Introduction to *Histories and Historians of the Ancient Near East,* a series of essays including Grayson, Hoffner, and Van Seters (see above).

Writings from the Ancient World. Atlanta, 1990–. Recently launched series of volumes, each devoted to a single group of texts, defined generically and/or linguistically.

DENNIS PARDEE

Inscriptions of the Classical Period

For the classical period inscriptions are found in Old Persian, Elamite, Akkadian, Hebrew, Phoenician, Aramaic, the Anatolian languages, Greek, and Egyptian. They were inscribed on almost all materials that are inscribable—ceramics, stone, marble, or bronze—and on a range of objects—ostraca, seals, jar handles.

Old Persian. Inscriptions are the primary source for the language of Old Persian and for accounts of the Persian Empire from the point of view of the Persians. (The historian Herodotus had excellent sources for the history of Persia, but he was Greek and he viewed the East from a Greek perspective.) The premier inscription in Old Persian from the classical period is the Bisitun monument. [*See* Bisitun.] The declaration of Darius (521–486 BCE) was cut into the native rock of a cliff face and inscribed in three languages (Persian, Elamite, Akkadian) in cuneiform. Darius gives his lineage, the organization of his empire, his dedication to Ahuramazda, his justification for the seizure of the throne (that Bardiya, the supposed brother of Cambyses, his predecessor, was an imposter), his quelling of rebellion, and advice to his successors. The inscription was composed on clay tablets and parchment first, then inscribed, read to Darius, and finally sent in translation to the satrapies. An Aramaic version survives that was discovered in Egypt. A Babylonian text known as the Cyrus cylinder, the officially approved declaration of the accomplishments and lineage of Cyrus, has survived only in a very fragmentary Old Persian version. A comparison of the Cyrus cylinder and the Bisitun monument suggests that Darius may have invented a common ancestor, "Achaemenes," to link his ancestry to Cyrus's. An equally well-known inscription of Darius's son and successor, Xerxes, records his pious (as an adherent of Ahuramazda) destruction of "the demons." Other Persian inscriptions record the building programs of the kings.

Languages of Syria-Palestine. Syria and Palestine provide few epigraphic remains that allow a prosopographical study to determine the area's ethnic composition in antiquity.

Hebrew. Inscriptions provide information about the development of the Hebrew language, alphabet, and morphology; about the background of the Hebrew Bible; and about local history and social organization. By and large, however, few Hebrew inscriptions exist from the period following Nebuchadrezzar's destruction of the Temple in Jerusalem (586 BCE). The few earlier inscriptions give an idea of the measures of defense taken against Nebuchadrezzar, present some religious opposition to the rule, and mention Greek mercenaries.

Phoenician. Inscriptions in this period are found in Old Phoenician at Byblos and Sidon, in the form of tomb curses and dedications. One of the best-known is the tomb inscription of King Eshmunazar, which gives some historical information. [*See* Byblos; Sidon; Eshmunazar Inscription.] Other inscriptions in the Phoenician language are found on Cyprus (sometimes bilingual, in Phoenician and Greek) and also are predominantly dedications or grave markers. Inscriptions in Phoenician are found on Rhodes, and in other places where Phoenicians traded. Although the inscriptions themselves contribute little historical information, their provenance attests to the activity of the Phoenicians.

Aramaic. Beginning in the second millenium BCE the Arameans, whose original language was Aramaic, began to infiltrate and in some places dominate Mesopotamia and Syria. Because the Arameans were merchants, their trading expeditions spread their language throughout the Near East. Aramaic alphabetic script appears to have been used along with cuneiform by the Assyrians. [*See* Cuneiform.] Monuments depict Aramaic scribes alongside cuneiform scribes, and some cuneiform tablets have filing notations in Aramaic. [*See* Scribes and Scribal Techniques.] During the siege of Jerusalem by the Assyrians in 701 BCE, negotiations were carried on in Aramaic. By the classical period, Aramaic was the international language of diplomacy, displacing Hebrew (it is the principal language also of the books of *Daniel* and *Ezra*). The first recorded reference to the house of David outside the Bible is in an Aramaic inscription discovered in 1993 at Dan, in Israel (Biran and Naveh, 1993). [*See* Dan.] Some scholars have argued that the Greek alphabet derived partly or largely from Aramaic and not from Phoenician. Persian officials used it among themselves throughout the Persian Empire. (Correspondence was dispatched in leather bags sealed with the name of the official in Aramaic.) As the common official language, inscriptions in Aramaic are found throughout the Persian Empire, although they are relatively rare. Dedicatory inscriptions are found in Cilicia, Lydia, and Lycia, though in Anatolia Aramaic was supplanted by Greek.

Anatolian Languages. Inscriptions establish the languages used in Anatolia in the classical period. They show relationships between languages and the spread of Greek.

Phrygian. The inscriptions in Phyrgian (the principle source for knowledge of the language) date from 750 BCE (rare) to the fifth century BCE and beyond and establish Phrygian as Indo-European. If the suggestion that Phrygian is somehow related to Latin could be established, scholars would have to reassess the ancient legends of the settlement of Italy from central Anatolia.

Lydian. Inscriptions in Lydian are all on stone and date from the sixth to the fourth centuries BCE. Bilingual inscriptions exist in Lydian-Aramaic and Lydian-Greek. They suggest that Lydian belongs to the Hittite-Luwian branch of Indo-European. Seal inscriptions show the spread of Persian influence in Sardis and throughout Lydia. [*See* Hittite; Luwians; Sardis.]

Lycian. A trilingual Lycian-Greek-Aramaic stela from Xanthos in year 1 of Artaxerxes (either 358 or 337 BCE) and a few funerary inscriptions survive. These inscriptions give enough information to identify the Lycian language as Indo-European, but not to assign it within the family of Indo-European languages. [*See* Lycia.]

Carian. Inscriptions of the seventh–sixth centuries BCE, including a few fragmentary bilingual texts using a Grecian-style alphabet, do not provide enough information to identify even the family to which Carian belongs. The names (from graffiti) of a group of mercenaries in Egypt in 591 BCE can be recognized as Carian. Carian gave way to Greek.

Greek. Hundreds of inscriptions from the Greek settlements in Asia Minor and the islands off its coast survive. They were public inscriptions, meant to inform citizens of their rights or obligations; they thus reveal the internal affairs of the separate cities, their relations with each other, and their relations with Persia and, finally, with Alexander. For instance, one of the earliest constitutions known, from Chios, from about 600 BCE, recognizes the rights of the people while allowing for some aristocratic privileges; another (early fourth century BCE) fixes the exchange rate between Mytilene and Phocea for the purpose of easing commerce. A letter from Darius (521–486 BCE) to his satrap on a marble stela in Magnesia on the Meander stressed his commitment to protect local religion and to the "greening" of the empire. An inscription on limestone from Xanthos (late fifth century BCE) shows a Lycian dynast to have been a member of the

Athenian Empire. In 391–388 BCE the cities of Miletus and Myus referred a boundary dispute to the arbitration of the Persian king. In the mid-fourth century BCE, Strato, the king of Sidon, vassal of the Persian Empire, developed a relationship with Athens. Inscriptions show how local, non-Greek rulers adopted Greek names, made Greek cities their capital, and employed Greek mercenaries, often against the Persian king. They also reveal the difficulties the Persian king had in controlling his far-flung subject (and satraps). Inscriptions also delineate Alexander's policy toward the Greek cities, restoring exiles, settling property disputes, and giving grants of freedom and land. [*See* Miletus.]

Egyptian. The classical period in Egypt is best known through the accounts of Herodotus (and other lesser writers), as Greeks began to visit Egypt not only as mercenaries and merchants, but also as tourists and students. Psammetichus II's campaign against Nubia in 593 BCE (or 591) is recorded in Egyptian and Greek inscriptions. The Greek inscription furnishes details of the organization of the Egyptian army (there were separate commands for Egyptians and foreigners) and together with the Egyptian inscriptions defines the extent of the expedition. Greeks were employed as mercenaries until the Persian conquest, and Greek merchants were settled at Naukratis. [*See* Naukratis.] An inscription of Nectanebo I (378–360 BCE) describes the financial arrangements: a 10 percent tax on silver, gold, and manufactured items. Inscriptions support the suggestion that the Egyptians learned about the specialized Greek warship, the trireme, from Greeks and employed these triremes with Greek and Carian crews.

INSCRIPTIONS: Classical Period. *Limestone grave stela from Abu Sir.* The subjects here appear Greek from the prothesis (laying out) depicted, but the style and the winged disk above are Egyptian. The assumption may be that this is a scene of Greeks in Egypt, except that the inscription (which we cannot read) is in Carian. Dated to 500 BCE. Height 27 cm. Berlin Staatliche Museum #19553. (Courtesy Pamela Lenck Bradford)

A reconstruction of the chronology of the Saite pharoahs, the line of pharoahs from the mid-seventh century to the Persian conquest in 525 BCE, is based on epigraphy. Inscriptions allow the account of Herodotus of the Persian conquest of Egypt (in which an "insane" king Cambyses slew the sacred bull Apis; 3.27–30.1) to be corrected. According to inscriptions, the sacred bull lived through the turmoil and conquest unharmed by the Persians; and Cambyses did reduce the income and expenditures of the temples, which turned the priestly caste against him. Darius I allowed the Egyptians to undertake building projects. The assimilation of the ruling classes can be traced through a Persian noble with the name *Tachos,* an Egyptian noble who was a general in the Persian army. Midway through the Persian occupation historical inscriptions largely end; they reappear, in significant numbers, only after Alexander's conquest.

Besides inscriptions in Egyptian, several corpora of inscriptions in Aramaic have been discovered in Egypt. These have provided information on Semites and Persians in Egypt, particularly on aspects of everyday life (marriage contracts, real-estate transactions, the workings of the Persian bureaucracy in Egypt). [*See* Egyptian Aramaic Texts.]

Without the inscriptions of the classical period, nothing would be known of the Old Persian language, of the kings' official records, or of the organization of the Persian empire. Inscriptions are the only sources for some ancient languages, and they allow origins and movements (e.g, of the Anatolian peoples) to be traced. Inscriptions are a means of tracing the increasing influence of Greeks in the Near East before Alexander and the chronology, organization, and society of the Egyptians before and during the Persian domination.

[*See also* Akkadian; Aramaic Language and Literature; Egyptian; Greek; Hebrew Language and Literature; Persian; *and* Phoenician-Punic.]

BIBLIOGRAPHY

Biran, Avraham, and Joseph Naveh. "An Aramaic Stele Fragment from Tel Dan." *Israel Exploration Journal* (1993): 81–98.

The Cambridge Ancient History. Vol. 3. Edited by John Boardman et al. 2d ed. Cambridge, 1982. Discusses the languages, materials, and sources of the classical period in historical context.

Fitzmyer, Joseph A. *A Wandering Aramean: Collected Aramaic Essays*. Missoula, 1979. Good introduction to the Aramaic language and available texts.

Gibson, John C. L. *Textbook of Syrian Semitic Inscriptions*. 3 vols. Oxford, 1971–1982. Complete collection of the significant Semitic documents of this period, with translations.

Harden, Donald B. *The Phoenicians*. 3d ed. Harmondsworth, 1980. Brief references to and descriptions of Phoenician inscriptions.

Jones, Clifford M. *Old Testament Illustrations*. Cambridge, 1971. Provides photographs of the major sources.

Kent, Roland G. *Old Persian: Grammar, Texts, Lexicon*. 2d ed. New Haven, 1953. A transliteration and translation of Persian texts.

Meiggs, Russell, and David Lewis. *A Selection of Greek Historical In-*

scriptions to the End of the Fifth Century BC. Oxford, 1969. Greek texts, some related to this period and area, principally the letter of Darius.

Pritchard, James B. *Ancient Near Eastern Texts Relating to the Old Testament.* Princeton, 1969. Translations of the principle documents.

The Sculptures and Inscriptions of Darius the Great of the Rock of Behistun in Persia. London, 1907. British Museum publication that provides texts in cuneiform, transliterations, and translations, as well as photographs and drawings of the monument.

ALFRED S. BRADFORD

Inscriptions of the Hellenistic and Roman Periods

Inscriptions for the period that begins with the death of Alexander the Great in 323 BCE and ends with the Muslim conquest of the Near East and northeast Africa after Muhammad's death in 632 CE have been found in large quantities. They occur on official buildings and houses, on temples and altars, synagogues and churches, on and in tombs, on ex-votos and potsherds, on rocks and mountains, on temple and church utensils—in short, on any surface suitable for writing. With this diversity, it is not surprising that epigraphic techniques vary according to the material used: marble, limestone, metal, wood, or pottery. Inscriptions are engraved on marble, whereas they are usually written with ink on wood or pottery. Inscriptions supply firsthand, direct sources of information, for they comment on all religious and secular aspects of tribes, nations, and empires, as well as on their different social levels.

When Alexander and his successors, the Seleucid and Ptolemaic dynasties, ruled the Near East, koine Greek became the official administrative language. [*See* Seleucids; Ptolemies; Greek.] However, Official Aramaic, the language of the Achaemenid chancelleries, also remained in use, especially in Mesopotamia and farther east. [*See* Aramaic Language and Literature.] Yet, even before Alexander's arrival, Greek was circulating—as the trilingual inscription in Aramaic, Lycian, and Greek from Xanthos in Lycia (337/36 BCE) attests. [*See* Lycia.] Many copies of royal edicts in Greek have been found inscribed on marble stelae or on the walls of temples (Welles, 1974). The Near East, including Anatolia and Egypt, has yielded an enormous number of Greek inscriptions continuing far into the Islamic period. The most famous example from Egypt is the Rosetta stone, a decree of the Egyptian priesthood passed in 196 BCE and written in Greek, hieroglyphic Egyptian, and Demotic—a combination that enabled the decipherment of hieroglyphic Egyptian by Champollion in 1820. [*See* Egyptian; Hieroglyphs; *and the biography of Champollion.*] The use of Greek also spread eastward to present-day Afghanistan, where two Greek inscriptions of the Indian king Aśoka were found in Kandahar. These are the only two Buddhist documents in Greek, and while the first has a parallel Aramaic text, they testify to the cultural prestige of Greek in those distant regions. Alongside Greek, the indigenous languages remained in use particularly for private purposes during the period of the Hellenistic dynasties until the arrival of the Romans in the person of Pompey in 63 BCE. Few of these inscriptions have survived from the period because of the relative scarcity of contemporary evidence (Millar, 1987).

The use of Greek alongside various indigenous, mainly Semitic, languages typified the basic bilingualism that characterized Near Eastern cultures in the Hellenistic and Roman periods and later. Many inscriptions are bilingual, mostly Greek and Aramaic, with the Greek often representing the official version and the Aramaic providing a translation of the text. Hence, Aramaic became, to a certain extent, hellenized through the adoption of Greek words and idiom, a phenomenon that particularly manifests itself in official public inscriptions (e.g., at Palmyra). [*See* Palmyra.] The beginning of the Roman period saw a resurgence of inscriptions and papyri written in the various local languages. [*See* Papyrus.] Jewish inscriptions in Palestine were written in Greek, Hebrew, and Aramaic. [*See* Hebrew Language and Literature.] The Jews in Edessa used Hebrew and Greek for their tomb inscriptions. By contrast the inscriptions from the synagogue at Aphrodisias are only in Greek. [Synagogue Inscriptions; Aphrodisias.] Other synagogues in Asia Minor also yielded mainly Greek inscriptions and very few in Hebrew.

The use of a certain language cannot be interpreted as indicative of a particular culture or religion. Language in these periods and in these areas does not function as an impermeable cultural barrier. Coastal areas have yielded Phoenician and Punic inscriptions alongside Greek ones. [*See* Phoenician-Punic.] Punic and Neo-Punic inscriptions also come from North Africa and Tripolitania. The Nabateans living in Petra, their capital (in modern Jordan), wrote their inscriptions in Nabatean, a form of Aramaic, but also used Greek. [*See* Nabateans; Nabatean Inscriptions.] A host of Nabatean graffiti has also been found along caravan routes in the Sinai and Negev deserts and on the Arabian Peninsula. The desert areas in modern Jordan, in Syria and in northern Arabia have also yielded Safaitic, Thamudic, Taymanite, Lihyanite, Dedanite, and Minaean inscriptions, as well as graffiti mainly consisting of Arab proper names of the various tribes and clans. [*See* Safaitic-Thamudic Inscriptions; Tayma'; Dedan.]

Northern Mesopotamia is the area of Old Syriac inscriptions, but Greek and Hebrew examples are also attested that date mainly from the second and third centuries CE. [*See* Syriac.] From that period, Aramaic inscriptions from Aššur and Hatra are known. [*See* Aššur; Hatra.] Palmyra, the caravan city in the middle of the Syrian desert, has supplied by far the largest number of Aramaic inscriptions, including many bilingual ones (Greek, Palmyrene) and even trilingual ones (Greek, Palmyrene, Latin). Dura-Europos, the fortress

INSCRIPTIONS: Hellenistic and Roman Periods. *The Pontius Pilate inscription.* (Courtesy ASOR Archives)

on the Euphrates River, has yielded texts in Greek, Latin, Palmyrene, and in Iranian languages, attesting the various cultures and powers that manifested themselves in that border area. [*See* Dura-Europos; Latin.] Despite the fact that the Romans ruled large parts of the Near East until the Muslim conquests, there are relatively few Latin inscriptions. Greek remained the official language of administration, while Latin inscriptions are mainly found on milestones along Roman roads or pertaining to the Roman army and other Roman officials. When the Romans over the centuries terminated the independence or quasi-independence of many cities and nations and incorporated them into the provinces into which the Near East was divided, inscriptions were basically no longer written in indigenous languages and local scripts. Greek remained dominant and Latin texts are very rare after Constantine the Great founded Constantinople in 330 CE, which became the seat of Roman government. Apart from Greek, only Syriac inscriptions are attested, but they are mainly concentrated in the eastern regions, where Syriac essentially became the language of Near Eastern Christianity. Greek was also used in the Iranian empires of the Parthians and Sasanians. [*See* Parthians; Sasanians.] The res gestae of the Sasanian king Shapur I (241–272 CE) are carved on a stone wall at Naqsh-i Rustam near ancient Persepolis in three languages: Middle Persian, Parthian, and Greek. [*See* Naqsh-i Rustam; Persian.] Other Aramaic languages—Mandaic and Talmudic Aramaic—alongside Syriac were used for incantation texts written on unglazed pottery bowls and lead strips that have been found in large quantities in modern Iraq, particularly at the site of ancient Nippur. [*See* Mandaic; Nippur.]

The thousands of inscriptions covering a wide range of languages and periods deal with all aspects of history and culture and consequently present a variety of literary genres. There are official documents and edicts issued by the Hellenistic rulers and city councils and also Greek versions of official Roman documents (Sherk, 1969). Legal texts are attested in a great variety, ranging from the so-called sacred laws that regulate behavior in temple areas to tax laws. An example of the last category is the bilingual tax law of Palmyra, written in Greek and Aramaic on four large stelae, that was passed in 137 CE. The entire inscription is preserved in the Hermitage at St. Petersburg, Russia, to which it was transported after its discovery in 1881. Building inscriptions commemorating founders, dates, and the functions of public and private buildings are essential to the archaeology of towns and villages, supplying the main structural elements of the historical chronology of urban development. Honorific inscriptions for meritorious citizens and public officials, as well as for emperors and priests, usually accompanied statues erected in the main colonnades of towns or within the sacred areas of temples. These give insight into the organization of the body social and into the public deeds of its important members.

A special category of inscriptions is the caravan texts honoring caravan leaders, the great entrepreneurs of Near Eastern antiquity, which often refer to their brave activities bringing the caravans home through the desert, where they were threatened by robbers and other dangers. The large majority of these inscriptions belong to the mercantile network of Palmyra and have been instrumental in reconstructing ancient trade routes and economies. Another significant group is tomb inscriptions commemorating the dead and cursing grave robbers. Such inscriptions provide the means for reconstructing families and clans, especially the wealthy, for whom the monumental tombs were built. [*See* Tombs.] The most impressive examples are again found at Palmyra, where wealthy citizens had hypogea and tower-tombs constructed that sometimes contained several hundred dead. Most tomb inscriptions are rather stereotyped, but the Edessene area in northern Mesopotamia offers a wide range of interesting texts on walls and inlaid in mosaics that covered the floor of the cave tombs. [*See* Mosaics.]

Because literary texts regarding the various cults of the Near East in Hellenistic and Roman times are rare (presumably Egyptian and Mesopotamian religious practices based on the ancient myths continued, but proper religious texts do not exist for Syria and Phoenicia), inscriptions on altars

INSCRIPTIONS: Hellenistic and Roman Periods. *Columnal monument.* Commemorating honors given Tiberius by the people of Sardis. (Courtesy ASOR Archives)

and ex-votos and dedications in temples, often combined with sculptures and reliefs, are the only sources of information about Near Eastern cults in this period. This dearth applies to the religion of the Nabateans, to the cities of Palmyra and Hatra and of the rest of the Levant, and to the important religious centers of Heliopolis/Baalbek, and Emesa/Homs. [*See* Baalbek; Homs.] On the other hand, the important religious center of Hierapolis/Mabbug has yielded Greek inscriptions and Aramaic texts on coins. The often enigmatic *De Dea Syria* of Lucian of Samosata, describing the history of the temple and its cult, is the only literary description of a Syrian cult that has been preserved. The religious practices of seminomadic desert dwellers can only be reconstructed from their inscriptions, graffiti, and petroglyphs.

Inscriptions differ in many aspects from literary texts in grammar as well as in idiom and lexicology. While the language of the public inscriptions is usually highly stylized and sometimes pompous, the private ones reveal the language of everyday life, local dialects, and variants of official languages. Inscriptions, therefore, are invaluable for studying the grammar, orthography, vocalization, pronunciation, and lexicology of Greek and the various Near Eastern languages. Some, like Palmyrene Aramaic and the languages of the Nabateans and Phoenicians, are only known through inscriptional evidence. Inscriptions are also the main source for studying the onomastics and prosopography of the Near East. Proper names often occur in Semitic texts as well as in Greek transcription; in this way, inscriptions provide insight into the pronunciation of the names, which are unvocalized in Semitic script. Many individuals in Mesopotamia and elsewhere also took a Greek name, which often contains a clue to the meaning of their Semitic name. Related to this practice is the so-called Greco-Babyloniaca, a group of clay tablets dating to the second century BCE or later. [*See* Tablet.] They transcribe cuneiform and Aramaic texts in Greek script. [*See* Cuneiform.] In this way they provide insight into the contemporary pronunciation of the languages transcribed.

The Greco-Roman world, including the Near East, produced copious amounts of inscriptions during the Hellenistic and Roman periods. Writing, often in public form, was a distinctive characteristic of Greco-Roman civilization in the west and east, and therefore was an almost incomparable cultural phenomenon. Consequently, inscriptions refer to vast provinces of life, social structures, and the thought and values of the ancient world; they contain vast amounts of information, but there is much they do not divulge. Their perspective is limited to what was deemed fit for the contemporary reader, and they present certain stylized conventions and practices. The primary challenge in using inscriptions as a source of history and culture is constructing an intelligible context within which the inscriptions can be interpreted. The problem is exacerbated when inscriptions are badly damaged or only partially preserved; it becomes chronic when the original context is lost. Without supporting archaeological evidence, inscriptions run the high risk of becoming stray texts whose meaning is elusive or enigmatic. Moreover, even when inscriptions can be read and interpreted easily, they often contradict other sources of information, such as histories or archaeological finds, although sometimes the information is complementary. Despite these difficulties, the publication of a single inscription can bring a new dimension to and totally change an established scholarly opinion. As such, inscriptions remain the main and most direct source of historical information on life and society in the Greco-Roman Near East. Indeed, as a result of the paucity of literary sources, inscriptions (and papyri) are the main instrument for writing the history of the Hellenistic and Roman Near East. Their value is recognized increasingly by scholars, who are combining inscriptions with archaeological and scanty literary evidence (Sherwin-White and Kuhrt, 1993; Millar, 1993).

The rapid spread of Christianity (one of the major changes in the Roman Empire) asserted by ecclesiastical authors is also challenged by inscriptional evidence, which suggests that it was, rather, a protracted and prolonged process. [*See* Church Inscriptions.] While the center of early East Roman Christianity can be traced to Antioch in northern Syria, the countryside remained for the greater part pagan until far into the fifth century (Liebeschuetz, 1977). A comparable situation prevailed at Edessa, capital of Osrhoene in northern Mesopotamia, and allegedly the center of Early Syriac Christianity, which became the first Christian kingdom in the world. All Syriac inscriptions from the first four centuries are pagan and provide conclusive proof that the process of christianization developed in the opposite way to what Christian writers have asserted. Inscriptions can therefore be a vital corrective to traditional views of the history of the Greco-Roman Near East—which are, moreover, sometimes steeped in scholarly prejudices. Inscriptional finds add new information to the scholarly file and are imperative for augmenting and embellishing the history of the Near East. Moreover, only finds of Greek and bilingual inscriptions can alleviate the problem—or at least supply a better understanding of Hellenism, the expression of Greek civilization that emerged in the Hellenistic and Roman period and about which there is still much vigorous debate.

[*See also* Writing and Writing Systems; *and* Writing Materials.]

BIBLIOGRAPHY

Bérard, François, et al. *Guide de l'épigraphiste: Bibliographie choisie des épigraphies antiques et médiévales.* Paris, 1986. Fairly comprehensive survey of tools and studies of epigraphy, with extensive and very useful bibliographies.

Dijkstra, Klaas. *Life and Loyalty: A Study in the Socio-Religious Culture of Syria and Mesopotamia in the Greco-Roman Period Based on Epigraphic Evidence.* Leiden, 1995.

Fitzmyer, Joseph A. "The Languages of Palestine in the First Century A.D." In Fitzmyer's *A Wandering Aramean: Collected Aramaic Essays,* pp. 29–56. Missoula, 1979.

Inscriptions grecques et latines de la Syrie. 10 vols. to date. Paris, 1929–. The most complete survey of Greek and Latin inscriptions found in Syria.

Inscriptions Reveal: Documents from the Time of the Bible, the Mishna, and the Talmud. Israel Museum Catalogue, no. 100. Jerusalem, 1972. Well-illustrated catalog with a wide range of inscriptions and clear commentary.

Liebeschuetz, J. H. W. G. "Epigraphic Evidence on the Christianisation of Syria." In *Limes: Akten des XI Internationalen Limeskongresses,* edited by Jenö Fitz, pp. 485–508. Budapest, 1977.

Millar, Fergus. "Epigraphy." In *Sources for Ancient History,* edited by Michael Crawford, pp. 80–136. Cambridge, 1983. Basic study of the use and function of inscriptions for historical research of the ancient world.

Millar, Fergus. "The Problem of Hellenistic Syria." In *Hellenism in the East,* edited by Amélie Kuhrt and Susan Sherwin-White, pp. 110–133. Berkeley, 1987.

Millar, Fergus. *The Roman Near East, 31 BC–AD 337.* Cambridge, Mass., 1993.

Neumann, Günter, and Jürgen Untermann, eds. *Die Sprachen im römischen Reich der Kaiserziet.* Beihefte der Bonner Jahrbücher, 40. Cologne, 1980. Excellent survey of all languages of the Roman Empire; good bibliography.

Robert, Louis. *Hellenica: Recueil d'épigraphie, de numismatique e d'antiquités grecques.* 13 vols. Paris, 1940–1965. Excellent studies dealing mainly with Asia Minor.

Robert, Louis. *Opera minora selecta: Épigraphie et antiquités grecques.* 4 vols. Amsterdam, 1969–1974.

Schmitt, Rüdiger. "Die Sprachverhältnisse in den östlichen Provinzen des römischen Reiches." In *Aufstieg und Niedergang der römischen Welt,* vol. II.29.2, edited by Wolfgang Haase, pp. 554–586. Berlin and New York, 1983. The best survey of the languages used in the eastern Roman Empire; excellent bibliography.

Seyrig, Henri. *Antiquités syriennes.* 6 vols. Paris, 1934–1966. Collection of articles on archaeology and the use of inscriptions, originally published in the journal *Syria.*

Seyrig, Henri. *Scripta varia: Mélanges d'archéologie et d'histoire.* Bibliothèque Archéologique et Historique, vol. 125. Paris, 1985.

Sherk, Robert K. *Roman Documents from the Greek East: Senatus Consulta and Epistulae to the Age of Augustus.* Baltimore, 1969.

Sherwin-White, Susan, and Amélie Kuhrt. *From Samarkhand to Sardis: A New Approach to the Seleucid Empire.* Berkeley, 1993.

Teixidor, Javier. *Bulletin d'épigraphie sémitique.* Paris, 1986. Surveys of semitic inscriptions with useful commentaries, originally published in the journal *Syria* (1964–1980).

Welles, C. B. *Royal Correspondence in the Hellenistic Period. A Study in Greek Epigraphy.* London, 1934; rpt., Chicago, 1974. Classic monograph of royal edicts in Greek.

H. J. W. Drijvers

Inscriptions of the Islamic Period

Thousands of inscriptions of the Islamic period are found in Arabia and in neighboring Arab and Islamic countries. Archaeological research has shown that the Arabic script used by Arabs and Muslims developed from Nabatean script, which was closely linked to Aramaic script. [*See* Aramaic.] The evolution of Arabic script from Aramaic is evident in the extensive texts and inscriptions found in Syria and dated to the early seventh century CE. In this period in Jerusalem and Mecca, those who were literate seem to have had knowledge of Aramaic. The alphabet of the Kufic Arabic of the Islamic period has similarities to alphabets found in some inscriptions of the pre-Islamic period, such as those at Umm el-Jimal I (250 CE), Umm el-Jimal II (sixth century CE), Harran (568 CE), Osays (423 CE), and in the an-Namarah (512 CE) and Zabad texts (328 CE). [*See* Umm el-Jimal.]

The basic sources of the Arabic inscriptions are the revelations about the emergence of Islam made to the prophet

Muhammad and the Qur'an, which were written in Arabic script. Other sources were the Prophet's correspondence and peace treaties. The revelations were memorized and then inscribed on different materials—on palm leaves and tree stumps, camel bones, hides, thin stone slabs, silk and other cloth, and woven bast. The inscriptions were primarily incised or engraved; some were embossed. After the Islamic conquest of Egypt, linen and papyrus were adopted for writing inscriptions.

Islamic inscriptions from the first century AH onward are found on tombstones, coins, mosques, palaces, and forts and are religious and civil in nature. Inscriptions generally have Qur'anic verses and supplications and furnish historical, biographical, or administrative details, depending on the place and purpose for which they were intended. They also furnish funerary details—for example, the name of the deceased, his or her ancestry, and date of death. These details contribute to the development of a demographic profile of a particular place. Some inscriptions are decorative. Tombstone inscriptions in particular are an important source for studying the evolution of Arabic script. Genealogical details on tombstones—for example, titles and positions held—are sources for studying regional history. The tombstones were engraved by Arab calligraphers, the most renown of whom was Mubarak al-Makki. His inscriptions, dated to AH 243/857 CE, are characterized by unusually long texts.

Inscriptions of paramount importance are those found in the Prophet's mosque at Medina, the al-Ḥaram mosque in Mecca, the Dome of the Rock and al-Aqṣa mosque in Jerusalem, the mosque of Ibn Tulun (Cairo); and the mosques at Qayrawan (Tunisia), and Cordoba and Gharnaṭah (Spain). [*See* Medina; Mecca; Jerusalem.] The largest group of tombstones (more than four thousand) and the earliest (dated to 31/651) come from Aswan and Cairo (Egypt). Registered and studied by Gaston Wiet (1936–1942; 1971) in 1932, they are preserved in the Islamic Art Museum, Cairo. [*See* Cairo.] Other studies have been carried out by Abdur Rahman Abd at-Tawwab and Solange Ory. Bernard Roy Paule Poinsset conducted the first studies of Islamic inscriptions from Qarawan in 1950–1958.

A large collection of inscriptions was found at the Gorjani cemetery in Tunisia. The collection of inscriptions on tombstones found in the Dhalak Islands in the Red Sea (Eritrea) is another important source for studying Arabic script. These have been published by Giovanni Oman (1976) and Madeleine Schneider (1983). Scores of tombstone inscriptions have been found at other locations, such as in Yemen, Oman, Syria, and Spain. Adolf Grohmann (1934–1955) listed forty-five inscriptions, dated to between 22/643 and 129/746. They include inscriptions not only from tombstones, but also from buildings, as well as supplications written on rocks, cloth, and papyrus. In addition to these early inscriptions, Grohmann cites examples of inscribed Early Islamic coins. [*See* Yemen; Oman; Syria, *article on* Syria in the Islamic Period.] Most of the inscriptions found are on religious and civic buildings in Syria, Egypt, and Iraq. In Arabia a very important inscription was found at the Saysad dam in Ṭa'if, built by Muawiyah ibn Abi Sufiyan in 58/677. It was published by George C. Miles in 1948.

Archaeological survey and research conducted in Saudi Arabia have brought to light scores of Islamic inscriptions. Inscriptions on rocks have been found in the Hijaz, Asir, Tihama, Ṭa'if, Mecca, and Medina. The inscription on Jabal Sal in the heart of al-Medina al-Munawarrah is considered to be the earliest in the Muslim world. Among the richest areas of early Islamic inscriptions (first–third century AH) in Arabia are Hanakiya, Suwaydra, Khybar, Ruwawa (near Medina; see figure 1), Jabal Hisma (west Tabuk), and Dawmat al-Jandal. A larger number of inscriptions have been found along the different pilgrim routes in Saudi Arabia.

A prominent corpus of inscribed tombstones was found in the region of Ashm and as-Sirrayn, along the coast of Tihama, south of Mecca. They are dated to between the third and seventh centuries AH/ninth–thirteenth centuries CE, and constitute an important source of regional history. Their inscriptions also reflect the development of Arabic script and its decorative aspects.

Examples of the earliest dated rock inscriptions in Saudi Arabia and their provenance follow. (The figures named are either those who wrote the inscriptions or those on whose behalf [or in whose name] the inscriptions were written.)

Khalid Ibn al-ʿAs, AH 40/660 CE (Darb Zubaydah)
Abdullah ibn Diram, AH 46/666 CE (Wadi Sabeel, Najran)
Jahm ibn ʿAli ibn Hubayrah, AH 56/676 CE (Darb Zubaydah)
Muawiyah ibn Abi Sufiyan, AH 58/677 CE (Saysad, dam, Ṭa'if)
Rabah ibn Hafs ibn Asim ibn ʿUmar ibn al-Khattab, AH 76/694 CE (Ruwawa, Medina)
Two inscriptions referring to Uthman ibn Wahran, AH 80/700 CE (Wadi Al Usaylah, Mecca)
Maymun Mawla abi Mariam Mawla Rabah, AH 80/700 CE (Syrian pilgrim route)
Ufayr ibn Al Mudarib, AH 83/703 CE (Syrian pilgrim route)
Abdullah ibn Amarah, AH 84/704 CE (Arafat area, Mecca)
Mukhlid ibn Abi Mukhlid Mawla ʿAli ibn Abi Ṭalib, AH 91/710 CE (Syrian pilgrim route)
Abu Jaʿfar ibn Hasan al-Hashimi, AH 98/716 CE (Arafat Region, Mecca)
Abu Salmah ibn Abdullah ibn Abdullah ibn ʿUmar ibn Uthman ibn Hafs, AH 100/718 CE (Ruwawa, Medina)
Muhammad ibn Yahya ibn al Tufayl, AH 112/731 CE (western Tabuk)
Al Hakam ibn ʿUmar ibn Farwah, AH 113/732 CE (southern Hijaz)
Uthman ibn Hafs, AH 120/738 CE (Ruwawa, Medina)

INSCRIPTIONS: Islamic Period. Figure 1. *Two inscriptions from Ruwawa, near Medina.* The top three lines are dated AH 140/750 CE. The bottom text is undated. (Courtesy S. Al-Rashid)

Abdullah ibn ʿUmar ibn Hafs, AH 121/739 CE (Ruwawa, Medina)
Asim ibn ʿUmar ibn Hafs, AH 124/740 CE (Ruwawa, Medina)
Harith ibn Ṣāghir, AH 121/739 CE (al-Jawf region)

There are several unpublished inscriptions dated to the Umayyad period in the region of Hijaz and Asir. Their eventual publication will add to the corpus of Early Islamic inscriptions and writings found outside the Arabian Peninsula and will be a fertile field for the study of the development of Arabic script.

Numerous ʿAbbasid inscriptions and writings are dated. The most important locations follow:

Restored Sanʿa mosque (Yemen), AH 136/754 CE
Masjid al-Bayʿah, AH 144/761 CE (Mina, Mecca)
Al-Ḥaram mosque (Mecca), from the time of Caliph al-Mahdi (one inscription is dated to AH 167/783 CE)
Carved milestone with the names *Khalifa al-Mahdi* and *Yaqteen ibn Mosa,* a minister (Darb Zubaydah)
Restored pilgrim road inscribed with the names *Khalifa al-Muqtadir Billah al-ʿAbbāsi* and *ʿAli ibn ʿIsa,* a minister, AH 304/916 CE (from Iraq to Mecca)

Several other dated ʿAbbasid inscriptions on rocks, buildings, and tombstones from different periods in the ʿAbbasid era have also been found. Ottoman foundation inscriptions are found in the fortresses scattered along pilgrim roads in Syria and Egypt and on some irrigation works.

BIBLIOGRAPHY

Arabic References

Faʿr, Muhammad Fahd Abdullah al-. *Tatawur al-Kitabat wa al-Nuqush fi-al-Hijaz mundhu fajr al-Islam Hatta muntasaf al-Qarn al-Sabi al-Hijri.* Jiddah, 1984.

Ghabbān, ʿAlī Ibrāhīm ibn ʿAlī Hāmid. *Islamic Archaeology of Northwestern Saudi Arabia* (in Arabic). Riyadh, 1993.

Ghabbān, ʿAlī Ibrāhīm ibn ʿAlī Hāmid. *Northwestern Saudi Arabia.* Part 1, *Studies in the History and Archaeology* (in Arabic). Riyadh, 1993.

Grohmann, Adolf. *Awraq al-Bardi bi Dar al-Kutub al-Masriyyah.* 2 vols. Translated by Hasan Ibrahim Hasan. Cairo, 1934–1955.

Munajjid, Ṣalāḥ al-Dīn al-. *Dirasat fi Tarikh al-Khatt al-Arabi mundhu Bidayatih ila Nihayat al-Asr al-Umawi.* Beirut, 1979.

Naqshabandi, Nasir. "Mansha al-Khat al-Arabi wa Tatawurah Lighayat Ahd al-Khulafa al-Rashidin." *Sumer* 3 (1947): 129–142.

Rashid, Saʿad al-. "Al-Athar al-Islamiyyah fi al-Jazirah al-Arabiyyah fi Asr al-Rasul wa al-Khulafa al-Rashidin." In *Studies in the History of Arabia,* vol. 3, part 2, pp. 145–199. Riyadh, 1989.

Rashid, Saʿad al-. "Naqsh muʿarrakh min al-ʿAsr al-Umawi majhul al-mawqi fi mantiqat Janub al-Hijaz." In *Dirasat fi al-Athar,* pp. 265–270. Riyadh, 1992.

Rashid, Saʿad al-. *Darb Zubaydah: Tariq al-Hajj min al-Kufa ila Makkah al-Mukarramah, dirasah tarikkiyyah haḍariyyah athariyyah.* Riyadh, 1993.

Sayoti, Jalal ad-Din Abd al-Rahman (b. Abi Bakr). *Tarikh al-Khulafa.* Edited by Muhammad Muhyi ad-Din Abdal-Hamid. 3d ed. Cairo, 1964.

Ush, Muhammad Abu al-Faraj al-. "Kitabat Arabiyyah Ghayr Manshurah Wujidat fi Jabal Usays." *Les Annales archéologique de Syrie* 3 (1963): 281–293.

English and Other Sources

ʿAbd al-Tawab, Abd al-Rahman. *Stèles islamiques de la Nécropole d'Assouan.* 3 vols. Cairo, 1977.

Grohmann, Adolf. *Arabic Inscriptions.* Bibliothèque de Muséon, vol. 50. Louvain, 1962.
Grohmann, Adolf. *Arabische paläographie,* vol. 2, *Das Schriftwesen, die Lapidarschrift.* Vienna, 1971.
Hamidullah, Muhammad. "Some Arabic Inscriptions of Medinah of the Early Years of Hijrah." *Islamic Culture* 13.4 (1939): 427–439, pls. 1–10.
Hawary, Hassan, and Rached Hussein. *Catalogue général du Musée Arabe du Caire.* Vol. 3. Cairo, 1932.
Miles, George Carpenter. "Early Islamic Inscriptions near Ta'if in the Hijaz." *Journal of Near Eastern Studies* 7 (1948).
Miles, George Carpenter. "'Ali B. 'Isa's Pilgrim Road: An Inscription of the Year 304 H (916–917 A.D.)." *Bulletin de l'Institut d'Égypte* 36 (1953–1954): 477–487.
Oman, Giovanni. *La necropoli islamica di Dahlak Kebir.* 2 vols. Naples, 1976.
Roy, Bernard, et al. *Inscriptions arabes de Kairouan.* 2 vols. Paris, 1950–1958.
Schneider, Madeleine. *Stèles funéraires musulmanes des Iles Dahlak.* 2 vols. Cairo, 1983.
Wiet, Gaston. *Catalogue général du Musée Arabe du Caire.* Vols. 2–10. Cairo, 1936–1942.
Wiet, Gaston. *Catalogue général du Musée de l'Art Islamique du Caire.* Cairo, 1971.
Zaylai, Ahmad Omar al-. "The Southern Area of the Amirate of Makkah (3rd–7th/9th–13th Centuries): Its History, Archaeology, and Epigraphy." Ph.D. diss., Duke University, 1983.

SA'AD ABDUL AZIZ AL-RASHID

INSCRIPTION SITES. Sites that yield inscriptions but do not have a history of permanent settlements are known throughout the ancient Near East from nearly every chronological period. The inscriptions they display can be classified into two distinct types: private inscriptions or graffiti on rough, unmodified rock surfaces and official proclamations often inscribed on a smoothed or otherwise modified surface, specifically for the purpose of public viewing. Inscription sites are best attested in Egypt and Syria-Palestine and on the Anatolian and Iranian plateaus. The paucity of examples from Mesopotamia is no doubt related to the character of its physical geography: Mesopotamia is a low-profile, alluvial plain with few outcroppings; the remainder of the Near East is generally more rugged and mountainous with ample rock surfaces suitable for inscriptions.

The first category of inscription sites is comprised mostly of graffiti. Thousands of private inscriptions have been cataloged throughout the Syro-Arabian desert and the Sinai Peninsula. As its name attests, Wadi Mukatteb ("wadi of the inscriptions") in the Sinai is particularly rich in inscriptions, among them, Nabatean, Arabic, Aramaic, Greek, Armenian, and occasionally Latin texts. [*See* Nabatean Inscriptions; Arabic; Aramaic Language and Literature; Greek; Armenian; Latin.] Sometimes the inscription is merely a name with a patronymic, but often a prayer or memorial is included. Earlier hieroglyphic Egyptian inscriptions are also attested in the Sinai, in the vicinity of ancient mines. [*See* Hieroglyphs.] Throughout the Syro-Arabian desert fringe hundreds of private inscriptions in Thamudic and Safaitic script have been found dating from the first through fourth centuries CE. [*See* Safaitic-Thamudic Inscriptions.] Most of these, consisting of names and prayers, are also in the form of graffiti.

The second category of inscription sites, official proclamations, is better attested outside Palestine, in Egypt and Lebanon and on the Anatolian and Iranian plateaus. These inscriptions are also commemorative in nature. Numerous Egyptian inscriptions recording mining expeditions and military exploits are known from Wadi el-Mughara, in the ancient mining region of western Sinai, and from Wadi Hammamat and Wadi el-Hudi in the eastern desert. All date to as early as the Old Kingdom. The inscription of Henu, steward of Mentuhotep I, for example, describes an expedition to the Red Sea and to Punt, as well as quarrying activity carried out in the wadi. A rock stela of Mentuhotep III describes miraculous events that accompanied the quarrying of a sarcophagus.

In Lebanon, at Nahr el-Kalb, three hieroglyphic inscriptions of Rameses II and adjacent cuneiform inscriptions of Tiglath-Pileser I, Shalmaneser III, and Esarhaddon overlook the sea on the road leading north from Beirut. They commemorate successful military campaigns into this area. [*See* Beirut.] Each inscription is accompanied by a figural relief of the victorious ruler. Other Greek, Latin, and Arabic inscriptions are attested as well at this strategically important site.

In the central and southern portions of the Anatolian plateau, late second- and early first-millennium hieroglyphic Luwian inscriptions dot the landscape. [*See* Luwians.] Many of them are associated with a particular population center, while others seem to function as boundary markers or, less frequently, as proclamation inscriptions. One of the most striking from the Hittite imperial period is the rock relief and hieroglyphic inscription of Ḫattušili found at Firaktin (perhaps beside what was a road in antiquity) depicting the Hittite king pouring a libation. [*See* Hittite; Hittites.] A more dramatic inscription site is that of Akpinar near Manisa in western Anatolia. The relief with accompanying inscriptions is cut into a niche high on an outcrop. These and others from the imperial period are perhaps primarily art sites and only secondarily inscriptions sites. The inscriptions are mostly names—labels accompanying the figural relief. Similar inscription sites are known from the postimperial period. Many inscriptions ostensibly removed from settlements are concentrated in the Halys River basin, along what may have been transportation routes near, for instance, Asarjik, Sausa (near ancient Karaburna), and Bulgarmaden.

One of the best-known inscriptions sites from antiquity is that of Bisitun in western Iran. [*See* Bisitun.] Its inscriptions and accompanying relief, cut high above the main east–west road connecting the Iranian plateau and the Mesopotamian alluvium near ancient Kermanshah, commemorate the accession and reign of Darius I. Like other inscription sites in this category, Bisitun can also be considered an art site.

Sites with graffiti are often found along roads or pilgrim routes (e.g., Darb el-Hajj, Darb Zubaydah) and memorialize an individual's participation in a holy journey. [*See* Darb Zubaydah.] The inscriptions are generally short and only occasionally have a figural representation (perhaps a cross or menorah). Proclamation inscriptions, while often isolated, are also generally found along traveled routes—be they major highways or a road to a mine. Their often dramatic location (at times high on a cliff or rock outcrop that required scaffolding) bespeaks a greater expenditure of resources than was possible for the average individual. They acknowledge the presence of a ruler and boast of his exploits or military prowess. The two types of inscription sites, while exhibiting marked differences in quality and content, bear much the same intent and message: they attest to humankind's desire for immortality and memorial.

[*See also* Art Sites; *and* Inscriptions.]

BIBLIOGRAPHY

Černý, Jaroslav. *The Inscriptions of Sinai*, part 2, *Translations and Commentary*. London, 1951.

Gelb, Ignace J. *Hittite Hieroglyphic Monuments*. Oriental Institute Publications, 45. Chicago, 1939.

Giveon, Raphael. "Nahr el-Kelb." In *Lexikon der Ägyptologie*, vol. 4, p. 319. Wiesbaden, 1982.

Porter, Bertha, and Rosalind Moss. *Topographical Bibliography of Ancient Egyptian Hieroglyphic Texts, Reliefs, and Paintings*, vol. 7, *Nubia, the Deserts, and Outside Egypt*. Oxford, 1951.

Stone, Michael E., ed. *Rock Inscriptions and Graffiti Project*. 3 vols. SBL Resources for Biblical Study, 28, 29, 31. Atlanta, 1992–1994.

JOHN S. JORGENSEN

INSTITUTE OF HOLY LAND STUDIES.

Founded in 1957 by G. Douglas Young, the Institute of Holy Land Studies had as its initial purpose providing graduate-level training in Israel in the archaeological, historical, geographic, linguistic, and cultural background of the Bible from a conservative Christian perspective. The institute first offered classes in 1959; in 1967 it moved to its present location on Mt. Zion, overlooking the Hinnom Valley. Sidney DeWaal was appointed as the institute's seventh president in 1993.

Currently, the institute offers both short- and long-term programs of study on undergraduate and graduate levels. The short-term program operates primarily in January and throughout the summer. The sessions are two to three weeks long and involve extensive field trips to major archaeological sites and the study of biblical background, modern Israel, or field archaeology. The long-term program has two major facets. The institute offers two-year Master of Arts degrees in biblical history, Hebrew language, and Middle Eastern studies; students enrolled in other undergraduate or graduate programs may spend a semester or a year at the institute. Through the long-term program, students may also take courses at the Hebrew University of Jerusalem. Nondegree study on the graduate level may lead to certificates in Middle-Eastern studies or biblical exegesis.

Prominent Israeli scholars and expatriate American scholars comprise the institute's faculty. Together, the faculty provide coursework in archaeology, historical geography, modern Hebrew, history of Judaism, Middle Eastern history, biblical and ancient Near Eastern languages, and biblical studies.

The institute is loosely associated with more than one hundred graduate and undergraduate institutions in the United States and Canada. More than nine thousand students from twenty-five countries have attended the institute since 1959, most in the short-term program.

CHARLES E. CARTER

INSTITUT FRANÇAIS D'ARCHÉOLOGIE DU PROCHE ORIENT.

The French Institute of Archaeology in Beirut was founded in 1946 by Henri Seyrig, the former director of antiquities of Syria and Lebanon under the French Mandate. Seyrig envisaged a center in which resident scholars and students from the East and West could openly interact. He chose an impressive nineteenth-century mansion that had belonged to the Beyhum family to house the institute. For it, he established one of the most complete libraries of Near Eastern archaeology and related subjects in the region.

Following Syria's independence from France, Seyrig continued his close cooperation with the Syrian Department of Antiquities and was granted a concession to continue archaeological work begun in 1936. The Mission de Haute Syrie, one of the institute's major archaeological projects, set out to map, study, document, and publish the seven hundred Roman-period and paleo-Christian villages and monuments in northern Syria, between Antioch and Aleppo. From the beginning, and until 1975, under the direction of the Russian architect Georges Tchalenko, the mission compiled a unique and comprehensive architectural and historical record and produced two major publications: a classic and fundamental reference work on the area (Tchalenko, 1953–1958) and another on the village churches (Tchalenko and Baccache, 1979–1990). Among the institute's other main projects were excavations at Palmyra, Baalbek, and the Crac des Chevaliers. From 1967 to 1972, the institute was directed by Daniel Schlumberger. He was followed by Ernest Will (1973–1980), who began the excavations at Tell ʿArqa in northern Lebanon and published the institute's contribution to the study of the desert city of Palmyra in

Syria (Seyrig, Amy, and Will, 1968–1975). The institute edits two periodicals: *Syria* (1920ff.), an annual journal of oriental art and archaeology; and *Bibliothèque Archéologique et Historique (BAH),* a monograph series that covers subjects from prehistory to the nineteenth century.

The institute was renamed Institut Français d'Archéologie du Proche Orient (IFAPO) in 1977, two years after the outbreak of hostilities in Lebanon. Two new centers were opened, in Amman, Jordan, and in Damascus, Syria, providing a base for the institute's archaeological projects in those countries. Between 1981 and 1992, the war in Lebanon precluded serious fieldwork there.

IFAPO's current program comprises survey, excavation, and restoration work in Syria and Jordan for the prehistoric through the Islamic period. The institute's 1989 exhibition in Damascus, "The French Contribution to Syrian Archaeology, 1969–1989," presented an overview of its work. The institute's last director, Georges Tate (1980–1990), and the present one, François Villeneuve, are involved in the rural archaeology of the periods preceding Islam in northern Syria (Tate, 1992), southern Syria (Dentzer, 1985), and Jordan. Two international colloquia held in Damascus under the institute's auspices discussed traditional water management in irrigated lands (Geyer, 1990) and houses in ancient Syria from the third millennium BCE to the beginnings of Islam (held in 1992).

IFAPO continues to record and preserve local architecture, such as the Hellenistic residence of a local potentate at ʿIraq el-Amir in Jordan (Will et al., 1991). The institute's historic contribution, particularly to architectural studies, continues to be exemplified in the work of Jacques Seigne at Jerash (Gerasa), in Jordan, and Palmyra. Interdisciplinary teamwork and close cooperation with the regional departments of antiquities and between Western and Middle Eastern professionals and institutions characterize the IFAPO's work as a foreign research center.

[*See also the biographies of Seyrig and Schlumberger.*]

BIBLIOGRAPHY

Dentzer, Jean-Marie, ed. *Hauran I: Recherches archéologiques sur la Syrie du Sud à l'époque hellénistique et romaine.* Bibliothèque Archéologique et Historique, vol. 124 Paris, 1985.

Geyer, Bernard, ed. *Techniques et pratiques hydro-agricoles traditionelles en domaine irrigué: Approche pluridisciplinaire des modes de culture avant la motorisation en Syrie; Actes du Colloque de Damas, 27 juin–1er juillet 1987.* 2 vols. Bibliothèque Archéologique et Historique, vol. 136. Paris, 1990.

Seyrig, Henri, Robert Amy, and Ernest Will. *Le temple de Bêl à Palmyre.* 2 vols. Bibliothèque Archéologique et Historique, vol. 83. Paris, 1968–1975. Fundamental study and presentation of Palmyra's principal sanctuary, major deity, and cult.

Tate, Georges. *Les campagnes de la Syrie du Nord du IIe au VIIe siècle.* Vol. 1. Bibliothèque Archéologique et Historique, vol. 133. Paris, 1992. Recent coverage of village communities in northern Syria; see in conjunction with Tchalenko (1953–1958).

Tchalenko, Georges. *Villages antiques de la Syrie du Nord: Le massif du Bélus à l'époque romaine.* 3 vols. Bibliothèque Archéologique et Historique, vol. 50. Paris, 1953–1958. Comprehensive presentation and interpretation of the growth, development, decline, and abandonment of the area's village communities.

Tchalenko, Georges, and E. Baccache. *Églises de village de la Syrie du Nord.* 3 vols. Bibliothèque Archéologique et Historique, vol. 105. Paris, 1979–1990. Detailed study and reconstruction of the North Syrian village churches characterized by a stone-built and sculpted, horseshoe-shaped arrangement of seats (=*bēmâ*) in their main nave. The first two volumes of architectural drawings and photographs illustrate the third text volume, *Églises syriennes à béma.*

Will, Ernest, et al. *ʿIraq al Amir: Le château tu tobiade Hyrcan.* 2 vols. Bibliothèque Archéologique et Historique, vol. 132. Paris, 1991.

HELGA SEEDEN

INSTITUT FRANÇAIS D'ARCHÉOLOGIE ORIENTALE. The oldest foreign archaeological organization in Egypt, the Institut Français d'Archéologie Orientale du Caire (IFAO) was founded in December, 1880, as the École Française du Caire. Its mission was to study Egyptian antiquities, history, and philology, as well as "oriental" antiquities (those of other Near Eastern cultures). Gaston Maspero, its first director, drafted a plan of organization and divided the staff between *pensionnaires,* newly graduated scholars with specific research projects, and *chargés de mission,* who work for various excavations and research projects. During the early years, members focused their attention on the copying of ancient Egyptian texts and monuments, and began publication of their research in 1883.

In 1898, under the directorship of Émile Chassinat, the name was changed to the Institut Français d'Archéologie Orientale du Caire. Chassinat inaugurated a vast program of excavations all over Egypt and founded the institute press which to date has published more than seven hundred volumes in twenty-five series.

The IFAO is one of the largest foreign archaeological institutes in Cairo. Its established position in Egypt has enabled it to carry out large long-term excavations and restoration projects at major sites ranging in date from prehistoric to Islamic times, supported by a permanent staff and a network of expedition headquarters throughout Egypt. IFAO excavations and documentation projects have included the complete temples of Edfu and Dendera, the tombs and workmen's village at Deir el-Medineh, the early Christian site at Kellia, the tomb of Seti I in the Valley of the Kings, the tomb of Ti at Saqqara, the treasury of Thutmose I at Karnak North, and sites in the oases of the Western Desert. During the 1960s, the IFAO participated in the UNESCO campaign for the salvage of the Nubian monuments, excavating at the temple of Rameses II at Wadi es-Sebua. It has also collaborated with the Egyptian Department of Antiquities and with other French and foreign institutions.

[*See also the biography of Maspero.*]

BIBLIOGRAPHY

Dawson, Warren R., and Eric P. Uphill. *Who Was Who in Egyptology.* 2d rev. ed. London, 1972. See entries for Maspero and Chassinat.

IFAO. *Un siècle de fouilles françaises en Égypte, 1880–1980, à l'occasion du Centenaire de l'École du Caire (IFAO).* Cairo, 1981. Catalog of exhibition honoring the centennial of the IFAO. Descriptive essays and good photographs for all the sites excavated by the IFAO.

Vercoutter, Jean. Introduction to *Le livre du centenaire de l'Institut Français d'Archéologie Orientale du Caire, 1880–1980.* Institut Français d'Archéologie Orientale du Caire, Mémoires, vol. 104. Cairo, 1980. History of the institute written for its centennial.

SUSAN J. ALLEN

INSTITUT FRANÇAIS D'ÉTUDES ANATOLIENNES D'ISTANBUL. Founded in 1930, and called the Institut Français d'Archéologie, the Institut Français d'Études Anatoliennes was created to promote studies in Islamic and Anatolian antiquities. The institute took its current name in 1975, in order to reflect its interest in Anatolia's civilizations through the modern period.

The institute's staff consists of a director, a scientific assistant, a student, and five researchers on stipends. Several of them are archaeologists who specialize in a wide range of periods, from the Prehistoric to the Byzantine.

The institute facilitates work and provides a logistical base for the various French expeditions working in Turkey, in which the institute's researchers frequently participate. The institute handles administrative matters, provides storage space for excavation equipment, and makes its vehicles available to expeditions. The institute also develops its own field projects, often in collaboration with Turkish archaeologists and other institutions such as the Centre National de la Recherche Scientifique (CNRS) and universities. For example, a major project in the Black Sea area is being carried out in partnership with the Groupement de Recherche 1056 of the CNRS.

The Institut Français d'Études Anatoliennes is an active partner in a wide range of other scientific activities being undertaken in Turkey, around which it organizes museum exhibits, colloquia, and discussions on such study topics as defensive systems in Anatolia and amphoras from the Black Sea. Its research appears in the journal *Anatolia Antiqua* and in volumes of the collection Varia Anatolica.

BIBLIOGRAPHY

Amandry, Michel, and Alain Davesne, eds. *Anatolie antique: Fouilles françaises en Turquie.* Collection Varia Anatolica, 4.1. Paris, 1989.

Balkan-Atli, Nur. *La néolithisation de l'Anatolie.* Collection Varia Anatolica, 7. Paris, 1994.

De Anatolia Antiqua. 3 vols. Bibliothèque de l'Institut Français d'Études Anatoliennes, 32, 38, 40. Paris, 1991–1994.

Grands ateliers d'architecture dans le monde égéen du VIe siècle av. J.-C.: Actes du colloque d'Istanbul, 23–25 mai 1991. Collection Varia Anatolica, 3. Paris, 1993.

Kassab, Dominique, and Tahsin Sezer. *Catalogue des lampes en terre cuite du Musée Archéologique d'Istanbul,* vol. 1, *Epoques préhistoriques, archaïques, classiques et hellénistiques.* Collection Varia Anatolica, 6. Paris, 1995.

Rémy, Bernard, ed. *Anatolia Antiqua/Eski Anadolu.* 2 vols. Collection Varia Anatolica, 1. Paris, 1987–1988.

Rémy, Bernard. *Les carrières sénatoriales dans les provinces romaines d'Anatolie au Haut-Empire (31 av. J.-C.–284 ap. J.-C.): Pont-Bithynie, Galatie, Cappadoce, Lycie-Pamphylie et Cilicie.* Collection Varia Anatolica, 2. Istanbul, 1989.

Rémy, Bernard, ed. *Pontica I: Recherches sur l'histoire du Pont dans l'antiquité.* Collection Varia Anatolica, 5. St. Étienne, 1991.

CATHERINE ABADIE-REYNAL

Translated from French by Melissa Kaprelian

INSTITUT FRANÇAIS D'ÉTUDES ARABES. Founded in 1922, the Institut Français d'Études Arabes de Damas (IFEAD) has as its focus Muslim archaeology and art as well as Arab and Islamic studies in the Bilad ash-Sham (Syria). Its works are published in the *Bulletin des Études Orientales (BEO),* created in 1931 and now published annually (vol. 46 in 1994), and in nonperiodical publications, currently 150 in number.

From its creation, the institute, under the direction of established directors and researchers, has maintained an interest in Syrian territory through urban studies, research involving the steppe and its inhabitants, and archaeological surveys conducted by Eustache de Lorey, Henri Seyrig, Jean Sauvaget, Jean Lassus, Robert Montagne, Michel Écochard, Albert de Boucheman, and Jacques Weulersse. Since the 1950s, historical research has been carried out on a wide variety of subjects, all with the same goal: to understand the country and its inhabitants in different periods.

The town has remained a recurring topic of research with, among others, the establishment of the Vieux Damas Extramuros (extramural Old Damascus) program. Work on the waqfs, Ottoman fiscal registers, and economic and dynastic texts has enhanced the approach to studying Islamic society (carried out by Sauvaget, Janine Sourdel-Thomine, Dominique Sourdel, Sami Dahan, Nikita Elisséeff, André Miquel, Khaled Moaz and Solange Ory, Jean-Claude David, J.-P. Pascual, Sarab Attassi, Robert Mantran, André Raymond, Henri Laoust, and Thierry Bianquis). Research on the contemporary period also constitutes a part of this study. Between 1970 and 1980, the institute devoted its attention to the archaeological areas in those towns that had served as rest stops for travelers along the right bank of the Euphrates River. Under the direction of Jean-Claude Golvin and Raymond, five salvage excavations were undertaken before the construction of the Assad dam at the site of Balis. De Lorey, G. Salles, and L. Cavro had conducted, but not completed, an excavation there in 1929–1931. Gilles Hennequin and Abd al-Faraj al-ʿUsh published the coins from the excavation (IFEAD, 1978). A Franco-Syrian team at Rahba-Mayadin, on a site 350 km (217 mi.) from Balis, excavated a town from the 'Abbasid and Mamluk periods in six seasons, under the direction of Bianquis. Arlette Nègre published the coins from this site (*BEO* 32–33 [1980–1981]). Marie-Odile Rousset has published an inventory of Islamic archaeological sites in Iraq with the institute (1992). A catalog of the pottery from Mayadin is in preparation.

Since 1983, the institute has devoted equal attention to archaeological research in rural Syria. Sophie Berthier has studied the Middle Euphrates in close collaboration with the anthropologist Olivier D'Hont, gathering information on the different types of human settlement along the banks of the river. The anthropological results appear in *Vie quotidienne des 'Agedat* (IFEAD, 1994). Alexandrine Guérin excavated the village site of Msayke in the Léjà, in southern Syria, in 1993 that followed numerous regional explorations conducted since 1991 (*BEO* 45 [1993]). This multidisciplinary study, involving archaeology, architecture, historical geography, and anthropology, followed the work of a team headed by Jean-Marie Dentzer (CNRS, Equipe de recherche associée 20) studying the Hauran in the pre-Islamic periods.

The institute's library is open to all researchers. With 950 periodicals, 400 of which are current subscriptions, and 50,000 volumes, it is one of the best French libraries for Arabic studies. The institute cooperates with Syrian researchers and local institutions such as the Académie de Langue Arabe, the University of Damascus, the Direction des Antiquités, and the al-Assad Library (national library). It also cooperates with the Syrian Antiquities Authority in joint ventures.

[*See also the biographies of Sauvaget and Seyrig.*]

BIBLIOGRAPHY

Renaud Avez, *L'Institut français de Damas au Palais Azem (1922–1946) à travers les archives*. Damascus, 1993. Includes information on the origins of the institute.

ALEXANDRINE GUÉRIN and JACQUES LANGHADE

Translated from French by Melissa Kaprelian

'IRA, TEL (Ar., Khirbet Ghara) a Negev desert site located in the Beersheba valley, 18 km (11 mi.) east of the city of Beersheba (31°14′00″ N, 34°59′20″ E, map reference 1487 × 0713). The tell, slightly more than 6 acres in area, covers the entire plateau of an isolated hill (514 m above sea level) surrounded by precipitous slopes.

The possibility that the site is referred to in the Bible remains debated. Yohanan Aharoni (1957) suggested identifying it with Qabse'el, which heads the list of Judahite cities in the Negev (*Jos.* 15:21) and is equivalent to Yeqqabse'el (*Neh.* 11:25). Eighteen years later, following Crüsemann (1973, p. 212 ff.), he suggested identifying Tel 'Ira with Zephath in *Judges* 1:17 (Aharoni, 1975, p. 119). F.-M. Abel (1938, p. 353), suggested Jagur in *Joshua* 15:21, and Yigael Yadin (1961, p. 110) Mmšt of *lmlk* seal impressions. Benjamin Mazar suggested that the site is Elto'lad (*Jos.* 15:30; see Avigad, 1990, p. 263). In consideration of Tel 'Ira's altitude, at 514 m above sea level, André Lemaire (1973, p. 361 ff.), Nadav Na'aman (1980, p. 146), and Anson F. Rainey suggested Ramat Negev (Heb., "height" of the Negev; *Jos.* 19:8). Remains from the Hellenistic to the Byzantine periods have so far shed no light on the site's ancient name.

David Alon surveyed the site under auspices of the Israel Department of Antiquities in the early 1950s. Aharoni's extensive 1956 survey on behalf of the Hebrew University of Jerusalem led him to conclude that Tel 'Ira had been the capital of the Negev in the Iron II period (Aharoni, 1957). The Institute of Archaeology at Tel Aviv University conducted excavations there between 1979 and 1987, most of them directed by Itzhaq Beit-Arieh. Avraham Biran and Rudolf Cohen directed an expedition from the Nelson Glueck School of Biblical Archaeology of the Hebrew Union College of Jerusalem, participating for one season in 1979.

The earliest settlement at Tel 'Ira dates from the Early Bronze III (stratum IX). From this period excavations exposed several floors, with clay vessels found in situ, and isolated segments of walls. The most common finds were pottery sherds scattered over the bedrock. Although the exact nature and extent of this earliest settlement could not be clarified, it appears that it was unwalled and fairly extensive, the southernmost settlement in Palestine during the period.

After a prolonged hiatus in occupation, an Israelite population settled at some undetermined time between the tenth and ninth centuries BCE. During that period a small, temporary settlement was established at the site, of which no architectural remains are preserved (stratum VIII).

Stratum VII is dated to the first half of the seventh century BCE. The Israelite city, whose remains are plainly visible today, covered the area. Most of this city was surrounded by a solid wall about 1.60 m thick and about 600 m long. A four-entryway gate structure and two towers (17 × 18 m) were erected at its eastern end. The gate belongs to the so-called Solomonic gate type known from Megiddo, Hazor, and Gezer. Some public buildings were also exposed in this area, including one with five rooms and a storehouse. To the north and east this area was surrounded by a casemate wall, which demonstrates that the two types of city wall existed side by side in stratum VII. The steep approach to the gate was protected by a large tower (6 × 9 m) that projected outward from the wall.

The storage building, evidently an official (royal) storehouse, contained a large quantity of pottery vessels, including some twenty-five large pythoi capable of holding large amounts of food. A conflagration destroyed stratum VII, shortly after which, in the second half of the seventh century BCE, the city was rebuilt and reinhabited (stratum VI). The

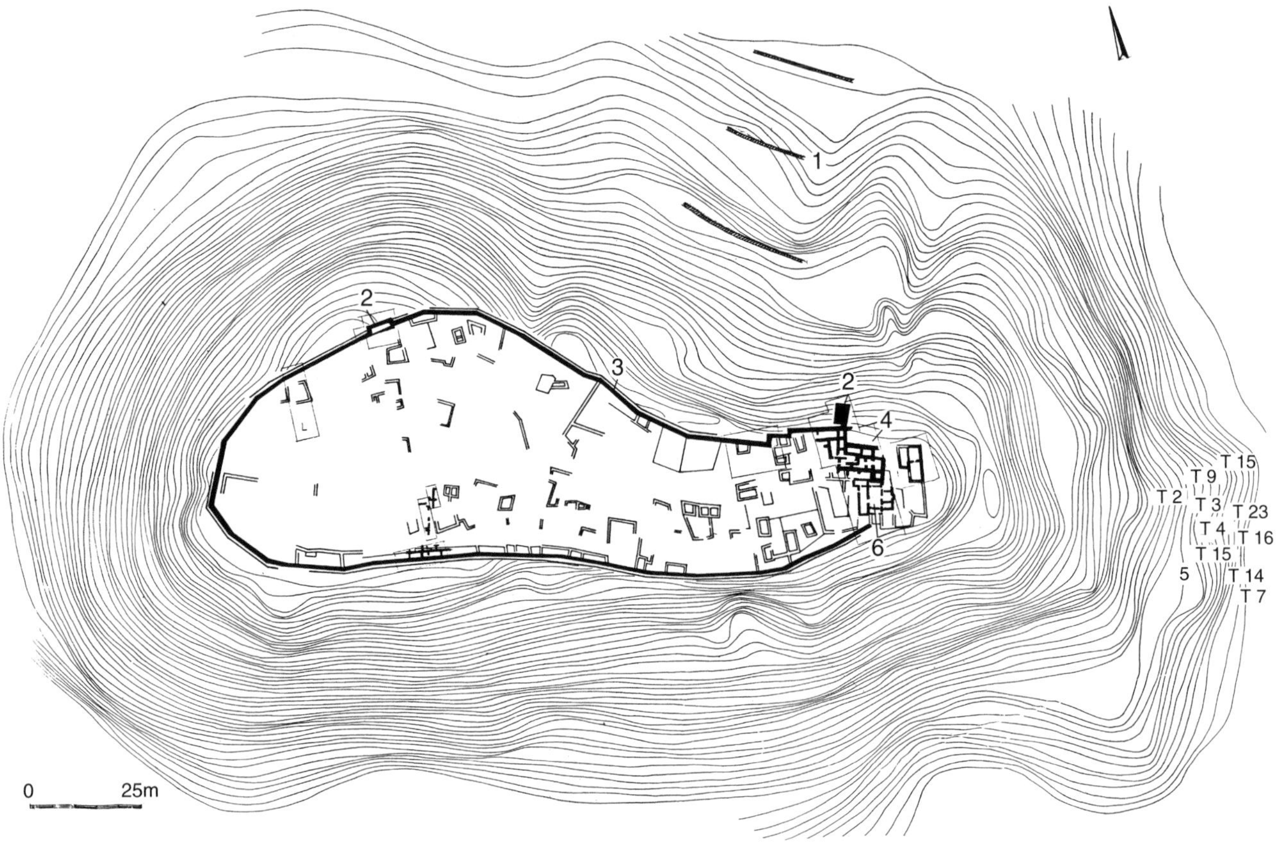

ʿIRA, TEL. *Plan of the site.* (Courtesy I. Beit-Arieh)

final destruction of the Iron Age city took place at the beginning of the sixth century BCE.

The cemetery of the Israelite city was discovered on the eastern slope. It comprises some twenty-five rock-cut bench tombs, then common in Judea (Judah). [*See* Burial Techniques.] The settlement's water supply relied on large cisterns also cut in the rock. Beyond the site, the groundwater was exploited by digging wells, a method still practiced by bedouin. [*See* Cisterns.]

According to the archaeological data, the city's economy was based on agriculture and sheep and goat herding. However, it can be assumed that in this semiarid region the central government, which was vitally interested in the city's continued existence, took the primary responsibility for its economic well-being.

In the strata of the Israelite settlement, large and varied amounts of typical Judean small finds were recovered—figurines, shekel weights, and jewelry. The written finds were scant—short inscriptions on jars; the opening phrase of a letter written in cursive Hebrew, *ʿbdk* ʾ[*mr*] ("your servant sa[id]" or "sa[ys]"); and an ostracon inscribed *mpqd brkyhw gbḥ mwqr šlmyhw*—a list of personal names.

As was the case elsewhere in the Negev, this site was resettled by the exiles returning from Babylon (Persian period, stratum V). The resettlement, however, was smaller than that of stratum VI. The site is represented in the Hellenistic period (stratum IV) by a large fortified city using the Iron Age city wall, whose remains extend to most of the excavated areas. The residences generally followed the plan of the Iron Age houses over which they were built, with some abutting of the Iron Age city wall. A smaller, but still fortified settlement appeared in the Early Roman Period (stratum III) that may have served as part of the Herodian limes.

The population of Tel ʿIra again grew in the Byzantine period (stratum II), inhabiting an area as larger—or larger—than the Iron Age city. A fairly well-preserved large monastery with a church was discovered on its east side. An eight-line inscription, still intact, indicates that the church complex was dedicated to St. Peter. The last occupation of Tel ʿIra took place in the Early Arab period (stratum I).

BIBLIOGRAPHY

Abel, Félix-Marie. *Geographie de la Palestine,* vol. 2. Paris, 1938.

Aharoni, Yohanan. "The Negev (South) of Judah." *Judah and Jerusalem: The Twelfth Archaeological Convention* (in Hebrew), pp. 46–58. Jerusalem, 1957.

Aharoni, Yohanan. "The Negev of Judah." *Israel Exploration Journal* 8 (1958): 26–38.

Aharoni, Yohanan, Volkmar Fritz, and Aaron Kempinski. "Excavation at Tel Masos (Khirbet el-Meshash)." *Tel Aviv* 2 (1958): 97–124.
Alon, David. "The Tribal Territory of Simeon." *Mibifnim* 17 (1953): 100–116 (in Hebrew).
Avigad, Nahman. "Two Hebrew 'Fiscal' Bullae." *Israel Exploration Journal* 40 (1990): 262–266.
Beit-Arieh, Itzhaq. "Tel ʿIra, a Fortified City of the Kingdom of Judah." *Qadmoniot* 18 (1985): 17–25.
Crüsemann, Frank. "Uberlegungen 245 Identification der Hirbet el-Msas." *Zeitschrift des Deutschen Palästina-Vereins* 89 (1973): 211–224.
Danin, A. *Desert Vegetation of Israel and Sinai.* Jerusalem, 1983.
Lemaire, André. "Les Ostraca hebreux de l'epoque royale israelite." Ph.D. diss., Paris, 1973.
Na'aman, Nadav. "The Inheritance of the Sons of Simeon." *Zeitschrift des Deutschen Palästina-Vereins* 96 (1980): 136–152.
Yadin, Yigal. "The Fourfold Division of Judah." *Bulletin of the American Schools of Oriental Research,* no. 163 (1961): 6–11.

ITZHAQ BEIT-ARIEH

IRAN. *See* Persia.

IRAQ. *See* Mesopotamia.

ʿIRAQ EL-AMIR (ancient Tyros), site located in the luxurious valley of Wadi es-Sir, 24 km (15 mi.) west of Amman, Jordan. To the northwest rise towering, rocky cliffs, in which two tiers of caves are hewn. To the east, in the modern village, the settlement that dates to the Early Bronze period (3,200–3,000 BCE) was excavated. To the southwest, on the old track to Jerusalem, are the ruins of the palace, the Qaṣr el-ʿAbd.

The site was first brought to the attention of scholars by the two British commanders, C. L. Irby and J. Mangles, in 1823 and by the French explorers Melchior de Vogüé and Felicien de Saulcy in 1864 and 1865, respectively. Charles H. Butler published the first reconstruction of Qaṣr el-ʿAbd in 1919, but it was not until 1961–1962 that the first excavations were conducted there by Paul W. Lapp, on behalf of the American Schools of Oriental Research. From 1976 to 1986, the Department of Antiquities of Jordan and the French Institute of Archaeology for the Near East (IFAPO) have sponsored a program of excavation and restoration of the *qaṣr,* made soundings at its main gate, and surveyed the irrigation system and environs of ʿIraq el-Amir (Villeneuve, 1988). [*See the biographies of Vogüé, Saulcy, Butler, and Lapp.*]

Historical Background. On two of the carved facades in the lower tier of caves, the name *Tobyah* is deeply engraved in Aramaic characters of the late fourth or early third century BCE. These are dwelling caves, originally a troglodite village, and would have been reused as shelters in times of danger. In the upper tier, silos and cisterns and a large cave (28 m deep × 6 m in width) with about eighty horse troughs carved along its inner straight side, suggest the presence of a stable for cavalry.

The name *Tobyah,* which means "Yahweh is my well-being," left as a signature on the two caves, may date to the period of the First Temple in Jerusalem (first millennium BCE). Under the Persian Achaemenids (sixth century BCE), "Tobyah the Ammonite servant," (*ʿabd* in West Semitic languages), is mentioned in the *Book of Nehemiah* 2:1 as one of the governors of "beyond the river." He, with Sanballat the Horonite, governor of Samaria, and Geshem, king of the Arabs in Idumea, yielded his authority to prevent the rebuilding of Solomon's Temple and the walls of Jerusalem (*Neh.* 2:19; 3:35). Nevertheless, Nehemiah, a cupbearer of King Artaxerxes I, who returned from exile in about 445 BCE, was appointed governor of Judea (Judah) and was able, with the king's support, to rebuild the walls of the city. He expelled Tobyah, a dignitary, from a spacious chamber in the Temple he had acquired through the complicity of the high priest Eliashib. Ezra, a scribe and priest who arrived after Nehemiah, in about 398 BCE, was commissioned by the king to restore the law of Moses and officially promulgated it in the Temple (*Neh.* 8:1–12). He excluded the Tobiads from the high priesthood because they were unable to trace their genealogy to a pure Israelite origin (*Es.* 2:60).

Little material culture has been discovered at ʿIraq el-Amir from the Persian period. In his report Lapp mentions a few objects shown to him from the village and dated to the period (Lapp, 1963, p. 30), and a lion protome was discovered in 1978 in a modern fence, in the northern part of the village. Its open mouth and menacing fangs are typical of the Babylonian and Achaemenid style.

In the Early Hellenistic period, under the reign of Ptolemy II Philadelphus (285–246 BCE), according to the Zenon papyri discovered at Gerza in the Faiyum of Upper Egypt, Tobias appears as a leading authority in Transjordan and one who commands a garrison of cavalry. He entertained friendly relations with Ptolemy II and his minister of finance, Apollonios. In papyrus 59005, Sourabitt, listed among the localities of Palestine and Transjordan, is usually identified with Ṣur of the *ʿabd,* "servant" (*Neh.* 2:1) or Ṣur of the Birtha (manor)—that is, Rabbath Ammon (Mittmann, 1970).

Flavius Josephus recounts in *Antiquities* 12.154–236 the tales of the Tobiads in the Hellenistic period with legendary episodes and several anachronisms. Yet, his is the only available account and its historicity cannot be denied completely (Wellhausen, 1897, pp. 245ff.). According to this report, Joseph the Tobiad, whose mother was a sister of the high priest of Solomon's Temple Onias II, leased the collection of taxes of Coele-Syria (Transjordan?), Samaria, Judea, and Phoenicia. He held this lucrative office for twenty-two years, probably from the end of Ptolemy's III reign (246–221 BCE) to the time of Ptolemy VI Philometor (c.177/76 BCE).

During one of several official journeys to Alexandria, Joseph the Tobiad fell in love with an Egyptian dancer whom he wished to marry. But his brother, who had accompanied Joseph, gave his daughter over to him one night while he was drunk. He fathered a son with her, Hyrcanus, who distinguished himself from childhood with precocious intelligence, whom he favored. As a young man, Hyrcanus, probably through bribery, had the king of Egypt appoint him to the office of his aging father (*Antiq.* 12.220). His half-brothers, colluding with their father, resolved to kill Hyrcanus on his return from Egypt. Hyrcanus escaped their ambush, killed two of his brothers, and sought refuge east of the Jordan River, at the family's ancestral estate of Tyros/ʿIraq el-Amir, in Wadi es-Sir (see below). He made his home there, levying tribute on the local inhabitants and making war on them. With the support of the high priest, he probably had deposited his fortune in the Temple of Jerusalem, as is attested by the episode of Heliodorus in *2 Maccabees* 3:1–40. Hyrcanus is described in 3:11 as "a man of great dignity," a reflection of just how influential he was at that time.

In fact, it was political conflicts that forced Hyrcanus to withdraw to Transjordan: in 200 BCE, Antiochus III, the Seleucid monarch of Syria, conquered Palestine, Phoenicia, and Transjordan from the Ptolemies. [*See* Seleucids.] The pro-Seleucid party in Jerusalem, headed by the high priest Simon and supported by Hyrcanus's older brothers, persecuted Hyrcanus, a partisan of the Ptolemies. It was then that he was obliged to withdraw to Tyros. He and his father continued to collect taxes for the Ptolemies, in accordance with the dowry agreement made with the king of Egypt: Antiochus III gave his daughter Cleopatra I Syra in marriage to Ptolemy V (193 BCE) and presented the royal couple with the tribute of the countries he conquered. This was certainly the occasion for a new auction of the taxes and Joseph the Tobiad won the bid for the second time by doubling the sum of 800 talents proposed by the other Syrian tax-farmers (*Antiq.* 12.145–155).

After the death of Joseph the Tobiad, factional strife arose in Jerusalem and the pro-Seleucid party, supported by Hyrcanus's older brothers and the high priest Simon, declared war on Hyrcanus, who was banished and swore never to return to Jerusalem. His final retreat can be estimated toward the end of Seleucus IV's reign, in about 177 BCE.

Archaeological Remains. In describing Hyrcanus's estate, Josephus was topographically accurate: "The place is between Arabia [the Nabatean kingdom] and Judea [Peraea] not far from Esbonistis" (*Antiq.* 12.233–34). The name *Tyros* given to the estate by Hyrcanus is the Aramaic transcription of *Ṣor,* meaning "rock" and preserved in modern Wadi eṣ-Sir; ʿIraq, in the local dialect is "rock," "cliff," or "cave." El-Amir ("the prince") is significant evidence of the persistence of local traditions attached to an ancient site in the East. Josephus describes the main monument built by Hyrcanus as a *baris uschura,* a "mighty manor." The term *baris* is borrowed from the Greek used in fourth-century BCE Asia Minor, in which it meant "domain," "fortified residence," or "manor" (Will et al., 1991, pp. 31–35). The description of the domain in *Antiquities* 12.233–34 is complex and incomplete for it omits the village that was the main settlement of the Tobiads, several important buildings, such as the Plaster Building (Lapp, 1963, pp. 8–39), the monumental gateway, and the defensive walls (Villeneuve, 1986, pp. 157–165). The other buildings mentioned by Josephus are *aulai,* probably "small villas," and *paradeisoi,* meaning "parks," rather than "hunting reserves." However, the outstanding structure was the *baris,* the actual Qaṣr el-ʿAbd, or "palace of the steward."

This two-storied rectangular monument (37 m north–south × 18.5 m east–west) was erected on an artificial terrace southwest of the village (see figure 1). Its lower level contained four storage rooms, pierced with seven windows, that opened on a long corridor on the east and west sides. A monumental entrance distyle in antis on the northern and southern facades gave access to the building. Two water basins at the northeastern and northwestern corners released the overflow of water through feline fountains. The upper story, which was originally designed as the owner's residence, was never completed. It included four corner towers, accessible through the northeastern stairway, two galleries with twenty-one fluted Corinthian columns on the east and west sides, and a central festival hall. There was, in addition, a balcony on each of the corner towers that was supported by a frieze of lions being followed by a lioness with her cubs. The frieze on the southern balcony (see figure 2) was unfinished and the water basins were unplastered—evidence that Qaṣr el-ʿAbd had been abruptly abandoned.

There are pre-Hellenistic antecedents for the Qaṣr el-ʿAbd: the two-storied Ammonite towers at Rujm el-Malfuf, North and South; the Umm Sweiwineh towers south of Amman; the Khilda towers to the west; and several other megalithic towers near Rabbat Ammon that date to the seventh century BCE but that were reoccupied from the Early Hellenistic to the Roman-Byzantine periods. Good parallels of fortified residences can be found in Iran at Shar-i Qumis near Hamadan and in northern Iraq at Jaddala, both dated to the Late Hellenistic period (Will et al., 1991, pp. 276–77). [*See* Hamadan.] An Aramaic inscription at Jaddala recounts that the residence was designed as a *birtha* or manor. The antecedent of these residences is the Neo-Hittite *bit-ḫilani,* which is characterized by a columned entrance usually flanked by two towers. Nevertheless, the architectural decoration of the *qaṣr,* with its Corinthian floral capitals, applied half columns, acroteria, and row of acanthus leaves on the base of the shafts are Alexandrian in origin. Later developments of this architecture are the Khazneh ed-Deir and especially the Palace Tomb at Petra, in southern Jordan. [*See* Petra.]

The date of the Qaṣr el-ʿAbd has been the subject of speculation. De Saulcy (1865) related the monument to the Am-

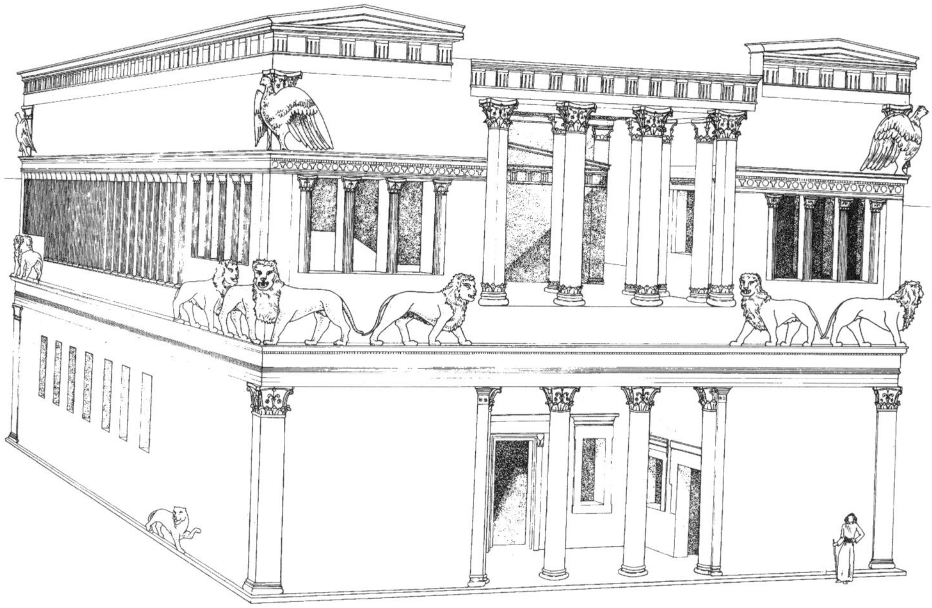

ʿIRAQ EL-AMIR. Figure 1. *Reconstruction of Qaṣr el-ʿAbd.* (After F. Larché)

monite period. No significant evidence was discovered in excavating the monument because it was never finished and therefore was not occupied in the Hellenistic period. However, the excavation of the main gateway revealed pottery sherds and coins of chronological importance: six bronze coins, dated to the end of Antiochus III's reign (c. 208–200 BCE), were associated with floor 1, which is not related to the architectural level of the gateway but to a later entrance system "prepared in haste" (Dentzer et al., 1982, p. 320; 1983, p. 141). Jean-Marie Dentzer and his colleagues conclude that construction of the *qaṣr* was begun "at the end of the reign of Seleucus IV (187–175 BCE) but was interrupted in 175 BCE. Their interpretation is not fully convincing, however: on the one hand, the assumption that Hyrcanus ended

ʿIRAQ EL-AMIR. Figure 2. *Unfinished lion relief in the sourthwestern balcony of Qaṣr el-ʿAbd.* (Courtesy F. Zayadine)

his life in 175 BCE does not rest on historical ground. Several authors date his suicide to the first campaign of Antiochus IV (169 BCE) and Antiochus's looting of the Jerusalem Temple treasure (Will et al., 1991, p. 21). On the other hand, if floor 1 of the gateway was a reuse, a reasonable conclusion would be that the gateway itself, and especially the *qaṣr*, are earlier than 200 BCE. With this evidence it is not possible to accept Momigliano's hypothesis that the *qaṣr* was standing in 259 BCE (Momigliano, 1931–1932; Gera, 1990, p. 25), but it is likely that Hyrcanus began building his fortified residence when he first fled east in about 209 BCE.

The later occupation of the *qaṣr* belongs to two phases: the first dates to the Late Roman period (third–fourth centuries CE), ending with the 363 earthquake, and the second from the fifth to the mid-seventh centuries. The latter is attested by both coins and pottery lamps. Byzantine and Umayyad iconoclasm was probably responsible for the destruction of the animal reliefs still standing in the eighth century.

There is no reason to accept Josephus's chronology and date Hyrcanus's end to the accession year of Antiochus IV in 175 BCE. The new king of Syria had to busy himself at first with consolidating his power, for he was opposed by his nephew Demetrius. He began to meddle directly in Jewish affairs in 174 BCE, when Joshua (Jason) offered a high price to buy the priesthood and with the arrival of Menelaus in the position 172 BCE. At the end of his first campaign in Egypt in 169 BCE, Antiochus was directly confronted with the factions fighting in Jerusalem. By pillaging the Temple treasure, and collecting Hyrcanus's fortune, he realized the role of that independent "princelet," but east of the Jordan. Hyrcanus had been fighting the Nabatean Arabs, who joined the Seleucid party after Antiochus III's campaign in 218 BCE. The dramatic end of Hyrcanus's adventure is recounted in *Antiquities* 12.236: "seeing how great the power which Antiochus had, and fearing that he might be captured by him and punished for what he had done to the Arabs, he ended his life by his own hand." This may refer to the capture of Jerusalem by the Seleucid king in 169 BCE and the execution of the enemies of the high priest Menelaus. Hyrcanus was most probably directly threatened by Antiochus IV and his army before his suicide. The revolt of the Maccabees in 167 BCE brought an end to Tobiad hegemony east and west of the Jordan.

BIBLIOGRAPHY

Butler, Howard Crosby, et al. *Publications of the Princeton University Archaeological Expeditions to Syria in 1904–1905 and 1909*. Division II, Section B: Northern Syria. Leiden, 1920. See pages 1–25.

Conder, Claude R. *The Survey of Eastern Palestine: Memoirs of the Topography, Orography, Hydrography, and Archaeology*. London, 1889. See volume 1, page 78.

Dentzer, Jean-Marie, et al. "Fouille de la porte monumentale à Iraq al-Amir: La campagne de 1978." *Annual of the Department of Antiquities of Jordan* 26 (1982): 301–321.

Dentzer, Jean-Marie, et al. "The Monumental Gateway and Princely Estate of Araq el-Amir." *Annual of the American Schools of Oriental Research* 47 (1983): 133–148.

Edgar, Campbell Cowan. *Zenon Papyri*. Catalogue Général des Antiquités Égyptiennes du Musée de Caire, 1. Cairo, 1925.

Gera, Dov. "On the Credibility of History of the Tobiads, Josephus Antiquities 12, 156–222." In *Greece and Rome in Eretz Israel*, edited by Aryeh Kasher et al., pp. 21–38. Jerusalem, 1990.

Goldstein, Jonathan A. "The Tales of the Tobiads." *Studies in Judaism in Late Antiquity* 12.3 (1973): 85–123.

Irby, Charles Leonard, and James Mangles. *Travels in Egypt and Nubia, Syria, and Asia Minor during the Years 1817 and 1818*. London, 1823. See page 146.

Josephus, Flavius. *Jewish Antiquities*. Translated by Ralph Marcus. Loeb Classical Library. London, 1958.

Lapp, Nancy L., et al. "The Excavations at Araq el-Emir." *Annual of the American Schools of Oriental Research* 47 (1983): 1–154 plans 1–5.

Lapp, Paul W. "Soundings at ʿArâq el-Emîr (Jordan)." *Bulletin of the American Schools of Oriental Research*, no. 165 (1962): 16–34.

Lapp, Paul W. "The Second and Third Campaigns at ʿAraq el-Emir." *Bulletin of the American Schools of Oriental Research*, no. 171 (1963): 8–39.

Lapp, Paul W. "The 1962 Excavation at ʿAraq el-Emir." *Annual of the Department of Antiquities of Jordan* 10 (1965): 37–42.

Marcus, Ralph. Preface to Flavius Josephus, *Jewish Antiquities*. Loeb Classical Library. London, 1958.

Mazar, Benjamin. "The Tobiads." *Israel Exploration Journal* 7 (1957): 137–145, 229–238.

Mittmann, Siegfried. "Zenon in Östjordanland." In *Archäologie und Altes Testament: Festschrift für Kurt Galling*, edited by Arnulf Kuschke and Ernst Kutsch, pp. 199–210. Tübingen, 1970.

Momigliano, Arnaldo. "I Tobiadi nella prehistoria del moto maccabaico." *Atti della Reale Accademia delle Scienze di Torino*, ser. 2, vol. 67 (1931–1932): 165–200.

Orrieux, Claude, and Édouard Will. *Ioudaismos-Hellenismos: Essai sur le judaïsme judéen à l'époque hellénistique*. Nancy, 1986. See pages 77ff.

Saulcy, Félicien de. *Voyage en Terre Sainte*. Paris, 1865. See pages 211–235.

Saulcy, Félicien de. *Mémoire sur les monuments d'Aaraq-el-Emyr*. Mémoires de l'Académie des Inscriptions et Belles-Lettres, 26. Paris, 1867.

Villeneuve, François.. "Recherches en cours sur les systèmes défensifs d'un petit site d'époque hellénistique en Transjordanie: Iraq al-Amir." In *La fortification dans l'histoire du monde grec: Actes du colloque international la fortification et sa place dans l'histoire politique, culturelle et sociale du monde grec, Valbonne, décembre 1982*, edited by Pierre Leriche and Henri Tréziny, pp. 157–165. Paris, 1986.

Villeneuve, François. "Prospection archéologique et géographique historique: la région d'Iraq al-Amir (Jordanie)." In *Géographie historique au Proche-Orient*, edited by P.-L. Gatier, B. Helly, and J.-P. Rey-Coquais, pp. 257–288. Notes et monographies techniques no. 23. Paris, 1988.

Villeneuve, François. "L'histoire des Tobiades chez Flavius Josèphe." In *Le monde du roman grec*, edited by Marie-Françoise Baslez et al., pp. 249–257. Études de Littérature Ancienne, vol. 4 Paris, 1992.

Vogüé, Melchior de. *Le Temple de Jérusalem*. Paris, 1864. See pages 34–38.

Wellhausen, Julius. *Israelitische und jüdische Geschichte*. Berlin, 1897. See page 254.

Will, Édouard. *Histoire politique du monde hellénistique*. Vol. 1. Nancy, 1966.

Will, Ernest, F. Larché, and Fawzi Zayadine, et al. *Iraq al Amir, le château du Tobiade Hyrcan.* Paris, 1991.

FAWZI ZAYADINE

IRBID, site located in northwestern Transjordan (map reference 674 × 062) and identified with biblical Beth Arbel (*Hos.* 10:14), classical Arbela, and Islamic Arbad. The site's name prior to the eighth century BCE remains unknown. In 1890, Gottlieb Schumacher recorded the site's classical remains, and in 1929, William Foxwell Albright noted its importance between the fourteenth and the tenth centuries BCE. Although considerable obfuscation of the remains has occurred in the last century, systematic excavations, survey, and the integration of textual ethnohistorical, and recently taken oral historical data have begun to clarify the occupational history of the tell and the surrounding area.

The site consists of an eliptically shaped tell (about 500 m × 400 m) and surroundings that encompass modern Irbid and Barha. Following an intensive survey of the tell and its vicinity in 1983–1984, systematic excavations were begun in 1984 that are still underway. Stratified occupational data are most secure for the period from about 3500 to about 700 BCE; however, there is also some stratified evidence for the first–ninth centuries CE, which are attested to textually as well. Excavations of the surrounding area, conducted by the Jordanian Department of Antiquities, and analysis of the survey data have helped to confirm the sequence of occupation attested to on the tell.

Evidence for the Late Chalcolithic and Early Bronze periods has been found on the southwest and western sides of the tell. Cisterns were cut into the bedrock near small-scale, probably domestic, structures. No city wall was found.

In the Middle Bronze Age (c. eighteenth–nineteenth centuries BCE), the tell was encircled by a boulder wall of basalt, which is indigenous to the region. To the east, part of a glacis was excavated. Structures relating to this period were badly disturbed by later occupation. However, the domestic nature of the pottery implies private dwellings, rather than public.

The Late Bronze and Early Iron Age occupation (c. 1300–1000 BCE) is the clearest to date. Domestic structures on the west reused or partially destroyed the Middle Bronze structures. On the northwest side of the tell and farther to the east was part of the necropolis, as shown by R. Dajani. The city wall was extended in the south by the addition of a chert and limestone hewn block wall. On the southwest, a public complex dating to the end of the Late Bronze Age, supported by carbon-14 dates, has been excavated. The structures were multistoried and enclosed by a perimeter wall. Cultic objects—an incense burner, goblets, cups and saucers, lamps, and a basalt libation stand—were found on storage shelves at the rear of the complex. One room contained large storage vessels that held lentils, olives, grains, and probably oil. A fire destroyed the complex, during which the wooden beam supports burned, causing the mud-brick superstructure to collapse into the randomly sized stone substructure. The destruction debris extended for about 100 m and was 4 m deep. The fire and destruction were caused by natural means.

Following the destruction, the debris was leveled but not removed. The stones were reused to build minor industrial and domestic structures and new construction techniques altered the area. Although other areas on the tell attest to the change in constructional techniques from the Late Bronze to the Iron Age, only the complex in the southwest was destroyed. The pottery corpus indicates a gradual change in typology, rather than a distinctive and fundamental change based on historical periodization.

As at other sites, the tell was incorporated into the plan of the Roman city. The site's function as the center for municipal structures continues to the present. Although its size surpassed that of Beit Ras/Capitolias, located 5 km (3 mi.) to the north, Irbid/Arbela's status was lower. That the sites were interconnected seems clear; accommodations must have been made regarding the surrounding arable land. Irbid's fame in early Islamic history emanates from Caliph Yazid II, who lived at Beit Ras and died at Irbid, probably at Barha, to the west, which then was probably a district of Irbid, as it is today.

BIBLIOGRAPHY

Albright, William Foxwell. "New Israelite and Pre-Israelite Sites: The Spring Trip of 1929." *Bulletin of the American Schools of Oriental Research,* no. 35 (1929): 1–14.

Lenzen, C. J., et al. "Excavations at Tell Irbid and Beit Ras, 1985." *Annual of the Department of Antiquities of Jordan* 29 (1985): 151–159.

Lenzen, C. J. "Tall Irbid and Bait Rās." *Archiv für Orientforschung* 33 (1986): 164–166.

Lenzen, C. J., and E. Axel Knauf. "Tell Irbid and Beit Ras, 1983–1986." *Liber Annuus/Studii Biblici Franciscani* 36 (1986): 361–363.

Lenzen, C. J., and E. Axel Knauf. "Irbid." *Revue Biblique* 95 (1988): 239–247.

Lenzen, C. J., and Alison M. McQuitty. "The 1984 Survey of the Irbid/Beit Rās Region." *Annual of the Department of Antiquities of Jordan* 32 (1988): 265–274.

Lenzen, C. J. "Tell Irbid and Its Context: A Problem in Archaeological Interpretation." *Biblische Notizen* 42 (1988): 27–35.

Lenzen, C. J., and Alison M. McQuitty. "An Architectural Study of the Irbid Region with Particular Reference to a Building in Irbid." *Levant* 21 (1989): 119–128.

Lenzen, C. J. "Irbid and Beit Rās: Interconnected Settlements between c. A.D. 100–900." In *Studies in the History and Archaeology of Jordan,* vol. 4, edited by Ghazi Bisheh, pp. 299–307. Amman, 1992.

Schumacher, Gottlieb. *Northern ʿAjlun, "Within the Decapolis."* London, 1890.

C. J. LENZEN

IRRIGATION. The history and extent of irrigation in the ancient Near East are difficult to trace because the physical evidence in many instances is located away from settled sites in the open countryside. It is only recently that regional surveys have been initiated to determine the extent of occupation beyond well-defined sites and the use made of natural resources. To help in this endeavor, space-age technology, using information gained through the LANDSAT system, is now being utilized to trace ancient waterworks (Adams, 1981, p. 33). Because many known waterworks were in use for more than just one period, however, determining their original date is complicated. These limitations in studying the history of irrigation, render the results incomplete.

Very soon after the domestication of plants in the Neolithic period, people realized that in certain regions cultivation required supplementing rainfall with water from other sources. Thus, in the Ubaid–Early Dynastic I periods in the valleys of the great rivers of Mesopotamia (Adams, 1981, pp. 52–129) and in predynastic Egypt (Hodges, 1970, p. 61), dense settlement was undertaken and flourished to the point of developing unique cultures. The nature of the floods in the Nile River valley and in Mesopotamia differed and required different responses. The Nile inundation occurs in early spring and recedes, after only a few days, after depositing a new, rejuvenating layer of soil in which sowing can take place immediately; the Tigris and Euphrates Rivers flood in the early summer, when it is too late for sowing. Thus, sowing in Mesopotamia took place before the flooding, and the fields had to be protected with dikes against the crops being washed away. In Egypt, canals were dug to irrigate the fields after the floodwaters had receded (Hodges, 1970, p. 60); this undertaking, which required a strong central authority because it involved more than just one community, probably led to the unification of Egypt.

In other regions, different existing water sources, such as springs and brooks, had to be tapped and wells and cisterns had to be built. Jericho, founded in the Neolithic period, is considered to be the earliest urban site; its settlement was made possible by a perennial spring nearby. Its earliest settlement was surrounded by a defense wall with a tower protecting the approach to the spring (Kenyon, 1979, p. 25), whose water was used for drinking, watering animals, and irrigating land.

Some of the earliest preserved waterworks are those at Jawa, the short-lived Early Bronze Age (late fourth millennium BCE) site in Jordan's Black Desert. While irrigation in the river valleys of the Nile and the Tigris and Euphrates relied on flooding, at Jawa water for irrigation became available from catchment basins created to collect runoff water that was in turn diverted into dams and gravity canals (Helms, 1981, pp. 135–198). The remains of these waterworks and those of the town and its fortifications suggest that they were designed and constructed by a highly organized population. [*See* Jawa.] Irrigation with runoff water was also practiced in other arid zones, such as the Negev desert, but in later periods. Remains of water-collection and distribution facilities dated to the Iron II period have been found at Ramat Maṭred and Mishor ha-Ruaḥ (tenth–ninth centuries BCE) in the central Negev, and in the Buqeiʿa (seventh century BCE), west of the northern tip of the Dead Sea (for bibliography, see Borowski, 1987 pp. 1–20). It seems that settlements throughout this period were initiated, or at least supported, by the central Judean government for economic as well as political and military reasons. During the Roman–Byzantine and Early Arab periods, agriculture in the Negev continued to rely on the same method of diverting water to terraced fields, cisterns, and pools. [*See* Cisterns.]

Throughout history, Mesopotamian agriculture relied on irrigation by canals that took their water from its great rivers. The great canal networks and their use and maintenance dictated strong, central political units first centering on city-states and later on territorial empires. The use and care of canal irrigation was state controlled and demanded a highly organized social system that relied on detailed recordkeeping (Adams, 1981, p. 165). In Girsu, Eanatum (c. 2500 BCE) and Entemenak (c. 2400 BCE) constructed weirs of baked bricks laid in bitumen (Jacobsen, 1982, p. 62); similar activities were carried out at Lagash (Hruška, 1988). Ur-Nammu, king of Ur, devoted his energies to many projects, among them a substantial program of irrigation works that assured the city's prosperity (Hallo and Simpson, 1971, p. 78). Gungunum of Larsa, as well as other kings of the Mesopotamian city-states of the first half of the second millennium BCE (Renger, 1990), was also occupied with the building and maintenance of canals for bringing fresh water to the south (Hallo and Simpson, 1971, p. 92). Mathematical texts from the Old Babylonian period (c. 2000–1600 BCE) suggest that the ancients were preoccupied with the volumes of water from different sources that were necessary to irrigate fields to a certain depth (Powell, 1988). [*See* Girsu and Lagash; Ur; Larsa.]

The subject of irrigation plays a prominent role in the earliest agricultural manual, known as the Sumerian "Georgica," composed in about 2100 BCE and still in vogue in about 1700 BCE (Jacobsen, 1982, p. 57). According to this manual, fields were irrigated in the summer (June–July) in preparation for weeding (July–August). After the ground was prepared (August–October) and sown (September–October), four irrigations were recommended during particular stages of crop development—the final one when the crop (barley) was ripening, to ensure an extra good yield (Jacobsen, 1982, pp. 59, 61).

The Mari (Syria) archives are another source of information about irrigation in this region of the Euphrates (Kupper, 1988). Included in the correspondence of the governors of the districts of Mari, Terqa, and Sagaratum are reports pertaining to new canals built under their supervision; information related to water control; irrigation terminology; and the enumeration of personnel involved in irrigation and canal maintenance. The amount of information available demonstrates the importance of irrigation to the kingdom's economy. Archaeological surveys and excavations show that the Mari region was already being cultivated and irrigated in the Early Bronze Age, at the beginning of the third millennium BCE (Margueron, 1988). [*See* Mari; Terqa.]

Unfortunately, the intensive irrigation of certain soils leads to salinization. In southern Mesopotamia, the soil is alluvial in origin, of fine-textured clays with a high salt content. In addition, irrigation with river water and capillary action from a shallow and saline water table add salt to the soil. High salt content affects germination and makes the soil impermeable (Jacobsen, 1982, pp. 5–7). Soil salinization in Mesopotamia led to the abandonment of wheat cultivation in favor of the more resistant barley. [*See* Cereals.]

Gradual salinity through irrigation in Mesopotamia's Diyala region slowly rendered the area unusable for normal cultivation and forced the abandonment of the region (Jacobsen, 1982, p. 71). The earliest occupation of the region occurred in about 4200 BCE, and it was very fertile and prosperous until much of it was abandoned during the Islamic period. Throughout its history, however, the Diyala region suffered several abandonments, the result primarily of the collapse of the political system in charge of the irrigation network. With the collapse of central authority, waterworks could not be maintained and the entire agricultural system collapsed, forcing the population to abandon it. [*See* Diyala.]

Since prehistoric times in the Iranian plateau, a water-transport system known as *qanat,* was developed (Olmstead, 1948, pp. 16–68). It consisted of a horizontal tunnel with vertical shafts that allowed entrance for maintenance and the release of air pressure (Landels, 1978, pp. 38–40). The water carried by these systems originated in the mountains as melted snow (Olmstead, 1948, p. 165). Early traditions concerning this system found their way into the Avesta (Olmstead, 1948, pp. 16, 20). Titles to plots watered by *qanats* were owned in fee simple (Olmstead, 1948, p. 68). During the time of Darius, the Persians introduced (c. 490 BCE) the *qanat* system into Egypt, where it was used at the Oasis of the South (Olmstead, 1948, p. 224).

The first pharaoh, the legendary Menes, is credited not only with uniting Upper and Lower Egypt, but also with being the first to try to control the Nile by building dikes and apportioning the water used for agricultural purposes (Hodges, 1970, p. 91). The centrality of government control of water continued throughout Egyptian history into the Hellenistic, Roman, and Byzantine periods (Bonneau, 1986). During certain periods, installations known as Nilometers were used to measure the level of floodwaters in order to compute the tax rate for the year; the higher the water level, the more abundant the crop, and thus the higher the tax rate. Nilometers were built along the river, mostly near temples. In addition to the archaeological recovery of remains of these installations, Nilometers are depicted on mosaics, such as those uncovered in Israel at Sepphoris and Beth-Shean and at Tabgha (Netzer and Weiss, 1992, p. 38). [*See* Sepphoris; Beth-Shean; Tabgha.] The annual flooding of the Nile required repeated land surveying, which taught the Egyptians how to lay out a right-angle triangle and solve other mathematical and geometric problems (Hodges, 1970, p. 132).

Gardening is a branch of agriculture that also requires controlled irrigation. In ancient Palestine it was practiced on a limited scope because of irrigation difficulties (including the terrain and minimal water sources). In Jerusalem in the First Temple period (c. 950–586), there were gardens in the Kidron Valley that were watered by an open canal, the Siloam channel, which originated at the Gihon Spring. [*See* Jerusalem.] It is known from Egyptian textual and artistic evidence, and from the Bible (*Dt.* 12:10–11) that gardening was well developed in Egypt. To be able to water gardens year-round, water had to be brought from the river to the fields (Endesfelder, 1982, p. 142). Initially, this was accomplished by hand, but later with an implement called *shaduf* in Arabic (see figure 1). A *shaduf* is a long horizontal beam on an upright pole; it has a vessel attached at one end and a weight at the other. When the vessel is immersed, water is drawn into a canal leading to the agricultural plot or into a large receptacle from where it can be carried by hand to other destinations. The *shaduf* is known from a Mesopotamian cylinder seal (c. 2000 BCE) and from Egyptian tomb painting (c. 1500 BCE; (Hodges, 1970, pp. 118–119). This method, although still in use, was later partially replaced, probably in the Roman period, by the screw pump invented by Archimedes. Another technical improvement for irrigation, which probably reached the region in the Early Roman period, is the waterwheel (or bucket) powered by draft animals (or humans). The waterwheel raises water from a low source, such as a river, to higher ground, where it can be distributed through canals. However, the height to which water could be raised was limited by the size of the wheel, a problem that was resolved with the invention of the bucket chain. This installation was made of an endless chain with buckets attached at set intervals. The chain was draped over the axle of a wheel that was operated in a manner similar to that of the waterwheel. The difference in elevations between the water source and the higher destination depended on the length of the chain (Landels, 1978, pp. 71–74).

Roman technological influence was strong in ancient Palestine beginning in the time of Herod the Great, who introduced new ways of transporting water from distant sources. In and around Jerusalem, for example, water was brought from "Solomon's Pools" at Artas, south of Bethlehem. Wa-

IRRIGATION. Figure 1. *A shaduf, a type of primitive irrigation pump on the river bank of the Nile.* (Erich Lessing/Art Resource, NY)

ter for urban and agricultural uses was brought by aqueducts utilizing arch-supported canals, bridges, tunnels, and siphons. [*See* Aqueducts.] Large irrigation projects were carried out around Jericho, Samaria, and Caesarea. The Romans utilized similar water systems in the second century CE in North Africa to bring vast areas under cultivation to grow high-quality wheat. Where cereals could not be cultivated, olive trees were planted.

In Roman Palestine, water rights for agricultural use were included in property deeds, as is seen in the documents belonging to Babatha's archive found in a cave near ʿEin-Gedi. These rights were enumerated according to days of the week, number of hours, and water sources for irrigation (Yadin, 1971, pp. 235–237).

Irrigation has always been a labor-intensive branch of agriculture that cannot survive without tight control by a central authority. When a political system was weakened, water management often disintegrated, the economy collapsed, and periods of disorder and scarcity took over.

[*See also* Agriculture; Hydraulics; *and* Hydrology.]

BIBLIOGRAPHY

Adams, Robert McC. *Heartland of Cities: Surveys of Ancient Settlement and Land Use on the Central Floodplain of the Euphrates.* Chicago, 1981. Excellent source for the study of ancient Mesopotamian irrigation and urban society.

Bonneau, Danielle. "Le souverain d'Égypte, juge de l'usage de l'eau." In *L'homme et l'eau en Méditerranée et au Proche Orient,* vol. 2, edited by Françoise Métral and Jean Métral, pp. 69–80. Lyon, 1986. Brief study of the legal role of the Egyptian king in matters of water control.

Borowski, Oded. *Agriculture in Iron Age Israel.* Winona Lake, Ind., 1987. Good bibliographical source for runoff irrigation in the Negev.

Endesfelder, Erika. "Zur Entwicklung der Bewässerungstechnik in Ägypten." In *Produktivkräfte und Gesellschaftsformationen in Vorkapitalistischer Zeit,* edited by Joachim Herrmann and Irmgard Sellnow, pp. 141–147. Berlin, 1982. Brief study of irrigation techniques in Egypt.

Hallo, William W., and William Kelly Simpson. *The Ancient Near East: A History.* New York, 1971. Concise history of Mesopotamia and Egypt.

Helms, S. W. *Jawa: Lost City of the Black Desert.* London, 1981. Excellent report on this site, including its ancient waterworks.

Hodges, Henry. *Technology in the Ancient World.* New York, 1970. Excellent study of ancient technology, including water pumps.

Hruška, Blahoslav. "Die Bewässerungsanlagen in den altsumerischen Königsinschriften von Lagas." *Bulletin on Sumerian Agriculture* 4 (1988): 61–72. Brief study of texts related to irrigation from the Sumerian period.

Jacobsen, Thorkild. *Salinity and Irrigation: Agriculture in Antiquity.* Bibliotheca Mesopotamica, 14. Malibu, 1982. Extensive study of the causes and effects of salinity in Mesopotamia.

Kenyon, Kathleen M. *Archaeology in the Holy Land.* 4th ed. New York, 1979.

Kupper, J.-R. "L'irrigation à Mari." *Bulletin on Sumerian Agriculture* 4 (1988): 93–104. Study of irrigation-related texts from the archives at Mari.

Landels, J. G. *Engineering in the Ancient World.* Berkeley, 1978. Excellent study of ancient technology, including water pumps, aqueducts, and *qanat.*

Margueron, Jean-Claude. "Espace agricole et aménagement régional à Mari au début du IIIe millénaire." *Bulletin on Sumerian Agriculture* 4 (1988): 49–60. Brief study of agriculture and irrigation in and around Mari in the Early Bronze Age.

Netzer, Ehud, and Zeev Weiss. "New Mosaic Art from Sepphoris." *Biblical Archaeology Review* 18.6 (1992): 36–43, 78. Some of the mosaics from Sepphoris, including the one depicting a Nilometer.

Olmstead, Albert T. *History of the Persian Empire: Achaemenid Period.* Chicago and London, 1948. Extensive history of the Persian Empire, including the history of *qanat.*

Powell, M. A. "Evidence for Agriculture and Waterworks in Babylonian Mathematical Texts." *Bulletin on Sumerian Agriculture* 4 (1988): 161–171. Brief study of mathematical texts related to irrigation.

Renger, Johannes. "Rivers, Water Courses, and Irrigation Ditches and Other Matters Concerning Irrigation Based on Old Babylonian Sources, 2000–1600 B.C." *Bulletin on Sumerian Agriculture* 5 (1990): 31–46.

Yadin, Yigael. *Bar-Kokhba: The Rediscovery of the Legendary Hero of the Last Jewish Revolt against Imperial Rome.* London, 1971. Popular description of the archaeological work around ʿEin-Gedi, with a chapter on the archive of Babatha.

ODED BOROWSKI

ISFAHAN, site located in modern Iraq, on the banks of the Zayandeh-Rud, some 17,160 m (5,200 ft.) above sea level, midway between Damascus and Aleppo in the west and Bukhara and Samarkand in the east (32°40′ N, 51°38′ E). Isfahan is an oasis surrounded by desert and semidesert. It boasts the most abundant water supply on the land-locked Iranian plateau, a condition that led to the early development of agriculture and urban growth there. Isfahan was a center for the exchange of goods and ideas perhaps as early as Achaemenid times.

Identified as ancient Gabae, Isfahan was cited by Strabo (15.3.3) as one of the Achaemenid royal residences. As an administrative center, it appears as the Parthian *G'b* and Middle Persian *Gdy/Gay* in the third-century CE inscription of the Sasanian king Shapur I at Naqsh-i Rustam (inscription on the Kaʿbah of Zoroaster, *KZ* ll. 27, 33). [*See* Naqsh-i Rustam.] These names, in turn, have been equated with *Aspahan/Asfahan/Isfahan* in late classical and later Arab sources; the abbreviation *ASP,* for Aspahan, occurs on Sasanian coins from the fourth century onward, while *Spahan* is found on Sasanian administrative seals as a province of the Sasanian Empire.

Spahan was the site of one of the many sacred fires established throughout the Sasanian Empire by the chief priest of the Zoroastrian state church, Kirder, in the third century. In Nestorian Christian accounts from the Sasanian period, Asfahan/Isfahan is mentioned as an episcopal seat.

The foundation of the present city appears to date to early in the Sasanian period, when it was centered on the town of Jayy (Gay), now Shahristan, a suburb 8 km (5 mi.) to the east. Jayy served as a citadel and place of refuge for the surrounding villages in times of war, as well as an archival and administrative center. According to later Arab and Persian sources, it was protected by a wall with one hundred towers and four gates aligned according to the seasonal positions of the sun. Outside one of the gates, a special open space, or *maidān,* served as a marketplace.

Three kilometers (2 mi.) to the west was Yahudiyya, where, according to one tradition, Jews had been settled in the sixth century BCE by the Babylonian king Nebuchadrezzar or, according to another, by the Sasanian ruler Yazdigird I (399–420 CE), at the request of his Jewish wife. With the Arab conquest of Iran in the middle of the seventh century, Jayy became the seat of an Arab governor and site of the first Friday Mosque in the region. Jayy declined after 767 (AH 150), when the ʿAbbasid governor shifted his administration and the mosque to Khusinan, a village closer to Yahudiyya. Shortly thereafter, Khusinan was absorbed by Yahudiyya, which is now the center of modern Isfahan and, since 773 (AH 156), the location of the third and present-day Friday Mosque.

The city continued to develop under the Buyids in the tenth century; it was walled and ovoid in shape, with twelve gates and a citadel. Within it, the Friday Mosque was fronted on the *maidān* and associated bazaar area—the religious, administrative, commercial, and intellectual center of the city. Another major period of construction was under the Seljuks in the eleventh and twelfth centuries. The me-

ISFAHAN. Figure 1. *The Sasanian bridge at Shahristan.* (Courtesy J. Lerner)

dieval history of Isfahan ended with the elevation of the city as the capital of Persia in 1598 (AH 1006) under the Safavid Shah 'Abbas, who was responsible for a grand architectural program.

No archaeological work has been done in Isfahan to document its pre-Islamic past. A ten-arched bridge spans the Zayandeh-Rud at Shahristan (see figure 1), the former Jayy; its stone piers are probably a Sasanian construction. Two Sasanian capitals, both bearing royal and divine busts in relief, have been known since at least the nineteenth century, when they were observed at the entrance to the Safavid pavilion on the Maidan-i Shah. By analogy with similar capitals from other sites in Iran, these date to the time of Khusrau II (591–628 CE) and attest to some unknown palatial structure. The capitals are unexcavated and were most likely moved from their original findspot. On a hill to the west of the city are the mud-brick ruins of what may be an *āteshgāh*, or Zoroastrian fire temple. Shah Diz, a mountaintop stronghold south of the city, may or may not date to the Sasanian period.

Other than the Friday Mosque, the minarets of Isfahan and the twelfth-century Sha'ya Mosque, none of Isfahan's pre-Safavid Islamic monuments have been published from an archaeological point of view. While restoration work in the Friday Mosque yielded no definitive pre-Islamic levels, the history of this major building is now better understood.

[*See also* Mosque; Persia, *articles on* Persia from Alexander to the Rise of Islam *and* Persia in the Islamic Period; *and* Sasanians.]

BIBLIOGRAPHY

Galdieri, Eugenio. *Isfahan: Masgid-i Gum'a.* 3 vols. Rome, 1972–1982. Documents the research and restoration activities in the Friday Mosque by the Istituto Italiano per il Medio ed Estremo Orient of Rome; good photographs.

Gaube, Heinz. *Iranian Cities.* New York, 1979. Examination of three typical Iranian cities—Isfahan, Herat, and Bam—using literary and physical evidence to describe their form and function in the different stages of their growth.

Godard, André. "Iṣfahān." *Athar-è Irān* 2 (1937): 7–176. Earliest publication of the *āteshgāh* and Shahristan bridge.

Golombek, Lisa. "Urban Patterns in Pre-Safavid Isfahan." In *Studies on Isfahan: Proceedings of the Isfahan Colloquium, Part 1,* edited by Renata Holod, pp. 18–44. Iranian Studies, 7. Chestnut Hill, Mass., 1974. Lucid reconstruction from literary sources and firsthand observation of the pre-Safavid city; useful bibliography.

Le Strange, Guy. *Lands of the Eastern Caliphate.* 2d ed. Cambridge, 1930. See Chapter 14 for a complete account of Arab and Persian medieval authors.

Luschey, Heinz. "Zur Datierung der sasanidischen Kapitelle aus Bisutun und des Monuments von Taq-i-Bostan." *Archäologische Mitteilungen aus Iran* 1 (1968): 129–142, pl. 52. Useful for photographs of the two Sasanian capitals said to come from Isfahan and similar capitals from other Sasanian sites.

Minasian, Caro O. *Shah Diz of Isma'ili Fame: Its Siege and Destruction.* London, 1971. Controversial interpretation of what has been identified as the remains of a citadel outside modern Isfahan.

JUDITH LERNER

ISIN, ancient capital of the first dynasty of Isin, situated about 200 km (124 mi.) south–southeast of Baghdad, Iraq, about 20 km (12 mi.) south of Nippur (31° 51′ N, 45° 17′ E). The ruins of Isin cover about 1.5 sq km and are 8 m high. The site's modern name is Išān al-Baḥrīyāt. (J. N. Postgate [1930] has proposed that during the third millennium the site was known as IN^{ki}.) The identification with the ancient city was made by K. Stevenson in 1923. The first brief excavation was carried out in 1924 by the excavators of Kish, A. T. Clay and Stephen Langdon (see P. R. S. Moorey, *Kish Excavations, 1923–1933,* Oxford, 1978). Their trench north of the highest point was rediscovered by a German expedition in 1986, working on behalf of the University of Munich and the Bavarian Academy of Science and supported financially by the German Research Council. From 1973 to 1989, before the Gulf War, eleven seasons of excavation had taken place.

The first king of the first dynasty of Isin, Ishbi-Erra (2017–1985/1953–1921 BCE; middle, or short, chronology) may also have been the founder of the city of Isin. During the first season of excavations by the German team, however, traces of an older occupation were found, especially from the Akkadian period, and quality objects recovered, the oldest of which belong to the Ubaid period (fourth millennium). Ishbi-Erra was a general during the reign of the last ruler of the Ur III dynasty, Ibbi-Sin, prior to becoming king of Isin. According to the Bible, he belonged to the tribe of the so-called Amorites. [*See* Amorites.] These people spoke a West-Semitic dialect as did the later Arameans, Hebrews, and Arabs. Nomads, they invaded southern Mesopotamia from Northern Syria at the end of the third millennium. King Shu-Sin of Ur III built a wall against the Amorites between the Euphrates and Tigris Rivers north of Baghdad, where the distance between the rivers is narrowest. [*See* Ur.] The ruins of this wall, constructed of earth and clay, can still be seen. One of the best-known subtribes of the Amorites (which means "west" in West-Semitic languages), or MAR.TU. (Sum., "west"), were the Benjaminites ("the sons of the south"), mentioned in the Bible with Abraham from Ur in Chaldea. [*See* Chaldeans.] From the Bible, and now also from cuneiform inscriptions, it is known that the home of the Benjaminites was both in the south near Ur and in the north near Harran (*Gn.* 35:18, 24; 42:4, 36; 43:14–16, 29; 34; 44:12; 45:12, 14, 22; 46:27; *Dt.* 33:12; *Jos.*18:20, 28; *Jgs.* 2:21). West-Semitic tribes may have migrated from there into Canaan at the same time the Amorites invaded Mesopotamia. As a result of the biblical name *Canaan,* West-Semitic people in this area were called Canaanites. [*See* Canaanites.]

The best-known of the Amorite kings in Mesopotamia was Hammurabi of the first dynasty of Babylon (1792–1750/1728–1686 BCE). Unfortunately, that level in the city of Babylon has not yet been excavated because the level of groundwater is still too high. [*See* Babylon.] In the sixteenth century BCE, Babylon was conquered by the Hittites under King Muršili I. [*See* Hittites.] The real winners, however, were the Kassites, who may have come from the east (the names of some of their gods resemble those in India in the second millennium BCE), although in Mesopotamia cuneiform letters were used for the Babylonian/Akkadian as well as the Sumerian languages. [*See* Kassites; Cuneiform; Akkadian; Sumerian.] Just before 1000 BCE another West-Semitic people came to Mesopotamia, the so-called Arameans, who established the second dynasty of Isin and whose principal capital was Babylon, rather than Isin. [*See* Arameans.] The Arameans ruled over Babylonia for a long period, until the invasion of the Achaemenids under King Cyrus the Great in 538 BCE.

The primary god of Isin was the goddess Gula, the main goddess of medicine in the Near East and specially favored by the Kassites in the second millennium BCE. [*See* Medicine.] Her temple (60 × 90 m) was discovered at the highest point on the tell. The temple contained two chapels, one of Gula and the other of her husband, Ninurta. The main period of use was during the Kassite period. One of the temple's courtyards was covered with burned clay slabs and had stamp inscriptions of a Kurigalzu of the fourteenth century BCE. The walls were built mainly of sun-dried bricks. This temple was probably founded in the Early Dynastic period (c. 2700 BCE) because at some places below the walls of the Kassite and the Old Babylonian levels burnt and sun-dried bricks, whose shape is plano-convex, were discovered. Clay and St. Langdon had found them in their trench in 1924, as well. The building's most important feature, however, was a large (4 × 3 m) staircase in front of the temple leading to the main entrance. Excavated in the last two seasons (1986, 1989), the staircase is composed of nineteen steps of sun-dried bricks paved with clay. Curiously, the steps showed no traces of use. In front of the staircase an altar or pedestal was built up with reused bricks inscribed with the names of kings of the first dynasty of Isin, such as Bur-Sin (1895–1874/1831–1810 BCE). This staircase was in place from the beginning of the second millennium BCE until the sixth century BCE, when Nebuchadrezzar II (604–562 BCE) restored the Temple of Gula for the last time.

The staircase suggested the existence of a temple tower, the so-called ziggurat, but according to cuneiform texts there was no ziggurat at Isin. [*See* Ziggurat.] The sacred building was also surrounded by a great wall, a temenos, founded by Ishme-Dagan of Isin (1953–1935/1889–1871 BCE) and rebuilt in the Kassite period. The 1986 expedition searched for the second-millennium BCE palace at several locations in the ruins. In the southeast an official building was found from that period with very well made and plastered walls. The buildings ground plan could be compared to that of one of the southern buildings at Tell Asmar, also a structure with official features and significance. At Isin an archive of about eighty tablets was found, mentioning some deliveries to King Enlil-bani (1860–1837/1796–1773 BCE). [*See* Libraries and Archives; Tablet.]

West of the Temple of Gula two larger buildings were excavated during the last two seasons, also with some hints of being a palace. Two inscriptions on seal-impressions mention the king's scribe and brewer. South of the temple, occupation levels from the beginning of the third millennium BCE were discovered just below the surface, with circular offering tables like those at Uruk and Ur from the same period. [*See* Uruk-Warka.]

Outside the city of Isin were several Early Islamic buildings that were in use until the Mongol invasion in the thirteenth century. One of the buildings seems to have been a caravanserai.

The site's small finds were numerous, and some are of very fine quality, especially the cylinder seal from the Akkadian period. [*See* Seals.] In the Temple of Gula a mace head of the Akkadian king Šar-kali-šarri (2223–2198 BCE) was found, dedicated to Gula, the Lady of Isin, an indication of the importance of Isin/IN^{ki} then. The terra-cotta reliefs of the Old Babylonian period found at Isin show new motifs (e.g., representations of ostriches). A curious find from the temple area is a figurine of a kneeling man with his left hand on his back, perhaps either pointing to where he has pain or to where he was healed. The excavation's anthropologist discovered some traces of arteriosclerosis in examining skeletons at Isin. Other corpses showed a blow to the head or stroke injuries. One skull had small artificial openings in the area of the right parietal bone, indicating that a Babylonian doctor had performed a trepanation, but probably only in a postmortem, for cult purposes.

Until the beginning of the twentieth century, the ruins at Isin were surrounded by water, like a marsh *(ḥōr)*, as the modern name shows: Išān al-Baḥrīyāt "monument *(išān)*, which was nearly covered by the sea (baḥrīyāt)." The bones of deer and razorback hogs found at Isin suggest that the region was also a swamp in the past, with brushwood and trees, as those animals could only have existed in such a biotope. Among the animal bones was also a whale bone, an intimation of the legend of the prophet Jonah, who was spewn out of the mouth of such an animal, although farther north, near the Assyrian capital of Nineveh. [*See* Nineveh.] A mosque bearing his name, *Nebi Yunus*, is a reminder of the event.

BIBLIOGRAPHY

Cassin, Elena, et al., eds. *Die Altorientalischen Reiche*. 3 vols. Fischer Weltgeschichte, vols. 2–4. Frankfurt, 1965–1967.

Edzard, Dietz O. *Die "zweite Zwischenzeit" Babyloniens*. Wiesbaden, 1957.

Hrouda, Barthel, ed. *Isin-Išān Baḥrīyāt I–IV*. 4 vols. Munich, 1977–1992.

Postgate, J. N. *Sumer* 30 (1974): 207ff.

BARTHEL HROUDA

ISKANDER, KHIRBET, 7.5-acre site on the northern bank of Wadi el-Wala, in modern Jordan, strategically located on the ancient King's Highway, approximately 24 km (15 mi.) south of Madaba, in what was once northern Moab.

In surveys (Glueck, 1939) and excavations (Parr, 1960) important remains from the Early Bronze IV period (c. 2350–2000 BCE) had been noted at the site. In 1981, 1982, 1984, and 1987, the American Schools of Oriental Research sponsored an excavation at Khirbet Iskander directed by Suzanne Richard, with Drew University, Upsala College, and Seton Hall University as affiliates. Roger Boraas served as associate director in 1982 and 1984. The project's primary research objective was to test the hypothesis that sedentism was an alternative subsistence choice to pastoralism in the Early Bronze Age. Excavation affirmed the hypothesis, even expanding the parameters of sedentism in this alleged "nomadic interlude" to include small fortified towns.

The stratigraphic profile that emerged is tentative and awaits additional excavation and final publication. The best stratigraphic sequence (seven phases thus far) comes from area B at the northwest corner of the site. The earliest, phase G, represented by fragmentary house walls, dates to EB I. Phase F house walls represent the basal EB IV settlement. Phases E–B constitute the EB IV settlement within fortifications. Phase A, therefore, is the final, postfortification EB IV settlement, after which the site was abandoned.

Four distinct phases of the site's fortifications are currently discernible: an inner wall (E), outer wall (D), and two domestic use phases (C–B). The inner wall, of stone and mud brick, was found in a collapsed state. The phase D rebuilding included the inner wall, a new outer wall, a rubble fill, and a square tower with steps, creating a 2.5-meter defense system. Excavation has revealed two interior-use phases thus far, a building complex in phase B and a limited sounding into an earlier domestic level (C). Two contiguous broadrooms formed part of a larger building complex in phase B. In one of the rooms benches line the walls and in the other a stone-lined bin (possibly a *favissa,* or repository for discarded cultic objects) is associated with a fire pit, hearth, decorated offering plate (with the foot of a bovine incised inside), and miniature vessels. These remains as well as the quality and quantity of vessels uncovered in situ suggest a public, possibly cultic function. Also discovered was a range of vessels, including large storejars containing grain, a vat, amphoriskoi, teapots, cups, and jugs.

Destruction debris encased the vessels in phase B, but the reuse of walls in phase A suggests an immediate recovery for the site. The settlement pattern changes from a fortified public complex to a domestic complex of interconnected long- and broadroom houses.

Several houses had blocked pillar walls that were once freestanding. Such pillar construction ties Khirbet Iskander to Negev desert sites such as Har Yeroḥam and Be'er Resisim. [*See* Be'er Resisim.] The style revives in the Iron Age I period. A study of three *tabuns,* querns, grinders, a mortar, and stone tables/benches within these buildings should provide insight into the still enigmatic domestic activities in EB IV.

In Area C, three phases (A–C) of the Gateway were investigated at the southeastern crest. After the destruction of the fortifications, settlement patterning changed here as well, but the transformation was from domestic to public. The excavation exposed twelve squares in the latest phase (C), which comprised monumental, well-constructed guardrooms on either side of a 2.25-meter-wide bench-lined entryway. There were two rows of steps at each end of the plaster-coated passage. This passage was the only access point into the interior of the town, which was discovered when the wall lines were traced that connect this area with the domestic quarter uncovered in area A to the west. The northern steps led to a courtyard and partially paved storage bin. Connected to the guardrooms on both sides is a series of rooms, one of which contained three stone platforms and extensive flint *débitage,* indicative of a specialized work area. Broadroom houses below, in phases B and A, testify to the area's previous domestic nature.

All of the EB IV tombs excavated were of the typical single-shaft, round or square chamber variety, and all contained secondary burials. The surprise discovery was a two-chambered EB I tomb containing thirteen skulls and a variety of pottery (e.g., false-spouted jars, dipper juglets, and duck-handled vessels). When combined with the omphalos base and band-slipped fragments found in phase G in area B, this new and tantalizing tell and tomb data serve to underscore the gap in occupation at Khirbet Iskander during the urban EB II–III periods.

BIBLIOGRAPHY

Glueck, Nelson. *Explorations in Eastern Palestine.* Vol. 3. Annual of the American Schools of Oriental Research, 18/19. New Haven, 1939.

Parr, Peter J. "Excavations at Khirbet Iskander." *Annual of the Department of Antiquities of Jordan* 4–5 (1960): 128–133.

Richard, Suzanne. "Toward a Consensus of Opinion on the End of the Early Bronze Age in Palestine-Transjordan." *Bulletin of the American Schools of Oriental Research,* no. 237 (1980): 5–34.

Richard, Suzanne, and Roger S. Boraas. "Preliminary Report of the 1981–82 Seasons of the Expedition to Khirbet Iskander and Its Vicinity." *Bulletin of the American Schools of Oriental Research,* no. 254 (1984): 63–87.

Richard, Suzanne. "Excavations at Khirbet Iskander, Jordan: A Glimpse at Settled Life during the 'Dark Age' in Palestinian Archaeology." *Expedition* 28.1 (1986): 3–12.

Richard, Suzanne. "The Early Bronze Age: The Rise and Collapse of Urbanism." *Biblical Archaeologist* 50 (1987): 22–43.

Richard, Suzanne, and Roger S. Boraas. "The Early Bronze IV Fortified Site of Khirbet Iskander, Jordan: Third Preliminary Report, 1984 Season." In *Preliminary Reports of ASOR-Sponsored Excavations, 1982–85,* edited by Walter E. Rast, pp. 107–130. Bulletin of the

American Schools of Oriental Research, Supplement no. 25. Baltimore, 1988.
Richard, Suzanne. "The 1987 Expedition to Khirbet Iskander and Its Vicinity: Fourth Preliminary Report." In *Preliminary Reports of ASOR-Sponsored Excavations, 1983–87,* edited by Walter E. Rast, pp. 33–58. Bulletin of the American Schools of Oriental Research, Supplement no. 26. Baltimore, 1990.

SUZANNE RICHARD

ISRAEL. *See* Palestine.

ISRAEL ANTIQUITIES AUTHORITY. Since the Antiquities Authority Law was passed in 1989, the Israel Antiquities Authority (IAA) has been empowered by the government of Israel to administer the nation's Antiquities Law (1978). The IAA assumed the duties of the former Israel Department of Antiquities (IDA) and bears responsibility for all archaeological matters. The IDA was founded in 1948, shortly after the establishment of the State of Israel, and initially was attached to the Ministry of Labor and Construction. It was subsequently transferred to the Ministry of Education and Culture. Under the British Mandate (1917–1948) all archaeological documentation (files, collections, maps, photographs, plans) belonging to the Department of Antiquities had been located in the Jordanian sector of Jerusalem, as was the Palestine Archaeological Museum and its research library. Starting from scratch, the IDA set up six departments responsible for inspection, conservation excavations and surveys, museums, archives and library, and research and publications. It enlisted the assistance of archaeology enthusiasts throughout the country in reporting discoveries of remains, increasing the department's ability to record sites and antiquities and enhance awareness of the need for antiquities protection.

In its formative years, IDA staff included Shmuel Yeivin, director; Immanuel Ben-Dor, deputy director; P.L.O. Guy, director of excavations and surveys; Jacob Pinkerfeld, conservator of monuments and acting chief inspector of antiquities; Michael Avi-Yonah, scientific secretary and acting inspector of antiquities in Jerusalem; Penuel Kahane, inspector of regional museums; Yaʿaqov Ory, inspector of antiquities in the southern district; Ruth Amiran, inspector of antiquities in the northern district; and Milka Cassuto, head library clerk. Through 1989, the IDA directors were Avraham Biran (1961–1974), Avraham Eitan (1974–1988), and Amir Drori (1988–1989). Technical support staff in the form of surveyors, photographers, illustrators, and restorers was brought into the department, as were physical anthropologists and lab personnel. In the 1980s a special team was assembled to prevent the robbery of antiquities from known and previously unknown sites.

Among the largest excavations in which the department was involved were those at Tel Dan, Tel Ashdod, ʿEin-Gedi, Ḥammath-Gader, Beth-Shean, and Beth-Guvrin. A large survey project, the Negev Rescue Survey, was in operation from 1978 to 1988, overseeing rescue excavations and surveys conducted as a result of the peace treaty with Egypt and the subsequent redeployment of the Israel Defense Forces in the Negev desert. Large rescue excavation projects were undertaken at Biqʿat ʿUvdah, Ramat Maṭred, and in the Tel Malḥata area during the survey.

The IDA had been involved in hundreds of rescue excavations, as well as in joint excavations with the Hebrew University and the Israel Exploration Society in Jerusalem and in other parts of the country. The Archaeological Survey of Israel began its work in 1964, and, since 1967, the office of the staff officer for archaeology for Judea and Samaria has also conducted numerous rescue excavations and surveys.

The Antiquities Authority Law enumerates the functions of the IAA as follows:

- *Custodianship of archaeological sites.* Some fifteen thousand sites are currently known as the result of large-scale archaeological surveys. The country is divided into four regional districts, each overseen by a district archaeologist and a team of archaeological assistants.
- *Excavations.* Land excavations, salvage excavations, underwater excavations, surveys, and the issuing of excavation permits for local and foreign expeditions are the jurisdiction of the IAA. In the eighteen months preceeding July 1993, the IAA was involved in more than two hundred salvage excavations, employing a staff of more than two hundred and fifty archaeologists. Large rescue excavations were conducted where housing was being prepared for Russian and other immigrants in Jerusalem, Beersheba, Ashkelon, and Beth-Shemesh. Long-term archaeological excavations directed by the IAA were conducted for purposes of tourism at Banias, Beth-Shean, Caesarea, Beth-Guvrin, Mareshah (Marisa), and ʿEin-Ḥaṣeva. Many important archaeological excavations have also recently been conducted by the archaeological institutes at Israeli universities (The Hebrew University of Jerusalem at Tel Dor and Tel Hazor; Tel Aviv University at sites in the Golan; Ben-Gurion University of the Negev at Tel Haror; and the University of Haifa at Ḥatula, Caesarea, and Tabun) as well as by academic institutions from the United States (the Harvard University expedition at Ashkelon), France (at Tel Yarmut), Japan (at ʿEin-Gev), and other countries. IAA staff includes experts in the fields of prehistory, physical anthropology, paleobotany, paleozoology, petrography, and carbon-14 dating.
- *Theft.* Preventing the theft of antiquities and monitoring antiquities dealers is the responsibility of a special IAA unit. There are regular patrols and inspection of all sites and regions as well as periodic visits to dealers.

- *Laboratories.* The IAA operates scientific laboratories for preservation and restoration. Metal, glass, and ceramic artifacts are preserved and restored as well as photographed and drawn for purposes of documentation.
- *Curatorship.* The curating, documentation, and storage of more than one million artifacts produced by excavations or by chance have been carried out by the IAA and tens of thousands have been lent to museums for permanent or temporary display. The Dead Sea Scrolls are part of this patrimony.
- *Documentation and recording.* Archaeological information is recorded and documented by site, including data from the period of the British Mandate. All archaeological material from IAA endeavors is organized, consolidated, and classified in a national database.
- *Public education.* The IAA is responsible for the initiation and management of projects designed to promote public awareness and care for antiquities both in the society at large and throughout the educational system.
- *Publications.* Major archaeological reports, articles, and notices are regularly published. Excavation reports were first published in *ʿAtiqot* in 1955; in the original format there were separate English and Hebrew volumes—nineteen English and ten Hebrew volumes were published through 1990. Seven volumes have appeared in the new combined English/Hebrew format. *Ḥadashot Arkheologiyot* has appeared in Hebrew since 1961 and the equivalent *Excavations and Surveys in Israel* (English translations) has appeared since 1982. Maps from the Archaeological Survey of Israel and the Negev Emergency Survey (six maps from areas in northern Israel, including ʿAtlit, Haifa, and Maʿanit; four maps from Judea (Judah) and the central part of the country, including Herodium and the hill country of Benjamin; and eight Negev maps that include the Sede Boqer and Miṣpe Ramon areas) have also been published. Guidebooks to sites such as Tiberias, Chorazin, and Maʿale Adumin and a book called *Highlights of Recent Excavations* have also been published.
- *Library.* A scientific library for the discipline of archaeology and related subjects is presently housed at the Rockefeller Museum in Jerusalem.
- *Preservation, restoration, and site development.* Several teams of restorers, architects, and engineers form the department responsible for preservation and restoration. Site development involves preparing the site for visitors and includes reconstruction activities as well as the preparation of explanatory signs and promotional material on the history of the site, and so forth.

The IAA's annual budget includes a $9-million base granted by Israel's Treasury Department through the Ministry of Education. A similar sum is generated by various excavations and projects through the Ministry of Tourism and by regional authorities for local development projects. The conservation and restoration of Israel's archaeological heritage has assumed primary importance among the IAA's tasks and has thus enjoyed a considerable portion of its resources. Some fifty sites throughout the country are currently under the care of IAA preservation teams, among them Tel Dan; Banias; Mt. Berenice in Tiberias; Caesarea; Beth-Guvrin, Mareshah (Marisa); an aqueduct on the Hebron Road, Malḥa (the new site of the Biblical Zoo), and Mamilla near the Jaffa Gate in Jerusalem; the synagogue at ʿEin-Gedi; Yeroḥam; ʿEin-ʿEvrona; and Timnaʿ. In managing and developing archaeological sites that will attract the general public and show visitors tangible evidence of Israel's past, the IAA attempts to minimize reconstruction and preserve site integrity. A new IAA project is the ʿEin-Ya'el Living Museum in the Jerusalem hills. The museum uses an archaeological site as the setting for educational seminars and workshops in ancient crafts. The IAA is involved in incorporating the many archaeological sites uncovered as a result of the rapid growth of new Jerusalem suburban neighborhoods into area parks.

[*Most of the sites mentioned are the subject of independent entries. See also* Israel Exploration Society; Survey of Israel; *and the biographies of Avi-Yonah, Guy, and Yeivin.*]

BIBLIOGRAPHY

See *Sefer HaChukkim* 885 (10 February 1978): 76–83, for the Antiquities Law, 5738–1978; and *Sefer HaChukkim* 1283 (3 August 1989): 88–94, for the Antiquities Authority Law, 5749–1989, both passed by the Israeli parliament.

RUDOLPH COHEN

ISRAEL EXPLORATION SOCIETY. On 7 November 1913, the first general meeting of the Jewish Palestine Exploration Society (which became the Israel Exploration Society in 1948) was convened by a group of Jewish intellectuals living in Ottoman Palestine. Until that time investigation of the ancient land of Israel had been the monopoly of foreign scholars and expeditions. In addition to a lecture that evening by Isaiah Press on "The History of Research in the Land of Israel," the program included an address by the society's chairman, the educator David Yellin, who stressed to the audience that the responsibility of a reborn people in the land of the Patriarchs was to recover its material past and to leave behind "for the generations to come" evidence of the "holy books," which are "the inheritance of the whole world."

Although the outbreak of World War I brought a halt to the society's activities, it was reestablished in 1920 under the direction of Nahum Slouschz, an archaeologist, historian, and scholar of Hebrew literature. The society's statutes proclaimed that it would hold lectures and seminars (many geared to the general public), establish a library and a museum in Jerusalem that would be the basis of an institute for the exploration of Palestine, organize tours, carry out scientific excavations, and publish a scientific periodical, books, and pamphlets.

To meet the society's most urgent need, the raising of funds, committees of philanthropic Jews were formed in the United States, London, Paris, The Hague, and Egypt. By 1923, the society could report to the American committee that three excavations were underway and that the ruins of the ancient synagogue at Hammath Tiberias had been cleared. The first ancient menorah discovered in Palestine was found at Hammath Tiberias (the Israel Exploration Society subsequently chose it for its logo). A museum with a specialized library that had been built in 1922 housed the finds from these first excavations, including the menorah and a fine collection of ancient Palestinian coins. This collection eventually formed the nucleus of the archaeology section of the country's national museum in Jerusalem, The Israel Museum. In 1926, the library was moved to the newly formed Department of Archaeology at the Hebrew University of Jerusalem.

In a story published on 6 March 1924, *The London Times Weekly Edition* gave international recognition to Slouschz's work in Absalom's Tomb and adjacent sepulchral monuments in Jerusalem's Kidron Valley. In 1925, also under the society's auspices, Eleazar Lipa Sukenik and L. A. Mayer began an excavation of the Third Wall in Jerusalem, a project critical to determining Jerusalem's boundaries in the first centuries BCE and CE.

Arab insurrections between 1929 and 1931 resulted in a temporary suspension of activity, but it was renewed in full force in the 1930s with excavations by Benjamin Maisler (Mazar) and Moshe Stekelis at Ramat Raḥel, and by Maisler at Beth-Sheʿarim, in addition to other, smaller projects. In 1934 the society opened the Institute for the Exploration of the Land of Israel in Tel Aviv, but renewed hostilities in 1936 made convening its classes unfeasible.

Within a decade of its foundation and despite shortages of funds, the society had issued five important publications, including two volumes of its *Qobetz* series and E. Brandenburg's comprehensive study on 160 caves in the Jerusalem area. What began with the *Qobetz* series was continued in 1933 by *Yediot: Bulletin of the Jewish Palestine Exploration Society,* the society's first attempt to publish a quarterly devoted entirely to studies of the Land of Israel. In 1968 it was replaced by a new quarterly, *Qadmoniot: Quarterly for the Antiquities of Eretz-Israel and Bible Lands.*

In the 1940s, lectures, conferences, and excavations were held without interruption, in spite of the world war and the hostilities that surrounded the founding of the State of Israel in May 1948. Scholars and the general public attended the society's first annual conference in Jerusalem in 1943; its fifth annual conference was held in war-scarred Jerusalem in 1948. With independence, the society became the Israel Exploration Society (IES), under the direction of Maisler (Mazar). For the IES, Maisler carried out the first excavation under the new state at Tell Qasile, near Tel Aviv. To communicate to foreign scholars the results of Israeli scientific investigations in the field, in 1951 the first volume of the English-language quarterly, the *Israel Exploration Journal (IEJ),* was published. In that same year, the IES initiated a Hebrew (with English summaries) festschrift series, *Eretz-Israel: Archaeological, Historical and Geographical Studies.* The names of many of the society's founding members, whose work was fundamental to research into the land of Israel, appear as editors and contributors on the covers of the issues.

In 1955 the IES mounted the first large-scale archaeological expedition carried out by local archaeologists at Hazor, under the direction of Yigael Yadin of the Hebrew University of Jerusalem. It was Israeli archaeology's first "field school" and its staff members now rank among the country's leading archaeologists. In 1960 the IES organized another large-scale expedition, this time to the Judean Desert Caves. Staffed by Yadin, Yohanan Aharoni, Pessah Bar-Adon, and Nahman Avigad; coordinated by the IES director, Joseph Aviram; and assisted by the Israeli army, the expedition was an organizational feat. Its purpose was to probe caves plundered by bedouins searching for ancient manuscripts. The IES subsequently played a central role in the excavation of the Israelite citadel and Early Bronze Age city of Arad, the Herodian palace-fortress at Masada, the Temple Mount and Upper City in Jerusalem, Beth-Shean, Aphek, Herodium, Lachish, Dor, Elusa, and other sites. Forty-seven years after it was issued a license to excavate the City of David, the ancient kernal of Jerusalem, on its southeastern hill, the IES sponsored Yigal Shiloh's archaeological expedition there. [*See* Jerusalem.]

In a country where numerous institutions deal with the study of the land, the publications of the IES represent authoritatively the fields of Palestinian archaeology and related studies. In addition to its periodicals (see above), the IES publishes excavation reports (Hazor, Masada, and the Judean Desert expeditions) and special studies both in Hebrew and English.

The IES's annual conferences are intended for the general public, and another annual meeting, during which the latest discoveries are reported, caters to the country's archaeologists. The IES has sponsored two international congresses on biblical archaeology (1984, 1990) in which the state of the art was reviewed and debated by the international scholarly community.

In 1989, seventy-six years after it was established and forty-one years after the creation of the State of Israel, the IES and its director, Joseph Aviram, received the prestigious Israel Prize. It acknowledged the IES as the country's principal and most effective institution for furthering knowledge of its archaeology and history both at home and abroad.

[*See also* History of the Field, *article on* Archaeology in

Israel; *and the biographies of Aharoni, Avigad, Mazar, Shiloh, Stekelis, Sukenik, and Yadin. In addition, most of the sites mentioned are the subject of independent entries.*]

BIBLIOGRAPHY

Amiran, Ruth. *Ancient Pottery of the Holy Land* (1963). New Brunswick, N.J., 1970.

Amiran, Ruth. *Early Arad,* vol. 1, *The Chalcolithic Settlement and Early Bronze Age City, First–Fifth Seasons of Excavations, 1962–1966.* Jerusalem, 1978.

Amitai, Janet, ed. *Biblical Archaeology Today: Proceedings of the International Congress on Biblical Archaeology, Jerusalem, April 1984.* Jerusalem, 1985.

Avigad, Nahman. *Hebrew Bullae from the Time of Jeremiah: Remnants of a Burnt Archive.* Jerusalem, 1986.

Aviram, Joseph, et al., eds. *Masada: The Yigael Yadin Excavations, 1963–1965, Final Reports.* 4 vols. Jerusalem, 1989–1994.

Ben-Tor, Amnon, ed. *Hazor III–IV: An Account of the Third and Fourth Seasons of Excavation, 1957–1958.* Jerusalem, 1989.

Biran, Avraham, and Joseph Aviram, eds. *Biblical Archaeology Today, 1990: Proceedings of the Second International Congress on Biblical Archaeology, Jerusalem, June–July 1990.* Jerusalem, 1993.

Finkelstein, Israel. *The Archaeology of the Israelite Settlement.* Jerusalem, 1988.

Judean Desert Caves, Survey and Excavations: The Expedition to the Judean Desert, 1960–1961. 2 vols. Jerusalem, 1960–1961.

Kempinski, Aharon, and Ronny Reich, eds. *The Architecture of Ancient Israel: From the Prehistoric to the Persian Periods.* Jerusalem, 1992.

Mazar, Benjamin. *The Early Biblical Period: Historical Studies.* Edited by Shmuel Ahituv and Baruch Levine. Jerusalem, 1986.

Stern, Ephraim, et al., eds. *The New Encyclopedia of Archaeological Excavations in the Holy Land.* 4 vols. Jerusalem and New York, 1993.

Yadin, Yigael, et al. *Hazor: An Account of the Excavations, 1955–1958.* 4 vols. in 3. Jerusalem, 1958–1961.

Yadin, Yigael. *The Finds from the Bar Kokhba Period in the Cave of Letters.* Jerusalem, 1963.

Yadin, Yigael. *The Temple Scroll.* 3 vols. Jerusalem, 1983.

JANET AMITAI

ISRAELITES. The name *Israel* is used to designate the entirety of the people as well as the political entity formed by this people. In every instance what the term embraces is subject to historically determined variations.

Nomenclature. "The people" is understood as the amalgamation of twelve tribes, each of which is traced back to a tribal father. Their common father is Jacob, who, as a logical consequence, is renamed Israel (*Gn.* 32:23–33). The Israelite people are thus fictitiously traced back to an ancestor of the same name. This construction presupposes the political union of the tribes under the kingdom; consequently, the use of the name as a designation for the people first dates from the period of the monarchy. At the same time, the name *Israel* is most often used for the ten northern tribes, in contrast to Judah (*2 Sm.* 3:10, 5:5, etc.). After the division of the kingdom in 927 BCE, the name *Israel* is used to designate the northern kingdom. With the demise of the northern kingdom in 722 BCE, the name is also used to refer to Judah (*2 Chr.* 11:3, 21:2). After the end of Judah in 587 BCE, Israel becomes a religious definition in order to differentiate the people who worship Yahweh from the surrounding peoples. [*See* Judah.]

In contrast to the more than twenty-five hundred references to Israel in the Bible, there are only a few extrabiblical ones. The oldest mention is found on the Israel stela of Pharaoh Merneptah (1213–1203 BCE), where the name was represented in the so-called group writing as *ysr'r* (*ANET* 378). According to Helmut Engel (arguing against Gösta Ahlström, 1986), the determinative points to the fact that, in contrast to the previously mentioned cities of Ashkelon, Gezer, and Yenoʿam, the reference is to a population group in the region of the land of Canaan. The spelling *yśr'l* in the Moabite Mesha inscription from the ninth century BCE (*ANET* 320ff.) and the Aramaic stela fragment from Dan (Biran and Naveh, 1993) corresponds to the biblical spelling and is evidence for the general use of the Assyrian form *sir-'i-la-a-a,* from the time of Shalmaneser III (shortly after 853 BCE) (*ANET* 278ff.). [*See* Moabite Stone; Dan.] The name is constructed with the theophoric element *El;* the verbal element is formed using the root *yśr,* whose meaning is unclear because of a lack of evidence. In the folk-etymological explanation in *Genesis* 32:29, the name is linked with *śrh,* "to fight." For the time being the etymology must remain open.

Origins. The name is not attested in the Bible for the prestate period; Israel as a nation-state is not historically understandable before 1000 BCE. However, the Egyptian reference shows that there must have been a population element with this name, although no closer determination is possible either ethnically or with respect to geographic settlement. The Song of Deborah (*Jgs.* 5:13–18) names a total of ten tribes, which to be sure did not form a political unity but were nevertheless pledged to common action in case of war on behalf of Yahweh. With two exceptions, the names are identical with those in the later system of twelve tribes: Ephraim, Benjamin, Machir, Zebulon, Issachar, Reuben, Gilead, Dan, Asher, and Naphtali. These tribes did not form a political unit and did not have control over a self-contained settlement area; however, they were later merged into the totality of the Israelite people.

The origin of the Israelite tribes is unknown. The biblical story of a long stay in Egypt is fiction. Locating the emergence of Israel as a people in Egypt in a time period lacking precise description shows that no unified tradition existed concerning the origin of the people. A reconstruction of Israel as an ethnic unit in the prestate period is purely hypothetical. Because the report in *Joshua* 1–12 of the conquering of the land is similarly not historical, two different models, with various modifications—the "revolution" model and the "immigration" model—have been developed recently to explain the occupation of the land; each also explains the origin of these new population groups, replacing older "conquest" models.

The revolution model (Mendenhall, 1962, 1970; Got-

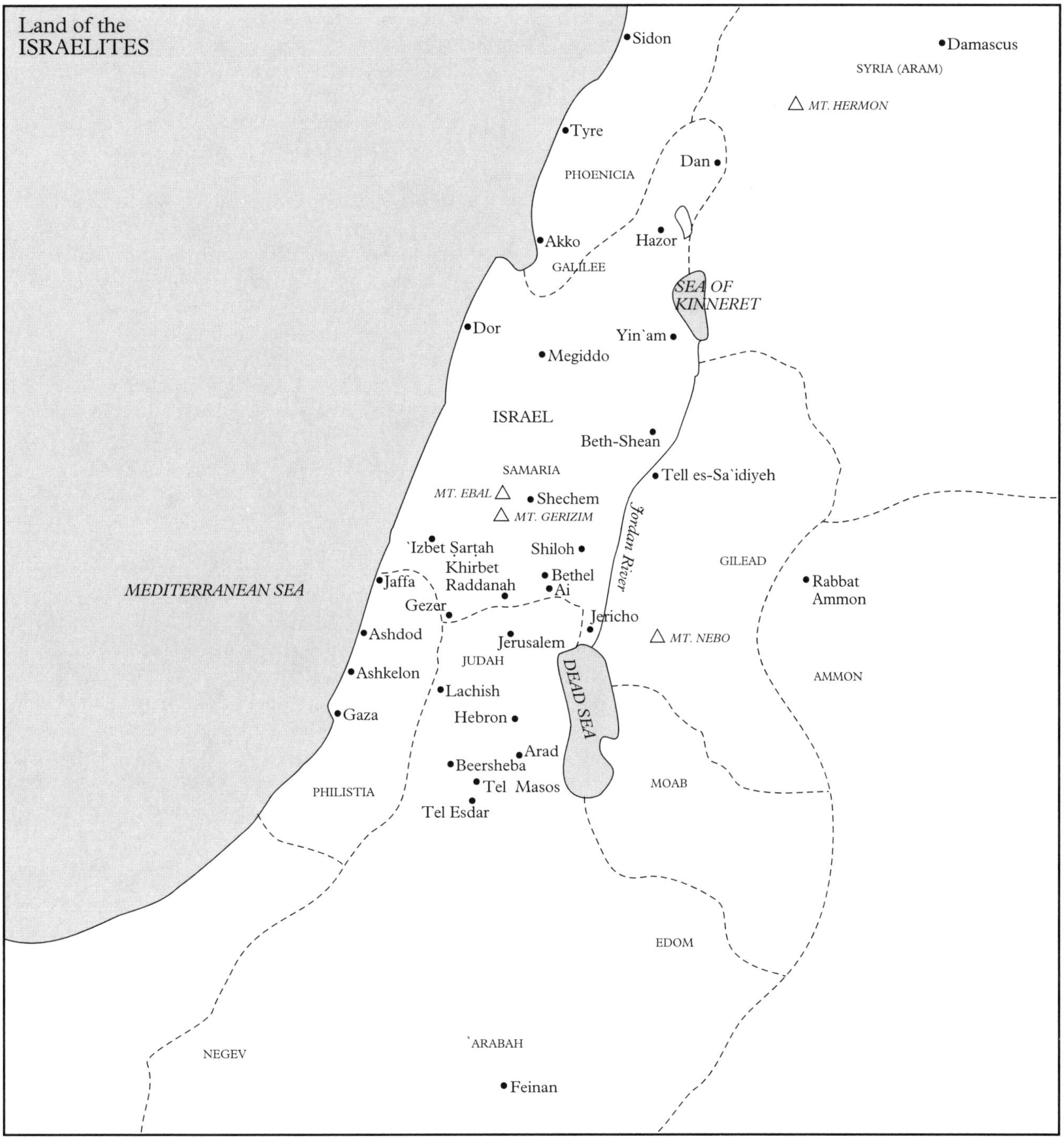

twald, 1979; Lemche, 1985) postulated a social revolution within the Canaanite city-states at the end of the Late Bronze Age. This radical change resulted in the ruling class losing power and the lower class becoming independent. The latter group then left the urban centers and founded new settlements outside the previously settled areas. This thesis explains the downfall of the city-states as a revolutionary event and identifies the population of the new settlements as Canaanites, who certainly modified their life-style and social structure but nevertheless retained their economic form and material culture. The immigration model (Alt, 1989; Finkelstein, 1988; Fritz, 1987) postulates a nomadic population outside of the Canaanite city-states, with which they engaged in economic and cultural exchanges. With the collapse of the urban centers, this symbiotic relationship of the nomadic groups and the cities necessarily came to an end. Therefore, the groups outside the cities were forced to form fixed settlements in order to feed themselves by practicing agriculture and stock breeding. Thus, a modification of the economic system was connected with a modification of lifestyle. The inhabitants of the new settlements were from elements formerly in the areas surrounding the cities, but it is impossible to determine their ethnic identity any more closely than that. Possibilities include the underprivileged groups called ʿApiru (Ḫapiru) in sources, or the nomads also named in the texts, of which the Shasu *(šȝsw)* were the most important group.

The historical processes for the Israelite tribes developing from the Canaanite population or from groups outside the city-states are, however, largely obscure, making it impossible to choose between the hypotheses. The archaeological remains also give no certain data regarding the origin of the inhabitants in the new settlements. The variety in settlement patterns and construction forms supports the idea of a mixed population. Thus, it seems entirely possible to combine the two hypotheses. Both forms of development are conceivable and could have taken place in a parallel fashion. Following the collapse of the Canaanite city-states, portions of the Canaanite population could very well have sought other habitation sites. At the same time, the nomadic populations in the vicinity of the cities could have been forced to occupy new settlement areas. In any case, the various elements of the population were not cut off from each other but were, rather, involved in many forms of exchange, which were continually altered in form and content. The final destruction of most of the cities, which took place no later than the first half of the twelfth century BCE, altered the previous ways of life so radically that all the groups living in the land were forced to give up their familiar way of life to found and occupy new settlement sites. Because the two hypotheses complement each other in explaining the development of the new settlements, they can also be used to reconstruct the historical processes.

Settlements. In comparison with the Late Bronze Age cities, the distribution of the Iron Age I settlements presents a completely different picture. Not only has the number of settlements greatly increased, but they are also generally located outside the spheres of influence of the former city-states, in areas that were only sporadically settled or completely unsettled during the second millennium BCE. The preferred regions for the settlements, which generally had a size of only 0.5–1 ha (1–2.5 acres), are Galilee, the central hill country, the Negev desert, and the cultivated strip along the middle of the east bank of the Jordan River. However, even in layout and size, the Early Iron Age settlements are fundamentally different from the Canaanite cities because of their lack of large-scale palaces and temples. [*See* Palace; Temples, *article on* Syro-Palestinian Temples.] In addition, the settlements are as a rule unfortified, even in those cases where the houses located on the perimeter are laid out in the form of a fortification ring. The settlements are characterized by an ad hoc plan, as well as by the presence of numerous silos and cisterns. [*See* Cisterns.] Three types of settlement can be differentiated on the basis of their layout.

1. *Ring-form settlements.* Houses organized in a circle or an oval, which created a central open area, are known as ring-form settlements. Examples were found at Tel Esdar stratum III, ʿIzbet Ṣarṭah stratum III, and Beersheba stratum VII.

2. *Nucleated villages.* Settlements characterized as having been built up randomly, either with individual houses or with complexes consisting of several buildings, are known as nucleated villages. There may be streets of varying width or irregularly shaped open areas between the various units. The arrangement of the houses is completely unplanned, and the settlement is open on the perimeter. The settlements of Ai, Khirbet Raddanah, ʿIzbet Ṣarṭah stratum II, Tel Masos stratum II, and Beersheba stratum VI are examples of this type.

3. *Farmsteads.* Individual buildings or a group of buildings surrounded by a wall and that may have had a certain protective function are known as farmsteads. The remains at Beit Jala and on Mt. Ebal are freestanding farmsteads.

Architecture. With the exception of the architecture, the material culture of the Early Iron Age shows a strong continuity with that of the preceding Late Bronze Age period. Only the house construction—the so-called "four-room" house—shows a certain originality. Even if the construction types are supposed not to have been deeply rooted in the Late Bronze Age, the almost complete lack of courtyard houses and the development of new forms of construction give the Iron Age I a distinctive cultural stamp. Irrespective of the differences in the type of settlement, it is possible to determine the development of a few house types that became common in Iron II as well.

1. *Broadroom houses.* While it is true that broadroom houses occur only occasionally, they are by no means restricted to ring-form settlements. Their distinguishing characteristic is the position of the entrance on the long side of the building. Originally, this type was a single-roomed house; however, it could also be divided by stone pillars along its length and was provided with small rooms separated by diagonal walls.

2. *Pillar houses.* As rare as the broadroom house, the pillar house is a rectangular building with the entrance on the narrow side. It is divided along its length by two rows of stone pillars. Of the three long rooms formed in this fashion, the middle room is wider than the two side rooms. This part was presumably not roofed and was therefore an open courtyard.

3. *Three- and four-room houses.* Residential architecture is primarily characterized by three- and four-room houses that often are arranged in a row next to each other. [*See* Four-room House.] The "four-room house" indicates a building that, like the pillar house, is divided by two rows of stone pillars along its length, but that has an additional room

situated on the side opposite the entrance. The room extends across the entire width of the house. The designation "four-room house" is misleading, insofar as the central area was an open courtyard providing air and light for the other rooms. The basic conception could be varied by interior and exterior structures, as well as by changes in construction; however, the ubiquitousness of the plan shows that it was a firmly established type. The three-room house is simply a variant of this construction form, in which there is only one side room next to the courtyard.

These three forms of residential house are closely related typologically, but no clear derivation has yet been established. In spite of their courtyards, the Iron Age houses are fundamentally different from the courtyard house in their use of stone pillars and in the arrangement of the rooms. Although the LB courtyard house cannot possibly be the model for the form of the residential house in the Iron Age, in LB cities there are occasional instances of buildings divided by rows of stone pillars. Even if this form of room construction represents an exception, it is still possible in the last analysis to trace the division of rectangular rooms by stone pillars back to the Canaanite culture. However, the predominance of this construction type and its almost exclusive use in the Early Iron Age is new. The broadroom house, the pillar house, and the four-room house are all characteristic of the Early Iron Age settlements. It is striking that up to the present time there is still no evidence of cult buildings for the period. There may have been sacred structures outside the settlements, but so far there is no clear proof of any.

Ceramics. The ceramic repertoire of the Late Bronze Age was taken over and developed in the Iron Age. In the process, decoration with geometric patterns and mythological motifs disappeared almost completely. Slip and burnish became new techniques for surface treatment. Apart from changes in its design, the cooking pot was provided with two handles, and a pot with a narrow opening was developed from the jug. Some forms, such as the jug with a spout and the collar-rim jar were not used after the end of Iron I. [*See* Ceramics, *article on* Syro-Palestinian Ceramics of the Neolithic, Bronze, and Iron Ages.]

Metallurgy. In metalworking as well the Canaanite tradition was carried on in the beginning; this is demonstrated especially by the Early Iron Age hoards found in the old urban centers of Megiddo, Beth-Shean, and Tell es-Saʿidiyeh. [*See* Megiddo; Beth-Shean; Saʿidiyeh, Tell-es.] However, even in the new settlements weapons and tools were manufactured from bronze using older methods and designs. As a new form, the bowed fibula was adopted from the Aegean area during Iron II. After the collapse of foreign trade at the end of the Late Bronze Age, the raw material presumably came from the only known deposits in the country, at Feinan, on the east edge of the ʿArabah. [*See* Feinan.] In the case of many tools and weapons, however, bronze was gradually replaced by iron. Above all knives, sickles, daggers, and swords were made exclusively from iron from the tenth century BCE onward because the blades could be sharpened better and were stronger. The prerequisite for this changeover was the development of a new technology for tempering iron. The early manufacture of steel resulted from forging in conjunction with heating in a charcoal fire, so that the iron was carburized. The carbon gave a greater strength to the iron, making it superior to bronze. [*See* Metals, *article on* Neolithic, Bronze, and Iron Ages.]

Language. In the Early Iron Age villages the population most probably spoke an early form of Hebrew. It is true that long inscriptions are lacking, but the core portion of the Song of Deborah (*Jgs.* 5:12ff.) permits the conclusion. In any case, this song remains the only text from the prestate period. From the tenth century BCE onward, the Hebrew language is attested by both biblical and extrabiblical sources. Like Canaanite, Phoenician, and Aramaic, Hebrew is one of the northwest group of Semitic languages. As numerous other Northwest Semitic idioms, Hebrew was written with an alphabetic script that consisted only of consonants. This had been developed in the southern Levant during the course of the second millennium BCE. In contrast to the syllabic script of Egypt and Mesopotamia, the alphabetic script represented an innovation and a simplification. Based on an acrophonic principle (every symbol reproduces the sound of the first letter of the word after which it is named), it reduces the written characters to the number of sounds present in a language. The oldest documentation for this form of writing in Hebrew is the ostracon from ʿIzbet Ṣarṭah. This abecedary, or handwriting exercise, consists of five lines scratched onto a fragment of pottery (ostracon); the bottom line reproduces the letters of the Hebrew alphabet—with the exception of *mem*—in the sequence still used today, although *ʿayin* and *pe* have traded places. [*See* Ostracon.] The letters are written by an unpracticed hand from left to right and are in the tradition of the Proto-Canaanite script, as it is attested by short inscriptions from the Canaanite cities. [*See* Hebrew Language and Literature.]

Urbanization. After the foundation of the kingdom, there was a wave of urbanization under David and Solomon that led to the dissolution of the village form of settlement in Iron II. This reurbanization continued during the course of the United Monarchy. Building the new cities corresponded to the requirements for the new state to consolidate its power internally and externally. Because different requirements governed the location of the city, there was continued development only in exceptional cases. To found a city it was necessary to have a nearby source of living water, arable land in the vicinity; and a strategic location in terms of defense and commercial and other traffic. These had been the prerequisites for the Canaanite cities, so it is not surprising that a number of Iron Age cities were founded on Bronze Age tells. Furthermore, the Canaanite settlements that had survived the collapse of the culture were included in the newly formed kingdom of David and Solomon.

Based on their layout, the cities can be divided into four groups: (1) residential cities; (2) cities with limited administrative or military function; (3) administrative or military centers; and (4) royal cities. [*For details, see* Cities, *article on* Cities of the Bronze and Iron Ages.] In spite of their differences, these various types of cities reveal a series of common characteristics. In plan they are round or oval, which is determined by the character of the topography (they were erected either on a mountaintop or on an older tell—sloping sites and or sites on spurs are rare. The city was surrounded by a strong ring of walls, where various fortification elements, such as massive walls, casemate walls, and projecting towers, could be utilized. As a rule, the city's single gate took on civil functions in the absence of other large buildings. In residential construction, the three- and four-room houses predominated, but public buildings were laid out as pillar houses; in addition there were palace structures. Numerous cities were equipped with their own water-supply systems, a significant technical achievement.

Urban foundations at the outset of the kingdom were planned. A state with the desire to expand must factor in the need for defense and take appropriate measures. The new phase of urbanization in Israel that coincided with the formation of the state reflects the strong desire to structure the country politically. The settlements were fitted inside a ring of walls in order to offer the inhabitants a certain measure of security in case of attack. The technical execution of those fortifications was adopted from the country's construction tradition and topography.

Economy. In the prestate period, as during the monarchy, the economy was based on farming and stock breeding. Agriculture was not restricted to growing grain, but included vineyards and olive groves. Sheep and goats were the primary livestock, although cattle accounted for about a fourth of the livestock raised. In any case, planting based on rainfall and a mixed economy must be assumed. The foodstuffs produced were mainly for direct consumption; any excess would have been exchanged for finished goods from craftspeople: primarily ceramics, weapons, bronze and iron tools, and jewelry.

Society. In the Early Iron Age settlements social differences seem not to have been very marked, inasmuch as the overall construction is very homogeneous. In spite of this uniformity, a certain social stratification must be postulated. Ownership is ownership of land, and this could vary in size. For example, the story of Nabal (*1 Sm.* 25) shows that there were already large landholders in Israel in the prestate period. The amount of land under cultivation determined economic strength, and this in turn determined social standing. With the advent of the kingdom, the social structure was modified to the extent that the king and his entourage occupied the highest position. Responsibilities connected to administration and military obligations demanded, on the one hand, the possession of land as crown estate and, on the other, a contribution from the people in the form of taxes in goods and services. This could lead to the appropriation of the property of the individual and in the long run to an overall restructuring of all relationships relating to property. In any case, changes in ownership, in the final analysis, necessarily resulted in a change in the social order.

The king had not only political, but also economic power; possession of land, contributions, and services secured his supremacy, in which the members of his entourage shared. Farmers could make up for the necessary contributions only by cutting back on their own needs or through increased cultivation. Because only large landholders were able to increase the amount of land in production and the size of their work force, the kingdom necessarily led to a two-class society: an economically powerful, but small, upper class and the mass of small farmers whom debt could reduce to the status of slaves.

Monarchy to Exile. Under pressure from the Philistines, the Israelite tribes formed a state by raising Saul to the kingship. In the beginning this consisted only of cooperation in common military endeavors. David was the first leader to provide the kingdom with the necessary stability by eliminating the Philistine threat and by subduing the neighboring states of Ammon, Moab, and Edom, as well as the small Aramaic principalities. [*See* Ammon; Moab; Edom; Arameans.] Through personal union David united not only the dominion over Judah, but also the kingdom of Israel over the northern tribes and the royal status of the city of Jerusalem that he had conquered (*2 Sm.* 2:1–4, 5:1–10). Under his son and successor, Solomon, there followed the consequent elaboration of the state in the realm of internal politics. With Solomon's death, the kingdom David had built fell apart because the vassals defected; its division into the two kingdoms of Israel and Judah followed (1 *Kgs.* 11, 12). Of the two kingdoms, Israel was at first the stronger economically, and all of Judah's attempts to reestablish the unity of the kingdom failed because of Israel's military superiority. A peace arrangement was not established until the ninth century BCE, when it was sealed by the marriage of Jehoram, heir to the throne of Judah, to the Israelite princess Athaliah, one of the daughters of Ahab (2 *Kgs.* 8:18). In the course of the western campaigns of the Assyrians in the eighth century BCE, Israel was conquered by Tiglath-Pileser III; a large portion of the territory of the state was incorporated into the Assyrian kingdom as the provinces of Dor, Megiddo, and Gilead. [*See* Assyrians; Dor; Gilead.] In 722 BCE, the conquest of the capital city of Samaria meant the end of the northern kingdom of Israel. The remaining area was set up under direct Assyrian administration as the province of Samaria. In Judah, the kingdom continued to exist under Assyrian rule until the Assyrians were replaced by the Babylonians. With the seizure of Jerusalem by Nebuchadrezzar in 586 BCE, however, the king was exiled to Babylon. With the Exile, the kingdom ruled by the dynasty David founded came to an end. After their loss of sovereignty, the populations of the states of Israel and Judah and their neighbors lived in exile both inside and outside the country under the changing rule of the great powers that succeeded each other in turn. Until its destruction in 70 CE, the Temple in Jerusalem that Solomon had founded and that was newly reerected after the Exile became the focal point of the people. [*See* Biblical Temple.]

BIBLIOGRAPHY

Ahlström, Gösta W. *Who Were the Israelites?* Winona Lake, Ind., 1986.

Ahlström, Gösta W. *The History of Ancient Palestine from the Palaeolithic Period to Alexander's Conquest.* Journal for the Study of the Old Testament, Supplement 146. Sheffield, 1993.

Alt, Albrecht. *Essays on Old Testament History and Religion.* Sheffield, 1989.

Biran, Avraham, and Joseph Naveh. "An Aramaic Stele Fragment from Tel Dan." *Israel Exploration Journal* 43 (1993): 81–98.

Borowski, Oded. *Agriculture in Iron Age Israel.* Winona Lake, Ind., 1987.

Coote, Robert B. "The Meaning of the Name Israel." *Harvard Theological Review* 65 (1972): 137–142.

Coote, Robert B., and Keith W. Whitelam. *The Emergence of Early Israel in Historical Perspective.* Sheffield, 1987.

Davies, Philip R. *The Origins of Israel in the Biblical Period.* Sheffield, 1992.

De Geus, C. H. J. *The Tribes of Israel.* Assen, 1976.

Donner, Herbert. *Geschichte des Volkes Israel und seiner Nachbarn in Grundzügen.* 2 vols. Göttingen, 1984–1986.

Engel, Helmut. "Die Siegesstele des Merenptah." *Biblica* 60 (1970): 373–399.

Finkelstein, Israel. *The Archaeology of the Israelite Settlement.* Jerusalem, 1988.

Flanagan, James W. *David's Social Drama: A Hologram of Israel's Early Iron Age.* Journal for the Study of the Old Testament, Supplement 73. Sheffield, 1988.

Frick, Frank S. *The Formation of the State in Ancient Israel.* Sheffield, 1985.

Fritz, Volkmar. "Conquest or Settlement? The Early Iron Age in Palestine." *Biblical Archaeologist* 50 (1987): 84–100.

Fritz, Volkmar. *Die Stadt im alten Israel.* Munich, 1990.

Gottwald, Norman K. *The Tribes of Yahweh: A Sociology of the Religion of Liberated Israel, 1250–1050 B.C.E.* Maryknoll, N.Y., 1979.

Halpern, Baruch. *The Emergence of Israel in Canaan.* Chico, Calif., 1983.

Hayes, John H., and J. Maxwell Miller, eds. *Israelite and Judaean History.* Philadelphia, 1977.

Herzog, Ze'ev. "Settlement and Fortification Planning in the Iron Age." In *The Architecture of Ancient Israel: From the Prehistoric to the Persian Periods,* edited by Aharon Kempinski and Ronny Reich, pp. 231–274. Jerusalem, 1992.

Hopkins, David C. *The Highlands of Canaan: Agricultural Life in the Early Iron Age.* Sheffield, 1985.

Kochavi, Moshe. "An Ostracon of the Period of the Judges from ʿIzbet Ṣarṭah." *Tel Aviv* 4 (1977): 1–13.

Lemaire, André. "Asriel, šr'l, Israel et l'origine de la confédération israélite." *Vetus Testamentum* 23 (1973): 239–243.

Lemche, Niels Peter. *Early Israel: Anthropological and Historical Studies on the Israelite Society before the Monarchy.* Supplements to Vetus Testamentum, 37. Leiden, 1985.

Margalith, Othniel. "On the Origin and Antiquity of the Name 'Israel.'" *Zeitschrift für die alttestamentliche Wissenschaft* 102 (1990): 225–237.

Mazar, Amihai. *Archaeology of the Land of the Bible, 10,000–586 B.C.E.* New York, 1990.

Mendenhall, George E. "The Hebrew Conquest of Palestine." *Biblical Archaeologist* 25 (1962): 66–87.

Miller, J. Maxwell, and John H. Hayes. *A History of Ancient Israel and Judah.* Philadelphia, 1986.

Naveh, Joseph. *An Early History of the Alphabet.* Jerusalem, 1982.

Shiloh, Yigal. "Elements in the Development of Town Planning in the Israelite City." *Israel Exploration Journal* 28 (1978): 36–51.

Soggin, J. Alberto. *A History of Israel: From the Beginnings to the Bar Kochba Revolt, A.D. 135.* London, 1984.

Stager, Lawrence E. "The Archaeology of the Family in Ancient Israel." *Bulletin of the American Schools of Oriental Research,* no. 260 (November 1985): 1–35.

Weippert, Helga. *Palästina in vorhellenistischer Zeit.* Handbuch der Archäologie, vol. 2. Munich, 1988.

Wilson, Robert R. *Prophecy and Society in Ancient Israel.* Philadelphia, 1980.

VOLKMAR FRITZ

Translated from German by Susan I. Schiedel

ISTANBUL. *See* Constantinople.

ISTITUTO ITALIANO PER IL MEDIO ED ESTREMO ORIENTE. The Italian Institute for the Middle and Far East, known as IsMEO, was founded in 1933 by Giovanni Gentile, who was its first president. Giuseppe Tucci, who had been close to Gentile, became president in 1947. He was succeeded by Sabatino Moscati in 1978 and by Gherardo Gnoli in 1979.

The institute was founded in response both to the foreign policy needs of the Italian government at the time and to the lagging development of oriental studies, particularly concerning areas beyond the Near East, as compared to that of other European countries. The stated aims of the institute, which operates under the supervision of the Ministry of Foreign Affairs, are concerned with cultural relations between Italy and Asian countries, as well as with the study of Asian civilizations. It originally also had the task of fostering economic relations, but that never came within the main focus of its efforts. Currently boasting more than 100 general members (who alone have voting rights in every decision taken), more than 150 associate members, and about 70 corresponding members in countries in Asia and Europe and in the United States, the institute's members are orientalist scholars and archaeologists from numerous universities and cultural institutions, as well as Italian diplomats.

IsMEO is currently engaged in archaeological work in Nepal, Oman, Pakistan, Russia, Thailand, Hungary, and Yemen. New projects will involve China, Jordan, India, and Mongolia. Its research is organized through agreements with Italian institutions (mainly the National Research Council and the Oriental Institute of Naples), as well as with foreign institutions in Europe (in Austria, France, Germany, the United Kingdom, Russia, and Hungary), the United States, and Asia (in China, Japan, Jordan, India, Kuwait, Oman, Pakistan, Thailand, Turkmenistan, and Yemen).

GHERARDO GNOLI

IVORY. *See* Bone, Ivory, and Shell.

ʿIZBET ṢARṬAH, hill country site located northeast of Rosh ha-ʿAyin, southwest of Kafr Qasim, and about 16 km (10 mi.) east of Tel Aviv (map reference 14675 × 16795). In the western margins of the western hill country, the site is situated on a hill that borders on and overlooks the coastal plain. Tel Aphek, site of a Canaanite city-state on the coastal plain, is about 3 km (2 mi.) to the west, across the Aphek Pass. With access to the Yarkon River controlled by Aphek, occupants of ʿIzbet Ṣarṭah had to store water in cisterns cut into the hillside. [*See* Aphek; Cisterns.]

An archaeological survey team from Tel Aviv University discovered the site in 1973. Excavations, directed by Moshe Kochavi, continued for four seasons (1976–1978) under the auspices of the Institute of Archaeology of Tel Aviv University and the Department for the Land of Israel Studies at Bar-Ilan University, with Israel Finkelstein serving as field director. The excavators distinguished three Iron Age strata: the two earliest date to Iron I; the latest, to the beginning of Iron II. Six other Iron I sites were identified nearby. Settlement patterns in the region and architectural features in every stratum of the site indicate that the occupants of ʿIzbet Ṣarṭah belonged to the population that settled hundreds of hill country sites in the early Iron Age.

An oval-shaped settlement established at the end of the thirteenth or at the beginning of the twelfth century BCE was uncovered at the earliest level, stratum III. The site was roughly half an acre in size, with a continuous outer wall. Access was from the northeast; where a narrow opening flanked by monolithic doorjambs led to stone-paved open space. At the center of the settlement was a courtyard in which several stone-faced silos were found. The courtyard was surrounded by a wall, to which a belt of contiguous broad rooms of various widths was attached. The rooms lacked internal doorways and had to be entered from the courtyard. Their walls, made out of large stones, were preserved to one course and most of the floors were bedrock.

Sherds from the entire settlement history of stratum III were uncovered, and the variety of pottery types indicates that the inhabitants interacted with the people of the nearby coastal plain. Because the site was situated on the border between the hill country and the coastal plain, ʿIzbet Ṣarṭah was affected by regional rivalries. At the beginning of the eleventh century BCE, the stratum III settlement was abandoned as a result of growing tensions between the people of the hill country and the Philistines on the coastal plain. [*See* Philistines, *article on* Early Philistines.]

Abandonment was apparently planned, as only a few complete pottery vessels, including three collar-rim storejars, were found. Among the earliest pieces were fragments of a Mycenaean stirrup jar, a krater of the "ibex-and-palm" type, and a krater with a "palm" ornamentation applied in relief; bases of "Canaanite" jars; cooking pots with an everted rim; and various bowls in pottery styles of the Late Bronze Age. The latest pottery pieces were rims of red-slipped bowls and fragments of jars with plain, unshaped rims.

ʿIzbet Ṣarṭah was resettled at the end of the eleventh century BCE, after the destruction of Aphek and probably as part of the Israelite westward expansion from the hill country to the coastal plain—perhaps under King Saul. There are indications that aspects of this stratum II settlement were planned. Its layout varies significantly from that of stratum III in size—it was roughly an acre—and in its internal configuration.

At the center of the settlement a large, four-room house (16 × 12 m) was preserved up to three courses of stone with outer walls as much as 1.4 m thick. Three long, connecting rooms were separated by two rows of stone pillars. An enclosed room was situated perpendicular to them along the south wall. The floors of the side rooms were made out of stone slabs; the rest were of bedrock or beaten earth. The only entrance was at the northern end of the long western wall, and a small room was attached to the house at its northwest corner (see figure 1).

Clustered around three sides of the house were forty-three silos that had been dug into a light-colored, mud-brick material, as well as the rooms of the earlier stratum. This brick substance, ubiquitous in stratum III, was reused as foundation material for the stratum II houses, which were built in a series along the edge of the site. Like the large central house, two of these smaller structures had four rooms. Although they were positioned near the slope of the hill, these structures did not function as a line of defense because they were not built contiguously.

The silos, which were lined with small and medium-sized stones, held an estimated volume of 1.3 cu m. Found inside of one of them (no. 605) was an ostracon in two fragments bearing eighty-six letters of Proto-Canaanite script, the longest Proto-Canaanite inscription uncovered in the country to date. Only one line of the five-line inscription, a Proto-Canaanite abecedary, is legible. [*See* Proto-Canaanite.]

The stratum II settlement was abandoned after only a few decades, perhaps in the wake of the Philistine consolidation of power in the region. ʿIzbet Ṣarṭah was reoccupied shortly thereafter, however, at the beginning of the tenth century BCE, perhaps when Israelite expansion westward was resumed under King David. The stratum I site was smaller than that of stratum II, but their plans were similar. The four-room house was rebuilt with partitions between the col-

ʿIZBET ṢARṬAH. Figure 1. *Four-room house after restoration.* (Courtesy ASOR Archives)

umns, and two rooms, with installations, were added at the north of the building. A few new silos also were added. In the process of rebuilding, the stratum II houses at the edge of the site were damaged. The same pottery types as those found in stratum II were uncovered in stratum I; only a statistical analysis can differentiate sherds from the two levels. [*See also* Four-room House; Granaries and Silos.]

Like stratum II, the stratum I site was abandoned after a brief occupation, this time because the fertile Yarkon basin had opened to Israelite settlement. ʿIzbet Ṣarṭah was never resettled, but during the later Byzantine period it was used as an agricultural site. Stones taken from stratum II structures were reused to build several walls, one of them around the top of the hill.

[*See also* Canaanites.]

BIBLIOGRAPHY

Cross, Frank Moore. "Newly Found Inscriptions in Old Canaanite and Early Phoenician Scripts." *Bulletin of the American Schools of Oriental Research,* no. 238 (1980): 1–20.

Demsky, Aaron. "A Proto-Canaanite Abecedary Dating from the Period of the Judges and Its Implications for the History of the Alphabet." *Tel Aviv* 4 (1977): 14–27.

Dotan, Aron. "New Light on the ʿIzbet Sartah Ostracon." *Tel Aviv* 8 (1981): 160–172.

Finkelstein, Israel. *ʿIzbet Sartah: An Early Iron Age Site near Rosh Haʿayin, Israel.* British Archaeological Reports, International Series, no. 299. Oxford, 1986.

Kochavi, Moshe. "An Ostracon of the Period of the Judges from ʿIzbet Sartah." *Tel Aviv* 4 (1977): 1–13.

Naveh, Joseph. "Some Considerations on the Ostracon from ʿIzbet Ṣarṭah." *Israel Exploration Journal* 28 (1978): 31–35.

LESLIE WATKINS

Based on material submitted by Israel Finkelstein

IZEH, a plain and a town located in the western Bakhtiari Mountains of Iran and known as Malamir in the later Islamic period until 1935. The plain, approximately 22 km (14 mi.) long and 10 km (6 mi.) wide, is mainly used for agriculture. An archaeological survey uncovered numerous ancient sites from as early as the third millennium, but no full-scale excavation has yet been carried out there (Wright, 1979). Reliefs carved on the surrounding rocks and boulders testify to the site's importance from the early second millennium BCE until the Parthian period. The rock carvings are presented here in a proposed chronological order. The numbering of the individual reliefs follows Louis Vanden Berghe (1963).

Elamite Period. In default of excavated finds, rock carvings are almost the only evidence for Elamite culture in the Izeh valley. They show people in cultic ceremonies. The earliest reliefs were manufactured in the Old Elamite period; the most important carvings range from the twelfth century BCE up to the Neo-Elamite period.

Shah Savar. At the southeastern end of the plain, a smoothed panel is cut in a vertical cliff. Only the upper part of the panel was used for a frieze in low relief. Four standing orants are introduced by a fifth to a seated deity. The structure (the pictoral frieze over a blank area) and the topic (orants with an enthroned god) can be compared with the Elamite rock reliefs at Kurangun and Naqsh-i Rustam, dated to the seventeenth and sixteenth centuries BCE, respectively. [*See* Naqsh-i Rustam.]

Hung-i Nowruzi (mod. Hung-Azhdar). At the northern end of the plain, two oblong panels are cut into a boulder. The relief is carved only in the lower space. Faint remains of at least seven standing figures can be discerned. The little that is preserved seems to resemble the Shah Savar panel and may date to the same period.

Shikaft-i Salman I–IV. At the southwestern border, there is a wide cave with a spring. Two reliefs (Shikaft-i Salman I and II) are carved on the outside, on the cliff at the right side of the cave, and two (III and IV) on the inside. Carved in relief I are two men, a child, and a woman who are standing and facing left, behind a thymiaterion (or censer); in II a man, a child, and a woman face left (see figure 1); in III a man faces right; and in IV a man wearing a long skirt faces right. All the figures face the place where water springs from the rock and where a huge water (?) channel comes from above. Their hands are posed in two different Elamite prayer gestures: one or both hands raised before the face or clasped at the waist (figure 1). The figures have stylistic parallels in a relief from Susa that was assembled by Pierre Amiet (*Arts Asiatiques* 32 [1976]; 13–28) from scattered glazed bricks; the Susa relief is dated to the time of Shilhak-Inshushinak (twelfth century BCE) by a contemporary inscription. The rock reliefs at Shikaft-i Salman are accompanied by cuneiform inscriptions that name Hanni son of Tahhi, chief of Ajapir, as having commissioned them. He is the same ruler who commissioned the inscription and relief Kul-i Farah I (see below); he may have lived anywhere between the late eighth and early sixth centuries BCE. Thus, the dates of manufacture of the reliefs and of the inscriptions are separated by several centuries, which can be explained only by means of a usurpation of older pictures by Hanni. Nevertheless, the late inscriptions may hint at the significance of the place. The large text to the left of relief III relates the dedication (?) of images of Hanni and his family to the goddess Mashti at a place called Tarrisha. As neither the deity's nor the place's name are mentioned in the Kul-i Farah inscription, both may be connected to Shikaft-i Salman, probably since deepest antiquity. This means that nameless men, women, and children from the end of the second millennium BCE may be represented at this cave with a spring venerating the goddess Mashti, mistress of Tarrisha.

Kul-i Farah I–IV. Opposite Shikaft-i Salman, at the

IZEH. Figure 1. *Shikaft-i Salman II relief.* (Photograph by Barbara Grunewald, Deutsches Archäologisches Institut, Tehran)

IZEH. Figure 2. *Kul-i Farah III relief, south side.* (Photograph by Barbara Grunewald, Deutsches Archäologisches Institut, Tehran)

northeastern border, a ravine called Kul-i Farah with reliefs on its slopes and on boulders shows processions (III and IV), animal sacrifices (I–III, V) and a banquet scene (IV). Together with other scattered rocks (either roughly worked as platforms or with cavities on the top, or with smoothed panels on one side), the whole arrangement points to a cultic use. Based on their style, it appears that the reliefs were manufactured at different dates.

Relief IV. The banquet scene, with about 150 figures, covers several rock faces that jut out at various angles along the south side of the ravine. The central figure is seated in front of a stand that holds three goblets; he faces a table and is surrounded by his servants. His arms bearer is positioned in the register below. From both sides, figures arranged in registers face the center. Most of these hold their right hand to their mouth in a gesture of eating or of veneration, and some are playing musical instruments. The banquet scene has parallels on Middle Elamite seals. The shape of the throne is known from a bead of Shilhak Inshushinak (twelfth century BCE); the goblets represented were in use no later than about 1000–900 BCE.

Relief III. The northern, southern, and the southwestern sides of a boulder are covered with processions moving east (see figure 2). The procession on the north is divided into three registers and headed by a man whose height fills all three registers. Encountering him are smaller individuals, similar to the participants in the procession, three of whom are playing harps. The southwestern and southern processions follow in four registers, a large figure supported by four kneeling men. He is preceded by three naked men and encountered by some ordinary people, as on the northern side. The destination of the processions seems to be the rounded east side, where three bulls and eighteen smaller animals are represented.

Relief VI. The same large figure supported by kneeling men is shown in relief VI. He is followed only by a few smaller individuals, among them the arms bearer (cf. Kul-i Farah IV, I).

Style and iconography place reliefs III, IV, and VI in one group. They therefore may originate in roughly the same period, at about the end of the second or the beginning of the first millennium BCE.

Relief I. A rectangular panel on the north wall of the ravine, relief I is the only inscribed monument at Kul-i Farah. On its upper part, a text of twenty-four lines covers the space unoccupied by the figures; short captions, or labels, are carved on or beside the human figures. The main figure is, according to the text on his skirt, Hanni son of Tahhi, chief of Ajapir, who dedicated his image to the god Tirutur. Behind him stand, in smaller scale, his arms bearer and another official in a long skirt. In front of Hanni in the upper part of the relief, are three musicians; in the lower part are four men engaged in sacrificial acts. The "one who delivers the sacrificial victim" leads a goat; the "priest" is occupied with a thymiaterion and the others with a bull; and three beheaded carcasses and loose heads of rams lie in between. The text contains invocations of Elamite deities, deeds of Hanni, and the dedication of the relief to the god Tirutur. For the text, Matthew Stolper suggests "a date within the seventh century" (Calmeyer and Stolper, 1988, p. 279). Although comparable Neo-Elamite art is scarce, there is no reason to doubt here—in contrast to Shikaft-i Salman—that the text and pictures are contemporaneous. In particular, the large figure of Hanni differs from the reliefs at Shikaft-i Salman and at Kul-i Farah III, IV, and VI in style and iconography. The headdress and the garment with its rosette border and fringes find their parallels in the clothing of the Elamite king Tepti-Humban-Inshushinak (Assyr, Te'umman), killed during a battle with Ashurbanipal in 653 BCE, that is pictured in Assyrian reliefs at Nineveh.

Reliefs II and V. Similar in subject to most of the Kul-i Farah reliefs, in reliefs II and V a large man, followed by four smaller figures, is directed to a slaughtering scene where a naked man is occupied with a bull lying on its back. With the bull are six smaller animals in the same position (i.e., in the same numerical relationship as on relief III). On relief V, the large man is praying over a thymiaterion. Too few details are given or preserved to allow a positive dating. In all probability they were carved after IV, III, and VI, but their temporal relation to relief I cannot be fixed. Certainly, they were made before Achaemenid times.

Kul-i Farah, seen through its reliefs, seems to be a place of ceremonies with animal sacrifices, processions with music, and symposia.

Parthian Period. The latest rock reliefs are Parthian. They are located on the northern side of the valley. The subject of these carvings is different from the Elamite ones. They show people of rank facing the sovereign.

Hung-i Nowruzi (Hung-i Azhdar). The boulder with the faint Elamite relief bears a Parthian relief on its back side, facing the cliff; in front of it, an isolated stone relief is lying on the ground. The rock relief shows a horseman with his attendant moving to the right and four standing men in front of him, in frontal view. The two parts of the relief differ in style and iconography. The rider is Greek in inspiration. Comparable heads can be found on Arsacid coins of the second half of the second century BCE. The four standing men have their closest parallels in Parthian reliefs from the beginning of the third century CE. Various proposals, the following among them, have been made to explain this discrepancy.

The entire relief has been dated based on the elements of the left side, the rider. Louis Vanden Berghe (1963) compares the head with that of Mithridates I (171–138 BCE) on a coin, interpreting the relief as the representation of Mithridates I as he is received by Elymaean nobles after the Parthian conquest of Elymais in 140/39 BCE. This would make the four men the oldest examples of frontal representation. To support this view, other scholars argue with sculptors from different schools or with the ecclecticism of Greco-Iranian art.

The entire relief has also been dated, based on the elements of the right side, the four standing men. Trudy S. Kawami (1987) argues that the artistic style and details of dress and hairstyle of the four nobles indicate a date in the Late Parthian period, at the end of second or third centuries CE. She suggests that a local ruler and his entourage are represented as they pay homage to their ancestor, sculptured in the fashion of the Hellenistic period.

Other scholars have harmonized the dating discrepancy by proposing a date between the two extremes (first century BCE and first century CE) for the entire relief. However, Hans E. Mathiesen proposes that an unfinished relief of the victorious Mithridates I (second century BCE) was "completed" by a Parthian or Elymaean king in about 200 CE, which means that the carvings on the left and right sides belong to different times. (The relief lying on the ground shows a man in frontal view, who may have been part of a larger nearby composition.)

Hung-i Yar-i Alivand. The weathered rock relief at Hung-i Yar-i Alivand shows two standing figures in frontal view. A shallow circular element between them suggests the interpretation that this is an investiture scene. The dating for the carving ranges from the first century BCE to the late second century CE.

Hung-i Kamalvand. The rock relief at Hung-i Kamalvand shows a horseman and a standing figure pouring a libation before him. An inscription names "Phraa]tes the priest, son of Kabniskir." The date of the carving is usually given as second century CE.

[*See also* Elamites; *and* Susa.]

BIBLIOGRAPHY

Calymeyer, Peter, and Matthew W. Stolper. "Mālamīr." In *Reallexikon der Assyriologie und Vorderasiatischen Archäologie,* vol. 7, pp. 275–287. Berlin and New York, 1988. Discussion of the Elamite reliefs and their inscriptions, with an extensive bibliography.

De Waele, E. "Travaux archéologiques à Šekāf-e Salmān et Kūl-e Farah près d'Iẕeh (Mālamīr)." *Iranica Antiqua* 16 (1981): 45–61, pls. 1–4. Geographical evaluation, being one of several preliminary reports based on an unpublished doctoral thesis.

Kawami, Trudy S. *Monumental Art of the Parthian Period in Iran.* Acta Iranica, vol. 26. Leiden, 1987.

Mathiesen, Hans E. *Sculpture in the Parthian Empire.* 2 vols. Aarhus, 1992.

Vanden Berghe, Louis. "Les reliefs Élamites de Mālamīr." *Iranica Antiqua* 3 (1963): 22–39, pls. 9–28. Treatise of the Elamite reliefs (exclusive of Khul-i Farah VI) with good illustrations.

Vanden Berghe, Louis, and Klaus Schippmann. *Les reliefs rupestres d'Elymaïde (Iran) de l'époque Parthe.* Iranica Antiqua, supp. 3. Ghent, 1985.

Wright, Henry T., ed. *Archaeological Investigations in Northeastern Xuzestan.* Ann Arbor, 1979.

Ursula Seidl

J

JACOBSEN, THORKILD (1904–1993), philologist, cuneiformist, and archaeologist; one of the great interpreters of Mesopotamian culture. Born in Denmark, Jacobsen studied Assyriology first at the university of his native Copenhagen and then, in the late 1920s, at the University of Chicago. Throughout his life, he was passionately and deeply committed to the study of ancient Mesopotamia, its land, cultures, and languages.

Jacobsen was a field assyriologist with the Iraq Expedition of the Oriental Institute (1929–1937), working closely with Henri Frankfort, its director, as well as with Pinhas Delougaz, Seton Lloyd, and Gordon Loud. He was the epigrapher at Khorsabad and in the Diyala region and led the excavation at Ishchali. Together with Lloyd, Jacobsen excavated Sennacherib's aqueduct at Jerwan. He was instrumental in introducing to Iraq the method of systematic surface ceramic survey.

Returning to Chicago in 1937, Jacobsen began a twenty-five-year affiliation with the university. From 1946 to 1951, he was director of the Oriental Institute and then dean of the Division of Humanities. As director, he gave new shape to the Assyriology faculty of the Oriental Institute and to American Assyriology, in general. Moreover, he set the agenda for American archaeology in Iraq by reestablishing American excavations at Nippur jointly with the University of Pennsylvania and setting in motion the surface surveys that would lead to his and Robert McC. Adams's important discoveries regarding waterways, salinization, and settlement patterns (Jacobsen and Adams, 1958). Disagreements over the policies, direction, and execution of the Chicago Assyrian Dictionary led to Jacobsen leaving Chicago in 1962 for Harvard University, where he taught until his retirement in 1974.

Jacobsen's unique blend of textual scholarship, knowledge of art and archaeology, quest for conceptual patterns, appreciation of the environment and way of life of ancient Mesopotamia, and his own deep human sympathy allowed him to fathom the meaning and recreate the image of a past civilization. He approached the task in an existential spirit and saw that alien and distant human life was something that not only existed in its own terms, but also mattered very deeply for the enduring human spirit.

[*See also* Assyrians; Diyala; Khorsabad; Nippur; Sumerian; Sumerians; Ur; *and the biographies of Frankfort and Lloyd.*]

BIBLIOGRAPHY

Jacobsen, Thorkild. *The Sumerian King List.* Oriental Institute, Assyriological Studies, 11. Chicago, 1939. Exemplary edition and analysis.

Jacobsen, Thorkild. "Mesopotamia." In *The Intellectual Adventure of Ancient Man: An Essay on Speculative Thought in the Ancient Near East,* by Henri Frankfort et al. New York, 1946. Groundbreaking and breathtaking interpretation of Mesopotamian religious thought.

Jacobsen, Thorkild, and Robert McC. Adams. "Salt and Silt in Ancient Mesopotamian Agriculture." *Science* 128 (1958): 1251–1258. Pioneering study of Mesopotamian irrigation and settlement patterns.

Jacobsen, Thorkild. *Toward the Image of Tammuz and Other Essays on Mesopotamian History and Culture.* Edited by William L. Moran. Harvard Semitic Series, vol. 21. Cambridge, Mass., 1970. A number of Jacobsen's seminal essays originally published between 1930 and 1965. The collection includes some of Jacobsen's most important writings on Mesopotamian religion and mythology, political and cultural history, and Sumerian and Akkadian grammar. See as well the bibliography of Jacobsen's writings to 1969 (pp. 471–474) and the assessment of his work by Moran (pp. v–vi).

Jacobsen, Thorkild. *The Treasures of Darkness.* New Haven, 1976. Develops the idea of divine intransitivity and transitivity; reconstructs the major stages in Mesopotamian religion over four thousand years; and analyzes significant segments of the religious literature.

Jacobsen, Thorkild. *Salinity and Irrigation: Agriculture in Antiquity.* Bibliotheca Mesopotamica, 14. Malibu, 1982.

Jacobsen, Thorkild, ed. and trans. *The Harps That Once . . .: Sumerian Poetry in Translation.* New Haven, 1987. Meticulous but profound and beautiful translations of religious poetry—myths, prayers, and laments.

Jacobsen, Thorkild. "The Sumerian Verbal Core." *Zeitschrift für Assyriologie* 78 (1988): 161–220. This study continues his earlier "About the Sumerian Verb" (included in Jacobsen, 1970), which was the first systematic and comprehensive utilization of the principle of fixed-rank order in studying the Sumerian verb and an explication of some of its intricacies.

Kramer, Samuel Noah. "Thorkild Jacobsen: Philologist, Archeologist, Historian." In *Sumerological Studies in Honor of Thorkild Jacobsen on His Seventieth Birthday, June 7, 1974,* edited by Steven J. Lieberman, pp. 1–7. Chicago, 1976. Assessment of Jacobsen's career by a contemporary who represented a different approach to Sumerian mythology and religion.

Tzvi Abusch

JAFFA, site located along the southern edge of modern Tel Aviv–Jaffa, on a promontory jutting into the Mediterranean Sea that forms one of the few ancient harbors along the coast of Israel (32°01′ N, 34°45′ E; map reference 162 × 127). Jaffa is referred to in Egyptian texts and the Hebrew Bible as Jaffa, and the name is preserved in Arabic as Yafa el-ʿAtiqa ("ancient Jaffa").

The Harris papyrus and reliefs on the Karnak temple refer to the conquest of Jaffa by Thutmosis III in the fifteenth century BCE. Jaffa is one of the Egyptian administrative centers through which the Egyptians controlled Syria-Palestine in the Late Bronze Age. The Amarna letters and Papyrus Anastasi I, dated to the fourteenth and thirteenth centuries BCE, respectively, mention Jaffa as an Egyptian stronghold. [*See* Amarna Tablets.] Additionally, an Akkadian letter sent from Ugarit and found at Aphek mentions Jaffa as the seat of an Egyptian official. [*See* Aphek.] In 701 BCE Sennacherib recorded the conquest of Jaffa on the Prism stela. The Hebrew Bible includes Jaffa within the tribal boundary of Dan (*Jos.* 19:46). The site is connected with the shipping of cedars from Lebanon in the construction of the First and Second Temples (*2 Chr.* 2:15; *Ezr.* 3:7). Jonah attempts to flee from God via Jaffa (*Jon.* 1:3).

Jaffa was excavated from 1945 to 1950 by P. L. O. Guy for the Department of Antiquities of Israel. John Bowman and B. S. J. Isserlin excavated in 1952 for the University of Leeds. The most extensive excavation was undertaken by Jacob Kaplan, between 1955 and 1974, for the Museum of Antiquities of Tel Aviv–Jaffa. During six seasons of excavation, Kaplan opened four areas (A, B, C, and Y). Eight archaeological strata have been discerned, from the Middle Bronze Age II through the Roman Period. [*See the biography of Guy.*]

Stratum VII dates to MB IIB/C. In area A, along with mud-brick walls, a small section of a typical MB IIB glacis was found. In area C, the eighth-century glacis may rest on the remains of an MB IIA glacis. In area Y, an infant jar burial and an MB IIB/C tomb were excavated.

The Late Bronze Age is well represented in area A. Architectural remains from stratum VI (LB I) are dated by Bichrome, Gray-Burnished, and Cypriot Base-Ring and Monochrome wares. In area Y, stratum VI is limited to pits dug into loam. Stratum V (LB IIA) is dated to the fourteenth century BCE by pottery found in a silo. Strata IVA and B both date to the Late Bronze IIB (cf. Kaplan, 1993). The earliest LB gate was founded in stratum IVB. This gate system includes mud-brick walls and sandstone doorjambs. Four doorjamb fragments were inscribed with titles of Rameses II, along with part of his name. Rivka Gonen (1992) has suggested that this gate may be freestanding and purely ceremonial. In stratum IVA a better-preserved gate on the same orientation was uncovered. At this point the city was fortified with a wall system that included a fortified structure or citadel. Bronze hinges from this stratum IVA gate were found in situ on the bottom left doorjamb. There is evidence of burning and destruction ending both strata IVA and B within the thirteenth century BCE.

Kaplan (1993) suggests that a small (4.4 × 5.8 m) rectangular structure next to the citadel is a temple. This poorly preserved building includes a white plaster floor and two column bases; almost no small finds or pottery, except for a lion's skull with a half scarab near its teeth, were recovered. The excavator dates this structure to the late thirteenth/early twelfth centuries BCE and compares it to the northern temple at Beth-Shean. Mariusz Burdajewicz (1990) suggests that it is only a small shrine and rejects the comparison to the Beth-Shean temple because of its small size. Initially Amihai Mazar suggested architectural parallels at Tell Qasile and in the Aegean. More recently however, Mazar (1992) has cast doubt on whether this structure is a temple at all.

The scant Iron Age (stratum IIIB) remains from area A include Philistine sherds found in pits and depressions that date the stratum to the eleventh century BCE. A rough stone wall and floor and two cattle burials with stone markers belong to stratum IIIA (eighth century BCE). In area C there is some indication of a glacis. Jaffa is now under the political control of Ashkelon.

Persian period (stratum II) remains include an ashlar wall dating to the fifth century BCE. Stone walls of large structures with mud-brick and stone paving were found throughout area A. In this stratum a construction technique using ashlar piers interspersed with fieldstone fills—a technique associated with the Phoenicians—was revealed. Stern (1992) suggests that Jaffa may mark the southernmost extent of Phoenician culture from the eighth century BCE to the Hellenistic period. Jaffa may have belonged to the Sidonians, as it was recorded in the Eshmunazar Inscription (fifth century BCE?) that the king of Persia presented Eshmunazar of Sidon with Dor and Jaffa. Fragments of Attic ware were found in area Y. [*See* Phoenicians; Sidon.]

Stratum I dates to the Hellenistic period. An ashlar corner of a fortress was found in stratum IB (third century BCE), along with the remains of an ashlar casemate wall. A possible cult hall with a fieldstone altar was also uncovered in this stratum. A third-century BCE catacomb was found in area C, and in area Y there was evidence of a monumental ashlar building with square rooms that may be part of a Hellenistic agora. The Zenon papyri mention the visit of an Egyptian treasury official during the reign of Ptolemy II, in 259/58 BCE. Under the Hasmoneans (stratum IA) the city was captured from the Seleucids and became a Jewish port. Guy found a hoard of more than eight hundred coins in his excavations dating to the reign of Alexander Jannaeus.

The only stratified remains from the Roman period were found in area C (levels VI–I). Fragments of a mosaic date to the sixth–seventh centuries CE (level I). Architectural fragments were excavated in levels II (fifth century CE), III (fourth century CE), and IV (third century CE). In level V (second century CE) better-preserved architecture was found, along with a hoard of bronze and silver coins dating no later than Trajan's reign (98–117 CE). A small glass factory and a well-constructed catacomb were also excavated. Two important Greek inscriptions found in level VI (first century CE) include a limestone inscription mentioning Judah, an *agoranomos* of Jaffa during the reigns of Nerva (96–98 CE) and Trajan. The second inscription is a third-century BCE votive that mentions Ptolemy IV Philopator. Additional inscriptions include jar handles with Greek and Latin inscriptions, a tile with a Tenth Legion stamp, and a pyramidal seal with the name *Ariston.* A marble door leaf (mid-second–mid-third centuries CE) was also found. Jacob Pinkerfeld (1955) suggests that this fragment is similar to mausoleum doors from the necropolis at Palmyra. [*See* Palmyra.] The city was destroyed by Cestius Gallus and Vespasian in 67 CE; it was later rebuilt and referred to as Flavia Ioppa. A Jewish cemetery from nearby Abu Kabir, east of Jaffa, dates from the first through the fifth centuries.

BIBLIOGRAPHY

Applebaum, Shimon. "The Status of Jaffa in the First Century of the Current Era." *Scripta Classical Israelica* 8–9 (1988): 138–144. Important historical overview of Jaffa in the Roman period.

Bowman, John, et al. "The University of Leeds, Department of Semitics Archaeological Expedition to Jaffa, 1952." *Proceedings of the Leeds Philosophical Society* 7.4 (1955): 231–250.

Burdajewicz, Mariusz. *The Aegean Sea Peoples and Religious Architecture in the Eastern Mediterranean at the Close of the Late Bronze Age.* Oxford, 1990.

Gonen, Rivka. "The Late Bronze Age." In *The Archaeology of Ancient Israel,* edited by Amnon Ben-Tor, pp. 211–257. Jerusalem, 1992.

Kaplan, Jacob. "The Archaeology and History of Tel Aviv–Jaffa." *Biblical Archaeologist* 35.3 (1972): 66–95. Thorough overview of the author's important research at Jaffa and its environs. His chronological conclusions and some of his interpretations are problematic and remain so in his updated article (below).

Kaplan, Jacob. "Jaffa." In *The New Encyclopedia of Archaeological Excavations in the Holy Land,* vol. 2, pp. 655–659. Jerusalem and New York, 1993.

Kindler, Arie. "The Jaffa Hoard and Alexander Jannaeus." *Israel Exploration Journal* 4 (1954): 170–185. Formal numismatic analysis with an emphasis on minting techniques.

Landau, Y. H. "A Stamped Jar Handle from Jaffa." *ʿAtiqot* 2 (1959): 186–187. Useful article about Jaffa in the classical period.

Mazar, Amihai. *Excavations at Tell Qasile,* part 1, *The Philistine Sanctuary: Architecture and Cult Objects.* Qedem, vol. 12. Jerusalem, 1980. Essential for understanding the validity of Kaplan's claims regarding the so-called Lion Temple. Must be used in conjunction with Mazar's article below.

Mazar, Amihai. "Temples of the Middle and Late Bronze Ages and the Iron Age." In *The Architecture of Ancient Israel: From the Prehistoric to the Persian Periods,* edited by Aharon Kempinski and Ronny Reich, pp. 161–187. Jerusalem, 1992.

Pinkerfeld, Jacob. "Two Fragments of a Marble Door from Jaffa." *ʿAtiqot* 1 (1955): 89–94.

Stern, Ephraim. "The Phoenician Architectural Elements in Palestine during the Late Iron Age and Persian Period." In *The Architecture of Ancient Israel: From the Prehistoric to the Persian Periods,* edited by Aharon Kempinski and Ronny Reich, pp. 302–309. Jerusalem, 1992.

J. P. DESSEL

JAR BURIALS. One of the many forms of human interment places the body of the deceased in a jar for burial. Infants and children were inserted into a single jar, while adults were positioned in one large jar or two facing jars. The neck of the jar frequently was removed to facilitate the insertion of an adult body. Jar burial is similar to the Late Bronze–Iron Age practice of anthropoid coffin burial: both employed ceramic vessels to contain (predominantly) primary interments with accompanying mortuary offerings. In contrast to these forms of primary interment, Iron Age Phoenician urn burials have yielded predominantly cremated remains (Tell er-Rugeish, Achziv, Khaldeh), and Chalcolithic and Hellenistic-Byzantine ossuaries encased secondary bone collections (Azor, Ḥaderah).

From the Natufian period through the Middle Bronze Age (c. 10,500–1550 BCE), infants and children were buried in jars or in large jars called pithoi, under house floors or courtyards (Aphek, Ashkelon, Yoqneʿam). During this same period, adolescents and adults were buried in caves or shaft tombs and pit or cist graves (Adeimeh, Bab edh-Dhraʿ, Jericho, Shiqmim). Infant jar burials beneath occupation surfaces have been reported from the fifth-millennium Pottery Neolithic site of Shaʿar ha-Golan. Stillborns, infants, and children up to approximately the age of nine were buried in pithoi at the more southerly sites of Naḥal Besor and Teleilat el-Ghassul during the Chalcolithic period (4300–3300 BCE).

Jar burial was reintroduced beginning in the MB IIA (2000–1500 BCE), when the northern coast and valleys were resettled. As in the earlier periods, children, now with a small number of provisions, including ointment juglets and jewelry, were interred in jars under occupation surfaces (Ashkelon, Yoqneʿam). The introduction of jar burial for adults, which first appeared in the Late Bronze II (1400–1200 BCE), is also attributed to northern influence. Extramural interments of exclusively mature individuals, inserted at the time of death into one or two large jars positioned to form a burial receptacle, have been reported from the four northern sites of Azor, Kefar Yehoshuʿa, Tell el-Farʿah (North), and Tel Zeror. The forty-year-old man buried at Kefar Yehoshuʿa was provided with flasks, other pottery vessels, a bronze blade, and cuts of sheep, ox, and pig for nourishment.

Jar burial continued through the Iron Age (1200–586 BCE), although with diminishing frequency. Eleven sites yielded jar burials in northern and coastal Cisjordan and on the Transjordanian plateau in Iron I (1200–1000 BCE), for example, at Afula, Amman, and Azor, whereas only six or

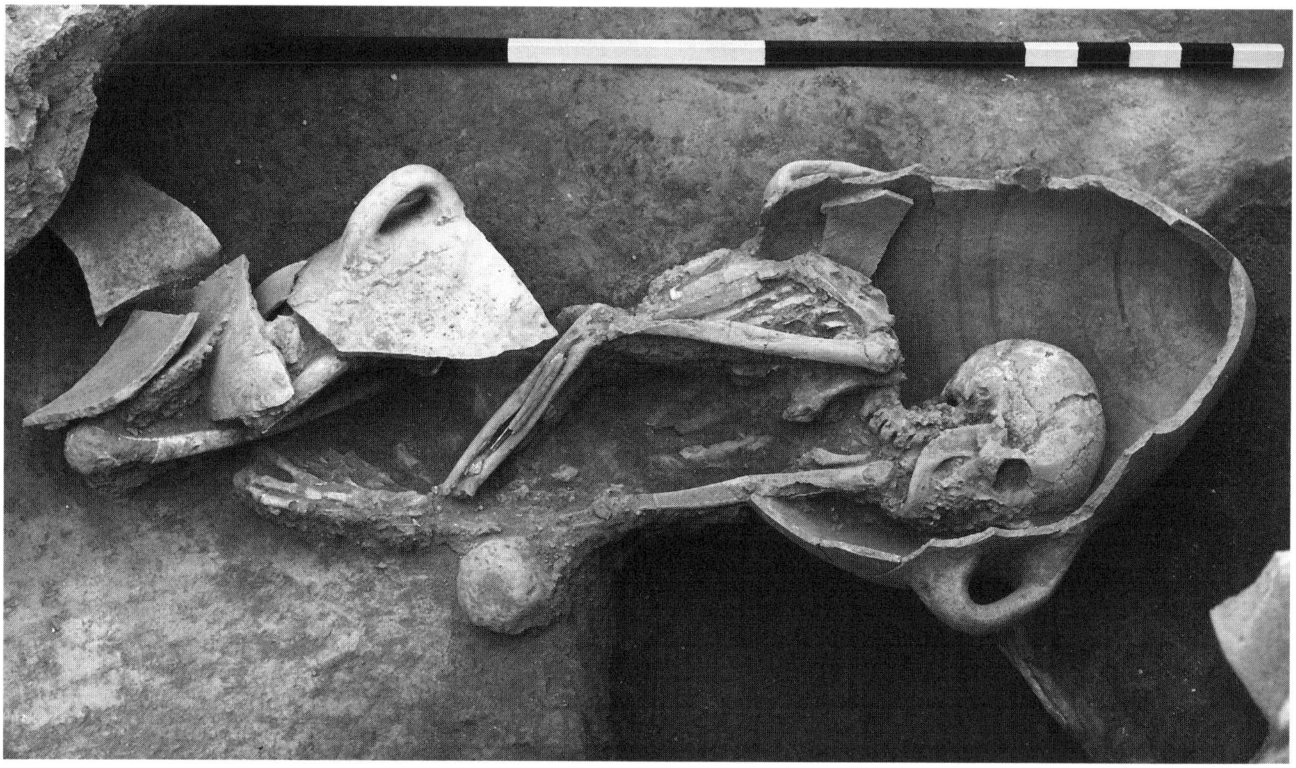

JAR BURIALS. *Double-pithos burial from Tell es-Saʿidiyeh.* (Courtesy ASOR Archives)

seven sites provided Iron II examples (1000–586 BCE). Small numbers of children continued to be interred in jars, which were usually buried in cave or chamber tombs along with adolescents and adults.

[*See also* Burial Techniques. *In addition, many of the sites mentioned are the subject of independent entries.*]

BIBLIOGRAPHY

Avi-Yonah, Michael, and Ephraim Stern, eds. *Encyclopedia of Archaeological Excavations in the Holy Land.* 4 vols. Englewood Cliffs, N.J., 1975–1978. Summary of excavations including results of all earlier expeditions to the sites.

Ben-Tor, Amnon, ed. *The Archaeology of Ancient Israel.* Translated by R. Greenberg. New Haven, 1992. Collection of essays with differing emphases on the Neolithic through the Iron Age II–III periods.

Bloch-Smith, Elizabeth. *Judahite Burial Practices and Beliefs about the Dead.* Journal for the Study of the Old Testament, Supplement 123. Sheffield, 1992. Summary and comprehensive catalog of the Iron Age burials.

Mazar, Amihai. *Archaeology of the Land of the Bible, 10,000–586 B.C.E.* New York, 1990. Comprehensive, detailed, well-illustrated survey of biblical archaeology, limited only by the traditionalist biblical interpretation.

Stern, Ephraim, ed. *The New Encyclopedia of Archaeological Excavations in the Holy Land.* 4 vols. Jerusalem and New York, 1993. Supplements Avi-Yonah and Stern (above), with results of more recent excavations and revised interpretations.

ELIZABETH BLOCH-SMITH

JARMO (or Qalʿat Jarmo), prehistoric site located in northern Iraq (35°33′ N, 44°57′ E), approximately 11 km (7 mi.) east of the town of Chemchamal, at an altitude of 8,250 m. Jarmo occupies a hilltop above a wadi locally known as Cham-Gawra, one of several that drain the higher slopes of the ridges enclosing an intermontane plain in the Iraqi foothills of the Zagros Mountains. This plain is bounded by the Kani Domlan-Jabal Tasak and the Kani Shaitan Hasan-Sarirma Dagh ridges, and is 16 km (10 mi.) wide by 56 km (35 mi.) long (Braidwood and Howe, 1960, pp. 26–27).

Jarmo, dated to the seventh millennium BCE (see below), was for many years the oldest known agricultural and pastoral community in the world. It was first located in the 1940s by the Iraqi Directorate of Antiquities, which recommended it to Robert J. Braidwood of the Oriental Institute at the University of Chicago when he inquired about ancient village sites in northern Iraq (Braidwood, 1974). Under the auspices of the Oriental Institute, Braidwood excavated at Jarmo from March to June 1948; September 1950 to spring 1951; and March to June 1955.

Excavation was undertaken to recover empirical evidence for the beginnings of agriculture and pastoralism. The site was the first in the Near East in which interdisciplinary field archaeology was applied to elucidating the origins of food production. In the second and third seasons of excavation, Braidwood's staff included natural scientists as well as archaeologists. The structure and functioning of these interdisciplinary teams investigating an important cultural and economic transition influenced subsequent archaeological projects in many parts of the Old and New World long after the Iraq-Jarmo Project's fieldwork was terminated.

As the first archaeologically known example of a very early agricultural and pastoral village, Jarmo's architectural and other cultural remains were for many years the only documentation available for the way of life of the world's first farmers and herders.

Braidwood's work at Jarmo was emulated by subsequent generations of archaeologists (several of whom were his students) in addressing the same problem in many other areas of western Asia. Braidwood himself has fielded a series of more recent projects in Iran and Turkey. Our understanding of the transformation from hunting-gathering-foraging economies to food-producing ones is now much different from that of the late 1950s when the Jarmo data were new and unique (for recent summaries see Bar-Yosef and Meadow, in press; Bar-Yosef and Belfer-Cohen, 1989; and Moore, 1985; see also Braidwood, 1974). Nevertheless, Jarmo continues to have significance in the history of world archaeology.

The archaeological work at Jarmo was interrupted after a nationalist revolution took place in Iraq in the summer of 1958. No excavation has been carried out since then. Information gained from analyses on the material recovered between 1948 and 1955 are detailed in two volumes (Braidwood and Howe, 1960; Braidwood et al., 1983). Braidwood dates the site to early in the seventh millennium BCE but freely admits that the various radiocarbon dates are not very helpful. Apparently, contamination by bitumen (locally available and used throughout the occupation) and complex site-formation processes affected the radiocarbon samples.

The village of Jarmo is thought to have been occupied by approximately 100 to 150 people at any one time (there is a maximum of some 7 m of deposit). Its population lived in rectilinear household complexes constructed of puddled adobe (Ar., *tauf*). The Jarmoan economy was based on domestic emmer and einkorn wheat, two-row barley, lentils, and vetchling. Available wild plants included field pea, pistachio nuts, acorns, and wild wheat and barley. The villagers kept dogs, domestic goats and sheep, and—in the later period of the site's occupation—domestic pigs. There was considerable hunting of wild animals. Cattle, onager, and small mammals were apparently taken for food. Bones of lion, leopard, a small wildcat, fox, and lynx have been identified among the Jarmo fauna. These carniverous species may have been killed for their pelts, or to protect the villagers and their flocks.

The Jarmo people were skilled flint and obsidian knappers, producing both normal-sized and microlithic tools, primarily from blade cores. The obsidian was imported from Anatolia, but not in large quantities. Other imports included marine shells and, perhaps, turquoise. Milling stones are well represented in the ground-stone categories, as are small celts and chisel-like implements, beads, pendants, and bracelets. Nicely made stone bowls were produced in some quantity from a wide variety of fine-grained local limestone; and a plethora of small clay figurines (human, animal, and geometric) are also characteristic of the Jarmo artifact assemblage. Bone tools, especially perforators, or awls, are abundant, and the bone industry also includes carefully made spoons and beads. The villagers made small quantities of pottery, an innovation that seems to have originated elsewhere and is only patchily found in the Jarmo deposit.

The Jarmo assemblage, once virtually the only one of its kind, can now be seen as an example of many such farming and herding communities scattered throughout the Zagros region in both Iraq and Iran in the Early and Mid-Holocene periods. As Braidwood pointed out forty years ago, these humble but vigorous settlements created the economic and social foundations for the rise of Mesopotamian civilization in the fourth millennium BCE.

[*See also* Paleobotany; Paleoenvironmental Reconstruction; *and* Paleozoology.]

BIBLIOGRAPHY

Bar-Yosef, Ofer, and Anna Belfer-Cohen. "The Origins of Sedentism and Farming Communities in the Levant." *Journal of World Prehistory* 3 (1989): 447–498.

Bar-Yosef, Ofer, and Richard H. Meadow. "The Origins of Agriculture and Animal Husbandry in the Near and Middle East." In *Last Hunters-First Farmers: New Perspectives on the Prehistoric Transition to Agriculture,* edited by T. D. Price and A. B. Gebauer. Santa Fe, N.M., in press.

Braidwood, Linda S., et al. *Prehistoric Archeology Along the Zagros Flanks.* University of Chicago, Oriental Institute, Publications, vol.105. Chicago, 1983.

Braidwood, Robert J. "The Iraq Jarmo Project." In *Archaeological Researches in Retrospect,* edited by Gordon R. Willey, pp. 61–83. Cambridge, Mass., 1974.

Braidwood, Robert J., and Bruce Howe, eds. *Prehistoric Investigations in Iraqi Kurdistan.* University of Chicago, Oriental Institute, Studies in Ancient Civilization, no. 31. Chicago, 1960.

Moore, Andrew M. T. "The Development of Neolithic Societies in the Near East." *Advances in World Archaeology* 4 (1985): 1–70.

Patty Jo Watson

JAWA, large fortified site located in northeastern Jordan, at the eastern margins of the Fertile Crescent, on the border between steppe and arable land (32°20′ N, 37°0′ E). The site was founded in the Early Bronze Age IA as a walled settlement sustained by an elaborate water-harvesting system of dams, canals, and pools. The system drew winter runoff from Wadi Rajil, one of the largest of the wadis draining southward from the volcanic peak of Jebel al-Druze in southern Syria. This first occupation was short lived, and the site was abandoned after a few decades. Jawa was occupied again at the beginning of the Middle Bronze Age (EB–MB/MB IIA) when a "citadel" and outbuildings were constructed on its summit, within the EB walls.

Because of its remote location, Jawa was not known to pioneer archaeologists in Syria and Palestine. The site was first recorded in an aerial photograph taken by Antoine Poidebard in the 1930s. Poidebard believed Jawa to be Roman because of the regular nature of the fortification walls. It was also visited by Aurel Stein at about this time. The first to recognize its true date was G. Lankester Harding, when he and Fred Winnett explored the area in the 1950s, looking for inscriptions. In the 1970s, Svend Helms began excavations at Jawa under the auspices of the British School of Archaeology in Jerusalem. His work provided a detailed record of the occupations and water systems associated with the site. [*See the biographies of Poidebard, Harding, and Winnett.*]

Jawa is located on a rocky island between the main gorge of Wadi Rajil and a tributary valley entering the main gorge from the west. The EB town consisted of an upper settlement, defended by massive fortifications that followed the edge of the rock scarp, and a lower part of the town, spread around the slopes of the hill and enclosed by an outer wall. The upper settlement was entered through a large chambered gateway on the west. Entrances to the lower town were found at the southern end of the site, while posterns around the walls allowed limited access at other places. The Jawa houses were rounded and built of stone and mud brick with packed-clay floors. The roofs were of mud and straw laid on timber beams.

The MB settlement was laid out within the upper fortification walls of the earlier town. In the center was a citadel, a complex comprising a rectangular unit divided into a series of interconnected cells. The cells were roofed with basalt slabs laid on stone piers. A ring of rectangular courtyard houses built of stone and also roofed with basalt slabs surrounded the citadel.

The site was supported by a complex water-harvesting system constructed in the Early Bronze Age. More than 8 km (5 mi.) of structural remains of stone gravity canals, diversions, earth-and-stone-lined dams, and reservoirs can still be seen along Wadi Rajil, and at Jawa itself. The water system was simple in principle. The annual winter discharge of Wadi Rajil was deflected into canals at three points, and these canals led the water to the main reservoirs in the valley, west of the site. Overflow and secondary diversion systems led water into other pools farther downstream.

Jawa had a limited cultural assemblage, probably reflecting its location on the edge of the steppe. Items at the site, most of them basic and functional, had to be made locally or transported from a long way off. The EB pottery assemblage can be divided into two repertoires, one reflecting Palestinian, and the other Syrian, influence. Holemouth jars are one of the most common forms. Most have a line of punctuate decoration (dots) below the rim and some have vestigial lug handles. Large Syrian-type jars with lug handles and punctuate decoration and smaller jars with stamp seal impressions on both the body of the vessel and on lug handles are also part of the assemblage. Bowls and platters are less common. Painting and plastic decoration appear on some of the jar forms. The MB pottery assemblage similarly reflects contact with both Palestine and Syria.

Other items found at the site include basalt saddle querns, rubbing stones and stone vessels, flint tools, stone and shell beads, and small clay animal figurines.

BIBLIOGRAPHY

Betts, Alison V. G., ed. *Excavations at Jawa, 1972–1986.* Edinburgh, 1991. Technical report on the stratigraphy, pottery, and other finds.

Gregory, Shelagh, and David Kennedy, eds. *Sir Aurel Stein's Limes Report.* British Archaeological Reports, International Series, no. 272.1–2. Oxford, 1985. Briefly mentions Aurel Stein's visit to Jawa.

Helms, S. W. *Jawa: Lost City of the Black Desert.* London, 1981. Semi-popular account of excavations at Jawa and the site's significance; slightly outdated, but a good summary for the lay reader.

Poidebard Antoine. *La trace de Rome dans le désert de Syrie.* Paris, 1934. Aerial photographs, including a view of Jawa.

Alison V. G. Betts

JEBEL QAʿAQIR, site located 12 km (7.5 mi.) west of Hebron at the juncture of the Central Hills and the Shephelah (map reference 1457 × 1034). It was discovered by William G. Dever and excavated by him on behalf of the Hebrew Union College in Jerusalem in 1967–1971.

The site is occupied almost exclusively in Early Bronze IV (c. 2200–2000 BCE). It consists mostly of typical shaft-tomb cemeteries with hundreds of tombs. Many had been robbed in 1967, but thirty-eight of these were excavated in Cemetery B (see figure 1), and some forty were cleared and planned elsewhere in Cemeteries A, B, C, D, and E. The tombs were all laid out systematically along steplike terraces on the lower slopes of the horseshoe-shaped ridge. They had round or oval shafts 1.00–1.75 m in diameter and as much as 2.00 m deep, and round dome-shaped chambers up to 2.00 m in diameter. Most were single-chamber tombs, but a few were bilobate. The doorways into the lateral chambers were blocked by large stones, often plastered into place. Shallow body-recesses and lamp-niches were often present, but the bones were never in the recesses or the lamps in the niches. These and other considerations, such as the fact that the lack of weathering of the rock in the shafts indicates only summer burials between the rains, leads to the conclusion that some groups living at the site prepared the tombs in large numbers in advance of their use by other groups.

Most tombs contained the bones of a single individual, but some had up to four. Frequently a headless sheep or goat carcass was included. Other offerings consisted of a few pieces of pottery, or a copper dagger, javelin, or awl. All the

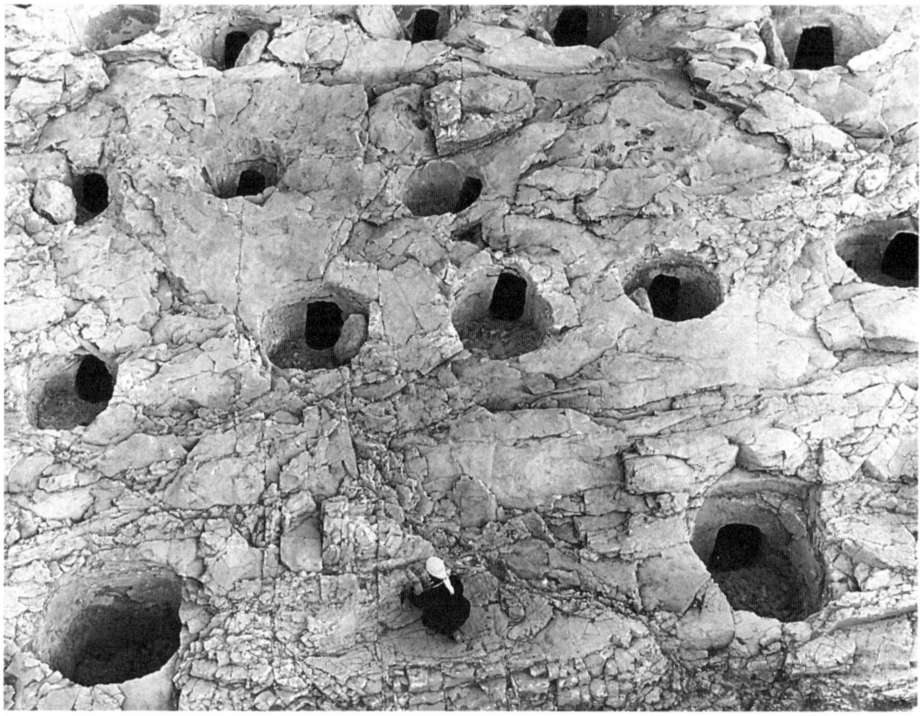

JEBEL QAʿAQIR. Figure 1. *EB IV shaft tombs in cemetery B, c. 2000 BCE.* (Photograph by Theodore Rosen)

bones, both human and animal, were disarticulated, indicating that these were secondary burials. Analysis of the human bones by Patricia Smith revealed that 17 percent were children, 17 percent adolescents, and the remainder adults of both sexes. The skeletal type was gracile Mediterranean, identical to local population groups of the third millennium BCE, but different from the more robust second-millennium BCE groups. The disarticulated burials no doubt indicate a seminomadic population, probably pastoralists who migrated seasonally and transported their dead for burial at ancestral cemeteries. Such customs may seem strange, but they are well documented ethnographically.

The only dwellings at the site were natural caves, sometimes enlarged and furnished with storage areas, hearths, and mortars cut into the bedrock. One cave, G 26, produced an assemblage of more than two dozen pots and stone tools. Another, Cave G 23, perhaps a dump, yielded sherds of more than 1800 vessels. These caves probably represent summer shelters of pastoralists camping briefly at the site.

On the ridge above the cemetery there were found a well preserved potter's kiln; a large dolmenlike structure; an enigmatic "high place" with standing stones; a dozen large cairns that were not, however, used as expected for burials; and a rambling boundary wall.

The significance of Jebel Qaʿaqir is that it is one of the few Early Bronze IV "domestic" sites of Dever's "Southern Family" thus far excavated, although it has extensive ceramic links with pastoral nomadic encampments in the Negev, like Be'er Resisim. It is best understood as a very small year-round settlement with a large influx of summertime pastoralists from the Negev who used the area as a burying ground.

[*See also* Burial Sites; Tombs.]

BIBLIOGRAPHY

Dever, William G. "Jebel Qaʿaqir." *Israel Exploration Journal* 21.4 (1971): 229–230.

Dever, William G. "A Middle Bronze I Site on the West Bank of the Jordan." *Archaeology* 25 (1972): 231–233.

Dever, William G. "New Vistas on the EB IV ('MB I') Horizon in Syria-Palestine." *Bulletin of the American Schools of Oriental Research,* no. 237 (1980): 35–64.

Dever, William G. "Cave G 26 at Jebel Qaʿaqir: A Stratified MB I Domestic Assemblage." *Eretz-Israel* 15 (1981): 22*–32*.

Gitin, Seymour. "A Ceramic Inventory of Cave G 23 at Jebel Qaʿaqir." *Eretz-Israel* 12 (1975): 46*–62*.

Horwitz, Liora K. "Animal Offerings from Two Middle Bronze Age Tombs." *Israel Exploration Journal* 37 (1987): 251–255.

Smith, Patricia. "The Physical Characteristics and Biological Affinities of the MB I Skeletal Remains from Jebel Qaʿaqir." *Bulletin of the American Schools of Oriental Research,* no. 245 (1982): 65–73.

WILLIAM G. DEVER

JEMDET NASR, site located 100 km (62 mi.) south of Baghdad, approximately halfway between the Euphrates and Tigris Rivers at the northern end of the south Mesopotamian plain (32°42′ N, 44°47′ E). The Proto-cuneiform symbols NI + RU or UB are possible representations of the site's ancient name. The UB sign, a five-pointed star, occurs on clay tablets, spindle whorls, a cylinder seal, and painted and incised pottery from the site. The modern name derives from *jemdet,* an Iraqi word for "small mound" and *"Nasr,"* the name of a modern local sheikh. Of the two mounds at Jemdet Nasr, mound A covers 1.5ha (3.7 acres) and mound B totals 7.5 ha (18.5 acres). Almost all excavation so far has taken place on mound B, which rises to a height of 3.5 m. Occupation commences in the Ubaid period (c. 4000 BCE) and flourishes from 3,400 to 2,800 BCE, during the Late Uruk, Jemdet Nasr, and Early Dynastic I periods. On the summit of mound A the foundations of a baked-brick building of Neo-Babylonian or Parthian date have been excavated.

Jemdet Nasr first came to notice in 1925, when artifacts from the site were brought to the nearby camp of the Oxford University–Field Museum (Chicago) Expedition to Mesopotamia excavating the Sumerian city of Kish under Stephen Langdon. Langdon conducted a season of excavations at Jemdet Nasr in 1926; Louis Watelin, field director at Kish, directed a brief second season in 1928. Material from these two seasons was hastily excavated and inadequately published. More recent excavations, in 1988 and 1989, were carried out by R. J. Matthews for the British Archaeological Expedition to Iraq.

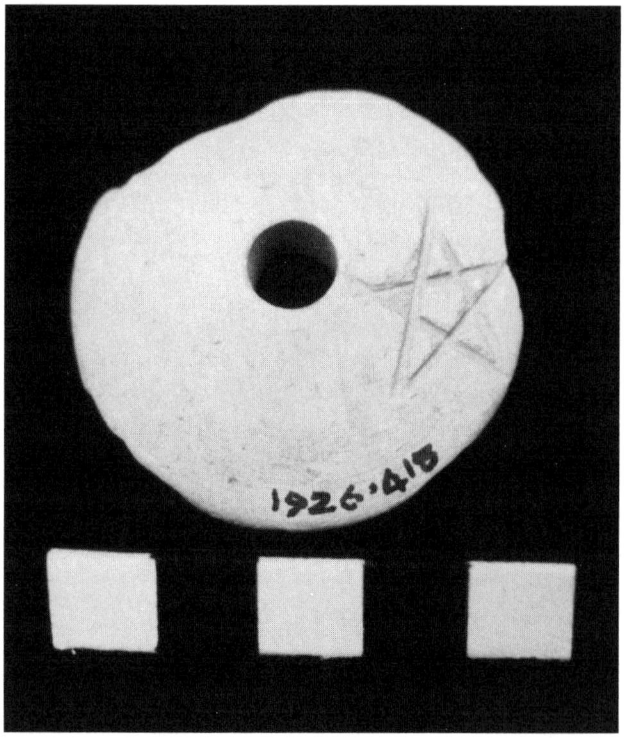

JEMDET NASR. *Spindle whorl.* Note the incised five-pointed star, the UB sign, a possible ancient representation of the name of Jemdet Nasr. From the 1926 excavation. (Courtesy R. J. Matthews)

The principal architectural feature at Jemdet Nasr is a large building (92 × 48 m) constructed of both sun-dried and baked mud bricks, with clay roofing and ceramic gutters or drains. The building consists of ranges of long, narrow rooms on three sides of a more open area, all resting on a brick platform. The contents of this large building, as well as its unusual size and plan, suggest that it functioned as an administrative organization of some significance, probably a temple. Artifacts from this building were considered distinctive enough to define a previously unknown period, called Jemdet Nasr (3200–3000 BCE). When this period was first identified, there was some uncertainty as to its nature and extent. It is now clear, however, that Jemdet Nasr, as a cultural definition, is a term which can only be applied to southern Mesopotamian communities of the late fourth millennium. In contrast to the preceding Late Uruk period, when a largely homogeneous material culture spread from southern Mesopotamia across great areas of the ancient Near East—from southwestern Iran to southern Anatolia and even reaching Egypt—the Jemdet Nasr period was a time of retrenchment and relative cultural isolation in southern Mesopotamia.

An extremely important group of more than two hundred inscribed clay tablets was found within the large building. Other tablets, now in museums in Europe, are thought to have been illicitly removed from the site. The Jemdet Nasr tablets are written in a Proto-cuneiform script comparable to that employed on tablets from the Eanna Archaic III levels at the site of Uruk-Warka, immediately postdating the Eanna Archaic IV tablets which are the earliest inscribed clay tablets from Mesopotamia. [*See* Uruk-Warka.] The language of these tablets is likely to bear some relation to the Sumerian language of later, Early Dynastic texts, although the lack of grammatical elements makes any language identification hazardous. The Jemdet Nasr tablets deal with the administration of an unidentified important institution, probably a temple, and concern the management of labor, measurement of land, herding of animals, and distribution of rations; they employ a range of numerical counting systems including sexagesimal and bisexagesimal. The tablets thus appear to deal exclusively with economic and administrative matters; many bear impressions made by cylinder seals which depict naturalistic scenes of humans, animals, architecture, and decorative motifs. One group of thirteen tablets bears a seal impression which lists the names of several early Mesopotamian cities, including Ur, Larsa, Nippur, Uruk, Kesh, Zabala, and Urum. [*See* Seals.] Similar lists of early Mesopotamian cities are known from contemporary contexts at Uruk-Warka, as well as from Early Dynastic and Old Babylonian tablets from Abu Salabikh and Ur. This evidence is the earliest indication of some form of intercity cooperation in ancient Mesopotamia, although its precise

JEMDET NASR. *Burial of the Late Uruk period.* Next to the contracted body are grave goods, including pots, a stone bowl, and many shells. From the 1989 excavation. (Courtesy R. J. Matthews)

nature remains unclear. The need for cities to act in concert in the Jemdet Nasr period may be an indication of military threats to southern Mesopotamia attendant upon the collapse of the Late Uruk cultural sphere.

Other artifacts include distinctive stone cylinder seals with abstract designs of ladders, spiders, and pig-tailed humans, very different from the seal impressions on the tablets. In a large rubbish dump of Early Dynastic I date, a group of 180 clay sealings was recovered. These sealings, which had originally sealed door locks and containers, were impressed with naturalistic scenes similar in many respects to those on the Proto-cuneiform tablets, thus demonstrating continuity from Jemdet Nasr into Early Dynastic times. The Jemdet Nasr pottery assemblage includes polychrome painted vessels which display distinctive plum, dark red, and black colors, and a range of plain pottery types subsequently found at other sites in southern Mesopotamia as far north as the Diyala valley and Hamrin mountains. Based on the ceramics, the main Jemdet Nasr period sites in southern Mesopotamia are Uruk-Warka, Ur, Fara, Nippur, and Tell Uqair. In sum, the material culture of Jemdet Nasr reflects the consolidation of administrative and social developments in the centuries following the invention of Proto-cuneiform writing in the Late Uruk period in southern Mesopotamia. These developments were to underpin the spectacular achievements of Sumerian civilization in the succeeding Early Dynastic period.

BIBLIOGRAPHY

Englund, Robert K., and J. P. Grégoire. *The Proto-Cuneiform Texts from Jemdet Nasr.* Materialien zu den frühen Schriftzeugnissen des Vorderen Orients, vol. 1. Berlin, 1991. The first volume in a series which aims to provide full coverage of all known Proto-cuneiform texts from Mesopotamia.

Finkbeiner, Uwe, and Wolfgang Röllig, eds. *Gamdat Nasr: Period or Regional Style?* Beihefte zum Tübinger Atlas des Vorderen Orients, Reihe B, vol. 62. Wiesbaden, 1986. Publication of a conference held to discuss the definition and significance of the site and period of Jemdet Nasr, containing many relevant and authoritative articles on Mesopotamia and surrounding areas; subsequent excavation has refined many of the details.

Matthews, R. J. "Excavations at Jemdet Nasr, 1988." *Iraq* 51 (1989): 225–248. Account of recent work.

Matthews, R. J. "Defining the Style of the Period: Jemdet Nasr, 1926–28." *Iraq* 54 (1992): 1–34. Analysis of material from the 1920s seasons, with special reference to the pottery.

Matthews, R. J. "Jemdet Nasr: The Site and the Period." *Biblical Archaeologist* 55 (1992): 196–203. Fully illustrated general survey of the 1920s and 1980s excavations within a wider Mesopotamian context.

Matthews, R. J. *Cities, Seals, and Writing: Archaic Seal Impressions from Jemdet Nasr and Ur.* Materialien zu den frühen Schriftzeugnissen des Vorderen Orients, vol. 2. Berlin, 1993. Full publication of the seal impressions on the clay tablets from Jemdet Nasr, with an analysis of their role within the administration and a discussion of "city name" seal impressions from Jemdet Nasr, Uruk, and Ur.

R. J. MATTHEWS

JEMMEH, TELL, site located in Naḥal Besor, about 10 km (6 mi.) due south of Gaza (map reference 097 × 088). W. J. Phythian-Adams and Sir William Flinders Petrie identified it as biblical Gerar. However, Benjamin Mazar has demonstrated that it is Yurza, a border town mentioned in New Kingdom topographical lists and in the Amarna texts. Yurza is also "Arṣa on the Brook of Egypt" of the Esarhaddon inscriptions. Yardha, Yurza, and Arṣa are not mentioned in the Bible. Phythian-Adams first sampled the site for one day in 1922, followed by Petrie for six months in 1926–1927. Gus Van Beek conducted major excavations in 1970–1978, and small, problem-solving digs in 1982, 1984, 1987, and 1990.

At virgin soil, the area of the site was approximately 12.15 acres; 15 m of occupational debris covered about 1,500 years of continuous occupation from the Middle Bronze III through the Early Hellenistic periods. Although the entire site was settled in most periods from the tenth to the eighth centuries BCE, and again in the Persian period, only the western half was occupied. A small Chalcolithic settlement was found on the east side. Occasional Crusader and twentieth century CE artifacts were found at the surface.

The site was resettled in the MB II–III, ending a 1,500-year hiatus. The climate had by then changed sufficiently to support rainfall agriculture in this marginal environment. The site was protected by an earthen revetment, and ass sacrifices were found buried beneath buildings. Imports show a brisk trade with Cyprus, and a Tell el-Yahudiyeh bull vessel relates Jemmeh to coastal and Jordan Valley Canaan.

The Late Bronze II was an extraordinarily active period at the site, indicated by debris accumulated to a depth of 6 m. The elite lived on the west side, where an enormous house of the thirteenth century featured a public area—with cobblestone floor, mud benches along the walls, a bread oven in one corner, and a plastered bathroom in another—and a domestic section complete with courtyard, ovens, and a private entrance. Camel bones first appear in this period, and African fauna are represented by vertebrae of an African ostrich and a horn core of a hartebeest.

A Philistine settlement followed and may have lasted to the end of the occupation. The most noteworthy find of the twelfth–tenth centuries is a very large, technologically sophisticated pottery kiln, so far unparalleled in Israel. The tenth-century settlement exhibited a method of minimizing damage to mud-brick buildings from earthquake by surrounding the mud-brick foundations with compressible sand.

In the seventh century BCE the Assryian king Esarhaddon conquered Arṣa and converted the town into a military base, protected by a casemate-wall system, for his assault on Egypt. He built new buildings following a common Assyrian plan, vaulted rooms with the pitched-brick method long known in Assyria, and outfitted one building with fine ceramic Assyrian Palace ware. Two ostraca were found, written in a script with Philistine characteristics, one of which contains an unusual series of names, in which six probable family names end in *šin*.

Petrie's largest building was probably a massive Persian fort guarding a small town. Petrie found ten and Van Beek two circular storage buildings with no house remains. This suggests that the site was a central storage facility during Ptolemaic rule in the late fourth–third centuries BCE. The ostraca indicate that produce, representing taxes paid to the state, was deposited in the structures according to kind—grain in some, wine in others.

Jemmeh is the first Palestinian excavation in which everything—bones, seeds, plaster, slag—was saved and attempts were made to restore all artifacts. This methodology eliminated collecting biases, yielded new forms and artifacts not heretofore seen, and made it easier to determine the functions of structures and areas.

BIBLIOGRAPHY

Aharoni, Yohanan. "The Land of Gerar." *Israel Exploration Journal* 6.1 (1956): 26–32.

Maisler (Mazar), Benjamin. "Yurza: The Identification of Tell Jemmeh." *Palestine Exploration Quarterly* 84 (1952): 48–51.

Naveh, Joseph. "Writing and Scripts in Seventh-Century B.C.E. Philistia: The New Evidence from Tell Jemmeh." *Israel Exploration Journal* 35 (1985): 8–21.

JEMMEH, TELL. *Granary, from the northeast.* The two piers are the springers of a radially arched crosswall supporting roofing beams. Superimposed mud-brick floors indicate use in two periods. (Courtesy G. W. Van Beek)

Oppenheim, A. L. "Babylonian and Assyrian Historical Texts, Esarhaddon." In *Ancient Near Eastern Texts Relating to the Old Testament,* edited by James B. Pritchard, pp. 289–294. 3d ed. Princeton, 1969.

Petrie, W. M. Flinders. *Gerar.* British School of Archaeology in Egypt, Publications of the Egyptian Research Account, no. 43. London, 1928.

Phythian-Adams, W. J. "Report on Soundings at Tell Jemmeh." *Palestine Exploration Fund Quarterly Statement* (1923): 140–146.

Schaefer, Jerome. "The Ecology of Empires: An Archeological Approach to the Byzantine Communities of the Negev Desert." Ph.D. diss., University of Arizona, 1979.

Van Beek, Gus W. "Archeological Investigations at Tell Jemmeh, Israel." *National Geographic Society Research Reports: 1975 Projects,* pp. 675–696. Washington, D.C., 1984.

Wilson, J. A. "Egyptian Historical Texts: The Asiatic Campaigns of Thut-mose III." In *Ancient Near Eastern Texts Relating to the Old Testament,* edited by James B. Pritchard, p. 235. 3d ed. Princeton, 1969.

Gus W. Van Beek

JERASH, site located in the region of Gilead, 34 km (21 mi.) north of Amman, Jordan, and 22 km (14 mi.) east of ʿAjlun (32°17′ N, 35°54′ E). The ruins at Jerash (Gk., Gerasa) attest to the city's prominence in the Hellenistic and Roman eras. Identification of the site is based on Roman-era public inscriptions that describe the city's inhabitants as Gerasenes. Coins and other inscriptions offer a more complete title for the city: "the city of the Antiochenes on the River Chrysorhoas, formerly [of] the people of Gerasa, holy and sacrosanct" (C. B. Welles, "Indices to the Inscriptions," in *Gerasa: City of the Decapolis,* New Haven, 1938 [hereafter Welles, 1938], no. 232). The Hellenistic title *Antioch* may have been bestowed in honor of Antiochus III (223–187 BCE) or IV (175 BCE) once Transjordan passed to the Seleucid dynasty (200 BCE). One account (*Etymologicon Magnicum,* col. 207) offers an etymology of the pre-Hellenistic name for Gerasa based on the tradition that when Alexander the Great captured the city, the younger men were killed and only the elderly *(geron)* survived. Another account (Stephanus Byzantius, *de Urbibus* 3.543) attributes the title to a company of *gerontes* ("veterans") that Alexander settled at the site. It is more likely that the name *Gerasa* was the hellenized version of an unknown Semitic name for the pre-Hellenistic settlement.

Although the German scholar Ulrich Seetzen first recognized the site in 1806, major excavation did not begin until 1925, when George Horsfield led an Anglo-American team sponsored by the British Mandatory Government. Their work continued until 1931 and was supplemented in 1928 by a joint expedition from the British School of Archaeology in Jerusalem and Yale University, led by John Winter Crowfoot. The American School of Oriental Research (ASOR) replaced the British school in 1930 under the direction of Clarence S. Fisher, and then Nelson Glueck in 1933–1934. Between 1925 and 1934, excavators uncovered the sanctuaries of Zeus and Artemis and the southern theater and cleared the *cardo* and many church foundations. The area of the city east of the bisecting Chryorhoas River has not been excavated because it runs under the modern town of Jerash. [*See the biographies of Horsfield, Crowfoot, Fisher, and Glueck.*]

Restoration continued in the 1940s and 1950s. The lower terrace of the Temple of Zeus and the oval plaza were partially restored in the 1940s, and restoration of the southern theater lasted until the 1960s. Otherwise, work during the 1960s was limited to removing debris from either side of the *cardo* and partially restoring the gates of the Temple of Artemis (see figure 1). An Italian expedition from the University of Turin resumed excavations at Jerash in 1975; it was subsumed in 1982 by The Jerash Archaeological Project, composed at various times of teams from Jordan, Great Britain, the United States, Australia, France, Poland, Spain, and Italy. The project has excavated many structures in the western half of the city, principally the Temples of Artemis and Zeus, as well as the hippodrome and tombs outside the city.

Pre-Roman sites outside the walls of Jerash have yielded Acheulean hand axes, numerous Neolithic flint implements, and hearths, as well as Chalcolithic flint implements and burial mounds. These finds, along with Bronze Age, Middle Bronze Age, and Iron Age pottery from inside and outside the city walls, suggest that the site and its environs had been intermittently inhabited since the earliest Stone Age settlement.

It is likely that a small Hellenistic or pre-Hellenistic settlement existed at Gerasa and became a polis after Antiochus III or IV won Transjordan. A Roman inscription states that a group of Macedonians, perhaps Greek veterans, were early inhabitants (Welles, 1938, no. 78). Various legends assign the founding of the city to a particular political figure (Antiochus IV, Alexander the Great, or one of Alexander's successors: Perdiccas or Antigonus). A Roman-era inscription (Welles, 1938, no. 137) states that a statue of Perdiccas, Alexander's general, was erected at Gerasa; it suggests that during the Roman era Perdiccas was regarded as the founder of the Hellenistic city.

By the mid-second century BCE both the Ptolemaic and Seleucid empires were weakening. [*See* Ptolemies; Seleucids.] Hostility toward Hellenism led to the Hasmonean revolt against the Seleucids in 173–164 BCE. Under Alexander Jannaeus, in 103 BCE, the Hasmoneans took control of the Decapolis cities. [*See* Decapolis.] Gerasa and Philadelphia, however, remained in the hands of Zeno and Theodorus, the "tyrants" of Philadelphia, who brought some of their treasure for safekeeping to the Temple of Zeus at Gerasa (Josephus, *War* 1.104; *Antiq.* 13.393). Indeed, excavation of the foundation walls of the temenos of the Temple of Zeus uncovered Rhodian stamped jar handles (c. 210–180 BCE),

JERASH. Figure 1. *View of the propylaea and staircase leading to the Sanctuary of Artemis.* (Courtesy E. C. Lapp)

confirming the existence of the sanctuary at that time. Alexander Jannaeus reportedly captured Gerasa at the end of his reign (102–76 BCE), however, and died while besieging Ragaba, in Gerasene territory (Josephus, *Antiq.* 13.398).

The Decapolis region, contested among local powers such as the Nabateans, Itureans, and Hasmoneans in the wake of Seleucid disintegration, succumbed to Rome with the arrival of Pompey in 63 BCE. The Decapolis cities, including Gerasa, were given back their autonomy by Pompey, but they remained under the hegemony of the Province of Syria to the north.

The city came to flourish with the broad security and prosperity that characterized the Pax Romana, possibly interrupted by Jewish uprisings. During the First Jewish Revolt against Rome (66–70 CE), the rebels reportedly attacked Gerasa, despite reports of peace between the Romans and Jews (*War* 2.458; 4.480). [*See* First Jewish Revolt.] Indeed, the continuity of the building program during the revolt suggests to most scholars that the Gerasa captured by the Romans (*War* 4.487–848) was not the Decapolis city. Architectural fragments attributed to a synagogue and found in the fill of Hadrian's arch suggest that the city's Jewish community was destroyed prior to 130, although not necessarily as a result of the Jewish uprising in the 60s (cf. Welles, 1938, nos. 56–57).

The renewed prosperity at the advent of the Roman era led to the renovation of the Temple of Zeus (22–24 CE). A terraced courtyard surrounding the temple was built on a hill in the southwest quarter of the city in 27/28 CE. Its vaulting required substantial retaining walls, so a major building project, perhaps during the reign of Augustus, preceded the courtyard. The second renovation (161–163 CE) added three successive terraces joined by stairs that ascend the hill toward the temple. The upper terrace, a flat, colonnaded platform (110 × 50 m), surrounds the temple proper. The temple rests on subterranean vaults, with eight columns along its facade and twelve along its sides. Two altar inscriptions dated to the 40s CE (Welles, 1938, nos. 2, 4) reveal that the temple was a local enterprise subsidized by Gerasenes and suggest a substantial degree of private wealth.

The basis for later urban development was also laid during the Early Roman era. Gerasa's orthogonal plan, with its bisecting *cardo maximus,* two *decumani,* and a city wall of uniform construction (101 towers spaced at 17–22 m intervals), was formulated by 75/76 (Welles, 1938, no. 65). Excavations against the inner face of the southern city wall indicate that the first Roman wall was built in 70 CE, although the present, thicker walls date to the fourth century. Six gates interrupt the wall; the most elaborate pair mark the north and south entrances, with two on the west and two water gates to accommodate the Chrysorhoas River. The 12-meter-wide, Ionic-colonnaded *cardo maximus* (see figure 2) extends for more than 800 m to the city's northern and southern extremes and intersects two 8–9-meter-wide *decumani.* The *cardo* also conceals the main artery of the underground sewage system and parallels the course of the Chrysorhoas, which is traversed by three bridges.

A Corinthian triple archway joins the *cardo maximus* to the oval plaza (first century), a unique precinct set in a natural depression northeast of the Temple of Zeus. Surrounding the elliptical (90 × 80 m) area's stone-slab pavement are 160 Ionic columns. Underneath the plaza lies the confluence of a network of water and drainage channels for the west and southwest of the city, and a small street joins the plaza with the city's south gate.

The south theater, just west of the Temple of Zeus, was dedicated in 90/91. The lower auditorium *(ima cavea)* was built into a natural slope and contained four divisions *(cunei)*, while the upper auditorium *(summa cavea)* stood above and contained eight. The theater held, in its eight sections of fifteen rows each, about three thousand spectators and displayed an elaborately decorated scaenae.

The next phase in Gerasa's growth followed Trajan's reorganization of the Roman east in 106, when the expansionist emperor annexed the Nabatean kingdom and founded the Roman Province of Arabia. [*See* Nabateans.] Gerasa became a central part of the new province, whose political and military capital was at Bosra. Gerasa continued to prosper in its role as a caravan city, then more profitably placed along a tributary of the major international route linking east–west trade, the Via Nova Trajana. By the end of the Hadrian's reign (117–138), the Roman road network in Syria-Palestine was complete. [*See* Roads; Transportation.] Jerash became a key junction along the route that connected Philadelphia with the Mediterranean cities. This boost in trade led to increased contact with the Nabateans, evidenced by Nabatean coins and jewelry styles and a Nabatean public inscription. A building spree followed Trajan's reorganization of the east and continued during the reign of Hadrian, who visited the city, heralded by a triumphal arch. Also at this time (until the reign of Alexander Severus), Gerasa began to strike its own coins bearing the image of Artemis or *Tyche* with the emperor.

JERASH. Figure 2. *View of the central colonnade next to the cardo.* (Courtesy E. C. Lapp)

In addition to considerable renovation of the Temple of Zeus (162–166) and monumentalization of the *cardo* with the northern and southern tetrapyla, expensive construction began during the second century on the Temple of Artemis. The new sanctuary to the city's patron goddess became the focal point of the city during the Middle Roman era and required thirty years of construction (150–180). Its size, complex architecture, and well-planned approach up its processional way rendered the Artemesion one of the most impressive sanctuaries in the Syro-Palestinian world. Beginning in the eastern half of the city, the processional way (11 m wide × 500 m long) bridges the river, approaches the *cardo* at an ornamental exedra, and ascends the retaining wall toward the eastern end of the colonnaded propylaeum. A staircase then leads to the outer court (161 × 121 m) of the temenos through a triple gate and finally to a colonnade (11 m wide × 100 m long) that leads to the temple court (124 × 88 m). The Temple of Artemis stands in this colonnaded court; two sets of stairs ascend the podium (40 × 22.6 × 4 m) to the temple. Of peripteral hexastylos design, the temple displays six Corinthian columns along its facade, with eleven along each of its sides.

Another extravagant structure, the triumphal arch, lies 400 m south of the city and is dated to 130 CE, just prior to Hadrian's visit. Its main passageway is flanked by subsidiary passages, and both facades contain four engaged Corinthian columns that bear an ornamented architrave and pediment. A passage running from side to side under the main arch indicates that the arch was intended to be a part of the city's southern wall, but the extension of the wall to meet the arch never took place.

Also outside the city walls, northwest of the triumphal arch, lies Gerasa's hippodrome (mid-second century CE). Despite an interior length of 244 m and a capacity for fifteen thousand spectators, it is the smallest circus in the east. At its southern end are ten well-preserved compartments from which the chariots started. Recent excavation redated (based on lamp fragments and inscriptions) the structure to this era from its formerly posited third-century date (Kehrberg, 1988; Seigne, 1988).

Telling evidence for the wealth of the city also appears in the duplication of structures. The northern theater, situated northeast of the Temple of Artemis and south of the northern *decumanus,* is smaller than its earlier, southern counterpart and dates to 162–166 CE. Features include vaulted entrances, at least four vomitoria, and two double passageways, or *paradoi.* Recent excavation suggests that the original building may have been a roofed odeum and estimate its capacity to some sixteen hundred spectators (Khouri, 1986). [*See* Theaters; Odeum.] The theater was expanded in a later phase (222–235) and rededicated then. Inscribed on some of the seats of the fourteen-row auditorium are eight legible names of Greek gods and one reference to Hadrian that may have represented the voting tribes *(phylai)* in the city's *boule.*

Temple C (110–150 CE) is the smallest temple in the city (24 × 27 m). The structure faces southeast, and the entrance to the T-shaped cella rests within a rectangular peristyle court (15.3 × 9.4 m). The vaulted chamber that lies underneath the podium suggests to some that the structure may have functioned as a *heroon* ("hero's shrine"; see Kraeling, 1938).

The western baths (150–200 CE), situated at the corner of the *cardo* and northern *decumanus,* comprise one of the largest structures in the city (50 × 75 m). Although unexcavated, surface finds suggest a plan similar to those at Timgad and Cyrene. [*See* Cyrene.] Entered from the east, the structure centered around a domed frigidarium flanked by apodyteria to the east and a *caldarium* to the west.

The nymphaeum (191 CE), a small (22 m wide) but finely decorated monument, also indicates the second-century expenditure on ornamental buildings at Gerasa. Placed south of the Artemision along the *cardo maximus,* the structure displays a two-level facade and central apse, with niches and a Corinthian colonnade spanning its length. The first, marble-covered level bears an elaborately carved entabulature; the second level, plastered and richly painted, bears pediments and a once-gilded or painted half dome. Water flowed from the statues of the lower story to a basin, through lion heads, to lower circular basins decorated with dolphin motifs and into an underground channel.

The decline of Jerash began early in the third century. Political instability and economic vulnerabilities loosened the cohesion of the empire so that Caracalla's promotion of the status of Gerasa, dubbing it Colonia Aurelai Antoniniana, was only an ostensible improvement in the city's fortunes. Trade diminished as the Nabateans began to relinquish their political and economic power to the aspiring Palmyrenes. [*See* Palmyra.] When Roman political instability succeeded in hampering international trade, Gerasa's fortunes faded rapidly. The widespread, lavish construction of previous eras gave way to the dismantling of standing structures for construction materials, although new construction projects did include the (as yet unexcavated) east baths, the festival theater at Birketein (1,200 m north of the city walls), and the expansion of the north theater. The imperial reforms of Diocletian offered a temporary reprieve from Gerasa's decline late in the third century. It was during that time that the city's walls were refortified and a small marketplace just west of the city's south gate was established.

In the absence of epigraphic evidence from the city between 307 and 440, little can be added to the city's history. The reign of Justinian (527–565), however, marks a renaissance in the life of the city. Reforms in civil and military administration, the protection of the frontiers, and the return of government spending on public buildings improved Gerasa's economic situation and the Gerasenes' standard of living.

The Christian character of the sixth-century city is exhibited in the variety and sophistication of its ecclesiastical structures: chapels, baths for parishioners, and churches. [*See* Churches.] Church interiors were decorated with mosaics and silver; a glass chalice and several Late Roman glass lamps have been recovered. [*See* Mosaics.]

A series of churches was built in the late fifth and early sixth centuries, beginning in 464/465 (Welles, 1938, no. 298) with the Apostles, Prophets, and Martyrs Church, situated in the northeast part of the city. The church exhibits a cruciform plan: each of its arms contains a nave and aisles, with the central area of the cross supported by Corinthian columns. Building continued with St. Theodore's (496), distinguished by a narthex-flanked nave that led to a rhomboid-shaped atrium to the west and a fountain court to the east. The Procopius Church (526) was the first sixth-century ecclesiastical structure, and the only church on the city's east bank. Its sparse remains suggest that it was basilical, with Corinthian-colonnaded side aisles; its mosaic floors depict floral and geometric motifs.

The complex of St. George, St. John the Baptist, and Sts. Cosmas and Damian dates to 529–533. The three churches actually comprise one structure (a central church with lateral churches). The Church of St. John was built in 531 (Welles, 1938, no. 306). It is circular, with an exedra facing each of the cardinal points. The apse is on the east, with the chancel in front of it, and the dome was supported by four columns. The two flanking churches are identical basilicas with apses in their eastern walls.

The Synagogue Church, built in 530–531, is so-named because the remains of a synagogue were found beneath the church. [*See* Synagogues.] Beneath the church's apse was the synagogue's narthex, whose floor had a mosaic depicting animals entering Noah's ark. From the narthex, three doors opened to the synagogue's hall, which was divided into a nave and aisles by two rows of columns. An inscription (Welles, 1938, no. 341) records the names of its three donors.

Sts. Peter and Paul (540) and the Mortuary Church (565),

found in the southwest quarter of the city, were excavated under Horsfield's direction in 1929. The former was a basilica with three apses and a colonnaded atrium at its western end, dated to 540 on the basis of mosaic parallels with other dated churches. The nearby Mortuary Church, a burial chapel, was a simple hall, terminating in an apse that opened on the south into a burial cave dating from the latter half of the sixth century. The Church of St. Genesius, a basilica with an exterior apse and a chapel on the southwest, is dated by an inscription (Welles, 1938, no. 331) to 611. Shortly after the construction of the church, the city was occupied by the Persians (614), and in 635 it fell to the Muslims. Jerash was occupied until a series of earthquakes struck in the mid- to late eight century. The ruined site may have hosted settlement periodically until its final destruction in 1122 by Baldwin III.

BIBLIOGRAPHY

Borkowski, Zbigniew. "Inscriptions on Altars from the Hippodrome of Gerasa." *Syria* 66 (1989): 79–83.

Browning, Iain. *Jerash and the Decapolis*. London, 1982. Broad and very readable account of early exploration at Jerash and excavations prior to the Jerash Archaeological Project, with a useful introduction to other Decapolis cities.

Gerasa 1: Report of the Italian Archaeological Expedition at Jerash, Campaigns 1977–1981. 2 vols. Mesopotamia, 18/19. Florence, 1983–1984.

Harding, G. Lankester. "Recent Work on the Jerash Forum." *Palestine Exploration Quarterly* 81 (1949): 12–20.

Harding, G. Lankester. *The Antiquities of Jordan*. London, 1959.

Kalayan, Haroutine. "Restoration in Jerash (with Observations about Related Monuments)." *Annual of the Department of Antiquities of Jordan* 22 (1977–1978): 163–171.

Kalayan, Haroutine. "The Symmetry and Harmonic Proportions of the Temples of Artemis and Zeus at Jerash, and the Origins of Numerals as Used in the Enlargement of the South Theater in Jerash." In *Studies in the History and Archaeology of Jordan*, vol. 1, edited by Adnan Hadidi, pp. 243–254. Amman, 1982.

Kehrberg, Ina. "Selected Lamps and Pottery for the Hippodrome at Jerash." *Syria* 66 (1988): 85–97.

Khouri, Rami G. *Jerash, a City of the Decapolis*. London, 1984.

Khouri, Rami G. *Jerash: A Frontier City of the Roman East*. London, 1986. Highly useful guide for touring the site, with introductions to exploration, history, and culture at Jerash from the Hellenistic to Islamic eras.

Kraeling, Carl H., ed. *Gerasa, City of the Decapolis*. New Haven, 1938. Standard reference, includes meticulous measurements and plans for all structures within and outside the city walls and Welles's (1938) compilation of inscriptions.

McCown, Chester C. "A New Deity in a Jerash Inscription." *Journal of the American Oriental Society* 54 (1934): 178–185.

Meshorer, Ya'acov. *City-Coins of Eretz-Israel and the Decapolis in the Roman Period*. Jerusalem, 1985.

Olávarri, Emilio. *Excavaciones en el Agora de Gerasa en 1983*. Madrid, 1986.

Parapetti, Roberto. "The Architectural Significance of the Sanctuary of Artemis at Gerasa." In *Studies in the History and Archaeology of Jordan*, vol. 1, edited by Adnan Hadidi, pp. 255–260. Amman, 1982. Uses archaeological evidence of the Artemion to demonstrate the importance of symmetry to the aesthetic of sanctuary architecture.

Pouilloux, Jean. "Deux inscriptions au théâtre sud de Gérasa." *Studium Biblicum Franciscanum/Liber Annuus* 27 (1977): 246–254.

Seigne, Jacques. "Le sanctuaire de Zeus à Jerash: Éléments de chronologie." *Syria* 66 (1988): 287–295.

Spijkerman, Augusto. "A List of the Coins of Gerasa Decapoleos." *Studium Biblicum Franciscanum/Liber Annuus* 25 (1975): 73–84.

Spijkerman, Augusto. *The Coins of the Decapolis and Provincia Arabia*. Jerusalem, 1978.

Thompson, Henry O. *Archaeology in Jordan*. New York, 1989.

Zayadine, Fawzi, ed. *Jerash Archaeological Project*, vol. 2, *Fouilles de Jérash, 1984–1988*. Paris, 1989. Compilation of essays reporting the results of the Jerash Archaeological Project; essential companion to Kraeling (above).

MELISSA M. AUBIN

JERBA, island off the coast of southern Tunisia, occupying a central position in the Mediterranean seaways (33°53′ N, 10°52′ E). Jerba (Djerba) is one of the first ports north and west of the Gulf of Syrte. It provides essential water and supplies for boats traveling from Tripolitania to the Maghrib. The island is relatively flat, with long beaches on the sea-front punctuated by small coves. The best harbor is now found at Houmt Souk; however, all of the coast to the southeast provides protected anchorages, and the major ports in antiquity seem to have been located there.

In Hellenistic and Roman times the island was known as Meninx, after its principal port. Pliny (5.41) reports that Eratosthenes, a Greek astronomer, identified the island with the land of the Lotus eaters visited by Odysseus. Meninx remained the largest town through the third century CE and in 251 Vibius Gallus and Volusius were proclaimed emperors there (Aurelius Victor, *Epit.* 31). However, by that time the name of the island was shifting to that of another city, Girba (Aurelius Victor, *Epit.* 31; Cuntz, 1929). This has been identified with modern Houmt Souk on the basis of an inscription found there that mentions the Respublica Girbitana (*Année Épigraphique*, 1987, 1032); however, some doubt may persist as to whether the ancient site was not farther inland. The Arab traveler al-Tijani, writing in the fourteenth century, speaks of the ruined city of Gerba with a splendid mosque and baths, some distance from the fortress at Houmt Souk (Gragueb, 1976, pp. 25–44).

Jerba has been settled since prehistoric times. The island formed part of the Numidian kingdom of Masinissa; a large city site at Henchir Borgou, marked by the ruins of a tower-tomb, appears to date from the early second century BCE. Jerba's economic potential was reinforced under the Antonines by the construction of a causeway linking it to the coast; the rapid development of Meninx during the Roman period seems to be related to this event. There is a strong possibility that the island was a center for the slave trade, dealing in slaves from south of the Sahara desert who were brought up to the coast through the valley of the Fazzan in southern Libya.

Byzantine remains, such as the small fort on the main road between the causeway and Houmt Souk, as well as the records of bishops of the island, qualified in Latin as *Girbitani,* suggest that occupation and some prosperity continued up to the Arab conquest. In the eighth century most of the original population appears to have converted to the Ibadi Muslim sect, which was, until recently, in the majority.

Jewish communities are found at Hara Sghrir and Hara Kebira, just inland from Houmt Souk. Tradition dates the Jewish settlement of the island to the destruction of the First Temple in Jerusalem in 586 BCE; it is said that a door of the temple and stones from a sanctuary were brought to Jerba by a group of *kōhănîm* (Heb., "priests") and built into the synagogue at Hara Sghrir, known as the Ghriba. This is the reason commonly given for the importance of the Ghriba as a pilgrimage site. Although there is no archaeological or documentary proof of this early origin, numerous Jewish communities in Roman North Africa are known. Furthermore, certain local customs, such as the recitation of a long *kiddush* (Heb., "sanctification") before Passover, find parallels in Morocco and Yemen and may predate the unification of Jewish ritual.[*See* Hebrew Language and Literature.] Thus, the origin of the community may well lie in the second, if not the first, diaspora. The existence of the Jewish community on Jerba is first demonstrated by documents from the Cairo Geniza dating to about 1030 CE. These merchants' records show that, by the eleventh century, Jerba was participating in a wide commercial network, trading agricultural products as well as slaves with Cairo, Sicily, Amalfi, Genoa, and Venice. The Norman conquest of the island probably did not damage this trade, although the effects of a massacre in 1154 will have to be evaluated by historians. Subsequently, the island was taken by the Aragonese, and from then on was the subject of a dispute between Christians and Muslims.

Two Aragonese forts are known from the medieval period. One, the Borj Ghazi Mustafa in Houmt Souk, has been excavated by the Tunisian Department of Antiquities. The earliest fortress, constructed between 1284 and 1289 by Roger de Loria, admiral of Aragon and Sicily, is defended by circular, square, and octagonal towers (the latter mentioned by al-Tijani in the fourteenth century). The second Aragonese fort is found at Borj Kastil, on the tip of a long sandspit on the southeast side of the island.

BIBLIOGRAPHY

Cuntz, Otto, ed. *Itineraria romana.* Vol. 1. Leipzig, 1929. See page 83 for Girba in the *Itinerarium maritimum.*

Ennabli, Abdelmajid. "Meninx." In *Princeton Encyclopedia of Classical Sites.* Princeton, 1976.

Gragueb, Anton. "Note sur le voyage de Tijani dans le Sud Tunisien." *Cahiers de Tunisie* 24 (1976) 25–44.

Valensi, Lucette, and Avram L. Udovitch. *Juifs en terre d'Islame: Les communautés de Djerba.* Paris, 1984. Study of the communities of Hara Sghrir and Hara Kebira, with an introduction to the history of the sites.

ELIZABETH FENTRESS

JERICHO (31°80′ N, 35°30′ E; map reference 192 × 142), site located in the Jordan Valley, northwest of the Dead Sea, about 2 km (1 mi.) northwest of the modern oasis of Jericho (Ar., er-Riḥa) and to the east of the mountains of Judea (Judah). Geographically, the first settlement occurred on the fertile plain of the Great African Rift Valley, some 250 m (825 ft.) below sea level, through which the Jordan River descends into the Dead Sea.

The first references to Jericho in the Hebrew Bible are in the books of *Numbers* (22:1, 26:3), where the encampment of Israel is described across the river from the town; of *Deuteronomy* (34:1, 3), where the site is named; and of *Joshua* (2:1–3, 5:13–6:26), where it is recorded that spies were sent to examine the city and that the town was surrounded and conquered. The modern name of the mound, Tell es-Sultan, is the medieval name given to the site because it is located at the spring of ʿAin es-Sultan ("Elisha's fountain"). During the period of the Judges, when the site was purportedly occupied by Eglon of Moab, the town was also known as the "city of palm trees" (*Jgs.* 3:13).

Archaeological History. Because of its biblical connections, the site of Jericho inspired considerable attention for nearly fifteen hundred years before the advent of modern archaeological research. Many pilgrims and travelers visited the area during the first millennium CE, the first written account, in 333 CE, being that of the Pilgrim of Bordeau (described in *Jerusalem Pilgrimage, 1099–1185*, by John Wilkinson, with Joyce Hill and W. F. Ryan, London, 1988, p. 4). It was not until 1868, however, that the first archaeological investigation of the mound was undertaken by Charles Warren, on behalf of the British Palestine Exploration Fund. Warren excavated east-west trenches on the mound and sank 2.4 sq. m shafts 6.1 m into the earth (Warren, 1869, pp. 14–16). Although Warren dug through the EB town wall and found artifacts, he did not consider that the excavated material remains (pottery and stone mortars) were very important occupational finds for dating successive historical periods. Warren's conclusion regarding Jericho and other similar sites was: "The fact that in the Jordan valley these mounds generally stand at the mouths of the great wadies, is rather in favour of their having been the sites of ancient guard-houses or watch-towers" (Warren, 1869, p. 210).

The site was more seriously investigated when Claude R. Conder and H. H. Kitchener made a topographical survey of Jericho and its surroundings, published in *The Survey of Western Palestine,* vol. 3 (London, 1883). The second archaeological expedition to the site was conducted by an Austro-German team directed by Ernst Sellin and Carl Watzinger between 1907 and 1909 and in 1911, under the sponsorship of the German Oriental Society (Deutsche Orient-Gesellschaft); the results appeared in *Jericho: Die Ergebnisse der Ausgrabungen* (Leipzig, 1913). The large portion of the mound excavated revealed much of the Middle Bronze Age glacis, which originally surrounded the town, as well as portions of the EB town walls. Houses belonging to the Israelite occupation of the town (eleventh–early sixth centuries BCE) were discovered on the southeast side of the mound. Controversy over the dating and capture of Jericho by Joshua has centered around two main schools of thought. The first theory conforms essentially to the biblical view that the Israelite occupation occurred with military attacks on Canaanite cities (a view primarily maintained by William Foxwell Albright, G. Ernest Wright, and John Bright). The second theory is that the conquest was a gradual and peaceful assimilation process that occurred in about 1200 BCE, at the beginning of the Iron Age (a view held by Albrecht Alt and Martin Noth and more recently discussed by Manfred Weippert [1971], and Israel Finkelstein [1988]).

In an effort to obtain further archaeological evidence concerning this question, excavations were conducted at Jericho from 1930 to 1936 by John Garstang. He led the Marston-Melchett Expedition on behalf of the University of Liverpool and the British School of Archaeology in Jerusalem. Garstang excavated many areas on the mound and also located a number of MB and LB tombs in the necropolis associated with the site (Garstang, 1932, pp. 18–22, 41–54; 1933, pp. 4–42; Bienkowski, 1986, pp. 32–102). Garstang originally claimed that the Israelites had indeed destroyed Jericho on the evidence of fallen walls he dated to the end of the Late Bronze Age, but he later revised their destruction to a much earlier period. Although the Joshua controversy was not solved, Garstang did reveal the very early Mesolithic and Neolithic stages of occupation on the site.

In an effort to resolve the Joshua problem and to clarify the results of Garstang's excavations, Kathleen M. Kenyon directed the most recent archaeological work at Jericho (1952–1958), sponsored by the British School of Archaeology in Jerusalem, the Palestine Exploration Fund, and the British Academy in collaboration with the American School of Oriental Research (now Albright Institute) in Jerusalem and the Royal Ontario Museum, Toronto (Kenyon, 1957, 1960, 1965, 1981; Kenyon and Holland, 1982, 1983). The Kenyon expedition excavated a large number of tombs in the necropolis dating from the Proto-Urban period (c. 3400–3100 BCE) to the Roman period. Although much of the ancient mound had already been dug by the previous two expeditions, Kenyon was able to plot three main trenches on the north (trench II), west (trench I), and south (trench III) slopes of the tell in order to obtain comparative stratigraphical cross-sections of the main fortification systems of different historical periods. She also excavated a number of large squares inside the walls of the town in order to cross-check the results of the former excavations as well as to expose larger areas of the Mesolithic and Neolithic periods of occupation; these squares are lettered and numbered A I–II (grid E4–5, on the highest part of the tell, 24 m high), D I, D II (grid H4–5, east end of trench I), E I–V (grid E–F6–7, northeast side of the tell), F I (grid G4–5, northeast end of trench I), H I–VI (grid H6–7, east side of the mound above the spring), L I (grid G5–6, center of the mound), and M I (grid F–G5, overlapping the EB town wall on the northwestern side of the mound).

Major Remains. Archaeological investigations of the site have shown that it is one of the earliest settled communities in the world. During the Mesolithic period (or Epipaleolithic, beginning c. 12,000 BCE), local hunters camped around the natural spring and constructed an oblong platform of clay directly on bedrock in square E I (Kenyon, 1981, pl. 144b). Kenyon indentified a group of three stone sockets associated with the platform as probable supports for "totem poles" used in a shrine or sanctuary, but Peter Dorrell (Kenyon and Holland, 1983, p. 489) later reclassified these stones as limestone mortars. Many Natufian flint and bone tools, including a small bone harpoon, were found in this area.

The next stage of growth at Jericho occurred during the Epipaleolithic/Neolithic 1 period (c. 8700–8500 BCE). Rudimentary clay "humplike" (or "hog-backed") bricks belonging to the bases of walls of shelters, with probable branch and skin superstructures, were found in squares D–F and M I (Kenyon, 1981, pls. 129, 295). The most important aspect of the flint industry was the occurrence of pale-gray obsidian tools. The obsidian for making the tools came from Çiftlik in eastern Turkey, thereby confirming that the inhabitants of Jericho had already evolved extensive trade relations, making it a major center of evolving civilization.

Although there was a gap in occupation between the Epipaleolithic/Neolithic 1 period and the next stage of development, the Neolithic 1 occupation (c. 8500 BCE), great advances had been made in architecture and town planning. The development of one-room, domed, round houses constructed with plano-convex mud bricks implies a permanent settlement and the beginning of a true town. For reasons not yet ascertained, the inhabitants built a major stone wall around the town, as well as a stone tower (diameter, 8.5 m; height, 7.75 m) against the inner side of the town wall in trench I (Kenyon, 1981, pls. 4, 6). The excavator suggested that these constructions were either for defense or protection from wild animals, but Ofer Bar-Yosef (1986, pp. 159–161) has hypothesized that the wall may have been necessary to keep the rising accumulation of ground debris out of the town. The tower may also have been used for some religious purpose. The presence of bone tools such as pins, awls, and a shuttle attest to both a skin-working industry and weaving (see figure 1).

The succeeding Neolithic 2 period (c. 7000 BCE) is architecturally notable in that there was a complete change in house construction from simple round rooms to rectangular rooms. Seventeen building levels were found that revealed that the houses were built around a central courtyard containing fireplaces. Impressions left in the clay floors gave evidence of different patterns of rush-made mats (Crowfoot in Kenyon and Holland, 1982, pp. 546–550, pls. 4–5). One very large room (about 6 m × 6 m) stands out because it contained a plaster-lined basin and a series of pits, as well as adjoining semicircular domed enclosures on its east and west sides (Kenyon, 1981, pls. 46b, 221). Because of its unique plan, Kenyon suggested that it probably served as a cult center or temple. However, the presence of bone tools could imply that it was a skin-working "factory," with the domed enclosures used as drying kilns. Other finds certainly suggest some form of cult practice or ancestor worship. A group of human skulls was plastered and painted to represent human faces, possibly to resemble the actual features of the deceased (Kenyon, 1981, pls. 50–59). Dated to the end of this period were two clay figures stylized to represent human figures; one had shells inlaid as eyes and painted features (Garstang, 1935, pl. 53) (see figure 2).

It is known that Jericho was abandoned at the end of Neolithic 2 because there were considerable layers of eroded material over the occupation remains of that period. The next sequence of settlements is known as the Pottery Neolithic A and B period, or Neolithic 3–4, because the newcomers to the site brought the art of pottery making with them. Two distinct styles of pottery indicate that there were two separate groups of settlers (Kenyon and Holland, 1982, figs. 1–19, 21–33 for the A and B period pottery types). While the Pottery Neolithic A people lived only in pit dwellings cut into the debris of the previous occupation, the arrival of the B people introduced the construction of hut dwellings and, later, of freestanding houses with stone foundations and handmade mud-brick superstructures. Crowfoot Payne has identified the new types of flint tools used as Yarmukian (Kenyon and Holland, 1983, pp. 706–716, figs. 332–341). An analysis of the plant remains from this period led Maria Hopf (Kenyon and Holland, 1983, p. 578) to conclude that the Pottery Neolithic, or Neolithic 3–4, people were primarily herdsmen and hunters.

Jericho was again abandoned for a considerable period of time at the end of the Pottery Neolithic period. The next occupation of the site, in Kenyon's terminology, is known as the Proto-Urban period (c. 3400–3100 BCE = EB I elsewhere), which she subdivided into periods A and B on the basis of different pottery styles found in the tombs of the necropolis belonging to this stage of occupation. Garstang's excavations in area E revealed the best information concerning the religious customs and architecture of this period; he found a broadroom building, with an entrance facing east, that he labeled shrine 420 (Garstang, 1936, pp. 73–74, pl. 41a). Stone objects associated with the shrine included a small libation altar and an oval-shaped smoothed stone Garstang thought could have been a prototype of the *maṣṣēbâ*.

The next occupation at Jericho is the Early Bronze Age (Kenyon's EB I–III, c. 3050–2300 BCE = EB II–III elsewhere), which gradually evolved out of the preceding Proto-Urban period. Defense of the town seems to have been uppermost in the thoughts of its EB occupants, as Kenyon found remains of two parallel town walls constructed of

JERICHO. Figure 1. *Neolithic moat, tower, and fortification wall.* (Erich Lessing/Art Resource, NY)

JERICHO. Figure 2. *Pre-Pottery Neolithic B head with inlaid seashell eyes.* (Courtesy ASOR Archives)

mold-made, unbaked rectangular mud bricks. During the later stages of the walls, the town was also protected by an external ditch. Architecturally, the earliest houses are either oblong with a curved end, or circular; later, rectangular designs were employed, as well as mud-brick built silos for storing grain. This was the first period at Jericho in which artificial irrigation was employed to produce food for self-sufficiency: large quantities of carbonized naked hexaploid bread-wheat remains were found (Hopf in Kenyon and Holland, 1983, p. 579). Multiple burials in the rock-cut tombs in the necropolis contained pottery vessels and personal ornamentation, attesting to some belief in an afterlife. International trade was thriving, as both pottery and objects were imported from eastern Turkey, Syria, and Egypt. The prosperity of this period ceased when the town was violently destroyed, probably as a result of a general collapse of the economy caused by deforestation of the region—which in turn made the town vulnerable to invasion as well as disease. The archaeological evidence shows that the town was then unoccupied for about two hundred years.

The town was partially reoccupied during Kenyon's Intermediate Early Bronze–Middle Bronze Age (c. 2100–1950 BCE) by a group of seminomadic newcomers who may be identified with the "Amorites" (other scholars identify this period at other sites as EB IIIB or EB IV, c. 2300–1950 BCE). The new pottery is related to types also found in north Syria (Kenyon, 1981, fig. 12). A new type of tomb plan was introduced that had a vertical shaft leading into rock-cut chambers below. Kenyon postulated that the newcomers were organized into tribal groups because seven different burial customs could be observed in the tombs. The tomb types are dagger, pottery, dagger/pottery, outsize, bead, composite, and multiple burial (Kenyon, 1960, 1965).

Kenyon divided the following MB period at Jericho into two major stages: MB I (1950–1850 BCE) and MB II (1800–1550 BCE). The town was very heavily fortified by three successive plastered ramparts placed against the steeply sloping sides of the mound, which had been created by previous occupation debris. Originally, the rampart was most likely crowned with a freestanding mud-brick defensive wall, but erosion has removed all traces of this. The houses Garstang and Kenyon excavated in grids H–K6 show good town planning in that the dwellings are well aligned with two streets and drains (Garstang, 1934, pp. 118–130, pls. xiii–xvi; Kenyon, 1981, pl. 336a). The objects of everyday use, as well as the burial customs, of the MB inhabitants are extremely well preserved because of the excellent state of preservation of the tombs in the necropolis (Garstang, 1932, pp. 41–54; 1933, pp. 3–37; Kenyon, 1960, pp. 263–515; 1965, pp. 167–478). This period in the history of Jericho was brought to a violent end by a major conflagration that may have been caused by an earthquake or by the Egyptians.

The Late Bronze Age period at Jericho (c. 1400–1325 BCE) is perhaps the most controversial with regard to its fortification system and its historical connections with the biblical Joshua story (the entry and settlement of the Israelites into Canaan). Many scholars (cf. Finkelstein, 1988) believe that the settlement was a peaceful and gradual infiltration of an already-established local population. Kenyon concluded, with reference to the military conquest theory and the LB walls, that there was no archaeological data to support the thesis that the town had been surrounded by a wall at the end of LB I (c. 1400 BCE; for recent arguments against this view, see Bryant G. Wood, 1990, and the rebuttal by Piotr Bienkowski, 1990). Also, Kenyon found very few remains on the mound that can be dated to this period in the site's history (see Kenyon, 1981, p. 371, fig. 14:6, pl. 199a, b; cf. Garstang, 1934, pp. 105–108, pl. xii). However, evidence from the necropolis, tombs 4 and 5, does indicate burials during this period (Bienkowski, 1986, pp. 71, 90, 102).

The reoccupation of Jericho does not occur until the Iron Age (c. 1200–587 BCE), in about the eleventh century. Pottery evidence from a tenth-century tomb, A 85 (Tushingham in Kenyon, 1965, p. 487, fig. 253), accords well with the biblical account in *1 Kings* 16:34 that Jericho was reoccupied and fortified by Hiel the Bethelite during the time of

Ahab. The town's main Iron Age occupation did not occur until the seventh century BCE, however. Extensive occupational remains were found by all three expeditions (see especially Franken, 1974, and Weippert and Weippert, 1976). The presence of a royal stamped jar handle impressed with a two-winged royal stamp implies that Jericho was administered by Judah at this time (Bartlett in Kenyon and Holland, 1982, p. 537, fig. 220:1, pl. 3a). The pottery evidence also suggests that the town remained occupied until the Babylonian Exile in 587 BCE.

As a result of erosion there is no evidence of any building remains on the ancient mound after the end of the Iron Age, if any such occupation occurred. Occupation from the Persian through the Byzantine periods was centered on two nearby mounds known as Tulul Abu el-ʿAlayiq. The town's position on the eastern flank of Judea probably continued to make it strategically important militarily. As a natural oasis it was also of great economic value to a succession of conquerers by providing them with food and medicinal plants. A bronze barbed arrowhead attests to at least the presence of Persian warriors or their subjugates (Kenyon and Holland, 1982, p. 569, fig. 229:18); a Rhodian stamped handle implies active trade during the Hellenistic period (Bartlett in Kenyon and Holland, 1982, p. 542, fig. 220:6); and Roman tombs and graves indicate the presence of Roman legionnaires either encamped on or near the ancient town.

[*See also* American Schools of Oriental Research; British School of Archaeology in Jerusalem; Herodian Jericho; *and the biographies of Conder, Garstang, Kenyon, Kitchener, Sellin, Warren, and Watzinger.*]

BIBLIOGRAPHY

Bar-Yosef, Ofer. "The Walls of Jericho: An Alternative Interpretation." *Current Anthropology* 27 (1986): 157–162.

Bienkowski, Piotr. *Jericho in the Late Bronze Age.* Warminster, 1986. The most comprehensive treatment to date of the Late Bronze Age at Jericho, based on the excavated material of both Garstang and Kenyon.

Bienkowski, Piotr. "Jericho Was Destroyed in the Middle Bronze Age, Not the Late Bronze Age." *Biblical Archaeology Review* 16.5 (1990): 45–46, 69. Recent archaeological treatments of Jericho and the "Joshua problem."

Finkelstein, Israel. *The Archaeology of the Israelite Settlement.* Jerusalem, 1988. Recent treatment of different theories concerning the evidence for the Israelite settlement in Canaan.

Franken, Hendrichs J. *In Search of the Jericho Potters: Ceramics from the Iron Age and from the Neolithicum.* Amsterdam, 1974. The best technical study of the manufacture of Iron Age Israelite pottery.

Garstang, John. "Jericho: City and Necropolis." *Liverpool Annals of Archaeology and Anthropology* 19 (1932): 3–22, 35–54; 20 (1933): 3–42; 21 (1934): 99–136; 22 (1935): 143–168; 23 (1936): 67–76. Final scientific reports on the Garstang expedition to Jericho.

Garstang, John, and J. B. E. Garstang. *The Story of Jericho.* 2d ed. London, 1948. The best general discussion of Garstang's excavations; well illustrated.

Holland, Thomas A. "Jericho." In *The Anchor Bible Dictionary,* vol. 3, pp. 723–737, 739–740. New York, 1992. The author's previous and most up-to-date general discussion of the archaeological finds from the Kenyon expedition, with fuller bibliography.

Kenyon, Kathleen M. *Digging Up Jericho.* London, 1957. The most comprehensive general discussion of the archaeology and history of Jericho relating primarily to the author's excavations; well illustrated.

Kenyon, Kathleen M. *Excavations at Jericho,* vol. 1, *The Tombs Excavated in 1952–54.* London, 1960. Final excavation report.

Kenyon, Kathleen M. *Excavations at Jericho,* vol. 2, *The Tombs Excavated in 1955–58.* London, 1965. Final excavation report.

Kenyon, Kathleen M. *Excavations at Jericho,* vol. 3, *The Architecture and Stratigraphy of the Tell.* 2 vols. Edited by Thomas A. Holland. London, 1981. Final excavation report with detailed plans, sections, and photographs of the occupation phases, as well as specialist reports on radiocarbon dates and the human skeletal remains.

Kenyon, Kathleen M., and Thomas A. Holland. *Excavations at Jericho,* vol. 4, *The Pottery Type Series and Other Finds.* London, 1982. Final excavation report, which includes drawings of the key pottery forms from each period and specialist reports on various objects.

Kenyon, Kathleen M., and Thomas A. Holland. *Excavations at Jericho,* vol. 5, *The Pottery Phases of the Tell and Other Finds.* London, 1983. Final excavation report, which includes drawings of pottery forms from each phase of occupation and specialist reports on various objects, studies of plant, charcoal, and animal remains, and additional radiocarbon dates for Jericho.

Warren, Charles. "Note on the Mounds at Jericho." *Palestine Exploration Fund Quarterly Statement* 1 (1869): 209–210.

Weippert, Helga, and Manfred Weippert. "Jericho in der Eisenzeit." *Zeitschrift des Deutschen Palästina-Vereins* 92 (1976): 105–148.

Weippert, Manfred. *The Settlement of the Israelite Tribes in Palestine: A Critical Survey of the Recent Scholarly Debate.* London, 1971. Standard reference work for assessing the Israelite "peaceful invasion" theory of Canaan.

Wood, Bryant G. "Dating Jericho's Destruction: Bienkowski Is Wrong on All Counts." *Biblical Archaeology Review* 16.5 (1990): 45, 47–49, 68–69. Must be used cautiously with regard to Bienkowski's 1990 rebuttal.

THOMAS A. HOLLAND

JERUSALEM, site located at an average height of 740 m above sea level, on the spine of the Judean range, 40 km (25 mi.) east of the Mediterranean coast (UTM map reference 7115 × 5183). The name of the city is derived from Canaanite, in which it means "the god Salem is its founder." This god is well known from Ugaritic texts (fourteenth century BCE), in which he is one of the two "agreeable and handsome gods" Šaḥar and Šalem—the gods of day and night, respectively. Because the oldest occurrences of *Jerusalem* are as *Urushalimun* in the Egyptian execration texts (nineteenth and eighteenth centuries BCE) and *Urusalim* (Amarna tablets, Egypt, fourteenth century BCE), some scholars dispute the derivation and meaning of the name. Archaeologically, the site of ancient Jerusalem can be divided into three sectors: the biblical City of David (the hill of Ophel), its historical nucleus, located south of the Old City and the Temple Mount (UTM map reference 7117 × 5184); the Old City itself, encircled by the sixteenth-century Ottoman walls; and the areas outside the walls, which include the ancient Jewish cemetery on the Mount of Olives, the Kidron

Valley below the City of David, and many Christian holy places. The ancient city is well defined by the Kidron and Hinnom valleys, which form the framework in which the city is engulfed from east, south, and west, leaving the northern side entirely exposed to attacks with no natural defense. The vulnerability of Jerusalem from the north is an important factor in its history. Another valley, named Tyropoean by Flavius, crosses the city from north to south, creating the western confine of the City of David as well as the Temple Mount.

History of Excavations. The first archeological excavations in Jerusalem were those of Félicien de Saulcy, who in 1860 cleared the so-called royal tombs north of the Old City. These excavations mark the beginning of a long list of nineteenth-century explorations of the city and its topography by individuals working without religious bias or superstition, investigations that yielded information of enduring relevance. More methodical exploration of the city began with the survey directed by Charles Wilson in 1864 and the excavations directed by Charles Warren in 1867–1870, that followed, on behalf of the Palestine Exploration Fund (PEF). Warren explored sections of the hill south of the Temple Mount (the Ophel), not realizing that he was digging the biblical city. It was only in 1881, after Hermann Guthe's excavations on the hill, on behalf of the Deutscher Verein zur Erforschung Palästinas, that it was identified as the core of the ancient city. In 1894–1897 Frederick Jones Bliss and Archibald Campbell Dickie, also for the PEF, excavated sections of the Ophel, uncovering not only the city's "First Wall" (see below), but also the remains of one of its early churches. In 1911 a group of engineers headed by Montague Parker cleared the immediate vicinity of the only perennial spring, the Gihon, located on the eastern slope of the City of David. There they discovered a group of three Early Bronze I tombs, since dubbed the Ophel tombs, as well as an elaborate tunnel system fed by the spring. [*See* Palestine Exploration Fund; *and the biographies of Saulcy, Wilson, Warren, and Bliss.*]

Louis-Hugues Vincent thoroughly studied Parker's explorations, correctly identifying the results of the work and giving them scholarly significance. More advanced and archeologically reliable excavations on the Ophel began with the work of Raymond Weill in 1913–1914 and again in 1923–1924. His excavations provided a more thorough view because he revealed strata from various periods, thus placing the hill and its water installations in historical context. Weill was followed by R. A. S. Macalister and J. Garrow Duncan (in 1923–1925), who discovered partial remains of the city's defenses and residential quarters. They were succeeded by John W. Crowfoot and Gerald M. FitzGerald (in 1927–1929) who, under the auspices of the British School of Archaeology in Jerusalem (BSAJ) and the PEF, uncovered, among other remains, the Valley Gate, thus defining the western boundary of the City of David. Their original plan was to dig a trench that would extend across the hill, the deep valley that borders it on the west (the Tyropoean), and the city's western hill (known today as Mt. Zion). Technical problems created by the accumulation of enormous fills over the centuries prevented them from achieving their goal. [*See* British School of Archaeology in Jerusalem; *and the biographies of Vincent, Weill, Macalister, and Crowfoot.*]

From 1961 to 1968, Kathleen M. Kenyon, under the auspices of the PEF and institutions in France, Canada, England, and Australia, reexcavated the City of David. In 1978, another team, headed by Yigal Shiloh on behalf of the Hebrew University of Jerusalem and the City of David Society, initiated a new series of excavations on the hill. This project was concluded in 1985 and, together with Kenyon's excavation results, succeeded in giving the scholarly world a comprehensive view of ancient Jerusalem's history and archeology. [*See the biographies of Kenyon and Shiloh.*]

Bronze Age. The earliest remains on the hill were found in Shiloh's excavation areas B, E1, and E3. The remains of the Chalcolithic period (late fourth millenium) consist mainly of pits dug into the natural bedrock and filled with debris and Early Bronze Age I (third millenium) pottery, which contributes important additional data for the period of the Ophel tombs (see above). In area E1 remains of a typical broadroom house were found; it had been built on bedrock, with its interior walls surrounded by stone benches. The later phases of the urban Early Bronze Age are not represented in Jerusalem. The Middle Bronze Age I (also designated EB IV), although not found in the City of David, is nevertheless represented by tombs dated to the period found by the Kenyon team, as well as by the nineteenth-century scholars who worked on the Mount of Olives and in the village of Silwan across the Kidron Valley from the City of David. (It is now also suggested that the grotto under the Dome of the Rock on the Temple Mount is also a burial cave that dates to this period [see Rivka Gonen, "On Ancient Tombs and Holy Places," *Cathedra* 34 (1985): 3–14].)

The transformation of Jerusalem into a fortified city took place in the Middle Bronze Age II period (eighteenth century BCE), when the site was surrounded by a city wall some 3 m thick (found by both Kenyon in her section A and Shiloh in his area E). In the following MB phases, bastions were added to the wall; it is highly probable that a tower flanking a gate, found in Kenyon's section A also belongs to the MB fortifications. Because the tower was found at a point where the wall is above the spring, and because the buildings there had been in use when the Babylonian army destroyed Jerusalem in 586 BCE, many scholars believe that the gate is the biblical Spring Gate (*Neh.* 2:14, 3:15, 8:3, 16). The eastern slope of the hill above the spring is very steep, demanding a resourceful solution to make construction possible there: a system of terraces proved to be the answer. It is probable, as Kenyon suggested, that these terraces are the structures referred to in the Bible as the *millô'* (Heb., "fill") built by David and repaired by Solomon and Hezekiah (Kenyon, 1974).

In the Late Bronze Age, Jerusalem is mentioned in the Amarna tablets (see above), which give the impression that the city was then quite prosperous and attempting to expand into the territories of the neighboring city-states. Excavations in the vicinity of the City of David seem to confirm this: in 1954, Sylvester J. Saller discovered a wealthy tomb on the Mount of Olives (Saller, *The Jebusite Burial Place,* Jerusalem, 1964, pp. 7–10). In 1935, on the Hill of Evil Counsel (south of the Hinnom Valley), D. C. Baramki discovered a cistern with a rich assemblage of LB finds (Baramki, "An Ancient Cistern in the Grounds of Government House, Jerusalem," *Quarterly of the Department of Antiquities in Jerusalem* 4 [1935]: 165–167) and in 1933, a tomb rich with grave goods was found in the Naḥlat Aḥim neighborhood northwest of the Old City (published by Ruth Amiran in *Eretz-Israel* 6 [1960]: 28–37 [Heb.], 27* [Eng.]). [*See the biographies of Saller and Baramki.*] At the summit of the southeastern hill in the City of David itself, a monumental LB structure was found that constitutes a series of terraces built of small stones on various levels to create a huge artificial mound. No doubt the work of the Canaanite kings of Jerusalem, the structure created a podium on which a citadel or a royal palace might suitably have been built. Later, in David's time, the podium was covered with an enormous stepped stone structure, the best-preserved structure dated to the time of that king (c. 1000–940 BCE).

Iron Age. The remains of the period immediately preceeding the Davidic conquest of Jerusalem, found in Shiloh's areas D1 and E1, were too poor to cast any light on the "Jebusites" who then dwelled in the city (*Jos.* 15:63; *Jgs.* 1:21, etc.). Except for the podium (see above), remains in the city from the tenth century are quite scant. Area G, where the stepped structure was found (Kenyon's section A) is located at the northeast corner of the City of David. The structure served as the city's citadel then. Kenyon found, as its western extention, a city wall of the casemate type, which is typical of tenth-century BCE fortifications (her area H). Slightly east of the stepped structure Kenyon also found a palmette ("Proto Aeolic" type) capital, which is an indicator of "royal" architecture at other cities in the country as well (e.g., Hazor). All the indications therefore are that the stepped structure belonged to the citadel of David, as his palace and fort are referred to in the Bible (*2 Sm.* 5:7; *1 Kgs.* 8:1). It was only in the time of his son Solomon that the city's civic and administrative center moved farther north to the Temple Mount. Because of its location, no archeological evidence of that center has yet been found. The condition of the stepped structure may be an indication of the process of erosion by millennia of winter rains. In the eighth–seventh centuries BCE, when the city reached its zenith, the stepped structure was utilized as an artificial hill on which some of the city's best-preserved private houses were built. Cult objects such as figurines representing various deities were found there—examples of the syncretistic religious inclinations of the city's inhabitants (Shiloh, 1984, p. 17).

An important feature of biblical Jerusalem is its water installations. The earliest are simple canals directing water from the Gihon Spring to pools—the Kings Pool and the Siloam Pool—farther down the Kidron and Tyropoean Valleys. The first installation, discovered by Warren in 1867, is known today as Warren's Shaft. The date of its construction is not clear because Warren destroyed its immediate archeological context. The shaft consists of three main parts: a tunnel that brings water from the spring toward the inside of the hill (22 m long); a vertical shaft (12.3 m long) to the tunnel that served as a well from which water could be drawn; and a long tunnel that begins at the lower part at the top of the shaft and ascends at first moderately (28 m long) and then steeply, necessitating steps (8 m high) to the surface (Shiloh, 1984, pp. 21–22, 24). Warren's shaft enlarged natural karstic cavities in the bedrock. It was designed for use when the city was under siege as an undisturbed and unseen source of water. Some scholars identify it as the *ṣinnôr* (Heb., "pipe") the Bible says was the passage through which David's men entered Jerusalem in order to conquer it (*2 Sm.* 5:18; *1 Chr.* 11:6). If, however, the water system should be dated to the time of Solomon, this identification is untenable.

The second water installation is Hezekiah's tunnel. During that king's reign, the city expanded westward, covering the hill west of the City of David. Hezekiah surrounded the newly settled environs of the city with a wall (see below) that included the Tyropoean Valley and the Siloam Pool within the city wall. These new topographic realities enabled Hezekiah to bore a water tunnel over half a kilometer long (because of later construction and quarrying on the hill it is impossible to be more precise, but 533 m is frequently conjectured). The tunnel slopes about 30 cm from the spring to the pool. At a certain point in Hezekiah's tunnel, an inscription (discovered by local children in 1880) was installed. It describes the moment when the two parties, hewing the tunnel from two ends, met. It is not a royal inscription, however, and the king is not even mentioned. The ascription of the tunnel to Hezekiah rests on the epigraphic dating of the inscription to the late eighth-century BCE and the biblical description of the deeds of that king. [*See* Water Tunnels; *and* Siloam Tunnel Inscription.]

The western limits of the City of David are still a matter of dispute because no substantial remains have been discovered. A section of a city wall about 8 m wide, in which a gate was incorporated was discovered by Crowfoot and Duncan in 1927–1928 (see above). They ascribed it to the biblical city, it is now dated to the second or first century BCE. North of the City of David, toward the Temple Mount, Benjamin

Mazar and Elat Mazar excavated a large public building (some parts of it were first excavated by Warren and other parts by Kenyon) and a second structure. Benjamin Mazar has identified the first one as *bēt millô'* (*2 Kgs.* 12:21); Elat Mazar believes the second structure to be a city gate (Mazar and Mazar, 1989, pp. 58–60; many scholars prefer to interpret it as a royal storehouse, however). Although these remains are later than the Solomonic period, they nevertheless indicate the great works carried out by the kings of Judea (Judah) in the immediate vicinity of the Temple Mount. Of the Temple itself, there are no remains from the biblical period. The present Temple Mount and its retaining walls date to the first century BCE, the Second Temple period, and they have obliterated or conceal all earlier remains. [*See the biography of Mazar.*]

The cemeteries of the Iron II period (most of the eighth–seventh centuries BCE), have recently become subject to thorough study. David Ussishkin surveyed the cemetery in the village of Silwan across the valley from the City of David in 1968–1971. His survey revealed more tombs similar to the ones known from Charles Clermont-Ganneau's 1874 survey and subsequent surveys (altogether, some fifty burial caves). [*See the biography of Clermont-Ganneau.*] Gabriel Barkay has identified rock-cut tombs on the grounds of the École Biblique et Archéologique Française as being part of the large cemetery north of the present Old City. Amos Kloner and Amihai Mazar produced more information about the latter, describing an additional fifteen caves, including the Garden Tomb. In 1990 Ronny Reich found another section of that cemetery west of the Old City. This and another cemetery discovered by Barkay farther south, in his excavations on the grounds of the Scottish church from 1979 to 1988, reveal the extent of the burial grounds around the ancient city. (See Barkay, Kloner, and Mazar, "The Northern Necropolis of Jerusalem during the First Temple Period, in Geva, ed., 1994, pp. 119–127; Barkay and Kloner, "Jerusalem Tombs from the Days of the First Temple," *Biblical Archaeology Review* 12 [1986]: 22–30; and Barkay, "Excavations at Ketef Hinnom in Jerusalem," in Geva, ed., 1994, pp. 85–106.) Research into these cemeteries concentrates on two problems: does the diffusion of the tombs reflect the size of Jerusalem at the end of the First Temple Period, and can the size of the cemetery help to deduce the number of inhabitants then living in the city?

Many remains of the First Temple period have been discovered on Jerusalem's western hill (see figure 1). The Jewish Quarter, in the Old City, was excavated during the quarter's reconstruction and rehabilitation. Directed by Nahman Avigad from 1968 to 1978, the excavations recovered a 65-meter-segment of the "Broad Wall," or Nehemiah's wall (Avigad, 1983). It forms a section of a 7-meter-deep city wall probably constructed by Hezekiah in the late eighth–early seventh centuries BCE. [*See the biography of Avigad.*] Many Judean refugees moved to Jerusalem at about that time, following the expansion of the independent pagan coastal cities; others were fleeing the Assyrian destruction of northern Israel. The expansion of the city, as well as the need to fortify the newly founded neighborhoods to its west, compelled Hezekiah to build the wall, which withstood the Assyrian siege of 701 BCE. The wall and adjacent remains of fortifications were surrounded by houses, some of which were demolished by the construction of the wall (cf. *Is.* 22:10). At the western edge of the hill more contemporary remains were uncovered at the Citadel, near the Jaffa Gate (by Hillel Geva, 1976–1980; and Renee Sivan and Giora Solar, 1980–1988; see Geva, "Excavations at the Citadel of Jerusalem, 1976–1980," and Sivan and Solar, "Excavations in the Jerusalem Citadel, 1980–1988," in Geva, ed., 1994) and on the southern slope of Mount Zion (by Bargil Pixner, Doron Chen, and Shlomo Margalit, 1977–1988; see Chen, Margalit, and Pixner, "Discovery of Iron Age Fortifications below the Gate of the Essenes," in Geva, ed., 1994, pp. 76–81). All these remains indicate the city's expansion toward the end of the First Temple period, although many questions remain unanswered.

Persian Period. During the fifth century BCE, when repatriates from Babylon came to Jerusalem, some reconstruction work was undertaken. This activity continued until the time of Ezra and Nehemiah (*Neh.* 3:1–32). The latter even reconstructed the city walls, although there is no archaeological proof of that activity. On the southeastern hill of the City of David, a few poorly constructed walls were found by Shiloh in his area G that had been used as terraces to support the debris of collapse from the 586 BCE Babylonian destruction (stratum 10). In his area D1–2, more contemporary remains were found, constituting, among other things, a quarry, possibly an indication of the works carried out in the city as a part of its rebuilding by Nehemiah.

Hellenistic Period. The period between Nehemiah (c. 445 BCE) and the second century BCE is one of the most obscure in the history of Jerusalem, although some literary sources that describe the city are available (e.g., the Letter of Aristeas). It seems that only after the Maccabean revolt against the Seleucids, when Jerusalem became independent again (164 BCE), does its expansion toward the western hill become its most prominent urban feature. From what can be deduced from the archaeological record, the city shrank during the Persian period to its earlier dimensions—when it was limited to the southeastern hill, the City of David. The remains of the biblical city were still prominent above ground on the western hill, however, and when the western hill was surrounded by a wall those remains were incorporated. Avigad's excavations (see above) defined the limits of the settlement of the western hill. It became, in the second century BCE, the center of the city, and remained so until the fall of Jerusalem in 70 CE.

The southeastern hill, the City of David, was surrounded by walls that partially reused the Bronze Age–Iron Age walls,

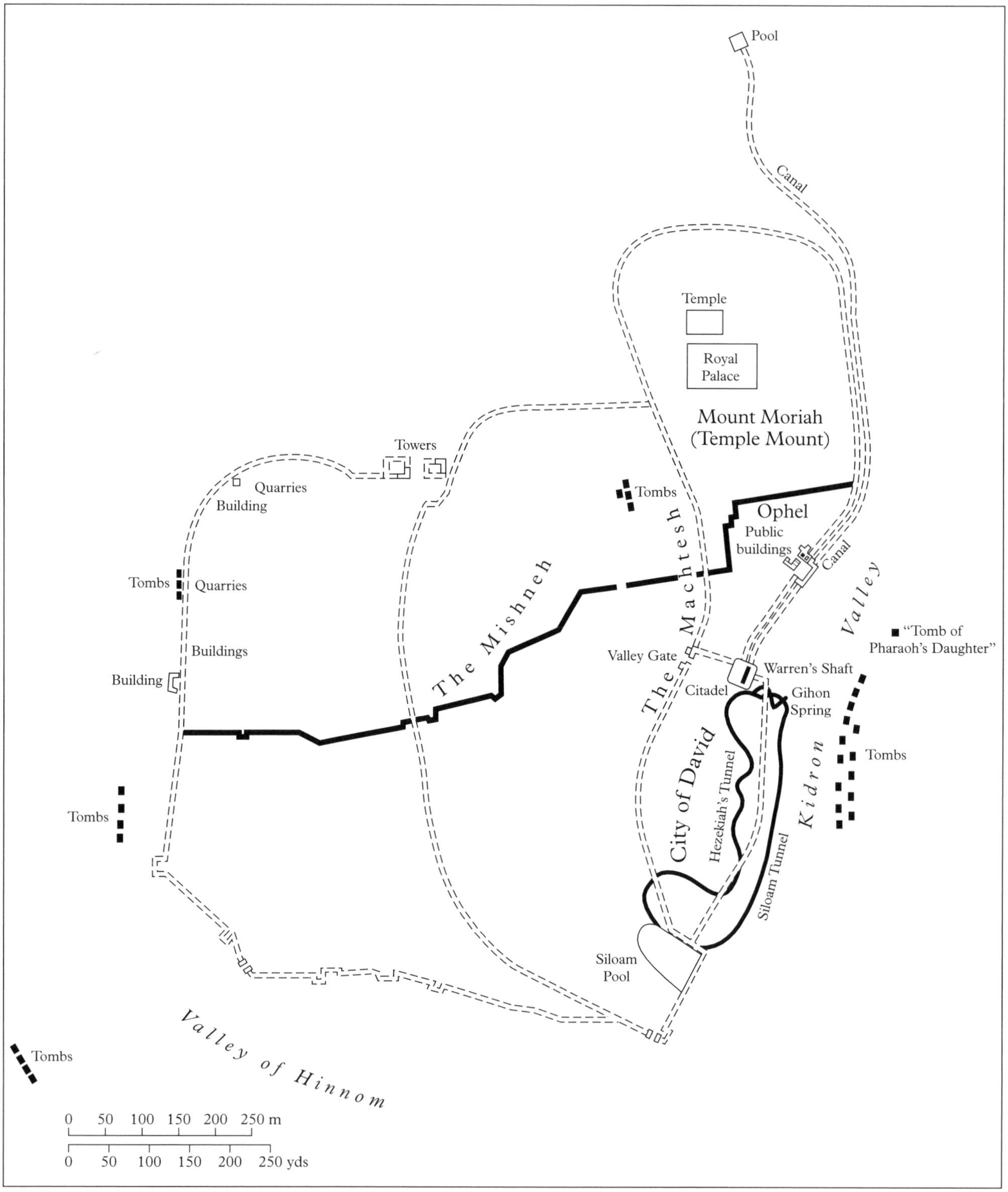

JERUSALEM. Figure 1. *Plan of the city, First Temple period.* (After Bahat, 1990)

but were modified by Nehemiah. His changes included removing the wall's eastern alignment from halfway up the slope to its summit, giving the city its smallest dimensions ever. Macalister and Duncan (see above) had excavated that city wall but misinterpreted it; Kenyon and Shiloh corrected the dating to the second–first centuries BCE. The remains include two towers and a section of a wall, along with other elements Macalister and Duncan had discovered on the eastern slope and by Bliss and Dickie (see above) along the southern slope of the same hill and on the southern slope of the western hill (Mt. Zion). From 1977 to 1988, Pixner, Chen, and Margalit reexcavated a small section in the wall examined by Macalister and Duncan, confirming their dating. In 1973–1976, farther north on the western slope of that hill, Magen Broshi excavated the entire length of the wall. He distinguished two phases: of the Maccabean period and of the Herodian period. The latter was a reinforcement of the earlier wall and was probably connected with the construction of the Herodian palace inside the wall at that point (Broshi, "Excavations along the Western and Southern Wall of the Old City of Jerusalem," in Geva, ed., 1994, pp. 147–155). Between 1934 and 1947, C. N. Johns had found another section of the wall in the Citadel, along with three towers incorporated into it. Later excavators (Ruth Amiran and Avraham Eitan in 1968–1969; Hillel Geva from 1976 to 1980; Sivan from 1980 to 1988) confirmed Johns's results and refined his discovery of the two phases of construction, Maccabean and Herodian (Amiran and Eitan, "Excavations in the Jerusalem Citadel," in Yadin, ed., 1975, pp. 52–54). It was in the latter phase that the Tower of David was constructed, still one of the city's dominant features (see figure 2). Avigad excavated the eastern extension of the wall above, and discovered a gate in it that, although irregular in form, still must be interpreted as a city gate—it is unarguably an opening in the wall. The entire length of the wall is, thus, now well understood. The first-century CE historian Josephus Flavius named it the "First Wall" (*War* 5.142–145).

The city confined within the First Wall yielded a great many archaeological finds: from the City of David, an inscribed stone that probably was originally installed above the lintel of a synagogue served by at least of three generations of the same family. Although from Josephus's descriptions some of the city's most sumptuous structures were located in the city of David, excavation has not revealed any structures of importance (Shiloh, 1984, pp. 29–30). The lack of monumental remains on the southeastern hill can be as-

JERUSALEM. Figure 2. *The citadel/tower of David.* (Courtesy Pictorial Archive)

cribed to the fact that in successive periods it served as a quarry. The remains of the Maccabean period on the western hill are better known from Avigad's excavations (see above). Although built over in the Herodian period, these survived—the lower parts of the houses revealed the lower parts of walls, cisterns, and baths, both for secular and religious purposes. In addition, many of the small finds indicate the character and size of the city in the Late Hellenistic period.

Roman Period. The Herodian period marks the apex in the development of the western hill (also called the Upper City and Zion by Josephus, *War* 5.137). Avigad's excavations revealed whole neighborhoods, including villas of great elegance—the Burnt House and the Western House—in the residential quarter, known as the Herodian Quarter, that occupied the entire western hill (see figure 3). Amiran and Eitan's excavation in the Citadel (see above) confirmed these findings. Two distictive strata were discovered in the Citadel representing the Maccabean and Herodian periods. From the small area excavated, the urban plan featured grids of crisscrossed streets flanked by houses, as was common in contemporary cities in the Greco-Roman world. This plan was also found in Broshi's 1972 excavations on Mt. Zion (see above), as well as in minor excavations on the lower parts of the eastern slope of the western hill (Bliss and Dickie in 1894–1897; Yitzhak Margovsky in 1969; Meir Ben-Dov in 1975–1977; See Margovsky in *Revue Biblique* 78 [1971], p. 597; Ben-Dov, "Excavations and Architectural Survey of the Archaeological Remains along the Southern Wall of the Jerusalem Old City," in Geva, ed., 1994, pp. 311–320). The houses on the western hill, which were built on a slope, all followed a similar plan: installations in their lower part—for storage, cisterns, and baths—supported the main floor. The main floor incorporated a central paved courtyard surrounded by rooms of various sizes. The houses were decorated with mosaic floors and frescoes. These adhered to the Jewish law forbidding human representation and display floral and geometric designs. Only one house was found in which the courtyard was surrounded by a colonnade (the Column House). Of special importance is the fact that furniture was found in some of the rooms, of which the most common type are stone tables in more than one design. The abundance of small finds includes terra sigillata ware, painted bowls, cups, trays, and beautiful glass and stoneware. The entire quarter was destroyed by the conflagration of 70 CE, whose traces were dramatic and ubiquitous (Avigad, 1983).

According to Josephus (*War* 5.176–183), Herod built a sumptuous palace on the western hill. In excavations carried out on its supposed site (by A. D. Tushingham from 1962 to 1967 and Dan Bahat and Broshi in 1971–1972) its foundations were exposed. The palace was large (130 × 330 m) and raised on an artificial platform constructed on a crisscross pattern of retaining walls that created compartments filled with earth to a height of more than 8 m. Some fragments of painted plaster found in secondary use in the Citadel may have belonged to the upper part of the palace.

Another city wall, which Josephus called the Second Wall (*War* 5.146), surrounded the northern quarter of the city. Dated to Herod's reign, some scholars believe that it may be earlier. Because the alignment of this wall underlies the present Old City, there is very little chance that archaeology will reveal traces of it. Its course has been a matter of dispute since the beginning of scholarship on Jerusalem. Avigad discovered a city gate in his excavations in the Jewish quarter (see above) that may be the Gate of Genneth Josephus mentions as the starting point of the Second Wall; Josephus maintains that its final point was at the fortress named Antonia (see below). The only clear trace of the wall is a small fragment of a thick wall, built of typical Herodian ashlars discovered by R. W. Hamilton (1949) while excavating the Damascus Gate in 1937–1938. Warren uncovered other remains in 1867–1870 in the so-called Muristan Quarter of the Old City he ascribed to the Second Wall. They were found to belong to the Late Roman period (see below). They were excavated under the nearby Church of the Redeemer by Ute Lux and K. Vriezen in 1971–1972. The same is true of the ancient remains exposed by N. Khitrowo in 1874 in the Russian Hospice east of the Church of the Holy Sepulcher. Moreover, Kenyon's excavations in the Muristan (her area C) found that the entire area had been used as a quarry, probably also in the Herodian period, as well as a burial ground. (In the Church of the Holy Sepulcher at least six burial caves were found, including the traditional tomb of Jesus.) No vestiges of the city's domestic quarters surrounded by the Second Wall have ever been found.

The city's northernmost extension was defended by another wall, the Third Wall (Josephus, *War* 5.147–148). Many sections of this wall were found forming a long (about one kilometer) east–west curtain. The remains of the wall were still visible in the nineteenth century and were described by Edward Robinson (in 1838; see his *Biblical Researches in Palestine,* 2 vols., Boston, 1841; for this wall, see vol. 1, pp. 465–467) and then by Wilson (in 1864). In 1925–1927 and again in 1940, Eleazar L. Sukenik and L. A. Mayer (1930) excavated a long section of the wall and some towers bonded to it. Because most of the stones were robbed in antiquity, only a few details are known of its construction. It was about 4.5 m wide and built with stones dressed with typically Herodian margins and bosses. The towers protruded northward for more than 7 m from the wall's northern face. The wall's foundations were a packed earthwork—whose remains are in many cases the only indication of the wall's existence. [*See the biographies of Robinson and Sukenik.*]

Another excavation, by Emmett W. Hamrick in 1965, yielded coins dating from the 50s CE found in the wall's foundation layer, suggesting that the wall was built near the time

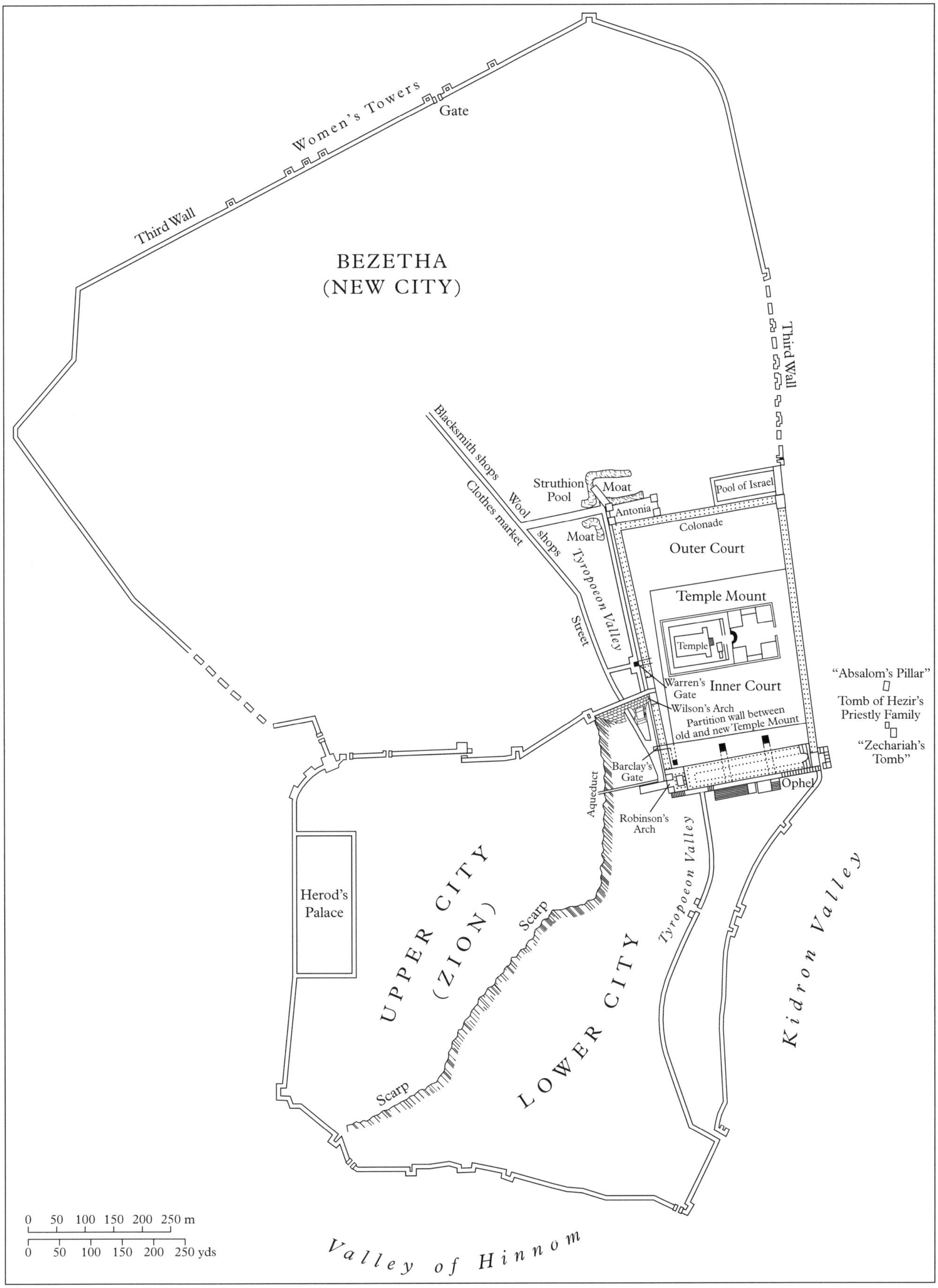

JERUSALEM. Figure 3. *Plan of the city, Herodian period.* (After Bahat, 1990)

of the First Jewish Revolt against Rome (67–70 CE), exactly as described by Josephus (*War* 5.148). In 1972–1974, Ehud Netzer and Sarah Ben-Arieh uncovered a house adjacent to the wall, finding evidence of the wall's destruction during the revolt ("Excavations along the 'Third Wall' of Jerusalem, 1972–1974," *IEJ* 24 [1974]: 97–107). Excavations along the line of the wall were resumed between 1990 and 1992 by four teams, who found signs of quarrying activity as well as a hoard of tools at the site and in some sections of the wall (see V. Tzaferis, N. Feig, A. Onn, and E. Shukron, "Excavations at the Third Wall, North of the Jerusalem Old City," in Geva, ed., 1994, pp. 287–292). In the area defended by the wall, a few contemporary remains were uncovered by Conrad Schick in 1879 and 1893 and by Netzer and Ben-Arieh in 1977: some partial remains of houses, one of which was excavated by Netzer and Ben-Arieh (see above) and a round structure, built in the *opus reticulatum* technique. The function of the round structure is unclear, although it is most likely a decorated tomb, possibly the one Josephus (*War* 5.108, 507) describes as Herod's Monument. [*See the biography of Schick.*]

Since the beginning of archaeological exploration in Israel the Temple Mount has been a focus of scholarly attention, both in survey and excavation (see figure 4). Of the Temple itself, however, practically no remains have survived. The present Temple Mount is essentially the one built by Herod the Great during the last two decades of the first century BCE. The first excavations along the outer face of the Temple Mount's retaining walls were carried out by Warren (in 1867–1870), who was following the lines of Wilson's 1864 survey. The next major studies were by Kenyon and Roland de Vaux in 1961–1968 (they reached the Ummayyad layer only in their area J) and then by Benjamin Mazar (see above), who excavated the western part of the southern retaining wall of the Temple Mount and the southernmost section of the western wall. [*See the biography of Vaux.*] In addition, Mazar's expedition investigated the tunnel that the Ministry of Religious Affairs had bored along the length of the Western Wall (the Kotel). Work in that tunnel was resumed in 1985 under Bahat's supervision. These excavations and surveys have, in combination, provided clear details of the Temple Mount: it is a large, irregular rectangle (488 × 320 × 280 × 470 m), 740 above sea level. The Herodian construction destroyed that of Solomon and of the temples built by the repatriates from Babylon and the Maccabeans. The Herodian foundations, which reach bedrock, thus conceal any earlier remains. The Herodian walls are built with bossed ashlars incised with double margins. The Herodian additions to the Temple Mount were installed along its north, west, and south sides. To construct the new areas level with the existing Maccabean platform, enormous fills became extensions on the south and north. The hill that held the Antonia fortress was partially cut away, and the valleys between it and the existing hilltop were also filled in.

JERUSALEM. Figure 4. *The Temple Mount.* (Courtesy Pictorial Archive)

Some stones in the wall weigh as much as several hundred metric tons, making the Herodian walls one of the marvels of the ancient world. Geoelectric analysis has revealed the thickness of the wall to be 4.60 m. Streets paved with large stones abutted the western and southern sections of the artificial hill. The street at the northernmost point of the Temple Mount was flanked by columns, although they were found in too limited an exposure to permit conclusions as to their purpose.

The platform's two southern gates, today called the Double and Triple Gates (erroneously named the Hulda Gates) and the four western gates (named after their discoverers—Robinson, James T. Barclay, Wilson, and Warren) were initially studied in the nineteenth century. The Double Gate still retains its Herodian decorated domes over the ancient passageway. Warren's expedition (see above) discovered subterranean passages under the Triple Gate, whose function is not yet clear. Two broad staircases, opposite the western gate (65 m wide) and eastern gate (about 15 m wide), explored by Mazar (see above), suggest the monumentality and beauty of the Herodian structures. The entire area just south of the southern wall was dotted with ritual baths, indicating an ardent need to preserve the laws of purity for the Temple. On the southern street many fragments of decorated stones were found that probably came from the magnificent royal stoa Herod built along the southern retaining wall of the Mount. Mazar's expedition cleared the majestic staircase that descends from the southern gate in the western wall and the pier supporting the large arch over which the stairs were installed (Robinson's Arch). Farther north, Barklay (in 1854) described another passage (5.60 m wide and about 8 m high) to the Temple Mount platform that still carries his name. Another gate even farther north was named as homage to Warren by Charles Wilson, who examined it from inside the passageway. During work in the tunnel along the western wall in 1985, Bahat studied its outer side (Bahat, "The Western Wall Tunnels," in Geva, ed., 1994, pp. 181–182). Between these two gates, a bridge was discovered by Titus Tobler in 1853 and investigated by Wilson in 1864. The existing easternmost vault (Wilson's Arch) is dated to the Umayyad period (eight century CE); it replaced a Herodian vault. Warren investigated the entire system of the bridge, which he called the Great Causeway (Conder and Warren, 1884, pp. 193–209). It consisted of a series of small vaults, all dating to the same period. The arch (or rather the bridge of which it formed a part) was rebuilt over an older one that had not only facilitated the walk from the western hill across the central valley (the Tyropoean) but supported the aqueduct conveying water from "Solomon's Pools" south of Bethlehem to the Temple. [*See* Aqueducts.] Under the bridge, a large room—which Warren called the Masonic Hall—is one of the country's best-preserved examples of Herodian architecture, although its function is not yet clear. At the northern end of the tunnel that was bored along the western wall, excavation revealed that Herod did not finish constructing the western wall: it ends in the partially cut away Antonia hill. Because the hill itself was left intact, some earlier pre-Herodian remains are preserved, including another aqueduct. (Warren had originally discovered that aqueduct in 1868, but it was subsequently forgotten.) Cisterns and the remains of foundation trenches for walls were also preserved—the last remains of the fortress built by the Maccabean rulers as a palace called Baris (see Bahat, in Geva, ed., 1994, p. 187). No traces of the Antonia fortress have hitherto been found in the tunnel. Many scholars have studied the rocky pinnacle on which the Antonia fortress was built. Vincent and, later, Marie Aline de Sion (in 1955) attempted to reconstruct the fortress from remains of the natural rock, which had been carved by Herod's workmen from four sides to create defensive scarps (de Sion, *La Fortress Antonia à Jérusalem et la question du Prétoire*, Jerusalem, 1955). On the northern side a deep moat was excavated in which Herod installed a large pool, still visible in the monastery of the Sisters of Zion. Farther east, another contemporary pool was found, the one known as the Sheep Pool or, in the Christian tradition, the Bethesda Pool. Originating in the First Temple period, it is really two pools, separated by a thick wall (50–60 × 95 m). The pools were partially excavated most recently (in 1981) by Marie-Joseph Pierre and Jourdain-Marie Roussée ("Saint Marie de la Probatique: États et orientations de recherche," *Proche Orient Chretien* 31 [1981]: 23–42). Another pool of the same date, adjacent to the northern wall of the Temple Mount, was filled in in the 1930s. It is known today as the Pool of Israel. Its ancient name is unknown, but it was the largest of the city's pools (110 × 38 m). The aqueducts that provided water to the city from Solomon's Pools were still in use in the twentieth century. [*See* Pools.]

Considerable scholarship has been focused on the city's many surrounding cemeteries, as well as its water systems. It is possible that almost a thousand burial caves have been found in those cemeteries from the Herodian period and described by scholars since the nineteenth century. The hills surrounding the city were once pockmarked with caves for a distance of about 3 km (2 mi.) from the city limits in all directions. Some won fame because of the great beauty of their facade decoration (Avigad, 1954; L. Y. Rahmani, "Ossuaries and Ossilegium (Bone-Gathering) in the Late Second Temple Period," in Geva, ed., 1994, pp. 191–205). Most of the tombs date to the first centuries BCE and CE. [*See* Burial Sites; Tombs.]

Following the period of Roman oppression and the First Jewish Revolt against Rome in 63–70 CE, the city was almost entirely destroyed. Only a few remains, such as the western section of the city wall and the Temple Mount, were preserved. It was only after the emperor Hadrian's visit in 129 CE that the decision was made to reconstruct the city. [*See* First Jewish Revolt; Bar Kokhba Revolt.] Most of the important remains of the Roman city date, therefore, to the second century CE. Under Hadrian (r. 117–138) a typical Roman city was planned—a plan that is retained in the Old City to the present.

The camp of the Tenth Roman Legion stationed in Jerusalem was installed in what is today the Old City's Armenian Quarter. Excavations in the Citadel (by Johns in 1934) and in the Armenian Garden (by Kenyon and Tushingham from 1962 to 1967) produced some evidence of the camp, namely many roof tiles bearing seals of the legion (which were also found in the Jewish Quarter, although not in situ). In the Citadel some fragments of walls were also found, but none that permit the reconstruction of any installation. In 1949, a workshop that had produced similar tiles was discovered by Michael Avi-Yonah about 3 km (2 mi.) northwest of the Old City that was recently (1992) excavated entirely. A considerable amount of information about this period has been gleaned from the inscriptions found in the city, all of them in secondary use in later installations, mostly epitaphs of legionnaires.

The city's fortifications in the Roman period pose a problem because there is no concrete evidence for precise archaeological dating; all hypotheses for dating the walls must therefore rest on historical evidence. Hamilton's excavations at the Damascus Gate in 1937–1938 revealed the city gate and its later abutting walls (Hamilton, "Excavations against the Northern Wall of Jerusalem," *Quarterly of the Department of Antiquities in Palestine* 10 [1994]: 1–54). On the east, the gate has the typical configuration of a large central gate with two smaller flanking gates. A fragment of an inscription mentions the name of the city then, Aelia Capitolina. No precise date could be obtained for this gate's construction, but it seems that it should be assigned to Hadrian's reign. Recent excavations (M. Magen, "Excavations at the Damascus Gate, 1979–1984," in Geva, ed., 1994, pp. 281–286) along the northern city walls suggest two possibilities for dating: either the walls were built toward the end of the third century, when the Tenth Legion left and the city was defenseless, or they were built in the first third of the fourth century, when, with the triumph of Christianity, Jerusalem became a central city within the framework of the Byzantine Empire. Archaeologically, the finds associated with the walls are conclusive. The Roman Damascus Gate may simply have been a triumphal arch if no wall was attached to it for at least 150 years. There were three more such arches in the city: two at the entrance to either of the fora that existed in Jerusalem (see below), and one about 400 m north of the Damascus Gate. Some contemporary streets have also been located. The city's main street, the *cardo,* was found, including a piazza, adjacent the Damascus Gate, by Menahem Magen in 1979–1984. Farther south, a small segment of pavement and a column belonging to the flanking portico were found by Margalit in 1978. Still farther south, Avigad, in the framework of the excavations in the Jewish Quarter (see above), located the extension of the *cardo,* constructed in the sixth century. Another, eastern *cardo* was found during development work in 1978 by Magen and Emanuel Eisenberg. Another street, today the main street in the Christian Quarter, was excavated for its entire length by Margalit in 1977. No remains of the *decumanus,* the east–west main street, that probably once existed, have been found, however, in spite of the deep trenches excavated in 1986 along its supposed line.

Altogether it seems that the Roman city had two distinctive features: a northern civil administration sector and a southern military sector occupied by the army. The present Jewish Quarter is still problematic regarding its function during the Roman period. Avigad (see above) discovered many fragments of tiles and other contemporary finds, but none in situ. It is thus assumed that the legion's camp was installed farther west, in the present Armenian Quarter. No definite line for the camp's western limits has ever been found. As already pointed out, a street grid was found for the northern half of the city, along with its two fora. The eastern forum was located north of the Temple Mount during construction of the monastery of the Sisters of Zion in 1868–1874. Although Vincent and Marie Aline (see above) misinterpreted the remains (believing them to belong to the Herodian Antonia fortress), in 1971, Pierre Benoit proved that they were a forum with a beautifully paved piazza, surrounded by various installations (columns, incisions on the floors, etc.) and a rocky scarp, all artificially hewn. A triumphal arch was erected on the west, toward the city. It was identified in the late medieval period as the Ecce Homo arch, where Jesus was taken from the Antonia fortress by Roman soldiers to be crucified. The entire complex had been erroneously identified as the Praetorium, where Jesus was tried by Pilate (*Mt.* 27:11–14; *Mk.* 15:2–5; *Lk.* 23:3–12). Part of the western forum has been excavated. In 1874 Khitrowo excavated the triumphal arch and a section of its pavement. Kenyon uncovered other sections of the pavement (her area C), and Lux and Vriezen (see above) excavated more under the Church of the Redeemer. North of this forum, the Temple of Aphrodite was built in Hadrian's time; during the Byzantine Empire, it became the Church of the Holy Sepulcher. The two superimposed edifices were excavated and studied between 1960 and 1969 by Charles Coüasnon (*The Church of the Holy Sepulchre in Jerusalem,* London, 1974) and later by Virgilio C. Corbo (*Il Santo Sepolcro di Gerusalemme,* Jerusalem, 1982), revealing that very few remains of the Roman temple are preserved. What is preserved are the retaining walls of the temple precinct, a large wall under the present facade of the church (the southern retaining wall), and wall remains in the nearby Russian Hospice, which include the enclosure's eastern facade. Broshi and Barkay discovered some of the temple's foundation under the church in 1975–1976 (Broshi and Barkay, "Excavations in the Chapel of St. Vartan in the Holy Sepulchre," *IEJ* 35 [1985]: 108–128). These scant remains do not permit a clear picture of the temple to be drawn. [*See the biography of Corbo.*]

In Mazar's excavations along the southern and western walls of the Temple Mount (see above), remains of at least three large public buildings, tiles of the Tenth Legion, and some inscriptions were also found that are attributed to the activity of the legion in this part of the city. Because the Roman city was built north of the City of David, it appears that the city's ancient core was used as a quarry where many of the stones needed to construct the new city were cut. At the southern end of this hill, the Romans rebuilt the Siloam Pool, transforming it into a square pool surrounded by colonnades (Bliss and Dickie, 1898, esp. pp. 132–177); a contemporary adjacent street was also found there, descending the valley from the city lying farther to the north. Tombs of the period were found surrounding the city, but no single burial ground has so far been discovered. On Salah edh-Din Street Hamilton and S. A. S. Husseini excavated some contemporary tombs in 1934. Netzer and Ben-Arieh also found tombs along the Third Wall (see above). At Naḥal Raqafot, about 3 km (2 mi.) west of the city, L. Y. Rahmani found some of the best-preserved tombs in 1972 (Rahmani, "Roman Tombs in Naḥal Raqafot, Jerusalem," *'Atiqot* 11 [1976]: 77–88). Some Roman tombs were found among the Iron Age tombs discovered between 1975 and 1994 at the Scottish Church. The only other temple discovered in Jerusalem was that of Aesclepius, excavated by the White Fathers on their property at the Church of St. Anne inside St. Stephen's Gate (the Lion's Gate) within the walls of the Old City.

Byzantine Period. The ascendancy of Christianity made Jerusalem a central city in the Byzantine Empire. Many clergymen, pilgrims, and others flocked to the city, which grew immensely in the fourth and fifth centuries and reached its apex in the sixth (see figure 5). Church building was the city's main area of development and the churches are the prominent features in the archaeology of the period. Foremost is the Church of the Holy Sepulcher, built by Emperor Constantine in the 320s. Built above the pagan Temple of Aphrodite, it has the same dimensions (see above). The church is divided into four parts: a central round structure regarded as the tomb of Jesus; the Holy Garden, an open courtyard with porticoes on three sides that incorporates the hill of Golgotha in the southwest corner; the basilica, which was actually the temple in which the Christian cult was practiced; and the atrium, or forecourt, which gave access to the church from the east—from the *cardo,* where the church's three gates were located.

Another church (fifth century), excavated by Bliss and Dickie (see above), was built at the Siloam Pool, incorporating the pool itself. In the excavations in the Jewish Quarter, Avigad partially exposed the "Nea" Church, revealing its immense size. The identification of the remains with the church, which is mentioned in contemporary literary sources, was further confirmed by the discovery of a building inscription in subterranean vaults. The vaults served to level the site for construction and as cisterns for the church and its numerous dependencies (e.g., hospices). The inscription mentions the founder, Emperor Justinian, and a date of about 549 CE (Nahman Avigad, "A Building Inscription of the Emperor Justinian and the Nea in Jerusalem," *IEJ* 27 [1977]: 145–151). The Church of Holy Zion, a fourth-century structure, was first discovered in 1898–1899 by H. Renard and then investigated by Eisenberg in 1983. The building had a basilical plan with five naves. The traditional tomb of King David is incorporated in it.

A church was discovered at a site where tradition locates a miracle—that of the healing of the paralytic (*Jn.* 5:2–9). The church, a typical basilica in plan was built on the large wall that divides the two Bethesda pools (see above), on 13-meter-high pillars that reach from the bottom of the pool to the surface. (C. Mauss in 1854, the White Fathers in 1914, and Rousée and Pierre in 1956).

The church of St. Stephen was built by the empress Eudocia in the fifth century. It was excavated by Marie-Joseph Legrange from 1885 to 1893 and entirely reconstructed for use by the Dominican fathers. On the Mt. of Olives, the emperor Constantine built a church named Eleona (Gk., "of the olives") that was discovered in 1910–1911 by Vincent and partially cleared and restored. Other churches on the slopes of the mountain have also been excavated, including the Dominus Flevit (probably the Late Byzantine Church of Gethsemane) by J. T. Milik and Billarmino Bagatti in 1955; the Church of Gethsemane built by Theodosius I in 385 and excavated by Gaudence Orfali from 1910 to 1919; two chapels on the site of the present Russian Church of the Ascension, investigated from 1870 to 1893 that include the tomb of the Virgin, even though the remains are mostly from the Crusader period; and two unidentified churches on top of the mountain, investigated by Bliss and Dickie in 1894. Many contemporary tombs have also been discovered on the mountain's slopes. Barkay found a church on the hill of the Scottish Church during his 1975–1989 excavations. To this repertoire belong burial chapels: one decorated with birds in a mosaic pavement found by Dickie in 1894 north of the Damascus Gate; the "Orpheus mosaic" found in the same area studied by Vincent in 1901; and the chapel recently discovered by Reich in his 1992 excavation in the Mamilla area west of the Old City (Reich, "The Ancient Burial Ground in the Mamilla Neighborhood, Jerusalem," in Geva, ed., 1994, pp. 117–118). [*See* Churches; Mosaics.]

The Byzantine period's primary contribution to Jerusalem's fortifications was the empress Eudocia's addition, in 446 CE, of a new southern city wall—actually a reconstruction of the First Wall (first century BCE). The empress, a resident of the city, rebuilt the wall to enclose the newly built churches of Siloam, Zion, and Peter in Galicantu, as well as the nearby residential neighborhoods. Bliss and Dickie excavated most of this new city wall in 1894–1897; Kenyon, Warren, Broshi, Macalister and Duncan, and others excavated more of it. Some evidence of the network of streets in that part of the city was revealed in every excavation that took place there (see Broshi, "Standards of Street Widths in the Roman–Byzantine Period," *IEJ* 27 [1977]: 232–235). A fragment of the city wall was also discovered in Sivan's excavations in the Citadel (see above). Evidence of the density of the residential quarter that wall encircled can be deduced from the excavations on the southeastern hill of the city of David by Macalister and Duncan in 1923–1925 and Crowfoot and FitzGerald in 1927 and from Mazar's 1967–1978 excavations along the southern wall of the Temple Mount. A well-planned residential quarter was revealed in which the streets were flanked by well-built houses in which a central open courtyard was the main feature. Only in Mazar's excavations did the location of the houses seem to be unplanned, although their embellishments reveal that the inhabitants were well-to-do. In the Jewish Quarter the extensions of the Roman *cardo* was found to belong to the Byzantine period. It was apparently built by the emperor Justinian to

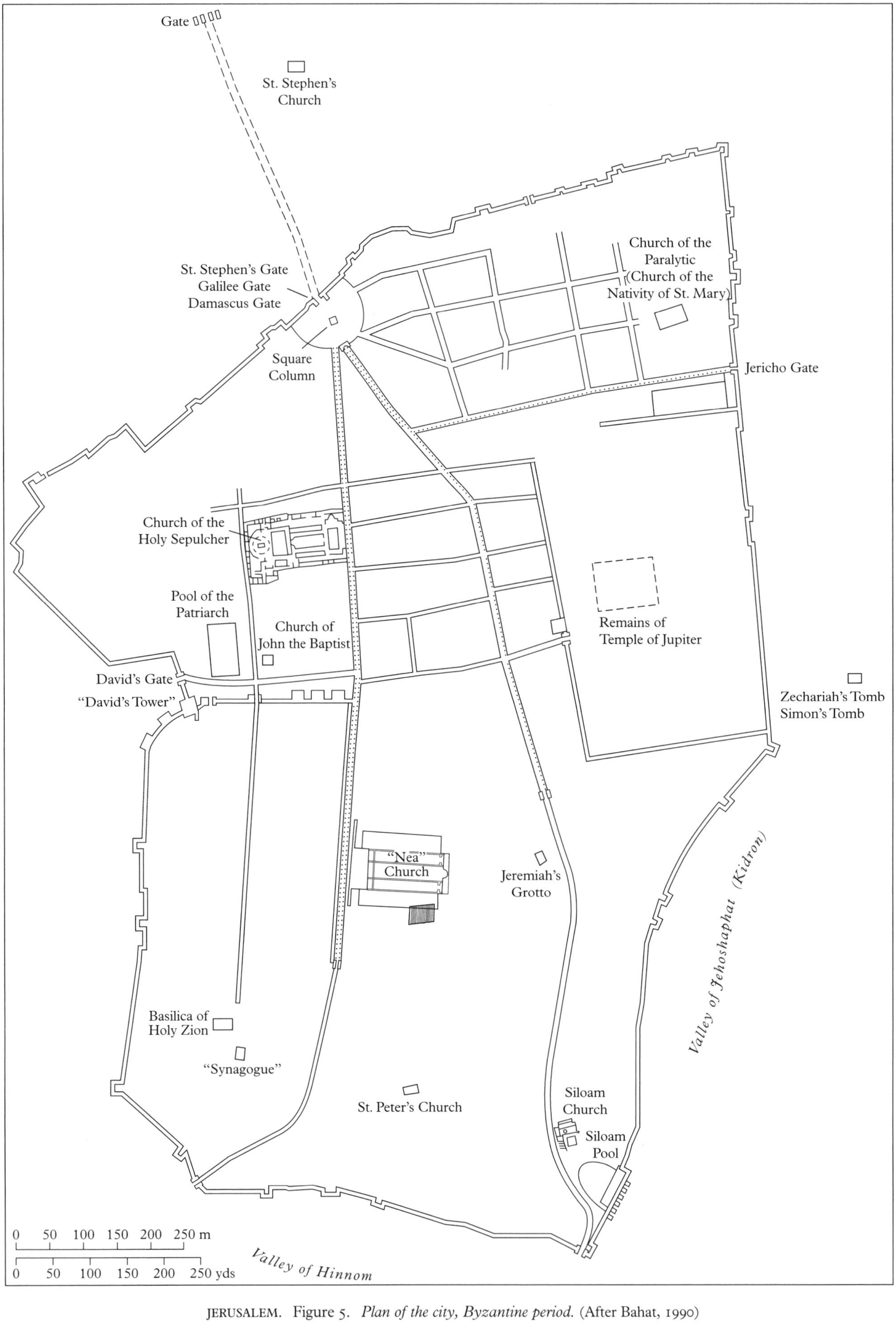

JERUSALEM. Figure 5. *Plan of the city, Byzantine period.* (After Bahat, 1990)

connect the Church of the Holy Spulcher to the newly built Nea church, probably for religious processions. Fragments of the eastern *cardo* may well belong to this period (see above).

Excavations that began in 1990 north of the Old City have revealed monasteries and chapels along the Third Wall (first century CE.) Similar structures were found in previous excavations along this wall—by Sukenik and Mayer (1930) in 1929 and by Netzer and Ben-Arieh in 1972–1974 (see above). The last of the Byzantine construction projects was the Golden Gate. It was built in 629 by the emperor Heraclius as a triumphal arch when he brought True Cross back to the city after its captivity among the Persians, who had conquered Jerusalem in 614.

Islamic Period. The Arab conquest of Jerusalem in 638 did not alter the city appreciably, but there were some alterations in its landscape as the Nea church had been destroyed. The period is characterized by considerable building activity on and around the Temple Mount. It was under the Umayyad dynasty (661–750) that the focus of the sanctity of the Holy City moved from the Church of the Holy Sepulcher back to the Temple Mount. The Dome of the Rock and the al-Aqṣa mosque were built in 691 and 711–713, respectively, along with other, minor structures on the Mount (see figure 6). An administrative compound was built south of the Temple Mount. It is unique of its kind because, although literary documents from the period reveal that similar compounds were constructed in all the main cities of Islam, the one in Jerusalem is so far the only one to survive. Excavated by Mazar between 1967 and 1978, it comprised six large palaces organized along the west and the south walls of the Temple Mount. Wall paintings, stucco, and vast dimensions are their main aesthetic features.

During the period earthquakes struck the country, creating decisive destruction in the city. The 747 or 749 quake left the Umayyad structures in ruin. Only the Dome of the Rock survived it. There are almost no architectural remains from the ʿAbbasid period that followed. The earthquake of 1033 also created major devastation in the city. It was during the reconstruction that followed it that the present southern alignment of the city wall was created. In his excavations in the Jewish Quarter, Avigad recovered a small section of this eleventh-century wall with a postern. The present northern city wall was repaired then and some fragments of that reconstruction have been found in excavation (by De Groot in 1979). J. Basil Hennessy's excavations at the Damascus Gate revealed two cisterns flanking the gate's entry that he ascribes to the Umayyad period (see G. J. Wightman, *The Damascus Gate, Jerusalem,* Oxford, 1989). As a result of the repairs after the 1033 earthquake, the southern part of the city was left outside the walls, and the inhabitants of that part of the city moved into the port city, which was included by the new walls. Other contemporary building projects include the repair work of the Temple Mount retaining walls and the installation of the so-called Solomon's Stables under the Temple Mount esplanade. The Byzantine neighborhood on the southeastern hill (the City of David) existed into the Arab period, but the architectural renovations they underwent were of inferior quality.

JERUSALEM. Figure 6. *Dome of the Rock.* (Courtesy Pictorial Archive)

Medieval Period. The Crusaders conquered Jerusalem on 15 July 1099. The alignment of the city walls then remained through subsequent repairs in the ʿAyyubid (1187–1250) and Ottoman (1517–1917) periods. It was during those periods that Jerusalem acquired its Oriental character, still apparent to the visitor. The Muslims made conscious efforts to change the city's Crusader/Christian features. [*See* Crusader Period.]

In the last few decades, many excavations have been carried out in the city to obtain a better understanding of the Late and post-Medieval periods: for example, the Citadel (by Geva in 1976–1980 and Sivan in 1980–1988); the Churches of St. Julian (by Bahat in 1972) and St. Peter in Vinculi and the Crusader southern market (by Avigad from

1969 to 1982); the Churches of St. Thomas of the Germans (by Bahat and Reich in 1976) and St. Mary of the Germans (by Asher Ovadiah and Netzer in 1968); the Holy Sepulcher (by Corbo, Coüasnon, Christos Katsimbinis from 1960 to 1969); the foundations of the chapel of St. Egidius (by Bahat in 1985); the cloister of St. Mary Magdalene (by Bahat in 1978); the Crusader royal palace (by Bahat and Broshi in 1970–1971; see their "Excavations in the Armenian Garden," in Yadin, ed., 1975, p. 56); the Templar wall, south of the Temple Mount (by B. Mazar from 1967 to 1978); and the Damascus Gate (by Hennessy in 1972).

Some ʿAyyubid remains have been uncovered as well. Many vestiges of this period are preserved in the city and are responsible for its special character. In 1961–1967, in the Armenian Garden, Tushingham found a large building in his area L that he interpreted as a caravanserai, although its plan may be better explained as an administrative structure. The building's centrality was underscored by the discovery of strong towers in the contemporary western and southern city wall built by the nephew of Salah edh-Din (Saladin) between 1202 and 1212. These towers (excavated by Broshi in 1971–1972, Avigad from 1969 to 1982, Margowsky from 1969 to 1972, and Ben-Dov from 1973 to 1977) were incorporated in a city wall of which only small sections are preserved. However, Bliss and Dickie (from 1894 to 1897) discovered a city wall crowning Mt. Zion that can be identified with a wall the literary sources report was built by Salah edh-Din, who also excavated a moat in front of it. The northwestern corner of the Old City preserves the remains of a tower and a section of the medieval city wall (explored by Bahat and Menashe Ben-Ari in 1972). Between 1968 and 1983 Michael H. Burgoyne did a survey of Mamluk buildings in the city for the BSAJ. The greatest change in the character of the city took place in the sixteenth century under the Ottoman sultan Süleiman the Magnificent. The city walls of Jerusalem (demolished by Saladin's nephew in the thirteenth century) were reconstructed, as were six fountains built by him in addition to the reconstruction of the aqueducts from Solomon's Pools south of Bethlehem. Public buildings were also added to the city and its present Muslim character was thus secured.

[*See also* Bibilical Temple.]

BIBLIOGRAPHY

Amiran, David H. K., and Arie Shachar. *Atlas of Jerusalem*. Berlin and New York, 1973.

Avigad, Nahman. *Ancient Monuments in the Kidron Valley*. Jerusalem, 1954.

Avigad, Nahman. *Discovering Jerusalem*. Nashville, 1983.

Avi-Yonah, Michael. *Sefer Yerushalayim* (in Hebrew). Vol. 1. Jerusalem, 1956.

Bahat, Dan. *The Illustrated Atlas of Jerusalem*. New York, 1990.

Ben-Dov, Meir. *In the Shadow of the Temple: The Discovery of Ancient Jerusalem*. Translated by Ina Friedman. New York, 1985.

Benvenisti, Meron. *Jerusalem, the Torn City*. Minneapolis, 1976.

Bliss, Frederick Jones, and Archibald Campbell Dickie. *Excavations at Jerusalem, 1894–1897*. London, 1898.

Burgoyne, Michael Hamilton, and D. S. Richards. *Mamluk Jerusalem: An Architectural Study*. London, 1987.

Conder, Claude R., and Charles Warren. *The Survey of Western Palestine*, vol. 5, *Jerusalem*. London, 1884.

Crowfoot, John W., and Gerald M. FitzGerald. *Excavations in the Tyropoean Valley, Jerusalem, 1927*. London, 1929.

Geva, Hillel, ed. *Ancient Jerusalem Revealed*. Jerusalem, 1994.

Hamilton, Robert William. *The Structural History of the Aqsa Mosque: A Record of Archaeological Gleanings from the Repairs of 1938–1942*. London, 1949.

Hollis, F. J. *The Archeology of Herod's Temple*. London, 1934.

Kenyon, Kathleen M. *Jerusalem: Excavating 3000 Years of History*. New York, 1967.

Kenyon, Kathleen M. *Digging Up Jerusalem*. London, 1974.

Lutfi, Huda. *Al Quds al-Mamlukiyya*. Berlin, 1985.

Macalister, R. A. S., and Duncan J. Garrow. *Excavations on the Hill of Ophel, Jerusalem, 1923–1925*. London, 1926.

Mazar, Benjamin, and Eliat Mazar. *Excavations in the South of the Temple Mount*. Qedem, vol. 29. Jerusalem, 1989.

Rosen-Ayalon, Myriam. *The Early Islamic Monuments of al-Haram al-Sharif*. Qedem, vol. 28. Jerusalem, 1989.

Shiloh, Yigal, et al. *Excavations at the City of David, 1978–85*. 3 vols. to date. Qedem, vols. 19, 30, 33. Jerusalem, 1984–1992.

Simons, Jan Jozef. *Jerusalem in the Old Testament*. Leiden, 1952.

Sukenik, Eleazar L., and Leo Mayer. *The Third Wall of Jerusalem: An Account of Excavations*. Jerusalem, 1930.

Tushingham, A. D., et al. *Excavations in Jerusalem, 1961–1967*. Vol. 1. Toronto, 1985.

Vincent, L.-H., and Félix-Marie Abel. *Jérusalem: Recherches de topographie, d'archéologie et d'histoire*, vol. 2, *Jérusalem nouvelle*. Paris, 1926.

Wilson, Charles W. *Ordnance Survey of Jerusalem*. London, 1865.

Yadin, Yigael, ed. *Jerusalem Revealed: Archaeology in the Holy City, 1968–1974*. Jerusalem, 1975.

DAN BAHAT

JEWELRY. Adornment and satisfying the wearer's vanity are only two of the contributions jewelry makes to an individual's well-being. Some pieces of jewelry, many of them shaped like deities, their attribute animals, or symbols, are at the same time meant to protect the individual and to demonstrate one's piety. Jewelry shaped like flowers or fruit reflects the time-honored use of plants as personal ornament, as well as the symbolic significance of their shape or divine associations (e.g., McGovern, 1985). The materials (gold = sun, silver = moon) usually are also weighted with symbolic significance. When worn, jewelry also serves to express human difference/inequality (see below). Lastly, jewelry is an investment, and in precoinage times (and later) could be used as money: many types have a standard weight and gold/silver content, their value being enhanced by fine work, whether viewed as personal effects or as money.

In the ancient Near East and elsewhere, the craving to bedeck oneself with jewels transcended gender. Excavated finds on skeletal remains of known gender, as well as artistic representations, reveal that by their appearance alone it is seldom possible to distinguish women's jewels from those of men (Marcus, 1993, p. 170). This may, at least in part, be an archaeological optical illusion: common sense suggests, and ample ethnological studies illustrate, that jewelry—along with other personal ornaments and accessories, clothing, and tattooing—did express differences, of wealth, gender, family and social status, official function, and ethnos (cf. Marcus, 1993), and that some of it was intended for special occasions such as weddings and festivals. Possessed of emotions and desires on a majestic scale, many gods display a knack for jewelry no less than that of mortals.

Jewelry is found least in habitational contexts—that is, on the floors; exceptions to this rule occur chiefly in cases of violent destruction not followed by plundering (Marcus, 1993, p. 159). Most jewelry is found in tombs, foundation deposits, temple favissae, or hoards.

While in the former three its function is plain enough, there are several possibilities for the preburial role of jewelry from hoards. It is often impossible to decide whether the pieces in a hoard belong to a jeweler/trader or are the property of a customer. Intact jewelry pieces may be identified as finished products/stock-in-trade of the former, and as personal ornaments or money of the latter. Broken jewelry pieces may be identified as spare parts/recyclables of the former, and as money of the latter.

Unfortunately, the archaeological context does not always permit one to distinguish a foundation deposit from a hoard, which might have been hidden in the face of danger. When it can be distinguished, a hoard will not only afford chronological, technological, and typological insight; it might offer an opportunity for economic interpretation (Balmuth, 1976; Curtis, 1984).

In Mesopotamia, archaeologists have unearthed the splendid jewelry of the third-millennium royal tombs of Ur; Egypt, in addition to the grave goods of Tutankhamun, has yielded a sizable sample of second-millennium and early first-millennium BCE royal jewelry. Students of ancient Palestinian jewelry have to content themselves with a far more modest corpus. In another contrast with Egypt there is hardly any piece that can be regarded as funerary in origin. Representational art (e.g. Neo-Assyrian reliefs) and textual mentions (like in *Ex.* 39 and *Is.* 3:18–24) complement the picture and lend it perspective.

Materials, Techniques, and Tools. The first known gold, usually considered to be of Egyptian origin (for a modest local source exploited much later, Wadi Ṭawaḥin near Eilat, see Wolff, 1993, pp. 160–162), appears in Palestine in the Chalcolithic period. Copper, thought to have been mined locally at Feinan and Timnaʿ, makes its appearance in Palestine in the same period. Silver, probably coming from Anatolia, is first found in jewelry of the Early Bronze I period (see Prag, 1978). Bronze makes its debut in jewelry, as well as in tools and weapons, in the Middle Bronze I period (see Eisenberg, 1985). Iron was not a popular metal in jewelry making; personal ornaments in this metal belong chiefly to the early Iron II.

Stones were valued chiefly for their colors, not because they refracted light (precious stones, such as diamonds and rubies, were not yet used). Lapis lazuli from Afghanistan and turquoise from Sinai, so popular in Egypt—the former also in Mesopotamia—were rare in Palestine. Carnelian (quartz with iron minerals, from the surrounding sandstone deserts) was used abundantly in Palestine in beads from the late Neolithic onward. Other quartzes, such as amethyst (quartz with manganese minerals, from near Aswan, Egypt), are found less frequently from the EB I onward. Animal and plant products were always available locally and were in use as jewelry long before the Chalcolithic period—such as wood, Mediterranean and Red Sea shells, ostrich-egg shell, and bone (e.g., in the PPNB Naḥal Ḥemar cave, Bar-Yosef and Alon, 1988, pp. 19–20). Elephant ivory, coming from Egypt and possibly Syria, and hippopotamus ivory, available also locally, was used in Palestine since the Chalcolithic, and amber since the Late Bronze. The source of the latter seems to be the Baltic region, probably attesting to indirect trade, with Greece the last leg of the relay before Syria-Palestine; the local amber product was of low quality (Todd, 1985; Bass, 1986, p. 286; Harding, 1987; Pulak, 1988, pp. 24–25; Sherratt, 1995).

Manufactured materials used in jewelry production included the alkaline glaze on "soapstone" beads, known since the Chalcolithic period; glazed faience (since EB I); and glass (since MB IIA; cf. McGovern et al., 1991, and the section on MB IIA below). Glass, like stones, was valued for its colors. A twelfth-century BCE sizable glass ingot discovered at Ashdod may attest to the local manufacture.

Innovative methods and technological breakthroughs in metallurgy are detectable in jewelry. In the Chalcolithic period, soldering and lost wax casting were introduced; since EB II–III (and possibly earlier) chasing and repoussé are employed to enhance pieces; in the MB IIB granulation, which depended on fine soldering, and cloisonné techniques appear in Palestine for the first time (on granulation see Hoffmann and Davidson, 1965, p. 46; Carroll, 1974); filigree is found rarely since the LB period, like gilding in Iron II (the exact technique for the latter is still unclear).

Jewelers used drills, anvils (Potts, 1985, p. 186), chasing hammers, doming blocks, and drawplates; the latter two are still missing from the archaeological record of Palestine, but hardstone beads are a possible alternative for drawplates. Also employed were stone dies for impressing a pattern into sheet metal, and stone molds (distinguishable by their pouring channels from dies) were probably used only for casting wax in the lost-wax technique. The finest soldering was done employing a brazier and blowpipe (documented in Egyptian tomb paintings of jewelers).

Chalcolithic Period. Until the fifth millennium (pre-Ghassulian cultures) jewelry finds consist mostly of beads and pendants, such as the carnelian, garnet and other stone beads from Kabri in Israel. From the Ghassulian Chalcolithic heavy gold rings (ingots?) were found in the Naḥal Qana cave (Gopher et al., 1990), which is roughly contemporary with the elite cemetery at Varna (Bulgaria), and its gold jewelry. Although no jewelry was recovered in the Naḥal Mishmar "Cave of the Treasure," there was ample evidence among the metal objects discovered for sophisticated soldering and the lost-wax technique (Shalev et al., 1992, 1993; Tadmor et al., 1995). A double-spiral wire pendant was discovered within a small copper hoard at Neve Noy near Beersheba, closely related to the Naḥal Mishmar finds (Baumgarten and Eldar, 1985; Negbi, 1976, pl. 47, shows how it was worn). A pendant with the same double-spiral motif in relief was found at Biqʿat ʿUvda in the southern Negev desert (Avner, 1984, pl. 16:2). This motif was widespread in the ancient Near East and in Old Europe and was probably related to fertility (Keel, 1987). An ivory hairpin surmounted by a bird was found among other ivories of Egyptian inspiration at Beersheba (Perrot, 1955, pp. 171–172, pl. 22B), and there is a similar example from Shiqmim. Unique among the finds from Palestine is a beadwork purse(?) from a cave in Naḥal Ṣeʿelim in the Judean Desert, made of white- and blue-glazed stone beads (Aharoni, 1961, p. 15, pl. 7A). Bracelets, of a type found also around much of the Indian Ocean rim, cut from Red Sea shells like Lambis truncata *sabae,* continue from the Chalcolithic (Levy and Alon, 1985, pp. 129–130) into the EB (Schaub and Rast, 1989, pp. 310–312).

Early Bronze Age. Among the rare gold finds from the EB I are wire spiral hair(?) rings (also found in electrum and silver) from tombs at Azor (Ben-Tor, 1975, p. 24; and excavation by A. Druks, exhibited in the Israel Museum, Jerusalem, unpublished), and a wire ring (earring?) and seamless, seemingly soldered tube from Tell en-Naṣbeh. Some of the earliest silver finds from the Levant are a pin (hairpin?), unearthed in an EB I tomb at Bab edh-Dhraʿ in Jordan (Schaub and Rast, 1989, pp. 312–313), and the items from Azor just mentioned. From a tomb at Azor two oblate amethyst beads (finished Egyptian imports) were among the twelve hundred beads found (Ben-Tor, 1975, p. 23). From an EB I tomb at Tell el-Assawir and from a contemporary domestic context at ʿEin-Besor come Egyptian or egyptianizing Ram's(?)-head pendant beads (Gophna, 1980, p. 15, pl. III:4). Faience beads were recovered in quantity from EB I tombs, e.g. at Jericho, that may have been produced locally.

Splendid isolated EB II–III finds hint at the richness and diversity of the jeweler's craft. In an unexpected find-spot, a modest habitational site at out-of-the-way ʿEin ha-Meʿara in the western Negev, were discovered three drop-shaped, hollow, gold pendant-beads (exact date within the EB uncertain; Haiman, 1989, p. 180), with comparable finds but not exact parallels in Egypt. In a late EB II or early EB III tomb excavated in 1941 at Kinneret, a locality on the Sea of Galilee, the finds include a repoussé gold disk, of uncertain use, and beads attesting to the advanced technology of the day: hollow cylinders with closed ends, thick ones whose soldering is visible and thin ones that may have covered now-decayed faience beads; tubular carnelian beads with gold caps and a band (with comparisons in contemporary Egypt and Mesopotamia); and a barrel-shaped electrum(?) bead with what may be hammered-on gold caps (Mazar et al., 1973; Amiran, 1993; see figure 1). Similar material—cylindrical gold beads and two repoussé gold plaques—was recovered from an EB III charnel house at Bab edh-Dhraʿ (Rast and Schaub, 1987, p. 48; Schaub and Rast, 1989, pp. 468–469). The jewelry from Kinneret was believed to show Anatolian inspiration, but when considered together with the Bab edh-Dhraʿ finds local origins are suggested. Three star-shaped spacer beads were found at Jericho in Tomb A (Garstang, 1932, pl. XXII); it is not clear whether they are local or imported. An ivory hairpin surmounted by an animal shape was found at Megiddo, stratum XVIII (Loud, 1948, pl. 201). Although granulation and cloisonné are known in third-millennium Mesopotamia, and cloisonné is known in contemporary Egypt, these two techniques are unknown in the EB II–III Levant. Nor are finger rings found in the region before the MB I.

Middle Bronze I. In this period bronze is introduced and is employed *inter alia* in jewelry and personal accessories, such as toggle pins. In fact the latter, used to fasten garments, made their debut in this period—in Mesopotamia toggle pins are found already in the Early Dynastic III period. MB I toggle pins made of bronze come, for instance, from ʿEinan. At the same site copper bracelets were found in situ on a woman's arm, as were finger rings, two of them in situ on the middle finger of a woman's right hand, and

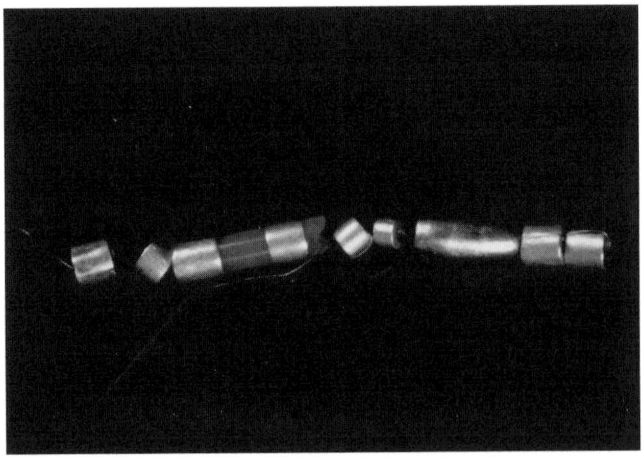

JEWELRY. Figure 1. *Gold, silver, and carnelian beads.* From an EB tomb at Kinneret, near the Sea of Galilee. (IAA 41.488, 41.498, 41.500, 41.501, 41.503, 41.516; courtesy Israel Antiquities Authority)

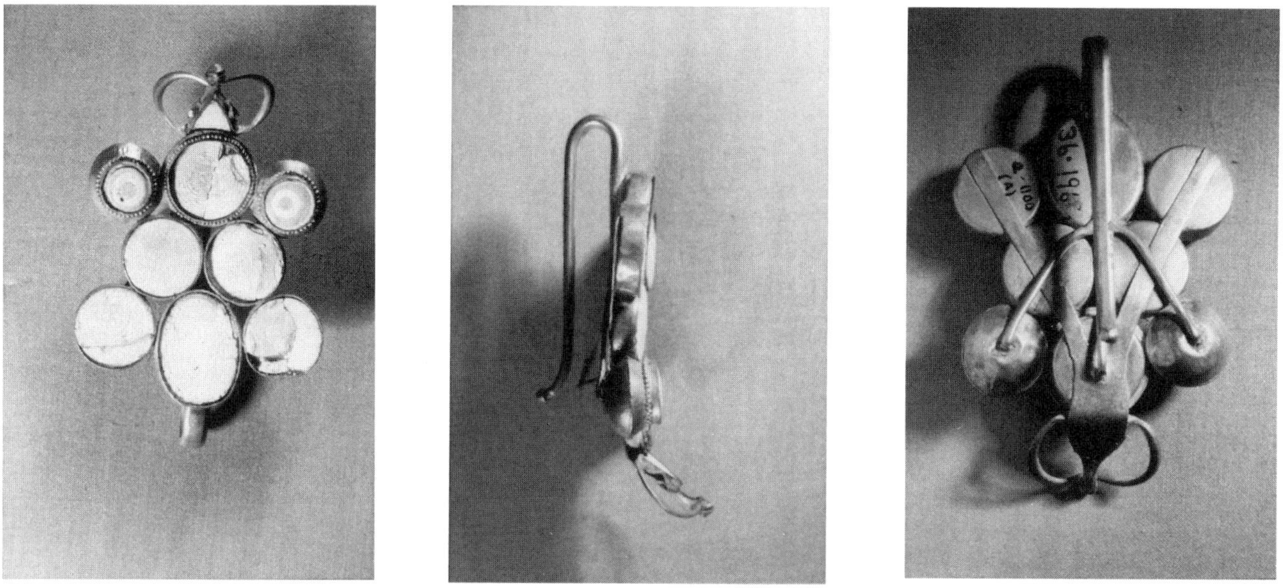

JEWELRY. Figure 2. *Three views of a gold and glass earring.* From a mid-second-millennium BCE tomb at Megiddo. (IAA 36.196; courtesy Israel Antiquities Authority)

spiral hair rings (Eisenberg, 1985, pp. 71–72). An MB I copper diadem was found on the skull in a tomb at Jericho (Kenyon, 1965, fig. 41:8), and an amethyst bead, a rare Egyptian import, at Maʿabarot (Dar, 1977, pp. 35–37). A silver bracelet was unearthed in a tomb of the same period at Hazoreaʿ (Meyerhof, 1989, p. 106, pl. 37), a very rare find in this metal besides the celebrated ʿAin es-Samiyeh goblet (Tadmor, 1986, 100–102).

Middle Bronze IIA. The MB IIA royal tombs at Byblos revealed the first Syro-Palestinian gold granulation, some of it made into elaborate figural motifs never since repeated (Maxwell-Hyslop, 1971, p. 103). Little jewelry datable to this period was recovered in Palestine. (Aphek in the Sharon, the type-site for the stratigraphy and pottery chronology of the Palestinian MB IIA, yielded hardly any jewelry at all.) The earliest glass find from Palestine belongs to this period: a bead from Tel Dan (Ilan et al., 1993); it is roughly contemporary with the substantial find from Aššur (Wartke, in Harper et al., 1995, pp. 54, 106).

Middle Bronze IIB to Late Bronze I. Throughout the second millennium gold finds outnumber silver in Syria-Palestine. The richest find in Palestine in the late MB/early LB period and the one that comes nearest to royal jewelry, or, rather, princely jewelry was made at Tell el-ʿAjjul (Negbi, 1970, using outdated chronology; Ziffer, 1990, pp. 54*–63* [English], 63–78 [Hebrew]). Egyptian influence, expressed for instance in scarabs mounted in gold and silver and in the use of amethyst (Ziffer, 1990, p. 74), is present amongst the mostly local work of the ʿAjjul assemblages, much of it exhibiting great skill in execution, such as in the fine granulation. There are partial parallels to the ʿAjjul material in the princely tombs at Ebla, with a few further comparisons from the Uluburun shipwreck, and at Tell ed-Dabʿa in the eastern Nile Delta. In this period (late MB/early LB) toggle pins became elaborate in design (Ziffer, 1990, p. 71). Crescent pendants, which began as an open form, gradually closed in the course of the Late Bronze Age (Ziffer, 1990, p. 58*; Tadmor and Misch-Brandl, 1980, p. 78). Solid crescentic (or "boat") earrings began to appear then and continued as a popular form for more than a millennium. Legume-shaped sheet-gold earrings from Tell el-ʿAjjul have symbolic significance because of their crescentic shape (Negbi, 1971). One pair was provided with a unique sliding lock (Ziffer, 1990, p. 55*). By adding a head and tail, and decorating the crescentic base-form in a semblance of feathers, the same shape was transformed into a bird with outspread, raised wings (Ziffer, 1990, pp. 65 vs. 64), tentatively identified by Tufnell (1983) as a wryneck. Most of these legume-shaped and bird-shaped earrings are decorated with granulation and wire (Lilyquist, 1993). Fly and fly-larva pendant beads (Tadmor, 1986, p. 123 bottom left), and flamboyant glass-inlayed multiple-eye (blue and yellow concentric circles) earrings with rams' heads soldered at the bottom have also been found at Tell el-ʿAjjul (Ziffer, 1990, pp. 56*, 66), and a similar pair turned up at Megiddo (see figure 2). Also from ʿAjjul are neck ornaments or belts made of multiple, hinged parts (Ziffer, 1990, p. 69) and a diadem or choker in the shape of a gold strap with evenly spaced tubes that may have held now-vanished gold flowers (Ziffer, 1990, p. 68, comparable to an intact item from Egypt, ibid., p. 67). In Megiddo was found a complex hinged silver bracelet of the late MB or early LB (Guy and Engberg, 1938, pl. 145:22). Sheet-metal repoussé pendants are rather common in Syria-Palestine, continuing from the MB II well into the LB period: circular examples with a "Cappadocian symbol" or double thunderbolt, the symbol of the storm god (e.g., from late MB Shiloh, Finkelstein and Brandl, 1985, pp. 23–24), or with an eight-pointed star, the symbol of the goddess Ishtar, and drop-shaped pendants with the schematic image of a naked goddess (examples of latter two from Tell el-ʿAjjul, Tadmor, 1986, pp. 123, 125).

Late Bronze II to Early Iron I. Just as MB IIB and LB I jewelry are inseparable, so the jewelry items of the fourteenth–twelfth centuries form a fairly coherent group. Jewelry lists were found for instance in Syria in the Ningal Temple at Qatna, and in the Amarna letters. Gold ingots were recovered at Beth-Shean, and bivalve stone molds (see above) for casting several items each—earrings, beads, pin—were found at Hazor stratum XIV (Yadin et al., 1961, pl. 158:31); Tell Abu Hawam stratum V (Hamilton, 1935, p. 58, no. 359); and Beth-Shemesh (Grant, 1931, pl. 13). Jewelry in the Late Bronze Age II reflects a mixture of local types—traditional plus innovative designs—and Egyptian types. Circular and goddess-shaped pendants begin to appear in glass (Megiddo, Lachish, Dan, Tel Mevorakh). Pomegranate-bud pendant earrings with the hoop separate are new, and have as their provenience Deir el-Balaḥ (Dothan, 1979, pp. 74, 76), a hoard from Beth-Shemesh (Tadmor and Misch-Brandl, 1980, p. 77; see figure 3), Tell el-Farʿah (South), Tel Nami (unpublished), Megiddo, and Ugarit. Beads and pendant-beads in palmette, drop, lotus-seed, and Egyptian *nefer* (hieroglyph denoting "good[ly]") shapes, made of gold, carnelian, and faience, and belonging to Egyptian-type necklaces or broad collars, were found at Deir el-Balaḥ (where red-tinted gold was also used; Dothan, 1979, pp. 78–80; Tadmor, 1986, p. 133), Dhahrat el-Humraya, Beth-Shean (Tadmor, 1986, p. 135) and Lachish. Inscribed massive Egyptian-type finger rings in metal, stone, and faience are known from several sites: from ʿAjjul comes a gold ring with the name of Tutankhamun; in Judur, Aphek, and Azor were discovered finger rings inscribed with good wishes in Egyptian hieroglyphs. Granulation in the LB II is less widespread than in the preceding period; whether this reflects a real decline of the technique or only the chances of discovery cannot be said. One example in silver or electrum, a pair of bracelet centerpieces, comes from Kamid el-Loz (Hachmann, 1983, p. 157); a pair of gold bracelets from the tomb of Tutankhamun constitutes a close parallel (Andrews, 1990, p. 157 right). The earliest known appearance of cloisonné is certainly inspired by Egypt (where this technique is at home), but the jewelry pieces thus made have a possibly local origin: isolated examples have been found at Lachish (Tufnell, 1958, pl. 25:9); Megiddo (Loud, 1948, pl. 224:27); and Kamid el-Loz (Miron, 1990, pp. 45, 168, 171, pl. I). An LB II filigree bead in gold from

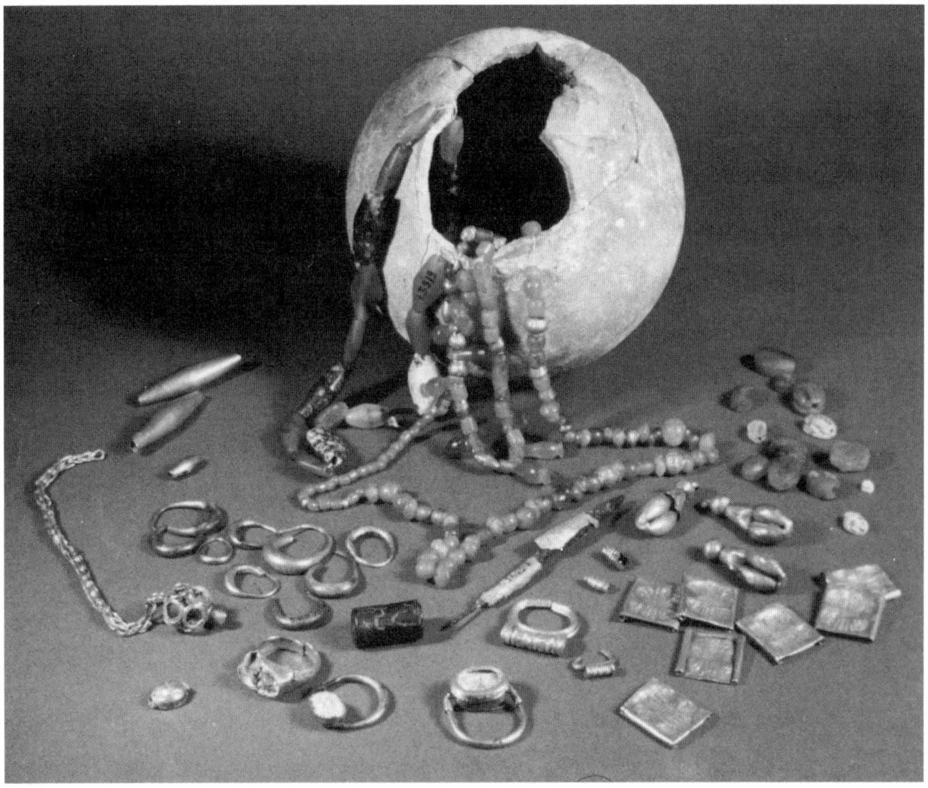

JEWELRY. Figure 3. *Part of a jewelry hoard.* Beth-Shemesh; thirteenth century BCE. Also shown is the ceramic vessel in which the hoard was found. (Courtesy Israel Antiquities Authority)

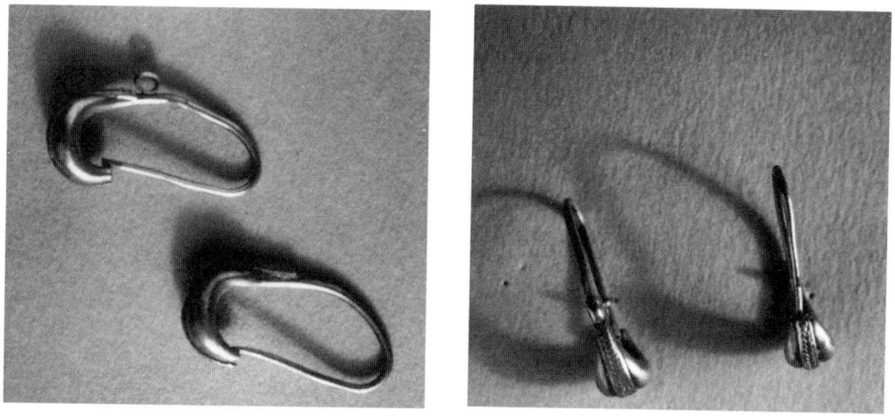

JEWELRY. Figure 4. *Two views of a pair of gold earings.* Tell Jemmeh, early first millennium BCE. (IAA J.1006; courtesy Israel Antiquities Authority)

the Beth-Shemesh hoard is the only local example of this rare technique (Tadmor and Misch-Brandl, 1980, p. 75). The bead has exact parallels in the Valley of the Kings in Thebes, Egypt, in a tomb of a daughter of Queen Tawosert (1188–1186 BCE) (Andrews, 1990, p. 127), and from Tell el-ʿAjjul comes an imitation in faience (Petrie 1933, no. 10 on p. 5, pls. 8, 10). Tapering metal-band finger rings in the Hittite style appear at Tell el-Farʿah (South) (Petrie, 1930, pl. 36; Macdonald et al., 1932, pl. 51) and Tel Nami (Singer, 1993). The earliest-known amber beads in Palestine, of Baltic origin, were found at Tell Abu Hawam and a few other sites in LB II contexts (Sherratt, 1995, p. 202; more references in "materials" section above). In early Iron I, LB traditions initially were continued, as is evidenced, for instance, at Tell el-Farʿah (South), where Flinders Petrie found a late twelfth- or eleventh-century gold crescent pendant and carnelian lotus-seed beads (Petrie, 1930, pls. 36, 37, 39).

Late Iron I to Early Iron II. As far as jewelry is concerned this period, the eleventh–ninth centuries, is to be regarded as a continuum. New local jewelry types introduced, perhaps by the Sea Peoples, are known chiefly from the Tell el-Farʿah (South) cemeteries. Tassel earrings in gold, electrum, silver, and bronze, whose prototype probably was floral (Maxwell-Hyslop, 1971, p. 225, photographs 198, 200), are also known, in addition to Tell el-Farʿah, from Madaba (Harding, 1953, p. 32, nos. 197–198), Timnaʿ (Rothenberg, 1988, pl. 55:15), the Judean Desert (unpublished), and Tawilan, the latter in a sixth–fifth-century context (Bienkowski, 1991, p. 102). Early examples of "basket" earring(?) pendants were unearthed in eleventh–ninth-centuries contexts, an example in gold at Tell el-Farʿah (South) (Petrie, 1930, pls. 36, 39) and in silver at Beth-Shean; these finds herald the much later Phoenician type (see below). The earliest examples of massive bracelets, armlets and anklets, the latter two distinguished by their size, also appear in late Iron I: iron examples were found at Tell el-Farʿah (South) and Tell Qasile (Mazar, 1985, p. 8–9).

Iron I types continued into the Early Iron II, pre-Assyrian period, as noted, and new developments are discernible. At Eshtemoaʿ a silver hoard was recovered (Yeivin, 1990) and at Tell Jemmeh there were silver and gold finds (Petrie, 1928), both apparently from the ninth century. Elongated gold crescent earrings with a herringbone wire decoration and a loop to hold a pendant, the latter now lost, were discovered at Tell Jemmeh (see figure 4), and silver specimens come from Arad and Eshtemoaʿ. Other earrings from Tell Jemmeh and elsewhere display a flattened crescentic hoop decorated with a row of granules (Yeivin, 1990, fig. 16:11), and use is made of granulation on items from the Eshtemoaʿ hoard (Yeivin, 1990, fig. 17:7). Iron and bronze bangles were found at Lachish and at other sites, but while the use of the bronze specimens continues, the interest in iron bangles appears eventually to diminish. Subsequently, at Tell el-Mazar, a burial was found with both bracelets and anklets in situ on the skeleton (Yassine, 1984, p. 93). Fibulas, invented in the Late Bronze Age Aegean, began to replace toggle pins in Syria-Palestine in the Early Iron II or perhaps as early as Iron I. Fibulas were also used for securing a seal with a chain, and there is a type of fibula which is cast in one piece with a seal (Curtis, 1994; Curtis, in Curtis and Reade, 1995, p. 174).

Late Iron II. From this period mostly silver jewelry is found; gold is rare. There appears to be little cloisonné work, though cloisonné decoration of ivory and wood carving is popular. New shapes in jewelry proliferated, displaying Syro-Assyrian and Phoenician as well as local styles. The former is probably the result of Assyrian deportations, certainly of Assyria's imperial rule, and one may be entitled to speak of a Syro-Assyrian koine, encompassing most of the Near East: parallels to jewelry finds from Palestine exist as far afield as Karmir Blur in Urartu. Late Iron II jewelry finds in the southern Levant are mainly from inland sites, e.g., Ketef Hinnom, Kamid el-Loz (Hachmann and Kuschke, 1966), Meqabelein, and Tel ʿIra. Some types continue into the sixth–fifth centuries, or else are difficult to differentiate; there are, for example, mixed seventh–fifth-centuries tombs in Jerusalem (Ketef Hinnom) and Amman (Adoninur). Abundant use is made of hollow shapes embellished with granulation and wire decoration, mainly in earrings. Cloisonné is found in Amman (the tomb of Adoninur) and Meqabelein in ring bezels. In Palestine, at Tel Miqne/Ekron, a sheet-silver pendant, incised with the images of Ishtar and a worshiper (Gitin, 1995, fig. 4.14), is a provincial rendering of North Syrian work paralleled at Zincirli. Triangular eye beads made of glass, of Assyrian type, were found at Gezer and other sites (Reich and Brandl, 1985, p. 49).

Though artifacts coming from or inspired by Phoenicia are common in Iron II Palestine, Phoenician influence in jewelry (some of it egyptianizing) has been first observed only in work done in the early 1990s on late Iron II finds from the coastal sites of Achziv and Tel Miqne/Ekron (former unpublished, latter in Gitin, 1995, fig. 4.12); inland jewelry shows Syro-Assyrian influence (see above). Parallels to the Miqne and Achziv jewelry come mainly from the Phoenician West. Among the finds are elaborate earrings, including some with multiple pendants (basket and lotus flower), and a rare example of gilding was observed on silver Horus eyes from Miqne. A silver finger ring from the same site, with a hieroglyphic inscription, should be noted. Few Phoenician/egyptianizing finds are also known from inland sites, such as a gold finger ring from Samaria, that has a parallel in a bracelet of Sheshonq found at Tanis. At Achziv a lion-shaped pin-head made of Baltic amber was found (Sherratt, 1995, p. 202; more references in "materials" section above).

Multiple hollow-ball earrings are probably of local inspiration, an offshoot of the MB–LB granule-cluster earrings, unless the Iron Age version was made by Iranian deportees to Palestine—somewhat similar earrings of the early first millennium BCE are known from Marlik and Hasanlu in Iran (Maxwell-Hyslop, 1971, photographs 135, 144). Examples of the local type found in a seventh-century BCE tomb at Tel 'Ira (Beit-Arieh, 1985, p. 23) testify to the date of their introduction; when they appear elsewhere it is often in post-Iron II or mixed contexts, e.g., at Ketef Hinnom and Kamid el-Loz (Hachmann and Kuschke, 1966, p. 64, fig. 20:6–7). Also found only locally are hoops of several earring types decorated with wound wire and tiny hollow balls.

An abundance of inexpensive Egyptian faience amulets in the shapes of deities and their symbols, such as Horus eyes (Herrmann, 1994), and local carved bone "club" and "hammer" pendants (Platt, 1978; Herrmann, 1994, p. 814) have been found, for example, at Lachish.

[*See also* Bone, Ivory, and Shell; *and* Metals. *In addition, many of the sites mentioned are the subject of independent entries.*]

BIBLIOGRAPHY

Aharoni, Yohanan. "The Expedition to the Judean Desert, 1960, Expedition B." *Israel Exploration Journal* 11 (1961): 11–24.

Amiran, Ruth. "The Kinneret Gold Plaque and the Alaca Royal Tombs Again." In *Aspects of Art and Iconography: Anatolia and Its Neighbors. Studies in Honor of Nimet Özgüç*, edited by Machteld J. Mellink et al., pp. 23–24. Ankara, 1993.

Andrews, Carol. *Ancient Egyptian Jewellery*. London, 1990.

Avner, Uzi. "Ancient Cult Sites in the Negev and Sinai Deserts." *Tel Aviv* 11 (1984): 115–131.

Balmuth, Miriam S. "Jewellers' Hoards and the Development of Early Coinage." In *Actes du 8ème congrès international de numismatique, New York–Washington, September 1973*, edited by Herbert A. Cahn and Georges Le Rider, pp. 27–30. Paris and Basel, 1976.

Bar-Yosef, Ofer, and David Alon. "Naḥal Ḥemar Cave." *'Atiqot* 18 (1988).

Barkay, Gabriel. *Ketef Hinnom: A Treasure Facing Jerusalem's Walls*. Israel Museum Catalogue, 274. Jerusalem, 1986.

Bass, George F. "Bronze Age Shipwreck at Ulu Burun (Kaş): 1984 Campaign." *American Journal of Archaeology* 90 (1986): 269–296.

Baumgarten Ya'aqov, and Iris Eldar: "Neve Noy: A Chalcolithic Site of the Beer-Sheba Culture." *Biblical Archaeologist* 48 (1985): 134–139.

Beit-Arieh, Yitzhaq. "Tel 'Ira—A Fortified City of the Kingdom of Judah." *Qadmoniot* 18 (1985): 17–25.

Ben-Tor, Amnon. "Two Burial Caves of the Proto-Urban Period at Azor, 1971." *Qedem* 1 (1975): 1–54.

Bienkowski, Piotr, ed. *Treasures from an Ancient Land. The Art of Jordan*. Liverpool, 1991.

Carroll, Diane L. "A Classification for Granulation in Ancient Metalwork." *American Journal of Archaeology* 78 (1974): 33–39.

Chernykh, Evgenii Nikolaevitch. *Ancient Metallurgy in the USSR: The Early Metal Age*. New York, 1992. First insight in English into the vast work done in the former USSR; invaluable for the history of technology.

Curtis, John E. *Nush-i-Jan*, vol. 3, *The Small Finds*. London, 1984. On hoards.

Curtis. John E. "Assyrian Fibulae with Figural Decoration." In *Beschreiben und Deuten in der Archäologie des Alten Orients: Festschrift für Ruth Mayer-Opificius*, edited by N. Cholidis, et al., pp. 49–62. Münster, 1994.

Curtis, John E., and Julian E. Reade, eds. *Art and Empire. Treasures from Assyria in the British Museum*. The Metropolitan Museum of Art, exhibition catalog. New York, 1995.

Dar, Shimon. *Early Settlements in 'Emeq Hefer*. Ma'abarot (Israel), 1977 (Hebrew).

Dothan, Trude. *Excavations at the Cemetery of Deir el-Balaḥ*. Qedem, vol. 10. Jerusalem, 1979.

Eisenberg, Emmanuel. "A Burial Cave of the Early Bronze Age IV (MBI) near 'Enan." *'Atiqot* 17 (1985): 59–74.

Finkelstein, Israel, and Baruch Brandl. "A Group of Metal Objects from Shiloh." *The Israel Museum Journal* 4 (1985): 17–26.

Garstang, John. "Jericho." *Liverpool Annals of Archaeology and Anthropology* 19 (1932): 3–22, 35–54.

Gitin, Seymour. "Tel Miqne-Ekron in the Seventh Century B.C.E.: The Impact of Economic Innovation and Foreign Cultural Influences on a Neo-Assyrian Vassal City-State." In *Recent Excavations in Israel: A View to the West. Reports on Kabu, Nami, Miqne-Ekron, Dor, and Ashkelon*, edited by Seymour Gitin, pp. 61–79. Archaeological Institute of American Colloquia and Conference Papers, no. 1. Dubuque, Iowa, 1995.

Gopher, Avi, et al. "Earliest Gold Artifacts in the Levant." *Current Anthropology* 31 (1990): 436–443.

Gophna, Ram. "Excavations at 'En Besor, 1976." *'Atiqot* 14 (1980): 9–16.

Grant, Elihu. *Ain Shems Excavations (Palestine, 1928–1929–1930–1931)*. Part 1. Haverford, 1931.

Guy, P. L. O., and Robert Engberg. *Megiddo Tombs*. Chicago, 1938.

Hachmann, Rolf, ed. *Frühe Phöniker im Libanon: 20 Jahre deutsche Ausgrabungen in Kamid el-Loz.* Mainz, 1983.

Hachmann, Rolf, and Kuschke, Arnulf. *Bericht über die Ergebnisse der Ausgrabungen in Kamid el-Loz (Libanon) in den Jahren 1963 und 1964.* Saarbrücker Beiträge zur Altertumskunde, vol. 3. Bonn, 1966.

Haiman, Mordekhai. "Preliminary Report on the Western Negev Highlands Emergency Survey." *Israel Exploration Journal* 39 (1989): 173–191.

Hamilton, Robert William. "Tell Abu Hawam." *Quarterly of the Department of Antiquities in Palestine* 4 (1935): 1–69.

Harding, Gerald Lankester. "An Iron-Age Tomb at Meqabelein." *Quarterly of the Department of Antiquities in Palestine* 14 (1950): 44–80.

Harding, Gerald Lankester. *Four Tomb Groups from Jordan.* Palestine Exploration Fund Annual, no 6. London, 1953. Madaba and Amman (Adoninur) tombs.

Harding, A. F. Review of Todd 1985. *Antiquity* 61 (1987): 333–334.

Harper, Prudence O, et al. eds. *Discoveries at Ashur on the Tigris. Assyrian Origins: Antiquities in the Vorderasiatisches Museum, Berlin.* The Metropolitan Museum of Art, exhibition catalog. New York, 1995.

Hermann, Christian. *Ägyptische Amulette aus Palästina/Israel.* Orbis Biblicus et Orientalis 138. Fribourg and Göttingen, 1994.

Hoffmann, Herbert, and Patricia F. Davidson. *Greek Gold: Jewelry from the Age of Alexander.* Mainz, 1965.

Horne, Lee. "Brasscasters of Dariapur: West Bengal Artisans in a Changing World." *Expedition* 29 (1987): 39–46. Lost wax technique.

Ilan, David, et al. "An Early Glass Bead from Tel Dan." *Israel Exploration Journal* 43 (1993): 230–234.

Keel, Othmar. "The Peculiar Headrests for the Dead in First Temple Times." *Biblical Archaeology Review* 13 (1987): 50–53.

Kenyon, Kathleen M. *Excavations at Jericho,* vol. 2, *The Tombs Excavated in 1955–58.* London, 1965.

Lechevalier, Jean, et al. "Technique de perforation par percussion de perles en cornaline (Larsa, Irak)." *Paléorient* 8 (1982): 55–65.

Levy, Thomas E., and David Alon. "The Chalcolithic Mortuary Site near Mezad Aluf, Northern Negev Desert: Third Preliminary Report." In *Preliminary Reports of ASOR-Sponsored Excavations,* edited by Walter E. Rast, pp. 121–135. Bulletin of the American Schools of Oriental Research, Supplement no. 23. Baltimore, 1985.

Lilyquist, Christine. "Granulation and Glass: Chronological and Stylistic Investigations at Selected Sites, ca. 2500–1400 B.C.E." *Bulletin of the American Schools of Oriental Research,* nos. 290–291 (1993): 27–92.

Loud, Gordon. *Megiddo,* vol. 2, *Seasons 1935–1939.* Chicago, 1948.

Lucas, Alfred. *Ancient Egyptian Materials and Industries.* 4th ed., rev. and enl. by J. R. Harris. London, 1962.

Macdonald, Eann, et al. *Beth-Pelet,* vol. 2, *Prehistoric Fara; Beth-Pelet Cemetery.* London, 1932.

Marcus, Michelle I. "Incorporating the Body: Adornment, Gender, and Social Identity in Ancient Iran." *Cambridge Archaeological Journal* 3 (1993): 157–178.

Maxwell-Hyslop, K. Rachel. *Western Asiatic Jewellery c. 3000–612 B.C.* London, 1971.

Mazar, Amihai. *Excavations at Tell Qasile,* part 2, *The Philistine Sanctuary: Various Finds, the Pottery, Conclusions, Appendixes.* Qedem 20. Jerusalem, 1985.

Mazar, Benjamin, et al. "An Early Bronze Age II Tomb at Beth Yerah (Kinneret)." *Eretz Israel* 11 (1973): 176–193, esp. 183, 186 (Hebrew; English summary p. 28*).

McGovern, Patrick E. *Late Bronze Palestinian Pendants: Innovation in a Cosmopolitan Age.* Sheffield, 1985.

McGovern, Patrick E., et al. "The Beads from Tomb B10a B27 at Dinkha Tepe and the Beginning of Glassmaking in the Ancient Near East." *American Journal of Archaeology* 95 (1991): 395–402.

Meyerhof, Ezra L. *The Bronze Age Necropolis at Kibbutz Hazorea, Israel.* British Archaeological Reports, International Series, no. 534. Oxford, 1989.

Miron, Renate. *Kamid el-Loz,* vol. 10, *Das "Schatzhaus" im Palastbereich. Die Funde.* Saarbrücker Beiträge zur Altertumskunde, vol. 46. Bonn, 1990.

Moorey, P. R. S. *Materials and Manufacture in Ancient Mesopotamia: The Evidence of Archaeology and Art: Metals and Metalwork, Glazed Materials, and Glass.* British Archaeological Reports, International Series, no. 237. Oxford, 1985.

Musche, Brigitte. *Vorderasiatischer Schmuck von den Anfängen bis zur Zeit der Achämeniden (ca. 10,000–330 v. Chr.).* Leiden, 1992.

Negbi, Moshe. "Crescent- or Legume-Shaped Ear-Rings?" *Israel Exploration Journal* 21 (1971): 219.

Negbi, Ora. *The Hoards of Goldwork from Tell el-Ajjul.* Studies in Mediterranean Archaeology, vol. 25. Göteborg, 1970.

Negbi, Ora. *Canaanite Gods in Metal: An Archaeological Study of Ancient Syro-Palestinian Figurines.* Tel Aviv, 1976.

Perrot, Jean. "The Excavations at Tell Abu Matar, near Beersheba—III." *Israel Exploration Journal* 5 (1955): 167–189.

Petrie, W. M. Flinders. *Gerar.* London, 1928.

Petrie, W. M. Flinders. *Beth Pelet.* Vol. I. London, 1930.

Petrie, W. M. F. *Ancient Gaza III.* London, 1933.

Platt, Elisabeth E. "Bone Pendants." *Biblical Archaeologist* 41 (1978): 23–28.

Potts, T. F. "Preliminary Report on a Sixth Season of Excavations by the University of Sydney at Pella in Jordan (1983/84)." *Annual of the Department of Antiquities of Jordan* 29 (1985): 181–210.

Prag, Kay. "Silver in the Levant in the Fourth Millennium B.C." In *Archaeology in the Levant: Essays for Kathleen Kenyon,* edited by P. R. S. Moorey and Peter J. Parr, pp. 36–46. Warminster, 1978.

Pulak, Cemal. "Bronze Age Shipwreck at Ulu Burun, Turkey, 1985 Campaign." *American Journal of Archaeology* 92 (1988): 1–37.

Rast, Walter E., and R. Thomas Schaub. "Bronze Age Cities along the Dead Sea." *Archaeology* 40/1 (1987): 42–49.

Reedy, Chandra L. "Modern Statues and Traditional Methods: A Casting Workshop in Chamba, Himachal Pradesh, Northwest India." *Expedition* 29 (1987): 47–54. Lost wax technique.

Reich, Ronny, and Baruch Brandl: "Gezer under Assyrian Rule." *Palestine Exploration Quarterly* 117 (1985): 41–54.

Rothenberg, Beno. *The Egyptian Mining Temple at Timna.* London, 1988.

Schaub, R. Thomas, and Walter E. Rast. *Bâb edh-Dhrâʿ: Excavations in the Cemetery Directed by Paul W. Lapp (1965–67).* Winona Lake, Ind., 1989.

Shalev, Sariel, et al. "A Chalcolithic Mace Head from the Negev, Israel: Technological Aspects and Cultural Implications." *Archaeometry* 34 (1992): 63–71.

Shalev, Sariel, and Peter J. Northover. "The Metallurgy of the Nahal Mishmar Hoard Reconsidered." *Archaeometry* 35 (1993): 35–47.

Sherratt, A. "Electric Gold: Re-opening the Amber Route." *Antiquity* 69 (1995): 200–203. Review of: C. W. Beck and J. Bouzek, *Amber in Archaeology: Proceedings of the Second International Conference on Amber in Archaeology, Liblice (Czech Republic), 1990* (Prague, 1993).

Singer, Charles J. *A History of Technology,* 8 vols. Oxford, 1954–1984.

Singer, Itamar. "A Hittite Signet Ring from Tel Nami." In *Kinattūtu ša dārâti: Raphael Kutscher Memorial Volume,* edited by Anson F. Rainey, pp. 189–193 Tel Aviv, 1993.

Tadmor, Miriam. "Catalogue numbers 13–67." In *Treasures of the Holy Land. Ancient Art from the Israel Museum.* The Metropolitan Museum of Art, exhibition catalog. New York, 1986, pp. 57–134.

Tadmor, Miriam, et al. "The Naḥal Mishmar Hoard from the Judean Desert: Technology, Composition and Provenance." *ʿAtiqot* 27 (1995): 95–148.

Tadmor, Miriam, and Osnat Misch-Brandl. "The Beth Shemesh Hoard of Jewellery." *The Israel Museum News* 16 (1980): 71–79.

Todd, Joan M. "Baltic Amber in the Ancient Near East: A Preliminary Investigation." *Journal of Baltic Studies* 16.3 (1985): 292–301. Special issue of the journal, "Studies in Baltic Amber," edited by Todd.
Tufnell, Olga. *Lachish IV: The Bronze Age*. London, 1958.
Tufnell, Olga. "Some Gold Bird Ornaments: Falcon or Wryneck?" *Anatolian Studies* 33 (1983): 57–66.
Tylecote, R. F. *A History of Metallurgy*. 2d ed. Brookfield, Vt., 1992.
Wolff, Samuel R. "Archaeology in Israel." *American Journal of Archaeology* 97 (1993): 135–163.
Yadin, Yigael, et al. *Hazor III–IV: An Account of the Third and Fourth Seasons of Excavations, 1957–1958*. Jerusalem, 1961 (plates).
Yassine, Khair. *Tell el-Mazar*, vol. 1, *Cemetery A*. Amman, 1984.
Yeivin, Ze'ev. "The Silver Hoard from Eshtemoa'." *'Atiqot* 10 (1990): 43–56 (Hebrew).
Ziffer, Irit. *At That Time the Canaanites Were in the Land. Daily Life in Canaan in the Middle Bronze Age 2, 2000–1550 B.C.E.* Eretz Israel Museum, Tel Aviv, exhibition catalog. Tel Aviv, 1990.

BENJAMIN SASS

JEWISH PALESTINE EXPLORATION SOCIETY. *See* Israel Exploration Society.

JEZREEL, TEL, a 15-acre mound situated in the eastern part of the Jezreel Valley on a ridge extending along its southern side. The site's a commanding position offers a breathtaking view of the valley. Although there is a large spring, 'Ein Jezreel, in the valley to the northeast, it seems that the numerous rock-cut cisterns that collected rainwater at the site and in its immediate surroundings served as the settlement's main water source.

Development works carried out nearby in 1987 revealed Iron Age monumental remains. Following limited salvage excavations by the Israel Antiquities Authority, systematic excavations were started by David Ussishkin and John Woodhead, on behalf of Tel Aviv University and the British School of Archaeology in Jerusalem, respectively. Six large-scale seasons of excavation took place between 1990 and 1995.

A few Late Neolithic flint implements of the Wadi Rabbah culture are the earliest finds collected at the site. A considerable number of Early Bronze Age I and III pottery fragments were also recovered on the surface and a few Middle Bronze Age II sherds were found. A considerable amount of Late Bronze Age pottery concentrated in the constructional fills of the Iron Age gate indicates the existence of a settlement in the central part of the mound during that period. The existence of a Canaanite settlement at Jezreel has a bearing on the origins of the name of the site and the valley, which first appears in late biblical accounts. Jezreel was located in the tribal inheritance of Issachar (*Jos.* 19:18). It is mentioned in the list of Solomon's district officers (*1 Kgs.* 4:12). Iron I pottery found in the constructional fills of the later Iron Age indicates that Jezreel was probably settled during the period of the United Monarchy.

During the reign of the Omride dynasty (882–842 BCE), Jezreel became a royal center of considerable importance in the kingdom of Israel, and a large enclosure was built there. The site's importance during this period is attested in two biblical stories: *1 Kings* 21 describes the story of Naboth the Jezreelite who had an orchard near King Ahab's "palace," and *2 Kings* 9–10 relates in detail the story of Jehu's revolt in 842 BCE. It was there that he received the decapitated heads of the members of Ahab's family sent to him from Samaria. *Hosea* (1:4) mentions "the blood of Jezreel upon the house of Jehu"—a possible indication that Jehu destroyed Jezreel at that time.

The royal enclosure, built on a grand scale and according to a uniform plan, is rectangular and surrounded by a casemate wall with projecting towers at the corners. Its outer maximal measurements are about 332 × 184 m, and the area inside the enclosure is about 45 dunams (11 acres). One of the long sides follows the slope and faces the valley. The gate, of the six-chambered type, is located in the opposite long side. The casemate wall is supported by a massive earthen rampart. On three sides—but not on the long side facing the valley—a rock-cut moat forms the outer ring of the fortifications. The moat is about 8–12 m wide and, at one point at which its bottom was reached in excavation, it is about 6 m deep. It was estimated on the basis of presently available data that about 26,800 cu m of rock were quarried in the moat and that at least 23,300 cu m of material were dumped in the ramparts. The area of the enclosure is largely destroyed or covered with later remains, and relatively little is known about the buildings inside. Remains of a domestic character were found in the casemates and adjoining structures.

Iron Age domestic remains probably dating to the eighth century BCE were found superimposed on the enclosure's ruined walls, an indication that it had only been used for a brief period. To this later settlement should be assigned a handle of a royal Judean storage jar; it bears a stamp with a two-winged emblem and the city name *m*[*mšt*], which dates to the time of Sennacherib's campaign in Judah in 701 BCE. The distribution of royal storage jars was limited to Judah, which makes this particular handle significant. [*See* Seals; Judah.]

A number of suggestions have been raised regarding the role of Jezreel in the period of the Omride dynasty. According to one, Israel had two capitals then—Samaria and Jezreel, one Samaria may have served as a "summer" capital and Jezreel in the winter. [*See* Samaria.] It has also been suggested that the kingdom had two religious centers—one Israelite and the other, Phoenician, the latter having been promoted by Jezebel, Ahab's wife. The present excavators have raised the possibility that Jezreel was built as a central military base for the royal Israelite army at the time of the Omride kings. This view is supported by the nature of the enclosure, the unusually massive fortifications, the poor quality of construction, and the poor domestic remains within its perimeter.

Following the destruction of the Iron Age enclosure, settlement at Jezreel apparently continued uninterruptedly until the twentieth century CE. Remains of the Persian, Hellenistic, and Roman periods have been found. During the Byzantine period, a densely populated settlement (Esdraela of Eusebius's *Onomasticon*) existed here. Structural remains were found all over the site and its outskirts, as well as inside the disused Iron Age moat.

During the period of the Crusades, a settlement belonging to the Templars, Le Petit Gérin, existed here. It is mentioned several times in association with battles of the period. Its center was apparently at the western side of the site, where an Ottoman tower is located, founded on Crusader walls—probably the remains of the crusader settlement's main building or fort. A church was built nearby. In later periods, the Arab village of Zerʿin developed on this part of the site.

BIBLIOGRAPHY

Ussishkin, David, and John Woodhead. "Excavations at Tel Jezreel, 1990–1991: Preliminary Report." *Tel Aviv* 19 (1992): 3–56.

Ussishkin, David, and John Woodhead. "Excavations at Tel Jezreel, 1992–1993: Second Preliminary Report." *Levant* 26 (1994): 1–48.

Williamson, H. G. M. "Jezreel in the Biblical Texts." *Tel Aviv* 18 (1991): 72–92.

DAVID USSISHKIN

JILAT, WADI EL-, tributary of Wadi ed-Dabi (Wadi Dhobai), which drains the southwestern sector of the Azraq basin, an internal drainage basin in north-central Jordan (31°30′ N, 36°25′ E). The wadi runs through low hills of Late Cretaceous and Early Tertiary limestones, marls, and cherts, at elevations of between 950 and 750 m. These are located in the present-day transition zone between steppe and desert, receiving about 100 mm of rainfall per year. The western drainage is covered by loessic soils held in place by perennial grasses and other vegetation; the eastern sector is actively deflating into a desert environment. A series of Pleistocene and Holocene fluvial, colluvial, and eolian deposits has been identified on the valley floor (Garrard et al., 1988). A gorge cuts through these deposits, in which water may be found after winter rains. This attracts bedouin who graze camel, sheep, and goats in this region between late autumn and spring.

In 1937–1938, John d'A. Waechter et al. (1938) conducted an archaeological survey in the valley, recording a number of Epipaleolithic and Neolithic sites, as well as a well-constructed dam of historic date. Waechter excavated soundings at two of the prehistoric sites (Ḍhobai B and K), which have recently been the subject of more intensive research. Between 1982 and 1989 six seasons of paleoenvironmental and archaeological survey and excavations were conducted in the valley focusing on the Paleolithic and Neolithic occupation (Garrard et al., 1994). More than thirty Stone Age sites were found in a 5-kilometer (3 mi.) stretch of the valley floor; soundings were excavated at eight of them and broader area excavations were undertaken at another five.

The most spectacular of the Epipaleolithic sites is Jilat 6 (Garrard and Byrd, 1992). The site forms a low mound and is covered by a dense canopy of flint artifacts for an area of 20,000 sq m (2 ha, or 5 acres). With the exception of Kharaneh 4, which is located 25 km (16 mi.) to the north, Jilat 6 is the largest site of its period known in the Near East. Although the scale may partly be the result of erosion, it is thought to represent a seasonal aggregation site used by hunter-gatherers in the period around 14,000 BCE. Animal and plant remains demonstrate that the groups subsisted on gazelle, wild ass, hare, and the seeds and tubers of the local steppic plants.

A series of Neolithic sites was excavated dating to between 7500 and 5500 BCE (Garrard et al., 1994). These are much smaller than contemporary sites in the better-watered areas to the west and were probably occupied seasonally. Excavations revealed semisubterranean circular or oval dwellings with external walls built from upright slabs of the local limestone. Roofs were probably constructed from perishable organic materials. The site of Jilat 26 (c. 6700 BCE) contained a semicircle of twenty such structures, with evidence of an outdoor activity area on the side sheltered from the wind. Plant remains from the Jilat Neolithic sites indicate that domestic wheat and barley were in use from the earliest levels onward; it is unclear, however, whether these were cultivated locally or imported from areas to the west. [*See* Cereals.] Presently the local climate is too arid for regular cultivation. The animal remains indicate that hunting of gazelle and hare remained important down to 6000 BCE. Later Neolithic sites contain substantial numbers of sheep and goat bones thought to derive from imported livestock. Their appearance provides a terminus ante quem for the process of caprine domestication in the southern Levant. [*See* Sheep and Goats.]

With the exception of a minor excavation at the Early Bronze Age site of Jilat 27 (Garrard, unpublished), no work has been done on later prehistoric sites and burial cairns in the region. However, the dam, which has been described as one "of the most impressive hydraulic architectural structures in Jordan," is the subject of an article by Konstantinos D. Politis (1993, quotation from p. 43). It was built across the main gorge and is 58 m long, 5 m wide, and 6 m in maximum height. Its downstream face is built from stepped ashlar masonry, supported by three buttresses. Politis found Nabatean sherds in the cement, but the presence of Byzantine and Umayyad sherds in the vicinity suggests that the present dam may have been built in this later period. The reservoir area has completely filled in with silt, which may have happened quite rapidly after its construction. It has been suggested that the dam may have been built as a showpiece or as a gift to local tribes in exchange for support (King et al., 1983).

BIBLIOGRAPHY

Garrard, Andrew N., et al. "Environment and Subsistence during the Late Pleistocene and Early Holocene in the Azraq basin." *Paléorient* 14.2 (1988): 40–49. Summary of environmental work in Wadi el-Jilat.

Garrard, Andrew N., and Brian F. Byrd. "New Dimensions to the Epipalaeolithic of the Wadi el-Jilat in Central Jordan." *Paléorient* 18.1 (1992): 47–62. Describes the main Epipaleolithic sites.

Garrard, Andrew N., et al. "The Chronological Basis and Significance of the Late Palaeolithic and Neolithic Sequence in the Azraq basin, Jordan." In *Late Quaternary Chronology and Paleoclimates of the Eastern Mediterranean*, edited by Ofer Bar-Yosef and Renee S. Kra, pp. 177–199. Radiocarbon, Tucson, 1994. Summary of recent prehistoric investigations.

Garrard, Andrew N., et al. "Prehistoric Environment and Settlement in the Azraq basin: An Interim Report on the 1987 and 1988 Excavation Seasons." *Levant* 26 (1994): 73–109. Description of the Neolithic sites.

King, Geoffrey R. D., et al. "Survey of Byzantine and Islamic Sites in Jordan: Second Season Report, 1981." *Annual of the Department of Antiquities of Jordan* 27 (1983): 385–436. A brief discussion of the dam.

Politis, Konstantinos D. "The Stepped Dam at Wadi el-Jilat." *Palestine Exploration Quarterly* 125 (1993): 43–49. Detailed discussion of the dam.

Waechter, John d'A., et al. "The Excavations at Wādi Dhobai, 1937–1938, and the Dhobaian Industry." *Journal of the Palestine Oriental Society* 18 (1938): 172–186, 292–298. Initial fieldwork in Wadi el-Jilat.

ANDREW N. GARRARD

JORDAN. *See* Transjordan.

JORDAN VALLEY. The Jordan Rift Valley lies between the Sea of Galilee and the Dead Sea. It is situated below sea level and encompasses the lowest spot on earth. The Jordan Valley is part of a much larger rift extending from Iskanderun in North Syria into Africa, beyond the Red Sea. It is bordered by two ranges of mountains with steep slopes on its west and east sides that rise to about 500–1200 m above sea level. Its eastern highland is interrupted by several side wadis running east–west and emptying into the Jordan River or the Dead Sea: Wadi el-Yarmuk, Wadi el-ʿArab, Wadi Ziqlab, Wadi el-Jirm, Wadi el-Yabis, Wadi Kafranja, Wadi Rajib, Wadi ez-Zerqa, Wadi Shuʿeib, Wadi el-Kafrain, Wadi er-Ramah, and Wadi Azeimah. [See Ziqlab, Wadi; Yabis, Wadi el-; Shuʿeib, Wadi.] These wadis, together with other water sources, account for the valley's continuous occupation. The valley varies in width. It is about 2 km across near Tell es-Saʿidiyeh and the modern village of Kraymeh, but it becomes much wider (about 18 km, or 11 mi.) to the south, around the plains of Sweimeh and Jericho. [*See* Saʿidiyeh, Tell es-.] The west side of the valley is narrower than the east side and has a smaller number of side wadis with perennial streams. There are also fewer modern villages and archaeological sites than on the east. The main wadis on the west are Nahr el-Jalud, Wadi el-Maliḥ, Wadi el-Farʿah, Wadi el-Auja, and Wadi el-Qelt. The Marj ibn Amir (Esdraelon Valley) cuts through the western highland to become the main connecting corridor between the Ghor and the Mediterranean Sea. The Ghor, the major part of the valley, is flat and has been cultivated throughout history. All the major wadis on both sides of the valley have carved courses for themselves through the floor of the Ghor, preparing suitable locations for many major and small settlements, including the northern Jordan Valley's important archaeological sites of Beisan (Beth-Shean) and Ṭabaqaṭ Faḥl (Pella). [*See* Beth-Shean; Pella.] The area between Wadi Shuʿeib and Wadi ez-Zerqa (a distance of about 15 km, or 9 mi.) was not irrigated until the Umayyad period, around Ghor Kibid, and then in connection with the modern extension of the East Ghor Canal. Irrigation meant bringing water from distant streams. [*See* Irrigation; Agriculture.]

The Jordan Valley consists of three main geographic zones: ez-Zor is the small valley cut by the Jordan River until it empties into the Dead Sea. The Zor is up to a kilometer wide, but it lacks major settlements because of flooding and the changing bed of the Jordan River in this zone. The second zone is called al-Katar, a region of barren, desiccated hills that separates the Ghor from the Zor. These hills date from the Pleistocene Age, and some were settled in the Neolithic Chalcolithic, Early Bronze, and Iron Ages. The major part of the valley is al-Ghor (see above).

Archaeological and ethnoarchaeological studies have shown strong connections between the Jordan Valley and the highlands in all periods. The inhabitants of the Jordan Valley have had to locate their settlements carefully, taking into consideration the availability of water, security, and roads. They have also had to avoid areas subject to floods and earthquakes, or adapt themselves to their occurrence. In most cases the Ghor's good soil was protected and settlements were placed on barren land or in the foothills. Those settlements were constructed mainly of mud bricks and reeds, in contrast to stone, the main building material in the highlands.

Agriculture has always been the main occupation of Ghor settlers, whose abundance was distributed beyond the boundaries of the Jordan Valley. Its tomatoes, cucumbers, and other products are still exported. During the Islamic period, it was the main source of cane sugar for the area of greater Syria (see below).

Deforestation on the foothills and salinization are critical environmental problems in the valley. In certain areas, the soil was washed down from the highlands and the slopes to form new soil layers. Evidence of highland *terra rosa* has been found as far away as the Katar hills along the Jordan River. Strong soil erosion and frost occasionally destroy the area's agricultural products. In addition to agriculture, the inhabitants of the valley have also produced pottery, metals, and textiles. Evidence of these industries has been found in excavations in the area.

The valley is comfortably warm to intolerably hot and humid. It receives rain mainly between the months of November and March, ranging between 38 and 41 cm (15–16 in.) annually. The valley's tropical character has been made green through water and irrigation systems, and malignant malaria and other epidemics were eradicated a few decades ago.

Two main, parallel roads were used in antiquity, running north–south on both sides of the valley, connecting its major settlements. The roads are dated by numerous Roman milestones, but they appear to have played a similar role as early as the first and second millennia BCE. They were open to the north, but ended in the south at the Dead Sea and the surrounding steep cliffs, disconnected from the Wadi ʿArabah and the Red Sea. Both roads were interconnected with a number of subsidiary roads.

Many archaeological surveys and excavations have been carried out in the valley, including those of William Foxwell Albright (1926) in the 1920s; Nelson Glueck (1951) in the 1930s–1940s; Henri de Contenson (1964) and James Mellaart in the early 1950s; and Moawiyah Ibrahim, James Sauer, and Khair Yassine in the 1970s (Ibrahim et al., 1976). Until the mid-1970s, large-scale excavations were restricted to a few sites: Teleilat el-Ghassul, Qumran, Tell es-Sultan (Jericho), Tulul Abu el-ʿAlayiq, Khirbat al-Mafjar, Tell Iktanu, Tell Deir ʿAlla, Tell es-Saʿidiyeh, Mallaḥa, Shaʿar ha-Golan (al-'Uqhuwanah), and Khirbet Kerak (Beth-Yeraḥ). [*See* Teleilat el-Ghassul; Qumran; Jericho; Mafjar, Khirbat al-; Iktanu, Tell; Deir ʿAlla, Tell; Shaʿar ha-Golan; Beth-Yeraḥ.] In addition, small excavations were conducted at Shuna (North), Pella, Tell Abu Ḥabil, Ghrubba, and Azeimah. [*See* Ghrubba.] Work has been resumed at old excavation sites in the east Jordan Valley, at Ghassul, Iktanu, Deir ʿAlla, Saʿidiyeh, Pella, and Shunah (North), while new excavations have begun at Tell Nimrin, Umm Ḥammad esh-Sharqi (et-Twal), Kataret es-Samra, Abu Sarbut, Tell el-Mazar, Abu Ḥamid, Abu en-Ni'aj, Tell el-Ḥayyat, Abu el-Kharaz, el-Maqbarah, and Dhraʿ el-Khan. [*See* Nimrin, Tell; Mazar, Tell el-; Ḥayyat, Tell el-.]

Paleolithic to Chalcolithic Periods. The earliest evidence of habitation in the Jordan Valley was found at the Paleolithic sites of Tell Abu Ḥabil, south of Wadi el-Yabis, and Wadi el-Ḥammeh, about 2 km (1 mi.) north of Ṭabaqat Faḥl (Pella). In the lower Wadi el-Ḥammeh basin, a sequence of Pleistocene deposits dating from about 80,000–11,000 years BP have been attested. Among these deposits were Upper Paleolithic, Kebaran, and Natufian sites. The Natufian occupation includes two isolated large oval enclosures and smaller structures (Edwards, 1989, pp. 409–412).

Natufian and Pre-Pottery Neolithic (PPN) evidence has also been found at Abu 'Urabi, Mhith, and Dhraʿ el-Khan, sites situated at the mouth of wadis close to foothills. The most impressive Natufian and PPN remains in the valley were excavated at Jericho and ʿAin Mallaḥa. The Natufian evidence at Mallaḥa included three levels with a large number of huts and plastered storage pits, in addition to pits with collective burials. At Jericho a clay platform with microliths and a bone harpoon-head were the main finds from the Natufian I period. Jericho is a unique PPN settlement, with its successive layers and distinctive defensive structures, which include a wall enclosing an area of 4 ha (10 acres) and a massive stone tower (Kenyon, 1960, 1965, 1981; Kenyon and Holland, 1982, 1983). Except for its defensive structures, Jericho's repertoire has close parallels at Wadi Himar, ʿAin Ghazal, and Wadi Shuʿeib. [*See* Jericho; ʿAin Ghazal.]

Jericho and Shaʿar ha-Golan, represent two groups in an early phase of the Pottery Neolithic (PN) in Palestine. Jericho's pottery includes distinctive coarse ware and decorated red-burnished ware; Shaʿar ha-Golan and other sites display the painted and incised pottery with simple geometric designs of the Yarmukian culture, in addition to distinctive examples of engraved and incised pebbles and human figures. Other sites include PN material: Ghassul, Ghruba, Ghannam, Dhraʿ el-Hesseini, Katar Zakari, Qa'dan, Pella, Baqurah, and Abu Ḥamid. Most show no distinction between PN and Chalcolithic material. Both periods seem to represent early village farming communities that were related to many other sites on the highland.

The Chalcolithic period that followed has been attested at many large, open settlements in the valley with coarse and painted handmade pottery, chisel axes, and fan scrapers. Large-scale excavations, such as at Ghassul and Abu Ḥamid, exposed large rectangular houses and storage facilities.

Bronze Age. Early phases of the Early Bronze Age (before the beginning of the third millennium) appear at open settlements such as Rweihah, Umm Ḥammad esh-Sharqi, and Kataret es-Samra. Other EB II–III sites were located in the foothills and have a defensive character. Khirbet Kerak (Beth-Yeraḥ) and Jericho are the main fortified towns in the valley. More recent excavations at Iktanu, Saʿidiyeh, Abu el-Kharaz, Pella, and Shunah (North) show scanty evidence of EB fortifications. In the following transitional period (EB IV–Middle Bronze I), there are numerous low sites with new locations in the Katar hills, foothills, and side wadis. Most lack architectural remains; the primary evidence is from shaft tombs, such as at Wadi el-Ḥammeh, Umm Ḥammad (et-Twal), and Jericho. [*See* Shaft Tombs.]

The MB period is well represented at many sites in the valley where excavation has revealed architectural complexes: Pella, Tell el-Ḥayyat, and Deir ʿAlla. Most striking are a series of four roughly square MB IIA–C temples at Tell el-Ḥayyat and defensive walls at Jericho, Deir ʿAlla, and Pella. Significant MB material has come from tombs at Jericho and Pella (Kenyon, 1960, 1965).

The prosperity of the Jordan Valley continued throughout the Late Bronze Age (1550–1200 BCE) and has been widely attested in settlements at Jericho, Deir ʿAlla, Pella, Abu el-Kharaz, Saʿidiyeh, and Kataret es-Samra. At some of these sites, LB tombs were also excavated. Egyptian, Cypriot, and Mycenaean materials demonstrate strong international contacts with other Mediterranean regions. An LB sanctuary on a high platform was excavated at Deir ʿAlla.

Iron Age. There seems to have been a smooth transition from the Late Bronze into the Iron Age. Most major LB sites were reoccupied in the main periods of the Iron Age. This cultural continuity can be demonstrated at Jericho, Nimrin, Deir ʿAlla, Mazar, Saʿidiyeh, Pella, and Abu el-Kharaz, although some recession in international contacts can be observed during Iron I.

Significant material from Iron II comes from excavations at Deir ʿAlla, phase IX (Franken, 1969, phase M). This phase includes a large architectural complex that may have served as a religious center and related workshops. A lengthy Ammonite/Aramaic plaster text attributed to Balaam Bar Beor, the Balaam mentioned in the Hebrew Bible appears to represent a tradition of religious practice in the Jordan Valley that may extend beyond the immediate region. [*See* Deir ʿAlla Inscriptions, Aramaic Language and Literature.] A strong earthquake toward the end of the ninth century BCE destroyed this settlement and perhaps others in the area.

Persian through Islamic Periods. At the end of the Iron Age, in about the mid-sixth century BCE, there is a decline in the material culture of the Jordan Valley, even though some sites reflect continuous occupation between the sixth and first centuries BCE. The best-known sites during this period are Nimrin, Deir ʿAlla, Mazar, Saʿidiyeh, and Pella; however, there is relatively little architectural evidence from them for the Persian and Early Hellenistic periods. Toward the end of the Hellenistic period (second and first centuries BCE), prosperity is demonstrated through building activities and the quantity of imported amphora handles with inscriptions. The Dead Sea Scrolls found at Qumran, at the northwest corner of the Dead Sea, and in the surrounding caves are the most dramatic discovery in the Jordan Valley. [*See* Dead Sea Scrolls.]

The Roman period is well represented throughout the Jordan Valley. More than fifty Roman sites are distributed in and near foothills, on the Ghor, and near the Katar hills. Many were situated along the Roman road, which is indicated by a number of milestones, some bearing Latin inscriptions. Sites located on the peaks of hills served defensive and military purposes, while other, open sites were supported by agriculture. Most of the Roman sites have been identified in surveys. A few were excavated: Tulul Abu el-ʿAlayiq, Abu el-Kharaz, and Pella. These investigations showed that the Roman occupation in the valley was strongly connected to urban sites in the highlands. Cultural, religious, and commercial activities are best represented at Pella, which Josephus Flavius (first century CE) referred to as a city of importance. Excavations at the site revealed a large civic complex and some tombs from the Roman period.

During the Byzantine era, population density was high, reflecting, to a large extent the preceding Roman period. Byzantine sites are found everywhere in the valley and indicate that agriculture was practiced on a large scale. Byzantine remains have been excavated mainly at Pella, the largest city in the area then. Excavation has uncovered three churches and large residential quarters. [*See* Churches.] The Byzantine city must have served as an administrative center for at least the northern Jordan Valley and parts of the eastern highland.

Islamic sites are represented in all parts of the valley, especially (but not exclusively) from the eleventh to the fifteenth centuries. Archaeological surveys have shown Ottoman sites to be underrepresented, although historical sources mention a significant number of settlements during the period. Interest in Islamic sites is increasing, and a number of them have been excavated. Hisham's palace at Khirbat al-Mafjar near Jericho for example, was built in the first years of the Umayyad caliph Hisham ibn ʿAbd al-Malik (724–743). It comprises a large central courtyard and a bath complex with painted mosaic floors, in addition to a mosque and a gatehouse (Hamilton, 1959). The most impressive archaeological evidence of a large Islamic settlement comes from Pella, however, where, as with many other sites in the area, the inhabitants' Christian and civic rights seem to have been maintained as a result of a peace covenant with the Muslim army led by Abu ʿUbaidah ʿAmir bin el-Jarrah. In Arab sources, Fahl (Pella) is mentioned as a center for the district of Transjordan (Jund el-ʿUrdun). The archaeological and the historical evidence reveals continuity from the Byzantine into the Umayyad and ʿAbbasid periods. The area experienced a severe earthquake in 747, whose effects could be traced in a number of locations at Pella. A sizable ʿAbbasid settlement, north of the mound, was established in the ninth and continued into the tenth century (Walmsley, 1989, pp. 436–438). [*See* Umayyad Caliphate; ʿAbbasid Caliphate.]

Most of the Islamic sites in the Jordan valley are agricultural and were sometimes connected to aqueducts and other elements in irrigation systems. There is clear evidence that sugar was produced on a large scale in the valley, based on the number of sugar mills associated with quantities of "sugar pots." Mosques, mausolea, and cemeteries are found all over the valley. [*See* Mosque; Mausoleum.] Monuments carry the names Nebi Musa, Abu ʿUbayad, Dirar, Sharhabil, Maʿadh, and Waqqas. They are difficult to date but were dedicated to prophets and to leaders of early Islam. Most are located at Early Islamic sites or in their immediate vicinity.

[*See also* Palestine; *and* Transjordan. *For further discussion of the western side of the valley, see* Judah *and* Judean Desert Caves.]

BIBLIOGRAPHY

Albright, William Foxwell. "The Jordan Valley in the Bronze Age." *Annual of the American Schools of Oriental Research* 6 (1926): 13–74.

Contenson, Henri de. "The 1953 Survey in the Yarmouk and Jordan Valleys." *Annual of the Department of Antiquities of Jordan* 8–9 (1964): 30–46.

Dollfus, Geneviève, and Zeidan A. Kafafi. "Preliminary Results of the First Season of the Joint Jordano-French Project at Abu Ḥamid." *Annual of the Department of Antiquities of Jordan* 30 (1986): 353–379.

Edwards, Philip C. "History of Pella." In *Archaeology of Jordan,* vol. 2, *Field Reports,* edited by Denyse Homès-Fredericq and J. Basil Hennessy, pp. 409–412. Louvain, 1989.

Franken, H. J., with contributions by J. Kalsbeek. *Excavations at Tell Deir ʿAllā,* vol. 1, *A Stratigraphical and Analytical Study of the Early Iron Age Pottery.* Leiden, 1969.

Glueck, Nelson. *Explorations in Eastern Palestine.* Vol. 4. Annual of the American Schools of Oriental Research, 25/28. New Haven, 1951.

Hamilton, Robert William. *Khirbat al-Mafjar: An Arabian Mansion in the Jordan Valley.* Oxford, 1959.

Helms, S. W. "Jawa, Tell Umm Hammad, and the EB I/Late Chalcolithic Landscape." *Levant* 19 (1987): 49–81.

Hennessy, J. Basil. "Teleilat Ghassul: Its Place in the Archaeology of Jordan." In *Studies in the History and Archaeology of Jordan,* vol. 1, edited by Adnan Hadidi, pp. 55–58. Amman, 1982.

Ibrahim, Moawiyah, James A. Sauer, and Khair Yassine. "The East Jordan Valley Survey, 1975." *Bulletin of the American Schools of Oriental Research,* no. 222 (1976): 41–66.

Kafafi, Zeidan A. "The Neolithic of Jordan (East Bank)." Ph.D. diss., Freie Universität, 1982.

Kenyon, Kathleen M. *Excavations at Jericho,* vol. 1, *The Tombs Excavated in 1952–54.* London, 1960.

Kenyon, Kathleen M. *Excavations at Jericho,* vol. 2, *The Tombs Excavated in 1955–58.* London, 1965.

Kenyon, Kathleen M. *Excavations at Jericho,* vol. 3, *The Architecture and Stratigraphy of the Tell.* 2 vols. Edited by Thomas A. Holland. London, 1981.

Kenyon, Kathleen M., and Thomas A. Holland. *Excavations at Jericho,* vol. 4, *The Pottery Type Series and Other Finds.* London, 1982.

Kenyon, Kathleen M., and Thomas A. Holland. *Excavations at Jericho,* vol. 5, *The Pottery Phases of the Tell and Other Finds.* London, 1983.

Leonard, Albert, Jr., ed. *The Jordan Valley Survey: Some Unpublished Soundings Conducted by James Mellaart.* Annual of the American Schools of Oriental Research, 50. Winona Lake, Ind., 1992.

Mittmann, Siegfried. *Beiträge zur Siedlungs- und Territorialgeschichte des nördlichen Ostjordanlandes.* Wiesbaden, 1970.

Pritchard, James B. *The Excavation at Herodian Jericho, 1951.* Annual of the American Schools of Oriental Research, 32/33. New Haven, 1958.

Sauer, James A. "Transjordan in the Bronze and Iron Ages: A Critique of Glueck's Synthesis." *Bulletin of the American Schools of Oriental Research,* no. 263 (1986): 1–26.

Smith, Robert Houston. *The 1967 Season of the College of Wooster Expedition to Pella.* Pella of the Decapolis, vol. 1. Wooster, Ohio, 1973.

Tubb, Jonathan N. *Excavations at the Early Bronze Age Cemetery of Tiwal esh-Sharqi.* London, 1990.

Walmsley, Alan. "The Early Islamic and ʿAbbasid Pella/Fahl, 635–c. 900." In *Archaeology of Jordan,* vol. 2, *Field Reports,* edited by Denyse Homès-Fredericq and J. Basil Hennessy, pp. 436–440. Louvain, 1989.

Yassine, Khair, ed. *Archaeology of Jordan: Essays and Reports.* Amman, 1988.

Moawiyah Ibrahim

JOTAPATA (Gk., Iotapata; Heb., Yodefat; Ar., Khirbet Shifat), site located in the Galilee, directly south of modern Moshav Yodefat and described by Josephus (*War* 3.158–160) as surrounded on three sides by steep ravines and accessible from the north, hidden by surrounding mountains, and having no natural water source (map reference 176 × 248). Jotapata was the site of the first major battle between Roman Jewish forces in the Jewish War that began in 66 CE. Josephus, the commander of the Jewish forces, describes in great detail the battle and his subsequent capture by Vespasian (*War* 3.145–288, 316–408). Archaeological remains provide a glimpse of the battle as well as a rare look at a first-century CE Galilean site undisturbed by building activities from later periods.

In 1847, E. G. Schultz (1849) first properly identified Jotapata; Edward Robinson associated the site with Jiphthahel (*Jos.* 19:14, 27), but the apparent absence of Late Bronze or Iron I pottery makes his identification unlikely. Claude R. Conder and H. H. Kitchener (1881) suggested that the site might also be the Gopatata of the Talmud (*Ecclesiastes Rabbah* 108a), Yodpat in the Mishnah (*ʿArakh.* 9.6), and Jotabe, an episcopal town in 536 CE. William Foxwell Albright associated it with biblical Yotva. A place called Yodefat existed in the time of Joshua, according to the Mishnah (*ʿArakh.* 9.6), but excavations in 1992 directed by Douglas Edwards, Mordechai Aviam, and David Adan-Bayewitz indicate that the first major occupation of the site occurred in the Hellenistic period.

The site consists of upper Yodefat, or Jotapata, and is approximately 480 acres in area when combined with lower Khirbet Shifat immediately to the north. Jotapata had a large outer fortification wall that experienced at least three building phases: in its earliest phase (probably belonging to the Seleucid period), an outer wall (2.5–3.5 m thick) extended around the north, east, and west sides. [*See* Seleucids.] The inner part of the fortification wall was built over an earlier building that produced large storage jars and a Ptolemaic coin on its floor, suggesting a founding date for the town in the Ptolemaic period. An inner wall at the northern part of the site increased the wall's thickness to more than 5 m. Its construction style resembles that of the Hellenistic city wall found at the coastal city of Dor. [*See* Dor.]

On the north, the city wall consists of large ashlars founded on bedrock; the ashlars were covered on their north face by chipped pieces of limestone, in some spots to a depth of almost 4 m. A series of narrow walls held the limestone chips in place, creating an artificial hill to the northwest that increased protection where the town was most vulnerable.

A portion of a ramp composed of mortar and crushed pottery, probably built by the Romans during their attack on Jotapata in 67 CE, was also found on the northwest. [*See* First Jewish Revolt.] Ballista, iron bow and catapult arrowheads, possible sandal nails, and Early Roman pottery embedded in or under the mortar that stabilized the ground in front of the wall are clear evidence of the first-century battle between the Roman army and the town's Jewish defenders. Another rubble wall 5 m inside the ashlar wall on the northeast created a casemate wall 5–6 thick. The casemate structure was built on top of the quarried limestone chips associated with the earlier wall (see above). This construction appears to date to the Early Roman period and may be associated with preparations for war against the Romans. Similar rubble walls extend south: one follows the contour of the hill and the other follows the upper hill. The upper wall appears to have been built during the Hellenistic period; the lower wall enclosed the lower plateau in the Roman period.

The language of at least some of the first-century CE inhabitants was Aramaic or Hebrew, as shown by an ostracon found in a first-century context. An unfinished olive press and an olive-press complex in a cave on the site's steep east side suggest the industry's importance in the town. Several stepped pools, possibly *miqvaot* or ritual baths, have been located near the oil-press operations. However, the pools may have simply served as settling pools. An Early Roman pottery kiln at the southern edge of the town indicates that Jotapata had a degree of self-sufficiency in ceramic manufacturing, although pottery from kilns at Kefar Ḥananyah show that Jotapata was part of a regional economic network that linked pagan cities (such as the coastal city of Akko) with Galilean cities, towns, and villages. [*See* Kefar Ḥananyah.]

Upper Yodefat, or Jotapata, was apparently not occupied after the Romans destroyed it in the first century. The lower part of the town, Khirbet Shifat, was apparently reestablished to the north in the late first or early second century CE. Pottery found down to floor surfaces indicates that this lower town continued at least into the medieval period.

[*See also* Galilee; *and the biographies of Albright, Conder, Kitchener, and Robinson.*]

BIBLIOGRAPHY

Adan-Bayewitz, David. *Common Pottery in Roman Galilee: A Study of Local Trade.* Ramat Gan, 1993.

Aviam, Mordechai. Article in Hebrew in *Cathedra* 28 (1983): 33–46.

Conder, Claude R., and H. H. Kitchener. *The Survey of Western Palestine: Memoirs of the Topography, Orography, Hydrography, and Archaeology,* vol. 1, *Galilee.* London, 1881. See pages 289, 311–313.

Edwards, Douglas R., Mordechai Aviam, and David Adan-Bayewitz. "Yodefat, 1992." *Israel Exploration Journal* 45.2–3 (1995): 191–197.

Josephus. *The Life.* Translated by Henry St. John Thackeray. Loeb Classical Library, Josephus, vol. 1. Cambridge, Mass., 1966. See 188, 234, 322, 350, 353, 357, 412, and 414.

Josephus. *The Jewish War.* Loeb Classical Library, Josephus, vols. 2–3. Cambridge, Mass., 1967–1968. See 2.573, 3.111–114, 3.141–339, 3.405–406, 3.432, 3.438, 4.1, 4.4, 4.624, and 5.544.

Meyers, Eric M., et al. "The Meiron Excavation Project: Archaeological Survey in Galilee and Golan, 1976." *Bulletin of the American Schools of Oriental Research,* no. 230 (1978): 1–24.

Schultz, E. G. "Mitteilungen über eine Reise durch Samarien und Galilaea." *Zeitschrift der Deutschen Morganländischen Gesellschaft* 3 (1849): 46–62.

Tsafrir, Yoram, et al. *Tabula imperii romani: Iudaea-Palaestina.* Jerusalem, 1994.

Wolff, Samuel R., et al. "Archaeology in Israel." *American Journal of Archaeology* 98 (1994): 481–519. See pages 509–510.

DOUGLAS R. EDWARDS

JUBAH, WADI AL-, isolated, yet protected, valley located at a mountain/sand desert interface in the modern Republic of Yemen, with the central highlands to the west and the Ramlat as-Sabʿatayn to the east. The upstream southwestern tail of the crescent-shaped wadi is at 14°57′ N, 45°15′ E; the eastern edge of the wadi is at 15°01′ N, 45°21′ E; and the northwestern reach, where the wadi vanishes into the sands of the desert, is at 15°12′ N, 45°17′ E, 25 km (15 mi.) south of Marib.

Precambrian metamorphic rocks intruded by plutons of Late Proterozoic diorite and granite underlie the area. Near the center of the structurally controlled erosional course of Wadi al-Jubah through these rocks, the roof of the diorite pluton was breached, forming a basin rimmed on all sides by mountainous barriers. Pleistocene and Holocene alluvial deposits within the basin created a fertile plain that became a rich savannah during more moist periods. With the advent in about 5000 BCE of the current more arid cycle, a grassy, arid savannah developed that persisted until early agriculturalists overgrazed and irrigated the region.

Except for squeezes taken from Sabaean and Qatabanian inscriptions by local inhabitants employed by Eduard Glaser during the late nineteenth century and a short epigraphic survey conducted by Albert Jamme of the Catholic University, Washington, D.C., in the area in 1975–1976, this wadi was unknown to archaeologists until 1982. In that year, the American Foundation for the Study of Man (AFSM) initiated an archaeological project in Wadi al-Jubah to continue the pioneering work done between 1950 and 1952 in nearby Wadi Beiḥan and at Marib, under the direction of Wendell Phillips and William Foxwell Albright. Between 1982 and 1987 the new AFSM team conducted six campaigns in Wadi al-Jubah, consisting of archaeological, geological, pedological, botanical, and epigraphic surveys, with test excavations at six sites. The project's initial goal was reconnaissance: to identify the types, extent, and dates of archaeological remains preserved in this region. The project was coordinated by James A. Sauer (chief archaeologist), Jamme (epigrapher), and Jeffrey A. Blakely (field director since 1983).

It is not known when hominids first reached the southern part of the Arabian Peninsula, but the presence of core and flake tools with Acheulean characteristics, found in secondary alluvial contexts within Wadi al-Jubah, indicates that hominids were in the wadi, at least periodically, by the Lower Paleolithic period. A few Upper Paleolithic and possibly Neolithic tools were also discerned only in secondary alluvial contexts. Hearths, cairns, and small structures attributed to the fifth, fourth, and early third millennia are present. Because the project was largely survey, these remains were not investigated in any detail. The AFSM located a large South Arabian Bronze Age site (late third–mid-second millennium) just to the north of Wadi al-Jubah but did not investigate it in detail.

The vast majority of the visible archaeological remains within Wadi al-Jubah date to the Sabaean and Qatabanian periods (approximately the fifteenth century BCE–first century CE). For much of this period Wadi al-Jubah was dominated by its one major site, Hajar ar-Rayḥani, more commonly called al-Hajar (15°05′ N, 45°18′ E); the remainder of the wadi appears to have supported small farming communities set across an intensively irrigated landscape. Starting in the mid-second millennium, a series of dams and canals fed water to a growing field system. Sediment in the irrigation water replenished soil nutrients but also raised the level of the fields and canals several meters until, apparently, the fields grew too high to receive adequate water and the system failed, in about the mid-first millennium BCE.

Hajar ar-Rayḥani appears to have been the central place within the wadi and to have served as a stop on the ancient South Arabian trade route, situated near where it crossed the border separating Qataban from Saba' (Sheba). Its ruins are located on top of a Bronze Age site and may represent continuous occupation from that period. It received a massive fortification wall in about the eighth century BCE and experienced a major destruction a few hundred years later. The site supported local ceramic, metallurgical, and lapidary industries, possibly until its abandonment early in the first or second century CE. Following this site's abandonment, Wadi al-Jubah was not occupied by a sedentary population living in permanent structures until the nineteenth century, when the wadi was repopulated and a new irrigation system was established on top of the older, eroded system.

[*See also* Marib.]

BIBLIOGRAPHY

Primary and Technical Reports

Blakely, Jeffrey A., et al. *The Wadi al-Jubah Archaeological Project,* vol. 2, *Site Reconnaissance in North Yemen, 1983.* Washington, D.C., 1985.

Glanzman, William D., and Abdu O. Ghaleb. *The Wadi al-Jubah Archaeological Project,* vol. 3, *Site Reconnaissance in the Yemen Arab Republic, 1984: The Stratigraphic Probe at Hajar ar-Rayhani.* Washington, D.C., 1987.

Overstreet, William C., et al. *The Wadi al-Jubah Archaeological Project,* vol. 4, *Geological and Archaeological Reconnaissance in the Yemen Arab Republic, 1985.* Washington, D.C., 1988.

Toplyn, Michael R. *The Wadi al-Jubah Archaeological Project,* vol. 1, *Site Reconnaissance in North Yemen, 1982.* Washington, D.C., 1984.

Secondary and Popular Reports

Blakely, Jeffrey A., and James A. Sauer. "The Road to Wadi al-Jubah: Archaeology on the Ancient Spice Route in Yemen." *Expedition* 27.1 (1985): 2–9. Initial popular statement describing work in Wadi al-Jubah, only partially superseded by Sauer and Blakely (1988).

Gwinnett, A. John, and Leonard Gorelick. "Bead Manufacture at Hajar ar-Rayḥani, Yemen." *Biblical Archaeologist* 54 (1991): 186–196. Narrowly focused but engaging account of beads and the technology of ancient bead manufacture based on stone and mineral beads found in Wadi al-Jubah.

Sauer, James A., and Jeffrey A. Blakely. "Archaeology along the Spice Route of Yemen." In *Araby the Blest: Studies in Arabian Archaeology,* edited by Daniel T. Potts, pp. 90–115. Copenhagen, 1988. The most up-to-date, popular statement describing work in Wadi al-Jubah; does not include the results of the 1987 season.

JEFFREY A. BLAKELY

JUDAH. Covering the southern third of Israel, Judah (Lat., Judea) designates, in certain late periods, an entire country. Both poor and remote, this small region was the cradle of the Hebrew Bible.

Geography. Judah extends over some 4,400 sq km (2,728 sq. mi.): 2,150 sq km (1,333 sq. mi.) are essentially desert; 1,500 sq km (930 sq. mi.) are partly cultivatable highlands; and 750 sq km (465 sq. mi.) tend to have good soil. The adjacent regions are, from the north, counterclockwise, the highland of Ephraim; Philistia (the coastal plain and the western Negev desert); the Negev highlands; and the Dead Sea and Jordan Valley.

The core of the region is the Jerusalem area (about 150 sq km or 93 sq. mi.) and the highlands of Judah (about 1,000 sq km or 625 sq. mi., including the ʿArqub in the northwest, and the central and southern parts, also known as the highlands of Hebron). The Land of Benjamin (the Benjamin highlands, about 350 sq km, or 217 sq. mi.), is north of these. All of these areas (the Judean highlands) comprise the southern part of modern Israel's central highlands. The altitude ranges from 600 m above sea level in the south to 1,020 m near Hebron. Mean annual rainfall ranges from 300 to 400 mm in the south, to about 700 mm (including snow) in the highest parts of the region, but it may fall to below 300–200 mm in the frequent drought years. Mean temperature is about 10–7°C (January) to 22–26°C (August). The Judean highlands, especially south of Jerusalem, are the highest, steepest, and poorest part of the central highlands.

East of the highlands, the Judean Desert slopes down to the Jordan Valley and the Dead Sea shore (about 400 m below sea level). The desert is large (about 1,150 sq km, or

713 sq. mi., not including Jericho) but very marginal: it has a mean annual rainfall of only 50–100 mm (200–400 mm on the higher desert plateau) and, in August, a mean temperature of only 26–34°C. To the south lies the Beersheba-Arad valley: the biblical Negev of Judah (only part of the modern Negev). This also is a fringe area, but it is not so marginal. An important natural route to the south and east, it extends for more than about 1,000 sq km (620 sq. mi.). Its mean annual rainfall is about 300–150 mm and its mean temperature is about 28–26°C (August) to 14–10°C (January).

Below, to the west, lies the Shephelah of Judah (about 750 sq km, or 465 sq. mi., excluding the western parts, which are connected to Philistia), the richest part of Judah, composed of moderately undulating hills. Its altitude is about 150–300 m in the lower (western) Shephelah and 300–600 m in the upper (eastern) Shephelah. This is the real biblical hill country of Judah, although some translations give that name to the highlands. Its mean annual rainfall is about 350–550 mm; its mean temperature is the same as the Negev's.

History and Methods of Research. Judah's ancient remains were first recorded by such nineteenth-century explorers as Edward Robinson, Victor Guerin, and above all Claude R. Conder and Horatio Herbert Kitchener, but they were unable to date most of the ruins. [*See the biographies of Robinson, Guerin, Conder, and Kitchener.*] Modern excavations have been conducted at several sites since the 1920s. The main stratigraphic excavations (mostly of more than one period) are in the Judean highlands: Jerusalem, Khirbet et-Tell (Ai), Tell el-Jib, Tell en-Naṣbeh, Tell el-Ful, Ramat Raḥel, Giloh, Herodium, Beth-Zur, Hebron, Susiya, and Khirbet Rabud (Debir); in the Shephelah: Beth-Shemesh, Tel Yarmut, ʿAzekah, Mareshah (Marisa)/Beth-Guvrin, Lachish, Tell Beit Mirsim, and Tel Ḥalif; in the Negev of Judah: Tel Beersheba, Tel Esdar, Tel Masos, Tel ʿIra, Arad, ʿAroʿer, Tel Malḥata, and Ḥorvat ʿUza; and in the Judean Desert: Masada, ʿEin-Gedi, Qumran, several caves and monasteries, and sites in the Buqeiʿa valley and along the Dead Sea shore. Major stratigraphic-ceramic sequences for the early periods have been published for Tell Beit Mirsim and Lachish.

The first modern archaeological survey, systematic but very selective, was conducted in the Judean Desert and highlands in 1967–1968 (Kochavi, 1972). More detailed surveys have been conducted since the early 1980s in the highlands and the Shephelah. The available data (Finkelstein and Magen, 1993) from the various subregions still differ significantly.

The highlands of Judah have been surveyed by Avi Ofer since 1982 (800 sq km, or 496 sq. mi., not including the ʿArqub). A sample of about a third of the area has been completed, enabling an estimation of the possible lacunae in the selective survey (completed for the entire region, including all ruins marked on maps). To fill in the gaps, 15 percent must be added to the settled area in the surveyed region, based on results from the wide sample areas. An additional 35 percent must be added for the ʿArqub. The size of each site in different periods is estimated following a standard technique: sherd scatters and maximum size of site. Diagnostic pottery rims from each period are counted, while the rims that can be dated to more than one period are assigned to them according to percentages. This counting is weighted according to the length of each period, which is indispensable for valid analysis. The weighted relative percentage of each period, compared with the maximum percentage, yields the relation of its size to the maximum size, or a calculated size estimate. For early periods, this estimate may be too low, as sherds could be covered by later debris. To minimize error, an average is made between the maximum and the calculated size, using a factor proportional to the extent of later debris. This averaged estimate may reduce possible errors and is the basis for further evaluations. In special cases, the estimate is changed according to other relevant data (e.g., sherd distribution over the site, which, however, generally is not useful). Several averages were calculated for each period and subregion, such as relative height above sea level as a security factor, distance from water sources and roads, and land use. The averages were calculated not only per site, but also per settled area, which is more significant. A rank-size analysis of all periods indicates possible changes in social integration. The intensity of pottery at every site and in every period was also analyzed, representing the intensity of human activity—population size relative to carrying capacity (an estimate based on settled area is, however, problematic because the coefficients of inhabitants per acre vary too much). By all these means, a purely archaeological history of the region was obtained, which will be compared to its documented history.

Many surveyors have explored the small Land of Benjamin (Finkelstein and Magen, 1993). In most cases the indispensable data are published (although unweighted), but most periods lack subdivisions, such as Iron II–III, and the data, evaluated separately for each arbitrary survey unit, have not been synthesized. Most of the Jerusalem area has been surveyed but not yet published. Yehudah Dagan (1992) has surveyed the Shephelah, covering about 75 percent of the area and almost all of its principal sites. Most of his data has not yet been evaluated or published, but the Iron Age sites are reasonably well known. In the desert there has not been much progress since Pessah Bar-Adon's work (1967 onward). Many scholars have explored the Negev of Judah, especially Yohanan Aharoni and his successors, but their work was not part of a systematic research program or publication, and most of their surveys were incomplete.

History of Settlement. A detailed archaeological analysis is so far available only for the highlands of Judah.

Prehistory. There have been almost no surveys of prehistoric Judah. However, René Neuville's work in the desert yielded some caves and rock shelters, important type-sites for the prehistoric cultures in Israel: Umm Qaṭafa (Early Paleolithic), ʿErq el-Aḥmar (Middle to Epipaleolithic), and el-Khiam (Middle Paleolithic to Neolithic). Other Neolithic sites are Naḥal Ḥemar, Abu Ghosh, and (nearby) Khirbet Rabud.

Protohistory (c. 4000–2000 BCE). During the Chalcolithic period, the Beersheba-Ghassul culture in the Shephelah and Negev flourished, including the type-sites in the Beersheba basin. The highest level of solid organization seems to have been small chiefdoms. The extensive human activity in the desert in the period includes a regional temple found above the oasis of ʿEin-Gedi; a magnificent hoard of bronzes was found in the nearby Cave of the Treasure. Signs of human activity are scant in the Judean highlands, however—perhaps the result of the environment. [*See* ʿEin-Gedi.]

The Early Bronze Age witnessed the first urban civilization. In the first stage (EB I) many sites were inhabited in all of the nondesert parts of Judah, significantly penetrating the highlands. Twenty-eight sites are known in the highlands of Judah, with a total size of about 42/17 acres (42 averaged, 17 calculated). To the north, ten more sites are recorded (about 37 acres in total) that are dominated by the site of Ai. The area south of Jerusalem may have been dominated by the great city at Tel ʿErani, on the southwestern edge of the Shephelah. During EB II, a large city existed at Arad, connected with copper mining and trade in the southern deserts (Sinai and the ʿArabah). In the southern highlands, between Arad and Ai, there seems to have been a decline in sites; the situation in the Shephelah is not yet clear. The transition to EB III witnessed a grave crisis in the south, perhaps connected to the strengthening of Egypt under the third dynasty and competition over copper sources. Arad and other centers were weakened or abandoned. In contrast, settlements in the highlands flourished. Ai (27 acres) was still the center of a unit extending north of the region. In the highlands of Judah, twenty-two sites (32/20 acres), most of them fortified, were headed by a large city (15 acres) at Ras Tawra, on the highest mountain in the region (1,010 m high). EB III culture comes to an end in the last third of the third millennium BCE. During the succeeding EB IV, pastoral society is found everywhere in the central highlands (it was not entirely nomadic, as was thought), represented by a few poor sites, with many cemeteries of typical shaft tombs, frequently unconnected to any particular site. [*See* Arad; Ai.]

Middle Bronze Age (c. 2000–1500 BCE). In the Middle Bronze Age a new urban culture flourishes. For the first time, documents are available, evidence of a dimorphic Amorite-Canaanite (West Semitic) society—that is, it combines urban and pastoral elements. The main city-states are found at Lachish in the Shephelah and Jerusalem in the Judean highlands. In the latter, twenty-three sites (a total of 34 acres) are centered in the fortified site of Hebron (6 acres). A cuneiform tablet from Hebron, unique in Judah, reveals the existence of an Amorite-Canaanite society, with a Hurrian element. It seems that Hebron was a third city-state, smaller than the other two and maneuvering between them. In the Negev, only two fortified sites were found (Tel Masos and Tel Malḥata), which may belong to a unit centered west of the region. [*See* Lachish; Hebron.]

Late Bronze Age (c. 1550–1150 BCE). Under the domination of the Egyptian Empire, the Late Bronze Age is a period of great decline, especially in the highlands and frontier zones. The main centers are still Lachish and Jerusalem, bordered on the west by Gezer and Gath (Tel eṣ-Ṣafi). The Amarna letters testify to this reality and to the existence of smaller centers (e.g., Qeʿilah in the Shephelah) maneuvering between the greater city-states. In the highlands of Judah there is only one significant site, Khirbet Rabud (Debir), which is small. An element of refugees (the *ḥapiru*) appears, mainly in the highlands. [*See* Gezer; Rabud, Khirbet.]

Iron Age IA–B (c. 1200–1050 BCE). Although the Iron I is generally defined as the twelfth–eleventh centuries, it seems that the late eleventh century belongs to the next phase. In Iron I, a mass of new settlements is evident all over the highlands: it appears to be a new society, just beginning to crystalize, without dominant centers. In the highlands of Judah some eighteen settlements appear (45/27 acres) in which the main site is Hebron. These sites are not very small, but their economic preferences tend toward horticulture. Northward, the same appears to be true for western Benjamin; it is uncertain, however, whether the eastern sites here antedate the tenth century BCE. In Iron I/IIA, the name Judah first appears, designating only the highlands of Judah. Looking westward, the settlers saw the hill country, which they referred to as "the lowland" (Heb., *shephelah*). That region was then completely abandoned, and the Philistine culture was emerging to the west. A few large villages appeared in the Negev: Tel Masos, Naḥal Yattir, and probably Beersheba, whose material culture was connected to the coast. [*See* Masos, Tel; Beersheba.]

The population in the central highlands seems to have been composed of northern groups emigrating from the crumbling Hittite Empire; local elements, such as the *ḥapriu;* and other settling pastoralists, called Proto-Israelites. Local centers were reestablished in Jerusalem by the Jebusites, in Hebron, and perhaps at other sites, such as Gibeon. [*See* Gibeon.]

Iron Age IC–IIA (c. 1050–800 BCE). The process of settlement accelerated in new directions in the Iron IC–IIA. The desert fringe became densely inhabited for the first time. Probably most of the tribal-pastoral elements that were to become the core of the Judahites only now began to settle. The Judean highlands were settled through a continuous process, changing once and for all from a fringe area to an integral part of the inhabited land. In the highlands of Judah, there are thirty-three known Iron IIA sites (85/50 acres altogether) and eighty-six Iron IIB sites (137/95 acres). The estimated total inhabited area toward 800 BCE was 237 acres; in Benjamin and the area surrounding Jerusalem, 187 acres; Jerusalem, 75 acres; the Shephelah, about 237 acres; and the Negev, 12 acres.

The continuous settlement increased integration among the settled groups, and foreign occupation by the Philistines accelerated the process. An Israelite national kingdom was established in all of the central highlands under King Saul, whose expansion may have stimulated the rise of other ethnic entities in the region. The most important event in the history of Judah, however, was the rise of King David, first in Hebron and then in Jerusalem, where he established the capital of his dynasty. David and his son Solomon built Jerusalem as their kingdom's impressive center. Judah first appeared as a unified entity extending over all of Judah in the schism following Solomon's death. The entity was then in transition from a city-state to a national kingdom, a process completed two centuries later.

Iron Age IIB (c. 800–701 BCE). The climax of Judah's settlement, in Iron IIB, is matched only in the later Byzantine period. In the highlands of Judah, 122 sites were surveyed (232/215 acres); in Benjamin, about 100 sites (225 acres); in the Shephelah about 340 sites (about 500 acres). The estimated total inhabited area in the highlands of Judah is 388 acres; in Benjamin, 300 acres; in the Shephelah, 625 acres; in the Negev, 20 acres; in the desert, 10 acres; and in Jerusalem about 150 acres. The total is about 1,500 acres, or 120,000–150,000 inhabitants (using traditional estimates). The Ceramic Intensity Index is much higher than for other periods (40 percent higher than in the Byzantine period), so figures should perhaps be higher. It seems that Judah became a fully integrated nation only toward this stage, which ended in catastrophe. In 701 BCE, the Assyrians, under Sennacherib, marched on Judah to suppress the revolt of King Hezekiah. They destroyed the country and killed or exiled most of the inhabitants of the Shephelah and about 50–70 percent of those inland. Only Jerusalem resisted.

Iron Age IIC–Iron III (c. 701–538 BCE). Following the Assyrian destruction Judah's recovery began in the highlands and then spread partially to the Shephelah. The Negev and the desert flourished. Toward the end of the seventh century BCE, the inhabited area is estimated as follows: the highlands of Judah, 300 acres (mostly in the north); Benjamin, 225 acres; the Shephelah, 225 acres (± 75); the Negev, 37 acres; and the desert, 25 acres. Jerusalem (still 150 acres) was more central, materially and spiritually. The Deuteronomic ideology flourished, heralding the coming transition to Judaism.

The recovery was disrupted by the events that led to the destruction of the First Temple and the termination of the kingdom by the Babylonians under Nebuchadrezzar. The destruction in the countryside was less severe than previously, but long-term processes led the Shephelah, Negev, and highlands of Hebron into continuous impoverishment. They were separated from Judah and incorporated in Edom (later Idumea). [*See* Edom.]

Persian Period (c. 538–332 BCE). With the return of the exiles, following the edict of King Cyrus, Judaism definitively replaced the old Judahite/Israelite national identity. It centered in the Yehud district (Heb., *medinah*), including Benjamin and part of the highlands of Judah. Half of the highlands sites (eighty-seven sites; 120/90 acres) are in that northern one-quarter of the district. The Second Temple was built and was regarded by the Jewish community as the only legitimate sanctuary. The western part of Idumea was inhabited by urban, Hellenized Phoenicians and the inland part by a rural society with autochthonous roots. With the tide of history turning, the old polis regime reappeared.

Hellenistic Period (c. 332–37 BCE). Both Jewish and Hellenistic culture flourished between 332 and 37 BCE throughout the highlands of Judah (ninety-eight sites; 132/75 acres), first under Ptolemaic and then under Seleucid kings. The Maccabean Revolt, beginning in 167 BCE, ended with the consolidation of the Hasmonean kingdom of Judah. At its zenith, under Alexander Jannaeus, it covered the whole land of Israel, including most of Transjordan and the Golan. When Pompey established Roman hegemony in 63 BCE, Judah was reduced to the mostly Jewish-populated areas in the highlands, parts of Transjordan, and the Galilee. [*See* Ptolemies; Seleucids; Hasmoneans.]

Roman I Period (c. 37–135 BCE). The kingdom of Judah reached its maximum expansion and wealth in the time of Herod the Great (40/37–4 BCE). Jerusalem, "most famous among [Near] Eastern cities" (Pliny), again became the center of a great kingdom. The Second Temple, rebuilt by Herod, was the period's outstanding monument, and Judah prospered (the highlands of Judah included ninety known sites, extending to 245/115 acres). The kingdom did not survive Herod, however, and Judah became the Roman province of Judea. Later, the great revolt of the Jews (66–70 CE) led to the country's destruction by the Romans under Vespasian and Titus. Jerusalem and the Temple were destroyed in 70 CE, as well as many other Judean sites (the last stronghold, Masada, is the most famous and most excavated). Following the destruction, Judea became the garrison of the Roman Tenth Legion. [*See* Masada.]

The period (Roman I) was one of great unrest. The main archaeological evidence comes from the Judean Desert sites, including Qumran. The canonization of the Hebrew Bible was completed; the Pharisees achieved hegemony in Judaism; the Saducees and Essenes disappeared; and Christianity emerged. Messianic yearnings led to the Bar Kokhba Revolt against the Roman emperor Hadrian, ending with the massive destruction of Judea in 135 CE and the end of its Jewish identity until the modern era. [*See* Judean Desert Caves; Qumran; Essenes; *and* Bar Kokhba Revolt.]

Roman II Period (c. 135–324 BCE). Following the destruction by Hadrian, the name Judea was changed to Syria-Palaestina (Philistia) and then to Palaestina Prima, in order to erase the memory of Judah (hence the name Palestine, which lasted until modern times). The Land of Judah never had a specific name after that. Jerusalem was rebuilt as Aelia Capitolina. In about 200 CE, Emperor Septimius Severus established Eleutheropolis (Beth-Guvrin), which dominated most of Judah, except for Aelia and its surroundings. In the highlands of Judah, ninety-five sites are known (150/90 acres). Its southern part remained predominantly Jewish (Heb., *dromah,* "southern") and the rest was mostly pagan.

Byzantine Period (c. 324–638 BCE). The Byzantine period is generally assumed to be the most heavily populated of the ancient periods in Israel. In the highlands of Judah 273 sites (425/350 acres) are known. However, the Ceramic Intensity Index is only about 70 percent Iron IIB, which is consistent with the settlements' uncrowded character. Christianity became the official religion in the Byzantine period and the society was composed mainly of religious communities: Christians, Jews, Samaritans, and pagans.

"Medieval Period" (c. 638–1516 BCE). In archaeological and especially in ceramic terms, the period between 638 and 1516 is not well known. It will only be discussed briefly here.

Early Arab period (*c.* 638–1099 CE). Following the Arab conquest in 638 CE, the Jund Philastin inherited Palaestina Prima. Judah was included within three subdistricts (Ar., *achwar*): Aelia (Jerusalem), Beit Jibrin, and the Dead Sea. Under the Umayyad, ʿAbbasid, and Fatimid dynasties, part of the population became Muslim, and some Arab bedouin tribes settled in the Land of Judah, mainly on the desert fringes. Ramla became the capital of Philastin. The al-Aqṣa mosque and the Dome of the Rock were built in Jerusalem, which became Islam's third important pilgrimage site. [*See* Umayyad Dynasty; ʿAbbasid Dynasty; Fatimid Dynasty; *and* Ramla.]

Crusader and Ayyubid period (*c.* 1099–1291 CE). Most of the Crusader remains known in Judah are in Jerusalem, although forts and fortified properties were built in the countryside as well. Between 1099 and 1291, the Frankish element of the society played an important role within the Kingdom of Jerusalem. Judah was the first royal domain, and then Hebron and Beth-Guvrin became independent principalities. Following the kingdom's end (in 1191 CE), Judah became predominantly Muslim.

Late Arab period (*c.* 1291–1516 CE). Under the Mamluks, the coastal plain was intentionally depopulated, turning it into a fringe area, while the population of the highlands increased. Judah was divided first between the districts of Jerusalem and Hebron (as a province of Damascus) and then the province of Gaza. The deterioration of the land reached its peak during this period. In 1376, Jerusalem became the seat of a minor governor.

Ottoman Period (1516–1917 CE). Following the Ottoman conquest in 1516, most of Judah was unified within the district of Jerusalem, including the city's subdistricts and Hebron. Parts of the Shephelah fell within the Ramla subdistrict. The land flourished in the sixteenth century, and Jerusalem was refortified with the wall that still encircles it. Ottoman administrative documents (Tk., *defteri*) give the best information on the economics of the land's traditional society. In the following centuries Judah sank into decline, while Jerusalem's position was strengthened, heralding the political and cultural importance it would know in the twentieth century.

[*See also* Jerusalem; Negev; Northern Samaria, Survey of; Shephelah; *and* Southern Samaria, Survey of. *In addition, the following sites not previously cross-referenced above are the subject of independent entries:* ʿAroʿer; Beit Mirsim, Tell; Beth-Shemesh; Beth-Zur; Esdar, Tel; Ful, Tell el-; Giloh; Herodium; ʿIra, Tel; Mareshah; Naṣbeh, Tell en-; Ramat Raḥel; Susiya; *and* Yarmut, Tel.]

BIBLIOGRAPHY

The *Atlas of Israel,* 3d ed. (Tel Aviv, 1985) contains geographic data relevant to the region. Detailed maps of Judah from ancient to Byzantine periods can be found in the second edition of *The Macmillan Bible Atlas* by Yohanan Aharoni and Michael Avi-Yonah (New York, 1993). The earliest (and still best) modern systematic description of ancient ruins in Judah is provided in Claude R. Conder and H. H. Kitchener, *The Survey of Western Palestine,* vol. 3, *Judaea* (London, 1883); see sheets 17–26. The dating is unreliable, however. Geographic histories include Yohanan Aharoni, *The Land of the Bible,* 2d ed. (Philadelphia, 1979), for biblical Israel and Judah, and Michael Avi-Yonah, *The Holy Land: From the Persian to the Arab Conquest, 536 B.C. to A.D. 640,* 2d ed. (Grand Rapids, Mich., 1977), for the classical periods. Aharoni's text is somewhat out of date and differs from this entry on many points.

For archaeological scholarship and excavation reports, the reader should consult the following:

Bar-Adon, Pessah. *Excavations in the Judean Desert.* ʿAtiqot, Hebrew Series, vol. 9. Jerusalem, 1989. Reports on the author's excavations; English summaries.

Dagan, Yehudah. "The Shephelah during the Period of the Monarchy in Light of Archaeological Excavations and Survey." M.A. thesis, Tel Aviv University, 1992. Until recently, the only publication of the author's comprehensive survey. Presents a list of 276 Iron Age sites, although the data and conclusions may be disputable. In Hebrew with English summary; may be obtained from Tel Aviv University.

Finkelstein, Israel, and Yizhak Magen. *Archaeological Survey of the Hill Country of Benjamin.* Jerusalem, 1993. Survey results.

Kochavi, Moshe, ed. *Judea, Samaria, and the Golan: Archaeological Survey, 1967–1968* (in Hebrew). Jerusalem, 1972. Report of selective surveys, including of Judah (but only of the highlands and the margins of the Shephelah), the Judean Desert, and the Land of Benjamin.

Ofer, Avi. "The Highland of Judah during the Biblical Period." Ph.D. diss., Tel Aviv University, 1993. Complete report of the survey in the area, with a detailed analysis of evaluation methods and historical data about biblical Judah. In Hebrew with English summary.

Ofer, Avi. "The Highland of Judah: A Fringe Area Becoming a Prosperous Kingdom." In *From Nomadism to Monarchy: Archaeological and Historical Aspects of Early Israel,* edited by Israel Finkelstein and Nadav Na'aman (in press). Archaeological and historical discussion of the Iron Age I in Judah, including survey methods and some information about other periods (especially the Bronze Age and Iron Age II). Based on the author's dissertation (see above).

AVI OFER

JUDEA. *See* Judah.

JUDEAN DESERT CAVES. Since the fourth century CE there have been reports of discoveries of scrolls and other artifacts in caves in the Judean desert (cf. Eusebius, *Ecclesiastical History* 6.16.1). Modern interest in these caves stems from the discovery of the Qumran scrolls in 1947. After bedouins had ransacked many of the caves in the area of Qumran, it was decided that a comprehensive and systematic search of the Judean Desert caves should be undertaken by archaeologists. This was done in 1952 under the direction of Roland de Vaux and G. Lankester Harding while they were digging at Qumran. There were also several follow-up excavations at the caves and sites in the immediate vicinity of Qumran, on the Jordanian side of the border with Israel, during the 1950s. Nonetheless, bedouin discoveries continued to preempt those of the archaeologists.

The eastern Judean desert is dissected by several east–west canyons that drain toward the Dead Sea. Expeditions on the Israeli side of the border in 1961–1962 focused on the area between Masada and ʿEin-Gedi and divided the region into four sectors with a team assigned to each sector. The four teams were directed by Yohaman Aharoni, Pessah Bar-Adon, Nahman Avigad, and Yigael Yadin; their task was to explore every cave and crevice in their sector (Avigad et al., 1960–1961). Exploration and excavation of these dark caverns was made difficult by the large rocks that cluttered the cave floors and by the occasional thick layers of animal droppings that covered the floors. Equally daunting was the fact that many caves were located in sheer cliffs far above the valley floor and could be entered only after a perilous climb (Yadin, 1963).

The discovery of materials from the Chalcolithic, Middle Bronze, Iron, and Roman periods made it clear that the caves had served as places of refuge throughout history for people forced to flee their homes. The artifactual and inscriptional remains from the Middle Bronze and Iron Ages are meager, indicating that the caves were only used intermittently and for short periods of time. The materials from the Chalcolithic and Roman periods, however, are considerable and impressive. While nearly all of the caves evidenced occupation during the Chalcolithic period, the most significant finds came from the Cave of the Treasure in Naḥal Mishmar (Bar-Adon, 1980). The vast amount of household vessels, tools, textiles, and foodstuffs found in this cave indicates that during the Chalcolithic period it was inhabited for regular and prolonged periods. The most spectacular discovery was a cache of more than four hundred copper items: tools, mace heads, baskets, crowns, and utensils. Many of these items are ornately decorated and can be seen in the Israel Museum in Jerusalem. The objects suggest that the owners were wealthy individuals who brought their treasures with them in the hope of returning home once the danger that forced them into the cave had passed. Unfortunately, they never again used their valuables in the luxurious surroundings for which they were obviously intended.

Equally noteworthy are the discoveries dating to the time of the Second Jewish Revolt against Rome led by Bar Kokhba (132–135 CE). [*See* Bar Kokhba Revolt.] While the leader of this revolt is traditionally identified as Bar Kokhba ("son of a star"), a title with messianic overtones, some Jewish traditions label him Bar Koziba ("son of a lie"). The Bar Kokhba letters, from the Cave of Letters in Naḥal Ḥever, identify the leader's actual name and title as "Simon ben Kosiba, prince of Israel." Both forms of his name, *Bar Kokhba* and *Bar Koziba*, are, therefore, tendentious corruptions of his real name and reflect two attitudes toward his revolt. Many Jewish rebels followed Bar Kokhba and fled into the desert to prosecute their war against the Romans.

The caves in the Judean desert have yielded a tremendous amount of information about these Jewish rebels and their way of life. The discovery of pottery, glass, and other luxury items from this period indicate that the inhabitants prepared the caves in advance for prolonged stays and entered them only when necessary. Once refugees were safely inside the caves, it would have been nearly impossible to attack or expel them forcibly. The Romans watched the rebels from camps they established above the caves and on the opposite sides of the canyons. This strategy enabled the soldiers stationed across a canyon to watch the rebels in the caves and relay the information to other soldiers stationed in the camp above the caves. The rebels waited in the caves and used the rations they had brought with them. Their plan, however, failed terribly. One cave, the Cave of Horror in Naḥal Ḥever, yielded more than forty skeletons of men, women, and children who perished there. In the end, the Romans outlasted the rebels by cutting off their supply lines and starving them.

The Cave of Letters in Naḥal Ḥever yielded two large collections of documents (Lewis et al., 1989; Yadin, 1963). The Bar Kokhba letters comprise more than a dozen dispatches in Hebrew, Aramaic, and Greek sent by Bar Kokhba to his commanders in other places (principally ʿEin-Gedi). [*See* ʿEin-Gedi.] This correspondence provides details about the rebels' chain of command, their observation of Jewish festivals, and Bar Kokhba's stern leadership style. The Archive of Babatha, the daughter of Simon, is a collection of thirty-five legal documents (marriage contract, loans, deeds, wills) in Nabatean, Aramaic, and Greek, dating from 93 to 132 CE. [*See* Nabatean Inscriptions.] Babatha, once a wealthy and prominent resident of Nabatea, moved to ʿEin-Gedi and eventually fled to the caves in advance of the Roman assault on Bar Kokhba's forces. Although traditions about this revolt were preserved in a variety of sources, the discoveries from the Judean Desert caves provided the first direct evidence of the rebels and their way of life.

Other caves in the region have yielded additional evidence

of occasional occupation from prehistoric times through the Middle Ages. Excavation and exploration of the caves continues under the direction of the Israel Antiquities Authority and the Society for the Preservation of Nature. A comprehensive survey of the region was conducted during the 1980s, and reports of artifactual and inscriptional finds continue to surface.

[*See also* Dead Sea Scrolls; Judah; Qumran; *and the biographies of Aharoni, Avigad, Harding, Vaux, and Yadin.*]

BIBLIOGRAPHY

Avigad, Nahman, et al. *Judean Desert Caves, Survey and Excavations: The Expedition to the Judean Desert, 1960–1961*. 2 vols. Jerusalem, 1960–1961.

Bar-Adon, Pessah. *The Cave of the Treasure: The Finds from the Caves in Nahal Mishmar*. Jerusalem, 1980.

Benoit, Pierre, et al. *Les grottes de Murabbaʿat*. 2 vols. Discoveries in the Judaean Desert, vol. 2. Oxford, 1961.

Lewis, Naphtali, et al. *The Documents from the Bar Kokhba Period in the Cave of Letters: Greek Papyri, Aramaic and Nabatean Signatures and Subscriptions*. Jerusalem, 1989.

Yadin, Yigael. *The Finds from the Bar Kokhba Period in the Cave of Letters*. Jerusalem, 1963.

Yadin, Yigael. *Bar-Kokhba: The Rediscovery of the Legendary Hero of the Last Jewish Revolt against Imperial Rome*. London, 1971.

J. EDWARD WRIGHT

JUDEIDEH, TELL EL- (Heb., Tel Goded), site located in the Shephelah (31°38′ N, 34°54′ E; map reference 141 × 115) on a natural hill about 398 m above sea level, and about 25.4 km (15 mi.) south of Gezer, 43.5 km (27 mi.) north-northeast of Beersheba, 34.5 km (21.5 mi.) east of Ashkelon, and 22 km (13.7 mi.) northwest of Hebron.

The site has generally been identified with the Moreshet-Gath of *Micah* 1:14, the home of the prophet Micah (*Mi.* 1:1; *Jer.* 26:18). *Micah* 1:13–15 implies that Moreshet-Gath was near Lachish (9.6 km [6 mi.] southwest of Tell el-Judeideh) and Mareshah (Marisa; about 4.5 km [2.8 mi.] south-southwest of the site). The Madaba map places Moreshet-Gath north of Beth-Guvrin (2 km [1 mi.] south of Judeideh). Both F.-M. Abel (*Géographic de la Palestine*, vol. 2, Paris, 1938, p. 392) and Yohanan Aharoni (*The Land of the Bible*, rev. ed., translated and edited by Anson F. Rainey, Philadelphia, 1979, p. 330) subscribe to this identification; Zecharia Kallai (1962), however, identifies Tell el-Judeideh with Libnah (cf. Negev 1990). Apart from the proposed identifications with cities mentioned in the Hebrew Bible and what can be reconstructed through excavation, the history of the site is unknown.

Tell el-Judeideh was excavated as part of a regional project in 1899–1900, under the direction of F. J. Bliss and R. A. S. Macalister, funded by the Palestine Exploration Fund. Because archaeology was then in its infancy and ceramic typology was yet to be understood, the results of that excavation are confusing and disappointing. Of the approximately 2.5-hectare (7-acre) site, Bliss and Macalister excavated about 87 sq m, finding few remains from the "pre-Israelite" period (the Bronze Age); the "Jewish" period (the Iron Age); and the "Hellenistic–Roman" period.

Many of the fragmentary wall remains from the Iron Age showed extensive evidence of fire. However, because of the excavation's limited exposure and the state of the art, it is impossible to assign a precise date to them. The excavation did not reveal a fortification system for the Iron Age, but it did uncover thirty-seven stamped *lmlk* jar handles. Among them were representations of both the two-wing and four-wing variety, as well as references to the four cities regularly attested: Ziph, Hebron, Socoh, and *mmšt*. These handles imply an occupation of the site in the late eighth century BCE.

The bulk of the remains date from the Roman period and consist of an oval enclosure encompassed by a wall approximately 228 m long and about 91.5 m wide. The wall is, on the average, about 3.35 m thick and is built of roughly dressed stones, dry laid in horizontal courses. Sixteen unevenly spaced internal buttresses strengthen it. Only some of the buttresses are bonded to the wall; they extend 1–1.5 m into the enclosure.

Four gates, each directed to a cardinal point, provide access to the enclosure. Internal square towers flank the gates. Some of the towers have interior chambers, and Bliss postulated that those that appear to have been solid were probably destroyed into their foundations below the chambers. Some of the gates retain their pillars, sockets, and thresholds, which indicate that they had double-wing doors. That a fifth gate, leading to the southeast, may have existed was inferred from Bliss's discovery of two large slabs of stone in the line of the city wall (1900, p. 93). The two streets extending from the gates—the north-south *cardo*, and the east-west *decumanus*—intersected at right angles just south of a large two-part building in the middle of the enclosure.

The western part of the building is square (13.6 m) with exterior walls that are 1 meter thick. Eight rooms that apparently had earthen floors and no exterior windows surrounded a courtyard. The eastern building was separated from it by a hallway. It had four rooms on its eastern side and one room or a columned porch on its south, all of which opened into a courtyard with a large pool. Eight columns originally surrounded the pool in an asymmetrical arrangement; six column bases were found in situ.

Broshi suggests (1977, p. 696) that the western building was a women's house (a *gynaeconitis*), and the eastern one was for men (an *andron*). On the basis of the architectural styles, he proposes a Herodian date for the structure.

[*See also the biographies of Bliss and Macalister.*]

BIBLIOGRAPHY

Bliss, Frederick Jones. "First Report on the Excavations at Tell ej-Judeideh." *Palestine Exploration Fund Quarterly Statement* (April 1900):

87–101. This source, and the following entries by Bliss, constitute the formal excavation reports available for Tell el-Judeideh. Their usefulness is hampered by the inadequate excavation techniques of the time.

Bliss, Frederick Jones. "Second Report on the Excavations at Tell ej-Judeideh." *Palestine Exploration Fund Quarterly Statement* (July 1900): 199–222.

Bliss, Frederick Jones, and R. A. S. Macalister. *Excavations in Palestine during the Years 1898–1900*. London, 1902.

Broshi, Magen. "Judeideh, Tell." In *The Encyclopedia of Archaeological Excavations in the Holy Land,* vol. 3, pp. 694–696. Englewood Cliffs, N.J., 1975–.

Kallai, Zecharia. "Libnah" (in Hebrew). In *Encyclopaedia Biblica,* vol. 4, pp. 421–423. Jerusalem, 1962.

Negev, Avraham, ed. "Goded (Tel)." In *The Archaeological Encyclopedia of the Holy Land,* p. 161. Rev. ed. Nashville, 1986 (3d ed. New York, 1990).

DALE W. MANOR

K

KABRI, TEL, a large mound of about 80 acres located in the foothills of the western Lower Galilee bordering the Jezreel Valley, 5 km (3 mi.) inland from Nahariya (map reference 1632 × 2681). The site may be ancient Reḥob, mentioned in the Egyptian Execration texts and in *Jos.* 19:28. Moshe Prausnitz carried out surveys and soundings for the Israel Department of Antiquities in 1957–1958; and Aharon Kempinski carried out major excavations in 1986–1993 for the Institute of Archaeology of Tel Aviv University, assisted by W.-D. Niemeier of Heidelberg University.

The site, well watered and in a very fertile area, was occupied extensively in the Neolithic period and into the Early Chalcolithic phases. Belonging to this horizon are Dark-Faced Burnished wares of the so-called Wadi Rabah culture.

The third millennium is represented by an Early Bronze IA–B phase (c. 3400–3100 BCE) characterized by large oval houses with central pillars; quantities of typical pottery, including Grain Washed; several rich tombs, one with a radiocarbon date of about 3494 BCE; and a sealing that is Mesopotamian in style and usually found only in EB II–III contexts. The EB II phase exhibits substantial broadroom houses and "metallic" wares that are northern in type.

The Middle Bronze Age saw the maximum expansion of Kabri, exhibiting two phases of fortifications. The first, with a shallow earthen rampart and an inner wall, belongs to MB I. A later phase, of MB II–III date, witnessed the addition of a massive city wall. The MB pottery includes vessels that are Anatolian in type, "North Syrian Painted Ware," and Cypriot imports. Several burials produced scarabs, including one with the name of a Hyksos king, *ykbm*. The most spectacular remains of this phase belong to a large, multiroom palace (no. 607) with a plastered "ceremonial hall" decorated with multicolored floral frescoes on both the floors and walls (more than 2,300 fragments). The closest parallels are from Middle Minoan II Crete (Phaistos); Late Minoan IA Knossos and Thera; and now Tell ed-Dabʿa in the Egyptian Delta. [*See* Dabʿa, Tell ed-.] The destruction of the MB levels may have occurred as early as 1600 BCE.

Later remains belong to the Iron Age, with Cypro-Phoenician and Phoenician pottery. The Iron Age was brought to an end by Assyrian and Babylonian destructions. Persian and Hellenistic occupations are also attested.

BIBLIOGRAPHY

Kempinski, Aharon, ed. *Excavations at Kabri: Preliminary Reports*. 6 vols. Tel Aviv, 1987–1992. Covers the 1986–1991 seasons.

Prausnitz, M. W. "Kabri." *Israel Exploration Journal* 9 (1959): 268–269.

William G. Dever

KAFRANJA, WADI, region of Jordan, located between Wadi el-Yabis and Wadi Rajib, that drains the western face of Jebel ʿAjlun (biblical Gilead), entering the Jordan River at Tell es-Saʿidiyeh. The region is well watered, receiving 300–600 mm (12–23.5 in.) rainfall annually and possessing numerous springs. Cereals, olives, and vines are cultivated on slopes and terraces near the wadi head, and its drier southwestern tail is suitable for grazing. Pine, pistachio, and oak forests cover the ridges dominating the valley. In medieval times iron was mined in the surrounding limestone hills and smelted locally. The sharply dissected topography with elevations up to 1100 m (3,610 ft.) isolate the region from the plains north, east, and south and the Jordan valley to the west.

There have been no systematic excavations in Wadi Kafranja. Qalʿat er-Rabad (map reference 2185 × 1922), built in 1284–1285 at Saladin's behest, is the principal monument. The castle was cleared and repaired during the British Mandate of 1921–1948 (Johns, 1932), but never excavated. In ʿAjlun village (map reference 2213 × 1940) the Department of Antiquities has carried out salvage excavations and the Department of Religious Affairs has restored a Mamluk mosque.

Nineteenth-century travelers visited Qalʿat er-Rabad and extolled the verdure of Wadi Kafranja (Merrill, 1881; Le Strange, 1886; Conder, 1892). Gottlieb Schumacher conducted the first concerted survey around 1900 (Schumacher and Steuernagel, 1924–1926). Nelson Glueck reconnoitered the wadi in 1942, but reported only four sites (1951; pp. 231–235). Augostino Augustinović and Bellarmino Bagatti (1951–1952) explored ʿAjlun village and the highlands east, north, and west, but did not descend into the wadi. Ernst Kutsch (1965) found evidence of ancient occupation at modern Anjara and Kafranja and at sites along the wadi bottom. Siegfried Mittmann (1970) incorporated this earlier work into a comprehensive study of ancient settlement in northern Transjordan. Wolf Dieter Hütteroth and Kamal Abdulfattah (1977) examined early Ottoman tax records for Wadi Kafranja in a study of the historical geography of the sixteenth-century CE southern Levant. The most recent archaeological survey of the Wadi Kafranja was completed in 1986 (Greene, 1996).

This superbly habitable but rather remote region was settled perhaps as early as the Chalcolithic, if the seven dolmen fields at the wadi's southern end date to that period, and not, as previously believed, to the Early Bronze. Early Bronze occupation in the wadi is well attested (eight sites), but the Middle Bronze is not (three sites). Late Bronze settlement is more widespread than initially supposed (five sites). The Iron Age saw a clear increase in settlement (Iron I, fourteen sites; Iron II/Persian; twenty-nine). There was a sharp decline in the Hellenistic (ten sites) but settlement grew again in the Roman period (twenty-two sites). The Byzantine collapse in the early seventh century was not accompanied by a serious retraction of settlement in Wadi Kafranja. Byzantine (sixteen sites) and Late Byzantine/Umayyad settlement (eleven sites) shows strong continuity and significant ceramic connections with contemporary Jerash nearby. There is a significant and surprising increase in ʿAbbasid settlement (twenty sites). Later, the construction of Qalʿat er-Rabad, intended to prevent Crusader incursions across the Jordan, enhanced security in the region. The castle was rebuilt in the ensuing Ayyubid–Mamluk period coinciding with the densest occupation (thirty sites). There was a simultaneous expansion of water-powered grist mills in the wadi. Remains of nineteen mills probably dating in this period line the wadi between ʿAjlun and Kafranja villages. Ottoman tax records indicate that at least sixteen mills were functioning in 1596 CE. Only one remained in use after World War II (Greene, 1995).

Wadi Kafranja and sites in it are not mentioned in biblical or other ancient Near Eastern texts, though such mentions are common in medieval Arabic literature (see the article "ʿAdjlun," in *Encyclopaedia of Islam,* new ed., Leiden, 1960–, vol. 1, p. 208). Ottoman tax accounts name settlements in the wadi corresponding to sites of Ottoman date recorded by archaeological survey.

[*See also* ʿAjlun.]

BIBLIOGRAPHY

Augustinović, Augostino, and Bellarmino Bagatti. "Escursioni nei dintorni di ʿAglun (Nord di Transgiordiana)." *Studium Biblicum Franciscanum/Liber Annuus* 2 (1952): 227–314. Archaeological, historical, and topographic survey of the highlands above Wadi Kafranja, east, north, and west of modern ʿAjlun village.

Conder, Claude R. *Heth and Moab: Explorations in Syria in 1881 and 1882.* 3d ed. London and New York, 1892. See chapter 6, "Mount Gilead," for the ʿAjlun region.

Glueck, Nelson. *Explorations in Eastern Palestine.* Vol. 4. Annual of the American Schools of Oriental Research, 25/28. New Haven, 1951. Part of Glueck's archaeological surveys east of the Jordan. See pages 23–25 for his work in Wadi Kafranja (four sites only).

Greene, Joseph A. "Water Mills in the Wadi Kafranja: The Relationship of Technology, Society, and Settlement in North Jordan." In *Studies in the History and Archaeology of Jordan,* vol. 5, edited by Safwan Tell, pp. 757–765. Amman, 1995.

Greene, Joseph A. "Ajlun-Kafranja Survey, 1986: Final Report." *Annual of the Department of Antiquities of Jordan* 42 (1996).

Hütteroth, Wolf Dieter, and Kamal Abdulfattah. *Historical Geography of Palestine, Transjordan, and Southern Syria in the Late Sixteenth Century.* Erlanger Geographische Arbeiten, 5. Erlangen, 1977. Reconstructs the wadi's medieval agricultural economy through study of the Ottoman tax records *(defters);* see pages 162–163 for Wadi Kafranja. Some villages mentioned in the documents have been located by archaeological survey.

Johns, C. N. "Medieval ʿAjlūn I: The Castle (Qalʿat er-Rabaḍ)." *Quarterly of the Department of Antiquities of Palestine* 1 (1932): 21–33. The fullest and still standard analysis of the history and architecture of this important Crusading-period fortification (only the first part was published).

Kutsch, Ernst. "Beiträge zur Seidlungsgeschichte des wādi kufrinği." *Zeitschrift des Deutschen Palästina-Vereins* 81 (1965): 113–131. The first detailed archaeological survey of Wadi Kafranja, with a discussion of settlement history. Summarized in English in Arnulf Kuschke, "New Contributions to the Historical Topography of Jordan," *Annual of the Department of Antiquities of Jordan* 6–7 (1962): 90–95, esp. 92–93.

Le Strange, Guy. "A Ride through ʿAjlûn and the Belkâ during Autumn of 1884." In Gottlieb Schumacher's *Across the Jordan: Being an Exploration and Survey of Part of Hauran and Jaulan,* pp. 268–323. New York, 1886. Enriched by the author's wide knowledge and frequent citation of medieval Arabic texts that mention ʿAjlun.

Merrill, Selah. *East of Jordan: A Record of Travel and Observation in the Countries of Moab, Gilead, and Bashan.* London, 1881. See chapters 27 and 28 for Wadi Kafranja.

Mittmann, Siegfried. *Beiträge zur Siedlungs-und Territorialgeschichte des nördlichen Ostjordanlandes.* Wiesbaden, 1970. Extensive survey of north Jordan. See pages 78-89 for a report of Mittmann's work in Wadi Kafranja, based on Kutsch (above).

Sapin, Jean. "Prospection géo-archéologique de l'Ajlûn, 1981–1982." In *Studies in the History and Archaeology of Jordan,* vol. 2, edited by Adnan Hadidi, pp. 217–227. Amman, 1985. Programmatic effort to integrate archaeological survey and paleolandscape studies in the ʿAjlun region, including Wadi Kafranja.

Schumacher, Gottlieb, and D. C. Steuernagel. "Der ʿAdschlūn." *Zeitschrift des Deutschen Palästina-Vereins* 47 (1924): 191–240; 48 (1925): 1–144, 191–392; 49 (1926): 1–167, 273–303. Originally prepared to accompany the *Karte des Ostjordanlandes* (1913–1921). Primarily a work of physical and historical topography with ethnography excurses, this is the earliest and most comprehensive exploration of the ʿAjlun region. See 1924: 234–237 and 1925: 300–327.

JOSEPH A. GREENE

KALAVASOS, village (34°46′ N, 33°18′ E) situated close to the southern coast of Cyprus, halfway between Limassol and Larnaca. The village area has been occupied since the Neolithic period (c. 4500 BCE), but its ancient name is unknown. Brief excavations at Tenta, south of Kalavasos, by Porphyrios Dikaios in 1947 under the auspices of the Cypriot Department of Antiquities revealed the presence of an Aceramic Neolithic settlement, then dated to 5800 BCE. Since 1976 the Vasilikos valley, centered on Kalavasos, has been the scene of multidisciplinary fieldwork designed to elucidate the sequence of occupation and nature of life in the valley from the earliest Neolithic until medieval times, some nine thousand years. Excavations have been undertaken at four sites, in conjunction with a field survey designed to recover information on the pattern of ancient settlement.

The Aceramic Neolithic village of Tenta, now dated to the seventh millennium, represents the earliest excavated settlement in the valley. Located on a small hill 2.3 km (1.4 mi.) south–southeast of Kalavasos, it consists of a cluster of curvilinear stone and mud-brick domestic buildings (see figure 1), surrounded by an outer settlement wall with a ditch cut in the limestone outside it. The reason for these defensive features and the origin and circumstances of the initial settlers are unknown. The population was small, perhaps fifty people. The dead were buried under house floors and in open areas outside. Stone was used for the manufacture of sophisticated vessels, domestic equipment, and items of personal adornment. Domesticated plants (emmer and einkorn wheat, barley, and lentils) and animals (sheep, goat, and pig) were known to the inhabitants, and fallow deer were hunted. Following the end of the Aceramic Neolithic, the site was reoccupied (c. 4500 BCE) after a considerable gap, but the remains are insubstantial.

The succeeding Early Chalcolithic period (c. 3500 BCE) is represented by the excavated site of Ayious, on the east side of the valley, opposite Tenta. No standing architectural remains were identified, only pits of various types, including several large ones connected by subterranean tunnels. Dikaios located similar pits at nearby Pamboules (site B) in 1947, which he interpreted as pit dwellings. It seems likely that the pits are the extant remains of a settlement that consisted mainly of lightly built structures. Finely painted pottery, ceramic figurine fragments, and domestic stone tools were found within the pits.

The later Chalcolithic period in the valley is known only from scattered surface finds of pottery at several sites. The nature of the succeeding Early Bronze Age remains to be established, but the Middle Bronze Age (c. 1950–1650 BCE) is well represented by numerous excavated subterranean chamber tombs within the confines of the village, especially in the area of the church and mosque. Large numbers of fine pottery vessels, bronze tools and weapons, and stone and faience beads were deposited with the dead. Excavation of a contemporary settlement has not yet been undertaken in the valley, but the field survey attested dense occupation of the Kalavasos region in the early second millennium BCE.

While there may have been a reduction in the density of settlement in the early Late Bronze Age, the large, town-sized settlement of Ayios Dhimitrios south of Tenta is indicative of the urban character of life in the thirteenth century BCE. The site occupies 11.5 ha (28.4 acres) of gently sloping ground overlooking an easy crossing of the Vasilikos River from its western side. The location is strategic because it also lies at the junction of two major routes—east–west along the southern coastal region of the island, and north–south from the copper mines north of Kalavasos down to the coast. In view of the known importance of copper in the LB economy of Cyprus, it can scarcely be doubted that the

KALAVASOS. Figure 1. *Kalavasos-Tenta.* Architecture on the upper part of the site, from the south-southeast. (Courtesy I. A. Todd)

Kalavasos mining region was of considerable significance for its copper deposits at the time Ayios Dhimitrios was occupied. The field survey did not prove beyond doubt the LB utilization of the Kalavasos mining area, but Bronze Age remains have been found within 500 m of the mining zone.

Initial excavations were undertaken at Ayios Dhimitrios within the line of the Nicosia–Limassol highway that has obliterated the settlement's central sector. Rectilinear structures (100–600 sq m in area) were found, fronting onto long, straight streets. Subsequent excavations at the north end of the site revealed a palatial complex, called building X. The plan of this square structure (30.5 m across) is tripartite around a central courtyard (see figure 2). Extensive use of finely cut, large stone blocks was made in the outer walls, and the building probably had an upper story. The most impressive architectural feature is a rectangular hall, with a central row of stone pillars to support the roof, used for storing olive oil (and perhaps other commodities) in rows of very large storage jars (pithoi). The fifty pithoi in the main hall had an estimated capacity of 33,500 liters (see below). The building's character is clearly public rather than private; an administrative purpose may be supported by the discovery within and adjacent to it of a number of small clay cylinders with signs inscribed in the Cypro-Minoan script, indicating a literate clientele.

Immediately west of building X, excavation revealed parts of another building (XI) in which olive oil was probably manufactured. A very large stone tank was set into the floor of one room, and gas chromatography analyses of its interior face suggested that it had contained olive oil, as was the case

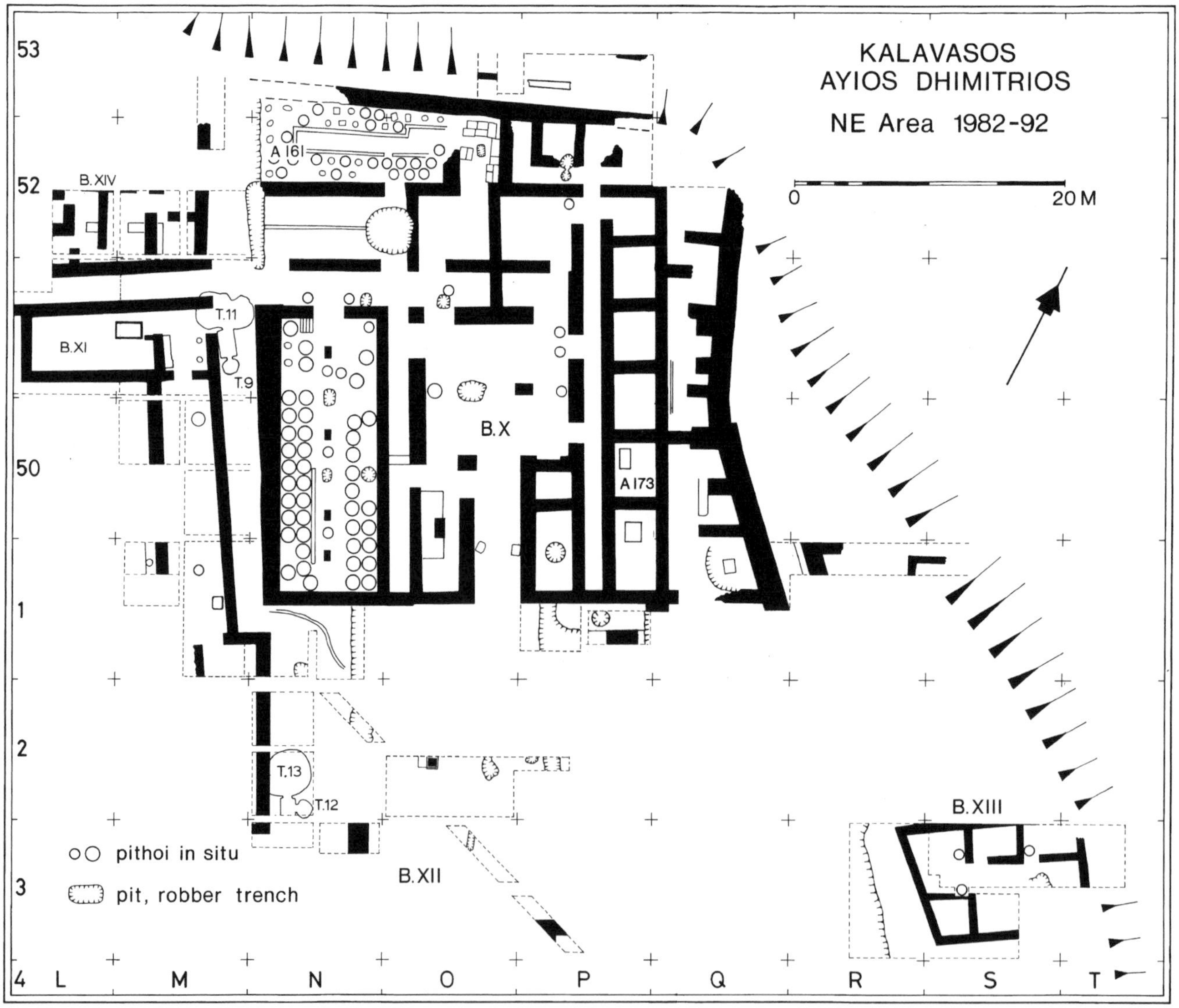

KALAVASOS. Figure 2. *Kalavasos-Ayios Dhimitrios.* General plan of building X and adjacent areas. (Courtesy I. A. Todd)

with some of the pithoi. Crushing and pressing equipment has not yet been found.

A series of rock-cut chamber tombs was also found within the settlement area; in the most significant of these, tomb 11 (c. 1375 BCE), three young women, a young child, and three infants were buried together with quantities of fine imported and local pottery, gold jewelry, and other exotic grave goods; the latest skeleton was found completely intact, with its associated grave gifts in situ. The apparent wealth of the inhabitants of Ayios Dhimitrios seems to have been derived from copper trading and olive-oil manufacture.

[*See also* Olives.]

BIBLIOGRAPHY

Dikaios, Porphyrios. "The Stone Age." In *The Swedish Cyprus Expedition.* Vol. 4. Stockholm, 1962. Invaluable summary of Dikaios's work in the Kalavasos area and elsewhere (see part 1, pp. 1–204), written after the initial formulation of the prehistoric Cypriot sequence. Now dated and must be used in conjunction with current literature.

South, Alison K. "From Copper to Kingship: Aspects of Bronze Age Society Viewed from the Vasilikos Valley." In *Early Society in Cyprus,* edited by Edgar Peltenburg, pp. 315–324. Edinburgh, 1989. See South (1992) for a more up-to-date, though less accessible, study.

South, Alison K., Pamela Russell, and Priscilla Schuster Keswani. *Vasilikos Valley Project,* part 3, *Kalavasos-Ayios Dhimitrios II: Ceramics, Objects, Tombs, Special Studies.* Studies in Mediterranean Archaeology, vol. 71. Göteborg, 1989. The first volume of the final excavation report covering material from the 1979–1983 excavations in the more central and southern sectors of the site, excluding the northern building X area and tomb 11.

South, Alison K. "Kalavasos-Ayios Dhimitrios 1991." *Report of the Department of Antiquities, Cyprus* (1992): 133–146. The latest results of excavations at this site, including notes on gas chromatography analyses by Priscilla S. Keswani.

Todd, Ian A., ed. *Vasilikos Valley Project,* part 1, *The Bronze Age Cemetery in Kalavasos Village.* Studies in Mediterranean Archaeology, vol. 71. Göteborg, 1986. Final report on the excavation of a series of thirteen MB tombs in Kalavasos village in 1978.

Todd, Ian A. *Vasilikos Valley Project,* part 6, *Excavations at Kalavasos-Tenta.* Vol. 1. Studies in Mediterranean Archaeology, vol. 71. Göteborg, 1987. The first of a two-volume final report on the Tenta excavations (the second volume is forthcoming).

IAN A. TODD and ALISON K. SOUTH

KAMID EL-LOZ, tell located at the southeastern edge of the Lebanese Biqaʿ (Bekaa) Valley, north of the modern road that branches off the north–south road from Qabb Ilyas to Mashgara, leading eastward via Jubb Jannin and joining the southbound road from Masna to Rashaya. Kamid el-Loz is strategically located at the place where two ancient main roads cross: the old road going from the Upper Jordan Valley through Wadi-at Taym, crossing the Biqaʿ into Syria, and another one from the Phoenician coast. Tell Kamid el-Loz is one of the largest (300 × 240 m) and highest (26 m) settlement hills in the Biqaʿ. Two springs are in close proximity to the tell: one to the north, the other at its western edge.

As early as 1897, A. Guthe suggested that the modern name of Kamid el-Loz implied that of ancient Kumidi. Egyptian sources of the second half of the second millennium BCE mention a location KMT *(Ku'-m'-t),* or Kumidi, several times, most probably an administrative center, that of a *rabu* (ruler) of an Egyptian province in Asia. This identification was confirmed in 1969 by the discovery of four clay tablets (followed by more between 1972 and 1978, letters written by the Egyptian pharaoh to the *rabu,* in which it is clear that Kumidi is a city in the southern Biqaʿ and that it is located at a cultural crossroad. This applies perfectly to Kamid el-Loz, the only tell in the southern Biqaʿ that meets all the requirements established for Kumidi.

In 1954, Arnulf Kuschke identified the site of Kamid el-Loz and began excavating it in 1963. Fieldwork between 1963 and 1965 was carried out by joint expeditions from the Universities of Johana Gutenberg of Mainz and the University of Saarbrucken, directed by Kuschke and Rolf Hachmann, respectively. Between 1964 and 1981, the University of Saarbrucken alone assumed the work. The excavation continued for six years into the Lebanese civil war (with the exception of the years 1975 and 1976) and closed prematurely in 1981. Since then, treasure hunters with bulldozers have destroyed the fragile architectural evidence and stratification of the second- and third-millennium town. Prior to 1981, excavation had cleared an area of 5,700 sq m.

The earliest archaeological remains cover the bedrock at the northern edge of the tell. They revealed an Early Neolithic settlement yielding plain Neolithic pottery, a few clay idols, and numerous lithic tools. The Chalcolithic level has not yet been found. All that is known about the existence of an Early Bronze Age town are some pottery sherds found out of context in later strata. The Middle Bronze Age was excavated over an area of 2,400 sq m. A number of urban settlements were uncovered whose size, building materials, and building techniques were superior to those of later periods. This probably indicates a politically more important settlement than any of the later Late Bronze Age towns. A fortified city wall was cleared on the tell's northern and eastern slopes. The location of the MB palace and temples is known; they lie, unexcavated, underneath the LB palace and temple.

The excavations concentrated mainly on the Late Bronze Age city, which was cleared for 3,800 sq m. A city wall surrounded the LB city. The temple was located in the northwestern part of the tell, separated from the palace by an esplanade that opened onto a street leading outside the city. The temple was destroyed and rebuilt four times. The distinctiveness of this temple is its double court. The western court was paved with mud-brick blocks and had three rectangular basins lined with plaster, probably used for sacrifices. Four temple models were found in the court. An annex to the temple consisted of two rooms where large number of clay vases and bronze figurines were found. The LB palace was located south of the temple. Like the temple, the palace was destroyed and rebuilt five times. The mud-brick walls of the entrance hall were preserved to a height of more than 3 m.

Only one building was excavated to the east of the oldest palace. Tombs of three people with rich funerary material, were found beneath it; it was probably the site's royal cemetery. [*See* Grave Goods.]

To this same period belong beautiful ivory objects and six Amarna tablets. [*See* Amarna Tablets.] Following this period, the city remained uninhabited for a time. An area of 4,400 sq m was excavated from the Iron Age I period. It yielded eight superposed levels of nonfortified villages consisting of small, irregular houses of one to two rooms, built out of wood. Poor residential materials were found inside. No Phoenician remains from the Iron II period were found. The excavator indicates that period could be present in the southern, unexcavated part of the tell. In the Persian period the deserted northwest sector of the tell was used as a cemetary. Modern occupation of the site covers part of the Persian, Hellenistic, and Roman cemeteries.

[*See also* Phoenicians.]

BIBLIOGRAPHY

Hachmann, Rolf, ed. *Kamid el-Loz, 1977–1981*. Bonn, 1986. See pages 205–211 for a complete bibliography.

Hachmann, Rolf, ed. *Kamid el-Loz, 1963–1981: German Excavations in Lebanon (Part I)*. Berytus, vol. 37. Beirut, 1989.

LEILA BADRE

KANEŠ (or Neša; mod. Tk., Kültepe [ashmound] and Karahöyük, the latter the name of a small village near the mound), site situated 21 km (13 mi.) to the northeast of Caesarea (modern Kayseri), the capital of the Cappadocian kingdom. The site is at the junction of several natural roads: an east–west road coming from Sebasteia (modern Sivas), a southeast–west road via Malatya, and a south–north road from Cilicia. This strategic location increased the importance of Kaneš in the commerce of the ancient world and is one of the main reasons it became one of the trading centers of ancient Syro-Mesopotamia.

Kaneš consisted of two parts; a city mound *(tepe)* and a lower city (*karum* or trade center in Assyrian terminology). The city mound includes an inner citadel and the areas in which the palaces and temples of the kings were built. The mound rises 20 m above the Kayseri plain and contains a series of occupation levels. With a diameter of 550 m, it is among the largest mounds in central Anatolia. Surrounding the mound and rising 2–2.5 m above the plain, and with a diameter of up to 3 km (2 mi.), is the lower city of Karum Kaneš, the center of the system of Old Assyrian trading colonies in Anatolia.

Kaneš is 124 km (77 mi.) from the Hittite capital Ḫattuša (Boğazköy) and 73 km (45 mi.) to the south of Alişar (ancient Ankuwa). The city mound of Kaneš had a long existence, while the Karum Kaneš only lasted for about three hundred years—it was founded much later than the site on the mound and was abandoned much sooner.

Kaneš-Kültepe became known in the archaeological literature when the first cuneiform tablets were found there in 1871. Ernest Chantre undertook the first excavations on the mound in 1893–1894. In 1906, Hugo Winckler and also Hugo Grothe carried out brief excavations on the mound only. In 1925, Bedrich Hrozny conducted excavations both on the mound and in the lower city for one season. He succeeded in discovering about one thousand tablets. The finds identified the center as Karum Kaneš, which had been suggested by Benno Landsberger as early as 1924.

Systematic excavations by a team under the direction of Tahsin Özgüç began in 1948 on behalf of the Turkish Historical Foundation and the General Directorate of Monuments and Museums; they are still underway regularly. Both the mound and the *karum* were excavated in parallel projects and yielded important monuments, now in the process of being restored.

Karum. The *karum* of Kaneš consists of four levels (I–IV): the upper level contains two phases, Ia and Ib. Levels IV (built on virgin soil) and III belong to the very beginning of the Middle Bronze Age (c. 2000–1920 BCE). They did not yield written documents, but the entire area of the *karum* was built up in both levels. The pottery used in these levels was monochrome wheelmade ware found side by side with handmade polychrome ware.

The most spectacular era at Kaneš is represented by *karum* level II (1920–1850 BCE), established in the period of the Assyrian king Erishum I, and the following phase of *karum* Ib (1800–1750 BCE). Level II was destroyed by a heavy conflagration in about 1850 BCE, in the time of the Assyrian king Puzur-Ashur. After an interval of at most two generations, the town of level Ib was established on the ruins. From historical and archaeological perspectives, the discoveries from these levels reveal two facts of major importance: cuneiform tablets record the beginning of Anatolian history, and the very lively commercial and cultural relations that existed among Anatolia, Mesopotamia, and North Syria, stimulated the development of native Anatolian art.

Karum level II presents a town with stone-paved streets, below which run functional drainage channels, and open spaces that mark divisions into various districts.

The *karum* of Kaneš in levels II and Ib was surrounded by a fortification wall whose diameter is the largest in the Near East.

In the period of the Assyrian trading colonies (levels II and Ib), Kaneš was a very strong city protected by two con-

KANEŠ. *Beak-spouted pitcher.* From level II; red slipped and highly polished. Note the pair of horses set on the wide band handle, which tend to be light brown in color. Height, including horses, is 26 cm. Museum of Anatolian Civilizations, Ankara. (Courtesy T. Özgüç)

centric fortification systems, the center of the kingdom of Kaneš.

In houses of two, four, or six rooms, most of them two-storied, tablets in Assyrian were found, in archives mostly belonging to Assyrian and, in fewer instances, to native merchants, on top of regularly aligned jars, boxes, rush matting, and bags and on wooden shelves. Fourteen thousand tablets and envelopes were discovered between 1948 and 1992. Because the fire that destroyed the city started very suddenly, the people of the town could just save their lives; all their belongings that were fireproof remained in place until they were excavated. Pottery in the Hittite style and cult objects in the shape of animals sacred to the gods—bulls, lions, eagles, antelopes, rabbits, and boars—reached a high level of development in this period. [*See* Hittites.]

In layout, *karum* level Ib follows that of level II, in which building techniques and plans are native Anatolian. In level Ib, in contrast to level II, commercial relations with Aššur weakened, while trade within Anatolia gained momentum. As in level II, ivory, bronze, faience, silver, lead, stone, and terra-cotta figurines of gods and goddesses and stone molds for their manufacture were discovered in houses and in tombs. These are the first examples of native Anatolian style. They became the source of the Hittite style that developed later in central Anatolia. In level Ia, Kaneš declined in importance, written records disappeared, and evidently trade relations were cut. The *karum* of Kaneš was not subsequently occupied.

In every level at Kaneš the dead were buried below the floors of the houses in pits, jars, or stone cists. The funeral gifts were rich and varied. Figurines imported from northern Syria and Mesopotamia, in metal and terra cotta, expand the evidence provided by tablets and cylinder seals to refine the dating for this period.

One of the richest groups of finds from the Assyrian trading colony period represented at Kaneš level II (1920–1840 BCE) is the glyptic group—cylinder seal impressions on baked clay envelopes containing tablets and on bullae. These seal impressions, clearly reflecting the cosmopolitan character of the trade with foreign peoples, are in Ur III Neo-Sumerian, Old Babylonian, Old Assyrian, and Old Syrian styles. Among the styles represented, Kaneš's native Anatolian group takes a very important and very informative place. Executed in a highly individual style, they consist of representational scenes executed in fine detail: processions of deities standing on sacred animals and hunting or war

KANEŠ. *Clay drinking vessel in the shape of a lion.* From level II. Filled through the spout located on its back, the outlet for the liquid was through an opening in the mouth. Length 21 cm, width 17.8 cm. Museum of Anatolian Civilizations, Ankara. (Courtesy T. Özgüç)

scenes. The surface of these seals is filled with multiple motifs and symbols. Stamp seals, which are typical of Anatolia, and appear in every level at Kaneš, reached their true development in levels II and Ib. With the end of the Assyrian trading period at Kaneš, cylinder seals went out of use. [*See* Seals.]

Mound. Excavations on the mound went down to the final phase of Early Bronze Age I, distinguishing a total of eighteen building levels. The final phases on the mound are two Roman building levels (1–2) and one Hellenistic level (3). At that time Kültepe was a small town overshadowed by Kayseri. A major part of the *karum* of Kaneš had become the site of the cemetery. Levels 4–5 represent the Late Hittite period. Kültepe then was the center of one of the kingdoms allied to the land of Great Tabal. In the tenth–eighth centuries BCE, Kültepe maintained a strong position, but toward the end of the eighth century BCE it was conquered and destroyed by the Assyrians, who shattered its hieroglyphic stelae, statues, and sculpted orthostats.

The concordance of the Middle Bronze Age levels on the mound and in the *karum* follow:

mound	*karum*
6	Ia
7	Ib
8	II
9	III
10	IV

In levels 7 and 8 a series of five royal rulers (one of them a queen) are known by name; they had palaces and temples that were built both on the inner citadel and in the surrounding area. Tablets from the palace archives reveal that one of those palaces belonged to Waršama son of Inar, king of Kaneš. It is evident that palaces in that period were built like Old Babylonian palaces, but temples were built in the native Anatolian style. [*See* Palace, Temples, *article on* Mesopotamian Temples.] A spearhead with an Akkadian inscription by King Anitta, who ruled over Neša, found in the official storage building of the Anitta palace, was the first authentic historical document found in situ at Kaneš.

Levels 11–13 represent the Early Bronze III period, an important prelude to the Assyrian trading colony era. Kaneš, equipped with monumental buildings, had developed extensive economic and cultural connections with Mesopotamia and North Syria, to which imported cylinder seals, pottery, and metal objects testify. Alabaster figurines of goddesses and gods, characteristic of this period, were discovered in the inner sanctum of temples and in tombs. Levels 14–17 represent Early Bronze Age II. Level 18 is the final phase of Early Bronze I.

[*See also* Kültepe Texts.]

BIBLIOGRAPHY

Balkan, Kemal. *Letter of King Anum-Hirbi of Mama to King Warshama of Karnish.* Ankara, 1957.

Garelli, Paul. *Les Assyriens en Cappadoce.* Paris, 1963.

Landsberger, Benno. "Assyrische Handelskolonien in Kleinasien aus dem dritten Jahrtausend." *Der alte Orient* 24.4 (1925): 1–34.

Larsen, Mogens T. *Old Assyrian Caravan Procedures.* Istanbul, 1967.

Orlin, Louis L. *Assyrian Colonies in Cappadocia.* The Hague, 1970.

Özgüç, Nimet. *The Anatolian Group of Cylinder Seal Impressions from Kültepe.* Ankara, 1965.

Özgüç, Nimet. *Seals and Seal Impressions of Level Ib from Karum Kanish.* Ankara, 1968.

Özgüç, Tahsin. *Ausgrabungen in Kültepe, 1948.* Ankara, 1950.

Özgüç, Tahsin, and Nimet Özgüç. *Ausgrabungen in Kültepe, 1949.* Ankara, 1953.

Özgüç, Tahsin. *Kültepe-Kaniş: New Researches at the Center of the Assyrian Trade Colonies.* Ankara, 1959.

Özgüç, Tahsin. *Kültepe and Its Vicinity in the Iron Age.* Ankara, 1971.

Özgüç, Tahsin. *Kültepe-Kaniş II: New Researches at the Trading Center of the Ancient Near East.* Ankara, 1986.

Özgüç, Tahsin. "New Observations on the Relationship of Kültepe with Southeast Anatolia and North Syria during the Third Millennium B.C." In *Ancient Anatolia: Aspects of Change and Cultural Development; Essays in Honor of Machteld J. Mellink,* edited by Jeanny V. Canby et al., pp. 31–47. Wisconsin, 1986.

Veenhof, Klaas R. *Aspects of Old Assyrian Trade and Its Terminology.* Leiden, 1972.

Tahsin Özgüç

KARATEPE PHOENICIAN INSCRIPTIONS.

Karatepe, a Neo-Hittite walled town overlooking the Ceyhan River, is situated approximately 100 km (62 mi.) northeast of Adana in Cilicia, Turkey. It was discovered in 1946 by the German archaeologist Helmuth T. Bossert, and a Turkish team began a series of excavations there in the following year. Those excavations and a meticulous restoration project culminated in the creation of an open-air museum at the site.

Karatepe basically consists of a walled enclosure approximately 1 km in circumference with two monumental gates. The lower part of the two gates is comprised of orthostats covered with bas-reliefs and inscriptions in Phoenician and hieroglyphic Hittite (Luwian). The Phoenician text appears in three places: there are two identical texts on each of the gate structures and a third, which is slightly different, on the statue of a divinity. Each gate also has a hieroglyphic version. Upon discovering the Phoenician inscriptions, Bossert sent copies to a dozen Semitic scholars, each of whom published a translation. Bossert himself began translating the more difficult hieroglyphic text, a task eventually completed in 1974 by Franz Steinherr, one of his students.

The author of the inscriptions, a certain Azatiwada (*'ztwd),* identifies himself as a vassal of Urikki, king of the Danunians (*'wrk mlk Dnnym).* He refers to the blessings he has brought to the Danunians, inhabitants of the Adana plain, while keeping Urikki's descendants on the throne. Thus, he appears to have played the role of a kind of palace prefect. He boasts of the part he has played in maintaining peace in the region, particularly by constructing a citadel, which he named after himself (Azatiwada), on the orders of the gods Baal and Rašap (Resheph), in whose honor he has established sacrifices. The inscription ends with a prayer to the gods to bless him, the city, and its inhabitants and with curses on anyone attempting to destroy his work.

These inscriptions are not without problems, one of the most crucial of which is their date. Indeed, the only indication of a specific time period is the mention of Urikki, the vassal of the Assyrian king, in the annals of Tiglath-Pileser III (738, 732 BCE) and in a letter found at Nimrud dating to 709. Because the inscriptions had to have been written after Urikki's death, they are probably from the very end of the eighth century, which would correspond to the paleographic analysis of the Phoenician text. Because the archaeological data appear to indicate an earlier date for the fortress (ninth century BCE), a great deal of debate has centered around this apparent discrepancy. The later date is now generally accepted for the inscriptions and the earlier one for the fortress. It is hypothesized that Azitawada constructed his citadel on the remains of previous construction. Nevertheless, the historical context remains unclear: the absence of any mention of Assyria is particularly surprising; it apparently implies a period of Assyrian retreat after the death of Sargon II (705).

These inscriptions are significant because they constitute the longest known Phoenician text to date. With the Kilamuwa inscription at Zincirli and the Cebel Ires Daği inscription, they reveal the status of Phoenician as an international language in Anatolia from the ninth to the seventh centuries BCE. The fact that the inscriptions are in two languages proved to be instrumental in deciphering the Hittite hieroglyph. Finally, they provide information about the Luwian pantheon in this period and the functional parallels in the Phoenician version.

[*See also* Hittite; Luwians; Neo-Hittites; *and* Phoenician-Punic.]

BIBLIOGRAPHY

Bossert, Helmuth T., and Halet Çambel. *Karatepe: A Preliminary Report on a New Hittite Site.* Institute for Research in Ancient Oriental Civilizations, Publications, no. 1. Istanbul, 1946.

Bossert, Helmuth T. *Karatepe kazilari.* Ankara, 1950.

Bron, François. *Recherches sur les inscriptions phéniciennes de Karatepe.* Geneva, 1979.

Deshayes, Jean, et al. "Remarques sur les monuments de Karatepe." *Revue d'Assyriologie* 75 (1981): 31–60.

Donner, Herbert, and Wolfgang Röllig. *Kanaanäische und aramäische Inschriften.* no. 26. Wiesbaden, 1963.

Gibson, John C. L. *Textbook of Syrian Semitic Inscriptions,* vol. 3, *Phoenician Inscriptions,* no. 15. Oxford, 1982.

Winter, Irene J. "On the Problems of Karatepe: The Reliefs and Their Context." *Anatolian Studies* 29 (1979): 115–151.

FRANÇOIS BRON

Translated from French by Monique Fecteau

KAR-TUKULTI-NINURTA. Site located about 3 km (2 mi.) north of Aššur in northern Iraq, on the east bank of the Tigris River. Since 1960, two villages have appeared within the old ruin: Tulul al-ʿAqir (its official modern name) and Naʿifeh. Serious archaeological work at the site was carried out in winter 1913–1914 by the architect Walter Bachmann, a member of Walter Andrae's team at Aššur. The identification of Tulul al-ʿAqir with ancient Kar-Tukulti-Ninurta, a residential city founded by the Middle Assyrian ruler Tukulti-Ninurta I (1233–1197 BCE), already suggested by Friedrich Sarre and Ernst Herzfeld (1911), was proved by the several foundation tablets Bachmann excavated. Unfortunately, Bachmann did not write a final report and the original field notes were considered lost. Based on the existing original plans and maps, it was at least possible for Tilman Eickhoff (1985) to publish a summary of Bachmann's work. Fieldwork under the direction of Reinhard Dittmann sponsored by the German Research Foundation was reopened at the site in 1986 and continued in 1989. The original data belonging to the early campaign were recovered in 1992, in Dresden, Germany. [*See* Aššur; *and the biography of Andrae.*]

The site is about 500 ha (1,235 acres) in area (only 250 ha, or 617 acres, have been surveyed and mapped thus far). The site's western limit is defined by the Tigris; its eastern one must be next to a large Middle Assyrian channel running parallel to the river that enters the plain about 25 km (16 mi.) to the north. The ruin's northern limit cannot be defined today because of recent leveling activities; the southern city wall was not traced until 1989. The city was subdivided into several quarters: an official royal-administrative one, separated from the others by a fortification wall and further subdivided by a smaller wall into western and eastern sections. This complex could be entered through at least four gates (figure 1: D, F, G, N). The western quarter, on the bank of the Tigris, includes the palace and temples. The eastern part is as yet functionally unidentified and partly overlaid by the two recent villages.

Of the original palace complex (minimum measurements 320 × 150 m), only two parts have been excavated so far. The so-called North Palace (figure 1: M) was accessed from a courtyard or an open space to the north through a monumental entrance that led to the representative rooms; this plan foreshadows the later Neo-Assyrian reception suite layout, in which access is given to a large unexcavated area, perhaps to a courtyard (or more than one) ending in a huge terrace originally about 18 m high (see the South Palace, figure 1: A). Fragments of elaborate wall paintings on the flanks of the eroded terrace indicate the former importance of the rooms on the top; assuming two stories, they were almost the same height as the top of the neighboring ziggurrat of the Aššur Temple (see figure 1: B, i.e., about 30 m high). South of the terrace are industrial-like installations.

Recent surveys, south of the terrace, makes likely the existence of a large (165 × 120 m) unexcavated structure. About 60 m north of the North Palace, recent excavations unearthed parts of another large complex with a room or courtyard paved with unique rhomboid bricks. The walls

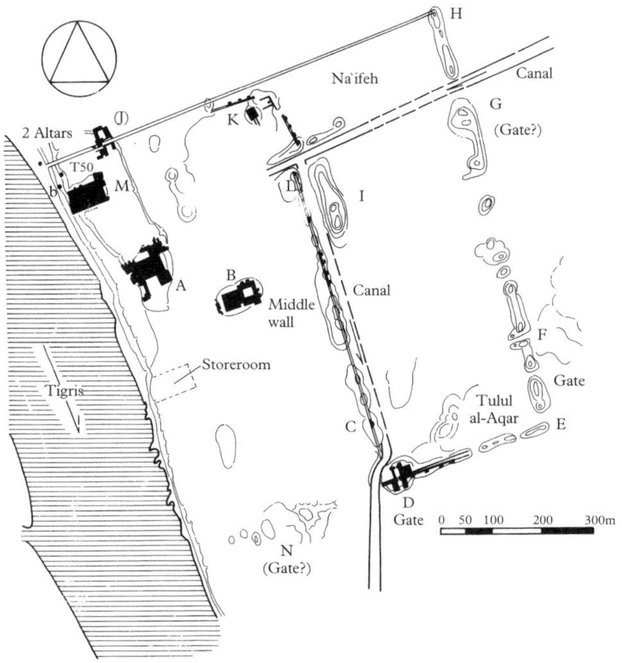

KAR-TUKULTI-NINURTA. Figure 1. *The official section of the town.* (Courtesy R. Dittmann)

had been decorated with glazed tiles in green and yellow, with frit panels with palmette motifs. The only large fragment found has a direct, contemporaneous parallel in the area of the Ishtar Temple at Aššur; in light of the three votive altars found in the immediate vicinity, this structure might be another temple and not part of the palace, as the stamps, marked É. GAL, on the bricks suggest. In the northeast corner of the western official part, a small (18.5 × 20 m), towerlike structure of unknown function has been excavated (figure 1: K).

The Aššur Temple with its ziggurat (figure 1: B, figure 2; measuring 30 × 30 m) at the base) is located immediately to the southeast of the terrace of the South Palace.The niche of its cella, whose layout is somewhat Babylonian, offers some enigmatic installations that could belong to a wood-panel construction once perhaps decorated with paintings. Because in the 1913–1914 excavations no other temple was found or traced on the ruin, the structures found in 1989 have now altered the assumption that the large oblong room next to the cella is the place where the gods mentioned in the texts (see Freydank, 1976–) as worshiped at Kar-Tukulti-Ninurta (in addition to Aššur: Adad, Shamash, Ninurta, Nusku, Nergal, Sebittu, and Ishtar), were assembled in the form of votive altars. Access to the ziggurat is unclear. Andrae and Bachmann identified a small structure west of the ziggurat as a staircase building from which, via a bridge-like construction, the first level of the ziggurat could be reached. Another hypothesis, based on the evidence of Tell er-Rimah (possibly ancient Karana), envisions access via the roof of the temple. [*See* Rimah, Tell er-.] The Aššur Temple at Kar-Tukulti-Ninurta has no staircase, and the possibility that there was no real access to the Middle Assyrian ziggurat needs to be considered. This would also be in harmony with the Aššur-Enlil Ziggurat at Aššur. [*See* Ziggurat.]

About 250 m north-northeast of the North Palace, a new small temple was excavated in 1989 at an elevation called Tell O. The deity worshiped is as yet unidentified; it is also unclear whether this structure belonged to the administrative sector of the city, to a residential area, or the suburbs. Midway between this temple and the palace is an area (about 150 × 150 m) with a dense concentration of pottery and a lot of grinding-stone fragments. The finds may indicate a grain-manufacture and storage unit, such as mentioned in the texts. Traces of large structures are found in the vast southern parts of the city along the channel, surely the place where the king settled the different peoples exiled there following his campaigns in neighboring countries.

It has been assumed that after the violent death of Tukulti-Ninurta I the ruin was either completely deserted or was no more than a hamlet. Survey evidence, as well as a critical

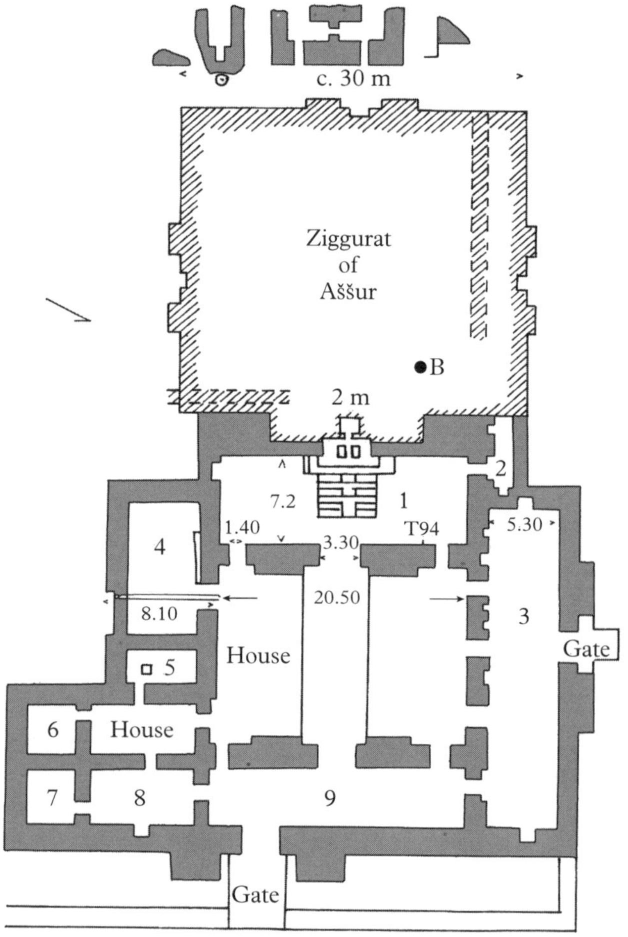

KAR-TUKULTI-NINURTA. Figure 2. *Plan of the Aššur temple with ziggurat.* (Sketch by W. Bachmann)

examination of the historical sources, shows that there was a brief interruption in the use of most of the public buildings (with the exception of the new temple in Tell O, which continued to be in use for a short time) and that in the one-year reign of Ninurta-Tukulti-Aššur (1133 BCE) parts of structures had been pulled down. So-called Ishtar hands, found in some quantities especially in the South Palace, attest to a partial reuse of the ruin in the ninth century BCE. Important traces of a Neo-Assyrian occupation have mostly been found in the official sector of the town (figure 1: J? and newly excavated areas). Historical records mention at least two official administrators of the town at the end of the ninth and the second half of the eighth centuries BCE. No traces of a post-Assyrian occupation have yet been found, with the exception of a few Parthian sherds and some medieval pottery.

BIBLIOGRAPHY

Bastert, Katrin, and Reinhard Dittmann. "Anmerkungen zu einigen Schmuckelementen eines mittelassyrischen Temples in Kar Tukultī-Ninurta (Iraq)." *Altorientalische Forschungen* 22 (1995): 8–29. Preliminary report on the excavation of the temple in Tell O in 1989.

Dittmann, Reinhard, et al. "Kar Tukultī-Ninurta/Al-ʿAqar 1986." *Sumer* (1989–1990): 86–97. Preliminary report on the campaign of 1986.

Dittmann, Reinhard, et al. "Untersuchungen in Kār-Tukultī-Ninurta (Tulūl al-ʿAqar), 1986." *Mitteilungen der Deutschen Orient-Gesellschaft* 120 (1988): 97–138. Preliminary report of the work at the site in 1986 and a critical review of the old data.

Dittmann, Reinhard. "Ausgrabungen der Freien Universität Berlin in Assur and Kār-Tukultī-Ninurta in den Jahren 1988–89." *Mitteilungen der Deutschen Orient-Gesellschaft* 122 (1990): 157–171. Second preliminary report on the new excavations.

Dittmann, Reinhard. "Assur und Kar Tukulti-Ninurta." *American Journal of Archaeology* 96 (1992): 307–312. Treats the campaigns of 1986 and 1989.

Eickhoff, Tilman. *Kar Tukulti Ninurta: Eine mittelassyrische Kult- und Residenzstadt.* Abhandlungen der Deutschen Orient-Gesellschaft, 21. Berlin, 1985. The first comprehensive compilation of the data from the old excavation.

Frame, Grant. "Assyrian Clay Hands." *Baghdader Mitteilungen* 22 (1991): 335–381. Compilation of data on the so-called Ishtar Hands.

Freydank, H. "Kār-Tukulti-Ninurta. A. Philologisch." In *Reallexikon der Assyriologie und Vorderasiatischen Archäologie,* vol. 5, pp. 455–456. Berlin, 1976–. Overview of the textual finds and historical information on the ruins.

Sarre, Friedrich P. T., and Ernst Herzfeld. "Der Djabal Makhūl." In *Archäologische Reise im Euphrat- und Tigris-Begiet,* vol. 1, pp. 212–214. Berlin, 1911. The earliest correct identification of the site and some pottery sherds, already indicating a Neo-Assyrian occupation.

REINHARD DITTMANN

KASSITES. A tribal people of unknown origin, the Kassites (Kaššu) are attested mainly in Babylonia and western Iran in the second and first millennia BCE. Apart from Kassite-Akkadian bilinguals and Kassite onomastica (Balkan, 1954, pp. 2–4), a Kassite presence in Babylonia is deduced from textual references to a "land of the Kassites" (Kessler, 1982, p. 57, no. 1), a "king of the Kassites" (Brinkman, 1976, p. 405), a "Kassite" dynasty (Babylonian king list A), and certain individuals designated as Kassite in administrative records.

The Kassite dynasty (fifteenth–twelfth centuries BCE) is bracketed by two "dark ages" which obscure what is known of its rise and the aftermath of its fall. Though often dismissed as a reign lacking in cultural identity, Kassite rule brought an extended period of relative political stability and economic prosperity to a unified Sumer-Babylonia, which attained international prestige, ranking with Assyria, Ḫatti, and Egypt in the Amarna correspondence of the fifteenth–thirteenth centuries BCE. [*See* Amarna Tablets.] The culture and literature of Babylonia, promoted by the Kassites in an effort to legitimize their rule at home, spread throughout the Near East, along with the widespread adoption of Babylonian as the language of diplomacy.

History. Texts of the eighteenth century BCE provide the first references to individuals and groups of Kassites linked primarily with Sippar and its tribal environs. As agricultural laborers and militiamen, these early Kassites appear in collaboration, but also in confrontation, with the Babylonians. By the end of the Old Babylonian period, a Kassite is attested as far west as Alalakh in the Orontes valley; their main concentration lay on the Middle Euphrates and Khabur river valleys, near Khana and Terqa. This area was ruled by a king with the Kassite name of Kashtiliashu, who may have been a Babylonian vassal (Podany, 1991–1993, p. 60, n. 60).

From the region of Khana, the Kassites gained control of northern Babylonia following the decline of the first dynasty of Babylon in the early sixteenth century BCE. With the departure of the Sealand kings and the conquest of their territories, the Kassites then ruled over a united Sumer-Babylonia between about 1475 and 1155 BCE. Most of what is known about the Kassites of this period relates to the ruling dynasty.

According to the Babylonian king list A, the Kassite dynasty consisted of thirty-six kings who, with minor interruptions, reigned an unprecedented 576 years. Little is known of the earlier kings until the reign of Agum II. In an inscription known from a later copy, which may be a scribal forgery, Agum II is said to have returned the statues of Marduk and his wife from Khani to Babylon twenty-four years after their removal by the Hittites in about 1595 BCE (middle chronology). The first Kassite monarch to rule the north as king of Babylonia was Burna-Buriash I (c. 1510 BCE), but it is not until the late fifteenth century BCE that there are contemporary sources for the Kassite kings. Royal inscriptions and the Amarna letters, dating largely between 1402 and 1347 BCE, document the intensification of international relations between Egypt and Babylonia—from the initial exchange of ambassadors and gifts under Kara-indash (c. 1415 BCE) to diplomatic marriages and large-scale trade during the reign of Burna-Buriash II (1359–1333 BCE).

The early years of Sumero-Babylonian unification and the establishment of the Kassite dynasty were marked by extensive building programs, associated in particular with Kara-indash and Kurigalzu I (c. 1390 BCE). With proceeds obtained largely from international trade, major restoration and reconstruction were undertaken in several old Sumerian cities, notably at Ur, Eridu and Uruk. A fortified capital or royal residence was erected at Dur Kurigalzu/ʿAqar Quf on the outskirts of modern Baghdad, presumably to defend the capital at Babylon against Assyria or Elam. With the decline of Mitannian hegemony in the mid-fourteenth century BCE, Babylon extended its boundaries northward to Kirkuk, where Kassites made up approximately 2 percent of the population in and around Nuzi (1440–1340 BCE), whose records provide the oldest archival corpus of Kassite onomastica. [*See* Mitanni.]

During the reign of Burna-Buriash II, the Kassite dynasty ranked among the major powers of the Near East, its monarch hailed internationally as a "Great King" and his family linked by diplomatic marriages to the courts of Ḫatti, Egypt, and Assyria, where the influence of Babylonian language, religion, and customs is apparent.

After 1335 BCE, the equilibrium was upset by occasional conflicts on the northern and eastern frontiers, with Babylonian incursions into Assyria and Iran and vice versa. A short-lived Assyrian interregnum under Ashur-Uballit I was followed by Tukulti-Ninurta I's more major conquest of Babylonia (c. 1225–1217 BCE), which recovered its independence before the Elamite invasion by Shutruk-Nahhunte brought about the end of the Kassite dynasty in about 1155 BCE. The deportation of prisoners and booty accounts for the presence of Kassites in northern Mesopotamia from the late thirteenth century BCE. They are still attested serving in various capacities in Neo-Assyrian records of the first millennium BCE. At this time, monarchs with Kassite names reigned in the northerly regions of Allabria and Na'iri. Large concentrations of Kassites had been settled to the east in the Namri (Namar)-Habban area, which fell under Assyrian influence in the ninth century BCE.

After the fall of the Kassite dynasty in the mid-twelfth century BCE, Kassites continued to reside in Babylonia, where they appear to have been fully assimilated. They bear Babylonian names and hold high governmental posts, until at least the ninth century BCE. Monarchs of Kassite descent occupied the throne under the second Sealand and Bazu dynasties in the late eleventh and early tenth centuries BCE. At that time, when trade relations to the west and north of Babylonia were being disrupted by the Arameans, there were close artistic and economic connections between Babylonia and the people living in the area of the Zagros Mountains, on either side of the Baghdad-Kermanshah road. It is there, in the piedmont hills of eastern Iraq and western Iran, that the majority of Kassites settled in the first millennium BCE. A warlike tribal people, they retained their independence from the Neo-Assyrian period through to Achaemenid and Hellenistic times, when the main textual sources are in Greek or Latin (Brinkman, 1968, 1972, 1976).

Language and Literature. Knowledge of the Kassite language and its syntax is limited, based as it is on bilingual lists and scattered references to Kassite deities, names, terms, and words. From what is known, it bears no relation to any other language or language family. Archives and texts dating to the Kassite dynasty have been found at numerous sites on the Middle Euphrates (Terqa); in the Hamrin (Tell Mohammed, Tell Imlihiye, Tell Zubaydi); in Sumer-Babylonia (Ur, Larsa, Uruk, Isin, Nippur, Babylon, Dur Kurigalzu, Sippar); at Susa; and on both Failaka (Kuwait) and Bahrain (Qalaʿat al-Bahrain). The bulk, largely unpublished, are written in Middle Babylonian and concern economic life. Dedicatory building inscriptions were, by contrast, written in Sumerian. [*See* Sumerian.] These, the letters, and the royal inscriptions (notably from Dur Kurigalzu) shed light on international affairs, the conventional titulary of the Kassite monarchs, and their public display of power and piety through major building projects. Boundary stones (*kudurru*) from the final quarter of the dynasty inform on the tax structure and provincial administration under Kassite rule.

In addition to restoring and maintaining national shrines, the Kassite kings also promoted the collection, composition, and recording of literary works, which were stored in temple libraries, such as those largely preserved at Ur, Uruk, Nippur, Babylon, and Sippar. Some of these were looted by Tukulti-Ninurta I, following his sack of Babylon in the thirteenth century BCE. It appears that many of the standard literary works found in the later Neo-Assyrian libraries of the seventh century BCE are copies of Kassite originals and compilations. Scribal families of the first millennium BCE claimed descent from famous Kassite forebears, one of whom, Sin-leqe-unnini, is credited with the authorship of the eleven-tablet Epic of Gilgamesh found in Ashurbanipal's library at Nineveh.

Sociopolitical Structure and Settlement Patterns. As ruler of a unified Sumer-Babylonia, the Kassite monarch replaced the old political structure of city-states with a national state and surpassed his predecessors in international prestige. In what appears to have been an attempt to appease the ancient Sumerian centers, the Kassite monarchs (who bore Kassite names until the reign of Kudur-Enlil [1254–1246 BCE], when some assumed Babylonian names) adopted Babylonian titulary, customs, religion, and language.

For much of its rule, the Kassite monarchy was dominated by a single family; the normal succession being father–son, but fraternal succession may also have occurred. The Amarna correspondence demonstrates that the palace engaged in foreign trade—though the extent of its involvement is uncertain—and royal participation in military maneuvers—which then incorporated the horse and chariot—is also attested.

Information on the government bureaucracy, provincial administration, and taxation derives mainly from *kudurrus* (boundary stones) of the last quarter of the dynasty. The individual provinces were governed by a *šaknu*/*šaknu mati* (governor/governor of the land) or, in the case of Nippur, the *šandabakku* (a unique title for the governor of Nippur), but little is known of their duties or the extent of their jurisdiction. Private ownership of land was recognized by the crown. Exemption from taxes in kind, corvée, and military service was normally obtained only by royal decree, which may have been granted to certain religious cities (e.g., Babylon) at this time.

Apart from the ruling dynasty, little is known of the Kassite aristocracy or the Kassite component within the population of Babylonia. Kassite social structure was tribal, based on a unit called House of So-and-So, after an eponymous ancestor. Each house or clan, comprising persons related in the male line, involved up to several villages with considerable agricultural land and was headed by a *bēl biti* ("lord of the house"). The Kassite tribal organization is best attested between 1200 and 850 BCE. There are, however, references to Kassite "houses" in the eighteenth century BCE, suggesting the existence of similar social units on the outskirts of Old Babylonian cities. These units seem to have retained their social structure throughout the period of the Kassite dynasty. The prominence of relatively small clan and tribal units in Kassite society may account for the steady rise in the percentage of small nonurban settlements (e.g., Tell Zubaydi) and the decline in urban complexes in Babylonia during the Late Bronze Age.

Economy. The extensive building and restoration programs undertaken by the Kassite monarchs in the fourteenth and thirteenth centuries BCE were largely financed by trade, in particular with Egypt. In its age-old role as middleman, Babylonia prospered at the center of a complex network of commercial contacts that spread throughout the Near East and beyond to the Aegean, as well as to present-day Afghanistan. Babylonian textiles, horses (steeds), and chariots were sent west to Egypt with transhipped luxury items such as lapis lazuli in exchange for gold and precious stones. The textual evidence for far-flung trade during the Amarna period is borne out in the archaeological record by the discovery of a Babylonian cylinder at Failaka and another in the Uluburun shipwreck, which was bound westward, where Kassite seals made of lapis lazuli were found in a hoard at Thebes in Boeotia (Porada, 1981). Evidence for foreign shipments within Babylonia include a Mycenaean-style ingot from Tell al-Abyad, as well as Egyptian jewelry found at Babylon, Tell ed-Der, and Nippur. As a result of this trade, the country's economy went on the gold standard, which lasted at least until the reign of Ada-shuma-iddina (c. 1222–1217 BCE). Under the last kings of the dynasty, trade had dwindled to such an extent that Babylonia briefly went on a copper standard.

Religion and Burial Customs. The official embrace of Mesopotamian religion and liturgy left little trace of the veneration of Kassite deities, and much of the evidence is textual. The investiture of the Kassite kings took place at Babylon in the shrine of their patron deities, Šuqamuna and his consort Šimalija, both mountain deities of foreign origin, whose names occur in Ugaritic literature and whose statues were still preserved in the seventh century BCE. There is an indication of a possible cult of a Kassite goddess (^{d}Kaššītu) in about the mid-first millennium BCE at Uruk and perhaps also at Babylon.

Other prominent Kassite deities include: Buriaš, the weather god; Ḫarbe, the lord of the pantheon—a god also venerated in Hurrian areas; Maruttaš (often equated with the Sumero-Akkadian Ninurta); Mirizir, a goddess identified with the generic Bēltu; Saḫ, a sun god; Šipak, the moon god; and Šuriaš, the more common solar deity. The names of some of the Kassite gods have been compared with Indo-European deities, but contact, if any, would have occurred prior to the arrival of the Kassites in Mesopotamia (Brinkman, 1976).

Material Culture. As with the religious and literary culture of the Kassites, there is little remaining in the way of architecture, industry, or art that is quintessentially Kassite. At the capital, Babylon, most of the Kassite occupation lies under the water table, but contemporary levels have been exposed at several ancient Sumerian cities (Nippur, Isin, Larsa, and Ur) and, most recently, in the Hamrin and Haditha regions. [*See* Hamrin Dam Salvage Project.] These provide evidence for Kassite town planning, as well as secular and religious architecture and burials—which, on the whole, adhere to Mesopotamian conventions. Much the same applies to the extant artwork of the Kassite period, which is characterized by the selective adaptation of established forms and iconography.

Architecture and architectural decoration. The earliest-known Kassite building is the Inanna temple built by Kara-indash at Uruk (late fifteenth century BCE). Its rectangular plan follows the Assyrian *langraum* scheme, with the entrance in the center of the short wall, directly opposite the altar. Its exterior decoration of baked, molded bricks is derived from unbaked variations at Old Babylonian and Old Assyrian temples. The alternating mountain and water deities, which decorate the facade, each have older prototypes, but their combination is unique. Fragments of molded-brick ornament have also been found at Ur, Nippur, Larsa, and Dur Kurigalzu. The technique was adopted and developed by the Elamites, Assyrians, Babylonians, and Persians.

Dur Kurigalzu was most probably founded by Kurigalzu I in the early fourteenth century BCE. The eroded remains of its ziggurat, which still rises about 57 m above the plain, was often mistaken by early travelers for the biblical Tower of Babel. [*See* Ziggurat.] Its mud-brick core was leveled and bonded with layers of reed matting and plaited ropes at regular intervals. Aside from this construction method, the ziggurat conforms to southern decoration and plan with an exterior facade of buttresses and recesses and a triple staircase giving access to the temple on top. Also reminiscent of Ur III and Isin/Larsa-period religious precincts is the adjoining complex of partially excavated courtyards and corridors—identified as temples though they lack a recognizable shrine.

The palace at Tell Abyad, 700 m northwest of the ziggurat, covered an area of about 300 sq m. It consisted of several courtyard blocks with four building levels, of which level II is associated with tablets of Kudur-Enlil (1254–1246 BCE) and Kashtiliashu IV (1232–1225 BCE); level I contained those of Marduk-apla-iddina (1171–1159 BCE). Wall painting, found in all four building levels, is especially well preserved in level IC, where individuals and groups are shown in procession. The procession motif prefigures the common theme of Assyrian palace decoration, and the fez, which is later adopted as the royal headdress in Assyria, appears here in connection with one group of Babylonian nobility or Assyrian subjects. [*See* Wall Paintings.]

Sculpture. The Kassites are credited with the introduction of the *kudurru,* an elaborately carved boundary stone which served to commemorate royal land grants (see figure 1). Most popular in the thirteenth–fourteenth centuries BCE, the oldest extant *kudurru* dates to the fourteenth century BCE; they continued to be made into the first millennium BCE. The text is generally accompanied by a relief decoration illustrating the symbols of the deities who witnessed the transaction. While most deities and symbols are Mesopotamian in origin, three symbols (a bird with its head reversed, a bird on a pole, and the cross) represent Kassite gods.

Glyptic. Kassite glyptic is conventionally divided into four main styles, whose regional and chronological distribution is difficult to determine on the basis of the evidence available to date. First Kassite has been traced to origins in the eighteenth century BCE although a number of seals from the Khana kingdom have now been redated to the sixteenth century BCE (Podany, 1991–1993). It is seen as an outgrowth of the late Old Babylonian style, continuing to at least the mid-thirteenth century BCE. Characterized by its hard-stone material and full-length inscriptions, this group includes most of the seals inscribed with royal names. [*See* Seals.] Comparisons between this group and the later paintings at ʿAqar Quf, on the one hand, and Kassite *kudurru* on the other, are considered unconvincing. Caps of granulated gold, once regarded as typically Kassite, are now known to have been used during the reign of Shamshi-Adad I of Assyria.

Second Kassite includes a variety of mainly symmetrical designs of which the most important is the "cthonic god" series. The scenes depicting a god rising from either water or mountains resemble the figural decoration on the Temple of Kara-indash at Uruk and find parallels at Aššur. Other typical designs are centered on an upright man, demon, or tree that is flanked by diagonal fish men, animals, or monsters. This group ranges from the fourteenth to late thirteenth centuries BCE. The related Third Kassite/Isin II group is posited in the twelfth century BCE, on account of its apparent derivation from Assyrian prototypes of the thirteenth century BCE. The scenes concentrate on the themes of animals, monsters, and trees and are identified above all by the volute tree and garland motif.

KASSITES. Figure 1. *A kudurru representing the mastiff of Gula.* (Courtesy J. C. Margueron)

Pseudo-Kassite is typified by its soft-stone or composite material, its truncated inscriptions, horizontal and vertical borders, and the twisted tree. A tentative origin in the mid-fourteenth century BCE is argued on the basis of impressions on dated tablets from Nippur. A hybrid group, pseudo-Kassite designs show influence form Babylonian, Mitannian, and Elamite traditions. (Matthews, 1992; Kühne, 1995).

Luxury products. The Kassite-period industry in luxury goods is characterized by the production of faience, sintered quartz, and glass wares, which, in common with other production centers of the Amarna Age, was largely restricted to local needs. A foreign, Egyptian influence is manifest in the jewelry of this period, as well as in the painted terra-cotta head from the palace at ʿAqar Quf.

[*See also* Mesopotamia, *article on* Ancient Mesopotamia. *In addition, most of the sites mentioned are the subject of independent entries.*]

BIBLIOGRAPHY

Language and Texts

Balkan, Kemal. *Kassitenstudien I: Die Sprache der Kassiten.* Translated from Turkish by F. R. Kraus. American Oriental Series, 37. New Haven, 1954.

Dosch, Gudrun, and Karlheinz Deller. "Die Familie Kizzuk. Sieben Kassitengenerationen in Temfena und Šuriniwe." In *Studies on the Civilization and Culture of Nuzi and the Hurrians,* edited by M. A. Morrison and D. I. Owen, vol. 1, pp. 91–113. Bloomington, Ind., 1981.

Kessler, Karlheinz. "Kassitische Tontafeln von Tell Imliḥiye." *Baghdader Mitteilungen* 13 (1982): 51–116.

Lambert, W. G. "Ancestors, Authors, and Canonicity." *Journal of Cuneiform Studies* 11 (1957): 1–14.

Prichard, James, ed. *Ancient Near Eastern Texts Relating to the Old Testament.* 3d ed. Princeton, 1969.

History

Brinkman, John A. *A Political History of Post-Kassite Babylonia, 1158–722 B.C.* Analecta Orientalia, 43. Rome, 1968. See pages 246–259.

Brinkman, John A. "Foreign Relations of Babylonia from 1600 to 625 B.C.: The Documentary Evidence." *American Journal of Archaeology* 76 (1972): 271–281.

Brinkman, John A. "The Monarchy in the Time of the Kassite Dynasty." In *Le palais et la royauté: Archéologie et civilisation; compte rendu de la 19e rencontre Assyriologique internationale,* edited by Paul Garelli, pp. 395–408. Paris, 1974.

Brinkman, John A. *Materials and Studies for Kassite History,* vol. 1, *A Catalogue of Cuneiform Sources Pertaining to Specific Monarchs of the Kassite Dynasty.* Chicago, 1976.

Edzard, Dietz O. "Die Beziehungen Babyloniens und Ägyptens in der mittelbabylonischen Zeit und das Gold." *Journal of the Economic and Social History of the Orient* 3 (1960): 38–55.

Podony, Amanda. "A Middle Babylonian Date for the Ḫana Kingdom." *Journal of Cuneiform Studies* 43–45 (1991–1993): 53–62.

Art and Archaeology

Baqir, Taha. *Iraq Government Excavations at 'Aqar Quf, 1942–1943.* London, 1944.

Baqir, Taha. *Iraq Government Excavations at 'Aqar Quf: Second Interim Report, 1943–1944.* London, 1945.

Beran, Thomas. "Die babylonische Glyptik der Kassitenzeit." *Archiv für Orientforschung* 18 (1957): 255–278.

Boehmer, Rainer Michael, and Heinz-Werner Dämmer. *Tell Imliḥiye, Tell Zubeidi, Tell Abbas.* Baghdader Forschungen, 7 Mainz am Rhein, 1985.

Invernizzi, Antonio. "Excavations in the Yelkhi Area (Hamrin Project, Iraq)." *Mesopotamia* 15 (1980): 19–49.

Kühne, Hartmut. "Der mittelassyriche 'Cut Style.' " *Zeitschrift für Assyriologie* 85.2 (1995): 277–301.

Matthews, Donald M. *Principles of Composition in Near Eastern Glyptic of the Later Second Millennium B.C.* Orbis Biblicus et Orientalis, Series Archaeologica, 8. Freiburg, 1990.

Matthews, Donald M. *The Kassite Glyptic of Nippur.* Orbis Biblicus et Orientalis, 116. Freiburg, 1992.

Porada, Edith. "The Cylinder Seals Found at Thebes in Boeotia." *Archiv für Orientforschung* 28 (1981): 1–70.

Seidl, Ursula. *Die babylonischen Kudurru-Reliefs.* Orbis Biblicus et Orientalis, 87. Freiburg, 1989.

Spycket, Agnès. "Kassite and Middle Elamite Sculpture." In *Later Mesopotamia and Iran: Tribes and Empires 1600–539 BC,* edited by John Curtis, pp. 25–32. London, 1995.

Tomabechi, Yoko. "Wall Paintings from Dur Kurigalzu." *Journal of Near Eastern Studies* 42 (1983): 123–131.

DIANA L. STEIN

KAZEL, TELL AL-, one of the largest five tells on the Syrian coast, situated on the ʿAkkar plain in the western part of the topographic depression of Homs, the easiest pass from Syria's interior to the sea. It dominates the al-Abrash River at a distance of about 3.5 km (22 mi.) from the sea, 8 km (5 mi.) north of Nahr al-Kabir al-Junubi (the Eleutheros) and about 25 km (16 mi.) southeast of Tortose and Arwad. The tell is shaped like an oval platform (310 × 280 m). Its summit is about 25 m above the surrounding plain and 50 m above sea level. Three ancient roads climb to the tell's upper terraces, which were used in antiquity. The modern village, which until recently occupied the center of the tell, was transferred to the plain.

The word *kazel* in this toponym is not Arabic or any other Semitic language. However, *casal,* which means "castle" in the toponymy of the Crusader period in Syria, may explain the name ("tell of the castle"). In fact there was a *casal* crowning the tell as early as the Roman period, whose tower was uncovered in 1956 during the excavations of Maurice Dunand and Nassib Saliby (see below). Ptolemy (5.15.4) mentions the Simyra *castellum,* as does Pomponius Mela (1.12). It is probable that Simyra was the name of the site in the Greco-Roman period, a likely variation of *Sumur,* the name of the city in the Amarna letters and *Sumri* in the Middle Assyrian records. [*See* Amarna Tablets.] Sumur, the capital of Amurru, is mentioned more than fifty times in the Amarna texts. It would correspond well to the privileged position of Tell al-Kazel in the historically important pass from the coast to inner Syria and at the center of a very fertile plain of about 500 sq km (310 sq. mi.)

From *Genesis* (10:18), Pliny (*Nat. Hist.* 5.20.17) and Strabo (*Geog.* 16.2.12) followed by W. M. Thomson (*Bibliotheca Sacra,* 1848, vol. 5, pp. 15–17) and Ernest Renan (*Mission en Phénicie,* Paris, 1864, p. 115) it is possible to conclude that the city of Simyra should exist on the plain between the Amrit (Marathus) River and the Nahr al-Kabir al-Junubi (the Eleutheros). These resources confirm the annals of Thutmosis III (Breasted, 1906, 11.108.465) and Tiglath-Pileser I (Luckenbill, 1926, p. 98, no. 302). The latter arrived from Arwad to "Sumri" in six hours (three double hours), which corresponds exactly to the distance between the two sites. Finally, the land to the north of Tell al-Kazel is still named Ard Simyrian ("land of Simyrian"), after the later name of the site (Simyra). From the archaeological point of view, Tell al-Kazel is the largest and the richest of the tells, and its stratigraphy is in accord with the known period of Sumur/Simyra. [*See the biography of Renan.*]

The primary argument against the identification of Sumur/Simyra with Tell al-Kazel considers that the Amarna letters mention "the ships of Sumur," and Tell al-Kazel is 3.5 km (2 mi.) from the sea. However, the Mediterranean sea has undergone frequent fluctuations throughout history, so that the coastline then may have been closer to the site. If this were true for the Amarna period, the river could have been used to bring the ship into a harbor in front of the city. In any case, many harbors, like Minet el-Beida and al-Mina, were far from the cities they served.

E. O. Forrer in 1939 and Robert Braidwood in 1940 (see "A Note on the Identification of Simyra," *Syria* 21 [1940]: 218–221) were the first to refer to Tell al-Kazel. In 1956 the tell was surveyed under the auspices of the Syrian Directorate General of Antiquities and Museums by Maurice Dunand and Nassib Saliby. In 1960–1961 and 1962, Dunand, Adnan Bounni, and Saliby undertook large-scale excavations there. In 1985, jointly with the museum of the American University of Beirut, the Syrian Directorate General resumed a season of excavations headed by Bounni and Leila Badre. Since 1986, Bounni granted the entire permit to the AUB team directed by Badre with the strict collaboration of Michel Al-Maqdissi from the Syrian Directorate General of Antiquities and Museums.

The riverbank at the foot of Tell al-Kazel is rich in stone artifacts from the Lower and Middle Paleolithic periods. The tell itself is on a natural promontory on which the first settlement was located in the Neolithic period. Neolithic stone implements for agriculture and hunting have been found on the surface, with scattered material from other periods before the end of the third millennium. The debris from these periods is 10 m thick.

Urban installations presumably began with the arrival of the Cananite-Amorite population. [*See* Amorites.] The city was then protected by a rampart. The extraction and reuse of stones from the tell both recently and in antiquity have greatly disturbed the archaeological sequences. Nevertheless, from the pottery and some undisturbed locations in the three excavated areas to the west, southeast, and northeast the history of the site since the Middle Bronze Age can be reconstructed:

1. *MB period.* The city wall in area III to the northeast was built of stone rubble and buttressed by a glacis made of hard yellow clay. The corresponding ceramics are mainly carinated black bowls and burnished flat-based jars.

2. *Amarna period.* The palace to the northwest and another LB III architectural remains produced local plain jars and utensils, white-slipped bowls, base-ring juglets, Mycenaean-type vessels with Canaanite garments, and weapons.

3. *Iron Age I.* The lower parts of large rooms were excavated, and local bichrome and sub-Mycenaean III C pottery were found (necklace beads and an Astarte plaque).

4. *Iron Age II.* A great quantity of red-slipped pottery was found in level A. Cypro-Geometric vessels were also well represented along with some Neo-Assyrian pottery sherds.

5. *Achaemenid period.* A rich level was excavated from the Achaemenid period with a monumental building and probably a Cananite temple (a Persian-style column base and one offering table). The principal corresponding types of pottery were Cananite jars and imported Attic ceramics (sixth–fourth centuries BCE). Noteworthy also was a large collection of terra-cotta heads of typical Cananite (Phoenician) priests. [*See* Phoenicians.]

6. *Hellenistic period.* The principal area excavated from the Hellenistic period was a large cemetery on the northeast terrace. It was very rich in local and imported pottery: Late Cananite small jars, imported Rhodian amphorae, local fish plates, Megarian bowls and bowls from Pergamon.

7. *Roman period.* On the southern side of the tell the lower part of a Roman tower was excavated, but there were few other traces of this period, except for quantities of Early and Late Roman pottery.

8. *Byzantine and Islamic periods.* Byzantine pottery and a variety of glazed Islamic vessels were found on the surface without a clear connection to any buildings, which had mostly been removed during agricultural activities.

BIBLIOGRAPHY

Badre, Leila. "Tell Kazel, 1987." *Archiv für Orientforschung* 36–37 (1989–1990): 258–260.

Badre, Leila, et al. "Tell Kazel–Syria Excavations of the AUB Museum, 1985–87: Preliminary Reports." *Berytus* 38 (1990): 9–124.

Badre, Leila. "Recent Phoenician Discoveries at Tell Kazel." In *Atti del II congresso internazionale di studi fenici e punici,* vol. 2, edited by Enrico Acquaro et al. Rome, 1991.

Badre, Leila, et al. "Tell Kazel (Syrie), Rapport preliminaire sur les 4e–8e campagne de fouilles (1988–1992)." *Syria* 71 (1994): 259–346.

Breasted, James H. *Ancient Records of Egypt: Historical Documents from the Earliest Times to the Persian Conquest.* Vol. 2. Chicago, 1906.

Dunand, Maurice, and Nassib Saliby. "À la recherche de Simyra." *Annales Archéologiques Arabes Syriennes* 7 (1957): 3–16.

Dunand, Maurice, Adnan Bounni, and Nassib Saliby. "Fouilles de Tell Kazel: Rapport préliminaire." *Annales Archéologiques Arabes Syriennes* 14 (1964): 3–14.

Elayi, Josette. "Les importations grecques à Tell Kazel (Simyra) à l'époque perse." *Annales Archéologiques Arabes Syriennes* 36–37 (1986–1987): 132–135.

Gubel, Eric. "Tell Kazel (Ṣumur/Simyra) à l'époque perse." *Transeuphratène* 2 (1990): 37–49.

Klengel, Horst. "Sumur/Simyra und die Eleutheros-Ebene in der Geschichte Syriens." *Klio* 66.1 (1984): 5–18.

Luckenbill, Daniel D. *Ancient Records of Assyria and Babylonia.* Vol. 1. Chicago, 1926.

Maqdissi, Michel al-. *Courriers de l'archéologie syrienne.* 2 vols. Damas, 1989.

Weiss, Harvey. "Archaeology in Syria." *American Journal of Archaeology* 95.4 (1991): 734–735.

ADNAN BOUNNI

KEFAR ḤANANYAH, Jewish village located on the lower slope of a hill east of the Ḥananyah Valley, in northern Lower Galilee, about 9 km (5.5 mi.) southwest of Safed (map reference 189 × 258). The identification of ancient Kefar Ḥananyah with modern Kafr ʿInan (Kufr ʿAnan) is based on geographic references in tannaitic literature, including mention of Kefar Ḥananyah as a boundary point between Upper and Lower Galilee (Mishnah Shev. 9.2); on archaeological and archaeometric evidence showing that the site was a pottery-manufacturing center during the Roman and Early Byzantine periods (see below); on the mention in a twelfth-century CE text of a rock-cut synagogue at Kefar

Ḥananyah (see below); and on the phonetic similarity of Kafr ʿInan (Kufr ʿAnan) to Kefar Ḥananyah.

Rabbinic sources dating to the first/second–fourth centuries CE refer to Kefar Ḥananyah as a well-known pottery-manufacturing center, mentioning several of its products and attesting to their durability under conditions of thermal stress. Rabbi Ḥalafta of Kefar Ḥananyah (second century CE) is quoted several times in tannaitic sources. The description by Jacob ben Nathanel, a twelfth-century (prior to 1187) traveler, of a synagogue at Kefar Ḥananyah "quarried from the hill with only one built wall" (Reiner, forthcoming, no. 1), seems to refer to more substantial remains then visible of the rock-cut structure at the site (see below). Menachem ha-Ḥevroni (c. 1215) mentions a synagogue in use by the residents of Kefar Ḥananyah (Reiner, forthcoming, no. 5). In two unpublished manuscripts (c. sixteenth century), and apparently also in a fragmentary third text (probably late fifteenth century), two synagogues are mentioned (in two cases the authors state that one of the synagogues is in use by the Jews of the settlement; Reiner, forthcoming, no. 10).

Joseph Braslavsky (Braslavi; 1933) identified remains of a rectangular rock-cut public structure (similar to that at Meiron) located east of the village of Kufr ʿAnan as an ancient synagogue. [*See* Synagogues.] In the early 1980s, Zvi Ilan (1981–1982) published a plan of that building, found remains of another public building he suggested was a second synagogue, and traced remains of an aqueduct to the site, suggesting an early date for its construction (it is apparently medieval, however; see below). [*See* Aqueducts.] Parts of several installations for olive-oil production have been studied by Rafael Frankel (1984). [*See* Olives.] A bronze polycandelon, bearing an Aramaic dedicatory inscription mentioning the "holy place of Kefar Ḥananyah" and inscribed with two seven-branched menorahs, each flanked by a lulav and shofar, was found at el-Makr in the western Galilee and published by Jean-Baptiste Frey (1952) and, subsequently, by Joseph Naveh (1978, 1988).

The pottery center at Kefar Ḥananyah was studied as part of an interdisciplinary regional project investigating the manufacture and local trade of common pottery in the Galilee and Golan in the Late Hellenistic, Roman, and Early Byzantine periods. The ongoing project, directed by David Adan-Bayewitz, was begun in 1981 by him and the late Isadore Perlman at the Hebrew University of Jerusalem, and has continued at Bar-Ilan University and the Lawrence Berkeley National Laboratory, with the collaboration of Frank Asaro, Robert D. Giauque, and Helen V. Michel of the latter institution, and Moshe Wieder, of the former.

Archaeometric work conducted between 1981 and 1985 showed that Kefar Ḥananyah supplied most of the kitchen pottery of the Galilee, and a significant minority of the cooking vessels of the Golan, from the Early Roman through the Early Byzantine periods (c. mid-first century BCE–early fifth century CE). The vessel forms made at Kefar Ḥananyah have been identified and dated, and their geographic and quantitative distribution described (Adan-Bayewitz, 1993).

In the wake of this analytical study, Adan-Bayewitz directed three seasons of excavation at Kefar Ḥananyah (1986, 1987, 1989), under the auspices of Bar-Ilan University. Unearthed were remains of a Late Roman pottery kiln with a stone-paved approach, a rock-cut pit containing a large quantity of ash along one side of the access pavement, and an outer structure (possibly a fuel store) supported by ashlar pillars. All four components were built in a trench (3–3.5 m wide) cut into the slope. Two successive plaster-lined structures, which may have served as clay-soaking pools, were found about 10.5 m west of the kiln.

The kiln is a common Roman type, circular in plan (about 2.9 m in diameter) with a round central pillar (1 m in diameter). At the north (rear) and east of the furnace chamber one or two courses of cut stones line the bedrock. The entrance to the furnace chamber is about 0.9 m wide, and its jambs are built of ashlars. Following the destruction in the Early Byzantine period of the apparently disused kiln and outer structure, the recessed area served as a dump for discarded vessels—including an estimated equivalent of 9,500–13,000 whole vessels, about 98 percent of which were of two Kefar Ḥananyah vessel forms. Recovered in the excavations were pottery wasters of Kefar Ḥananyah vessels dating to the Early, Middle, and Late Roman–Early Byzantine periods.

The trench cut into the bedrock slope, in which the kiln and associated structures were built, also cut through an earlier roof-tile layer, above an Early Roman accumulation. A number of the tiles bore the impression of the Legio VI Ferrata (LEGVIF). No architectural remains associated with the roof-tile layer have been found.

Probes excavated in the final in situ section of the Kefar Ḥananyah aqueduct (see above) showed that that part of the aqueduct had not been constructed prior to the medieval period.

[*See also* Galilee, *article on* Galilee in the Hellenistic through Byzantine Periods; *and* Golan.]

BIBLIOGRAPHY

Rabbinic Sources, the Polycandelon Inscription, and the Medieval Texts

Frey, Jean-Baptiste. *Corpus inscriptionum iudaicarum,* vol. 2, *Asie-Afrique.* Rome, 1952. Presentation and discussion of the polycandelon inscription (see pp. 164–165, no. 980).

Klein, Samuel, ed. *Sefer ha-Yishuv.* Volume 1. Jerusalem, 1939. Collection of rabbinic texts on Kefar Ḥananyah (see p. 92).

Naveh, Joseph. *On Stone and Mosaic: The Aramaic and Hebrew Inscriptions from Ancient Synagogues* (in Hebrew). Tel Aviv, 1978. Presentation and discussion of the polycandelon inscription (see pp. 34–36, no. 16).

Naveh, Joseph. "Lamp Inscriptions and Inverted Writing." *Israel Exploration Journal* 38 (1988): 36–43. Magical elements of the polycandelon inscription.

Reiner, Elchanan, ed. *Sefer ha-Yishuv*. Vol. 3, *Division: Sacred Places*. Forthcoming. See "Kefar Ḥananya." Definitive publication and study of the texts on Kefar Ḥananyah dating to 1099–1517.

Safrai, Shmuel. "Notes on Palestine Studies" (in Hebrew). In *Benjamin de Vries Memorial Volume*, edited by Ezra Zion Melamed, pp. 328–333. Jerusalem, 1968. Reprinted in Shmuel Safrai, *'Eretz Yisra'el va-Ḥakhameha bi-Tekufat ha-Mishna ve-ha-Talmud*, pp. 105–112. Jerusalem, 1983. Collection of rabbinic texts on Kefar Ḥananyah (see p. 109).

Surveys and Studies

Braslavski, Joseph. "Kefar Ḥananya" (in Hebrew). *Bulletin of the Jewish Palestine Exploration Society* 1 (1933): 18–23. Important early study of the rock-cut public building, medieval Jewish settlement, and venerated tombs.

Frankel, Rafael. "The History of the Processing of Wine and Oil in Galilee in the Period of the Bible, the Mishna, and the Talmud" (in Hebrew). 2 vols. Ph.D. diss., Tel Aviv University, 1984. Studies of parts of several installations for olive-oil production at Kefar Ḥananyah.

Ilan, Zvi. "Kfar Hananya: History and Remains of a Jewish Village in Galilee." *Israel Land and Nature* (Winter 1981–1982): 61–69. Useful popular survey of literary sources and surface remains at the site.

Ilan, Zvi. "Ḥ. Kefar Ḥananya, Survey." *Israel Exploration Journal* 33 (1983): 255. Brief scientific report on the author's survey at Kefar Ḥananyah, including a plan of the rock-cut public building.

Ilan, Zvi. "A Survey of Ancient Synagogues in Galilee" (in Hebrew). *Eretz-Israel* 19 (1987): 170–198. Report on presentation of the survey of the two public buildings at Kefar Ḥananyah, including a plan of both structures (see pp. 184–186).

Ilan, Zvi. "The Aqueduct to Kefar Hanania" (in Hebrew). In *The Aqueducts of Ancient Palestine*, edited by David ʿAmit et al., pp. 97–100. Jerusalem, 1989.

The Archaeometric Study and the Archaeological Excavations

Adan-Bayewitz, David, and Isadore Perlman. "Local Pottery Provenience Studies: A Role for Clay Analysis." *Archaeometry* 27 (1985): 203–217. Initial analytical study of the Kefar Ḥananyah pottery.

Adan-Bayewitz, David. "Studies in Talmudic Archaeology 1: The Kavkav" (in Hebrew). *Sinai* 99 (1986): 164–177.

Adan-Bayewitz, David. "Studies in Talmudic Archaeology: Krozin" (in Hebrew). *Sidra* 5 (1989): 5–16. This and the study above identify specific products of Kefar Ḥananyah with vessels mentioned in rabbinic literature.

Adan-Bayewitz, David. "Kefar Ḥananya, 1989." *Israel Exploration Journal* 41 (1991): 186–188. Report on the third season of excavation at Kefar Ḥananyah.

Adan-Bayewitz, David. *Common Pottery in Roman Galilee: A Study of Local Trade*. Ramat Gan, 1993. Comprehensive work on the manufacture and distribution of Kefar Ḥananyah pottery, including discussions of the socioeconomic, ecological, and historical implications of the analytical data and detailed treatment of the rabbinic sources.

David Adan-Bayewitz

KEISAN, TELL, a high, prominent mound of about 15 acres, situated on the Akko plain between Haifa and Akko. Although the site is today about 8 km (5 mi.) inland, it originally connected the Mediterranean coast with the hills of Lower Galilee. It has been identified tentatively with biblical Achshaph (*Jos.* 11:1, 12:20, 19:25).

Tell Keisan was excavated by John Garstang and Alan Rowe in 1935 and 1936 and again from 1971 to 1980 by Roland de Vaux, Jacques Prignaud, Jacques Briend, and Jean Baptiste Humbert for the École Biblique et Archéologique Française in Jerusalem. [*See* École Biblique et Archéologique Française.]

There are scattered Neolithic remains, but the tell was first settled in the Early Bronze I–III period (stratum XVI, following the system of the 1935 excavation), with a city wall 5 m wide. Even more massive walls, embankments, and a glacis characterize the Middle Bronze Age strata (XV–XIV) city. A Late Bronze Age occupation, while attested, is not well documented (strata XIII–XI). The later excavations, however, delineated an important LB II/Iron I transitional horizon (Garstang and Rowe's stratum 13) characterized by both Egyptian imports and Late Mycenaean IIIC pottery. It came to a violent end in a destruction in the early twelfth century BCE plausibly attributed to the "Sea Peoples."

The Iron I levels at Tell Keisan (strata 12–9), some 3 m thick, are especially significant. Stratum 12 may represent a mid-twelfth-century BCE rebuilding by a northern group of the Sea Peoples (the Sherden?), with some Philistine Bichrome ware. Stratum 11 represents a more substantial urban establishment, in the late twelfth century BCE, that ended either in destruction or abandonment. Stratum 10 reflects the mixed cultural influences of Lower Galilee and the northern coast in the eleventh century BCE, with Philistine ware continuing alongside locally made pottery of Mycenaean and Cypriot derivation. The recent excavators refer to it as Levanto-Mycenaean, but it could be a forerunner of the slightly later Phoenician coastal ceramic repertoire. Some of the vessels were used in the manufacture of purple dye, for which the Phoenicians were well-known. Strata 9C–A, which cover much of the eleventh century BCE, revealed substantial well-planned, multiroomed structures laid out on a rectangular grid, although no city wall was in evidence. Philistine Bichrome ware disappeared by the end of stratum 9A, overlapping with distinctive Phoenician Bichrome jugs that begin in stratum 9B. Stratum 9 ends in about 1000 BCE in a conflagration that is also in evidence at other northern sites (Tel Abu Hawam IV; Hazor XI; Megiddo VIA); however, the destruction is more likely to be the result of local events than to any northern campaigns of King David (*2 Sm.* 8:3–12). Stratum 9 is perhaps best understood as marking the Phoenician ascendency in the area. [*See* Abu Hawam, Tell; Hazor; Megiddo; Phoenicians.]

Strata 8–6 (Iron II period) witnessed major changes. The settlement of stratum 8, which was relatively impoverished, initially reused some earlier walls and did not expand; this settlement continued from about 1000 BCE into about the mid-eighth century BCE with no notable feature but remarkable continuity. By the beginning of stratum 7, the old LB traditions were finally exhausted, and the subsequent pottery was typical Iron Age domestic ware, noteworthy only for scattered Cypro-Phoenician and Samaria wares. When stratum 5 ended, it was without any clear indication of the Assyrian destructions of the late eighth century BCE.

Strata 5–4 belong to the period of Assyrian conquest and domination (referred to by the later excavators as Iron III), when Tell Keisan underwent a sort of renascence. An Assyrian influence is then apparent and is reflected in "Palace" and other wares, as well as in Assyrian-style seals. [*See* Seals.] Stratum 4, with two phases, is characterized in its plan by a new rectangular grid. The later excavators see, especially in the pottery, a Phoenician culture combined with Neo-Assyrian elements. Numerous Phoenician amphorae found throughout the eighth–sixth centuries BCE point to maritime trade: links with Cyprus are especially close, but by late in stratum 4 (4A) large quantities of Aegean, Rhodian, and Ionian wares were also imported. Stratum 4A ended in destruction in the mid-seventh century BCE, perhaps the work of a punitive expedition to Akko in 643 BCE mentioned in the annals of Ashurbanipal.

Strata 3–1 are Persian and Hellenistic, respectively, and are characterized by Greek imports. The strata ended by the late second century BCE. In the Byzantine period a small Christian community occupied the site until the seventh century CE.

BIBLIOGRAPHY

Briend, Jacques, and Jean-Baptiste Humbert. *Tell Keisan, 1971–1976: Une cité phénicienne en Galilée.* Fribourg and Paris, 1980.

WILLIAM G. DEVER

KENYON, KATHLEEN MARY (1906–1978), archaeologist born in London, the elder daughter of Frederic Kenyon the papyrologist and director and principal librarian of the British Museum (1909–1930). Kathleen M. Kenyon was educated at St. Paul's Girls' School in London and at Somerville College, Oxford, where she specialized in history. She became a member of the Oxford Archaeological Society and was its first woman president. She was a good student and a fine athlete, with the energy and drive to make her a natural leader.

On graduation in 1929 she accompanied Gertrude Caton-Thompson (who had been a student and colleague of William Flinders Petrie) as general assistant, photographer, and driver, to excavate the stone ruins of Zimbabwe, in what was then Southern Rhodesia. Upon her return to England, she was recruited by R. E. Mortimer Wheeler and his wife Tessa to participate in a major excavation (1930–1936) of the Romano-British city of Verulamium (St. Albans).

From the Wheelers Kenyon learned the principles and techniques of the new stratigraphic method they had been developing since before World War I. It involves excavation by trenches, or squares, and very careful observation, interpretation, and recording (as excavation proceeds) of the soil strata encountered (distinguished by color, texture, and composition). When the vertical faces of the trenches and of balks running up to them are recorded and drawn to scale, it is possible to plot, in three dimensions, the stratigraphic positions and relationships of all structures and finds, and to assign relative dates to them. Absolute dates could be assigned on the basis of the pottery or coins contained in the pertinent strata. When the carbon-14 method of dating became available, the remanent radioactivity in preserved organic materials such as bone or wood could provide absolute dates. Although the method requires meticulous technique, the evidence for the conclusions educed is preserved for all to see and, if necessary, to reassess. Kenyon, who describes this method in *Beginning in Archaeology* (1952), introduced it to the Near East during her work with John W. Crowfoot at Samaria (1931–1933).

Back in England she was closely associated with Wheeler in the founding of the University of London Institute of Archaeology (1934). Before and after World War II (during which she served with the Red Cross) she worked at British sites. From 1948 to 1951, she joined John Ward-Perkins, director of the British School in Rome, in excavations at Sabratha in Tripolitania. Soundings into the essentially Romano-Byzantine city reached important Phoenician levels.

In 1951, Miss Kenyon became honorary director of the British School in Jerusalem. John Garstang had made important discoveries at Jericho (1931–1936) but raised problems requiring further investigation. Kenyon's excavations there (1952–1958) made Jericho the type-site in Palestine for the application of the Wheeler-Kenyon stratigraphic method.

In 1961 Kenyon began what would be seven years of excavation in Jerusalem. The site was an exceedingly difficult one because of its topography (its steeply sloped terrain), its history (the accumulated debris of centuries), and its being a living city (with its houses and roads in daily use). She was able to establish for the first time a historic framework for the city over its 3,800 years of existence.

In 1962 Kenyon became principal of St. Hugh's College, Oxford. When she retired in 1973, after a tenure of great practical and creative advantage to the college, she was able to concentrate on publication. Her detailed annual reports in the *Palestine Exploration Quarterly* during her excavations of Jericho and Jerusalem were supplemented by popular (but by no means superficial) general works. Of the definitive publications on Jericho, only two volumes of her *Excavations at Jericho* (1960, 1965) were released before her untimely death. However, she left much virtually completed work, which was subsequently edited and, where incomplete, augmented as volumes 3–5 (1981–1983). Since her death, three volumes on the Jerusalem expedition have been published (vols. 1, 2, and 4; 1985, 1990, and 1995). Kenyon made important contributions to the new (third) edition of the *Cambridge Ancient History*. While archaeological data were the chief sources for these works, in them and in her *Amorites and Canaanites* (1966), she attempted to relate the cultural, social, and political conditions reflected in written as well as archaeological documentation. The fourth and much-revised edition of her *Archaeology in the Holy Land* (1960) appeared, posthumously, in 1979.

Kathleen M. Kenyon is not only remembered for her dynamic and imaginative leadership in the field and the significance of her discoveries, but for the encouragement and training she devoted to scores of young students who, in turn, have made their reputations in archaeology all over the world. Her accomplishments led to many academic and international honors but the appreciation of her own country was marked most vividly by the DBE (Dame of the Order of the British Empire) conferred on her by Queen Elizabeth II in 1973.

[*See also* British School of Archaeology in Jerusalem; Jericho; Jerusalem; Samaria; *and the biographies of Caton-Thompson, Crowfoot, Garstang, and Wheeler.*]

BIBLIOGRAPHY

Crowfoot, John W., Kathleen M. Kenyon, and Eleazar L. Sukenik. *The Buildings at Samaria.* Samaria-Sebaste: Report of the Work of the Joint Expedition in 1931–1933 and of the Work of the British Expedition in 1935, no. 1. London, 1942.

Crowfoot, John W., Grace M. Crowfoot, and Kathleen M. Kenyon. *The Objects from Samaria.* Samaria-Sebaste: Report of the Work of the Joint Expedition in 1931–1933 and of the Work of the British Expedition in 1935, no. 3. London, 1957.

Franken, H. J., and Margaret L. Steiner. *Excavations in Jerusalem, 1961–1967,* vol. 2, *The Iron Age Extramural Quarter on the South-East Hill.* Oxford, 1990.

Kenrick, Philip M. *Excavations at Sabratha, 1948–1951: Report on the Excavations Conducted by Dame Kathleen Kenyon and John Ward-Perkins.* London, 1986.

Kenyon, Kathleen M. "Notes on the History of Jericho in the 2nd Millennium B.C." *Palestine Exploration Quarterly* (1951): 101–138.

Kenyon, Kathleen M. "Excavations at Jericho." *Palestine Exploration Quarterly* (1952): 4–6, 62–82; (1954): 45–63; (1955): 108–117; and (1960): 88–108.

Kenyon, Kathleen M. *Beginning in Archaeology.* London, 1953.

Kenyon, Kathleen M. *Digging Up Jericho.* London, 1957.

Kenyon, Kathleen M. *Archaeology in the Holy Land* (1960). 4th ed. New York, 1979.

Kenyon, Kathleen M. *Excavations at Jericho,* vol. 1, *The Tombs Excavated in 1952–54.* London, 1960.

Kenyon, Kathleen M. "Excavations in Jerusalem." *Palestine Exploration Quarterly* (1962): 72–89; (1963): 7–21; (1965): 9–20; (1966): 73–88; (1967): 65–73; and (1968): 97–111.

Kenyon, Kathleen M. *Excavations at Jericho,* vol. 2, *The Tombs Excavated in 1955–58.* London, 1965.

Kenyon, Kathleen M. *Amorites and Canaanites.* London, 1966.

Kenyon, Kathleen M. *Jerusalem: Excavating 3000 Years of History.* New York, 1967.

Kenyon, Kathleen M. *Digging Up Jerusalem.* London, 1974.

Kenyon, Kathleen M. *Excavations at Jericho,* vol. 3, *The Architecture and Stratigraphy of the Tell.* 2 vols. Edited by Thomas A. Holland. London, 1981.

Kenyon, Kathleen M., and Thomas A. Holland. *Excavations at Jericho,* vol. 4, *The Pottery Type Series and Other Finds.* London, 1982.

Kenyon, Kathleen M., and Thomas A. Holland. *Excavations at Jericho,* vol. 5, *The Pottery Phases of the Tell and Other Finds.* London, 1983.

Kenyon, Kathleen M. *The Bible and Recent Archaeology.* Revised by P. R. S. Moorey. London, 1987.

Moorey, P. R. S. *A Century of Biblical Archaeology.* Cambridge, 1991. See pages 63, 94–99, 122–126.

Moorey, P. R. S. "British Women in Near Eastern Archaeology: Kathleen Kenyon and the Pioneers." *Palestine Exploration Quarterly* (1992): 91–100.

Prag, Kay. "Kathleen Kenyon and *Archaeology in the Holy Land.*" *Palestine Exploration Quarterly* (1992): 109–123.

Tushingham, A. D., et al. *Excavations in Jerusalem, 1961–1967.* Vol. 1. Toronto, 1985.

Tushingham, A. D. "Kathleen Kenyon." *Proceedings of the British Academy* 71 (1985): 555–582.

Wilkes, John. "Kathleen Kenyon in Roman Britain." *Palestine Exploration Quarterly* (1992): 101–108.

A. D. TUSHINGHAM

KERAK (al-Karak; often Karak), site commanding the intersection of the main north–south route along the Transjordanian plateau with an important east–west route from the desert to the Dead Sea and the west bank of the Jordan River (31°11′ N, 35°42′ E).

The town occupies an irregular plateau (850 m north–south × 750 m east–west), at the north end of a ridge, naturally protected by steep escarpments. To the south, the ridge narrows into an isthmus (200 m long × 110–140 m wide) isolated from the rest of the ridge by deep ditches cut to the north and south: a castle (see below) occupies the resulting island.

Early History. Kerak was an important Moabite center. A Moabite inscription names Mesha, or his father Chemosh-yat, mid-ninth-century BCE kings of Moab, and suggests that Kerak had a temple to the god Chemosh. The place names Qîr-Mô'āb (*Is.* 15:1), Qîr-Ḥereś (*Jer.* 48:31, 48:36; *Is.* 16:11), and Qir-Ḥăreśet (*Is.* 16:7; *2 Kgs.* 3:25) are thought to refer to Kerak, perhaps because the Isaiah Targum renders Qîr-Mô'āb by the Aramaic Karkāʿ dĕ-Mô'āb. If correct, then Kerak was an important fortress in the revolt of Mesha against Israel and the site of the dramatic siege in 2 *Kings* 3:25–27. Kerak cannot be the Qarḥoh on Mesha's stela, which was evidently a quarter of Dibon.

Kerak was the administrative center of Moab during the Persian period (539/520–332 BCE). Nabatean pottery is commonly found there and Nabatean-Roman *spolia* (architectural and decorative fragments) are reused in the castle (see below). In about 130 Hadrian granted polis status to Kerak, which later had its own mint. The Madaba map (mid sixth-century CE) shows [Khara]khmōba as a walled, hilltop city. [*See* Madaba.]

Crusader Kerak and the Lordship of Oultrejourdain. Early in the twelfth century CE, the kings of Jerusalem built a line of fortifications to protect their revenue from Transjordan and to dominate the trade routes: al-Ḥabīs (Crusader, Cava de Suet, Cave de Sueth; Ar., ʿAyn Ḥabīs, al-Ḥabīs, Ḥabīs Jaldak), pre-1109(?); Montreal (Crusader, Mons regalis, Mont royal, Montreal; Ar., al-Shawbak), 1115; Ayla (Crusader, Helim) and Ile de Graye (Ar., Jazīra Fara'ūn, al-Qurayyah), 1116–17(?); Li Vaux Moys (Crusader, Li Vaux Moys, Castellum Vallis Moysis; Ar., al-Wu ayra); and two other castles in the Petra region, Celle (Ar., al-Ṣalʿā[?]) and Hormoz (Ar., al-Ḥabīs [?]), 1127(?). Castles were also built at Amman (Crusader, Ahamant) and Tafīla (Crusader, Taphila). [*See* Qurayyah; Amman.]

Oultrejourdain was kept mostly in the royal domain until about 1126 when it was granted to Pagan the Butler (Romain de Puy was not the first lord of Oultrejourdain but held lands in the Balqāʿ). The crown retained some castles and lands until 1161, when Baldwin III invested Philip de Milly with all royal property from Wadi Zarqa to the Red Sea. The lordship was crucial to the defense of the kingdom and was economically important: it exported bitumen, dates, grain, oil, salt, sugar, and wine. Kerak had its own Dead Sea port. Tolls were levied on caravans and bedouin passing through the region.

In 1142, Pagan built Kerak castle (Crusader, Chrac, Crac [not to be confused with Crac des Chevaliers in Syria], Crac de Montreal/Mont royal, Cracum Montis regalis, Petra Deserti, Pierre dou Desert, Civitas Petracensis; Ar., al-Karak, Karak al-Shawbak) to replace Montreal as the center of Oultrejourdain (see figure 1). His successors, Maurice and Philip de Milly, strengthened it. Philip entered the Templars in about 1165 and was succeeded by his daughter's husbands, first Miles de Plancy (1172–1174) and then Reynald de Châtillon (1177–1187). Nur al-Din and Salah ad-Din attempted to take Kerak in 1170 and 1173. When Reynald used Kerak as a base for raids on caravans protected by treaty and on al-Hijaz, Salah ad-Din launched systematic assaults (1183, 1184, 1187). Reynald was killed after the Battle of Hattin in July 1187. In November 1188, after a siege of eight months, Kerak capitulated.

Middle Islamic Kerak. Under the Ayyubids (1193–1263), Kerak usually belonged to the independent Syrian principality of Damascus, although al-Nāṣir Dāwūd (1227–1249) and al-Mughith ʿUmar (1250–1263) ruled Kerak as a semiautonomous principality. Al-ʿĀdil (1193–1198) refortified the castle, converted the cathedral into a mosque, and founded a mosque in Wadi Kerak. Al-Muʿaẓẓam (1198–1227) repaired the castle after the earthquake of 1211, constructed the western entrance tunnel, and ordered the improvement of the Ḥajj road from Damascus to al-Hijaz (work at Mu'ta and Maʿān was completed). Further refortification was carried out under al-Nāṣir Dāwūd, who built a palace within the castle. Al-Mugith ʿUmar repaired damage caused by the 1261 earthquake.

Under the Mamluk sultans (1263–1517), Kerak became the chief town of an administrative province stretching from Ziza to ʿAqaba and from the Dead Sea to the desert. Kerak's prosperity was largely dependent on the patronage of the sultans, although the region continued to export agricultural products, especially sugar. Baybars I (1260–1277) visited Kerak frequently and undertook its major refortification (see below). In the late thirteenth and fourteenth centuries, Kerak was used as a school where the sons of the dynasty could be educated in Arab ways and as a place of exile for

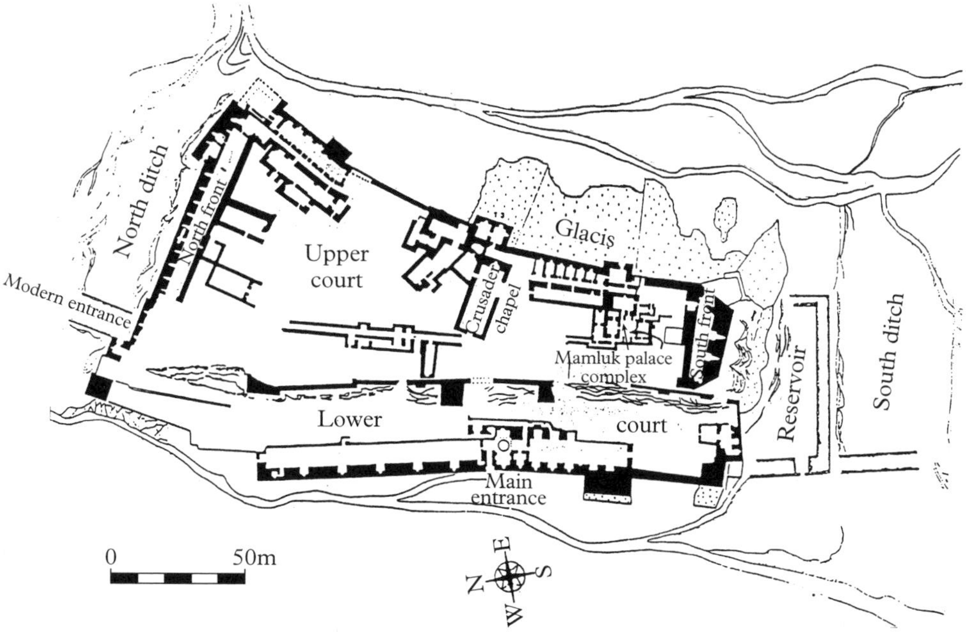

KERAK. Figure 1. *Plan of Kerak Castle.* (Courtesy J. Johns)

troublesome members of the ruling family. Al-Nāṣir Muḥammad spent two periods of exile in Kerak (1294–1298, 1308–1310) and in 1311 had a palace, bath, school, khan, hospital, and mosque built there. For a few months in 1342, under al-Nāṣir Aḥmad, Kerak became the capital of the Mamluk state. During the fifteenth century, Mamluk interest in Kerak waned, and local tribes increasingly came to dominate the town.

In 1517, an Ottoman governor was installed at Kerak. The Ottomans attempted to retain control of the town throughout the sixteenth century, but soon after 1600 it was in Arab hands. Successive Ottoman expeditions (1655–1656, 1678–1679, 1710–1711) failed to regain control.

Remains. The town's walls and towers are well preserved. Burj al-Ẓāhir is a massive salient, very similar to the castle's south front, and defends the northern extremity of the plateau. A foundation inscription of Baybars I appears on its interior face (*RCEA* 4733). *Burj al-Banawī,* a round tower on the south wall, also carries a foundation inscription of Baybars flanked by two heraldic "lions of Baybars" (*RCEA* 4734). *Burj al-Ṣaʿūb* is an elaborate tower with a machicolated parapet and a talus defending a postern at the easternmost point of the circuit. Entrance to the town was originally through two subterranean passages: northeast of the Burj al-Ṣaʿūb and west of the Burj al-Ẓāhir, the latter dated to 1227 (*RCEA* 3965).

The Crusader cathedral was converted into the *jāmiʿ* (congregational mosque) under al-Malik al-ʿĀdil. The early twentieth-century mosque on the same site preserves two Arabic inscriptions in the prayer hall: one records the foundation of the *jāmiʿ* in 1198 (*RCEA* 3800A); the other records repairs carried out in about 1380 (Albert de Luynes, *Voyages d'exploration à la Mer Morte,* 3 vols. Paris, 1871–1876, vol. 2, pp. 200–201, no. 18). A third inscription, on the minaret, records Sultan Barqūq's perpetual exemption of the Kerakis from all property taxes (*ibid.*, pp. 201–202, no. 19).

The Greek church (of St. George?) is a mid-nineteenth-century reconstruction of a Byzantine structure. The smaller Greek church of St. George is apparently medieval in date. In the cemetery below Burj al-Ẓāhir is a nineteenth-century (?) *qubba* (domed tomb) identified as the tomb of Noah, a claimed shared by Kerak Nūh in Lebanon. At nearby Mazar, the mausoleum of Jaʿfar ibn Abū Ṭālib, a companion of the prophet who fell at the Battle of Mut'a, is incorporated into the modern mosque: two Arabic inscriptions record work on the mausoleum in 1327 and 1351 (*ibid.*, pp. 206–208, nos. 23–24).

The constructional history of the castle has yet to be thoroughly investigated. No standing remains are indisputably pre-Crusader. Two distinct phases of Crusader construction may be distinguished, however, and the south and west defenses were extensively rebuilt under Baybars I. There is considerable amount of postmedieval alteration of the interior apartments.

The castle consists of a large upper court occupying the crest of the ridge and a lower court built on a terrace to the west. The north front, built of huge limestone blocks, was originally flanked by two massive salients: of these only the eastern survives; the modern entrance is through the ruined west corner. The much-damaged Crusader chapel and adjoining sacristy lie in the middle of the upper court. South and west of the chapel, below the court, are the apartments of the Mamluk palace. Of particular note are a small entrance court decorated by a plaque with an intricate inlaid geometric design (originally one of a pair); a reception hall; and what may be a small mosque. The south end of the castle is dominated by the massive south front overlooking the castle reservoir and the south ditch: the foundation inscription of Baybars I is on the exterior face. The lower court is separated from the upper court by a curtain wall. In Mamluk times, the principal entrance was through a monumental gate in the west wall, into a long gallery beneath the lower court. There are also small posterns in the north and south fronts. The central salient in the west wall of the lower court bears a much-damaged foundation inscription of Baybars I.

[*See also* Ayyubid-Mamluk Dynasties; Crusader Period.]

BIBLIOGRAPHY

Brown, Robin M. "Excavations in the Fourteenth Century A.D. Mamluk Palace at Kerak." *Annual of the Department of Antiquities of Jordan* 33 (1989): 287–304. Brief excavation report.

Canova, Reginetta. *Iscrizioni e monumenti protocristiani del paese di Moab.* Sussidi allo Studio delle Antichità Cristiane, 4. The Vatican, 1954. Fundamental guide to the Christian inscriptions and monuments of Kerak.

Deschamps, Paul. *Les Châteaux des Croisés en Terre-Sainte,* vol. 2, *La défense du royaume de Jérusalem.* Bibliothèque Archéologique et Historique, vol. 34. Paris, 1939. Still the only attempt at a thorough survey of the castle and town fortifications.

Ghawanmah, Yusuf D. *Imārat al-Karak al-Ayyūbiyyah.* Kerak, 1980. The only existing study of Ayyubid Kerak; includes an English summary. Alternatively, see Humphreys below.

Ghawanmah, Yusuf D. *Tar'īkh sharqī al-Urdunn fī ʿaṣr dawlat al-Mamālik.* 2 vols. Amman, 1979. The only existing study of Mamluk Kerak; includes an English summary. Alternatively, see Irwin and Thorau below.

Gibson, John C. L. *Textbook of Syrian Semitic Inscriptions,* vol. 1, *Hebrew and Moabite Inscriptions.* Oxford, 1971. See pages 71–83 for the Mesha stela and the Moabite inscription from Kerak.

Humphreys, R. Stephen. *From Saladin to the Mongols: The Ayyūbids of Damascus, 1193–1260.* Albany, N.Y., 1977. Useful synthesis based on the primary sources, containing much information about Ayyubid Kerak.

Irwin, Robert. *The Middle East in the Middle Ages: The Early Mamluk Sultanate, 1250–1382.* Carbondale, Ill., 1986. Short, lively account of the early Mamluk sultanate, with useful material on Kerak.

Mayer, Hans Eberhard. *Die Kreuzfahrerherrschaft Montréal (Sobak) Jordanien im 12. Jahrhundert.* Wiesbaden, 1990. Thorough account of the history of Crusader Oultrejourdain; see also Tibble below.

Pringle, Denys. *The Churches of the Crusader Kingdom of Jerusalem: A Corpus.* Vol. 1. Cambridge, 1993. The first of three volumes. See especially the entries "ʿAin al-Ḥabīs" (p. 26), "Jazīrat Faraʿūn" (pp.

274–275), and "Karak" (pp. 286–295), which include useful and copious bibliographies.

Répertoire chronologique d'épigraphie arabe (RCEA). 18 vols. to date. Edited by Étienne Combe, Jean Sauvaget, and Gaston Wiet. Cairo, 1931–. Standard collection of Arabic epigraphy.

Thorau, Peter. *The Lion of Egypt: Sultan Baybars I and the Near East in the Thirteenth Century*. London, 1992. Biography of the first Mamluk sultan, containing many useful references to Late Ayyubid and Early Mamluk Kerak.

Tibble, Steven. *Monarchy and Lordships in the Latin Kingdom of Jerusalem, 1099–1291*. Oxford, 1989. Useful supplement to Mayer (above). Tibble's reinterpretation of the early years of Oultrejourdain (c. 1115–c. 1126 CE) is preferable to Mayer's.

JEREMY JOHNS

KESTEL, an Early Bronze Age tin mine and its associated specialized mining areas, located 4 km (2.5 mi.) from the town of Çamardı and situated upslope from several rivers coursing through the Niğde Massif, a large volcanic dome formation in south-central Turkey (37°50′ N, 34°58′ E). The Kuruçay stream, with the highest analyzed cassiterite (tin oxide) sediments, carrys with it sediments rich in pyrite, hematite, garnet, tourmaline, magnetite, scheelite, cinnabar, titanite, rutile, apatite, monazite, and gold. The tin appears as sand-sized brilliant red, orange, yellow, and (rarely) black cassiterite grains that can be easily separated by manual means such as a pan or a vanning shovel and very little water. Because of their high specific gravity, tin particles sediment out from the less dense magnetite, hematite, and quartz. This simple process was replicated a number of times at Celaller village in 1992 by Bryan Earl from Cornwall, England. The Kestel mine is characterized by intense tectonic movement and is in a major subduction zone, where mineralization is common. The mine was cut into a slope composed of granite, marble, gneiss, and quartzite. The site of the Early Bronze Age miner's village, Göltepe, lies 2 km due south of the Kestel tin mine, across the valley on a prominent hilltop that overlooks the Kuruçay stream.

Cassiterite was found at the Kestel mine by the Turkish Geological Research and Survey (MTA) after sifting through 80 tons of alluvial stream sediments in the course of a major five-year research project investigating the sources of heavy minerals. K. Aslıhan Yener investigated and excavated the tin mine from 1987 to 1989 and in collaboration with Lynn Willies from 1990 to 1992. Only subeconomic material remains unmined today. The most convincing evidence of former tin production is the one ton of metallurgical debris, such as crucible fragments with tin-rich slag accretion, found in excavation at the neighboring site of Göltepe and at the entrance to the Kestel mine. Recent analyses by atomic absorption spectroscopy from veins remaining unmined inside the Kestel mine indicated that even after extensive mining in antiquity, the veins still contained more than 1.5 percent tin. [*See* Spectroscopy.] There have been two primary mineralizing episodes: an early tin-bearing one and a later one of hematite with weak tin. Willies notes that evidence of ore extraction continues below the marble into the underlying quartzitic schist and granitic pegmatites. As of the 1992 excavation season, the depth of the Kestel mine measured 1.5 km in its greatest known extent.

As presently understood, the Kestel mine was originally in operation in about 3000 BCE, probably as an open-pit-mining operation. During the early EB I–II, the mine expanded into shaft and gallery systems, workshops were set up outside the mine entrance, and Göltepe was settled. Göltepe grew into what may have been a substantial walled town and tin-processing workshop toward the middle of the third millennium (EB II), at the same time that bronze was being widely used in Anatolia and was increasing in use in Syria and Mesopotamia. The settlement and the mine attained their largest extent during this and the early part of the EB III period. At that time, they comprised one of a number of centers lining the strategic passes through the Taurus Mountains. The sites may have controlled resources, production, and intermontane traffic during the pre-Akkadian period.

Aside from the original four soundings done in 1987–1988, the soundings made in 1991 and 1992 in the Kestel mine were to obtain a chronological sequence for the mine and to determine the extent and nature of the tin mineralization. Mined by fire setting in antiquity, five samples of charcoal from excavated contexts inside the Kestel mine gave radiocarbon determinations of 2070–1880 BCE, calibrated to 2870–2200 BCE, dating its use firmly in the Early Bronze Age. Another six dates recently obtained suggest an even earlier beginning for the mine (2740 BCE ±100 calibrated 3240–3100 BCE).

In order to test the assumption that cassiterite was the targeted mineral in the Bronze Age, four small-scale soundings 1 × 2 m in size were initiated inside the galleries in 1988 and 1989. The assumption was that the detritus of mining activity would yield important information about dating the mine and about the original ore body composition. Sounding S.2 (1.5 × 1 m) was placed in chamber VI at the confluence of five upsloping galleries, some of which measured a scant 60 cm in diameter. These galleries had circular cross sections and differed morphologically from chambers I and II, which have larger entrances. Careful study of the stratified assemblage indicated that the mining debris dates to the Bronze Age. Also supporting this view were the massive layers of rubble with third-millennium ceramics that were overlaid by thin horizons dating to the Byzantine period, but without any associated mining debris. Thus, the fact that there are Byzantine-period strata in the mine, dated by ceramics and radiocarbon (charcoal samples from sounding S2, at −30 cm = 380 ±60 CE, calibrated 347–609 CE), does not indicate that mining took place during these later periods.

The discovery of a large diabase mortar or anvil with two circular hollows on one surface provided information about the specific tools of extraction and beneficiation in this chamber. The EB sherds are mostly dark-burnished and unburnished varieties, with a red-burnished and micaceous finish. Some cruder examples, such as a holemouth jar and several straw-tempered types, also emerged in the lowest strata, suggesting the existence of a Late Chalcolithic phase in this mine as well.

Sounding S2 has established several discernible features about this chamber. First of all, cassiterite was being mined in the third millennium. The technique entailed fire setting and then battering the ore with heavy hammerstones. Mortars, pestles, and bucking stones indicate that some ore beneficiation was also taking place inside the mine. It is apparent from the stone tool types found inside that hammerstones for battering and pulverizing the ore were being utilized. Surprisingly, however, bucking stones, a stone with one flat surface and a hollow in the middle, indicate that grinding also took place. The debris may have been used as backfill in the mine. The presence of beneficiation suggests that some fine-scale processing was essential for extraction and may indicate that veins were small or that testing of the particular area of the deposit by empirical means was necessary and was more efficiently carried out within the mine. It may also be that some tools were stored or discarded in the mine. Therefore, the ore was battered, pecked, and enriched there. Second, the presence of pottery with open forms, the domestic fauna, and a hearth suggest that a certain minimal amount of domestic activity also took place inside the mine. Larger ceramic forms, presumably to contain water for beneficiation and drinking or cooking, may have been used for such short-term storage.

The soundings in the mine have provided important information about the tools employed in the technology of Bronze Age mining and ore pulverization; they also indicate that the mine probably provided some amount of habitation or shelter. The Kestel excavations have helped define an interactive system between the mine and Göltepe, with its specialized sectors devoted to smelting tin. Tin smelting entailed an initial ore enrichment at Kestel, followed by grinding and washing phases at Göltepe. Fired in crucibles of various sizes, the resulting tin metal was fabricated into ingots by pouring the molten metal into molds. The data from this project have led to the irrefutable conclusion that tin was mined at Kestel and processed at Göltepe in the third millennium. Reconstruction can now proceed to question where the products went and what the impact of this strategic industry was on the bronze producers.

In the process of mapping and excavating test trenches inside the galleries, a mortuary/burial chamber was discovered in several abandoned mine shafts. Mortuary traditions as well as data on status, diet, and population can be derived from the excavation of this new evidence. One extensive mortuary chamber contained a number of different burial traditions—pithos burials, stone-built tombs, simple internment, and rock-cut chamber tombs—spanning a date from the Late Chalcolithic/EB I to the end of the third millennium. [*See* Burial Practices.] Broken fragments of human skeletal material occurred throughout the chambers. A preliminary assessment has identified a minimum of eight individuals interred in the chamber, based on counts and aging information from femurs, mandibles, and a few pelvises. So far, this small demographic sample contains children, men, and at least one woman, mirroring a true population composition. One is an infant fewer than two years old. Three are subadults younger than eighteen years of age: one twelve–fifteen-year-old, one from five–ten years old, and the other approximately eight. Four adults are represented, including one female and one probable male. [*See* Demography; Paleopathology.]

Pottery in association within the burial chamber has chronological and stylistic parallels with the Göltepe and Kestel assemblages. Red- and black-burnished wares, light-clay minature lug ware, painted Anatolian metallic wares, and imported ceramics such as Syrian bottles and Syrian metallic wares link the mine not only with the processing site, Göltepe, but with neighboring regions as well. A copper spiral akin to examples dating to the end of the third millennium, as well as Syrian bottles, plain simple ware, and Syrian metallic wares, indicate interregional connections with Syria and Mesopotamia, as well as the Mediterranean coast.

In addition to Kestel representing the earliest and largest shaft-and-gallery systems related to tin mining, the 1992 research indicated that an earlier phase of occupation existed on the slope of the mine, most likely dating to the Late Chalcolithic/EB I. Data on initial settlement in this area and the earliest extraction phase for the mine can be derived from this area. It is clear that the mortuary chamber will be an important source of data and will be critical to understanding each of the settlements and the interaction among them. So far no comparable examples of burials in mine chambers are known from other regions.

[*See also* Göltepe; Metals, *article on* Artifacts of the Neolithic, Bronze, and Iron Ages; *and* Taurus Mountains.]

BIBLIOGRAPHY

Sayre, E. V., et al. "Statistical Evaluation of the Presently Accumulated Lead Isotope Data from Anatolia and Surrounding Regions." *Archaeometry* 34.1 (1992): 73–105.

Willies, Lynn. "An Early Bronze Age Tin Mine in Anatolia." *Bulletin of the Peak District Mines Historical Society* 11 (1990): 91–96.

Willies, Lynn. "Report on the 1991 Archaeological Survey of Kestel Tin Mine, Turkey." *Bulletin of the Peak District Mines Historical Society* 11 (1991): 241–247.

Willies, Lynn. "Reply to Hall and Steadman." *Journal of Mediterranean Archaeology* 5.1 (1992): 99–103.

Yener, K. Aslıhan, et al. "Kestel: An Early Bronze Age Source of Tin Ore in the Taurus Mountains, Turkey." *Science* 244 (1989): 200–203.

Yener, K. Aslıhan. "Stable Lead Isotope Sudies of Central Taurus Ore Sources and Related Artifacts from Eastern Mediterranean Chalcolithic and Bronze Age Sites." *Journal of Archaeological Science* 18 (1991): 541–577.

K. ASLIHAN YENER

KETEF HINNOM, Iron Age cemetery located along a high scarp on the southwestern bank of the Hinnom Valley, south and southwest of Jerusalem (31°40′ N, 35°15′ E; map reference 173 × 131). This necropolis is located on the grounds of St. Andrew's Scottish Church and Hospice. The site is known by its Hebrew name, which means "shoulder of Hinnom."

Three major necropoli served Iron Age Jerusalem: the eastern necropolis in the village of Silwan, the northern necropolis north of the Damascus Gate, and the western necropolis along the slopes of the Hinnom Valley. The southern and southwestern extents of the Hinnom Valley were utilized in response to the growth of the city in the eighth and seventh centuries BCE. Thirty-seven tombs have been located along the length of the valley. This area of ancient Jerusalem and its environs were partially surveyed by R. A. S. Macalister in 1900. [*See the biography of Macalister.*] More recently, bench tombs at Ketef Hinnom were excavated by Gabriel Barkay (1979–1988), under the auspices of Tel Aviv University. These tombs date to the end of Iron II (late eighth–sixth centuries BCE). Some of the cave tombs may have been used in the Second Temple period as well, however.

A variety of burial types were found at Ketef Hinnom, including plain pit graves and bench tombs. [*See* Tombs; Burial Sites; Burial Techniques.] These bench tombs are typical of Judah in the Iron II and include features such as sarcophagi carved into the bedrock, burial benches carved along the walls, projecting cornices, carved headrests, and the use of two Egyptian cubit standards. [*See* Sarcophagus.] Typically, bench tombs consist of a single or multichambered tomb in which a series of benches is cut along the chamber walls. A small entrance opens to a forecourt that leads into a central hall. Burial chambers are arranged around this central hall. The body was laid out on a bench, into which headrests were often carved. When a new body was interred, the earlier bones and grave goods were gathered and placed in repositories under the burial benches. It is believed that in this way extended families were buried for generations in the same chamber tomb. [*See* Grave Goods.]

Barkay excavated nine bench tombs at Ketef Hinnom, all of which were cut into the bedrock. None of the roughly square tombs was intact, as their ceilings had collapsed. Additionally, the area had been used as a quarry in antiquity. Five of the tombs were single chambered, with benches along three sides. Carved stone headrests were found in several tombs. In cave 13 the headrests were so arranged as to hold two parallel sets of bodies ordered head to foot. Cave 20 is distinctive in its plan, dimensions, and decorative details. It is a multichambered tomb with parallels in Jerusalem's northern necropolis and at Beth-Shemesh tombs 5–8. [*See* Beth-Shemesh.] This tomb also used the short Egyptian measurement system (the *amah*), as opposed to the long, or royal, one used in the other tombs. Many of the tombs throughout Jerusalem utilized such a standardized system of measurement, suggesting the use of a set of plans or blueprints. The Israelite system of measurement, the cubit, was based on the Egyptian system.

The most spectacular find from Ketef Hinnom was the undisturbed repository in room 25, located in burial cave 24. Cave 24 is a complex, multichambered tomb with five chambers off the central hall. A variety of features were used in interring the dead, including benches, headrests, and deep grooves. In room 25 the six headrests could accommodate six bodies arranged side by side. This chamber is roughly 3 × 1.8 m and 2 m high. A cache of mortuary goods was found in the repository that the excavator dates from the seventh century BCE to some time after the Babylonian destruction in 586 BCE (Barkay, 1984). The remains of more than ninety-five individuals were found along with more than one thousand objects. The burial goods included 263 whole ceramic vessels, a bathtub coffin, Scythian iron arrowheads, bronze axheads, bone objects, alabaster vessels, beads, a glass bottle, more than one hundred pieces of silver jewelry, silver seals, and gold objects. A sixth-century BCE coin from the Aegean island of Kos found in this tomb is one of the earliest coins found in Israel. Most significant was the recovery of two small silver amulets inscribed with priestly blessings. The silver amulets were delicately incised, and the largest is only 97 mm long and 27 mm wide. They date to the mid-seventh or early sixth centuries BCE. One amulet records the name *Yahweh*. The wording of both scrolls is almost identical to the priestly benediction in *Numbers* 6:24–26 (Barkay, 1983). This represents the earliest surviving biblical passage, antedating the Dead Sea Scrolls copies by some four hundred years. [*See* Dead Sea Scrolls.]

The importance of this tomb is immeasurable. Its material greatly expands what is known of the nature of the Jewish community in Jerusalem after the Babylonian destruction. Hillel Geva (*New Encyclopedia of Archaeological Excavations in the Holy Land,* edited by Ephraim Stern, vol. 2, p. 715, Jerusalem and New York, 1993) suggests that the western necropolis was used for the lower classes and the eastern necropolis of Silwan for nobility and high officials. While the proximity and architectural elaboration found in the Silwan necropolis indeed supports this suggestion, the notion of a lower-class necropolis at Ketef Hinnom must be reassessed in light of the finds in room 25 of cave 24.

[*See also* Jerusalem.]

BIBLIOGRAPHY

Barkay, Gabriel. "The Divine Name Found in Jerusalem." *Biblical Archaeology Review* 9.2 (1983): 14–19. Popular account of the excavation, conservation, and interpretation of the silver amulets.

Barkay, Gabriel. "Excavations on the Hinnom Slope in Jerusalem" (in Hebrew). *Qadmoniot* 17 (1984): 94–108. One of the only detailed scholarly articles regarding the Tel Aviv excavations at Ketef Hinnom. Not, however, a final report; a more complete report of the material culture from cave 24 is still needed.

Barkay, Gabriel, and Amos Kloner. "Jerusalem Tombs from the Days of the First Temple." *Biblical Archaeology Review* 12.2 (1986): 23–39. Popular account and review of Iron Age tombs from the northern necropolis.

Barkay, Gabriel. *Ketef Hinnom: A Treasure Facing Jerusalem's Walls.* Israel Museum Catalogue, no. 274. Jerusalem, 1986. See pages 34–35 for a brief review of the finds.

Bloch-Smith, Elizabeth. *Judahite Burial Practices and Beliefs about the Dead.* Journal for the Study of the Old Testament, Supplement 123. Sheffield, 1992. Excellent scholarly work providing a detailed analysis of Iron Age Judean burials; recommended for any serious research on this subject.

King, Philip J. *Jeremiah: An Archaeological Companion.* Louisville, Ky., 1993. Semipopular book that intertwines the archaeological data from the seventh and sixth centuries BCE with the biblical narrative from the same period. A very useful background volume for Iron II.

Mazar, Amihai, and Gabriel Barkay. "The Iron Age." In *The Archaeology of Ancient Israel,* edited by Amnon Ben-Tor, pp. 258–373. New Haven, 1992. Contains an overview of the significance of Ketef Hinnom in Iron II–III (see esp. pp. 369–371).

Ussishkin, David. *The Village of Silwan.* Jerusalem, 1993. Excellent detailed architectural analysis of Jerusalems' eastern necropolis at Silwan, with historical background for the study of Iron Age mortuary practices and the archaeology of Iron Age Jerusalem.

J. P. DESSEL

KHABUR. The Khabur River catchment of northern Syro-Mesopotamia can be divided into the Khabur Triangle, or Upper Khabur, and the Lower Khabur. The former, where precipitation ranges annually from 500 mm northeast of modern Qamishli at the Syro-Turkish border to 250 mm just south of Hassekeh, is a broad agricultural region formed by a number of tributaries, the most important of which is Wadi Jaghjagh. The narrow alluvial valley of Lower Khabur cuts through very dry areas (from 250 mm to less than 150 mm annual precipitation) on its course to the Euphrates River.

Modern exploration of the Upper Khabur began in 1850 with Austin Henry Layard, who uncovered a Neo-Assyrian *lammasu* ("winged bull") at Tell Araban, today known as Tell Agaga, ancient Shadikanni. In campaigns in 1899, 1911–1913, and 1927–1929, M. von Oppenheim explored the western Khabur and excavated Tell Ḥalaf. Between the world wars, Antoine Poidebard pioneered aerial reconnaissance in his study of the Roman limes system along the Lower Khabur and Wadi Jaghjagh to Nisibin. In 1934–1935 Max Mallowan surveyed portions of the Khabur Triangle and began excavations at Tell Brak and Chaghar Bazar. Recent surveys have been conducted by Frank Hole and by D. J. W. Meijer in the northeast part of the Khabur Triangle and by B. Lyonnet in its central area. Hartmut Kühne has surveyed the lower Khabur and, in anticipation of a new dam, J. Monchambert has surveyed the Middle Khabur. [*See the biographies of Layard, Poidebard, and Mallowan.*]

These surveys, and excavations at approximately thirty sites, document occupation from the Neolithic period to the present; it reached a peak in the late third and early second millennia BCE, both in number of sites and population, estimated from total hectares occupied. Some Bronze Age sites are quite large, ranging from 30 to more than 100 ha (74–247 acres): Mozan, Hamoukar, Barri, Leilan, Chuera, Mabtuh (East), Hamidi, Brak, Beydar, Chaghar Bazar. [*See* Mozan, Tell; Leilan, Tell; Chuera, Tell; Brak, Tell.] In the western part of the Upper Khabur about a dozen Bronze Age tells are surrounded by large earthworks; von Oppenheim first noted this unusual feature and coined the term *kranzhügel,* "wreath-shaped tell," for them. Settlement was relatively sparse from the end of the Middle Bronze Age until the twentieth century.

The earliest excavated remains from the Khabur date to the Pre-Pottery Neolithic B (PPNB) at Tell Feyda, followed by Hassuna material from Kashkashuk II. Von Oppenheim first encountered painted Halafian ceramics of the Chalcolithic period in deep soundings at the ware's namesake, Tell Ḥalaf. [*See* Ḥalaf, Tell.] Important Uruk (late fourth millennium) remains, including the beveled-rim bowl, related to styles from southern Mesopotamia, have been found throughout the Khabur catchment. At Tell Brak, Mallowan excavated the Eye temple from the Uruk period; it contained scores of small stone amulets with exaggerated eyes.

It has been posited that there was a break in occupation in the early third millennium and that the first complex polities—that is, secondary-state formation—in the Khabur, rather than being an outgrowth of Uruk influence, occurred in the mid-third millennium at dry-farming sites such as Tell Leilan. At issue is ceramic chronology: a style of painted and incised pottery called Ninevite 5, which dates to the first half of the third millennium, is found in the eastern part of the Upper Khabur to beyond the Tigris River. Chronologically problematic Metallic/Stone ware is distributed throughout the western Khabur and beyond. It is moot whether the significant increase in number and size of sites during the second half of the third millennium marks the transition to complex society. Nevertheless, this sudden increase in sites and the location of many of them, such as Tell Chuera and other *kranzhügel* tells such as Tell Beydar, where "Ebla" style tablets have been found, in agriculturally marginal areas, remains to be explained, as does their substantial decline beginning in the second quarter of the second millennium BCE. Several research teams have sought to reconstruct climatic and environmental conditions in the Khabur. A group led by Harvey Weiss of Yale University now suggests that there were climatic fluctuations during the third millennium, climaxed by a severe drought at the end of the Akkadian period, that lasted for several hundred years during the last quarter of the millennium.

On the banks of the lower Khabur River several sites served as storage centers for grain; they were found during salvage excavations in anticipation of a dam to be constructed south of Hassekeh. At Tell Raqai (excavated by Glenn Schwartz and Hans Curvers for Johns Hopkins University and the University of Amsterdam) a circular mud-brick building was identified as a granary complex, and at Tell 'Atij (excavated by Michel Fortin of Laval University) there are storage facilities but little evidence for domestic habitation. Similar configurations are known at Ziyada (excavated by Giorgio Buccellati, Daniela Buia, and Steven Reimer for the University of California, Los Angeles) and at Kerma (excavated by Muntaha Saghié of the Lebanese University in Beirut). It has been proposed that these sites were collection points for grain to be shipped downstream to Mari, or for pastoralists during the summer months when fodder was scarce. [*See* Mari.]

At Tell Brak, the palace of the Sargonic king Naram-Sin, discovered by Mallowan (1947), has been augmented by large mud-brick public buildings in area SS (excavated more recently by David and Joan Oates. Weiss's soundings at Tell Leilan provide a ceramic sequence for much of the third millennium and show that the site greatly increased in size in about 2600 BCE.

During the early second millennium BCE, in the Middle Bronze Age (Old Assyrian, Old Babylonian periods), historical evidence for the Khabur is greatly expanded from archives of the period that tell of the Old Assyrian trade network that passed through the Khabur between Aššur and Anatolia: from the Mari archives of the Old Babylonian period, and recently from post-Mari archives at Tell Leilan (ancient Shubat-Enlil, once the seat of power for Shamsi-Adad, who briefly controlled much of Northern Mesopotamia). [*See* Assyrians; Aššur; Anatolia, *article on* Ancient Anatolia.] With his demise and the destruction of Mari by Hammurabi of Babylon, the Khabur Triangle came under the influence of Yamḫad, ancient Aleppo, for a time. [*See* Aleppo.] Habur ware dates to this period, a painted pottery Mallowan first identified at Chaghar Bazar. The presence of Hurrians increased during this period, one early center of which was Urkish (possibly Tell Mozan, being excavated by Buccellati and Marilyn Kelly-Buccellati). [*See* Hurrians.]

By the middle of the second millennium BCE, the Hurrian-dominated kingdom of Mitanni had emerged as the main power of northern Syro-Mesopotamia; its capital Waššukanni, located in the Khabur Triangle, has not been positively identified, although Tell Fakhariyah is one candidate. [*See* Mitanni; Fakhariyah, Tell.] During this period settlement was relatively sparse, and neither at Brak nor Chuera are Mitanni occupation remains extensive. At Tell Brak there was a palace (that can be reconstructed as a *ḫilani*) and an accompanying temple. During the fourteenth century BCE, Mitannian power collapsed in the face of Hittite pressure, but the main beneficiary in the Khabur region was Aššur, center of the Assyrians, who, after displacing the Mitanni, fought campaigns against pastoralists there. Their struggle led to the establishment of a number of Middle Assyrian settlements, including the fortress of Dur Katlimmu at Tell Sheikh Ḥamad on the Lower Khabur. Kühne recovered a small archive from his excavation at Tell Sheikh Ḥamad, and dates the first irrigation canals on the Khabur to that period. Two painted wares of the Late Bronze Age are Late Ḫabur (Khabur) ware and Nuzi (Mitanni) ware, but the majority of the pottery is plain. [*See* Sheikh Ḥamad, Tell; Nuzi.]

Early in the Iron Age (1200–333 BCE) a major center of the Aramean kingdom of Bit-Baḫiani was the city of Guzana (modern Tell Ḥalaf), which has provided a significant collection of early Aramean art and architecture. [*See* Arameans.] Von Oppenheim excavated two palaces on the acropolis. The so-called temple-palace has the plan of a *ḫilani*. Roman occupation obscures another major Aramean center at Tell Fakhariyah, where McEwan excavated a palace. Recently, a statue of *Hdys'y*, with a bilingual (Aramaic and Akkadian) inscription was discovered there by chance.

In the eighth–seventh centuries BCE, the Khabur region was incorporated into the Assyrian Empire. Neo-Assyrian palace ware was found at Tell Ḥalaf, and major settlements were located at Tell Beydar in the Khabur Triangle and on the Lower Khabur at Tell Agaga and Tell Sheikh Ḥamad. Tell Agaga, where Layard began his explorations in the Khabur, has recently been reexcavated by Assad Mahmoud. A major Neo-Assyrian fortress and administrative center was built at Tell Sheikh Ḥamad, ancient Dur Katlimmu. In the lower city, building F has a *ḫilani* plan, and rooms in building G were decorated with painted lotus friezes.

Settlement in the Neo-Babylonian, Persian, and Hellenistic periods is not well documented archaeologically in the Khabur. During the Roman period, the Khabur Triangle was a frontier between Roman and Parthian/Sasanian (Persian) control. Poidebard's reconstruction of the limes system is currently undergoing reevaluation. In the Byzantine and Islamic periods, settlement was modest in the southern parts of the Khabur catchment, but important settlements existed at Dara, Nisibin, and Diyarbakir. The limited settlement after the mid-second millennium BCE may have been related to the following conditions: its position as a march between kingdoms and empires where combat was endemic and conditions did not favor sedentary life, or its position as an agriculturally marginal zone where slight fluctuations in climate or human-induced environmental degradation inhibited settlement.

BIBLIOGRAPHY

Anon. "Mille et une capitales de Haute-Mésopotamie: Récents découvertes en Syrie du Nord." *Les Dossiers d'Archéologie,* no. 155 (December 1990). Short reports in a popular format.

Anon. "Lost Civilizations of the Desert: Recent Archaeological Research in Third Millennium North Syria." *Bulletin of the Canadian Society for Mesopotamian Studies* 21 (May 1991). Middle Khabur storage facilities and their significance.

Eichler, Seyyare, et al., eds. *Tall al-Ḥamīdīyā 2: Recent Excavations in the Upper Khabur Region.* Orbis Biblicus et Orientalis, Series Archaeologica, 6. Göttingen, 1990. The first section contains preliminary reports in English from a 1986 symposium in Bern on other Khabur excavations.

Fortin, Michel. "Résultats de la 4ème campagne de fouilles à Tell Atij et de la 3ème à Tell Gudeda, Syrie." *Echos du Monde Classique/ Classical Views* 37 n.s./12 (1993): 97–121.

Kühne, Hartmut. *Die Keramik vom Tell Chuera und ihre Beziehungen zu Funden aus Syrien-Palästina, der Türkei und dem Iraq.* Vorderasiatische Forschungen der Max Freiherr von Oppenheim-Stiftung, 1. Berlin, 1976. The first detailed study of third-millennium ceramics, now dated.

Kühne, Hartmut, ed. *Die Rezente Umwelt von Tall Šēḫ Ḥamad und Daten zur Umweltrekonstruktion der assyrischen Stadt Dūr-katlimmu.* Berichte der Ausgrabung Tall Šēḫ Ḥamad/Dūr-katlimmu (BATSH), vol. 1. Berlin, 1991. Scientific studies on the past and present environment of the Middle and Lower Khabur, and evidence for a Middle Assyrian canal system (English summaries).

Lebeau, Marc. "Esquisse d'une histoire de la Haute Mésopotamie au début de l'Âge du Bronze." *Zeitschrift für Assyriologie und Vorderasiatische Archäologie* 80 (1990): 241–296.

Mallowan, M. E. L. "Excavations at Brak and Chagar Bazar." *Iraq* 9 (1947): 1–266. Site and survey report; see as well Mallowan's reports in *Iraq* 3 and 4 and recent volumes of the journal for preliminary reports on Tell Brak by David and Joan Oates.

Moortgat-Correns, Ursula. *Die Bildwerke vom Djebelet el-Beda in ihrer Raumlichen und Zeitlischen Umwelt.* Berlin, 1972. Reviews Oppenheim's discussion of *kranzhügels.*

Oates, David and Joan Oates. "Tell Brak: A Stratigraphic Summary, 1976–1993." *Iraq* 56 (1994): 167–193. See also earlier preliminary reports in *Iraq.*

Orthmann, Winfried. *Tell Chuera: Ausgrabungen der Max Freiherr von Oppenheim-Stiftung in Nordost-Syrien.* Damascus, 1990. Short synthesis of excavation results, in German and Arabic.

Poidebard, Antoine. *La trace de Rome dans le désert de Syrie: Le limes de Trajan à la conquete Arabe: Recherches aeriennes (1925–1932).* Paris, 1934. Brilliant early use of aerial photography, but his interpretation of the Roman *limes* is now undergoing revision.

Rouault, Olivier, and Maria-Grazia Masetti-Rouault, eds. *L'Eufrate e il tempo: Le civiltà del medio Eufrate e della Gezira sirana.* Milan, 1993. Catalog of an archaeological exhibition for the Khabur and Middle Euphrates, with synthetic articles and brief site reports.

Schmidt, Hubert, et al. *Tell Halaf.* 4 vols. Berlin, 1943–1962. Monographs by individual authors containing primary source material, although the discussions are now dated.

Schwartz, Glenn M. *A Ceramic Chronology from Tell Leilan, Operation 1.* Yale Tell Leilan Research, 1. New Haven, 1988.

Schwartz, Glenn M., and Hans H. Curvers. "Tell al-Raqā'i 1989 and 1990: Further Investigations at a Small Rural Site of Early Urban Northern Mesopotamia." *American Journal of Archaeology* 96 (1992): 397–419. Discusses the final seasons of excavations and their implications. See bibliography for earlier reports.

Stein, Diana L. "Khabur Ware and Nuzi Ware: Their Origin, Relationship, and Significance." *Assur* 4.1 (1984): 1–65.

Warburton, David A. "Previous Archaeological Work in the Habur Region." In *Tall al-Ḥamīdīyā 1: Vorbericht 1984,* edited by Seyyare Eichler et al., pp. 13–30. Orbis Biblicus et Orientalis, Series Archaeologica, 4. Göttingen, 1985. One of the few reviews in English.

Weiss, Harvey, ed. *The Origins of Cities in Dry-Farming Syria and Mesopotamia in the Third Millennium B.C.* Guilford, Conn., 1986.

Weiss, Harvey, et al. "The Genesis and Collapse of Third Millennium North Mesopotamian Civilization." *Science* 261 (1993): 995–1004.

THOMAS L. MCCLELLAN

KHAFAJEH, one of the important sites to the east of modern Baghdad and slightly north of the confluence of the Tigris and Diyala rivers (33°38′ N, 44°40′ E). Archaeologically this section of modern Iraq is known as the Lower Diyala region. Because of the areas' proximity to Baghdad, the sites of the Lower Diyala have been known to scholars and travelers since Western interest in early Mesopotamia began in the nineteenth century. Henry Rawlinson mentioned Khafajeh and equated it with the ancient city of Opis. [*See the biography of Rawlinson.*] Modern interest in Khafajeh came about because of a number of illicitly dug antiquities that had appeared on the market in Baghdad that could be traced to the Lower Diyala region. Khafajeh was excavated by the Oriental Institute of The University of Chicago, The University Museum of the University of Pennsylvania, and the American Schools of Oriental Research from 1930 to 1938, followed by some minor work in 1950 by the Directorate General of Antiquities of Iraq. The directors of these excavations were Conrad Preusser, Pinhas Delougaz, and Ephraim A. Speiser. [*See the biography of Speiser.*] The excavation and recording techniques evolved by the excavators of Khafajeh and the other sites of the Lower Diyala became standards for American archaeological excavation in Mesopotamia for many years.

Covering some 216 ha (533.5 acres), Khafajeh is composed of a number of mounds; the four major mounds were labeled A through D by the excavators. These mounds rise from approximately 4 to 6 m (13–19.6 ft.) above the present plain level. Mound A, the largest, is situated in the northern part of the site and is the mound closest to the modern course of the Diyala river. Occupation began in the Uruk and Jemdet Nasr periods and lasted into the Akkadian period when A was abandoned. Mounds B and C are joined and are parts of a single settlement in the southwest. The excavated materials from these mounds are dated to the Old Babylonian period and perhaps to the early Kassite era. Mound D, located in the southeast, is the smallest mound and is dated to the Isin-Larsa and Old Babylonian periods.

Information derived from a hoard of tablets from a temple

of Sin in mound D of the Old Babylonian period allows for the identification of the mound with ancient Tutub, which was a town known in the Akkadian period (Harris, 1955). The name occurs in an Old Akkadian tablet from Eshnunna; therefore, it is likely that mound A, the earliest mound, was also known as Tutub during at least part of its history. An inscribed clay cylinder from Mound B found in the foundations of a room in a massive fortification indicates that in the Old Babylonian period mound B, and probably mound C as well, became known as Dur Samsuiluna. Samsuiluna of Babylon, the ruler after Hammurabi (1792–1750 BCE), constructed a fortress there in the twenty-third year of his reign. It is not known how long these ancient names survived, but it seems probable that in the early part of the first millennium during the Neo-Assyrian period, Khafajeh was located in a region known at one time as Tupliash.

Of the four mounds of Khafajeh, mound A was the most extensively excavated. The building sequences include the so-called Sin temple, the private houses, the small temple in square O 43, the Nintu temple, and the Temple Oval. It is most unlikely that the "Sin temple" was really sacred to the god Sin, but the name is so entrenched in the early literature describing the building that it would be confusing to rename the structure. A sounding beneath the Sin temple probably reached virgin soil and indicated that occupation in the area of the sounding began with the late Uruk period. The excavations of the actual temple are extremely important as they provide an unbroken series of levels of one building dating from the Jemdet Nasr period through the Early Dynastic period. It was one of the archaeological sequences in the excavations of the Lower Diyala region that provided a definition of the Early Dynastic period. Levels I through V of Sin are dated to "Protoliterate c and d," a terminology used by the excavators. This occupation is the equivalent of the Jemdet Nasr period. The chronological situation is somewhat more complicated in that it is now known that Protoliterate d of the Diyala region is actually contemporary with Early Dynastic I of southern Mesopotamia. Sin VI and VII are also Early Dynastic I, Sin VIII and IX are Early Dynastic II, and Sin X dates to Early Dynastic III. The plan of the earliest temple is based on the classic tripartite Sumerian temple type of southern Mesopotamia. By Sin IV the temple is built upon a terrace and is reached by a flight of steps. The plan also incorporates a large court to the east. In the Early Dynastic period plano-convex bricks are used and the building becomes increasingly monumental.

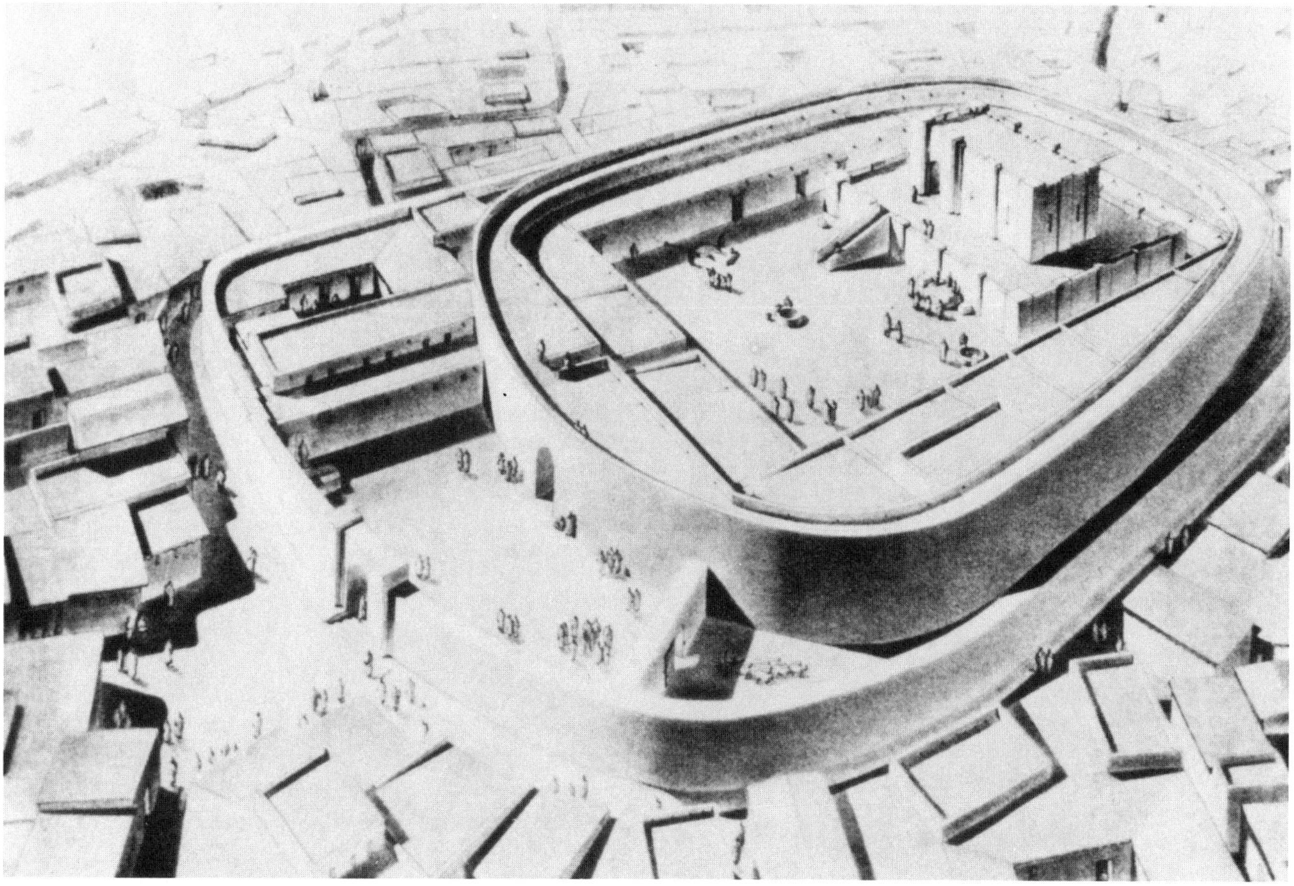

KHAFAJEH. *Reconstruction of the Temple Oval.* ED II period. (Courtesy Oriental Institute, Chicago)

To the west and south of the Sin temple and stratigraphically related to it were the remains of a long sequence of twelve levels of Early Dynastic private houses as well as the smaller Nintu temple and a temple located in square O 43 on the survey map of Khafajeh. These sequences greatly enriched our knowledge of the Early Dynastic period in the Diyala region and underlined the fact that there was an extraordinary diversity of architectural approaches to temple construction at Khafajeh during the third millennium. An additional new type of temple architecture was provided by the excavation of the very large Temple Oval further to the west of the private houses and in close proximity to the town wall. Three different levels of this Early Dynastic temple were excavated. Because the building must have dominated the southern part of mound, it is unfortunate that the deity to whom this temple complex was dedicated is not known. It was originally built on top of a foundation pit filled with some 7 m (23 ft.) of clean sand. The cella (inner part of the temple), which was not preserved, stood on top of a raised platform and was reached by a flight of steps rising from a courtyard surrounded by rooms and a large irregular oval wall. This wall in turn was surrounded by another curved wall. Its length was over 100 m (328 ft.), and in the south a residential type building called house D (no houses A, B, or C exist) was built in the space between the inner and outer curved walls. House D must have served in the administration of the temple. Most of the material found in mound A belongs to the Early Dynastic period, although some Akkadian finds were made in a private house area in the northern part of the mound.

Mention has already been made of the clay-foundation cylinder, which identified the excavated remains of mound B as Dur Samsuiluna, a fortress built by Samsuiluna around 1726. A portion of a 4.7-meter-thick buttressed wall of this fortification was exposed as well as parts of two different buildings. The plan of the larger of the two buildings has two parts that imply a dual function for the building's use, and the excavator suggests that it may have been the residence of a governor or ruler of the fort (Hill, 1990, p. 210). Perhaps to be included in Dur Samsuiluna is mound C. A few soundings on this mound were undertaken but nothing of importance was recorded.

KHAFAJEH. *Scarlet Ware jar.* ED I period. (Courtesy I. Theusen)

Large-scale excavations were carried out on mound D, which may be dated to the Isin-Larsa and Old Babylonian periods. Part of a massive fortification wall 7 to approximately 12 m (23–39 ft.) thick surrounded what has been termed "the citadel." The shape of the space defined by this wall was very irregular. A street led from an outer gate excavated in the northeastern part of the enclosure to a large temple building surrounded by private houses in the center of the citadel. The excavators defined an earlier and later phase of construction. An Old Babylonian tablet hoard found in a room of the later phase identified this building as a temple of the god Sin and provided for the identification of Khafajeh with ancient Tutub.

[*See also* Diyala.]

BIBLIOGRAPHY

Delougaz, Pinhas. *The Temple Oval At Khafajah.* University of Chicago, Oriental Institute Publications (OIP), 53. Chicago, 1940.

Delougaz, Pinhas, and Seton Lloyd. *Pre-Sargonid Temples in the Diyala Region.* OIP, 58. Chicago, 1942.

Delougaz, Pinhas. *Pottery from the Diyala Region.* OIP, 63. Chicago, 1952.

Delougaz, Pinhas, et al. *Private Houses and Graves in the Diyala Region.* OIP, 88. Chicago, 1967.

Ellis, Richard S. *A Bibliography of Mesopotamian Archaeological Sites.* Wiesbaden, 1972. See pages 43–44 for citations of preliminary reports.

Frankfort, Henri. *Sculpture of the Third Millennium B.C. from Tell Asmar and Khafājah.* OIP, 44. Chicago, 1939.

Frankfort, Henri. *More Sculpture from the Diyala Region.* OIP, 60. Chicago, 1943.

Frankfort, Henri. *Stratified Cylinder Seals from the Diyala Region.* OIP, 72. Chicago, 1955.

Harris, Rivkah. "The Archive of the Sin Temple in Khafajah (Tutub)." *Journal of Cuneiform Studies* 9 (1955): 31–88; 91–120. Identifies Khafajeh as Tutub.

Hill, Harold D., et al. *Old Babylonian Public Buildings in the Diyala Region.* OIP, 98. Chicago, 1990.

DONALD P. HANSEN

KHALDEH (Kobbet Choueifat), site located about 12 km (7 mi.) south of Beirut, Lebanon, along the highway connecting Beirut to Sidon. The site is formed by two promontories, about 10–15 m above sea level, that slope toward the sea for a length of 500 m. A milestone discovered at the site gives its distance as 239 Roman miles from Antioch and about 12 from Berytus (Beirut). Khaldeh is identified with ancient *Hi-il-du-ya* (in Akkadian), a city of the kingdom of Sidon annexed by Esarhaddon in 677/76 BCE (see *Archiv für Orient Forschung,* Berlin, 1926–, vol. 9, p. 48, col. 3.2). It is known as Mutatio Heldua in the itinerary of the Bordeaux pilgrim of the Roman period; *Khaldeh* is its modern Arabic name.

The site has been known since 1847, when Henn Guys mentioned it in *Beyrouth et le Mont Liban.* In 1960, during construction of the highway near the airport, the Lebanese Department of Antiquities uncovered some Phoenician tombs. Subsequently, archaeological excavations were carried out at the site under the direction of Roger Saidah (1961–1962) under the auspices of the Lebanese Department of Antiquities.

The excavations unearthed stratigraphic levels from the Byzantine-Roman, Early Roman, Greco-Persian, Late Bronze, and Late Chalcolithic periods. A complex of urban houses (villas with mosaic floors and baths) as well as industrial and agricultural quarters (olive presses and cisterns) dating to the Byzantine-Roman period (fourth–sixth centuries CE) were found covering the surface of the mound. The main discoveries from the Early Roman period are terra-cotta sarcophagi, characteristic terra sigillata and Megarian ware, and a number of coins of the imperial period. [*See* Sarcophagus.] The finds indicate a time span from the Late Hellenistic to the Early Roman period. The Greco-Persian period is represented by a few wall foundations constructed of limestone blocks.

About 422 tombs were discovered in the Iron Age (tenth–eight centuries BCE) Phoenician necropolis that shed light on the funerary practices. They were of two types: the majority were inhumations, in which the body was placed directly on the ground between two rows of stones and surrounded by grave goods—mainly Iron Age pottery. A lesser number of burials were in funerary urns found containing some calcinated bones, indicating the practice of incineration. [*See* Phoenicians; Burial Techniques; Grave Goods.] this extensive cemetery points to a large settlement, as yet unfound—possibly the first one in the Phoenician homeland to bear witness to that golden era in Phoenician history.

The Late Bronze Age (thirteenth–eleventh century centuries BCE) is attested by sherds discovered in the area of the cemetery. The Phoenician tombs apparently disturbed earlier LB settlements probably abandoned toward the end of the thirteenth century BCE. As the excavations neared their end, a few oval structures and funerary jars were discovered that are dated to the Late Chalcolithic period (beginning of the third millennium).

BIBLIOGRAPHY

Callot, Oliver. "Remarques sur les huileries de Khan Khaldé (Liban)." In *Archéologie au Levant: Recueil à la mémoire de Roger Saidah,* pp. 419–428. Lyon, 1982. See, as well, the contributions by Pierre Bordreuil (pp. 190–191), N. Duval and J.-P. Calliet (pp. 311–394), and J.-P. Rey-Coquais (pp. 402–408).

Gebara, Chérine. "Remarques sur la sigillée orientale d'après les fouilles de Khan Khaldé (Heldua)." In *Archéologie du Levant: Recueil à la mémoire de Roger Saidah,* pp. 409–417. Lyon, 1982

Guys, Henri. *Relation d'un séjour de plusieurs années à Beyrough et dans le Liban.* Paris, 1847.

Saidah, Roger. "Fouilles de Khaldeh." *Bulletin du Musée de Beyrouth* 19 (1966): 51–90; 20 (1967): 155–180.

Saidah, Roger. "Archaeology in the Lebanon 1968–69." *Berytus* 18 (1969): 130–134.

Saidah, Roger. "Objects grecs d'époque géométrique découvert récemment sur le littoral libanais (à Khaldé près de Beyrouth)." *Annales Archéologiques Arabes Syrienne* 21 (1971): 195–198.

LEILA BADRE

KHAWLAN AṬ-ṬIYAL, region situated on the internal slope of the Yemenite mountains, southeast of Yemen's capital, San'a. It occupies approximately the northwest sector of the basin of Wadi Dhanah (15°00′–15°15′ N, 44°30′–45°00′ E). This great watershed area, which the ancient Sabeans once closed with a dike near their capital, Marib (see below), drains into the desert to the east.

The name Khawlan is very ancient and comes from the name of a Himyarite tribe that occupied the region in the pre-Islamic era (first–second centuries CE). The appellation is derived from the high mountain (Jabal Ṭiyal, about 3,500 m high) dominating the chain that delimits the region on the north; the name distinguishes it from Khawlan bin ʿAmir, located farther north, near the city of Ṣaʿdah. The region is sparsely populated today, and the few villages (al-Kibs, Jiḥanah, ʿAsal, Banī Sulayḥ, aḍ-Ḍayq, al-Watadah) are distributed along the alluvial valleys (Wadi Miswar, Wadi Ḥababiḍ, Wadi ʿAṭfah, Wadi Shirwab), cutting into the bare hills of Precambrian granite that slopes toward the desert.

Except for the brief exploratory voyage made by Eduard Glaser at the end of the 1800s, no archaeological research had been done in the area prior to the beginning of the reconnaissance surveys carried out by the Italian Archaeological Mission in 1981.

In addition to a series of extensive Mousterian (Middle Paleolithic) workshops in Wadi Ḥababiḍ that produced flint tools, numerous Neolithic settlements characterized by isolated oval houses and by a sophisticated stone-working industry have been discovered. Several excavations conducted at site 3 in Wadi ath-Thayyilah (1984–1986) have given proof of the beginning of domestication. They have allowed the hypothetical reconstruction of the methods of exploiting resources that were used by the first sedentary Yemenites from about 5000 to 3500 BCE, in an environment more humid than the present one.

The reconnaissance surveys also led to the discovery—for the first time on the southern Arabian Peninsula—of a Bronze Age, datable to the third–second millennium. More than fifty sites from this period were discovered between

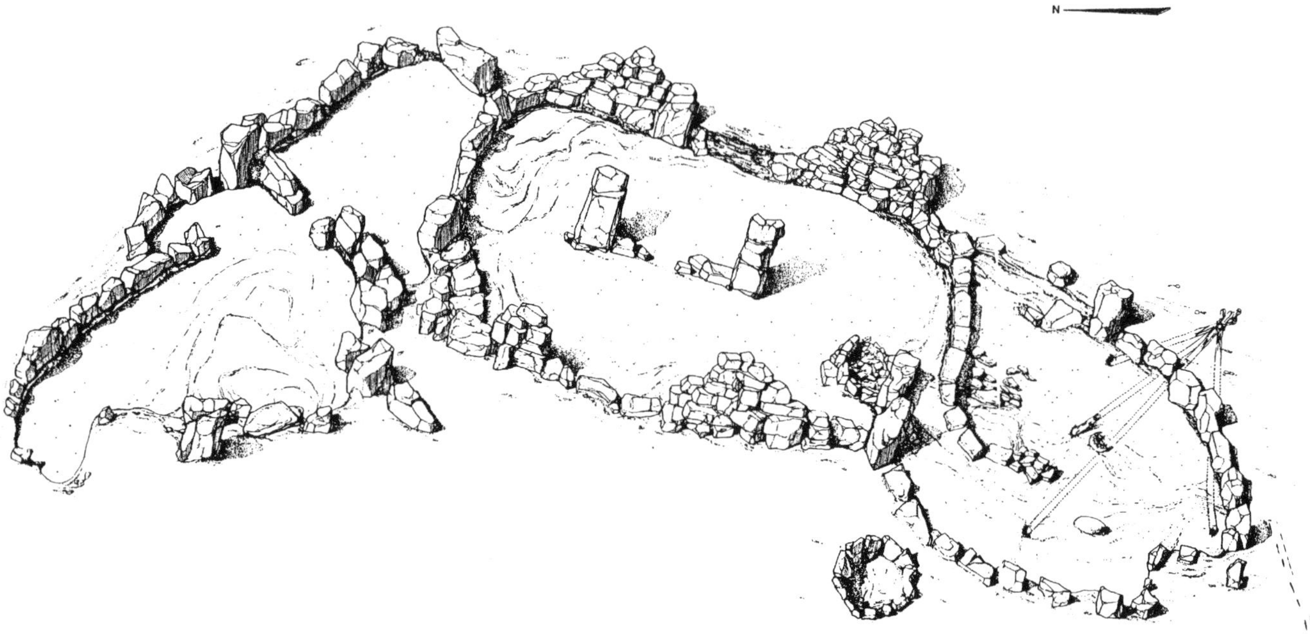

KHAWLAN AṬ-ṬIYAL. Figure 1. *Axonometric plan of loci 1-5, Wadi Yanaʿim.* (Courtesy A. de Maigret)

1981 and 1985 in the regions of Aʿrush and Suhman (western Khawlan) and Jabal Aʿmas (al-Ḥada). The data from the explorations and from the excavations conducted in four of the principal settlements (Wadi Yanaʿim, Wadi Najid el-Abyaḍ, al-Masannah, ar-Raqlah) offer a quite clear picture of the culture that preceded the Sabaeans.

This picture shows agricultural villages with oval houses centered around areas of common activity (see figure 1). Raised mud walls were perched on foundations of unworked blocks, and central pilasters supported the ceilings. Excavation led to the discovery of stone utensils, objects of bronze and semiprecious stones, grinding stones, pestles, and an abundance of animal bones on ceramic tile floors. The examination of seeds found in the clay of the tiles and of the bones show that the inhabitants cultivated millet, wheat, and barley and raised cattle, sheep, and pigs.

The ceramic ware, which shows evident parallels with Early Bronze Age Syrian-Palestinian wares, is clearly different from that of the following Sabaean period. It may suggest that the origins of the kingdoms of the southern Arabian Peninsula are to be found outside Yemen.

Paleoenvironmental studies have demonstrated that Bronze Age culture came to an end (at least in this area) toward the middle of the second millennium: the geohydrologic equilibrium upon which the economic success of these agricultural communities was based entered into a period of crisis. A drier, more irregular climate ensued, and the Khawlan, now traversed by more ephemeral and violent streams of water, was abandoned. Human occupation shifted toward the desert border to the east and began to be integrated into the emerging Sabaean culture. At that time, imposing hydraulic works were developed that were able to manage the irregular quantities of water coming from the mountains, and large stretches of the desert were cultivated with very intricate systems of irrigation. The dike at Marib is only the largest example of such new technology. [*See* Hydraulics.]

Thus, in the Sabaean period, only the most eastern part of the Khawlan was occupied. This was demonstrated by the Italian mission's discovery in 1985 of a large archaic Sabaean city (ancient Ḥafary) in Wadi Yala, about 30 km (19 mi.) southwest of Marib. A brief excavation conducted there in 1987 made it possible to ascertain that the city was first founded in the thirteenth–twelfth centuries BCE. Such a date should probably be assumed to mark the beginning of Sabaean culture in Yemen and the point of transition between prehistory and history in Khawlan and on the southern Arabian Peninsula.

[*See also* Marib.]

BIBLIOGRAPHY

Maigret, Alessandro de. "A Bronze Age for Southern Arabia." *East and West* 34 (1984): 75–106.

Maigret, Alessandro de, ed. *The Sabaean Archaeological Complex in the Wādī Yalā (Eastern Ḫawlān aṭ-Ṭiyal–Yemen Arab Republic): A Preliminary Report.* Istituto Italiano per il Medio ed Estremo Oriente, Centro Studi e Scavi Archeologici in Asia, Reports and Memoirs, 21. Rome, 1988.

Maigret, Alessandro de. *The Bronze Age Culture of Ḫawlān aṭ-Ṭiyal and al-Ḥadā (Republic of Yemen).* Istituto Italiano per il Medio ed Estremo Oriente, Centro Studi e Scavi Archeologici in Asia, Reports and Memoirs, 24. Rome, 1990.

Müller, David H., and Nicolaus Rhodokanakis, eds. *Eduard Glasers Reise nach Mārib.* Sammlung Eduard Glaser, 1 Vienna, 1913.

ALESSANDRO DE MAIGRET

Translated from Italian by Susan I. Schiedel

KHELEIFEH, TELL EL-, site located approximately 500 m from the northern shore of the Gulf of ʿAqaba, roughly equidistant between the modern cities of Eilat and Aqaba. Tell el-Kheleifeh was first surveyed in 1933 by the German explorer Fritz Frank, who identified the site with the biblical city of Ezion-Geber (*Nm.* 33: 35–36; *Dt.* 2: 8; *1 Kgs.* 9: 26–28; 22: 47–48; *2 Chr.* 8: 17–18). In 1937, Nelson Glueck conducted a surface survey of this low, mud-brick mound and concluded that the site had been occupied between the tenth and eighth centuries BCE. Glueck directed three seasons of excavation at Tell el-Kheleifeh for the Smithsonian Institution and the American Schools of Oriental Research (ASOR) between 1938 and 1940. He discerned six major periods of occupation, which he dated between the Iron I and Persian periods. Glueck wrote a number of articles about Tell el-Kheleifeh (see Vogel, 1970) but never published a final excavation report. He accepted Franks' Tell el-Kheleifeh/Ezion-Geber identification. (For a recent reappraisal of Glueck's excavations, see Pratico, 1985, 1993.)

Casemate Fortress. Two major architectural phases could be discerned in the mud-brick ruins at Tell el-Kheleifeh: the first, and earliest, was a casemate fortress; the later one was a fortified settlement. The former was composed of a square (45 m on each side) of casemate rooms. A large building, constructed on the so-called four-room house plan (Shiloh, 1970) was located in the center of this casemate square. This structure, identified by the excavator as a citadel or granary, measured 12.30 × 13.20 m. It was composed of three contiguous units at the northern end of the fortress. Each of these units, or small rooms, was roughly square. Extending to the south were three larger rectangular rooms (approximately 7.40 m long and 2–3 m wide) whose walls were preserved to a height of 2.70 m. An open space between the casemate fortification and this monumental building was, devoid of architecture and used as a courtyard until the later fortified settlement was built (see below).

In light of the excavated data, the chronology of the casemate fortress cannot be established. The only pottery that can be assigned to this level with certainty is Negevite ware, a handmade Iron Age tradition for which a refined typology has yet to be established. The chronology of Negevite pottery can only be determined on the basis of its association with datable wheelmade forms.

The fortress's plan is intriguingly similar to an architectural tradition well attested in the central Negev southward to the site of Tell el-Qudeirat (Qadesh-Barnea). Recent surveys and excavations have documented an extensive network of early Iron Age fortresses (eleventh and/or tenth centuries BCE) with notable similarities to the Tell el-Kheleifeh fortress, including the casemate construction and nearby buildings exhibiting the four-room plan (Cohen, 1979). Given the fact that Tell el-Kheleifeh's pottery and inscriptional materials do not predate the eighth century BCE (see below), this observation of the striking similarities between the Tell el-Kheleifeh fortress and those of the central Negev must be, for the present, one of comparative architecture and not chronology.

Fortified Settlement. When the casemate fortress was destroyed, a fortified settlement of considerable size (56 m [north] by 59 m [east] by 59 m [south] by 63 m [west] replaced it. This new, larger settlement was surrounded by a solid offset/inset wall with a different alignment that gave access through a four-chambered gate on the south. Unlike the casemate fortress with its open courtyards between the casemate wall and the central structure, the spaces inside the new offsets/insets wall were now occupied with buildings.

In part, the earlier casemate fortress was incorporated into the new plan. The edifice that once stood in the center of the casemate square was now located in the northwest corner of the fortified settlement. Some of the old casemate rooms, primarily those on the southern and eastern sides of the old fortress, continued in use. The casemate rooms of the western and northern sides, however, were now outside the new fortification perimeter.

The chronology of the fortified (offsets/insets) settlement can be established with reasonable certainty on the basis of the wheelmade pottery recovered (c. eighth–early sixth century BCE). The same chronology is also suggested by a small but important collection of stamp impressions that appear on the handles of storage jars. The inscriptions read "belonging to Qawsʿanal, servant of the king" *(lqwsʿnl ʿbd hmlk).* The script dates to the seventh or early sixth century BCE.

The offsets/insets settlement represents the last major architectural level at the site. There is fragmentary evidence for later occupation, after the sixth century BCE (a few Phoenician and Aramaic ostraca of the fifth and fourth centuries, a small collection of Greek body sherds and some pottery of the fifth century BCE). The building remains of the later occupation are poorly preserved.

Identification. Reappraising Glueck's work at Tell el-Kheleifeh has verified a number of his conclusions, but has also indicated the need for some significant revisions and refinements, particularly for the site's chronology and identification. Reappraisal has suggested later chronological horizons for the site than originally proposed by Glueck. As noted above, Tell el-Kheleifeh's wheelmade pottery is dated to between the eighth and early sixth centuries BCE, creating a problem in terms of the biblical references to Ezion-Geber (see above): the question is whether the ruins of Tell el-Kheleifeh do indeed preserve the story of biblical Ezion-

Geber and/or Eilat. The revised chronology provides no clear archaeological evidence for the period of Israel's wilderness traditions (*Nm.* 33: 35–36) or even for the time of Solomon's reign in the tenth century (*1 Kgs.* 9: 26–28). Additionally, the site provides only questionable evidence for the ninth century BCE (*1 Kgs.* 22: 47–48). Assuming the correctness of the revised chronology, the identification of Tell el-Kheleifeh is both an archaeological and a historical problem.

BIBLIOGRAPHY

Cohen, Rudolph. "The Iron Age Fortresses in the Central Negev." *Bulletin of the American Schools of Oriental Research*, no. 236 (1979): 61–79.

Glueck, Nelson. "The First Campaign at Tell el-Kheleifeh." *Bulletin of the American Schools of Oriental Research*, no. 71 (1938): 3–17.

Glueck, Nelson. "The Topography and History of Ezion-Geber and Elath." *Bulletin of the American Schools of Oriental Research*, no. 72 (1938): 2–13.

Glueck, Nelson. "The Second Campaign at Tell el-Kheleifeh (Ezion-Geber: Elath)." *Bulletin of the American Schools of Oriental Research*, no. 75 (1939): 8–22.

Glueck, Nelson. "The Third Season of Excavation at Tell el-Kheleifeh." *Bulletin of the American Schools of Oriental Research*, no. 79 (1940): 2–18.

Glueck, Nelson. "Ezion-Geber." *Biblical Archaeologist* 28 (1965): 70–87.

Glueck, Nelson. "Some Edomite Pottery from Tell el-Kheleifeh, Parts I and II." *Bulletin of the American Schools of Oriental Research*, no. 188 (1967): 8–38.

Glueck, Nelson. "Tell el-Kheleifeh Inscriptions." In *Near Eastern Studies in Honor of William Foxwell Albright*, edited by Hans Goedicke, pp. 225–242. Baltimore, 1971.

Meshel, Zeev. "On the Problem of Tell el-Kheleifeh, Elath, and Ezion-Geber" (in Hebrew). *Eretz-Israel* 12 (1975): 49–56.

Pratico, Gary D. "Nelson Glueck's 1938–1940 Excavations at Tell el-Kheleifeh: A Reappraisal." *Bulletin of the American Schools of Oriental Research*, no. 259 (1985): 1–32.

Pratico, Gary D. "Where Is Ezion-Geber? A Reappraisal of the Site Archaeologist Nelson Glueck Identified as King Solomon's Red Sea Port." *Biblical Archaeology Review* 12.5 (1986): 24–35.

Pratico, Gary D. *Nelson Glueck's 1938–1940 Excavations at Tell el-Kheleifeh: A Reappraisal.* Atlanta, 1993.

Shiloh, Yigal. "The Four-Room House: Its Situation and Function in the Israelite City." *Israel Exploration Journal* 20 (1970): 180–190.

Vogel, Eleanor K. "Bibliography of Nelson Glueck." In *Near Eastern Archaeology in the Twentieth Century: Essays in Honor of Nelson Glueck*, edited by James A. Sanders, pp. 382–394. Garden City, N.Y., 1970.

GARY D. PRATICO

KHIRBEH (Ar., *khirbet,* joined with a noun, meaning "ruin"). The term *khirbeh* indicates that at least some portion of a ruined structure or city is visible: for example, a wall line, cistern, or architectural fragment(s). Eighteenth- and nineteenth-century Western travelers to the Near East observed that a Palestinian *khirbeh* was a ruined city of ancient Palestine. Many such sites had names descriptive of their location: for example, Khirbet Qumran ("ruin of the grayish spot") and Khirbet el-Busl ("ruin of the onion"). [*See* Qumran.] Other descriptors referred to a current or previous owner: Khirbet el-Huseinat ("ruin of the Husein clan"). The names of still others represented their specific archaeological features: Khirbeh ed-Deir ("ruin of the monastery") and Khirbet es-Sukriyeh ("ruin of the sugar factories").

The *khirbeh* sites that attracted the most interest in the nineteenth century were those with Arabic place names that appeared to preserve "corrupted" versions of their ancient Hebrew, Greek, or Latin names: for example, Khirbet Seilun (biblical Shiloh) and Khirbet ʿAjlan (biblical Eglon). [*See* Shiloh.] Recognizing linguistic transformations between languages led to the identification of many biblical sites and to the creation of the first more-or-less comprehensive historical geography of biblical Palestine in the mid-nineteenth century. [*See* Historical Geography.]

Subsequent archaeological research, beginning in 1890 with the work of Flinders Petrie, showed that most of the ruined sites did not date to the period of the Hebrew Bible at all; they were, rather, ruined Roman-, Byzantine-, Crusader- or Islamic-period sites that in turn might preserve an earlier biblical place name from the immediate region but not necessarily of the site itself: the Roman, Byzantine, and Islamic site of Khirbet ʿAbdeh was Oboda/Avdat and Khirbet Kaisariyeh was Caesarea, but Khirbet el-Jezery was only adjacent to biblical Gezer. [*See* Avdat; Caesarea; Gezer.] Overzealous attempts to see biblical place names in Arabic place names produced erroneous results. The aforementioned Khirbet ʿAjlan, for example, probably had nothing to do with biblical Eglon, but rather was named in the seventh century CE by ʿAmr ibn al-ʿAṣ. Once scholars realized that the Palestinian *khirbeh* sites were post biblical (and often Islamic in date), interest in them as worthy of study on their own merit vanished.

Historical documentation identifies many *Khirbeh* sites as active villages through the sixteenth century and suggests that they were abandoned and ruined in the seventeenth and eighteenth centuries. Others were only seasonal habitation spots founded in the early nineteenth century. These also attracted the name *khirbeh,* in these instances meaning "temporary site." Finally, some of the Arab villages abandoned in 1948 and now located within modern Israel have also come to be referred to as *khirbeh.* Most *khirbeh* sites in modern Israel were given Hebrew names prefaced by the word *ḥorvat* ("ruin") and thus have two "modern" names. Many of the new Hebrew names do not preserve a tradition: some are modern identifications of the site's ancient name, when one can be suggested, and may not be accurate; and others may be named after a modern kibbutz and have no antiquity, such as Ḥorvat ʿUza, the modern name of Khirbet Aiyadiyah.

[*See also* History of the Field, *overview article;* Site Survey; Tell; *and the biographies of Petrie, Robinson, and Smith.*]

BIBLIOGRAPHY

Aharoni, Yohanan. *The Land of the Bible: A Historical Geography*. Translated and edited by Anson F. Rainey. 2d ed. Philadelphia, 1979. Classic account describing the geography of biblical lands but with interesting methodological discussions of how the sites were identified.

Hütteroth, Wolf Dieter, and Kamal Abdulfattah. *Historical Geography of Palestine, Transjordan, and Southern Syria in the Late Sixteenth Century*. Erlanger Geographische Arbeiten, 5. Erlangen, 1977. The best study of sixteenth-century Palestine. Many of the nineteenth-century *khirbeh* sites are seen at this time as active villages and towns.

Palmer, Edward H. *Arabic and English Name Lists*. Survey of Western Palestine, vol. 7. London, 1881. The name list from the Survey of Western Palestine identifying and translating Palestine's nineteenth-century Arabic place names.

Robinson, Edward. *Biblical Researches in Palestine, Mount Sinai, and Arabia Petraea*. 3 vols. Boston, 1841. Robinson's classic travel journal of Palestine in 1838, containing descriptions of many *khirbeh* sites.

JEFFREY A. BLAKELY

KHIRBET ______. *For toponyms beginning with this element (also spelled* Khirbat*), see under latter part of name. For a general definition of the term, see* Khirbeh.

KHORSABAD, modern village on the site of the ancient city of Dur Sharrukin ("fortress of Sargon"), is located in northern Iraq about 20 km (12 mi.) northeast of Nineveh (36°31′ N, 43°14′ E). The ancient city was founded by Sargon II, king of Assyria (721–705 BCE), who purchased the site from the inhabitants of a local village, Magganubba, and built a city there to be his new capital. The reasons for Sargon's decision to build a new capital are not clear. If he usurped the throne, as has often been thought, he may have wished to create a new administrative center away from hostile elements in the older Assyrian cities. He may, however, have simply wished to display his power and wealth by creating a splendid new capital for the expanding Assyrian Empire. With prisoners of war as laborers, work on the new city began in 717, and celebrations in honor of the king and the gods taking up residence were held in 707. Construction of the city remained unfinished at the time of Sargon's death in 705. Sennacherib, his son and successor, moved the capital to Nineveh, but Dur Sharrukin appears to have remained a provincial capital until its final abandonment when the empire fell in about 612 BCE. [*See* Nineveh.] The identity of the site did not disappear from memory, however; the medieval Arab geographer Yaqut referred to "a city called ruins of Ṣarʿon" located beside the contemporary village of Khorsabad.

Khorsabad was the first site in Mesopotamia to be extensively excavated, and it has produced a wealth of archaeological material. Excavation at the site began in the early 1840s, with the work of Paul Émile Botta, the French consul at Mosul. Disappointed at not finding anything of particular interest during earlier digging at Kuyunjik (the citadel of ancient Nineveh), Botta turned his attention to Khorsabad, where inscribed bricks were reported to have been found by the local inhabitants. His excavations were immediately successful. Between 1843 and 1844, numerous large stone slabs with pictorial reliefs were unearthed that had lined the walls of an immense palace. [*See* Palace.] Botta thought that he had uncovered the biblical city of Nineveh. Eugène Flandin, an artist sent by the French government to assist Botta, made drawings of the wall reliefs that were later published. When some of the discoveries were exhibited in Paris, they caused a sensation and spurred a European hunt for Mesopotamian antiquities.

Excavation at Khorsabad was resumed from 1852 to 1854 by Victor Place, Botta's successor as French consul at Mosul. Place cleared about two hundred rooms in the palace and he, too, found numerous stone wall reliefs and statues, most of which were lost in 1855: the boat and rafts conveying them down the Tigris River on the start of their journey to Paris sank near Qurna, after being attacked by rebellious tribesmen. Fortunately, drawings of many of the reliefs and architectural plans had been made by Félix Thomas, Place's draftsman, and these were later published. In addition, photographs (calotypes) of some of the archaeological work at Khorsabad, as well as of other places in Mesopotamia, were taken by Gabriel Tranchard, an engineer and friend of Place. Among the photographs, the most impressive are those showing the various stages in the excavation of a city gate: its arched entrance displays a border of glazed bricks along its upper facade and a flanking pair of stone colossi in the form of human-headed winged bulls.

Systematic excavations at Khorsabad were not resumed until 1929, when the Oriental Institute of the University of Chicago sent an expedition under Edward Chiera. The institute carried out excavations at the site until 1935, with the most important seasons (1932–1935) under the direction of Gordon Loud. Their work centered on the main citadel area, a second smaller citadel (palace F), and one of the city gates (gate 7). In 1957, the Iraqi Directorate General of Antiquities carried out excavations at the temple of the Sebittu (a group of seven beneficent deities) under the direction of Behnam Abu al-Soof.

The city wall surrounding Dur Sharrukin was constructed of mud brick on top of a stone base; it was about 14 m thick and 12 m high and enclosed an area roughly square in plan (approximately 1,800 × 1,700 m—about 300 ha, or 740 acres). Seven monumental gates (gates 1–7) provided entry into the city, and each gate was given a name honoring a Mesopotamian deity (e.g., "The Goddess Ishtar Is The One Who Makes Its People Flourish"). Two gates were located on each side of the city, except on the northwest, where there was only one (gate 7). At the time of excavation, this last gateway was blocked, suggesting that the doors had never been brought into position.

The area serving as the city's main citadel was located against the northwest city wall. The citadel was on the same level as the remainder of the city but was walled off from it and made accessible by two gates (A and B). Within the citadel, the palace complex and the temple to the god Nabu were placed on platforms, raising them above the level of the other structures uncovered there (buildings J, K, L, and M). The form and placement of several of the units within the citadel seem to be somewhat haphazard and irregular. This is surprising because the city was planned and built within a brief period of time.

The royal palace (*é-gal-gaba-ri-nu-tuku-a,* "palace without rival"), with its residential, administrative, ceremonial, and religious sections, was made up of approximately 240 rooms, courtyards, and corridors, and covered about 10 ha (25 acres). The palace complex was placed on a raised terrace about 12 m high that partly jutted beyond the main line of the city wall; its inhabitants thus received the prevailing wind and also obtained a view of the nearby mountains. Access to the terrace was by means of a broad ramp that led from an open square or plaza up to the main entrance of the palace. The palace of Sargon II is perhaps the best known of all the Neo-Assyrian palaces. It was planned around three large courtyards, with the throne-room suite located between the second and third courtyards. The main entrance, on the southeast, had three monumental gateways, each of which was guarded by pairs of colossal winged bulls (see figure 1). This entrance led into the first and largest courtyard, XV (103 × 91 m). Administrative offices were probably located around this courtyard; to its northeast was the palace service area, with kitchens, storerooms, and possibly workshops. The walls of the second major courtyard (VIII), reached by passing through two chambers, were lined with stone reliefs. The ceremonial and official sections of the palace were probably located around this courtyard. On the southwest side of this courtyard, three monumental entrances led into a typical Neo-Assyrian throne-room suite. The large rectangular throne room (about 10 × 47 m) had a stone throne dais against its narrow southeastern end and was embellished with stone wall reliefs and painted decoration. Beyond the suite of rooms adjacent to the throne room was the third and innermost courtyard, around which the palace's residential quarters were probably located.

A somewhat isolated complex of rooms was discovered in the southwest corner of the palace. It was first uncovered by Place, who thought it was the palace harem (Place, 1867–1870). Subsequent work by the Oriental Institute, however, showed that this area contains six sanctuaries, and their subsidiary rooms, grouped around three courtyards (Loud, 1936). The three largest sanctuaries were dedicated to the deities Sin, Shamash, and Ningal, and the three smaller ones to Ea, Adad, and Ninurta. Nearby was a ziggurat that, according to Place, was about 43 × 43 m and could be ascended by means of a stairway that spiraled around it. [*See* Ziggurat.] Place also reported that each level of the ziggurat was about 6 m high and painted a different color; the four preserved levels are white, black, reddish, and bluish (Place, 1867–1870).

KHORSABAD. Figure 1. *Winged bull with a human head, guardian figure from the gate of the palace of Sargon II.* Dated to the second half of the eighth century BCE. Musée du Louvre, Paris. (Alinari/Art Resource, NY)

Sargon claimed (e.g. Fuchs, 1994, p. 294, l. 64) that he built a structure for his palace in the image of a Syrian *bit-ḫilani,* which is generally thought to have included a pillared portico. Although various locations have been suggested for this structure, including an unusual building at the northwest corner of the palace terrace, no firm identification can be made at present. Great care was taken with the construction and decoration of the palace, and Sargon boasted (Fuchs, 1994, p. 294, l. 63) that various woods and precious materials had been employed for those purposes. Important doorways were guarded by colossal statues of winged bulls with human heads and figures of protective deities. The walls of numerous public rooms were faced with stone slabs carved with scenes depicting the king's military accomplishments, ceremonial activities, and religious scenes (see figure 2).

The only independent temple in the citadel at Khorsabad was dedicated to Nabu, the god of writing and wisdom, as was the most important temple discovered on the citadel at Nimrud (ancient Kalḫu). [*See* Nimrud.] South of the palace terrace, and connected to it by a corbeled stone bridge, was a lower, separate platform on which a large and imposing temple of Nabu (building H) was found. The temple contained about forty-five rooms and corridors arranged around five courtyards. The two major cellae were placed next to one another, the larger one dedicated to Nabu and the slightly smaller one probably dedicated to his spouse, Tashmetu. Two important facades inside the temple were embellished with glazed-brick decoration in bright colors, depicting lions, eagles, bulls, fig trees, and ploughs. Similar decoration was also found on the courtyard facades leading into the palace's Sin, Shamash, and Ningal sanctuaries.

In addition to the palace complex and the Temple of Nabu, at least four large residences were situated in the citadel (buildings J, K, L, and M). These resembled the palace in general layout but were less complex. An inscription found on three stone threshold slabs in the largest residence (building L) indicates that it belonged to Sargon's brother, the vizier Sin-aḫa-uṣur. Although not completely excavated, the structure may have had about two hundred rooms, courtyards, and corridors. No stone wall reliefs were found in these residences, but remains of impressive painted wall decoration were found in the main reception room of building K. [*See* Wall Paintings.]

A second, smaller citadel (palace F) was discovered against the southwest city wall, near one of the city gates. Similar to the palace complex, it was raised above the level of the city and extended beyond the normal line of the city wall. This area has been only partially excavated and was originally thought to be the palace of the crown prince. However, a comparison with Fort Shalmaneser at Nimrud makes it likely that it served as the city's arsenal and military barrack.

Limited excavation has been carried out in the city itself (as distinct from the two citadels), but one large residence located near gate B (building Z; Loud and Altman, 1938), a structure near the center of the city (building G; Place, 1867–1870), and a temple situated between gate 7 and gate A (Safar, 1957) have been uncovered. The temple was ded-

KHORSABAD. Figure 2. *Relief of an offering scene.* (Alinari/Art Resource, NY)

icated to the Sebittu (see above), and in it were found approximately fifteen stone altars of offering tables, each with the same shape: a round top and tripod base, with the bottom corners of the base carved in the form of a lion's paw.

Inscriptions of Sargon II describing his military campaigns and building activities were discovered throughout the royal palace, placed on the front and back of stone wall reliefs, on stone thresholds, on winged-bull colossi, on numerous clay barrel cylinders, and on small metal tablets, among other items. Among the other important inscriptions found at the site was the Khorsabad king list: it lists the rulers of Assyria from earliest times down to 748 BCE and was discovered in the Nabu temple by the Oriental Institute excavations.

The American excavators found few small objects in proportion to the scale of the site, a lack they attributed to the short life of the city and its orderly abandonment following Sargon's death, when most of the inhabitants moved to the new capital of Nineveh (Loud and Altman, 1938). Nevertheless, the site has produced a variety of miscellaneous objects, including carved ivories (similar to ones found at Nimrud, Arslan Tash, and Samaria), fragments of embossed bronze door bands (comparable to the ones found at Balawat), small bronze bells, and weights in the shape of ducks.

[*See also* Assyrians; Mesopotamia, *article on* Ancient Mesopotamia; Nineveh; *and the biography of Botta.*]

BIBLIOGRAPHY

Albenda, Pauline. *The Palace of Sargon, King of Assyria.* Paris, 1986. Brief history of the excavations at Khorsabad, followed by a detailed presentation and study of the wall reliefs found by Botta.

Amiet, Pierre. *Art of the Ancient Near East.* Translated by John Shepley and Claude Choquet. New York, 1980.

Botta, P. E., and Eugène Flandin. *Monument de Ninive.* 5 vols. Paris, 1846–1850. Description of Botta's work and discoveries (vol. 5) and copies of the reliefs and inscriptions found (vols. 1–4).

Fontan, Elisabeth, ed. *De Khorsabad à Paris: La découverte des Assyriens.* Notes et Documents des Musées de France, vol. 26. Paris, 1994. Series of popular essays treating various aspects of the French and American discoveries, published in connection with the reopening of the Assyrian galleries in the Louvre.

Frankfort, Henri. *The Art and Architecture of the Ancient Orient.* 4th ed. Harmondsworth, 1970. Dated but still useful synthesis of information on Mesopotamian art and architecture (see esp. pp. 143–152).

Fuchs, Andreas. *Die Inschriften Sargons II. aus Khorsabad.* Göttingen, 1994.

Loud, Gordon. *Khorsabad,* part 1, *Excavations in the Palace and at a City Gate.* Oriental Institute Publications, 38. Chicago, 1936. Includes chapters by Henri Frankfort and Thorkild Jacobsen.

Loud, Gordon, and Charles B. Altman. *Khorsabad,* part 2, *The Citadel and the Town.* Oriental Institute Publications, 40. Chicago, 1938.

Place, Victor. *Ninive et l'Assyrie.* 3 vols. Paris, 1867–1870. Description of Place's work, with drawings of the major finds; lavishly produced but almost impossible to find except in the best libraries.

Safar, Fuad. "The Temple of the Sibitti at Khorsabad." *Sumer* 13 (1957): 219–221, figs. 1–4.

GRANT FRAME

KISH, site located in Iraq northeast of modern Hilla and approximately 15 km (9 mi.) to the east of Babylon (32°33′ N, 44°39′ E). Kish is a region that comprises many mounds of different sizes covering an area some 8 × 2.5 km (50 × 15.5 mi.). Particularly important for archaeology were the mounds called Tell Uhaimir in the eastern part of this wide expanse and Tell Ingharra in the west. From early in the second millennium BCE part of the site (Tell Ingharra) seems to have been referred to as Ḫursagkalama; however, the geographical extent of Ḫursagkalama and its exact relationship to Kish (Tell Uhaimir) is by no means clear. Kish was one of the most important cities of ancient Mesopotamia and was considered to be the first seat of kingship after the Flood. The title "king of Kish" was of major importance in the early historic periods, and it was from Kish that Sargon set out to create the kingdom of Akkad. Diverse parts of the site were occupied from the Ubaid period into the time of the modern Ottomans.

Since the nineteenth century, scholars and travelers have been interested in Kish, and as early as 1852, minor excavations were undertaken by Fulgence Fresnel and Jules Oppert of the Expédition scientifique et artistique de Mésopotamie et Médie that was followed much later in 1912 by a fairly large-scale French expedition under the direction of Henri de Genouillac. Only one season of excavation was completed before the onset of the World War I. After the war a new major long-term joint expedition of the Field Museum of Natural History of Chicago and the Ashmolean Museum of Oxford University began work in 1923. Between 1923 and 1933 eleven campaigns were completed under the direction of Stephen Langdon. Ernest Mackay was the first field director and was succeeded in 1926 by Louis Watelin. In 1989 a Japanese expedition of Kokushikan University (Tokyo) under the leadership of Hideo Fuji started work again at Kish. Only one season of excavation was completed before the commencement of the Gulf War.

The evidence for occupation at Kish prior to the Early Dynastic period (c. 2900–2335) is scarce, but it is evident from the so-called Y-sounding in the major mound Tell Ingharra that the earliest strata excavated contained painted pottery of Jemdet Nasr type. This suggests that there was occupation in Tell Ingharra during the Jemdet Nasr period. On top of these early strata there was a domestic settlement probably of considerable size built with plano-convex bricks in Early Dynastic I. Above and partially sunk into these plano-convex brick levels was a cemetery also dating to Early Dynastic I. The grave materials were particularly rich, and some of the objects from the graves indicated that an advanced state of metal technology was employed. Also found in the Y-sounding were a group of graves containing chariots or carts perhaps drawn by both bovids and equids. Because of the quantity and quality of the objects found in the graves at Kish, these important burials are less famed than the graves from the Royal Cemetery of Ur; however, at least four burials in Kish indicate that the Ur burials were not unique. They may even predate the Ur cemetery, but it has proved difficult to determine the exact date of the Kish burials because of a series of very complex problems. Dates have ranged from Early Dynastic I to Early Dynastic IIIA.

Probably dating to Early Dynastic III are the remains of two solid structures at Tell Ingharra that have been called ziggurats. One is larger than the other, but both are constructed of plano-convex bricks with some of the successive courses of bricks forming a herringbone pattern, a characteristic building technique of the Early Dynastic period. The plans of these ziggurats are not known completely, and it is not clear whether they were built as a single platform or whether they had more than one stage. They were probably stepped and are of considerable interest for the history of the development of the temple platform and tower. They may well be worthy of further investigation.

More extensive remains of the Early Dynastic period were recovered from Mound A located to the south of the main part of Ingharra but considered to belong to it. Significant is a large building of plano-convex bricks that has been called a palace, clearly the most impressive of the monumental buildings of Early Dynastic Sumer. The entire complex is not known, but the excavated remains include a main north wing, an added south wing, and an eastern primary gateway constructed between the north wing and an eastern wing (?) no longer preserved. Apparently the original staircase was covered by a ramp when the southern wing or annex was built. The drawn plans of the palace complex have been regularized, and certain parts are not easy to interpret as some of the walls and rooms seem to have been improperly dug. A curious feature of the main northern wing is the use of long corridors forming a double enclosure around the rooms and courts of the building. Such corridors are known from other monumental building complexes in Sumer such as the so-called palaces at Eridu. [*See* Eridu.] The southern addition also has a special feature. Columns are used within a large room near the west end of the building and also in a porch on the eastern end. A residential area of the building is not clearly evident from the plan, and it has not been fully ascertained how such a complex as the Kish palace or other monumental buildings functioned as an expression of Sumerian kingship.

Like many of the early remains of Kish, the date of the palace has been much debated. Some have sought to date the building to Early Dynastic II on the basis of the perceived style of a group of inlay pieces. Even if it were possible to limit the style chronologically, such dating is fraught with difficulties. More cogent is the find of a tablet beneath a mud brick bench built in one of the rooms. The tablet is of the "Fara" type, representing a stage in the development of writing attributable to the early part of Early Dynastic IIIA and indicates that the building was in use during that period. Before the end of Early Dynastic IIIA the palace complex had already been abandoned and had at least partially disintegrated. Another cemetery known as Cemetery A was sunk into the palace area, and some 150 graves rich in pottery and seals were excavated. The A cemetery was short lived but is important for our understanding of the archaeology of Early Dynastic III. The change from palace area to cemetery area would imply some type of population shift.

Another monumental building probably also dating to the same time as the palace is the so-called Plano-Convex Building excavated in Area P to the north of Tell Ingharra. The building has very thick buttressed exterior walls and was probably heavily fortified. It has many storage rooms as well as long surrounding corridors in part of the complex. Unfortunately the plan of the entire building is not known.

Graves, pottery, tablets, some objects, a few architectural remains, and textual references from other sources all attest to the continued occupation and importance of Kish from the Akkad through the Old Babylonian and Kassite periods. At Tell Uhaimir was located the ziggurat and temple to the important god of Kish, Zababa. Apparently begun in the Old Babylonian period, the ziggurat underwent several rebuildings, and lasted into the Neo-Babylonian period when the exterior surface was enlivened with a complicated series of brick niches and buttresses. The actual temple seems to have been located on the northeast side of the ziggurat where bricks were found that were part of the reconstruction of the temple undertaken by Hammurabi of Babylon (1792–1750).

Significant to the history of Neo-Babylonian architecture is the uncompleted double temple excavated on Tell Ingharra near the early ziggurats. The main, large part of the temple measures some 92 × 83 m (57 × 51.5 ft.). There is a direct axis approach to the cella (the inner part of the temple housing the image of deity) leading from the main entrance in the northern wall through a large courtyard and then through two antecellas. The broad room cella is flanked on both sides by smaller dependent rooms. Bricks from a foundation box and fragments of a barrel cylinder suggest that the temple was originally built by Nebuchadrezzar II (604–562). In the Achaemenid period this temple no longer was used even though Kish continued to be occupied and many economic texts of the period were found. Fragmentary remains of the settlements in the later Parthian and Sasanian periods have also been preserved.

[*See also* Temples, *article on* Mesopotamian Temples; *and* Ziggurat.]

BIBLIOGRAPHY

The final publications of the Kish excavations include:

Genouillac, Henri de. *Fouilles françaises d'El-ʿAkhymer: Premières recherches archéologiques à Kish.* 2 vols. Paris, 1924–1925.

Langdon, Stephen H. *Excavations at Kish I, 1923–1924.* Paris, 1924.

Mackay, Ernest. *Report on the Excavation of the "A" Cemetery at Kish, Mesopotamia.* Chicago, 1925.

Mackay, Ernest. *A Sumerian Palace and the "A" Cemetery at Kish, Mesopotamia.* Chicago, 1929.
Watelin, Louis Charles, and Stephen H. Langdon. *Excavations at Kish III, 1925–1927.* Paris, 1930.
Watelin, Louis Charles, and Stephen H. Langdon. *Excavations at Kish IV, 1925–1930.* Paris, 1934.

Important syntheses with extensive bibliographies of the Kish excavations include:
Gibson, McGuire. *The City and Area of Kish.* Miami, 1972.
Gibson, McGuire. "Kiš. B. Archäologisch." In *Reallexikon der Assyriologie und vorderasiatischen Archäologie,* vol. 5, pp. 613–620. Berlin and New York, 1980.
Moorey, P. R. S. *Kish Excavations, 1923–1933.* Oxford, 1978.

DONALD P. HANSEN

KITAN, TEL, two-acre site located on a hillock on the west bank of the Jordan River, approximately 12 km (7.5 mi.) north of Beth-Shean (map reference 2043 × 2270). The site's occupational history was first explored by Nehamiah Tzori in the Beth-Shean Regional Survey. In 1970 Adam Druks cut a stratigraphic section through the tell, on behalf of the Israel Department of Antiquities and Museums. Between 1975 and 1978 Emmanuel Eisenberg conducted five seasons of excavation at the site, also on behalf of the department. In the course of those explorations, ten occupational levels were investigated.

The first settlement at Tel Kitan was in the Chalcolithic period (strata X–VIII). It consisted of several houses, occupied for an extended period of time, and underground silos. One house also contained an enormous buried storejar, one of the largest of its kind found in Israel. Over time, new buildings were constructed over the original houses. The ceramic assemblage at this Chalcolithic site is considered a northern variant of the Ghassulian culture. The excavator suggested that this long-lived village was an extension of the contemporary 60-acre settlement at nearby Neveh Ur.

The late Early Bronze Age I (stratum VII) unwalled village at Tel Kitan included a number of densely packed dwellings. Floors were often below ground level, and plastered benches ran along many interior walls. The rich repertoire of EB I materials found at Tel Kitan is attributed to the sudden destruction and abandonment of the site.

Tel Kitan was reoccupied in Middle Bronze I (stratum VI). While the first sanctuary was constructed in MB II (stratum V), it is likely that sacred activities took place in stratum VI as well. The exterior of the mud-brick sanctuary measured 5.5 × 6.9 m. Piers extended from two walls to form a shallow entryway, and two pillars flanked the entrance.

Five meters in front of the sanctuary facade stood a row of stone stelae; large holes between them may have once contained the socles of other standing stones. The central stela depicts a nude goddess cupping her breasts; her facial features are distinct. Two larger stelae stood elevated behind the front row of stones. Residential buildings, many containing infant jar burials, were located nearby.

Care was taken to preserve the stratum V sanctuary when a new sanctuary was constructed over it later in MB II. The exterior of the stratum IV building measured 11.5 × 14.3 m. In the courtyard, piles of ash filled with animal bones were heaped around a semicircular bench, and four crudely carved stone figurines lay near two basalt bases and a basalt slab. The settlement, which also included several houses, was surrounded by a fortification wall. The site was destroyed at the end of MB II.

In Late Bronze I (stratum III), a new sacred complex was constructed over the earlier one. Many precious and ritual objects were found in the sanctuary, which then consisted of a main hall and two small service rooms. Piles of broken pottery and a small pebble structure were found in the courtyard. As before, houses were located nearby. This occupation came to a sudden end, and Tel Kitan remained unoccupied for nearly two millennia. The thin-walled houses of the Early Arab period (stratum II), situated along a street, were badly eroded. During the Ottoman period (stratum I), a Muslim cemetery was located on the top of the mound.

BIBLIOGRAPHY

Eisenberg, Emmanuel. "The Temples at Tell Kittan." *Biblical Archaeologist* 40 (1977): 77–81.
Eisenberg, Emmanuel. "The Middle and Late Bronze Age Temples at Tel Kittan." In *Temples and High Places in Biblical Times,* edited by Avraham Biran, p. 159. Jerusalem, 1981.
Eisenberg, Emmanuel. "Tel Kittan." In *The New Encyclopedia of Archaeological Excavations in the Holy Land,* vol. 3, pp. 878–881. Jerusalem and New York, 1993.

BETH ALPERT NAKHAI

KITCHENER, HORATIO HERBERT, first Earl Kitchener of Khartoum and Broome (1850–1916), surveyor for the Survey of Western Palestine (1871–1877). As a young lieutenant in the British Royal Engineers, Herbert Horatio Kitchener was seconded in 1874 to the Survey of Western Palestine being conducted under the auspices of the Palestine Exploration Fund (PEF). A devout Christian, Kitchener brought to the survey a detailed knowledge of the Bible, which, combined with a military eye for topography, led him, like Claude R. Conder, to attempt numerous identifications of biblical sites. Many of his judgments were erroneous, as for example, in placing Ai at Khirbet Haiyan (*The Survey of Western Palestine: Memoirs of the Topography, Orography, Hydrography, and Archaeology,* vol. 3, London, 1883, p. 33). Kitchener's main contribution to the archaeology of Palestine was twofold. First, he surveyed about one-third of the country himself, recording in careful plans many structures which no longer exist. Second, as a keen amateur photographer, he took many photographs (preserved in the PEF archives). Twelve of his photographs were published in London in 1876 under the title *Guinea Book of Biblical Photographs* (also known as *Photographs of Biblical Sites*).

Much of Kitchener's work was published in the volumes of *Memoirs* which accompanied the maps of the Survey of Western Palestine; his reports and letters were published in the PEF's *Quarterly Statement* between 1874 and 1878. Kitchener went on to survey Cyprus and, in 1883, his fluent knowledge of Arabic led to his being recommended by Charles Wilson to carry out the trigonometrical survey of the Wadi ʿArabah during Edward Hull's geological reconnaissance of the Sinai Peninsula, also under the auspices of the PEF.

Kitchener made his professional name in the administration of Egypt, Sudan, South Africa, and India. He was distinguished as a Knight of the Garter, Knight Grand Cross of the Bath, and Knight Grand Cross of St. Michael and St. George and earned the order of merit. At the time of his death, he held the post of secretary of state for war.

[*See also* Palestine Exploration Fund; Sinai; *and the biographies of Conder and Wilson.*]

BIBLIOGRAPHY

Information on Kitchener's life and work is available in the Archives of the Palestine Exploration Fund, London. For a full-length biography, see Magnus (below).

Conder, Claude R., and H. H. Kitchener. *The Survey of Western Palestine: Memoirs of the Topography, Orography, Hydrography, and Archaeology*. 8 vols. and set of maps. London, 1881–1885.

Crace, J. D. "Lord Kitchener." *Quarterly Statement of the Palestine Exploration Fund* (July 1916): 122–123.

Kitchener, H. H. *Photographs of Biblical Sites*. London, c. 1876.

Magnus, Philip. *Kitchener: Portrait of an Imperialist*. London, 1958. Still the most authoritative study of Kitchener, although only a few pages are devoted to his work in Palestine.

YOLANDE HODSON

KITION, name of a kingdom and a site, today below the city of Larnaka, on the southeast coast of Cyprus (34°54′ N, 33°39′ E), north of the Salt Lake (Aliki). The historical territory of the Cypro-Phoenician kingdom of Kition was bounded by the sea on the south and southeast and was adjacent to the territories of Salamis on the northeast and Amathus on the west. To the north, the rich agricultural region of Idalion was annexed after 450 BCE. Tamassos, to the northwest, with its copper mines, belonged to Kition for several years in the fourth century BCE. [*See* Salamis; Amathus; Idalion.]

The name is attested in Hebrew (from the eighth century BCE) in the ethnic plural *kittîm* (cf. *Nm.* 24:24; *Is.* 23:1; *Ez.* 27:6). The identification with Qartihadasht ("new city"), mentioned in Assyrian on the prism of Esarhaddon from Nineveh and in Phoenician (Cyprus, *CIS* 1.5) has been questioned but is defensible. [*See* Nineveh; Phoenician-Punic.] The name of the city in Phoenician is *Kt(y)*; in alphabetic Greek Kit(t)ion; in syllabic Greek *Ke-ti-o-ne* (genitive); and in Latin, Citium. After the Middle Ages, the names *Scala, Larnaka,* and *Salines* occur.

Kition's location and ancient remains were noted by numerous early travelers in descriptions and schematic plans, among them Richard Pococke (1745), Giorgio Mariti (1769), and Carsten Niebuhr (1837). Pococke copied thirty-three Phoenician inscriptions that are now lost. In the nineteenth century, travelers, merchants, and such scholars as Max Ohnefalsch-Richter and Melchior de Vogüé discovered or occasionally purchased exceptional objects from the area and sent them to museums in Europe and the United States: from Bamboula, the stela of Sargon II from 707 BCE (Vorderasiatische Museum, Berlin) and large Hathoric capitals (Berlin; the Louvre Museum); from the Salt Lake, inscriptions to Eshmun-Melqart of Batsalos (Metropolitan Museum of Art, New York City); figurines from the sanctuary of Artemis Paralia (Louvre; British Museum); and figurines and sarcophagi from various areas of Larnaka, including [*See* Sarcophagus.] Kamelarga and Ayios Giorghos. The work of the British administration in 1879, carried out to do away with the unhealthy environment by filling the marshes with the material from the archaeological mound of Bamboula, irrevocably destroyed important historical remains (cf. Ohnefalsch-Richter, 1879; Sinclair, 1969–1970). Several documents were saved, such as the inscription in Phoenician of the accounts of the Temple of Astarte, now in the British Museum. In *CIS* 1 (1881), the majority of the Phoenician inscriptions from Cyprus are from Kition. The first precise plan of the site appears in the *CIS* (p. 35).

Scientific excavation at Kition began in 1929 with Einar Gjerstad's brief sounding for the Swedish Cyprus Expedition at Bamboula. He located a sanctuary of Herakles Melqart with a bothros filled with figurines. Excavations by the Cypriot Department of Antiquities directed by Vassos Karageorghis began in 1959 at Kathari, north of Larnaka. They uncovered an area with exceptional Late Bronze Age sanctuaries (temples 1–5), evidence of bronze metallurgy, and fortifications (see below). The newly arrived Phoenicians reoccupied and rebuilt the area in the ninth century BCE (temples 1 and 4). The expedition recovered evidence of metallurgy and inscriptions (see below).

In 1976, a resumption of work at Bamboula by a French expedition from the University of Lyon 2 directed by Marguerite Yon uncovered the sanctuaries of Melqart and Astarte (ninth–end eighth centuries) and a naval port with sheds (see figure 1) and boat slips (fifth–fourth centuries). In 1990, a Phoenician inscription was found by chance north of the town of Larnaka describing a monument that had been set up in the port after a naval victory by King Milkyaton in 392 BCE.

The earliest occupation of the area is attested by Early Bronze Age tombs at several places in Larnaka, but no settlement earlier than the thirteenth century BCE has been located. In this period, because silting had closed off the Salt Lake, rendering the port of Hala Sultan Tekke useless, a new settlement was established 1 km to the north on the seacoast at Kition, to find better access to the sea and continue the maritime activities. [*See* Hala Sultan Tekke.] A group of sanctuaries next to the fortification at Kathari and several tombs date to this period (see below).

Several traces of habitation remain from the Geometric I period, including a domestic establishment on the edge of the fortification to the north of Bamboula that was abandoned in the tenth century BCE. In the ninth century the Phoenicians established an important colony in Kition (cf. Justin, 18.5–6) that preserved its Phoenician character until the third century CE (Cypro-Geometric III, Archaic, and classical periods). The period is attested archaeologically at the sites of Kathari, Bamboula, Ayios Giorghios (on the edge of the Salt Lake), and various other locations in Larnaka. It is attested textually (literary texts and inscriptions), especially in the fifth–fourth centuries. Inscriptions and coin legends in Phoenician give the names of several kings, including Baalmilk I, Azibaal, and Baalmilk II (fifth century BCE); and Milkyaton and Pumayyaton (fourth century BCE). Because of their navy, these kings played a role in the maritime rivalries between the Greeks and the Persians in the eastern Mediterranean basin. The wealth of the kingdom depended on that maritime commercial activity, which was supported by the resources of the countryside (corn, olive oil, timber, copper, etc.). The most celebrated Kitian is the philosopher Zenon, founder of Stoicism, who was born there in the fourth century BCE. Ancient authors, such as Cicero (*De finibus* 4.20.56), recognized the Kition's Phoenician character.

At the end of the fourth century BCE, Ptolemy I Soter seized control of the city (Diodorus 19.79.4), and a new "era of Kition" began (in 311). Kition then followed the fortunes of the Lagid possessions and, after 50 BCE, of the Roman province to which Cyprus belonged.

Monuments are visible at different locations in the town: at Kathari, there are remains of temple 1 (Karageorghis, *Excavations at Kition*, vol. 5, 1987) constructed of cut stone blocks (thirteenth century BCE) and transformed into a Phoenician temple in the ninth century BCE; the remains of other temples and workshops that constituted the sacred area were found next to the fortification.

At Bamboula, various sanctuaries from the ninth century BCE to the classical period survive. The civic works from the beginning of the fourth century include a drainage system with a main sewer. The sanctuary is bounded on the north by the naval port, with sheds and slips for the ships (see Calvet, 1993).

There are tombs in various parts of Larnaka: Early Bronze Age tombs at Ayios Prodromos; LB tombs at Chrysopolitissa with grave goods of rich furnishings and local and imported luxury products; Archaic period tombs at Phaneromeni; beautifully built tombs from the Classical/Hellenistic period from Tourabi and Metropolis and from Ayios Ioannis and Ayios Giorghios, where the tombs continue to yield sarcophagi and funerary furnishings.

[*See also* Cyprus; *and* Phoenicians.]

KITION. Figure 1. *Ship sheds in the naval port.* (Courtesy Mission Française de Kition)

BIBLIOGRAPHY

Calvet, Yves. "Kition: Travaux de la mission française." In *Kinyras: L'archéologie française à Chypre,* pp. 107–138. Lyon, 1993. Includes bibliography of the French mission.

Cobham, Claude Delaval. *Excerpta Cypria: Materials for a History of Cyprus.* Cambridge, 1908.

Gjerstad, Einar, et al. *The Swedish Cyprus Expedition: Finds and Results of the Excavations in Cyprus 1927–1931.* Vol. 3. Stockholm, 1937. See "Kition" (pp. 1–79).

Hill, George F. *Catalogue of the Greek Coins of Cyprus.* London, 1904.

Hill, George F. *A History of Cyprus,* vol. 1, *To the Conquest by Richard Lion Heart.* London, 1940.

Karageorghis, Vassos, ed. "Chronique des fouilles et découvertes archéologiques à Chypre." *Bulletin de Correspondance Hellénique* 83 (1959): 336–361, and subsequent volumes.

Karageorghis, Vassos, ed. *Fouilles de Kition.* 5 vols. Nicosia, 1974–1987.

Karageorghis, Vassos. *Kition: Mycenaean and Phoenician Discoveries in Cyprus.* London, 1976.

Mariti, Giorgio. *Viaggi per l'Isola de Cipro.* Vol. 1. Florence, 1769.

Masson, Olivier, and Maurice Sznycer. *Recherches sur les Phéniciens à Chypre.* Paris and Geneva, 1972.

Nicolaou, Kyriakos. *The Historical Topography of Kition.* Göteborg, 1976.

Niebuhr, Carsten. *Reisen durch Syrien und Palaestina, nach Cypern.* Vol. 3. Hamburg, 1837.

Ohnefalsch-Richter, Max. "Neue Funde aus Cypern." *Ausland* 52 (1879): 970–974.

Pococke, Richard. *A Description of the East and Some Other Countries.* Vol. 2.1. London, 1745.

Reyes, A. T. *Archaic Cyprus: A Study of the Textual and Archaeological Evidence.* Oxford, 1994.

Sinclair, L. "Report on Excavations at the Bamboola-Larnaca." In D. Bailey, "The 'Village Priest's Tomb' at Aradippou in Cyprus." *British Museum Quarterly* 34 (1969–1970): 37–40.

Yon, Marguerite, ed. *Kition-Bamboula.* 4 vols. Paris, 1982–1993.

Yon, Marguerite. "Le royaume de Kition: Époque archaïque." In *Phoenicia and the East Mediterranean in the First Millennium B.C.,* edited by Éduard Lipiński, pp. 357–374. Studia Phoenicia, 5. Louvain, 1987.

Yon, Marguerite. "Le royaume de Kition: Époque classique." In *Numismatique et histoire économique phéniciennes et puniques,* edited by Tony Hackens and Ghislaine Moucharte, pp. 243–260. Studia Phoenicia, 9. Louvain, 1992.

MARGUERITE YON

Translated from French by Nancy Leinwand

KOLDEWEY, ROBERT (1855–1925), archaeologist whose work revolutionized Mesopotamian archaeology. Koldewey studied architecture, archaeology, and ancient history in Berlin, Munich, and Vienna. His first archaeological experience came on the acropolis at Assos. The German Archaeological Institute subsequently commissioned him to excavate on Lesbos. In 1887, Koldewey worked with Robert Moritz at Surgul and al-Hiba, near Sumerian Telloh, in southern Mesopotamia. There Koldewey refined excavation techniques for following mud-brick walls, finding many small houses separated by twisting, narrow streets. He also followed foundation trenches by observing dark discolorations in the soil, an unheard-of technique at the time. For years, this talented archaeologist worked as an architectural instructor at the university in Gorlitz, Germany, while excavating at classical sites in Italy, Sicily, and Syria. He started large-scale excavations in Babylon in 1899. He remained there for the next eighteen years, only leaving during World War I, when the British advance up the Tigris River threatened to cut off his last route to safety. Koldewey developed sophisticated techniques for tracing that city's myriad mud-brick structures, training teams of diggers to distinguish the texture of room fill and mud brick after careful scraping and picking. Starting with a general knowledge of the city gleaned from cuneiform tablets, Koldewey identified King Hammurabi's city (1790 BCE) and then cleared a large part of Nebuchadrezzar's (604–562 BCE) capital, tracing the course of the paved Procession Street, reconstructing the Ishtar Gate, and untangling the long history of the city's citadel and ziggurat. Koldewey's excavation techniques recovered the general layout of the royal city and enabled him to reconstruct the magnificent enameled friezes that adorned the Ishtar Gate and Procession Street. His methods influenced the techniques of later excavators like Leonard Woolley at Ur. Koldewey did tend to overlook the potential of pottery and small artifacts for dating stratified layers, an oversight his successors regretted.

[*See also* Babylon.]

BIBLIOGRAPHY

Koldewey, Robert. *The Excavations at Babylon.* London, 1914. Koldewey's account of the Babylon excavations, aimed at the general reader.

Koldewey, Robert. *Das Wieder erstehende Babylon* (1913). Leipzig, 1925. Another description of the royal city.

Lloyd, Seton. *Foundations in the Dust: The Story of Mesopotamian Exploration.* Rev. and enl. ed. London, 1980. General history of Mesopotamian archaeology that offers an assessment of Koldewey's work.

Oates, Joan. *Babylon.* London, 1979. Definitive popular account of Babylon, drawing on both historical and archaeological sources, with numerous plans and illustrations.

BRIAN FAGAN

KOŞAY, HAMIT ZÜBEYR (1897–1984), Turkish archaeologist, ethnologist, and museologist. Koşay was born in the village of Tilenkçi Tamak attached to the Ufa district in Russia's Idil-Ural province. After graduating from high school in 1916, Koşay became interested in ethnographic studies and, planning to study in Budapest, began to learn Hungarian. In Budapest he studied history and languages (1917–1921). He subsequently received a Ph.D. in Turkology and philology from the Eötrös College in Budapest. In 1923–1924 he took courses in ethnography at Berlin University.

Upon his return to Turkey in 1924, Koşay became involved in various government-sponsored projects related to ethnography, archaeology, and museology. Between 1927 and 1931 he created the Ethnography Museum in Ankara and served as its director. He was eventually in 1931 appointed general director of all museums and in 1945 director general of the Department of Antiquities and Museums.

Koşay's involvement in archaeological field projects began in the early 1930s. Atatürk, the leader of the then young Turkish republic, favored government-sponsored archaeological projects directed by Turkish archaeologists. He asked Koşay to excavate in the vicinity of Ankara, the capital of the republic. Thus, in 1933, Ahlatlıbel, southwest of the capital, became Koşay's first archaeological project. A year later he excavated Kumtepe, near Troy. His excavations at Alaça Höyük (1935–1948, 1963–1967) revealed important aspects of Hittite and pre-Hittite civilizations in Anatolia. The site's spectacular finds earned him a reputation as one of Turkey's most experienced and knowledgable field archaeologists. During his long career, Koşay carried out numerous other excavations and field surveys: in the 1930s he excavated the Phrygian site of Pazarlı in Çorum; in the 1940s, at Karaz Höyük in Erzurum and the Late Chalcolithic site of Büyük Güllücek in Çorum; in the 1960s, at the Early Bronze Age settlements at Güzelova and Pulur in Erzurum, and Pulur (Sakyol) in the Keban region; and, in 1972, at Yeniköy, also in the Keban.

Koşay published more than 35 books and 150 articles on Anatolian civilization. His work represents an important data bank on Early Bronze Age, Hittite, and Phrygian cultures in Anatolia.

BIBLIOGRAPHY

Koşay, Hamit Zübeyr. *Les fouilles de Pazarli.* Ankara, 1941.

Koşay, Hamit Zübeyr. *Ausgrabungen von Alaca Höyük.* Ankara, 1944. The first archaeological report on the excavations at Alaca Höyük.

Koşay, Hamit Zübeyr, and Mahmut Akok. *Ausgrabungen von Büyük Güllücek.* Ankara, 1944. Archaeological report on the 1942 and 1944 campaigns at Büyük Güllücek.

Koşay, Hamit Zübeyr. *Les fouilles d'Alaca Höyük.* Ankara, 1951. Preliminary report on the 1937–1939 excavations at Alaca Höyük.

Koşay, Hamit Zübeyr, and Hermann Vary. *Die Ausgrabungen von Pulur.* Ankara, 1964. Report on the 1960 season of excavations at Pulur.

Koşay, Hamit Zübeyr. *Guide d'Alaca Höyük.* Ankara, 1965.

Koşay, Hamit Zübeyr, and Mahmut Akok. *Ausgrabungen von Alaca Höyük.* Ankara, 1966. Preliminary report of the 1940–1948 excavations at Alaca Höyük.

Koşay, Hamit Zübeyr, and Hermann Vary. *Ausgrabungen von Güzelova.* Ankara, 1967. Archaeological report on the Güzeolova excavations.

Koşay, Hamit Zübeyr, and Mahmut Akok. *Alaca Höyük Excavations.* Ankara, 1973. Preliminary report on research and discoveries, 1963–1967.

Koşay, Hamit Zübeyr. *Keban Project Pulur Excavations, 1968–1970.* Ankara, 1976. Final report of the Pulur excavations in the Keban area.

JAK YAKAR

KOURION (Roman Curium), southern Cypriot city lying on a 70-meter bluff overlooking the Bay of Episkopi (34°40′ N, 32°51′ E). A sanctuary of Apollo Hylates (i.e., Apollo of the Woodlands) 2.5 km (1.5 mi.) west of the city that attracted worshipers, and a Roman stadium, perhaps of the second century CE, lay north of the city. Various sites have been found at the foot of the bluff adjacent to the stadium, but only a fraction of Kourion has been excavated.

KOURION. *General view of the site.* (Photograph by Noelle Soren)

Settlements of the Neolithic, Chalcolithic, and Bronze Age periods are within 7 km (4.3 mi.) to the north and east, but the earliest site at Kourion is Episkopi-Kaloriziki 2 km (1.2 mi.) east of the city. A cemetery spanning the Late Bronze Age and the Cypro-Classical period has revealed evidence of Greek settlers (Arcadians?), a new type of square-chamber tomb and Greek artifacts, including the famous falcon-headed, gold, and enamel scepter of Kourion (see Swing, 1982, p. 53, fig. 44; see also George McFadden, "A Late Cypriot III Tomb from Kourion," *American Journal of Archaeology* 58 [1954]: 131–142). Although no settlement was found at Kaloriziki, it seems that the nearby Late Bronze Age site Episkopi-Bamboula diminished in importance as inhabitants moved to Kourion.

Kourion is cited in the Prism of Esarhaddon (673–672 BCE), an important octagonal and cylindrical text, as a city under Assyrian control. Under Persian hegemony, which began around 550, Kourion took part in the Ionian Revolt of 499, when King Stasanor aided the Greeks, but then deserted to the Persian side (Herodotus, 5.113), allowing Kourion to stay independent after the revolt was crushed. In 351 Kourion was one of nine kingdoms of Cyprus (Diodorus, 16.42.4). In 332 Pasicrates, last king of Kourion, aided Alexander the Great against the Persians at the battle of Tyre (Arrian, *Anabasis* 22.2).

Little is known about Ptolemaic Kourion, but it revived considerably under the Romans, particularly in the Julio-Claudian and Trajanic periods. Kourion probably did not exceed twenty thousand inhabitants in the high empire and was supposedly visited by St. Paul and Barnabas (*Acts of Barnabas* 44) during their first missionary journey (45–48 CE). Kourion was destroyed by earthquakes; the most notable of them appears to have occurred on 21 July 365 CE, forcing the abandonment of the area for at least eighteen years. At the beginning of the fifth century, a small community had developed with two impressive early Christian basilica complexes and a palatial dwelling (the Eustolius complex) that featured private baths and fine mosaics with detailed inscriptions. The site was abandoned following Islamic raids of the mid-seventh century.

Excavations at the sanctuary of Apollo were conducted by George McFadden, aided by Bert Hodge Hill, for the University of Pennsylvania Museum (1934–1953). The results were summarized by Robert Scranton in 1967. New excavations began in 1978 by the Walters Art Gallery, Baltimore, under Diana Buitron and the University of Missouri under David Soren. The sanctuary functioned continuously from at least the seventh century BCE to the fourth century CE. Early features included a circular rubble altar in the archaic precinct, which was surrounded by votive terra-cotta figurines. Gold and silver statuettes of bulls found in the altar are now in the Cyprus Museum. Several major caches of votive terra cottas have been found in votive pits at the periphery of the precinct; one group of more than ten thousand horses and riders, chariots, and charioteers was recovered in 1981.

A large circular monument, initially constructed in the seventh or sixth century BCE and rebuilt in the Roman period, was found west of the altar and principal street of the sanctuary. It was placed on a flat, elevated terrace originally surrounded by plantings in rock-cut channels but later entirely walled in during the Julio-Claudian period. Unique in Mediterranean archaeology, it may have been used for sacred dancing. It was hypaethral (i.e., unroofed) and featured seven pits carved in the bedrock in its central area, possibly for date palms (sacred trees?). A wall blocked uninitiates from the proceedings. The precinct surrounding the monument may have been the *alsos* (holy grove) with sacred deer described by Aelian (*De Natura Animalium* 11.7).

The site also featured a temple dedicated by the Roman emperor Nero (54–68 CE) and erected over a simpler rectangular structure of the seventh or sixth century BCE. Thus, in the sixth century BCE it was possible to enter the sanctuary from the south, walk north on the main street, and go from the central court area straight to the rectangular proto-temple, and right to the archaic precinct or left to the circular monument. First uncovered by McFadden in 1934, the temple was restudied by Scranton in 1967. Detailed studies by the Soren team in 1979 led to a proposed reconstruction but Stefanos Sinos partially rebuilt it in situ in 1981 in a manner that differs slightly in the arrangement of front and anta capitals from the reconstruction proposed by Soren. As part of the Roman revisions, the sanctuary received a *palaestra* (low building with central court for exercising and athletics, esp. wrestling), baths, and an apparent visitor center (the South Building).

At the city site of Kourion, McFadden, J. F. Daniel, and Roger Edwards conducted excavations, which began in 1934. The ruins are scattered over a full kilometer and include a well-preserved theater remodeled under Nero but originally built in the late second century BCE. Since 1975 Demos Christou of the Cypriot Department of Antiquities has conducted important excavations in the northern area of the city revealing buildings of the forum including a possible stoa and a monumental building of the first century CE identified as a *nymphaeum* (monumental public forum). The opulence and size of these structures suggests that Kourion must have been of considerable importance in the Roman imperial period.

A. H. S. Megaw of the British School at Athens has unearthed the remains of a large Christian basilica of the early fifth century intended as the key structure for the post-earthquake revitalization of Kourion. Some materials were borrowed from the abandoned Apollo sanctuary. A baptistery, auxiliary chapels, and courtyards have also been unearthed.

Beginning in 1984, David Soren, excavating for the University of Arizona, restudied work by J. F. Daniel in 1934 and revealed a large house and possible market complex in which the skeletons of nine humans and one mule were found in the debris of the earthquake of 365 CE. This area of the site was never rebuilt. A small museum located in Kourion House in nearby Episkopi village features objects from Kourion and nearby areas.

BIBLIOGRAPHY

Benson, Jack L. *The Necropolis of Kaloriziki.* Studies in Mediterranean Archaeology, vol. 36. Göteborg, 1973.

Buitron, Diana. "Terracotta Figurine Deposit Unearthed." *American Schools of Oriental Research Newsletter* 35.4 (1984): 1–3.

Christou, Demos. "Excavations at Kourion: First Preliminary Report, 1975–1982." *Report of the Department of Antiquities of Cyprus* (1983): 266–280.

Megaw, A. H. S. "Excavations at the Episcopal Basilica of Kourion in Cyprus in 1974 and 1975: A Preliminary Report." *Dumbarton Oaks Papers* 30 (1976): 345–371.

Mitford, Terence B. *The Inscriptions of Kourion.* Philadelphia, 1971.

Scranton, Robert L. "The Architecture of the Sanctuary of Apollo Hylates at Kourion." *Transactions of the American Philosophical Society* 57 (1967): 3–85.

Sinos, Stefanos. *The Temple of Apollo Hylates at Kourion and the Restoration of Its South-west Corner.* Athens, 1990.

Soren, David. *The Sanctuary of Apollo Hylates at Kourion, Cyprus.* Tucson, 1987.

Soren, David. "The Day the World Ended at Kourion: Reconstructing an Ancient Earthquake." *National Geographic* 174 (July 1988): 30–53.

Swiny, Helena W., ed. *An Archaeological Guide to the Kourion Area and the Akrotiri Peninsula.* Nicosia, 1982.

Young, John H., and Suzanne H. Young. *Terracotta Figurines from Kourion in Cyprus.* Philadelphia, 1955.

DAVID SOREN

KRAELING, CARL HERMANN (1897–1966), historian of religion, prominent educator, archaeologist, and authority on the Near East. Kraeling began his career at the Lutheran Theological Seminary in Philadelphia, where he taught for nine years (1920–1929) and produced his first piece of scholarly research, *Anthropos and Son of Man: A Study in the Religious Syncretism of the Hellenistic Orient* (1927). After completing a Ph.D. from Columbia University (1927), Kraeling joined the faculty of the Yale Divinity School (1929). He earned a Th.D. from the University of Heidelberg (1935). At Yale he served as editor of the *Journal of Biblical Literature* (1931–1933) and was Buckingham Professor of New Testament Criticism and Interpretation (1941).

In the 1930s, Kraeling's interests shifted to archaeology and history. He participated in the British and American excavations at the site of Gerasa (Jerash) in Jordan and edited their findings in *Gerasa, City of the Decapolis* (1938). In 1947, Kraeling founded the Department of Near Eastern Languages and Literature at Yale University and served as its first chair for three years. He then moved to the University of Chicago as professor of Oriental archaeology. An indication of his efforts to promote interest in Near Eastern archaeology was his service as president of the American Schools of Oriental Research (1948–1955) and then as president of the American Oriental Society (1958–1959).

Kraeling served as the director of the Oriental Institute in Chicago from 1950 to 1960. He was responsible for the institute's excavations in Egypt and other parts of the Near East, and he directed the excavations at the Roman site of Ptolemais in Cyrenaica, publishing *Ptolemais, City of the Libyan Pentapolis* (1962). In addition to his administrative duties, he published a volume on *John the Baptist* (1951) and a study on the Dura synagogue (1956). In 1958 he assembled scholars from all over the world for a week-long seminar on the topic of urbanization in the ancient Near East. The proceedings were published as *City Invincible* (1960). From 1946 until 1965, he was a member of the board of directors of the Byzantine Research Institute of Harvard University at Dumbarton Oaks, in Washington, D.C., where he also lectured.

[*See also* American Schools of Oriental Research; Dura-Europos; Gerasa; *and* Ptolemais.]

BIBLIOGRAPHY

Kraeling, Carl H. *Anthropos and Son of Man: A Study in the Religious Syncretism of the Hellenistic Orient.* New York, 1927.

Kraeling, Carl H., ed. *Gerasa, City of the Decapolis.* New Haven, 1938.

Kraeling, Carl H. *John the Baptist.* New York, 1951.

Kraeling, Carl H. *The Synagogue.* The Excavations at Dura-Europos, Final Report 8, part 1. New Haven, 1956. Discussion of the houses at Dura-Europos.

Kraeling, Carl H., and Robert M. Adams, eds. *City Invincible: A Symposium on Urbanization and Cultural Development in the Ancient Near East.* Chicago, 1960.

Kraeling, Carl H. *Ptolemais, City of the Libyan Pentapolis.* Chicago, 1962.

Kraeling, Carl H. *The Christian Building.* The Excavations at Dura-Europos, Final Report 8, part 2. New Haven, 1967.

VICTOR H. MATTHEWS

KSAR 'AKIL, rockshelter situated 10 km (6 mi.) east–northeast of Beirut in Wadi Antelias, and 2 km (1 mi.) inland from Lebanon's present Mediterranean coastline (33°54′40″ N, 35°36′20″ E). Wadi Antelias has two branches that descend steeply through rugged limestone hills to the sea. Ksar 'Akil is on the northern branch, slightly above its junction with the southern fork. The copious Antelias spring lies half a kilometer downstream and, after heavy rain, a stream fills the wadi below the site. The site was inhabited from the Middle through the Upper Paleolithic into the Epipaleolithic period. Its unusually long, and apparently complete, sequence of occupation has made it the site of reference for the later Paleolithic in the Levant.

The site of Ksar 'Akil has been known since the early years of the twentieth century. Two major excavations have taken place there, one from 1937 to 1938 that was resumed in 1947 and 1948, and another from 1969 to 1975 that came to a premature end because of the outbreak of civil war. The first series of excavations was undertaken by Joseph G. Doherty, with the assistance of J. Franklin Ewing, under the auspices of Boston College and Fordham University. They dug a deep trench against the back wall of the rockshelter, through the entire sequence of occupation, down to the natural surface 23 m below (Ewing, 1949). The site was never fully published. The second series of excavations was conducted by Jacques Tixier for the Centre National de Recherche Scientifique in France, to obtain detailed information about human activity at Ksar 'Akil and to construct a well-dated sequence of environmental change for the successive periods of occupation there. The site had come under threat from large-scale limestone quarrying in Wadi Antelias, which provided an additional impetus for the work. Tixier's excavation was limited in scale: two sections were cut through the Epipaleolithic and the later Upper Paleolithic levels, to a depth of 7 m, before the excavation was concluded (Tixier and Inizan, 1981).

The sequence revealed in the original excavations was especially important for the development of the Upper Paleolithic, usually designated as the Levantine Aurignacian culture. It has inspired a series of studies on the chipped-stone assemblages from Ksar 'Akil and their geomorphological context. The cultural sequence at Ksar 'Akil began with a Middle Paleolithic of Levalloiso-Mousterian affinities that, after a lengthy intermediate episode, was succeeded by the Levantine Aurignacian. Ewing (1949) had called the intermediate phase a mixed or transitional zone, but it has been renamed Ksar 'Akil, phases A and B, by recent commentators. Ksar 'Akil was inhabited for the entire Upper Paleolithic—that is, Levantine Aurignacian, phases A and B—and through another transitional stage, Levantine Aurignacian C, or the Athlitian, into the Kebaran culture of the earlier Epipaleolithic.

Recent studies of the material from the earlier excavations and inferences derived from Tixier's work suggest that, while the basic sequence still holds, its interpretation should be modified. Anthony E. Marks and P. Volkman (1986) have suggested that the basal deposits may date to the early and middle Levalloiso-Mousterian, and that there may have been a hiatus in occupation between the Middle and Upper Paleolithic at Ksar 'Akil. Christopher Bergman (1987) has concluded that, although the Ksar 'Akil Upper Paleolithic sequence is still the longest known in the Levant, it should be regarded as discontinuous, with periods of human use separated by episodes of abandonment. Tixier had found preserved living surfaces containing hearths, food remains (animal bones), and flint artifacts.

The last phase excavated by Tixier, attributed to the "proto-Kebaran," ended in about 22,000 BP, in radiocarbon years. The lowest levels reached by him, corresponding to the upper part of the Levantine Aurignacian B in the older sequence, dated to about 32,000 BP. It is estimated that the Levantine Aurignacian at Ksar 'Akil began at least 40,000 years ago, whereas the Levalloiso-Mousterian levels probably date to well before 50,000 BP. This suggests that the Upper Paleolithic may have begun earlier in the Levant than in Europe.

Ksar 'Akil was used as a shelter by humans for much of the last cold episode of the Pleistocene. It is known from independent sources, principally deep-sea caves, ice cores, and pollen sequences (for example, Dansgaard and Oeschger, 1989; Shackleton and Opdyke, 1976; and Wijmstrar, 1969), that, although the climate was generally cooler throughout than today, temperature and humidity fluctuated considerably. Those fluctuations are reflected in the long sedimentary sequence in the rockshelter, though they are scarcely apparent in the collections of animal bones from the site. The faunal remains, studied by D. A. Hooijer (1961), are dominated by fallow deer. This suggests that the foothills of the mountains of Lebanon, which formed the environs of Ksar 'Akil, remained wooded, despite the numerous fluctuations in climate that occurred.

BIBLIOGRAPHY

Azoury, Ingrid. *Ksar Akil Lebanon,* vol. 1, *Levels XXV–XII.* British Archaeological Reports, International Series, no. 289. 1–2. Oxford, 1986. Analysis of the chipped-stone assemblages from Ksar 'Akil A and B and the Levantine Aurignacian A levels, with much background information on the history of research at the site.

Bergman, Christopher A. *Ksar Akil Lebanon,* vol. 2, *Levels XIII–VI.* British Archaeological Reports, International Series, no. 329. Oxford, 1987. Analysis of the chipped-stone assemblages from the Levantine Aurignacian levels, with illustrations of the first series of excavations.

Dansgaard, W., and Oeschger, H. "Past environmental long-term records from the Arctic." In *The Environmental Record in Glaciers and Ice Sheets,* edited by H. Oeschger and C. C. Langway, Jr., pp. 287–317.. Chichester, 1989.

Ewing, J. Franklin. "The Treasures of Ksâr 'Akil." *Thought: Fordham University Quarterly* 24 (1949): 255–288. Popular account of the first series of excavations.

Hooijer, D. A. "The Fossil Vertebrates of Ksâr ʿAkil, a Palaeolithic Rock Shelter in the Lebanon." *Zoologische Verhandelingen, Uitgegeven door het Rijksmuseum van Natuurlijke Historie te Leiden* 49 (1961): 1–68. Definitive study of the faunal remains.

Marks, Anthony E., and P. Volkman. "The Mousterian of Ksar Akil: Levels XXVIA through XXVIIIB." *Paléorient* 12.1 (1986): 5–20. Study of the chipped-stone assemblages from the Middle Paleolithic levels and a discussion of their significance.

Mellars, Paul, and Jacques Tixier. "Radiocarbon-Accelerator Dating of Ksar 'Aqil (Lebanon) and the Chronology of the Upper Palaeolithic Sequence in the Middle East." *Antiquity* 63 (1989): 761–768. Series of radiocarbon dates that provides data for a revision of the site's chronology.

Ohnuma, Katsuhiko. *Ksar Akil Lebanon,* vol. 3, *Levels XXV–XIV.* British Archaeological Reports, International Series, no. 426. Oxford, 1988. Restudy of technological change in the chipped-stone assemblages from Ksar 'Akil, phases A and B.

Shackleton, N. J., and Opdyke, N. D. "Oxygen-isotope and paleomagnetic stratigraphy of Pacific core V28-239. Late Pliocene to latest Pleistocene." In *Investigations of Late Quaternary Paleoceanography and Paleoclimatology,* edited by R. M. Cline and J. D. Hays, pp. 449–464. Washington, D.C., 1976.

Tixier, Jacques, and Marie-Louise Inizan. "Ksar 'Aqil, stratigraphie et ensembles lithiques dans le paléolithique supérieur: Fouilles 1971–1975." In *Préhistoire du Levant,* edited by Jacques Cauvin and Paul Sanlaville, pp. 353–367. Paris, 1981. Summary of the results of Tixier's excavations with a preliminary interpretation.

Wijmstra, T. A. "Palynology of the first 30 metres of a 120 m deep section in northern Greece." *Acta Botanica Neerlandica* 18.4 (1969): 511–527.

A. M. T. MOORE

KÜLTEPE TEXTS.

The body of some twenty-thousand cuneiform tablets written in Old Assyrian script and language discovered in the fields at Kültepe ("ash mound"), the modern name for the ruins of the ancient city of Kaneš (also called Neša), in ancient Anatolia, is currently known as the Kültepe texts. The site is located about 19 km (12 mi.) northeast of modern Kayseri. [*See* Kaneš.] Nearly all the tablets, which are dated to the twentieth–eighteenth centuries BCE, were discovered in the walled lower city, called *kārum* ("commercial quarter"), an area of more than one square kilometer northeast of the mound. The tablets were found in the houses of traders, usually in so-called sealed rooms or safes, stored on wooden shelves or kept in jars and sealed tablet coffers. A limited number of tablets have been discovered on the city mound, mainly in the ruins of the local palace.

Discovery and Publication. The first tablets appeared in about 1880 via the antiquities market. Until 1948, an estimated four thousand tablets were acquired in this way for collections. Most have been published, at least in cuneiform copies (Veenhof and Klengel-Brandt, 1992). In 1925 their presumed provenance was established during excavations by the Czech scholar Bedřich Hrozný and another one thousand discovered (now in the Archaeological Museum at Istanbul). Since 1948 systematic excavations at Kültepe by Tahsin Özgüç for the Turkish Historical Society, presently directed by Kutlu Emre, yielded about fifteen thousand tablets; they and many other artifacts, are now in the Anatolian Civilizations Museum in Ankara. Publication of these excavated texts begin in 1990 with the appearance of the first volume of the series *Ankara Kültepe Tabletleri,* under the auspices of a "Kültepe Tablets Publication Committee" (Bilgiç, 1990).

History of Trade. Mesopotamian traders in Anatolia are mentioned in epics about Old Akkadian kings (twenty-fourth–twenty-third centuries BCE). Both texts and excavations distinguish two periods. The first is identical to level 2 at *Kārum* Kaneš, based on the total number of year eponyms known today, and may have lasted eighty years, perhaps until 1840/35 BCE, covering three generations of traders and Assyrian kings. Most of the Kültepe texts are from this period (to its last fifty years). It ended with the destruction of Kaneš. After a relatively short interval (perhaps less than one generation), the *kārum* was again inhabited and trade flourished. This second period may have lasted from about 1810 until 1740 BCE (*kārum* level 1b), but although Assyrian traders were still present and the system still functioned more or less, a lot had changed: the role of native Anatolian traders surpasses that of the Assyrians, different articles of trade appear (no tin was imported), and commercial activity, as reflected in the fewer than three hundred texts from this period, reveal that trade took place primarily within the borders of Anatolia.

Old Assyrian Trade in Anatolia. The tablets reveal intensive and sophisticated overland trade between Aššur and central Anatolia, where Assyrian traders had settled in the last quarter of the twentieth century BCE. [*See* Aššur.] The more important settlements were called *kārum* ("commercial quarter"), the designation of important trading stations under the walls of usually bigger Anatolian cities; alongside about fifteen *kārums* there existed about a dozen smaller factories, called *wabartum* ("settlement"). *Kārum* Kaneš administered the network and was equipped with a building ("house," with office and storage facilities and a shrine of Aššur), a secretary, and an assembly (which also acted as a court of law), led by a limited number of important traders. The colonies functioned somewhat as a province of Aššur, subject to its assembly and ruler, maintaining contact via both official letters and "envoys of the city" (who transmitted orders and verdicts and supervised diplomatic contacts with the Anatolian rulers).

Assyrian donkey caravans brought large quantities of expensive woolen textiles and tin into Anatolia. These commodities, acquired rather cheaply in Aššur, could be converted into Anatolian silver with great profit. (The gross profit on tin was at least 100 percent and on textiles at least 300 percent.) Family firms, whose members also used capital invested by rich Assyrians, temples, and commercial moneylenders (interest at 30 percent per year), conducted the trade. Partnerships, service contracts, mutual representation, commission, and credit were vital instruments of trade. Secure and regular communications and a permanent presence in Anatolia guaranteed reliable information on the local markets, which made it possible to grant long-term credit and to direct the flow of merchandise or keep it temporarily in stock.

Written documents played a vital role in the trade, maintaining communication with Aššur and with people in other commercial settlements. Thousands of contracts were validated by the seal impressions of parties and witnesses applied to the clay envelopes in which the tablets were encased: debt notes (originating from credit sales and consignment), service contracts with personnel, transport contracts with caravan leaders, and numerous quit claims. Most are dated by the week, month, and eponym year (in all some 120).

KÜLTEPE TEXTS. *Tablet with its envelope.* Top: The tablet on the right (British Museum, BM 113572) is a business letter of the Assyrian trader Ennum-Aššur son of Šalmah. The envelope on the left is impressed on the top and bottom with the seal of the sender. Bottom: Detail drawing of the seal impression on the envelope (BM 113572a). (Courtesy K. R. Veenhof)

Contracts served evidentiary purposes and were used in the numerous lawsuits among traders. Hundreds of witnessed records of private summonses show that an attempt was first made to solve problems privately or by arbitration before formally appealing to local Assyrian courts (usually a *kārum*). The latter resulted in records of interrogations, negotiations, sworn oaths, and finally formal verdicts, ultimately by the city and the ruler of Aššur, the highest judicial authorities, which could also issue binding procedurial orders and assign attorneys to plaintiffs.

Finally, the archives contain numerous notes, lists, and memoranda: accounts of caravan expenses, lists of merchandise in stock or given in consignment, and individual transactions. They were needed to keep track of the many, often simultaneous and complicated transactions and of payments not in cash but by book transfer (via the *kārum* office), which required periodic general settlements of accounts under the auspices of the *kārum.*

Contacts with native Anatolians, living inside or outside the *kārum,* resulted in the oldest written historical data on Anatolia some two centuries before the Old Hittite Empire emerged. The country consisted of a fair number of city-states, each with its ruler and a varying number of officials, most of whom were designated as "the one in charge of . . ." (lit., "great one of . . ."). The most important were the *rabi simmiltim* ("great one of the stairway"), the second man after the king, frequently the crown prince, and the *rabi sikkitim,* presumably a military official. In addition, the texts introduce priests of various local gods, some that also occur in the names of the festivals mentioned as dates of payments in loans or credits granted to locals. Some rulers of important and powerful cities, such as Kaneš and Purushanda, appear as overlords of smaller ones.

The still-limited number of purely native Anatolian contracts (in the Assyrian script and language mastered by some local scribes) deal with the sale and purchase of houses and slaves, marriage and divorce, adoption and inheritance, debt, slavery, and security. The society was, to all appearances, primarily agricultural, but also characterized by trade and metallurgy. Assyrian traders were allowed to work and settle in *Kārum* Kaneš on the basis of sworn agreements ("oaths") between the authorities and local rulers. Such agreements granted the right to trade, Assyrian jurisdiction, and protection of the caravans in exchange for the payment of import and transit taxes (5 percent on textiles, four pounds of tin per donkey load), and a right of preemption of ten percent of the textiles. Anatolian rulers promised to make good losses from brigands and occasionally (?) to prevent other (Babylonian) traders from entering their territory. Assyrians who tried to dodge the taxes by smuggling could be fined and jailed, and local rulers and officials harming Assyrians or refusing to pay their debts could be boycotted. On the whole, losses and conflicts were exceptional because both parties, profiting from the trade, stuck to the agreements. The linguistic analysis of the large body of Anatolian personal names occurring in the texts reveals that the bulk of the population spoke a language closely related, though not identical, to Old Hittite or (as the Hittites themselves said) "Nešite," probably in a more archaic form. In addition there were proto-Hattian and Hurrian population groups.

Seal Impressions. Several thousand Kültepe tablets, particularly contracts and judicial records, have been found in sealed envelopes and validated as legal documents by seal impressions (see above). In addition, many fragments of envelopes belonging to letters have been discovered (opened to be read) that had been sealed by their senders. Excavations have yielded hundreds of bullae originally attached to a variety of containers and packets in order to protect, identify, or validate them (e.g., by the official seal of the "city office" in Aššur, applied as proof of clearance after payment of the export tax). Some served as labels for transport, others for storage, and still others to close and seal the doors of storerooms. The perhaps two thousand different seal impressions known today exhibit a great mixture of elements of styles and techniques from various traditions and workshops. While most Anatolians used stamp seals, some of them, and all Assyrians, used cylinder seals. Old Assyrian, Babylonian, Syrian, Anatolian, and Syro-Anatolian styles can be distinguished; some older seals were recut and reused. Seals and sealings, which are subjects for iconographic studies, had legal significance on certain types of records. Once the owner of a seal is identified (only some 15 percent are inscribed), it becomes possible to discover links between the seal and its owner's ethnicity, status, or wealth.

[*See also* Kaneš.]

BIBLIOGRAPHY

Bilgiç, Emin, ed. *Ankara Kültepe Tabletleri,* vol. 1. Türk Tarih Kurumu Yayınları 6/33. Ankara, 1990. The first volume with texts officially excavated and preserved in the museum at Ankara.

Eisser, Georg, and Julius Lewy. *Die altassyrischen Rechtsurkunden vom Kültepe.* 2 vols. Mitteilungen der Vorderasiatisch-Aegyptischen Gesellschaft, vols. 33 and 35.3. Leipzig, 1930–1935. First systematic and still reliable edition of 340 legal documents including commentary.

Garelli, Paul. *Les Assyriens en Cappadoce.* Paris, 1963. The first comprehensive study of all aspects of the Kültepe texts and the Old Assyrian trade, with extensive analysis of the Anatolian population, chronology, the political relations between Assyrians and Anatolian rulers, and a full bibliography.

Larsen, Mogens T. *Old Assyrian Caravan Procedures.* Istanbul, 1967. Reconstruction of the system based on standard texts: transport contracts, caravan accounts, and notifying messages.

Larsen, Mogens T. *The Old Assyrian City-State and Its Colonies.* Copenhagen, 1976. Analyzes the political structure of Aššur and the government of the colonies, with a long historical introduction.

Michel, Cécile. *Innāya dans les tablettes paléo-assyriennes.* 2 vols. Paris, 1991. Studies the family and business of two traders and includes a full edition of 280 texts used as sources.

Orlin, Louis L. *Assyrian Colonies in Cappadocia.* The Hague, 1970. General survey and interpretation, outdated by Garelli's book (above).

Özgüç, Nimet. *Seals and Seal Impressions of Level Ib from Karum Kanish.* Ankara, 1968.

Özgüç, Tahsin. *Ausgrabungen in Kültepe: Bericht über die im Auftrage der Türkischen Historischen Gesellschaft, 1948 durchgeführten Ausgrabungen.* Ankara, 1950.

Özgüç, Tahsin. *Kültepe-Kaniş: New Researchers at the Center of the Assyrian Trade Colonies.* Ankara, 1959.

Özgüç, Tahsin. *Kültepe-Kaniş II: New Researchers at the Trading Center of the Ancient Near East.* Ankara, 1986. Report on the excavations between 1959 and 1983.

Teissier, Beatrice. *Sealing and Seals on Texts from Kültepe Kārum Level 2.* Leiden, 1994. Study of sealing practices and seals on the basis of a sample of nearly seven hundred seal impressions, presented in tables and drawings.

Veenhof, Klaas R. *Aspects of Old Assyrian Trade and Its Terminology.* Leiden, 1972. Investigates the material aspects of caravan transport, taxes, smuggling, trade in wool and textiles, and forms of sale and purchase, including the markets.

Veenhof, Klaas R., and Evelyn Klengel-Brandt. *Altassyrische Tontafeln aus Kültepe: Texte und Siegelabrollungen.* Vorderasiatische Schriftdenkmäler der Staatlichen Museen zu Berlin, vol. 26. Berlin, 1992. The latest publication of cuneiform texts and seals in photos and drawings, with general and detailed descriptions of types of texts and the iconography of the seals.

Klaas R. Veenhof

KUNTILLET ʿAJRUD (Heb., Ḥorvat Teman), site located in the northeast Sinai Desert (30°11′ N, 34°25′ E; map reference 0940 × 9560), approximately 50 km (30 mi.) south of Qadesh-Barnea and a few kilometers west of Darb Ghazza, an ancient route and modern track leading to Eilat and southern Sinai. The mound rises prominently from the broad valley of Wadi Qurayyah, which forms a natural east–west route. The top of this isolated hill is a narrow plateau, with ruins at its western end. Shallow wells at the foot of the hill still make the site an important one.

Kuntillet ʿAjrud has been explored by Edward H. Palmer (1869), Alois Musil (1902), Beno Rothenberg (1967), and Ze'ev Meshel (1970); Meshel directed three seasons of excavation between October 1975 and April 1976 under the auspices of Tel Aviv University, the Israel Department of Antiquities, and the Exploring the Land Division of the Kibbutz Movement. There are two structures on the site: a main building at the western end of the plateau, and a secondary one 10 m to its east. The state of preservation of the second one is very poor, as were its finds.

The main building, a rectangle with four corner rooms, covers an area of approximately 15 × 25 m. The entrance was through a small exterior court area ringed with stone benches and then through a small gate room leading to a narrow chamber divided into two wings. In each wing plastered stone benches surrounded the walls. Except for a narrow passage between the wings, the benches fill the spaces. The bench room extends north–south across the entire width of the building and apparently was the most important part of the site. Certainly its function was associated with the benches.

Plaster fragments that had detached from the walls were found in the bench room. Some of the fragments are inscribed with black ink: two Hebrew inscriptions in Phoenician script (see below) and a partial third inscription. The third inscription was found in situ, about 1.5 m above floor level, on the northern doorpost of the entrance leading to the main courtyard. The bench room, the corner rooms abutting its two wings, and the adjoining parts of the main building produced most of the other significant finds. Two pithoi adorned with inscriptions and pictures and stone bowls of various sizes, four of which had the names of donors incised on their rims. Bases of pithoi and large storage jars were found, still in situ, in the two long rooms located to the south and west of the main courtyard. These areas served as storerooms for food supplies.

The Hebrew inscriptions and the cosmopolitan style and motifs of the drawings found at the site attest to its unique significance. Some of the inscriptions are written in ancient Hebrew script and some in Phoenician script, on plaster, stone, and pottery.

1. *Plaster fragments.* Three partial inscriptions, written in ink in Phoenician script but in the Hebrew language, were

KUNTILLET ʿAJRUD. *Aerial view of the site.* (Photograph by Avraham Hay; courtesy Z. Meshel)

found on plaster fragments in the bench room; portions of two others, written in ancient Hebrew script, were found in the debris at the entrance to the western storeroom. One of the Phoenician inscriptions reads: "your days may be prolonged, and you shall be satisfied . . . give YHWH of Teman and his Asherah . . . YHWH of Teman and his Asherah favored. . . ."

Another inscription is a piece of an ancient theophany describing the revelation of God in language echoing the Hebrew Bible: "and when El rose up . . . and hills melted . . . and peaks were pounded . . . bless Baal in (the) day of war . . . the name of El in (the) day of war. . . ." It is noteworthy that Baal and God (Heb., *'el*) are mentioned here in poetic parallelism, in connection with a possible reference to a "day of war" *(yôm milhāmā).*

2. *Stone bowls.* Among the four inscriptions incised on the rims of stone bowls, the most complete one reads: "(donated) by Ovadyo son of ʿAdnah; may he be blessed by YHW(H)." These stone bowls were apparently dedicated to the god of Israel by donors who sought his blessing.

3. *Pottery.* One or two letters are incised on the shoulders of most of the pithoi. The letter *'aleph* is found most frequently, while the letter *yod* is found least often; the combination *qoph-resh* appears in two instances. It is assumed that these letters are abbreviations indicating types of offerings and tithes, a practice described a millennium later in the Mishnah and Tosefta. These letters were incised on the pithoi prior to firing. Neutron activation analysis of their clay established that they were made in the vicinity of Jerusalem, perhaps reinforcing the suggestion that priests lived at the site and received supplies in the forms of sacrifices and tithes. Among the seven inscriptions incised on the shoulders of storejars after firing are four reading *lśr ʿr,* to be read *leśar ʿir,* "(belonging) to a city official." The jars may either have held commodities consigned to an official at the site or registered by him.

Among the inscriptions written in red ink on two large pithoi that are also decorated with pictures are four repetitions of the alphabet, a list of personal names, and two blessings that resemble the priestly benediction. One of these was written above two figures of the Egyptian god Bes and may be reconstructed as follows: "A[shy]o m[lk] (the king) said: tell [x, y, and z], may you be blessed by YHWH of Shomron (Samaria) and his Asherah." If this reconstruction is sound, it is possible that *'(sy)w (hm)lk* ("Ashyo the king") is a transposition of the name *yw'š*, "Joash," referring to the king *(hmlk)* of Israel who reigned from Samaria (c. 801–786 BCE); this may provide an important synchronism for dating the site. The second inscription is reconstructed as "Amaryo said: tell my lord, may you be well and be blessed by YHWH of Teman and his Asherah. May he bless and keep you and be with you." The two inscriptions not only shed light on the religious character of the site, but also provide revealing glimpses into the history of Israelite religion.

Various divine, human, and animal figures are drawn on the two storejars. On one of them, alongside two representations of Bes, a seated figure, perhaps Asherah, plays a lyre. The familiar motif of the tree of life, flanked by two ibex, also appears on this vessel, along with drawings of a lion, a procession of animals, and a cow licking the tail of a suckling calf. On the other vessel five figures are depicted raising their hands in a gesture of supplication, and an archer raises his bow. Most of these motifs, are well-represented elsewhere in Syria/Phoenicia.

The subject matter of the inscriptions, the references to various deities, and the presence of dedicated vessels all suggest that Kuntillet ʿAjrud was not a temple but a kind of religious center. Given its location (it may have been associated with journeys of the Israelites to Eilat and to Ezion-Geber and perhaps with those of pilgrims to southern Sinai), the absence of ritual appurtenances usually associated with cult or sacrifices (e.g., altars), as well as its architectural plan, it may have been a wayside shrine. A journey south along the Darb Ghazza from Qadesh-Barnea might have included stopping at this well-side station to make dedications to Israel's god in the bench room of the main building.

Kuntillet ʿAjrud was only occupied for a few years. The interpretation of the evidence points to an occupation by a small group of priests from Israel, with an officer *(śr ʿr)* at their head. The reference to "Yahweh of Samaria" on one of the large decorated pithoi, the Phoenician-style writing, the decorative and pictorial artwork, the pottery types, and the onomastic conventions (names ending in *-yau,* and not *-yahu*), suggest that the site was in sustained contact with the northern kingdom of Israel. In return for provisions, primarily from Judah, priests would have rendered various blessings and other services to travelers.

The date of the site, determined by typological and paleographic analysis, and by the need to identify a historical period in which Israelite influence over Judah was especially strong, points in the excavator's opinion, not to the time of the reigns of Jehoram, Ahaziah, and Athaliah (850–837 BCE), but to the period of Joash, king of Israel (c. 801–786 BCE), who captured King Amaziah of Judah, broke down the wall of Jerusalem, and seized the treasures of the Jerusalem Temple and palace (*2 Kgs.* 14:1–16; *2 Chr.* 25:1–24). It is possible that Joash intended to gain direct access to the Red Sea, and that this was the reason for the war between the two kings. The victory of Joash may be reflected in the construction of the buildings at Kuntillet ʿAjrud.

BIBLIOGRAPHY

Chase, Debra A. "A Note on an Inscription from Kuntillet ʿAjrūd." *Bulletin of the American Schools of Oriental Research,* no. 246 (1982): 63–67.

Dever, William G. "Asherah, Consort of Yahweh? New Evidence from Kuntillet ʿAjrud." *Bulletin of the American Schools of Oriental Research,* no. 255 (1984): 21–37.

Emerton, J. A. "New Light on Israelite Religion: The Implications of the Inscription from Kuntillet ʿAjrud." *Zeitschrift für die alttestamentliche Wissenschaft* 94 (1982): 2–20.

Lemaire, André. *Les écoles et la formation de la Bible dans l'ancien Israël.* Fribourg, 1981. See pages 26–28.

Lemaire, André. "Date et origine des inscriptions hébraïques et phéniciennes de Kuntillet ʿAjrud." *Studi Epigrafici e Linguistici* 1 (1984): 131–143.

McCarter, P. Kyle, Jr. "Aspects of the Religion of the Israelite Monarchy: Biblical and Epigraphic Data." In *Ancient Israelite Religion: Essays in Honor of Frank Moore Cross,* edited by Patrick D. Miller, Jr., et al. Philadelphia, 1987.

Meshel, Ze'ev. *Kuntillet ʿAjrud: A Religious Centre from the Time of the Judaean Monarchy on the Border of Sinai.* Jerusalem, 1978.

Meshel, Ze'ev. "Did Yahweh Have a Consort? The New Religious Inscriptions from Sinai." *Biblical Archaeology Review* 5.2 (1979): 24–34.

Tigay, Jeffrey H. *You Shall Have No Other Gods: Israelite Religion in the Light of Hebrew Inscriptions.* Atlanta, 1986. See pages 26–29.

Tigay, Jeffrey H. "A Second Temple Parallel to the Blessings from Kuntillet ʿAjrud." *Israel Exploration Journal* 40 (1990): 218.

Weinfeld, Moshe. "Kuntillet Ajrud Inscriptions and Their Significance." *Studi Epigrafici e Linguistici* 1 (1984): 121–130.

ZE'EV MESHEL

KURNUB, a fortified settlement in the central Negev desert, also known as Mampsis, located 40 km (25 mi.) southeast of Beersheba, at the junction of the roads from Aila (Eilat) to Jerusalem and Gaza (map reference 156 × 046). Kurnub is the site's Arabic name. At the end of the first century BCE, the site was settled by the Nabateans as a secondary stop on the trade route from Petra to the Mediterranean Sea. The settlement prospered into the second century CE, when it and the rest of the Nabatean kingdom became part of the Roman Provincia Arabia and horse breeding replaced trade as the primary economic activity. (In contrast to other Nabatean sites in the Negev, agriculture at Kurnub was never an important part of the economy, primarily because of the dearth of arable land.) In the Late Roman period Kurnub became a garrison in defense of the Jerusalem—Aila road. Its strategic importance continued into the Byzantine period, primarily because of its proximity to Transjordan. The mosaic Madaba map portrays it (under the Greek name *Mampsis*) as a fortified city—an arched gateway flanked by towers. [*See* Madaba.] It is also mentioned as Mamphis in the military papryi of Neṣṣana, another sixth-century source. [*See* Neṣṣana.] Because the latest coins found at the site date to the mid-sixth century CE, it is believed that the town was destroyed by Arab invaders sometime before the Muslim conquest of Palestine in 636 CE.

Following numerous late nineteenth- and early twentieth-century surveys and preliminary explorations, Kurnub was extensively excavated between 1965 and 1967, in 1971–1972, and again in 1990 by a team led by Avraham Negev on behalf of the Hebrew University of Jerusalem. Architectural remains at Kurnub are more extensive than at any other site in the Negev, and the quality of that construction is striking. More than two-dozen public buildings have been excavated, among them, two Byzantine churches with mosaic pavements. A Late Roman city wall surrounded the town, which also had an extensive water-collection system and three distinct cemeteries with burials dating from the Nabatean through the Byzantine periods.

Kurnub was not one of the early Nabatean settlements in the Negev. Remains from the Middle Nabatean period (c. 30 BCE–70 CE) are the earliest found there. Studying this period is further hampered because the town was completely rebuilt, following a new plan in the second century CE. The largest of the Middle Nabatean buildings, all of which were built of hammer-dressed stones, was a fortress situated at the site's highest elevation, in the northeast.

The Late Nabatean/Late Roman period (70 CE–mid-fourth century CE) begins with the reign of Rabel II (70–106 CE) and continues into what is known historically as the Late Roman period. (It can, however, be classified as Late Nabatean because the same structures continued in use from the second through the mid-fourth centuries—and in most cases beyond, into the Byzantine period.) The Late Roman finds consist primarily of pottery and coins and the remains of the city wall. Built at the end of the third century or at the beginning of the fourth, the wall was about 900 m long and enclosed an area of about 15 acres. It had two gates and was defended by two towers. The main gate was on the north; the western gate gave access to Naḥal Mamshit.

Many Late Nabatean buildings were constructed on or incorporated into the foundations of earlier buildings. A large Middle Nabatean structure, for example, was uncovered beneath the city wall. Use of the Late Nabatean public pool at the northeastern edge of the city extended into subsequent periods. The pool (18 × 10 × 3m) apparently had a wooden roof supported by pillars. Next to it was the public bathhouse, which consisted of a courtyard that may have been used as a dressing room, two cold baths, a tepid bath, and a three-room hot bath. [*See* Baths.]

Water for the pool, bathhouse, and city cisterns was supplied by a network of water-collection systems constructed at various points for which the Nabateans are known. [*See* Cisterns.] Water was collected primarily by damming Naḥal Mamshit but also by conducting rainwater from a nearby mountain slope. Three dams in Naḥal Mamshit were kept under observation from a high (5 m), square tower (10 × 10 m) situated at the western edge of the town. This structure had a paved courtyard with a roofed water reservoir as well as storerooms, a guest suite (a separate, self-contained dwelling unit), and a square, characteristically Nabatean staircase tower. [*See* Reservoirs.]

A very large building (35 × 20 m), believed to have been the governor's palace, was uncovered northeast of the tower, at the center of the western edge of town. The building's internal courtyard (19 × 6 m) housed a guardroom, reception hall, and library, as well as servant quarters, a kitchen, storerooms, and storage cellars. The colonnade running along the western and northern walls of the courtyard supported arches that in turn supported a balcony onto which the upper rooms opened. This "l"-shaped arrangement has not been found elsewhere in the Negev. A separate residential area—its rooms distinguished by stone floors—was accessed via an arched vestibule.

Also unique to the Negev is the stable found in a large rectangular building (27 × 35 m) in the town's southwestern corner. Three rooms were partitioned such that a wide central area was flanked by two elongated aisles. Animals housed in these aisles were fed from troughs dug into the sills of four arched openings cut out of both the western and eastern walls of the central hall. A stable of the same type—though much larger and more elaborate—was found in a building complex in the eastern section of the city. A square structure (40 × 40 m), it had only one entrance, which led through a vestibule into a large irregularly shaped courtyard. The building comprised numerous units, including workshops, a lavatory, a residential wing and visitors' suite, a stylobate bearing columns with Nabatean capitals, and a treasure room. Both of these buildings contained cisterns.

Traders found respite at the large khan, or caravanserai (23 × 42 m), located to the northwest, just beyond the later Roman city wall. This rest house, which included large courts, halls, and rows of rooms along its northern and eastern sides, resembles the one found at Avdat. [*See* Avdat.] About 50 m from the caravanserai, the excavators uncovered two buildings thought to have been schools in which Nabatean architecture and construction were taught. The earlier building, which was square (30.30 × 30.25 m), contained pottery dating from the Middle Nabatean through the Byzantine periods. Various imported wares indicate that some of its occupants were wealthy. Adjoined to this structure's western wall was a larger, rectangular building (35.80 × 45.25 m) dated to the early second century CE. Destroyed by the mid-fourth century, its remaining pillars and arches were later ruined in an earthquake, perhaps that of 363. Later in its history, this building may have been a barrack for a locally recruited militia.

During the Byzantine period (mid-fourth–early sixth centuries CE) many Late Nabatean buildings continued in use; the primary Byzantine remains, however, are two churches, designated the east church and the west church. Both date to the second half of the fourth or the beginning of the fifth century. The east church complex (55 × 35 m) contained a chapel, baptistery, annexes (housing a bath and perhaps a monastery), and a square bell tower. [*See* Baptisteries; Baths; Monasteries.] Access to the complex was through a large atrium (15 × 18 m) abutting the basilica on the west. The church (27.5 × 15 m) was entered through one of three openings in the atrium's eastern wall. Both of its aisles were paved in stone. A mosaic floor in the nave was decorated with geometric designs; two large crosses were executed in front of the bema. [*See* Mosaics.] The church had a single, central apse flanked by rectangular rooms; neither room contained an apse, but relics were found inside of both. Extending around the interior of the semicircular apse was a bench with three steps that supported the base of the bishop's throne. Numerous Arabic invocations were engraved on the apse, an indication that Arab tribesmen occupied the site temporarily after it was conquered early in the seventh century.

The west church, situated in the southwestern corner of the city, was built over part of a large Late Nabatean building. Like the east church, it had a colonnaded atrium with a central cistern and three openings that led into the basilica. The interior (17.5 × 10 m) was smaller than that of the east church, but its plan was identical and its aisles were also paved in stone. Bird, fruit, and geometric motifs were executed in the nave's colored-mosaic pavement, which also featured six undated Greek inscriptions.

Most of the city's marketplace, comprising three rows of shops situated along two streets, is dated to the Byzantine period. Its southern portion was constructed on the foundations of a large Middle Nabatean building; and at some point in its history, the structure apparently served as a monastery. The marketplace is one of the few buildings that survived the Muslim conquest of Kurnub.

[*See also* Churches; *and* Nabateans.]

BIBLIOGRAPHY

Negev, Avraham. "The Nebateans and the Provincia Arabia." In *Aufstieg und Niedergang der römischen Welt,* vol. II.8, edited by Hildegard Temporini and Wolfgang Haase, pp. 631–633, 647–658. Berlin, 1977.

Negev, Avraham. "Housing and City-planning in the Ancient Negev and the Provincia Arabia." In *Housing in Arid Lands: Design and Planning,* edited by Gideon Golany, pp. 3–32. London, 1980.

Negev, Avraham. *The Greek Inscriptions from the Negev.* Jerusalem, 1981. See pages 69–72.

Negev, Avraham. *Tempel, Kirchen und Zisternen.* Stuttgart, 1983.

Negev, Avraham. *Nabatean Archaeology Today.* New York, 1986.

Negev, Avraham. *The Architecture of Mampsis Final Report.* 2 vols. Jerusalem, 1988.

Negev, Avraham. "Mampsis: The End of a Nabatean Town." *Aram* 2.1–2 (1990): 337–365.

Negev, Avraham. "The Mampsis Gymnasia and Their Latter History: Preliminary Report and Interpretation." In *Early Christianity in Context: Monuments and Documents,* edited by Frederick Manns and Eugenio Alliata, pp. 241–264. Studium Biblicum Franciscanum Collectio Maior, 38. Jerusalem, 1993.

Wenning, Robert. *Die Nabatäer: Denkmäler und Geschichte.* Göttingen, 1987. Contains a full bibliography (pp. 159–172.).

Avraham Negev

KURSI (Ar., Khirbet el-Kursi), site located at the mouth of Naḥal Samakh on the eastern shore of the Sea of Galilee (map reference 2481 × 2102). It and the fertile valley that surrounds it were identified long ago by surveyors and researchers as the land of the Gergesenes of the Gospels, related to the story of the stampeded Gadarene swine (*Mt.* 8:28–34; *Mk.* 5:1–20; *Lk.* 8:26–39). The identification was based mainly on the site's topographical setting, as well as on the modern name *Kursi,* which may be a distortion of the original name, *Gergesa.* Archaeological surveys and excavations conducted in the area after 1967 by Dan Urman and S. Bar-Lev proved the identification beyond doubt (see below). The early Christians identified the site with the place where the miracle took place, according to the Synoptic Gospels. From a topographical point of view, it corresponds to the biblical description of the land of the Gergesenes.

From 1970 to 1974, Vassilios Tzaferis, under the auspices of the Israel Department of Antiquities, excavated a site located some 300 m east of the shore of the Sea of Galilee, partly on the valley side and partly on the slopes overlooking the sea. After three seasons of excavation (1969–1972) a religious settlement consisting of a church and the remains of a walled monastery was revealed. The monastery (140 × 120 m in area) was enclosed by walls on all four sides. At the center of the enclosed area was a magnificent early Christian basilica (25 × 45 m), one of the largest discovered in the vicinity of the Sea of Galilee.

At a distance of several meters to the east of the monastery, halfway up the slope of Naḥal Samakh, another building was discovered that included a small chapel paved with colorful mosaics and a rectangular room with a natural conglomerate stone boulder standing in the center. It was probably this room, with its natural rock, that the early Christians saw as the place of the miracle, at least in the writings of the church fathers from the fourth century onward.

Based on the archaeological evidence, three phases (levels) can be distinguished in the settlement, basilica, and chapel: the earliest dates from the second half of the fifth century to the middle of the sixth century CE; the second lasted from the second half of the sixth century to the beginning of the seventh; and the third began in the seventh century and continued until the middle of the eighth.

In the earliest stage of occupation (level 1) the settlement was a compact and well-organized community with streets, dwellings, and drainage channels. It no doubt functioned as a purely religious community, as evidenced by the magnificent church in its center, its most important element. At approximately the same time, the chapel dedicated to the "miracle" was erected.

In the second stage (level 2) many changes took place within the church and the monastery, probably as the result of an increase in the Christian population in the region and of changes in liturgical customs. Prosperity ended abruptly with the Persian invasion in 614 CE; the monumental character of the church was altered and its area greatly reduced. Some of the chapels on its two long sides were converted to industrial use: one was used as a storeroom and another held an oil press. Within the residential quarter, new buildings of less refined construction were built on the earlier remains.

The third stage (level 3) was the last occupation before the entire complex was destroyed, probably by an earthquake, and abandoned. New settlers came who were not sensitive to the site's religious significance or to the architectural importance of the church. This final settlement was short-lived, lasting only until the second half of the eighth century. The monastery and the church, as well as the chapel dedicated to the miracle, were destroyed, abandoned, and subsequently laid in ruins.

[*See also* Churches; Monasteries.]

BIBLIOGRAPHY

The Excavations at Kursi-Gergesa. ʿAtiqot (English Series), vol. 16. Jerusalem, 1983.

Urman, Dan. "The Site of the Miracle of the Man with the Unclean Spirit." *Christian News from Israel* 22 (1971): 72–76.

VASSILIOS TZAFERIS

KUWAIT. Located at the head of the Arab-Iranian Gulf, the State of Kuwait bounds with Saudi Arabia to the south, Iraq to the west and north, and the Gulf to the east. Kuwait consists of 17,000 sq km (10,540 sq. mi.) of the Arabian desert, the Gulf littoral, and several uninhabited off-coast islands, of which Bubiyan and Warba are the largest and lie near the Shatt al-Arab. Other islands to the south—Kubbar, Qaruh, Auha, Umm al-Marindin, and Umm an-Nammal in Kuwait Bay—are bare and small. The principal archaeological remains are found on Failaka Island at the entrance to Kuwait Bay, which has been inhabited since 2000 BCE.

The mainland is characterized by a mostly flat, stony desert plain broken by escarpments and hills. Particularly in the north, the wadi systems drain internally, except along the east coast, where they drain into the Gulf. Wadi al-Batin, the relic of an ancient watercourse, rising in Arabia to the south, is a prominent feature defining the state's western boundary. Shallow, depressed basins (playas) in the central, north, and west of Kuwait are important collection stations for winter rains. Typical coastal sand dunes occur in the southern part of the region.

The earliest inhabitants of the Arabian Peninsula and Gulf must have derived from populations enacting a developed Olduwan culture in Tanzania and Kenya more than one million years BP. Arabian-bound emigrants probably crossed from Africa near Bab al-Mandeb (Ethiopia) to Yemen at the mouth of the Red Sea. Acheulean sites are known in North Arabia at Shuway Hittiyah 644 km (400 mi.) due west of Kuwait) and at more than two hundred lakes sites in central, west, and southwest Arabia dating between 700,000 and 100,000 BP. Wadis running north from central Arabia were natural corridors for the peoples who were to inhabit the Gulf and the whole of the Near East. Wadi al-Batin, framing Kuwait on the west, and still archaeologically unknown, is an obvious route. By 50,000 BP, Mousterian culture had developed on the Arabian Peninsula. The Gulf was a fertile valley, well-watered by an extension of the Shatt al-Arab emptying into the Gulf of Oman (Indian Ocean) at Hormuz. In 15,000 BCE, the Gulf began to fill from the south, forcing the resident populations of the Shatt valley to seek higher ground north and west.

Between 8000 and 5000 BCE, a Mesolithic hunting culture was established in the Burgan Basin, where characteristic microliths have been found in association with bitumen pools. Drawings of animals (horned quadrupeds with elongated bodies, giraffelike creatures) and a palm tree, executed in a reddish-yellow pigment, decorate the underface of a prominent flat rock near Mudaira (on the north side of Kuwait Bay) that may date to this period.

Neolithic (5000–3500 BCE) sites are distributed along all of the Gulf's western littoral. One site identified in Kuwait at Sabiyah (on the north side of Kuwait Bay) exhibits pottery, fishing gear, celts, and small blades, a rather deprived version of the contemporaneous Ubaid culture flourishing in Sumer. [*See* Ubaid.] The Neolithic may have continued for some time in Kuwait, although no artifacts have been discovered on the mainland or islands to suggest any continuity of habitation.

There is no evidence of an Early Bronze culture. Nevertheless, somewhere along the mainland littoral a society based on a fishing culture must have existed because the economic surplus provided by fishing would have created the initial stimulus for trade. Two of the types of boats that would have been utilized still survive: the *warjia* (a reed craft) and the *houri* (a dugout); the bones of large sea mammals from the second-millennium BCE excavations on Failaka Island indicate the use of a frame or plank boat essential for deep-water fishing.

Other recognized archaeological remains in the State of Kuwait are to be found on the tiny island of Umm an-Nammal, located very close to the tip of Cape Asharij, which juts into the rear position of Kuwait Bay. The island is accessible to the mainland at low tide, and they were no doubt joined in antiquity. The staff of the Kuwait National Museum have completed a thorough survey of the island and conducted test excavations at several of the more substantial locations.

Four sites containing meager Bronze Age remains are clustered near the center of the island. One of the sites is identified as a kiln, and sherds of ceramic wares are comparable to material from excavations at Qalʿat al-Bahrain that has been dated to the end of the third millennium and the first half of the second millennium BCE. Other small sites on the island contained Late Kassite, Late Hellenistic, and Late Islamic period material.

The Sabiyah peninsula has been briefly surveyed along the Khor Sabiyah, the channel separating the mainland from Bubiyan Island. Four sites were located, devoid of architecture but identified by pottery dating mainly from the Middle and Late Islamic periods.

[*See also* Failaka.]

BIBLIOGRAPHY

Dickson, H. R. P. *Kuwait and Her Neighbors*. London, 1956.

Howard-Carter, Theresa. "Kuwait." In *Reallexikon der Assyriologie,* vol. 6, pp. 389–397. Berlin, 1983.

Howard-Carter, Theresa. "The Johns Hopkins University Reconnaissance Expedition to the Arab-Iranian Gulf." *Bulletin of the American Schools of Oriental Research,* no. 207 (1972): 6–40.

Howard-Carter, Theresa. "The Tangible Evidence for the Earliest Dilmun." *Journal of Cuneiform Studies* 33 (1981): 210–223.

Kassler, P. "The Structural and Geomorphic Evolution of the Persian Gulf." In *The Persian Gulf: Holocene Carbonate Sedimentation and Diagenisis in a Shallow Epicontinental Sea,* edited by B. H. Purser, pp. 11–33. Berlin and New York, 1973.

McClure, Harold A. *The Arabian Peninsula and Prehistoric Populations.* Coconut Grove, Fla., 1971.

THERESA HOWARD-CARTER

L

LACHISH (Ar., Tell ed-Duweir), a prominent mound of about 31 acres located near a major road leading from Israel's coastal plain to the Hebron hills. The site's location, the fertile land in the area, and an ample water supply from numerous wells contributed to its development as an important settlement.

In 1929 William Foxwell Albright identified ancient Lachish with Tell ed-Duweir. With the absence of inscriptions, this identification, which is generally accepted, is based on circumstantial evidence and archaeological data. Tel Lachish was first excavated (1932–1938) by a British expedition directed by James L. Starkey, assisted by G. Lankester Harding and Olga Tufnell. The excavations were terminated when Starkey was murdered by Arab bandits. Starkey published only brief excavation reports, and Tufnell completed the publication work (Tufnell, 1953; Tufnell et al., 1940; Tufnell et al., 1958).

Starkey carried out large-scale excavations on the summit of the mound and in the surrounding area. Most of the remains uncovered on the summit date to the Iron Age and later. Earlier remains were uncovered in a section cut near the northeast corner of the site and on the nearby slope. The Canaanite Fosse Temple was discovered near the northwest corner of the mound, and numerous graveyards and a Bronze Age settlement were uncovered in the area surrounding the mound. Few of Starkey's stratigraphic conclusions (with the exception of the Assyrian siege ramp) were challenged by later excavators. For purposes of interpretation and publication, the most recent excavation (see below) has kept Starkey's stratigraphic divisions and terminology, except for the Middle and Late Bronze Age phases in levels VIII and VII in which his divisions are not sufficiently flexible.

In 1966 and 1968 Yohanan Aharoni (1975), under the auspices of the Hebrew University of Jerusalem, undertook limited excavations in the solar shrine area. In 1973, Tel Aviv University initiated full-scale excavations under the direction of David Ussishkin, assisted by Gabriel Barkay, Christa Clamer, Yehudah Dagan, John Woodhead, and Orna Zimhoni (Ussishkin, 1978, 1983). A reconstruction program for the Iron Age city gates is being carried out by Dagan, who also surveyed the surrounding region (Dagan, 1992). [*See* Restoration and Conservation.]

Neolithic, Chalcolithic, and Early Bronze Ages. An assemblage of flint implements and a single pottery sherd found on the mound probably indicate the existence of a Pottery Neolithic site in one of the surrounding valleys. Chalcolithic Ghassulian pottery was found on the mound, suggesting a settlement. Remains from the end of the Chalcolithic period and the beginning of the Early Bronze Age were uncovered on the northeast corner of the mound and on a ridge northwest of the site, where settlers lived in caves. A dolmen on the northwest ridge is probably related to this settlement. EB remains were found on the northeast corner, in Area D (in the center of the mound) and in tombs, indicating that the site was extensively settled during this period.

Intermediate Bronze Age. Except for a small settlement and its cemetery (cemetery 2000) on the ridge to the northwest there is no sign of habitation in the Intermediate Bronze Age (EB IV); 120 rock-cut single-chambered tombs were excavated. [*See* Tombs.] The period's pottery assemblage belongs to Ruth Amiran's southern Family A (Amiran, 1960) and to William G. Dever's Families J and S (Dever, 1980).

Middle Bronze Age. To date no evidence has been recovered for the MB I Canaanite city, but there was new settlement on the mound and Lachish was an important city-state by MB II–III. A glacis with a lime-plastered sloping surface constructed around the site in the Middle Bronze Age is responsible for the existing mound's configuration, but no remains of a freestanding city wall on top of the glacis have been found. Along the bottom of the glacis, on the west, a fosse was cut into the bedrock. In the center of the mound the northwest wing of a large palace with massive brick walls and perhaps a second story was excavated in area P. The palace probably belonged to the city's ruler. Huge stone slabs in secondary use from an earlier, similar structure were also used in its construction. Destroyed by fire, this palace was subsequently repaired and reused for domestic and industrial purposes. [*See* Palace.] Remains of a cult place were found in area D, but the structure is badly preserved and its character and plan are unknown. Many votive vessels and animal bones indicate its ritual function. Starkey's level VIII in the northeast corner of the site dates to this period. Many rock-cut tombs were found outside the site, richly furnished with pottery, weapons, and scarabs. [*See* Grave Goods; Weapons and Warfare.]

Late Bronze Age. The settlement decreased in size and declined in importance following the MB destruction. It did not regain prominence until the later part of the Late Bronze Age, then becoming one of the most significant city-states in Canaan. Papyrus Hermitage 1116A, dated to the reign of Amenhotep II (1453–1419 BCE), is the earliest written source referring to Lachish. It records food presentations to envoys from Lachish and other Canaanite cities. Several cuneiform tablets containing letters from kings of Lachish to their overlords, Pharaohs Amenhotep III and Amenhotep IV, in the fourteenth century BCE were found at Tell el-Amarna in Egypt. [*See* Cuneiform; Amarna Tablets.] Another letter, discovered at Tell el-Ḥesi, was apparently sent by an Egyptian official stationed at Lachish. [*See* Ḥesi, Tell el-.]

LB Lachish apparently was unfortified, and a temple was erected in the abandoned fosse near the northwest corner of the mound (Tufnell et al., 1940). It was rebuilt twice (phases I–III) and the finds were rich in each successive temple and in the surrounding pits, into which offerings had been thrown. The original fosse temple was modest; fosse temple II was larger. Fosse temple III, the largest, was destroyed by fire; it was apparently contemporaneous with the level VII domestic structures on the mound in area S. All were destroyed at the same time, probably toward the end of the thirteenth century BCE (Ussishkin, 1985). Buildings belonging to levels VII and VI (thirteenth–twelfth centuries BCE) were uncovered near the upper periphery of the mound, indicating that there was no city wall there then. However, the buildings along the upper edge of the site may have been adjoining, forming a line of fortifications around the city. In any case, by the fourteenth century BCE, the entire area excavated in area S up to the edge of the mound was open ground.

Information about the settlement between the end of the Middle Bronze Age and level VII is scarce. Some remains were uncovered in the northeast (Starkey's level VII) as well as in area P and in area S beneath level VII. In addition, many tombs contained pottery vessels, including Cypriot imports, and scarabs.

Level VI. The last prosperous Canaanite city is represented in level VI. It demonstrates a cultural continuity from level VII, but the city was rebuilt along different lines: in area S the level VII domestic structures were replaced by a public building; the fosse temple was not rebuilt, and a new sanctuary was built on the acropolis (see figure 1), possibly as part of the royal palace. The main complex of the acrop-

LACHISH. Figure 1. *Main hall of the Late Bronze Age acropolis temple, from the north.* (Courtesy Institute of Archaeology, Tel Aviv University)

olis temple consists of an antechamber, a main hall, and a cella, climbing the slope in that order. The entrances to the three units are on a straight axis that passes through the center of the complex. The main hall is rectangular; its ceiling was supported by cedar of Lebanon beams resting on two huge columns. The plan of the temple shows affinities to shrines at Tell el-Amarna and Deir el-Medineh in Egypt. [*See* Amarna, Tell el-.] Various architectural elements, such as painted plaster, the stone staircase leading to the cella, and octagonal columns, indicate a strong Egyptian influence. Nevertheless, a gold plaque portraying a naked Canaanite goddess (Clamer, 1980) and a graffito of a Canaanite deity indicate that a Canaanite cult was performed there.

The level VI finds attest to strong ties with Egypt, in particular during the reign of Rameses III (1182–1151 BCE, low chronology of Wente and Van Siclen, 1976). Several bowl fragments inscribed in hieratic script document (as do similar inscribed bowls from Tel Seraʿ) a harvest tax paid to an Egyptian religious institution, probably associated with a local temple (Goldwasser, 1984). [*See* Seraʿ, Tel.] The recording of the harvest tax on votive bowls reflects the economic exploitation of southern Canaan by Egyptian authorities and their religious establishment, suggesting that Lachish was under direct Egyptian control. The level VI city was completely destroyed by fire, its inhabitants were liquidated or driven out, and the site was abandoned until the tenth century BCE. With the absence of inscriptions, the identity of the conquerors cannot be established. One possibility is that Lachish was destroyed by the Sea Peoples, who settled at about that time on the coastal plain. [*See* Philistines, *article on* Early Philistines.] (Significantly, Philistine painted pottery—monochrome as well as bichrome—has not been found at Lachish, except for some sherds in a cave on the slope.) The alternative possibility is that level VI was destroyed by the Israelites, as described in *Joshua* 10:31–32. The biblical record, which describes a large Canaanite city destroyed in a swift attack, fits the archaeological evidence. On the other hand, the motive for the destruction remains obscure: the Israelites did not settle at the site or in the surrounding region (Dagan, 1992) until much later.

A cache of bronze objects, one of which contains a cartouche of Rameses III, was found in area G beneath the level VI destruction debris. Thus, level VI could not have been destroyed before the later part of his reign—in about 1160 BCE. The destruction of Lachish may have coincided with Egyptian loss of control over southern Canaan (c. 1130 BCE), as without Egyptian protection unfortified Lachish could not defend itself.

Seven or eight brief inscriptions written in Canaanite alphabetic script have been recovered (Puech, 1986–1987), making Lachish the cardinal site in Canaan proper for studying this script. The earliest inscription includes four letters incised on an MB bronze dagger. [*See* Proto-Canaanite.]

Level V. The settlement was renewed, but unfortified, after a long period of abandonment in level V. It is usually assigned to the period of the United Monarchy and its destruction to Pharaoh Shishak (Sheshonq)'s campaign in about 925 BCE. Small domestic buildings were uncovered in different parts of the site. Aharoni (1975) discovered a cult room in the solar shrine area; its cultic equipment included a stone altar and pottery incense burners and chalices. The cult room was destroyed by fire; remains of destruction may also have been detected in area S. Level V cannot be dated with certainty because the date of the pottery characterizing it remains problematic.

Level IV. A large fortified city was constructed in level IV, probably because of Judah's new strategic needs (Solomon's divided kingdom). [*See* Judah.] Lachish is cited in *2 Chronicles* 11:5–12,23 as one of the cities fortified by Rehoboam, but the list may refer to construction works by a later Judean king. Level IV appears to have been constructed by one of the early kings of Judah—Rehoboam (928–911 BCE), Asa (908–867 BCE), or Jehoshaphat (870–846 BCE).

The city was surrounded by massive fortifications. The city gate on the southwest included a roadway ascending into the city, an outer gate built as a projecting bastion, a six-chambered inner gate, and an open courtyard between the two gates (see figure 2). An outer revetment surrounded the site halfway down the slope; it supported a glacis that reached the bottom of the main city wall extending along the mound's upper periphery. Whether the outer revetment functioned merely as an obstacle preventing attackers from reaching the main wall or was a city wall that could have been manned in time of siege cannot be determined.

A huge palace-fort (palace B), apparently the residence of the Judean governor, crowned the center of the city. The edifice was built on a raised foundation podium whose superstructure is missing. The foundation podium has two differently constructed parts, A and B. It is generally believed that podium A belonged to an earlier edifice (palace A of level V) that was incorporated in level IV into the newly erected palace B. It seems more probable, however, that podium A was originally an integral part of palace B, and that it was constructed as a separate unit and, for technical reasons, in a different style. Palace B had two annexes. The northern building was probably a storehouse, while the southern one (labeled the "government storehouse" by Starkey) was either a stable or a storehouse (see below). A massive wall (the enclosure wall) connected the corner of the palace-fort and the main city wall.

A great shaft, a rock-cut installation (about 22.50 m deep) on the eastern side of the site, was partially cleared by Starkey. It may be an unfinished water system, but it is more likely the quarry that supplied the stones for the level IV monumental structures. A deep well uncovered at the site's northeast corner was probably the city's main water source, at least in the Iron Age. The beginning of level IV lacks domestic structures. In a later phase, however, a house was built in area S; some domestic remains were also found near the city gate, indicating the beginning of settlement in open areas of the fort.

2 Kings 14:19 and *2 Chronicles* 25:27 record that King Amaziah (798–769 BCE) fled to Lachish when a revolt broke out in Jerusalem. The rebels followed him to Lachish and killed him. The king's choice of Lachish as a refuge indicates the city's importance in the kingdom of Judah. It is not known whether this event took place in level IV or III.

Palace B, the city gate, the "enclosure wall," and the residence in area S (but apparently not the city walls) were rebuilt in level III, indicating their destruction at the end of level IV. As no remains of willful destruction were discerned, these structures may have been destroyed by an earthquake, such as the one that occurred in about 760 BCE, during the reign of Uzziah (*Am.* 1:1; *Zec.* 14:5).

Level III. The rebuilding of the city gate, the palace-fort compound, and the enclosure wall mark level III. The number of settlers at Lachish must have increased, as many buildings of domestic character were found in the areas south of the palace-fort and along the road from the city gate into the city. Of note is the enlarged palace-fort compound. Podiums A and B of former palace B, as well as an extension (podium C), formed an enlarged raised foundation for the new palace C. Its superstructure has not survived, except for some floor segments. The palace-fort and its two annexes opened into a large courtyard.

The southern annex was enlarged in level III. Its ground plan (and that of the smaller level IV building) resembles the controversial stable compounds at Megiddo and the storehouse at Tel Beersheba and probably served similar functions. [*See* Megiddo; Beersheba.] If these buildings were stables, the large courtyard might have been a training and parade ground for chariots from the Judean garrison. The lamentation of *Micah* (1:13) associates Lachish with chariots, and the Lachish reliefs (see below) portray burning vehicles, probably chariots, being thrown on the Assyrian attackers.

Assyrian conquest. The level III city was destroyed in 701 BCE by Sennacherib, king of Assyria. Campaigning in Judah, Sennacherib established his camp at Lachish (*2 Kgs.* 18:14, 17; *Is.* 36:2, 37:8; *2 Chr.* 32:9) and from there sent a task force to challenge King Hezekiah in Jerusalem. [*See* Jerusalem.] When the destruction of Lachish was complete, its inhabitants were deported. The region of Lachish was probably included in the Judean territory Sennacherib turned over to the Philistine kings. The well-dated, large assemblages of pottery vessels sealed beneath the destruction debris of the level III structures form the basis for dating the pottery of Judah in that period (Tufnell, 1953; Zimhoni, 1990).

LACHISH. Figure 2. *Excavation of the Iron Age city gate, from the south.* (Courtesy Institute of Archaeology, Tel Aviv University)

The main Assyrian attack was carried out in the southwest corner of the city. The archaeological data make possible the reconstruction of the battle that took place here (Ussishkin, 1990). The Assyrian army laid here a huge siege ramp (the oldest siege ramp, and the sole Assyrian one known). [*See* Assyrians.] Starkey unknowingly removed a substantial part of it. Made of boulders heaped against the slope of the mound, its top reached the bottom of the outer revetment. It is estimated that 13,000–19,000 tons of stone were dumped there. The stones of the upper layer were joined with mortar to create a compact surface. An earthen platform on top of the siege ramp provided level ground for the siege machines.

As a countermeasure, the defenders laid a counterramp against the inner side of the city wall, opposite the siege ramp. It was composed of mound debris topped by a layer of limestone chips. At its apex it is about 3 m higher than the top of the city wall, forming a basis for a new defense line apparently erected there. When the defense positions on top of the city walls collapsed, the Assyrians had to extend the siege ramp in order to attack the new, higher defense line. The second stage of the siege ramp is also composed of boulders.

Remains of weapons, ammunition, and equipment have been recovered, mostly at the point of attack at the southwest corner: a bronze helmet crest, scales of armor, slingstones, iron arrowheads, a few carved bone arrowheads; a fragment of an iron chain, and twelve large, perforated stones apparently used by the defenders to unbalance the siege machines.

Starkey uncovered a mass burial—the scattered, disarticulated skeletons of about fifteen hundred individuals—in a few adjoining caves that may be associated with the Assyrian attack. D. L. Risdon (1939) has studied 695 skulls belonging to men, women, and children; three had been trepanned. Curiously, the crania bear a close racial resemblance to the contemporary population of Egypt.

Lachish reliefs. A series of stone reliefs commemorating the conquest of Lachish existed in Sennacherib's palace at Nineveh (Kuyunjik), decorating the walls of a large room (Ussishkin, 1982). [*See* Nineveh.] The palace was excavated in 1847–1851 by Austen Henry Layard, who sent most of the reliefs to the British Museum in London. The original length of the relief series was 26.85 m; 18.85 m were sent to London and thus preserved. From left to right, the series depicted Assyrian horses and charioteers, Assyrian infantry attacking the city, the besieged city itself, Assyrian soldiers carrying booty, deported families leaving the city, Judean captives, Sennacherib seated on his throne, the royal tent and chariots, and the Assyrian camp. The city is portrayed in detail: the city gate and city walls under attack (see figure 3), the huge siege ramp on which five siege machines are deployed, and a large structure in the center of the city, possibly the palace-fort. The perspective, in schematic Assyrian style, appears to be from a point on the slope of the hill southwest of the mound. It may be the point, probably in front of the Assyrian camp, from which Sennacherib watched the battle from his throne, as depicted in the relief.

Royal Judean storage jars. Tel Lachish is a key site for studying royal Judean storage jars and their stamps. By 1994, 403 royal stamps and 63 personal stamps from Lachish had been amassed: 85.60 percent of the royal stamps are of the four-winged type, and 73.96 percent of the identifiable royal stamps include the city name *Hebron.* All the stamped handles belong to storage jars of type 484, following Tufnell's classification (Tufnell, 1953), but many jars of this type were not stamped. Neutron activation analysis has shown that these jars were produced of similar clay, originating in the region of Lachish, indicating that they were manufactured at a single regional center.

Ten jars with stamped handles and many unstamped jars were restored. It appears that jars of all the types found were used concurrently. The restorable jars were uncovered beneath the destruction debris of level III and thus date to shortly before 701 BCE. This date fits the view that the royal storage jars were produced by Hezekiah's government as part of the preparations to meet the Assyrian invasion. The capacity of the stamped jars varies, so that the stamps would not have been a royal guarantee of capacity. The personal stamps were also impressed on jars with royal stamps (Ussishkin, 1976), suggesting that the owners of the personal stamps were either potters or officials otherwise associated with the production of the jars. There is no consistent pattern to where on a handle the stamps were applied; many stamps were applied carelessly and were not ment to be read.

Level II. Following a period of abandonment, Lachish was rebuilt and refortified, probably during the reign of Josiah (639–609 BCE). The level II city was poorer and less densely inhabited, and its fortifications weaker than those of levels IV–III. The palace-fort was not rebuilt, and its ruins loomed over the center of the city. Numerous small houses were uncovered in different parts of the site.

A smaller city gate was built on the ruins of the earlier one. It contained an outer and an inner gate, with a rectangular courtyard surrounded by small rooms between them. The Lachish letters uncovered in one of these rooms hint that the city's headquarters were located in the city-gate complex. [*See* Lachish Inscriptions.] The outer revetment was repaired, and a new main stone city wall was erected on the remains of the previous wall.

Numerous Hebrew ostraca, inscriptions on pottery vessels, bullae, seals, and inscribed weights were found in level II. Most important are the Lachish letters, a group of ostraca interpreted as correspondence mostly sent to "my lord Yaush," an army commander at Lachish, by a subordinate

LACHISH. Figure 3. *Detail of the Nineveh reliefs of the siege of Lachish.* An Assyrian battering-ram attacking the city wall. (Courtesy Institute of Archaeology, Tel Aviv University)

stationed at some point not far from the city, shortly before the Babylonian conquest (Torczyner et al., 1938). Yigael Yadin (1984) believed that the letters are copies or drafts of letters sent from Lachish to the commander in Jerusalem. Several inscriptions on vessels were found in a storeroom near the city gate, two of which define types of wine kept in the vessels. Two jar inscriptions mention dates—probably the regnal years of Zedekiah (596–586 BCE). Seventeen bullae stamped with Hebrew seals were found in the solar shrine area; another, stamped with the seal of "Gedaliah who is over the house"—possibly Gedaliah son of Ahikam (*2 Kgs.* 25:22)—was found on the surface of the mound.

Level II was destroyed in 588/86 BCE by Nebuchadrezzar, king of Babylon. Shortly before, Jeremiah (34:7) had named Lachish as one of the remaining Judean strongholds. A considerable amount of pottery—including storage jars stamped with a rosette emblem—was sealed beneath the debris of the houses, providing an indicative pottery assemblage for the period (Zimhoni, 1990).

Level I. After a period of abandonment following the destruction of level II, Lachish was rebuilt as a Persian government center. Level I covers the Babylonian, Persian, and the beginning of the Hellenistic periods. The fortifications were restored, and a small palace (the Residency), a temple (solar shrine), and a few large buildings were constructed. Judeans returning from the Babylonian Exile settled there (*Neh.* 11:30). The Residency was constructed on the foundation podium of the Judean palace-fort, which was cleared of the debris from the level III palace-fort. The Residency was smaller than the earlier edifice. Its plan combined that of an Assyrian open-court house and that of a North Syrian *bit-ḫilani;* the square column bases in the porticos were carved in Achaemenid style. At a later phase of level I, the Residency was settled by squatters. The solar shrine, whose entrance faced east, was built in a style similar to it, and they are probably contemporaneous. The finds indicate that the shrine was in use until the Hellenistic period. The Persian-period finds include about two hundred small limestone altars found outside the mound near the southwest corner. [*See* Altars.] One altar bears an inscription mentioning incense. [*See* Incense.] It is not clear whether these altars were associated with the cult practiced in the solar shrine.

Later Remains. The settlement was abandoned during the Hellenistic period. For unknown reasons, Marisa/Mareshah and then Eleutheropolis/Beth-Guvrin replaced Lachish as the region's central settlement. [*See* Mareshah.] A segment of the Roman road from Eleutheropolis to Gaza, which passed near the site, was uncovered by Starkey. Numerous coins from different periods were found on the surface, indicating that the summit was continuously cultivated. The western part of the summit contained burials, devoid of any burial offerings, which probably belonged to bedouins. The latest remains include trenches, cartridges, and coins from Israel's War of Independence in 1948.

[*See also the biographies of Aharoni, Harding, Layard, Starkey, and Tufnell.*]

BIBLIOGRAPHY

Aharoni, Yohanan. *Investigations at Lachish: The Sanctuary and the Residency (Lachish V).* Tel Aviv, 1975.

Amiran, Ruth. "The Pottery of the Middle Bronze Age I in Palestine." *Israel Exploration Journal* 10 (1960): 204–225.

Clamer, Christa. "A Gold Plaque from Tel Lachish." *Tel Aviv* 7 (1980): 152–162.

Dagan, Yehudah. *Archaeological Survey of Israel: Map of Lakhish (98).* Jerusalem, 1992.

Dever, William G. "New Vistas on the EB IV ("MBI") Horizon in Syria-Palestine." *Bulletin of the American Schools of Oriental Research,* no. 237 (1980): 35–64.

Goldwasser, Orly. "Hieratic Inscriptions from Tel Sera' in Southern Canaan." *Tel Aviv* 11 (1984): 77–93.

Puech, Émile. "The Canaanite Inscriptions of Lachish and Their Religious Background." *Tel Aviv* 13–14 (1986–1987): 13–25.

Risdon, D. L. "A Study of the Cranial and Other Human Remains from Palestine Excavated at Tell Duweir (Lachish) by the Wellcome-Marston Archaeological Research Expedition." *Biometrika* 35 (1939): 99–165.

Torczyner, Harry. *Lachish I: The Lachish Letters.* London, 1938.

Tufnell, Olga, et al. *Lachish II: The Fosse Temple.* London, 1940.

Tufnell, Olga. *Lachish III: The Iron Age.* London, 1953.

Tufnell, Olga, et al. *Lachish IV: The Bronze Age.* London, 1958.

Ussishkin, David. "Royal Judean Storage Jars and Private Seal Impressions." *Bulletin of the American Schools of Oriental Research,* no. 223 (1976): 1–13.

Ussishkin, David. "Excavations at Tel Lachish, 1973–1977: Preliminary Report." *Tel Aviv* 5 (1978): 1–97.

Ussishkin, David. *The Conquest of Lachish by Sennacherib.* Tel Aviv, 1982.

Ussishkin, David. "Excavations at Tel Lachish, 1978–1983: Second Preliminary Report." *Tel Aviv* 10 (1983): 97–175.

Ussishkin, David. "Levels VII and VI at Tel Lachish and the End of the Bronze Age in Canaan." In *Palestine in the Bronze and Iron Ages: Papers in Honour of Olga Tufnell,* edited by Jonathan N. Tubb, pp. 213–230. London, 1985.

Ussishkin, David. "The Assyrian Attack on Lachish: The Archaeological Evidence from the Southwest Corner of the Site." *Tel Aviv* 17 (1990): 53–86.

Wente, E. F., and C. C. Van Siclen. "A Chronology of the New Kingdom." In *Studies in Honor of George R. Hughes,* edited by J. H. Johnson and E. F. Wente, pp. 217–261. Studies in Ancient Oriental Civilization, 39. Chicago, 1976.

Yadin, Yigael. "The Lachish Letters: Originals or Copies and Drafts?" In *Recent Archaeology in the Land of Israel,* edited by Hershel Shanks, pp. 179–186. Washington, D.C., 1984.

Zimhoni, Orna. "Two Ceramic Assemblages from Lachish Levels III and II." *Tel Aviv* 17 (1990): 3–52.

DAVID USSISHKIN

LACHISH INSCRIPTIONS. The site of Tell ed-Duweir or Tel Lachish has provided one of the most important corpora of Hebrew inscriptions: thirty-six are presently known and the ongoing excavations may well discover others. In addition, important Proto-Canaanite inscriptions, *lmlk* sealings and other seals and sealings (Diringer, 1953, pp. 340–348; Aharoni, 1968: 165–167), inscribed weights (Diringer 1953, pp. 348–356; Aharoni, 1968, p. 165), several Egyptian inscriptions (Goldwasser, 1991), and a three-line Aramaic inscription on a Persian-period altar (Diringer, 1953, pp. 358–359) have been recovered at the site.

The first group of Hebrew texts, numbering twenty-one, was discovered in 1935 and 1938 and published almost immediately by Harry Torczyner (Torczyner, 1938, texts 1–18; Torczyner, 1940, texts 19–21). During a trial excavation carried out at the Solar Shrine at Lachish in 1966, a single ostracon was found (Aharoni, 1968, text 22). In the excavations that have been ongoing since 1973 under David Ussishkin, another ten inscriptions have come to light (Lemaire, 1976, text 23; Ussishkin, 1978, texts 24–30, pp. 81–88; and Ussishkin, 1983, texts 31–32, pp. 157–160). For reasons that are unclear, this sequential numbering of the Hebrew inscriptions omitted four brief texts, not written on ostraca, that Diringer reedited (1953, pp. 356–358).

It is the first group of texts, the so-called Lachish letters, that have made the collection famous, for several of these documents are relatively long and well preserved. There can be no doubt that this group is at least partially homogeneous, for five of the ostraca are sherds from the same vessel (G. Lankester Harding in Torczyner, 1938, p. 184). Whether this means that the documents are drafts of letters written on the site and sent elsewhere (Yadin, 1984) is open to debate (Rainey, 1987). The most important documents in this group are letters from an inferior to his superior in an administrative and/or military context (e.g., text 3, ll. 1–2: "Your servant Hoshayahu hereby reports to my lord Yaush"). The letters are generally dated to the period before the fall of Judah, in 586 BCE, perhaps in 589. The concerns of that time appear to be reflected in the mention in text 3 of a high-level embassy to Egypt (the envoy is Konyahu, general of the army [*śr hṣb'*]) and of an unnamed prophet *(hnb').* Although attempts to identify this prophet as Jeremiah are pure speculation, the extrabiblical attestation of the term *nb'* itself is important; the circumstances of these letters also are not unlike the situation in the time of Jeremiah, as described in the Hebrew Bible (Dussaud, 1938: 256–271; Lemaire, 1977, p. 109).

Several of this first group of texts are of less historical interest than the letters; they are either simple lists of names (texts 1, 11, and 19) or are too poorly preserved to allow meaningful analysis (texts 10, 12, and 17). Text 20, a brief jar inscription, is important because it may include an element of dating: if *btšʿyt* means "in the ninth (year)," it may refer to the ninth year of Zedekiah, king of Judah, which would correspond to 589–588 BCE, the date indicated in the Hebrew Bible for the beginning of the siege of Lachish (*Jer.* 39:1; cf. Lemaire, 1977, pp. 134–135).

The documents found since 1966 are more heterogeneous and include an ostracon with a list of names (text 22), other fragmentary inscriptions on ostraca (texts 23 and 31), and several inscriptions originally written with ink or incised on whole jars (texts 24–30 and 32). The four inscriptions from the earlier excavations not included in the sequential numbering fall into the heterogeneous category, but two are important: a royal *bat* jar inscription, useful in attempting to ascertain the quantity designated by the term *bat,* and a partial alphabet (Diringer, 1953, pp. 356–358).

These inscriptions provided the first reasonably extensive body of texts in Judean Hebrew written in cursive script. They provided, therefore, an important contribution to early descriptions of extrabiblical cursive paleography (Dussaud, 1938, pp. 270–271), orthographic practice (Cross and Freedman, 1952, pp. 51–56), and grammar. Some of the texts discovered since, at Tel Arad, have shown that orthographic conventions could vary (e.g., they reveal a more extensive use of *matres lectionis*), but that the basic language of these two primary corpora was identical and for all intents and purposes was also identical with standard biblical Hebrew. One of the primary contributions of the Lachish letters to the study of Hebrew syntax has been to show how frequently nonverbal elements were fronted in the spoken language (e.g., text 4, ll. 6–7: *wsmkyhw lqḥh šmʿyhw wyʿlhw hʿyrh,* "Now as for Semakyahu, Shemayahu has seized him and taken him up to the city").

The Lachish letters also provided the first body of extrabiblical data regarding epistolary usages in preexilic Hebrew (Pardee et al., 1982, pp. 67–114, 145–164). These data have more recently been expanded by the letters from Tel Arad (*ibid.*, pp. 24–67). Because the total number of letters known from the period is still small, however, many details of epistolary usage remain unknown.

[*See also* Arad Inscriptions; Hebrew Language and Literature; *and* Lachish.]

BIBLIOGRAPHY

Aharoni, Yohanan. "Trial Excavation in the 'Solar Shrine' at Lachish: Preliminary Report." *Israel Exploration Journal* 18 (1968): 157–169. *Editio princeps* of text 21, with a hand copy.

Cross, Frank Moore, and David Noel Freedman. *Early Hebrew Orthography*. New Haven, 1952.

Diringer, David. "Early Hebrew Inscriptions." In *Lachish,* vol. 3, *The Iron Age,* by Olga Tufnell et al., pp. 331–359. London, 1953.

Dussaud, René. "Le prophète Jérémie et les lettres de Lakish." *Syria* 19 (1938): 256–271.

Goldwasser, Orly. "An Egyptian Scribe from Lachish and the Hieratic Tradition of the Hebrew Kingdoms." *Tel Aviv* 18.1 (1991): 248–253.

Lemaire, André. "A Schoolboy's Exercise on an Ostracon at Lachish." *Tel Aviv* 3 (1976): 109–110. *Editio princeps* of text 23, with a photograph (pl. 5/2).

Lemaire, André. *Inscriptions hébraïques,* vol. 1, *Les ostraca.* Littératures Anciennes du Proche-Orient, 9. Paris, 1977. Excellent philological and historical treatment of texts 1–22.

Pardee, Dennis, S. David Sperling, J. David Whitehead, and Paul E. Dion. *Handbook of Ancient Hebrew Letters.* Society of Biblical Literature, Sources for Biblical Study, vol. 15. Chico, Calif., 1982. Comprehensive bibliography on epistolary documents (up to 1978).

Rainey, Anson F. "Watching Out for the Signal Fires of Lachish." *Palestine Exploration Quarterly* 119 (1987): 149–151.

Torczyner, Harry. *Lachish,* vol. 1, *The Lachish Letters.* London, 1938. *Editio princeps* of texts 1–18, with a photograph, hand copy, and commentary.

Torczyner, Harry. *Tʿwdwt lkyš: Mktbym mymy yrmyhw hnbyʾ.* Jerusalem, 1940. Hebrew edition of previous entry, with the addition of texts 19–21, discovered in 1938.

Ussishkin, David. "Excavations at Tel Lachish—1973–1977: Preliminary Report." *Tel Aviv* 5 (1978): 1–97. Includes *editio princeps* of texts 24–30, with hand copies and photographs (pls. 26–32).

Ussishkin, David. "Excavations at Tel Lachish, 1978–1983: Second Preliminary Report." *Tel Aviv* 10 (1983): 97–175. Includes *editio princeps* of texts 31–32, with hand copies and photographs (pls. 41).

Yadin, Yigael. "The Lachish Letters—Originals or Copies and Drafts?" In *Recent Archaeology in the Land of Israel,* edited by Hershel Shanks, pp. 179–186. Washington, D.C., 1984.

DENNIS PARDEE

LAGASH. *See* Girsu and Lagash.

LAGRANGE, MARIE-JOSEPH (1855–1938), founder of the École Biblique et Archéologique Française in Jerusalem. Lagrange took a doctorate in law at the University of Paris before entering the Toulouse province of the Dominican Order in 1879. After seminary studies at the University of Salamanca in Spain (1880–1884), he taught there and in Toulouse (1884–1888) before undertaking graduate studies at the University of Vienna (1888–1890). He opened the École Biblique on 15 November 1890, and within a decade he had recruited and trained scholars of the caliber of M. A. Jaussen (1871–1962), L.-H. Vincent (1872–1960), A. M. Savignac (1874–1951), F.-M. Abel (1878–1953), and P. E. Dhorme (1881–1966), whose original research quickly demanded an outlet. In 1892 he founded the *Revue Biblique* and in 1900 the monograph series *Études Bibliques,* both of which still flourish.

Lagrange carried out pioneering topographical research in Palestine, Sinai, and Petra but is best known as a historian, a biblical commentator, and the author of twenty-nine books. In addition to full-scale commentaries on *Judges* (1903), *Mark* (1911), *Romans* (1916), *Galatians* (1918), *Luke* (1921), *Matthew* (1923), and *John* (1925), his research produced major works on the canon and textual criticism of the New Testament, messianism, and intertestamental Judaism. Many of his 248 articles made highly original contributions in areas as diverse as the theology of inspiration, patrology, and Palestinian topography. His 1,500 book reviews reveal a fruitful and sustained dialogue with authors specializing in all facets of biblical studies.

Lagrange's programmatic book *La méthode historique* (1903) won him enemies among Roman Catholic traditionalists during the Modernist crisis, but his loyalty and perseverance eventually established the critical method as fundamental to Catholic biblical studies. Before poor health obliged him to leave Jerusalem in 1935, he had initiated a second generation of brilliant scholars, notably, Pierre Benoit (1906–1987), Bermara Couroyer (1900–), and Roland de Vaux (1903–1971).

[*See also* École Biblique et Archéologique Française.]

BIBLIOGRAPHY

Braun, François-Marie. *L'oeuvre du Père Lagrange: Étude et bibliographie.* Fribourg, 1943. Indispensable for its exhaustive bibliography.

Murphy-O'Connor, Jerome, with a contribution by Justin Taylor. *The Ecole Biblique and the New Testament: A Century of Scholarship, 1890–1990.* Novum Testamentum et Orbis Antiquus, vol. 13. Fribourg, 1990. See chapter 2 for a critical evaluation of Lagrange's contribution to New Testament scholarship.

Lagrange, Marie-Joseph. *Père Lagrange: Personal Reflections and Memoirs.* Translated by Henry Wansbrough. Foreword by Pierre Benoit. New York, 1985. An approach to an autobiography for the years 1855–1913, edited by Pierre Benoît as *Le Père Lagrange, au service de la Bible: Souvenirs personnels* (Paris, 1967).

JEROME MURPHY-O'CONNOR, O.P.

LAHAV (Tel Ḥalif; Ar., Tell Khuweilifeh), 3-acre mound at Kibbutz Lahav in southern Israel, on the southwestern flank of the Judean hills, 8 km (5 mi.) south of Tell Beit Mirsim, 15 km (9 mi.) north of Tel Beersheba, and 25 km (15 mi.) west of Tel Arad (31°23′ N, 34°52′ E; map reference 1373 × 0879). The site's prominent geomorphological location, at the juncture between the coastal plain, Judean mountains, and Negev desert, commands the route from the seacoast north of the Beersheba drainage east into the Judean hills.

Identification. Based on the proximity of Tel Ḥalif to its satellite site, Ḥorvat Rimmon (Ar., Khirbet Umm er-Rammamin), less than 1 km south of it, Félix-Marie Abel, in his 1938 geographical survey, identified Tel Ḥalif with biblical Ziklag, the city that the Philistine overlord Achish ceded to King David (*1 Sm.* 27:6 ff.). In the nineteenth century, Claude R. Conder and H. H. Kitchener identified Ḥorvat Rimmon as the Iron Age Rimmon mentioned in the territorial lists of Judah in *Joshua* 15:32 and 19:7. Accepting this hypothesis, Abel also identified Ḥalif with Tilla, a Byzantine-period settlement that Eusebius, in his *Onomasticon* (99.26), had located near Rimmon, 26 km (16 mi.) south of Beit Jibrin. More recently, noting the absence of Iron Age remains at Ḥorvat Rimmon, Amos Kloner (1980) argued that Ḥalif itself was biblical Rimmon, suggesting that its Byzantine-period satellite later co-opted its name. Nadav Na'aman (1980) has also suggested that Tel Ḥalif is biblical Ḥormah. [*See the biographies of Abel, Conder, and Kitchener.*]

Exploration. Archaeological exploration at Tel Ḥalif began in the 1950s, following the establishment of Kibbutz Lahav on its eastern slopes. The first formal investigations were intermittent salvage operations conducted by the Israel Department of Antiquities. These included investigations of tombs of the Roman/Byzantine settlement at site 66 below the tell on the northwest in 1962 (Gophna and Sussman, 1974) and of the Iron Age at site 72 on the slopes facing the tell to the south in 1964 and 1972 (Biran and Gophna, 1964; Seger, 1972.)

The Lahav Research Project launched an integrated study of Tel Ḥalif and its environs in 1976 that included excavation, regional survey, and ethnographic study. The project was carried out by a consortium of American scholars and institutions under the direction of Joe D. Seger. Field research seasons were conducted in 1976, 1977, 1979, and 1980 (phase I); 1983, 1986, 1987, and 1989 (phase II); and in 1992–1993 (phase III.) These explorations recovered evidence of ancient settlement on the tell itself, on its lower eastern terrace, and at a number of satellite sites. Traces of occupation from the Chalcolithic period (c. 3500 BCE) through the late Byzantine and Islamic periods were found, along with remains of nineteenth- and early twentieth-century CE Arab dwellers.

Settlement History. The first settlers at the site utilized the lower terrace area just above the valley to the east. Excavations at terrace sites 101 and 301 produced evidence of Chalcolithic (stratum XVII) and Early Bronze I (stratum XVI) occupation; they revealed that Ḥalif steadily developed as a significant village site between 3500 and 2900 BCE. Ḥalif's architecture and small finds from the end of the EB I indicate that it was a regional center in commercial contact with early dynastic Egypt.

Ḥalif was not occupied until the end of EB II. Nearby Arad flourished in the EB II, but when it declined at the end of the period, the main tell at Ḥalif underwent vigorous new settlement. In field I, on the eastern slopes, the EB III settlement is marked by four substantial architectural phases (strata XV–XII). The stratum XV city was defended by large fortification walls. Its defenses included a 7.5-meter-wide tower fronted by a well-prepared crushed limestone glacis. The final stratum XII EB settlement was destroyed in the twenty-fourth century BCE, possibly in the course of late fifth-and sixth-dynasty Egyptian forays in the area.

After the eclipse of the stratum XII city, Ḥalif lay unoccupied until just before 1500 BCE. The stratum XI resettlement, in the late Bronze IA period follows closely on the mid-sixteenth-century destruction of city D at nearby Tell Beit Mirsim. In field I at Ḥalif, four LB phases were identified (strata XI–VIII). In strata X and IX, during LB IB and IIA, the presence of a large Egyptian style "residency" building and its associated remains indicates that the settlement was a trading station along the route into the southern Judean hills.

With stratum VIII (LB IIB) all of the field I architecture was converted into a storage complex with numerous stone-lined bins. Elements of an adjacent domestic building in area B10, with three subphases of room resurfacing, testify to the intensity of this thirteenth-century occupation. Stratum VIII ends in destruction in about 1200 BCE.

Modest occupation continues into the Iron I period (stratum VII), as indicated by several later surfacing phases in the area B10 structure in field I, along with evidence from probes in fields II and III. However, significant rebuilding begins again only during stratum VI in the Iron II period. This was a period of extensive growth and expansion at Ḥalif, presumably under the aegis of the Judean monarchy. Traces of the Iron II settlement were found virtually everywhere at and around the site. These included the extensive site 72 cemetery on the slopes of the hill southwest of the tell.

On the summit of the tell, large-scale architectural exposures from the Iron II period were made in fields II, III, and IV. The first major Iron II redevelopment (stratum VIB) took place in the early ninth century BCE. Investigation in fields III and IV indicated that they included casematelike fortification walls associated with intramural domestic buildings and an outlying flagstone paved glacis. The stratum VIB city experienced massive destruction at the end of the eighth century BCE, probably by Sennacherib in his campaign in 701. A subsequent squatter phase of reoccupation (stratum VIA) represents a brief resettlement during the first quarter of the seventh century BCE. After this, occupation ceases until the Persian era.

In stratum V, reoccupation by a regional Persian administration is indicated by pits and surface deposits all across the tell. Significant architecture was encountered only in field II, where elements of a large building (the foundations of its walls are a meter wide) and related artifacts suggest that it was a barrack or other military structure.

Above the Persian remains two subphases of another large building were found. These date to the Hellenistic period (stratum IV). Initial construction is dated to the mid-fourth century BCE. A second-century Ptolemaic coin sealed in a grave beneath final-phase floors shows continuity of settlement until at least about 200 BCE. An occupational hiatus in the Early Roman period followed.

With the flight of Jews and Christians from Jerusalem during the first- and second-century CE wars with Rome, the site recovered dramatically, however. A substantial Roman/Byzantine village (Tilla) was established on the tell and on the terrace below its northeast slopes (stratum III.) This included the cemetery at site 66 below the tell to the northwest. Tilla is part of an intensive regional pattern of Roman/Byzantine resettlement that includes significant satellite villages at Ḥorvat Rimmon to the south, Khirbet Zaʿaq to the north, and Khirbet Abu Hof to the southwest.

Traces of later occupation representing the early Islamic (stratum II) and modern Arabic periods (stratum I) are found mainly on the lower terrace areas. Excavated remains in cave complex A, just below field I, indicate an early Islamic presence from Mamluk times (c. 700 CE) until well into the period of the Crusades. The more prominent remains, however, belong to the late nineteenth- and twentieth-century settlement of Khirbet Khuweilifeh. Excavations and ethnographic research indicate that until about 1940, cave complexes and other structures in the Khuweilifeh village were used seasonally by Arab *fellahin*—sharecroppers, shepherds, craftsmen, and traders—working as clients of bedouin who claimed ownership of the region.

BIBLIOGRAPHY

Abel, Félix-Marie. *Géographie de la Palestine.* Vol. 2. Paris, 1938.

Biran, Avraham, and Ram Gophna. "An Iron Age Burial Cave at Tel Halif." *Israel Exploration Journal* 20 (1970): 151–169.

Borowski, Oded. "The Biblical Identity of Tel Halif." *Biblical Archaeologist* 51.1 (1988): 21–27.

Gophna, Ram, and Varda Sussman. "A Jewish Burial Cave of the Roman Period at the Foot of Tel Halif" (in Hebrew). *Atiqot* 7 (1974): 11–12.

Jacobs, P. "Tell Halif: Prosperity in a Late Bronze Age City on the Edge of the Negev." In *Archaeology and Biblical Interpretation: Essays in Memory of D. Glenn Rose,* edited by Leo G. Perdue et al., 67–86. Atlanta, 1987.

Kloner, Amos. "Hurvat Rimmon, 1979." *Israel Exploration Journal* 30 (1980): 226–228.

Na'aman, Nadav. "The Inheritance of the Sons of Simeon." *Zeitschrift des Deutschen Palästina-Vereins* 96 (1980): 136–152.

Seger, Joe D. "Tell Halif (Lahav)." *Israel Exploration Journal* 22 (1972): 161.

Seger, Joe D., and Oded Borowski. "The First Two Seasons at Tell Halif." *Biblical Archaeologist* 40 (1977): 156–166.

Seger, Joe D.. "Investigations at Tell Halif, Israel, 1976–1980." *Bulletin of the American Schools of Oriental Research,* no. 252 (1983): 1–23.

Seger, Joe D. "The Location of Biblical Ziklag." *Biblical Archaeologist* 47.1 (1984): 47–53.

Seger, Joe D., et al. "The Bronze Age Settlements at Tell Halif: Phase II Excavations, 1983–1987." In *Preliminary Reports of ASOR-Sponsored Excavations, 1983–87,* edited by Walter E. Rast, 1–32. Bulletin of the American Schools of Oriental Research, Supplement no. 26. Baltimore, 1990.

JOE D. SEGER

LAMPS. The oil lamp was the most common means of lighting in the ancient Near East. It basically consisted of a reservoir, a wick, and fuel; any other features were but variants or embellishments. The wick was an absorbent cord that could be made from a variety of fibrous plants, of which flax was particularly suitable and widely available. Animal fat was an early fuel, but vegetable oils—particularly those derived from olives, castor beans, and sesame seeds—became the most widely used fuel, providing a steady flame that was relatively free from smoke and odor. The labor-intensive agricultural practices of the ancient world dictated frugality with lamp oil in most periods and regions, even though lamps could burn satisfactorily on a grade of oil that was unsuitable for human consumption.

As early as the Epipaleolithic and Pre-Pottery Neolithic in the Near East, concave shells and stone bowls were utilized as lamps. By the fifth and fourth millennia BCE small, handmade ceramic bowls began to serve the same purpose, though as yet there was little attempt to create distinctive lamp forms. The wick was usually draped over the rim of the bowl or floated on the fuel. Because oil would, in time, seep wastefully and messily through the ceramic ware, a lamp was sometimes placed in a saucer of water before or during use.

In Egypt throughout the dynastic period, cylindrical vessels of stone or pottery were used as lamps. They had no wick spouts, the flame rising near the center. Herodotus's description of Egyptian lamps, written in about 400 BCE, would have been appropriate to describe traditional Egyptian lamps at almost any time during the previous two millennia or more: they were "small vases filled with salt and olive oil, on which the wick floated" (*Hist.* 2.62). Even the magnificently carved alabaster lamps in the tomb of the pharaoh Tutankhamun were essentially only large cups. In Mesopotamia the Sumerians made vessels of metal or carved stone in the form of a conch shell, but it is not certain that these always served as lamps.

In the Levant during the Early Bronze Age, ordinary small bowls continued to serve as lamps, as traces of carbon black on their rims indicate, but a potter would sometimes pull out the rim slightly to form a small triangular wick channel. Toward the end of the third millennium the partially nomadic people of the southern Levant used a distinctive flat-bottomed saucer lamp, handmade or turned on a slow wheel, that had four prominent wick channels spaced at equal intervals around the sides.

The Middle Bronze Age in the Levant (c. 1800–1550 BCE), which was closely linked with the Canaanite culture, saw the introduction of a wheelmade saucer lamp that generally had a round bottom but in some regions was given a slightly flattened base. Although there were some typological developments over the successive centuries, this type of lamp continued to be the customary form of Canaanite lamp during the Late Bronze Age (1550–1200 BCE). In addition to their primary function in everyday life, lamps were sometimes placed in the ceremonial foundation deposits of buildings. They also were placed in rock-cut family tombs along with food and objects of daily life, as provisions for the afterlife, and sometimes were left outside the entrances to tombs in memorial rites. Even at this early date—if, indeed,

LAMPS. *Lamps of the Bronze-Iron Ages and the Hellenistic period.* Top row, l to r: MB oil lamp, c. 2000 BCE; two LB oil lamps, c. 1400 BCE; Iron Age I oil lamp, c. 1000 BCE. Bottom row: typical Iron Age II oil lamps, c. 800 BCE; Hellenistic pinched oil lamps, c. 100 BCE. (Courtesy Pictorial Archive)

not before—lamps were recognized not simply as devices for producing light, but as symbols of life.

Saucer lamps continued to be used, in modified form, in the Levant throughout the Iron Age (c. 1200–600 BCE) and Persian period (c. 600–300 BCE). The Phoenicians—seafaring descendants of the Canaanites—carried the saucer lamp, sometimes in a dual-spout form, to Cyprus, North Africa, and elsewhere. Among the varieties of saucer lamp used in central Palestine were a stump-base type in the Iron II period (c. 900–300 BCE) and an extremely shallow version with a large, everted rim that was popular in the Persian period. Occasionally, and perhaps for special purposes, saucer lamps were molded of bronze. Lamps continued to be placed in tombs, sometimes in considerable quantities. Some lamps, having seven wick channels equidistant around the rim and occasionally provided with pedestal bases, may have been used in religious rites. The forms of the lamps in the Temple in Jerusalem were different from those of household specimens and may have changed with passing time; the description of Solomon's Temple (*1 Kgs.* 7:49) alludes to ten gold lampstands, and the priestly account of Israel's ideal cult paraphernalia includes a distinctive seven-branch lampstand (Heb., *menorah*) of gold (*Ex.* 25:31–40).

In Mesopotamia there were, along with varieties of saucer lamps, ceramic specimens harking back to the archaic shape of the conch shell, and some specimens were made of bronze or iron. By the twelfth century BCE, however, the Assyrians were using a new form of wheelmade lamp that had a globular oil reservoir with a flat base and a filling hole at the top, as well as a tubular wick channel that curved upward from the lower part of the reservoir. This lamp form served as the glyphic representation of Nusku, the Assyrian god of fire. Assyrian tombs customarily were provided with a niche in which a lamp was placed. This distinctive lamp continued to be used in Mesopotamia during the Babylonian and Persian periods, and its form appears to have influenced a Palestinian closed lamp during the time of Persian domination.

As early as the seventh and sixth centuries BCE, Greek traders began to bring black-glazed wheelmade lamps into the Near East. The earliest imports had shallow, open bodies, but before long a new style of Greek lamp appeared with a globular oil reservoir, a filling hole at the top, and a short wick channel that extended horizontally from the upper part of the body. Although found most often at commercial settlements on the coast of Asia Minor, the Levant, and Egypt, these sturdily made, handsome lamps sometimes found their way to places farther inland.

The revolution in material culture that swept through the Near East following the conquests of Alexander the Great in the late fourth century BCE brought the rapid alteration of previous lamp traditions. During the third century most lamps were in the new international Hellenistic style, which still relied on the potter's wheel. In the second century BCE, however, molded lamps consisting of joined upper and lower halves largely supplanted the wheelmade tradition throughout the Hellenistic world. A much-favored color for these lamps and other molded vessels was gray, with a glossy gray-black finish, but wares and finishes in other colors sometimes were used. Molding made possible a vast variety of shapes and decorative designs that had been impossible to fabricate on a potter's wheel; factories at Ephesus and at other localities that exported to distant regions sometimes restricted their production largely to a single distinctive form for which they became well known. Decorative designs on molded lamps were largely confined to the area around the filling hole and on the top of the nozzle and tended to be floral or geometric. Loop handles were attached to some specimens. Lamps with multiple nozzles were not uncommon, and elegant bronze lamps were manufactured for special purposes. Typological differences among Hellenistic lamps often provide archaeologists with a useful chronological sequence that contributes to the dating of contemporaneous artifacts.

Despite the immense popularity of molded lamps, wheelmade types continued to be made in some regions of the Near East during the Late Hellenistic period. Small saucer lamps in the Iron Age tradition were manufactured in Egypt in the late dynastic period. In Palestine some potters made a distinctive lamp by pinching together two places on the rim of a small, flat-bottomed bowl so as to form a wick hole. In a different but similarly conservative vein, potters at the Jewish sectarian community of Qumran in the Jordan Valley fashioned distinctive closed lamps on a wheel.

When the Roman period succeeded the Hellenistic era in the mid-first century BCE, the vast majority of lamps continued to be molded; however, a new type of common lamp associated with imperial Rome soon supplanted the Hellenistic forms. The oil reservoir became flattened, with a concave discus on the top, the filling hole was reduced to a small puncture, the wick channel was shortened, and a design in low relief was added to the circular top surface. No longer restricted largely to linear patterns, artisans created a variety of striking designs for the discus, among which were scenes of gladiatorial combat, mythological and animal representations, and abstract patterns. Such lamps often were produced in factories located around the Mediterranean basin that were devoted solely to the manufacture of molded ceramics; the name of the factory sometimes was embossed on the flat base.

In spite of the dominance of the imperial and related lamp types, there was a considerable variety of forms during the early years of the Roman period. Oversized specimens with elaborate decorative handles, sometimes fabricated in bronze or iron, were used in public buildings, cult centers, and the residences of the wealthy. Hellenistic artistic traditions continued to influence both the form and the decoration of finer lamps. Sculptural lamps in an international style also were popular, taking such varied shapes as human

LAMPS. *Roman, Byzantine, and Early Islamic lamps from Sepphoris.* (Courtesy E. M. Meyers)

figures, animals, gods, boats, gladiator helmets, and shoes. Wheelmade lamps sometimes reappeared, though only in provincial contexts; among these was a type with a wheelmade, knife-pared body and a stubby, scimitar-shaped nozzle that was popular in Palestine and Transjordan in the Herodian era. In Mesopotamia molded lamps with short nozzles were often glazed. By this time crude oil (called naphtha) was being used in parts of Mesopotamia as an alternate fuel for lamps. During the Late Roman period (c. 135–335 CE) lamps frequently degenerated, especially as designs were repeatedly copied, with an increasing loss of precision in form and decoration. Specimens tended to develop regional characteristics, some of which have proved useful to archaeologists as indicators of date and provenience. Mesopotamian lamps sometimes continued to reflect their more remote ancestry in the Nusku lamp.

The Byzantine period (c. 335–635 CE) brought new typological developments to lamps in the Near East. In many regions the body and nozzle often merged into an almond shape, with a wide filling hole; decorative elements often were placed, much as in the Hellenistic period, on the shoulder and between the filling hole and the wick hole. The Christian tradition found expression in the frequent display of the cross and other religious motifs and Jewish tradition in the menorah. In Palestine some molded lamps displayed Christian sentiments in Greek, which became increasingly garbled with time. At Carthage, discus lamps in a distinctive red-orange ware retained the small filling hole of Roman lamps so that the discus could be boldly decorated with religious symbols, figures of saints, or pagan motifs. Churches and synagogues were illuminated with large, ornate bronze lamps on tall tripod bases or suspended from chains, and cup-shaped glass lamps came into widespread use in sanctuaries.

By this time a transformation in the function of lamps interred with the dead had undergone a change. There was no longer great concern to provide physical necessities for the dead, but there was much interest in symbolic burial gifts. Epitomizing life, as they so readily did, lamps came to constitute a considerable proportion of funerary gifts. The variety of specimens found in some tombs suggests that each mourner may have brought a lamp to be left burning in the tomb. In Egypt frog-shaped lamps may have been manufactured primarily for use in burials, inasmuch as in popular Egyptian tradition the frog was believed to represent immortality.

After the Islamic conquest of the Near East in the seventh century CE, Byzantine lamps gradually evolved into distinctively Islamic types; however, the almond shape was long retained, and even the simple saucer shape reappeared in the tenth and eleventh centuries in Egypt and the Levant. During the caliphates of Cairo and Baghdad, new forms emerged; among the many diverse medieval types were green-glazed pedestal lamps and slipper-shaped lamps decorated with blue underglaze. It is only in recent centuries that oil lamps have been superseded by artificial illumination.

BIBLIOGRAPHY

An exhaustive bibliography of studies of lamps in the ancient Near East would include several hundred titles, but no comprehensive overview of the technology and typological history of lamps yet exists for the entire region. Academic interest has chiefly been on lamps of the Greco-Roman and Byzantine periods and their great variety. Geographically, the most extensive research has dealt with the lamps of Palestine, which have been treated in numerous excavation reports, catalogs of museum collections, and scholarly articles. Among the latter are the author's series of articles on "The Household Lamps of Palestine" (*BA* 27 [1964]: 1–31, 101–124; 29 [1966]: 2–27); unlike most lamp studies, which are limited to discussions of lamp typology, chronology, and motifs, these articles discuss the archaeological evidence in light of historical texts, technology, and cultural practices. The lamps of other regions of the ancient Near East have been much less adequately published and studied; for some regions, such as Arabia, there is scarcely any literature. An unusually diverse range of Near Eastern lamp types will be found in Renate Rosenthal and Renee Sivan's *Ancient Lamps in the Schloessinger Collection,* Qedem, vol. 8 (Jerusalem, 1978). Some useful information about the technology of ancient lamps, as well as brief comments about some major lamp types from Egypt, the Levant, and Mesopotamia, will be found in *A History of Technology,* vol. 1, *From Earliest Times to the Fall of Ancient Empires,* edited by Charles Singer et al., pp. 235–237 (London, 1954). An extensive bibliography pertaining to lamps in the ancient Near East can be found in *Les lampes de terre cuite en Méditerranée des origines à Justinien,* edited by Thérèse Oziol and René Rebuffat, Travaux de la Maison de l'Orient, no. 13 (Lyon, 1987).

ROBERT HOUSTON SMITH

LAPITHOS, important village on the north coast of Cyprus approximately 14 km (8.5 mi.) west of the town of Kyrenia and 70 km (43.5 mi.) from the south coast of Turkey (35°22′ N, 33°09′ E). Lapithos falls within the Kyrenia district of the Republic of Cyprus, but came under Turkish occupation during the summer of 1974 and is currently (1995) part of the self-proclaimed and internationally unrecognized Turkish Republic of Northern Cyprus. Its historically predominant ethnic-Greek population has now been replaced by Turkish Cypriot and mainland Turkish settlers.

The village is built on terraces on the lower northern slopes of the Kyrenia mountain range, above the fertile coastal plain, in an area well watered by perennial springs and abundant rainfall. Lapithos has long been noted for its citrus groves and other thriving agriculture. It has also been a traditional center for such crafts as woodcarving, pottery, and embroidery. Although Lapithos lacks a large natural harbor, its shoreline is protected from the prevailing northeasterly winds and would have been adequate for ancient shipping.

The modern village was founded in 654 CE by settlers from the nearby coastal town of Lambousa, who sought protection from Arab raids. However, according to tradition, Lapithos was founded by Laconians in the aftermath of the Trojan War. Archaeology suggests that the vicinity was the center of extensive occupation at least since the Chalcolithic period (c. 3800 BCE).

The area has been the focus of considerable archaeological investigation, beginning with the explorations of John L. Myres in 1913 and Menelaos Markides in 1917 on behalf of the Cyprus Museum. In 1927 the Swedish Cyprus Expedition, under the direction of Einar Gjerstad, conducted extensive excavations in the area, which were fully published in volume 1 of *The Swedish Cyprus Expedition* (1934) and formed the basis for a substantial portion of the syntheses in volume 4 of the same work (1948–1972). This activity was followed in 1931–1932 by an expedition from the University Museum of the University of Pennsylvania, which was directed by B. H. Hill. The results are still largely unpublished, except for the study of one tomb. Little evidence for settlements has been recovered as excavations to date have concentrated on cemeteries.

Lapithos demonstrates the characteristic Cypriot settlement pattern in which successive sites move from place to place within a limited region, presumably all utilizing common resources, such as a water source. The earliest-known habitation is the Chalcolithic settlement at the locality *Alonia ton Plakon,* excavated by the Swedish Cyprus Expedition. This occupation is followed after an apparent hiatus by the extensive Early–Middle Bronze Age (c. 2100–1600 BCE) necropolis near the coast at *Vrysi tou Barba,* explored by Myres, Markides, the Swedish Cyprus Expedition, and the University Museum. Here chamber tombs contained rich offerings of pottery and metal, including the earliest import to Cyprus from the Aegean, a Middle Minoan I jar.

Following another apparent hiatus, Late Cypriot (c. 1300–1050) tombs of two different types were constructed higher up the slopes, at *Ayia Anastasia* and *Kylistra.* These cemeteries were followed by new ones at *Kastros, Kato Kastros, Plakes,* and near the sea, dating from the early Cypro-Geometric to the beginning of Cypro-Archaic (c. 1050–700), another exceptionally rich phase. Classical (fifth–fourth century) and Roman-period remains have also been found in the area.

[*See also the biographies of Gjerstad and Myres.*]

BIBLIOGRAPHY

Adelman, Charles M. *Cypro-Geometric Pottery: Refinements in Classification.* Studies in Mediterranean Archaeology, vol. 47. Göteborg, 1976. See chapter 2, "Lapithos."

Gjerstad, Einar *Studies on Prehistoric Cyprus.* Uppsala, 1926. See pages 8, 58–87.

Gjerstad, Einar, et al. *The Swedish Cyprus Expedition: Finds and Results of the Excavations in Cyprus, 1927–1931.* 4 vols. Stockholm, 1934–1972.

Grace, Virginia R. "A Cypriote Tomb and Minoan Evidence for Its Date." *American Journal of Archaeology* 44 (1940): 10–52.

Herscher, Ellen. "New Light from Lapithos." In *The Archaeology of Cyprus: Recent Developments,* edited by Noel Robertson, pp. 39–60. Park Ridge, N.J., 1975.

ELLEN HERSCHER

LAPP, PAUL WILBERT (1930–1970), archaeologist and a director and professor of archaeology at the American School of Oriental Research (ASOR) in Jerusalem (1960–1968). Lapp died in an accident on Cyprus, so that his archaeological career spanned fewer than thirteen years. His major publication, *Palestinian Ceramic Chronology, 200 B.C.–A.D. 70* (1961), grew out of his early field experience at Shechem/Balaṭah (1957, 1960) and Beth-Zur (1957) and his Harvard Th.D. dissertation. It was the first systematic study of Late Hellenistic and Early Roman pottery and is still the basic work for that period.

Developing the field methodology and pottery analysis he studied under William Foxwell Albright at Johns Hopkins University and G. E. Wright at Harvard University, and in close consultation with Kathleen M. Kenyon of the British School of Archaeology in Jerusalem and Roland de Vaux of the École Biblique et Archéologique Française, Lapp attempted to combine the best approaches to field archaeology at that time. At ASOR he concentrated on small excavations to give short-term residents at the institute a variety of field experienes: at ʿIraq el-Amir (1961, 1962), Wadi ed-Daliyeh (1963, 1964), Dhahr Mirzbaneh (1963), Tell el-Ful (1964), Tell er-Rumeith (1962, 1967), and Bab edh-Dhraʿ (1965, 1967). He directed more extensive excavations at Taʿanach (1963, 1966, 1968), in association with the Concordia schools of the Missouri-Synod Lutherans.

Lapp's prompt publication of preliminary reports from his ʿIraq el-Amir, Bab edh-Dhraʿ, and Taʿanach excavations set a standard. The final publication of Dhahr Mirzbaneh appeared in 1966; publication of Wadi ed-Daliyeh, and Tell el-Ful, portions of the ʿIraq el-Amir excavations, and his Bab edh-Dhraʿ excavations were completed by Nancy L. Lapp and other of his colleagues. In addition to excavation reports, Lapp published several synthetic studies.

[*See also* Bab edh-Dhraʿ; Daliyeh, Wadi ed-; Ful, Tell el-; ʿIraq el-Amir; Rumeith, Tell er-; *and* Taʿanach.]

BIBLIOGRAPHY

Harvard Theological Review 64.2–3 (1971): *Studies in Memory of Paul Lapp.* Articles by an international group of biblical scholars and archaeologists, with a Memorial Minute and a bibliography of Lapp's works.

Lapp, Nancy L., ed. *The Third Campaign at Tell el-Fûl: The Excavations of 1964.* Cambridge, Mass., 1981.

Lapp, Nancy L., et al. *The Excavations at Araq el-Amir.* Winona Lake, Ind., 1983.

Lapp, Nancy L. "Rumeith." In *Archaeology of Jordan,* vol. 2, *Field Reports,* edited by Denys Homès-Fredericq and J. Basil Hennessy, pp. 494–497. Louvain, 1989.

Lapp, Paul W. *Palestinian Ceramic Chronology, 200 B.C.–A.D. 70.* New Haven, 1961.

Lapp, Paul W. "Tell er-Rumeith." *Revue Biblique* 70 (1963): 406–411; 75 (1968): 98–105.

Lapp, Paul W. *Biblical Archaeology and History.* New York, 1969. Oberlin College Haskell Lectures, 1966.

Lapp, Paul W. *The Dhahr Mirzbâneh Tombs: Three Intermediate Bronze Age Cemeteries in Jordan.* New Haven, 1966.

Lapp, Paul W., and Nancy L. Lapp, eds. *Discoveries in the Wâdī ed-Dâliyeh.* Cambridge, Mass., 1974.

Lapp, Paul W. *The Tale of the Tell.* Edited by Nancy W. Lapp. Pittsburgh, 1975. Introductory chapters on archaeological method and on each of the excavations Lapp directed, reprinted from semipopular sources. Contains a complete bibliography of his works.

Perspective (Pittsburgh) 12.1–2 (1971): *Essays in Memory of Paul W. Lapp.* Includes a bibliography.

Rast, Walter E. *Taanach I: Studies in the Iron Age Pottery.* Cambridge, Mass., 1978.

Schaub, R. Thomas, and Walter E. Rast. *Bâb edh-Dhrâʿ: Excavations in the Cemetery Directed by Paul W. Lapp, 1965–67.* Winona Lake, Ind., 1989.

NANCY L. LAPP

LARSA (modern Tell Senkereh), the royal capital of an important realm in southern Mesopotamia at the beginning of the second millennium BCE, located about 20 km (12 mi.) from ancient Uruk and 100 km (62 mi.) from the modern city of Nasiriyyah.

The site was noticed in the mid-nineteenth century by travelers exploring this desert region, specifically by William K. Loftus, who carried out several soundings for the Assyrian Excavation Fund in 1853–1854 that confirmed its identity with Larsa. In 1903 Walter Andrae, the excavator of Aššur, located the outlines of walls that demonstrated the existence of a great monument at the heart of the city. [*See the biography of Andrae.*] The arrival on the antiquities market of numerous beautiful objects, sometimes inscribed, and cuneiform tablets drew the attention of specialists to Senkereh, which had been systematically plundered. André Parrot, under auspices of the National Museums of France, conducted the first campaign to Senkereh in 1933. [*See the biography of Parrot.*] Iraq's denunciation of the partition regime (under which half the objects found at a site stayed in

Iraq and the other half went to the institution that financed the mission) and the discovery of Mari that served to detain Parrot in Syria delayed further excavation until 1967, during which Parrot conducted two campaigns aimed at completing a large sounding at the center of the tell. In 1969 and 1970, under the direction of Jean-Claude Margueron, the excavations reached the palace of Nur-Adad and the temple E.babbar, dedicated to the sun god Shamash (Utu in Sumerian). In 1976, Jean-Louis Huot assumed responsibility for the excavations and, until the Gulf War of 1991, conducted eight campaigns at the site, attending in particular to the religious complex formed by the E.babbar and the ziggurat that occupied the center of the city. [*See* Ziggurat.]

The area of the ruins extends for 2 km north–south and 1.8 km west–east; it reaches an elevation of 22 m. An oval, its perimeter is generally higher than its center, which is occupied by a relatively level plateau; the accumulation of the ruins of the various levels of the E.babbar (see below) forms its highest point.

The city's history is as yet imperfectly known. A number of indices (e.g., the high frequency of fragments of terracotta sickles) suggest that the foundation reaches back to the Ubaid period, although as yet no phase earlier than the third millennium has been found in situ. [*See* Ubaid.] A large building from the Early Dynastic period was located, but its excavation is as yet incomplete; it attests simply to a certain importance of the city in that period. The documentation becomes much richer by the beginning of the second millennium BCE. The texts of that period, sometimes found in excavation, more often coming from the antiquities trade, reveal the city in the period of the Amorite dynasties, when Larsa contended with other Sumero-Babylonian cities, such as Isin, to assume the heritage of the third dynasty of Ur and rebuild the empire. [*See* Isin; Ur.] Larsa played an important role in the nineteenth century BCE and at the beginning of the eighteenth, but it was finally Hammurabi who unified Mesopotamia to the advantage of Babylon. [*See* Babylon.] Larsa survived its imperial dream and remained a place dominated by its sanctuary. Its economic activity was periodically more or less important until the Parthian period, the last represented at the site.

As yet, little is known of the city, but aerial photographs nevertheless permit some understanding of its plan. Excavations have concentrated on its religious core, dominated by the E.babbar and the ziggurat. After conquering the city, Hammurabi endowed it with a monumental complex more than 300 m long that consisted of a linear succession of buildings and great courts. The architecture was ornamented with a series of semiengaged spiral columns that connects with the axis of the ziggurat (see figure 1), itself provided with a court oriented to the northeast. Chapels and workshops lined the courts. The entire grandiose complex was constructed symmetrically on a southwest–northeast axis. The sanctuary (see figure 2) was restored several times

LARSA. Figure 1. *Decorative semi-engaged spiral columns.* North wall, grand court of the E.babbar. (Courtesy J.-C. Margueron)

and survived until the eleventh century BCE. In the Neo-Babylonian period, a more restrained structure stood on the site of the earlier cella. Occupation is attested again in the Seleuco-Parthian period.

The palace of Nur-Adad (1865–1850 BCE) presents the peculiarity of never having been occupied; it is probable that it remained incomplete as a result of the difficulties that king encountered at the end of his reign. Even incomplete, the building embodies the administrative organization of the period, when the system of the palatial economy prevailed in a pure state: the architectural thought of the Amorite period,

LARSA. Figure 2. *Stairway descending into the sanctuary of the temple of the E.babbar.* (Courtesy J.-C. Margueron)

in the form of the palace. [*See* Palace.] The complex composed of the administrative quarters and the throne room is the best expression of what was customary in this sphere. Several fine houses from the Old Babylonian period were also uncovered.

BIBLIOGRAPHY

Huot, Jean-Louis, ed. *Larsa (8eme et 9eme campagnes, 1978 et 1981) et Oueili (2eme et 3eme campagnes, 1978 et 1981): Rapport préliminaire.* Paris, 1983.

Huot, Jean-Louis, ed. *Larsa (10e campagne, 1983) et Oueili (4e campagne, 1983): Rapport préliminaire.* Paris, 1987.

Huot, Jean-Louis, ed. *Larsa, travaux de 1985.* Paris, 1989.

Margueron, Jean-Claude. "Larsa, rapport préliminaire sur la quatrième campagne." *Syria* 47 (1970): 261–277.

Margueron, Jean-Claude. "Larsa, rapport préliminaire sur la cinquième campagne." *Syria* 48 (1971): 271–287.

Margueron, Jean-Claude, with Jean-Louis Huot. "Larsa." In *Reallexikon der Assyriologie und vorderasiatischen Archäologie,* vol. 6, pp. 500–506. Berlin and New York, 1984.

JEAN-CLAUDE MARGUERON

Translated from French by Nancy W. Leinwand

LATAMNE, open-air Paleolithic site located on a slope above the middle reaches of the Orontes River, 23 km (14 mi.) northwest of the town of Hama, in Syria (35°14′ N, 36°36′32″ E). Latamne is a rare example of an undisturbed camp of the Middle Acheulean culture, one of a very few known anywhere in the world. It has yielded important evidence concerning human activities during the Middle Pleistocene epoch.

Willem J. van Liere, a Dutch geomorphologist, found handaxes and associated bones of Middle Pleistocene animals in deposits exposed by quarrying at Latamne in 1960. A Dutch archaeologist, Pieter J. Modderman, of the University of Groningen, conducted additional investigations of the locality in 1961 and 1962; some of the artifacts he recovered were in such good condition they could only have come from an intact site. Accordingly, the Paleolithic archaeologist J. Desmond Clark of the University of California at Berkeley was invited to excavate the site in 1964 and 1965. Excavation revealed that the Acheulean campsite had once been situated on a sandy bank beside a stream (Clark, 1968). Soon after it was abandoned, however, it was covered by silt, which preserved its cultural remains in situ.

At the time of excavation the site consisted of a single layer of debris 12 × 19 m in extent covered by a thin deposit of sand. The most distinctive remains were numerous limestone blocks grouped in clusters and rows and concentrated mainly in the southwestern part of the site. Other blocks were scattered over the rest of the habitation area. In the center of the camp and toward the northeast were concentrations of flint artifacts and debris. The stone blocks and artifacts had all been brought to the site by its inhabitants from sources nearby. Clark believes that the blocks were used as weights to anchor a shelter made of perishable materials (1967).

The artifacts were unusually varied for a site of such antiquity. They comprised large flint cutting tools, notably handaxes, a number of heavy-duty tools, particularly choppers and scrapers, and some smaller scrapers. Some of them were manufactured at the site while others were brought there in a finished state. Several of the limestone blocks were used as anvils to make flint tools. The evidence suggests that the site was used as a camp by a group of Acheulean people for one or two seasons about 500,000 years ago.

A few bones and animal teeth were found on the site, but considerably more were found in contemporary geologic deposits in the vicinity. The main species were large and medium-sized animals: elephant, hippopotamus, rhinoceros, large deer, gazelle, bison, antelopes, camels, and horses. Some of these animals would have been hunted by the inhabitants of the Latamne campsite. Among the predators were hyenas and jackals. The environment in which these creatures lived would have consisted of open woodland and grasslands, with gallery forest, that is, a narrow band of trees, fringing the Orontes River and its tributary streams.

BIBLIOGRAPHY

Clark, J. D. "The Middle Acheulian Occupation Site at Latamne, Northern Syria (First Paper)." *Quaternaria* 9 (1967): 1–68. Comprehensive account of the preliminary investigations of the Latamne locality, of the first season of excavations at the campsite, and a summary of its place in world prehistory.

Clark, J. D. "The Middle Acheulian Occupation Site at Latamne, Northern Syria (Second Paper), Further Excavations, 1965: General Results, Definition, and Interpretation." *Quaternaria* 10 (1968): 1–60. Full description of the second season of excavations with an interpretation of the site's function.

A. M. T. MOORE

LATIN. An inflectional language, Latin averages three morphemes per word. As in Spanish and Russian, the Latin vowel system has a two-dimensional structure involving three heights with the added contrast of front-back or unrounded bottom: high (*i*, *u*), mid (*e*, *o*), low (*a*), front unrounded (*i*, *e*), back rounded (*u*, *o*).

Latin has fifteen to eighteen consonantal phonemes in native words, a phoneme being a *significantly* different and distinct sound. Latin orthography did not distinguish between short and long vowels (which are phonemically distinct) nor between consonantal and vocalic *i* and *u*. The Latin phonemic system underwent a number of changes. Early Latin had from twenty-seven to thirty-one phonemes (depending on the distinction between long and short vowels), and by the mid-first century BCE, the phonemic inventory was from thirty-one to thirty-six phonemes.

Verbs have two voices, active and passive. A verbal form is a "sentence/word," that is, a word that contains the nuclear construction of the favorite sentence-type of the language, in this case a predicate constitute. Nouns and adjectives share the inflectional category of number and case; nouns have a gender, and adjectives are inflected for gender. The eight cases of Indo-European were reduced to seven in Latin: nominative, accusative, vocative, genitive, dative, ablative, locative.

Although archaic Latin had a stress accent falling on the first syllable of a word, classical Latin developed a system of accentuation based in part on Greek models. Words of two syllables are accented on the first syllable. Words of more than two syllables are governed by the "penultimate rule." They are accented on the penult (next to the last syllable) if long (e.g., *a-mī´-cus,* "friend"; *con-fi´-ci-o,* "invention") or on the antepenult (syllable before the penultimate) if the penult is short (e.g., *do´-mi-nus,* "lord"; *a´-lăc-ris,* "eager").

History of Latin. The term *Latin* was derived from a group of related tribes called *Latini,* who settled in the region of Latium, where Rome eventually came to occupy a significant position. The Latini originated in central Europe and settled in Latium by the tenth century BCE. Latin belongs to the Italic group of the Indo-European family of languages, and is divided into two groups, Oscan-Umbrian and Latin-Faliscan. Oscan was the standardized common language of central Italy until the area was subjugated by the Romans. Originally the language of Latium and the city of Rome, Latin eventually displaced the other Italic languages as a result of the increasing political and military power which Rome exerted first in central Italy, then throughout the Italian peninsula, then in the western Mediterranean and finally throughout the ancient world.

By the end of the Republic (31 BCE), Greeks dominated Roman education (grammar, rhetoric, philosophy); Greek literature, mythology, and history were basic to Roman education; and Greek was the first language of Roman education. By the first century BCE, young male Roman aristocrats were regularly educated in Greece. Nonetheless, educated Romans were privately bilingual but never boasted publicly of their appreciation of Greek culture or fluency in Greek. By the first century CE, only a small percentage of the population of the residents of Rome were of Roman or Italian ancestry, perhaps 10 percent. Within Rome itself various national groups often maintained linguistic and cultural traditions; the extensive Jewish community, for example, which numbered from thirty thousand to fifty thousand, was a Greek-speaking community, doubtless because of the hellenization of Palestine. Of the 534 Jewish catacomb inscriptions, 76 percent are in Greek, 23 percent are in Latin, and one is in Aramaic. Roman emperors were generally bilingual. Marcus Aurelius, for example, chose to write his *Meditations* in Greek. By the fourth century CE, however, most educated Romans in the west were monolingual and understood little or no Greek. The formal end of classical Latin may be dated to 813, when Charlemagne officially recognized the colloquial forms of Latin as independent Romance languages.

Writing Systems. The Latin alphabet of twenty-one letters was ultimately derived from the Greek alphabet of twenty-six letters. The Greeks in Italy did not use a single, uniform alphabet, but five different alphabets. Of these, the Ionic alphabet of Tarentum was used in some south Oscan inscriptions, and an alphabet from central Greece was the basis for the primitive Etruscan, Oscian, and Umbrian alphabets, as well as those of Rome and Latium. The Latin system, derived from the early twenty-six-letter Etruscan alphabet, originally consisted of twenty letters; The capital letters *C* and *G* were both represented by the *C.* C as an initial capital letter served for both letters in abbreviations for the *praenomina* (forenames) Gaius (C.) and Gnaeus (Cn.), and *z* and *y* were added as phonemes in transliterated Greek words. Later the Latin alphabet was increased to twenty-one letters with the distinction between *c* and *g.* The Roman alphabet lacked *j* (the consonantal version of *i*), *u* (the vocal version of *v*), and *w.* During the first century CE, emperor Claudius attempted to add three new letters to the Latin alphabet, but for the most part these innovations did not long survive his decease (Quintilian, 1.7.26; Suetonius, *Claudius,* 41.3; Tacitus, *Annals,* 2.13–14).

Latin in the West. Although Rome does not appear to have had a formal language policy, Latin was the primary language of Rome (a polyglot city with a substantial Greek population), of all colonies founded by Rome (the first Roman colony outside Italy was Narbo in Gaul, founded in 118 BCE), and of the Roman army and Roman provincial civilian administrations. Italy had previously been multilingual, but Latin increasingly predominated until by the first century BCE it was the dominant language of the peninsula. In the western empire outside Italy and the Roman colonies, the army was one of the main vehicles for the spread of Latin, both through contact with the local population and the learning of Latin by non-Latin speaking auxiliaries. In Italy there were two different kinds of Latin, the formal, polished, correct Latin spoken by the educated and surviving in public speeches and most of extant Latin literature, and common colloquial Latin. Plautus is a major exception. There were striking phonological differences between regional varieties of Latin. (Cicero, *Brutus,* 171–172; Jerome, *Epistles,* 107.9; see Omeltchenko, 1977; Whatmough, 1970), that is, there were a number of vulgar types of Latins. Though some of these vulgar forms developed into the Romance languages, it is hardly appropriate to speak of Latin dialects during the earlier period.

In many of the provinces in which Latin was the language of the army, administration, and culture, there were also native tongues which inevitably exerted influence on Latin phonology (*Historia Augusta Septimus Severus,* 19.9). In North Africa, the indigenous language was Libyan (Berber, from the Greek term *barbaroi,* "foreign"). From the eighth century it was the language St. Augustine called the *lingua Punica,* that is, a Semitic language based on Phoenician. Libyan was the first language of both the emperor Septimus Severus (145–211 CE) and Augustine (354–430 CE). Although there are some inscriptions in Libyan, many in Punic, and some bilinguals in Punic-Latin and Libyan-Latin, the more than thirty thousand Latin inscriptions from North Africa are most numerous.

The relationship between Rome and the many Greek colonies in the western Mediterranean was complex. Many Greek settlements in Magna Grecia lost their Greek population and language through the conquests of the Samnites. After its capitulation to Rome in the Pyrrhic War in 272 BCE, Tarentum and many other cities were either destroyed or depopulated during the remainder of the Republican period until the inauguration (in 27 BCE and following) of Augustus's policy of the romanization of Italy obliterated the remaining pockets of Greek culture and language. Neapolis was the last city in the western Mediterranean to abandon Greek as an official language, and public and private inscriptions were written in Greek until the late first century CE, perhaps because Roman aristocrats found it convenient to have a Greek city near Rome. During the Second Punic War (218–201), Sicily was captured and plundered by the Romans and later (132 BCE) became the first Roman province. Subsequently, Augustus founded six colonies in Sicily in which Latin was the first language. This development was accompanied by a conscious program of Romanization which resulted in the gradual elimination of the Greek language during the first few centuries CE. Before Augustus, most public inscriptions and legends on coins were in Greek, thereafter, Latin was used almost exclusively. The replacement of Greek by Latin in old Greek colonies occurred primarily in the Augustan age.

Latin in the East. Roman immigration to the East, which was under Greek control, began during the third century BCE and peaked during the second century. Although Macedonia, which was established in the second century (148) was the first Roman eastern province, official Roman colonization in the Greek East did not begin until the mid-first century.

By 14 CE there were about thirty colonies in the Greek East: four in Greece, fifteen in Asia Minor, six in Macedonia, one in Crete, and two in Syria. In addition by the mid-first century CE there were sixteen Roman provinces in the East: four in Greece (Achaea, Epirus, Macedonia, Thracia), six in Asia Minor (Asia, Bithnyia and Pontus, Galatia, Lycia and Pamphylia, Cilicia, Cappodocia), and four in Syria (Syria, Iudaea [Judea], Mesopotamia, Arabia), as well as Egypt and Crete and Cyrenaica (the latter two forming one province).

Latin was the first language of all Roman colonies. Although these settlements were eventually hellenized, the colonists formed a socially separate, privileged group, and the native populations had an inferior social status, lacking Roman citizenship. Both public and private inscriptions as well as legends on coins were exclusively Latin in such colonies.

Syria-Palestine. Following the Roman conquest of Palestine in 63 BCE, Latin was used in Palestine primarily by the Romans for whom it was the language of the army as well as of the civilian administration. Inscriptional evidence for Latin includes dedications on aqueducts and buildings, funerary texts, milestones on Roman roads, and large numbers of bricks and tiles with stamp impressions of abbreviations for the Tenth Legion, Fretensis. The excavation of Caesarea Maritima has uncovered many Latin inscriptions, including a dedicatory slab erected by Pontius Pilate (prefect of Judea around 26–36 CE) for a cult center for Tiberius and a inscription of the Tenth Legion, which repaired the high-level aqueduct during the time of Hadrian. The multilingual character of Jerusalem is attested by the signs posted within the Temple in Greek and Latin forbidding foreigners to enter the holy place.

Two fragmentary Greek copies of this inscription have been found (*Supplementum Epigraphicum Graecum* 8.169; 20.477). The inscription on the cross of Jesus was written in Aramaic, Latin, and Greek (*Jn.* 19:20).

Egypt. The Romans generally regarded Egyptians with contempt, and often made no distinction between native Egyptians and Egyptian Greeks. Egypt had three Greek cities, Naukratis and Alexandria in Lower Egypt and Ptolemais in Upper Egypt. Alexandria was populated primarily by Greeks and Jews who engaged in intermittent conflict. The Greek language predominated in the administration of Roman Egypt. The papyri containing imperial constitutions, edicts, rescripts (orders) and decrees are 75 percent Greek and 25 percent Latin. Generally, imperial rescripts sent to private individuals, including Romans, as well as those for public promulgation in Egypt, are written in Greek, and communications and mandates addressed to Roman officials and instructions to the army are written in Latin. Edicts of the Roman prefect of Egypt and other Roman magistrates in Egypt are almost exclusively promulgated in Greek. Egyptian provincials who were not Roman citizens always used Greek in legal documents. Roman citizens necessarily used Latin for many types of legal documents (e.g., birth certificates, marriage contracts, petitions to the prefect, and wills).

Genre and Text. Latin literature is customarily divided into three major periods: (1) the formative period, that is, Livius Andonicus to Cicero (c. 240–80 BCE); (2) the classical period or Golden Age, to the death of Augustus (c. 80 BCE–14 CE); (3) the Silver Age, to the death of Apuleius (14–180 CE). (Gian Biagio Conte's *Latin Literature* [1994] contains a masterful survey.)

Data for the formative period of Latin literature are limited because of the few texts that antedate the third century

BCE. In the view of both ancient and modern scholars, Latin literature began during the late third century with Livius Andronicus, a Greek from Tarentum who became a school teacher in Rome and translated the *Odyssey* into Latin for a school text. Gnaeus Naevius, a Greek from Sardinia, was trilingual (Greek, Oscan, Latin), and wrote an epic on the first Punic war between Carthage and Rome in Latin. Another Greek, Quintus Ennius of Rudiae near Tarentum, adapted Greek metrical form to the Latin language. Latin prose has its beginning with Ennius's translation of Euhemerus preserved by the Christian rhetorician Lactantius. There was hardly a single author of Latin prose or poetry who actually came from the city of Rome. That means that no Latin literature is completely native. The earliest extensive body of literature that has survived, however, consists of the twenty-one plays of T. Maccius Plautus (late third–early second centuries), from Umbria, who became Rome's greatest dramatist. Terence (c. 195–159), a native of North Africa wrote comedies based closely on Greek originals, particularly Menander. Latin prose began with M. Porcius Cato (234–149 BCE), who wrote orations and essays. Only his *De agricultura* has survived. Prose Roman history, which had its beginnings in the *Annales* or yearly records compiled by the current *pontifex maximus* (the highest priestly office in Rome), was written in Greek beginning in the late third century BCE by Q. Fabius Pictor and his successors.

The classical period or Golden Age of Latin literature began with the admired didactic poem of Lucretius (94–55 BCE), *De rerum natura,* which focused on Epicurean physics. The most innovative author of the period, however, was Marcus Tullius Cicero (106–43 BCE), a politician and orator whose prose compositions, consisting primarily of primarily speeches, letters, and philosophical essays, became literary and rhetorical models for later writers. Other influential writers of this period include Cicero's contemporaries, M. Terentius Varro (116–27), who wrote the now-lost *Roman Antiquities* and his single extant work, *De re rustica* (On Agriculture); Julius Caesar (100–44), who wrote *De bello Gallico* (On the Gallic War), and *De bello civili* (On the Civil Wars) in crisp, unadorned prose; and Sallust (86–35), who also wrote historical works. During the empire period (31 BCE–476 CE), the poet of greatest stature was Vergil (70–19 BCE) whose most important work was the epic *Aeneid,* a modernized *Iliad* and *Odyssey* that promulgated the ideals of the Augustan principate. Other eminent Latin poets include Horace (65–8 BCE), Propertius (late first century), and Ovid (43 BCE–17 CE), who wrote in elegaic meter. Livy (59 BCE–17 CE) wrote a history of Rome in 142 volumes, of which thirty-five have survived.

During the early Imperial period the Latin literature produced during the classical period became models, but to be imitated and reacted against, during the following centuries. After varying degrees of intellectual and literary repression following the death of Augustus in 14 CE, Latin literature again exhibited creativity during the Silver Age, that is, from the end of the first to the middle of the second century CE. Authors of the Silver Age by turns imitated or reacted against the works of the Golden Age. Some of the more important literary figures are Seneca (c. 4 BCE–65 CE), an important writer of literary tragedies, philosophical essays, and letters, and his nephew Lucan (39–65 CE), who wrote *Pharsalia;* both were forced by the emperor Nero to commit suicide. Pliny the Elder (c. 23–79 CE), Pliny the Younger (c. 61–112); and Tacitus (born c. 56), who wrote *Germania, Agricola, Histories,* and *Annals.* The accomplished comic novelist Apuleius (c. 123–180 CE) wrote the *Golden Ass.*

Inscriptions. The earliest surviving Latin inscriptions date to the sixth century BCE. They often resemble Greek letter forms and are sometimes written in the so-called *boustrophedon* ("turning like oxen when plowing") style in which alternate lines written from left to right then right to left. An example is perhaps the earliest Roman inscription from possibly the sixth century BCE (*Corpus Inscriptionum Latinarum,* vol. 1, pt. 2, no. 1). While an early Latin inscription from Praeneste from the seventh century survives (*Inscriptiones Latinae Selectae,* no. 8561), its authenticity is now doubtful (Gordon, 1983, p. 75f.). The Romans began to inscribe texts in the sixth century BCE, while most of the literary and inscriptional evidence for Latin begins to accumulate toward the end of the third century BCE. In addition to stone, bronze was commonly used, particularly for legal texts (Pliny, *Nat. Hist.,* 16.237; 34.99). More perishable wooden boards were frequently used for public notices, such as Caesar's famous short text displayed at his triumph in 47 BCE: *VENI VIDI VICI* "I came, I saw, I conquered" (Suetonius, *Caesar,* 37.2). Vespasian tried to replace the more than three thousand bronze tablets that were destroyed by a fire on the Capitoline in Rome in 69 CE (Suetonius, *Vespasian,* 8.5).

More than three hundred thousand Roman inscriptions are known, mostly carved in capital letters, which reached their fullest development toward the end of the first century CE. The most extensive collection of Latin inscriptions is the *Corpus Inscriptionum Latinarum* (Berlin, 1862–), which consists of eighteen volumes to date, primarily arranged geographically. Hermann Dessau edited a selection of nine thousand texts published as *Inscriptiones Latinae Selectae* (Berlin, 1892–1916). In the western Mediterranean, the language of these inscriptions was primarily Latin, and in provinces east and south of the Adriatic, Greek—the *lingua franca* of the Levant—predominated. The evidence for the use of Oscan is limited to about two hundred inscriptions from the last two centuries BCE. Knowledge of Umbrian is largely restricted to the Iguvine tablets from the first century BCE. The main categories of inscriptions are (1) laws, treaties, and other public documents (often on bronze panels); (2) commemorations of the construction of a building; (3) honorific texts for individuals (often on a statue base); (4)

altars and religious dedications; (5) gravestones; and (6) curse tablets.

BIBLIOGRAPHY

Allen, W. Sidney. *Vox Latina: A Guide to the Pronunciation of Classical Latin.* Cambridge, 1965. Important discussion of the reconstructed phonetics of classical Latin.

Altheim, Franz. *Geschichte der lateinischen Sprache von den Anfängen bis zum Beginn der Literatur.* Frankfurt am Main, 1951.

Balsdon, John P. V. D. *Romans and Aliens.* Chapel Hill, N.C., 1979.

Conte, Gian Biagio. *Latin Literature: A History.* Translated by Joseph B. Solodow. Revised by Don P. Fowler and Glenn W. Most. Baltimore, 1994. One of the best short English-language introductions to Latin literature.

Fitzmyer, Joseph A. "The Languages of Palestine in the First Century A.D." In Fitzmyer's *A Wandering Aramean: Collected Aramaic Essays,* pp. 29–56. Missoula, 1979. Slightly updated version of the important article originally published in *Catholic Biblical Quarterly* 32 (1970): 501–531.

Gordon, Arthur E. *Illustrated Introduction to Latin Epigraphy.* Berkeley, 1983. Extremely informative for all aspects of the study of Latin inscriptions.

Keppie, Lawrence. *Understanding Roman Inscriptions.* Baltimore, 1991.

Lewis, Naphtali. *Life in Egypt under Roman Rule.* Oxford, 1983.

Meinersmann, Bernhard. *Die lateinischen Wörter und Namen in den griechischen Papyri.* Leipzig, 1927.

Millar, Fergus. "Local Cultures in the Roman Empire: Libyan, Punic, and Latin in Roman Africa." *Journal of Roman Studies* 58 (1968): 126–134.

Omeltchenko, Stephen W. *A Quantitative and Comparative Study of the Vocalism of the Latin Inscriptions of North Africa, Britain, Dalmatia, and the Balkans.* Chapel Hill, N.C., 1977.

Pinkster, Harm. *Latin Syntax and Semantics.* London and New York, 1990.

Schmitt, Rüdiger. "Die Sprachverhältnisse in den östlichen Provinzen des römischen Reiches." In *Aufstieg und Niedergang der römischen Welt,* vol. II.29.2, edited by Wolfgang Haase, pp. 554–586. Berlin and New York, 1983.

Sherk, Robert K. *Roman Documents from the Greek East: Senatus Consulta and Epistulae to the Age of Augustus.* Baltimore, 1969.

Whatmough, Joshua. *The Dialects of Ancient Gaul.* Cambridge, 1970.

Wilson, Alan J. N. *Emigration from Italy in the Republican Age of Rome.* Manchester, 1966.

David E. Aune

LAWRENCE, THOMAS EDWARD (1888–1935)

LAWRENCE, THOMAS EDWARD (1888–1935), British archaeologist born in Tremadoc, Caernarvonshire, Wales, the illegitimate son of Thomas Chapman and Sarah Lawrence. Educated at City of Oxford High School for Boys and Jesus College, Oxford University, Lawrence, by his late teens had developed a passion for medieval history. He was heavily influenced by the Pre-Raphaelites and the work of William Morris. Lawrence cycled widely as a boy and sailed on his father's yacht when the family lived in France. In 1908, as part of his research for his thesis at Oxford, Lawrence undertook a cycling tour of France, from St. Malo to Marseille and back to Le Havre. The following year he undertook a walking tour of the Crusader castles of Syria, from Beirut into northern Palestine and then north to Aleppo. From 1911 to 1914, Lawrence took part in the British Museum's excavations at Carchemish, a period he regarded as one of the happiest of his life. In spring 1914, Lawrence and his colleague on the Carchemish excavations, C. L. Woolley, were engaged by the Palestine Exploration Fund to carry out an archaeological survey of Palestine's Negev desert.

When World War I broke out in 1914, Lawrence enlisted and, because of his knowledge of the area, was posted in military intelligence in Cairo. Sent as military adviser to the Hashemite army in Transjordan, then in revolt against the Ottoman Turks, he came to play an important role in the war in Palestine but was badly affected by the experiences. His role in the war and in the peace settlement that followed, and the noteriety arising from the publications of Lowell Thomas, prevented Lawrence from returning to archaeology, as Woolley had been able to do. In 1922 Lawrence enlisted in the Royal Air Force (RAF), under the name John Hume Ross, in an attempt to escape from the constant publicity and speculation about his wartime activities. His identity was quickly revealed, and he was discharged. In 1923 he enlisted in the tank corps under the name T. E. Shaw and in 1927 officially changed his name to Shaw. In 1925 he was able to return to the RAF. Late in 1926 he was posted to Karachi, India, and in 1928 to Miranshah on India's northwest frontier, where he remained until his presence was exposed in 1929. He returned to England and from 1929 to 1935 worked as part of an RAF team testing designs for a speedboat to tend seaplanes. Lawrence left the RAF in February 1935, retiring to his cottage at Clouds Hill, Dorset. He died in a motorcycle accident.

[*See also* Carchemish; Negev; Palestine Exploration Fund; *and the biography of Woolley.*]

BIBLIOGRAPHY

Dann, Uriel. "T. E. Lawrence in Amman, 1921." *Abr-Nahrain* 13 (1972): 33–41.

James, Lawrence. *The Golden Warrior: The Life and Legend of Lawrence of Arabia.* London, 1990.

Lawrence, Arnold W., ed. *T. E. Lawrence, by His Friends, a New Selection of Memoirs.* New York, 1937.

Lawrence, Thomas Edward. *Seven Pillars of Wisdom.* London, 1926.

Lawrence, Thomas Edward. *Revolt in the Desert.* London, 1927.

Storrs, Ronald. "Lawrence, Thomas Edward." *Dictionary of National Biography 1931–1940,* pp. 528–531. London, 1949.

Wilson, Jeremy. *Lawrence of Arabia: the Authorized Biography of T. E. Lawrence.* New York, 1992.

Rupert Chapman

LAYARD, AUSTEN HENRY (1817–1894)

LAYARD, AUSTEN HENRY (1817–1894), excavator of Nineveh and Nimrud. Layard's career as an archaeologist occupied less than a decade of his life but was the basis of his considerable fame and successful career in the British government. Beginning in 1840, he spent several years in Mesopotamia—after 1842 with the assistance of Stratford Canning, then British ambassador to Turkey. Layard's initial excavation was but one of a range of slightly stealthy activities performed through the ambassador.

Commencing operations at the great mound of Nimrud in November 1845, Layard almost immediately came upon portions of two palaces, one being that of Ashurnasirpal II. His finds of Late Assyrian reliefs, statuary, and other artifacts marked the first major English discoveries in Mesopotamia; within two years the discoveries were on display at the British Museum. By the time Layard returned to England, in 1847, he had discovered portions of eight Assyrian palaces.

Layard's discoveries came two years after those of his colleague and rival, the Frenchman Paul-Émile Botta at Khorsabad. Yet, in a second campaign (1849–1851) Layard succeeded, as Botta had not, at the mound of Kuyunjik (Nineveh), excavating artifactual and textual remains of the great palace of Sennacherib. [*See the biography of Botta.*] Excavations begun by Layard at Kouyunjik and Nimrud were continued and expanded by Hormuzd Rassam and William Kennett Loftus, through 1855, under the auspices of the British Museum and the (private) Assyrian Excavation Fund.

Layard's activities as an archaeologist and also a publicist were central to the fledgling enterprise of Assyriology. The exhibition of his discoveries inspired a host of emulatory representations in, among other media, jewelry, panoramas, theatrical production, painting, poetry, and architecture. Layard's account of the first campaign, *Nineveh and Its Remains* (1849, popular edition 1851) was arguably Britain's greatest archaeological bestseller of the entire nineteenth century.

Layard's work provoked extensive discussion by theologians, historians, and art critics. His discoveries did much to change, as well as complicate, prevailing notions of biblical credence, historical progress, and artistic form. Layard thus contributed significantly to the intellectual growth of the antiquarian science of his time.

[*See also* Nimrud; Nineveh.]

BIBLIOGRAPHY

Bohrer, Frederick N. "The Printed Orient: The Production of A. H. Layard's Earliest Works." *Culture and History,* no. 11 (1992): 85–105.

Fales, Frederick M., and Bernard J. Hickey, eds. *Austen Henry Layard: Tra l'Oriente e Venezia.* Rome, 1987. Essays on various aspects of Layard's life and interests, with a catalog of an exhibition.

Layard, Austen Henry. *Discoveries in the Ruins of Nineveh and Babylon.* London, 1853.

Layard, Austen Henry. *Autobiography and Letters.* 2 vols. London, 1903. Focused disproportionately on the period in Mesopotamia.

Saggs H. W. F. Introduction to Layard's *Nineveh and Its Remains* (1849), 1–64. New York, 1970. Independent critical assessment, based on significant archival and intertextual work.

Waterfield, Gordon. *Layard of Nineveh.* New York, 1963. The standard biography of Layard.

Frederick N. Bohrer

LEAD ISOTOPE ANALYSIS. Measuring the relative isotopic abundances of lead to characterize its isotopic composition has become a frequently used analytical method in determining the provenance of archaeological finds. In conjunction with diagnostic evaluations of an object's stylistic attributes and method of fabrication, the isotopic data can be used to address archaeological and art historical questions of authenticity, as well as to study the production and distribution of metal. Lead isotope analysis can provide information about the sources of the materials used and their trade patterns, information with valuable socioeconomic and political implications. The technique is applicable to a wide range of lead-containing materials such as glass, glazes, metals (copper, silver, bronzes, brasses, and pewter), paint pigments, and lead ores.

The technique has traditionally been used as an analytical tool in geological studies to measure the geochronological age of the Earth or to determine the age of an ore deposit. Elemental lead is composed of four stable isotopes whose masses are 208, 207, 206, and 204. Stable isotopes differ from each other only by the number of neutrons in their atomic nucleus, referred to as their mass number. Three of the four isotopes of lead (Pb 208, Pb 207, and Pb 206) are derived in part as the stable end products from the radiogenic decay of thorium 232, uranium 235, and uranium 238, respectively, and in part from primordial lead created at the time of the Earth's formation. The fourth isotope (Pb 204) exists in its original form (at the earth's beginning) and is dependent only on the amount originally present in the formation of the deposit. Thus, the isotopic composition of lead in ores is dependent upon the geochemical constituents of the mineralization and its age and emplacement history. These variances in the isotopic composition of lead create a distinct "isotopic signature" in ore deposits containing lead.

Because the differences in isotopic composition are very small, a measurement of high precision and high accuracy is required. Chemical-separation techniques under clean conditions, involving acid dissolution, ion-exchange chromatography, and anodic electrodeposition are used to extract and purify the lead. Thermal ionization mass spectrometry is the analytical tool generally used to measure the relative isotopic abundances in naturally occurring elements. This involves the introduction of a sample into a mass spectrometer, where it is thermally ionized, accelerated by electrostatic forces through a magnetic field, and separated according to mass. The various masses are then electronically detected and measured.

Archaeological evidence has demonstrated that the isotopic signature present in the ore is preserved in the object, unaffected by the object's metallurgical history or subsequent weathering. In theory, this unique isotopic composition can be used to identify the object's geographic source or to eliminate others. However, the method has its limitations: mixing and overlapping are factors that pose complications in interpretating the data. In antiquity, lead was frequently salvaged, remelted, and reused. During this recycling, certain materials could have been mixed, thus erasing their original lead signatures. The overlapping factor arises from the fact that ores in different regions, sometimes widely separated geographically, can have similar isotopic compositions if formed at the same time under geologically similar conditions. Still used in conjunction with other analytical methods, such as trace-element analysis and multivariate and probability statistical analysis, lead isotope analysis has proven to be an important technique in archaeology.

[*See also* Analytical Techniques.]

BIBLIOGRAPHY

Faure, Gunter. *Principles of Isotope Geology*. New York, 1986.

Gale, N. H. "Lead Isotope Studies Applied to Provenance Studies: A Brief Review." In *Archaeometry: Proceedings of the 25th International Symposium,* edited by Yannis Maniatis, pp. 496–502. Amsterdam, 1989.

Gulson, Brian L. *Lead Isotopes in Mineral Exploration*. New York, 1986.

Russell, Richard D., and R. M. Farquhar. *Lead Isotopes in Geology*. New York, 1960. A good reference for understanding the basic principles and early history of lead isotope analysis but outdated on present methodology. The reader is urged to consult scientific literature for more up-to-date measurement techniques.

Sayre, E. V., et al. "Statistical Evaluation of the Presently Accumulated Lead Isotope Data from Anatolia and Surrounding Regions." *Archaeometry* 34.1 (1992): 73–105. Covers the debate on the use of multivariate and probability statistical analysis, methodology, selection of data, treatment of outliers, etc. For continuing discussion, see *Archaeometry* 34.2 (1992): 311–336, and 35.2 (1993): 241–263.

EMILE C. JOEL

LEATHER.

In virtually all ancient cultures of the Near East, animal hides must have been used for a variety of purposes as early as Paleolithic times. In the art and texts of the early civilizations of Mesopotamia and Egypt we see leather used for clothing, gloves, footwear, tents, containers or pouches, military implements and armor, fittings for animals, ropes, boats and sails, balls, musical instruments, cushions, furniture, and writing materials. The standard of Ur shows early examples of leather harnesses and kilts with the fleece worn in or out as items of clothing (Henri Frankfort, Harmondsworth, 1954, figs. 76 and 77; C. Leonard Woolley, *Ur Excavations,* Philadelphia, 1927–1976, vol. 2, *The Royal Cemetery,* pl. 92).

The value and versatility of leather as opposed to cured raw skin lies in its qualities of strength, flexibility, and durability, which is achieved only through the process of tanning. Wall paintings in a number of Egyptian tombs illustrate the various aspects of leather production. Among these are a tomb at Beni Hasan, and the tomb of Rekmire at Thebes. After the corium or middle layer of skin was cleaned of hair and flesh through scraping and soaking in solutions of lime and pigeon droppings, the tanning process changed the raw skin or corium into leather resistant to water and to decay through the use of one of three substances: tannic acid commonly derived from the bark, leaves, or fruit of the pomegranate, acacia, or tamarisk; alum and salt to produce a white leather in a process called *tawing;* and third, fish oils in a process called *chamoising*.

A number of ancient texts on tablets from sites in Mesopotamia describe leather products, the processing of leather, and the wages and rights of tanners and shoemakers. Very few clearly identifiable tanners' workshops have been discovered, however, in archaeological excavations of any period in the Near East (at Pergamon—see Machteld J. Mellink, "Archaeology in Anatolia," *American Journal of Archaeology* 96 [1992]: 144–145, and Wolfgang Radt, *Archäologische Anzieger* 1991, pp. 410–412; and at Ḥorvat Sumaq—see Samuel R. Wolff, "Archaeology in Israel," *American Journal of Archaeology* 97 [1993]: 157–158). Tools and objects made of leather have been recovered from Egyptian tombs (including sandals and a stool from the tomb of King Tutankhamun) and from the tombs at Ur, and in caves in Palestine.

Because of the unpleasant smells associated with the processing of hides, tanneries were usually located on the outskirts of town. Among the Hebrews, tanners were considered to be of low status, although leather products were in great demand. In Egypt and Assyria, for example, where warfare was a major activity, tanneries could be owned by the state, especially for the production of the quantities of leather goods required by the army and navy. Independent artisans who produced luxury items were also important, however, and in the Hellenistic and Roman periods tanners had their own guilds in many cities of the Near East.

Among the most famous producers of fine leather in the Islamic world were the tanneries in Morocco. The workshops of Fez, established by the tenth century CE and still functioning, were among the strongest and most influential guilds in the city with one hundred workshops under the Merinide dynasty. A constant source of water, a supply of animal skins, and inspiration and techniques derived from Persia and Moorish Spain account for the importance and success of the industry in Fez. Unlike tanners in other ancient cultures, the tanners of Fez had high status as artisans, whereas olive oil producers and metal workers were accorded the lowest status.

BIBLIOGRAPHY

Forbes, R. J. *Studies in Ancient Technology*. Leiden, 1966. Summarizes the evidence for ancient techniques from texts and leather artifacts (see vol. 5, pp. 2–46).

Le Tourneau, Roger, and L. Paye. "La corporation des tanneurs et l'industrie de la tannerie a Fès." *Hesperis* 20.1–2 (1935): 167–240. Detailed account of the history, techniques, and organization of the tanneries in Fez, Morocco.

Reed, R. *Ancient Skins, Parchments, and Leathers*. London, 1972. Early methods and scientific basis of skin processing.

Waterer, John W. *Leather Craftsmanship*. London, 1968.

VIRGINIA R. ANDERSON-STOJANOVIĆ

LEBANON. *See* Phoenicia; Syria.

LEHUN, site located in central Jordan, in the Madaba district (biblical Moab), 80 km (50 mi.) south of Amman, 7 km (4 mi.) east of Dhiban (biblical Dibon) and 3 km (2 mi.) east of ʿAraʿir (biblical ʿAroʿer), on the northern plateau of Wadi Mujib (the biblical Arnon River). The site is quite extensive: 1,100 m north–south by 600 m east–west. It ranges in altitude between 719 and 748 m above ʿAqaba sea level and is divided north–south and east–west by seasonal wadis, delimitating natural areas (excavation sectors A–D), alternatively chosen by settlers in antiquity. The region is fertile, largely open to the steppe and the desert, and has a semiarid Mediterranean microclimate. No literary sources mention Lehun, but some travelers and archaeologists have either visited or otherwise noted it, such as Rudolf-Ernst Brünnow (1904), Nelson Glueck (1933), and Raphael de Savignac (1936).

Excavations at Lehun were sponsored by the Belgian Committee of Excavations in Jordan, whose directors from 1977 to 1984 was P. Naster and since 1977 is Denyse Homès-Fredericq. The site is characterized by permanent settlements from prehistoric to modern times. The southern sectors (B3, C1, D) are its most strategic area: they are well protected by the cliffs of Wadi Mujib and overlook the whole region. Remains of the Early Bronze, Late Bronze, and Iron Ages were found there. In the northern sectors (A, B1–2, C1), on the northern, more fertile slopes of Wadi Lehun, in the vicinity of the fertile fields of the Moabite plateau, some settlements appeared in more peaceful and commercial periods: in the Nabatean and Roman periods, as well as in Islamic, Ottoman, and modern times. [*See* Moab.]

The area has been inhabited since the Paleolithic period, as is attested by nearly one thousand tool samples collected over an area of 225,000 sq m. The range of tools assembled is impressive: racloirs, burins, scrapers, flakes (sometimes Levallois flakes), nuclei, and core fragments in sector C1. The Chalcolithic period is represented by some surface flints and a few sherds.

The first permanent sedentarization (sector B3) appears in the Early Bronze Age. Remains of a large settlement (still to be excavated) and an adjacent water reservoir, similar to the town of Jawa in northern Jordan, have been located. [*See* Jawa.] Separated by the Wadi Lehun, a disturbed family tomb was excavated under an earth layer some 40–60 cm deep. It contained more than 130 specimens of often undamaged and homogeneous handmade ceramics that are comparatively dated by material from Bab edh-Dhraʿ IA–B. [*See* Bab edh-Dhraʿ.] In the transition period of the Late Bronze–Iron Ages (1300–1000 BCE), a fortified village (170 m north–south × 37–60 m east–west) was built following the borders of the well-protected plateau in sector D. The settlement belongs to a period when the Moabite kings were developing and defending their kingdom. Different residential complexes, sometimes of the pillared-house type (see figure 1), were discovered. [*See* Four-room House.] Their wheel-made pottery and artifacts indicate an agricultural environment (storage jars, cooking pots, pilgrim flasks, grinding stones, pestles). A beautiful faience scarab from the twentieth dynasty (1186–1070 BCE) represents a sphinx with a ram's head and an atef before an upraised uraeus and an open lotus flower. Its base is inscribed with a deficient hieroglyph name of Amun-Re, which suggests that Lehun was still inhabited at the end of the second millennium BCE. The village seems to have been temporarily abandoned.

The buildings on the southern part of the plateau were later leveled and their stones used as the foundation for an Iron Age fortress. This fortress, with its central courtyard, probably belonged to the belt of military installations along the northern Moabite plateau: it measures 33–37 m east–west by 43 m north–south and is strategically located, overlooking the whole region and would have controlled all traffic on the King's Highway, in the nearby valleys, and on the southern Moabite plateau. It was protected by the cliffs of northern Moab. Its four inner-corner watchtowers are unique in central Jordan because they were built inside the fortress. Breaks in the fortification's walls and the stone fill found in some of its casemate rooms attest to the building's having been attacked. The wheel-made pottery, some silos, and ovens suggest that this settlement was also agricultural. The fortress probably served an economic purpose as well: fortified storage buildings are known in ancient Palestine and in Assyria, possibly for supplying grain and wheat to garrisons—in this case, to Moabite ʿAroʿer or Dibon. [*See* ʿAroʿer; Dibon.] An Egyptian new year flask of the Saite period (seventh–sixth centuries BCE) reflects international relations in the Near East during the twenty-sixth dynasty.

In the Nabatean period, Lehun must have been a religious center of some importance: it is a small, square temple (6.25 × 6.25 m), built of embossed local limestone blocks, that corresponds to the single-chambered Nabatean sanctuaries that are Oriental in origin. It was probably used by traders and caravaneers traveling one of the byroads of the King's Highway. Ceramic fragments found in the temple date to the first century CE and are of smooth or ribbed common pottery and distinctive Nabatean painted fine ware. The temple and its altar have been restored and reconstructed. An intrusive Nabatean grave was discovered in the Pillar

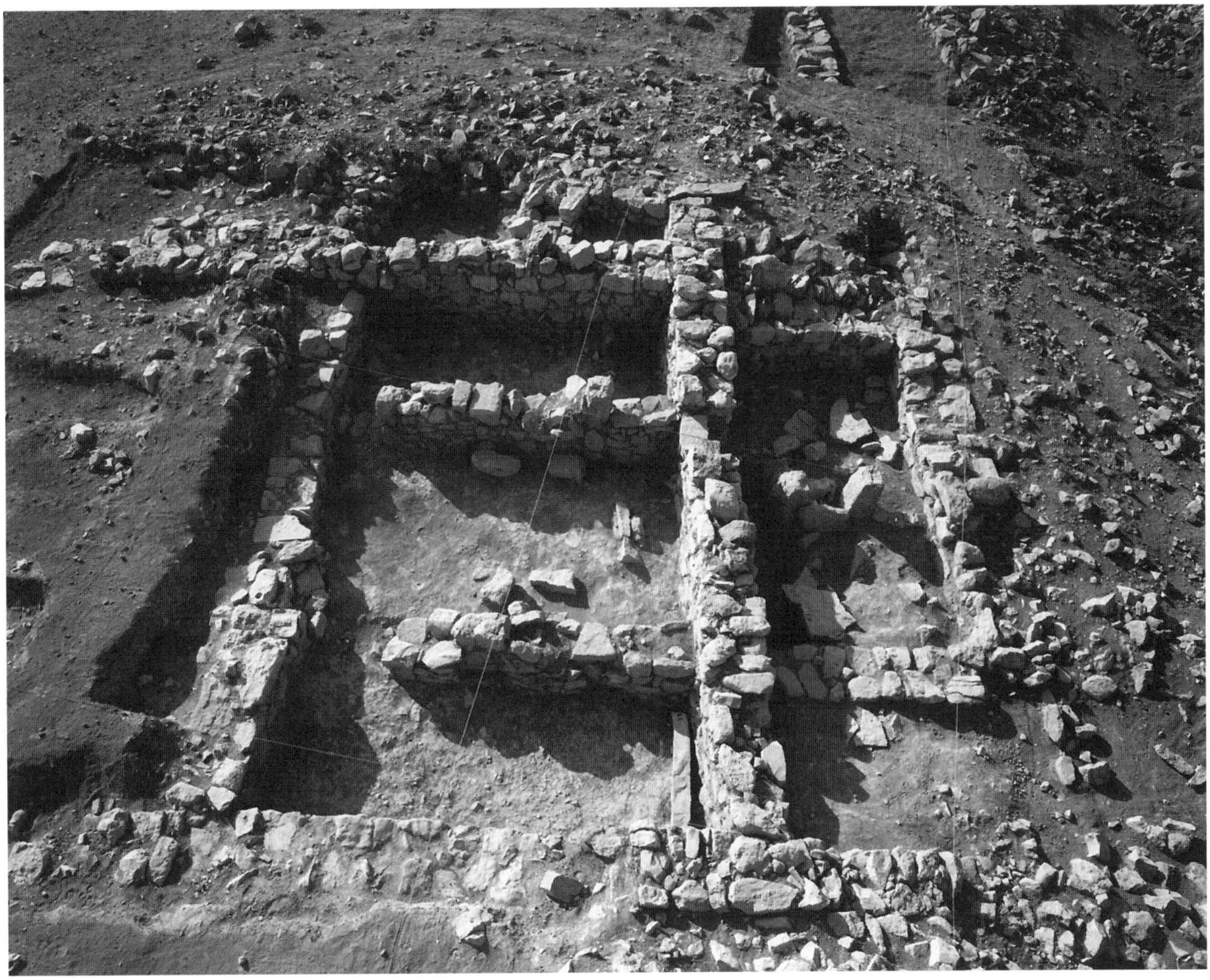

LEHUN. Figure 1. *Pillar House I, sector D.* (Courtesy D. Homès-Fredericq)

House I in sector D: it belonged to a woman and is dated by the pottery and jewelry (a bead necklace, bronze fibula, earrings, and bracelets). [*See* Nabateans; Grave Goods.]

The Islamic period is represented by a small rural mosque of the late Mamluk period. A bronze coin found on its floor gives a post quem date as late as the fourteenth century. The mosque was built near a small village. A large agricultural complex with a cave has been partially excavated north of it. Three collapsed Ottoman houses (sector C2) are still used as granaries by the villagers of modern Lehun.

BIBLIOGRAPHY

Homès-Fredericq, Denyse. "Un goulot de bouteille de Nouvel An, trouvé à Lehun (Jordanie)." In *Studia Paulo Naster Oblata,* edited by Simone Scheers, pp. 79–90, pls. 8–9. Orientalia Lovaniensia Analecta, 12–13. Louvain, 1982.

Homès-Fredericq, Denyse. "Lehun." In *Pottery and Potters, Past and Present: 7000 Years of Ceramic Art in Jordan,* edited by Denyse Homès-Fredericq and H. J. Franken. Tübingen, 1986.

Homès-Fredericq, Denyse, and J. Basil Hennessy, eds. *Archaeology of Jordan,* vol. 1, *Bibliography and Gazetteer of Surveys and Sites;* vol. 2, *Field Reports: Surveys and Sites.* Louvain, 1986–1989.

Homès-Fredericq, Denyse. "Lehun (El/Khirbet el)." In *Archaeology of Jordan,* vol. 2, *Field Reports,* edited by Denyse Homès-Fredericq and J. Basil Hennessy, pp. 349–359. Louvain, 1989.

Homès-Fredericq, Denyse. "Late Bronze and Iron Age Evidence from Lehun in Moab." In *Early Edom and Moab: The Beginning of the Iron Age in Southern Jordan,* edited by Piotr Bienkowski, pp. 187–202, figs. 16.1–11. Sheffield Archaeological Monographs, 7. Sheffield, 1992.

DENYSE HOMÈS-FREDERICQ

LEILAN, TELL, a roughly 90-ha site located at the confluence of Wadi Jarrah and Wadi Siblah on the eastern half of the Khabur Plains of northeastern Syria (36°57′41.8″ N, 41°30′35.6″ E). Leilan's location on the present-day 440-mm isohyet that stretches across the lowland plains of northern Mesopotamia unites the site with Tell al-Hawa, Tell Taya, Tell er-Rimah, and Mosul/Nineveh to the east and Tell Aid,

Farfara, Tartab, and Tell Mozan to the west. [*See* Taya, Tell; Rimah, Tell er-; Nineveh; Mozan, Tell.] This north Mesopotamian geoclimatic and cultural region was known in the third millennium as Subir, at which time Leilan's name was Shekhna, and in the early second millennium BCE as Subartu, when Leilan's name was Shubat-Enlil.

Prehistoric Periods. Leilan was founded upon a small ridge alongside Wadi Jarrah, in the late Ubaid (Leilan VI) period. [*See* Ubaid.] At this time the Leilan region was already experiencing the forces of early spatiofunctional hierarchization: Leilan was about 20 ha in size and a center for the forty-nine Halaf/Ubaid small village sites located within 15 km (9 mi.) of it. Climatic conditions during this period were significantly more humid than at present, to judge from the Halaf/Ubaid villages in the Wadi Radd region, 20 km (12 mi.) to the south, that is now agriculturally marginal.

Severe, and perhaps sudden, aridification (F. Sirocko et al., "Century-Scale Events in Monsonal Climate in the Past 24,000 Years," *Nature* 364 [1993]: 322–324) occurred during or at the end of the succeeding Leilan V period that may have played a role in local and southern Mesopotamian social stratification and the Late Uruk period expansion process and its sudden collapse. Regional settlement shrank during period V to eight sites. To judge from its Leilan IV period ceramic assemblage, Leilan was then one of the enigmatic Late Uruk period "colonies." The succeeding collapse was followed by the Leilan IIIa (painted Ninevite 5) period, which lasted for about one hundred years. During this period and the next two hundred years (c. 2900–2600 BCE), local settlements were of fewer than 10 ha and widely distributed along the perennial streams of the Khabur River. There is no evidence within individual settlements for social stratification or political organization at the state level. The distinctive cylinder seals used during this period unite the region with the dry-farming stretches of the Zagros piedmont and the proto-Elamite culture area of southwestern Iran. [*See* Seals; Agriculture; Elamites.] Very few sealings from these northern seals have been retrieved in southern Mesopotamia.

Early Historic Periods. In the Leilan IIId period (c. 2600–2400 BCE), Leilan suddenly expanded more than sixfold, growing from an acropolis-based settlement of fewer than 15 ha to the approximately 100 ha comprising most of the lower town and some settled areas outside its later walls.

LEILAN, TELL. Figure 1. *Operation 5, lower town south, residential quarter and street.* Dated to 2600–2000 BCE. (Courtesy Harvey Weiss)

LEILAN, TELL. Figure 2. *"Subarian" style cylinder seal impression showing a seated musician playing a lyre.* Dated about 2600 BCE. L87-1493 (Courtesy Harvey Weiss)

The lower town (south) exposure shows that the Leilan settlement in the IIId period was a planned city—that is, straight streets (4.5 m wide) were laid out with straight street walls providing only limited access to cross alleys (see figure 1).

On the Leilan acropolis (northwest), the small domestic structures of the earlier Leilan IIIc period were now replaced with a public cultic quarter that was to be maintained, renovated and rebuilt during the next four hundred years, to the end of the Akkadian imperialization of the region. [*See* Cult; Akkadians.] The activity center of this quarter was a mud-brick sacrificial altar situated in the center of a mud-brick platform (10 × 15 m). [*See* Altars.] Around the platform were elaborate rooms to the east, including one with more than twenty bones of human adults, juveniles, and infants in an ash-filled submural pit sealed by a late period IIa floor; a ramp and stairway to the south; and, also to the west, storage rooms filled with cylinder-seal impressions.

The cylinder seals in the storage rooms are local Khabur Plains ("Subarian style") imitations of Sumerian late Early Dynastic II/early Early Dynastic III banquet scenes that replaced the local "piedmont Jemdet Nasr" sealing tradition (see figure 2). This contact with southern Mesopotamia, whatever its nature, may have stimulated sudden regional secondary state formation and urbanization. Across the Leilan lower town, as well as on the Leilan acropolis, the ceramics in use during this period were those of the terminal Ninevite 5 incised tradition—that is, the radical social and economic alterations of the period were not accompanied by synchronous changes in traditional ceramic manufacture technologies.

In the Leilan IIa period (c. 2400–2300 BCE), the consolidation of state power within the cities of Subir is marked by the first construction of a defensive wall around the Leilan acropolis (northwest) cultic quarter. It protected and isolated the elite, their wealth, and administrative power from the residents of the Leilan lower town and Leilan-region villages. The acropolis (northwest) cultic quarter wall, of mud brick, was 2.5 m wide. The Leilan lower town, however, still lacked a wall throughout the period. Substantial changes took place during this period in ceramic technology: the tradition of the Ninevite 5 period incising disappeared almost completely, and ceramic production moved toward simplified, less labor-intensive production techniques. This alteration suggests that containers were serving new purposes influenced or controlled by state authority for state standards of measurement—capacities and areas for agricultural production, distribution, collection, taxation, storage, and reinvestment. Economic and political relationships with southern Mesopotamia intensified during this period with cuneiform archives documented at nearby Tell Beidar. [*See* Libraries and Archives.]

The Leilan period IIb (c. 2400–2200 BCE) witnessed the Akkadian conquest and imperialization of Subir by Naram-Sin. This event was conditioned by the availability on the Subarian side of a rich cereal-agriculture region, already urbanized and organized regionally for efficient production, and by the need on the Akkadian side to replace the conquer-plunder-destroy syndrome of previous southern monarchs with a more efficient and longer-lasting system of accessible, adjacent-region exploitation. Naram-Sin's conquest of the Khabur Plains was accompanied by the installation of a complex Akkadian imperial administration penetrating deeply across the urbanized landscape of Subir. At Leilan the Akkadian presence is documented epigraphically by two inscribed artifacts retrieved at the acropolis northwest cultic quarter: one is a fragmentary Old Akkadian tablet, the second a fragmentary Old Akkadian sealing with the Old Akkadian inscription: "Hayabu the shabra official."

Six features of Akkadian imperialization have been identified archaeologically at Tell Leilan:

1. *Population redistribution.* The Akkadian imperialists streamlined the regional administration of production by reducing the number of Leilan-region settlements from twenty-two to thirteen. Tell Mohammed Diyab, the large secondary center only 8 km (5 mi.) southeast of Leilan, was reduced in size from 50 to 10 ha, its population apparently nucleated within Leilan. Do Gir, the comparable satellite site to the north of Leilan, suffered a similar fate.

2. *Regional population control.* Regional control to prevent insurrection and to protect imperial administration and stores required the deployment of local populations for defensive/protective and legitimizing construction works. Substantial numbers of laborers were, for the first time, deployed to construct a massive city wall around Tell Leilan. At the eastern edge of the Leilan lower-town settlement the rock-hard calcitic virgin soil was first excavated to depths of .5–1.5 m. Two concentric walls of mud brick, each 8 m wide (a casemate wall), were then set into these excavations. A middle wall, perhaps a walkway between the two, was one meter wide. On the northern side of the city, where a natural

depression and rise afforded protection, an imposing earthen rampart was constructed by excavating a 10-meter-wide/deep ditch and then mounding the excavated virgin soil.

3. *Agricultural redistribution.* Botanical remains within 50–100 percent samples of each lower-town (south) house floor's debris are missing nodal stems, rachises, and nonseed plant parts. The domesticated cereals and pulses, mostly barely and lentils, had already undergone primary and secondary processing and were clean, ready for storage, cooking, and consumption, suggesting that they are the remains of rations previously processed and stored elsewhere prior to distribution. [*See* Cereals.]

4. *Introduction of Akkadian mensuration and Leilan* sila *bowls.* The Leilan IIb (Akkadian) lower-town ceramic assemblage includes a bowl type of distinctive appearance and standardized capacities. The bowl is dark green, with no visible temper; it is wheel made and has a flat base and simple rim with straight sides. Along with 557 sherds of this vessel type that have been retrieved and measured, 27 complete or fragmentary stacked kiln wasters (SKWs) of these vessels have also been retrieved and measured (see figure 3). The SKWs have a trimodal capacity distribution: about 55 percent range between .2 and .4 l; 38 percent between .8 and 1.2 l; and 6 percent at 1.5 l. The rim sherds of the fragmented vessels in general, however, suggest that most derive from vessels of 1-liter (Sumerian *sila*) capacity. These vessels are the only vessels within the Leilan IIb assemblage for which wasters have been retrieved. It seems likely that they are an administrative artifact of Akkadian imperialism: standardized *sila* bowls for ration distribution according to the Akkadian imperial standards.

5. *Akkadian intensification of agroproduction.* As part of the Akkadian reorganization of production, water courses were stabilized by channelization—deepening and straightening water-course channels—to counter the effects of rapid siltation and to maintain efficient water flow. On the western side of Tell Leilan this water management is recorded within a 4-meter sequence of repeated entrenchments into calcic virgin soil, embankments of large basalt blocks, and masses of water-borne silt and pebbles cleared from the channel. Leilan period IIb potsherds were stratified on the beds of the stabilized channels. Channelization prevented wasteful water-course meandering and may have permitted supplemental summer crop production. Akkadian canal-management expertise may have been the source of this intensifier of northern agroproduction.

6. *Akkadian cult practices.* The white-plastered walls of the Leilan IIa acropolis (northwest) cultic quarter were truncated, and surfaces of mud brick and thick mud plaster were prepared over them and over ashy room deposits. Two constructions were set upon these prepared surfaces: stone walls, up to 1.2 m wide, constructed of coarsely prepared basalt boulders (some of these walls had 3–5 courses of mud brick on them, while others were simply topped with a surface of mud plaster and large potsherds); and a large, mud-brick building with three-brick-thick walls, most of which remains to be excavated. The exterior surfaces of these structures covered the period-IIa platform, leaving only the burnt-altar surfaces at floor level. The Akkadians thereby maintained the cultic locus of previous state rulers while instituting their own cult practices.

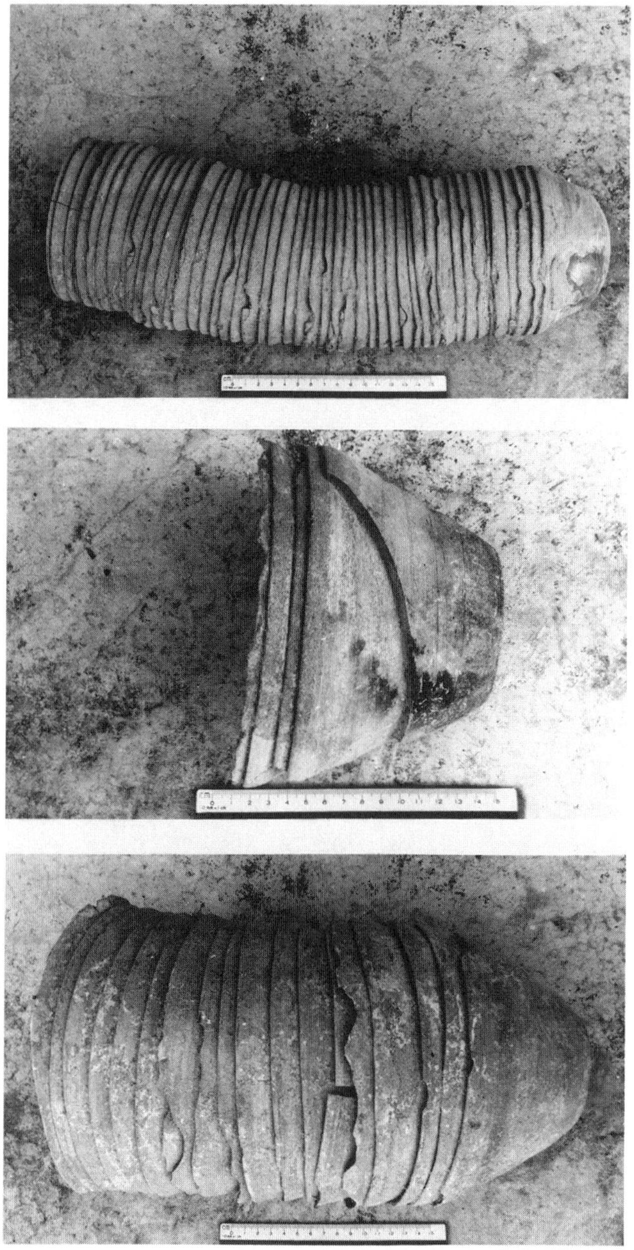

LEILAN, TELL. Figure 3. *Period IIB "sila" bowls of three standardized volumes.* Top: forty-six fused wasters, each 0.265 liters; middle: five fused wasters, each 1.052 liters; bottom: eighteen fused wasters, each 1.522 liters. (Courtesy Harvey Weiss)

Desertification and desertion (c. 2200–1900 BCE) characterize the collapse of Akkadian imperialism. The extractive organization imposed by the Akkadian dynasty was interrupted by urban collapse in the south and collapse, reorganization, and abandonments in the north. There is no evidence for settlement at Tell Leilan between periods IIb and I—that is, between 2200 and 1900 BCE. (Similarly, there was no sedentary settlement at Tell al-Hawa, Tell Taya, Tell Khoshi, Chaghar Bazar, Tell Mohammed Diyab, or at the hundreds of other settlements within northern Mesopotamia. A reduced local power, using the title "King of Urkish and Nawar," emerged at this time to control briefly the remnant Khabur Plains populations of Mozan and Brak. [*See* Mozan, Tell; Brak, Tell.] A few sherd types retrieved through regional surface surveys (and unassignable with certainty to other periods) may document some village-level sedentary human activity.

Soil micromorphology studies (thin sections of datable pedostratigraphic units) undertaken at Tell Leilan and sites within the surrounding countryside have revealed a rapid alteration of climatic conditions for this period: a sudden intensification of wind circulation; an increase in atmospheric dust; and the establishment of arid conditions. The wind erosion and dust deposition are also documented in southern Mesopotamia and the Persian Gulf. A relatively massive displacement of sedentary agriculturalists and seasonally transhumant pastoralists is suggested by the Leilan and other Khabur Plains settlement abandonments. Synchronous population expansion in southern Mesopotamia, as well as tribal Amorite incursions into the sedentary heartland of southern Mesopotamia, suggest the amplitude of population transfer at this time. [*See* Amorites.]

Only at the end of this desertification period, with the reestablishment of favorable climatic conditions in the nineteenth century BCE, was sedentary settlement reestablished on the Khabur Plains by those previously displaced. Amorite chiefs, acculturated in southern Mesopotamia after decades of sedentary life there, led the resettlement; under the paramountcy of Shamshi-Adad, they selected the abandoned urban center at Tell Leilan to be the new Khabur Plains regional administrative center, Shubat Enlil, "the dwelling place of Enlil." Inscriptions of servants of Shamshi-Adad and his successors were retrieved at Leilan within the temples excavated on the northeastern quadrant of the acropolis in 1979, 1980, and 1982. These inscriptions were the first Leilan evidence for the historical identification of the site. Additional epigraphic data have been retrieved from the lower town palace (east) and the lower town palace (north). [*See* Palace.]

On the Leilan acropolis three levels of temple construction were identified. The last, building level I, was a badly eroded, partial rebuilding of building level II. Building level II was an elaborate "long-room" temple with a central cella featuring impressive northern and southern facades decorated with intricate columns and column decoration. The northern facade of building level II was decorated with semi-attached, spiral mud-brick columns (see figure 4); the same building's southern facade was decorated with a variety of columns embellished with mud-plaster incising and relief (see figure 5). Building level II was a foreshortened rebuild of building level III, where interior spiral columns set on each side of a central column were retrieved. An associated building level "X," stratigraphically linked probably to building level II (but almost entirely eroded except for its deeply set wall foundations), provided a range of administrative tablets and sealings linked with officials' and rulers' letters and sealings retrieved in 1985 and 1987 within the lower town palace (east).

The topography of the lower town suggests that the lower town palace (east) covered an area of 9 or 10 ha and therefore was one of the largest early second-millennium BCE palaces in Mesopotamia. Twenty-five rooms already retrieved include a baked-brick court with a central throne area along the wall opposite the room's main entrance. Side exits from the throne wall lead to smaller rooms, including some with six hundred cuneiform tablets and several hundred tablet fragments, major portions of the palace's royal archives, resting both on the rooms' floors and within their roof and wall collapse. [*See* Cuneiform.] These documents include dated archival, royal administrative texts and royal letters and treaties, many bearing the impressions of inscribed seals of royal servants. Large fragments of a locally copied recension of the Sumerian King List document both the level of scribal activity within the palace complex during this period and relationships with southern Mesopotamian scribal activity. [*See* Sumerians.]

The archives chronicle the activities of the local dynasty that succeeded Shamshi-Adad at Tell Leilan, but sealings of Shamshi-Adad and his sons retrieved in one partially excavated room at the northeast limit of the 1987 exposure suggest that the palace was built and used initially during the reign of Shamshi-Adad himself. The lower town palace (north) was retrieved, in part, in 1991 and provided an archive of 590 tablets devoted exclusively to the administration of receipts for royal beer-preparation supplies and beer disbursement. The disbursement documents are sealed with the seal of an official of the king of Andarig; they suggest that after the death of Shamshi-Adad, the king of Andarig, a powerful neighbor of Shubat-Enlil, had direct or indirect control over the former capital city.

Six soundings in the Leilan lower town and on the acropolis have revealed impressive public architecture associated with the reign of Shamshi-Adad and his successors. The only domestic structures retrieved have been small units piled against the early second-millennium BCE city wall. These data and the topography of the site suggest a relatively small agricultural population within the capital city during this period. Regional survey indicates that the resettlement of the Khabur Plains under the rule of Shamshi-Adad was

LEILAN, TELL. Figure 4. *Northeast acropolis showing the north facade of the period I, level 2 temple.* Nineteenth century BCE. (Courtesy Harvey Weiss)

LEILAN, TELL. Figure 5. *Sculpted mudplaster decoration on a semiattached column.* From a period I building, level 2 temple on the northeast acropolis. (Courtesy Harvey Weiss)

focused at the village level: the reoccupied Leilan administered a densely occupied empire (more than sixty villages within 15 km, or 9 mi.), extending from the Euphrates to the Zagros. [*See* Mari.] The city was conquered and destroyed by Samsuiluna of Babylon in a military campaign in 1728 BCE. The site was only reoccupied in the early twentieth century CE by Kurdish villagers.

[*See also* Mesopotamia, *articles on* Prehistoric Mesopotamia *and* Ancient Mesopotamia; *and* Temples, *article on* Mesopotamian Temples.]

BIBLIOGRAPHY

Akkermans, P. A., and Harvey Weiss. "Tell Leilan 1987 Operation 3: Preliminary Report on the Lower Town Palace." *Annales archéologiques arabes syriennes* 38 (1989): 1–19.

Akkermans, P. A., et al. "An Administrative Building of the King of Andarig at Shubat Enlil." *NABU* [= *Nouvelles assyriologiques breves et utilitaires*] 4 (1991): 68–70.

Charpin, Dominique. "Šubat Enlil et le pays d'Apum." *Mari: Annales de Recherches Interdisciplinaires* 5 (1987): 129–140. Publication of Mari epigraphic data that confirms Leilan data for identification of Leilan as Shubat-Enlil and Shekhna.

Eidem, Jesper. "Tell Leilan Tablets 1987: A Preliminary Report." *Annales archéologiques arabes syriennes* 38–39 (1989): 20–40. With the following items by Eidem, preliminary publication of the royal letters and treaties from the lower town (east) palace.

Eidem, Jesper. "Les archives paléo-babyloniennes de Tell Leilan." *Les Dossiers d'Archéologie* (Paris) 155 (1990): 50–53.

Eidem, Jesper. "An Old Assyrian Treaty from Tell Leilan." In *Marchands, diplomates, et empereurs,* edited by Dominique Charpin and Francis Joannès, pp. 185–207. Paris, 1991a.

Eidem, Jesper. "Tell Leilan Archives 1987." *Revue d'assyriologie et d'archéologie orientale* 85 (1991b): 109–135.

Ismail, Farouk. "Altbabylonische Wirtschaftsurkunden aus Tall Leilān." Ph.D. diss., University of Tübingen, 1991. The administrative texts from the lower town (east) palace.

Parayre, Dominique. "Les sceaux et empreintes de sceaux découverts à Tell Leilan en 1987." *Annales archéologiques arabes syriennes* 38–39 (1989): 41–55. With the following items by Parayre, third- and second-millennium Tell Leilan seal impressions and their internal and external administrative and iconographic relationships.

Parayre, Dominique. "Seals and Seal Impressions from Tell Leilan, 1985." *American Journal of Archaeology* 94.4 (1990): 556–567.

Parayre, Dominique. "Notes sur la glyptique de Tell Leilan à l'époque paléo-babylonienne." In *Marchands, diplomates, et empereurs,* edited by Dominique Charpin and Francis Joannès, pp. 389–395. Paris, 1991.

Parayre, Dominique. "Ninevite 5 Seal Impressions from Tell Leilan." In *The Origins of North Mesopotamian Civilization: Ninevite 5 Chronology, Economy, Society,* edited by Harvey Weiss. New Haven, forthcoming.

Schwartz, Glenn. *A Ceramic Chronology from Tell Leilan Operation 1.* Yale Tell Leilan Research, 1. New Haven, 1988. Much of the Tell Leilan ceramic sequence, with statistical analysis for chronological purposes.

Senior, Louise, and Harvey Weiss. "The Akkadian Reorganization of Subarian Agro-Production." *Orient-Express* 2 (1992): 16–24. Leilan *sila* bowls explained.

van de Mieroop, Marc. "Tell Leilan Tablets, 1991: A Preliminary Report." *Orientalia* 63 (1994): 305–344. Report on the administrative archive retrieved from the lower town (north) palace in 1991.

Vincente, Claudine. "The 1987 Tell Leilan Tablets Dated by the Limmu of Habil-kinu." Ph.D. diss., Yale University, 1991. Administrative texts from the lower town (east) palace.

Weiss, Harvey. "Tell Leilan on the Habur Plains of Syria." *Biblical Archaeologist* 48.1 (March 1985): 5–34. Precis of Leilan settlement history and significance.

Weiss, Harvey. "Tell Leilan and the Shubat Enlil." *Mari: Annales de Recherches Interdisciplinaires* 4 (1985): 269–292. The relationship between the site and the ancient second-millennium capital.

Weiss, Harvey. "The Origins of Tell Leilan and the Conquest of Space in Third Millennium Mesopotamia." In *The Origins of Cities in Dry-Farming Syria and Mesopotamia in the Third Millennium B.C.,* edited by Harvey Weiss, pp. 71–108. Guilford, Conn., 1986. North Mesopotamian climate, agroproduction, and transport economics.

Weiss, Harvey. "Tell Leilan 1989: New Data for Mid-Third Millennium Urbanization and State Formation." *Mitteilungen der Deutschen Orient-Gesellschaft zu Berlin* 122 (1990a): 193–218. Report on the lower town (south) excavations, including the initial IIId period settlement through the IIb abandonment.

Weiss, Harvey. "'Civilizing' the Habur Plains: Mid-Third Millennium State Formation at Tell Leilan." In *Resurrecting the Past, A Joint Tribute to Adnan Bounni,* edited by Maurits van Loon, Paolo Matthiae, and Harvey Weiss, pp. 387–407. Leiden, 1990b. Definition of the acropolis (northwest) settlement periodization and the significance of the Leilan IIId seal impressions for understanding North Mesopotamian secondary state formation in 2600 BCE.

Weiss, Harvey, and Maria-Agnes Courty. "Entre droite épigraphique et gauche archéologique, y-a-t-il une place pour la science?" *Les Nouvelles de l'Archéologie* 57 (1994): 33–41. Polemic and explanation of the third-millennium climate change and collapse data.

Weiss, Harvey, Gil Stein, P. A. Akkermans, Dominique Parayre, and Robert Whiting. "1985 Excavations at Tell Leilan, Syria." *American Journal of Archaeology* 94.4 (1990): 529–581. Excavations on the Leilan acropolis, at the city wall, and at the lower town (east) palace, with analysis of cuneiform tablets archives and cylinder seal assemblages.

Weiss, Harvey, Maria-Agnes Courty, Wilma Wetterstrom, Louise Senior, Richard Meadow, François Guichard, and Anna Curnow. "The Genesis and Collapse of Third Millennium North Mesopotamian Civilization." *Science* 261 (1993): 995–1004. Analysis of third-millennium settlement, agriculture, abrupt climate change, and socioeconomic collapse.

Weiss, Harvey, Maria-Agnes Courty, and Melinda Zeder. "Tell Leilan 1993." *Annales Archéologiques Arabes Syriennes,* forthcoming. Report of the Leilan IIId–IIb acropolis (northwest) cultic quarter.

Wetterstrom, Wilma. "Diet and Cooking in a Workmen's Quarter in the Mid-Third Millennium B.C. at Tell Leilan." Paper delivered to the Society for American Archaeology, Pittsburgh, 9 April 1992.

HARVEY WEISS

LEPTIS MAGNA, important Roman harbor situated adjacent to the eastern side of the modern town of Homs, 120 km (74.5 mi.) east of Tripoli in Tripolitania, the western province of Libya (32°48′ N, 14°17′ E). The topographical development of Leptis appears to have been more complex than previously demonstrated. The early Punic levels (Carter, 1965) may be only a part of the full picture. It appears from the *Stadiasmus Maris Magni* (*Geographi Graeci Minores I,* edited by K. Muller, Paris, 1955, pp. 93, 94) that a distinction should be made between the *hormos* (protected harbor) and the actual settlement of Leptis. The latter lay at the mouth of the Wadi Lebda from at least sometime in the sixth century BCE. By the early second century (accepting the conventional dating of the *Stadiasmus*), however, Leptis still lacked a port and was named *Neapolis,* "new town." The *Stadiasmus* refers to another site called Cape Hermaios at a distance of 15 stades (about 2.7 km or 1.5 mi.) west of Neapolis, and this clearly points to the promontory on which modern Homs is situated. Although silting has occurred at Homs, a small harborage still exists on the east side of the promontory, offering protection from onshore northerly winds. A port, even a small one at this point, also avoids the problem of seasonal floods descending from the Wadi Lebda, a feature of late autumn and winter. Some part of the early history of Leptis is perhaps to be sought here, particularly if the name *Hermaios* is interpreted as cognate with the modern Homs.

This hypothesis has gained greater credibility from recent discoveries to the west of the present waterfront at Homs. Excavations for a new building in 1972 revealed the very extensive remains of a villa belonging to the mid second century CE (Di Vita, 1974). The evident prosperity of the villa with its substantial bath suite is a striking reflection of the wealth at the disposal of the Leptitane upper class. More relevant in this context, however, was the discovery of a harbor mole sealed by the remains of the villa. It was suggested that the remains of the quay with its stone mooring rings were of Hellenistic date. The position of the quayside below the later villa clearly testified to the Homs waterfront having been extended in an eastward direction, perhaps as the result of silting. The date of the mole seems to be before the first century CE, but more precise dating within the Hellenistic period is lacking. Discussion of the chronology involved depends on the use of mooring stones made of Ras el-Ḥammam limestone, an argument that Antonino Di Vita (1969, p. 196) also deploys in his proposed late Hellenistic dating of the layout of the Forum Vetus at Leptis proper. Despite the lack of precision, the sequence of development appears to coincide with the situation implied in the *Stadiasmus.* Until the Hellenistic period Leptis lacked adequate port facilities and relied on use of the *hormos* available at Homs, where some early Phoenician evidence might reasonably be expected to emerge. Whether this (material) is forthcoming remains to be seen, but the reference to Leptis as Neapolis leads to the inference that there was a change of emphasis from Homs to Lebda nearly 3 km (2 mi.) to the west at the mouth of the Wadi.

The next question concerns the possible identification of the early settlement. Study of aerial photographs of Leptis shows quite clearly that north of the old forum important evidence survives towards the triangular promontory ultimately adapted into part of the Severan harbor (Jones, 1989). On morphological grounds the jumbled houses and courtyards visible under a covering of sand may date at least to the period of the late Punic settlement. The detailed plan of the buildings therefore suggests that a small but apparently early quarter of Leptis survives and needs to be incorporated into our view of the evolution of the city.

This reconstruction accords with the picture implied by the *Stadiasmus* for at least early second century BCE. As Di Vita (1974, p. 229) has argued, Homs may have remained the major transshipment port until the little understood harbor development at the mouth of the Wadi Lebda epigraphically attested under Nero (Bartoccini, 1958). The development of the core of Leptis is known primarily from the evidence of the Punic graves located under the stage area of the Roman theater (where the earliest evidence is a Corinthian sherd of c. 500 BCE) and from a deep sondage through the floor of the old forum (Carter, 1965). The results are of great interest, but the development of ceramic studies now make it difficult to accept wholly either the attribution of the various phases to relatively strict chronological dates or the precise dating of the pottery.

Although the early history of this great coastal city still contains many gaps in our knowledge, its development in the early and later Imperial period is uniquely well understood in North Africa. There are two reasons: the manifest changes in the layout and extent of the city, and the wealth of epigraphic and architectural evidence from the early Imperial period (31 BCE–69 CE) when the Punic aristocracy was first assimilated into the Roman provincial system. Two centuries later Septimius Severus, a son of one of Leptis Magna's greatest provincial families, became the emperor of the Roman world and founded a brief African dynasty.

LEPTIS MAGNA. *West gate, Municipal Palace.* Roman period. (SEF/Art Resource, NY)

These two groups from the early and later empire contributed to the architectural growth of the city in a variety of magnificent buildings. Their excavation was undertaken by Italian archaeologists in the years when Tripolitania was under Italian control 1911–1942. Italian involvement has continued along with British survey work, and Libyan archaeologists are continuing to uncover the great amphitheater to the west.

The early core of the town appears to have centered, as one might expect, around the old forum area. Harbor facilities on site must initially have been the foreshore at the mouth of the Wadi Lebda which was protected in part by an offshore island. The three temples of the old forum lay on the north side, and opposite, across the square, lay a *curia,* or council chamber, and a basilica. The date of the formal paving of the area is disputed but the visible paving probably dates to the Augustan period. The changes of alignment in the principal spine road to the southwest reflect the development of the city. The arch of Tiberius stands at the end of the first section close to three remarkable buildings built by local benefactors in the early Julio-Claudian period. The market with its two circular kiosks was constructed by the rich patron Annobal Rufus in 9–8 BCE. He also was responsible for the construction of the famous theater in 1–2 CE. The structure comprises the usual semicircular auditorium or *cavea* fronting a stage through whose ornamental backdrop *(scaenae frons)* an arch revealed a view of an integrated temple to the northeast. This small temple to the deified Roman emperors was constructed through the patronage of Annobal's relative Iddibal Tapapius and dedicated in 43 CE. Between the two major buildings discussed above lay the site of the so-called Chalcidicum, a long, columned portico behind which lay a rectangular open space surrounded by porticos, possibly to serve as another market. It was dedicated by Iddibal Caphada Aemilius in 11–12. The names of the early imperial patrons are of particular interest; they demonstrated the cultural assimilation of Roman nomenclature by a local aristocracy that retained latinized versions of their Libyo-Punic names. These three spectacular buildings sprung up early in the first century CE presumably in areas where development was still possible at the time. The relationship of the central core of the city to the presumably later city walls is not understood at present.

The harbor area, as an inscription (*Inscriptions of Roman Tripolitania,* no. 341) implies, underwent some formalization during the reign of the emperor Nero. The principal developments, however, occurred further west along the coast at the site of the now eroded circus and the magnificent amphitheater, which is slowly emerging from its covering of sand. By the turn of the century the layout of the Chalcidicum and the adjacent arch of Trajan shows that the road to the southwest ran past a formalized street grid of dwelling blocks to the crossroads with the main east–west route along the North African coast. It is evident from both the original

LEPTIS MAGNA. *The scaena, ruins of a Roman theater.* (SEF/Art Resource, NY)

Italian survey and subsequent examination of air photographs that the northwestern coastal area beyond the city walls with an impressive east gate was extensively occupied. Although most of the evidence has been destroyed by the growth of modern-day Homs, beyond the Hunting Baths of second-century CE date with their famous surviving murals there lay a series of major warehouses and storerooms on either side of the road to Tripoli. These structures undoubtedly represent storage areas for agricultural products, notably massive amounts of olive oil from the Gebel hinterland awaiting shipment in Tripolitanian-style amphorae to the markets of southern Italy and above Rome where Tripolitanian oil may have accounted for up to 10 percent of the market.

The first imperial intervention in this setting was the construction across the southeastern quarter of the residential area of the magnificent baths of Hadrian, with a formal palaestra, or colonnaded courtyard, to the north. Still greater remodeling was to come in the last decade of the second century when the emperor Septimius Severus (193–211) glorified his native town with extensive renovation. A four-way arch with scenes depicting his state visit to his native town formalized the junction of the spine road with the great coastal highway. From the eastern side of the Hadrianic baths a colonnaded street was constructed northeast toward the harbor area. Partly to disguise the Wadi Lebda at this point a magnificent nymphaeum opposite the Hadrianic baths acted as a backdrop overlooking a small piazza at a change in the angle of the colonnaded street. Along its northern side Severus's architect cleverly inserted a huge forum and a separate basilica integrated within an irregular area of former streets. At its southeast gate the forum was focused on the Severan temple to the imperial cult, and an entrance through a series of shop facades led directly into the great basilica completed in 213 CE by Severus's son, the emperor Caracalla (198–217). Its two-story construction and clerestory roof led to its eventual conversion into a Christian cathedral, and it can be argued that this magnificent building had a seminal influence on the later development of the basilican church form. The interior retained not only the twin culmination (with its dedicatory inscription along the entablature) but also the original pilasters with scroll decoration containing largely Bacchic scenes.

The sculptural techniques evident in the forum and the inhabited scrolls of the basilica were generally thought to reflect the school of Aphrodisias in western Anatolia, but isotopic analysis of marble types imported to Leptis Magna along with much Egyptian granite has broadened the picture. Although the Proconnesian origin of the inhabited scrolls in the basilica has been confirmed, the origins of the other marbles used have now been shown to include examples from Dokimeion, Naxos, and Thasos/Aliki around the Aegean and Carrara in Italy. Furthermore, it has been argued that the layout of the Severan buildings flanking the colonnaded street extended in the intended original form farther north toward the Flavian temple. Whether this arrangement was an integral part of the original project is not certain but, if it was, another element needs to be recognized in the already massive urban remodeling brought about under the brief star of the African emperor and his sons (Walda and Walker, 1984, p. 81; 1988, p. 55; Di Vita, 1982, p. 84).

The single largest development in the program was undoubtedly the construction of the Severan harbor around the mouth of the Wadi Lebda. A mole was constructed linking the area of the promontory beyond the old forum with the offshore island on the tip of which a lighthouse was built. The southern mole contained a second lighthouse and a temple of Portumnus together with a range of warehouses flanking the excavated quayside overlooking the now silted interior.

Relatively little work has been devoted to the latest stages of Byzantine Leptis but there is a hint of possible urban continuity from the recovery of seventh-century CE coinage from recent examination of the Flavian temple area. The much-reduced Byzantine wall circuit is generally believed to have encircled the back of the old forum temples and the basilica and then to have crossed the wadi to the south mole. The implications of this reduction may have to be rethought in the light of the possible identification of an outer, T-shaped arm on the eastern side of the Severan harbor. If this extension was in use in the Byzantine period and if the inner harbor perhaps substantially silted, then it would force a considerable adjustment of our view of the inhabited area available within the Byzantine wall circuit. This question, like so many in the vast unexplored area of Tripolitania's greatest city, remains for future decades to unravel.

BIBLIOGRAPHY

Bartoccini, Renato. *Il Porto Romano di Leptis Magna.* Rome, 1958.

Bianchi Bandinelli, Ranuccio, et al. *The Buried City: Excavations at Leptis Magna.* New York, 1966.

Birley, Anthony R. *Septimius Severus: The African Emperor.* 2d ed. New Haven, 1988.

Caputo, Giacomo. *Il Teatro Augusteo di Leptis Magna: Scavo e restauro, 1937–1951.* Rome, 1987.

Carter, Theresa H. "Western Phoenicians at Lepcis Magna." *American Journal of Archaeology* 69 (1965): 123–132.

Degrassi, Nevio. "Il mercato Romano di Lepcis Magna." *Quaderni di Archeologia della Libia* 2 (1951): 27–70.

Di Vita, Antonino. "Le date di fondazione di Leptis e di Sabratha sulla base dell'indagine archaeologica e l'eparchia cartaginese d'Africa." In *Hommages à Marcel Renard,* vol. 3, edited by Jacqueline Bibauw, pp. 196–202. Collection Latomus, 103. Brussels, 1969.

Di Vita, Antonino. "Un passo della Stadiasmos tes magales thalasses ed il porto ellenistico di Lepcis Magna." In *Mélanges de philosophie de littérature et d'histoire ancienne offerts à Pierre Boyancé,* pp. 229–249. Rome, 1974.

Di Vita, Antonino. "Il progetto originario del forumnovum Severianum a Leptis Magna." *Mitteilungen des Deutschen Archäologischen Instituts, Abteilung Römische* 89 (1982): 84–106.

Di Vita–Evrard, Ginette. "Municipium Flavium Lepcis Magna." *Bulletin Archéologique du Comité des Travaux Historiques,* n.s. 17B (1984): 197–210.

Floriani Squarciapino, Maria. *Leptis Magna.* Basel, 1966.

Floriani Squarciapino, Maria. *Sculture del Foro Severiano di Leptis Magna.* Rome, 1974.

Goodchild, Richard G., and J. B. Ward-Perkins. "The Romans and Byzantine Defences of Lepcis Magna." *Papers of the British School at Rome* 21 (1953): 42–73.

Haynes, Denys E. L. *An Archaeological and Historical Guide to the Pre-Islamic Antiquities of Tripolitania.* Tripoli, 1959.

Jones, G. D. B., and Robert Kronenburg. "The Severan Buildings at Lepcis Magna." *Libyan Studies* 19 (1988): 43–53.

Jones, G. D. B. "The Development of Air Photography in North Africa." In *Into the Sun: Essays on Air Photography in Archaeology in Honour of Derrick Riley,* edited by David L. Kennedy, pp. 25–43. Sheffield, 1989.

Torelli, Mario. "Per una storia della classe dirigente di Leptis Magna." *Rendiconti Accademia Nazionale dei Lincei: Classe di Scienze Morali* 28 (1974): 377–410.

Walda, H., and S. Walker. "The Art and Architecture of Lepcis Magna: Marble Origins by Isotopic Analysis." *Libyan Studies* 15 (1984): 81–92.

Walda, H., and S. Walker. "Isotopic Analysis of Marble from Lepcis Magna: Revised Interpretations." *Libyan Studies* 19 (1988): 55–59.

Ward-Perkins, J. B. *The Severan Buildings of Lepcis Magna.* London, 1993.

Whittaker, C. R. "The Western Phoenicians: Colonisation and Assimilation." *Proceedings of the Cambridge Philological Society* 20 (1974): 58–79.

G. D. B. JONES

LEVANT. The regional designation Levant is derived from the Latin *levare,* "to raise," the participle being *levans*

(-antis); it is similar in derivation and use to "to orient," for "the lands to the east" (from the European perspective). The term is sometimes employed to designate the lands around the eastern shores of the Mediterranean—the Near/Middle East, as opposed to the Far East. The Levant would thus include modern Asiatic Turkey, Syria, Lebanon, Israel, Jordan, and possibly Egypt (but not necessarily Cyprus).

The term *Levant* was popular in the nineteenth century in such fields as history, geography, economics, political science, and ethnography, especially in French scholarship. More recently, however, "Levantine" has taken on negative connotations, like "Byzantine," to suggest the mysterious mind, bureaucratic intrigue, and unsavory business practices of an Oriental world inferior to the West. Accordingly, the term has been all but abandoned, except in a few very recent attempts to revive it in Anglo-Saxon Near Eastern archaeology. There the term *Southern Levant* is sometimes used alternatively to refer to ancient Syria-Palestine. Such usage among younger archaeologists may be encouraged by the adoption of *Levant* as the name for the annuals of the British School of Archaeology in Jerusalem.

[*See also* Syria-Palestine.]

William G. Dever

LEVI DELLA VIDA, GIORGIO (1886–1967), Semitist and Islamist, called "one of the greatest Orientalists of our times" (Moscati, 1968, p. 1). Levi Della Vida's main works include the publication of Syriac and Arabic manuscripts, the edition of important Western Semitic inscriptions (e.g., from Karatepe in Turkey and all the Punic inscriptions from Tripolitania, North Africa) and historical syntheses of the ancient Semitic and Islamic worlds. His analytical works display profound erudition, subtle intuition, and an exemplary philological method; in his work as a historian he combined positivistic methodology with the idealistic tendencies of contemporary philosophy and historiography.

Levi Della Vida had been a pupil of Ignazio Guidi at the University of Rome. His collaborator, as early as 1911, in his translation of the Arabic sources for *Annali dell' Islam* was Leone Caetani. In 1913 Levi Della Vida became professor of Arabic at the Istituto Universitario Orientale in Naples and in 1916 was a professor of Semitic languages at the University of Turin; in 1920 he succeeded Guidi in teaching Hebrew and Semitics at Rome. In 1931 he refused, with only eleven other Italian professors, to swear allegiance to the fascist government and was consequently removed from his office. From 1932 to 1939 he was employed in the Vatican Library, charged with studying Arabic and Syriac manuscripts, but as a result of political and religious persecution, he was forced to leave Italy. He went to the United States, where he taught Semitics at the University of Pennsylvania until 1945 (and again in 1946–1947). At the end of World War II he returned to Rome, where he taught the history of Islamic institutions until 1956, when he retired. He was a member of the most prominent academies in Europe and America; he received a doctorate *honoris causa* at the universities of Paris (Sorbonne), Algiers, and Jerusalem, and he received Lidzbarski's prize for Semitic epigraphy. His name and image appear on a medal awarded by the University of California to students of Islam.

BIBLIOGRAPHY

Garbini, Giovanni, ed. *Giorgio Levi Della Vida nel centenario della nascita, 1886–1967.* Studi Semitici, n.s. 4. Rome, 1988. Includes a bibliography of works by Levi Della Vida.

Gordon, Cyrus H. *The Pennsylvania Tradition of Semitics.* Atlanta, 1986. See especially pages 62–64.

Michelini Tocci, Franco. "La storiografia orientalistica in Italia fra otto e novecento." In *La cultura storica italiana tra otto e novecento,* edited by M. Martirano and E. Massimilla, vol. 2, pp. 113–144. Naples, 1991.

Moscati, Sabatino. *Ricordo di Giorgio Levi Della Vida.* Orientis Antiqui Collectio, 7. Rome, 1968. With a bibliography of Levi Della Vida's works.

Tessitore, Fulvio. "Giorgio Levi Della Vida nella storiografia italiana tra otto e novecento." Introduction to Giorgio Levi Della Vida, *Arabi ed Ebrei nella storia,* edited by Francesco Gabrieli and Fulvio Tessitore, pp. 11–56. Biblioteca di Saggistica, 17. Naples, 1984.

Maria Giulia Amadasi Guzzo

LIBRARIES AND ARCHIVES. The emergence of writing in the ancient Near East, shortly before 3000 BCE, resulted in two kinds of texts, as the Mesopotamian evidence shows: groups of records drawn up for administrative purposes and texts used in training scribes. The former are usually designated archival texts; the latter, commonly called school texts, in time formed the contents of libraries.

Archival texts were drawn up by scribes/managers as an aid to memory and proof of transactions, to take stock of goods and personnel, to register transfers, and to meet the demands of accountability. Eventually, contracts, letters, and a variety of reports and notes were included, written to control economic and political processes and kept for consultation. Such collections, unearthed during excavations, are called archives. School texts, reflecting the complexity of cuneiform script, comprise a variety of sign and word lists together with student exercises. [*See* Cuneiform.] In the middle of the third millennium school texts were joined by the earliest literary texts (e.g., hymns, incantations, proverbs), written by and for the scribes responsible for the archives and usually found in the same locales. They attest the scholarly scribal activity that eventually developed libraries: collections of nonadministrative, scholarly, and traditional texts written and collected for educational purposes and professional needs. [*See* Scribes and Scribal Techniques.] They keep turning up in houses (schools and dwellings of master scribes), temples, and even palaces, always connected with the literati who collected and used them and who usually lived or worked in the places the texts were found.

Archives. The definition of *archives* as collections of records accumulated during the period of a particular administrative task performed by a person or institution may be too broad. Some would add to it "performed ex officio and still present with those who made and used them." Others would even wish to reserve the term for "a collection or repository of records no longer in use but preserved for their historical value and stored under special conditions." In the ancient Near East, such restrictions were usually ignored. Coherent bodies of administrative and legal records from large private households are in principle no different from those created by officials of a palace or temple—both of which also functioned as a large household. [*See* Palace.] Many archives have been found in situ, left behind when a disaster struck the building in which they were kept and used. A convincing example is the archive in room L 2769 of palace G at Ebla (c. 2400 BCE). [*See* Ebla.] Thousands of tablets had been stored on wooden shelving along walls that collapsed. The room was only accessible from adjoining room L 2875, a typical scriptorium, with low benches along the walls on which tablets could be laid out. [*See* Tablet.] Similar discoveries have been made elsewhere: in the houses of Assyrian traders in Kaneš (Anatolia, nineteenth century BCE), in the residence of Ur-Utu at Sippar/Amnanum (Tell ed-Der, destroyed c. 1630 BCE), and in the house of Shilwatesshub at Nuzi (house A on the northeastern mound, destroyed c. 1330 BCE). [*See* Kaneš; Sippar; Der, Tell ed-; Nuzi.]

Many complete or partial archives have been found in secondary locations: old records, having lost their value, might be discarded or put to secondary use as fill for walls and mud-brick benches or for leveling floors (not surprising in a country without building stone). Reconstruction and terracing suggest that parts of older buildings were displaced together with their contents, including archives. The bulk of the archival texts of the Temple of Inanna at Nippur (Ur III period, twenty-first century BCE) were discovered in distinct pockets in the fill of the foundation platform of a temple (?) erected there two thousand years later. [*See* Nippur.] Hundreds of records of the same period were discovered at Ur, stacked five to six layers deep under the pavement of a building dated to the Kassite period (c. 1300 BCE). [*See* Ur; Kassites.] Archival texts from the period of Assyrian domination of Mari were used as fill for mud-brick benches built in the palace of the next king, Zimrilim (eighteenth century BCE). [*See* Mari.] The so-called Persepolis fortification tablets (Achaemenid period) by their very name perpetuate their secondary use as fill for walls. [*See* Persepolis.]

Remains of archives and coherent files have even been recognized among the oldest administrative records known, those from level IV at Uruk (before 3000 BCE), where they had been deposited as part of the general debris in trash pits or used as architectural fill. [*See* Uruk-Warka.] Such hoards may be treated as archives if they exhibit enough coherence, but as random parts of larger collections, they must be used with caution for historical reconstructions. The best example of an archive as a respository of records no longer in use was found in the archival building of the "tablet hill" at Girsu (Telloh). [*See* Girsu and Lagash.] The archive originally contained some thirty thousand tablets dating to the end of the third millennium, they were carefully filed, in chronological order, in five or six layers on benches in two adjacent galleries. Such huge archives and repositories must have been restricted to large institutions, where, it may be assumed, administrative continuity and storage facilities were accompanied by qualified scribes who respected old records.

Even when violent destruction disturbed an original locale and scattered tablets, the findspot and the contents of the records can help to identify the source. Records dealing mainly with land transfer, dating to the fourteenth century BCE, were found in debris filling the area of court IV in the southern part of the palace at Ugarit (destroyed c. 1180 BCE). Found in the higher levels of the debris, they proved to have fallen from an upper story and had to be distinguished from records dating to the second half of the thirteenth century BCE found in the same area near the floors (particularly in archive rooms nos. 30 and 31). Upper stories could of course also have held current archives, as was the case at Maşat Höyük (Tapigga, with a Hittite palace), Mari, Nineveh, and Ḫattuša/Boğazköy (in building E of the citadel, where they had fallen down the slope). [*See* Nineveh; Boğazköy.]

Another source of confusion is archives having been transferred in antiquity. Tablet labels with Babylonian dates show that the diplomatic correspondence of Zimrilim of Mari was moved to a room (no. 115) adjoining the palace's interior court, where it was inspected by the scribes of the conqueror Hammurabi. In the wake of building new capitals or palaces, the chancery archives of Assyrian kings were moved, as was deduced by Simo Parpola (1983) from the sometimes remarkable location and composition of certain archives. Such operations imply selection because the collections exhibit gaps.

All the examples mentioned thus far concern cuneiform archives. There is no reason to doubt that these observations are also valid for archives consisting of records on papyrus, leather, or wood. [*See* Papyrus.] Destruction (with conflagration) and climate have almost completely robbed history of such collections. They can only be inferred from the existence of the clay sealings or bullae originally attached to certain records that have survived. [*See* Seals.] This applies also to the hundreds of wax-coated wooden writing boards (codices) used in Mesopotamian chanceries and libraries, whose existence is known from colophons and library records. Hoards of bullae with royal seals have been discovered at Ḫattuša/Boğazköy, in the so-called western building at Nişantepe, in building D at Büyükkale, and in the City of David, Jerusalem, once attached to official documents. Sealed bullae, discovered in Judah from about 600 BCE are considered to be remnants of a burned archive (Avigad, 1986), and the numerous bullae found in an archival chamber with extensive shelving, room 61, of Sennacherib's palace at Nineveh are the remains of an archive containing records on papyrus originating in Egypt and the Levant.

Only under special circumstances have parts of archives not written on clay survived. From ancient South Arabia records in the shape of inscribed wooden sticks are known that survived in the dry climate (Ryckmans et al., 1994). The so-called Samaria papyri (fourth century BCE) were discovered in a cave in Wadi ed-Daliyeh near the Jordan River, (Cross, 1969) and several hoards, including the Babatha archive (c. 100 CE), carefully packed in a leather bag, have been discovered in caves west of the Dead Sea (Yadin, 1971). [*See* Dead Sea Scrolls.] Such hoards had been carried to refuges in inhospitable and dry places. A few hoards of inscribed potsherds (ostraca) are also known that could be called archives: the Samaria ostraca (eighth century BCE), the Lachish ostraca (c. 600 BCE), and the Arad ostraca (i.e., the archive of Elyashib, c. 600 BCE). [*See* Samaria Ostraca; Lachish Inscriptions; Arad Inscriptions.] The first consist of administrative bookings (later digested in a papyrus ledger?); the second and third comprise small groups of letters. The following observations apply almost exclusively to clay tablets because of the lack of substantial archives of noncuneiform texts found in situ.

Storage and filing. A small, private archive could be stored in a jar or basket in a residence. Large institutions had special archival rooms for the systematic storage of records. Large archives, with valuable and sensitive records, were kept in sealed rooms and admission was restricted (ex officio or by mandate). Special committees were appointed to enter the sealed rooms of absent or dead Assyrian traders in Kaneš (Veenhof, 1986, p. 12). The location of archival rooms was often dictated by practical considerations: archives for registering regular deliveries and expenditures near the entrance of a palace (e.g., the eastern and western archives of the palace at Ugarit); the archive of "the king's meal" in the kitchen area of the palace (e.g., at Mari); a chancery archive near the rooms where the king and his counselors met; tablets with international treaties in the archival room of a temple, where they had been deposited before the gods who had to guarantee them (e.g., at Ḫattuša). [*See* Ugarit.] This implies that large institutions usually had several archival rooms for different spheres of domestic and international activity: agriculture, industry, husbandry, commerce, the military. At Archaic Uruk (Eanna, level IV, area of the Red Temple) "substantially coherent and discrete administrative . . . archives, that is, tablets from an individual accounting . . . unit" have been observed (Englund, 1994, p. 14ff.). Practical considerations may explain archival decentralization—for example, in the case of production centers (for textiles, leather, metals, and even agricultural production) outside temples and palaces, such as the Isin Craft Archive (c. 2000 BCE, with nearly a thousand records). This may account for the absence of archives in Early Dynastic temples (however, that may also be because such patrimonial organizations knew only a limited separation of official and private spheres, and thus administrative archives are to be found in the houses of its high officials).

Three methods of storage are usually distinguished: a container system, an open-shelf system, and a pigeonhole system. Many written sources mention jars, baskets, boxes out of wood or reed, trays and leather bags. The first are found regularly in excavations. Some containers even have an inscription identifying the contents, as was the case with some of the ten jars holding the archive of the regular offerings of the Aššur temple (c. 1100 BCE, found in storeroom 3′, under the responsibility of Ezbu-leshir). Traces of baskets and boxes are more elusive, but their use can be deduced from the remains of wood (Gasche, 1989, p. 30ff.; Stein, 1993, p. 24ff.) and metal (copper nails in the archival room of Shilwa-Tesshub at Nuzi). The use of shelves is well attested in Mesopotamia and elsewhere (at Ugarit and Ḫattuša; in buildings A and K at Büyükkale [Veenhof, 1986, p. 13]). Along three walls of the main archival room in the palace at Ebla were clear traces of where triple shelving had been fixed to the walls. Mud-brick benches for storing containers holding tablets may have been an alternative to shelves and were suitable for laying out tablets for inspection. Room 17 of Ur-Utu's residence (see above) was equipped with benches. The pigeonhole system was used in the library room of the Nabu temple at Khorsabad, in Sennacherib's palace at Nineveh (room 61, used for papyrus records), and in the Neo-Babylonian Temple of Shamash at Sippar (room 355, with fifty-six niches built of mud brick, wood, and reeds, in three tiers along three walls). Less sophisticated were brick boxes used as filing cabinets (in the scribal office of the northwest palace at Kalḫu).

Tablets in large archives could be classified by format, size, and style: there are links between the physical appearance and the contents of records (e.g., multi- or single columned, square, round or oblong, with or without a sealed envelope). In the Ur III period, for example, so-called round tablets are used in Lagash for recording the assessment of fields and (their) expected yield (Veenhof, 1986, p. 14). From the seventh century BCE onward, key words, summaries, dates, and names were written in Aramaic on the edges for quick identification. Containers and stacks of tablets could be identified by their labels, in use since the third millennium and particularly common during the third dynasty of Ur. The labels were usually attached to baskets, trays, and boxes with tablets called *pisan-dub-ba*, "tablet" *(dub)* basket *(pisan)* in Sumerian (Veenhof, 1986, p. 16ff.). The texts written on them identify the subject, transaction, occasion, date (they frequently cover an accounting period of one month or one year), and place of the group of records. Unfortunately, almost all of them (their number approaches five hundred) lack an archaeological context, so they cannot be linked to particular files. The variety of forms bears witness to systems with different, at times ad hoc criteria of classification. Some labels, moreover, may be transport rather than filing or storage labels. Clay bullae, with seal impressions and short inscriptions are also used. Old Assyrian traders used them also to identify records by provenience, format (sealed or not), type (letters, copies), and subject matter, frequently adding personal names.

Contents. Archives differ widely as to scope, size, and institutional setting. Archives of great institutions may cover various areas and levels of administrative activity, such as production (agriculture, husbandry, crafts), trade, foreign relations (gifts, tribute, booty), jurisdiction, personnel management, the army, cult. The huge archive at Drehem (Puzrish-Dagan, Ur III period), however, only registered, painstakingly, the delivery and disbursement of livestock in the public sphere. The so-called customs archive from Mari consisted only of letters of clearance received by traders entering Mari's territory upon payment of an import duty. The letters were submitted to the overseer of the traders upon the latter's arrival in the city. Private persons and families usually kept a single archive, covering many activities. This could result in large holdings, with at times more than a thousand records (Old Assyrian traders in Kaneš [Veenhof, 1986, p. 9, n. 33], the Teḫip-tilla family in Nuzi [Maidman, 1979], the Murashû firm at Nippur [Stolper, 1985]). Large archives of high officials can be a mixture of records received or kept ex officio and those bearing on private affairs. That of Shamash-hazir, an official of King Hammurabi of Babylon in Larsa charged with the allotment and administration of crown land, contained more than a hundred letters of the king's, as well as his wife's, correspondence. The business reflected in the huge archive of the chief lamentation priest (Ur-Utu) of the goddess Annunitum at Sippar/Amnanum (see above) also reflects his responsibilities as administrator of the temple. Archives of expert scribes and scholars, risen to the ranks of senior officials, may contain private archival records in combination with public records and a personal library of scholarly texts, as was the case with that of Rap'anu at Ugarit.

Administrative records of institutions, which aim at controlling the movement of goods and persons, frequently exhibit standardized formats, styles, and layouts. They comprise both a small tablet for registering single, daily events and monthly and yearly summaries and balanced accounts—ledgers drawn up for the purpose of accountability. The transactions recorded are deliveries, transfers, expenditures, distributions, and accounting. There are always lists of personnel (receipt of rations, wages, fields), of material in stock (inventories), of special expenditures (offerings, gifts), as well as letter orders (as proof of disbursements). Such administrative archives usually cover a limited period—one or two generations at most—with a clear numerical preponderance of records of the last few years before their abandonment or destruction. Many records, especially of daily transactions, after having been consulted could be discarded, stored separately or "erased" (with red lines over the tablets, as at Mari); legal documents (notes of debt) in due time could be "broken" or "killed" (in the language of the texts). Rules for discarding documents as such are not known and may have varied from one administration to another. Certain records, such as a comprehensive yearly account, cadastral texts, and some legal documents, were kept longer, for later reference. The size of a public archive is also conditioned by the measure of bureaucratic control, which of course was never complete and showed remarkable fluctuations from deliberate measures and historical developments. Increased standardization and central control are already attested during the Old Akkadian period (Naram-Sin) and the Ur III period (from the middle of the reign of Shulgi, c. 2050 BCE).

A royal chancery archive, such as that from the Neo-Assyrian period, had a wide scope: political correspondence, legal documents (treaties, grants, conveyances), records concerning the military (conscription, booty, equipment), official religion (expenditures for the cult, building of temples), and the court (royal family, harem, courtiers, officers, specialists, lists of disbursements of luxury items such as wine, oil, and garments). A variety of reports supplied information on military campaigns, conquered areas, production and works, and on ominous features relevant to the royal house (signs on earth and in the heavens, dreams, prophecies). Such palace archives could also contain private records of palace officials, either because they kept them in their offices, or because the king wished to exercise control over powerful and potentially dangerous individuals, such as officers of the guard, royal charioteers, and those controlling the harem (Parpola, 1983). Royal archives usually also contain selections of historical state documents, such as earlier royal correspondence. Thus, such archives could take on the character of a royal reference library.

Institutional and state archives are a mine of information for the historian interested in recovering a past administration's main features, discovering how power was wielded, and the status, duties, and careers of the main officials. Dated records allow the reconstruction of historical events, and the statistical evaluation of large archives make quantitative approximations possible. The king's obligations toward the cult and the temples make such archives a source for the study of religion and of the king's role in it.

Private archives contain a variety of records reflecting the activities of their owners as traders, landowners, priests, and officials. Among these there are nearly always letters, both those received in function (administrative duties, contractual links with the authorities) and those of a private nature. Letters were essential for overland traders (see above) and make up half of the records of the Old Assyrian traders. Because of their informative and virtual legal value (sealed message tablets contained orders and authorizations) archival copies were kept. In Babylonia, recipients of such letters were advised "to preserve them as proof of my order" and the same may be true of the Sumerian letter orders of the Ur III period. [*See* Sumerian; Sumerians.] Private archives always contain a number of long-term legal documents, such as marriage, adoption, and inheritance contracts and especially title deeds of real property. They were carefully preserved in their sealed envelopes and may go back several generations (some even more than two hundred years). They were the core of the small archive of Silli-Ishtar from Kutalla, which he left wrapped in reed mats and covered by mud bricks when he had to flee from his house in about 1740 BCE, never to return. When Ur-Utu's house in Sippar/Amnanum was destroyed by fire, someone tried to salvage a box of such records but lost them on the way out and they were found before the door to the court (Gasche, 1989, p. 32 with pl. 12.1).

Lawsuits over property rights were occasions to consult and produce tablets, and verdicts confirming the rights they embodied became part of such archives. When lost, they could be "revived" and rewritten on the basis of oral testimony before the judges. When real property was sold, such earlier title deeds—which contained valid descriptions of the property—had to be handed over to the new owner. This explains the presence of seemingly out-of-place records found in private archives. They might also have contained contracts ceded, given as pledge, or deposited there for safekeeping by friends. Also discovered in private archives are small hoards of records belonging to junior members or employees of a household (who had no houses of their own). Without careful excavation and recording (many private archives have been dug illicitly), such data and links are lost. Excavated archives that did not undergo conservation procedures (numbers lost), were poorly published (ignoring the links between textual and archaeological data), or were divided among various museums (e.g., archives from Aššur, Nippur, Nuzi, Ur) are responsible for the loss of essential information.

Well-analyzed private archives are a mine of information for social history. The large variety of legal contracts and judicial records are the main source of what is known of ancient law. Official archives as a rule contained few contracts; only in certain periods and cases (notably records dealing with the transfer of real estate, especially when encumbered with servicies and duties) were private contracts registered or abstracted by the authorities. Official courts of law occasionally kept copies of verdicts (e.g., the collection of tablets with final verdicts passed by city governors in the Ur III period). However, the general rule was that those verdicts and the files to which they belonged would be given to the winning party to store. The enormous variety of letters sheds light on many aspects of daily life, without which what is known of family life, trade, and personal religion would have been rather scant. Such letters, moreover, are a prime source for studying ancient languages, especially idioms.

Libraries. Collections of scholarly and traditional texts written and used by scribes during and after their training developed into libraries. The texts were also used in training pupils, which explains why such collections, especially in early periods, are frequently found in or near the archival rooms where the scribes worked (e.g., at Shuruppak/Fara, Abu Salabikh, Ebla). [*See* Fara; Abu Salabikh.] Expert scribes, with specific duties and interests and perhaps more free time, eventually began writing down or composing additional texts to serve their personal needs, such as ritual, divinatory, liturgical, medical, and astrological texts and incantations not part of the school's standard curriculum. Some worked as master scribes in a palace (chancery) or temple, others earned their living by running a school in their house, where a mixture of school and professional texts and private archival records is usually discovered. Schools in a capital city may have had links with the chancery (where official inscriptions and royal hymns must have been composed). This may explain why some royal texts (hymns, letters, inscriptions—especially of the kings of Ur III and Isin) found their way into the curriculum. When Sumerian disappeared as a spoken and soon after as a written language (after 2000 BCE), it remained indispensable for scholars as the basis of the writing system. [*See* Writing and Writing Systems.] Schools and scholars devoted a great deal of attention to copying traditional Sumerian texts, which led to the growth of a kind of standard corpus, eventually arranged in a normative sequence. This corpus, registered by the first lines of compositions in various catalogs, and to a varying degree actually discovered in schools (especially in Nippur), can be considered a kind of standard library. Texts outside this corpus, written and kept for specific professional needs (e.g., collections of incantations or omens) could be added.

Akkadian compositions (epic and mythical texts, prayers, wisdom texts, historiographic compositions) were composed, written down, and copied in these schools, but what is known of this Akkadian corpus as part of school and scholarly libraries is more limited. [*See* Akkadian.] In the following centuries many such libraries are known, usually in the houses or work places of master scribes. Convincing examples have also come to light at Ugarit, discovered in private houses, such as those of Rap'anu (see above), of "the high priest" (Mesopotamian lexical texts, Hurrian texts, mythical and epic texts in the alphabetic cuneiform script of Ugarit, written by the scribe Ili-malku), and of "the

Hurrian priest" (Hurrian and Ugaritic texts in alphabetic script). [*See* Hurrian; Ugaritic.] Such libraries are also found in temples, where the scholars who wrote and used them worked (e.g., Temple M_1 at Emar/Meskene on the Middle Euphrates, c. 1200 BCE). [*See* Emar.] The many divinatory and incantation texts it contained reveal the specialization of its owner, who also had a small sample of literary texts (wisdom, Epic of Gilgamesh, a ballad). The same pattern is observable in Babylonia after the end of the second millennium BCE. The traditional corpus was by then more or less fixed (the term *canonized* has been used in this context). Many collections discovered in houses and rooms of temples contain a sampling of this standard corpus, together with more specialized texts (e.g., incantations, divinatory and medical texts). Good examples are the library of the incantation priest in Aššur, the one found in a house in the Assyrian town of Huzirina (Sultantepe, four hundred different texts), and that of Anu-bēlshunu, a scholar attached to the Bit-Resh Temple of Seleucid Uruk. [*See* Aššur.] The closest approximation of a temple library (without an admixture of archival texts) was discovered in 1986 in room 355 of the Shamash temple in Sippar (c. 500 BCE), stored in more than fifty niches in the walls; however, its full size remains unknown (Al-Jadir, 1987).

The evidence for palace libraries is very limited. The postulated library of Tiglath-Pileser I in Aššur (c. 1100 BCE) has been shown to be the collection of an Assyrian scribal family from the first decades of the twelfth century BCE. The palace chancery may have incorporated in part some important older state documents (palace edicts, perhaps also the Middle Assyrian laws), but that does not make it a library. That important documents were carefully preserved, perhaps as separate collections, is not surprising. A collection of treaty tablets was stored in the great temple at Ḫattuša, probably because they had been deposited there before the gods who had to watch over them. In the same city, in building A of the citadel house, an important collection of older judicial decisions and royal edicts was found registered in a catalog, perhaps in the royal reference library.

The only real palace library, and perhaps the only library that fully deserves the name, was created by King Ashurbanipal in about the middle of the seventh century BCE in Nineveh. It was discovered and excavated by Austen Henry Layard and his successors between 1850 and 1932. [*See the biography of Layard.*] From royal letters and colophons on tablets it is known that the king wished to collect all scholarly and religious texts considered important. He may have built on an already existing royal collection, but his own contributions were very substantial. Scribes were sent out to collect and copy tablets and, after his victory over Babylonia, hundreds of texts (both on clay tablets and on wax-coated writing boards, including polyptychs) were confiscated from houses and temples. Tablets copied for the library were inscribed with special colophons (some in ink, on existing tablets) that state the king's intentions and identify them as royal property. All of these texts are now in the British Museum, as the K(uyunjik) Collection. The total number of different tablets (many compositions are represented by several—at times up to five or six—copies) has been estimated at around fifteen hundred, with perhaps two hundred thousand lines of text. The collection comprises the whole of the canonical corpus, the stream of tradition.

Catalogs (also those listing all the individual tablets in a lengthy series, with tablet numbers and catch lines) and labels made the library accessible. The majority of tablets consist of magical, medical, divinatory, and ritual texts, indicating that it focused on what was "good for the kingship," especially texts that would protect the king and his family against evil. There is also a substantial group of literary texts, however. Notwithstanding all this information supplied by the king's scribes, it is still not easy to reconstruct the library: in the nineteenth century the rich harvest of texts from at least two palaces and a temple seems to have been mixed up: the southwest palace (rooms 40, 41), built by Sennacherib in about 700 BCE, Ashurbanipal's own northwest palace (the successor to the older Succession Palace), and the Temple of Nabu. In addition, there was a certain amount of mixing of archival records with library texts. It seems that the king considered certain royal archival documents worth preserving alongside scholarly and literary texts. This means that, although there is no doubt that Nineveh contained a large, specifically royal library, the border between royal archive and royal library must have been somewhat fluid—how fluid can only be established if the originally separate royal text collections can be distinguished. A thorough analysis of the libraries of Nineveh remains a task for the future.

BIBLIOGRAPHY

Al-Jadir, Walid. "Une bibliothèque et ses tablettes." *Archéologia* 224 (1987): 18–27.

Arnaud, Daniel. *Recherches au pays d'Astata. Emar VI/4: Textes de la bibliothèque*. Paris, 1987. Full edition of all texts found in temple M_1, as a sample of a library of a priest-specialist.

Avigad, Nahman. *Hebrew Bullae from the Time of Jeremiah: Remnants of a Burnt Archive*. Jerusalem, 1986.

Charpin, Dominique. *Archives familiales et propriété privée en Babylonie ancienne: Étude des documents de "Tell Sifr."* Geneva, 1980. Paradigmatic analysis of a small private archive of the Old Babylonian period discovered in ancient Kutalla.

Courtois, Jacques-Claude. "Ras Shamra (Ugarit). I. Archéologie." In *Supplément au Dictionnaire de la Bible*, fasc. 52–53, cols. 1222–1280. Paris, 1979. Illustrated overview of the various archives and libraries discovered at Ugarit.

Cross, Frank M. "Papyri of the fourth Century B.C. from Daliyeh." In *New Directions in Biblical Archaeology*, edited by David Noel Freedman and Jonas C. Greenfield, pp. 41–62. New York, 1969.

Englund, Robert K. *Archaic Administrative Texts from Uruk. The Early Campaigns*. Archaische Texte aus Uruk, Bd. 5. Berlin, 1944. Edition and analysis of the earliest cuneiform records, from c. 3200 BCE.

Foster, Benjamin R. "Archives and Record Keeping in Sargonic Mesopotamia." *Zeitschrift für Assyriologie* 72 (1982): 1–27. Basic analysis of early archival practice, with good evidence on filing systems.

Gasche, Hermann. *La Babylonie au 17e siècle avant notre ère: Approche archéologique, problèmes et perspectives.* Ghent, 1989. Chapter 2 describes and analyzes the large and carefully excavated archive of Ur-Utu at Tell ed-Der.

Gibson, McGuire, and Robert D. Biggs, eds. *The Organization of Power: Aspects of Bureaucracy in the Ancient Near East.* Studies in Ancient Oriental Civilizations, no. 46. Chicago, 1987. Pays ample attention to administrative archives as instruments of bureacracy, especially during the Ur III period in Mesopotamia.

Hunger, Hermann. *Babylonische und assyrische Kolophone.* Alter Orient und Altes Testament, 2. Kevelaer, 1968. Presents and analyzes the information on the tradition and copying of literary cuneiform tablets incorporated in libraries.

Jones, Tom B. "Sumerian Administrative Documents: An Essay." In *Sumerological Studies in Honor of Thorkild Jacobsen on His Seventieth Birthday, June 7, 1974,* edited by Steven J. Lieberman, pp. 41–62. Chicago, 1976.

Krecher, Joachim. "Kataloge, literarische." In *Reallexikon der Assyriologie und vorderasiatischen Archäologie,* vol. 5, pp. 478–485. Berlin, 1976–.

Lieberman, Steven J. "Canonical and Official Cuneiform Texts: Towards an Understanding of Assurbanipal's Personal Tablet Collection." In *Lingering over Words: Studies in Ancient Near Eastern Literature in Honor of William L. Moran,* edited by Tzvi Abusch et al., pp. 305–336. Atlanta, 1990.

Maidman, M. P. "A Nuzi Private Archive: Morphological Considerations." *Assur* 1 (1979): 179–186.

Nissen, Hans J., et al. *Archaic Bookkeeping: Writing and Techniques of Economic Administration in the Ancient Near East.* Chicago, 1993. Highly informative presentation, in word and image, of the earliest records for describing and interpreting the earliest administrative systems (third millennium BCE).

Oppenheim, A. Leo. *Ancient Mesopotamia: Portrait of a Dead Civilization.* Chicago, 1964. The introduction and chapter 5 deal with the scribes, their creative efforts, libraries, and recording.

Parpola, Simo. "Assyrian Library Records." *Journal of Near Eastern Studies* 42 (1983): 1–30. Presents the records of acquisitions from Ashurbanipal's library in Nineveh from confiscations in Babylonia.

Posner, Ernst. *Archives in the Ancient World.* Cambridge, Mass., 1972. Describes and analyzes the data from the ancient Near East in the wider framework of what is known from antiquity.

Ryckmans, Jacques, W. W. Müller, and Y. ʿAbdallah. *Textes du Yémen Antique inscrits sur bois.* Louvain-la-Neuve, 1994.

Shawe, J. "Der alte Vorderorient." In *Handbuch der Bibliothekwissenschaft,* edited by F. Milkau and G. Leyh, vol. 3, pp. 1–50. Weisbaden, 1955.

Sigrist, Marcel. *Drehem.* Bethesda, 1992. Overview and analysis of the largest administrative archive (dealing with livestock) of the Ur III period.

Soldt, W. H. van. *Studies in the Akkadian of Ugarit: Dating and Grammar.* Alter Orient und Altes Testament, 40. Neukirchen-Vluyn, 1991. A meticulous reconstruction and analysis of the archives and libraries discovered at Ugarit (see pp. 47–231).

State Archives of Assyria. 10 vols. to date. Helsinki, 1987–. Full edition of the Assyrian state archives discovered at Nineveh, with introductions and translations, including royal correspondence, astrological reports, oracular queries, treaties and loyalty oaths, prophecies, legal transactions, administrative records, and court poetry.

Stein, Diana L. *Das Archiv des Šilva-Teššub,* vol. 8, *The Seal Impressions.* Wiesbaden, 1993. Overview of the various archives discovered at Nuzi as introduction to a detailed analysis of one archive, with the use of texts and seal impressions.

Stolper, Matthew W. *Entrepreneurs and Empire: The Murašû Archive, the Murašû Firm, and Persian Rule in Babylonia.* Istanbul, 1985.

Veenhof, Klaas R., ed. *Cuneiform Archives and Libraries: Papers Read at the 30e Rencontre Assyriologique Internationale, Leiden, 4–8 July 1983.* Leiden, 1986. Papers devoted to many archives in the ancient Near East by some of the best specialists in the field, with a general introduction and much bibliographic data.

Weitemeyer, Mogens. "Archive and Library Technique in Ancient Mesopotamia." *Libri* 6 (1956): 217–238. Careful study by a professional Assyriologist and librarian.

Yadin, Yigael. *Bar-Kokhba: The Rediscovery of the Legendary Hero of the Last Jewish Revolt against Imperial Rome.* London, 1971. The discovery and contents of the remains of papyrus archives in caves west of the Dead Sea.

Zettler, Richard L. *The Ur III Temple of Inanna at Nippur.* Berliner Beiträge zum Vorderen Orient, 11. Berlin, 1992. Comprehensive analysis of an early temple on the basis of its archives.

KLAAS R. VEENHOF

LIBYA. Situated at the northeast corner of Africa, Libya consists of three regions: Cyrenaica, Tripolitania, and Fezzan (ancient Phazania). Cyrenaica and Tripolitania are semiarid Mediterranean coastal zones on opposite sides of the Gulf of Syrte. Arid Fezzan, dotted with oases, separates them at the Sahara's northern edge.

For the ancient Greeks, Libya was all of northern Africa between the Nile River and Gibraltar; to them, its light-skinned inhabitants were all "Libyans," though they distinguished subgroups such as Garamentes, Maures, and Numidians. Phoenicians traded with Libyans beyond the Pillars of Hercules (Herodotus 4.196). [*See* Phoenicians.] The *Periplus of the Erythraean Sea* of Hanno the Carthaginian, a partly fanciful, partly factual account of a sea voyage to "Libyan lands beyond the Pillars of Hercules" (presumably the Atlantic coast of Morocco), mentions Libyphoenicians, punicized native peoples. [*See* Phoenician-Punic.] The name also bears tenuous connection with biblical Lehabim (Table of Nations, *Gn.* 10:13) and Lubim (*2 Chr.* 12:3).

The Greeks may have learned the name from the Egyptians, for whom, from the Old Kingdom onward, Libya formed a hostile western desert frontier. In his mortuary complex at Abu Sir, Sahure (fifth dynasty) boasted a victory over Libyans. The Story of Sinuhue (twelfth dynasty) mentions Tehune-Libyans vanquished by Egypt. Rameses II (nineteenth dynasty) built a chain of forts in the western desert against Libyan incursions. On reliefs at Medinet Habu, Rameses' son Merneptah recorded his defeat of a coalition of Sea Peoples and Libyans (written RBW or LBW, vocalized *Lebu* or *Libu*). During the twenty-second–twenty-third dynasties (c. 945–725 BCE), pharaohs with Libyan names like Sheshonq and Osorkon controlled Lower Egypt.

Cyrenaica took its name from Cyrene, the earliest Greek foundation in Africa (631 BCE, following Herodotus 4.150–151). Cyrenaica was also known as Pentapolis for its five major cities: Apollonia (Sosuza), Cyrene (Shahat), Ptolemais (Tolmeta/Barce), Tauchira (Arsinoe/Tocra), and Euesperides (Berenice/Benghazi) (Stillwell, 1976). The Persians under Cambyses possessed the region, and Ptolemy I annexed it after Alexander's death. In 96 BCE Ptolemy Apion bequeathed Cyrenaica to Rome, after which it was united with nearby Crete as a Roman province. [*See* Cyrene; Ptolemais.]

Tripolitania ("three cities"), colonized by Phoenicians in the seventh century BCE, had three principle cities: Leptis Magna (Labdah), Oea (Tripoli/Trablus), and Sabratha (Stillwell, 1976). [*See* Leptis Magna.] Until 146 BCE, Tripolitania formed the eastern province of a west Phoenician realm dominated by Carthage. [*See* Carthage.] After Carthage's destruction, Rome ceded Tripolitania to its Numidian allies. Tripolitania later became a Roman province famous for olive oil production.

The monumental urban ruins at Cyrenaica and Tripolitania have attracted archaeologists, as have traces of Paleolithic and Neolithic peoples that once inhabited a less desiccated Fezzan. The archaeology of later native North Africans, the Berbers, is still poorly understood, though their language and inscriptions are known (Camps, 1986). One remedy for this neglect has been the UNESCO Libyan Valleys Survey, devoted to the archaeology of rural Tripolitania. The survey has discovered extensive Roman-period (though not necessarily Roman-designed) floodwater irrigation systems. [*See* Irrigation.] These supported a significant inland occupation based on mixed agriculture (grape, olive, cereals) integrated with mobile sheep/goat pastoralism, the prevailing mode of subsistence before and after the Romans (*Journal of Libyan Studies,* 1989).

[*See also* North Africa.]

BIBLIOGRAPHY

Camps, Gabriel. "Libyco-Berber Inscriptions." In *Encyclopaedia of Islam,* new ed., vol. 5, pp. 754–757. Leiden, 1986.

Journal of Libyan Studies 20 (1989). Special issue entitled "Libya: Studies in Archaeology, Environment, History, and Society, 1969–1989," edited by D. J. Mattingly and J. A. Lloyd.

Stillwell, Richard, ed. *Princeton Encyclopedia of Classical Sites.* Princeton, 1976.

JOSEPH A. GREENE

LIMES ARABICUS. The Latin term *limes Arabicus* means "Arabian frontier" and appears in literary sources in the fourth century CE. By this period the eastern frontier of the Roman Empire was divided into frontier districts (Lat., *limites*), each under the command of a *dux.* South of the Euphrates River these districts extended along the edge of the North Arabian desert and formed the empire's southeastern frontier. The limes Arabicus extended from the region just south of Damascus to Wadi el-Hasa, near the southern end of the Dead Sea. By the fourth century the frontier zone south of Wadi el-Hasa was the *limes Palaestinae,* which in turn extended to the Red Sea at Aila ('Aqaba). The limes was defended by Roman garrisons based in forts and towns along the frontier. Their primary mission was to protect the sedentary provincial population and the lucrative caravan traffic that passed through the region against the raids of nomadic Arab tribes (Saraceni, or Saracens) from the adjacent desert. [*See* Hasa, Wadi el-; 'Aqaba.]

Only two literary sources explicitly refer to the limes Arabicus. The church historian Rufinus (*Hist. Eccl.* 2.6), describing the assault on the frontier by the Saracen queen Mavia during the reign of Valens (364–378 CE), refers to the "towns and cities of the limes Arabicus." The historian Ammianus Marcellinus (31.3.5), describing events leading up the battle of Adrianople in 378 CE, refers to a certain Munderichus, who was later *dux limitis per Arabiam,* "duke of the limes through Arabia."

The Roman frontier in this region was created by Trajan, who annexed the Nabatean kingdom in 106 CE as the new province of Arabia. [*See* Nabateans.] Trajan then built a major road (Via Nova Trajana) that extended from southern Syria to the Red Sea. Most forts of the later limes Arabicus were built along or a short distance east of this road, which was completed between 111 and 114. The original Roman provincial garrison consisted of Legio III Cyrenaica, based at the provincial capital of Bosra in the north, and perhaps ten auxiliary units based in towns and forts along the frontier. [*See* Bosra.] Some strengthening of the Arabian frontier occured under the Severan dynasty (193–235). Inscriptions document the construction of several forts around the northwest outlet of Wadi Sirḥan, a natural migration route between southern Syria and the interior of the Arabian Peninsula, and by many milestones reflecting road repairs. The frontier appears to have faced an increased Saracen threat by the late third century, when the frontier defenses were significantly strengthened by Diocletian (284–305). He rebuilt the road system, constructed or rebuilt many new fortifications, and reinforced the provincial army with new units. He also redrew the provincial boundaries, transferring southern Transjordan, the Negev, and Sinai (formerly part of Arabia) to the province of Palestine. [*See* Negev; Sinai.] The military frontier advanced to the desert fringe and Roman forces campaigned deep in the desert, apparently as far as Jawf (Duma) at the southeastern end of Wadi Sirḥan. The *Notitia Dignitatum* (*Oriens* 37), dated to about 400 CE, reveals that the *dux Arabiae* commanded two legions, eight elite cavalry vexillations, six cavalry units or *alae,* and five infantry cohorts. These forces were styled *limitanei*—that is, troops that manned the limes. The limes Arabicus appears to have remained well fortified until the late fifth century, when there is evidence for the abandonment of some forts and a decline in the quality of its garrisons. In about 530, Justinian effectively demobilized most of the remaining units by stopping their pay and turned over primary responsibility for the defense of the southeastern frontier to the Ghassanids, Christian Arab clients. By this date the limes Arabicus, in the sense of a military frontier, effectively ceased to exist.

Although descriptions of some individual sites were made by several nineteenth-century travelers to the region, the first systematic survey of most of the Arabian frontier was conducted by Rudolf-Ernst Brünnow and Alfred von Domaszewski in the 1890s. Their focus was largely architectural and epigraphic. As a result of the subsequent destruction of many sites, their work remains fundamental. Subsequent surveys identified many other smaller sites, such as watchtowers, that formed part of the frontier system. As late as the mid-1970s, however, no fort of the limes had been excavated and no comprehensive survey had been conducted. The Limes Arabicus Survey, directed by S. Thomas Parker in 1976 under the auspices of the American Schools of Oriental Research, collected pottery from most major sites along the entire length of the frontier in Transjordan. This evidence, combined with excavation results from several key sites (e.g., el-Lejjun/Betthorus and Umm el-Jimal), led to the first historical synthesis of the Roman frontier (Parker, 1986). [*See* Umm el-Jimal.] Since the late 1970s several scholars have focused on more limited sectors or individual sites on the frontier, producing important new evidence. A lively debate has begun about the nature of the frontier, with some questioning the level of the Saracen threat while others defend the traditional notion about the purpose of the frontier system.

The fortifications of the limes include watchtowers, *castella* (forts), fortresses, and fortified cities. The last category is beyond the scope of this discussion, but various sources suggest that Roman army units were based within some towns and cities. Hundreds of structures identified as towers exist along the frontier; they seem to date to many periods, but they were not all military structures. The Romans often reused existing Iron Age and Nabatean structures but also built some new towers at key locations. Few have been excavated, further complicating their dating. Analysis of surface pottery and architecture has, however, permitted some understanding of these structures: many were erected on elevations with extensive views, usually intervisible with

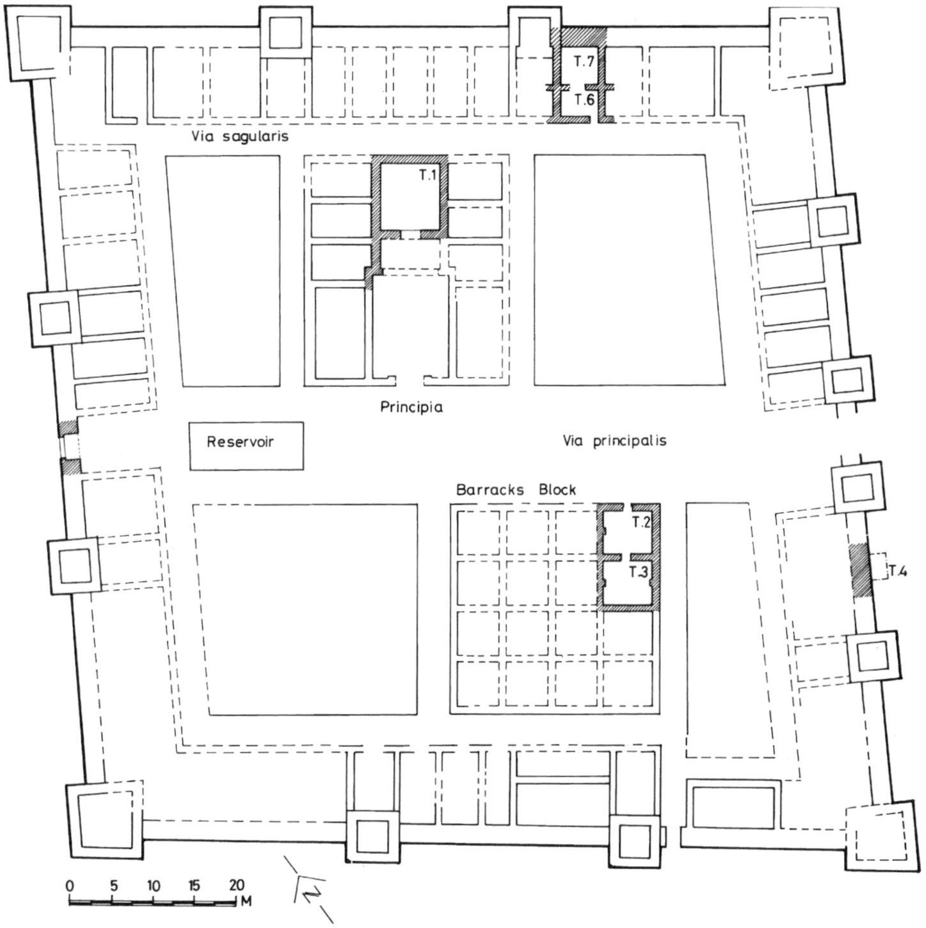

LIMES ARABICUS. Figure 1. *Plan of Da'janiya.* Roman fort built around 300 CE along the Arabian frontier. (Courtesy S. T. Parker)

other towers, and thus presumably served as the "eyes and ears" of the frontier system.

A number of *castella* have now been excavated, including forts at Umm el-Jimal, Qaṣr al-Ḥallabat, Khirbet es-Samra, Umm er-Rasas/Kastron Mefaa, Qaṣr Bshir, Khirbet el-Fityan, Daʿjaniya (see figure 1), and Ḥumeima. [*See* Qaṣr al-Ḥallabat; Umm er-Rasas; Ḥumeima.] The most common type of *castellum* is the so-called *quadriburgium,* or rectangular fort with towers projecting from the four corners. This type may date as early as the early third century, as evidenced by Qaṣr al-Ḥallabat, dated epigraphically to 213 CE. Perhaps the best-preserved and most securely dated *castellum* is Qaṣr Bshir (see figure 2), on the Kerak plateau east of the Dead Sea. [*See* Kerak.] This *quadriburgium* is dated to 293–305 CE by an in situ Latin inscription. The interior plan consists of ranges of two-storied rooms surrounding a central courtyard; the ground-floor rooms served as stables and the second-story rooms housed a garrison of about 150 men. Most other excavated *castella* also date to the tetrarchy, including those at Umm el-Jimal, Khirbet es-Samra, Khirbet el-Fityan, and Daʿjaniya. Recent excavation by John Oleson of the large (approximately 3 ha, or 7 acres) fort at Ḥumeima, on the Via Nova Trajana between Petra and Aila, suggests a second-century date and is thus the earliest-known Roman fort along the frontier.

By the fourth century at least three and possibly four legions were based along the Arabian frontier. The *castra* of the Legio III Cyrenaica has been identified as an annex attached to the city wall of Bosra but is as yet unexcavated. Arabia's second legion, IV Martia, was based in a fortress at el-Lejjun, east of the Dead Sea on the Kerak plateau. At 4.6 ha (11 acres), el-Lejjun is typical of Late Roman legionary fortresses with its massive projecting U-shaped interval towers and semicircular corner towers. Erected in about 300 CE, the fortress seems to have been designed for a garrison of about two thousand men, but this was later reduced to about one thousand, following a reconstruction in the late fourth century. The fortress is the most extensively excavated Roman military site along the frontier, with portions of the fortifications, headquarters, barracks, bath, church, and other structures exposed. The legion remained in garrison until the Justinianic demobilization of the early sixth century. The fortress itself was destroyed in an earthquake in 551 CE.

Farther south, on the limes Palaestinae, the Legio X Fretensis was transferred from Jerusalem to Aila (ʿAqaba) by the end of the third century. Its fortress at Aila has not been identified. Just east of Petra is the great fortress at Udruḥ, which is virtually a twin of el-Lejjun in terms of its size (4.7 ha, or 12 acres) and the number and plan of its gates, interval towers, and angle towers. The original internal plan of Udruḥ was obscured by later Islamic occupation. Although the excavator, Alistair Killick, has proposed a Trajanic date for its construction, no specific evidence has been advanced

LIMES ARABICUS. Figure 2. *Qaṣr Bshir.* Roman fort built between 293 and 305 CE east of the Dead Sea. (Courtesy S. T. Parker)

to support this early date. Rather, the close architectural parallels with el-Lejjun and other late third–early fourth-century fortifications strongly suggest that the extant fortifications at Udruḥ were erected in the Diocletianic era. It has plausibly been suggested that this fortress was originally erected for Palestine's other legion, VI Ferrata, which may have been transferred from northern Palestine to Udruḥ in about 300 CE but was disbanded or destroyed during the fourth century. Neither the legion nor the site appear in the relevant chapter in the *Notitia* (*Oriens* 34).

[*See also* Fortifications, *article on* Fortifications of the Hellenistic, Roman, and Byzantine Periods; Roman Empire; *and* Transjordan, *article on* Transjordan in the Persian through Roman Periods.]

BIBLIOGRAPHY

Banning, E. B. "Peasants, Pastoralists, and *Pax Romana:* Mutualism in the Southern Highlands of Jordan." *Bulletin of the American Schools of Oriental Research,* no. 261 (1986): 25–50.

Brünnow, Rudolf-Ernst, and Alfred von Domaszewski. *Die Provincia Arabia.* 3 vols. Strassburg, 1904–1909. Still indispensable survey of the architectural evidence for the limes Arabicus.

Graf, David F. "Rome and the Saracens: Reassessing the Nomadic Menace." In *L'Arabie préislamique et son environnement historique et culturel: Actes du Colloque de Strasbourg,* edited by Toufic Fahd, pp. 341–400. Leiden, 1989.

Isaac, Benjamin. *The Limits of Empire: The Roman Army in the East.* Rev. ed. Oxford, 1992. Revisionist study that downplays the level of external nomadic threat, emphasizing instead the problem of internal security.

Kennedy, David L. *Archaeological Explorations on the Roman Frontier in North-East Jordan.* British Archaeological Reports, International Series, no. 134. Oxford, 1982.

Kennedy, David L., and Derrick N. Riley. *Rome's Desert Frontier from the Air.* Austin, 1990. Lavishly illustrated with aerial photos and plans of many key sites along the Arabian frontier.

Mayerson, Philip. "The Saracens and the *Limes.*" *Bulletin of the American Schools of Oriental Research,* no. 262 (1986): 35–47.

Parker, S. Thomas. "Peasants, Pastoralists, and *Pax Romana:* A Different View." *Bulletin of the American Schools of Oriental Research,* no. 265 (1986): 35–51. Reply to Banning's article.

Parker, S. Thomas. *Romans and Saracens: A History of the Arabian Frontier.* American Schools of Oriental Research, Dissertation Series, 6. Winona Lake, Ind., 1986. Historical and archaeological survey of the limes Arabicus.

Parker, S. Thomas, ed. *The Roman Frontier in Central Jordan: Interim Report on the Limes Arabicus Project, 1980–1985.* 2 vols. British Archaeological Reports, International Series, no. 340. Oxford, 1987. Report on excavations at el-Lejjun, Khirbet el-Fityān, Rujm Beni Yasser, and Qaṣr Bshir and survey of the Roman frontier east of the Dead Sea.

Parker, S. Thomas, ed. *The Roman Frontier in Central Jordan: Final Report on the Limes Arabicus Project, 1980–1989.* 2 vols. Washington, D.C., forthcoming. Results on excavations at el-Lejjun and Daʿjāniya, survey of the frontier east of the Dead Sea, and a historical synthesis of this sector.

Parker, S. Thomas. "The Nature of Rome's Arabian Frontier." In *Roman Frontier Studies 1989: Proceedings of the XVth International Congress of Roman Frontier Studies,* edited by Valerie Maxfield and Michael Dobson, pp. 498–504. Exeter, 1991. Review of recent scholarly debate on the subject.

Sartre, Maurice. *Trois études sur l'Arabie romaine et byzantine.* Collection Latomus, vol. 178. Brussels, 1982. The first essay deals with the borders of the province; the second with the region's Arab tribes.

Speidel, Michael P. "The Roman Army in Arabia." In *Aufstieg und Niedergang der römischen Welt,* vol. 2.8, edited by Hildegard Temporini and Wolfgang Haase, pp. 687–730. Berlin, 1977. Definitive study of the Roman army in this province.

Speidel, Michael P. "The Roman Road to Dumata (Jawf in Saudi Arabia) and the Frontier Strategy of *Praetensione Colligare.*" *Historia* 36 (1987): 213–221. Important epigraphic evidence about the penetration of Roman forces deep into the Arabian desert during Diocletian's reign.

S. THOMAS PARKER

LIONS. Not found in the fossil record of the Levant until the Late Pleistocene, lions *(Panthera leo)* arrived as tropical elements entering an already diverse fauna. If artistic and literary evidence are any guide, lions were known all over the ancient Near East. With more than 150 citations in the Hebrew Bible, they apparently were familiar in biblical times. Lions were finally hunted to extinction in Palestine in the nineteenth century CE. Elsewhere in the region they were not exterminated until after World War I. Several subspecies of lion ranged throughout the greater Near East until modern times, but it is impossible to determine which were closest to ancient Levantine populations.

Lion imagery was ubiquitous in the cultures of the ancient Near East. In religious and royal symbolism the lion appears as aggressor, victim, and protector of gods and kings. Given its prominence in literature and iconography, it is surprising that the bones of lions are such very rare finds at archaeological sites. The most spectacular discovery has been the skull and mandibles of a lioness found on the floor of a twelfth-century BCE Pre-Philistine temple in Jaffa, Israel. Half a scarab seal found in close proximity led the excavators to suggest that a lion cult was practiced in the temple. The right mandible has two sets of deep cut marks that are consistent with opening the oral cavity from the basal surface of the jaws while leaving the head attached to the skin. Two lion bones associated with Iron I pottery in a noncultic Iron II building were recovered from Tel Miqne/Ekron. A third lion bone was of Iron II date. At Tel Dan, one lion foot bone was recovered from the mid-ninth-century BCE deposit in the altar room complex in the sanctuary; the cut marks on this bone are consistent with skinning. A fragment of a mandible was found in a metalworking area of Iron I date at the same time. These bones are in collections studied by Paula Wapnish and Brian Hesse (see Wapnish and Hesse, 1991).

At the site of Ḥesban, in Jordan, an ankle bone of Roman date and a shoulder from a lion cub (date uncertain) were recovered. Farther afield, from the site of Habuba-Kabira in northern Syria, four lion bones were noted, two from the Uruk period (fourth millennium) and two from the Middle Bronze Age. From Lidar Höyük in southeastern Anatolia, a lower jaw and lower leg bone were discovered in Late Bronze deposits, and one first phalanx noted from the Hellenistic period.

Documentation of the lion in ancient Egypt comes almost exclusively from artistic representations, from the Old Kingdom onward. However, the remains of seven partial lion skeletons are reported from the grave complex of Hor-Aha in Umm el-Qaab. These bones date from the first dynasty (early third millennium), and are mostly of young animals, suggesting to the investigators that they might have been kept in captivity.

BIBLIOGRAPHY

Boessneck, Joachim. *Die Tierwelt des Alten Ägypten.* Munich, 1988.

Boessneck, Joachim, and A. von den Driesch. "Besprechung der Tierknochenfunde aus dem Grabkomplex des Horus-Aha im Umm el-Qaab bei Abydos." *Internationale Archäologie* 1 (1991): 55–62.

Cornelius, Izak. "The Lion in the Art of the Ancient Near East: A Study of Selected Motifs." *Journal of Northwest Semitic Languages* 15 (1989): 53–85. The latest study of a much covered topic, useful for its bibliography.

Kaplan, Jacob, and Haya Ritter-Kaplan. "Jaffa." In *The New Encyclopedia of Archaeological Excavations in the Holy Land,* edited by Ephraim Stern, vol. 2, pp. 655–659. Jerusalem and New York, 1993. Illustrates the lion skull from the Pre-Philistine temple. No photographs of the mandible have been published.

Wapnish, Paula, and Brian Hesse. "Faunal Remains from Tel Dan: Perspectives on Animal Production at a Village, Urban and Ritual Center." *Archaeologica* 4 (1991): 9–86. Reports on the lion foot bone found in the altar complex at Tel Dan.

PAULA WAPNISH

LITERACY. The subject of literacy in the ancient Near East touches on all major aspects of civilization, not the least being the recording of history, for the invention of writing some five thousand years ago signaled the emergence of humanity from the darkness of the prehistoric age. Writing radically changed all earlier forms of communication, the transmission of tradition, formal education, accounting, and man's perception of the world.

This epic event then, dated to about 3100 BCE, marks the beginning of the historical period. Writing was preceded by oral and iconographic means of communication—including the arduous process of accounting by using tokens and counters bearing agreed-upon designs that may have evolved into pictographic logograms (Schmandt-Besserat, 1984). Those other means of social intercourse coexisted and interacted with literate forms, as they continue to do.

The earliest form of writing is found in ancient Uruk, in southern Mesopotamia. Probably invented by Sumerian accountants as a mnemonic device, it was a system of pictographic signs depicting concrete objects—that is, logograms, or word signs. [*See* Sumerian.] (The $, or dollar sign, used to express the idea of "dollar" is a logogram.) Because it is inherently brief, a pure logographic system lacks the flexibility to reproduce visually the subtleties of language—the ultimate object of writing. Ancient scribes realized this limitation and very early on introduced the phoneticization of writing by depicting syllables, which are called syllabograms. For instance, they would take a logogram such as the original pictographic star-shaped *AN*—meaning "star," "heaven," and "god"—and read it as the syllable *an,* unrelated to the word sign. This is an early application of the rebus principle whereby an object is depicted whose name has the same sound as in the words represented (e.g. two gates and a head = "gateshead"). They could thus reproduce any word phonetically—whether it was a concrete object, a personal name, or a verb. Actually, the conservative Mesopotamian literati chose to write in a combination logosyllabic system, including class determinatives and phonetic complements, comprising a total of about six hundred signs. (Only two hundred or so signs would have been used by any one scribe at any one time, however.) [*See* Writing and Writing Systems; Scribes and Scribal Techniques.]

The external form of the signs evolved from the initial pictograph into a stylized linear representation. With the widespread use of soft clay as a writing surface in Mesopotamia, the signs were reproduced by a prism-shaped split reed that created the wedged-shaped signs now called cuneiform. [*See* Writing Materials; Cuneiform.] These signs evolved over a period of three thousand years, becoming the hallmark of Mesopotamian culture and influence.

The idea of writing in both its essence as a logosyllabic system and in its external form as a pictograph and then in cuneiform had a profound effect on all types of writing in the ancient Near East. It stimulated Egyptian hieroglyphic writing (literally "sacred carvings"), which dates to about 3000 BCE, and its adaptation into linear hieratic, as well as Proto-Elamite. [*See* Hieroglyphs; Egyptian.] The Sumerian system was used to write other languages, such as Akkadian (Babylonian and Assyrian) and Hittite. [*See* Akkadian; Hittite.] The prestige and influence of cuneiform script is apparent in its adoption in Ugarit and Canaan between about 1400–1200 BCE for their innovative alphabetic scripts and in its use in representing the syllabic script of Old Persian, devised in about 520 BCE in the time of Darius the Great. [*See* Ugaritic; Proto-Canaanite; Phoenician-Punic; Persian.]

Scribes. The evolution of writing in ancient Mesopotamia, and the parallel development of ancient Egyptian scripts and their influence in the contemporary Near East, reflects the growing stature and organization of the scribal class in antiquity. Scribes set the standard and defined literacy in its institutionalized form in the school and at court. By the second millennium BCE, they had created a canon of literature that exemplified the great civilizations of Mesopotamia and Egypt and established a code of ethics for the professional scribe. The sum total of their studies, station in society, and literary productivity might aptly be called scribal culture (Oppenheim, 1964, chap. 5; Hallo, 1991).

The literature (and iconography) of both Mesopotamia and Egypt describe that form of limited literacy that characterized the specific professional class holding the monopoly on writing. While there were differences in language and scripts, the literati of these two great civilizations shared many traits, among them a position of authority and respect, an education, and a conservative and elitist ideology regarding their literate status and privileged position in society and in the eyes of their patron deities.

Already in the Ur III (c. 2110–2000 BCE) and Old Babylonian (nineteenth–eighteenth centuries BCE) periods, scribal schools attracted the sons of the aristocracy and high administration, thus maintaining the profession's privileged status. The children studied in the *edubba,* "the tablet house." The headmaster was the *adda edubba,* or "father of the tablet house," sometimes called the *ummia* > *ummānu,* or "master." In the hierarchy of the school could be found the disciplinarian *(ugula),* the teacher's helper or aid (*sheshgal*—i.e., "the big brother"), and the teachers of the various subjects the *dumu edubba,* "the son of the tablet house," would learn.

The tens of thousands of documents written in cuneiform and in Egyptian hieroglyphics and in hieratic scripts are the output of the scribal class, a small percentage of their respective societies. John Baines (1983) has estimated that in ancient Egypt the scribal class numbered between 2 and 5 percent of the total population. In addition to the light shed by iconographic and archeological data, most of what is known about these ancient civilizations is derived from and shaped by the work of the scribe.

By the end of the third millennium, a considerable body of literature had come into being in Mesopotamia that was soon incorporated into the curriculum of the Sumerian schools. [*See* Sumerian.] These texts were studied and recopied, forming the basis of a canon. Mesopotamian scribal culture was to become bilingual. At the end of the second millennium BCE, when Sumerian ceased to be a spoken language and was replaced by Akkadian, it continued, much like Latin in the Middle Ages, to be taught, spoken, and even written in scribal schools.

In addition to belles lettres, the written scholarly output included lists of legal phraseology and formulae, linguistic material and encyclopedic data, and *omnia compendia* (collections of unusual natural phenomena). At a later period, mathematics and astronomy texts became more common. Letters and contracts were the scribes' main fare.

The privileged status of the scribes is one of the central themes in the school texts of Mesopotamia and Egypt. The theme was obviously a pedagogic device to support the student through the many required years of tedious study, drill, and discipline. It inculcated the idea of elitism and pride in a profession that claimed immortality in addition to the benefits of this world. One of the best-known texts is the Egyptian composition "In Praise of Learned Scribes":

> As for those learned scribes from the time of those who lived after the gods . . . their names have become everlasting, (even though) they are gone . . . they made heirs for themselves in the writings and in the (books of) wisdom which they composed. They gave themselves [the papyrus roll as a lector] priest, the writing board as a son-he-loves, (books of) wisdom (as) their pyramids, the reed pen their child and the back of a stone for a wife. From great to small were made into his children . . . their names are pronounced because of their books which they made, since they were good and the memory of him who made them (lasts) to the limits of eternity. Be a scribe, put it in your heart, that thy name may fare similarly. More effective is a book than a decorated tombstone or an established tomb wall. . . . It is better than a (well-) founded castle or a stela in a temple" (*ANET,* pp. 431–432).

A Babylonian scribe of the mid-second millennium BCE would probably have felt at home in any number of scribal centers throughout Mesopotamia, Syria, Canaan, and even Egypt. For example, the el-Amarna archive, which contains the diplomatic correspondence of the Egyptian court of the early fourteenth century BCE, as well as some literary and scholarly texts, was written in cuneiform, in the Middle Babylonian dialect, in Akkadian. Half of these letters were from the Canaanite vassal states whose local scribes struggled with the lingua franca. [*See* Amarna Tablets.] Judging from the cuneiform texts found at Canaanite sites, local scribes received a classical, albeit provincial, education.

In ancient Egypt the scribal school, called the *ʿt n sb3* > *ansebe,* composed many texts that made up the curriculum (including wisdom literature and onomastica) that opened with the key word *sb3yt,* "instructions." A scriptorium could be found adjoining the temple that bore the significant name *pr ʿnḫ* "the house of life."

There is no real proof for widespread literacy in these great civilizations. At different times, there may have been more literati or greater interest in writing and its benefits. In the Old Babylonian period, for example, an increased number of documents is indicated, especially personal ones, such as letters. In addition, in the Old Assyrian period, an attempt was made to reduce the number of signs to a more manageable hundred or so.

It is noteworthy that in Mesopotamia's long history only three kings claimed literacy: Shulgi of Ur (2094–2047 BCE), who was praised as the ideal king; Lipit-Ishtar (1953–1924 BCE) of Isin, known also as a legislator; and Ashurbanipal (668–627 BCE), a king of Assyria. The first two were praised for their patronage of the scribal schools, and the last was renown for his extensive library, discovered at Nineveh. [*See* Nineveh.] Whatever their real expertise in reading and writing cuneiform, their claim is to have mastered the scribal art and education. Writing never became a prerequisite for kingship or its idealization, as we find in Israel (*Dt.* 17:18–19). Ashurbanipal declared on a tablet:

> The profession of Adapa I learned, the hidden treasure of all the scribal art. I studied the signs of heaven and earth, I argued matters in the assembly of the wise. I discussed (the series) *Šumma Amut Matlat Šame* ("if the liver reflects the heavens") with the scholars. I solved difficult (problems) of division and multiplication that had no solution. I read the artistic script of Sumer and Akkadian writing which is difficult to understand. I collated the sealed, dark, and confused antediluvian inscriptions on stone (D. D. Luckenbill, *Ancient Records of Assyria and Babylonia,* Chicago, 1926–1927, vol. 2, pp. 378–379).

On the other hand, in Egypt the princes seem to have received scribal training. The early Prophesy of Neferti, dated to the Middle Kingdom (c. 1970–1750), narrates how pharaoh "extended his hand to the scribe's case and withdrew for himself a papyrus scroll and a scribal ink board. Then he wrote that which he was told by the lector-priest Neferti" (*ANET,* p. 444). The kings take a prominent place in wisdom literature. For instance, the tenth-dynasty king Merikare in his "Instructions" to his son said, "Do not kill a man when thou knowest his good qualities, one with whom thou once didst sing the writings . . ." (*ANET,* p. 415).

The uses of writing in the civilizations of the ancient Near East, according to A. Leo Oppenheim (1964, pp. 230ff.), fall into three categories: (1) Recording data for future use—administrative records, legal codification, sacred lore (myths, rituals, and local theology), royal annals (historic inscriptions and chronologies), and scholarly data and documentation; (2) communicating data on a synchronic level—letters, royal edicts, public announcements, and school texts and exercises; and (3) ceremonial purposes (documents not meant for human eyes)—Egyptian mortuary texts, cuneiform foundation inscriptions, monumental engravings on mountainsides (e.g., the Bisitun trilingual inscription), letters to the gods, magical writs and incantations on amulets and bowls, and execration texts for sympathetic magic. [*See* Bisitun.] From this catalog it is possible to conclude that the literary productivity of these great civilizations was turned inward—that is, it was meant for the use, education, and enjoyment of the scribal class exclusively. When indeed they felt they should have a wider audience, the scribes created a divine readership, as some of the above ceremonial inscriptions indicate.

Exacting methods of copying texts, the difficulty in acquiring and mastering the use and preparation of the different writing surfaces and implements, and the storing of texts in libraries and archives did not allow for widespread literacy in those ancient societies. Colophons are an important source for understanding scribal practice. Very often the writer added *kima labirshu shaṭirma bari,* "according to its original, it was written and checked." The Ashurbanipal library colophon was *shaṭir shaniq bari,* "written, collated, and checked." Sometimes, the amanuensis would emphasize his source by noting *ki pi ummani,* "dictated by the master," or *ki pi tuppi qabari shaṭir,* "copied from an old text."

On the basis of the literary output and the learned methods of transmission and preservation of these texts, it appears that literacy in these societies was limited to the professional scribes. While there are other examples of limited literacy, as in second-millennium BCE Mycenaean Greece, where Linear B was used for administrative purposes, ancient Mesopotamia and Egypt produced the scribal culture that shaped the entire ancient Near East.

Alphabet. The Canaanite invention of the alphabet in the first half of the second millennium BCE was the most important development in the history of writing since its inception and phonetization, as well as in the spread of literacy in antiquity (for strictures on the use of the term *alphabet* to describe the Canaanite invention, see Gelb, 1963). For more than five hundred years, it evolved from an almost completely pictographic script to a standardized linear signary, conventionally written from right to left. It became the official medium of writing in the emerging Northwest Semitic societies of the Early Iron Age. By the end of the seventh century BCE, the alphabet had become the dominant script of the ancient Near East and literate Mediterranean. The social and cultural consequences of its spread were manifold, ultimately leading to greater popular literacy and the democratization of higher culture.

In essence, the "alphabetic revolution" was the radical reduction of writing from a system of hundreds of logographic and syllabic signs to that of between twenty-two and thirty consonants, according to the phonetic inventory of the language being written. The conception of the alphabet was based on a sophisticated analysis of the phonemic system of Canaanite. Each phoneme received an appropriate sign that was originally a pictograph, for which it was named. In other words, as Alan H. Gardiner assumes, the letter names originally represented a word beginning with that particular phoneme, which he calls the acrophonic principle. For example, the bucranium, or ox head, is called *'alf,* "ox" in Canaanite, and represents the initial phoneme *'a.* Similarly, *bet,* "house," represents the sound *b.* Gardiner demonstrates this principle in his decipherment of the Proto-Sinaitic inscriptions found in and around the turquoise mines of Serabit el-Khadem in southern Sinai. He interprets four recurrent signs as *bʿlt,* "lady," a plausible Canaanite epithet for the Egyptian goddess Hathor, "the lady (of turquoise)," worshipped at that site. The acrophonic principle suggests that not only the letter forms, but their names, are intrinsic aspects of the invention of the alphabet. In fact, an abecedary found at Ugarit from the fourteenth century BCE, interpreted by Frank M. Cross and Thomas O. Lambdin (1960) as listing Babylonian syllabic equivalents, supports the contention that the alphabetic letter names are at least that old.

From the epigraphic evidence, it must be assumed that the alphabet was conceived in Canaanite scribal circles in the first half of the second millennium BCE. The earliest alphabetic texts seem to have been found at Gezer, Lachish, and Shechem (seventeenth century BCE). [*See* Gezer; Lachish; Shechem.] Even the above-mentioned Proto-Sinaitic script (which some date to the fifteenth century BCE) was probably written by Canaanite merchants (not slaves) or their secretaries, who had set up camp at the mines. The Canaanite genius who invented the alphabet was probably familiar with several systems of writing—the Egyptian having the greatest influence on his choice of the consonantal values of the signs and some of the hieroglyphic forms he adopted.

The invention of the alphabet seems to be the result of deliberate reflective thought on how to improve upon an existing technique. As Alan R. Millard suggests, the discovery "required thorough analysis of the phonemic stock of his language, an analysis perhaps facilitated by the common practice of listing words as part of school training" (Millard, 1986, p. 394).

Very early on, a set order of the letters was established accompanied by a mnemonic song facilitating the learning process and easy dissemination of the alphabet. Actually, there were two basic orders of the alphabetic letters. The first is the *abecedarium* in all its variations. The earliest examples are the thirty-letter Ugaritic alphabet written in cuneiform; then the reduced twenty-two linear Canaanite alphabet that became the source through Greek and Latin for all the European alphabets and via Aramaic to the scripts of the East—not the least important being the alphabet of classical Arabic. The latter, while rearranged according to external form and supplemented with diacritically differentiated identical signs, is still taught as the *abjedhawa,* recalling the first six letters of the Old Canaanite abecedary.

The second system for ordering the letters is generally called the South Semitic alphabet of twenty-eight letters: h l ḥ m q w š r ġ/b t s k n kh ś f ʼ ʻ ḍ g d b/ġ ṭ z ḏ y ṯ ṣ/ẓ. This order is known from Geʻez and seems to have come originally to Ethiopia by way of South Arabia, where it was used as a means of writing local dialects. A. G. Lunden (1987) discovered this order in a Canaanite cuneiform tablet dated to the thirteenth century BCE from the excavations at Beth-Shemesh in the 1930s. [*See* Beth-Shemesh.] It now becomes apparent that there were at least two basic patterns of ordering the letters of the alphabet in ancient Canaan. For whatever reason, the *ABC* order was preferred over the *HLḤM* order that moved to the periphery of the Semitic world. These innovations in education and communication were introduced by and meant for a very conservative body of professionals, heirs to a tradition of writing fifteen hundred years old. [*See* Alphabet.]

Two Patterns of Literacy. Two basic patterns of literacy existed in the ancient Near East. The predominant form was the limited literacy of the highly trained professional scribes in the main cultural and political centers of Mesopotamia and Egypt and their satellites. Redefining a term introduced by Henri I. Marrou (1956), this form of literacy can be called scribal culture. The second form is the one found in the emerging literate societies—Iron Age Syria, Phoenicia, ancient Israel, and classical Greece—where simple reading and writing skills were learned by laymen employing the local alphabetic scripts. No doubt there was contact and influence between the bearers of both types of culture. It is the former pattern that has left most of the written evidence, indicating greater influence in areas of formal education and defining the categories of "wisdom." Belonging to the restricted "scribal culture" meant not only mastering the techniques of writing, but also learning the rudiments of such subjects as mathematics, astronomy, and engineering, as well as imbibing an esprit de corps of the literati. However, it was the second pattern that ultimately triumphed, inheriting its cultural legacy and becoming the medium that shaped classical antiquity.

Much of the discussion regarding popular literacy and its diffusion and measurement has centered around ancient Israel. This is because of the variety and quality of the literary and epigraphic sources. The Bible, in particular, reflecting a period of some thousand years of Israelite history, remains a basic source for the study of alphabetic literacy. Even so, because of the objective problem of defining *literacy* in antiquity, there is a wide difference of scholarly opinion on the matter. For instance, is literacy the ability to read and write—or just one of them? What level of expertise constitutes "literacy": writing or reading one's name, a simple sentence, or a complex document? Is there a means to determine a gradation in the ability to write that would distinguish between a professional scribal hand, a layman's script, a craftsman's markings, and graffiti in a vulgar style? How can widespread literacy as a social phenomenon be measured? The nature of the problem is that there are variables in the level and extent of literacy in every society. In other words, the problem is methodological because there are no direct, absolute, or objective criteria for defining and measuring broad-based literacy prior to the Industrial Revolution, let alone for antiquity.

Furthermore, regarding ancient Israel, subjective issues have been raised by different disciplines of research regarding the historicity of the Bible and its transmission and the value of epigraphic evidence and paleography to answer social and cultural historical questions. For instance, Swedish scholars identified with the Uppsala school of biblical research claim that the Bible, for the most part, was composed orally and only later, in reaction to the national tragedy of the Exile, was put into writing: thus, in the First Commonwealth period, except for a limited number of scribal administrators, the population would have been illiterate (Engnell, 1969). However, some paleographers claim hard evidence for widespread literacy during the period of the monarchy (Millard, 1985). It has become increasingly clear that research on the topic must synthesize literary and epigraphic evidence. Issues of composition, transmission, and publication of ancient texts and the typology of formal and occasional inscriptions must be placed in a social context that fits the historical developments of that period of antiquity (Demsky, 1985, 1988).

An attempt in that direction is visible in studies of school and education systems in ancient Israel. There is literary and epigraphic evidence of some formal education for scribes, priests, royalty, women, artisans, and laity (Demsky, 1971). However, it is not clear whether there were actual educational institutions like the Mesopotamian *edubba* or more informal settings like the home or workshop. There is no biblical word for *school.* The term *bēt-hassēfer*/*hassōfēr,* "the house of the book or of the teacher (scribe)," is Late Hebrew. For that matter, terms like *bēt-midrash* and *yeshivah* are found first in *Ben Sira* 51:23, 29, while *bēt migra* and *bēt talmud* for elementary and higher education are rabbinic.

Following Mesopotamian models, scholars have described the ancient Israelite school by reconstructing the supposed curriculum taught there on the basis of literary and epigraphic evidence. André Lemaire (1981) has gone to one extreme in finding schools throughout the country, while Menahem Haran (1988) has gone to the other extreme of denying their existence. There is no doubt that certain subjects made up a program of formal education—that the simpler the subject the more widespread its adaption. For instance, learning the letters of the alphabet by repetition of the abecedary and accompanying exercises was basic for a general urbanite's education. It would have been of particular use for artisans, who introduced writing into their craft—for which there is evidence from potters, ivory joiners, and builders.

It is of interest that the biblical term *yôdēʿa sēfer* and its opposite, *ʾašer lōʾ yôdēʿa sēfer,* within the prophetic context of *Isaiah* 29:11–12, are the only direct references to the ability to read in the Bible. The former has been translated "one who can read," or "a knower of a book," indicating a reasonable ability to read. This interpretation is seemingly confirmed by Lachish letter 3:8–10, in which a garrison commander is asked: *lōʾ yādaʿtâ qĕrōʾ sēfer,* "Don't you know how to read?" [*See* Lachish Inscriptions.] Actually, *yôdēʿa sēfer* means "to know writ" (Bib. Heb., *sēfer* = Late Heb. and Aram., *ktāb*), implying that with some knowledge of writing it is also possible to read. This Hebrew term for minimal literacy should be compared to the internationally well-known terms for professional scribes: *sōfēr* (Ugar./Phoe., *spr;* Aram., *sāfar*), *šoṭer* (Akk., *šaṭaru*), or *ṭifsar* (Assyr., *ṭupsarru;* Sum., *dup.šar*). Not only a basic knowledge of writing seems to have been common in Israelite urban centers from the eighth century BCE onward, but also some understanding of elementary arithmetic and the ability to inscribe numbers (*Is.* 10:19).

Spread of Literacy. The factors that influence such a complex aspect of life as written communication and the storage of data affect all levels of society to different degrees. This was true in antiquity as well. There factors probably act in concert: the technical innovation of an alphabetic script; changes in the power structure in society; and the degree of motivation in some societies to attempt to change their world.

An alphabet of no more than thirty signs that can be learned in a matter of days—as opposed to a writing system of hundreds of logosyllabic signs, each of which may have multiple values—would, seemingly, allow for wider literacy. However, there were periods of illiteracy or semiliteracy in societies in which the alphabet was used: in Medieval Europe and, as H. C. Youttie (1973) has shown, in Hellenistic-Roman Egypt. On the other hand, when there is high motivation or centralized government control, the masses can learn an even more complex system, as the modern Chinese have proven.

The second factor is social: if there are interest groups that find it necessary, for self-preservation, to prevent or forestall innovations in the field of literacy or communication, there will be limited literacy. For example, from the dual system of administration at the beginning of the Assyrian Empire (end of the eighth century BCE), the iconographic motif found on royal stelae and in wall paintings is of two scribes—the Assyrian *ša zigni,* representing the conservative establishment and writing in cuneiform, and the Aramaic eunuch, the *ša reši,* standing behind him writing his innovative alphabetic script on a leather scroll. This dual system is further corroborated by contemporary Aramaic notations on cuneiform tablets. Of course, the opposite can also occur. The retreat of the great empires from Syria and Canaan in the thirteenth century BCE left a void in administrative methods and staff. The new peoples, like the Arameans and Israelites, had no comparable scribal tradition or organization. As a result, their leaders readily adopted and encouraged the rapid development of the local Canaanite alphabet. This brought about the standardization of the script, of the direction of writing, and of letter stance and order. It did not take long before they recognized the advantages of this medium to store and recall information (see *Jgs.* 8:14).

The third factor in the spread of literacy is motivation—a drive to control or influence people politically, economically, or religiously through the written word, even within the same ethnic, religious, or national community. The Assyrians realized that in order to succeed in asserting administrative control over their newly established empire (745–611 BCE) and in integrating its many conquered peoples it was wise to adopt the Aramaic language and its written medium, the utilitarian alphabet. Aramaic dialects were spoken widely throughout Syria, parts of Anatolia, and as far as south Chaldean Babylon. After the destruction of Aram Damascus in 732 BCE, the last and strongest independent Aramean kingdom, the Aramaic language was free of national ties and local culture. It became the *Reichsprach,* a most unusual example of a conquered people's language becoming an instrument of the conqueror in empire building. Besides its obvious advantages—many speakers, grammatical simplicity, and no national and geographic ties—Imperial Aramaic had its own facile and utilitarian script that was quickly adopted along with an unemployed professional scribal class. It was under the Neo-Babylonians (609–539 BCE) and Persians (539–333 BCE) that Aramaic became the lingua franca of the ancient Near East and its script the medium of government and civilian life. [*See* Aramaic Language and Literature.]

An example of what may be the economic motivation in the spread of writing might be found in the history of the Phoenicians, those great entrepreneurs who traded off the products of one land for those of another (cf. *Ez.* 27). Egypt, a major client, supplied them with sundry raw materials and goods, among which was papyrus. [*See* Papyrus.] It was probably through Byblos (Phoen., Gebal; Egyp., Keben), which had the longest-standing business relationship with Egypt, that the potential of exporting papyrus throughout the Mediterranean lands was realized (recounted in the early eleventh-century BCE "Journey of Wenamun to Phoenicia," *ANET,* pp. 25–29). However, the market for papyrus as a writing surface had to be created. Perhaps it was this economic need that motivated the Phoenicians to introduce and teach their own Canaanite alphabet as well. It certainly was not for political or religious reasons that it was spread throughout the Mediterranean lands. Herodotus (5.58) in the fifth century BCE, defined the boundaries between the civilized world and the barbarians by who wrote on papyrus (the former) and who on animal skin (the latter). It is worth noting that the Greek word for *book, biblion,* and its cognates in the European languages are derived from the place name *Byblos.* [*See* Byblos.]

There is no need to prove the Greeks' indebtedness to the Phoenicians for their *alpha-beta,* attributed by some to Cadmus (i.e., *qedem,* "the easterner"), who took up residence in mainland Thebes. Opinions differ widely about when this borrowing of the Canaanite alphabet occurred. Joseph Naveh (1987) has proposed an early, eleventh-century BCE date on the basis of comparative paleography. Rhys Carpenter and L. H. Jeffery (1961) argue for an early seventh-century BCE date, with the earliest datable Greek epigraphy. Indeed, there may have been several channels of influence, spread over a long period. However, it seems that the best contact was within the historical framework of the early tenth century BCE and the beginning of Phoenician colonization of the western Mediterranean. [*See* Phoenicians.]

An established religion, especially one using an alphabetic script, can be a catalyst in the spread of literacy. This becomes more obvious with the advent of Israelite monotheism, where, to rephrase Jack R. Goody (1986), there is an intrinsic connection between its features and the literate modes in which its beliefs and behavior are formulated, communicated, and transmitted. Biblical monotheism is characterized by the cardinal belief in the deity who reveals his will through an inscription on stone and in a scroll using the literary form of a vassal covenant to express his special relationship to his chosen people, Israel. This covenant is to be read publically every seven years before all men, women, and children (*Dt.* 31:10–31) in what seems to be the first recorded case of religious education for the masses. It is no wonder that Ezra, in the mid-fifth century BCE, used this commandment as his model for the public Torah reading that would become the centerpiece of synagogue worship (*Neh.* 8:1ff.). The Torah even became the symbol of the divine and the direct object of veneration (cf. *Ps.* 119, esp. verse 48). [*See* Hebrew Language and Literature.]

By the mid-eighth century BCE, apostolic prophets were commanded to write down their message for the sake of communicating it to the masses (e.g., *Is.* 8:1; *Jer.* 29:1, 36:2; *Ez.* 37:16) or as a means to safeguard it for future generations (e.g., *Is.* 30:8; *Jer.* 30:2–3, 32:10ff.). These are the "writing prophets"—beginning with Amos, Hosea, Isaiah, and Micah—and they continue down to the mid-fifth century BCE, with the last of the classical prophets—Haggai, Zechariah, and Malachi. These prophets use various literate means to enhance and publicize their message, a sure sign that their urban audience appreciated and understood this method of instruction. For example, in order to hold his listeners' attention, Jeremiah (25:26, 51:1, 41) introduces the *atbash* exercise familiar to all beginners (in which, after having learned the order of the letters, the student matches letters from opposite ends of the alphabet, e.g., the first [*'aleph*] with the last [*taw*], the second [*beth*] with the next to last [*shin*], etc.). Nahum resorts to an alphabetic acrostic (1:2ff.) familiar from late biblical poetry, and Zechariah (6:10, 14) plays on an alphabetic mnemonic for storing information. Thus, in ancient Israel it seems that writing was an integral part of the religious experience.

This is not to say that writing was absent from pagan religions. The ancient scribes regarded writing like the other arts, as the invention of the gods. The Sumerian Nisaba, the Babylonian Nabu, and the Egyptian Thoth were the patron deities of the scribal profession and assigned similar roles in the divine assembly. Books of wisdom and esoteric divination were attributed to various deities. The idea of the heavenly Tablet of Destiny, the *ṭup šimati,* where all creation's fate was recorded, is a recurrent motif in Mesopotamian mythology. In the second-millennium BCE *Enuma elish,* the Babylonian story of creation, Tiamat empowers her second consort, Kingu, by presenting him with the Tablet of Destiny. For the Mesopotamian literati, this motif reflects belief in the primordial existence and the efficacy of the written word. In fact, the *Sitz im Leben* of the creation epic is in its being read by the high priest in the inner sanctum before the statue of Marduk on the fourth day of the Akitu new year festival. This literate aspect of cult no doubt superceded an oral dramatic presentation of the myth and reflects the growing influence of the scribal community even in matters of religion.

A closer comparison of the differences between how Mesopotamian paganism used cuneiform writing and how Israelite monotheism applied the alphabet demonstrates the nature of religion as a catalyst for the spread of literacy. In Babylon, the creation story is about the deeds of Marduk. Its private reading is intended to remind the deity of his duties toward the world in subduing the forces of chaos. Although there is no evidence for how widely the text was known, it certainly was not meant for mass consumption. Cuneiform writing in general is a closed and secret art turned inward upon the scribal class. Similarly, the Tablet of Destiny remains a figment of mythic imagination.

In Israel, conversely, the Torah, or a portion thereof, was to be read publicly before the entire populace every seven years. The text is meant for the edification of all the people and not for initiates alone. It is turned outward. Biblical monotheism is a national religion. The Sinai theophany is described as a public experience and the text is meant to preserve its memory in the literary form of a covenant (*Dt.* 29:13–14). Not only the public reading of the text, but also its private and communal study (*Ps.* 1:2, 19:8ff., 119; *Neh.* 8:13ff.) became religious values for the laity, stimulating the further desemination of the written word and the spread of literacy. Private schools (*Eccl.* 12:9f.; *Ben Sira* 51:23ff.; *Avot* 1:4) and, later, public schools established by Shim'on ben Shetah (c. 100 BCE) and by the high priest Joshua ben Gamla (B.T., *B.B.* 21a) are not secular; they are, rather, institutions for religious instruction (cf. B.T. *Shab.* 104a).

Furthermore, for comparison's sake, the description of the Tablets of the Covenant, written by the finger of God, avoids the introduction of divine mythic writing implements (*Ex.* 32:15f.; 34:1). Moses even shapes the stone writing surface of the second set of tablets. While preserved beyond the view of the populace, they did have a direct obvious influence on the architecture of the desert sanctuary and the Jerusalem Temples, and that influence is felt to this day in the layout of the traditional synagogue and the place of the holy ark. [*See* Synagogues.]

The idea of a revealed written document is so closely associated with the essence of historical monotheism and its mission that Christianity and Islam were able to compete with the authority of the Mosaic Torah only by replacing it with the belief in another superior divinely revealed work. The "holy" is found in Scripture and in the technique of writing and not in nature, as paganism would have it. Literate terms are central to the self-identification of the monotheistic faiths. Early Christianity (as well as the Dead Sea covenanters) borrowed Jeremiah's prophesy of the "new covenant/testament" to be written upon the heart (*Jer.* 31:30ff.) and concretized it into a corpus of naratives, missives, and apocalyptic revelations recorded in the Greek koine. Breaking with tradition, not only in regard to the languages of revelation (Hebrew and Aramaic), but also in abandoning the cumbersome scroll for the compact and portable codex, Christianity's message could now reach out to a wider audience of Greek-speaking Jews and gentiles, heirs to the Hellenistic education that set the standard for literacy in antiquity (Marrou, 1956; Innes, 1950).

Islam's *al-Qur'an,* "the reading/recitation," revealed by the archangel Gabriel (cf. *Dn.* 9:21ff.), was in a language that had almost no written tradition prior to that time. Subsequently, the Arabic of the holy writ would become the model for literate expression. Marking this turning point, the Qur'an proclaims Muhammad "the seal of the prophets" (38.40)—the capstone of all earlier written revelation. Especially noteworthy is the coining of the generic term for members of the monotheistic religions, in particular Judaism, as *'Ahl al-Kitab,* "the people of the book." [*See* Arabic.]

This survey of the history of literacy in the ancient Near East from the end of the fourth millennium BCE until the advent of Islam in the first half of the seventh century CE has touched on great cultural achievements not only in the realm of communication, education, and the storage of information, but also in the areas of politics, government administration, and economics—not to mention established religion. The study of literacy during the first half of this period is primarily the attempt to understand the art of writing as learned and practiced by a limited professional scribal class and how it spread throughout the ancient Near East. For the latter half of this period—beginning in the first millennium BCE—momentous social and religious developments are documented that indicate the gradual democratization of higher literary culture and the formation of literate societies in which laymen and artisans could read and write. It is a period when Mosaic monotheism is integrally associated with a holy book leaving its indelible impression on the formative stages of Christianity and Islam. One of the consequences of these literary developments was the creation of an institutionalized religious service around the public reading and exposition of that holy text. Commentary and translation of the revealed book further encouraged the dissemination of literature culture to the masses in antiquity.

BIBLIOGRAPHY

Baines, John. "Literacy and Ancient Egyptian Society." *Man* 18 (1983): 572–599.

Černý, Jaroslav. *Paper and Books in Ancient Egypt.* London, 1952.

Cross, Frank Moore, and Thomas O. Lambdin. "A Ugaritic Abecedary and the Origins of the Proto-Canaanite Alphabet." *Bulletin of the American Schools of Oriental Research,* no. 160 (1960): 21–26.

Demsky, Aaron. "Education in the Biblical Period." *Encyclopedia Judaica,* vol. 6, cols. 382–398. Jerusalem, 1971.

Demsky, Aaron. "On the Extent of Literacy in Ancient Israel." In *Biblical Archaeology Today: Proceedings of the International Congress on*

Biblical Archaeology, Jerusalem, April 1984, edited by Janet Amitai, pp. 349–353. Jerusalem, 1985.

Demsky, Aaron, and Me'ir Bar-Ilan. "Writing in Ancient Israel and Early Judaism." In *Mikra: Text, Translation, Reading, and Interpretation of the Hebrew Bible in Ancient Judaism and Early Christianity,* edited by M. J. Mulder, pp. 1–38. Philadelphia, 1988.

Demsky, Aaron. "The Education of Canaanite Scribes in the Mesopotamian Cuneiform Tradition." *Bar Ilan Assyriological Studies* 1 (1990): 157–170.

Driver, Godfrey R. *Semitic Writing: From Pictograph to Alphabet.* 3d ed. London, 1976.

Engnell, Ivan. *A Rigid Scrutiny.* Nashville, 1969.

Gardiner, Alan H. "The Egyptian Origin of the Semitic Alphabet." *Journal of Egyptian Archaeology* 3 (1916): 1–16.

Gelb, Ignace J. *A Study of Writing.* 2d ed. Chicago and London, 1963.

Goody, Jack, ed. *Literacy in Traditional Societies.* Cambridge, 1968.

Goody, Jack. *The Logic of Writing and the Organization of Society.* Cambridge, 1986.

Hallo, William W. "Isaiah 28:9–13 and the Ugaritic Abecedaries." *Journal of Biblical Literature* 77 (1958): 324–338.

Hallo, William W. "The Concept of Canonicity in Cuneiform and Biblical Literature: A Comparative Appraisal." In *The Biblical Canon in Comparative Perspective,* edited by K. L. Younger, Jr., William W. Hallo, and B. F. Batto. Scripture in Context, 4. Lewiston, 1991.

Haran, Menahem. "On the Diffusion of Literacy and Schools in Ancient Israel." *Supplements to Vetus Testamentum* 40 (1988): 81–95.

Harris, William V. *Ancient Literacy.* Cambridge, Mass., 1989.

Hunger, Hermann. *Babylonische und Assyrische Kolophone.* Alter Orient und Altes Testament, 2. Kevelaer, 1968.

Innes, Harold A. *Empire and Communication.* Oxford, 1950.

Jacobsen, Thorkild. "Mesopotamian Religious Literature and Mythology." In *The New Encyclopaedia Britannica,* 15th ed., vol. 11, pp. 1007–1012. Chicago, 1974.

Jeffery, L. H. *The Local Scripts of Archaic Greece.* Oxford, 1961.

Kramer, Samuel Noah. *The Sumerians: Their History, Culture, and Character.* Chicago, 1963.

Landsberger, Benno. "Scribal Concepts of Education." In *City Invincible: A Symposium on Urbanization and Cultural Development in the Ancient Near East,* edited by Carl H. Kraeling and Robert McC. Adams, pp. 94–123. Chicago, 1960.

Lemaire, André. *Les écoles et la formation de la Bible dans l'ancien Israël.* Fribourg, 1981.

Lunden [Loundine], A. G. "L'abécédaire de Beth Shemesh." *Le Muséon* 100 (1987): 243–250.

Marrou, Henri Irénée. *A History of Education in Antiquity.* New York, 1956.

Millard, A. R. "An Assessment of the Evidence for Writing in Ancient Israel." In *Biblical Archaeology Today: Proceedings of the International Congress on Biblical Archaeology, Jerusalem, April 1984,* edited by Janet Amitai, pp. 301–312. Jerusalem, 1985.

Millard, A. R. "The Infancy of the Alphabet." *World Archaeology* 17 (1986): 390–398.

Naveh, Joseph. *An Early History of the Alphabet.* 2d ed. Jerusalem and Leiden, 1987.

Oppenheim, A. Leo. *Ancient Mesopotamia: Portrait of a Dead Civilization.* Chicago, 1964.

Schmandt-Besserat, Denise. "Before Numerals." *Visible Language* 18 (1984): 48–60.

Youttie, H. C. "AGRAMMATOS: An Aspect of Greek Society in Egypt." *Scriptiunculae* 11 (1973): 611–627.

Youttie, H. C. "*Bradeos graphon:* Between Literacy and Illiteracy." *Scriptiunculae* 11 (1973): 629–651.

AARON DEMSKY

LITHICS. [*This entry surveys the history of stone artifacts with reference to the technologies used to create them, the uses to which they were put, and their overall role in the cultures and societies in which they figured. It comprises three articles:*

Typology and Technology
Artifacts of the Chalcolithic Period
Artifacts of the Bronze and Iron Ages

The first serves as an overview, providing a discussion of the importance of typology for identification purposes and the development of specific typologies. The other articles treat the artifacts of specific periods and regions.]

Typology and Technology

Stone tool manufacture is essentially a reduction process wherein a block of raw material is chipped and/or ground, either to a desired shape or to produce flakes that are further modified to a desired shape. The simplest techniques involve the splitting open of cobbles and the removal of a few flakes to produce a sharp cutting or chopping edge, with little attention paid to general morphology. More sophisticated core-reduction techniques involve preparing the core (the original block of raw material) such that the shape of the flakes is predetermined—for example, to points, blades, bladelets, and special flakes.

The removal of flakes (knapping, flaking) can be accomplished using several techniques: direct percussion—that is, a direct blow on the core using a hard (stone) or soft (antler, bone) hammer; indirect percussion—a blow applied to a punch placed in the desired point on the core; block-on-block and anvil techniques; and pressure techniques, such as a chest punch. Further modification (retouch), usually of flakes, can also be accomplished using several methods, most notably direct percussion and pressure retouch.

The preferred, although not exclusive, materials for stone chipping or knapping (the predominant mode of lithic manufacture in prehistoric times) were either amorphous (e.g., obsidian) or cryptocrystalline (e.g., flints, cherts, chalcedonies) in structure. These materials fracture conchoidally, and thus the shape and direction of the chippage can be controlled by the knapper. In contrast, crystalline (e.g., quartz) materials break along cleavage lines. Other advantages of these materials include hardness and sharpness. Beginning in the Late Epipaleolithic, and continuing through historic times, softer, more friable materials (e.g., limestone, dolomite, basalt, phosphorite, schist) were often exploited for various types of grinding stones and stone vessels, although harder materials (e.g., flint, granite) could also be used.

The products of lithic manufacture can be divided into two general classes, waste and tools. Tools are defined by the presence of retouch, or secondary modification, and not by assumed function. Unretouched pieces may indeed have

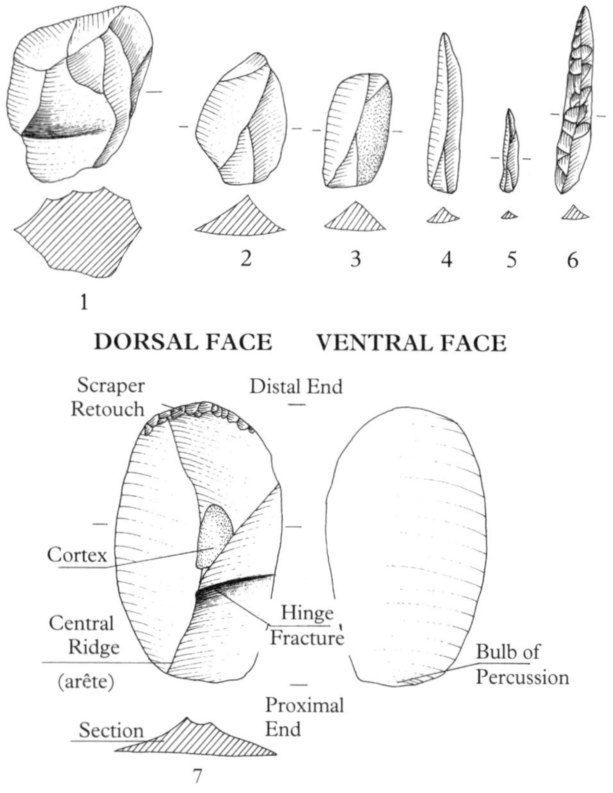

LITHICS: Typology and Technology. Figure 1. *Idealized lithic tool types and attributes.* (1) core; (2) flake; (3) primary flake, with cortex; (4) blade; (5) bladelet; (6) ridge-blade, core trimming element; (7) scraper and selected flake elements and attributes. (Courtesy S. A. Rosen)

been used. Waste products can be further divided into cores, amorphous debris, and debitage (flake products). Cores and some types of debitage, like tools, are often characteristic of specific cultural units. In general, waste provides information on modes of manufacture. Specific typologies for both waste and tools have been developed for different periods.

Scales of Analysis. On the most detailed level, analyses focus on microscopic edge wear and damage on stone tools in order to ascertain elements of function, such as direction of movement, intensity of utilization, or type of material worked. Experimental studies have suggested potential success rates as high as 80 percent for identifying some elements of function (Keeley, 1980). However, there has been debate over the efficacy of the method, given the nonpristine state of most lithic assemblages and the possibility of multiple uses.

Analyses of macroscopic attributes incorporate metric attributes such as length, width, thickness, and various angular measurements; nominal features such as type of striking platform, planar shape, or location of retouch; and presence/absence attributes, such as sickle gloss, edge retouch, and cortex. Attributes can be chosen to reflect specific factors so that, for example, edge angle is often assumed to reflect function (i.e., scraping versus cutting), whereas wings on arrowheads are usually assumed to be stylistic.

On the level of the artifact, virtually all scholars utilize various agreed-upon types, both waste and retouched tools, in order to expedite analysis. Types are assumed to represent intuitively obvious sets of covarying attributes. Debate exists over the legitimacy of specific tool types and whether they indeed represent types as recognized by early *Homo*. However, a more appropriate measure of their legitimacy is their analytic efficiency—whether they serve a reasonable archaeological goal. Types are usually organized in a hierarchical framework, with several levels of subtypes, and statistical attribute analyses may be conducted to subdivide the types further or to confirm their independent existence.

The assemblage (e.g., Clarke, 1978) is a higher unit of analysis consisting of the collection of artifacts from a physically definable location, usually from a specific stratum or substratum from an archaeological site, although conceivably from a specific locus within a site. In theory, assemblages should represent the final discard stage of the original lithic tool kit employed on the site (assuming little postdepositional disturbance). However, given the difficulties in defining the processes of discard, and the often disturbed nature of many assemblages, interpretation is not straightforward. The key point is that assemblages do not represent frozen or fossilized actions. In a large sense, they are the products of a multitude of actions, both cultural and noncultural, and reflect a range of factors. The classic debate over the interpretation of Mousterian (Middle Paleolithic) variability centered precisely over the issue of which factors dominated the formation of assemblages and the morphology of tool types.

Higher-level analyses involve the definition of "cultures," "industries," and "complexes," but precise definition of these terms has not been achieved. This is probably the result of both the inherent variability in sets of assemblages and the resulting problems in defining borders, as well as the difficulties of restricting normal English terms like *culture* and *industry* to very specific phenomena. Cultures are assumed to represent the equivalent of ethnographically definable tribes or groups and are reconstructed on the basis of what are assumed to be stylistically sensitive attributes, or types. Attempts to define cultures are often disputed by adducing functional or other explanations for the allegedly stylistic traits. Cultures are most easily definable in the later periods of prehistory, when tool standardization is such that regional and chronological variability are easily defined.

In essence, the first well-defined lithic cultures in the Near East occur in the Epipaleolithic—for example, the Natufian, Ḥarifian, and Negev Kebaran. Thus, several "complexes" have also been defined for the Epipaleolithic—the Kebaran complex, the Geometric Kebaran complex, and the Mushabian complex. Each is divided into several, often unnamed, clusters of assemblages that essentially correspond to cultures. In the case of the Epipaleolithic, the intermediate-level culture is definable; however, for earlier periods there is usually a jump from the assemblage to the complex or industry. This is primarily a consequence of the great variability inherent among assemblages, difficulties in chronology, and often, a relative scarcity of sites. Of course, it may also be that pre-*Homo sapiens sapiens* simply did not exhibit cultural behavior as it is presently recognized.

Causes of Variation. Variability in stone tool morphology, technology, and type frequencies in the archaeological record can be caused by any of a range of factors, either individually or in combination. These are reviewed briefly below.

Raw materials. Both the properties and availability of raw materials affect patterns of exploitation. For example, flint can be of coarse or fine grain, may show many or few impurities, and may come in different-sized nodules that are distributed unevenly over the landscape. Different flint chipping technologies (e.g., flakes, blades, bladelets) may require different qualities of raw material. The same is true of other raw materials, such as basalt and quartzite. Thus, in general, different periods, with different lithic technologies, show exploitation of different types of stone.

Access to and availability of raw materials play a role here. Quantitative variability in assemblage or industrial attributes may be a function of relative expense of acquisition of appropriate raw materials (e.g., Dibble, 1987). Patterns of trade and exchange may often be reconstructed through quantitative analysis of distributions of raw material and completed artifacts.

Function. The different functions of stone tools affect the nature of variation. Function may be reflected on a range of scales, from microscopic edge damage to the general configuration of tool kits. Different types of function can also be defined, so that beyond utilitarian use, stone tools may have subsidiary social and ideological functions. Obvious examples are ritual objects. Other social functions, particularly involving strengthening of group identity, may also obtain.

Style. Stylistic attributes are those that reflect nonutilitarian elements in the design of a stone tool. These may be decorative, or they may be reflected in the choice of different but equivalent technologies for the same utilitarian function. Style is often assumed to reflect ethnic tradition, and stylistic attributes are thus used to reconstruct various units of culture. There is clear overlap between style and socioideological functions.

Biological abilities. Technological evolution is also affected by developments in coordination and intellectual capabilities. Development of the precision grip in later hominids allowed for finer coordination and execution of the knapping process. The evolution of abstract thought is represented in the increasing symmetry of tools, the development of what appear to be paradigmatic types (e.g., handaxes), and in the generally increasing complexity of lithic technologies.

Archaeological biases and postdepositional processes. Biased collection techniques and the deliberate selection of special or supposedly diagnostic types can render assemblages noncomparable, as well as result in the loss of much information. Natural processes such as deflation and erosion can affect lithic analysis on several levels, from the presence of abrasion on individual artifacts to the disappearance of smaller artifacts as a result of natural sorting processes.

Chronological Overview. The following sections review briefly the general development of lithic technology from the first evidence for stone tool manufacture in the Near East up to the apparent final displacement of chipped stone implements in the Iron Age. Notably, ground stone implements and vessels continue in common use more or less up through recent times.

Lower Paleolithic. In the Levant, the Lower Paleolithic industries are core-tool and flake based; the core tools, especially bifaces, comprise the diagnostic elements. The presence of bifaces in virtually all Middle Pleistocene assemblages places the entire Levantine Lower Paleolithic in the Acheulean complex. At ʿUbeidiya (c. 1.4 million years ago) high proportions of chopping tools, spheroids, polyhedrons, and trihedrals among the bifaces distinguish the assemblage from the later Acheulean (Bar-Yosef, 1975).

Middle and Late Acheulean assemblages, such as from Berzine, Birkat Ram, ʿEmeq Rephaim, ʿEvron, Kissufim, Latamne, Maʿayan Baruch, Tabun, and Umm Qaṭafa show much higher proportions of handaxes. The site of Gesher Benot Yaʿaqob shows a significant addition of relatively numerous basalt cleavers to the lithic repertoire. Many of these sites are surface collections and/or were investigated early in the history of research and may reflect collection bias. In general, within the Acheulean there is a trend toward shorter and more finely manufactured bifaces (Gilead, 1970). In the Late Acheulean, the Levallois technique for specialized flake manufacture makes its first appearance.

Interpretation of trends and variability are problematic, especially given the difficulties of chronology in these early periods, and of collections from early excavations. However, given the immense time span of the Acheulean complex, and the fact of physical evolution during this period, it is likely that changes in physical and intellectual abilities played a major role, at least in the long-term trends. The cleavers at Gesher Benot Yaʿaqob have been interpreted by some, for example, Ofer Bar-Yosef, to reflect a direct connection to Africa.

Middle Paleolithic. The rise of diagnostic flake tools, especially those manufactured using Levallois technologies, and the concomitant decline and eventual disappearance of bifaces are the primary defining characteristics of the Middle Paleolithic (Copeland, 1975; Bordes, 1961). Two pre-Mousterian industries can be defined: the Yabrudian (including the Acheulo-Yabrudian) and the Pre-Aurignacian (ʿAmudian), found at Tabun, Yabrud, Zumoffen, Bezez, Zuttiyeh (Yabrudian only), and Masloukh (Yabrudian only). Many scholars place these industries in the terminal Acheulean or refer to them together as the Mugharan complex (Jelinek, 1982). The Yabrudian is a flake industry characterized especially by the presence of Quina-type scrapers (thick, canted, stepped retouch). Pre-Aurignacian assemblages, sometimes sandwiched between Yabrudian layers, are characterized by high proportions of blade tools and other "Upper Paleolithic" types (burins, endscrapers)—hence the name Pre-Aurignacian. Neither shows high Levallois indices.

The heavy use of the Levallois technique for the manufacture of flakes, blades, and points is the hallmark of the Mousterian in the Levant. A basic unilineal typological framework was established by Dorothy Garrod's (Tabun, Skhul, el-Wad) and René Neuville's (ʿErq el-Aḥmar, Abu Sif, Qafzeh) excavations. More recent excavations and studies at numerous sites (e.g., Ksar 'Akil, Kebara, Qafzeh, Tabun, Rosh ʿEin-Mor, Quneitra, Fara, Tirat ha-Carmel) have focused more on functional and technological questions. Assemblages have been viewed as tool kits, and groups of similar assemblages as functionally similar (Binford, 1986).

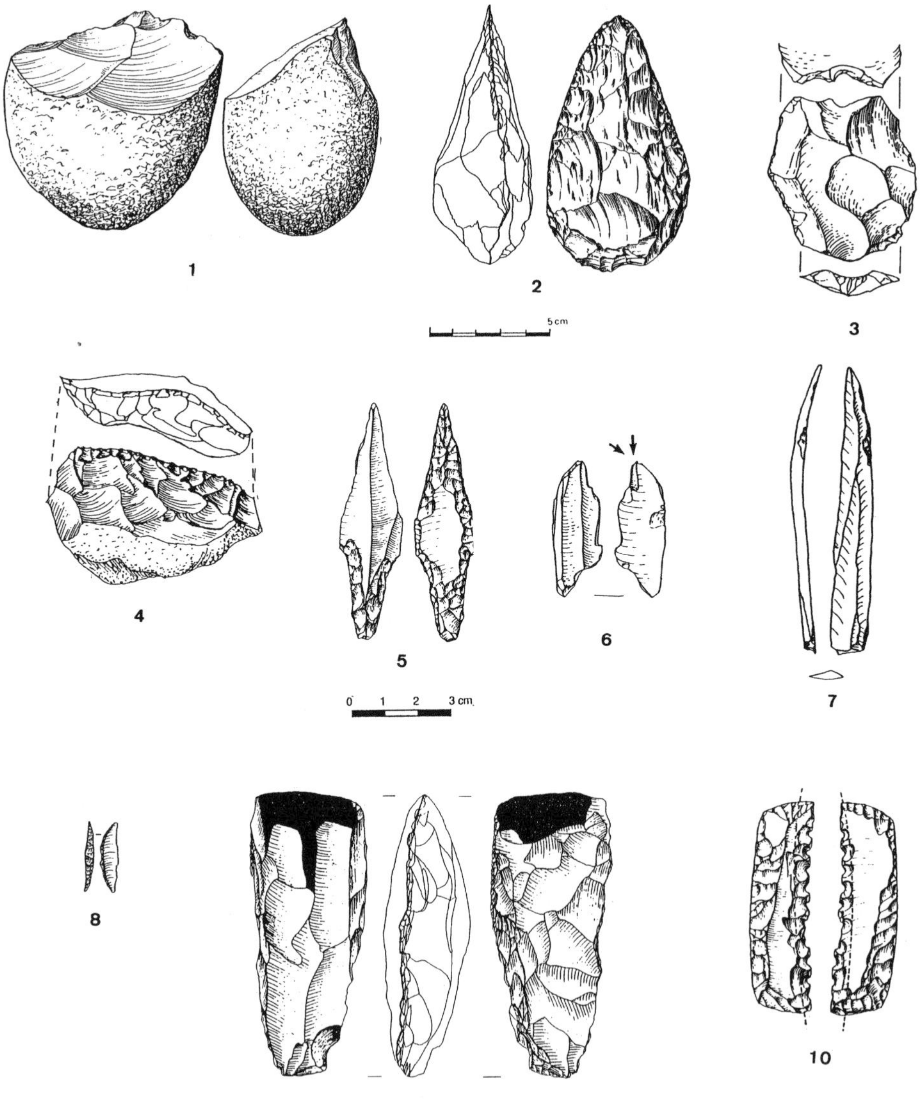

LITHICS: Typology and Technology. Figure 2. *Examples of lithic tools.* (1) chopping tool; (2) handaxe; (3) Levallois flake; (4) Quina (Yabrudian) scraper; (5) arrowhead; (6) burin; (7) El Wad point; (8) lunate; (9) adze; (10) sickle blade. (For sources, see bibliography)

Tool morphology has been interpreted in light of reduction sequences and different patterns in the exploitation of raw materials (Dibble, 1987). A general trend toward increasingly gracile flakes (greater width–thickness ratio) has also been demonstrated and interpreted to reflect gradual evolution in physical coordination (Jelinek, 1982).

Upper Paleolithic. The dominance of blade technologies in Upper Paleolithic industries replacing the Levallois technique, endscrapers (instead of sidescrapers), burins, and blade tools distinguishes them from those in the Middle Paleolithic. Local transition from the Middle to the Upper Paleolithic has been demonstrated typologically at Ksar 'Akil in the production of Upper Paleolithic scrapers and other types using Levallois blanks (Azoury, 1986). The technological transition has been demonstrated at Boqer Taḥtit and Boqer using conjoinable-piece analysis. It shows the development of Upper Paleolithic prismatic blade cores from Levallois blade cores (Marks, 1983).

Two apparently partially contemporary complexes are defined: the Levantine Aurignacian (e.g., Antelias, el-Wad, Ksar 'Akil, Arkov, Hayonim, ʿErq el-Aḥmar) and the Aḥmarian (e.g., Boqer A, Gebel Lagama sites, Qadesh-Barnea sites, ʿErq el-Aḥmar, Qafzeh, Ksar 'Akil). They differ in the dominance of fine-blade technology and tools in the Aḥmarian (from ʿErq el-Aḥmar), as opposed to flake and blade technologies, and the dominance of burins (for working wood and bone) and endscrapers in the Aurignacian (Gilead, 1991). The significance of the contrasts is disputed; suggestions include differing cultural traditions, ecological adaptations related either to geographical location (the Aḥmarian more evident in the desert, the Aurignacian in the Mediterranean zone) or climatic fluctuations, and chronotechnological developments.

Epipaleolithic. The dominance of bladelet technology and the development of the specialized microburin technique for bladelet truncation in the later Epipaleolithic are the defining technological characteristics of the period. Typologically, complexes and cultures have been defined on a range of standardized microlithic tool types (Goring-Morris, 1987; Henry, 1989). Variation within these tool types, as in length and the presence of Helwan backing retouch on Natufian microlithic lunates (e.g., Hayonim, el-Wad, ʿEinan), provide the means for finer subdivision. As in the Upper Paleolithic, the functions of stone tools seem to reflect hunting (points, barbs) and processing (scrapers, burins). The addition of sickles to the repertoire, as evidenced by the lustrous edges of some blades and bladelets, is an important precursor to later Neolithic agriculture. The terminal Epipaleolithic Ḥarifian culture also witnesses the introduction of small arrowheads.

Of special technological significance in the Epipaleolithic is the development of a range of stone pestles, cup marks, mortars, and bowls, the results of a combination of chipping of rough-outs and the grinding of final products. Beyond their utilitarian significance for processing grains, the decorative elements on the pestles and bowls probably held symbolic meaning. Breached stone mortars and bowls have been found with some burials (e.g., Neveh David, Naḥal Oren).

Neolithic. With respect to lithic analysis, this period is notable for the introduction of ground-stone celts, true grinding stones, and heat treatment in the manufacture of long blades. Much of this complex is directly related to the evolution of agriculture. Blades were utilized for arrowheads and sickles. Chronological and geographic distinctions are based on the wide variety of types and attributes in both classes (Gopher, 1994). The end of the Neolithic shows a decline in the use of arrowheads, except in the desert regions, probably related to the decline of hunting in the latest Neolithic economies.

Neolithic industries also include a range of flake tools (scrapers, notches, denticulates), burins, and other blade tools. Technologically, flakes dominate the waste assemblages from most sites, although the diagnostic elements (for the Pre-Pottery Neolithic B and the early Pottery Neolithic) are long, prismatic blades manufactured from bipolar naviform cores.

Stone vessels and art (masks, figurines) have also been discovered (e.g., Shaʿar ha-Golan, Naḥal Ḥemar), presumably of symbolic significance. Of additional interest is the long-distance exchange of obsidian, from sources in Anatolia to as far south as Sinai and the central Negev.

Post-Neolithic. The two major trends in lithic industries following the Neolithic are the increasing specialization in manufacture of all kinds, and a general decline in the importance of chipped-stone artifacts (Rosen, 1989). Specialization is especially evident in sickle and ground-stone vessel manufacture. The decline in chipped-stone tools is reflected both in a decrease in types (and presumably in functions) and an absolute numerical decrease. By the Iron Age, only sickles are present in the chipped-stone tool repertoire (although threshing-sledge teeth may also be present, they are difficult to identify). Iron sickles replace flint toward the end of the Iron Age.

Ground-stone vessels and grinding stones are of increasing importance during the historical periods, as agricultural technologies and economies improve. The introduction of bronze and iron tools provides more efficient means of stoneworking on a larger scale, resulting in a range of objects such as sarcophagi, olive presses, mills, and millstones. [*See* Sarcophagus; Olives.] Many stone vessels incorporate both utilitarian and symbolic functions, as in Chalcolithic basalt fenestrated and decorated bowls and mortars, or in limestone cups from the Second Temple period in Israel.

Summary. Lithic artifacts are the primary remains of material culture available from prehistoric periods. They are thus the primary means for reconstructing basic cultural history, as well as other elements of the cultural process. In the proto- and early historical periods, they provide a valuable addition to other realms of material culture, especially in making it possible to define specialized modes of manufacture and exchange based on analysis of waste. Study of these artifacts also provides insight into their various functions, usually utilitarian; often, however—but especially in the case of ground-stone vessels—they hold important symbolic meaning.

[*See also the biographies of Garrod and Neuville. In addition, many of the sites mentioned are the subject of independent entries.*]

BIBLIOGRAPHY

The sources for the ten illustrations in figure 2 are as follows: (1) Ofer Bar-Yosef and N. Goren, *The Lithic Assemblages of 'Ubeidiya*, Qedem 34, Monographs of the Institute of Archaeology, Hebrew University (Jerusalem, 1993), fig. 26:3; (2) R. Schild and F. Wendorf, "New Explorations in the Egyptian Sahara," in *Problems in Prehistory: North Africa and the Levant,* edited by F. Wendorf and A. E. Marks (Dallas, 1975), fig. 9:2; (3) P. Boutie and S. A. Rosen, "Des gisement Mousteriens dans le Neguev central / resultats preliminaires de prospections recentes," in *Investigations in South Levantine Prehistory,* edited by O. Bar-Yosef and B. Vandermeersch (Oxford, 1989), fig. 3:1; (4) L. Copeland, "The Middle and Upper Paleolithic of Lebanon and Syria in Light of New Research, in Wendorf and Marks, eds., 1975 (see above), fig. 3:5; (5) A. Gopher, *The Flint Assemblages of Munhata (Israel)* (Paris, 1989), fig. 12:12; (6) *ibid.,* fig. 21:3; (7) I. Gilead and O. Bar-Yosef, "Prehistoric Sites in the Area of Qadesh Barnea," in *Sinai,* edited by G. Gvirtzman et al. (Tel Aviv, 1987), fig. 5:1; (8) A. E. Marks, "An Outline of Prehistoric Occurrences and Chronology in the Central Negev, Israel," in Wendorf and Marks, eds., 1975 (see above), fig. 9:d; (9) unpublished, from the author's analysis of lithic assemblages at Sataf; (10) Gopher, 1989 (see above), fig. 40:10.

Azoury, Ingrid. *Ksar Akil, Lebanon: A Technological and Typological Analysis of the Transitional and Early Upper Palaeolithic Levels of Ksar Akil and Abu Halka,* vol. 1, *Levels XXV–XII.* Oxford, 1986. Primary reference from one of the most important cave sites in the Levantine Paleolithic.

Bar-Yosef, Ofer. "Archaeological Occurrences in the Middle Pleistocene of Israel." In *After the Australopithecines,* edited by Karl W. Butzer and Glynn L. Isaac, pp. 571–604. The Hague, 1975. Although somewhat dated, this is still one of the most important syntheses of the Lower Paleolithic in the Levant.

Bar-Yosef, Ofer. "Prehistory of the Levant." *Annual Review of Anthropology* 9 (1980): 101–133. Concise review of Levantine prehistory by one of its leading scholars.

Binford, Sally R. "Variability and Change in the Near Eastern Mousterian of Levallois Facies." In *New Perspectives in Archaeology,* edited by Sally R. Binford and Lewis R. Binford, pp. 49–60. Chicago, 1986. Classic summary of the "Mousterian functional argument" on Near Eastern data.

Bordes, François. *Typologie du Paléolithique ancien et moyen.* Bordeaux, 1961. The basic descriptive typology used by virtually all scholars for the Middle Paleolithic in Europe and the Near East; well illustrated.

Bordes, François. *A Tale of Two Caves.* New York, 1972. Classic example of standard typological analysis in the Paleolithic.

Clarke, David L. *Analytical Archaeology.* 2d ed. New York, 1978. Still a primary reference for archaeological systematics.

Copeland, Lorraine. "The Middle and Upper Paleolithic in Lebanon and Syria in Light of Recent Research." In *Problems in Prehistory: North Africa and the Levant,* edited by Fred Wendorf and A. E. Marks, pp. 317–350. Dallas, 1975. Although somewhat dated, there have been few Paleolithic excavations in Lebanon and Syria since it was written and it remains an important summary.

Dibble, Harold L. "The Interpretation of Middle Paleolithic Scraper Morphology." *American Antiquity* 52 (1987): 109–117. An important technological perspective in tool technologies.

Garrod, Dorothy A. E., and Dorothea M. A. Bate. *The Stone Age of Mount Carmel: Excavations at the Wady al-Mughara.* Vol. 1. Oxford, 1937. Primary reference for Levantine prehistory and typology.

Gilead, David. "Handaxe Industries in Israel and the Near East." *World Archaeology* 2 (1970): 1–11. Gilead's work was original and exhaustive and remains a primary reference on Acheulean industries in the Near East.

Gilead, Isaac. "The Upper Paleolithic Period in the Levant." *Journal of World Prehistory* 5 (1991): 105–154. The most up-to-date review of this period available.

Gopher, Avi. *Arrowheads of the Neolithic Levant: A Seriation Analysis.* American Schools of Oriental Research, Dissertation Series, no. 10. Winona Lake, Ind., 1994. Perhaps the definitive study of arrowhead typology and seriation in the Neolithic, with discussion of other aspects of the lithic industries as well.

Goring-Morris, A. Nigel. *At the Edge: Terminal Pleistocene Hunter-Gatherers in the Negev and Sinai.* 2 vols. Oxford, 1987. Model presentation of the materials, with much emphasis on lithic analysis and numerous illustrations.

Henry, Donald O. *From Foraging to Agriculture: The Levant at the End of the Ice Age.* Philadelphia, 1989. Elegant summary of the origins of agriculture, including a considerable amount of data and analysis of lithic materials.

Jelinek, Arthur J. "The Tabun Cave and Paleolithic Man in the Levant." *Science* 216 (1982): 1369–1375. In the absence of a final report, this is the best summary of the recent excavations, including important technological analyses.

Keeley, Lawrence H. *Experimental Determination of Stone Tool Uses: A Microwear Analysis.* Chicago, 1980. Classic in microscopic analysis of stone tools.

Marks, A. E. "The Middle and Upper Paleolithic Transition in the Levant." *Advances in World Archaeology* 2 (1983): 51–98. Seminal analysis of technological continuity between the two periods.

Neuville, René. *Le Paléolithique et le Mésolithique du désert de Judée.* Archives de l'Institut de Paléontologie Humaine, Mémoire 24. Paris, 1951. Neuville's work remains a cornerstone in Levantine prehistory.

Rosen, Steven A. "The Analysis of Early Bronze Age Chipped Stone Industries: A Summary Statement." In *L'urbanisation de la Palestine à l'âge du Bronze ancien: Bilan et perspectives des recherches actuelles; Actes du Colloque d'Emmaüs, 20–24 octobre 1986,* edited by Pierre de Miroschedji, pp. 199–224. Oxford, 1989. The only recent synthesis of lithic industries and analysis at the beginning of the Bronze Age.

Valla, François R. *Les industries de silex de Mallaha (Eynan) et du Natoufien dans le Levant.* Mémoires et Travaux du Centre de Recherche Préhistoriques Français de Jérusalem, no. 3. Paris, 1984. Primary and exhaustive technological and typological study of the lithic industries of Natufian culture.

STEVEN A. ROSEN

Artifacts of the Chalcolithic Period

The lithic assemblages from the Chalcolithic period, like those from the preceding Neolithic and the later Early Bronze Age, can be divided into two broad technological spheres: ground stone and chipped stone. These are not exclusive categories; some chipped-flint tools (such as celts) may be finished by grinding, and many ground-stone tools were initially chipped (such as basalt vessels).

Chipped-Stone Industries. Chalcolithic domestic sites usually exhibit at least five different chipped-stone technologies: flake tools, blade tools, tabular scrapers, celt tools, and microlithic tools. In addition to these common chipped-stone technologies, rare tool types may occur at some sites, such as prismatic blades and perforated star-shaped disks, the latter known primarily from sites in the Golan region of modern Israel. [*See* Golan.] All of these types are typically manufactured from cryptocrystalline silicates (chert or flint) of varying quality and color, though chipped-limestone tools have been recovered from sites such as Grar and Gilat. [*See* Gilat.]

Predominant at most sites are the ad hoc tools that represent the domestic production of flint for a wide range of everyday needs. Within the ad hoc tool category a variety of subtypes is commonly recognized, such as notches, denticulates, borers, scrapers, sidescrapers, and choppers, as well as retouched and/or utilized flakes and débitage. The majority of these exhibit a range from standardized to nonstandardized and were produced locally with the common flake technology, requiring no specialized skills or flint.

Blade tools during the Chalcolithic are primarily limited to the manufacture of sickle blades, although some blades were made into awls or other less standardized tools. Sickle blades, identified by the lustrous "sickle sheen" (a result of plant silica deposition) along the working edge, are typically rectangular to trapezoidal in outline, with one side backed (invasive longitudinal retouch). There is evidence for prismatic blade manufacture in the Chalcolithic, but it constitutes a significant part of the flint-tool assemblage only in the Early Bronze Age.

Celt tools, a broad category encompassing axes, adzes,

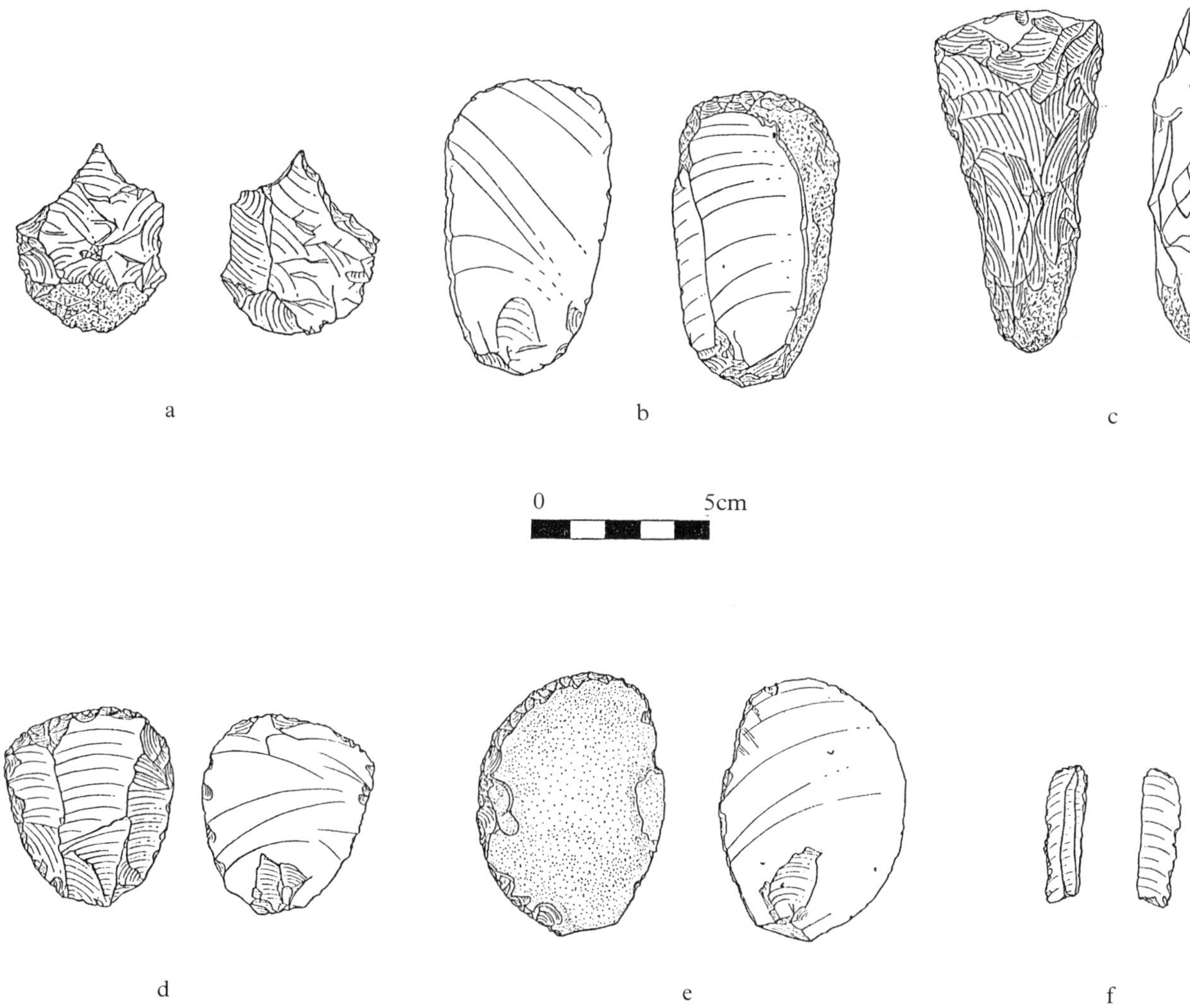

LITHICS: Chalcolithic Period. *Typical chalcolithic flint artifacts.* (a) borer or perforator; (b, d) endscrapers; (c) axe; (e) "tabular" scraper; (f) micro-endscraper. All tools are from the northern Negev site of Shiqmim. (Courtesy Y. M. Rowan)

and chisels, are generally made from bifacially flaked cores, although flakes are occasionally used. Axes and adzes, differentiated primarily by the adze's asymmetric bit (working edge), as opposed to the axe's symmetric bit, are common at most Chalcolithic sites. Less frequently seen are chisels, often called the Ghassulian chisel after the type-site of Teleilat el-Ghassul, which are generally narrower at the bit and body than axes and adzes. [*See* Teleilat el-Ghassul.]

Tabular scrapers, also known as Ghassulian fan scrapers, only rarely exhibit the classic fan shape. Although they are called scrapers, microwear analyses have suggested that some were used as knives. Manufactured from large cortical flakes of fine-grained flint, these pieces are usually retouched along all edges, often with the intentional removal or thinning of the bulb of percussion. The result is a large, thin flake that sometimes exhibits grinding on the cortical surface (incisions begin only in the Early Bronze Age). Debris from the production of tabular fan scrapers is found only at a few sites, indicating possible specialized production, selectivity in flint procurement, and some form of exchange.

Microlithic tools such as microendscrapers, transverse arrowheads, and microborers are found only at some sites, particularly those on the southern coastal plain, such as Gilat, Grar, and the Wadi Gaza sites; they are less frequent at the Beersheba sites in the northern Negev desert. [*See* Beersheba; Negev.] Microendscrapers (small bladelet tools with slight retouch primarily along the distal tip) are manufactured from a very fine semitranslucent flint. Transverse arrowheads manufactured from bladelets are primarily limited to southern Negev and Sinai sites. [*See* Sinai.] Microborers are not commonly recovered from most sites, but it is difficult to know if this is a result of geography, chronology, or recovery methodology.

Obsidian, more common during the Pre-Pottery Neolithic, is known from a few Chalcolithic sites, such as Gilat, Teleilat el-Ghassul, Tel Kabri, and Sinai site A301, and is indicative of some long-distance trade with Anatolia. [*See* Kabri, Tel; Anatolia, *article on* Prehistoric Anatolia.] A number of sites identified as specialized flint-tool production areas indicate trade in chipped-flint tools. Tabular scraper procurement and production sites are known from the western Negev and Sinai. A number of Wadi Gaza sites specialized in flint-tool production; Wadi Gaza sites A, B, and D show evidence of celt-tool production and possibly export. Site A also produced many stages of tabular scraper production. Only a few sites have recovered large numbers of microborers, sometimes with a scarcity of other flint tools. Unfortunately, microborers, which are probably related to bead production, are extremely small (about 10–20 mm) and may be overlooked during excavations.

Ground-Stone Artifacts. The majority of ground-stone assemblages are grinders manufactured from beach rock, limestone, or basalt, with the material selection typically a function of a site's proximity to a source. Virtually ubiquitous at domestic sites, grinding stones as well as an array of mortars and pestles affirm the increased reliance on an agricultural subsistence base. Hammerstones and pounding stones, varying from pecked and battered round cobbles to ground and worn stones, are found at virtually all sites. Large stone rings are frequently discovered, alternatively interpreted as digging-stick weights or weights, or, at coastal sites, as anchors or net weights.

Basaltic vessels, a few examples of which are known from the Neolithic period (Tel Dan), achieve the highest craftsmanship during the Chalcolithic period. [*See* Dan.] Two types of basaltic (sometimes actually phosphoritic) vessels are common—the large bowl and the pedestaled, fenestrated stand (or "incense burner"), both represented by similar ceramic forms. Basaltic vessels are often decorated with chevron incisions along a thin, flared rim and with an incised band around the base of a bowl. In addition to vessels, basaltic pillar figurines with anthropomorphic or zoomorphic features are found in the Galilee and Golan regions, presumably manufactured from the locally available basaltic lava flows. However, at sites in the northern Negev and coastal plain regions, basaltic origins are unknown; the Dead Sea area, the Golan, and the Galilee regions all remain potential source areas (geologists have eliminated the Maktesh Ramon in the Negev as a potential basalt source area). The lack of evidence for basaltic artifact production at all sites indicates specialized production and exchange.

A wide range of other artifacts also was manufactured from ground stone, some of it from distant sources. Ground-stone mace-heads, while rare, are also found produced from limestone, diorite, gabro, granite, and haematite, some resembling predynastic Egyptian forms. These artifacts are conceivably items of warfare but may also represent symbols of power, authority, and divinity, as is known from later textual and pictographic evidence from both Egypt and Mesopotamia. Spindle whorls, commonly limestone or ceramic, are infrequently found made of other materials, such as basalt, sandstone, flint, or chlorite schist. These artifacts, flat and circular to elliptical, attest to the increased importance of spinning wool. Other small, perforated ground-stone artifacts are frequently found, alternatively called loom weights or stone rings, which also may relate to the spinning craft.

Decorative items such as beads and pendants, typically manufactured from locally available materials such as limestone and chalk, are sometimes also made of carnelian, malachite, calcite, and amazonite. Palettes, rectangular to trapezoidal in shape and biconvex to concave in cross section, are known made from granite, scoria, chlorite schist, and limestone; some were probably used to grind ocher, an iron oxide pigment used for ceramic paint, and cosmetic or medicinal preparations. Evidence from predynastic Egyptian contexts also supports a possible commemorative function.

Even more rare are the abstract violin-shaped figurines,

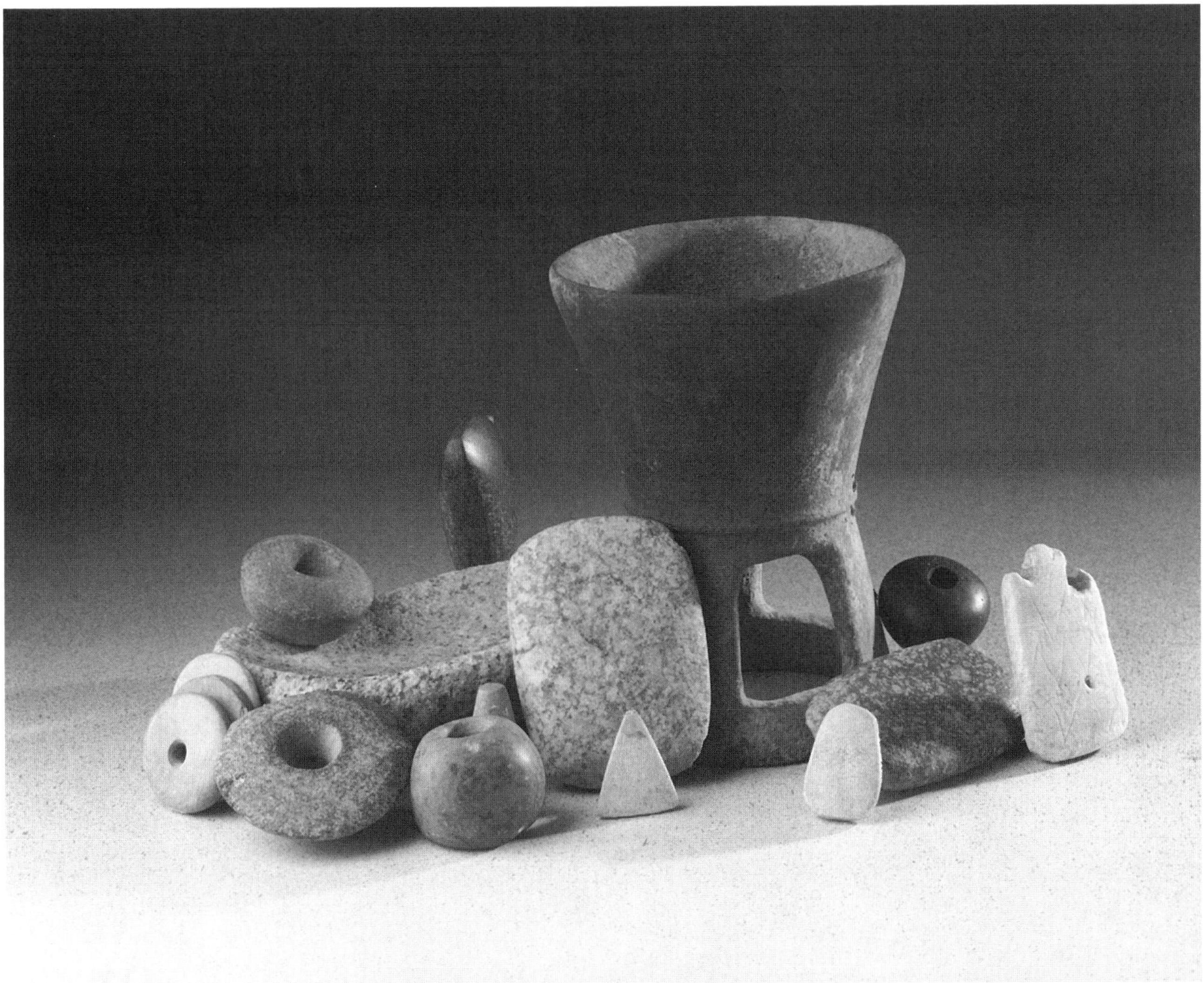

LITHICS: Chalcolithic Period. *Assorted ground stone artifacts from the chalcolithic site of Gilat.* Shown are spindle whorls, maceheads, palettes, a votive axe, a basalt fenestrated stand, and a pendant. (Courtesy Y. M. Rowan)

in the southern Levant found only in Chalcolithic contexts, which are often made of similar materials, including granite, chlorite schist, mica schist, limestone, and calcite. By far the greatest number of these enigmatic figurines were found at Gilat, where a plethora of other nonlocal stone materials was also recovered. These abstract, geometric figurines have been interpreted as having served a cultic and/or an economic function. They were manufactured by chipping, grinding, and polishing, and the lack of manufacturing detritus indicates that they were imported.

BIBLIOGRAPHY

Alon, David, and Thomas E. Levy. "The Archaeology of Cult and the Chalcolithic Sanctuary at Gilat." *Journal of Mediterranean Archaeology* 2.2 (1989): 163–221.

Amiran, Ruth, and Naomi Porat. "The Basalt Vessels of the Chalcolithic Period and Early Bronze I." *Tel Aviv* 11 (1984): 11–19. The only synthesis of basalt vessels from Chalcolithic sites in the southern Levant.

Gilead, Isaac, and Yuval Goren. "Petrographic Analyses of Fourth Millennium B.C. Pottery and Stone Vessels from the Northern Negev, Israel." *Bulletin of the American Schools of Oriental Research,* no. 275 (1989): 5–14. Important work suggesting that stone vessels found at Chalcolithic sites in the northern Negev originated in Transjordan around the eastern areas of the Dead Sea.

Macdonald, Eann, et al. *Beth-Pelet,* vol. 2, *Prehistoric Fara; Beth-Pelet Cemetery.* British School of Archaeology in Egypt, Publications of the Egyptian Research Account, no. 52. London, 1932. Primary reference on the results of early excavations in the Wadi Ghazzeh region, with ample illustrations and photographs.

Neuville, René. "Objects en silex." In *Teleilāt Ghassūl I,* by Alexis Mallon et al., pp. 55–65. Rome, 1934. Though dated, this work remains an important reference from what is still regarded one of the more important Chalcolithic sites.

Rosen, Steven A. "The Potentials of Lithic Analysis in the Chalcolithic of the Northern Negev." In *Shiqmim*, vol. 1, *Studies Concerning Chalcolithic Societies in the Northern Negev Desert, Israel, 1982–1984*, edited by Thomas E. Levy, pp. 295–312. British Archaeological Reports, International Series, no. 356. Oxford, 1987. The only methodical synthesis of Chalcolithic chipped-stone tools from the southern Levant published to date.

Rosen, Steven A. "The Analysis of Early Bronze Age Chipped Stone Industries: A Summary Statement." In *L'urbanisation de la Palestine à l'âge du Bronze ancien: Bilan et perspectives des recherches actuelles; Actes du Colloque d'Emmaüs, 20–24 octobre 1986*, edited by Pierre de Miroschedji, vol. 1, pp. 199–222. British Archaeological Reports, International Series, no. 527. Oxford, 1989. Primarily concerned with EB flint analysis but refers to the Chalcolithic period, including important changes between them.

YORKE M. ROWAN

Artifacts of the Bronze and Iron Ages

Lithic assemblages of the Bronze and Iron Ages can be divided into two classes: chipped-stone industries and ground-stone industries. Chipped-stone tools are types of small cutting, boring, and scraping utensils manufactured using various knapping methods, usually on cryptocrystalline materials (e.g., flints). The ground-stone industry comprises a wider range of implements, including various kinds of grinding stones, stone vessels and mortars, weights, palettes, polished objects such as votive axes, and lapidary (a technology in itself, and not dealt with here). Production methods include knapping and chiseling; coarse and fine abrasion, or polishing; pecking; cutting; splitting; and drilling. Raw materials include limestones and chalks, basalt, alabaster, steatite, diorite, some cryptocrystalline materials, and semiprecious stone.

Aside from the obvious typomorphological differences between the two classes, there is a contrast between their utilitarian and social functions, technology, raw materials, and general developmental trajectory. Whereas the chipped-stone industries show increasing production specialization and restriction in functions through the Bronze and Iron Ages, the ground-stone assemblages seem to reflect relative stability in production mode and, in fact, show increased diversity in function. To a degree, both of these phenomena can be associated with the introduction of metal tools. Over the three-millennia-long course of this period, metal tools slowly replaced most chipped-stone tools. In contrast, they facilitated the manufacture of other stone implements, allowing better implements, as well as a wider range of them, to be produced. Unlike chipped-stone tools, there is little functional overlap between ground-stone tools and vessels and metal tools in these periods.

In addition to the examination of basic technologies and utilitarian functions of lithic assemblages, these artifacts can also be used to reconstruct other aspects of culture. In particular, the large quantities of production waste associated with both classes of artifacts and the relative scarcity of sources of some raw materials (e.g., basalt or obsidian) allow patterns of production, specialization, and exchange to be analyzed. In some cases, stylistic motifs, reflective of different aspects of cultural traditions, can also be traced.

Chipped-Stone Industries. Although chipped-stone industries have been the subject of detailed reports and synthesis (e.g., Rosen, 1989), the same is not true for other stone implements. Syntheses of other stone technologies, even on the level of the site, are rare, and collections have focused on art objects, sometimes to the near exclusion of other elements.

Early Bronze Age blade industries. Long prismatic blades, usually trapezoidal in section, struck from large uniplatform cores, are characteristic of the Early Bronze Age across virtually the entire Near East. Early excavators in the Levant referred to these blades as ribbon knives, but they were later more formally described and analyzed by René Neuville and John W. Crowfoot, who referred to them as Canaanean blades. No good antecedents for this technology have been found in the Levantine Chalcolithic, nor do they continue into the succeeding Middle Bronze Age, although they are abundant in the EB IV–MB I horizon in northern Israel.

These blades were used primarily for sickle manufacture. Up to 15 cm or more in length, and traditionally of fine-grained brown flint, they were usually snapped into shorter sections, truncated, and hafted. The recovery of relatively fresh pieces with sickle gloss suggests that pieces were retouched or sharpened only after the primary edge dulled. Segments were often reversed in the haft, as reflected in the double-edged gloss on some pieces. Bitumen preserved on the edges of some segments is indicative of a hafting mode, and although most show lateral hafting of short segments, some complete blades were apparently utilized as reaping knives and not sickles in the narrow sense.

The near absence of corresponding cores and debitage at most sites, the recovery of packets of complete, unworked blades deriving from the same core, and the discovery of a few workshops (e.g., at Har-Haruvim and Lahav in Israel, Saida-Dakkerman in Lebanon, and Hassek Höyük in Turkey), indicate exchange and a degree of production specialization.

In addition to Canaanean blades and sickles, two other blade industries are present in the Early Bronze Age. Egyptian bitruncated and/or backed blades have been discovered at some sites in the northern Negev and the Shephelah (e.g., Tel ʿErani). These are smaller, less regular in section, and manufactured on different flint from the Canaanean blades. Utilized in part for sickle manufacture, they seem also to have been used for knives.

In the Negev, especially at Biqʿat ʿUvda, small, relatively crude blades served as blanks for backed sickles and arched backed blades—perhaps functionally knives. These types are virtually absent from northern assemblages.

Other blades were also manufactured, apparently as ad-

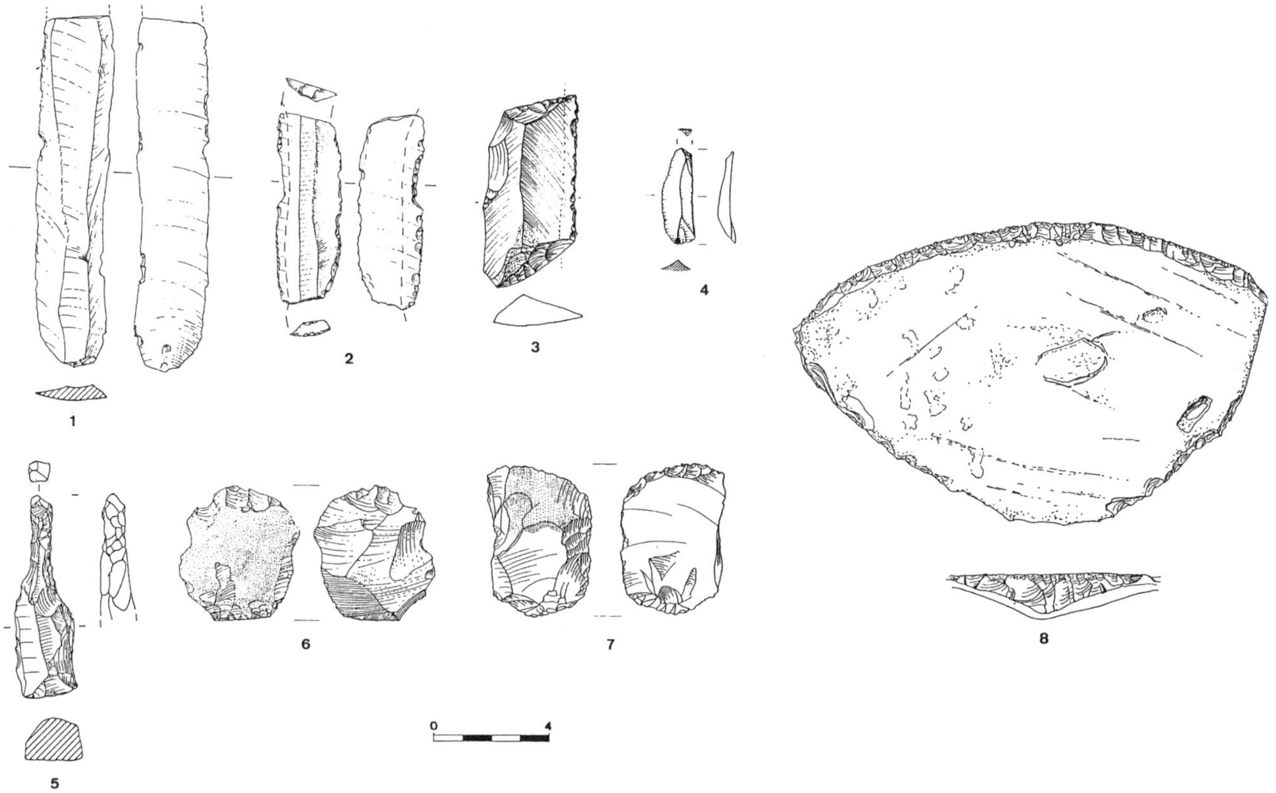

LITHICS: Bronze and Iron Ages. Figure 1. *Chipped stone tools.* (1) Canaanean blade, broken at end; (2) Canaanean sickle segment; (3) large geometric sickle segment from Iron Age Tell el-Ḥesi; (4) microendscraper; (5) borer; (6) denticulate/notch; (7) scraper; (8) fanscraper (tabular scraper). (For sources, see bibliography)

juncts or ad hoc substitutes for Canaanean blades. These are smaller and less standardized than their prismatic counterparts. They also show little evidence for production specialization.

Early Bronze Age bladelet industries. The earliest stages of the Early Bronze Age seem to show a continuation of the Chalcolithic bladelet industries. This is reinforced by the presence of Egyptian twisted bladelets in the south. These tools seem to drop out of the repertoire later in the period. In the desert regions, bladelet technology is present in the form of microlithic transverse arrowheads and lunates, as in the assemblages from the *nawamis* tombs of ʿEin-Hudera, Gebel Guna, and associated sites.

Early Bronze Age tabular scraper industry. Tabular scrapers are large, flat, cortical flakes showing different kinds and locations of retouch. The classic type, the fan scraper, is a transverse scraper with distal retouch, a faceted striking platform, and in many cases, bulbar thinning. However, the classic type is relatively rare and there is much variation in shape and preparation. The primary characteristic is the retention of the cortex and even that may have exceptions.

Production techniques seem to have included block-on-block, direct, and indirect percussion. EB types may exhibit cortical incisions in various patterns—for example, the "protoaleph." Microscopic analysis of edge wear has indicated that at least some of these tools functioned as knives. Also, there appears to be some spatial association with ritual loci, suggesting some cultic functions for the class.

EB tabular scrapers as a class clearly originated in the preceding Chalcolithic period or in the terminal Neolithic. They disappear with the end of the EB III and have not been found in reliable contexts at EB IV–MB I sites. In common with Canaanean blades, evidence for the manufacture of these pieces is absent from all but a few sites. Unlike the blades, workshop sites have been found exclusively in the southern deserts, and the quantitative distribution of these pieces shows a geometric decline with distance from the assumed source area. This suggests some kind of down-the-line exchange system similar to that postulated for Anatolian obsidian during the Neolithic period.

Early Bronze Age ad hoc industry. The bulk of most EB assemblages is comprised of a range of retouched and utilized flakes and debris. They may be further subdivided into types: scrapers, notches and denticulates, choppers and hammerstones, and retouched pieces. Within these types there is little standardization. Microwear analyses and the wide range in morphology and attributes of the general class indicate a wide range of functions, including hide scraping, plant processing, whittling, boneworking, piercing, cutting and shredding of soft materials, and pounding and chopping.

In contrast to other industries, there is abundant evidence for local on-site manufacture for the entire range of these artifacts. Cores and debitage from simple flake manufacture are the most abundant element on virtually all sites, and these tools constitute the most common tool class. There is no evidence for specialized manufacture or exchange of these items, and the raw materials exploited are local.

A similar ad hoc industry dominates Chalcolithic assemblages, although the crude and generalized nature of the technology precludes the assumption of cultural continuity on this basis. These tools are common in the EB IV–MB I horizon as well.

Special classes. Special imported pieces, such as Egyptian bifacial knives and scrapers (ʿEin-Besor, Tel ʿErani) are also occasionally recovered. Various obsidian artifacts have been found, especially in the north, and should be treated as a special class because of their potential in defining trade relations.

Post–Early Bronze Age sickles. Following the Early Bronze Age, Canaanean sickle technology was replaced by a flake industry for the production of Large Geometric sickles. This type continues through the middle of the Iron Age, with minor typological variations, until flint sickles are replaced by iron. The technotypological and chronostratigraphic discontinuity between the Canaanean and Large Geometric sickles should be emphasized.

Large Geometric sickles were manufactured by backing and truncating medium-sized flakes (usually 5–7 cm long). Shapes such as rectangles, trapezoids, triangles, and parallelograms were fixed by the angles of the truncations. The bulb of percussion was often deliberately removed, apparently to facilitate hafting. Bitumen and possibly resin-based adhesives have been discovered on the backs of some sickles. Sickles were used first without edge retouch and were later sharpened with a serration retouch.

No obvious cores from Large Geometric sickles have been recovered, but several secondary workshops or caches have been excavated. In several caches at Gezer these consisted of a large number of unretouched flakes appropriate for sickle manufacture, numerous incomplete and unused sickles, a few used sickles, and a horn core for knapping and retouch. Such caches are clear evidence for the specialized manufacture of these sickles.

The continued use of flint sickles even into the Iron Age is a reflection of their effectiveness, the ready availability of the raw material, and the efficiency of the specialized production-distribution system.

Post-EB ad hoc industry. A good definition of the post-EB ad hoc industry is difficult to develop because of the scarcity of well-collected assemblages from unmixed MB II contexts. By the Late Bronze and Iron Ages the industry is considerably reduced, both numerically and typologically. Typically, as at Deir el-Balaḥ, sickles constitute some 80 percent of the assemblage—the rest are comprised for the most part of retouched flakes. The decline of this industry is probably the result of the increasing availability of bronze, and later iron, for small utensils.

Ground-Stone Industries. As mentioned above, ground stone implements in the Bronze and Iron Ages constitute a more diverse class functionally than do the chipped stone tools. The following review touches only on the primary types.

Grinding stones. The standard grinding stones throughout the Bronze and Iron Ages at virtually all sites are saddle querns and associated rubbing stones. The raw material used is usually basalt, sandstone, limestone, or flint. Shapes vary depending on the original block, but rubbing stones are often loaf shaped. Querns from EB Jericho average roughly 30 cm in length and 15–20 cm in width; rubbing stones have about half those dimensions (Dorrell, 1983). At Arad they are somewhat larger (Amiran, 1978). By the Iron Age, as at Tell Qasile, larger rubbing stones and grinding slabs, occasionally with rectangular bases, appear. These allowed more efficient processing of larger quantities of grain. The rotary quern seems not to have been introduced until the second century BCE, and occasional finds from earlier periods are likely to be intrusions. However, large rollers, presumably complementary to rubbing stones, have been found in Iron Age contexts at Megiddo. The absence of chipping debris and rough-outs at virtually all sites, along with the common use of nonlocal raw materials, such as basalt and sandstone, is indicative of production specialization and exchange.

Vessels. The EB basalt vessel industry, as at Arad, Jericho, and other sites, shows a qualitative decline from its Chalcolithic predecessor. Fenestrated bowls disappear (perhaps replaced by ceramic copies), and the fine finish and decorative incisions common in the Chalcolithic are rare or absent in the Early Bronze Age (Braun, 1990; Amiran and Porat, 1984). The most common types show thick, flat bases and high splayed rims. A subtype shows one or, more rarely, several lug-type handles.

In addition to these vessels, crude mortars, often of limestone, are also common, and small, shallow cup marks have also been found. Door sockets, morphologically similar to crude mortars have also been discovered.

MB, LB, and Iron Age basalt vessels, as at Hazor and Megiddo, show a resurgence in basalt vessel craftsmanship. This is especially evident in the introduction of tripod-based bowls and variants with decorative elements. Simple bowls and mortars are also present, and at Jericho they dominate. Various platters, palettes, and shallow bowls, of both coarse (limestone, basalt) and fine (alabaster, calcite, steatite) materials have been found at numerous sites.

As with the grinding stones, the apparent absence of production debris and use of nonlocal materials are indicators

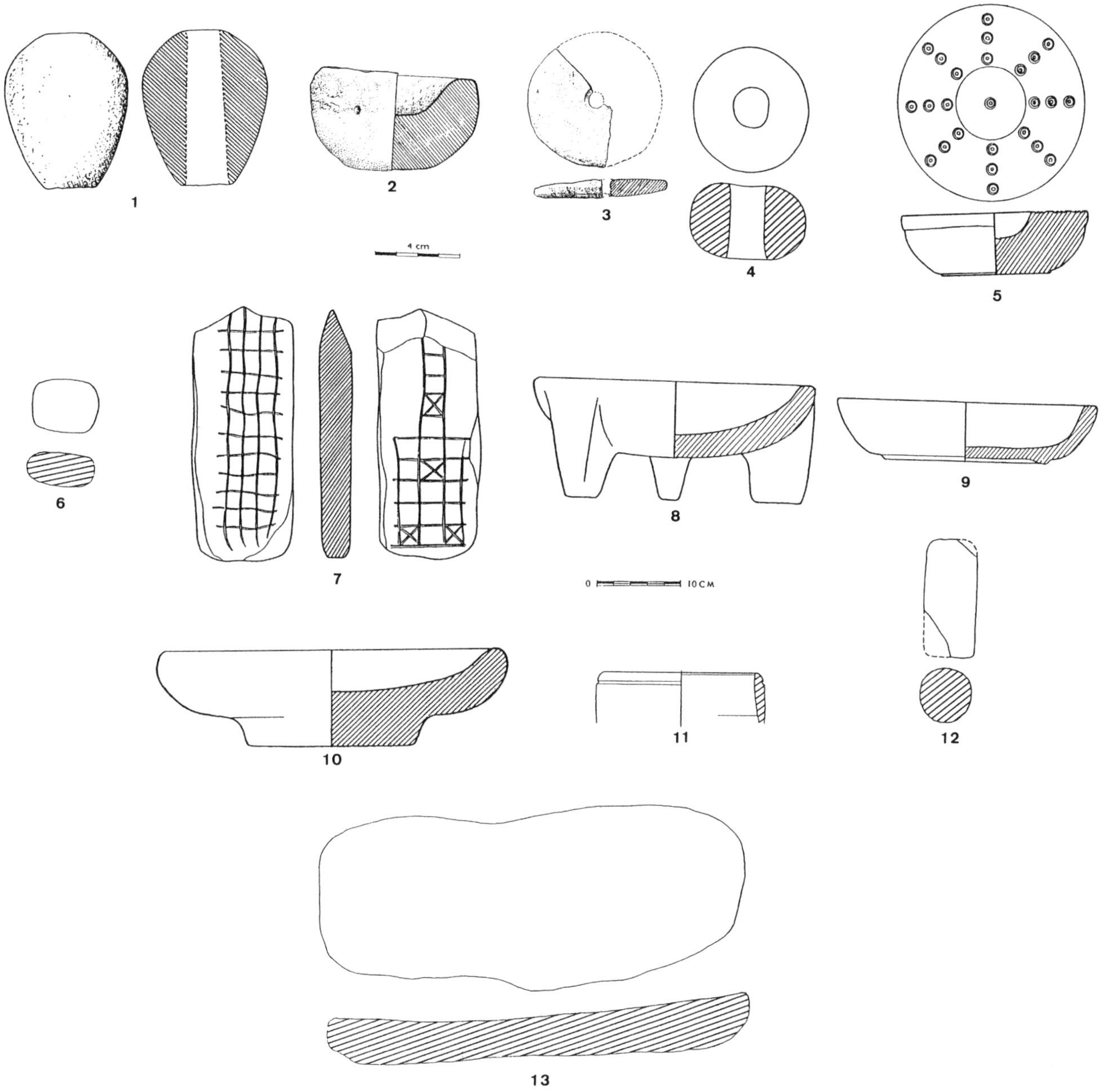

LITHICS: Bronze and Iron Ages. Figure 2. *Stone vessels and other artifacts.* (1-5) upper scale, (6-13) lower scale. (1) limestone macehead; (2) light brown travertine mortar; (3) white limestone perforated disc fragment; (4) limestone macehead; (5) cosmetic stone palette; (6) limestone grinding/rubbing stone; (7) stone gameboard; (8) basalt tripod mortar; (9) basalt bowl; (10) basalt bowl; (11) limestone bowl; (12) limestone pestle; (13) basalt basal grinding stone. (For sources, see bibliography)

of trade and production specialization. Some vessels, of alabaster and calcite, are clearly luxury goods imported from Egypt.

The functions of this class of utensils are varied. Mortars were used for processing grain, and a large mortar at Tell Qasile may be associated with a brewery. Other vessels may also have served as mortars, although many were associated with ritual, perhaps on a domestic level. Door sockets, presumably for attached hinges, have already been noted. Many of the finer palettes and platters were for the preparation and use of cosmetics.

Pestles and pounding stones. Manufactured out of limestone and basalt, the most common type of grinding stone at Jericho was small and almost dome shaped. Pounding stones, hammerstones, and hammers are also found in large numbers in all periods. Hammerstones range from simple cobbles with signs of pecking through fully rounded, fist-sized balls that show deliberate pecking all around.

Hammerheads, as at Megiddo, show worked waists for hafting. This class of tools probably had many uses, including food processing, hammering, the reduction of metal ores (as at Timnaʿ) and possibly as ballistas and weights or measures. The more finely worked basalt objects were probably connected to some type of exchange network, but most were locally manufactured.

Pierced objects. Ranging in size from small beads to large stone rings, pierced objects vary considerably in form, workmanship, and function. All show a central hole, probably drilled out with a bow drill. Typologically they include large stone rings, finely polished mace-heads, spindle whorls, loom weights, and beads. Raw materials are varied, both between types and within them. Thus, spindle whorls at Megiddo are of limestone, basalt, steatite, and hematite, and weights are of hematite, limestone, and sandstone. Large stone rings at Arad are of basalt, limestone, and sandstone, but the mace-heads are almost exclusively of limestone. The different types are found throughout the Bronze and Iron Ages, and it is difficult to ascertain any chronotypological change.

The function of the large stone rings is unclear; suggestions include their use as digging-stick weights, net weights, and measuring weights. Ship anchors have been recovered from sites on the coast. [*See* Anchors.] The mace-heads may have been weapons, or alternatively, ritual objects. Their Chalcolithic copper antecedents were certainly not weapons and thus lend credence to a symbolic role, especially in the Early Bronze Age. Spindle whorls and looms generally should be associated with textile manufacture, although, in some cases, use as small measuring weights cannot be ruled out. [*See* Textiles.]

As with other stone implements, the pierced objects seem to reflect varying degrees of production specialization and exchange. A fundamental problem with these objects is the scarcity of good collection and synthetic study.

Miscellaneous objects. Beyond the general groups of ground-stone tools, a wide range of other types is found at all sites: stone disks (sometimes pot lids), casting molds, gaming boards, grooved stones (whetstones), potters' wheels, polished votive axes, and figurines. [*See* Games.] As with other types, most of these reflect degrees of specialization and exchange.

[*See also the biographies of Crowfoot and Neuville. In addition, many of the sites mentioned are the subject of independent entries.*]

BIBLIOGRAPHY

The sources for the eight illustrations in figure 1 are as follows: (1) S. A. Rosen, "Notes on the Flint Implements from Tel Yarmuth," in *Yarmouth I,* by P. de Miroschedji (Paris, 1988), pl. 52:6; (2) *ibid.,* pl. 51:14; (3) unpublished, from the author's own research; (4) I. Gilead, "Grar: A Chalcolithic Site in the Northern Negev, Israel," *Journal of Field Archaeology* 16.4 (1989), fig. 10:2; (5) R. Cohen, *Archaeological Survey of Israel Map of Sede Boqer-East (168) 13–03,* (Jerusalem, 1981), fig. 2, p. 26; (6) Rosen, 1988 (see above), pl. 50:6 (7) *ibid.,* pl. 50:7; (8) J. C. Payne, "The Flint Industries of Jericho," in *Excavations at Jericho V* (London, 1983), fig. 348.

The sources for the thirteen illustrations in figure 2 are as follows: (1) W. G. Dever et al., *Gezer II* (Jerusalem, 1974), pl. 39:8; (2) P. de Miroschedji, *Yarmouth I* (Paris, 1988), pl. 49:9; (3) *ibid.,* pl. 49:2; (4) R. Amiran, *Early Arad* (Jerusalem, 1978), pl. 76:5; (5) Y. Yadin et al., *Hazor II* (Jerusalem, 1960), pl. CV:24; (6) Amiran, 1978 (see above), pl. 80:11; (7) Yadin, 1960 (see above), pl. LXXVIII:6; (8) *ibid.,* pl. LXXVII:4; (9) *ibid.,* pl. LXXVII:9; (10) *ibid.,* pl. CIV:6; (11) Amiran, 1978 (see above), pl. 77:1; (12) *ibid.,* pl. 80:12; (13) *ibid.,* pl. 79:3.

Amiran, Ruth. *Early Arad,* vol. 1, *The Chalcolithic Settlement and Early Bronze Age City, First-Fifth Seasons of Excavations, 1962–1966.* Jerusalem, 1978. Includes a discussion of the full range of stone artifacts recovered from the site, including a note on the chipped-stone tools by Tamar Schick.

Amiran, Ruth, and Naomi Porat. "The Basalt Vessels of the Chalcolithic Period and Early Bronze I." *Tel Aviv* 11 (1984): 11–19. Incorporates petrographic analysis into a standard typological study, with important results on sources of stone vessels.

Braun, Eliot. "Basalt Bowls of the EB I Horizon in the Southern Levant." *Paléorient* 16.1 (1990): 87–96. One of the rare synthetic studies of stone vessels.

Brézillon, Michel N. *La dénomination des objets de Pierre Taillée.* Gallia Préhistoire Supplément, 4 Paris, 1971. Classic introduction to stone-tool technology and typology; especially well illustrated.

Dorrell, Peter G. "Appendix A: Stone Vessels, Tools, and Objects." In *Excavations at Jericho,* vol. 5, edited by Kathleen M. Kenyon and Thomas A. Holland, pp. 485–575. London, 1983. The most complete study of nonchipped-stone artifacts available from a single site.

El-Khouli, Ali. *Egyptian Stone Vessels: Predynastic Period to Dynasty III.* 3 vols. Mainz am Rhein, 1978. Exhaustive catalog and study of stone vessels of all types from the indicated time period in Egypt; extensive bibliography.

Lamon, Robert S., and Geoffrey Shipton. *Megiddo I.* Chicago, 1939. A wealth of information on different types of stone implements and vessels is scattered throughout the volume.

McCaslin, Dan E. *Stone Anchors in Antiquity: Coastal Settlements and Maritime Trade-Routes in the Eastern Mediterranean ca. 1600–1050 B.C.* Studies in Mediterranean Archaeology, vol. 61. Göteborg, 1980. Covers not only the technology and typology of stone anchors, but attempts social and economic reconstructions based on provenance and distribution.

Rosen, Steven A. "The Analysis of Early Bronze Age Chipped Stone Industries: A Summary Statement." In *L'urbanisation de la Palestine à l'âge du Bronze ancien: Bilan et perspectives des recherches actuelles; Actes du Colloque d'Emmaüs, 20–24 octobre 1986,* edited by Pierre de Miroschedji, pp. 199–224. Oxford, 1989. The only recent synthesis and analysis of EB lithic industries.

Semenov, S. A. *Prehistoric Technology.* London, 1964. English translation of the seminal work on microscopic analysis and functional determination.

Yadin, Yigael, et al. *Hazor III.* Jerusalem, 1960. One of a handful of site reports that record a range of stone implements, especially vessels of different periods.

Steven A. Rosen

LLOYD, SETON HOWARD FREDERICK (1902–1996), archaeologist who worked extensively in Iraq and Turkey. Born in Birmingham, England, Lloyd qualified as an architect in 1926. In 1929 he replaced a colleague as the architect on Henri Frankfort's excavations at Tell el-Amarna in Egypt; he subsequently assisted Frankfort on the Oriental Institute of Chicago's excavations in Iraq: he worked at first millennium BCE sites at Khorsabad and Jerwan in Assyria; in the Diyala region east of Baghdad, he recorded sequences of temples and palaces from about 3100–1750 BCE by tracing their mud-brick walls. In these excavations he made innovative use of kite photography. In 1937–1938 Lloyd worked with John Garstang at the prehistoric site of Mersin on Turkey's south coast and conducted a survey around Sinjar, in northern Iraq, that provided a model for archaeological surveys and the basis for subsequent excavations (e.g., Tell er-Rimah and Yarim Tepe). During World War II, as adviser to the Directorate General of Antiquities in Iraq, Lloyd worked with Iraqi archaeologists at sites (Hassuna, Uqair, and Eridu) selected to fill gaps in the chronologies of northern and southern Iraq from about 5800 to 2000 BCE. Lloyd also helped to reorganize the collections of the Iraq Museum in Baghdad. In 1949 Lloyd went to Turkey as the first director of the British Institute of Archaeology at Ankara. His excavations at Polatlı, Beycesultan, and Sultantepe provided sequences from the Chalcolithic to the Iron Ages. He also conducted architectural surveys of Islamic Harran and Seljuk Alanya. In 1962 Lloyd became professor of Western Asiatic archaeology at the Institute of Archaeology in London, where he taught until 1969. Lloyd has since added to what was already an extensive list of publications, ranging from guidebooks for troops during World War II to excavation reports and handbooks for students. He has been the recipient of many academic honors and is a Fellow of the British Academy.

[*See also* British Institute of Archaeology at Ankara; Diyala; Eridu; Hassuna; Rimah, Tell er-; *and the biographies of Frankfort and Garstang.*]

BIBLIOGRAPHY

Lloyd, Seton. *The Interval: A Life in Near Eastern Archaeology*. Faringdon, 1986.

Lloyd, Seton. "Seton Lloyd." In *The Pastmasters: Eleven Modern Pioneers of Archaeology*, edited by Glyn E. Daniel and Christopher Chippindale, pp. 61–88. London, [1989?]. Based on "Archaeological Retrospective 4: Seton Lloyd," *Antiquity* 56 (November 1982): 181–188.

Lloyd, Seton. *Ancient Turkey: A Traveller's History of Anatolia*. London, 1989.

Lloyd, Seton. "Back to Alanya." *Anatolian Studies* 40 (1990): 219–221.

"Seton Lloyd: A Bibliography." *Iraq* 44 (1982): 221–224. Omissions and additions are listed in *The Interval* (p. 179).

DOMINIQUE COLLON

LOCUS. The technical term archaeologists use to describe certain excavated features is *locus*. The word refers specifically to discrete archaeological entities created by human hand or through postoccupational decay. The locus is the basic unit of excavation; additionally, it provides a means of relating associated artifacts and ceramic materials to those archaeological entities.

Complicating our understanding of the locus is the fact that this basic unit may be defined differently by different archaeologists. Older works may utilize the term locus, but they often neglect to define it at all. More recently, Americans and Europeans have generally used locus to refer to architectural elements, to built features, and to layers of soil, while for Israelis, the term often describes rooms in their entirety.

The locus is a tool that enables an excavator to maintain a three-dimensional perspective. It challenges the excavator of each square, each area, each field, and each site to consider stratigraphic relationships among the various features within each square, among contiguous squares, and throughout a site. Excavation with attention to loci requires the continual evaluation and reevaluation of the stratigraphic relationship among architectural features, for example, walls, revetments, socles, and cisterns, along with soil levels, including surfaces, fills, and postoccupational debris layers. The value of the locus is best seen in archaeological plans and sections, in which the rendering of loci enables the excavator to demonstrate visually the relationship among a site's various architectural and depositional features.

Typically, each discrete archaeological entity is assigned a locus number when it is first encountered in the excavation process. This locus number places the newly discovered feature into the record of excavated features, or loci, in the square in which it was found. The recording of the locus ensures that the new feature is accurately and completely described in the excavation note book. This description usually includes elevation, size, construction materials, color, contents, extent of preservation, a discussion of nearby features to which the locus relates, and other appropriate topics.

The locus number then becomes the reference number for all pottery and artifacts associated with the excavated feature—whether at the time the locus number is originally assigned or later in the excavation process. Sometimes pottery and artifacts that had been excavated in contexts that were ambiguous can later be assigned locus numbers that clarify their contexts. In this way, there is a record for each excavated area describing the association of features and objects.

This record, in which architectural elements, debris layers, artifacts, and pottery are described and related, provides a basic resource for archaeologists in their discussion of stratigraphic and chronological relationships throughout a site. It permits the reevaluation of decisions, should new evidence warrant it. Additionally, it allows those who were not participants in an excavation to review its basic building blocks and the interpretive process that was applied to them.

[*See also* Balk; Stratigraphy.]

BIBLIOGRAPHY

Aharoni, Yohanan. "Remarks on the 'Israeli' Method of Excavation." *Eretz-Israel* 11 (1973): 48*–53*.

Joukowsky, Martha Sharp. *A Complete Manual of Field Archaeology: Tools and Techniques of Field Work for Archaeologists.* Englewood Cliffs, N.J., 1980.

Lance, H. Darrell. "The Field Recording System." In *A Manual of Field Excavation: Handbook for Field Archaeologists,* edited by William G. Dever and H. Darrell Lance, pp. 73–107. Cincinnati, 1978.

Mazar, Amihai. *Archaeology of the Land of the Bible, 10,000–586 B.C.E.* New York, 1990.

Wright, G. Ernest. "The 'New' Archaeology." *Biblical Archaeologist* 38 (1975): 104–115.

BETH ALPERT NAKHAI

LOWER EGYPT, the northern part of the country, comprising the Nile Delta south to Cairo. The nome (provincial) divisions that characterized Upper (southern) Egypt from very early times developed later in Lower Egypt where they followed the division of the Delta into long lenticular land areas separated by the branches and drainage channels of the Nile River. Eventually, Lower Egypt was divided into twenty nomes, as indicated in the lists from the Ptolemaic and Roman temples of Edfu and Dendera. Memphis in the first nome of Lower Egypt was a major religious capital and the administrative center of Egypt throughout much of its history. The great pyramid cemeteries in the western desert, from Abu Roash in the north to Dahshur on the southern border with Upper Egypt, belong to Memphis. In one of the offices of the civil government, there was a northern vizier for Lower Egypt who lived at Memphis.

Merimde Beni Salame has long been the most important Neolithic site in the Delta, located along its southwestern edge. Recent research indicates that the material from Merimde is part of a predynastic cultural tradition, named after the sites of Maadi and Buto, that developed separately from the predynastic Naqada culture (c. 3850–3000 BCE) in the upper Nile Valley (Bruce Trigger, "The Rise of Egyptian Civilization," in Trigger et al., 1983). The ceramic tradition is exemplified by small shallow bowls and black and brown polished jars with incised and impressed decoration. Late Predynastic and Early Dynastic iconography and texts from Upper Egypt and Saqqara indicate that Buto was an important religious center and perhaps the political capital of Lower Egypt in the Predynastic period.

In early times the ancient Egyptians associated the northeastern Delta with Asiatics, particularly Canaanites from southern Palestine, just as the western Delta may have been continually infiltrated by Egypt's western neighbors, the Libyans. Throughout the three thousand-year history of ancient Egypt there was a continual interplay between southern Palestine and Egypt, beginning with strong Palestinian influence at the Predynastic site of Maadi in the southeastern Delta followed by Egyptian penetration of southern Palestine in the early first dynasty (c. 2920–2770). The lower corners of the flat and expansive Nile Delta were at all periods Egypt's soft points that allowed non-Egyptian cultures—Canaanite, Libyan, Assyrian, Persian, Greek, and Roman—to penetrate and dominate the Egyptian Nile Valley.

An influx of Syrian traders and southern Palestinian immigrants in the late Middle Kingdom (second half of the twelfth dynasty, c. 1845–1783) led to a secondary state in the northeast Delta ruled by non-Egyptians. The Egyptians called them *ḥeka khasut,* "rulers of foreign countries," from which the Greeks derived the more familiar term *Hyksos.* Ruling from Avaris, the site of Tell ed-Dabʿa in the northeast Delta, the Hyksos comprise the fifteenth and sixteenth dynasties. Over the course of nearly three decades of excavation, Manfred Bietak of the Austrian Archaeological Institute in Cairo has found a complete chronological range of Middle Bronze II Canaanite culture, with ceramics, warrior graves, and temples that, in size and classic MBII features, match those found anywhere in Syria or Palestine (Bietak, 1968, 1975).

During the Hyksos domination the Egyptian state, ruled by the kings of the seventeenth dynasty (c. 1640–1550), was restricted to Upper Egypt south of Hermopolis. After the Egyptians defeated and expelled the Hyksos, the eighteenth dynasty (1550–1307) and later New Kingdom rulers (eighteenth–twentieth dynasty) initiated an active program of settlement in Delta sites such as Heliopolis, Saïs, Athribis, and Tanis. The eastern Delta became the staging area for campaigns into Syria and Palestine, the latter area coming under Egyptian control through the eighteenth and nineteenth dynasties. The nineteenth dynasty rulers, particularly Rameses II (1290–1224), built new Delta cities, the most important of which was Per-Rameses, at Qantir just north of the old Hyksos capital at Tell ed-Dabʿa. This new city became the new administrative center of the kingdom.

With the disintegration of the New Kingdom in the Third Intermediate period, a line of ethnic Libyan rulers rose to power from Tell Basta, where Libyans may have been moved by Rameses III after he defeated them in the west. Tell Basta, the capital of the eighteenth Lower Egyptian nome, located southeast of modern Zagazig was important since the Old Kingdom as the cult center of the cat-headed goddess Bastet. During the twenty-second and twenty-third dynasties (c. 945–712), the Delta was fragmented into separate principalities ruled by "Great Chiefs of the Ma" or Meshwesh, one of the Libyan peoples attested in the New Kingdom. Tanis, located at the site of San el-Hagar in the northeastern Delta, became a major religious center. Many royal statues and parts of royal monuments were moved to Tanis for reuse in its temple precinct, which also became the burial ground for the twenty-second dynasty rulers who retained the title "king of Upper and Lower Egypt" even during the times of greatest political fragmentation.

Toward the end of the Third Intermediate period (twenty-first–first half of twenty-fifth dynasty, c. 1070–712) the entire western Delta was taken by Tefnakht, the leader of another Libyan contingent known as the Libu. His descendants remained in some control through the period of nominal Nubian rule under the twenty-fifth dynasty. Eventually descendants of Tefnakht moved their control from west to east across the Delta and down the Nile Valley to establish their own kingdom over a unified Egypt as the twenty-sixth dynasty (c. 664–525). The capital was now Saïs, which had been a major Delta center since late Predynastic times.

In the Ptolemaic and Roman periods the Delta, which had returned to fragmented political control under the Persian domination, there were many settlements with the accoutrements of hellenized cities, including temples for both Greek and native Egyptian divinities. A large town of the Ptolemaic and Roman periods was found at Tell er-Ruba, which was part of the city of Mendes, the capital of the nome in the east central Delta. Mendes is an example of a true *tell* (mound) site, with settlement extending back to the late Predynastic period. Athribis hosted a Roman spa. In the western Delta Naukratis had been established as a major trading center during the reign of Amasis (c. 570–526) of the twenty-sixth dynasty. Kom Abu Bellou in the western Delta has proved one of the richest sites for burials of the Ptolemaic, Roman, and early Coptic periods (c. 332 BCE–sixth century CE).

Located at the extreme northwest of the Delta, Alexandria grew from a small native Egyptian fishing village, Rakotis, to become the capital of the Ptolemies, the preeminent city in Lower Egypt, one of the major ports of the Mediterranean coast, and the transit point between old native Egypt and the hellenized world.

[*See also* Alexandria; Dabʿa, Tell ed-; Delta; Heliopolis; Hyksos; Merimde; Naukratis; Saqqara; *and* Upper Egypt.]

BIBLIOGRAPHY

Baines, John, and Jaromír Málek. *Atlas of Ancient Egypt*. New York, 1980.

Bietak, Manfred. *Studien zur chronologie der nubischen C-Gruppe. Ein Beitrag zur frühgeschichte unternubiens*. Vienna, 1968.

Bietak, Manfred. *Der Fundort im Rahmen der archäologischen-geographischen untersuchungen über das ägyptische osrdelta, Tel el-Dabʿa*. Vienna, 1975.

Butzer, Karl W. *Early Hydraulic Civilization in Egypt: A Study in Cultural Ecology*. Chicago, 1976.

Emery, Walter B. *Archaic Egypt*. Baltimore, 1961.

Gardiner, Alan H. *Egypt of the Pharaohs*. Oxford, 1961.

Hayes, William C. *Most Ancient Egypt*. Chicago, 1965.

Kees, Hermann. *Ancient Egypt: A Cultural Topography*. Translated by Ian F. D. Morrow. London, 1961.

Trigger, Bruce G., et al. *Ancient Egypt: A Social History*. Cambridge, 1983.

ZAHI HAWASS

LUWIANS. Essentially an ethnolinguistic term, Luwian (or Luvian) is used to refer to population groups that became widespread in Anatolia during the second millennium BCE and spoke a common language. Scholars are still uncertain about both the original homeland of the Luwian-speaking peoples and the nature and period of their entry into Anatolia. There is, however, fairly general agreement that they settled in Anatolia during the third millennium BCE, initially occupying extensive areas in the west.

In the first half of the second millennium, a large part of western Anatolia seems to have been called Luwiya. However, the term was probably used only in a broad geographic sense, with no strong political connotations. By the middle of that millennium, *Luwiya* was replaced in the Hittite texts, most explicitly in the Hittite laws, by the term *Arzawa*. The latter, though varying in its geographic limits, nonetheless had distinct political connotations. During the Hittite New Kingdom, it embraced a number of Hittite vassal states known collectively as the Arzawa lands.

Luwian speakers extended far beyond the boundaries of Arzawa. The migrations that had led to their settlement in western Anatolia continued well into the second millennium, and by the middle of that millennium, Luwian-speaking groups occupied much of the southern coast of Anatolia, from the region later known as Lycia, in the west, to Cilicia, in the east. Lycia was the homeland, or part of the homeland, of the Luwian-speaking Lukka people, one of the Lycians' main Bronze Age ancestors. Luwian speakers also settled in Cilicia, particularly in the region of Bronze Age Kizzuwatna. Kizzuwatna also came under strong Hurrian influence and, presumably, Luwian and Hurrian cultural and ethnic elements mingled there.

Our understanding of the spread of Luwian speakers in western and southern Anatolia is based primarily on linguistic and onomastic evidence: a range of place names (names ending in *-assa*, for example) and personal names, as well as the names of Luwian deities. Thus, cults of the Luwian gods Tarḫunt and Šantas (Sandon) are attested in Kizzuwatna, and to the north of Kizzuwatna cults of the Luwian deities Šahašara, Ḫuwaššana, and Kuniyawanni are in evidence in the region of the classical Tyanitis, part of the Hittite Lower Land.

The most tangible evidence of the Luwian presence in Anatolia is provided by two types of inscriptions: cuneiform and hieroglyphic. The cuneiform texts are inscribed on clay tablets, dating to the fourteenth and thirteenth centuries BCE and found in the Hittite archives at Boğazköy/Ḫattuša. In these inscriptions (the bulk of which are published in Heinrich Otten, *Keilschrift Urkunden aus Boghazköi*, vol. 35, Berlin, 1953) the language used is identified as *lu(w)ili*, literally "(written) in the manner of Lu(w)iya." From the inscriptions, which deal mainly with ritual and cultic matters, it is clear that Luwian belongs to the Indo-European language family and has close affinities with the "Hittite" (more strictly Nešite) language. The hieroglyphic texts appear on a number of royal seals and rock monuments. The earliest known example of the script appears on a seal of Išpuhtahšu, a fifteenth-century king of Kizzuwatna. However, the majority of texts date from the thirteenth through the eighth centuries BCE.

Decipherment of the hieroglyphic script was greatly facilitated by the discovery in 1939 of a bilingual text, in Phoenician and Luwian hieroglyphs, at Karatepe, in eastern Cilicia. More recent work on the language of the inscriptions has established its virtual identity with that of the Luwian cuneiform texts. The character of the script, which was perhaps initially inspired by the monumental script of Egypt, made it a more appropriate medium than cuneiform for recording important achievements on public monuments. In the thirteenth century, increasing use seems to have been made of the script for this purpose, as is illustrated by the discovery in 1988 of a built stone chamber, commonly referred to as the Südburg structure, in the Hittite capital of Ḫattuša. The monument, which dates to the reign of the last Hittite king, Šuppiluliuma II (c. 1205–), bears a hieroglyphic inscription listing the king's military conquests in southern Anatolia.

Luwian elements survived the collapse of the Late Bronze Age civilizations, reemerging in the first millennium BCE. Indeed, the majority of hieroglyphic inscriptions, attributable to the rulers of Early Iron Age kingdoms in southeast Anatolia and northern Syria, date to the first two centuries or so of this period. In Lycia and Cilicia Aspera, Luwian personal names are attested as late as the classical and Roman imperial periods. The Lycian language was a direct descendant of the Luwian language, and Luwian deities figure prominently in the Lycian pantheon.

[*See also* Anatolia, *article on* Ancient Anatolia; Boğazköy; Cilicia; *and* Lycia.]

BIBLIOGRAPHY

Houwink ten Cate, Philo H. J. *The Luwian Population Groups of Lycia and Cilicia Aspera during the Hellenistic Period.* Leiden, 1961. Study of the survival of Luwian elements in southern Anatolia during the first millennium BCE.

Laroche, D. L. "Luwier, Luwisch, Lu(w)iya." In *Reallexikon der Assyriologie und vorderasiatischen Archäologie,* vol. 7, pp. 181–184. Berlin, 1928–. General discussion of the chief features of the Luwian language and the spread of Luwian-speaking peoples in Anatolia during the second and first millennia BCE.

Laroche, Emmanuel. *Dictionnaire de la langue louvite.* Paris, 1959. Luwian word list, with meanings (where known), Hittite equivalents (where applicable), and sources of reference.

Otten, Heinrich, and Christel Rüster. *Texte in hurritischer Sprache.* Keilschrifttexte aus Boghazköi, vol. 35. Berlin, 1993.

TREVOR R. BRYCE

LYCIA. The kingdom of Sarpedon and Glaukos in Homeric tradition, Lycia was located in the southwest corner of Asia Minor. This region was almost certainly part of the homeland of the Late Bronze Age Lukka people, remnants of whom formed one of the main population groups in Lycia in the first millennium BCE. Another population group may have come from Crete.

Lycia figures prominently in Homer's *Iliad* as Troy's most important ally in the Trojan War. However, the earliest archaeological evidence so far for settlement in the country dates only to the late eighth century BCE. A number of buildings of this period have been excavated on the acropolis at Xanthos, which was to become Lycia's largest and most important city.

In about 540 BCE, Lycia became a subject state of the Persian Empire. Shortly afterward, a local ruling dynasty was established at Xanthos that exercised authority over much of the country until the early decades of the fourth century BCE. In 367 BCE, Lycia took part in the abortive satrap rebellion. When the rebellion was crushed, the country was once more forced to submit to Persian overlordship and remained subject to Persia until Alexander the Great invaded the country in 334/33 BCE. After Alexander's death in 323, Lycia came first under the control of Antigonus of Macedon and subsequently under Ptolemaic and Seleucid rule. However, with the defeat of the Seleucid king Antiochus III by the Romans at the battle of Magnesia in 190 BCE, Lycia was brought within the Roman sphere of influence. In 43 CE, the emperor Claudius joined Lycia with the neighboring country of Pamphylia and made it a Roman province.

The language spoken by the native Lycians is closely related to the Late Bronze Age Luwian language. The script used was a modified form of the Greek alphabet. Our knowledge of this rests primarily on 170 inscriptions carved on stone, from the late fifth to the late fourth century BCE. The majority are sepulchral inscriptions, carved on the facades of rock-cut tombs—which often replicate features of the wooden houses in which the Lycians lived. Because in many cases these were family tombs, they often provide important information about Lycian family structure, including some support for Herodotus's claim that there were matrilineal elements in Lycian society. Although much of the content of the inscriptions is still unintelligible to us, the discovery in 1973 of a trilingual inscription—in Lycian, Greek, and Aramaic—has thrown new light on the language.

The inscriptions identify a number of Lycian gods and goddesses. The most prominent of these was "the mother of the gods," a direct descendant of the Luwian mother goddess. Under Greek influence, she was equated with the goddess Leto, who became increasingly important in Lycian religion. By the Roman imperial period, she and her children, Apollo and Artemis, were honored as the country's national gods. National religious festivals were held at the Letoon, the center of their worship. Apollo was also closely associated with the famous oracle at Patara. Lycia was in general well known for its oracular centers.

Early in the second century BCE, the Lycians formed a political federation of their cities. It was known as the *koinon,* or Lycian League, and met under the presidency of a *lykiarch.* Although under Roman rule the league lost much of its autonomy, it continued to exercise important administrative functions throughout the period of the Roman Empire.

Following the Roman Empire's adoption of Christianity, a number of bishoprics were established in Lycia. The city of Myra, where there are remains of a sixth-century church (with later additions), was the seat of Nicholas, the most famous of the Lycian bishops. Other remains from the early Christian period can be found in the Letoon, where a large church, also from the sixth century, was excavated in the 1970s.

Under Roman rule, Lycia enjoyed a relatively peaceful and prosperous existence. Products for which it was well known included perfume, wine, and, most importantly, timber cut from its cypress and cedar forests. The Arab invasions that began at the end of the seventh century brought major changes to Lycia. Yet, a number of the ancient Lycian cities, including Xanthos, survived and were still in evidence in the eleventh century, when the Seljuk Turks arrived.

[*See also* Anatolia; *and* Luwians.]

BIBLIOGRAPHY

Bean, George E. *Lycian Turkey.* London, 1978. General survey of Lycian history and archaeological sites.

Borchhardt, Jürgen, et al. *Götter, Heroen, Herrscher in Lykien.* Munich, 1990. Contributions by a number of scholars on a wide range of aspects of Lycian history and civilization from the Archaic through the Byzantine periods.

Bryce, Trevor R. *The Lycians,* vol. 1, *The Lycians in Literary and Epigraphic Sources.* Copenhagen, 1986. Study of Lycian history and society as revealed through inscriptions and literary sources, up to the time of Alexander's conquests.

TREVOR R. BRYCE

LYCOPOLIS. *See* Asyut.

M

MAʿAGAN MIKHA'EL. In fall 1985, while diving along the shore at Kibbutz Maʿagan Mikha'el, 32 km (20 mi.) south of Haifa, Israel, Ami Eshel noticed, in water less than 2 m deep, a pile of stones not native to the Levantine coast. Pieces of wood and pottery sherds protruded from the stones. Shifting local sand and a diver's keen sense of observation resulted in the discovery of the remains of an ancient merchantman.

Preliminary investigations were carried out soon after the discovery by Shelley Wachsmann, under auspices of the Israel Antiquities Authority. Based on the examination of an oil lamp and storage jar handles, a tentative date of the late fifth century BCE was assigned to the finds. In the following year, during further exploration by Elisha Linder and Avner Raban, several hull planks were observed while a test trench was being cut. The timbers were in an excellent state of preservation because they had been buried in the sand, an anaerobic environment, and protected under a thick layer of stones that turned out to be part of the ship's ballast. Excavation was undertaken by the Center for Maritime Studies of the University of Haifa, under the direction of Elisha Linder.

Survey and Excavation Techniques. To determine the extent of the remains, define the ballast area, and measure the depth of the sand that had accumulated over the site, a probe pipe was inserted into the sea bottom by means of a water jet, which disclosed a clay layer about 4 m below the present sea level. Test trenches aided in locating the vessel's endposts, which were nearly 8 m apart. For recording purposes, datum poles were inserted to define the plan of the site; they remained in place throughout the excavation to facilitate triangulation measurements in recording artifacts.

The ship lay in shallow water at a walking distance of less than 60 m from the shoreline. The surge made working conditions difficult, as sand continually drifted back into the excavation areas, affecting visibility. To prevent interference, a horseshoe trench was dredged around the site, its outside wall lined with some fifteen hundred sandbags, but that failed to eliminate the surge and sand migration; even waves less than a meter high made it impossible to work safely and to avoid movements that would endanger the delicate procedures. In three seasons of excavation (autumn 1988, spring and autumn 1989), out of a total of 160 days at the site, sea conditions allowed only thirty-two days of actual excavation of the hull and its contents.

The first task was to remove the ballast stones, whose total weight was more than 12 tons; some of the stones weighed more than 50 kg (100 lbs.) each. They consisted of three lithological groups: metamorphic, magmatic, and sedimentary rock. The first group, comprising 65 percent of the total, was mostly blue schist. The origin of the stones pointed first to the central Mediterranean seacoast, near Corsica and Calabria. Closer analysis determined a more likely location, however, farther east, in the Greek islands. Beginning at the offshore end of the ship, which the finds indicated was the stern, where the galley would normally be located, the excavation proceeded slowly toward the bow, using a dredger operated by a powerful water pump. Because damage by storm waves was feared, only one section of the inner hull was excavated at a time. Its contents were recorded, mapped, and photographed before they were removed.

Hull Structure. The vessel's original measurements were approximately 12 m long and 4 m wide. More than 11 m of its bottom were recovered, including its keel and the lower portions of its stem- and sternposts. The starboard side was found in a better state of preservation than the port side, rising at its highest to more than a meter above the bottom of the keel. The ship was constructed in the shell-first method: the hull was completely built before the internal frames were installed. The planks were attached to one another by a series of pegged mortise-and-tenon joints. Surprisingly, however, the ends of the planks were also lashed to the end posts by cords. Other structural components included full frames secured to the planks by copper nails, a longitudinal stringer supporting vertical stanchions, and a massive mast step, forward of the middle of the ship, that carried a single mast for a large square sail. The lower end posts were attached to the keel and consisted of a single timber nearly 8 m long with a false keel, or shoe. All of the hull's structural components were of pine, except the tenons, the treenails, and the false keel, which was of oak. The wood was in an excellent state of preservation, the external timbers unblemished by erosion or teredo worms. The ship appeared almost new and may therefore have been on its maiden voyage when it sank.

Ship's Contents. In addition to the heavy load of ballast and a great deal of dunnage (twigs and branches that buffered the ship's hull from the ballast stones), an impressive array of artifacts was intact in the hull or scattered around it. A complete one-arm anchor, made of oak, with a lead-filled wooden stock was discovered off the ship's starboard bow. The anchor's shank and arm were carved from a single timber. Remains of rope were found around its crown and lifting loop. The find is unique and thus essential to understanding the evolution of the anchor in antiquity.

Among the ceramic items were basket-handle storage jars; utensils the sailors used daily, such as jugs, plates, lamps, and a water "pithos"; and miniature juglets and cups or painted pottery that were probably the sailors' personal belongings. Also in the latter category are three beautifully carved wood artifacts: a heart- or leaf-shaped "jewel box" with a swivel top and two violin-shaped "cosmetic palettes." A collection of carpenter's tools consisting of wood handles belonging to cutting and boring tools, parts of bow drills, a carpenter's square, scores of treenails and tenons, and a whetstone, was found scattered around a woven basket that was probably the shipwright's tool kit. A few meters of rope, in widths varying from 2-40 mm and in a three-strand left-handed twist, were found intact, in undisturbed bundles, with some knots still detectable. Grape and fig seeds and olive pits were identified, as well as barley. A preliminary study of the pollen samples indicates an eastern Mediterranean coastal variety of plants that grow during the summer. The metal finds included what seemed to be a small copper incense scoop and copper and iron nails. A single lead ingot was recovered that was probably a source of raw material for use on board.

Shipbuilding Technology. Only a very few hull remains have been discovered in the Mediterranean in a reasonable good state of preservation from the general same period as the Maʿagan Mikha'el ship. Two are of particular interest: the late fourth-century BCE merchantman excavated and raised from the sea at Kyrenia, Cyprus, and the early sixth-century BCE shipwreck found near the coast of Gela, Sicily, which is still being explored. Considering the many similarities and some of the basic differences among these ships, it now appears that the Maʿagan Mikha'el ship is a missing link in hull construction between the other two vessels. One example points to the extensive use of lashing the timbers by means of cords in the Gela ship, a method that was only partially applied in the Maʿagan Mikha'el ship and disappeared altogether in the Kyrenia vessel. The conservation process of the Maʿagan Mikha'el hull timbers and perishable artifacts lasted three and a half years. Plans are underway for the ship to be reconstructed and displayed at the University of Haifa, in a newly built museum hall.

Summary. The Maʿagan Mikha'el ship plied the Mediterranean in about 400 BCE, a peak period of maritime activity and trade by the Phoenicians and Greeks. In its mode of construction it follows two Mediterranean traditions: mortise-and-tenon joints and cord lashing. More than half of the ship's displacement was comprised of ballast stones not native to the Levantine coast. Whether these were loaded at the port of departure or picked up en route, in a secondary use, is not known. The pottery remains one of the main clues by which the ship is dated and its sailing route traced. Presently, the leads point to Cyprus and Eastern Greece. Who carved the ship's unique wood anchor and where parallels for the carved wooden "boxes" are to be found are not yet known. Because it seems to have been on its maiden voyage, it is possible that the vessel itself was the merchandise. Further investigation and the results of laboratory testing may be able to fill in the existing information gaps.

BIBLIOGRAPHY

Eiseman, Cynthia J. E., and Brunilde Sismondo Ridgway. *The Porticello Shipwreck: A Mediterranean Merchant Vessel of 415–385 B.C.* College Station, Texas, 1987.

Frost, Honor. "The Punic Ship: Final Excavation Report." In *Atti della Accademia Nazionaledei Linecei,* supp. 30. Rome, 1976.

Linder, Elisha. "The Maʿagen Michael Shipwreck Excavation: First Season." *Center for Maritime Studies News* (Haifa University) 16 (1989).

Linder, Elisha. "Excavating an Ancient Merchantman." *Biblical Archaeology Review* 18.6 (1992): 24–35.

Rosloff, Jay. "The Maʿagan Michael Shipwreck Excavation, 1989 Season." *Center for Maritime Studies News* (Haifa University) 17 (1990).

Rosloff, Jay. "A One-Armed Anchor of c. 400 B.C.E. from Maʿagan Michael Vessel, Israel: A Preliminary Report." *International Journal of Nautical Archaeology* 20.3 (1991): 223–226.

Steffy, J. Richard. "The Kyrenia Ship: An Interim Report on Its Hull Construction." *American Journal of Archaeology* 89.1 (1985): 71–101.

Elisha Linder

MACALISTER, ROBERT ALEXANDER STEWART

MACALISTER, ROBERT ALEXANDER STEWART (1870–1950), archaeologist born in Dublin into an academic family, his father being a professor of anatomy at Cambridge. Some of Macalister's early training was in architecture and surveying, but his lifelong interests were broad and included not only Near Eastern archaeology but also Celtic archaeology and antiquities, ecclesiastical art and vestments, and music. In pursuit of the latter, he became an accomplished organist and choirmaster and composed hymns, a number of which were relatively well known. He never married and remained a staunch Protestant in Catholic Dublin. After his early fieldwork in Palestine, Macalister returned to University College Dublin, where, as professor of Celtic archaeology, he occupied the first chair in European archaeology in any university (1909–1943), a post he held until his retirement. In later life, he became somewhat notorious for his impatient field methods at Irish national monuments like Knowth, as well as for his cantankerous responses to any negative reviews of his books on many subjects.

Macalister carried out archaeological surveys and soundings in the Judean Shephelah (1898–1900) with Frederick J. Bliss, at the mounds of Tell es-Zakariyeh, Tell eṣ-Ṣafi, Tell es-Ṣandaḥanna, and Tell el-Judeideh, published in 1902 as *Excavations in Palestine during the Years 1898–1900*. It was Macalister's excavations at Gezer (1902–1909), however, sponsored by the British Palestine Exploration Fund (PEF), that made his reputation. These were among the first large-scale excavations carried out in Palestine, and they were promptly published by the PEF in 1912 in three sumptuous, handsomely illustrated volumes as *The Excavation of Gezer*. Nevertheless, Macalister's insistence on working year-round, alone without proper staff, his neglect of proper stratigraphic methods, and his adoption of a highly idiosyncratic chronology marred what appeared to many to be admirable and innovative work. The fact, revealed by the American excavations of G. Ernest Wright, William G. Dever, and Joe D. Seger in 1964–1974, is that Macalister discerned no more than one-third of the strata present at Gezer, and that his final publication is largely useless for reconstructing the site's actual history. Macalister later worked on the Ophel in Jerusalem with A. C. Dickey (1923–1925); there, his relative chronology of the city walls, although challenged by Kathleen Kenyon, was confirmed by the subsequent excavations of Yigal Shiloh. Macalister's later publications on Celtic archaeology are now regarded as little more than historical curiosities.

[*See also* Gezer; Jerusalem; Judeideh, Tell el-; Palestine Exploration Fund; *and the biography of Bliss*.]

BIBLIOGRAPHY

Bliss, Frederick Jones, and R. A. S. Macalister. *Excavations in Palestine during the Years 1898–1900*. London, 1902.

Dever, William G. "Excavations at Gezer." *Biblical Archaeologist* 30.2 (1967): 47–62.

Macalister, R. A. S. *The Excavation of Gezer, 1902–1905 and 1907–1909*. 3 vols. London, 1912.

Thomas, Page A. "The Success and Failure of Robert Alexander Stewart Macalister." *Biblical Archaeologist* 47 (1984): 33–35.

WILLIAM G. DEVER

MACCABEES. *See* Hasmoneans.

MACHAERUS. The modern village of Mukawer in Jordan, situated 30 km (19 mi.) southwest of Madaba on the south bank of Wadi Zerqa Ma'in (map reference 2092 × 1084), preserves the name of the Hasmonean-Herodian fortress of Machaerus built on the southern border of Jewish Peraea against the Nabateans. The site consists of two distinct areas: the ruins of the fortress on the isolated spur of Qal'at al-Mishnaqa (see figure 1), and the ruins of the Roman-Byzantine village of Machaberous northeast of it that is connected with the high plateau.

According to Josephus (*War* 7), Alexander Jannaeus (103–76 BCE) built the fortress of Machaerus and Gabinius, in 57 BCE, destroyed it. After fleeing from Rome, Aristobulus and his son Alexander sought refuge in its ruins. Herod the Great rebuilt it (after 37 BCE). It was composed of an upper and a lower city. According to Josephus, John the Baptist was thrown into the prison of the fortress, where he was put to death by order of the tetrarch Herod Antipas (*Antiq.* 18.5.1–2). At the outbreak of the First Jewish Revolt against Rome, the Roman garrison abandoned the fortress to the rebels, who held it for six years (until 72 CE). [*See* First Jewish Revolt.] Lucilius Bassus built the siege works around the fortress. The besieged of the upper city surrendered and the lower city was taken by force and burned.

In 1807 Ulrich Jasper Seetzen recorded the name of the village (Seetzen, 1854–1859, vol. 2, pp. 330–334; vol. 4, pp. 378–382) and in 1864 the Duke de Luynes explored its ruins (Luynes, 1874). In 1965 the Jordanian Department of Antiquities partially excavated a Byzantine church there. Joseph Vardaman began excavating the fortress in 1968. In 1973 August Strobel, of the German Evangelical Institute, surveyed the siege works around Qal'at al-Mishnaqa, the *vallum*, the camps, and the towers. In 1978–1981, work was resumed on the fortress by an archaeological team from the Studium Biblicum Franciscanum (SBF), directed by Virgilio Corbo. [*See the biography of Corbo*.] In 1989, a second Byzantine church was excavated in the village. A Greek inscription, with the name of the deceased, was retrieved from one of the plundered tombs of the Roman-Byzantine cemetery hewn in the rock on the east side of the village.

One of the main results of the SBF excavations has been the identification of the upper city on the top of Qal'at al-Mishnaqa with the palace-fortress (with a total surface of about 4,000 sq m) and of the lower city on the mountain's precipitous north slope with the housing for the palace-fortress personnel (an area of 5,000 sq m; only a few of those dwellings, which were destroyed by fire, have been excavated). In the palace-fortress, two main phases and a subphase of occupation were detected and identified with the Hasmonean fortress (three towers with part of the defensive wall), the Herodian fortress, and the fortifications of the Zealots during the First Jewish Revolt (the polygonal surrounding wall and ovens inside the fortress).

To the Hasmonean fortress belong three towers on the crest of the mountain, part of the defensive wall on its southeast side, and some rooms reused as a substructure for the thermae in the Herodian fortress. The tower at the northwest corner of the lower city also belongs to this period. In the tower's small rooms a large number of Late Hellenistic jars, bowls, and lamps were collected along with Hasmonean coins. The tower was connected to a huge rock-cut water

MACHAERUS. Figure 1. *Qal'at al-Mishnaqa-Mukawer.* (Archive Studium Biblicum Franciscanum; photograph by Michele Piccirillo)

reservoir 8 m deep that is perfectly preserved. The original entrance to the reservoir was carefully masked and blocked in antiquity. [*See* Fortifications, *article* on Fortifications of the Hellenistic and Roman Periods; Cisterns; Reservoirs.]

The central Herodian palace-fortress measures 110 m east–west and 60 m north–south. A corridor stretching north–south divides the palace into two blocks: the eastern block has a paved courtyard in the center flanked by the thermae on the south; it has an additional laconicum and rectangular rooms on the north; the western block has a peristylar columination on the north erected on a water cistern and a possible double triclinium on the south. The *apoditherium* of the thermae and the other rooms inside the fortress show traces of mosaic floors. The fortress shows no signs of successive reuse, except for two coins from Trajan's reign (97–117). An aqueduct (15 m high) collected the rainwater from the plateau into a series of plastered cisterns hewn on the northern slope of the mountain. A lower channel directed the rainwater from Wadi al-Mishnaqa in the lower series of cisterns. [*See* Aqueducts.]

Three Byzantine churches have been located in the ruins of the village: the north church was built and its mosaics executed in 603 CE; the central church is from the time of Bishop Malichos (possibly the first half of the seventh century); but the third church has not yet been investigated. [*See* Churches.]

BIBLIOGRAPHY

Corbo, Virgilio. "La fortezza di Macheronte: Rapporto preliminare della campagna di scavo, 8.09–28.10.1978." *Studium Biblicum Franciscanum/Liber Annuus* 28 (1978): 217–231, pls. 57–70.

Corbo, Virgilio. "Macheronte, la reggia-fortezza erodiana: Rapporto preliminare alla II campagna di scavo, 3.09–20.10.1979." *Studium Biblicum Franciscanum/Liber Annuus* 29 (1979): 315–326.

Corbo, Virgilio. "La fortezza di Macheronte (al Mishnaqa): Rapporto preliminare alla III campagna di scavo, 8.09–11.10.1980." *Studium Biblicum Franciscanum/Liber Annuus* 30 (1980): 365–376.

Corbo, Virgilio, and Stanislao Loffreda. "Nuove scoperte alla fortezza di Macheronte: Rapporto preliminare alla IV campagna di scavo, 7.09–10.10.1981." *Studium Biblicum Franciscanum/Liber Annuus* 31 (1981): 257–286.

Loffreda, Stanislao. "Preliminary Report on the Second Season of Excavations at Qal'at al-Mishnaqa-Machaerus." *Annual of the Department of Antiquities of Jordan* 25 (1981): 85–94.

Luynes, Duc de. *Voyages à la Mer Morte, à Pétra et sur la rive gauche du Jourdain I: Relation du Voyage.* Paris, 1874.
Piccirillo, Michele. "First Excavation Campaign at Qalʿat al-Mishnaqa-Meqawer (Madaba)." *Annual of the Department of Antiquities of Jordan* 23 (1979): 177–183.
Seetzen, Ulrich J. *Reisen durch Syrien Palästina Phönicien die Transjordan-Länder, Arabia Petraea und Unter Ägypten,* edited by F. Kruse. Berlin, 1854–1859.
Strobel, August. "Machaerus: Geschichte und Ende einer Festung im Lichte archäologisch-topographischer Beobachtung." In *Bible und Qumran,* pp. 198–225. Berlin, 1968.
Strobel, August. "Observations about the Roman Installations at Mukawer." *Annual of the Department of Antiquities of Jordan* 19 (1974): 101–127.
Strobel, August. "Das römische Belagerungswerk um Machärus: Topographische Untersuchungen." *Zeitschrift des Deutschen Palästina-Vereins* 90 (1974): 128–184.
Vardaman, E. J. *Machaerus: Project for Excavation.* Unpublished manuscript, Louisville, Ky.

MICHELE PICCIRILLO

MACKENZIE, DUNCAN (1861–1934), Scottish archaeologist, excavator, and explorer of various sites in the Aegean, Palestine, Sardinia, and the Sudan. Mackenzie received his undergraduate degree in philosophy from Edinburgh University in 1889, conducted postgraduate studies in classics and archaeology at the universities of Munich and Berlin, and earned a doctorate from the University of Vienna in 1895.

Mackenzie is known primarily for his work at Phylakopi on the island of Melos (1896–1899) and, especially at Knossos, Crete, as assistant to Sir Arthur Evans (1900–1910, 1920–1929). From 1910 to 1912 Mackenzie worked for the Palestine Exploration Fund, directing the excavations at ʿAin Shems (Beth-Shemesh). Mackenzie also traveled and recorded prehistoric monuments in Sardinia in 1906 and 1907 and worked in the Sudan for Sir Henry Wellcome on the excavations at Dar el-Mek and Saqadi in 1913. During World War I he assisted Evans in Oxford with the publication of *The Palace of Minos at Knossos* and with the reorganization of the Aegean collections in the Ashmolean Museum.

Mackenzie published little. His most important works are a chapter in a volume on Phylakopi (1904), articles on the pottery of Knossos (1903, 1906) four articles on Cretan palaces (1905–1908), and his reports on the excavations at ʿAin Shems published by the Palestine Exploration Fund (1911–1913). His main contributions to archaeology are his daybooks of the excavations at Phylakopi, Knossos, and ʿAin Shems. These daybooks not only contain valuable, unpublished information on these important sites but also, together with his surviving correspondence, show a precision in the recording of archaeological excavations and an attention to problems of methodology and interpretation that are quite outstanding for the period.

[*See also* Beth-Shemesh; Crete; Sardinia; *and the biography of Evans.*]

BIBLIOGRAPHY

Mackenzie, Duncan. "The Pottery of Knossos." *Journal of Hellenic Studies* 23 (1903): 157–205.
Mackenzie, Duncan. "The Successive Settlements at Phylakopi in Their Aegeo-Cretan Relations." In *Excavations at Phylakopi in Melos,* by T. D. Atkinson et al., pp. 238–272. London, 1904.
Mackenzie, Duncan. "Cretan Palaces and the Aegean Civilization." *Annual of the British School at Athens,* no. 11 (1904–1905): 181–223; no. 12 (1905–1906): 216–258; no. 13 (1906–1907): 423–445; no. 14 (1907–1908): 343–422.
Mackenzie, Duncan. "The Middle Minoan Pottery of Knossos." *Journal of Hellenic Studies* 26 (1906): 243–267.
Mackenzie, Duncan. *The Excavations at ʿAin Shems, 1911.* Palestine Exploration Fund Annual, no. 1, pp. 41–94. London, 1911.
Mackenzie, Duncan. *Excavations at Ain Shems (Beth-Shemesh).* Palestine Exploration Fund Annual, no. 2. London, 1912–1913 (double volume).
Momigliano, Nicoletta. "Duncan Mackenzie: A Cautious Canny Highlander." In *Klados: Essays in Honour of J. N. Coldstream,* edited by Christine Morris, pp. 163–170. London, 1994.

NICOLETTA MOMIGLIANO

MADABA, city located in central Jordan, 30 km (19 mi.) south of Philadelphia/Amman (map reference 2256 × 1249). The city of Madaba was built on a natural elevation of the Transjordan high plateau with steep slopes on the west, south, and southeast. The Roman-Byzantine town spread to the north over an area that slopes more gently toward the surrounding plain.

The site's ancient name is preserved in the mosaic floor inscriptions of the Church of the Virgin Mary ("the people of this city of Madaba") and in the west courtyard of the "cathedral." In the mosaic floor of the Hippolythus hall, the city is represented as a Tyche seated on a throne. In the Bible, Madaba is recorded among the Cities of the Plain in Moab conquered and occupied by the Israelite tribes (*Nm.* 21:30; *Jos.* 13:9–16). [*See* Moab.] In the environs of the city the battle between King David's army and the coalition of Ammonites and Arameans (*1 Chr.* 19:7ff.) took place. According to the Mesha inscription, the town was liberated by the Moabite king in about the second half of the ninth century BCE (1.7–9). [*See* Moabite Stone.] In later biblical texts, Madaba is mentioned among the cities of Moab (*Is.* 15:2). During the Maccabean revolt (second century BCE), "the sons of Jambri" went out of the city and laid an ambush for the Jewish convoy led by John, one of the brothers of Judas Maccabeus, plundering and killing them. John's death was immediately avenged by Jonathan and Simon (*1 Mc.* 9:36ff.). Later, John Hyrcanus conquered Madaba after a long siege (Josephus, *Antiq.* 13.9.1); it remained in the hands of the Hasmoneans, even during the reign of Alexander Jannaeus (*Antiq.* 15.4). Hyrcanus II, in exchange for the help he asked for in the war against his brother Aristobulus, promised to restore the city to the Nabatean king Aretas of Petra, together with other cities in the region (*Antiq.* 14.1.4). Madaba became a city of the Provincia Arabia after 106 CE.

In 37 CE, in the time of Aretas IV, the strategos of the city, a certain Abdobodat built a funerary monument for his father Itaybel and his son, also named Itaybel, of the ʿAmirat tribe (*banu ʿAmrat,* possibly "the sons of Jambri" of *Mc.* 9:36ff.). A bilingual inscription in Greek and Nabatean records that in the third year of the new Provincia Arabia (108/109 CE), another member of the same tribe, Abgar/Isyon son of Monoath, built a tomb for his son Selaman. In a Greek inscription found at el-Mushaqqar, on the road between Esbus/Ḥesban and Livias/Tell er-Rameh, the priest Zaidallah Petrigenous, *boleuta* (of the city council) of Madaba, is mentioned, who offered the monument in honor of an unknown Roman emperor.

Together with Greek and Latin inscriptions of the second–third centuries mentioning centurions of the Tertia Legio Cyrenaica stationed in the province, a dedicatory inscription was recently found with the name of the governor (Flavius) Iulianus at the time of Emperor Elagabalus (219 CE; see Piccirillo, 1989). Madaba had a local mint at the time of the emperors Septimius Severus, Caracalla, Geta, and Alexander Severus. The main typologies used were the Helios and the Tyche (standing or seated), of the Medabenon (inhabitants of Madaba) and the baetyl in a tetrastyle temple. So far, the main portions of the *decumanus,* the primary paved east–west road of Roman Madaba, and possibly the Tychaion, the temple of the city's Tyche along that road (whose carved architectural elements were reused in the city's Byzantine churches), have been identified.

Ulrich J. Seetzen crossed the ruins of the then abandoned tell of Madaba in 1807. In 1872, coming from the south, the expedition of Canon Tristram arrived at Madaba and camped among the ruins for four days. Explorers from the Palestine Exploration Fund arrived in 1881. Their arrival had been preceded, in December 1880, by ninety Christian bedouin families who had established themselves among the ruins allotted to them by the Turkish authorities. It is to this reoccupation of the site that the greater part of the following discoveries is owed. In 1887, the Latin missionary Don Biever sent to Jerusalem the transcription of the first inscriptions of the mosaic floor from the Church of the Virgin Mary. Gottlieb Schumacher, in October 1891, and P.-M. Séjourné, in 1892, drew the first general plan of the ruins. It was later updated by Frederick J. Bliss, in 1895; Giuseppi Manfredi, in 1899; A. Paulouskji and N. K. Kluge, in 1903; Alois Musil, in 1905; and by Melezios Metaxakis from 1905 to 1907. The Madaba mosaic map was seen in December 1896 in the new church built by the Greek Orthodox patriarchate by Cleofas Kikilides and published the following year. The event focused the attention of scholars from all over the world on Madaba (see figure 1). In 1897 mosaics also were discovered in the crypt of St. Elianos, in the Church of the Prophet Elias, and elsewhere. From that year on, Madaba became "the city of mosaics." [*See* Palestine Exploration Fund; *and the biographies of Schumacher and Bliss.*]

In 1965, a German mission under the direction of H. Donner restored the Madaba map mosaic. In 1966, Ute Lux of the German Evangelical Institute excavated the Church of al-Khadir and, in 1967, the Church of the Apostles (Lux, 1967, 1968). Beginning in 1968, the Department of Antiquities of Jordan conducted excavations in the cathedral and in the Salayta Church. In collaboration with the Department of Antiquities, Michele Piccirillo of the Studium Biblicum Franciscanum (SBF) conducted several archaeological campaigns, as of 1979, in the area of the Church of the Virgin Mary and of the Hippolythus hall, in the "burnt palace" along the paved Roman street, and in the cathedral church on the south side of the tell. [*See* Deutsches Evangelisches Institut für Altertumswissenschaft des Heiligen Landes; Franciscan Custody of the Holy Land.]

The finds from two tombs discovered in the necropolis area west of the tell are the only archaeological evidence that Madaba was inhabited at least from the thirteenth century BCE (the final phase of the Late Bronze Age). A second tomb, from the Iron Age I–II, was found on the slopes of the hill in front of the tell on the south.

The main edifices so far excavated are several churches and palaces of the Byzantine and Umayyad periods. It is known that Christianity spread rapidly in the Provincia Arabia. Eusebius mentions Qurayat as "a village of only Christians flourishing near Madaba" (*Onomasticon* 112.14). Monks lived on Mt. Nebo, west of Madaba, at least in the second half of the fourth century. [*See* Nebo, Mount.] However, it is only from the Acts of the Council of Chalcedon, held in 451, that the existence of a Christian community at Madaba is known, with a bishop under the authority of the metropolitan archbishop of Bosra. [*See* Bosra.] The *Life of St. Euthymius,* written by Cyril of Scythopolis, recounts that Gaianus, a disciple of the saint, was consecrated bishop of Maiumas in Gaza. In the fifth century Peter the Iberian, bishop of Maiumas, entered and stopped in Madaba on the road to the hot baths of Baarus (modern Hammamat Maʿin).

The inscriptions in the mosaics of the churches in Madaba and its environs are the principal and practically the only source of historical information available for the first decades of the sixth century through the eighth century. Phidus and Cyrus probably were the bishops of Madaba in the first decades of the sixth century. In the time of Phidus, the lower Chapel of the Priest John at Khirbet el-Mukhayyat was built and a mosaic executed. In the time of Cyrus, the *photisterion* ("baptistery") of the cathedral in Madaba received a mosaic, as did the Church of Kaianos in the Valley of ʿAin Musa north of Mt. Nebo. The mosaics in the diaconicon-baptistery of the Sanctuary of Moses and in the Church of

MADABA. Figure 1. *Detail of the Madaba Map mosaic, showing the Jordan River.* (Archive Studium Biblicum Franciscanum)

St. George in the village of Nebo mention that Elias was bishop in 531 and 536. [*See* Baptisteries.]

In 562, when John was bishop of the diocese, the Chapel of St. Theodore, in the atrium of the cathedral, received a mosaic. During John's episcopate, a small chapel was built in the southeast sector of the city, to which the Church of the Apostles was later added. In the village of Nebo, the upper Chapel of the priest John and the Church of the Holy Martyrs Lot and Procopius were built and paved with mosaic floors.

Just outside the north wall of the city of Madaba in the time of the emperor Justinian, a great reservoir was dug to provide the city's water. In the valley southwest of the tell, another great reservoir (about 100 sq m and 10 m deep) was already in use. The mosaic in the Hippolythus hall, the best example of the city's classical renaissance, is dated to this period, the first half of the sixth century (see figure 2). The hall was part of a mansion that had been added to the west side of the Roman temple (the Tychaion) on the north side of the paved road (the *decumanus*) in the center of the city's northern quarter. The mosaic pavement (7.30 × 9.50 m) is lavishly decorated with Nilotic and mythological motifs inspired by Euripides's tragedy *Hippolytus*. The personifications of the Tychai of the christianized cities of Rome, Gregoria, and Madaba also appear, each one holding a cross on a long staff. In the mosaic's central panel, the characters in the tragedy are accompanied by labels with their respective names: the handmaidens assist Phaedra, while the wet-nurse turns toward Hippolytus, who is accompanied by his ministers and by a servant who holds his mount by the bridle. In a second figurative panel, the goddess Aphrodite, seated on a throne next to Adonis, threatens with her sandal a winged Eros, who is being presented to her by a Grace. A second Eros supports Aphrodite's bare foot, while a third Eros looks on and a fourth is intent on emptying a basket full of flowers representing beans. A second Grace grasps a foot of still another Eros, who takes refuge among the branches of a tree, and a third Grace runs after the sixth

MADABA. Figure 2. *The Church of the Virgin and the Hippolytus Hall.* (Archive Studium Biblicum Franciscanum; photograph by Michele Piccirillo)

Eros. A peasant girl coming from the country observes the scene and locates the scene in the countryside.

From 576 to the end of the century, Sergius was bishop of Madaba. The inscriptions chart the period's building activities, which were especially busy in the diocese during his episcopate. He continued the renovations begun by his predecessor John, and in 576 brought to completion the restoration of the atrium of the cathedral, with its cistern and new baptismal chapel. In 578, the mosaicist Salaman signed mosaic floor of the Church of the Apostles, which was built on the southeast corner of the acropolis. At the same time, at Umm er-Rasas/Kastron Mefaa, 30 km (19 mi.) east of Madaba, the northern church (named the Church of Bishop Sergius), the Church of the Lions, the Church of the Rivers, and the Church of the Priest Wa'il were built and lavish mosaics were laid down. [*See* Umm er-Rasas.] The most important building program in the diocese was the construction of the Basilica of Moses on Mt. Nebo, completed in 597/98. At the same time, a sacred complex that included the Church of the Virgin and the Church of the Prophet Elias was begun in the city. Before the death of Sergius in 595/96, the crypt of the Church of the Prophet Elias was completed.

In 603, Bishop Leontius, "sweetest and true friend of peace," as he was remembered in inscriptions, had already succeeded Bishop Sergius. A room with mosaics, to the north of the church in the cathedral complex, is dated to 603. In the southern territory of the diocese, the west church in the village of Mukawer was decorated with mosaics and dedicated in 603. [*See* Machaerus.] In 608 the building program of the two churches on the main street, begun in the time of Sergius's predecessor, was finished with the aid of funds donated by two brothers, Menas son of Panphilus, and Theodosius. A chapel dedicated to the Virgin Theotokos was added to the baptistery on the southern wall of the Basilica of Moses on Mt. Nebo.

To these dated monuments should be added, for stylistic reasons, several other churches discovered at Madaba and in the nearby villages. They were either built or restored in the second half of the sixth century–beginning of the seventh century, at the time of the Bishops John, Sergius, and Leontius. It was the period during which the most intense ecclesiastical building activity took place: the northern church with the mosaic map of Palestine, the church of al-Khadir, the Hippolytus hall, and the Burnt palace.

The basilica near the city's north gate had been identified before the Madaba map mosaic was discovered and published. In the 1880s the Greek Orthodox community had chosen the area to build a chapel and a house for its priest. Then in 1896 a new church was built there, during which the left sections of its mosaic floor were uncovered. Within the three-naved church, the mosaic composition did not extend much farther than the limits of those sections, which are each 15.70 m wide and 5.60 m long. The nearly 150 geographic captions in the mosaic's left sections refer mainly to Syro-Palestinian territory from the region of Tyre and Sidon on the north, to the Egyptian Delta on the south, and from the Mediterranean Sea to the Syrian desert. The mosaic's figurative high point is the vignette of Jerusalem, which, in a way is the ideal center of the composition even if it is not in the exact physical center. The city, seen in a bird's-eye view, is represented with its walls, gates, streets, and principal buildings, some of them still identifiable. The map is oriented east, as are its cities and their buildings—so are the captions, which can be seen and read by whomever enters the church and walks toward the altar. In spite of the approximations the map's small area required in order to distribute the localities along the region's road network, the sites are quite clearly indicated, by captions and vignettes that suggest the importance of each locality. From the captions of the toponyms (mostly taken from the *Onomasticon* of Eusebius), and especially from the direct references to the Israelite tribes, it becomes clear that the map is, in the first place, a document of biblical geography. The addition of New Testament localities and the preeminence of Christian sanctuaries and churches and of the basilica of the Holy Sepulcher in the heart of Jerusalem, make the map a Christian rereading of the history of salvation in its geographic framework. Seen in this perspective, the map is a document of the faith of the Christians who executed it. Artistically, the map and the mosaics of Madaba and its environs should be seen in the context of the classical renaissance of the Justinian period.

After a period of historical silence, recent excavations have clarified that the Christian community of Madaba was still vital during the Umayyad period. On the acropolis of Maʿin, "a large village near the hot baths of Baaru" (*Onomasticon* 44.21), a church was rebuilt with a mosaic pavement in 719/20. The pavement depicted a series of buildings representing the cities and villages in Palestine and Transjordan.

At Umm er-Rasas/Kastron Mefaa the church of St. Stephen was rebuilt and paved with the same kind of architectonical representations at the time of Bishop Sergios II—certainly in the eighth century, although the exact year cannot be fixed. In 756, under Bishop Job, the presbytery of the same church was repaved. In 762, also under Bishop Job, the mosaic of the chapel of the Virgin Theotokos in the monastery of ʿAyn al-Kanisah on Mt. Nebo was restored.

In 767, at the time of Bishop Theophane, the mosaic of the church of the Virgin in the center of Madaba was repaved. This is the last date for the Christian community and for the city. Archaeological evidence points to a scanty occupation in the later periods until the modern resettlement in December 1880.

[*See also* Churches; *and* Mosaics.]

BIBLIOGRAPHY

Alliata, Eugenio. "Nota sulla ceramica." *Studium Biblicum Franciscanum/Liber Annuus* 32 (1982): 403–408.

Alliata, Eugenio. "Nota sulla ceramica dello scavo." *Studium Biblicum Franciscanum/Liber Annuus* 36 (1986): 328–334.

Avi-Yonah, Michael. *The Madaba Mosaic Map.* Jerusalem, 1954.

Bagatti, Bellarmino. "Il significato dei mosaici della scuola di Madaba (Transgiordania)." *Reallexikon für Antike und Christentum* 33 (1957): 139–160.

Di Segni, Leah. "The Date of the Church of the Virgin in Madaba." *Studium Biblicum Franciscanum/Liber Annuus* 42 (1992): 251–257.

Gatier, Pierre-Louis. *Inscriptions de la Jordanie,* vol. 2, *Région centrale (Amman, Hesban, Madaba, Maʿin, Dhiban).* Inscriptions Grecques et Latines de la Syrie, 21. Paris, 1986.

Gatier, Pierre-Louis. "Une inscription latine à Madaba." *Studium Biblicum Franciscanum/Liber Annuus* 37 (1987): 365–367.

Harding, G. Lankester. *Four Tomb Groups from Jordan.* Palestine Exploration Fund Annual, no. 6. London, 1953.

Lux, Ute. "Eine altchristliche Kirche in Madeba." *Zeitschrift des Deutchen Palästina-Vereins* 83 (1967): 165–182.

Lux, Ute. "Die Apostel-Kirche in Madeba." *Zeitschrift des Deutschen Palästina-Vereins* 84 (1968): 106–129.

Piccirillo, Michele. "Una tomba del Ferro I a Madaba (Madaba B–Moab)." *Studium Biblicum Franciscanum/Liber Annuus* 25 (1975): 198–224.

Piccirillo, Michele, with Eugenio Alliata. *Chiese e mosaici di Madaba.* Studium Biblicum Franciscanum, Collectio Maior, 34. Jerusalem, 1989.

Piccirillo, Michele. "Un'iscrizione imperiale e alcune stele funerarie di Madaba e di Kerak." *Studium Biblicum Franciscanum/Liber Annuus* 39 (1989): 105–118.

Saller, Sylvester J. "The Works of Bishop John of Madaba in the Light of Recent Discoveries." *Studium Biblicum Franciscanum/Liber Annuus* 19 (1969): 145–167.

Thompson, Henry O. "An Iron Age Tomb at Madaba." In *The Archaeology of Jordan and Other Studies Presented to Siegfried H. Horn,* edited by Lawrence T. Geraty and Larry G. Herr, pp. 331–363. Berrien Springs, Mich., 1986.

Michele Piccirillo

MADINAH. *See* Medina.

MAFJAR, KHIRBAT AL-, site located near Jericho in the Jordan Valley, where excavations carried out between 1934 and 1948 brought to light the richest and the most original of all princely establishments associated with the early Islamic dynasty of the Umayyads (661–750 CE). After 1948 additional sections of the site were cleared and a process of continuing renovation was initiated to preserve the existing ruins and to make them easier for visitors to understand. The vast majority of the finds from the site and most of the records of the excavations are kept in Jerusalem, in the former Palestine Archaeological Museum, now known as the Rockefeller Museum, where several sculpted ensembles have been reconstructed.

Khirbat al-Mafjar is also known as Qaṣr Hisham, because a graffito found in its ruins carries the name of that particular caliph who ruled between 724 and 744. There is in fact no valid reason to associate Khirbat al-Mafjar with Hisham and, even though a reasonable and tempting hypothesis can be made about the patron of the complex (see below), it cannot be demonstrated.

The site had been identified as a significant settlement as early as 1873 by the British surveyors of Palestine. For a while it was considered to be the biblical Gilgal and the Early Christian Galgala. In fact, its excavators first believed that they had found a Christian ecclesiastical establishment. It turned out to be an Umayyad palace that was probably never completed. Its construction seems to have been abandoned rather abruptly—either because of one of the several earthquakes that affected Palestine in the middle of the eighth century or because a patron suddenly disappeared or lost interest.

There are five parts to the establishment:

1. *Two-storied square castle.* Roughly 70 m to the side, the complex has a porticoed courtyard with single rooms, large halls, or apartments known in Arabic as *bayt*s around it (see figure 1); although their exact functions cannot be established, these halls clearly were meant for a diverse set of activities, a relative rarity in palaces of the same type. The entrance complex is unusually large and was decorated with a striking array of stucco sculptures, ranging from traditional geometric and vegetal designs to an unusual number of representations of personages and animals, and mural paintings, some representational, on the second floor. [*See* Palace; Furniture and Furnishings, *article on* Furnishings of the Islamic Period.]

2. *Mosque.* To the north of the castle, a small and architecturally sober mosque had a direct passage to the second floor of the living quarter. [*See* Mosque.]

3. *Bath.* A sequence of rooms—an enormous (30 × 30 m) common room covered by an extraordinary roof of vaults and domes, a small suite of bathing rooms, a large latrine, a heavily decorated small private room, and a monumental entrance—corresponds to the usual system that issued from Roman architecture. The respective sizes of the components and especially the decoration found in them are unique in three ways: by the techniques used (mosaics, paintings, and sculptures); by the subjects depicted (princes, half-clad women, animals in all sorts of guises, a most elaborate geometry, rich vegetation), even though many of the topics have not yet been properly identified; and by the styles of depiction (its models are found in the Mediterranean world as well as in Buddhist Central Asia). A small room in the northwest corner, whose exact function is unclear, is a museum of mosaic and sculpture masterpieces. [*See* Baths; Mosaics; Wall Paintings.]

MAFJAR, KHIRBAT AL-. Figure 1. *General view of the excavated palace.* (Courtesy Pictorial Archive)

4. *Forecourt.* Unifying the bath, mosque, and castle as a single composition, even though they were built at different times, is a forecourt. Toward the center of the courtyard an octagonal domed pavilion stood over a small pool.

5. *Walled and irrigated area.* A large walled and irrigated area surrounding the complex may have been used for cultivation or for hunting.

Khirbat al-Mafjar's architectural planning is awkward in many details, but the ensemble differs from other Umayyad castles through the imagination and originality of some of its construction (vaults in the bath hall, a pavilion in the forecourt), through its elaborate and luxurious decoration, and through the technical quality of most of its decoration. One of its excavators, Robert W. Hamilton (1988), has made a most persuasive argument that the licentious, poetic, and exhilarating life of the prince-poet and short-lived caliph Walid II (assassinated in 744) fits admirably with the setting and decoration of Khirbat al-Mafjar and that he should be considered the palace's patron. Like most sites in Syria and Palestine, Khirbat al-Mafjar was reoccupied in the twelfth–thirteenth centuries, when a caravanserai was built out of its ruins.

[*See also*; Umayyad Caliphate.]

BIBLIOGRAPHY

Creswell, K. A. C. *A Short Account of Early Muslim Architecture.* Rev. ed. Aldershot, 1989. See pages 179–200 for Khirbat al-Mafjar.

Ettinghausen, Richard. *From Byzantium to Sasanian Iran and the Islamic World.* Leiden, 1972. See chapter 3, "The Throne and Banquet Hall of Khirbat al-Mafjar" (pp. 17–65).

Grabar, Oleg. *The Formation of Islamic Art.* Rev. and enl. ed. New Haven, 1987.

Hamilton, Robert William. *Khirbat al-Mafjar: An Arabian Mansion in the Jordan Valley.* Oxford, 1959.

Hamilton, Robert William. *Walid and His Friends: An Umayyad Tragedy.* London, 1988.

Whitcomb, Donald S. "Khirbat al-Mafjar Reconsidered: The Ceramic Evidence." *Bulletin of the American Schools of Oriental Research,* no. 271 (1988): 51–67.

OLEG GRABAR

MAGDALA (Ar., Majdal), site located on the western shore of the Sea of Galilee, 3 km (2 mi.) north of Tiberias and 5 km (3 mi.) south of Capernaum (32°49′ N, 35°31′ E; map reference 198 × 247) and identified as ancient Migdal by its Arabic name.

No remains of city walls have yet been found at the site, but its borders are known on three sides: to the east, the Sea of Galilee; to the south, a cemetery; and to the west, the mountains. It seems that it was a small town in the early Hellenistic to Byzantine periods, also called Tarichea ("salted fish") and Migdal-Nunia ("the fish tower")—names that reflected the main occupation of its citizens—fishing. [*See* Fishing.] An underwater survey carried out by Ehud Galili for the Israel Antiquities Authority in 1991 raised the possibility that the town was named after a tower built in the water, south of the town, with natural rock as its base.

Magdala was a Jewish town founded in the Late Hellenistic (Hasmonean) period. The town came under siege and a heavy battle was fought there during the First Jewish Revolt against Rome, when Titus attacked it from the Sea of Galilee (Josephus, *War* 3.10.3). [*See* First Jewish Revolt.] According to Josephus, six thousand people were killed. The town is known later, in Christian tradition, as the birthplace of Mary Magdalene, a follower of Jesus (e.g., *Mt.* 27:56). The town survived the Roman defeat of the Jews, and its name appears a few times in Jewish sources (J.T. *Ber* 9.3, *Meg.* 3.1; B.T. *Yoma'* 1.2; see also Manns, 1976).

The largest excavations at the site were carried out by Franciscans, directed by Virgilio Corbo (1976), in 1971–1973 and 1975–1976. Five levels were unearthed. The first features a well-designed building (9 × 7 m) called a mini-synagogue by its excavators. It is a one-room structure, with a flight of steps the excavators interpreted as benches. On three sides of the rectangular building, three rows of pillars 33 cm in diameter and with Doric capitals were arranged in a U shape, with heart-shaped pillars in the corners. The excavators identified two floors, one above the other, with a fill about 30 cm deep. They dated the first floor to the first century BCE and the later floor to the first century CE. Water canals around the walls support Ehud Netzer's identification of the building as a springhouse, rather than a very small and unusual synagogue. [*See* Synagogues.]

West of the structure a group of pools and a water tower are dated to the Early–Late Roman period. The installations are connected to the spring that supplied water to the town. To the north an "urban villa" was excavated, and to the south a large building with twenty-four rooms and a large "piazza" adorned with pillars. [*See* Villas.] These elements point to a well-designed small town in the Roman period. According to the excavators, the eastern side of the town was badly damaged during the Jewish Revolt.

It is possible that the shipwreck found in the Sea of Galilee close to Magdala and dated to the first century CE is also a relic of that war. [*See* Galilee Boat.] The boat was found not far from the location of the town's ancient quay; both inside and near the quay a few arrowheads and a typical first-century CE cooking pot and oil lamp were recovered by Shelley Wachsmann.

A small salvage excavation carried out by the Israel Antiquities Authority in 1991, directed by Hana Abu-Uqsa (1993), uncovered the remains of a private building whose floors held storage jars, cooking pots, and assorted small finds. The earliest coins, as in the Franciscan excavations, are Hasmonean. It seems that the building was damaged during the First Revolt but was later rebuilt and remained in use until the second century. A Byzantine monastery was excavated at the site, which, as at neighboring Tiberias, demonstrates the social change that took place in formerly Jewish Galilee in the Byzantine period. [*See* Monasteries.]

A few hundred meters south of the site, a number of decorated sarcophagi were unearthed that date to the third-fourth centuries CE. [*See* Sarcophagus.] A hoard of 188 bronze coins minted in different cities was found nearby as well in 1973 (Meshorer, 1976).

[*See also the biography of Corbo.*]

BIBLIOGRAPHY

Abu-Uqsa, Hana. "Migdal." *Excavations and Surveys in Israel* 13 (1993): 28.

Corbo, Virgilio. "Città romana di Magdala: Rapporto preliminare dopo la quarta campagna di scavo, 1975." In *Studia Hierosolymitana in onore del P. Bellarmino Bagatti*, vol. 1, *Studi archeologici*, edited by Emmanuele Testa, pp. 355–378. Studium Biblicum Franciscanum, Collectio Maior, 22. Jerusalem, 1976.

Corbo, Virgilio. "Piazza e villa urbana a Magdala." *Studium Biblicum Franciscanum/Liber Annuus* 28 (1978): 232–240.

Corbo, Virgilio. "La mini-synagogue de Magdala." *Le Monde de la Bible*, no. 57 (1989): 15.

Loffreda, Stanislao. "Alcune osservazione sulla ceramica di Magdala." In *Studia Hierosolymitana in onore del P. Bellarmino Bagatti*, vol. 1, *Studi archeologici*, edited by Emmanuele Testa, pp. 338–354. Studium Biblicum Franciscanum, Collectio Maior, 22. Jerusalem, 1976.

Manns, Frédéric. "Magdala dans les sources littéraires." In *Studia Hierosolymitana in onore del P. Bellarmino Bagatti*, vol. 1, *Studi archeologici*, edited by Emmanuele Testa, pp. 307–337. Studium Biblicum Franciscanum, Collectio Maior, 22. Jerusalem, 1976.

Meshorer, Ya'acov. "A Hoard of Coins from Migdal." *'Atiqot* 11 (1976): 54–71.

Schneider, A. M. *The Church of the Multiplying of the Loaves and Fishes at Tabgha on the Sea of Gennesaret and Its Mosaics*. London, 1937. Translation of the original German edition (Paderborn, 1934).

Stefanski, Y. "Migdal." *Excavations and Surveys in Israel* 5 (1986): 71. Discusses the ancient town's northern border.

Wachsmann, Shelley. *The Excavations of an Ancient Boat in the Sea of Galilee (Lake Kinneret)*. 'Atiqot vol. 19. Jerusalem, 1990.

MORDECHAI AVIAM

MAGHREB. *See* North Africa.

MAGNETIC ARCHAEOMETRY.

A nondestructive geophysical investigation technique that reacts to magnetic characteristics in natural and worked materials, of use at archaeohistorical sites, is known as magnetic archaeometry, or magnetic survey analysis. Differences between ambient forces and those induced by human agencies such as heat, compaction, organic decay, and architecture are measurable if their magnetic properties are not the same.

While this form of site study is faster and less expensive than excavating test trenches, nearby vehicles, trains, buildings, and power lines can interfere with testing. Anomalies, which are measurable variations, existing between environmental rocks and sediments and human habitats with trenches, structures, paths and roads, and areas and materials that were fired can be located with instruments in the field.

The ambient magnetic field anywhere on the planet can be observed in the behavior of a suspended magnetized needle. Cartographers call the angle on the earth's surface between the earth's north rotational axis and the magnetic vector, the declination. The inclination is the dip angle between the horizontal at the point of measurement and the magnetic force field within the earth. This magnetic field has wandered through geologic time; it has, in fact, reversed its polarization from time to time.

The intensity of this natural magnetic field is a function of the greatest pull (or vector) on such a "needle" or detector by the forces in any given area on earth. The unit of magnetic field strength expressed by most researchers is the gamma (γ). For example, in the United States the magnetic field varies from 49,900 to 59,500 γ; its inclination varies from 60 to 75° below the horizontal (Weymouth and Huggins, 1985, p. 193). Strength variations occur during solar magnetic storms and over 24-hour periods.

Current magnetic surveys may employ one of three instrumental techniques: the rubidium or cesium magnetometer; the fluxgate magnetometer; or the proton free-precession magnetometer. In the first, atomic electrons of rubidium and cesium (vaporized) capture the magnetic response. The second method detects the vector field forces along the axis of its electromagnetic coil design. Most researchers employ the last—the least costly—mode of instrumentation. The detector of the proton magnetometer is a coil submerged in a liquid (water or kerosene) source for hydrogen. A current in the coil produces an intense magnetic field in the liquid much greater than the natural/or ambient forces. The nuclear protons (actually spinning magnetic dipoles) of the hydrogen are partially polarized. The coil current is cut off and the nuclear protons precess (by a change in the axis of rotation) in the magnetic flux of the earth at that location. The protons briefly precess together, inducing a measurable voltage in the coil. The results are read in gamma units upon amplification of the voltage and determination of the frequency. Instrumentation has been designed to exhibit cycle times in about one second and to have a sensitivity level of 0.1 γ or less.

Environmental materials such as bedrock, residual and transported soils, and iron objects can be magnetized by the effect of applied magnetism. This physical property, known as induced magnetization, disappears when the magnetic forces cease. Those magnetic characteristics displayed in the absence of any applied field are described as remnant magnetization. Heated material, such as certain rocks and most clays, that cools in a magnetic field posseses a thermoremnant magnetization. Some minerals, such as hematite and magnetite, exhibit properties of remnant magnetism. Hematite, for example, is susceptible to conversion to the more highly magnetic magnetite by heating or in organic decay loci in the absence of oxygen.

Subtle variations in the magnetic field over a site probably indicate the presence of human activities. These data are mapped using block portions of the site area—the blocks may vary in area up to a limit controlled by the frequency of the ambient magnetic changes, usually 100 m × 100 m quadrangles. Sample positions may be set at 1- or 2-meter grid-line spacings within each quadrangle, depending on the desired resolution of the data imagery when mapped. Sensor (detection) height is chosen so as to lower input ("noise") from the subtle magnetic properties of soils: 40–60 cm is regarded as optimal for a one-meter grid. Control points act as references to track the diurnal, or daily, variations in the environment under study. Careful monitoring of these control points (usually every 15–20 minutes) assures greater accuracy of the method and its precision.

The greatest accuracy is achieved when two proton magnetometers are employed in either of the following configurations: one instrument is maintained at a fixed point on the site while the other records values at the grid points; or both instruments are operated together with a fixed spacing between them. When setting up the measurement operations, every natural (geological) and human (archaeological) feature must be recorded. These conditions contribute to the plans for the analytical procedures and to the final understanding of the data. The results of magnetic analysis are best presented as a matrix of corrected site magnetic values. Computer processing is essential in which a dot-line printer is used with characters of different shades, each recorded at representative grid-point intervals. The lightness or darkness of each dot character is a function of the magnetic field force at each point. The maps produced are easily read and interpreted.

BIBLIOGRAPHY

Aitken, Martin J. *Physics and Archaeology.* 2d ed. Oxford, 1974.

Arnold, J. B. "A Magnetometer Survey of the Nineteenth-Century Steamboat Black Cloud." *Bulletin of the Texas Archaeological Society* 45 (1974): 225–230.

Atkinson, R. J. C. "Méthodes électriques de prospection en archéologie." In *La découverte de passé,* edited by Annette Laming, pp. 59–70. Paris, 1952.

Black, Glenn A., and Richard B. Johnston. "A Test of Magnetometry as an Aid to Archaeology." *American Antiquity* 28 (1962): 199–205.

Breiner, Sheldon. *Applications Manual for Portable Magnetometers.* Palo Alto, Calif., 1973.

Ezell, Paul, et al. "Magnetic Prospecting in Southern California." *American Antiquity* 31 (1965): 112–113.

Graham, I. D. G., and Irwin Scollar. "Limitation on Magnetic Prospection in Archaeology Imposed by Soil Properties." *Archaeo-Physika* 6 (1976): 1–124.

Lerici, C. M. "Archaeological Survey with the Proton Magnetometer in Italy." *Archaeometry* 4 (1961): 76–82.

Mason, R. "Large-Scale Archaeomagnetic Surveys of the Barton and Vinton Townsites." Paper delivered at the Fourteenth Annual Meeting of the Society for Historical Archaeology, New Orleans, 1981.

Ralph, Elizabeth K., et al. "Archaeological Surveying Utilizing a High-Sensitivity Difference Magnetometer." *Geoexploration* 6 (1968): 109–122.

Scollar, Irwin. "Magnetic Prospecting in the Rhineland." *Archaeometry* 4 (1961): 74–75.

SYMAP. *Synagraphic Computer Mapping.* Harvard University, Laboratory for Computer Graphics and Spatial Analysis. Cambridge, Mass., 1975.

von Frese, R. R. B. "Magnetic Exploration of Historical Archaeological Sites as Exemplified by a Survey at Ft. Quiatenon (12T9)." Master's thesis, Purdue University, 1978.

Weymouth, John W., and Robert Huggins. "Geophysical Surveying of Archaeological Sites." In *Archaeological Geology,* edited by George Rapp, Jr., and John A. Gifford, pp. 191–235. New Haven, 1985.

REUBEN G. BULLARD

MAKKAH. *See* Mecca.

MALLON, ALEXIS (1875–1934), best known in the field of Syro-Palestinian archaeology as the excavator of the Chalcolithic type-site of Teleilat el-Ghassul. Mallon was born in La Chapelle-Bertin, France. As a young priest, he was sent to Ghazir in Lebanon. Mallon earned a Ph.D. in Egyptian hieroglyphics and Coptic, and in 1904 he published a grammar of Coptic and a number of articles. After studying theology in England (1905–1909), he returned to Lebanon, where he taught and published numerous articles on Egyptology and Coptic studies in the "Melanges de la Faculte orientale de Beyrouth." Thereafter, his intellectual interests shifted to prehistory and biblical archaeology.

In 1913, the Pontifical Biblical Institute (PBI) acquired land in Jerusalem for a study center and Mallon was selected to oversee the Vatican's building program there. During World War I he returned to Rome, where he wrote "Les Hebreux en Égypte" (1921) and participated in the prehistoric research of Father Bovier-Lapierre. His interest in prehistory lasted until the end of his life.

Mallon returned to Jerusalem in 1919 to continue the PBI construction project, which had ceased during the hostilities. He conducted a number of surveys in the Dead Sea region with the French prehistorian René Neuville, publishing them in a number of concise and erudite reports in the journal *Biblica.* However, his most lasting achievement is the publication of his 1929–1932 excavations at Teleilat el-Ghassul, which appeared shortly after his death (Mallon, Koeppel, and Neuville, 1934).

Mallon's excavations at Teleilat el-Ghassul fundamentally altered Palestinian archaeology through the discovery of a new archaeological culture. William Foxwell Albright, who examined the new material with Mallon, labeled the assemblage Chalcolithic (Albright, 1932). Among the reasons

Mallon's work stands as a lasting achievement is his having been one of the pioneers in a multidisciplinary approach to archaeological fieldwork and analysis. His book on Teleilat el-Ghassul is still the most significant publication of the site, for the scale and care that Mallon and his team achieved.

[*See also* Teleilat el-Ghassul; *and the biography of Neuville.*]

BIBLIOGRAPHY

Albright, William Foxwell. "The Chalcolithic Age in Palestine." *Bulletin of the American Schools of Oriental Research,* no. 48 (1932): 10–13.

Mallon, Alexis. *Les hébreux en Égypte.* Rome, 1921.

Mallon, Alexis, Robert Koeppel, and René Neuville. *Teleilāt Ghassūl.* 2 vols. Rome, 1934–1940. Detailed geological studies; contextual summaries of the range of architectural features found at the site; descriptions of the flint, pottery, and small finds assemblages; chemical analyses of the paint used in the site's now well-known murals; and a study of megalithic mortuary remains in the Dead Sea environs.

THOMAS E. LEVY

MALLOWAN, MAX EDGAR LUCIEN (1904–1978), one of the principal archaeologists to work in the Near East. Mallowan received his B.A. in classics at Oxford and was immediately hired as Leonard Woolley's assistant at the Ur excavations, a position he held for six successive seasons (1925–1930). It was at Ur that Mallowan met his wife and archaeological companion of the next forty-five years, the mystery writer Agatha Christie. In 1931 he completed his apprenticeship by joining R. Campbell Thompson's excavations at Nineveh.

Mallowan's interests included all areas of the ancient Near East and the Indus Valley as well, but he excavated exclusively in northern Mesopotamia. He first chose to dig, in 1933, at Arpachiyah where the well-preserved Halaf deposits proved to contain a series of substantial circular buildings (Mallowan's conceivably domed tholoi) and an outstanding range of finely painted Middle and Late Halaf pottery. When subsequent political developments kept British teams from working in Iraq, Mallowan chose to explore the little-known region of the Khabur and Balikh Rivers in nearby northeastern Syria. Following an initial survey, he excavated at Chaghar Bazar in the Khabur basin where, in the course of two full seasons (1935 and 1936), he not only revealed a long Halaf sequence but also an early second millennium occupation associated with Khabur Ware and cuneiform tablets from the time of Shamshi-Adad I (c. 1813–1781 BCE). His second major excavation in the region was at Tell Brak where he discovered the richly appointed Eye Temple of Late Uruk date and an Akkadian palace attributable to Naram-Sin.

Mallowan's final large-scale excavation took place at Nimrud (1949–1957), where he first concentrated on the main buildings of the Neo-Assyrian citadel before turning his attention to outlying Fort Shalmaneser, a royal residence, arsenal and treasury in which an exceptional range of early first-millennium BCE ivories came to light. As an excavator Mallowan was always dependent on fresh finds for future funding and, in response to this pressure, he persisted in digging, well into the 1950s, with a small staff and a large work force. In his own words (*Memoirs,* 1977) he remained "an unashamed supporter of the bygone days of digging."

As the first Professor of Western Asiatic Archaeology at the Institute of Archaeology of the University of London (1947–1960), Mallowan's natural gifts as a teacher were especially valued. Knighted in 1968, he also continued throughout his later years to foster the activities of the British School of Archaeology in Iraq and the British Institute of Persian Studies, two institutions that owe a particular debt to his energy and initiative.

[*See also* Brak, Tell; British Institute of Persian Studies; British School of Archaeology in Iraq; Ḥalaf, Tell; Khabur; Nineveh; Ur; *and the biography of Woolley.*]

BIBLIOGRAPHY

Curtis, John E., ed., *Fifty Years of Mesopotamian Discovery: The Work of the British School of Archaeology in Iraq, 1932–1982.* London, 1982.

Mallowan, M. E. L. *Twenty-Five Years of Mesopotamian Discovery, 1932–1956.* London, 1956.

Mallowan, M. E. L. *Nimrud and Its Remains.* 2 vols. London, 1966.

Mallowan, M. E. L. *Mallowan's Memoirs.* London, 1977.

Reade, Julian. "Revisiting the North-West Palace, Nimrud." *Orientalia* 63.3 (1994): 273–278.

Stronach, David. "Sir Max Mallowan." *Iran* 17 (1979): v–vii.

DAVID STRONACH

MALTA. Only by some stretch of the imagination is Malta a Near Eastern land. Although Malta and its sister island Gozo are only 80 km (50 mi.) from Sicily, they are 290 (180) from Tunisia, 335 (210) from Libya, 620 (385) from Greece, 1060 (660) from Turkey, and 1,895 (1,175) from the Syrian coast. The Mediterranean Sea can join, however, as well as divide. At several points in their long history, either directly or with North Africa as intermediary, Malta and Gozo have been linked with Southwest Asia, occasionally quite closely.

Although the concept of diffusion is out of fashion in archaeological interpretations, the origins of farming in the ancient Near East, and its spread from there across Europe, are universally accepted. However, since it took one thousand years to reach Malta, around 5000 BCE, by a route that took it through Greece, Italy, and Sicily, eastern influence was much diluted. Nonetheless, it should not be forgotten that the wheat and barley, sheep and cattle, upon which the earliest Maltese farming was based, originated in the Near East.

In the long and largely indigenous development of Maltese prehistory, there are only two hints of eastern contact.

Associated with the spectacular megalithic temple architecture of 3500–2500 are numerous representations in stone and clay of grossly corpulent and strangely asexual human figures, popularly known as "fat ladies." They are well illustrated in John D. Evans's work on Malta (1971). Although similarities with much earlier examples from Çatal Höyük in Turkey have been noticed, they are in all probability accidental.

Rather more convincing are a series of open straight-walled bowls with flat base, single handle, and lip characteristically thickened on the inner side, discussed by David Trump (1966). The lip is also flat, insloping, and frequently decorated with incised triangles, which are dot-filled or diagonally hatched. A few have been found in temple-period deposits, and they become common in the succeeding Bronze Age, whose cultural affiliations lie with western Greece. Close parallels for this form and its decoration were found in Early Bronze Age Thermi on Lesbos, and occurred also on the nearby mainland at Troy. It is certainly exotic in Malta at much the same period, but the Turkish connection will not be certain until confirmed by clay analyses. All other foreign imports before the first millennium, whether raw materials or manufactured goods, can be traced to Sicily or elsewhere in southern Europe.

Phoenician and Punic Influences. A great change came with the expansion of Levantine, or more specifically Phoenician, trade. Although the first contacts were formerly dated to the ninth century, it is now generally felt that firm evidence goes back no further than the later eighth, though this would not rule out occasional earlier visits. Cultural influence increased strongly when Carthage took over control of Phoenician enterprise in the west in the mid-sixth century. The Punic period in Malta lasted to the arrival of the Romans. They sacked the islands in the First Punic War in the 250s and annexed them in the second war in 218.

Written evidence for the Punic period is remarkably scarce. Diodorus Siculus mentions the Phoenicians' occupation of Malta and Gozo, and Latin writers report the wresting of them from the Carthaginians. Apart from some dedications on potsherds, the earliest of which may date from the third century, epigraphic evidence is confined to the Roman period and will be described below. As a result, our only significant information is from the archaeology.

Direct evidence for settlements of the Punic period is scanty in the extreme. A thin stratum with Phoenician red-slipped sherds but no structures was identified beneath the main square of Victoria, Gozo, stratified between Bronze Age and Roman levels. In limited excavations within the acropolis, known now as the Gran Castello, all earlier deposits had been destroyed by medieval and recent occupation. Mdina, in the center of Malta, produced some Roman structures and a little residual Bronze Age pottery. No excavation has been attempted in Vittoriosa beside Grand Harbour. All these places must have had substantial Phoenician and Punic occupation on the evidence of surrounding cemeteries.

A special case is provided by a strange building of fine ashlar (dressed stone) masonry with an Egyptian-gorge cornice at Zurrieq in the south of the island. This architectural ornament can hardly be anything but Punic work, though excavation has produced no dating evidence in the badly disturbed deposits. It has been variously suggested that this structure could be the remains of a country house, a monumental tomb, or a temple (Houel, 1785; Mayr, 1909; Ashby, 1915; Isserlin, personal communication).

Two more securely religious sites have been discovered on dramatic cliff-bound headlands on the west coasts of Malta and Gozo, at Ras ir-Raheb and Ras il-Wardija. The former has not been properly studied but has yielded a stone *thymaterion* or incense burner and a bone relief carving of a boar. The latter consists of an alcoved rock-cut chamber, including a symbol of the Phoenician goddess Tannit, but no deposits. Both sites had massive water cisterns cut in the rock beneath them.

By far the most important building of the Punic period in the islands is the temple at Ta Silg, excavated by an Italian mission from 1963 to 1970 and reported by Michelangelo Cagiano de Azevedo and colleagues (1965–). A prehistoric temple had been erected on the site in the third millennium and activity continued through the Bronze Age to approximately 1000. About 700 the Phoenicians incorporated the earlier structures in a rectangular temple of their own, with a courtyard and temenos. Alterations such as the enlargement of the enclosure and the addition of a colonnaded portico and further structures were made, particularly in the fourth to second century. These changes show strong Hellenistic influence. Later remodelings under the Romans, and especially in the Byzantine period, further complicate the earlier phases.

The finds from Ta Silg underline the eastern Mediterranean connection, including architectural fragments with Egyptian and proto-Aeolic motifs, a fine ivory carved in openwork relief with palmette and lotus designs, and another fragment of an incense burner. Numerous dedications in Phoenician to Astarte and in Greek to Hera were recovered too. They were incised in pottery before firing and were thus clearly made to serve as votive offerings. These objects strongly support the identification of the site with the temple of Juno, which was looted by Gains Verres (governor of Sicily 73–71), as recorded in Cicero's speech for his prosecution. A second temple dedicated to Hercules/Melkart was mentioned by the geographer Ptolemy, but it has not been identified.

Of other epigraphic material, two marble *cippi* (votive pillars), one in the National Museum of Malta, one in the Louvre, have bilingual dedicatory inscriptions in Punic and Greek. The Louvre specimen assisted the original transliteration of the Phoenician script in the eighteenth century.

They also were probably found in the ruins of Ta Silg. A small and very elegant slab from Gozo, now broken, records work on public buildings and temples. Its second-century date emphasizes an important fact—that Punic culture survived Roman military conquest by two centuries or more. The Maltese people were *barbaroi* at the time of St. Paul's visit about 60 CE, which in the context must surely mean Phoenician-speaking.

This cultural overlap is particularly obvious from the tomb material, which gives us our most detailed evidence concerning the Phoenician impact on Malta. Some tombs undoubtedly date back to the Punic or even Phoenician period. A well-excavated burial from Ghajn Qajjet near Mdina was published by J. G. Baldacchino and T. J. Dunbabin (1953) and can serve as an example. A square shaft was cut into the soft rock and a trapezoidal chamber, which measured 3 × 3.6 m (9.9 × 11.8 ft.), opened from its foot. A stone slab sealed its entrance. A larger horizontal slab inside the chamber served as a bed for two skeletons, one male, one female. They were accompanied by seven bracelets, two of bronze and five of silver; four silver rings; a bronze lampstand top; and four key-shaped loops of iron, probably fittings on a bier. Thirty-three pieces of red-slipped Phoenician pottery included amphorae, an oinochoe (wine vessel), jugs, cups, dishes, plates, and *bilychnis* lamps (saucers with two pinched spouts). In addition, there were two imported Greek cups, a proto-Corinthian kotyle (deep drinking cup) of a little before 700 and a Rhodian bird-bowl of the mid-seventh century. Because the former was noticeably worn, the latter gives the more reliable date for the burial. There was also a plain jar of a form datable to the second century, and it contained cremated human bone. Clearly the tomb had been reopened to take this later interment. This reuse for later burials is only one of the problems in studying the several hundred tombs known from Malta and Gozo.

There are other intact tomb groups, but very few with datable imports. A fine fourth-century Megarian bowl from another tomb at Hamrun is a good example. Usually only locally made pottery was included, making close dating difficult. Gradually red slip was abandoned, though narrow hoops of red or purple paint were often applied to the buff ware. Larger jars and egg-shaped amphorae appear. As an example, in a tomb chamber at Tal Horr, Pawla, a young man was accompanied by two each of amphorae, jugs, bowls, and saucers, all with simple red rings, and a plain two-handled jar. He wore a silver signet ring bearing a palm tree within a cabled border.

Much less informative are the great majority of tombs, which were looted long ago. On the other hand, there are quantities of material, some of it high quality, in private collections of antiquities without provenance or secure association, which must originally have been recovered from these tombs. Fragments of decorated gold foil, a terra-cotta mummiform sarcophagus, numerous amulets in faience, bronze and gold, and silver rings with faience scarab bezels testify to close trading links with the Levant (Gouder, 1991, pp. 8–14).

Later still, the tombs become larger, with one or two rectangular chambers on the same axis as a rectangular shaft. Cremation is now the more usual burial custom, as in the secondary interment at Ghajn Qajjet near Mdina. Most of the tombs must date to the period of Roman occupation. From 100 BCE–100 CE, the whole suite of material of Phoenician derivation is gradually replaced by Roman provincial pottery and glass.

The coin evidence, which has been reviewed by Charles Seltman (1946), should also be mentioned. Whereas trade easily explains coins from Sidon, Aradus, Carthage, and the Greek cities of Sicily, the local issues are much more puzzling. Of these, some were inscribed with the names Anan and Gawl in Phoenician, others had the corresponding Melitaea and Gauliton in Greek, although the Greeks never held the islands. The conclusion from all this evidence is that, although Phoenician and Punic culture became firmly established among the inhabitants of Malta and Gozo, archaeological information from the islands is very restricted, and can add little to that from areas where it is better preserved, in the Levant, North Africa, Spain, Sardinia, and Sicily.

Arabic Influence. The next period of eastern influence comes with the Arab invasion of 870 CE under Ibn Khafadsha, after which Malta was held as a dependency of Tunis until the Arabs were expelled by Count Roger of Sicily in 1090. Historical records are scanty and give no further details. Epigraphy is confined to gravestone inscriptions, a fine one pertaining to Majmuna, a twelve-year-old girl from Gozo, and a number from Rabat, outside the walls of the Arab capital in Mdina. Where datable, most of these tombstones are later, often much later, than the Christian reconquest of 1090. The pattern of slow culture change follows a remarkably similar pattern to that under the Romans.

Maltese traditional pottery shows strong North African influence, presumably going back to the ninth–eleventh-century occupation. It includes lamps, strainer jars for water, and bipartite globular jars. Decoration consists of fine, geometric red painting on white slip or coarser white on burnished red, both again with North African parallels. Unfortunately, intact deposits earlier than the fifteenth century have not yet been found; therefore, such influences and their survival cannot be studied in detail.

That influence is clearest linguistically. Maltese is basically a North African Arabic dialect with considerable additions from Sicilian Italian. That it took such firm root in the two centuries of Arab occupation may be explained, it has been suggested, if in 870 the Maltese were already Semitic speakers, as would have been the case if they were still using Phoenician. Because no contemporary records exist, proof of this hypothesis is not forthcoming. It does remind us, however, that, although Malta is isolated from the Near East, the sea routes of the Mediterranean allowed eastern influences to make a lasting mark on the culture of the Maltese islands.

[*See also* Phoenicians.]

BIBLIOGRAPHY

Ashby, Thomas. "Roman Malta." *Journal of Roman Studies* 5 (1915): 49.

Baldacchino, J. G., and T. J. Dunbabin. "Rock Tomb at Ghajn Qajjet, near Rabat, Malta." *Papers of the British School at Rome* 21 (1953): 32–41.

Cagiano de Azevedo, Michelangelo, et al. *Missione archeologia italiana a Malta*. Rome, 1965–1973.

Ciasca, Antonia. "Malta." In *The Phoenicians,* edited by Sabatino Moscati, pp. 206–209. New York, 1988.

Evans, John D. *The Prehistoric Antiquities of the Maltese Islands*. London, 1971.

Gouder, T. C. *Malta and the Phoenicians*. Malta, 1991.

Harden, Donald B. *The Phoenicians*. London, 1962. Contains scattered references to Malta.

Houel, Jean. *Voyage pittoresque des Isles de Sicile, de Malte et de Lipari*. Paris, 1785. See vol. 4, pp. 97–98, pl. 259.

Mayr, Albert. *Die Insel Malta in Altertum*. Munich, 1909. See pp. 89–90, fig. 30.

Seltman, Charles. "The Ancient Coinage of Malta." *Numismatic Chronicle* 6 (1946): 81–90.

Trump, D. H. *Skorba: Excavations Carried Out on Behalf of the National Museum of Malta, 1961–1963*. London, 1966.

D. H. TRUMP

MAʿLULA, modern village located in the Qalamun Mountains, 60 km (37 mi.) north of Damascus, Syria, and 110 km (68 mi.) south of Homs. The village is 1,650 m above sea level, at the bottom of a valley bordered on three sides by cliffs. If the evidence provided by the inscriptions found by W. H. Waddington and Heinrich Moritz (inscriptions 2563–2565) in the nearby caves is reliable, the site has been occupied since the Roman period; two of the inscriptions give dates of 107 and 167 CE. The existence of the site is, in any case, attested by George of Cyprus (Gelzer, 1890, p. 188, n. 993) as Magloulon. It was then a part of Lebanese Phoenicia. The Arab historian Yaqut mentions Iklim as one of the many villages that are a part of Maʿlula.

The village houses are arranged on the slopes of the valley like the tiers of seating in an immense amphitheater. Behind the summit of the cliff lies the Mar Sarkis Church and, since 1988, a modern hotel, from which there is a magnificent panoramic view. Three quarters of the village's inhabitants are Christians—Greek Orthodox or Greek Catholic; the remaining quarter are Sunni Muslims. Maʿlula is cited as the seat of a seventeenth-century Melchite bishopric, but in 1724 it was reunited with Said Naya. [*See* Said Naya.] It is perhaps its isolation (although it is not far from Damascus it is in the mountains) that has enabled Maʿlula to maintain its predominantly Christian population, unusual in Syria. This isolation did not, however, completely protect it from the hazards of politics. The city was sacked in 1850 by Turkish troops under Mustafa Pasha, whose men were pursuing the survivors of the revolt of the emir of Baalbek who had come to Maʿlula seeking refuge; the village was attacked and besieged again in 1860 and 1925. [*See* Baalbek.]

Nevertheless, in many respects the village remains a living conservatory of the most ancient traditions of Syrian civilization. To begin with, the inhabitants continue to speak a Western Aramaic dialect related to Judeo- and Syro-Palestinian Aramaic. It is therefore not injudicious to surmise that it represents the last example in Syria today of the language spoken in Syria-Palestine in the time of Jesus. [*See* Aramaic Language and Literature.] In comparison, the Aramaic spoken in the villages of the Jezireh and the Ṭur ʿAbdin is much further removed, notably in the area of morphology. Maʿlula also retains in use many churches dating to the most ancient Christian past. In the Church of St. Elie, a mosaic from the fourth century has been uncovered. The best-known monasteries in Maʿlula are of Mar Sarkis (St. Serge, whose cult was very widespread in Syria) and St. Takla. The Church of Mar Sarkis was probably constructed on the ruins of a pagan temple; it is a small basilica with columns and a central nave flanked by two aisles. Even though basilicas with cupolas do not appear before the fifth century, the monks of the monastery propose a date for the church before the Council of Nicaea (325 CE); it was then that the altar tables found in pits in the central apse and the northern side chapel were outlawed—because their origin was believed to be pagan. [*See* Basilicas; Churches.] Carbon-14 analysis dates certain wooden elements from the wall supports of the central nave to the fourth century. None of these arguments is entirely convincing. Carbon-14 technology, in particular, does not permit such precise dating. In the absence of an executed scientific study, it is impossible to date this church with certainty. It is, however, entirely possible that its most ancient parts belong to the fourth or fifth century, as tradition holds. Since 1732 the monastery and church have belonged to the Basilien Salvatorien order and the Greek Catholic community.

BIBLIOGRAPHY

Gelzer, Heinrich. *Georgius of Cyprus: Descriptio orbis romani*. Leipzig, 1890.

Le Bas, Philippe, and W. H. Waddington. *Inscriptions grecques et latines de la Syrie*. Paris, 1870.

Moritz, Heinrich. *Die Zunamen bei den Historikern und Chronisten*. 2 vols. Landshut, 1897–1898.

Reich, Sigismund S. "Histoire de Maʿlula: Raisons pour la conservation et la disparition de cet idiome." In Reich's *Études sur les villages araméens de l'anti-Liban*. Documents d'Études Orientales de l'Institut Français de Damas, 7. Damascus, 1937.

GEORGES TATE

Translated from French by Melissa Kaprelian

MALYAN (Anshan), site located in Fars Province, Iran, 50 km (31 mi.) north–northwest of Shiraz at an elevation of 1,611 m above sea level (30°01′ N, 52°25′ E). Malyan is often mentioned with Susa in the royal titulary of Elamite kings. [*See* Susa.] Its ancient city wall, constructed in the Proto-Elamite period, enclosed 200 ha (494 acres), but the occupation mound within the wall has an area of only 130 ha (321 acres). The Archaeological Department of Fars opened soundings under the direction of Feridun Tavaloli in about 1961 and the University Museum of the University of Pennsylvania sponsored five field seasons there (1971–1978) under the direction of William M. Sumner. Excavations focused on the Proto-Elamite (Banesh) period, the Kaftari-Qale period, and the Qale-Middle Elamite period. Ceramic evidence indicates that the site was occupied nearly continuously from about 6000 BCE into the Islamic period.

Proto-Elamite Period (3400–2800 BCE). Proto-Elamite deposits were excavated in four main operations. Large horizontal exposures were excavated in operation ABC, located near the center of the main mound, and in operation TUV, on a small isolated mound near the northeast corner of the city wall. More limited excavations were undertaken in a narrow trench across the city wall (BY8), and in the H5 deep sounding below later Kaftari buildings in operation GHI.

ABC operation. Four Proto-Elamite buildings from building levels 2–5 were excavated in the ABC operation (20 by 30 m, reduced to 10 by 13 m in the lowest level). Building Level 5, founded at the level of the plain, was made of unfired mud bricks, like all the buildings excavated at Malyan. Building Level 4 was constructed directly on the remains of the razed walls of Building Level 5. The earliest Proto-Elamite tablet and glyptic art came from this level. In Building Level 3 (15 by 25 m), with seventeen rooms, had walls decorated with painted rosette, swirl, and nested-step motifs executed in red, white, yellow, gray, and black plaster. Finds included fragments of incised and painted plaster bowls and drum-shaped ceramic vessels with floral and animal decoration in relief. The bricky fill between this building and the floors of Building Level 2 produced a collection of tablets and sealings in the classic Proto-Elamite style that is related to administrative activities in or near Building Level 3.

Building Level 2 was a fifteen-room warehouse (18 by 26 m) containing thirteen large (about 2 m high) Jemdet Nasr-style painted storage jars. Finds included Proto-Elamite tablets, sealings, concentrations of specular hematite, mother-of-pearl geometric inlay, and unworked shells from the Persian Gulf.

TUV operation. Operation TUV was occupied only in the Proto-Elamite period. Building Level 3 (247 sq m) was founded on the ruins of earlier Banesh buildings. The building had a number of rooms, a circular burned structure, and an alleyway; it was later modified for the construction of a pyrotechnical installation for copper smelting. Finds include Proto-Elamite sealed and inscribed tablets (see figure 1), jar and door sealings in several styles, solid clay balls with seal impressions, tools, and raw materials and by-products associated with the production of personal ornaments in metal, stone, and shell. Building Level 3 was razed to make room for the construction of Building Level 2 (455 sq m), which had plaster-lined bins, storage jars, hearths, milling stones, wells, and trash pits. Level 1, which was immediately below the mound surface and partly eroded, included the remains of two buildings separated by an alley. Finds in levels 2 and 1 indicate a continuation of the domestic activities and craft production found in the earlier buildings.

BY8 trench and H5 sounding. The Proto-Elamite wall (Operation BY8, 30 × 4–8 m) was a series of rooms reinforced along its inner face with a mud-brick platform; the rooms were protected on the outer face by a mud-plaster glacis built on a stone foundation. A sounding in operation H5 produced Middle Banesh ceramics below trash deposits with Late Banesh or Early Kaftari ceramics. This is the only context at Malyan that might represent a transition between the Banesh and Kaftari ceramic styles.

Kaftari Period (2200–1600 BCE). The city reached its maximum extent, some 130 ha within the reconstructed city wall, during the Kaftari period. Kaftari deposits were excavated in five main operations: large horizontal excavations in operations ABC and GHI, smaller excavations in two 10

MALYAN. Figure 1. *Proto-Elamite tablet.* Operation TUV, BL3. (Courtesy W. M. Sumner)

MALYAN. Figure 2. *Kaftari stamp seal.* Operation B. (Courtesy W. M. Sumner)

MALYAN. Figure 3. *Kaftari figurines.* Operation ABC. (Courtesy W. M. Sumner)

× 10 m squares (GGX98, FX106), and in the upper strata of a trench across the city wall (BY8).

ABC operation. The upper strata in operation ABC (20 × 30 m) consisted of Kaftari trash layers resting on the eroded surface that had truncated Proto-Elamite level 2. Within this trash deposit were a number of surfaces, pits, wells, fragmentary buildings, and many finds, including seals (see figure 2), tablets, figurines (see figure 3), flints, metal objects, raw materials, and production by-products.

GHI operation. Building Levels 3 and 4 were explored in a reduced area of excavation at the bottom of operation GHI. Building Level 2 was a courtyard building with access to the adjacent street, which was littered with a dense trash deposit. Finds included administrative texts in Sumerian, a lenticular school text, seals and sealings, figurines, and a bronze buckle in the form of hands grasping a bar. Level 1 belonged to the Qale–Middle Elamite period.

FX106 and GGX98 operations. Evidence of five Kaftari building levels was revealed in operation FX106 (10 × 10 m). Building Level 2 was a domestic structure with signs of extensive repair and rebuilding, an exterior well, a drainage ditch, and a walkway paved with square and trapezoidal baked bricks. Finds included figurines, cylinder seal blanks, flint tools, and by-products of metallurgical production. Operation GGX98 (10 × 10 m in area) produced two Kaftari building levels and a large intrusive Kaftari pit that contained a number of black-on-red canteen sherds, inscribed sealings, and a sun-dried-brick production site with rows of bricks left standing to dry in a herringbone pattern.

Qale-Middle Elamite Period (1600–1000 BCE). The EDD operation (1,000 sq m) uncovered a large burned Middle Elamite building with a central courtyard (10 × 14 m), surrounded by a corridor and a series of rooms. Finds from the floors of the destruction level included administrative tablets recording transfers of metals, finished objects, grain, flour, and animal products. The tablets and sealings were impressed with punctate designs representing diamond patterns, cuneiform signs, and naturalistic motifs. Other finds included glazed knobs and tiles, stone door bolts, crude flint flakes, and unworked calcite, hematite, and bitumen. Pottery kilns, constructed after the fire, produced Qale painted and plain ware. A small domestic complex, reusing some of the standing walls of the burned building, was also constructed after the fire. Ceramics and an Elamite tablet, similar to the finds from the burned level, suggest that there was a relatively short time lapse between the later and earlier levels. A burial above the latest building level may date to the Neo-Elamite period.

Late Periods. There is no evidence of an Achaemenid occupation, in spite of the frequent mention of the name *Anshan* in tablets from Persepolis. [*See* Persepolis.] A Sasanian kiln, several late burials, and Islamic ceramics found on the surface represent the final use of the site.

[*See also* Elamites.]

BIBLIOGRAPHY

Alden, John R. "Excavations at Tal-I Malyan. Part 1: A Sasanian Kiln." *Iran* 16 (1978): 79–86. Describes a Sasanian kiln and associated ceramics.

Balcer, Jack Martin. "Excavations at Tal-I Malyan. Part 2: Parthian and Sasanian Coins and Burials (1976)." *Iran* 16 (1978): 86–92.

Blackman, M. James. "The Mineralogical and Chemical Analysis of Banesh Period Ceramics from Tal-e Malyan, Iran." In *Scientific Studies in Ancient Ceramics,* edited by M. J. Hughes, pp. 7–20. British Museum Occasional Paper, 19. London, 1981.

Blackman, M. James. "The Manufacture and Use of Burned Lime Plaster at Proto-Elamite Anshan (Iran)." In *Early Pyrotechnology: The Evolution of the First Fire Using Industries,* edited by Theodore A. Wertime and Steven F. Wertime, pp. 107–115. Washington, D.C., 1982.

Blackman, M. James. "Provenance Studies of Middle Eastern Obsidian from Sites in Highland Iran." In *Archaeological Chemistry III,* edited by Joseph B. Lambert, pp. 19–50. American Chemical Society, Advances in Chemistry Series, no. 205. Washington, D.C., 1984.

Carter, Elizabeth, and Matthew W. Stolper. "Middle Elamite Malyan." *Expedition* 18.2 (1976): 33–42. Preliminary report on the Middle Elamite building in historical context.

Hansman, John. "Elamites, Achaemenians, and Anshan." *Iran* 10 (1972): 101–125. The historical and geographic evidence concerning the identification of Malyan as Anshan.

Miller, Naomi F. "The Interpretation of Some Carbonized Cereal Remains as Remnants of Dung Cake Fuel." *Bulletin on Sumerian Agriculture* 1 (1984): 45–47.

Miller, Naomi F. "Paleoethnobotanical Evidence for Deforestation in Ancient Iran: A Case Study of Urban Malyan." *Journal of Ethnobiology* 5.1 (1985): 1–19.

Nicholas, Ilene M. *The Proto-Elamite Settlement at TUV.* Malyan Excavation Reports, vol. 1. Philadelphia, 1990.

Nickerson, Janet W. "Malyan Wall Paintings." *Expedition* 19.3 (1977): 2–6.

Nickerson, John L. "Investigating Intrasite Variability at Tal-e Malyan (Anshan), Iran." *Iranica Antiqua* 26 (1991): 1–38. The evidence for craft specialization during the Kaftari period.

Stolper, Matthew W. *Texts from Tall-i Malyan,* vol. 1, *Elamite Administrative Texts (1972–1974).* Occasional Publications of the Babylonian Fund, 6. Philadelphia, 1984.

Stolper, Matthew W. "Proto-Elamite Texts from Tall-i Malyan." *Kadmos* 24.1 (1985): 1–12.

Sumner, William M. "Excavations at Tall-i Malyan, 1971–72." *Iran* 12 (1974): 155–180.

Sumner, William M. "Excavations at Tall-i Malyan (Anshan), 1974." *Iran* 14 (1976): 103–115.

Sumner, William M. "The Proto-Elamite City Wall at Tal-i Malyan." *Iran* 23 (1985): 153–161.

Sumner, William M. "Proto-Elamite Civilization in Fars." In *Ǧamdat Naṣr: Period or Regional Style?,* edited by Uwe Finkbeiner and Wolfgang Röllig, pp. 199–211. Beihefte zum Tübinger Atlas des Vorderen Orients, Reihe B, vol. 62. Wiesbaden, 1986. An interpretation of the Proto-Elamite levels at Malyan in a regional and chronological context.

Sumner, William M. "Maljān, Tall-e (Anšan)." In *Reallexikon der Assyriologie und Vorderasiatischen Archäologie,* vol. 7, pp. 306–320. Berlin and New York, 1988. Summary of excavations at Malyan, with an extensive bibliography.

Zeder, Melinda A. "The Equid Remains from Tal-e Malyan, Southern Iran." In *Equids in the Ancient World,* edited by Richard H. Meadow and Hans-Peter Uerpmann, pp. 366–412. Beihefte zum Tübinger Atlas des Vorderen Orients, Reihe A, vol. 19.1. Wiesbaden, 1986.

Zeder, Melinda A. *Feeding Cities: Specialized Animal Economy in the Ancient Near East.* Washington, D.C., 1991.

WILLIAM M. SUMNER

MAMLUK DYNASTY. *See* Ayyubid–Mamluk Dynasties.

MAMPSIS. *See* Kurnub.

MANASSEH, SURVEY OF. *See* Northern Samaria, Survey of.

MANBIJ, provincial town in northern Syria, located 78 km (48 mi.) northeast of Aleppo, the economic and administrative center of a fertile plain south of the Sajur River and near its junction with the Euphrates River. Commonly identified with the Assyrian settlement Nappigi/Nampigi, known as Hierapolis throughout the classical period, the traditional Arabic name, meaning "gushing water," mirrors the abundance of the freshwater supply. Even in antiquity, the water was distributed mainly through subterranean channels (*qanats*) to the irrigated gardens surrounding the city.

The area's fertility has encouraged continuous settlement since prehistory. An important urban center developed there, famed for a large temple dedicated to Atargatis and Hadad, alongside a sacred pool. These, together with other monuments of the Hellenistic period—a theater, the site's circular defensive walls, and several churches, described in some detail by medieval geographers—had already disappeared by the time Gertrude Bell (1911) visited the site in 1910. Buildings from the Islamic era, known from Arabic sources and occasionally from building inscriptions, have also vanished without trace, as has an oratory from AH 463/1070–1071 CE, two madrasas from the mid-twelfth century, and the Great Mosque, of uncertain date, to which a minaret was added in 581/1185–1186. The minaret was still standing, adjacent to some other ruins, in 1879, when Eduard Sachau (1883) passed through Manbij. Soon after, in 1304/1886–1887, the monument was replaced by a modern mosque, constructed by order of the Ottoman sultan Abdülhamid for a newly settled community of Circassians.

Historically, Manbij was an important stronghold at the heavily contested traditional border between Anatolia, Syria, and Mesopotamia, marked by the Upper and Middle Euphrates. Already established as a military base in the Hellenistic period, it formed part of the Roman limes of Chalcis. Later on, in the Early Byzantine period, it was an advance fortification against the Sasanians, who nevertheless succeeded in sacking the town in 540. Conquered by the Muslims in 16/637, the fortified city was renamed Manbij according to the ancient name. On orders from the ʿAbbasid caliph Harun al-Rashid, it was established as the capital of the border provinces (*ʿawāṣim*) in 170/786, the starting point of the yearly military campaigns into the areas of the Byzantine Empire. The site's key position on the major roads connecting the Syrian metropolis of Aleppo with Baghdad in central Mesopotamia and with Mosul in northern Mesopotamia motivated frequent raids by its Christian neighbors, the Byzantines (in 962, 966, 974), and the Crusaders (in 1168–1071, 1111, 1120, 1123, 1124), until a semiautonomous principality was established there under the Ayyubids in the late twelfth century. Devastated by the Mongols in 657/1259, the area was soon depopulated and Manbij was consequently reduced to the status of a provincial settlement.

The nearest crossing point on the Euphrates, 29 km (18 mi.) farther northeast, called Jisr Manbij, was protected by a strongly fortified castle, the Qalʿat Najm, rebuilt in the mid-twelfth century by the Zangid ruler Nur al-Din Maḥmud. The castle was further enlarged by the Ayyubid ruler of Aleppo, al-Ẓahir Ghazi, in 605/1208–1209 and subsequently enriched with a palace, a bath, and a mosque (612/1215). This citadel and a ruined Ayyubid madrasa or mosque, together with a nearby domed mausoleum, are the only surviving architectural witnesses to the important role the region played in history.

BIBLIOGRAPHY

Bell, Gertrude Lowthian. *Amurath to Amurath.* London, 1911. See pages 19–26. Should be compared with the earlier account by Sachau (below).

Elisséeff, Nikita. "Manbidj." In *Encyclopaedia of Islam,* new ed., vol. 6, pp. 377–383. Leiden, 1960–. The best summary available on the Islamic period.

Goossens, Godefroy. *Hiérapolis de Syrie: Essai de monographie historique.* Publication of the University of Louvain, Recueil de Travaux d'Histoire et de Philologie, 3d ser., fasc. 12. Louvain, 1943. Still the standard reference on pre-Islamic Manbij.

Sachau, Eduard. *Reise in Syrien und Mesopotamien.* Leipzig, 1883. The most complete description of lost monuments, including the only published inscriptions of Qalʿat Najm (see pp. 146–155).

Sanlaville, Paul, ed. *Holocene Settlement in North Syria.* British Archaeological Reports, International Series, no. 238. Oxford, 1985. Report of archaeological surveys conducted in 1977 and 1979.

MICHAEL MEINECKE

MANDAIC. The national and religious language of the Mandaeans, the only surviving Gnostics, is Mandaic. The language emerged simultaneously with this religious community in southern Mesopotamia in the third century CE. The Mandaeans still live in their ancient communities on both sides of the Persian Gulf. As an ethnic group with an esoteric national religion, they are a foreign element in their environment. According to their own mythologico-legendary traditions, contained in their holy books (*Ginzā Rabbā,*

"The Great Treasure"; *Drašī d-Yahyā*, "Sermons of John [the Baptist]"; the Liturgies; and a later pseudohistorical treatise, the legend *Harrān Goweyṯā*), they had to flee from their original homeland, Palestine, because of Jewish persecution. In spite of the lack of external evidence, these myths and legends appear to have a solid historical kernel. All of this religion's basic and central notions and even its technical terms are decidedly Palestinian, not Babylonian (cf. the use of the root *ṣḇy*, "to baptize," with the Christian Palestinian *ṣḇʿ*, as opposed to the Syriac *ʿmd; yardᵉnā*, "Jordan," the technical term for "river," in which the baptism is performed; *naṣorāya* "observant (of the Law); spiritual leader." All typical technical terms of the *Gospel of John* (light, darkness, way, truth, life, vine), are fundamental expressions of the Mandaean faith and indicate that a strong Proto-Mandaean movement must have existed in the milieu of the author of the fourth Gospel.

Like the Babylonian Jews, the Mandaeans also had to adopt a local Aramaic idiom in their new country. It was a South Babylonian Aramaic dialect closely related to the Aramaic language of the Babylonian Talmud. Minor differences may be explained by the strictly separate life of the two communities, their traditional inimical attitude toward each other, and their diametrically opposite religious ideologies. It is not surprising that the language of Mandaean incantation texts (lead scrolls and magic bowls) is very close to that of Jewish phylacteries—both are written in a sort of Babylonian-Aramaic koine common to Mandaeans, Jews, and Christians (see figure 1). Another reason for the differences between the Mandaic and the Talmudic languages is their literary style. All of the classical Mandaean literature is exclusively poetic, whereas the Talmudic is entirely prosaic.

Once in Mesopotamia, the Mandaean Naṣoraeans had to invent an alphabet and to fix the orthographic rules for the language in which they wanted to propagate their religious ideas (they could not use the Jewish-Aramaic alphabet because of their enmity with the Jews). There are some Elymaean inscriptions (named after Elymaïs, an ancient name of the southern Iranian province of Khuzistan) from the second half of the third century CE that already show prototypes of the Mandaean book script at a time when the Mandaeans are supposed to have immigrated to southern Mesopotamia. The problem of whether the Mandaeans brought this script into this region when they immigrated or took it over has not yet been definitively solved. There are arguments for both sides of the question (Macuch, 1971). Nevertheless, it is noteworthy that the first copy of the Mandaean Liturgies should have been redacted at about that time, according to the colophons from Early Islamic times.

At any rate, the use of this script for Mandaic was an effective invention of the Naṣoraeans, and the speed with which it was adapted to all the practical needs of the language shows that its adoption was clearly premediated. Mandaean scholars broke with many scribal practices of Imperial Aramaic, introducing simple phonetic spelling with a complete *scriptio plena* that has no analogy among the various Aramaic writing systems. Like the Greeks, they used the signs for the laryngeals, which were no longer pronounced, to express vowels: ʾ for *a*/*ae*, *-ẖ* (original Aramaic *ḥ*) for the final *-ī* as a suffix of the third-person singular masculine, and ʿ for initial *e*/*i* or as a support for *o*/*u*. In all other positions the back and the front vowels *o*/*u* and *e*/*i* were expressed by the semivowels *w* and *y* used regularly as *matres lectionis*.

1.	ࡀ	æ/a/å, ā/â
2.	ࡁ	b/ḇ
3.	ࡂ	g/ġ
4.	ࡃ	d/ḏ
5.	ࡄ	h
6.	ࡅ	w/u
7.	ࡆ	z
8.	ࡇ	-ī
9.	ࡈ	ṭ
10.	ࡉ	y/e/i/ī
11.	ࡊ	k/x
12.	ࡋ	l
13.	ࡌ	m
14.	ࡍ	n
15.	ࡎ	s
16.	ࡏ	i/ī/e-, or graphical support for o/u: ࡏࡅ
17.	ࡐ	p/f
18.	ࡑ	ṣ
19.	ࡒ	q
20.	ࡓ	r
21.	ࡔ	š
22.	ࡕ	t/ṯ
23.	ࡖ	(a)d (only as relative particle)
24.	ࡀ	(= 1)

MANDAIC. Figure 1. *The Mandaic alphabet.*

Nevertheless, the inventors of this simple Mandaic writing system remained captives of the Imperial Aramaic orthography in three respects: the masculine plural ending *-ia* (< **-ayyā*), pronounced simply *-ī*, is still consistently written with the silent final *a(leph);* the silent *q* (< Proto-Semitic *ḍ*) still appears in the script as in Imperial Aramaic; and similarly, *z* (< Proto-Semitic *ḏ*) is still written, although with frequent (later) variants betraying the actual pronunciation.

Mandaic can be divided into three distinct periods: classical (third century CE–Early Islamic period); postclassical (medieval); and modern.

Classical Period. In the golden era of the Mandaic language and literature, the founders of the Mandaean community developed a South Babylonian Aramaic dialect as an expressive poetic tool for their Gnostic mythology and liturgy. This fundamental period, in which all basic Mandaean writings were written, is of extreme importance in both historico-religious and linguistic respects. Mandaeans are the only Gnostic sect that completely preserved its sacred literature; because it has been preserved as a liturgical language, its traditional recitation, partly supported also by the living colloquial pronunciation, gives welcome means to the study of the ancient phonetic phenomena of South Babylonian Aramaic.

The phonetics of classical Mandaic rest on a Late Babylonian substrate, of which the loss of the laryngeals (ʾ, ḥ, ʿ) and the dissimilation of geminates (*bb* > *mb, dd* > *nd, zz* > *nz)* are especially characteristic. The only laryngeal that remained is *h.* Both phenomena mentioned are already attested in the names of these people and their religion, *mandāyā* ("Mandaean"), an adjective deriving from *mandā,* "knowledge par excellence, or *gnōsis,*" hence originally *gnōstikos*—although it simply designates laymen as believers in *mandā d-heyyī, gnōsis tēs zōēs,* the "redeemer of the Mandaean religion." The word derives from *madd*ᵉʿ*ā* (root *ydʿ,* "to know") and is attested in its dissimilated form, but still with the original laryngeal, *mandaʿ,* four times in the *Book of Daniel* (2:21; 4:31, 33; 5:12). Through the coinage of this technical term for the central notion of the Mandaean religion, the infix *n* was quasi-sanctified. It was often written even where it was not originally pronounced (e.g., *kunza* for *kūza,* "jar"), or pronounced where it was not written.

Mandaic is known for the fluid state of its phonetics, especially the free or combinatory variations of the liquids *l, r, n;* the disappearance of the laryngeals; the syncope of dentals, sibilants, and palatals; and the metathetical words and roots that created numerous homonyms and facilitated wordplays in polemics against other religious.

Classical Mandaic morphology is simple. Because the Mandaeans did not write silent letters, as did the Syro-Arameans, the phonetically written form of the third-person plural perfect tense became homographic with the same person in the singular: *g*ᵉ*ṭál,* "he killed" and "they killed." Although the grammatical number was clear from the syntactic construction, in the medieval and modern periods, a full plural form, *g*ᵉ*ṭalyōn,* "they killed," developed. Otherwise, classical Mandaic morphology is easily comparable to Syriac and other Aramaic dialects.

Classical Mandaic syntax is very archaic, as Theodor Nöldeke (1964) rightly noted in his grammar. This may be the result in part of the predominantly poetic character of ancient Mandaic writings.

Postclassical Period. Compared to the classical period, the postclassical period is extremely prosaic, and in it the classical language was no longer fully understood. The medieval Naṣoraeans wrote down their speculations about the beginning of the world, their historico-geographic imaginings, casuistic commentaries, and astrological and pseudoscientific treatises (most of them published by Drower, 1937) in a new language that may have been closer to the spoken idiom of their time; however, their writings were not aimed at common believers and remained confined to priestly libraries. The writings lack the regularity of the language of the classical period and their syntax is burdensome, obscure, and much inferior to the clear and simple poetic syntax of the Naṣoraeans of the classical period.

Modern Mandaic. Lacking a proper literature, modern Mandaic is found in written form only in the colophons of the last few centuries in Iraq. Mandaic ceased to be spoken before the end of the nineteenth century. In the province of Khuzistan, where the Mandaeans are concentrated, it partly survived under harsh conditions in the cities of Ahwaz and Khorramshahr, to which the Mandaeans of the strongest community of Shustar immigrated because of Muslim persecutions at the beginning of the twentieth century. According to an estimate by Sālem Čoḥeylī from Ahwaz (personal communication, 1991), among the approximately thirty thousand Mandaeans in Iran there are fewer than one thousand who are still able to speak Mandaic.

BIBLIOGRAPHY

For a list of editions of Mandaic texts, see Rudolf Macuch (1965b, 1976) below. The reader may also consult the following:

Drower, Ethel S. *The Mandaeans of Iraq and Iran: Their Cults, Customs, Magic, Legends, and Folklore* (1937). Leiden, 1962. Firsthand observations, with folk tales in English translation.

Drower, Ethel S., and Rudolf Macuch. *A Mandaic Dictionary.* Oxford, 1963. The only dictionary of classical and postclassical Mandaic.

Lidzbarski, Mark. *Das Johannesbuch der Mandäer.* 2 vols. Giessen, 1905–1915. Reprint, Berlin, 1966. Critical edition and German translation of the Sermons of John [the Baptist].

Lidzbarski, Mark. *Mandäische Liturgien mitgeteilt, übersetzt und erklärt* (1920). Hildesheim, 1962. Includes a transliteration in Hebrew characters and a German translation. Superseded by Ethel S. Drower's complete edition, *The Canonical Prayerbook of the Mandaeans* (Leiden, 1959).

Lidzbarski, Mark. *Ginzā: Der Schatz oder das große Buch der Mandäer übersetzt und erklärt.* Göttingen and Leipzig, 1925. Classical translation of the main religious book of the Mandaeans based on Petermann's 1867 edition (see below).

Macuch, Rudolf. "Anfänge der Mandäer." In *Die Araber in der alten Welt,* edited by Franz Altheim and Ruth Stiehl, vol. 2, pp. 76–190. Berlin, 1965a. Reconstruction of early Mandaean history.

Macuch, Rudolf. *Handbook of Classical and Modern Mandaic.* Berlin, 1965b. Parallel grammatical description of the literary and the spoken language, with a complete bibliography up to 1965, an English-Mandaic vocabulary of the vernacular, and an addenda and corrigenda to Drower-Macuch (1963).

Macuch, Rudolf. "The Origins of the Mandaeans and Their Script." *Journal of Semitic Studies* 16.2 (1971): 174–192.

Macuch, Rudolf, ed. *Zur Sprache und Literatur der Mandäer.* Berlin and New York, 1976.

Macuch, Rudolf. "Hermeneutische Akrobatik aufgrund phonetischen Lautwandels in aramäischen Dialekten." *Orientalia Suecana* 33–35 (1984–1986): 269–283.

Macuch, Rudolf. *Neumandäische Chrestomathie mit grammatischer Skizze, kommentierter Übersetzung und Glossar.* Wiesbaden, 1989. First collection of Neo-Mandaic texts, with a detailed introduction and grammatical outline.

Nöldeke, Theodor. *Mandäische Grammatik* (1875). Darmstadt, 1964.

Classic grammar of classical Mandaic, with a detailed morphology and syntax; phonetics superseded by Macuch (1965b).

Petermann, Julius Heinrich. *Thesaurus S. Liber Magnus vulgo "Liber Adami" appellatus, opus Mandaeorum summi ponderis*. 2 vols. Leipzig, 1867. The only edition of the main religious work of the Mandaeans, the *Ginzā Rabbā*.

RUDOLF MACUCH

MANUAL OF DISCIPLINE. *See* Rule of the Community.

MARDIKH, TELL. *See* Ebla.

MARESHAH (Ar., Tell es-Ṣandaḥanna), site located about 1.5 km (1 mi.) south of Beth-Guvrin and 39 km (24 mi.) east of Ashkelon (map reference 1405 × 1113). The site was identified as biblical Mareshah (Gk., Marisa) by Edward Robinson, William Flinders Petrie, Frederick Jones Bliss, and others on the basis of biblical references and the writings of Josephus and of Eusebius. The identification has been confirmed by excavation. Ancient Mareshah comprised a high mound, a lower city with ancillary cave complexes, and a necropolis that encompassed the entire site.

Mareshah is first mentioned in the Bible as a city in Judah (*Jos.* 15:44). After the destruction of the First Temple it became an Edomite city. In the Late Persian period, it was the capital of Idumea at which time a Sidonian community settled there. It is also mentioned in the Zenon papyri (259 BCE). During the Hasmonean wars, Mareshah was a base camp for assaults on Judah and suffered retaliation by the Maccabees. After John Hyrcanus I took and destroyed Mareshah in 112 BCE, the region remained under Hasmonean control (*Antiq.* 13.396). The Parthians completely devastated the "strong city" in 40 BCE, and it was never rebuilt.

Mareshah was first excavated on behalf of the Palestine Exploration Fund in 1900 by Bliss and R. A. S. Macalister, who uncovered a planned and fortified Hellenistic city surrounded by a wall with towers. They also identified two Hellenistic and one Israelite strata. From 1989 to 1993, Amos Kloner cleared the northwestern tower on behalf of the Israel Antiquities Authority, revealing two Hellenistic building phases. Beneath those fortifications were Persian and Iron Age constructions. The earlier tower, dated to about 300 BCE, was built into debris of the Persian period. A new tower, dated to about 200 BCE, and built over the earlier Hellenistic tower, was probably destroyed toward the end of that century. Finds from the Israelite stratum found during the 1900 excavations include seventeen *lmlk* impressions. Among the numerous Hellenistic finds were 328 Rhodian amphora handles and three inscriptions. Sixteen small lead figurines and fifty-one limestone execration tablets attest magic practices at Hellenistic Mareshah.

Lower City. Ceramic evidence dates the original construction of the lower, partially walled city, which surrounds the mound in a belt of varying width, to the Hellenistic period. The lower city consisted of private houses, baths, workshops, and stores laid out in insulae with lanes and streets. The Southern House above Macalister's cave 53 was almost entirely excavated in 1989. It was erected in the mid-third century BCE and continued in use until the final destruction of the city. A staircase led to a second story and a corridor descended to a network of cisterns. [*See* Cisterns.] A juglet found under a floor contained twenty-five coins of 122–113/112 BCE. Similar dwelling units and caves were excavated in 1992–1993 in area 61, in the eastern part of the lower city. More units and caves beneath them were excavated in 1994 in areas 939–940.

Caves. The lower city had been constructed above hundreds of caves hewn into the soft chalky limestone of the hillsides. Macalister listed sixty-three cave complexes in his survey, and recent investigations have revealed ninety more. The principal uses of these caves were for the manufacture of olive oil and for pigeon breeding. Twenty-one Hellenistic oil presses have been discovered, of which two—comprising a crushing installation, three pressing beds, storage areas, a cistern, and a cultic niche—have been excavated. [*See* Olives.] More than seventy columbaria have been identified, the finest in caves 30 and 61. Cave 21 was excavated by Kloner in 1972 and 1981 and dated to the third–first centuries BCE. Each columbarium comprises halls with many small niches carved in the upper part of the walls; there are probably about fifty thousand such niches in all of Mareshah. There is no evidence for these having been used as repositories for human ashes. It is likely that the niches were intended initially as dovecotes; their subsequent functions are unclear. The caves were also used as stables, animal stalls, storerooms, cisterns, bathhouses, and ritual rooms. Cave 70, examined in 1980, consists of thirty-one rooms and contained various cereal grains and olive pits. Cave 75, explored in 1988, was occupied in the Iron Age, Persian, and Hellenistic periods.

Necropolis. In the eastern necropolis there are fifteen tombs, of which seven were first excavated in 1902 by John P. Peters and Hermann Thiersch (1905). Tomb I is the largest and most lavishly decorated, with a painted frieze of hunting scenes and animals adorning its walls. Greek inscriptions and graffiti date the tomb to 196–119 BCE. Tomb II, also painted, contains inscriptions dating it to 188–135 BCE. The northern necropolis contains twenty loculus tombs dated to the third–second centuries BCE. One tomb in the southwestern necropolis was excavated in 1989. Greek inscriptions and varied pottery assemblages date it to the third and second centuries BCE. Other tombs were cleared in

1989–1994. These tombs indicate that the inhabitants of Mareshah in the Hellenistic period (Idumeans, Sidonians, and Greeks) practiced secondary burial, added loculi for primary burial, and built family tombs.

[*See also* Necropolis; Tombs; *and the biographies of Bliss, Macalister, Petrie, and Robinson.*]

BIBLIOGRAPHY

Bliss, Frederick Jones, and R. A. S. Macalister. *Excavations in Palestine during the Years 1898–1900*. London, 1902.

Kloner, Amos, and Orna Hess. "A Columbarium in Complex 21 at Mareshah." *'Atiqot* 17 (1985): 122–133.

Kloner, Amos. "Mareshah." *Qadmoniot* 24.3–4 (1991): 70–85.

Kloner, Amos, and Nahum Sagiv. "The Technology of Oil Production in the Hellenistic Period at Mareshah, Israel." In *Oil and Wine Production in the Mediterranean Area*, edited by Marie-Claire Amouretti and Jean-Pierre Brun, pp. 119–136. Paris, 1993.

Peters, John P., and Hermann Thiersch. *Painted Tombs in the Necropolis of Marissa*. London, 1905.

Amos Kloner

MARI (mod. Tell Hariri), a Mesopotamian royal city that existed from the beginning of the third millennium to the beginning of the second millennium BCE, located on the right bank of the Euphrates River, close to the present-day border between Syria and Iraq. At Mari, the Euphrates traverses a quasi-desert steppe, where rainfall agriculture is impossible because of insufficient precipitation. However, surveys conducted since 1980 have located several canals, a number of which clearly supported agriculture—in particular, the one located on the terrace on the right bank of the river. The flow there seems to have been assured by a dammed lake constructed in Wadi es-Souab. The most important canal was on the left bank; it was connected to the Khabur River and flowed into the Euphrates just short of the lock at Baghouz. This canal (120 km, or 74 mi., long, with a channel that is 11 m wide for its entire length) appears to have been navigable, designed to facilitate the fluvial link between the active Mesopotamian plain and the foothills of the Taurus Mountains (Khabur and northern Syria). [*See* Taurus Mountains.] The birth of Mari—far from the other settlements and great population zones that the plain of the Khabur River, Mesopotamia itself, and western and northern Syria represent—can, thus, be explained in the context of the need for a city as a control point for river traffic, and perhaps also for caravan travel. The payment of taxes would have assured revenues, which explains Mari's wealth in certain periods. Thus, although the network of irrigation channels was designed to assure the subsistence of the population, it was not the primary reason the city was settled.

History of Excavation. In August 1933, Syrian peasants, while digging a grave, excavated a statue carved in the Sumerian style. The find drew the attention of Mesopotamian specialists to Tell Hariri, the source of the object. By December 1933, André Parrot, under the auspices of the National Museums of France, had made the first soundings. In January 1934, in a new trench at the western edge of the tell, in a temple dedicated to the goddess Ishtar, a statuette bearing on its shoulder the inscription "Lamgi-Mari" ("king of Mari") was recovered. The inscription securely identified the site with one of the cities mentioned in the Sumerian king lists as the seat of the tenth dynasty after the Flood and gave the name of an unknown king of Mari—a discovery of great importance. During the second campaign, in 1935, a Royal Palace from the beginning of the second millennium BCE was discovered. This exceptionally well-preserved monument had walls as high as 4 or 5 m and was full of material abandoned by the conquering Hammurabi of Babylon when he destroyed the city in 1760 BCE. The palace was unearthed in the course of five campaigns preceeding World War II. By the onset of the war, Parrot had discovered the palace, several phases of the Temple of Ishtar, and several sanctuaries in the city's sacral quarter, in particular the Temple of the Lions (incorrectly thought to be the sanctuary of Dagan, the great god of the Euphrates).

Parrot understood a new sequence of four campaigns for the Commission on Excavations of the Ministry of Foreign Affairs between 1951 and 1954, shortly after Syrian independence. He turned his attention to the area called the Red Mound, a high terrace from the third millennium, as well as to the temples of Ishtarat and Ninni-Zaza, which yielded a superb collection of statuettes. From 1961 onward, work focused on the structures situated north of the "ziggurat," identified at the time as annexes of the third-millennium Temple of Dagan; in 1964, however, the third-millennium palace under the second-millennium palace was located, leading Parrot to concentrate his efforts there until 1974, when he stopped digging. The work was continued in 1979 by Jean-Claude Margueron, with modified objectives: the whole valley was to be studied, with the aim of understanding the reasons and means by which the capital of the Euphrates was installed in a desert zone. Ten campaigns have been conducted since 1979.

Settlement Periods. Based on the most recent research, the origins of the city are to be placed at the beginning of the third millennium, during the Early Dynastic I period. Written sources attest that the city was destroyed by Hammurabi of Babylon in 1760 BCE (middle chronology). It thus existed for a millennium during which it participated, actively it seems, in the history of Syro-Mesopotamia, with periods of splendor and decline. It is probable that those fluctuations followed changes in the level of trade, which was international, in spite of the anachronism of the term. The various phases of Mesopotamian history are well represented at Mari: The Early Dynastic period (twenty-ninth or twenty-eighth–twenty-fourth centuries BCE); the Akka-

MARI. *Steatite statue of Idi-ilum, governor of Mari.* (Courtesy ASOR Archives)

dian period (to the time of Naram-Sin; twenty-fourth/twenty-third century); the third dynasty of Ur, designated here as the period of the *shakkanakku* (see below), a title meaning "governor" and denoting the holder of power at Mari (twenty-third or twenty-second century–twentieth century? BCE); and the moment at which the Amorite kings dominated the country (end of the nineteenth and beginning of the eighteenth centuries BCE).

The destruction of 1760 BCE, put an end to Mari as the capital of a realm playing a major role in the interchange of the cities of the ancient Near East. However, the traces of later structures attest that the city did not disappear overnight. People continued to live in the ruins of the city Hammurabi devastated. The remains of that epoch, the Khana period (seventeenth–sixteenth centuries BCE), are generally rather poor; it is in the neighboring city of Terqa that life continued. [*See* Terqa.] The Middle Assyrian period (thirteenth–twelfth centuries BCE) is represented by a modest structure located on the tell's northwest promontory and chiefly by a cemetery installed in the ruins of the Royal Palace, which demonstrates a certain affluence for the population. Another cemetery belongs to the Seleucid, or Parthian, period and it seems that Tell Hariri was then occupied by a modest village dependent on Dura-Europos. It seems that from that time onward, except for a contemporary cemetery on the northeast, the site was deserted.

Early Dynastic period. The first centuries of the city are still poorly understood. Because the earliest level, that of the initial settlement, was reached only in two soundings, one on the northern border of the tell (trench B) and the second in the central space of the sacred precinct of the pre-Sargonic palace, it is not possible to describe the organization of the city at its inception. It is known, however, that its plan was circular (1,900 m in diameter) and that it was surrounded by a dike to protect the city from the occasional floods that could ravage the valley. A canal linked to the Euphrates assured the city's water supply and also permitted boats to enter the port. No house plan has emerged clearly, and not enough material was recovered to engage in a general study concerning the first town of Mari. It is not until Early Dynastic III that a coherent whole emerges: the house

MARI. *Necklace of gold wire, lapis lazuli, and other precious stones; pendant with nude goddess.* Late middle Syrian period from tomb 125. National Museum, Aleppo, Syria. (Erich Lessing/Art Resource, NY)

of trench B with its tablets; the houses of the so-called pre-Sargonic quarter, with a small market around a porticoed square; the temples of Ishtar, Ninni-Zaza, and Ishtarat, as well as the one associated with the high terrace called the Red Mound; and especially the rooms of the palace and its Sacred Precinct. A flourishing city is revealed whose characteristics seem very original. At the end of the period, a school of sculptors at Mari made it a primary site of Near Eastern artistic production. The event or events that brought about the end of this phase are not known. It is probable that terrible destructions brought about the end of Mari during the Akkadian period, perhaps at the beginning of the twenty-third century BCE.

City of the shakkanakku. A new phase in the history of the city began near the end of the Akkadian period. The new dynasty is known by the name Shakkanakku (see below) because it undoubtedly resulted from the governors who directed the city for the benefit of the kings of Akkad, when they seized Mari for a short time. Enormous construction projects were undertaken that obliterated, in whole or part, the buildings of the latest levels of the Early Dynastic period. A new Royal Palace was built on top of the ruins of the earlier one, but following a completely new plan—except that the Sacred Precinct was preserved. The plan of the official apartments—a courtyard called the Court of the Palm closely associated with two successive long rooms, the second one being the Throne Hall—is a characteristic formula for royal palaces from the Third Dynasty of Ur (twenty-first century BCE) to the end of the Old Babylonian period (mid-second millennium). A second palace was built to the east of the temple area. Smaller in size, it would have sheltered the king while the new palace was being constructed. It was built over two hypogea that had clearly functioned as burial chambers for the former king and royal family. Unfortunately, they were completely pillaged by robbers in antiquity, perhaps when Hammurabi took Mari. At the heart of the city's sacred area, a new high terrace (sometimes mistakenly called a ziggurat) was erected in association with the Temple of the Lions. It covered over the area that had connected the Sacred Precinct with the temple on the Red Mound (see above).

MARI. *Frieze with mother of pearl inlays, schist, and ivory.* Depicted is a procession of priests and women decorating a bench with bull's legs. National Museum, Damascus, Syria. (Erich Lessing/Art Resource, NY)

Amorite domination. Excavation of the Royal Palace resulted in the recovery of very precise information about how life was organized in a great Amorite palace at the beginning of the second millennium BCE, thanks to the archives and other material abandoned by the Babylonian soldiers. [*See* Palace.] The palace was the political and administrative heart of all Mesopotamian cities. At Mari it was 2.5 ha (6 acres) in area, with nearly three hundred rooms at ground level—a number that could be doubled because there was a second story over most of the building, as proved by the height of the remaining walls (5 m), the position of objects in the filling levels, and the presence of stairs. The palace included the following features.

- House of the king, with an official area (Court of the Palm 106, Room of the Goddess with the Flowing Vase 64, throne room 65), storerooms, a staff (servant and slave) area, kitchen, and administrative quarters
- Second house, for the women in the court (queens, female workers), consisting of a residential zone (the house centered on room 31), staff quarters, and storerooms
- Temple area at the site of the former Sacred Precinct
- Great storerooms, partially unrecoverable in the southern part of the structure.

The life of the realm was revealed through the recovered archives, of which there are some fifteen thousand documents that cover daily life at the palace (incoming and outgoing merchandise, food and other goods, food rations as payments, the king's meals); administrative relationships between the king and his servants in the cities that made up the realm (the king gave his orders and received reports and other information from his governors); and the relationships among different realms, or international activities, with other cities in Mesopotamia and Syria. [*See* Mari Texts.]

It is not known what led Hammurabi to attack the capital

of the Middle Euphrates because he and Zimrilim seem to have maintained a long political alliance. All that is known is that the Babylonian king gave the name of the capture of Mari to the thirty-first year of his reign and the destruction of its walls to the thirty-third year, according to their tradition of naming a year by a significant event of the previous year. During the several months he occupied Mari, he systematically pillaged the palace and all the official buildings; he transferred his booty to Babylon, abandoning several stray objects in place (to the joy of the archaeologists). He then burned all the monumental buildings as a statement that Mari no longer held its place in the concert of realms of the twenty-eighth century BCE. Because the trade routes connecting Syria with Mesopotamia no longer principally passed the Euphrates, this destruction marked the end of the role Mari had played for a millennium.

Conclusions. In its diversity, the epigraphic documentation from Mari is one of the richest in the Near East. It gives an exceptionally concentrated picture of the Syro-Mesopotamian world during the brief period that preceded the fall of the city. The quality of Mari's preserved architecture and the richness of the surviving furnishings give an idea of what a city in the first Babylonian Empire, under the kingship of Hammurabi, may have looked like (the excavation of Babylon has not yielded finds from that period). The Royal Palace at Mari remains a unique example of a Bronze Age palace.

In the amplitude and the audacity of its conception, the architecture of the third-millennium palace expresses the inventive power of the Mesopotamian population. The perfection of some of its statues reveals that workshops at Mari were of the first rank for artists, perhaps because they had contact with two close, but not identical, realms—Mesopotamia and Syria.

Finally, the magnitude of the regional organization—resulting from the wealth from trade with the edge of the Taurus Mountain range, its Anatolian hinterland, western Syria, and alluvial or deltaic Mesopotamia—over whose control Mari was created to be the key, illustrates the dynamism of the Sumerian population at the dawn of history in a unique way, revealing all of its true depth in the first of the great urban civilizations. No other site has been so rich in evidence of a millennium of Mesopotamian civilization.

[*See also* Akkadians; Amorites; Babylon; Khabur; Mesopotamia, *article on* Ancient Mesopotamia; Sumerians; Syria, *article on* Syria in the Bronze Age; Temples, *article on* Mesopotamian Temples; *and the biography of Parrot.*]

BIBLIOGRAPHY

Durand, Jean-Marie, and Jean-Claude Margueron. "La question du harem royal dans le palais de Mari." *Journal des Savants* (October–December 1980): 253–280.

Heintz, Jean-Georges, et al. *Bibliographie de Mari: Archéologie et textes.* Wiesbaden, 1990. Complete list of publications about Mari, 1933–1988, supplemented by Heintz et al., "Bibliographie de Mari, Supplément I [1985–1990]," *Akkadica* 77 (March–April 1992): 1–37.

Margueron, Jean-Claude. *Recherches sur les palais mésopotamiens de l'âge du Bronze.* 2 vols. Paris, 1982. Demonstrates that the palace "of Zimrilim," to which the author devotes 170 pages of analysis, is the result of constructions and renovations that continued for more than two hundred years; twenty pages are reserved for the pre-Sargonic palace at Mari; general conclusions offered.

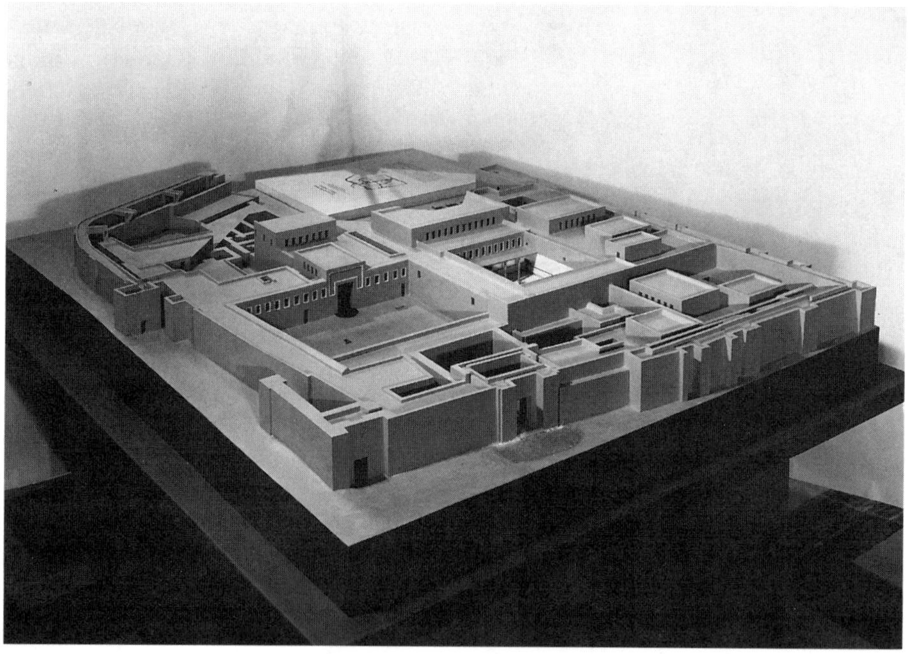

MARI. *Reconstruction of the second-millennium palace.* (Maguette Vuillet/Louvre)

Mari: Annales de Recherches Interdisciplinaires. Paris, 1982–. Reports of excavations conducted since 1979, as well as all the studies concerning Mari, archaeological and philological; published approximately every two years.

Parrot, André. *Mission archéologique de Mari II: Le palais,* vol. 1, *Architecture;* vol. 2, *Peintures murales;* vol. 3, *Documents et monuments*. Paris, 1958–1959. Many of the excavators' interpretations are now out of date. Volume 2 is a catalog.

Parrot, André. *Mission archéologique de Mari III: Les temples d'Ishtarat et de Ninni-Zaza*. Paris, 1967.

Parrot, André. *Mission archéologique de Mari IV: Le "Trésor" d'Ur*. Paris, 1968.

Parrot, André. *Mari, capitale fabuleuse*. Paris, 1974. Popular account of the excavations.

Young, Gordon D., ed. *Mari in Retrospect: Fifty Years of Mari and Mari Studies*. Winona Lake, Ind., 1992.

JEAN-CLAUDE MARGUERON

Translated from French by Nancy Leinwand

MARIB (Sabaean, Maryab), the pre-Islamic capital city of Saba' (biblical Sheba), located on the north bank of Wadi Dhanah, on its large silt delta, in northeastern Yemen, (15°29′ N, 45°28′30″ E). According to tradition, this was the city where the Queen of Sheba (1 *Kgs*. 10) lived and from which she ruled her kingdom. The site is rectangular in plan, with its long axis parallel to the wadi. It measures about 580 m in length (northeast–southwest) by 400 m in width (northwest–southeast), for an approximate area of 232,000 sq m, or 23.20 hectares (57.30 acres). It is the largest known pre-Islamic site in southern Arabia and has about 10 m of occupation debris. Centered in the northeastern area of the site a small, circular, secondary tell stands on the lower, rectangular tell. This piggyback tell contains the remains of successive occupations beginning in the Islamic period; it was occupied until portions were destroyed in Yemen's civil war in the 1960s and the remaining buildings in an earthquake in 1982. The piggyback tell had a surface area of 2.53 hectares or (6.26 acres) and a prewar population of about 765 people. Using a formula that assumes 10 percent occupation by public buildings for the large, pre-Islamic tell would yield a population of about 6,635 in pre-Islamic Marib.

Exploration and Excavation. The first European to visit Marib was Louis Arnaud (1843), who was followed by Joseph Halevy (1869). Of the early explorers, Eduard Glaser contributed the most by copying more than two thousand South Arabian inscriptions during four separate visits (1882–1884, 1885–1886, 1887–1888, 1892–1894). Ahmed Fakhry visited Marib in 1947 and copied inscriptions, photographed ruins, and sketched plans. In 1964 Gus Van Beek measured the site, studied the dam, and collected sherds in the ancient irrigated zone and on the tell.

The first excavations at Marib were directed by Frank P. Albright, on behalf of the American Foundation for the Study of Man (1951–1952), with Albert Jamme, an epigrapher. During an abruptly terminated three-month field season, the entrance hall of the 'Awwam Temple was cleared and a mausoleum adjacent to the precinct wall was excavated. Jamme published 283 South Arabic inscriptions from the excavations; he had been restrained by the local governor from working at the site for almost four weeks, so that the 283 was by no means all of the inscriptions found. The German Archaeological Institute, under the direction of Jürgen Schmidt, has been working at the site, chiefly excavating Temple Bar'an, since the 1980s.

'Awwam Temple. Known as Ḥaram Bilqis, or locally as Maḥram Bilqis, the 'Awwam Temple was dedicated to the moon god, 'Ilumquh, the primary deity at Marib. It is located on the valley floor, about 3.23 km (2 mi.) south–southeast of the Marib tell, straight across Wadi Dhanah. It consists of a large oval enclosure wall, accessed through a peristyle entrance hall on the northeast side and a narrow doorway on the west.

The oval wall encloses an area about 100 m long by 75 m wide and remains unexcavated, although Glaser reported walls and bedrock inside. The casemate oval wall stood about 9.5 m high by about 4.0 m at the base, tapering to 3.6 m at the top. It was constructed of limestone ashlar blocks finished with marginally drafted, pecked surfaces. The inner and outer walls were linked by sixty pairs of crosswalls; the resulting compartments were filled with stones, soil, and sand. The outer surface of the wall on the west side had no fewer than seven beautifully cut South Arabian inscriptions, each dedicating a portion of the construction of the wall to the gods and naming the king who ordered the work. In letters about 23 cm high, the cumulative length of the lines in the seven inscriptions runs to 143.64 m. The longest single inscription (Ja 555) has a total length of 42.37 m. Such inscriptions are unparalleled in the ancient world in pre-Roman times. The earliest inscription belongs to the mid-seventh century BCE, although the oval wall may have an earlier phase or phases.

The entrance hall was built into an opening in the oval wall, probably in the second half of the fifth century BCE by Tubbaʿkarib. Constructed as a casemate wall with masonry similar to that of the oval wall, it measured 23.97 by 19.15 m inside and consisted of an open court surrounded by a peristyle hall. The court was entered from the outside through a series of outer structures: through a line of eight monolithic, square piers, 7.65 m high; then through a small court with a peristyle on three sides; and finally through a triple doorway formed by two massive pylons with recessed corners on their outer sides. The roofed area of the peristyle was supported by the outer walls of the entrance hall and a series of thirty-two rectangular piers—all monoliths, except for two consisting of two stones—and the two pylons. The inner surface of the walls of the entrance hall was decorated with sixty-four false windows with successive recesses intricately carved to represent wooden lattice. Above the latticework was a series of five raised tegular panels, superficially resembling dentils, with a horizontal grill at the top. Above each window, the tegular panels and grill were repeated in the wall. Similar windows appeared on the outer surface of the north wall, but without regard to the placement of the inside windows. Three steps led to the entrance to the oval wall area. Two pylons formed the doorway and apparently supported a large water tank, from which a stream of water fell on the steps, eroding a large hole through the first and part of the second limestone steps. This may have been a final purification or washing area through which worshipers passed before entering the sacred oval area. The runoff water flowed through a channel to a bronze basin (230 × 69 cm) that bears an inscription on one edge indicating a fifth-century BCE date. A flight of stairs led to a roof room and possibly to a balcony. Other additions were built in various places in the entrance hall, chiefly after the first century CE, and continued to be repaired and repaved as late as the fourth century. Hundreds of inscribed stones, many with lengthy inscriptions, were found on the floor of the peristyle and the surrounding court. Stone bases of votive statues, bronze plaques with mounting dowels on the back edges, and painted inscriptions on the walls illustrate the religious customs and devotion of the Sabeans.

Mausoleum. Built of limestone blocks, a mausoleum touched the northwest corner of the oval wall. The structure (8.34 × 7.73 m) was entered through a doorway in its north wall. Four monolithic rectangular piers (3.60 m high), each finished with a capital with two rows of raised tegular panels, carried the roof, which consisted of granite joists spanning from pier to wall, rabbeted on its upper long edges to support limestone roof panels. A total of sixty burial compartments was arranged in tiers; the compartments were closed by means of two limestone panels fitted into grooves on either side and joined in the middle by a lap joint. The upper front edge was decorated with a grill, with the partitions finished with four or five parallel vertical grooves; both are common South Arabian architectural designs. In the northwest and southwest corners, underground burial chambers had been built. The mausoleum yielded several incense burners, including one of bronze, a gold globule, human skeletal material, and potsherds. Compartment-closing panel fragments contained the names of the deceased, two of whom were kings, proving that this was a royal mausoleum: Sumhuʿalay Yanaf and Yithʿʾamara Bayyin, son of Yakrubmalik Watar, both of the second half of the fifth century BCE.

South Tombs. A group of mausolea, located about 100 m south of the royal mausoleum, are more similar in plan and design to the mausolea at Heid Bin ʿAqil, Timnaʿ, and Qataban. The burials were badly disturbed, but especially noteworthy is a boustrophedon inscription painted on a wall and dated paleographically to the eighth century BCE.

Temple Bar'an. The Temple of Bar'an is located away from the tell; it is marked by a row of six rectangular, monolithic piers with capitals. An inscription indicates that the name of the temple was Bar'an, and that it was dedicated to the moon god 'Ilumquh. The temple is immediately west of the piers.

Marib Dam. The dam at Marib is one of the best-known monuments of the ancient Near East and the largest dam known from antiquity. It is located about 6 km (3.73 mi.) in a straight line west of the tell. It was built across the narrow defile of Wadi Dhanah, where the wadi emerges into a valley that increasingly widens to its borders, which are formed by black volcanic hills. Wadi Dhanah carries torrents of water during the southwest monsoon in the late winter and spring. The dam functioned as a barrage to deflect the waters into two sluices, one on the south and the other on the north side of the wadi. It was built of soil heaped to a 7-meter-high structure, triangular in section, with a facing on the west side of stones set vertically, cemented in place, and stretching 593 m across the wadi. The dam was anchored to a rock outlier on the south side, and the builders cut a channel through the bedrock to permit water to flow to the fields on the south side of the wadi; this took place during the reign of Sumuhuʿalay Yanaf, according to an inscription on the rock in channel, in the second half of the fifth century BCE. Later, a tower wall with a long wall paralleling the axis of the wadi was constructed of ashlar; after two thousand years, it still stands to more than 6 m. On the north side of the wadi, the terrain was flat, so that the north sluice was built with a long wall, angled to abut on the curving dam on the north end. Two sluice openings lead to the primary canal, followed by a massive wall at right angles, to deflect water into the sluices. This sluice in its present form dates from the fourth century CE, during the reign of Shammar Yuharʿish; it underwent repeated repairs in 449 and 450 CE, as well as by the Abyssinian viceroy, Abraha, in about 542 CE. The sluice was finally destroyed in about 575 CE. So far as is known, the installation was abandoned then.

The primary canal on the north side is partially intact for about one kilometer. Sluices located in the fields distributed the flow as quickly as possible by means of secondary and tertiary channels. On the south side, the primary canal was probably located on the higher ground, near the base of the rock outliers, and is now covered with sand.

The Qur'an (surah 34:14, 15) refers to "gardens, the one on the right hand and the other on the left," which are the fields on the north and south sides of the wadi, irrigated by this system. In aerial photographs, these fields show heavy rectangular erosion and extend eastward well beyond the tell and the 'Awwam Temple. Together they provided a combined area of at least 1619 ha (4,000 acres) of cultivable land.

Thus far, nothing from the time of the Queen of Sheba has been recovered at Marib; the earliest dated material belongs to the eighth century BCE, only two hundred years after her time. The great tell at Marib has not yet been excavated, however, and it is there that remains of the tenth century and perhaps of earlier centuries will surely be found.

[*See also* Qataban; Sheba; *and* Timnaʿ (Arabia).]

BIBLIOGRAPHY

Albright, Frank P. "Excavations at Mârib in Yemen." In *Archaeological Discoveries in South Arabia,* edited by Richard Le Baron Bowen and Frank P. Albright, pp. 215–287. Publications of the American Foundation for the Study of Man, vol. 2. Baltimore, 1958. Definitive publication of the American excavations at Marib and several important ancillary studies.

Bowen, Richard Le Baron. "Irrigation in Ancient Qatabân (Beiḥân)." In *Archaeological Discoveries in South Arabia,* edited by Richard Le Baron Bowen and Frank P. Albright, pp. 43–131. Publications of the American Foundation for the Study of Man, vol. 2. Baltimore, 1958. The most complete description of the ingenious flash-flood irrigation systems in southern Arabia.

Jamme, Albert. *Sabaean Inscriptions from Maḥram Bilqis (Marib).* Publications of the American Foundation for the Study of Man, vol. 3. Baltimore, 1962. Definitive scholarly study of the South Arabic inscriptions, including transliteration, translation, commentary, and historical interpretations of the large collection recovered by the American excavations at Marib.

Phillips, Wendell. *Qataban and Sheba: Exploring the Ancient Kingdoms on the Biblical Spice Routes of Arabia.* New York, 1955. Delightful semipopular book describing the research expeditions of the American Foundation for the Study of Man.

Schmidt, Jürgen, et al. *Antike Technologie: Die sabäische Wasserwirtschaft bon Marib.* 2 vols. Archäologische Berichte aus dem Yemen, vols. 5–6. Mainz am Rhein, 1991.

Van Beek, Gus W. "South Arabian History and Archaeology." In *The Bible and the Ancient Near East,* edited by G. Ernest Wright, pp. 229–248. New York, 1961. Summary of the history of exploration and excavation in southern Arabia and a general description of what was known as of the mid-1950s.

Van Beek, Gus W. "The Land of Sheba." In *Solomon and Sheba,* edited by James B. Pritchard, pp. 40–63. London, 1974. Fairly comprehensive description of the culture of Sheba, derived from archaeology; explores what is known historically and how the Solomon-Sheba relationship is viewed by Jewish, Ethiopic, Muslim, and Christian traditions.

Van Beek, Gus W. "A Population Estimate for Marib: A Contemporary Tell Village in North Yemen." *Bulletin of the American Schools of Oriental Research,* no. 248 (1982): 61–67. Population is calculated using aerial photographs to determine house density and data from a 1975 census to determine the average number of persons per house.

Gus W. Van Beek

MARIETTE, AUGUSTE (1821–1881), French founder of the Egyptian Antiquities Service and its national museum of antiquities (both firsts for the Arab world). Mariette began his career in archaeology by discovering the Serapeum at Saqqara—the vast catacomb containing the burials of the sacred Apis bulls—uncovering as well the approach avenue lined with sphinxes and two temples with hundreds of objects.

Although the initial finds from the Serapeum discovery went to the Louvre, which had sent Mariette to Egypt to procure Coptic and Syriac manuscripts, it became his aim to stop the rampant pillaging of Egypt's monuments. With the aid of Ferdinand de Lesseps, Egypt's ruler, Said Pasha, was persuaded to appoint Mariette director of an antiquities service. In this capacity Mariette then launched a massive archaeological rescue effort under his own exclusive authority to excavate throughout Egypt and recover portable objects for the nation, to be housed in what became the first of a series of ever-enlarging museums. At one point, Mariette had simultaneous expeditions in thirty-seven different locales. Certainly, without his supervision at each site, only the most obvious was found, and much of the work consisted of clearing buildings such as the Edfu, Dendera and Deir el-Baḥari temples. More than three hundred tombs were opened at Giza and Saqqara, and from there and Karnak came much of the collection of the current Egyptian Museum in Cairo.

Mariette's energies were also sapped by diplomatic demands from both France and Egypt, international exhibitions, and the publication of some of his work, such as five volumes on the temple of Dendera (1875), and a catalogue of antiquities discovered at Abydos (1880). Although he could not totally stop the illegal digging and export of antiquities, Mariette did raise international awareness of the importance of protecting the heritage of the past.

BIBLIOGRAPHY

Dawson, Warren R., and Eric P. Uphill. *Who Was Who in Egyptology.* 2d rev. ed. London, 1972.

Fagan, Brian M. *The Rape of the Nile: Tomb Robbers, Tourists, and Archaeologists in Egypt.* New York, 1975.

Vercoutter, Jean. *The Search for Ancient Egypt.* Translated by Ruth Sharman. New York, 1992.

Barbara Switalski Lesko

MARISA. *See* Mareshah.

MARI TEXTS. The bedouin discovery of Mari on 3 January 1934, at Tell Hariri in Syria revealed the location of a city that had become mythical after its fall. It was known to Assyriologists only by its mention in the Sumerian King Lists as the seat of one the dynasties after the Flood. From 1934 to 1938, six fruitful excavations took place there under the direction of André Parrot. In the first year twenty-five hundred whole tablets and fragments were unearthed. In the following year, no fewer than thirteen thousand inventory numbers were assigned for texts alone. When World War II brought an end to this period of research, some twenty thousand documents had been uncovered. Excavation was resumed after the war (with another long interruption during the Suez expedition in 1956), and another thousand texts were recovered. Tablets are still being discovered, although in more modest numbers, under the direction, since 1979, of Jean-Claude Margueron. [*See the biography of Parrot.*]

For the most part, Parrot excavated tablets in the royal palace and the area immediately southeast of it (the "ziggurat"); in excavations since 1979 tablets have also been found in the small palace of the Šakkanakku (a governing official) northeast of the tell (the House of Asqudum and the House of Queen Šibtu (where she was installed at the end of the reign of Zimrilim), as well as in areas B (from the period of Ebla), D, E, and F (reign of Yakhdunlim). [*See* Ebla.] In the palace of Zimrilim, the archives were divided among many small rooms, sorted according to administrative categories, indicating the function of different parts of the palace. [*See* Palace.] The most important of these rooms are numbers 108 and 115; 115, situated between the palm-tree court (room 106) and the court of the Temple of Ishtar (room 130) preserved administrative and diplomatic correspondence; 108 held the main body of administrative documents. A good part of the harem archives were recovered in room 72. Although the archives of the palace seem to have remained in their original arrangement, the Babylonians, who systematically sacked Mari, sorted through them to remove any that concerned them. [*See* Babylonians.] Thus, the records of international correspondence are limited. Many groups of documents were recovered from construction fill, such as the texts from the harem of Yasmakh-Addu (1798?–1776 BCE) found in 1982 in the retaining wall of an oil storeroom, and the private archives of Yakhdunlim (1815?–1799? BCE).

Contrary to Parrot's hopes, no library was found at Tell Hariri. The excavated texts belong to the administration of the state or the private archives of the people living in the palace. They give evidence of the daily life, the movement of palace supplies, and the affairs of the kingdom—known as the Banks of the Euphrates—and contact with foreign courts. The letters (e.g., from servants of the king, or his allies) are more important than the administrative texts (e.g., records of the import and export of goods and food, inventories, audits of accounts). The absence of archives concerning the kingdom's tax system suggests that such documents were housed outside the palace (the palace has been completely excavated and such archives would have held no interest for pillagers). There is a limited group of legal texts, as well as texts of an ideological or religious character, such as the "nail" of Yakhdunlim from room 18, or nine bricks inscribed with a single text from the Temple of Shamash that describes that king's expedition to Lebanon, and models of inscribed oracular livers. The (unpublished) epic of Zimrilim, written on a large tablet broken into three pieces, was discovered in room 115. [*See* Tablet.] It is the only work found that can properly be described as belletristic. Many magico-religious texts were found (e.g., incantations—a fragment of one dated to the third millennium was discovered in area B—and penitential and ritual psalms).

The first epigraphist for the French team was François Thureau-Dangin. He was soon superseded by C.-F. Jean and then by Georges Dossin, who turned "mariology" into an important field of study by the number and quality of his publications. In 1979, Jean-Marie Durand and Dominique Charpin took charge of editing the Mari texts, reinvigorating the project. The series *ARM (Archives Royales de Mari)*, founded by Dossin and Parrot, was initially devoted to the epistolary archives and was arranged by the authors of the letters: *ARM* 1, 4, and 5 concern Shamshi-Adad and his sons; *ARM* 3 contains the letters of the governor of Terqa, and 6 and 14 those of others, from Mari and Sagaratum; *ARM* 13 is based on the same principle, but the lots have less breadth. Volume 2 is the only one with any diversity, providing a better sampling of the documents. Some volumes are arranged thematically, such as *ARM* 10, women's correspondence, and, more recently, *ARM* 27, dedicated to the governors of the city of Qaṭṭunan.

Administrative texts were published initially by room: *ARM* 7 (room 170), *ARM* 9 (room 5), *ARM* 21 (rooms 134, 160), and *ARM* 24 (rooms Z, Y). Under Durand and Charpin it was decided that all epistolary and administration documents would be arranged by theme—the better to extract their historical and lexical interest and to allow for the poor data regarding find spots of the documents unearthed by the earlier excavations. *ARM* 26 (in three volumes) marks a significant evolution: the documents published (or republished) are grouped according to thematic or historical criteria (divination, religion, the military affairs of Sindjar and of the Upper Jezireh) without breaking with tradition (e.g., within these categories the letters are arranged by author). Because ARM 23 is a collective work, the administrative documents have been grouped according to themes such as texts dealing with garments or texts dealing with luxury crockery. The commentaries are more abundant and more systematically treated, according to the principle that, for the sake of comprehending the text, purely philological analysis cannot be separated from the reconstruction of the context. Many texts from Mari have also been published individually or in small lots in various journals and collections, such as *Syria* and the *Revue D'Assyriologie (RA)*. Since the 1980s there has also been a specialized journal, *MARI (Mari: Annales de Recherche Interdisciplinaires)*, as well as the occasional series *Florilegium Marianum*.

At first glance, the chronological range of the Mari texts seems fairly large: from the third millennium to 1761 BCE (the latest documented date). In reality, the useful historical span is no more than the twenty–fifty years that document the Amorite dynasty; these are the last decades of Mari. [*See* Amorites.] Earlier, the documents are too rare or brief to reconstruct a historical thread. What characterizes Mari archives is thus a great density of information over a very short period of time: two generations, during the reign of Zimrilim (1775–1761 BCE) and the end of his predecessor's, Yasmakh-Addu. No other period in antiquity is so extensively described and detailed.

The Near East appears in all its picturesqueness and complexity. The palace is revealed in all its different aspects: its gardens and courts where one day a princess exposed herself dangerously to the sun, its sanctuaries, its various administrative functions, its storehouses, and its workshops. The harem, which occupied its northwestern part, was inhabited by a great number of women, from the queen mother and principal royal wife, to slaves and captives, including concubines, who were the designated musicians, scribes, cooks, water drawers, and floor sweepers. At the entrance to the palace, prophets came to proclaim the truths that a divinity had revealed to them.

The king, in constant consultation with the gods, demanded that his subjects tell him everything they knew, even their dreams about him. It was naturally the divination priests, the governors of the kingdom, and the servants at the palace who had the most occasion to write letters. The chancellor's office maintained diplomatic correspondence with a number of small, turbulent states (principally in the Upper Jezireh) and the great powers of the day: to the west, Aleppo; to the southeast, Qatna; to the east, Eshnunna, Babylon, and Elam (whose Sukkalmah is the avowed suzerian of the Mesopotamian princes); and to the northeast, the monarchies of Sindjar and Ekallatum. [*See* Aleppo; Eshnunna; Babylon.] International exchanges—political, commercial, and cultural—as well as the movements of armies and diplomats, were intense and favored a certain awareness of the unity of the Near East on the part of the guiding classes, at least until family or racial solidarity came into question. Racism was not absent, particularly among the conquering Elamites. [*See* Elamites.]

The written language of Mari was Classical Akkadian, which differs little from that used in Babylon and elsewhere in the Near East. [*See* Akkadian.] More precisely, the syllabic writing and language came from the scribal tradition of Eshnunna, whose practice was adopted at Mari under Zimrilim. Nevertheless, strong influences from Western Semitic are recognizable. Akkadian lexicography and onomastics are also enriched with Hurrian words. [*See* Hurrian.] Peculiarities of syntax in the letters reveal as much the level of language as of any real dialect.

Mari's geographic horizon extended beyond the strict boundary of local politics. Thus Zimrilim could undertake a peaceful voyage, for religious reasons, to the Mediterranean coast. Mari maintained contacts with the island of Bahrain/Dilmun, thanks to passing merchants; with Kaneš/Kayseri in Anatolia; and with the Arab tribes. [*See* Bahrain; Dilmun; Kaneš.] The Mariotes nevertheless needed interpreters when they encountered Cretans on the quays of Ugarit or the people of Marhaši/Parahši in the Iranian mountains.

The Mari documentation testifies to a period in the history of the Near East when relationships among the great powers were more or less in balance, a balance of which there was a clear awareness. However, tensions among states rarely ceased and a king often had to mount a military expedition or extend a strong hand to his allies. There were constant quarrels within the kingdom and at the borders over pasture rights and territory; rivalries existed between nomadic and sedentary groups and among the confederations of bedouins; and occasionally there were great wars, when the armies of Eshnunna or Elam descended. The definitive destruction of Mari marked the end of this equilibrium in the Near East.

[*See also* Mari.]

BIBLIOGRAPHY

Charpin, Dominique. "La Syrie à l'époque de Mari: Des invasions amorites à la chute de Mari." In the catalog *Syrie: Mémoire et civilisation,* pp. 144–149. Flammarion, 1993. This is the best synthesis (in French) on the history of Mari. There are also other studies on Mari in this richly illustrated catalog.

Charpin, Dominique and Jean-Marie Durand. *Mari, Ébla et les Hourrites.* A series of fundamental syntheses on the age and the documents of Mari. Paris, 1996.

Durand, Jean-Marie. *Les déclarations prophétiques dans les lettres de Mari.* Supplement to Cahier Évangile, 1988–1994, pp. 8–74. The most recent synthesis in French on the theme of the prophets of Mari and the texts of Mari in translation.

Durand, Jean-Marie. *Les documents épistolaires du palais de Mari.* Forthcoming. A thematic collection (in French) of all the letters of Mari, translated and annotated, published before 1988 (*ARM* I–XVIII and uncollected).

Durand, Jean-Marie. *La religión en Siria durante la epoca de los reinos amorreos según la documentación de Mari.* Mitología y religión del Oriente Antiguo, 2.1, edited by G. del Olmo.

Heinz, J.-G., et al. *Bibliographie de mari: Archéologie et textes* (1933–1988). Weisbaden, 1990. Fundamental work for any study of Mari. Should be amplified with the supplements of the Belgian journal *Akkadica*: Supplement 1 (1989–1990), *Akkadica* 77 (1992): 1–37; Supplement 2 (1991–1992), *Akkadica* 81 (1993): 1–22; Supplement 3 (1992–1993), *Akkadica* 86 (1994): 1–23.

Malamat, A. *Mari and the Early Israelite Experience: The Schweich Lectures.* Oxford, 1989. A synthesis of very important comparative works dealing with the Bible and Mari.

MICHAËL GUICHARD

Translated from French by Melissa Kaprelian

MARLIK, late second to early first millennium BCE site, located in the region of Rahmatabad of Rudbar in Gilan province in northern Iran, about 50 km (31 mi.) from the town of Rasht on the Caspian Sea (at approx. 37° N, 50° E). During the 1940s and 1950s, the highlands of the northern slopes of the Elburz Mountains south of the Caspian were subject to much clandestine and illegal digging. It produced beautiful spouted pottery vessels, bronze and pottery animal figurines, bronze weapons, and even some silver and gold objects, all belonging to an unknown culture. This material was distributed throughout the world to collections and museums under the term *Amlash,* from the name of the market town to which the objects were taken to be sold to dealers.

In fall 1961, a team from the Iranian Archaeological Service began a survey in the foothills of the Elburz Mountains with the aim of mapping the area's archaeological sites and eventually of conducting systematic and scientific excavations to identify the people responsible for the masterpieces of art and technology. In the course of the survey the team entered the valley of the Gohar Rud (Crystal River), a tributary of the Sefid Rud (White River). There they found five apparently related mounds, Pileh Qal'a, Jazem Kul, Dure Bejar, Zeinab Bejar, and Marlik (or Cheragh-Ali Tepe, after its last owner). The mounds were surveyed one by one. The team eventually reached Marlik, a large mound that appears natural. It has a rocky crest surrounded by olive groves and wild pomegranate bushes and overlooks the rice paddies that blanket the lower slopes of the valley. Its surface was covered by brush and revealed few artifactual traces; one slope bore the scars of several ditches dug by unsuccessful antiquities hunters.

When a test trench produced a range of objects, including two small bronze animal figurines, two cylinder seals, and fourteen gold buttons, the need for immediate scientific excavation was met by the Iranian Archaeological Service, in cooperation with the Institute of Archaeology of the University of Tehran. Their team worked without interruption for fourteen months, from October 1961 to November 1962. Although at first the team had little idea of what might lie beneath the surface, gradually it became clear that Marlik contained the Royal Cemetery of a long-forgotten kingdom. Scattered over its crest were fifty-three tombs filled with a fascinating variety of objects of gold, silver, bronze, and pottery, testifying to the wealth and sophisticated craftsmanship of this three-thousand-year-old culture. Although the richest tombs were concentrated in the Royal Cemetery, the whole lower valley of the Gohar Rud was also essentially a contemporary burial ground for persons of lesser importance. Buried in simpler graves, with fewer grave goods, they had, perhaps, been attracted by the presence of the royal tombs. [*See* Tombs; Grave Goods.]

At Marlik, the tombs were formed basically of walls of broken stone and mud mortar built between the mound's large natural rocks. Some of the tombs were very roughly constructed, while others showed more care. For the most part, the natural stone of the surrounding area was used for construction. For some of the tombs, however, slabs of yellowish stone had been brought from the headwaters of the Gohar Rud, about 15 km (9 mi.) away. This stone might occur only in a single wall or in the form of slabs placed at the bottom of the tomb, but some of the richest tombs were built entirely of it.

In most of the tombs the skeletons had completely disintegrated, but in those few that still contained any, an elaborate burial ritual was revealed in which the body was carefully laid out on a long stone slab and surrounded by precious and ordinary objects their owners would need in the afterlife. With or without skeletal remains, the tombs were filled with a wide range of objects, including ritual vessels, human and animal figurines, jewelry, weapons and tools, domestic utensils, and some models of oxen with yoke and plow and toys.

The metal vessels found in the tombs were of gold, silver, and bronze, in many sizes and shapes—cups, bowls, pots with long spouts, beakers, and vases. They range from plain and unadorned forms to vessels with highly elaborate, sometimes narrative designs done in different techniques, including dotted linear engraving, repoussé in low and high relief (see figure 1), and, on one silver vessel, gold inlay. The workmanship ranges from simple, crude patterns on some vessels to highly elaborate naturalistic or stylized portraits of real and mythical animals and humans on others. In addition to these metal ritual vessels are several beautifully made in glass mosaic and frit.

Striking human and animal figurines were found in the tombs, made of pottery and of metal, including bronze, silver, and gold. The ceramic human figurines, most of them hollow, are highly stylized, as are several solid bronze figurines and one of gold. Some of the animal figurines are also highly stylized, such as the humped bulls, while others are more naturalistic. In addition to the bulls are figurines of stags, mountain goats, mules, horses, rams, bears, leopards, dogs, and wild boars and models of yoked oxen, tiger heads, and birds. The large number and high quality of the Marlik bronze figurines reflect the flourishing state of the bronze

MARLIK. Figure 1. *Gold bowl from Marlik.* An example of repoussé technique. (Courtesy E. O. Nagahban)

industry in the Elburz highlands during the late second and early first millennia BCE.

An extremely rich collection of jewelry was found in the tombs, including necklaces, pendants, buttons, bracelets, earrings, rings, forehead bands, leaves, hair binders, pins, and fibulae. Much of this jewelry came from tombs that appear to have belonged to women. Some ornamental items were, however found in tombs that may have belonged to warriors since they contained large numbers of weapons and hunting items. Most of the jewelry is of gold, sometimes combined with carnelian, agate, or other materials. Small amounts of jewelry out of shell, bone, frit, glass, lime gypsum, and bronze were also found. Some are masterpieces of great delicacy and beauty: pendants and earrings with fine granulation, pomegranate, quadruple spiral, and animal-head beads; and embossed rosette buttons, demonstrating the well-developed technology and skill of the Marlik craftsmen. [*See* Jewelry.]

Both cylinder and stamp seals were found in the tombs. There are fourteen definite and several possible cylinder seals, made of frit, gypsum, various stones, and even gold. The majority are of frit, with surfaces so badly damaged that in some cases the designs have entirely disappeared. Two of the cylinder seals are inscribed, the only evidence of writing found at Marlik, but the writing is legible on only one of them and it is fragmentary. The five stamp seals found are of cast bronze and have simple geometric designs. [*See* Seals.]

The pottery from the tombs seems, for the most part, to have a specifically funerary purpose. Although it does not differ too widely from the site's domestic pottery, it tends to be more elaborate and ornamental. The vessels are red, brown, and gray and of very fine clay tempered with fine grit. The firing was very well controlled and the surface treatment is of high quality. Especially notable among the many stylized forms are beautiful spouted vessels finished with burnishing and sometimes with a pattern-burnished decoration. Among the vessels in the tombs were bottles, jars, pitchers, chalices, mugs, cups, pots, bowls, basins, plates, vases, sieves, and lamps.

Of almost a thousand fairly complete weapons found in the tombs, fewer than forty were made of some material other than bronze, including about twenty-five of stone and a lesser number of iron. By the beginning of the Marlik period, the use of stone for weapons was already outdated. By the end of the Marlik occupation, iron was just beginning to be introduced, although it was still far from common. The large number of weapons in the tombs seems to reflect the role of the deceased as a formidable warrior, although some items, such as the many bronze arrowheads, could also have been used for hunting. Their inclusion with the pottery and bronze figurines of wild game suggests that the occupant of the tomb had been a great hunter. Among the other weapons found in the tombs were mace heads, swords, daggers, spearheads, and arrowheads, along with such military equipment as shields, helmets, cymbals, quivers, belts, and wristbands, almost all of them bronze (see figure 2). [*See* Weapons and Warfare.]

MARLIK. Figure 2. *Bronze macehead.* The form is that of a stylized human head. (Courtesy E. O. Nagahban)

The large collection of finds from Marlik has been assigned typologically to a date between the fourteenth and tenth centuries BCE, a date supported by a carbon-14 date of 1457 ± 55 years BCE. Marlik apparently represents the Royal Cemetery of an Indo-Iranian culture that first settled in the highlands of the northern slopes of the Elburz Mountains in the mid-second millennium BCE and flourished there for several centuries. This highly developed culture, especially notable for its bronze industry, covered the southern zone of the Caspian Sea and the northern slopes of the Elburz Mountains. Its influence was felt throughout the ancient world. The Marlik excavation thus provides information on a dark period of the early Indo-Iranian movement into northern Iran, illustrating the daily life, industry, craftsmanship, and religious beliefs and traditions of this previously unknown people.

BIBLIOGRAPHY

Negahban, Ezat O. "Marlik, a Royal Necropolis of the Second Millennium." *Archaeologia Viva* 1 (September–November 1968): 58–79.

Negahban, Ezat O. "Pottery Figurines of Marlik." In *Memorial Volume of the Fifth International Congress of Iranian Art and Archaeology, Tehran, Isfahan, Shiraz, 11th–18th April 1968,* vol. 1, pp. 153–163. Tehran, 1972.

Negahban, Ezat O. *Marlik: A Preliminary Report on Marlik Excavation, Gohar Rud Expedition, Rudbar, 1961–1962.* 2d ed. Tehran, 1977. See especially, "Seals of Marlik" (pp. 2–25).

Negahban, Ezat O. "Pottery and Bronze Human Figurines of Marlik." *Archäologische Mitteilungen aus Iran* 12 (1979): 157–173, pls. 29–34.

Negahban, Ezat O. "Maceheads from Marlik." *American Journal of Archaeology* 85.4 (1981): 367–378, pls. 59–64.

Negahban, Ezat O. *Metal Vessels from Marlik.* Prähistorische Bronzefunde, 2.3. Munich, 1983.

Negahban, Ezat O. "Mosaic, Glass, and Frit Vessels from Marlik." In *Essays in Ancient Civilization Presented to Helene J. Kantor,* edited by Albert Leonard, Jr., and Bruce Beyer Williams, pp. 221–227, pls. 34–37. University of Chicago, Oriental Institute, Studies in Ancient Oriental Civilization, no. 47. Chicago, 1989.

Negahban, Ezat O. "Pendants from Marlik." *Iranica Antiqua* 24 (1989): 175–208.

Negahban, Ezat O. "Horse and Mule Figurines from Marlik." In *Archaeologia Iranica et Orientalis: Miscellanea in honorem Louis Vanden Berghe,* vol. 1, edited by Leon De Meyer and E. Haerinck, pp. 287–309. Ghent, 1989.

Negahban, Ezat O. "Silver Vessel of Marlik with Gold Spout and Impressed Gold Designs." In *Iranica Varia: Papers in Honor of Professor Ehsan Yarshater,* pp. 144–151. Leiden, 1990.

Ezat O. Negahban

MARQUET-KRAUSE, JUDITH

MARQUET-KRAUSE, JUDITH (1906–1936), Palestinian archaeologist born in Ilanya (Sejera, 13 km, or 8 mi., west–southwest of Tiberias), the first daughter of Eliyahu Krause and Ḥaya (née Ḥankin). Marquet-Krause spent her early childhood in Sejera before the family's move in 1914, to the Miqweh-Israel agricultural school, east of Jaffa, where her father became director. She received her secondary education in Tel Aviv and subsequently studied in Paris, at the Sorbonne, the École des Hautes Études, and the École du Louvre, where she acquainted herself with Palestinian archaeology. On her return to Palestine she worked for a season at Jericho under John Garstang.

Her broad knowledge of Oriental archaeology and command of ancient and modern languages, as well as her enthusiasm and energy, brought her the appointment of director of the Baron Edmond de Rothschild Expedition to Ai (et-Tell). She conducted three seasons of excavation there (1933–1935), establishing that the site had been destroyed and abandoned more than a millennium before the Israelite settlement, and that a small, unfortified village had existed there in the Early Iron Age. These discoveries demonstrated that the account in *Joshua* 7:2–5 and 8:1–29 was an "etiological" legend. The excavations also revealed very important remains from the Early Bronze Age IC–IIIB (3000–2400 BCE): a palace (perhaps originally a temple), a temple that yielded a rich and important assortment of cult objects and Egyptian First Dynasty alabaster vessels, and fortifications that included an elliptical tower and postern. Her excavation of the cemetery recovered significant assemblages of EB pottery.

Judith Marquet-Krause's death from an incurable illness ended the short career of a very promising young scholar. She had planned to excavate at Ai for a few more seasons and then to turn her attention to Hazor. She was the first native Jewish archaeologist in Palestine, the first local woman archaeologist, and the director of the first large-scale expedition carried out by a Jewish team in Palestine.

[*See also* Ai; Jericho; *and the biography of Garstang.*]

BIBLIOGRAPHY

Callaway, Joseph A. "Ai." In *The New Encyclopedia of Archaeological Excavations in the Holy Land,* vol. 1, pp. 39–45. Jerusalem and New York, 1993. Summary of the excavations at Ai, with a useful coordination of Marquet-Krause's results and subsequent excavations at the site.

Dussaud, René. "Mme Judith Marquet-Krause." *Syria* 17 (1936): 319–320. Obituary, with an incorrect birthdate.

Marquet-Krause, Judith. *Les fouilles de ʿAy (Et-Tell), 1933–1935.* 2 vols. Paris, 1949.

Dan Barag

MARSEILLE TARIFF

MARSEILLE TARIFF. A fragmentary Punic inscription of the third century BCE, engraved on two stones, was found in 1844/45 near a cemetery in Marseille. Now housed in the Musée Borély, in Marseille, they are known as the Marseille Tariff. The stones and text reveal that the inscription originated in Carthage, for fragments of the same type of text have been found in the Punic metropolis. It is not known when or under what circumstances the inscriptions were brought to France.

In antiquity, the tariff was affixed to the gate of the Carthaginian temple of Baal Ṣaphon, the protector of seagoers. It served to regulate fees as well as the parts of the offerings that were designated for the priests and for those who presented the offerings (individuals, religious associations, and clans). The amounts given to each varied according to the type of sacrifice and victim and according to the role played by the priest in the different ceremonies.

The sacrificial material consisted primarily of bovids, ovids/caprids, and birds, but other offerings are attested as well, such as cakes, milk, oil, and various vegetal products. The sacrificial victims are divided into four categories according to age and size: oxen; calves and deer; sheep; and lambs, kids, and other small animals. A distinction seems to have been made between domestic and wild birds.

The text mentions three types of sacrifices: *kll, ṣwʿt,* and *šlm kll,* but their nature and their distinguishing characteristics are far from clear. In the case of the *kll,* which can be a burnt offering, all kinds of animals could be offered, with the exception of birds; the offerer did not receive any part of the victim and was moreover required to pay a fee, in amounts of silver that decreased according to the size of the beast, from the ox to the smaller animals. Some parts of the victim were assigned to the priest. The *ṣwʿt* sacrifices consisted of the same animals as in the *kll*, but the victim was divided between the offerer(s) and the priests, nothing being due directly to the god(s). The *šlm kll* admitted all kinds of victims. The priests received various amounts of silver, but neither they nor the offerer(s) was allowed to eat the flesh of the slaughtered animals (birds excluded).

It is frequently assumed that the Marseille Tariff has strong affinities with the normative texts of the Hebrew Bible *(Leviticus)*, not only in matters of vocabulary but in actual practice as well. A sound analysis of the inscription, however, points up more differences than similarities between the Hebrew and the Punic ritual traditions. Moreover, the aim of the Punic text, with its clear administrative concerns, is not theological but practical. Because of this emphasis on the administration of the cult, both the theologically oriented biblical texts and the tariff itself must be used with care in reconstructing the religion of ancient Carthage.

[*See also* Phoenician-Punic.]

BIBLIOGRAPHY

Amadasi [Guzzo], Maria Giulia. *Le iscrizioni fenicie e puniche delle colonie in Occidente*. Rome, 1967. Text, translation, and philological commentary; see, in particular, pages 169–182.

Amadasi Guzzo, Maria Giulia. "Sacrifici e banchetti: Bibbia ebraica e iscrizioni puniche." In *Sacrificio e società nel mondo antico*, edited by Cristiano Grottanelli and Nicola F. Parise, pp. 97–122. Rome, 1988. Comparative evaluation of both biblical and Punic ritual traditions.

Baker, D. W. "Leviticus 1–7 and the Punic Tariffs: A Form-Critical Comparison." *Zeitschrift für die alttestamentliche Wissenschaft* 99.2 (1987): 188–197. Reconsiders the relationship between *Leviticus* and the Carthaginian rites.

Delcor, M. "Le tarif dit de Marseille (CIS I, 165): Aspects du système sacrificiel punique." *Semitica* 38.1 (1990): 87–94. Terminological and historical-religious problems.

Donner, Herbert, and Wolfgang Röllig. *Kanaanäische und aramäische Inschriften*. 3 vols. Wiesbaden, 1962–1964. Text, translation, and philological commentary.

Xella, Paolo. "Quelques aspects du rapport économie-religion d'après les tarifs sacrificiels puniques." *Bulletin Archéologique du Comité des Travaux Historiques et Scientifiques*, n.s. 19B (1983): 39–45. Study of the ritual typology, kinds of victims, and character of the text (administrative rather than theological).

PAOLO XELLA

MARTYRION. In early Christian usage, *martyrion* denotes a place, shrine, sanctuary, sacred monument, or building marking a "place of witness." The term is comprised of the Greek stem *mart*, to which the denominative suffix *i-on* is appended. In the narrow sense, the Early Christian writers who use the term envisage a place or building that houses the physical remains of a blood witness. The concept developed from the predication of the Greek term *martys* ("witness") to Stephen (*Acts* 20:22), to Antipas (*Rv.* 2:13), and to other unnamed persons (*Rv.* 17:6) who, like Stephen and Antipas, testified to Jesus by giving up their lives. Jesus was the archetype of the blood witness; in Christian tradition, Peter, Stephen, and Paul follow close upon the archetype. In the broader sense, however, a martyrion is any place hallowed by tradition and associated with legendary heroes and heroines, both blood witnesses others.

The term is not a Christian neologism. Herodotus, Aeschylus, and Thucydides use it to denote testimony or physical proof. The plural, martyria, appears in *Exodus* 25:16, 21 as a synonym for the tablets of the Decalogue. It is also true, however, that, although attested in earlier contexts, the word is invoked with much greater frequency in later antiquity (second–sixth centuries) than in any other period of ancient history. Throughout later antiquity the term commonly implies a material place (usually a building), in contrast to earlier usages, where it carried legislative or judicial associations.

Beginning in the Constantinian period (305–337), the term comes to acquire a broad sphere of associated meanings. This fact makes it difficult to identify just exactly which building types should be classified under the martyrial rubric. For example, the Palestinian buildings constructed to mark and commemorate events in the lives of Jesus, John the Baptist, and Mary the mother of Jesus are denominated martyria. Also attested as martyria are certain shrines, sanctuaries, and sacred monuments marking either a theophany or an epiphany of a saint or an apostle or a figure from the Hebrew Bible. The best-known Palestinian example was the Constantinian construction (no longer extant) at Mamre, on a site where, according to tradition (*Gn.* 18:1), the Israelite God appeared to Abraham. In addition, the terms *memoria* and *tropaion* ("commemorative memorial," or "monument"; cf. Eusebius, *Church History* 2.25.7; 7.18.1), though used infrequently in patristic literature, are close functional equivalents to martyrium.

Yet another association the term comes to acquire, also beginning in the fourth century, is *martyrium* used as a synonym for various words denoting church buildings, including *ekklesia, kyriakon,* and *hieron*. This is a consequence of the real-life assimilation of two functionally different kinds of structures—the one for the eucharistic worship of the living community and the other for the commemoration and veneration of the dead. Christian cults of martyrs and holy sites expanded dramatically during the fourth century, and the martyrial structures associated with those cults were often used in multiple capacities, including the performance of liturgical functions unrelated to the cult of the dead. In short, the term *martyrion* was predicated of church buildings with increasing frequency from the fourth century onward.

On questions concerning origins and putative models, André Grabar (1946) hypothesized the derivation of Early Christian martyrial structures from Hellenistic and Greco-

Roman funerary antecedents, notably hero shrines (*herooa*) and mausolea. Grabar's view of this subject is closely tied to his invention of a sevenfold architectural typology of martyrial structures. He subsumes the full range of martyrial types under this scheme. Grabar distinguishes the types of plans: square structures; rectangular structures; structures with one apse on the periphery; triconch structures (or with a cella trichora); structures with a transverse hall or transept; structures built on a circular or polygonal plan; and martyrial buildings constructed on a cruciform grid. Of these seven plan types, the first three may be said to exhibit Hellenistic and Greco-Roman antecedents; for the remaining four, however, the evidence is at least problematic—some would say nonexistent. Thus, although Grabar's monograph is still the basic starting point for any serious study of martyrial structures in later antiquity, his seven-part typology, designed to support a theory of derivation from pagan prototypes, actually requires substantial modification and redefinition. It is necessary to consult more recent publications, especially those listed Kleinbauer's (1992) bibliography. It has been suggested that Christian martyrial structures may have influenced later, non-Christian architectural traditions, notably Islamic saints' shrines (see "Ḳubba," in *Encyclopaedia of Islam,* new ed., vol. 5, pp. 289–296, Leiden, 1986).

Early Christian martyrial structures situated in Near Eastern settings are products of the fourth through sixth centuries. Constantine endowed four martyrial buildings in the Holy Land: two in Jerusalem, one in Bethlehem, and another in Mamre); one in Constantinople (Holy Apostles); and another in Rome (St. Peter's). In the late fourth century, what Constantine had begun was continued in Palestine (Anastasis and Imbomon, both in Jerusalem) and in other martyrial buildings constructed in Rome and in provincial Italy, North Africa, the Rhineland, and Syria (i.e., St. Babylas in Antioch.) [*See* Jerusalem; Bethlehem; Constantinople; Antioch on Orontes.]

In the fifth and sixth centuries, more martyrial structures were built in virtually all the lands that had been conquered by Christianity. In addition to the places already mentioned, this includes the northern and central Aegean on the Greek side and along the Turkish coast; the interior of Anatolia, Egypt, Jordan, and especially Syria, which became the great Near Eastern center of martyrial architecture. On Syrian soil, the two most-impressive centers of martyrial cult and martyrial architecture are the shrine of the ascetic St. Simeon (d. 24 July 459) at Qalʿat Simʿan and the shrine of the Roman soldier St. Sergius (who, according to tradition, was tortured and martyred [with Bakchos] by his fellow soldiers during the Diocletianic period) at Rusafa/Sergiopolis in northeastern Syria, south of the Euphrates River. [See Qalʿat Simʿan; Rusafa.]

The following survey, organized alphabetically by region, provides a selected inventory of martyrial buildings in the Near East.

Anatolia/Turkey. (In addition to the items listed below, cf. Robert Edwards, "Yanıkhan (Cilicia in Turkey)" in *Encyclopedia of Early Christian Art and Archaeology* [hereafter *EECAA*], forthcoming.)

Antioch/Kaoussié: Martyrion of St. Babylas, late fourth century (cf. Pauline Donceel-Voûte, *Les pavements des églises byzantines de Syrie et du Liban: Décor, archéologie et liturgie I,* Louvain, 1988, pp. 21–31).

Der Kubbuk (southeast of Midyat in Ṭur ʿAbdin): square funerary structure, possibly a martyrion, fifth or sixth century (cf. G. Wiessner, *Göttingen Orientforschungen. Reihe II* 3 [1993]: 116–120).

Ḥaḥ (Anıtlı, 20 km (12.5 mi.) northeast of Midyat in Ṭur ʿAbdin): Martyrion of el-ʿAdrha; two-storied rectangular structure, possibly sixth century (cf. R. Krautheimer, *Early Christian and Byzantine Architecture,* 4th ed., New York, 1986, fig. 263.).

Isauria, Meriamlik, south of Seleucia/Silifke: Martyrial Church of St. Thekla, c. 375; rectangular plan on a longitudinal axis, narthex, nave and two aisles, central apse projecting from the east wall flanked by pastophory and diakonikon (cf. F. Hild, H. Hellenkemper, and G. Hellenkemper-Salies, "Kommagene—Kilikien—Isaurien," in *Reallexikon zur byzantinischen Kunst,* 1984–1989).

Arabian Peninsula. There are no surviving examples of martyrial buildings from the period of later antiquity.

Armenia. (In addition to the items listed below, cf. Robert Edwards, "Armenia," in *EECAA.*)

Aghoudi: two vaulted mausolea, fifth or sixth century (cf. A. Khatchatrian, *L'Architecture Arménienne du IVe au VIe siècle,* Paris, 1971, p. 30, pl. 3, fig. 8).

Aghts: hypogeum of the Arsacid kings, fourth century; vaulted, rectangular burial chamber with two arcosolium burials and an apse projecting from one of the short ends of the chamber (cf. *ibid.,* pp. 29–30, pl. 3, fig. 7).

Ardvi: mausoleum, fifth or sixth century (cf. *ibid.,* p. 31).

Nakhtjavan: hypogeum of the Kamsarkan lords, fifth century (cf. *ibid.,* p. 30).

Vagharchapat: Church of St. Hripsime, martyrial crypt, fourth century (cf. *ibid.,* p. 32, pl. 4, fig. 12; A. B. Eremian, "La chiesa di S. Hripsimé," *Ricerca sull'architettura armena* 6 [1972]: 1–140).

Zvart'nots: Church of St. Gregory (with the epithet Loosavorich, "the Illuminator"), mid- to late seventh century; aisled tetraconch constructed at a site that commemorates the epiphany of St. Gregory to King Tiridates III (cf. W. E. Kleinbauer, "Zvart'nots and the Origins of Christian Architecture in Armenia," *Art Bulletin* 54 [1972]: 245–262).

Cyprus. There are numerous martyrial traditions attributed to early Christian Cyprus, including the apostle Barnabas who is said to have been killed by Jews at Salamis and whose body is said to have been discovered in 488 (see Raymond Janin, "Chypre," *Dictionnaire d'histoire et géographie ecclèstiastique,* Paris, 1953).

Politiko: martyrion of St. Herakleides, late fourth century or earlier (cf. A. Papageorghiou, *E palaiochristianikē kai Byzantinē technē en Kuprō kata to 1964,* Nicosia, 1965, p. 6).

Egypt

Abu Mina: multiple phases of a martyrial structure, the earliest of them a small rectangular building dated to the late fourth century (cf. Peter Grossmann, "Abu Mina," and A. S. Atiya, "Martyrs, Coptic," both in *The Coptic Encyclopedia,* New York, 1991).

Ethiopia. There are no surviving examples of martyrial buildings from the period of later antiquity (cf. Marilyn Heldman, "Ethiopia," in *EECAA*).

Iran and Iraq. There are no surviving examples of martyrial buildings from the period of later antiquity (see Judith Lerner, "Christianity in Pre-Islamic Persia: Material Remains," in *Encyclopedia Iranica,* New York, 1992).

Israel

Bethlehem: Church of the Nativity, domed octagonal martyrion at the east end of the building commemorating the place where by tradition Jesus was born, mid-fourth century (cf. J. E. Taylor, *Christians and the Holy Places,* Oxford, 1993, pp. 96–112). [*See* Bethlehem.]

Jerusalem: Church of the Holy Sepulcher, domed triconch martyrion at the western end of the building commemorating the place where by tradition Jesus was buried, mid-fourth century (cf. Joseph Patrich, "The Early Church of the Holy Sepulchre in the Light of Excavations and Restoration," in *Ancient Churches Revealed,* edited by Yoram Tsafrir, Jerusalem, 1993, pp. 101–117). [*See* Jerusalem.]

Jerusalem, Mount of Olives: Eleona (Imbomon) Church; rectangular structure, apse at the east end over the cave from where by tradition Jesus ascended to heaven, late fourth century (cf. Taylor, 1993, pp. 143–156).

Mamre/Terebinthos (Ramat el-Khalil): small rectangular martyrial sanctuary where the three angels (the Trinity in Christian exegesis) appeared to Abraham (*Gn.* 18:1–22), fourth century (cf. Taylor, 1993, pp. 86–95).

Mount Gerizim: Church of Mary Theotokos; octagonal martyrial structure with an apse projecting to the east, late fifth century (cf. Y. Magen, "The Church of Mary Theotokos on Mt. Gerizim," in Tsafrir, 1993, pp. 83–89).

Jordan

Madaba: the so-called Cathedral Church, Chapel of the Martyr Theodore; rectangular chapel in the southwest corner of the building, dated 562 (cf. Michele Piccirillo, *The Mosaics of Jordan,* Amman, 1993, pp. 109–113–117). [*See* Madaba.]

Mount Nebo, Siyagha peak: Memorial Church of Moses; triconch martyrial sanctuary, late fourth century (cf. Piccirillo, 1993, pp. 144–145). [*See* Nebo, Mount.]

Lebanon. For martyrial remains in Lebanon, see index V, "Martyrium," in Pauline Donceel-Voûte, *Les pavements des églises byzantines de Syrie et du Liban* (Louvain, 1988).

Syria

Bosra: Church of Sts. Sergius, Bacchus, and Leontios; aisled tetraconch, c. 500 (cf. R. F. Campanati, "Considerazioni sulla chiese dei ss. Sergio, Bacco e Leonzio di Bosra dopo gli ultimi scavi (1977, 1978)" *Römisch-Germanisches Zantralmuseum Monographien* 10.1 [1986]: 133–142; Campanati, "Die italienischen Ausgrabungen in Bosra (Syrien). Der spätantike Zentralbau der Kirche des Hll. Sergius, Bacchus und Leontius," *BOREAS* 9 [1986]: 173–185; Jean-Marie Dentzer, "Bosra," in *EECAA*). [*See* Bosra.]

Qalʿat Simʿan: Church of St. Simeon; octagonal central structure with the base of Simeon's column at the center of the octagon; four rectangular wings project from the perimeter of the octagon, creating a cruciform plan, 474–491 (cf. J.-P. Sodini, "Qalʿat Semaʿan," in *EECAA*). [*See* Qalʿat Simʿan.]

Qanawat (Kanatha): Triconch martyrial chapel, fifth or early sixth century (cf. Donceel-Voûte, 1988, pp. 244–249).

Qartamin: Monastery of Mar Samuel, Mar Simeon, and Mar Gabriel; octagonal structure (possibly a martyrion) at the northwest corner of the main church, early to mid-sixth century (cf. E. J. W. Hawkins, M. C. Mundel, and Cyril Mango, "The Mosaics of the Monastery of Mār Samuel, Mār Simeon, and Mār Gabriel, near Kartmin," *Dumbarton Oaks Papers* 27 [1973]; see fig. 2, plan of the monastery).

Rusafa/Sergiopolis: Church (possibly the martyrion) of St. Sergios, located 150 m northwest of the basilica; tetraconch, before 553 (cf. Thilo Ulbert, "Rusafa," in *EECAA*). [*See* Rusafa.]

[*See also* Churches; Mausoleum; Palestine, *article on* Palestine in the Byzantine Period; Syria, *article on* Syria in the Byzantine Period; *and* Transjordan, *article on* Transjordan in the Byzantine Period.]

BIBLIOGRAPHY

Grabar, André. *Martyrium: Recherches sur le culte des reliques et l'art chrétien antique.* 2 vols. Paris, 1946. The basic work on the architecture of early Christian martyria.

Kleinbauer, W. Eugene. *Early Christian and Byzantine Architecture: An Annotated Bibliography and Historiography.* Boston, 1992. Now the indispensable lexical tool for the study of Early Christian architecture. Immensely informative. See entries 1804–1829 for a survey of literature on martyria, including the material culture of martyr sites and the cult and ideology surrounding them. NB: Kleinbauer citations refer to entry numbers.

Krautheimer, Richard, and Slobodan Curcic. *Early Christian and Byzantine Architecture.* 4th ed. New Haven, 1986. Concise introduction to Early Christian architecture, with numerous examples of martyrial structures.

Ward-Perkins, J. B. "Memoria, Martyr's Tomb, and Martyr's Church." *Journal of Theological Studies* 17 (1966): 20–38. Reprinted in *Art, Archaeology, and Architecture of Early Christianity,* edited by Paul Corby Finney, pp. 306–403. New York, 1993. Questions Grabar's derivation of Christian martyria solely from pagan funerary antecedents; his architectural typology, which divides martyrial structures into seven categories; and his developmental model, which he imposes on the Early Christian architectural evidence.

PAUL CORBY FINNEY

MASADA, a mesa located at the edge of the Judean Desert on the western shore of the Dead Sea, approximately 25 km (15.5 mi.) south of ʿEin-Gedi. Rising about 440 m above the Dead Sea, Masada's summit covers 23 acres. The cliffs surrounding Masada contain evidence of human activity beginning in the Chalcolithic period, but the site's main occupation was during the late Second Temple period. The history of Masada under the Hasmoneans and through the First Jewish Revolt (66–74 CE) is documented archaeologically and by the Jewish historian Josephus Flavius. Masada was last inhabited during the Byzantine period, when a small church occupied the site. [*See* Churches.]

Josephus' discussions of Masada (*War* 1.13, 15; 2.17, 22; 4.7, 9; 7.7–10; *Antiq.* 14.13–15) provide the basis for all histories of this site. As early as 1838 the American explorer Edward Robinson correctly identified Masada with the site called es-Sebba, basing his identification almost exclusively on information drawn from Josephus's account. Samuel W. Wolcutt visited the mesa in 1842 and identified the Roman walls and camps that encircle it. Félicien de Saulcy was the first to excavate at Masada and in 1851 uncovered the mosaic floor of a Byzantine chapel. [*See* Mosaics.] Claude R. Conder published plans of buildings on the summit and of one Roman camp in 1875. The first in-depth study of the Roman camps was carried out by Alfred von Domaszewski in 1909.

Major studies of the site were begun in 1932 when Adolf Schulter spent a month investigating and sketching the plans of the buildings and Roman camps. The exact location of the so-called Snake Path was established by Shmaryahu Gutman who, later, with A. Alon, surveyed the site's Herodian water system. Gutman then partially excavated and reconstructed some of the Roman camps.

In 1953 the Israel Exploration Society, the Israel Department of Antiquities and Museums, and the Hebrew University of Jerusalem identified structures on the northern and western sides of Masada and drafted corrected maps of the site. The major excavation of the site was carried out by Yigael Yadin in two seasons from 1963 to 1965. The buildings on top of the mesa were the primary focus of investigation, but Yadin also made trial soundings in one of the Roman camps. Using Josephus's record as his primary guide, Yadin excavated 97 percent of the area on the summit.

Josephus ascribed the first construction project on Masada to "Jonathan" (*War* 7.285), whom archaeologist Ehud Netzer (1991) associates with Jonathan Maccabaeus. Others associate him with Alexander Jannaeus. Josephus attributes the major building phase to Herod the Great, who from 37 to 31 BCE expanded the preexisting Hasmonean fortress (*War* 7.300). After a nearly disastrous siege by Antigonus Mattathias, the last of the Hasmonean kings (c. 40 BCE), Herod refortified the site.

Little information remains of the occupation of Masada after Herod's death; however, Josephus writes that rebels, whom he characterizes as *sicarii,* the "short-knived ones" captured the site from a Roman garrison (*War* 2.408, 433–434). This record, coupled with pottery with Latin inscriptions found in excavation, suggests that the fortress housed a Roman garrison following Herod's death. During the First Jewish War (66–74 CE) the site was occupied by the rebel group. In 73 CE the Roman Tenth Legion, led by Flavius Silva, marched against the Masada defenders led by Eleazar ben Ya'ir ben Judah (*War* 2.447; 7.252–253).

Though Josephus describes extensive Hasmonean construction on Masada, the only clear physical evidence of a Hasmonean presence is an assemblage of coins dating to Alexander Jannaeus and plaster dated to the period from some of the cisterns on the summit. No architecture can be attributed to the period, suggesting that Herodian construction destroyed earlier Hasmonean structures.

A casemate wall, dated to the Herodian period, enclosed the summit except on the north, where a palace forms the outer fortifications. The wall, built of local dolomite stone, about 13,000 m long; the casemates are about 5 m wide. There are four gates, seventy rooms, and thirty towers in the casemate wall. To supply fresh water, a series of aqueducts and cisterns was built. These supplied an abundance of water to the elaborate bathhouses, pools, and (during the Jewish Revolt) ritual baths. [*See* Aqueducts; Cisterns; Baths; Pools; Ritual Baths.]

The four palace complexes contain the most spectacular of all the architecture at Masada. The best known of these, the Northern Palace-Villa complex on the northernmost point of the summit, was built in three tiers near the edge of the cliff (see figure 1). [*See* Villa.] The upper level comprised living quarters with a semicircular porch.

The middle terrace, approximately 20 m below the upper terrace, contained a circular building. That building's foundations incorporated two concentric circular walls; the diameter of the outer wall was 16 m and of the inner wall 10 m. Yadin (1965) and Netzer (1991) propose that two rows of columns supported a roof. A staircase, hidden from view, connected the middle and upper terraces.

The lower terrace, built on a raised area at the cliff's edge, lies 16 m beneath the middle terrace. Building foundations

MASADA. Figure 1. *North end of the site showing the Herodian domestic palace, bath house, and storerooms.* (Courtesy Pictorial Archive)

revealed a central area that had been surrounded by porticoes and an inner columned wall. This terrace contained a small bathhouse with a simple paved mosaic floor and a structure with decorated plaster walls and columns. [*See* Wall Paintings.] Painted and mosaic elements on Masada use geometric patterns. They lack "graven" images, perhaps in accordance with a strict interpretation of the Second Commandment. In this, the art of Masada parallels contemporary art in Jerusalem and elsewhere in Judah. [*See* Jerusalem; Judah.]

The Western Palace, near the casemate wall, is the largest (4,340 m) residential building on Masada. Four distinct blocks of rooms constitute this palace: "royal" apartments, workshops and a service wing, storerooms, and an administrative section near what Yadin (1966) and Netzer (1993) call the residences of the palace officials. The opulence of the surviving architecture may have influenced Yadin's identification of this structure as royal apartments: its walls were decorated with plaster, and an indentation in the floor suggested a throne area to Yadin (1966) and Netzer (1993). The floor was covered with a richly colored mosaic with a central medallion of geometric and plant designs. A Roman-style bath was located in the northeast corner of a wing of this palace.

Situated southeast of this complex were three small palaces whose central courts and two-columned halls reflect the layout of the Western Palace. Herodian ceramics and coins found within the complex provide a reliable chronological indicator. Of special interest was the discovery of a wine amphora inscribed in Latin "to Herod, king of Judea."

Evidence of the Jewish occupation of Masada during the Jewish Revolt of 66–74 is extensive. Two blocks of long rooms (approximately 30 × 3 m) were attached to a building complex at the north end of the site. Yadin (1966) and Netzer (1993) date the remains of flour, oil, wine, dates, olives, and other foodstuffs recovered from these structures to the period of the revolt. Another group of storerooms west and south of the northern building contained caches of weapons. [*See* Weapons and Warfare.] Casemate rooms and palaces underwent conversion into living quarters, and cooking ovens, new walls, and benches were added in many of the Herodian buildings. Ritual baths were apparently built at this time, and in the northern casemate wall a synagogue was constructed in a room that had previously served as a stable. Numerous religious documents were discovered, many of them recovered in, or in close proximity to, the synagogue. The texts included biblical books, the *Book of Ben Sira (Ecclesiasticus),* and "The Songs of the Sabbath Sacrifice." The latter text was also discovered at Qumran. [*See* Qumran.]

The artifacts from the period of the revolt were of special interest to Yadin: items of everyday life (textiles and textile artifacts, ceramics, and baskets), hoards of Jewish coins dating to the fourth year of the revolt (70 CE), and ostraca of various types. [*See* Ostracon.] The ostraca include personal names, designations of priestly tithes, names of foodstuffs, and records of supplies and payments.

Following Josephus (*War* 7.395), Yadin excavated a group of ostraca he identified with the "lots" used by the defenders in carrying out their mass suicide (Yadin, 1966). These ostraca were found near the Water Gate in a group of eleven (a twelfth appears simply to be an incomplete ostracon sherd). Each carries a single name, including the name *Ben-Ya'ir,* who has been associated with Eleazar ben Ya'ir ben Judah. Not all scholars share this identification. Among those who have raised serious questions is S. J. D. Cohen (1982), who doubts the historicity of Josephus's description of the rebels and their mass suicide. Josephus reports that the Sicarii set fire to the "palace" during the final stage of the siege, though evidence of a conflagration was discovered (*War* 7.315–319, 397, 403–406).

Josephus reports that Flavius Silva built an extensive siege wall and a series of camps encompassing Masada (*War* 7.304–314), which archaeological exploration has verified.

Both the wall and several of the camps are still visible. Gutman excavated camp A and the assault ramp and Yadin (1965) made soundings in camp F. After the fall of Masada a Roman garrison remained at the site, but only a few related coins have been recovered that reflect this occupation. The site appears to have been abandoned until the Byzantine period (fifth–sixth centuries). An apsidal church was built northeast of the Western Palace that may have been part of a monastic complex.

[*See also* First Jewish Revolt; Hasmoneans; Israel Antiquities Authority; *and the biographies of Conder, Robinson, Saulcy, and Yadin.*]

BIBLIOGRAPHY

Cohen, S. J. D. "Literary Tradition, Archaeological Remains, and the Credibility of Josephus." *Journal of Jewish Studies (Essays in Honour of Yigael Yadin)* 33 (1982): 385–405. Revisionist reevaluation of the literary and archaeological evidence for the last days of Masada, bringing to bear parallels in Greco-Roman literature.

Josephus. *The Jewish War.* Books 1–7. Translated by Henry St. John Thackeray. Loeb Classical Library. London, 1927–1928. The standard edition of Josephus's writings.

Josephus. *The Jewish Antiquities.* Books 12–14. Translated by Ralph Marcus. Loeb Classical Library. London, 1943.

Knox, Reed, et al. "Iron Objects from Masada: Metallurgical Studies." *Israel Exploration Journal* 33 (1983): 97–107. Argues that specific metal objects discovered on Masada were produced by the rebels during the Jewish Revolt against Rome.

Masada 1–4: The Yigael Yadin Excavations, 1963–1965, Final Reports. Jerusalem, 1989–. Definitive, readable series of site reports that retains much of Yadin's original interpretations while reevaluating the discoveries. The series includes Yigael Yadin and Joseph Naveh, *Masada 1: The Aramaic and Hebrew Ostraca and Jar Inscriptions* (Jerusalem, 1989), published with *The Coins of Masada* by Ya'acov Meshorer; Hannah M. Cotton and Joseph Geiger, *Masada 2: The Latin and Greek Documents* (Jerusalem, 1989); and Ehud Netzer, *Masada 3: The Buildings, Stratigraphy, and Architecture* (Jerusalem, 1991). *Masada 4* (Jerusalem, 1994) includes Dan Barag and Malka Hershkovitz, *Lamps;* Avigail Sheffer and Herd Granger-Taylor, *Textiles;* Kathryn Bernick, *Basketry, Cordage, and Related Artifacts;* Nili Liphschitz, *Wood Remains;* and Andrew Holley, *Ballista Balls.*

Netzer, Ehud. "The Last Days and Hours at Masada." *Biblical Archaeology Review* 17.6 (1991): 20–32. Further discussion and exploration of the defenders' siege walls and Roman engines.

Netzer, Ehud. "Masada." In *The New Encyclopedia of Archaeological Excavations in the Holy Land,* vol. 3, pp. 973–985. Jerusalem and New York, 1993.

Newsom, Carol, and Yigael Yadin. "The Masada Fragment of the Qumran Songs of the Sabbath Sacrifice." *Israel Exploration Journal* 34 (1984): 77–88. Publication of the Masada fragment, comparing it to the version discovered at Qumran.

Yadin, Yigael. "The Excavation of Masada, 1963/64: Preliminary Report." *Israel Exploration Journal* 15 (1965): 1–120.

Yadin, Yigael. *Masada: Herod's Fortress and the Zealots' Last Stand.* New York, 1966. Fairly detailed, popular account of the excavation and finds at Masada.

GLENDA W. FRIEND and STEVEN FINE

MASHKAN-SHAPIR, ancient city in Mesopotamia identified with the site Tell Abu Duwari, located at 32°24′7″ N and 45°12′17″ E. The identification of Tell Abu Duwari with Mashkan-shapir was made firm when more than 150 fragments of baked clay cylinders bearing an inscription dedicating Mashkan-shapir's city wall were found in 1989 in association with one of the site's city gates.

In the broader scope of Mesopotamian settlement, the occupation of Mashkan-shapir was quite brief. Its name, which can be translated as "the encampment of the overseer," indicates its humble beginnings. The first textual reference to this town, dated to the Akkadian period (2334–2154 BCE) shows it to have been a place of refuge for a runaway slave girl. Mashkan-shapir continued for several centuries as an obscure outpost of Mesopotamian civilization, concerned more with raising sheep than the larger issues of state. Indeed, had the unification of southern Mesopotamia, which characterized most of the Akkadian and Ur III periods (2334–2004 BCE) persisted, Mashkan-shapir would probably have remained no more than a small rural hamlet.

The succeeding Isin-Larsa period was characterized by political fragmentation, however, with Larsa claiming dominance over the south, Isin the center, and (somewhat later) Babylon the territories of northern Babylonia. Given the absence of native sources of stone, metals, and high-quality timber for construction, this political fragmentation resulted in a disruption in the trade routes so vital to the Mesopotamian economy. Larsa, although in clear control of trade coming up from the Persian Gulf, was cut off by Isin from the usual trade route up the Euphrates River. Larsa therefore turned its attention to the territory between it and the Tigris River—the alternate route to the north.

It is here that Mashkan-shapir becomes significant. Mashkan-shapir was located—as can be seen on satellite images of the area—beside all or some of the path of the Tigris River in the early second millennium BCE. It was thus in a strategic position to control trade moving from areas east and north of Babylonia into the southern heartland.

The interest of the Larsa kings in Mashkan-shapir is made clear both by objects found at the site and by the more extensive textual record. Zabaya (1941–1933 BCE), one of the more obscure of the early Larsa kings, left a record of building activity at the site in the form of an inscribed clay nail; however, it was not until the reign of Sin-iddinam (1845–1843 BCE) that Mashkan-shapir became a major city. Sin-iddinam built the wall around Mashkan-shapir with the express intent "to increase its dwellings," as he says in his dedicatory inscription (see above). Archaeological evidence indicates that his city wall enclosed an area in excess of 70 hectares (173 acres)—an area larger than that walled in at Ur. From this time forth, Mashkan-shapir rose from obscurity and began to play a key role in trade between the key eastward trade route along the Diyala River and the kingdom of Larsa, and this was only the beginning. Within a decade of Sin-iddinam's death, the rulership of the parent city of Larsa was taken over by a family from Mashkan-shapir. Mashkan-shapir then became the second capital of the Larsa kingdom, playing key roles in justice and international diplomacy, especially following Rim-Sin's defeat of Isin in 1794 BCE. Mashkan-shapir fell when Hammurabi finally moved against Larsa in 1763 BCE. The shift in the allegiance of its armies to Hammurabi precipitated Larsa's downfall.

While Hammurabi's conquest ended Mashkan-shapir's role as a political capital, it remained an important city—as is testified by its inclusion in the prologue of Hammurabi's law code. However, conditions deteriorated in southern Babylonia under Hammurabi's successor, Samsuiluna (1749–1712 BCE). By 1720 BCE the cities of southern and central Babylonia lay abandoned, including Mashkan-shapir—probably the result of a combination of political upheaval and ecological degradation. While in Kassite times (between perhaps 1400 and 1150 BCE) new canals brought water back to old centers of Sumerian culture, Mashkan-shapir was either too far east or had had too brief a tradition for it to be included. It remained lost in the desert until its recent discovery by archaeologists.

The first archaeologist to visit Mashkan-shapir was Robert McC. Adams, who included the site in his survey of the area around Nippur, giving it the identification number 639. Based on his description of the site, Elizabeth C. Stone selected it as a likely candidate for excavation. To date, three seasons of work have been conducted there, two three-week seasons in 1987 and 1988–1989, and a three-month season in 1990.

The brevity of Mashkan-shapir's floruit is what gives its archaeological manifestations particular significance. Apart from an underlying Uruk occupation (3500–3000 BCE) and a very limited Parthian settlement (250 BCE–228 CE), the remains of Mashkan-shapir provide a snapshot of an early second-millennium Mesopotamian city that is unparalleled. Only 2 m above plain level on average, the major features of this ancient city have not been obscured by erosion or later occupation, as is so often the case at longer-lived examples.

Because the primary aim of the Mashkan-shapir project was to recover a sense of the overall city plan, the bulk of the work conducted to date has been devoted to reconnaissance—both aerial and surface surveys. In addition, several small soundings were excavated to test the validity of conclusions drawn from surface survey work alone; one extensive area, covering 1,000 sq m, was excavated in 1990.

The survey work conducted at Mashkan-shapir has not only revealed the site's major features—canals, temple platforms, city walls—but also some that are more subtle—roads, manufacturing areas, and special-purpose zones identified on the basis of their surface objects. Together, these provide a comprehensive view of the ancient city's organization, albeit a somewhat provisional one pending further excavation.

Mashkan-shapir was divided into its component parts by four major canals. Its south, central, western, eastern, and northern parts have different characteristics and apparently served somewhat different functions. A fifth major canal (possibly somewhat later in date) flowed through the northern portion of the site, but no differences in patterning have been observed on either of its banks. Minor canals were also located within the areas in the east and north that appear to have been associated with manufacturing—especially of ceramics. Where the main central canal intersected with the eastern and western branches, the area was opened into two harbors, each covering an area of approximately one hectare. It is not clear whether these harbors should be identified with the main Mashkan-shapir harbor (mentioned in one cuneiform text as holding 270 boats preparatory to an attack on the city of Kish) or if that center of international trade was located a kilometer or so away, on the banks of the Tigris River.

The site's religious quarter was located in the south; there, a quite small area is characterized by both baked-brick and mud-brick platforms that must once have supported temples. Associated with these platforms are some seventy fragments of life-sized and half-sized terra-cotta statuary in the shape of humans, lions, and horses. These statues doubtless guarded the entrance to a temple in the same way that similar statues guarded the entrances to the contemporary temples at Khafajeh, Isin, and Tell Harmal. Tentative evidence suggests that the immediate temple precinct was walled off from the rest of the southern portion of the city, but this conclusion awaits confirmation. [*See* Temples, *article on* Mesopotamian Temples.]

Also on the periphery of the site, but in this case in the southern part of the west mound, is the area that seems to have been devoted to secular administration. Aerial photographs reveal a walled building complex made up of a number of regularly built structures characterized by large courtyards. Large numbers of fragments of models of chariots have been found in this area, but their association with administrative practices is unclear. Two soundings and one larger excavation yielded numerous unbaked clay sealings, an administrative tablet, and some other inscribed materials that confirm the impression that this was an administrative area. The tablet suggests concern with trade and shipments of goods. Numerous fragments of the bitumen (natural asphalt, used for waterproofing) covering of reed and matting wrapped bundles may also be testimony to such activity, but more excavation is needed before the full scope of the area's activities can be assessed.

The third distinctive part of the city lies in the southern portion of the central mound. This was apparently the core of the early settlement. A sounding revealed residential structures dating to early in the Isin-Larsa period, before the city's rise to power. The evidence suggests that this early mound was left unoccupied for the last century or so of Mashkan-shapir's occupation and was used as a cemetery. Numerous fragments of large burial jars and typical grave goods—jewelry, cosmetic palettes, and weapons—litter the surface of the area (as do the traces of the work of illicit diggers at the site). Like the administrative area and perhaps also the religious quarter, this cemetery area was walled off from the rest of the central mound. Enclosed within this wall is another platform that presumably also supported a temple. It is possible that Mashkan-shapir's dedication to Nergal, the Mesopotamian god of death, may have led to this association between a cemetery and a temple—an association not seen at other Mesopotamian cities.

The rest of the site seems to have been largely residential in character. In some areas aerial photographs reveal the street pattern: major roads paralleled the canals, leaving space for a single row of houses between a street and a canal. Larger areas, though, were bisected by roads that connected with quays or bridges to allow passage across the canals.

The evidence suggests that there was a fairly even distribution of wealth over the spread of the residential districts. Artifacts associated with high status—cylinder seals, stone bowls, and even metal objects—are found all over the city. Also found everywhere are traces of baked-brick architecture and graves—an indication that not everyone was buried in the cemetery.

It is in the residential districts that evidence for manufacturing activities is found. Three such industries have been identified: copperworking, pottery production, and lapidary work. The first two are indicated by the presence of their residues—copper slag, kiln fragments, and wasters—while the third is marked by concentrations of unworked stones found with numerous small, mostly cuboid grinders. It appears that all crafts were represented in all parts of the city, but that there was some specialization. Most of the copper-production centers were located in the central part of the site; ceramic production was focused on the small canals in the north and east; and lapidary work was concentrated in the southeast.

The whole was surrounded by Sin-iddinam's city wall, in which three gates have been identified: a water gate and two gates located beside the canals where their flow enters the city. In many places, the densely occupied portion of the city never reached the wall. Instead, the empty space left held a few large, but scattered, buildings. In plan, some of these suggest storage facilities, so it is possible that the city's granaries were located near the city gates.

Although the exploration of Mashkan-shapir is still in its infancy, its unique occupational history has allowed a quite complete picture of the organization of this Mesopotamian city. Noteworthy are the role the canals played in dividing the city and the peripheral character of its main institutions, with religious and administrative centers located toward its edges.

[*See also* Isin; *and* Larsa.]

BIBLIOGRAPHY

Charpin, Dominique. "Les représentants de Mari à Babylone (I)." In *Archives épistolaires de Mari 1/2*, edited by Dominique Charpin et al., pp. 139–205. Archives Royales de Mari, vol. 26. The latest evidence on the role played by Mashkan-shapir in the political infighting leading up to the conquest of Larsa by Hammurabi.

Leemans, W. F. *Foreign Trade in the Old Babylonian Period as Revealed by Texts from Southern Mesopotamia.* Studia et Documenta, vol. 6. Leiden, 1960. Standard work on trade relations in early second millennium BCE Mesopotamia. See pages 166–172 for a discussion of Mashkan-shapir.

Stone, Elizabeth C. "The Tell Abu Duwari Project, Iraq 1987." *Journal of Field Archaeology* 17 (1990): 141–162. Preliminary report of the first season of work.

Stone, Elizabeth C., and Paul E. Zimansky. "Mashkan-shapir and the Anatomy of an Old Babylonian City." *Biblical Archaeologist* 55.4 (1992): 212–218. Discussion of the organization of Mashkan-shapir for a popular audience.

Stone, Elizabeth C., and Paul E. Zimansky. "The Second and Third Seasons at Tell Abu Duwari, Iraq." *Journal of Field Archaeology* 21 (1994): 437–455. Preliminary report of the last two seasons of work at Mashkan-shapir.

ELIZABETH C. STONE

MASKHUTA, TELL EL-, town in the eastern Nile Delta (see figure 1), occupied in the late Middle Bronze II and from about 610 BCE into the Early Roman period, with gaps in the Late Persian period, and in about 100 BCE–100 CE (30°33′ N, 32°06′ E).

The name of the site in the Second Intermediate period is unknown. Inscriptional and literary evidence indicates that after 610 BCE it was known as Per-Atum Tukw (the "estate of Atum in *Tkw*"); as biblical Pitom or Pithom (*Ex.* 1:11), in the region of *Tkw;* or as biblical Succoth (*Ex.* 12:37, 13:20; *Nm.* 33:5–6). The biblical references are anachronistic, probably arising from the antiquarian interests of Jeremianic refugees resident in the eastern Delta. [*See* Delta.] Though the older name was preserved into the Hellenistic period, it was more commonly known by its Greek name, Heroon polis (Eroopolis, Heroon; the Greek translation of *Gn.* 46:28, "near Heroopolis in the land of Rameses"). The Romans shortened it to Ero (Hero).

The first to excavate the site was Édouard Naville for the Egypt Exploration Society. (1893). Jean Clédat excavated many objects on behalf of the Service des Antiquités (about 1900–1910), but contributed little else. The Egyptian Antiquities Organization excavated in the northern cemetery, along the Ismailia canal, a necropolis area of the Persian period south of the temple precinct, and near the present village (c. 1970–1985). A major series of excavations (1978–1985) was undertaken by the University of Toronto's Wadi Tumilat Project, directed by John S. Holladay, Jr., with funding from the Smithsonian Institution and the Social Science and Humanities Research Council of Canada.

Second Intermediate Period (Middle Bronze IIB). The earliest occupation at the site, about 1700/1650–1600 BCE, was a small, unfortified Asiatic ("Hyksos") village of possibly only 2 ha (5 acres). [*See* Hyksos.] It was of short duration, with a total depth of stratification of about 2 m divided into seven archaeological phases. In its architecture

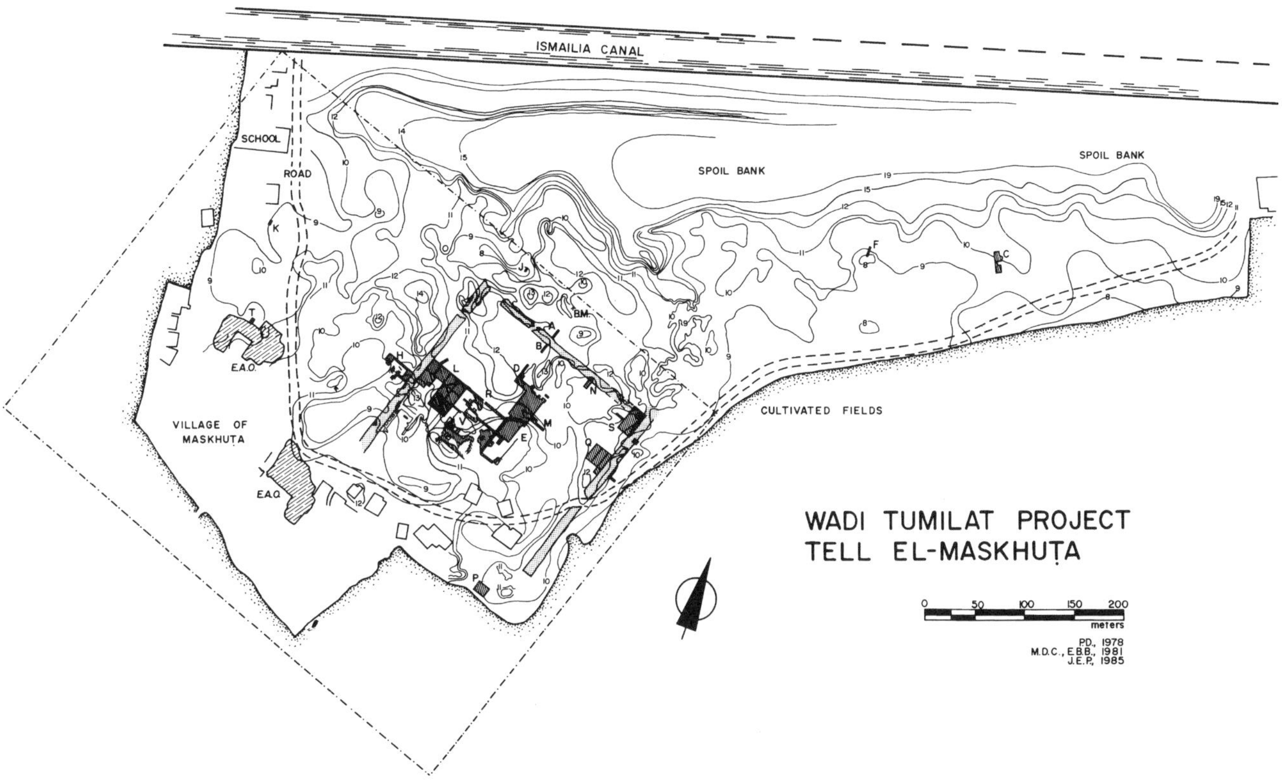

MASKHUTA, TELL EL-. Figure 1. *Plan of the site.* (Courtesy J. S. Holladay)

and burial practices, it resembled Tell ed-Dabʿa and presumably functioned as a Hyksos outpost (see figure 2). [*See* Dabʿa, Tell ed-.]

The pottery, some of it made on site, is a subset of that found at Tell ed-Dabʿa and is a mix of MB IIB and earlier Levantine forms together with local Egyptian forms. Significantly, the Asiatic aspects of the corpus do not resemble typical corpora from either Syria or Palestine. Despite the site's small size, the "urban" character of its architecture and layout is comparable to that at Tell ed-Dabʿa, in plot demarcation by sinuous boundary walls, house styles and construction, and a progression in area use from storage facilities (aboveground circular silos) and burials to an increasingly dense pattern of houses and associated features (relating to agricultural, animal husbandry, cooking, and industrial activities). Surprisingly, paleobotanical evidence shows that the site was seasonal, occupied only during the winter (through wheat harvest), with relocation elsewhere (to campsites?) during the summer. [*See* Paleobotany.] The economy was dominated by herding and plow-assisted dry farming (wheat, barley), apparently on more than a subsistence basis. Donkeys, sheep, goats, pigs, horses, hartebeest, and gazelle were present, and a wide variety of small game and birds were hunted. [*See* Hunting.] Crafts include pottery making; secondary bronze smelting and tool/weapon making; textile production using the warp-weighted loom; sickle production with preformed blades; and perhaps silversmithing. One enigmatic workshop housed high-temperature hearths and an industrial process for which multiple stakes had been driven into the floor, and in which red and yellow ocher, cobble-sized grinders, palettes, hammerstones, and reused chert slingstones played significant roles. Large quantities of water had repeatedly been sluiced over the floors. What was involved seems to have been the intensive manufacture of a composite product: possibly leather with metal fittings or ornaments, or elite products that involved precious metals.

Burials include "warrior's tombs," marked by burials of a single donkey and weapons, women's tombs, and small mud-brick tombs for infants and adolescents. [*See* Tombs; Burial Practices.] The tombs contained relatively rich offerings: gold and silver headbands, armbands, and earrings; scarabs; amulets; and food offerings. [*See* Grave Goods.] There were infant jar and cist burials and simple inhumations with few or no grave goods.

The evidence for seasonality, the site's short life-span, ending before the final phase of Hyksos domination, the high level of technological production, the great disparity between the agriculturalist-pastoralist orientation of the domestic economy, the rich burials of the town's residents, and the central-to-eastward trending of settlement in Wadi Tumilat all argue that the village was the primary reception, provisioning, and debarkation point for donkey caravans bearing products northwestward: presumably incense,

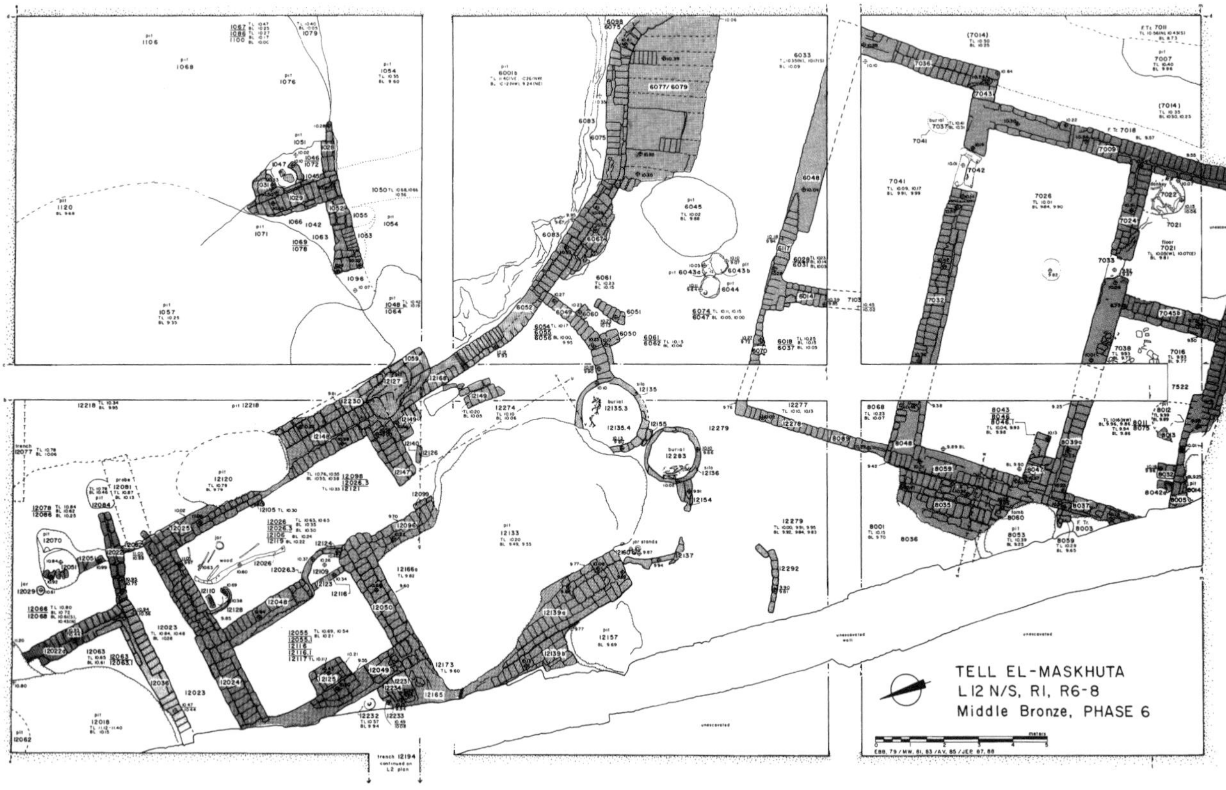

MASKHUTA, TELL EL-. Figure 2. *Plan of the final building phase of the MB IIB (Hyksos) occupation.* (Courtesy J. S. Holladay)

spices, ivory, gold, gemstones, precious woods, and animal pelts; commodities transported to the southeast were most likely copper, tin, silver, coniferous woods, linen, fine woolens, alabaster, medicinal drugs, weapons, and tools. The Hyksos settlement at Tell er-Retabah probably functioned as the region's principal military and administrative center and as a way station for caravans to the port city of Tell ed-Dabʿa. Such operations had military implications and relied on the cooperation of the indigenous pastoral people of the Sinai. Presumably, this extension of Hyksos settlement to the east occurred when the Nile River was closed to communications between Nubia and the Delta during the fifteenth dynasty. Or, given the hostility between Thebes and Karnak during the late fifteenth dynasty, it is possible that the overland traders operating between the Horn of Africa and its eastward-looking trade connections either were inadequately servicing the traffic into Nubia or began making exorbitant demands, causing Avaris to seek more direct connections with South Arabia. A third possibility is that the development, by the Late MB IIB or Early MB IIC, of overland trade connections between South Arabia and southern Palestine caused the merchant princes of Avaris to want some portion of that overland trade diverted to their own emporium.

Saite Period. With the advent of Necho II (610 BCE) and his sea-level canal connecting the Pelusiac branch of the Nile with the Red Sea via Wadi Tumilat, the site's exposed frontier position, unsettled since the Late MB II period, again became an asset. Following the use of the terrace as a work camp for canal-building and the sacrifice and burial of a large number of bulls (presumably as foundation sacrifices; see figure 3), houses and mid-sized aboveground granaries were built, accompanied by outdoor bread ovens, which also roasted fowl. [*See* Granaries and Silos.] Central planning is suggested by the shared design features in both the houses and silos. Following Necho's defeat and expulsion from Asia in 605 BCE, a 8–9-meter-wide defensive wall was erected. It cut through elements of the original town plan, including newly built houses enclosing an area of roughly 200 m per side. The adequacy of this 4-hectare (7-acre) space for the townsite is demonstrated by the lack of Saite occupational levels in all sectors of the enclosure. Two destruction phases followed, apparently in 601 BCE and in 568 BCE, both carried out by Nebuchadrezzer II. A minor presence of Judean pottery associated with a house destroyed in 568 BCE may attest to the settlement of some Jeremianic refugees from the 582 BCE dispersion. Another destruction marked the Persian conquest of Egypt in 525 BCE. A large Atum temple was founded at the beginning of this period, probably in association with bull sacrifices.

During the Saite period, expanded trade via the canal is evidenced by massive quantities of Phoenician "crisp ware" amphorae, Greek amphorae from Thassos and Chios, and imported mortaria, probably of Anatolian origin. A Phoenician terra-cotta statuette of a seated pregnant goddess (Asherah/Tannit?) found in a small limestone shrine is probably testimony to the presence of expatriate Phoenician traders. [*See* Phoenicians.] That Phoenician ships were the primary carriers seems evident, given the Egyptian reluctance to venture far from the mouth of the Nile, and given the quantity of Phoenician trade amphorae. The Greek and other amphorae, mortaria, and other heavy cargoes formed a substantial part of the ballast under which the keelless ships of the times sailed. [*See* Ships and Boats.] The ballast could then be sold at any port at which other heavy, large bulk products were to be on-loaded. Red Sea and Indian Ocean trade was not witnessed by material finds, but must be inferred from the wealth of evidence for widespread trade connections at what otherwise would be nothing but a small provincial town at the midpoint of a long canal terminating near Suez.

Persian Period. The site expanded to fill the entire enclosure area in the Persian period, with an elite necropolis to the southwest. The four great quadrilingual stelae near Tell el-Maskhuta and southward (the largest Persian monuments in Egypt), attest to Darius the Great's successful completion of the canal to the Red Sea. Outside the enclosure wall a stone-built well had been deliberately blocked and filled in the rebellion of 487 BCE. With evidence for a water sweep operating with a different well, and no evidence for any gateway in this area, these remains indicate well-supported horticultural and pastoral activities. [*See* Agriculture.] Belowground beehive granaries of no more than small-estate size point to some of the production being controlled by minor elites during this period. Given the massive numbers of Persian storage pits in southern Palestine, Persian agricultural intensification and bulking of agricultural surpluses for the eastern Nile Delta are likely.

Industrial and storehousing activities were concentrated near the enclosure wall on the eastern side of town, near the canal. What may have been priestly quarters are densely built near the temple. A bulla of Darius the Great mentioning the district of *Tkw* suggests that administrative quarters might have been located nearby. Fragmentary monuments from the thirtieth Nectanebid dynasty may be later imports to the site, or may indicate continued Nectanebid administration of the canal.

During the Persian period (c. 525–330), there was an increase in goods imported in Phoenician trade amphorae—probably mostly wine—and in Thassian and Chian amphorae. *Dipinta* (painted) inscriptions on jar fragments are mostly in Demotic, with a few in Phoenician script. Either Egyptian-based Phoenician traders labeled the storage jars in Demotic for local trade or Egyptians controlled most of the trade. Mortaria were imported in quantity, and small cubic limestone altars, ultimately of South Arabian inspira-

MASKHUTA, TELL EL-. Figure 3. *The third bull burial discovered at the site.* The burial pit was cut by the enclosure wall (top right) foundation trench, around 605 BCE. (Courtesy J. S. Holladay)

tion and probably not of local manufacture, suggests the spread of incense use to domestic cultic installations. [*See* Altars.] A cache of thousands of Athenian tetradrachmas points to trade gifts to the Atum temple, as do the "Tell el-Maskhuta bowls," inscribed "to the lady"—presumably Hathor—from Qainu the son of Gashmu, a princely Arabian name witnessed in the Bible (*Neh.* 2:19). Minute Ḥimyaritic silver coins bearing the archaic owl of Athena probably come from this period, further attesting trade relations with South Arabia.

Zoological and botanical analysis shows a great variety in the agricultural economy, reflecting a local intensification, the interests of the Persian rulers of Egypt, and greater availability of nonlocal species and varieties presumably because of traffic on the canal.

Ptolemaic Period. Following a diminished Late Persian and an Early Hellenistic occupation, the site's fortunes turned upward under Ptolemy II (282–246), who rebuilt the canal; he celebrated some of his imports (including elephants) in a stela found by Naville (1903). A new six-chambered granary with an attached bank of bread ovens was constructed and a Late Persian storehouse was restored. Nearby, work went on in support of the renewal of the Atum temple complex: sculptors' "trial pieces," scraps of quality limestone, and evidence of secondary bronze smelting were found in excavation.

It seems unlikely that the series of massive storehouses discovered by Naville (1903) began quite this early. Excavations demonstrated the successive building and wholesale replacement of three differently oriented large storehouses. This series dates from about the second half of the third century to about 150–125 BCE. Other, even more massive storehouses remain to be investigated. The material stored in these structures presumably were part of the trading activities between the Mediterranean basin and South Arabia and the Horn of Africa. During this period it is clear that Tell el-Maskhuta was either a major point of shipment for some heavy, high-volume capacity (e.g., wheat), or a turnaround spot for ships because only a few ships were needed for continuing on into the Red Sea (some choice Greek wines made the journey all the way to India). Alternatively, it is possible that cargoes were deliberately lightened for the southbound leg of the trip, with the transshipment of relatively low-bulk, high-value cargoes to fast triremes at the head of the Red Sea for better handling of the combined northern Red Sea problems of shallow water, adverse winds, and pirates. Transshipment to these Red Sea triremes could have taken place at Per Atum. The returning ocean-going ships could have taken on high-value, lightweight southeastern products (spices, incense, ivory, rare woods, etc.) for value and local products (grain, hides, dried meat) for partial ballast. They could then have gone tightly ballasted as far as Pelusium, where the ballast weight required for ocean travel could be made up of locally accumulated amphorae, metal and glass ingots, and choice building stone. During this period the site outgrew the enclosure area.

Roman Period. The Christian pilgrim Egira mentions a Roman military post at Hero in about 381 CE, but few remains of this period exist. By this time, the military garrison may have been located to the northeast. Following a break in occupation from the first century BCE to the first century CE, the site experienced its greatest period of expansion, probably associated with Trajan's reconstruction of the canal.

Only two small fields in the Roman cemetery were investigated. However, Roman materials overlaid much of the field E storehouse, and a number of Roman limekilns were sunk in pits penetrating MB and Saite levels. Limekilns had already been intensively used for the large and heavily plastered Hellenistic storehouses. The bricks for the latest field E storehouse contained lime flecks, which indicates that they were made of mud recycled from earlier buildings whose plaster had been stripped. Given the rarity of quality limestone in the Delta, it is notable that many large piles of limestone chips remained at the site. No traces of dressed or inscribed outer surfaces appeared, suggesting either that limestone chips were imported for lime making, or that new blocks for the Atum temple were made at locations well east of the temple.

A lack of typically Roman figured lamps and other late indicators suggests a relatively early date for the end of occupation in the late third–early fourth centuries CE. To the east, a Roman cemetery occupied the location of a former Hellenistic suburban village, filling it with squarish, largely subterranean, mud-brick tombs with vaulted roofs. The tombs were entered from a walled dromos centered on the eastern side, the arched tomb entrance being bricked in after each burial. The tomb burials were found stratified, owing to the constant exfoliation of mud-brick materials from the tomb vault. These tombs were looted during their active use-life, clearly by the attendants, and afterward. Traces remained of relatively rich burial goods (gold foil and a gold earring, glass vessels, carved bone hairpins). Simple inhumations lacking durable grave goods were cut into the open spaces between the tombs, and a children's cemetery of amphora burials, possibly slightly later, occupied the southeastern end of the excavation area. Among the latter was one Christian burial—oriented toward Jerusalem—marked by a Coptic epitaph and two chi-rho symbols on a Gaza amphora. A few other inhumations sharing this orientation may also be Christian; most other inhumations were oriented west. Indications of trauma and the mortality curve of adult males are consistent with a military population. [*See* Tombs; Burial Techniques; Grave Goods.]

In the Roman period, the defense and regulation of overland traffic seem to have heightened in importance because increasingly large Roman freighters were unable to operate safely in the northern Red Sea. [*See* Seafaring.] However, Trajan's reopening of the canal (see above) argues for its continued use as a viable military transit or commercial facility. For the latter activity, a more complicated system of assembling cargoes at Quṣeir or at points farther south in the Red Sea may be posited.

Islamic Period. In about 641 BCE the silted-up canal was reopened by Amr ibn al-ʿAṣ, the conqueror and first governor of Egypt. It was used until 767, when the second ʿAbbasid caliph, Abu Jafar al-Mansur, closed it, to keep supplies from reaching the rebellious cities of Mecca and Medina.

BIBLIOGRAPHY

Ball, John. *Egypt in the Classical Geographers.* Cairo, 1942.

Bennett, William J., Jr., and Jeffrey A. Blakely. *Tell el-Hesi: The Persian Period (Stratum V).* Winona Lake, Ind., 1989.

Bietak, Manfred. "Egypt and Canaan during the Middle Bronze Age." *Bulletin of the American Schools of Oriental Research,* no. 281 (1991): 27–72.

Clédat, Jean. "Deux monuments nouveaus de Tell El-Maskhoutah." *Recueil de Travaux Relatifs à la Philologie et à l'Archéologie Égyptiennes et Assyriennes* 32 (1910): 40–42.

Clédat, Jean. "Notes sur l'Isthme de Suez (monuments divers)." *Recueil de Travaux Relatifs à la Philologie et à l'Archéologie Égyptiennes et Assyriennes* 36 (1914): 103–112.

Holladay, John S. *Tell el-Maskhuta.* Cities of the Delta, part 3. Reports of the American Research Center in Egypt, vol. 6. Malibu, 1982.

Holladay, John S. "The Wadi Tumilat Project: Tell el-Maskhuta." *Bulletin of the Canadian Mediterranean Institute* 7.2 (1987): 1–7.

Holladay, John S. "A Biblical/Archaeological Whodunit." *Bulletin of the Canadian Mediterranean Institute* 8.2 (1988): 6–8.

Holladay, John S. "The Eastern Nile Delta during the Hyksos and Pre-Hyksos Periods: Towards a Systemic/Socio-Economic Understanding." In *Proceedings of the University of Pennsylvania Hyksos Seminar, Spring 1992,* edited by Eliezer D. Oren. Philadelphia, forthcoming.

Holladay, John S., and Carol Ann Redmount. *The Wadi Tumilat Project I: Surveys in the Wadi Tumilat, 1977 and 1983, Results and Archaeological Interpretation.* Forthcoming.

Naville, Édouard. *The Store-City of Pithom and the Route of the Exodus.* 4th ed. London, 1903.

Oren, Eliezer D. "Migdol: A New Fortress on the Edge of the Eastern Nile Delta." *Bulletin of the American Schools of Oriental Research,* no. 256 (1984): 7–44.

Paice, Patricia. "A Preliminary Analysis of Some Elements of the Saite and Persian Period Pottery at Tell el-Maskhuta." *Bulletin of the Egyptological Seminar* 8 (1987): 95–107.

Pritchard, James B., ed. *Ancient Near Eastern Texts Relating to the Old Testament.* 3d ed. Princeton, 1969.

Redford, Donald B. "Exodus I 11." *Vetus Testamentum* 13 (1963): 401–418.

Redford, Donald B. "Pithom." In *Lexikon der Ägyptologie,* vol. 4, cols. 1054–1058. Wiesbaden, 1983.

Redmount, Carol Ann. "On the Egyptian/Asiatic Frontier: An Archaeological History of the Wadi Tumilat." Ph.D. diss., Oriental Institute, University of Chicago, 1989.

Stern, Ephraim. "Limestone Incense Altars." In *Beer-Sheba I: Excavations at Tel Beer-Sheba, 1969–1971 Seasons,* edited by Yohanan Aharoni, pp. 52–53. Tel Aviv, 1973.

Veenhof, Klaas R. *Aspects of Old Assyrian Trade and Its Terminology.* Leiden, 1972.

JOHN S. HOLLADAY, JR.

MASOS, TEL

MASOS, TEL (Khirbet el-Meshash), site situated about 12 km (7 mi.) east of Beersheba in Israel's Negev desert (map reference 147 × 069). The name still indicates the areas rich water sources, in which groundwater is easily accessible by means of wells. The site consists of three different components, located on both sides of the wadi: a small tell; and remains of a large village to the northeast; as well as the artificial hills of an enclosure on the southern bank. The tell's existence has been known since the nineteenth century, when it was mapped by Claude R. Conder and H. H. Kitchener in the Survey of Eastern Palestine (1874). The other two sites were discovered during intensive surveys by Yohanan Aharoni (1964, 1967).

In spite of the existence of both the long lists of cities in the Negev in *Joshua* 15:21–32 and Shishak's list, the ancient name of Khirbet el-Meshash has not yet been ascertained. Its identification with Ḥormah by Aharoni (Aharoni et al., 1975, pp. 123–125 in particular) is unlikely because it seems that Ḥormah was a rather important city in the time of the Israelite Monarchy. During that period, except for a few decades at the end of the seventh century BCE, the archaeological record shows that Khirbet el-Meshash was deserted. The same applies to the suggested location of Ziklag by Frank Crüsemann (1973, especially pp. 222–224). The identification by Nadav Na'aman with Baʿalat Be'er, as in *Joshua* 19:8, is entirely arbitrary (Na'aman, 1980, p. 146). Taking into account that the name may have been mentioned in the list in 1 *Samuel* 30:27–31a, dated to the end of the eleventh century BCE, Sifmot and Rachal should be considered possible candidates for the ancient name.

The history of the site was revealed in 1972–1975, during the course of extensive excavations by a joint German-Israeli expedition led by Volkmar Fritz and Aharon Kempinski on behalf of the University of Mainz and Tel Aviv University. Tel Masos was settled only for short periods of time during different periods, with large gaps in occupation, which explains why the several settlements were spread out at a distance from one another.

The tell owes its formation to a settlement dated to the end of Iron II (seventh century BCE); resettlement took place, however, at the end of the Byzantine period. There is a former Iron I village (1200–1000 BCE) situated northeast of the tell, with some remains dating to the Chalcolithic period. The fortified enclosure on the southern bank of the wadi was constructed during the Middle Bronze Age II–III and was abandoned during the same period. Altogether, five periods of occupation can be distinguished: Chalcolithic earth dwellings; a fortified MB II–III enclosure; an Early Iron Age village; a settlement from the seventh century BCE; and a monastery dating from the seventh–eighth centuries CE.

The Chalcolithic material is meager and neither the pottery nor the implements exhibit any peculiarities. The funds come mainly from one subterranean dwelling dug into the

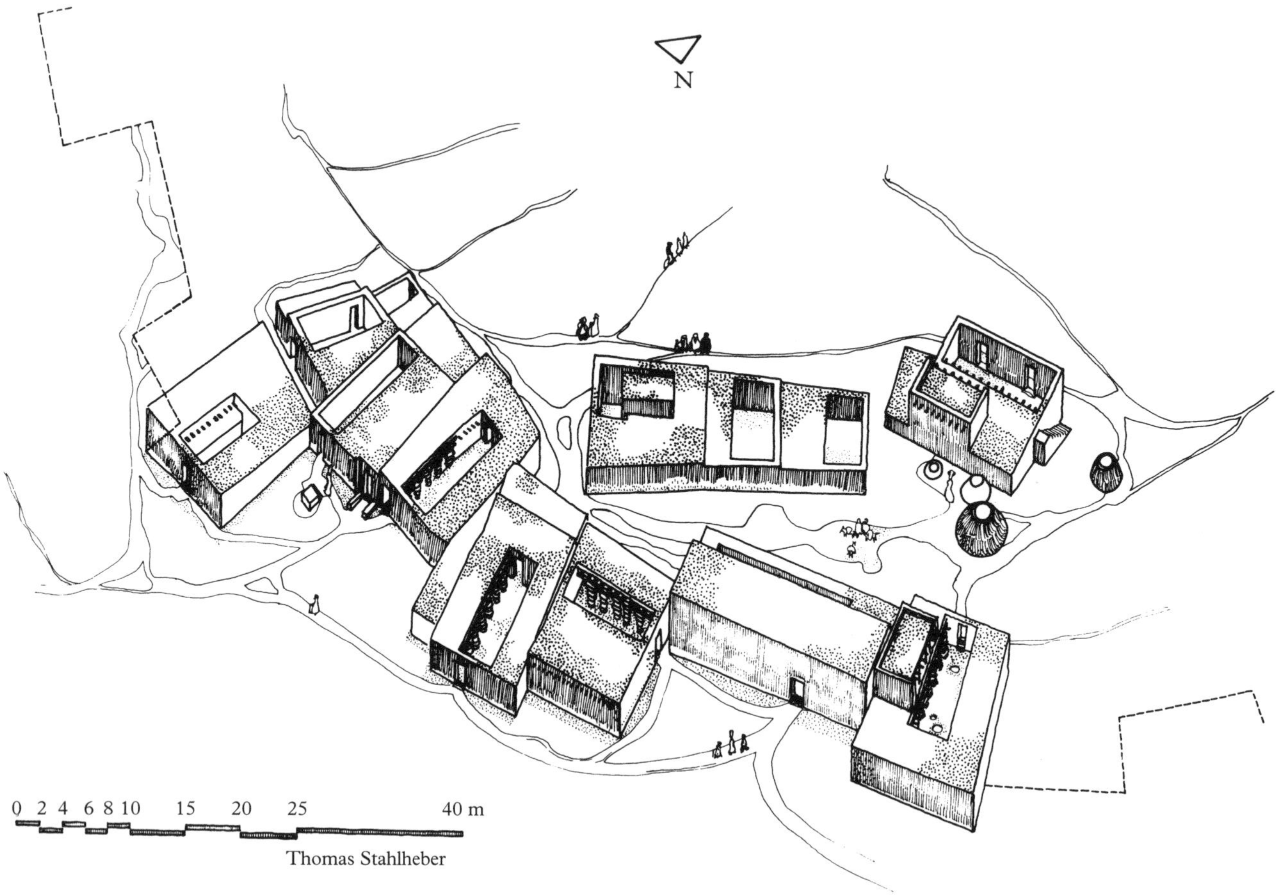

MASOS, TEL. *Reconstructed plan of the village.* (Courtesy V. Fritz)

loess; later, in the Iron I, a house was built on top of it. No exact date within the range of the period from 3600–3200 BCE can be given. The site belongs to the so-called Beersheba culture, known throughout the Negev.

Within the MB enclosure, two fortified settlements can be distinguished, the older of which was demolished when the subsequent one was built. The embankment enclosed a square with sides approximately 100 m in length, but a large part of the site had been washed away by the wadi that runs next to it. These settlements probably represent an attempt on the part of the coastal cities to control the route leading to the east; they yielded homogeneous ceramics that date to the seventeenth century BCE.

The Early Iron Age village covers an area of approximately 200 × 150 m and is the largest known site of this period in the country. Altogether, three strata with a total of five phases can be distinguished; they indicate continuous habitation from about 1200 until the beginning of the tenth century BCE. In the earliest phase, stratum IIIB shows some signs of nomadic occupation; there are floors, pits, and hearths, but no architecture. The building of actual houses begins in stratum IIIA, in about the middle of the twelfth century BCE. During the two phases of stratum II, the site was more densely built up, with a large variety of building types. Besides the dominant four-room house, there are three-room houses, broadroom houses, a courtyard house, and the so-called Amarna house, an Egyptian type of dwelling (cf. Fritz, 1988). Various other buildings had some sort of public function. The large variety of structures indicates that the population was by no means homogeneous. Stratum I is badly eroded but seems to mark a certain decline. The site was entirely abandoned at the beginning of the tenth century BCE.

The finds from Tel Masos include both local and imported ceramic wares; an example of early Phoenician ivory art; and a remarkably large number of copper and bronze objects. The imported ware include bichrome-style vessels from the Phoenician coast; sherds of Philistine pottery from the coastal plain; so-called Midianite ware originating in northwest Arabia; and fragments of Egyptian "flowerpots." The diverse nature of this assemblage shows that the village had wide-ranging connections in every direction. The large quantity of copper and bronze implements indicates that copperworking played an important role. A scarab made of steatite bears the motif of a pharaoh defeating his foes and can be assigned to the reign of Seti II (1204–1194 BCE).

During the second half of the seventh century BCE, a small settlement was constructed southwest of the former village, which had already been deserted for more than three hundred years. At its center stood a large building, whose size and arrangement of rooms suggest that it served as a caravanserai—a station along the trade routes passing through the area. The settlement was probably fortified and existed only for a short period of time. It was destroyed during the Edomite conquest at the beginning of the sixth century BCE.

The last occupation on the mound took place at the end of the period of Byzantine rule in Palestine, when Nestorian monks selected the top of the tell to build a small monastery. The monastery itself was built on the north, while the plateau to the south of it was used as a large courtyard with a surrounding wall. The entrance into the building led from this courtyard into a small hall, from which the central courtyard, around which the various rooms were grouped, was accessible. A chapel was incorporated into the building and could be reached from the entrance hall by a stairway with five steps. The apse was rectangular, a unique occurrence among Nestorian churches that is characteristic of Syrian churches. The altar was discovered in a room next to the chapel, not in situ. East of the chapel a crypt with a separate entrance contained seven graves. Each grave contained either two or three skeletons, all interred facing east. No artifacts of any kind were found, but the rubble inside the graves included pieces of plaster with fragments of inscriptions in Syriac script, which was written by the Nestorians in the eighth century CE. Other inscriptions incised in Syriac on stone were found throughout the building. The monastery was founded in the seventh century CE, but it did not last long. It suffered a sudden and violent destruction during the first half of the eighth century CE.

BIBLIOGRAPHY

Aharoni, Yohanan, et al. "Vorbericht über die Ausgrabungen auf der Ḫirbet el-Mšāš (Tel Māśôś), 2. Kampagne 1974." *Zeitschrift des Deutschen Palästina-Vereins* 91 (1975): 109–130.

Ahlström, Gösta W. "The Early Iron Age Settlers at Ḫirbet el-Mšāš (Tēl Māśōś)." *Zeitschrift des Deutschen Palästina-Vereins* 100 (1984): 35–52.

Crüsemann, Frank. "Überlegungen zur Identifikation der Ḫirbet el-Mšāš (Tēl Māśôś)." *Zeitschrift des Deutschen Palästina-Vereins* 89 (1973): 211–224.

Fritz, Volkmar. "The Israelite 'Conquest' in the Light of Recent Excavations at Khirbet el-Meshăsh." *Bulletin of the American Schools of Oriental Research,* no. 241 (1981): 61–73.

Fritz, Volkmar, and Aharon Kempinski. *Ergebnisse der Ausgrabungen auf der Hirbet el-Msas (Tel Masos), 1972–75.* 3 vols. Wiesbaden, 1983.

Fritz, Volkmar. "Tel Masos: A Biblical Site in the Negev." *Archaeology* 36.5 (1983): 30–37.

Fritz, Volkmar. "Die Verbreitung des sog. Amarna-Wohnhauses in Kanaan." *Damaszener Mitteilungen* 3 (1988): 27–34.

Kempinski, Aharon. "Tel Masos: Its Importance in Relation to the Settlement of the Tribes of Israel in the Northern Negev." *Expedition* 20.4 (1978): 29–37.

Na'aman, Nadav. "The Inheritance of the Sons of Simeon." *Zeitschrift des Deutschen Palästina-Vereins* 96 (1980): 136–152.

VOLKMAR FRITZ

MASPERO, GASTON (1846–1916), great French Egyptologist and most prolific author in the history of Egyptology. Maspero studied hieroglyphs on his own as a youth and then under Professor Emmanuel de Rougé, whose successor he became at the Collège de France in 1874 at the age of twenty-eight. In 1881 he succeeded Auguste Mariette as director of both Egypt's Bulaq Museum and the antiquities service. At this time he copied newly discovered religious texts inscribed inside late Old Kingdom pyramids for subsequent translation and publication.

Circumstances forced Maspero to raise funds in Europe in order to undertake such work as the excavation of the Great Sphinx and the temple of Luxor. He resigned and returned to France in 1886 to produce a number of books including one on Egyptian archaeology and another on Egyptian literature. Maspero's three-volume *Histoire ancienne des peuples de l'orient classique* (Paris, 1895–1899), which appeared in English as *The Dawn of Civilization: Egypt and Chaldaea* (London, 1894), exhibits his masterful broad command of history.

Maspero returned to Egypt in 1899 to become the director of the newly established Egyptian Museum in Cairo and remained in this position until 1915. There he organized its already vast holdings and produced the first guide for visitors. He supervised the conservation of such temples as Karnak, Edfu, Dendera, and Kom Ombo and the archaeological survey of Nubia to the south, threatened by the building of the first Aswan dam. Maspero's most useful archaeological project was undoubtedly his editorial direction of the catalog of the Egyptian Museum in Cairo, fifty volumes of which appeared during his tenure as director.

Maspero expanded and reorganized the Egyptian antiquities service into five inspectorates. His appointments and honors from the scientific and scholarly worlds were numerous. His English knighthood was a response to his unqualified support for the fledgling Egypt Exploration Fund in London, which went on to do so much important excavation in Egypt under Flinders Petrie, Édouard Naville, and others.

BIBLIOGRAPHY

Dawson, Warren R., and Eric P. Uphill. *Who Was Who in Egyptology.* 2d rev. ed. London, 1972.

Maspero, Gaston. *Histoire ancienne des peuples de l'Orient classique.* 3 vols Paris, 1895–1899. Translated as *History of Egypt, Chaldea, Syria, Babylonia, and Assyria.* 9 vols. Edited by A. H. Sayce. Translated by M. L. McClure. London, 1906.

Maspero, Gaston. *Egyptian Archaeology.* Translated by Amelia B. Edwards. New York, 1887.

Maspero, Gaston. *Le Musée égyptien: Recueil de monuments et de notices sur les fouilles d'Égypte.* Cairo, 1904–1924.
Maspero, Gaston. *Art in Egypt.* New York, 1912.
Maspero, Gaston. *Guide du visiteur au Musée du Caire.* 4th ed. Cairo, 1915.
Maspero, Gaston. *Manual of Egyptian Archaeology and Guide to the Study of Antiquities in Egypt.* New York, 1914.
Naville, Édouard. "Sir Gaston Maspero." *Journal of Egyptian Archaeology* 3 (1916): 227–234.

BARBARA SWITALSKI LESKO

MAṬARA, site of an Axumite urban center, located at the eastern edge of the northern Ethiopian escarpment about 3 km south of the modern town of Senafe, Eritrea (14°43′ N, 39°26′ E). It sat beside the route that once led from Adulis, a port on the Red Sea, to Axum on the western side of the Ethiopian plateau. This unwalled provincial center was abandoned sometime after the early seventh century CE, although there is no evidence of fire or massive destruction to suggest a violent end to inhabitation.

Excavations conducted by the Ethiopian Institute of Archaeology uncovered several typical Axumite mansions (similar to the great structure of Dungur at Axum) and a section of densely built popular housing, the latter datable to the sixth century CE.

The site has only one dressed (finished) monolithic stela (about 5 m or 16.4 ft. high), the original position of which is uncertain. Its rounded top is decorated with the disk and crescent, the religious symbol of pre-Christian Axumite coins. (Axum's King Ezana converted to Christianity about 333 CE.) Its brief inscription in unvocalized Geʿez script may date to the end of the third century. Although its sense is not clear, it refers to a military victory. Stelae at Axum are uninscribed.

The mansion of Francis Anfray's complex A is datable to the third century. Its remains exemplify the Axumite building style. The square central pavilion, which is 12.6 × 11.2 m (41.4 × 36.7 ft.) sits upon a stepped podium (platform) of stone-faced, mud-mortared rubble. Walls and podium have projecting and re-entrant sections, and corners are reinforced with dressed-stone blocks. The pavilion, reached by a flight of stone stairs at the center of the west facade, sits within a courtyard. It may be compared with the contemporary complex C and the somewhat later complex B of Maṭara. Additions to complex A are post-Ezana in date, as indicated by the associated cross-marked pottery.

The mansion complexes at Maṭara are aligned along the cardinal compass points. Complex C, a central pavilion raised on a stepped platform and with surrounding annex rooms, is partially overlaid by complex D. The central pavilion is subdivided into nine square sections, creating eight rooms and a staircase that led to upper story.

Complex B, which is larger in size (59.5 × 49 m or 195 × 161 ft.) and later in date, is more regular in plan. The rubble-stone and mud-mortared fabric of the central pavilion's podium includes reused stone fragments from the Ethio-South Arabian period. The central pavilion with monumental stairs on its north, east, and west sides is divided into nine "rooms"; stairs at two corners indicate an upper story. The surrounding rectangular courtyard is shaped by an exterior wall to which is attached a string of rooms opening off the courtyard. Associated finds included red pottery marked with a cross and Axumite coins of silver and bronze ranging in date from the reigns of Ezana to Gersem (seventh century).

Architectural complex D presents a new scheme. Although its general plan—central pavilion within a courtyard shaped by an enclosure wall lined with annex rooms—resembles the typical Axumite mansion, the central pavilion with grand western staircase has a crypt built of large, dressed-stone blocks. Above the lintel stone is a stone block carved with a cross. This chapel with subterranean tomb chamber is similar to the two subterranean tombs with superstructure at Axum, the so-called tombs of Kaleb and Gabra Masqal, which appear to date to the mid-sixth century CE.

Maṭara's complex F includes a typical, probably galleried Christian basilica, which was built in Axumite style. Immediately to the east of the church is a characteristic "keyhole"-shaped baptistery basin.

Axumite structures of Maṭara were built upon earlier constructions. Anfray found evidence of four levels. The lowest of them, which was associated with objects of a marked South Arabian character and pottery, belongs to the Ethio-South Arabian period (fifth–fourth century BCE). The next, his period II, belongs to the intermediate period and is characterized by schist walls and pottery similar to that found at Yeha, a major Ethiopian pre-Axumite site located east of Axum. It is unclear whether Maṭara was totally abandoned at the end of this intermediate period. Monuments of complexes A and C belong to Anfray's period III, the pre-Christian Axumite period with which is associated red and black Axumite pottery with no Christian symbols. Monuments of complexes B and D belong to his period IV (fifth–seventh century CE).

[*See also* Axum.]

BIBLIOGRAPHY

Anfray, Francis. "Première campagne de fouilles à Maṭarā (Nov. 1959–Jan. 1960)." *Annales d'Éthiopie* 5 (1963): 87–166.
Anfray, Francis, and G. Annequin. "Maṭarā: Deuxième, troisième et quatrième campagnes de fouilles." *Annales d'Éthiopie* 6 (1965): 49–142.
Anfray, Francis. "Maṭarā." *Annales d'Éthiopie* 7 (1967): 33–88.
Anfray, Francis. "Deux villes axoumites: Adoulis et Matara." In *IV Congresso Internazionale di Studi Etiopici—Roma 1972,* pp. 745–766, pls. 1–6. Accademia Nazionale dei Lincei, Quaderno no. 191. Rome, 1974.

MARILYN E. HELDMAN

MATARIA BOAT. In 1987 excavations for utility construction in Mataria (ancient Heliopolis or On), a suburb of Cairo, Egypt, exposed the remains of a boat, which dates to the fifth century BCE about 10 m (39 ft.) below ground level. Archaeologists recorded the existing 8 × 4 × 1.2 m (26 × 13 × 4 ft.) after about one-third of the hull was destroyed by heavy machinery. In addition, despite the efforts of the Conservation Department of the Egyptian Museum, Cairo, to record and preserve the fragments of the shallow, broad rivercraft, many of the planks of the surviving hull section broke apart. Most of the extant fragments today are 35–50 cm long. Barren sand immediately beneath the hull suggests that the craft was beached near an old river channel. Roman artifacts were found in the layers above the boat, but archaeologists discovered nothing directly related to the boat. Wood samples from the hull components include sycamore fig, sidder, acacia, and tamarisk, all local Egyptian woods.

The boat from Mataria is the latest-known Egyptian hull. Its builders lived in a prosperous, yet unstable time when Egypt was ruled by the Persians (twenty-seventh dynasty, c. 525–404 BCE). A Greek colony at Naukratis in the Nile Delta dates to the sixth century, and increasing numbers of foreigners came to Egypt thereafter, providing the opportunity for Egyptians to observe different technologies. The Mataria hull reflects Egyptian nautical traditions that incorporated a feature of Mediterranean shipbuilding found in boats dating from the Late Bronze Age to the Byzantine period but never seen in the older Egyptian hulls: the occasional use of pegs driven perpendicularly through tenons to lock mortise-and-tenon joints. Although this type of fastening is known as early as the Egyptian first dynasty (c. 2920–2770) in the manufacture of furniture, coffins, and statues, the Mataria boat marks the first recorded use of pegged mortise-and-tenon joints in Egyptian shipbuilding.

The mortises were up to 3 cm thick and 14 cm deep, larger than those of the seven known earlier Egyptian hulls. The use of treenails or pegs may reflect shipbuilding techniques adopted by the Egyptians about 1250 BCE. As the Mataria boat indicates, however, Egyptian shipbuilders did not imitate the practice followed elsewhere in the Mediterranean of locking every joint in place with pegs on either side of a plank seam. Not all mortise-and-tenon joints were pegged, and the current condition of the planking fragments prevents an analysis of the relation of the pegs to the construction. Because the peg length was greater than plank thickness, however, we must consider the possibility that the pegs functioned as treenails for fastening now-lost frames to the hull.

As for other important technological features, the planking of the Mataria boat continues the Old Kingdom and Middle Kingdom traditions of hull construction. In the Mataria boat planks of .8–6.0 × .2 × .08 m (2.5–19.5 × .65 × .25 ft.) were edge-joined to create a shell. Plank ends appear to have been butted against each other to form lines of planking called *strakes,* each side having about fifteen of them. Although the Mataria vessel traveled on the Nile about the time that the fifth-century Greek historian Herodotus described Egyptian boat construction (Haldane and Shelmerdine, 1990), the Mataria planks are much longer than those of his account. The basic method of construction, however, was the same. Interestingly enough, planks of the same dimensions as those of the Mataria boat were recorded for Upper Egyptian watercraft of the 1950s.

BIBLIOGRAPHY

Casson, Lionel. *Ships and Seamanship in the Ancient World.* Princeton, 1986.

Haldane, Cheryl, and Cynthia W. Shelmerdine. "Herodotus 2.96.1–2 Again." *Classical Quarterly* 40 (1990): 535–539.

Haldane, Cheryl. "The Lisht Timbers: A Report on Their Significance." In *The Pyramid Complex of Senwosret I,* by Dieter Arnold et al., pp. 102–112. Metropolitan Museum of Art, Egyptian Expedition, South Cemeteries of Lisht, vol. 3. New York, 1992.

Patch, Diana C., and Cheryl Haldane. *The Pharaoh's Boat at the Carnegie.* Pittsburgh, 1990.

CHERYL W. HALDANE

MAURITANIA. *See* North Africa.

MAUSOLEUM. The term *mausoleum* refers to a type of sepulchral monument that takes its name from the tomb of Mausolus of Halikarnassos, a Carian king who died in 353 BCE. The exact reconstruction of the mausoleum at Halikarnassos (modern Bodrum in Turkey) is disputed because of its poor state of preservation and the different descriptions given by ancient sources. However, all the evidence indicates that it consisted of a rectangular building surrounded by an Ionic colonnade on a base that may or may not have been a stepped pyramid. The building was capped by a stepped pyramid bearing a sculpted quadriga group. Mausolus commissioned some of the most famous artists of the fourth century BCE, including Scopas, Leochares, Bryaxis, and Timotheus, to sculpt the frieze that decorated the monument.

The Mausoleum at Halikarnassos was ranked among the seven wonders of the ancient world. It provided the inspiration and model for other highly decorated monumental tombs, especially in Asia Minor. One characteristic of these structures is the arrangement of a square base (or podium) that supports a building (or cella) that is surrounded by a colonnade and surmounted by a pyramidal roof. One such tomb was erected at Belevi near Smyrna, perhaps for Antiochus II of Syria, who died there in 246 BCE. The marble monument has a square podium with a Doric entablature containing the tomb chamber. The building on the podium was surrounded by Corinthian columns, between which stood larger-than-life-sized statues. The roof was probably pyramidal. Another tomb of this type, though smaller in size, is preserved at Mylasa in southwestern Turkey.

Mausolea are also found in the Syro-Phoenician realm. The tomb of Hamrath, at Suweida in Syria's Hauran, erected in about 75 BCE, has a square base with engaged Doric columns capped by a stepped pyramidal roof and is constructed of stone. The sepulchral monuments at Hermel and Kalat Fakra in Lebanon are two-storied structures with smooth-sided, pyramidal roofs, also constructed of stone.

Flavius Josephus (*Antiquities* 13.6.6) describes a mausoleum made of "polished white marble" erected in the second century BCE by Simon the Hasmonean at Modiʿin (near modern Lod in Israel) for his father and brothers. Although this monument no longer exists, two Jewish mausolea of the first century BCE and first century CE still stand in Jerusalem's Kidron Valley. The so-called Tomb of Zechariah and the Tomb of Absalom are monoliths cut out of the limestone of the rocky hillside. Each has a cubic central portion encircled by engaged columns. The Tomb of Zechariah has a smooth pyramidal roof, while the Tomb of Absalom is capped by a cylindrical "tholos." A Roman mausoleum built of rough stone dressed only on its outer face of the third or fourth century is located at the site of Mazor, also near Lod. Its lower part, which still stands virtually intact, has two burial chambers and a front porch with Corinthian columns. A mausoleum of the same date was found next to catacomb 11 in the Jewish necropolis at Beth-Sheʿarim. It was constructed of ashlar masonry and decorated with a carved animal frieze.

[*See also* Burial Techniques; *and* Tombs.]

BIBLIOGRAPHY

Avigad, Nahman, and Benjamin Mazar. "Beth Sheʿarim." In *The New Encyclopedia of Archaeological Excavations in the Holy Land,* vol. 1, pp. 236–248. Jerusalem and New York, 1993.

Dinsmoor, William Bell. *The Architecture of Ancient Greece.* 3d ed. New York, 1950. Contains a brief discussion of the development of the mausoleum in the classical and Hellenistic worlds.

Fedak, Janos. *Monumental Tombs of the Hellenistic Age: A Study of Selected Tombs from the Pre-Classical to the Early Imperial Era.* Toronto, 1990. Excellent, up-to-date survey of monumental tombs throughout the Hellenistic world.

Kaplan, Jacob. "Mazor." In *The New Encyclopedia of Archaeological Excavations in the Holy Land,* vol. 3, pp. 991–992. Jerusalem and New York, 1993.

Jodi Magness

MAZAR, BENJAMIN (1905–1995), Israeli historian and archaeologist. Born in Cechanovitz, Poland, Mazar (originally Maisler) studied Assyriology at the University of Giessen, Germany, and received his Ph.D. in 1927. In 1928 he moved to Jerusalem. His research interests covered wide-ranging aspects of the history, archaeology, and historical geography of the land of Israel and of the ancient Near East. In the years before World War II he was inspired by William Foxwell Albright, with whom he worked at Tell Beit Mirsim. From 1936 to 1939 he undertook excavations for the Israel Exploration Society at Beth-Sheʿarim, where he uncovered a Jewish necropolis of the second–fourth centuries CE. In 1943 he became a member of the academic staff of the Hebrew University of Jerusalem, where he established a department for the Historical Geography of the Land of Israel. He excavated at Beth-Yeraḥ (1945), Tell Qasile (1949–1951, 1956), and ʿEin-Gedi (1961–1964). His largest and most important enterprise was the excavations south and west of the Temple Mount in Jerusalem (1968–1978), where he uncovered public architecture from the Iron Age, Second Temple Period, and the Early Islamic period. His publications, teaching, and work over many years as editor in chief of the Hebrew *Encyclopedia Biblica* combined his broad knowledge and ability to synthesize data from the various fields of ancient Near Eastern studies, biblical studies, and archaeological research. This synthesis of disciplines was his main legacy to three generations of scholars in Israel, and many of his students became scholars in his numerous fields of interest.

From 1952 to 1961, Mazar was rector and president of the Hebrew University. Under his leadership the university overcame the crisis of the 1948 War of Independence, when the campus on Mt. Scopus was detached from the western part of Jerusalem, and entered a period of rapid academic development. He was also involved for many years in determining the general direction and quality of academic life in the State of Israel. Mazar earned many prizes and honorary degrees, among them the Israel Prize.

[*See also* Beit Mirsim, Tell; Beth-Sheʿarim; Beth-Yeraḥ; ʿEin-Gedi; Israel Exploration Society; Jerusalem; Qasile, Tell; *and the biography of Albright.*]

BIBLIOGRAPHY

A survey of Mazar's most important works is provided below, along with several collections of major and minor essays.

Untersuchungen zur Alten Geschichte und Ethnographie Syriens und Palästinas. Geissen, 1930.

History of the Archaeological Research in Palestine (in Hebrew). Jerusalem, 1936. Covers the history to 1925.

History of the Land of Israel (in Hebrew). Part 1. Tel Aviv, 1938.

En-Gedi: The First and Second Seasons of Excavations. ʿAtiqot, 5. Jerusalem, 1966. Co-authored with Trude Dothan and Immanuel Dunayevsky.

The Excavations at Beth Sheʿarim (1945). 3 vols. New Brunswick, N.J., 1973–1976.

Cities and Districts in Eretz-Israel (in Hebrew). Jerusalem, 1975. Collected essays.

The Mountain of the Lord. Garden City, N.Y., 1975.

Canaan and Israel: Historical Essays (in Hebrew). Jerusalem, 1980.

Excavations and Discoveries (in Hebrew). Jerusalem, 1986. Collected essays.

The Early Biblical Period: Historical Studies. Edited by Shmuel Ahituv and Baruch Levine. Jerusalem, 1986.

Biblical Israel: State and People. Edited by Shmuel Ahituv. Jerusalem, 1992. Collected essays.

AMIHAI MAZAR

MAZAR, TELL EL-, site located in modern Jordan in the middle of the Jordan Valley, approximately 3 km (2 mi.) north of Tell Deir ʿAlla and 6.5 km (4 mi.) south of Tell es-Saʿidiyeh (32°13′20″ N, 35°36′22″ E; map reference 1812 × 2074). The mound is relatively small (.75 acres) but rises an impressive 24 m above the surrounding plain (the elevation of the summit is 228.67 m below sea level). The site does not appear to have been founded on a natural hill but is comprised strictly of accumulated occupational debris. The absence of major fortifications strongly suggests that throughout its history, Tell el-Mazar was dependent on the larger villages in the region for both its security and economic prosperity.

Associated with Tell el-Mazar is a small mound—referred to as mound A in the excavation reports—located 220 m northwest of the main tell (map reference 1813 × 2073). Mound A rises only 1.8 m above the plain, has a maximum elevation of 249.10 m below sea level, and covers an area of just over an acre. The name *Mazar* (Ar., "place of visitation or pilgrimage") may be derived from the nearby mosque and grave of Abu Obeidah, an early Islamic general. Tell el-Mazar is not attested in ancient sources, including the Hebrew Bible.

Tell el-Mazar was noted and briefly examined by Nelson Glueck (1951) in 1942 and by Moawiyah Ibrahim, James Sauer, and Khair Yassine (1976) in 1975. These surface surveys collected pottery from the tell proper dating to the Middle and Late Bronze Ages and Iron I–II, Persian, Early Roman, Byzantine, and ʿAbbasid periods. Glueck (1951) refers to mound A as Tell el-Ghazala (his site no. 177) and collected LB, Iron II, Roman, and Byzantine pottery from the surface.

The first excavations at the tell and on mound A were initiated by Yassine for the University of Jordan in 1977. A total of four, two-month seasons were conducted on the tell (1977–1979, 1981). Mound A was also investigated during the 1977–1979 campaigns.

Stratigraphy. Although both surface surveys found MB and LB pottery, the earliest stratified material discovered thus far dates to Iron I. Five distinct strata have been identified on the summit of the main tell, covering an occupational sequence from the eighth through the late fourth centuries BCE, as follows:

Stratum I: fourth century BCE (Late Persian/Early Hellenistic)
Stratum II: fifth century BCE (Persian)
Stratum III: sixth–seventh centuries BCE (Late Iron II)
Stratum IV: seventh century BCE (Iron II)
Stratum V: eighth century BCE (Early Iron II)

Because of successive episodes of destruction, rebuilding, and pitting, architectural plans for the five strata at Tell el-Mazar are incomplete. Nevertheless, the overall occupational sequence is relatively clear. Mound A yielded evidence of an eleventh–tenth-century BCE occupation followed by a four hundred-year hiatus and then a reuse in the fifth century BCE as a cemetery.

Major Finds. The earliest occupational layer uncovered thus far (stratum V) consists of a large, flagstone-paved courtyard surrounded by rooms that contained loom weights, storage jars filled with grain, a beer mug, and a variety of animal bones. The excavator suggests that the fiery destruction at the end of the eighth century BCE may be attributed to Sennacherib's invasion of the region in 701 (Yassine, 1983, pp. 510–512).

In the early seventh century BCE a series of domestic structures (stratum IV) was built on the debris of stratum V. The modest walls and the rooms, which contained domestic utensils, suggest that the structures were private houses rather than part of a public or military installation. The stratum IV occupation appears to have ended peacefully. A large structure, designated the palace-fort, was built on top of the stratum IV houses. Its central portion consisted of a raised platform, or podium (10 × 15 m), surrounded by a thick (1.70 m) mud-brick wall and was divided into three large rooms. To the east, a stairway led to rooms at a lower level. Those rooms were used for a variety of domestic activities, including cooking, meat processing, food storage, and weaving. The stratum IV courtyard located north of the palace-fort is at the same elevation as the lower rooms and was reused in stratum III (Yassine, 1983, pp. 507–510).

Shortly before an intense fire destroyed the palace-fort, a series of partition walls was added in the podium rooms in an extensive remodeling. These newly formed rooms were the scene of increased domestic activity in this part of the structure. The excavator suggests that the destruction of the palace-fort in the early sixth century BCE may be attributable to Nabuchadrezzar II's campaign in 582 (Yassine, 1983, pp. 503–507).

The beginning of the fifth-century BCE occupation (stratum II) is marked by massive filling and leveling over the destruction debris of stratum III. A number of poorly constructed mud-brick rooms and adjoining courtyards appear to be modest private houses built roughly on the same orientation as the stratum III structures. The stratum II inhabitants of Tell el-Mazar used mound A as their cemetery. Objects from both the tell and the cemetery display a distinctive Archaemenid Persian influence (Yassine, 1983, pp. 501–503).

The Tell el-Mazar settlement seems to have slowly dwindled during the early fourth century BCE. By late in that century, the summit of the mound was covered with numerous pits and silos measuring up to 2 m in diameter and 4 m deep. [*See* Granaries and Silos.] The absence of any architectural remains from this phase (stratum I) indicates that the tell was then used exclusively as a granary (Yassine, 1983, pp. 498–500).

The earliest stratum on mound A revealed the fragmentary remains of a large (24 × 12.60 m) tripartite structure with stone foundations, mud-brick walls 1.20 m thick, and an associated courtyard 16 m wide. Constructed in the eleventh century BCE and destroyed in the late tenth century BCE, the building contained a variety of ceramic vessels (including storage jars, kraters, bowls, and chalices) and a fenestrated incense stand. Although no contemporary occupational layers have been found on the summit of main tell, it seems probable that they might be encountered beneath stratum V. Iron I layers and architecture have been uncovered on the tell's south slope. Citing parallels from Beth-Shean, Lachish, Megiddo, Ta'anach, and Deir 'Alla, the excavator has interpreted this structure as an open-court sanctuary with seven distinct phases of use, corresponding to phases F–K at Deir 'Alla (Yassine, 1984b). [*See* Beth-Shean; Lachish; Megiddo; Ta'anach; Deir 'Alla, Tell.]

In the fifth century BCE, mound A was used as a cemetery, apparently by the people who occupied the homes of stratum II on the tell. Eighty-five graves have been excavated (Yassine, 1984a). Three main types of burials are represented: simple interments (pit graves); pits lined with mud bricks; and pits lined with stones on one side. In addition, there was one infant jar burial (no. 47) and one larnax (clay coffin) burial (no. 23). The graves were approximately 1 m deep, .70 m wide, and 1–2 m long, each containing a single burial. Most, but not all, of the burials were oriented east–west, with the head at the east end of the grave, facing south. Males were buried in an extended position, whereas females were placed in a flexed position. Typical female grave goods consisted of silver and copper earrings, kohl sticks, shells, and beads. Males were often buried with iron arrowheads, spearpoints, and knives/daggers as well as stamp and cylinder seals made from limestone and such semiprecious stones as marble, agate, jasper, and lapis lazuli. Copper and ceramic vessels and copper/bronze pins, rings, and fibulae were found with both males and females. The cemetery was used throughout the fifth and possibly into the early fourth centuries BCE. [*See* Burial Sites; Tombs; Grave Goods; Jewelry; Weapons.]

BIBLIOGRAPHY

Glueck, Nelson. *Explorations in Eastern Palestine.* Vol. 4. Annual of the American Schools of Oriental Research, 25/28. New Haven, 1951. See pages 302–307.

Ibrahim, Moawiyah, et al. "The East Jordan Valley Survey, 1975." *Bulletin of the American Schools of Oriental Research,* no. 222 (1976): 41–66.

Yassine, Khair. "Ammonite Seals from Tell el-Mazar." In *Studies in the History and Archaeology of Jordan,* vol. 1, edited by Adnan Hadidi, pp. 189–194. Amman, 1982.

Yassine, Khair. "Tell El Mazar, Field I. Preliminary Report of Area G, H, L, and M: The Summit." *Annual of the Department of Antiquities of Jordan* 27 (1983): 495–513, pls. 100–112.

Yassine, Khair. *Tell el-Mazar,* vol. 1, *Cemetery A.* Amman, 1984a.

Yassine, Khair. "The Open Court Sanctuary from the Iron I at Tell el-Mazār Mound A." *Zeitschrift des Deutschen Palästina-Vereins* 100 (1984b): 108–118.

Yassine, Khair, and Javier Teixidor. "Ammonite and Aramaic Inscriptions from Tell el-Mazar in Jordan." *Bulletin of the American Schools of Oriental Research,* no. 264 (1986): 45–50.

Yassine, Khair, ed. *Archaeology of Jordan: Essays and Reports.* Amman, 1988.

DAVID W. MCCREERY and KHAIR YASSINE

MCFADDEN, GEORGE (1907–1953), pioneer of American archaeology in Cyprus. A graduate in architecture from Princeton University, McFadden was deeply interested in the broad span of classical Greek civilization from literature to archaeology. He inspired, supported, and co-directed the first major field project from the New World to excavate on Cyprus.

The University of Pennsylvania Museum (now the University Museum) had previously sponsored a brief excavation on Cyprus in 1931 directed by Bert Hodge Hill, but it lacked the means to underwrite more fieldwork. With McFadden's generous contribution the museum's Kourion Expedition was established to trace the history of human occupation in the area from earliest times through the breakup of the Roman Empire. Beginning in 1934, McFadden and Hill directed extensive excavations at several localities; at the city-site of Kourion they uncovered the theater, basilica, stadium, and temple of Apollo, now regarded as some of the island's most spectacular archaeological discoveries.

The expedition also sponsored an archaeological survey of the region and the excavation of and the publication by the Cypriot Department of Antiquities of Sotira *Teppes,* a Ceramic Neolithic settlement north of Kourion.

McFadden would have been well pleased to know that the archaeological tradition he established was to thrive after his accidental death. His fine house in the village of Episkopi, a short distance from Kourion, was partially converted into a museum displaying local archaeological finds, and the rest of the building has accommodated, over the years, expeditions associated with a wide range of sites. Some projects investigated the earliest human occupation of Cyprus on the Akrotiri peninsula, and others, at the far end of the chronological spectrum, have explored the medieval origins of Episkopi, McFadden's adoptive village, overlooking the bay where he drowned. Since 1969, the American School of

Classical Studies at Athens has offered many fellowships in McFadden's memory.

[*See also* Cyprus; Kourion.]

BIBLIOGRAPHY

Davis, Thomas W. "A History of American Archaeology on Cyprus." *Biblical Archaeologist* 52 (1989): 163–169. The most detailed overview to date of American archaeological research on the island.

Friend, A. M., Jr. "Necrology." *American Journal of Archaeology* 58 (1954): 154.

McFadden, George. "A Tomb of the Necropolis of Ayios Ermoyenis at Kourion." *American Journal of Archaeology* 50 (1946): 449–489, pls. 34–49.

McFadden, George. "A Late Cypriote III Tomb from Kourion Kaloriziki No. 40." *American Journal of Archaeology* 58 (1954): 131–142. McFadden's most important publication of material excavated by the Kourion Expedition.

Swiny, Helena W., ed. *An Archaeological Guide to the Ancient Kourion Area and the Akrotiri Peninsula.* Nicosia, 1982. Contains many references to McFadden's role in the Kourion excavations and describes his house and museum in Episkopi Village.

STUART SWINY

MECCA (more properly, Makkah), city located in an arid valley in al-Hijaz in western Saudi Arabia (21°27′ N, 39°39′ E) and about 73 km (45 mi.) from the Red Sea port of Jeddah, which serves the pilgrims to Mecca. To the southeast is the town of Ṭa'if, 88 km (55 mi.) away. Mecca must have existed since ancient times as the Ka'bah (see below) was established in the nineteenth century BCE (Salama, 1994); it has been known by different names, such as Bakka, Umm al-Qura, Makkah, al-Balad al-Amim (surah 95.3 in the Qur'an), or "the safe land." The climate is very hot. Around the Mecca Valley are mountains and wadis. The famous Mecca mountains, which have been frequently mentioned in autobiographies and geographical sources are Jabal Abi Qobais on the east, Jabal Qunaiga' on the west and Jabal Ḥira'. A few of the main antiquities of Mecca and its environs are mentioned below.

Both Bakka and Mecca are mentioned in the Qur'an. The holy mosque *(al masjid al-Ḥaram)* with the Ka'bah at its center is the holiest place of Islam for Muslims. It is the first house of worship that Allah appointed (3.96; 48.24). During ancient times Mecca was famous for Arabia's foremost sanctuary, the Ka'bah, which was built by Ibrahim (Abraham), and pilgrims thronged to it from distant places. The building of the Ka'bah by Abraham and Ismail is mentioned in the Qur'an (2.125–127, 119–121). Local clans, such as the Jurhom, Khuzaa', and Quraysh, controlled it from time to time. All Muslims face the Ka'bah for prayers. It was rebuilt several times. Mecca was the birthplace of the prophet Muhammad, and the Qur'anic revelations were originally addressed to the people of Mecca to reform them socially and morally. It was at Jabal Ḥira' on which the angel Gibril (Gabriel) descended from heaven and revealed Islam to the prophet Muhammad and directed him to spread it. Jabal Ḥira' is located some 6 km (3.7 mi.) to the northeast of Mecca. Jabal Thawr is also situated at the same distance to the southeast. In this mountain Muhammad hid himself before his migration to Medina.

When Caliph Umar made a pilgrimage to Mecca in AH 17/638 CE, a wall was built around the Ka'bah. This was enlarged by Caliph 'Uthman in 26/646 and arcades were built. Since then the holy mosque has been under constant expansion and rebuilding and has achieved the current extent under the government of Saudi Arabia.

The names of the extant old quarters are Ajyad, al-Mesfala, al-Shubaika, al-Hojon, al-Ma'abida, Shi'b-'Ali, Shi'b-'Amir, and Kudai. Of the several cemeteries in Mecca, al-Ma'lat, north of the Ka'bah, contains the burials of several venerable companions of the Prophet as well as of other followers and Muslim scholars; it has numerous inscribed tombstones, which provide important biographical information.

Because of Mecca's strategic location, it developed into an important commercial center where all principal trade and pilgrim routes, both internal and external, converged, linking Arabia, Egypt, Syria, Yemen, and the cities of Basra, and Kufah.

Since antiquity quarrying and masonry have been known at Mecca. Mecca has long accommodated markets, mosques, baths, and different industries. The valleys near Mecca have been exploited for farming; the most important are Wadi Fatimah, Wadi Nu'man, and Wadi 'Oranal.

During the twentieth century, Mecca has expanded considerably, becoming a cosmopolitan city. Millions of pilgrims and other visitors arrive annually. Because of the continuous structural expansions for al-Ḥaram mosque, many of the cultural landmarks have disappeared from the center of the holy city. However, some of the remains still reflect ancient architecture of mixed elements, both local and foreign.

Islamic antiquities at Mecca and its vicinity are numerous. The two ancient mosques associated with the Ka'bah and pilgrimage rites are Namira at Arafat and al-Khaif at Mina. During the cleaning of the Zemzem well in 1979, which springs from the eastern part of the Ka'bah area a large number of antiquities were recovered, such as pottery vessels, ceramics, metal objects, and Islamic coins (some of them are dated to the Ottoman era and the beginning of the modern Saudi state).

Some Kufic inscriptions on columns in the al-Ḥaram mosque dated to the reign of the 'Abbasid caliph al-Mahadi (158–169/775–785) survive. These texts document the comprehensive expansion of the al-Ḥaram mosque during al-Mahadi's rule. Some inscriptions of the Mamluk and Ottoman periods are also found in the mosque, recording the expansion and amendments of al-Ḥaram by other caliphs and sultans. Various ancient reservoirs and dams remain in and around Mecca. Near Mina three dams were erected by al-Hajjaj ibn Yusuf al-Thagafi, who ruled the Mecca emirate on behalf of the caliph Abdul Malik ibn Marwan for three years (73–75/692–694). Sad Athal, the biggest dam, which is built in stone, is about 140 m (460 ft.) long, 5.6 m (18.4 ft.) high, and 6 m (19.6 ft.) wide. One of the surviving water structures to date is at ʿAin Zobaida, which was financed and erected by al-Sayida Zobaida, the wife of Caliph Harun al-Rashid. It covers an area of 40 km (24.8 mi.) southeast of Mecca, extending to Arafat and Mina as well. It was used until the beginning of the twentieth century.

[*See also* Medina.]

BIBLIOGRAPHY

Angawi, Sami Muhsin. "Makkan Architecture." Ph.D. diss., University of London, 1988.

Arslān, Shakīb. *Al-irtisāmāt al-liṭāf fī khāṭir al-ḥājj ilā aqdas maṭāf.* Cairo, c. 1931.

Atlal: The Journal of Saudi Arabian Archaeology 1–2 (1977–1978).

Azraqī, Abū al-Walīd Muḥammad ibn ʿAbd Allāh. *Akhbār Makkah wa-mājāʾa fīhā min al-ʿathār.* 2 vols. Mecca, 1965.

Barakati, N. Abdulla al-, and Muhammed N. Sulayman Mannaʿ. *Dirasa Tarikh iya Limasagid al-Mashaʿr al-Moqadasa.* Jeddah, 1988.

Bāsalāmah, Ḥusayn ʿAbd Allāh. *Tārīkh ʿimārat al-Masjid al-Ḥarām.* Cairo, 1964.

Bilādī, ʿĀtiq ibn Ghayth al-. *Maʿālim Makkah al-tārīkhīyah wa-al-atharīyah.* Mecca, 1980.

Burton, Richard F. *Personal Narrative of a Pilgrimage to al-Madinah and Meccah.* 2 vols. New York, 1964.

Esin, Emel. *Mecca the Blessed, Madinah the Radiant.* London, 1963.

Faʿar, M. Fahad al-. *Tatawor al-Kitābāt wa-al-Nuqush fī al-Ḥijāz.* Jeddah, 1984.

Fākihī, Muḥammad ibn Isḥāq al-. *Akhbār Makkah fī qadīm al-Dahr wa-ḥadī thih.* 6 vols. Edited by ʿAbd al-Malik ibn ʿAbd Allāh ibn Duhaysh. Mecca, 1986–1988.

Fāsī, Taqī al-Dīn Muḥammad ibn Aḥmad al-. *Al-ʿiqd al-thamīn fī tārīkh al-Balad al-Amīn.* 8 vols. Cairo, 1958–1969.

Ibn Jubayr, Muḥammad ibn Aḥmad. *Riḥlat Ibn Jubayr.* Beirut, 1968.

Kawshak, Y. Hamza. *Zemzem ṭaʿāmun ṭaʿim wa-sharabun ṣogem.* Jeddah, 1983.

Salama, Awatif Adib. *Quraysh Khabal Islam.* Dar al-Mariq, 1414/1994.

Snouck Hurgronje, Christiaan. *Makkah in the Later Part of the Nineteenth Century.* Leiden and London, 1931.

Zailaʿī, Aḥmad ʿUmar al-. *Makkah wa-ʿAlāqātuhā al-Khārijīyah.* Riyadh, 1981.

SAʿAD ABDUL AZIZ AL-RASHID

MEDA'IN SALEH ("cities of Saleh"), site located in northwestern Arabia (26°51′ N, 37°58′ E), directly on the caravan route between Syria and Yemen. The site is universally identified with Hegra (or Egra), the Nabatean administrative and military center in the southern part of their kingdom, second in importance only to their capital, Petra. It is mentioned by Strabo (16.4.24) and also by Pliny (6.32.156) and Stephanus of Byzantium (*Ethnika* 260, 11–12). In Islamic tradition, as al-Hijr, it is associated with the Thamud, one of the early peoples of Arabia, whom God sought to convert from polytheism by sending the prophet Saleh to them. When the Thamud rejected him, their town was destroyed. Meda'in Saleh lies in a spectacular setting of isolated sandstone stacks, weathered into fantastic shapes, surrounding a broad, sand-filled basin. The basin is fed by winter storms and flash floods which provide ample supplies of water easily tapped by wells and cisterns. The site was familiar to thousands of Muslim pilgrims traveling to Mecca, and it is mentioned by many of the medieval Arab geographers. It was not until 1888 that it was brought to the attention of the Western world, however. Charles M. Doughty wrote about it in *Travels in Arabia Deserta* (Cambridge, 1888); however, it was not until 1909 that Antonin Jaussen and Raphael Savignac's very full description of the monuments and the inscriptions was published, with many photographs, drawings, and a sketched plan (*Mission archéologique en Arabie,* 2 vols., Paris, 1909 and 1914). More recent work has added a little to their account, but it remains basic for any consideration of the history of the site.

The earliest datable archaeological evidence appears to be seven monumental South Arabian inscriptions on reused building blocks, presumably the work of the Minean merchants established at Dedan, some 20 km (12 mi.) to the south, in about the fourth–third centuries BCE. [*See* Dedan.] There are also some Lihyanite graffiti from about the same period. The kingdom of Lihyan, based at Dedan, probably fell to a Nabatean adventurer, Masʿudu, in the second or early first century BCE. It must have been at this time that Meda'in Saleh was chosen by the rulers of Petra as the site for their southern base. The earliest datable pottery lying on the surface of the site—the distinctive fine Nabatean painted ware—dates to this time. Nothing more is known about this early period of occupation and development; Strabo's reference relates to about 24 BCE and alludes to the site as a village in the territory of King Obodas II. Judging from the inscriptions on the tombs (see below), the site flourishes in the first century CE, when its principal role was to collect payments from the Arabian trade caravans and protect the routes. When the Nabatean kingdom was annexed by Rome in 106 CE, it is unlikely that Hegra's strategic position was forgotten. Epigraphic evidence points to both a section of the Third Legion and a number of local auxiliary troops being stationed there during the second and possibly the third centuries CE. Nothing is known after that, and by the time of the Muslim conquest in the seventh century CE the "cities of Saleh" were the subject only of pious speculation.

Very little is visible on the surface of what was probably a prosperous and cosmopolitan town. The most striking remains are the approximately eighty Nabatean tomb facades carved in the sandstone cliffs (see figure 1). The facades are very similar to those at Petra, although the very ornate "classical baroque" tombs at Petra are absent at Meda'in Saleh. [*See* Petra.] They range in style from relatively plain, flat, vertical surfaces surmounted by one or two rows of crenel-

MEDA'IN SALEH. Figure 1. *Tomb facades.* (Courtesy P. J. Parr)

lations carved in low relief, to more elaborate facades with deeply cut moldings, pilasters, capitals, architraves, and pediments. They reproduce in the living rock the appearance of the entrance to a freestanding building. This architectural ornamentation is derived from a wide variety of sources, including ancient Mesopotamia, Egypt, and the classical world; it demonstrates that eclecticism which is the hallmark of Nabatean art and which makes it unique. Unlike the tombs at Petra, almost half of those at Meda'in Saleh bear inscriptions over their doorways, in the Nabatean script. The inscriptions are essentially legal texts, copies of which seem also to have been deposited in a temple. The inscriptions give the epitaph of the owner, the date of construction (in the form of the regnal year of the Nabatean king), and, in some cases, the occupation of the owner and the name of the stonecutter employed (interestingly not called an architect). The importance of these inscriptions is twofold: they prove that the types of Nabatean facades represented here were being carved contemporaneously between 1 and 76 CE (the varying degrees of embellishment primarily reflect social status, and thus the wealth of the owner). They also demonstrate a concentration of high-ranking military personnel in the city, presumably on account of its importance for guarding the southern limits of the Nabatean realm.

[*See also* Nabatean Inscriptions; Nabateans.]

BIBLIOGRAPHY

Bowersock, Glen W. *Roman Arabia.* Cambridge, Mass., 1983. Standard work on the subject, including the best short account of Nabatean history, with many references to Meda'in Saleh.

Bowsher, J. M. C. "The Frontier Post of Medain Saleh." In *The Defence of the Roman and Byzantine East,* edited by Philip Freeman and David Kennedy, pp. 19–30. Oxford, 1986. Succinct account of the military organization of the site in Nabatean and Roman times, derived from the texts.

McKenzie, Judith. *The Architecture of Petra.* London, 1990. Includes a chapter on the Meda'in Saleh tombs, with emphasis on the development of the architectural ornament and its relevance for dating the tombs at Petra.

Negev, Avraham. "The Nabataean Necropolis at Egra." *Revue Biblique* 83 (1976): 203–236. Very useful survey of the dated tombs, discussing both the architecture and the owners' social status.

PETER J. PARR

MEDEINEH, KHIRBET EL-, site located on the eastern bank of Wadi al-Moʿarradjeh, branch of the Mujib River, 7 km (4 mi.) east of Smakieh and about 16 km (10 mi.) from Qaṣr, a village situated on the Madaba-Kerak road in modern Jordan. The site was only recently identified with the Moabite cities attested in the Hebrew Bible and the historical records. Excavations were undertaken by Emilio Olávarri for the Casa Santiago in Jerusalem in 1976 and 1982.

The ruins cover a town surrounded by a solid wall that conforms to the oval configuration of the surface of the hill. A single wall 4 m wide defended the steep slopes to the north and south. The eastern slope, whose gradient is softer and more vulnerable, had a double parallel defense wall. In the town, the residential structures were attached to the inner face of the defense wall, leaving open space, perhaps a small plaza, in the center. One of these houses, which measures 10 × 6 m, was excavated in the 1976 campaign. Its four rooms are separated longitudinally by eight monolithic pillars on which the poles that held up the roof were probably affixed. Regular stone benches are attached to the walls of the rooms. In the 1982 campaign, another house was cleared with the following interior distribution: an open court at the entrance whose door is on the north wall; two rooms separated by three monolithic stone pillars that supported a terrace; an interior room with a window opening to the court; and a triangular enclosure with a staircase leading up to the terrace. This house clearly resembles the four-room Iron Age I pillared houses found elsewhere in the area. [*See* Four-room House.]

On the eastern side of the hill, the outer defensive wall was reinforced with two rectangular towers, one in its northern corner and the other in the middle of its course. A third tower at the southern corner, detached from the town wall, defended the main entrance. Near it, the doorway consisted of two rectangular towers delimiting an interior hall (2 × 10 m) in which stone benches were attached to the towers' interior walls. At the farthest end of the hall, a staircase with three steps served either as a place to dismount or as the presidential seat during the city's senate assembly (cf. *Gn.* 23:10, 34, 20 ff.; *Prv.* 31:23).

The pottery is a uniform repertoire assignable to a brief, single period of occupation (twelfth–eleventh centuries BCE). Predominant are the fragments of large jars with collared rims, craters, and characteristic cooking pots. The domestic housewares generally have a white slip. No remains of painted decoration or red-slipped burnished sherds were found.

Khirbet el-Medeineh, then, was small town, strongly fortified, belonging to the old kingdom of Moab. It was founded in the twelfth century BCE and abandoned in about 1075–1050 BCE. Its structures and pottery indicate a clear affinity with the contemporary urban environment in Canaan in the first phase of Iron Age I. Its strategic placement echoes the pressing interest with which the kings of Moab defended their eastern frontier from nomadic incursions coming from the eastern plateau. It was during this time that the Israelite tribes, bound for Canaan and sharing a vaster and increasing movement toward sedentarization, passed Khirbet el-Medeineh, on Moab's eastern frontier (*Nm.* 21:11; *Jgs.* 11:18).

BIBLIOGRAPHY

Miller, J. Maxwell. "Archaeological Survey South of Wadi Mujib: Glueck's Sites Revisited." *Annual of the Department of Antiquities of Jordan* 23 (1979): 79–92.

Olávarri, Emilio. "Sondeo arqueológico en Khirbet Medeineh junto a Smakieh (Jordania)." *Annual of the Department of Antiquities of Jordan* 22 (1977–1978): 136–149, pl. 84.

Olávarri, Emilio. "La campagne de fouilles 1982 à Khirbet Medeinet al-Mu'arradjeh près de Smakieh (Kerak)." *Annual of the Department of Antiquities of Jordan* 27 (1983): 165–178, pls. 28–31.

EMILIO OLÁVARRI

MEDES. The heartland of ancient Media is located in the central Zagros Mountains of western Iran. The Medes first appear in Assyrian cuneiform sources in the middle of the ninth century BCE. These early sources speak of many Median tribes and Median kings. Eventually, possibly late in the seventh century BCE, a unified Median state was formed. Allied with the Babylonians, the Medes captured Nineveh in 612 BCE, which led to the collapse of the Assyrian Empire in 610 BCE. [*See* Nineveh.] Median power then stretched from the Halys River in Anatolia to perhaps as far east as northeastern modern Iran. They are said to have ruled over the Persians, another Iranian tribe. They were conquered by Cyrus the Great of Persia in 550 BCE, and throughout Achaemenid times they were the second-most important people in the empire after the Persians themselves.

Median history and culture are complex. Herodotus (1.95–130) recounts that originally the Medes were village dwellers. They were united, at their request, under the kingship of one Deioces, who founded the capital city of Ecbatana (modern Hamadan). [*See* Ecbatana.] He then reigned for fifty-three years. Deioces was followed on the throne by his son Phraortes, who conquered the Persians, ruled for twenty-two years, and died fighting the Assyrians. His successor, Cyaxares, ruled for forty years and reorganized the Median army, separating spearmen, archers, and cavalry into separate units. In 612 BCE, in alliance with the Babylonians, Cyaxares conquered Nineveh. He was succeeded by his son Astyages, who reigned for thirty-five years and was overthrown by Cyrus in 550 BCE.

Herodotus (1.103–106) also recounts that Cyaxares's attacks on Assyria were interrupted by the conquest of Media by the Scythians, who ruled "Upper Asia" for twenty-eight years until they were finally driven out by Cyaxares. [*See* Scythians.] Herodotus's story may be a true account of a Median national epic history. Other written and archaeological sources on Median history, however, confirm Herodotus only in part. There is no record of either Deioces or Phraortes independent of Herodotus, and convoluted efforts by imaginative scholars to prove otherwise have failed. Astyages, on the other hand, is clearly the Ištuwigu of the cuneiform Babylonian chronicle and probably came to the throne of Media in 585 BCE. Cyaxares is the Umakištar of an earlier Babylonian chronicle that tells of the fall of Nineveh and the collapse of Assyria. Using Herodotus's chronology, Cyaxares came to the throne in 625 BCE. Thus, the latter half of Herodotus's story of the Median royal house is, in part, corroborated.

From archaeological and Assyrian cuneiform sources it is possible, independently of Herodotus, to reconstruct something of the early history of Media. The Assyrian sources give a clear picture of the Medes as an important people widespread throughout the central western Zagros from the mid-ninth to the mid-seventh century BCE and ruled by numerous "kings." Not all Medes lived in what, in these early times, can be called Media. The geographical Media, as known to the Assyrians, seems to have been located along the so-called High Road in the neighborhood of modern Kermanshah and eastward. Other peoples, some Iranian, some not, also lived in this area, but the sources suggest that, once as far east as the Hamadan plain, there were only Medes. Thus, the heartland of geographic Media would seem to lie east of Mt. Alvand (the mountain against whose eastern flank the city of Hamadan/Ecbatana lies). The people called Medes in the Assyrian texts are clearly a very diverse people in terms of culture and social and political organization.

The archaeological sources, such as they are, tend to confirm this picture. This is the Iron Age III period in Iranian archaeology (c. 850–500 BCE in central western Iran). The principal sites that can be considered Median are Tepe Nush-i Jan, Godin period II, and Baba Jan. Nush-i Jan was apparently primarily a religious establishment; Godin II the fortified palace of an important Median khan or tribal chief, such as are often mentioned in the Assyrian sources; and Baba Jan may have been the seat of a lesser tribal ruler. [*See* Godin Tepe.] Though broadly similar in many cultural characteristics, there are nevertheless marked differences among these sites that are in part the result of chronology and in part of functional variation, but that may also represent the diversity among the so-called Medes found in the Assyrian sources.

Herodotus's story of the earliest Medes living in "villages"—meaning, to the Greeks, that they had no cities and no central government and were, thus, uncivilized—appears, then, to be partially corroborated. On the other hand, there is no evidence for a unification of the Median state under Deioces or anyone else as early as the late eighth century BCE, as Herodotus recounts. There is also no evidence outside of Herodotus for a Scythian interregnum in Median history, although there is abundant evidence in Assyrian sources for the presence of Scythians in western Iran in the seventh century BCE.

The Assyrian sources fall silent on western Iran in about 640 BCE. Because Hamadan remains unexcavated, there is no available archaeological evidence of any centralization of the Median state. It is possible to conclude, however, that such a central state came into being sometime in the reign of Cyaxares, prior to the Median participation in the collapse of Assyria. In dealing with Cyaxares and Astyages, the Babylonian chronicle speaks of only one Median king. Cyaxares was clearly a powerful figure. Under him the Medes are reported to have sacked Harran in north Syria in 610 BCE and are at war with the Lydians deep in Anatolia in 585 BCE. The situation clearly changed markedly from the picture received from the texts of Sargon II of Assyria (721–705 BCE) of a Media of many tribes and many kings. Thus, some kind of Median political unity was created late in the seventh century BCE, possibly as a case of secondary state formation under pressure from Assyria.

This undoubted political unification of Media also had important cultural implications: it led to the "iranianization" of the central and northern Zagros Mountains. The Assyrian records speak of many ethnic groups and polities beside Medes in these regions in the eighth century BCE. Among other non-Iranian people were the Namrians, Ellipi, and Manneans. Yet, by the time the Babylonian chronicler is writing, all these people had disappeared from the written record and he knew the area simply as Media, occupied by Medes. The Manneans, as allies of the Assyrians at the seige of Nineveh, are, in fact, the last people from central western and northwestern Iran, other than Medes, mentioned in cuneiform sources.

By the end of the seventh century BCE, Media had emerged as one of the four principal powers of the ancient Near East, alongside Babylonia, Lydia, and Egypt. Cyrus the Great, by conquering Astyages and the Medes, thus, in one stroke, brought the other major Iranian group, the Persians, to world power. As noted above, however, the Medes remained a privileged group in the Persian Empire as the second-most important people ruled by the "king of kings." Indeed, these two Iranian groups were so identified that the Greeks spoke sometimes of Medes and sometimes of Persians when referring to the Achaemenid Iranians. For a Greek to become too closely associated with Iranian culture was to become medianized, not persianized. Medes played an equal role in the imperial guard with Persians and were equally responsible for the defense of the Achaemenid Empire.

It is also clear that Median culture, perhaps particularly in matters of religion, became thoroughly embedded in broader Iranian culture. The Median language, Old Northwest Iranian (as reconstructed by certain loanwords in Modern Persian such as *sag*, the word for "dog"—there are no texts in Median), is very likely the ancient form of modern Kurdish. If this is true, then part of ancient Media is still occupied by the descendents of the Medes.

Median art and architecture remain subjects of some controversy. Assuming that Godin II and Nush-i Jan were indeed Median sites, they provide in their architecture a clear link between the tradition of columned audience halls first documented in Iran at Hasanlu IV in Azerbaijan and the great columned audience halls of Achaemenid Persia at Pasargadae, Persepolis, and Susa. [*See* Hasanlu; Pasargadae; Persepolis; Susa.] In origin, the concept of the columned audience hall may not have been Iranian, but the concept certainly became thoroughly imbedded in Iranian architectural traditions, probably because the Medes adopted it. (A more recent manifestation of the tradition can be seen at

Chehel Situn, "the hall of forty columns," built in Isfahan in the seventeenth century CE.)

The Median contribution to the small arts of Iran is more problematical. Numerous objects in museums and private collections throughout the world have been ascribed to the Medes. Yet, not one comes from an archaeological excavation. All, if genuine, are the products of antiquities looting. Thus, the very existence of Median art, as opposed to architecture and ceramics, is a construct of the imagination and cannot be given scholarly credence.

In sum too little is known of Median history and culture. From both textual and archaeological bits and pieces, it is clear that it is much more than just a history of the Medes: it is a history of many peoples, Iranian and non-Iranian. From this mosaic came the first Iranian state, the kingdom of the Medes. The evidence is that this state rose to world power in the late seventh century BCE. As a young state it soon succumbed to the power of Cyrus the Great of Persia, but it nevertheless made a profound, and lasting, contribution to the greater world of Iranian culture.

[*See also* Assyrians; Persians.]

BIBLIOGRAPHY

Brown, Stuart C. "Media in the Achaemenid Period: The Late Iron Age in Central Western Iran." In *Achaemenid History IV: Centre and Periphery,* edited by Heleen Sancisi-Weerdenburg and Amélie Kuhrt, pp. 63–76. Leiden, 1990. Good summary of what is known and not known about the archaeology of Media.

Cameron, George G. *History of Early Iran.* Chicago, 1936. In large part out of date, but a pioneering study of ancient Elam and Media on which all subsequent studies have built.

Culican, William. *The Medes and Persians.* London, 1965. Somewhat out-of-date, readable semipopular work with value for the layperson.

Diakonoff, Igor M. "Media." In *The Cambridge History of Iran,* vol. 2, edited by Ilya Gershevitch, pp. 36–148. Cambridge, 1985. Somewhat idiosyncratic but thorough and scholarly review of Median history with a good bibliography.

Dyson, Robert H., Jr. "The Architecture of Hasanlu: Periods I to IV." *American Journal of Archaeology* 81 (1977): 548–552. Best short summary of Hasanlu's Iron Age architecture.

Goff, Clare L. "Excavation at Baba Jan, 1968: Third Preliminary Report." *Iran* 8 (1970): 141–156. Final preliminary report on this important site. See also specialist reports on aspects of the site in *Iran* 15 (1977): 103–140; 16 (1978): 29–65; and 22 (1985): 1–20.

Helm, Peyton R. "Herodotus' Medikos Logos and Median History." *Iran* 19 (1981): 85–90. Excellent analysis of what Herodotus may have been talking about in his sections on Media and the Scythians.

Herodotus. *The History.* Translated by David Greene. Chicago, 1987. The starting point for all ancient Iranian history.

Levine, Louis D. "Geographical Studies in the Neo-Assyrian Zagros." *Iran* 11 (1973): 1–27; 12 (1974): 99–124. The most thorough and complete attempt to reconstruct the historical geography of western Iran, including Media, in the Iron Age. Essential for understanding the cultural dynamics of the region and period.

Stronach, David. "Tepe Nush-i Jan: The Median Settlement." In *The Cambridge History of Iran,* vol. 2, edited by Ilya Gershevitch, pp. 832–837. Cambridge, 1985. Excellent brief summary of the archaeology of the Median levels at Nush-i Jan.

Young, T. Cuyler, Jr., and Louis D. Levine. *Excavations of the Godin Project: Second Progress Report.* Toronto, 1974. The most complete report yet published on the Median structure of Godin period II.

Young, T. Cuyler, Jr. "The Early History of the Medes and the Persians and the Achaemenid Empire to the Death of Cambyses." In *The Cambridge History of Iran,* vol. 4, edited by John Boardman, pp. 1–52. Cambridge, 1988. A longer discussion of Median history and archaeology, from which the present article is largely drawn.

T. CUYLER YOUNG, JR.

MEDICINE. As a general reference to healing practices, medicine has a long and complex history in the ancient Near East. It is useful to think of healing practices as part of a healthcare system that includes, but is not limited to, beliefs about the causes of illness, the options available to patients, and the role of governments in healthcare.

Public hygiene, which refers broadly to the organized efforts of a community to promote health and prevent disease, is also part of any healthcare system. Brief synopses are provided here of the healthcare systems in the major geocultural areas of the Near East (see below) from earliest times to the Early Islamic period (c. 1250 CE).

Prehistory. Little is known about the treatment of illness during the Paleolithic, the first period of human material culture, which ended approximately between 20000 and 16000 BCE in the Near East. By the end of the period, it is speculated, humans practiced therapeutic rituals and may have recognized the medicinal value of some plants. At Shanidar I (c. 45000 BCE), a rock-shelter in Iraq, the skeleton of a "Neanderthal" adult male suggests that he had received substantial care from his community because he had lived for years with osteoarthritis and other serious injuries. [*See* Shanidar Cave.]

In the Neolithic (c. 8500–4300 BCE) period, the domestication of animals introduced some new pools of diseases into human populations. Thus, bovine tuberculosis may have become more prevalent in human beings after cattle began to be kept for milk and food. Human tuberculosis is reflected in skeletal material from Egypt and Bab edh-Dhraʿ (Jordan) as early as the fourth millennium.

Some researchers conclude, on the basis of comparisons in dental attrition (among other features), that hunter-gatherers (e.g., Natufians at el-Wad, Jordan) in some Epipaleolithic cultures (c. 19000–8000 BCE) were generally healthier than agriculturalists at places such as Jericho and Tell Abu Hureyra, a large settlement in northern Syria. Yet, some studies of the Levant estimate the average life-span in the Neolithic at thirty-four years, compared to thirty years in the Epipaleolithic period. At Çatal Höyük, a large Neolithic town in Anatolia, skeletal remains of some individuals were estimated to be more than sixty years old. [*See* Çatal Höyük.]

Because many diseases need relatively high population densities in order to thrive, a number of diseases that were insignificant in hunter-gatherer bands became significant with the rise of urbanization. Other serious threats to public health in most cities of the ancient Near East probably included the unequal distribution of food and the contamination of food and water supplies by the inadequate disposal of human and animal wastes. Increases in trade, military expeditions, and migration helped to spread diseases among populations.

The frequency of enamel hypoplasia (thin enamel) and other skeletal features in the urban populations of the Early Bronze Age (c. 3300–2300 BCE) in the Levant may indeed indicate a decline in health status relative to the Epipaleolithic and Neolithic. High rates of hypoplasia are also found at Azor (near Tel Aviv) and elsewhere in the Chalcolithic period (4300–3300 BCE).

Throughout all prehistoric periods the family was probably the main caretaker for the ill. The appearance of survivable surgical procedures on the skull (trephination) is already evident in the Pre-Pottery Neolithic at Jericho (c. 8500–6000 BCE). The reasons for trephination are still unclear, but if it is a medical procedure, it may be one of the earliest representatives of the development of specialized healing crafts. The most effective treatment, however, was probably simple rest.

A discussion of the major geocultural areas in the Near East follows for the periods prior to the Islamic conquest in the eighth century CE. We shall proceed alphabetically: Anatolia, Cyprus and the Aegean, Egypt, Mesopotamia, and Syria-Palestine.

Anatolia. By the Neolithic period various groups had already built impressive towns (e.g., Çatal Höyük) in Anatolia. It is the Hittites, a group of Indo-European speakers, who are perhaps the best-known residents of the region, especially in the Late Bronze Age. The Hittite healthcare system is difficult to reconstruct because sources are very fragmentary. However, extant sources show that Hittite medicine included Luwian and Hurrian traditions. Many of the best-known Hittite medical texts are translations or adaptations of Mesopotamian models. [*See* Hittites; Luwians.]

The inadequate disposal of waste was probably a major public health problem, especially in urban areas. Concern with public health may be partly responsible for the clay pipes and drainage channels found at Boğazköy, Alaca Höyük, and other LB cities. Some of the wealthier households in Boğazköy and other cities were apparently equipped with toilets. [*See* Boğazköy.]

Illnesses mentioned in Hittite texts include disorders of the eyes, mouth, throat, and intestines. There are reports of illnesses afflicting King Šuppiluliuma (who died in about 1335 BCE of a plague brought back by his soldiers after a campaign in Syria) and King Ḫattušili III (c. 1278 BCE). The Plague Prayers of Muršili II (c. 1335–1308 BCE), which refer to an unidentified epidemic lasting some twenty years, recognize that diseases could affect the socioeconomic stability of an entire empire.

For Hittites, illnesses could be caused by numerous factors, including the sins of past generations. Evil and illness could resemble physical substances that needed to be removed by washing and other methods. Known therapeutic rituals emphasize an analogy between ritual actions, especially the act of speaking itself, and the effects on an illness. Many gods and goddesses (e.g., Išḫara, Šaušga, Kamrušepa) could be healers. There are no known Hittite temples that were used as sanitoria, but prayers and divinatory rituals related to illness may have been performed at temples.

Hittite physicians are already attested in the Old Hittite period (c. 1700–1500 BCE), and at least some probably were pupils of Assyrian healers. The materia medica included various plants and minerals. Hittite kings, like many sovereigns in the Near East, attempted to maintain a reliable and efficient organization of healers. Various texts also attest to the importance of female midwives and healers/diviners, some of whom had their own organizations. Hittite letters also mention the importation of professional healers from Egypt and Mesopotamia, especially in the fourteen–thirteenth centuries BCE. The general population, however, probably consulted a variety of folk practitioners who were not organized.

Cyprus and the Aegean. Although it is difficult to determine the earliest instances of healing activities in the Aegean area, some scholars argue that female figurines on Cyprus indicate the possible existence of fertility therapy by the Chalcolithic period (c. 3800–2500 BCE). Various Middle and Late Minoan period sites (e.g., Mt. Jouktas, Traostalos) on Crete have produced figurines of body parts that may have been associated with healing cults.

According to Vassos Karageorghis (*Cyprus,* London, 1982), medical activities may be detected in at least some LB temples at Kition on Cyprus. [*See* Kition.] At Mycenae, skeletal remains show that in the fourteen–thirteenth centuries BCE the elite were probably better fed and healthier than the general population.

Greeks generally believed that illness could be sent by a large number of deities who also could heal. Such deities included Apollo, whose arrows could cause epidemics (à la Resheph in the Levant), and Artemis, the goddess of women. The most famous healing god, Asclepius, who had the dog and serpent as emblems, was regarded as the patron of all physicians. Unlike most other gods, Asclepius rarely sent illness.

By the late first millennium BCE there is ample textual and archaeological evidence for the use of *asclepieia* (temples of Asclepius) as healing centers, particularly in Athens, Cos, Pergamon, and Epidauros. Patients usually were believed to be healed in a night's stay at the *asclepieion.* Figurines of afflicted (or healed) body parts were left in these temples. Probable scalpels and other surgical instruments have been discovered at the *asclepieion* in Pergamon.

City-states invested in the care of the chronically ill by building *asclepieia* and other healing temples. Community investments in *asclepieia* in Athens and Rome may be linked to local epidemics in 429 BCE and 292 BCE, respectively. Patients, especially wealthy ones, also supported the temple with thanksgiving offerings and other donations.

Hierarchies in healing options are attested in some Greek texts. For example, patients might first attempt to pray to a god at home. If that did not bring relief, a local physician might be consulted. If the latter was unsuccessful, the patient might go to the *asclepieion*. Comparable therapeutic hierarchies were probably used in most areas of the ancient Near East.

By the third century BCE, Hippocrates and other figures are credited with developing the first systems of "rational" medicine. For example, the Hippocratic treatise "On Airs, Waters, and Places" links climate and environment, not gods, with illness. Yet, such natural explanations can be found alongside supernatural ones in *asclepieia*. The Roman Empire helped to spread Greek concepts of healthcare throughout the Near East.

Egypt. Egyptian medical texts were among the first discovered and published by modern Near Eastern archaeologists. The Ebers papyrus (c. 1550 BCE), which contains a general collection of remedies, was published in 1875. Mummies from Egypt began to be studied medically as early as 1820. The thousands of skeletons from Egypt provide examples of various illnesses, including mandibular abscesses, skeletal deformities, and likely cases of tuberculosis.

Private tombs, especially in the Old Kingdom (c. 2575–2134 BCE), depict people with dwarfism, scoliosis, and other physical deformities. Some scholars argue that excavated human remains reflect a life expectancy of forty–fifty years and high infant mortality, regardless of social level.

Herodotus speaks of the scrupulous personal hygiene of the Egyptians, but Egypt probably suffered from poor public sanitation. Latrines existed in at least some upper-class households (and even in some second dynasty tombs, c. 2700 BCE), but excavations at Tell el-Amarna and elsewhere indicate that even some of the most luxurious homes were surrounded by heaps of garbage and open sewers.

Although the Ebers papyrus and other texts reflect the notion that irregularities in the system of vessels that carried air and fluids within the body could cause illness, Egyptians believed that illness could be sent and/or cured by a large number of deities, including Heket, Hathor, Imhotep, Isis, and Sekhmet ("the lady of pestilence"). Some temples specialized in healing, a notable example being the sanitorium established in the Ptolemaic period (304–30 BCE) at Deir el-Baḥari on the site of the "birthing temple" (where royal women gave birth) of Queen Hatshepsut (1473–1458 BCE).

Medical professions and skills may have developed quite early in Egypt. Probable dentists (known as "toothers") appear in about 3000 BCE. One of the earliest known physicians, Hesy Re of the third dynasty (c. 2600 BCE), is described as the "chief of the dentists and physicians" to the pyramid builders in a wooden panel found in his tomb at Saqqara. Two bodies from tombs from the fifth dynasty (c. 2465–2323 BCE) attest to the setting of fractured limbs by means of splints and bandages.

Scholars usually identify the *swnw,* attested in the main medical papyri and in other texts, as the principal type of healing practitioner. The Edwin Smith papyrus indicates that medical examinations were simple, direct, and meant to determine, among other things, whether patients would benefit from treatment. Most treatments probably used incantations along with drugs and physical procedures. In some periods, Egyptian practitioners were valuable commodities exported to Anatolia and other lands of the Near East.

In at least some periods the state seems to have invested in medical care in order to ensure the maintenance of a healthy labor force. Some records noted illness-related absences from state projects, and physicians (e.g., Hesy Re) were assigned to particular groups of laborers. Of course such investments probably varied with time and circumstance. For the majority of Egyptians, however, healthcare was probably provided by folk healers and administered in the home.

Mesopotamia. As elsewhere in the Near East, healing practices in Mesopotamia probably predate writing. Mesopotamian healers are mentioned in texts by the middle of the third millennium. As indicated by the earliest attested collection of medical prescriptions (Ur III period, c. 2050 BCE), the development of writing created new systems of collecting, storing, and distributing medical information.

Diagnostic manuals, letters, and other types of texts speak of the threats to public health posed by dirty water, urban epidemics, and famine (see Martinez, 1990). Some texts speak of taboos against contacting persons with certain skin diseases. Malaria and other diseases probably posed constant problems for people living near canals or near areas with poor water drainage. Eye ailments, impotence, and digestive problems are among the most frequent problems mentioned in Akkadian texts.

Marduk, Ea, and Ishtar were among the deities consulted for illness. Recent excavations at Isin and Nippur have renewed attention on the importance of Gula (Ninisina), a healing goddess associated with dogs (see figure 1). Dogs probably had a role in Gula's therapeutic rituals, and a dog cemetery, dated to about 1000 BCE, is associated with her temple at Isin. Although no known Mesopotamian temple functions as a large sanitorium, various temples (e.g., the temple of Gula at Isin in various periods) may have stored medical information, and priests may have performed therapeutic and diagnostic rituals in them.

Many Assyriologists have followed Edith K. Ritter (1965) in positing two main healing specialists in Mesopotamia, the *āšipu* and the *asû* (see figure 2). In this scheme, the former uses magical means while the latter does not. An alternative

MEDICINE. Figure 1. *Figurine from Isin of a patient and dog.* This may depict a ritual mentioned in texts in which a dog, associated with Gula, is touched by the patient for medicinal purposes. (Courtesy H. Avalos)

MEDICINE. Figure 2. *A panel of an Assyrian bronze plaquette, probably showing a healing ritual.* Note the figure on the couch and healers, perhaps *asipus* dressed in fish-garb, attending to him. (Musée du Louvre/Antiquités Orientales)

view argues that both professions operated within a framework that assumed magical causation. The distinction was rooted in the simple distribution of labor in the healthcare system—namely, the *asû* specialized in the direct application of herbs and bandages and the *āšipu* in contacting and appeasing the divine beings deemed responsible for the illness.

Intensive therapeutic labor resulted, in part, from polytheism itself. For example, a single illness might require the assembly of paraphernalia, plants, and incantation texts for each of the numerous supernatural beings that might be entreated or repelled. Complex therapeutic rituals could even leave kings waiting days without the desired treatment. Diagnostic manuals may have helped to set labor priorities by identifying patients who were expected to die regardless of therapy.

Patients chose consultants on the basis of availability, economics, and a host of other factors. Kings could affect the distribution of physicians by monopolizing their services or sending them to other lands. Kings and town officials could also help to manage the distribution of materia medica.

Some Mesopotamian laws reveal the state's efforts to set prices for medical services and malpractice (e.g., laws 215–221 of the Code of Hammurabi). Extant laws and contracts also show that the state attempted to place the responsibility for long-term healthcare on the families of the afflicted. In fact, care at home was prevalent throughout the history of Mesopotamia.

Persia. The healthcare systems in ancient Iran, especially in the Achaemenid period (550–332 BCE), are among the most difficult to reconstruct. Excavations of Persian palaces and houses in Persepolis, Susa, Pasargadae, and elsewhere indicate that Persians probably encountered the same urban health problems found elsewhere in the Near East.

Because Old Persian texts are few, the usual sources for the study of Persian medicine include Greek authors and the Videvdad, a Zoroastrian sacred text whose composition is dated by some scholars to within the Arsacid period (224 BCE–224 CE).

Zoroastrianism is a monolatrous religion popularized during the Achaemenid, Parthian/Arsacid, and Sasanian (224–652 CE) periods in Iran. In general, Zoroastrianism ascribed good and evil to two primordial principles: Angra-Mainyu, the principle of evil, is credited with creating thousands of diseases, while Ahuramazda is credited with creating healing substances, including *homa* ("wine").

The Videvdad outlines elaborate codes of purity that viewed physiological processes such as birth, menstruation, and death as generators of impurity that could be transmitted by touch. This theology apparently led to the use of elaborate rituals to purify those afflicted by illness. Various diseases, including chronic skin ailments, rendered the patient an outcast in society.

The Videvdad mentions at least three types of healing specialists (herbalists, surgeons, and incantation priests).

The same work notes procedures meant to certify physicians and outlines fees for various medical services. The medical school founded in the Sasanian period at Gundaishapur (Iran) foreshadowed Islamic hospitals and medical schools.

It is difficult to judge the extent to which Zoroastrian monolatry and purity laws were applied in the Achaemenid period. An Old Persian text does indicate that Xerxes I (485–465 BCE) destroyed the temples of "false gods," a policy that presumably would restrict the options for patients if such gods were healing deities. Yet, Greek reports indicate that Achaemenid kings valued or preferred Greek and Egyptian physicians. Interest in public health reportedly prompted Darius (522–486 BCE) to subsidize the medical professions in Egypt and elsewhere.

Some scholars argue that it was only in the Sasanian period that Zoroastrianism became a state religion. If so, it is only speculation that the state encouraged the removal of various types of patients from society and restricted therapeutic options, insofar as not all deities were seen as legitimate. While the persecution of Christians is attested in the Sasanian period, however, Christianity and many other religions survived and retained their healing traditions.

Syria-Palestine. The trephinated skulls found at Jericho from the Neolithic period and the implantation of a bronze wire in a tooth found at ʿEin-Ziq, a small Nabatean fortress in Israel's northern Negev desert in the Hellenistic era, attest to the long existence of specialized medical consultants in Syria-Palestine. Liver models found at LB Hazor and Megiddo may have been used in medical consultations or in hepatoscopy. The Amarna tablets (fourteenth century BCE) mention epidemics and the traffic of physicians in Canaanite royal courts.

As in most areas of the Near East, the inadequate disposal of garbage and human waste was a threat to public health in Syria-Palestine. City-states (e.g., Gibeon) in areas where rainfall was poor had to construct cisterns, which were vulnerable to contamination. By the Middle or Late Bronze Ages, parts of various cities (Jericho, Tell Beit Mirsim) apparently had drains, some of which may have carried sewage. Recent excavations in Jerusalem have recovered toilet seats, one of which was found in a separate cubicle in a house dated to about 586 BCE. However, it is not certain how widespread such amenities were in the city at the time.

Although there are many textual references to washing and related hygienic activities (*Gn.* 18:4; *Ps.* 60:8), it is likely that personal hygiene was generally poor in the absence of abundant water supplies. In the Bible, bathing was sometimes seen as a significant event (*Ru.* 3:3).

As in many areas of the ancient Near East, insect infestation was probably a significant problem in Syria-Palestine. Incense may have been useful in repelling some insects, and ivory and wooden combs found at various sites from various periods (e.g., at LB Megiddo) may have effectively removed lice. Shaving the body and covering it with oil also may have combatted lice and other ectoparasites. [*See* Incense.]

Archaeoparasitologists recently established the likely existence of certain intestinal diseases (e.g., tapeworm and whipworm infections) in ancient Israel, but the precise identification of most diseases in the Bible has been notoriously difficult, especially in cases of epidemics (*Nm.* 25; *1 Sm.* 5:6–12). Nonetheless, biblical stories recognize that epidemics can alter the course of history (e.g., the plagues on Egypt in *Ex.* 7–10), and many plagues are viewed as the result of Israel's contact with outside groups (e.g., Midianites in *Nm.* 25).

The condition usually translated as "leprosy" (Heb., *ṣāraʿat*) receives the most attention in the Bible (*Lv.* 13–14), but it does not have a simple modern equivalent because it probably encompassed a large variety of diseases, especially those manifesting chronic discoloration of the skin. Infertility was viewed as an illness that diminished the social status of the afflicted woman (*Gn.* 30:1–20).

As the Kirta epic and other Ugaritic texts indicate, El, the supreme god at Ugarit, was concerned with healing, especially infertility. In Tyre, Sidon, and other Phoenician city-states of the early first millennium BCE, Eshmun, who was sometimes identified with the Greek Asclepius, was a healing god whose temples may have provided therapeutic services. Many gods in the ancient Near East, including Yahweh and Resheph, were gods of disease and healing.

The Hebrew Bible has at least two principal explanations for illness. *Deuteronomy* 28 affirms that health (Heb., *šālōm*) encompasses a physical state associated with the fulfillment of covenantal stipulations that are fully disclosed to the members of the society. Illness stems from the violation of those stipulations, and therapy includes reviewing one's actions in light of the covenant. The *Book of Job* offers a contrasting, yet complementary, view arguing that illness may be rooted in divine plans that may not be disclosed to the patient at all—and not in the transgression of published rules. The patient must trust that God's undisclosed reasons are just.

Perhaps the most distinctive feature of the Israelite health-care system depicted in the canonical texts is the division of the patient's consultative options into legitimate and illegitimate. This dichotomy is partly the result of monolatry, insofar as illness and healing rest ultimately upon Yahweh's control (*Jb.* 5:18) and non-Yahwistic options are prohibited.

Because it was accessible and inexpensive, prayer to Yahweh was probably a patient's most common legitimate option. Petitions and thanksgiving prayers uttered from the viewpoint of the patient are attested in the Bible (*Ps.* 38; *Is.* 38:10–20). Other treatments mentioned in the Bible include "mandrakes" for infertility (*Gn.* 30:14), "bandages" (*Ez.* 30:21), and "balsam" from Gilead (*Jer.* 46:11). The last text shows awareness of the importance of Gilead in the production of medicinal substances consumed in Egypt.

Illegitimate options, which were probably widely used by Israelites, included consultants designated as *rōpĕʾîm* (*2 Chr.* 16:12), non-Yahwistic temples (*2 Kgs.* 1:2–4), and probably a large variety of "sorcerers" (*Dt.* 18:10–12). Female figurines found throughout monarchic Israel, especially in domestic contexts, may have been involved in fertility rituals. The largest known dog cemetery in the ancient world, recently uncovered at Ashkelon, may be associated with a healing cult of the Persian period. [*See* Ashkelon.]

The foremost legitimate consultants in the canonical texts are commonly designated prophets, and they were often in fierce competition with "illegitimate" consultants. Stories of healing miracles (e.g., *2 Kgs.* 4:8) may reflect an effort to promote prophets as the legitimate consultants. Their function was to provide prognoses (*2 Kgs.* 8:8) and intercede on behalf of the patient (*2 Kgs.* 5:11). Unlike some of the principal healing consultants in other Near Eastern societies, the efficacy of Israelite prophets resided more in their relationship with god than in technical expertise. The demise of the prophetic office in the early Second Temple period probably led to the wide legitimation of the *rōpĕ'îm* (cf. *Sir.* 38). Midwives (*Ex.* 1:15–21) may actually have been the most common healthcare consultants, especially for pregnant women.

Another accepted option for some illnesses, particularly in the preexilic period, was the Temple. In *1 Samuel,* Hannah visited the temple at Shiloh to help reverse her infertility. *2 Kings* 18:4 indicates that prior to Hezekiah the bronze serpent made by Moses as a therapeutic device (*Nm.* 21:6–9) was involved in acceptable therapeutic rituals in the Temple in Jerusalem. Bronze serpents have been found in temples (e.g., the *asclepieion* at Pergamon) and are known to have been used for therapy during the first millennium BCE. Bronze serpents, such as those found in or near shrines at LB Timnaʿ, Tel Mevorakh, and Hazor, may have been involved in therapeutic rituals, but other functions cannot be excluded.

The Priestly code, which may be viewed as an extensive manual on public health that centralizes in the priesthood the power to define illness and health for an entire state, severely restricted access to the Temple for the chronically ill (e.g., lepers in *Lv.* 13–14; cf. *2 Sm.* 5:8 on the blind and the lame) because of fear of "impurity."

The theology of impurity, as a system of social boundaries, could serve to remove socioeconomically burdensome populations, and especially the chronically ill, from society. "Leprosy" alone probably encompassed a wide variety of patients. In effect, the Priestly code minimizes state responsibility for the chronically ill, leaving the eradication of illness for the future (*Ez.* 47:12; cf. *Is.* 35:5–6).

Thanksgiving or "well-being" offerings (*Lv.* 7:11–36) after an illness were probably always acceptable and economically advantageous for the Temple. Offerings after an illness also may have served as public notice of the readmission of previously ostracized patients to the society (*Lv.* 14:1–32).

Relative to the Priestly code, the community responsible for the Dead Sea Scrolls added to the list of illnesses excluded from the normal community and expanded the restrictions for "leprosy," the blind, and the lame (1QSa II.4–9). Socioeconomic reasons, as well as the fear of magical contamination, may be responsible for such increased restrictions.

Perhaps the most significant consequence of the Priestly code was the growth of chronically ill populations with little access to the Temple. Because Jesus and his disciples appear to target these populations (*Mt.* 10:8; *Mk.* 14:3), early Christianity may be seen, in part, as a critique of the priestly healthcare system. In early Christianity illness may be caused by numerous demonic entities who are not always acting at Yahweh's command (*Mt.* 15:22; *Lk.* 11:14), and not necessarily by the violation of covenant stipulations (*Jn.* 9:2). Emphasizing that the cure for illness may be found in this world, early Christianity preserved many older Hebrew traditions regarding miraculous healings (*Acts* 5:16, 9:34) and collective health (*Jas.* 5:16), although the influence of Hellenistic healing cults (e.g., the Asclepius cult) also may be seen.

In the Roman Empire, famous therapeutic baths were constructed or enlarged. Near the Sea of Galilee, the large thermal bath complex that thrived from the second century to the end of the first millennium CE at Ḥammath-Gader is explicitly associated in inscriptions with therapy and may have been used by Romans, Christians, Jews, and Muslims. [*See* Ḥammath-Gader.] A mass grave near the Jordan River apparently contains the remains of sick visitors in search of healing (c. 614 CE) in the famous waters (see *2 Kgs.* 5). Ritual bath installations called *miqva'ot* (sg., *miqveh*), dating from the Second Commonwealth onward, have been uncovered in many Jewish communities (e.g., the Jewish Quarter in Jerusalem, Masada), but they probably were not used for ordinary therapeutic reasons. [*See* Ritual Baths.]

In the Byzantine period, and especially under the empress Eudocia (d. 460), various leprosaria were founded in the Judean Desert (e.g., at the Monastery of Theodosius). These leprosaria may reflect the state's attempt to channel populations of chronically ill patients to peripheral areas of the empire rather than simply to the outskirts or to special areas of major cities. In sum, prior to the rise of Islam, Syria-Palestine and most of the Near East already had a wide array of healthcare systems and facilities deriving from Greek, Roman, Jewish, Christian, Persian, and Arab traditions.

Islamic Period. Because Islam encompassed most of the geographic areas under discussion, the Islamic period merits a unified treatment. Between the ninth and fourteenth centuries CE, many of the most important works in medicine by Jews, Christians, Zoroastrians, and Muslims were written in Arabic, a language spread by Islam. Arabic medical texts are abundant, so that archaeology is not the primary source of information about healthcare in Islamic countries.

Little is known of the healthcare systems of the pre-Islamic cultures (e.g., Midianites, Nabateans) associated with the northwestern Arabian Peninsula, the homeland of Islam. It is possible to speculate that some diseases (e.g., malaria)

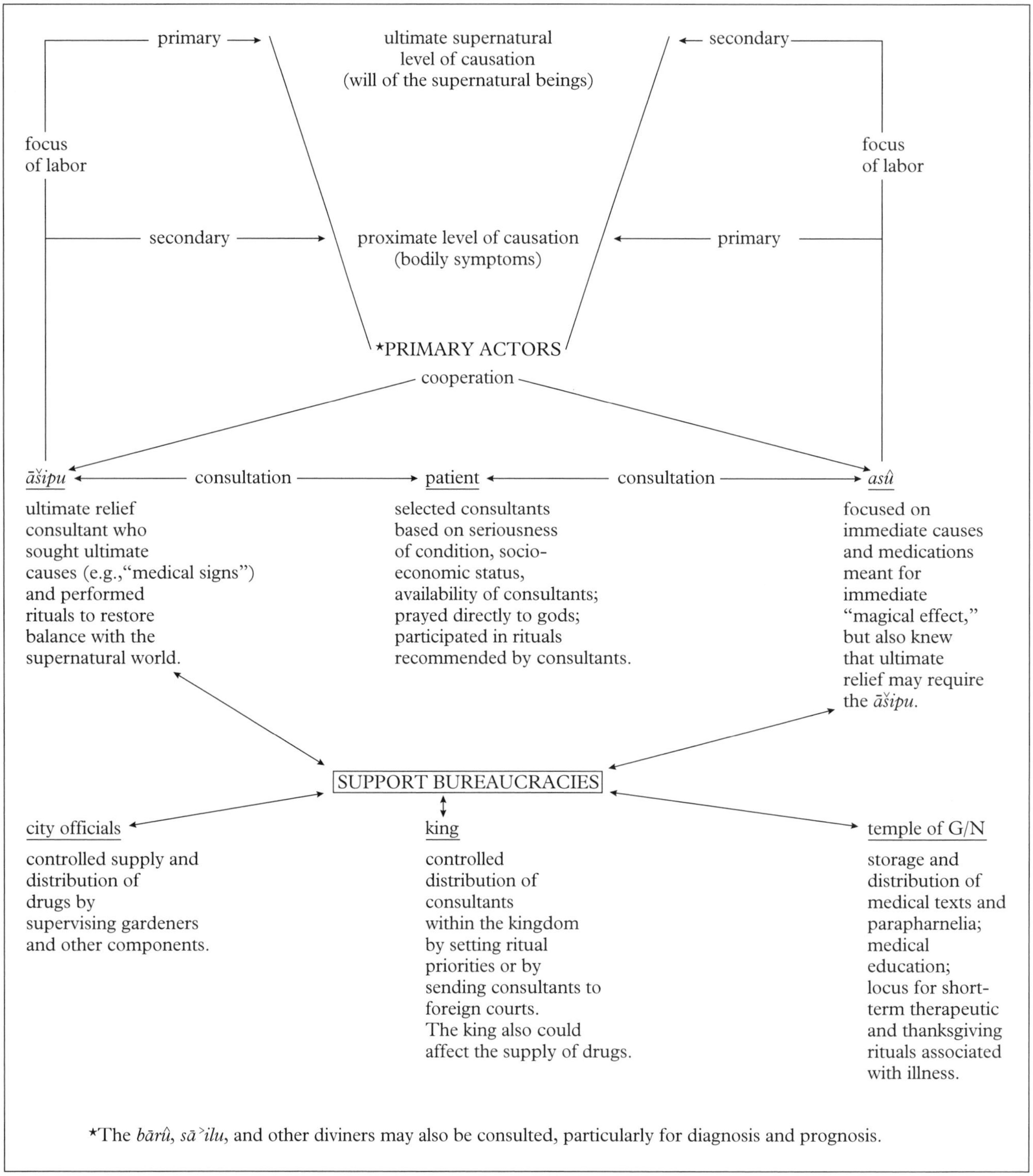

MEDICINE. Figure 3. *Synopsis of the Mesopotamian health care system.* (Courtesy H. Avalos)

were insignificant in arid regions. Analogies with healing practices elsewhere in the Near East probably existed (e.g., prayer; the use of special consultants). Jews and Christians lived in northwestern Arabia at the time of Islam's rise in the seventh century and presumably had their own healing traditions.

Some scholars argue that Islamic medicine was essentially Greek medicine. Others argue that while the Greek traditions are obvious, Islam synthesized various traditions and made new contributions. The famed Ibn Khaldun (1332–1406), in his *Muqaddimah,* acknowledges that Islam inherited a body of nonrevealed medical tradition from the bedouins, Sasanians, and other sources.

Under the word *salām,* the Qur'an speaks of the broad well-being of a person. Sickness encompassed the whole organism rather than just the soul or the body. Greek influence, however, helped to maintain the soul/body dualism in many Islamic traditions. Thus, Ibn Sina (980–1037), whose *Canon* was, for hundreds of years in the West and the East, one of the most authoritative medical textbooks, thought that the mind could heal or sicken the body.

As a monotheistic religion, Islam resulted in a dichotomous healthcare system insofar as patients could not use options sponsored by gods other than Allah. Although natural causes for illness seem to be recognized, ultimately illness and health are created by Allah's will and purposes. Prevention of illness was an essential component of Islamic medical practice, and a proper diet, which excluded pork, was seen as perhaps the most essential factor in maintaining good health.

The major traditions of Islam (e.g., Sunni, Shiʿah) developed some distinctive notions of treatment. For example, some scholars argue that Sunni tradition encourages patients to seek treatment at any time, whereas Shiʿi tradition encourages them to seek treatment only if the illness becomes unbearable. While major traditions prohibit the use of alcohol, other traditions (e.g., the Hanafi school) prohibit only intoxication.

Various Muslim states encouraged heavy investment in public health. For example, a rare, if not unprecedented, healthcare policy was promulgated in Iraq by Walid I (705–715), who reportedly provided stipends and attendants for lepers. In the early tenth century in Iraq special teams were established to visit prisons, and mobile dispensaries brought healthcare to the countryside, where doctors were scarce. The management of lepers during the Umayyad caliphate (755–1031) in Córdoba (Spain) included their segregation in "the suburb of the sick" (Ar., *Rabaḍ al-marḍā*). Endowments (Ar., *waqf*), often by wealthy individuals, for hospitals were generally encouraged.

The most famous general hospitals emerged during the ʿAbbasid caliphate (750–1257), especially in Baghdad, Mecca, and Damascus. There were also some hospitals for mental patients. The administrators and medical personnel of the first hospitals were often Nestorian Christians, who translated medical texts from Greek into Arabic (sometimes via Syriac). The principal doctors, who were also teachers, reportedly made rounds within the hospital and visited the court daily. The hospital founded in the twelfth century in Damascus reportedly kept detailed patient records. It also had protocols to separate patients who would be admitted from those who would be sent home after receiving treatment. In general, the Islamic period presents perhaps the best documented examples of how monotheistic societies integrated a variety of approaches to healthcare.

Synthesis. The advance of "civilization," and of urbanization in particular, posed new challenges to human health. Challenges included managing chronically ill populations, determining the level of state investment in public health, and maintaining a supply of consultants and medications, especially for the elite. Ancient governments recognized that epidemics could hasten the demise of an entire city or empire. The parallel and overlapping healthcare systems in the Near East provided a variety of responses to these challenges. In fact, many of the basic problems and responses pertaining to healthcare (e.g., level of state investment, regulation of medical fees) were first articulated in the ancient Near East.

Many aspects of a healthcare system are related to a culture's basic religious framework. Polytheistic systems (e.g., in Mesopotamia, Anatolia, and Egypt) allowed a broader range of alternatives for patients than monolatrous ones (see figure 3). Yet, the large number of gods that could be appeased or repelled could also lead to complex rituals that denied speedy attention even for the elite.

The development or imposition of monolatry tended to bifurcate a healthcare system into legitimate and illegitimate options. Although monolatrous systems (e.g., in Israel and Islam) could simplify the search for a healing deity, other factors could render the therapeutic process as variegated and complex as in polytheism (see figure 4).

Most healthcare systems had a variety of options that were probably arranged hierarchically, depending, in part, on the patient's needs and means. Prayer was probably one of the first, and most economical, options chosen by patients in all systems. Care at home was probably the preferred and most common option, even in cultures that centralized and localized healthcare to some extent (e.g., *asclepieia;* Islamic hospitals).

It is difficult to evaluate one healthcare system as better than another because precise data are lacking with which to measure their effectiveness. Some institutions meant to cure may actually have spread diseases by concentrating sick people in small spaces (e.g., *asclepieia*). The best medical technology (e.g., scalpels, forceps, dental drills, and splints) may have helped only simple problems (e.g., extraction of lodged weapons). In general, in most cultures, trauma (from accidents, strife), malnutrition, and disease maintained life

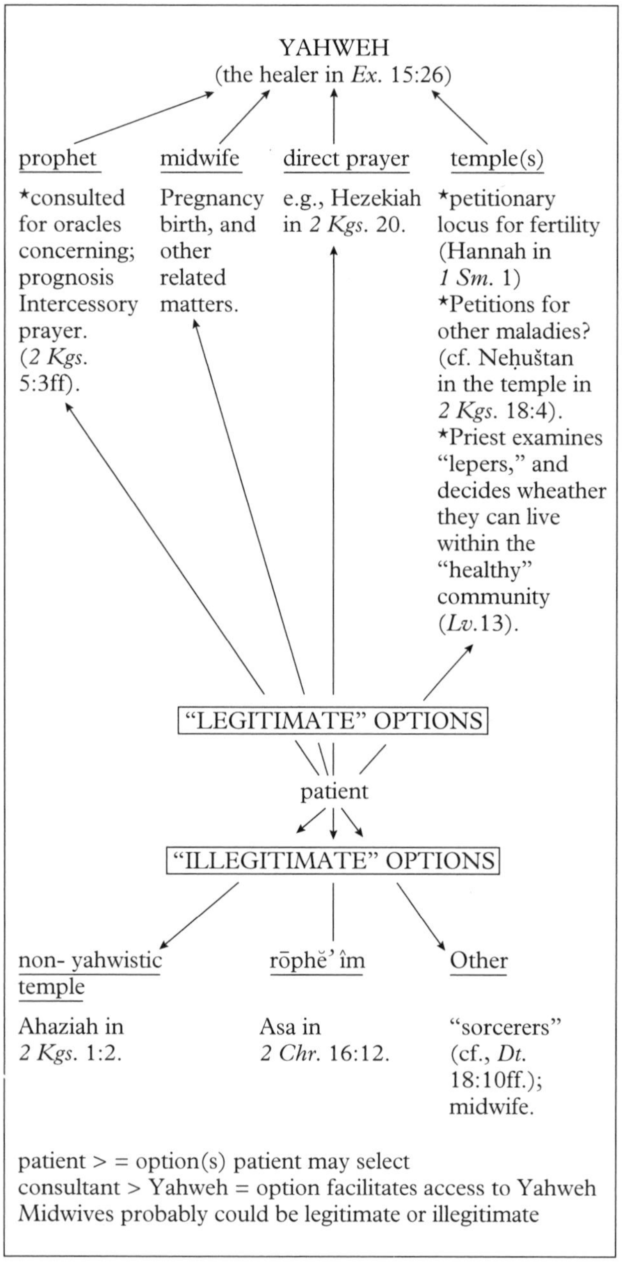

MEDICINE. Figure 4. *System of consultation options reported in the biblical texts.* (Courtesy H. Avalos)

expectancy to under forty years from the Paleolithic to the Early Islamic period.

Much of the information preserved in archaeological and textual sources pertains to the urban and literate segments of Near Eastern cultures; however, as is the case in many modern nonwestern cultures, the majority of patients lived outside of cities and had as healing consultants midwives and other types of folk healers who were illiterate—and thus did not document their practices.

Nonetheless, archaeology still has much to contribute to what can be known of ancient and modern healthcare. More importantly, by focusing on healthcare as a system that interacts with theology, politics, economics, and the environment, new questions can be posed about the textual and archaeological data already available.

[*See also* Paleopathology; Personal Hygiene. *In addition to the sites cross-referenced above, many others mentioned are also the subject of independent entries.*]

BIBLIOGRAPHY

Angel, J. Lawrence. "Ecology and Population in the Eastern Mediterranean." *World Archaeology* 4 (1972): 88–105. A paleopathologist discusses the general incidence of disease in the eastern Mediterranean.

Avalos, Hector I. *Illness and Health Care in the Ancient Near East: The Role of the Temple in Greece, Mesopotamia, and Israel.* Atlanta, 1995. The comprehensive study of healthcare systems in the relevant areas from a medical anthropological perspective also includes a short history of the study of medicine in the Near East.

Beckman, G. "Medizin. B. Bei den Hethitern." In *Reallexikon der Assyriologie,* vol. 7, pp. 629–631. Berlin, 1990. Survey in English of Hittite medicine.

Biggs, Robert D. "Medizin. A. In Mesopotamien." In *Reallexikon der Assyriologie,* vol. 7, pp. 623–629. Berlin, 1990. Survey in English of Mesopotamian medicine.

Bolger, Diane. "The Archaeology of Fertility and Birth: A Ritual Deposit from Chalcolithic Cyprus." *Journal of Anthropological Research* 48.2 (1992): 145–164.

Boyce, Mary. *Zoroastrians: Their Religious Beliefs and Practices.* 2d ed. London, 1986. Includes a discussion of medical practices.

Chosky, Jamsheed K. *Purity and Pollution in Zoroastrianism: A Triumph over Evil.* Austin, 1989.

Cohen, Mark Nathan, and George J. Armelagos, eds. *Paleopathology of the Origins of Agriculture.* New York, 1984. Anthology of essays discussing health in prehistoric cultures around the world, including various areas of the Near East.

Cohen, Mark Nathan. *Health and the Rise of Civilization.* New Haven, 1989. Survey of the impact of cultural evolution on human health.

Elgood, Cyril. *A Medical History of Persia and the Eastern Caliphate from the Earliest Times until the Year A.D. 1932.* Cambridge, 1951. Dated but useful summary.

Ghalioungui, Paul, and Zeinab El-Dawakhly. *Health and Healing in Ancient Egypt.* Cairo, 1965.

Grmek, Mirko. *Diseases in the Ancient Greek World.* Baltimore, 1989. One of the most comprehensive surveys on the topic.

Kleinman, Arthur. *Patients and Healers in the Context of Culture: An Exploration of the Borderland between Anthropology, Medicine, and Psychiatry.* Berkeley, 1980. Indispensable introduction to the study of healthcare as a system.

Majno, Guido. *The Healing Hand: Man and Wound in the Ancient World.* Cambridge, 1975. Richly illustrated discussion of medicine in Egypt, Mesopotamia, and Greece.

Martinez, R. M. "Epidemic Disease, Ecology, and Culture in the Ancient Near East." In *The Bible in Light of Cuneiform Literature,* edited by William Hallo et al., pp. 413–457. New York, 1990. This concise discussion of epidemics in Mesopotamia and elsewhere in the Near East includes extracts of Mesopotamian sources translated into English.

McNeill, William H. *Plagues and Peoples.* Garden City, N.Y., 1976.

Study of how diseases may have influenced the course of history in the ancient Near East and elsewhere.
Preuss, Julius. *Biblical and Talmudic Medicine* (1911). Translated by Fred Rosner. New York, 1978. Dated but important survey of Jewish medical practices, especially in the first half of the first millennium CE.
Rahman, Fazlur. *Health and Medicine in the Islamic Tradition.* New York, 1987. Excellent and concise summary by one of the world's leading scholars on Islam.
Ritter, Edith K. "Magical Expert (= *Āšipu*) and Physician (= *Asû*): Notes on Two Complementary Professions in Babylonian Medicine." In *Studies in Honor of Benno Landsberger on His Seventh-Fifth Birthday, April 21, 1965,* edited by Hans G. Güterbock and Thorkild Jacobsen, pp. 299–321. Chicago, 1965.
Seybold, Klaus, and Ulrich B. Mueller. *Sickness and Healing.* Translated by Douglas W. Stott. Nashville, 1981. Survey on the topic in the Bible.
Sigerist, Henry E. *A History of Medicine.* New York, 1961. Despite its date, still one of the most comprehensive and readable treatments of ancient medicine, especially in Egypt, Mesopotamia, Persia, and Greece.
Smith, Patricia M. "The Skeletal Biology and Paleopathology of Early Bronze Age Populations in the Levant." In *L'urbanisation de la Palestine à l'âge du Bronze ancien: Bilan et perspectives des recherches actuelles; Actes du Colloque d'Emmaüs, 20–24 octobre 1986,* vol. 1, edited by Pierre de Miroschedji, pp. 297–313. British Archaeological Reports, International Series, no. 527. Oxford, 1989.
Zias, Joseph. "Death and Disease in Ancient Israel." *Biblical Archaeologist* 54.3 (1991): 146–159. Survey from the prehistoric periods through the Byzantine era, with numerous bibliographic references.

HECTOR IGNACIO AVALOS

MEDINA (al-Madinah), city located in the Hijaz region of Saudi Arabia (24°28′ N, 39°36′ E), lying about 350 km (217 mi.) north of Mecca (Makkah) and about 425 km (263.5 mi.) from Jeddah.

Before Islam, Medina was known as Yathrib and was famous for its oasis on the trade routes from southern and northern Arabia and its commercial contacts with important trading centers. Around it are mountains and it is famous for its numerous wadis or water coarses across the oasis. According to Arabic sources, it was known by ninety-five names. Apart from Yathrib, the following were the most popular: Ṭaiba, Manzil al-Waḥyi, and ʿUsh al-Fuqaha'. The prophet Muhammad named the city Ṭaiba and Medina.

The settlement is spread out in four main areas—Al-ʿAwali, Quba, al-ʿUṣba, and ancient Yathrib. At the time of the prophet Muhammad's Hijrah (pilgrimage) in 622 CE, it was divided into nine independent quarters, which were described as neighboring states like villages. After the Hijrah the quarters expanded, linked to each other. Thus the city of Medina evolved, acquiring political and socioeconomic importance as the capital of the first Islamic city-state.

For this new city-state, Muhammad provided all amenities for the welfare of the people. New commercial specialized markets for different commodities were established. These centers included markets for livestock, grain, fruit, oil, vegetables, meat, perfume, cloth, and second-hand items. There were also auction places. Mosques (including the Prophet's Mosque), residential houses, forts, and rest-houses were constructed. This building activity continued in all directions, involving every aspect of life during the times of the caliphs. It reached its zenith during the Umayyad and ʿAbbasid periods, when palatial palaces were built in Medina.

After the assassination of Caliph ʿUthman, ʿAli succeeded him, and to counter the political moves of the opposition he shifted the capital in 651 from Medina to Kufah. Subsequently, the caliph Muʿawiyah made Damascus the capital in 661. Thus Medina lost all its splendor, retaining, however, its importance as a religious and cultural center as well as commercial hub for the trade coming from Yemen, Iraq, Syria, and Egypt.

The city was protected by the erection of a defensive wall, with seven entrances in 876, which was later rebuilt. Under the Ottomans the wall was raised to a height of 25 m (82 ft.). It had forty towers overlooking the outskirts of the city. However, to facilitate the free movement of traffic the wall was demolished in 1948.

During the Hijrah to Medina, the Prophet built the first mosque at Qubba, south of the city. After entering the city, a suitable larger site near al-Bakiʿ was selected and the Prophet's mosque was built.

MEDINA. *The Qalʿat Quba.* (Courtesy S. al-Rashid)

Since the Prophet's time, his mosque has been expanded from time to time to meet the growing needs of the ever-increasing number of visitors. Consequently the residential and commercial areas in the vicinity of the mosque were absorbed into its complex.

The number of mosques in Medina multiplied; forty were built during the Prophet's lifetime. Some of the mosques that were built by ʿUmar ibn ʿAbdul ʿAziz, ruler of Medina during the time of Caliph al-Walid ibn ʿAbdul Malik, (AH 86–96/705–715 CE) on spots in which the Prophet prayed survive to this day.

Despite the expansion and rebuilding of the ancient mosques, their distinctive characteristic features have been preserved. The Ottoman additions to the Prophet's mosque are outstanding in their architecture, porcelain arabesque decoration, and Qur'anic inscriptions. One of the most outstanding features surviving is the *miḥrab* (niche) erected by Mehrab al-Suleimany in 948/1541. One of the oldest inscriptions on the wall of the inner *miḥrab* of the Prophet's mosque is dated to 888/1483 in the reign of Sultan Gaitabi. It consists of five sentences written in Mamluk Thuluth script.

Medina was famous for numerous splendid Umayyad and Ottoman palaces, which are located near the Wadi al-ʿAqiq. Literary sources mention that there were seventy palaces built of stones and bricks. They were spacious and had high walls. Some of the surviving palaces belonged to the following rulers: Hisham ibn ʿAbdul Malik, ʿUrwa ibn Zubair, 'Asim ibn ʿUmar, Saʿid ibn al-ʿAṣ, and al-Marajel. Portions of these palaces are in private collections. ʿAbdul Quddas al-Anṣary has described the two-story palace of Saʿid ibn al-ʿAṣ as magnificent. Its architectural features resembled the classic Islamic style of Umayyad palaces in Syria, especially the Geran palace of Damascus.

Medina is famous for its many forts. During the Prophet's time they numbered 199. Of these, 127 belonged to Medinite Anṣars (helpers); 11 to the Mahajirs (immigrants from Mecca); and 159 to other tribes of Medina. Remains of many forts survive in good condition. One such example is the fort of Ka'b ibn al-Ashraf in the southeastern part of the city.

Numerous Arabic rock inscriptions, primarily graffiti, are found in and around Medina (al-Rashid, 1993). Some of these texts reveal the urban life and settlement of the people during the early Islamic periods. The most ancient inscription is found on Jabal Sal, northwest of the Prophet's mosque. Inscriptions of the early Umayyad period are located in the vicinity of the palaces. At Ruwawa about 50 km (31 mi.) south of the Prophet's mosque, fifty-five inscriptions have been discovered (al-Rashid, 1993). They are dated to first three centuries of the Hijrah and furnish family details about Caliph ʿUmar and others. Five are dated to the Umayyad period and four to the ʿAbbasid period.

[*See also* Inscriptions, *article on* Inscriptions of the Islamic Period; *and* Mecca.]

BIBLIOGRAPHY

ʿAbbāsī, Aḥmad ibn ʿAbd al-Ḥamīd al-. *Kitāb ʿUmdat al-akhbār fī Madīnat al-Mukhtār.* Edited by Muḥammad al-Ṭayyib al-Anṣāri. N.p., 198–.

ʿAlī, Jawād. *Al-mufaṣṣal fī tārīkh al-ʿArab Qabla al-Islām.* 10 vols. Beirut, 1968–1973.

ʿAlī, Ṣāliḥ Aḥmad al-. *Al-Ḥijāz fī ṣadr al-Islām.* Beirut, 1990.

Amahzoon, Muhamad. *Al-Madīnah al-Munawwarah fī Riḥlat al-ʿAyāshi, Dirāsāh wa-Taḥqīq.* Kuwait, 1988.

Anṣārī, ʿAbd al-Quddūs. *ʿĀthār al-Madīnah al-Munawwarah.* Medina, 1935.

ʿAyyāshī, Ibrāhīm ibn ʿAlī al-. *Al-Madīnah bayna al-māḍī wa-al-ḥaḍir.* Medina, 1972.

Batanūnī, Muḥammad Labīb al-. *Rīḥlah al-Ḥijāzīyah.* Cairo, 1911.

Burton, Richard F. *Personal Narrative of a Pilgrimage to al-Madinah and Meccah.* 2 vols. New York, 1964.

Ḥāfiẓ, ʿAlī. *Fuṣūl min tārīkh al-Madīnah al-Munawwarah.* Jeddah, 1984.

Ḥamdān, ʿĀṣim Ḥamdān ʿAlī. *Ḥārat al-Aghawāt.* Jeddah, 1992.

Ḥarbī, Ibrāhīm al-. *Kitāb al-manāsik wa-amākin ṭuruq al-ḥājj wa-maʿālim al-Jazīrah.* Edited by Ḥamad al-Jāsir. Riyadh, 1969.

Ibn Idrīs, ʿAbd Allāh ibn ʿAbd al-ʿAzīz. *Mujtamaʿ al-Madīnah fī ʿahd al-Rasūl.* Riyadh, 1982.

Khiyārī, Aḥmad Yāsīn Aḥmad al-. *Tārīkh maʿālim al-Madīnah al-Munawwarah Qadīman wa-ḥadīthan.* Edited by ʿUbayd Allāh Muḥammad Amīn Kurdī. N.p., 1990.

Al-Manhal 54 (1992). Special issue: "Al-Madīnah al-Munawwarah."

Marāghī, Abū Bakr ibn al-Ḥusayn al-. *Taḥqīq al-nuṣrah bi-talkhīṣ maʿālim Dār al-hijrah.* Edited by Muḥammad ʿAbd al-Jawād al-Aṣmaʿī. Medina, 1955.

Muṣṭafā, Ṣāliḥ Lamʿī. *Al-Madīnah al-Munawwarah: Taṭawūruhā al-ʿumrānī wa-turāthuhā al-miʿmārī.* Beirut, 1981.

Rashid, Saʿad al-. *Kitābāt Islamīyah Ghayr Manshūrah min "Ruwawah" al-Madīnah al-Munawwarah.* Riyadh, 1993.

Rifaʿt, Ibrāhīm. *Mirʾāt al-Ḥaramayn.* 2 vols. Cairo, 1925.

Sayyid, ʿUbayd Madani al-. "Oṭoom al-Madīnah al-Munawwarah." *Bulletin of the Faculty of Arts, University of Riyadh* 3 (1973–1974): 226–213.

Shāmi, Muḥammad ibn Yūsuf al-. *Faḍāʾil al-Madīnah al-Munawwarah.* Edited by Muḥyi al-Dīn Mattu. Beirut and Damascus, 1990.

Winder, R. Bayly. "Al-Madīna." In *Encyclopaedia of Islam,* new ed., vol. 5, pp. 994–1007. Leiden, 1960–.

Zailaʿī, Aḥmad ʿUmar al-. "Naqsh ta'sisi min Ḥārat al-Aghawāt bil-Madīnah al-Munawwarah Mu'rrakh sanat 706 H./1306–1307 A.D." *Dirāsāt fī al-ʿAthār* (1992): 271–303.

SAʿAD ABDUL AZIZ AL-RASHID

MEGIDDO (Ar., Tell el-Mutesellim; "the tell of the governor"), site located on the western side of the Jezreel Valley (Plain of Esdraelon), not far from the point where the brook of Naḥal Iron (Wadi Ara) crosses Mt. Carmel and enters the Jezreel Valley. In antiquity the main highway (Via Maris) from Egypt to Syria passed the narrow Naḥal Iron, militarily the best point for controlling the road, giving Megiddo special strategic importance. Megiddo is mentioned in the *Book of Revelation* (16:16) as Armageddon (probably Har Megiddo, "the Mount of Megiddo"), where the final battle between the people of God and the gentile armies will take place at the end of days.

Excavations. The first excavations at Megiddo were carried out between 1903 and 1905 by Gottlieb Schumacher (1908), an architect from Haifa, on behalf of the Deutscher Palästina-Verein. An analysis of the finds was later published by Carl Watzinger (1929). In 1925 the Oriental Institute of the University of Chicago began large-scale excavations, aimed at completely excavating the mound by horizontally digging one city level after the other. The program was too ambitious, and they subsequently excavated only parts of the site. The project ended with the onset of World War II in 1939. No attempt was made to correlate the work with the German finds or with Schumacher's crucial architectural data. Clarence S. Fisher (1929) directed the excavations from 1925 to 1927. He concentrated the work on the eastern side of the summit, further uncovering Schumacher's *Tempelburg*, a monumental Iron Age structure. From 1927 to 1934, P. L. O. Guy (1931) cleared more of the area to the east of the site, uncovering remains of early periods (Engberg and Shipton, 1934) and many tombs (Guy, 1938). He excavated the first-millennium BCE levels across the summit, including the city gate, palaces, and stable compounds (Lamon and Shipton, 1939) and cleared the water system (Lamon, 1935). From 1935 to 1939, Gordon Loud directed the work, concentrating on digging the lower strata in limited areas (AA–DD; Loud, 1948). A deep trench that reached bedrock was excavated in area BB at the site's eastern edge.

Between 1960 and 1972, Yigael Yadin (1970) of the Hebrew University of Jerusalem carried out soundings on the northeast and west to clarify the Iron Age stratigraphy and particularly the fortifications. In 1965 Immanuel Dunayevsky and Aharon Kempinski (1973), also of the Hebrew University, studied the stratigraphy of the cultic area in BB, and in 1974 Avraham Eitan (1974) studied, on behalf of the Hebrew University, the Iron Age remains on the eastern slope. A long-term project of systematic excavations initiated by Israel Finkelstein and David Ussishkin of Tel Aviv University and Baruch Halpern of Pennsylvania State University followed exploratory soundings in 1992 and 1993. They carried out a full-scale excavation season in 1994 on the lower terrace, on the summit near the Assyrian palaces, and in the cultic area in BB.

Early Settlement. Remains of settlement of the earlier periods were uncovered on the site in a limited area on the eastern slope, and it is unclear whether the settlement extended over the entire site or not.

Neolithic and Chalcolithic periods. The earliest settlement, on bedrock, was uncovered in area BB. Habitation remains in one cave date to the Pre-Pottery Neolithic (PPN) period (stratum–XX). Remains of stone and brick walls, floors, pits, and fireplaces cut in the surface of the rock belong to the earliest proper settlement here (stratum XX). Toothed flint sickle blades and pottery fragments of the Yarmukian culture date the settlement to the PPNB. Some remains dating to the Ghassulian culture of the Chalcolithic period were uncovered immediately above bedrock in the upper part of the slope in area BB: rock-cut pits, installations, and possibly a curving wall. The pottery contains a relatively large number of cornets and small bowls, a possible indication of cultic activity.

Early Bronze Age I. Remains of the Early Bronze Age I discerned in a surface survey northeast of the mound and on the lower terrace were uncovered in stages VII–IV in the area east of the mound (Engberg and Shipton, 1934) and in area BB (stratum XIX). The remains indicate that a huge unfortified EBI settlement existed there that extended over a large area east and northeast of the mound. The pottery is characterized by gray-burnished Esdraelon ware and grain-washed pottery. Two "curving" buildings—rectangular with a rounded end—and a number of cylinder seal impressions stamped on pottery vessels were uncovered in stage IV. [*See* Seals.]

A temple compound was excavated on the eastern slope of the mound in area BB. It was studied by Dunayevsky and Kempinski (1973) and again examined in the excavations since 1992. The temple was the first of successive sanctuaries built in this general area (the "sacred area") before the Iron Age. The shrine faced east, and a courtyard extended in front of it on the slope. The recent excavations indicated that there were two superimposed temples there, the upper one possibly dating to EB II. A stone pavement along the slope belonged to the earlier structure; some of the stone slabs are incised with figures of men, animals, and decorative patterns.

Early Bronze Age II–III. The EB II–III, are covered by strata XVIII–XV in area BB. Attempts to elucidate their stratigraphy and chronology were made by a number of scholars, in particular Kathleen M. Kenyon (1958), Dunayevsky and Kempinski (1973), and Douglas Esse (1991, pp. 67–90). A massive stone city-wall (about 4–5 m wide) was built in stratum XVIII; it marks the beginning of a smaller, but fortified, settlement. The wall's construction date is not clear; it is preserved to about 4 m in height. It turns inward at the edge of area BB, indicating that it did not surround the site. In stratum XVII it was widened to about 8 m. Kenyon (1958) suggested that it was merely a retaining wall supporting an edifice built higher on the slope.

Altar 4017, apparently the focal point of the sacred area, was built on the summit in stratum XVII and was later rebuilt. A circular, stone-built structure (8 m in diameter and 1.5 m high), it has seven steps leading to its top. An enclosure wall surrounded it, and large amounts of bones and pottery were found within it. Three temples, uniform in plan and measurements, were built near the altar in stratum XV. Each consisted of a rectangular cella entered through a porticoed porch and a side room. Two pillar bases were found in the center of each cella, and a raised altar stood against the rear wall. The temples were probably dedicated to three different deities; with the round alter they formed an impressive cultic compound. Their stratigraphy and chronology are unclear, but it seems they were constructed later than the altar, although they were in use contemporaneously. Loud assigned the temples to the Intermediate EB–MB period. It is now generally assumed that temple 4040 is earlier than the other two and that they all date to EB III. Excavations in 1994 revealed an EB III domestic layer beneath temple 4040, which needs to be factored into the dating.

Intermediate EB–MB period. During the EB–MB period, settlement continued but declined. Temple 4040 was reused: the cella was largely filled with rubble, leaving a small cultic cell in the center. A pavement with cultic vessels was found above the earlier round altar. A number of rock-cut tombs were uncovered to the southeast (Guy, 1938), many of them characterized by their plan: a vertical shaft leads into a central chamber surrounded by three smaller chambers. [*See* Tombs.] The pottery in the tombs represent wheel-made, gray vessels decorated with wavy white bands, defined by Ruth Amiran (1960) as Family C and by William G. Dever (1980) as Family NC in their classifications of the period's pottery.

Canaanite City. The beginning of the Middle Bronze Age (twentieth century BCE) marks the development of Megiddo (in stratum XIII) as an urban settlement—the center of a Canaanite city-state that existed, without interruption, until its destruction (in stratum VIIA) at the end of the Late Bronze Age (twelfth century BCE). The entire period was affected by Egyptian interests and influence, whose domination of Megiddo was a strategic prerequisite for hegemony in Canaan.

The custom then of constructing tombs within the city limits, the difficulty in clarifying the tombs' association with city levels, the site's continuous occupation, and the near absence of destruction by fire makes interpreting the stratigraphy and finds difficult. Many scholars have attempted to elucidate the stratigraphy, in particular Claire Epstein (1965), Kenyon (1969), Dunayevsky and Kempinski (1973; Kempinski, 1989), Patty Gerstenblith (1983, pp. 23–28, 114), and Rivka Gonen (1987). It seems that the settlement was extended during this period by the addition of a large area to the northwest. The lower city, demarcated by steep slopes, is clearly discernible today. In 1994 excavations were begun in the lower city (area F); whose uppermost level dates to the Late Bronze Age, indicating that the lower city was abandoned at the end of this period.

Middle Bronze Age. The MB I parallels the Middle Kingdom period in Egypt, when the twelfth dynasty renewed Egyptian interest in Syria and Canaan. The nature of the relationship between Egypt and Megiddo then is not clear. The Execration texts do not mention Megiddo (interpreted as an indication of Egyptian domination). Part of a stone statuette of Thuthotep, a contemporary high Egyptian official, was found—with two other broken statuettes—embedded in the raised platform of the stratum VIIB temple 2048. It is assumed that the statuettes stood in an earlier temple built at the spot and were broken when the temple was plundered; they may also have been buried later as an act of reverence. The historical implications of this find are similarly unclear. Some scholars assign strata XIII–XII to MB I (e.g., Kempinski, 1989), while others (e.g., Gerstenblith, 1983; Graham Davies, 1986) assign stratum XII to MB II. During MB II–III (strata XI–X), the Second Intermediate period in Egypt, Egyptian associations with Megiddo weakened, and scarabs are the main expression of Egyptian influence.

Massive fortifications characterize the MB city. At least three phases were uncovered at the north edge of the mound in area AA. In stratum XIII a city gate was uncovered with a stepped approach, narrow doorways, and an indirect passage (indicating that it was planned for pedestrians). The gatehouse and associated city wall were built of bricks on stone foundations and were supported on the outside by a glacis of limestone chips. In stratum XII the city gate must have been moved and a new wall supported by a glacis added. In stratum XI a new massive glacis was laid against the earlier fortifications, extending the mound on the north. The glacis leaned against a wall with buttresses constructed along its inner face. On the east, this wall segment ended in a tower that apparently either formed part of the city gate or flanked a monumental road leading to the upper city.

A continuation of the area AA strata XIII–XII walls was found in areas BB and CC, also of bricks on stone foundations. The unplastered brick walls were preserved to a considerable height, indicating that they were supported by a glacis and a constructional fill and were hidden from view. Schumacher uncovered remains of one or more glacis along the slope that supported massive brick walls, probably associated with the same fortification systems, in seven narrow trenches in different parts of the mound (Schumacher, 1908, pp. 23–36). Significantly, the lower city was apparently also fortified; the 1994 excavation revealed the existence of a massive city wall built of large stone blocks that probably dates to this period.

The MB royal acropolis at Megiddo was probably located at the center of the site. It included the *Nordburg*, a large building Schumacher uncovered in his main trench (1908, p. 37–66), and a building with thick stone walls uncovered in strata XI–X in area BB. Adjoining the southern side of the *Nordburg* Schumacher uncovered another building, the *Mittelburg*, which contained three unique stone-built tombs, apparently belonging to royalty or nobility. The largest was empty and hence was not considered by Schumacher to be a tomb. All the chambers are vaulted by fine stone rudimentary corbeling—an early example of this building technique.

The EB sacred area in BB continued to function. Loud (1948) uncovered buildings of strata XIII–IX around the sacred area but did not identify any contemporary building in the sacred area itself. He assigned an area with standing stone stelae (above altar 4017) to stratum XII and a series of superimposed rubble pavements to stratum IX. The new temple (no. 2048) was assigned to the Late Bronze Age. It is now generally agreed that this temple was founded in the Middle Bronze Age, in stratum X or even later. Temple 2048 has three superimposed phases. The earliest structure was preserved at foundation level only. It is a massive rectangle (21.50 × 16.50 m) containing a single hall with a niche opposite the entrance; two towers flanked the entrance. The temple is tower temple or fortress temple type and can best be compared to the contemporary temple at Shechem. [*See* Shechem.]

MB domestic buildings were uncovered in the various strata in areas AA and BB, indicating that Megiddo was densely populated then. The custom of intramural burial, inside and outside the houses, in graves and in stone-built tombs, was very common. [*See* Burial Sites; Burial Techniques.] Typical of the end of the period and of the beginning of the Late Bronze Age is bichrome ware—decorated pottery either imported from Cyprus or locally made.

Late Bronze Age. The expulsion of the Hyksos from Egypt and the campaign of Ahmose to Canaan in about 1550 BCE mark the beginning of the Late Bronze Age and the renewal of Egyptian influence in the country. It seems that Megiddo was not destroyed but was conquered in about 1479 BCE, during Thutmosis III's first Asiatic campaign. Events at Megiddo were recorded in detail in Thutmosis's monumental inscription carved on the walls of the Temple at Karnak and can be reconstructed (Davies, 1986, pp. 51–56). While the Egyptian army progressed northward along the coastal highway, the army of the Canaanite kings, led by the king of Qadesh on the Orontes River, concentrated near Megiddo. They prepared to challenge Thutmosis where the pass leading through the narrow Naḥal Iron opens to the Jezreel Valley (see above). Thutmosis III learned of his opponents' plan, but decided to follow the direct route and took the Canaanite armies by surprise. The Egyptians won the ensuing battle, and the Canaanites fled to Megiddo, which Thutmosis conquered after a seven-month siege. The battle established Egyptian domination over Megiddo. It probably continued until the end of Canaanite Megiddo, which is marked by the destruction of stratum VIIA (twelfth century BCE).

Megiddo is not mentioned in the descriptions of the campaigns of Amenhotep II (1427–1401 BCE), apparently because the city was already dominated by Egypt. One of the Taʿanach letters mentions the Egyptian commander at Megiddo. [*See* Taʿanach.] Papyrus Hermitage 1116A, dating to the reign of Amenhotep II, records presentations by Egyptian officials of grain and beer to envoys of various Canaanite cities, including Megiddo. Eight letters found in the el-Amarna archive and dating to the reigns of Amenhotep III (1391–1353 BCE) and Amenhotep IV (1353–1335 BCE) were sent from Megiddo. [*See* Amarna Tablets.] Six letters were sent by Biridiya, the ruler of Megiddo, who expressed his loyalty to the Egyptian pharaoh and discussed his struggle with Labayu, the ruler of Shechem, and the cultivation of estates in Shunem by forced labor. Egyptian domination probably continued into the thirteenth century BCE, but there is no documentation other than Papyrus Anastasi I, in which Megiddo appears as a place name in Canaan. Of particular interest is a fragmentary cuneiform tablet that includes the Epic of Gilgamesh; although found on the surface beyond the site (Goetze and Levy, 1959), it may derive from a scribal school at Megiddo.

A new royal palace was built in stratum IX on the north, probably replacing the earlier royal acropolis at the center of the settlement. Four successive palaces were excavated (area AA) in strata IX–VIIA. Particularly impressive is the stratum VIII palace. The stratum VIIA palace was decorated with wall paintings, an indication of Egyptian influence. [*See* Wall Paintings.] According to Loud (1948), the strata VIIB and VIIA palaces met with violent destruction; however, it seems possible that only the latest palace was destroyed by fire. A second palatial complex was built farther east, in area DD, but the relationship between the two is unclear.

The stratum VIIA palace included an annex—a three-chambered cellar. In its rear chamber, sealed by destruction debris, an assemblage of ivory objects and other precious items was found (Loud, 1939). The assemblage included 382 carved ivories of assorted types in the locally carved Canaanite style and imported Egyptian, Aegean, Assyrian, and Hittite examples. It is the richest assemblage of Bronze Age ivories found in the Near East.

A wide, paved roadway supported by a retaining wall led to a city gate near the palace. Built in stratum IX (or even stratum X) and used until stratum VIIA, it was a three-entry monumental gatehouse built with ashlars but without foundations. The gatehouse is not connected to a city wall and was probably erected where the stratum XI roadway or gatehouse was, incorporated in the line of the MB glacis. In 1993 the gatehouse, which the Chicago expedition had partially blocked after its excavation, was recleared, further excavated, and then restored by Israel National Parks Authority. The Chicago excavators believed that the gate had two floors, representing two phases, but the recent excavation has not verified this conclusion. Three large ovens where found on the floor, indicating that in its latest period of use it did not function as a gate.

The absence of a Late Bronze Age city wall has puzzled scholars, particularly because Thutmosis III laid a siege to the city (Gonen, 1987, pp. 97–98). It seems that the glacis of the previous period continued to function also in the Late Bronze Age. Also, houses built along the upper periphery of the mound may have formed a defense line around the city.

Temple 2048, uncovered in Area BB, which was probably founded in the Middle Bronze Age, continued to be in use. It was destroyed by fire at the end of the period. A number of valuable objects, including bronze figurines and two clay liver models, probably originate in the temple.

An ivory object bearing a cartouche of Rameses III was found in the assemblage of ivories in the stratum VIIA palace. It proves that stratum VIIA was not destroyed prior to the reign of that pharaoh (1182–1151 BCE; low chronology of Wente and Van Siclen). A statue of Rameses VI (1141–1133 BCE; low chronology), found buried in a pit in Area CC was probably placed in a temple; it indicates the continuation of Egyptian domination of Megiddo during Rameses VI's reign. The destruction of stratum VIIA probably occurred shortly afterwards, in about 1130 BCE. As it seems this destruction coincides with the end of Egyptian rule in Canaan, and the two events may well have been connected.

Strata VIB–A. Following the destruction of the Canaanite metropolis, a poor settlement was built in stratum VIB that was subsequently replaced by a larger, richer settlement in VIA. It was unfortified, but the excavators believed the later stratum VA/IVB (see below) city gate to have originated there. The buildings, mostly domestic in nature, were built of bricks on stone foundations. The sole public structure is building 2072, near the site's northern edge. Metal objects, mostly of bronze, reflecting a long tradition (probably Canaanite) of bronzework, are typical of this settlement; of particular interest are a number of bronze stands and iron blades uncovered by Schumacher (1908, pp. 84–87). The settlement was destroyed by fire.

Historical correlations. The Philistine bichrome pottery uncovered in stratum VI suggests a Philistine presence or influence. Albrecht Alt (1953), Mazar (1976), and Yadin (1970) believed stratum VIA represented the eleventh-century Canaanite-Philistine city David conquered, and Trude Dothan considers the fragments of Philistine pottery reported from that stratum to be an early indication of the Sea Peoples' presence; however, they are more likely merely stray sherds. [*See* Philistines, *article on* Early Philistines.]

The king of Megiddo is mentioned in *Joshua* 12:21 in the list of kings defeated by Joshua. *Joshua* 17:11–12 and *Judges* 1:27 record that the Canaanites continued to live in Megiddo until their later subjugation by the tribe of Manasseh (cf. *1 Chr.* 7:29). Albright (1936) believed that the expression "in Ta'anach, by the waters of Megiddo" (*Jgs.* 5:19) in the Song of Deborah refers to a time when Megiddo was not settled, assigning the poem and the events described in it to the period immediately following the destruction of the stratum VIIA city. Aharoni (1982) suggested that the Israelites destroyed the stratum and that stratum VIB was a small Israelite settlement. His view was supported by the presence of Collared-rim storage jars, usually associated with the Israelite conquest of Canaan, in stratum VIA.

Israelite City. Remains of domestic buildings of stratum VB were uncovered in various parts of the site. The stratum VB settlement was unfortified, except for one building, possibly a fort. It is usually considered to be Israelite, dating to the reign of David.

Solomonic city. Megiddo was included with Ta'anach and Beth-Shean in the fifth administrative district of Solomon (*1 Kgs.* 4:12). Apparently the district governor, Baana son of Ahilud, resided at Megiddo. [*See* Beth-Shean.] Megiddo is mentioned with Jerusalem, Hazor, and Gezer in *1*

MEGIDDO. Figure 1. *Aerial view of the southern Solomonic palace at the time of its excavation.* (Courtesy The Oriental Institute, University of Chicago)

MEGIDDO. Figure 2. *Suggested reconstruction of the stratum VA-IVB city gate.* Dated to the ninth century BCE. (Courtesy The Oriental Institute, University of Chicago)

Kings 9:15 as a central city built by Solomon and financed by levies. [*See* Jerusalem; Hazor; Gezer.] Monumental Solomonic remains were uncovered in all the excavations. Their interpretation is not easy and is, in many ways, controversial. Of special importance is Yadin's work (1970), which resulted in redating city wall 325 and "Solomon's stables" to the ninth century BCE.

Stratigraphically, the Solomonic city level includes the structures located above the stratum VB building remains and immediately beneath city wall 325 of stratum IVA and associated structures. Solomonic remains were assigned by the University of Chicago excavators to different strata: V (later VA), IVB, and IV. Albright (1943, pp. 29–30, no 10) observed that the remains of strata VA and IVB belong to a single city level (his VA/IVB), the superimposed stratum was labeled IVA. This terminology is largely used today, but some scholars label these levels VA and IV, respectively. Aharoni (1972; 1982) dated stratum VA/IVB to David's reign and IVA to Solomon's (cf. Kenyon, 1964, and Wightman, 1985).

Stratum VA/IVB includes three palaces (nos. 1723, 6000, 338) built along the upper periphery of the site on the south (see figure 1), north, and east, respectively. Situated in large courtyards, their facades face the center of the site. A large building (no. 1482), interpreted as an administrative in function, was built near the compound of the southern palace (no. 1723). Large quarters of domestic buildings were uncovered along the east and north, including a sanctuary (no. 2081) along the upper periphery on the north.

The buildings on the upper periphery formed a line of defense Yadin (1970) interpreted as a casemate city wall. The city gate, on the north, was a small, two-entry gatehouse, approached by a wide, lime-paved ramp (Loud, 1948, pp. 39–45) (see figure 2); the so-called Solomonic four-entry gatehouse is later in date and belongs to stratum IVA. In addition, a small postern (gallery 629) was built on the west, above the spring. Originally dated to the twelfth century BCE (Lamon, 1935), it was correctly assigned by Yadin (1970) to stratum VA/IVB.

Ashlar masonry was used lavishly in constructing the monumental buildings, both in their foundations and superstructure. Proto-Ionic stone capitals, mounted on pilasters and freestanding pillars, decorated their entrances. Unfortunately, the buildings were mostly destroyed when the ashlars were taken for reuse in stratum IVA. Construction with ashlars originated in Egypt and first appears in Canaan in the LB city gate and temple at Megiddo. It was introduced on a large scale during Solomon's reign. At Solomonic Megiddo, it fits the description of ashlar masonry in Solomon's palace in Jerusalem (*1 Kgs.* 7:9–12) and reflects the Phoenician influence on Solomon's building activities.

Palace 6000, uncovered by Yadin (1970, pp. 73–77), was rectangular (28 × 21 m). Most of its stones were removed following its destruction by fire. It was apparently a cere-

MEGIDDO. Figure 3. *Cult objects.* The objects were found in a cache in small sanctuary no. 2081 of stratum VA–IVB; dated to the reign of Solomon. (Courtesy The Oriental Institute, Univ. of Chicago)

monial palace built as a *bit-ḫilani* (a type of a ceremonial palace typical to North Syria in this period). It contained a porticoed entrance and a large central hall. Palace 1723 (Lamon and Shipton, 1939, pp. 11–24) was built in a spacious courtyard and entered through a monumental gatehouse (no. 1567) that was largely uncovered by Schumacher (1908, pp. 91–104). The nearly square palace (about 22 × 23 m) was mostly preserved at foundation level; hence, its aboveground plan is unknown. It seems probable that it contained both a ceremonial section built as a *bit-ḫilani* and a residential section (Ussishkin, 1966). If so, Solomonic Megiddo contained at least two *bit-ḫilani* palaces as, for instance, on the acropoli of Tell Taʿyinat and Zincirli (ancient Sam'al) in North Syria, which date to this general period. Other scholars restore only palace 6000 as a *bit-ḫilani* (Yadin, 1970; Kempinski, 1989).

Building 338, at the highest point in the city, was constructed on an aboveground foundation podium. It was first excavated by Schumacher (1908, pp. 110–124), who identified it as a sanctuary and associated it with the stratum II fortress (his *Tempelburg*). Fisher (1929, pp. 68–74) excavated it further and identified it as the Temple of Astarte; Guy (1931, pp. 30–37; Lamon and Shipton, 1939, pp. 47–59) interpreted it as the residence of the military commander of the eastern part of the city and assigned it to stratum IV (i.e., IVA). Guy's views are generally accepted today. However, while part of the building probably served a secular function, it seems that Schumacher rightly identified a shrine, characterized by two large stelae, in unit 340, in the southern part of the building (Ussishkin, 1989). Model shrines and stone altars uncovered inside and to the south of the building by Schumacher and Fisher (May, 1935) probably belong to this shrine. A wing of the building uncovered by Schumacher and later destroyed was ignored by the University of Chicago excavators; it apparently antedates city wall 325; hence, building 338 dates to stratum VA/IVB. Sanctuary 2081 contained a cache of cultic equipment (Loud, 1948, pp. 45–46) (see figure 3). Several stones carved in the shape of an eight segment of a sphere found nearby (Lamon and Shipton, 1939, pp. 24) suggest that a large horned altar erected of ashlars, similar to the Tel Beersheba altar, stood in the sanctuary's courtyard. [*See* Altars; Beersheba.]

It seems that stratum VA/IVB was destroyed by fire, but it is presently unclear when and by whom. Indications of destruction were uncovered in a number of places, primarily palace 6000, building 10, the gatehouse to the compound of palace 1723, and structures on the north.

Megiddo is mentioned in the list of cities conquered by Sheshonq I (biblical Shishak) during his campaign to Israel and Judah in about 925 BCE. Furthermore, Fisher (1929) found a fragment of a stone-carved stela erected by that pharaoh at Megiddo. It is estimated that the complete stela was about 3.30 m high and 1.50 m wide; it had stood not far from its findspot on the eastern side of the site. Albright (1943, p. 29, no 10) proposed that Solomonic Megiddo was destroyed by Sheshonq I, but it seems more likely that the pharaoh erected his stela in an existing city with the intention of holding it in the future (so that stratum VA/IVB must have been destroyed later).

Two decorated seals inscribed in Hebrew were uncovered by Schumacher in gatehouse 1567 in the palace 1723 compound: "(belonging) to Asaph" and "(belonging) to Shema, Servant of Jeroboam." They probably belonged to royal Israelite officials. Two more inscribed seals were found nearby, in Schumacher's dumps. The Shema seal is usually ascribed to the reign of Jeroboam II (784–748 BCE), but some scholars (e.g., Ussishkin, 1994) ascribe it to the period of Jeroboam I (928–907 BCE). If that is so, the compound of palace 1723, and probably all of the stratum VA/IVB city, would not have been destroyed prior to 928–907. [*See* Seals.]

Stratum IVA. The city of stratum IVA differs radically from that of VA/IVB because the role of the city changed with the Divided Monarchy. The city of stratum VA/IVB, a civilian district center characterized by palatial compounds, became a fortified stronghold in stratum IVA. Its date of construction is not clear. In view of the identification of the "stable compounds" as stable for horses (see below), many scholars date this city level to the reign of Ahab (873–852 BCE), known from Assyrian records of the battle of Karkar to have had strong cavalry and chariotry. Ahaziah, king of Judah, may have died at Megiddo in stratum IVA, fleeing before Jehu's men (*2 Kgs.* 9:27).

City wall 325 (about 3.6 m thick), stone built with insets and offsets, surrounded the city. The entrance was through a complex city gate—the so-called Solomonic gate (Loud, 1948, pp. 46–57). A roadway led to an outer gatehouse; the latter opened to an open court, and behind it was the inner, four-entry gatehouse that adjoined the city wall. The inner gatehouse rested on massive foundations built with ashlars in secondary use that were supported by a constructional fill. The foundations and ground plans of the gate complex are similar to the tenth–ninth century BCE gates at Hazor, Gezer, Ashdod, Lachish, and probably Tel Batash (ancient Timnah). [*See* Ashdod; Lachish; Batash, Tel.]

The construction date of the city gate is controversial. Stratigraphically, it adjoins city wall 325 and is contemporary with it—and thus belongs to stratum IVA. A growing number of scholars, notably Aharoni (1972), Ze'ev Herzog (1986), Ussishkin (1980), Kempinski (1989), and Finkelstein, concur. It follows that the gate complex dates to the period of the Divided Monarchy. Yadin (1958, 1970, 1980) believed that the four-entry gatehouse originated in stratum VA/IVB and was built by Solomon's architects. This dating is primarily based on the similarity in plan between this gate and the four-entry gates at Hazor and Gezer. All three were built by Solomon (*1 Kgs.* 9:15). Yadin (1970; 1980) offered a new interpretation of the stratigraphy to explain how the gatehouse antedates city wall 325 (which in fact adjoins it) this stratigraphy and dating are followed by most scholars.

A large water system was built to protect, as well as to facilitate, the approach to the spring at the bottom of the west slope (Lamon, 1935). It was originally assigned to the twelfth century BCE, but Yadin (1970) redated it. Gallery 629 (the stratum VA/IVB postern leading to the spring) and the approach to the spring from outside were then blocked. A vertical shaft was dug from the surface, its lower part hewed out of the rock, and steps were prepared along its sides. A rock-cut horizontal tunnel led from the bottom to the spring. In a later stage the horizontal tunnel was deepened, enabling the water to flow to the bottom of the shaft. [*See* Water Tunnels.]

Two "stable compounds" were uncovered (Lamon and Shipton, 1939, pp. 32–47) and identified by Guy (1931, pp. 37–48) as stables for horses—associating them with Solomon's "cities for chariots and cities for horses" (*1 Kgs.* 9:19). Several scholars (e.g., Lamon and Shipton, 1939; Yadin, 1976; Holladay, 1986; Davies, 1986) supported the identification of the structures as stables, while others (e.g., Pritchard, 1970; Herzog, 1973; Herr, 1988) argued for their different use as barracks, public storehouses, or marketplaces. This discussion assumes that they were stables for horses. The southern compound contains five stabling units. Each unit (about 21 × 11 m) contains a central lime-paved passage and two side, stone-paved aisles. Each aisle is separated from the central passage by a row of stone pillars alternating with stone mangers made of ashlars taken from the Solomonic palaces. The side aisles served as stalls for the horses, each pillar and the adjoining manger marking the position of one horse. Many pillars had holes in their corners for tethering. Each aisle could accommodate 15 horses—hence, each unit contained 30 horses and the entire complex had 150. The stables opened into a spacious, lime-paved square courtyard (about 55 × 55 m). It has been suggested (Lamon and Shipton, 1939, p. 35) that a unit of chariots was stationed in this compound and the courtyard used for its training. The northern complex contained similar stabling units, but they were not built uniformly around a large courtyard. It could hold 300–330 horses; altogether, 450–480 horses were garrisoned at Megiddo.

A large stone storage pit (no. 1414), uncovered midway between the two stable compounds, was assigned to stratum III (Lamon and Shipton, 1939, pp. 66–68). However, it probably belongs to stratum IVA, where it was the central silo for the horses' provisions (Ussishkin, 1994, pp. 424–426). The pit was at least 7 m deep; its diameter at the bottom is 7 m (for a capacity of about 450 cu m). Remains of chaff and grains were found inside. Assuming that each horse consumed about 9.6 l of food a day, the pit could have held supplies for 300–330 horses for about 130–150 days.

Stratum III. In 732 BCE, Tiglath-Pileser III annexed northern Israel to Assyria, and Megiddo became the capital of the Assyrian province Magiddu (stratum III). [*See* Assyrians.] City wall 325 continued in use, but a new city gate was constructed. Remains of one or two gatehouses superimposed above the four-entry inner gatehouse were uncovered. The upper one was a stratum III two-entry gatehouse. To the west of the city gate, two or three public buildings (nos. 1052, 1369, 1853) were uncovered that display Assyrian architectural features, in particular central, rectangular courtyards. It is clear that they were administrative or residential centers. Excavations resumed in this area in 1994 revealed a number of building stages. The buildings had not been destroyed by fire, but few finds were recovered. The absence of finds, in particular of Assyrian objects, is puzzling because the buildings were Assyrian provincial centers. Residential quarters extended over large areas of the city, with houses arranged in blocks separated by evenly spaced and parallel streets.

Strata II and I. Stratum II dates to the seventh century BCE. Its remains, uncovered across the site, include mainly domestic structures that follow the stratum III pattern. The stratum III Assyrian public buildings may have continued in use in stratum II. Remains of buildings uncovered near the site's upper periphery indicate that city wall 325 had fallen into disuse in stratum II or I sometime before the settlement ended.

A large structure (about 69 × 48 m), with a large central court, at the eastern edge of the site, was uncovered by Schumacher (1908, pp. 110–121) as part of the *Tempelburg* and by Fisher, who identified it as a stratum II fortress (Lamon and Shipton, 1939, pp. 83–86). The stone walls are about 2.5 m thick at foundation level. According to Lamon and Shipton (1939), the fortress was built above the disused city wall 325, the settlement's only fortification. (Both conclusions are doubtful.)

In 609 BCE, Pharaoh Necho reached Megiddo on his way to Carchemish to aid Assyria against Babylon. Josiah, king of Judah, met Necho at Megiddo and was executed by him (*2 Kgs.* 23:29–30; *2 Chr.* 35:20–24). Stratum I represents ordinary remains (many small houses, three long storerooms near the city gate, and a number of stone-built cist tombs) of the last settlement in the Babylonian and Persian periods. Tel Megiddo was abandoned in the fourth century BCE, possibly when Alexander the Great conquered the region in 332 BCE.

Later Periods. A Jewish village, Kefar 'Otnay, existed south of the site in about 100 CE. During Hadrian's reign (117–138 CE) the Legio II Traiana was stationed there and was later replaced by the Legio VI Ferrata. Kefar 'Otnay, renamed Legio after the occupying force, became the center of an administrative district whose name is preserved in the name of the later Arab village, Lejjun. Schumacher (1908) investigated extensive remains of the Roman and Arab periods, including aqueducts, a theater, tombs, and a possible site of a Roman camp to the south. He also uncovered some late remains, notably an Ottoman watchtower on the east.

[*See also the biographies of Aharoni, Albright, Alt, Dunayevsky, Fisher, Guy, Kenyon, Mazar, Schumacher, Watzinger, and Yadin.*]

BIBLIOGRAPHY

Aharoni, Yohanan. "The Stratification of Israelite Megiddo." *Journal of Near Eastern Studies* 31 (1972): 302–311.

Aharoni, Yohanan. *The Archaeology of the Land of Israel.* Philadelphia, 1982.

Albright, William Foxwell. "The Song of Deborah in the Light of Archaeology." *Bulletin of the American Schools of Oriental Research,* no. 62 (1936): 26–31.

Albright, William Foxwell. *The Excavation of Tell Beit Mirsim.* Vol. 3, *The Iron Age.* Annual of the American Schools of Oriental Research, 21–22. New Haven, 1943.

Alt, Albrecht. "Megiddo im Übergang vom kanaanäischen zum israelitischen Zeitalter." *Kleine Schriften zur Geschichte des Volkes Israel,* vol. 1, pp. 256–273. Munich, 1953.

Amiran, Ruth. "The Pottery of the Middle Bronze Age I in Palestine." *Israel Exploration Journal* 10 (1960): 204–225.

Davies, Graham I. *Megiddo.* Cambridge, 1986.

Dever, William G. "New Vistas on the EB IV ("MB I") Horizon in Syria-Palestine." *Bulletin of the American Schools of Oriental Research,* no. 237 (1980): 35–64.

Dunayevsky, Immanuel, and Aharon Kempinski. "The Megiddo Temples." *Zeitschrift des Deutschen Palästina-Vereins* 89 (1973): 161–187.

Eitan, Avraham. "Notes and News: Megiddo." *Israel Exploration Journal* 24 (1974): 275–276.

Engberg, Robert, and Geoffrey Shipton. *Notes on the Chalcolithic and Early Bronze Age Pottery of Megiddo.* Studies in Ancient Oriental Civilizations, no. 10. Chicago, 1934.

Epstein, Claire. "An Interpretation of the Megiddo Sacred Area during Middle Bronze II." *Israel .Exploration Journal* 15 (1965): 204–221.

Esse, Douglas. *Subsistence, Trade, and Social Change in Early Bronze Age Palestine.* Studies in Ancient Oriental Civilizations, no. 50. Chicago, 1991.

Fisher, Clarence S. *The Excavation of Armageddon.* Oriental Institute Communications, 4. Chicago, 1929.

Gerstenblith, Patty. *The Levant at the Beginning of the Middle Bronze Age.* ASOR Dissertation Series, 5. Winona Lake, Ind., 1983.

Gonen, Rivka. "Megiddo in the Late Bronze Age: Another Reassessment." *Levant* 19 (1987): 83–100.

Goetze, Albrecht, and Shalom Levy. "Fragment of the Gilgamesh Epic from Megiddo." *'Atiqot* 2 (1959): 121–128.

Guy, P. L. O. *New Light from Armageddon.* Oriental Institute Communications, 9. Chicago, 1931.

Guy, P. L. O. *Megiddo Tombs.* Oriental Institute Publications, 33. Chicago, 1938.

Herr, Larry G. "Tripartite Pillared Buildings and the Market Place in Iron Age Palestine." *Bulletin of the American Schools of Oriental Research,* no. 272 (1988): 47–67.

Herzog, Ze'ev. "The Storehouses." In *Beer-Sheba I,* edited by Yohanan Aharoni, pp. 23–30. Tel Aviv, 1973.

Herzog, Ze'ev. *Das Stadttor in Israel und in den Nachbarländern.* Mainz am Rhein, 1986.

Holladay, John S., Jr. "The Stables of Ancient Israel." In *The Archaeology of Jordan and Other Studies, Presented to Siegfried H. Horn,* edited by Lawrence T. Geraty and Larry G. Herr, pp. 103–166. Berrien Springs, Mich., 1986.

Kempinski, Aharon. *Megiddo: A City-State and Royal Centre in North Israel.* Munich, 1989.

Kenyon, Kathleen M. "Some Notes on the Early and Middle Bronze Age Strata at Megiddo" (in Hebrew). *Eretz-Israel* 5 (1958): 51–60.

Kenyon, Kathleen M. "Megiddo, Hazor, Samaria, and Chronology." *Bulletin of the Institute of Archaeology* 4 (1964): 143–155.

Kenyon, Kathleen M. "The Middle and Late Bronze Age Strata at Megiddo." *Levant* 1 (1969): 25–60.

Lamon, Robert S. *The Megiddo Water System.* Oriental Institute Publications, 32. Chicago, 1935.
Lamon, Robert S., and Geoffrey Shipton. *Megiddo I: Seasons of 1925–34, Strata I–V.* Oriental Institute Publications, 42. Chicago, 1939.
Loud, Gordon. *The Megiddo Ivories.* Oriental Institute Publications, 52. Chicago, 1939.
Loud, Gordon. *Megiddo II: Seasons of 1935–1939.* Oriental Institute Publications, 62. Chicago, 1948.
May, Herbert Gordon. *Material Remains of the Megiddo Cult.* Oriental Institute Publications, 26. Chicago, 1935.
Pritchard, James B. "The Megiddo Stables: A Reassessment." In *Near Eastern Archaeology in the Twentieth Century: Essays in Honor of Nelson Glueck,* edited by J. A. Sanders, pp. 268–276. Garden City, N.Y., 1970.
Schumacher, Gottlieb. *Tell el-Mutesellim,* vol. 1, *Fundbericht.* Leipzig, 1908.
Ussishkin, David. "King Solomon's Palace and Building 1723 in Megiddo." *Israel Exploration Journal* 16 (1966): 174–186.
Ussishkin, David. "Was the 'Solomonic' City Gate at Megiddo Built by King Solomon?" *Bulletin of the American Schools of Oriental Research,* no. 239 (1980): 1–18.
Ussishkin, David. "Schumacher's Shrine in Building 338 at Megiddo." *Israel Exploration Journal* 39 (1989): 149–172.
Ussishkin, David. "Gate 1567 at Megiddo and the Seal of Shema, Servant of Jeroboam." In *Scripture and Other Artifacts: Essays on the Bible and Archaeology in Honor of Philip J. King,* edited by M. D. Coogan, J. C. Exum, and Lawrence E. Stager, pp. 410–428. Louisville, 1994.
Watzinger, Carl. *Tell el-Mutesellim,* vol. 2, *Die Funde.* Leipzig, 1929.
Wightman, Gregory J. "Megiddo VIA–III: Associated Structures and Chronology." *Levant* 17 (1985): 117–129.
Yadin, Yigael. "Solomon's City Wall and Gate at Gezer." *Israel Exploration Journal* 8 (1958): 80–86.
Yadin, Yigael. "Megiddo of the Kings of Israel." *Biblical Archaeologist* 33 (1970): 66–96.
Yadin, Yagael. "The Megiddo Stables." In *Magnalia Dei: The Mighty Acts of God. Essays on the Bible and Archaeology in Memory of G. Ernest Wright,* edited by F. M. Cross, W. E. Lemke, and P. D. Miller, Jr., pp. 249–252. Garden City, N.Y., 1976.
Yadin, Yigael. "A Rejoinder." *Bulletin of the American Schools of Oriental Research,* no. 239 (1980): 19–23.

David Ussishkin

MEIRON, one of four major villages in Upper Galilee (Tetracomia), located just 1 km (1.6 mi.) north of the closest village, Khirbet Shema', at 750 m above sea level (33°00′ N, 35°27′ E; map reference 191 × 265). The site lies on the eastern ridge of the Meiron range (Jarmaq) and enjoys a plentiful water supply from rainwater (about 75 cm or 30 in. per year) and from the Spring of Meiron in the wadi to its south. The site is not to be confused with Merot in Josephus (*War* 2.573, 3.39), which is located just north of Safed. Rather, Meiron is to be identified with the Talmudic village associated with Simeon bar Yochai. The ruins of Meiron attracted Jewish pilgrims in medieval times, attention being focused on the traditional grave sites of sages and the ruin of the ancient synagogue. The Jewish feast of Lag B'Omer has been celebrated at the site since the thirteenth century CE.

The synagogue ruin was cleared and surveyed by Heinrich Kohl and Carl Watzinger (*Antike Synagogen in Galiläa,* Leipzig, 1916, pp. 80–88) at the beginning of the twentieth century. However, because the synagogue's western wall and floor are cut from natural rock, not much has survived except one of the southern portals (the others were restored by the Israel Department of Antiquities in the 1950s). [*See* Synagogues.] Excavations were sponsored by the American Schools of Oriental Research from 1971 to 1977, directed by Eric M. Meyers. They represent the only systematic work done at the site, which has suffered greatly from modern construction and pilgrimage during Lag B'Omer. The 1971 and 1972 seasons were conducted concurrently with the excavations at Khirbet Shema'. [*See* Shema', Khirbet.] After 1972, work at Meiron, Gush Ḥalav, and Nabratein was conducted under the framework of the Meiron Excavation Project. [*See* Gush Ḥalav; Nabratein.]

Soundings made up against the eastern closing wall of the synagogue produced limited results. Several rooms or annexes were uncovered with clear debris of the late third century CE and may be associated with the founding of the synagogue structure. Unfortunately, most of the synagogue's architectural elements had been robbed, so that the expedition was only able to alter slightly Kohl and Watzinger's plan. The building is a standard basilica with a portico with two rows of columns running north–south. [*See* Basilicas.] The facade, with three doorways on the south wall, possibly with a Torah shrine, was certainly the wall of orientation, and a gallery for extra seating can be reconstructed from existing architectural fragments. Significant medieval remains once covered the eastern end of the destroyed synagogue, but their poor state of preservation makes it impossible to identify their purpose.

The main focus of the excavation was the domestic areas located considerably downslope on the east, where preservation was better and the depth of debris considerable (2–4 m). Although pockets of Late Hellenistic and Early Roman debris were found, the major periods of occupation were the second–fourth centuries CE, with a clear floruit in the third–fourth centuries. Of special interest in the lower city was the insula, or block, known as MI. In this area a courtyard served as a major open space; it adjoined an interior space used for chores and specific trades (e.g., carpentry, as evidenced by small finds such as a bronze plane). The second story was most probably used as a sleeping space. An earlier ritual bath and cistern(s) also were discovered in this area. [*See* Ritual Baths; Cisterns.] Important details of everyday life, while ample, are difficult to reconstruct fully because of the poor state of preservation caused by extensive rock tumble.

Several houses in the next insula, MII, provided further details of domestic existence in Late Roman contexts. Of note is that a common space apparently connected two distinct units, both of which utilized the site's natural topography to full advantage. In both dwellings in this area, as in

MI, evidence was recovered of a fourth-century abandonment, especially in a sealed room whose contents were apparently purposely charred and set aside (as *hekdesh*, i.e., for the future Temple). The foodstuffs identified were wheat, barley, legumes, *fûl* beans, and walnuts. The courtyard, with an oven in the larger unit, is particularly well preserved. Soundings to the north of the settlement revealed cultivation areas and small field structures that would have been used to store supplies and for other agricultural activities.

The excavation of a tomb farther up the slope and to the west provided numerous small finds, intact pottery, and skeletal remains from the Late Hellenistic, Early Roman, and Late Roman periods. Secondary reburial of remains from *kokhim* or loculi predominate, while important evidence of endogomy was posited from the skeletal remains, suggesting family continuity over a very long period. Fairly extensive pottery remains were uncovered from the cisterns throughout the site. [*See* Burial Sites; Tombs; Burial Techniques.]

The significance of the Meiron excavations is their concentration on domestic/private rather than public buildings. The picture of everyday life revealed is consistent with life in rural, mountainous Upper Galilee. The large corpus of material culture published is one of the major building blocks available for reconstructing daily life in Roman Palestine.

BIBLIOGRAPHY

Meyers, Carol L., et al. "Excavations at Meiron in Upper Galilee, 1971, 1972: A Preliminary Report." *Bulletin of the American Schools of Oriental Research,* no. 214 (1974): 2–25.

Meyers, Eric M., et al. "Excavations at Meiron in Upper Galilee, 1974, 1975: Second Preliminary Report." *Annual of the American Schools of Oriental Research* 43 (1978): 73–98.

Meyers, Eric M., et al. "The Meiron Excavation Project: Archaeological Survey in Galilee and Golan, 1976." *Bulletin of the American Schools of Oriental Research,* no. 230 (1978): 1–24.

Meyers, Eric M., et al. *The Excavations at Ancient Meiron, Upper Galilee, Israel, 1971–1972, 1974–1975, 1977.* Cambridge, Mass., 1981. Final report on the excavations; contains plans, photos, and artifacts.

ERIC M. MEYERS

MEMPHIS, site located on the west bank of the Nile (29°51′ N, 31°15′ E) some 25 km (15 mi.) south of Cairo; one of ancient Egypt's longest-occupied settlements. According to the fifth-century BCE Greek historian Herodotus, Menes (probably best identified as King Aha, first dynasty, c. 3100 BCE), founded the initial settlement of Memphis. The city's occupation continued well after the dynastic period, although the founding first of Alexandria and then Fustat (an area in Cairo) seriously lessened its significance. Originally the town was called the "white fortress" *(jnb ḥḏ),* but during the late Old Kingdom the city acquired its most widely used name, Mennefer *(mn nfr).* The Greeks called it Menophreos, the derivation of the modern name, Memphis. Mennefer, an abbreviation for "(town of) the pyramid of Pepi Merenre," referred to the settlement housing the builders of Pepi I's pyramid at Saqqara, one of several nearby cemeteries serving the local population. Memphis acquired other names, but they generally refer to specific quarters or structures, not to the entire community. Mit Rahina is the name of the modern village nearby.

Memphis was the capital of the first Lower Egyptian nome (province), and during the Old Kingdom, it was the country's only capital. The city was a primary residence of the king and the seat of a vizier. Throughout Egyptian history, Memphis was a great center of political, economic, and religious prominence, even when the royal residence was located elsewhere. Today the archaeological remains of the city are visible only over 2.5 km (1.6 mi.) of floodplain, but ancient Memphis was certainly much larger. Cemeteries as far north as Abu Roash and south to Dahshur contained occupants who had lived in Memphis. The city encompassed civic structures such as palaces, temples, manufacturing zones, a port, and probably markets, as well as private estates with land and clusters of houses with gardens.

Several factors were responsible for Memphis's dominance over other Egyptian settlements. Its location at the apex of the Delta allowed effective control over communication between Lower and Upper Egypt as well as foreign trade. Archaeological and textual remains indicate that Memphis was a prominent religious site. A temple identified with Ptah, the creator god, is known from the first dynasty, and in later times it was the focal point of Memphis. Ptah was a deity of utmost importance, and during the reign of Shabaka (twenty-fifth dynasty, c. 770–657) a text now known as the *Memphite Theology* documents universal creation through Ptah's speech and thought. The priests associated with the Ptah temple were particularly powerful, having responsibilities that included the coronation, the Apis rites, and maintaining the country's archives, including the flood records. These duties, in conjunction with the potency of the Memphite theology, earned the Memphite priesthood a reputation for wisdom and knowledge.

Ptah was part of a triad that included his consort Sekhmet and his son Nefertum. By the end of Egyptian history, the Apis bull, an animal sacred to Ptah, was highly venerated at Memphis. Other important deities with recorded temples, shrines, or monuments at the site include Hathor, Tatenen, Neith, Amun, Sokar, Imhotep, and the foreign divinities, Baal, Reshep, Astarte, and Qudshu (Qadesh).

Flinders Petrie, working for the British School of Archaeology in Egypt between 1908 and 1913, was the first person to undertake an organized excavation of the site's archaeological remains, although the site's importance had been recognized earlier. His work focused upon the large Ptah temple and the palace of Apries. Clarence S. Fisher of the University Museum of the University of Pennsylvania worked at Memphis between 1915 and 1923. He discovered a large ceremonial(?) palace with much of the layout and wall decoration still preserved, dating to the reign of Merneptah. Fisher also seems to have excavated extensively (approximately 3000 sq m [32,283 sq. ft.]) among the settlement strata, but little has been published. [*See the biographies of Petrie and Fisher.*]

Rudolph Anthes, also of the University Museum, and John Dimick worked for two seasons at Memphis (1954–1956) and mapped extensively (Anthes, 1959, 1965). The Egypt Antiquities Organization (EAO) excavated the remains of shrines belonging to Sety I and Rameses II, the embalming house of the Apis bulls, and thirteenth dynasty tombs of the high priests of Memphis. Later, between 1982 and 1986, a team from New York University further explored the embalming house.

In 1982 to celebrate its centenary, the Egypt Exploration Society (EES) of London commenced a survey and test excavations at Memphis under the direction of David Jeffreys and Harry S. Smith (Jeffreys et al., 1983–1993). The principal goals of this ongoing project are to produce a detailed map of the city, investigate the site's history, record both new and previously discovered monuments and inscriptions, and develop an understanding of the damage caused to the archaeological remains by the local environment. These excavations have identified settlement strata from the Middle and New Kingdoms, and coring has allowed the archaeologists to develop a better understanding of the eastern shift of the settlement reflecting the Nile's changing course, which is now more than 3 km (2 mi.) away from the site.

BIBLIOGRAPHY

Anthes, Rudolf. *Mit Rahineh, 1955*. Museum Monographs. Philadelphia, 1959. *Mit Rahineh, 1956*. Museum Monographs. Philadelphia, 1965. These publications discuss the work of Anthes and his colleagues at the southwest corner of the Ptah temple enclosure wall, including the small Rameses II temple there, and work on Kom el-Qal'a. The first volume has a large scale topographic map of this area of Memphis.

Fisher, Clarence S. "The Eckley B. Coxe, Jr. Egyptian Expedition." *The Museum Journal* 8 (1917). A very brief discussion of his finds from Kom el-Qal'a at Memphis, focusing principally on material from Merenptah's palace.

Kees, Hermann. *Ancient Egypt: A Cultural Topography*. Translated by Ian F. D. Morrow. London, 1961. Contains a somewhat out of date but very readable discussion of Memphis' role in the history and culture of ancient Egypt.

Jefferys, David G., et al. "The Survey of Memphis." *Journal of Egyptian Archaeology* 69–79 (1983–1993). Preliminary reports of the annual excavation by the Egyptian Exploration Society, principally authored by Jefferys, Lisa L. Giddy, and H. S. Smith.

Jeffreys, David G.. *The Survey of Memphis. Part I: The Archaeological Report*. Occasional Publication, 3. London, 1985. Summary of the first years of Egypt Exploration Society's new work at Memphis; provides numerous maps and plans.

Jones, Michael, and Angela Milward Jones. "The Apis House project at Mit Rahinah: Preliminary Report of the Fifth Season, 1984–85." *Journal of the American Research Center in Egypt* 24 (1987): 35–46. Summarizes information on the structure's architecture in conjunction with data from the 1941 EAO excavations.

Kamil, Jill. "Ancient Memphis: Archaeologists Revive Interest in a Famous Egyptian Site." *Archaeology* 38.4 (1985): 25–32. Well-written article for popular consumption on the history and archaeology of the site.

Mahmud, Abdulla el-Sayed. *A New Temple for Hathor at Memphis*. Egyptology Today, 1. Warminster, England, 1978. One of the few publications available about work undertaken by the Supreme Council of Antiquities (Egyptian antiquities organization).

Petrie, W. M. Flinders. *Memphis I*. British School of Archaeology in Egypt, vol. 15. London, 1909. *The Palace of Apries (Memphis II)*. British School of Archaeology in Egypt, vol. 17. London, 1909. *Meydum and Memphis (III)*. British School of Archaeology in Egypt, vol. 18. London, 1910. *Roman Portraits and Memphis (IV)*. British School of Archaeology in Egypt, vol. 20. London, 1911. *Tarkhan I and Memphis V*. British School of Archaeology in Egypt, vol. 23. London, 1913. *Riqqeh and Memphis VI*. British School of Archaeology in Egypt, vol. 25. London, 1915. Site reports of Petrie's work in the various areas of Memphis. Most are quite brief in their content.

Redford, Donald B. "Memphis." In *The Anchor Bible Dictionary*, vol. 4, pp. 689–691. New York, 1992. Solid historical overview, with a focus directed to an audience of biblical specialists.

Zivie[-Coche], Christiane M. "Memphis." In *Lexikon der Ägyptologie*, vol. 4, cols. 24–41. Wiesbaden, 1982. A more detailed entry (in French) than Redford's on the history and archaeology of the site.

DIANA CRAIG PATCH

MERIMDE. In 1928, archaeological survey along the Nile Delta's western margin northwest of Cairo located a prehistoric site (30°19′ N, 30°51′ E) now known as Merimde Beni Salame, or Merimde. Against a background of small hills, Merimde sits on a low sandy rise overlooking the Delta's floodplain, adjacent to the Rosetta branch of the Nile River. The Viennese Academy of Science sponsored the initial work at Merimde under Hermann Junker (1928–1935); Josef Eiwanger (1977–1983) conducted later excavations for the German Archaeological Institute in Cairo.

The site encompasses a large area, approximately 20–25 ha (50–62 acres) of which only about 7,500 sq m (80,700 sq. ft.) have been exposed. It is unlikely that the entire site was occupied at any one time, making population estimates difficult. A previous estimate of sixteen thousand inhabitants is unlikely, and even a more reasonable estimate of 900–1300 people is still large for a Neolithic village (Hoffman, 1979; Hassan; 1988).

Merimde's roughly 2-meter-deep deposit consists of five levels (I–V), covering at least four hundred years (c. 4800–4400 BCE), and perhaps as much as one thousand years (c. 5200–4100) of occupation. The first two layers are discontinuous; the last three are defined by differences between assemblages. The cultural assemblages found in these layers have not been identified at any other site, although some artifact types have parallels in Faiyum A sites, at el-Omari, and in the earliest levels at Buto.

Merimde's inhabitants practiced a mixed economy of hunting, fishing, and agriculture. Plant remains include domesticated emmer wheat, barley, lentil, and fodder vetch. Individual houses had granaries that were often lined with baskets or matting. Meat came from domesticated animals, especially pigs, and also cattle, sheep, goat, and wild animals including hippopotami, crocodiles, and antelopes (?). Remains of other Nile fauna, such as fish, turtles, and freshwater mussels, have also been recovered.

The earliest occupation (I) produced sparsely scattered, insubstantial structures whose outlines suggest that they may have been houses and windbreaks. In the next level (II), the oval and horseshoe-shaped houses were made from wooden poles, covered by woven materials and possibly skins. The latest levels (III–V) contained small, sturdy, semisubterranean structures of straw-tempered mud. A step, made from a hippo tibia or wooden post, allowed easy access to the interior. These houses also contained a hearth and a large water jar. Placed side by side, these dwellings enclosed the living space, and in some locations, their layout suggests that communal passageways had been included in the settlement's design. Burials, principally of women and children, have been found scattered throughout the site, probably in abandoned sections of the settlement. They have few grave goods.

Polished wares dominate the ceramic finds, although the upper levels produced large quantities of coarse wares. A variety of lithic tools have been recovered, including arrowheads, knives, sickle flints, and axes. Bone and ivory tools are also common, but personal objects, such as statuettes, representing humans or animals, and jewelry are rare.

The earliest level (I), whose most distinctive feature is pottery decorated with an incised herringbone motif, has a blade assemblage corresponding strongly to material found in Pottery Neolithic A sites in Palestine. Pear-shaped maceheads, slings, semisubterranean houses, and flaked axes in later levels may also illustrate Palestinian contact. Other objects, however, suggest early ties to Saharan cultures.

BIBLIOGRAPHY

Baumgartel, Elise J. "What Do We Know about the Excavations at Merimda?" *Journal of the American Oriental Society* 85 (1965): 502–511. Adequate summary of Hermann Junker's excavation reports.

Eiwanger, Josef. "Merimde-Beni-Salame." In *Lexikon der Ägyptologie*, vol. 4, cols. 94–96. Wiesbaden, 1982. Abbreviated summary of the site's most important characteristics, including data from Eiwanger's work.

Hassan, Fekri A. "The Predynastic of Egypt." *Journal of World Prehistory* 2.2 (1988): 135–185. Contains an excellent summary of the Neolithic and Predynastic periods in Egypt, with important information on dating and population estimates for Merimde Beni Salame.

Hayes, William C. *Most Ancient Egypt*. Chicago, 1965. Chapter 3 contains a succinct summary of the earliest excavations at this site.

Hoffman, Michael A. *Egypt before the Pharaohs*. New York, 1979. Part 4, chapter 12 summarizes Junker's work.

Kemp, Barry J. "Merimda and the Theory of House Burial in Prehistoric Egypt." *Chronique d'Égypte* 43 (1968): 22–23. Although the focus of this article is not Merimde, Kemp reviews the data concerning house structures and burials there.

Diana Craig Patch

MEROË (ancient Bedewe/Medewe), site near modern Begrawiya (Northern Province, Sudan), the earliest large-scale city known in Africa outside of Egypt (16°54′ N, 33°44′ E). A substantial town under the Napatan rulers of Nubia (c. 760–270 BCE), Meroë became the royal, administrative, and religious capital of the Meroitic kingdom (270 BCE–350 CE). Mentioned by Herodotus and other early writers, Meroë was accurately located by James Bruce (1722) and archaeologically identified by John Garstang's excavations (1909–1914). The only subsequent excavations of significance were Peter Shinnie's (1965–1985), but from 1920 to 1923 George Reisner excavated Meroë's royal cemeteries, lying east of the city. Earlier Giuseppe Ferlini recovered spectacular examples of Meroitic royal jewelry (in gold and semiprecious stones) from one of the pyramids. The treasure was hidden in the upper part of a 31-meter-high stone pyramid, which Ferlini almost completely demolished in a fruitless search for additional treasure. [*See the biographies of Garstang and Reisner.*]

Several factors made Meroë a central place. It lay on the Nile, a major commercial and strategic route and, enjoying significant rainfall, possessed substantial agricultural and grazing lands. Significant local resources included sandstone for buildings, iron ores for the extensive smelting industry at Meroë, and clay deposits for pottery. Most importantly, Meroë was the node for far-flung trade and military routes linking Nubia to Egypt and the Mediterranean; to the Gezira (between the Blue and White branches of the Nile River); and to the wealthy trading kingdom of Axum (in modern Ethiopia) and the Red Sea. [*See* Axum.]

Founded by 1000, Meroë expanded significantly around 590; the earliest-known inscriptional reference dates to the Napatan ruler Iriki-Amanote (c. 431–405). Meroë may have been a—or even *the*—royal residence in Napatan times, but no rulers were buried nearby until Arkamaniqo (Gk., Ergamenes) about 270–260. Thereafter, Meroë flourished, remaining the royal burial ground until the end of the Meroitic state (350 CE); occupation may have continued, but ultimately the site was completely abandoned.

Meroë city occupied about 2.59 sq km (640 acres or 1 sq. mi.). On the west, a large stone-walled enclosure sheltered several palaces and ancillary buildings and abutted on its east a much-renovated and expanded temple to Amun, an Egyptian god long taken over by the Nubians. Extremely large (137 m [450 ft.] long), the temple included a colonnaded court; columned halls; and a sanctuary. A processional route led to a so-called Temple of the Sun outside the city; this temple was an enclosed area containing a single-chambered cult building surrounded by a colonnade. Both

MEROË. Figure 1. *Pyramid field at the site.* (Frédéric Caillaud, *Voyage à Méroë,* Paris, 1826)

stood on a platform. (To the city's southeast was a temple of Apedemak, a lion-headed Nubian deity). Smaller cult-structures flanked the processional route, including a temple that had been perhaps renovated to house a life-sized bronze statue of the Roman emperor Augustus. The Meroites had plundered the statue from Aswan in southern Egypt in 23 BCE.

Sprawling east of the royal enclosure were extensive agglomerations of residential zones and industrial and manufacturing areas. Deposits of slag from iron smelting are conspicuous along the city's eastern edge, and a cavelike quarry produced kaolin for a distinctive, white-fabric pottery. Other typical ceramic types included handmade black wares; a statistically dominant wheel-made brown ware for domestic purposes; and imported fabrics.

Meroë's burial grounds are rich and important sources of information. Immediately east of the city lie three discrete cemeteries; the northernmost dates to about 100 BCE–200 CE. The two others are later. Most graves were marked by a mound of sand or gravel, and were for relatively prosperous people. The commoners' cemeteries perhaps remain to be found.

Farther east, three other cemeteries are arranged in a triangle. The western cemetery (between the others and the city) included pyramid tombs of lesser royalty, and the northern and southern held the pyramid tombs of virtually all Meroë's rulers after Arkamaniqo (see figure 1). Other graves, marked by pyramids, mastabas (benchlike superstructures) or mounds were for queens, princes, and members of the elite. Pyramids, which were built of stone masonry, later of brick or rubble, often had an attached chapel (those of the kings were embellished with a pylon, a double-towered gateway in Egyptian style). Chapels were provided with scenes and texts of a funerary nature. Despite severe plundering, the surviving traces of royal and elite wealth are astounding. Hoards of golden jewelry have been found, as well as a wide range of imported objects (especially from Egypt and the Mediterranean), some of superb quality.

BIBLIOGRAPHY

O'Connor, David. *Ancient Nubia: Egypt's Rival in Africa.* Philadelphia, 1993.

Priese, Karl-Heinz. *The Gold of Meroë.* Translated by Russell Stockman. New York, 1993.

Robertson, J. H. "History and Archaeology of Meroe." In *An African Commitment: Papers in Honour of Peter Lewis Shinnie,* edited by Judith Sterner and Nicholas David, pp. 35–50. Calgary, 1992.

Shinnie, Peter L. *Meroe: A Civilization of the Sudan.* London, 1967.

DAVID O'CONNOR

MERRILL, SELAH (1837–1910), American clergyman, archaeologist, and diplomat; active promoter of biblical archaeology in the United States. Born in Canton Center, Connecticut, Merrill was educated at Yale and ordained at the Yale Divinity School. After service as a Union chaplain in the Civil War and as a minister in New York and California, he studied Semitic languages at the University of Berlin (1868–1870) and traveled widely in Egypt, Syria, and Palestine. In 1874, he was appointed archaeologist for the second expedition of the American Palestine Exploration Society (APES); he assumed command after the resignation of the expedition's leader, James C. Lane.

During three long excursions through Palestine and Transjordan, Merrill supervised the collection of hundreds of archaeological, ethnological, botanical, and geological specimens and directed the preparation of a rough map of ancient sites in the ancient kingdoms of Ammon and Moab. Though this work fell far short of the standard established by the British Palestine Exploration Fund in its Survey of Western Palestine, Merrill's popular account of the American explorations, *East of the Jordan* (1881), was well received by the general public.

After the disbanding of APES, Merrill briefly joined the faculty of the Andover Theological Seminary. Through family connections, he was appointed U.S. consul in Jerusalem in 1882 and served in that position during every Republican administration until his transfer to British Guiana in 1907. In Jerusalem, Merrill continued his collecting activities and became an outspoken critic of the historical traditions connected with the Church of the Holy Sepulchre. His book on the subject, *Ancient Jerusalem* (1908), is an early attempt to reconstruct the topography of Herodian Jerusalem and identify the location of its walls through archaeological finds.

Merrill sold his large collection of Palestinian antiquities and natural specimens to the Harvard University Semitic Museum in 1896. He was also an active supporter of the American School of Archaeology in Jerusalem, established in 1900 as the first major overseas enterprise of the American Schools of Oriental Research.

[*See also* American Palestine Exploration Society; American Schools of Oriental Research.]

BIBLIOGRAPHY

King, Philip J. *American Archaeology in the Mideast: A History of the American Schools of Oriental Research.* Philadelphia, 1983.

Merrill, Selah. *East of the Jordan: A Record of Travel and Observation in the Countries of Moab, Gilead, and Basham.* London, 1881.

Merrill, Selah. *Ancient Jerusalem.* New York, 1908.

Moulton, Warren J. "The American Palestine Exploration Society." *Annual of the American Schools of Oriental Research* 8 (1928): 55–69.

Vester, Bertha Spafford. *Our Jerusalem: An American Family in the Holy City, 1881–1949.* Garden City, N.Y., 1950.

NEIL ASHER SILBERMAN

MEṢAD ḤASHAVYAHU, fort located on the *kurkar* (sandstone) ridge south of Yavneh-Yam, about 100 m from Israel's Mediterranean coast (map reference 1207 × 1462). The site is not identified with any place known from historical records. It received its name in modern times after an ostracon inscribed in Hebrew with the name Ḥashavyahu was found in the first season of excavation at the site. Subsequently, in 1960–1961, Joseph Naveh conducted two seasons of excavations there. A third season, a rescue dig following damage to the site, was carried out in 1986 by Ronny Reich on behalf of the Israel Antiquities Authority.

The fort is L-shaped in outline; its maximum measurements are 77–95 m. It is surrounded by a wall about 3.2 m thick that is strengthened by exterior buttresses. A single gate on the west, protected by two towers, faces the sea. Except for the gate area, the fort represents a single stratum of construction, pointing to a short period of occupation. It is dated by its pottery to the last quarter of the seventh century BCE. Raised floor levels in several rooms in the gate area indicate a second, partial occupation in the Early Persian period, however. The fort's large western area was found to be almost devoid of buildings, except near the gate and abutting it from the inside. This part of the site is situated on a relatively steep slope, and the *kurkar* is exposed over almost all of it, so that it is possible that any early construction was washed into the sea by winter rains. The eastern area is divided into three blocks by two parallel alleys; each block is further subdivided into seven buildings. It seems that the eastern part of the fort was carefully planned to accommodate these blocks of buildings. The perimeter wall and the buildings are of mud brick on a foundation of *kurkar* stones; the gate and towers are constructed entirely of *kurkar*.

Two groups of pottery vessels were found: local Judean pottery (cooking pots, storejars, and juglets) and pottery that had originated in the Aegean world. The latter includes vessels containing a large amount of mica grit, used in the temper mixed with the clay, a characteristic element in Greek pottery. This group also includes typical Greek shapes, such as skyphoi and amphorae, and objects decorated in the Wild Goat style. Chunks of hematite ore, an unusual find, were discovered in several places on the site. Sir William Flinders Petrie reported similar finds in his excavations in the Nile Delta, at Daphne and Naukratis, that clearly belonged to their Greek inhabitants (for citation, see Reich, 1989, p. 232).

The rather large quantity of Greek pottery, relative to the amount of Judean pottery, and the presence of foreign iron ore raise the question of the use of the site and the reasons for a Greek presence here. Although Greeks were active in establishing merchant colonies in the Mediterranean at the time, it seems more likely that the Greeks here were mercenaries hired by the Judean king Josiah. Meṣad Ḥashavyahu would then offer clear evidence of Josiah's successful attempt to enlarge the kingdom of Judah to the west.

Several Hebrew ostraca were found near the gate area. [*See* Ostracon.] As noted above, one bears the name *Ḥashavyahu,* after which the site was named in modern times. The other names all indicate inhabitants from Judah. A document of special importance is a fourteen-line ostracon, also written in Hebrew, found in the guardroom at the gate. It is a letter or petition written by or on behalf of a worker employed in the vicinity for the harvest. The worker complains that as a punitive action his garment was confiscated—an action biblical law prohibits (*Ex.* 22, 26–27). An exhaustive bibliography on the reading and interpretation of this document has accumulated since its discovery.

BIBLIOGRAPHY

Naveh, Joseph. "A Hebrew Letter from the Seventh Century B.C." *Israel Exploration Journal* 10.3 (1960): 129–139.

Naveh, Joseph. "More Hebrew Inscriptions from Meṣad Ḥashavyahu." *Israel Exploration Journal* 12.1 (1962): 27–32.

Naveh, Joseph. "The Excavations at Meṣad Ḥashavyahu: Preliminary Report." *Israel Exploration Journal* 12.2 (1962): 89–113.

Naveh, Joseph. "Some Notes on the Reading of the Meṣad Ḥashavyahu Letter." *Israel Exploration Journal* 14.3 (1964): 158–159.

Reich, Ronny. "Third Season of Excavations at Meṣad Ḥashavyahu." *Eretz-Israel* 20 (1989): 228–232. In Hebrew with English summary on page 203*.

RONNY REICH

MEṢAD ḤASHAVYAHU TEXTS. During two campaigns in 1960 at the site of Meṣad Ḥashavyahu, located approximately one mile south of Yavneh-Yam, Israel, seven Hebrew inscriptions were discovered: one group of seven ostraca belonging to what was originally a single document, five other individual ostraca, and an inscription originally incised on the shoulder of a jar (Naveh, 1960, 1962). Among the same finds was a stone weight inscribed only with symbols. The modern name of the site was assigned on the basis of the appearance of the name *ḥšbyhw* in the incised inscription.

The most important of these documents is the first mentioned, for it is comparatively well preserved and of great historical interest. Its fifteen lines contain the plea of a harvest worker *(qṣr)* whose garment *(bgd)* has been confiscated by a certain Ḥawsha ʿyahu ben Shobay, otherwise unidentified. The plea is addressed to a local official *(śr)*, who goes unnamed, in standard inferior-to-superior phraseology ("May my lord the official hear the word of his servant . . ."). The worker claims that he has fulfilled his quota and that he has committed no wrong; he asks the official to have his garment returned either for these reasons or out of pity. In spite of some difficulties in interpretation, the language of the inscription is essentially that of the Judean Hebrew inscriptions (e.g., those from Arad and Lachish) and is closely related to standard biblical Hebrew.

The primary unresolved questions about the document are literary and sociohistorical. The document was first identified as a letter, but because of the absence of epistolary formulae that identification has either been qualified (Pardee et al., 1982, p. 23) or rejected (Smelik, 1992). There is general agreement on identifying it as a plea; the question is whether the form of the plea is epistolary. If the definition of a letter as "a written document effecting communication between two or more persons who cannot communicate orally" (Pardee et al., 1982, p. 2) be accepted, the document may qualify as a plea in epistolary form. It is in any case doubtful that a plea should constitute a literary category on the same level as a letter.

Joseph Naveh, the editor of the inscription, hypothesized that all of these documents should be assigned to the time of Josiah and be taken as evidence for a previously unrecorded Judean control of the coastal area (Naveh, 1960, p. 139), an opinion that became widespread in works on the history of the late seventh century BCE. In recent years, however, other origins have been proposed for the texts—for example, a Judean occupation under Jehoiakim (Wenning, 1989) or Judean mercenaries serving in an Egyptian fortress (Naʿaman, 1991, 44–47). Tied in with the political question are issues regarding the precise position of the *śr* (local governor or military or administrative official?), of the harvest worker (servant, slave, corvée-worker?), and of the one who seized the garment (directly under the *śr* or in another chain of command?). The biblical parallels for the required return of a confiscated garment (*Ex.* 22:25–26; *Dt.* 24:12–15, 17) raise the question of how widespread the requirement may have been.

[*See also* Yavneh-Yam.]

BIBLIOGRAPHY

Booij, Th. "The Yavneh Yam Ostracon and Hebrew Consecutive Imperfect." *Bibliotheca Orientalis* 43 (1986): 642–647. Discussion of several grammatical and lexical features.

Naʿaman, Nadav. "The Kingdom of Judah under Josiah." *Tel Aviv* 18 (1991): 3–71.

Naveh, Joseph. "A Hebrew Letter from the Seventh Century B.C." *Israel Exploration Journal* 10.3 (1960): 129–139. *Editio princeps* of the inscribed sherd and letter.

Naveh, Joseph. "More Hebrew Inscriptions from Meṣad Ḥashavyahu." *Israel Exploration Journal* 12.1 (1962): 27–32. *Editio princeps* of the other ostraca and the weight.

Pardee, Dennis, et al. *Handbook of Ancient Hebrew Letters.* Society of Biblical Literature, Sources for Biblical Study, vol. 15. Chico, Calif., 1982. Comprehensive bibliography up to 1978.

Smelik, K. A. D. "The Literary Structure of the Yavneh-Yam Ostracon." *Israel Exploration Journal* 42.1 (1992): 55–61.

Wenning, Robert. "Meṣad Ḥasavyahu." In *Vom Sinai zum Horeb: Stationen alttestamentlicher Glaubensgeschichte,* edited by Frank-Lothar Hossfeld, pp. 169–193. Würzburg, 1989. Discussion of historical context.

DENNIS PARDEE

MESHA INSCRIPTION. *See* Moabite Stone.

MESKENE. *See* Emar.

MESOPOTAMIA. [*This entry provides a broad survey of the history of Mesopotamia as known primarily from archaeological discoveries. It is chronologically divided into four articles:*

Prehistoric Mesopotamia
Ancient Mesopotamia
Mesopotamia from Alexander to the Rise of Islam
Mesopotamia in the Islamic Period

In addition to the related articles on specific subregions and sites referred to in this entry, see also History of the Field, *article on* Archaeology in Mesopotamia.]

Prehistoric Mesopotamia

The geographical area that will be treated in this article roughly corresponds with the territory of modern Iraq, where in the middle of the fourth millennium the southern part (Babylonia) and slightly later, the northern part (Assyria) became the scene of the emergence and development of Mesopotamian urban civilization. In the earlier periods, however, Mesopotamia was tied to larger developments in the Near East, in particular in Syria, Anatolia, and Iran. For the beginning of the domestication of plants and animals, of sedentary life, the evidence is better documented in other areas. The scant material recovered in Mesopotamia's northeastern mountain zones suffices only to show that people did live there and took part in the general cultural changes.

For the early millennia the carbon-14 dates used for all of the Near East are not always reliable. However, because the many dates available for the end of the Aceramic Neolithic seem to converge at about 6000 BCE, this may be a relatively secure anchor. It is only with the last cultural phase that will be discussed, the Late Uruk period, that through close parallels with early Egypt, dates become more stable, placing the end of the Uruk period at about 3100 BCE. The dates used in this discussion are at present the ones most commonly accepted.

Ecologically, Mesopotamia is highly diversified. The north and northeast share with other regions of the Near East those features that made possible the domestication of plants and animals and the controlled migration patterns that led toward sedentary life: highly adaptable, and thus domesticable, plants and animals and small-scale environments with sharp differences in climate and thus in different exploitable flora and fauna. The region's landscape forms (topography) range from narrow valleys in the high mountains to small plains in the piedmont to the alluvial plain. Thus, each level of agricultural ability found its appropriate landscape: mountain valleys are surrounded by a diversified environment, permitting survival by food gathering when agriculture failed; at the other end of the spectrum, the alluvial plain was open to those agricultural specialists who accumulated profound experience over thousands of years. The existence of an ever more demanding topography to challenge people, whenever their experience and resourcefulness rose to a point where higher social and economic risks could be faced, seems largely responsible for the continuity of early development in Mesopotamia and throughout the Near East.

Life is determined by the accessibility of water. Like hunters and gatherers early agriculturalists also depended upon areas with sufficient rainfall. Techniques of supplying additional surface water to enhance the growth of plants became necessary once advanced experience allowed the occupation of areas that were larger and more fertile but had less stable rainfall patterns, or never got enough rain. [*See* Irrigation.] The accessibility of water divides Mesopotamia. While a large part of Assyria lies in an area of sufficient precipitation, agricultural production in Babylonia depends entirely on an artificial supply of water.

The area's paleoclimate has been shown on average to have been similar to today's, but with shorter or longer deviations. While the fifth millennium seems to have been moister than average, another change, resulting in a slightly cooler and dryer climate, seems to have begun in the mid-fourth millennium and probably became influential in the formation of early urban society toward the end of that millennium.

Paleolithic and Epipaleolithic Periods. Evidence for the presence of paleolithic life in Mesopotamia is scarce but exists and, as elsewhere, is restricted to the mountainous zones. Best known is the Shanidar cave, with its burials of Mousterian Neanderthal-type humans. [*See* Shanidar Cave.] Stray finds dating to this period as well as to the Upper Paleolithic (the local name for the period in the Zagros Mountains is Zarzian) attest to its presence throughout the mountain ranges. From about 16,000 BCE onward (the Epipaleolithic period), flint tools tended to become more specialized, while the diet became more diversified perhaps a result of more efficient tools being used in hunting and gathering. In the Zarzian period, at the Shanidar and Zarzi caves, eastern Anatolian obsidian appears, attesting to long-distance contacts.

Aceramic Neolithic (c. 9,000–7,000 BCE). Sites showing the salient features of the Neolithic: incipient domestication and sedentarization, but no pottery, are few in Mesopotamia and lack the sequence of layers that would allow a sketch of the cultural development between the Epipaleolithic and the Pottery Neolithic. There is only Jarmo, with its aceramic layers beneath early pottery ones, that testifies to the latest part of that time-span. By that time, food production was already well advanced, and there is no doubt about an all-season occupation. In every respect, aceramic Jarmo is part of the greater Zagros horizon. [*See* Jarmo.]

Pottery Neolithic (c. 7,000–6,000 BCE). The best representative for the Pottery Neolithic part of the greater Zagros development is also the site of Jarmo. As elsewhere, the introduction of pottery vessels is not accompanied by major changes in the tool kit or the diet. Pottery, with its ability to adapt to minute changes in taste or needs to differentiate, and its ubiquity, henceforth becomes an indispensable tool in comparing or contrasting temporal and spatial cultural entities through similarities in shape and decoration.

Although basal Umm Dabaghiyeh, southwest of Mosul, seems to be contemporary with Pottery Neolithic Jarmo, other sites, like Hassuna or the lowest levels at Tell Soto, Matarrah, Shamshara, and Nineveh begin later. [*See* Hassuna; Nineveh.] In contrast to the others that still lie in hilly (ecologically diversified) terrain, Nineveh is the first lowland site, settled in the area of rain-fed agriculture. [*See* Agriculture.] Multiple storerooms combined with the evidence from paleobotanical and paleozoological analyses, seem to indicate that Umm Dabaghiyeh was a specialized hunting place; too little is known of the other sites to be more specific.

Ḥalaf (c. 5,500–5000 BCE). While the eponymous site of Ḥalaf lies in modern Syria, the area in which this specific kind of pottery is found also includes the northwestern part of Mesopotamia. [*See* Ḥalaf, Tell.] In fact, the finest specimens come from the site of Arpachiyah, northeast of Mosul. Other sites settled in this period are Yarim Tepe and basal Tepe Gawra. [*See* Tepe Gawra.] Pottery production reveals an advanced technology in the Ḥalaf period: the firing process could be controlled. The result was a firing-induced polychromy and lustre, on complex shapes with carinations and pedestals.

In architecture, besides small, multiroomed dwellings round structures are found that often have a long-rectangular antechamber attached. No public buildings of character can be singled out either by size or plan in this period. In the art of the Ḥalaf period animal figurines seem to strive for realism whereas human figures are abstract in style. Peculiarly shaped clay "counters" and stamps with linear incisions are part of the Ḥalaf cultural horizon. They indicate a kind of economic situation where it was necessary to keep records and mark items as personal property.

Samarra (c. 6,000–5,000 BCE). Unlike Ḥalaf, the Samarra cultural horizon is more confined to Mesopotamia, though Baghouz on the Syrian Euphrates, close to the Iraqi border, and Chogha Mami on the Iranian piedmont zone of the Zagros mountains indicate a possibly larger distribution. The few instances of the overlapping of the two zones do not allow greater specificity beyond indicating that these entities were contemporaneous, at least partially. The Samarra ceramic assemblage shows a matt painting on mostly simple, open shapes. The pottery is completely different from that of Ḥalaf, as is the architecture. Houses that are similar in size and plan prevail; they are large enough to be called dwellings of extended families, which may indicate a higher level of division of labor and social stratification than seen before or at contemporary Ḥalaf. There are again, however, no indications of public buildings. Small decorated statuettes of humans and animals in stone or clay were found both in the houses and private graves. [*See* Grave Goods.] It is only at Tell es-Sawwan in the area of Samarra that a wall and a moat were found surrounding the settlement. However, as yet no other settlement of the period has been explored as extensively as Samarra. [*See* Samarra.]

Eridu and Hajji Mohammed (c. 6,000–5,000 BCE). So far, all cultural developments have occurred either in the mountainous zones or in those areas in which rain-fed agriculture was possible. There is no indication that up to this point the southern plain took part in the steps toward sedentary life. The pottery found on a site close to Uruk (Uruk-Warka Survey no. 298) and matched by pre-Eridu material from basal Tell el-'Oueili, southeast of Larsa, is contemporary with Samarra, as is the material from the lower parts of the sequences at Eridu and Tell el-'Oueili. The corpus is enriched for the later part of the period by pottery from the short-lived Hajji Mohammed, southwest of Uruk. [*See* Uruk-Warka; Eridu; 'Oueili, Tell el-.] Initially using simple, mostly open shapes the phase of Hajji Mohammed pottery adds a sharp carination to deep bowls, reminiscent of Ḥalaf shapes. Patterns of painted decoration, however, differ from both Ḥalaf and Samarra pottery. The Eridu–Hajji Mohammed sequence is seen as contemporary with Ḥalaf/Samarra. To date, the occurrence of Eridu pottery is restricted to the extreme south of Mesopotamia and only the Hajji Mohammed pottery from Ras al-Amiya, south of Kish, suggests a larger distribution.

The areas excavated at Eridu/Hajji Mohammed were too small to reveal any architectural contexts, except in the temple sounding at Eridu where, in the second-lowest layer, a small freestanding square building was found. In the next phase, it received a niche opposite the entrance, which is usual for shrines in later Mesopotamian tradition. Measuring barely 3 × 3 m, it may not be a public building; but neither is it a dwelling. The level of subsistence and the economy more or less equal that of the contemporary periods in the north.

Ubaid (c. 5,000–4,000 BCE). Wares similar to those first identified in southern Babylonia at Ubaid, Ur, Eridu, and Uruk were subsequently found over large areas of the Near East. Simple open and closed forms bear a dark, monochromatic decoration of multiple concentric bands alternating with geometric designs like hatching, wavy lines, and garlands. The patterns were applied to the vessel rotated on a pivotted platform. Early wares with the full range of this complex decoration (Standard Ubaid) are followed by vessels with simplified designs, often restricted to one or two concentric bands (Late Ubaid). Because such elements are already found in the Eridu/Hajji Mohammed assemblages, Ubaid pottery is assumed to be a sequel to those groups, and hence, a native development of Babylonia.

The sequence of temples at Eridu is continued in the

Ubaid period. Temples were set on platforms for the first time. A central space was expanded with subsidiary rooms, indicating a specific order for the rituals conducted in it. Platforms in front of a niche in the rear wall may have served as altars (cf. the similar so-called Anu-Ziggurrat at Uruk). [*See* Ziggurat.]

The architecture at Tell Abada in the Hamrin dam salvage area differs markedly from that attested in earlier periods. The houses are of the Central Hall type (irregular smaller rooms attached to an elongated space) beginning a tradition found systematized in the large so-called temples of the Late Uruk period at Uruk-Eanna. A central building with a similar configuration was found, but because of its size and artifacts, a cache of clay counters, it may have been used for economic activities. As in the earlier periods, artistic expression is confined to small figurines of animals and erect humans.

To the north, at Tepe Gawra, east of Mosul, levels containing pottery resembling that of the Ubaid period were found overlying Ḥalaf levels. Although the shapes differ from those found in the south, as do the paste and the basic color, they share the principle of rotary decoration: their Ubaidlike appearance may be the result of a transformation of the local tradition by means of the new technique for applying decoration to a rotating vessel. This development shows a similar problem awareness, as this new technique certainly was an answer to a mutual challenge by the growing division of labor.

The architecture at Tepe Gawra uses the same type of central hall structure as the main component of what seems to have been large compounds composed of sheds and storage facilities. No public building was immediately evident, and a large round structure situated inside the habitation area remains enigmatic.

Early Uruk (c. 4,000–3,500 BCE). Though presumably of major importance, the Early Uruk phase is known only from a deep sounding at Uruk with limited exposures; hence, no broad architectural context was recovered. At first, this phase seems to mark only the rather sudden fading of Ubaid-style painted pottery and the emergence and rapid increase in the use of unpainted pottery made largely on the true potter's wheel, which enabled a different set of vessel shapes.

Late Uruk is the first urban civilization. It features monumental buildings and art, a high level of economic and political organization and the first script. These features were not present in late Ubaid. Yet, when they appear they are fully developed, without a sign of initial hesitation, so that the basic steps must have taken place in the Early Uruk phase.

Although not much has been recovered in excavations, Early Uruk pottery is an established entity identified in archaeological surface surveys, like Late Uruk. Based on such data, a major increase in settlement activity is noted in middle, and probably northern, Babylonia in the Early Uruk phase; the southern region, notably the hinterland of Uruk, remained at the low level of settlement activity of the Late Ubaid. Unfortunately, none of these Early Uruk sites has been explored.

In the northern part of Mesopotamia, the Ubaid pottery tradition passed over into local developments without apparent ties to the south. This is demonstrated by the stratigraphic sequence of Tepe Gawra, which, because it was excavated on a large scale, revealed some interesting architectural features. Of particular importance is a rectangular square surrounded by four public structures, that, on the basis of contemporary structures at Eridu, proved to be temples. Most conspicuously, this square occupies a quarter of the surrounding habitation area. Its size indicates that it was more than the center of the settlement. It is thus assumed that this central feature served a large surrounding area suggesting the existence of a structured settlement system.

Late Uruk (c. 3500–3100 BCE). A full array of archaeological evidence becomes available in the latest phase of the Late Uruk sequence at Uruk, or, in archaeological terms, in level IVa of archaic Eanna. Excavated on a large scale, Eanna features a number of monumental public buildings. Thousands of fragments of clay sealings and written tablets found there proved to be the means of control for an expanding economy. This area is characterized as the seat of a central economic (and political?) administration. [*See* Seals; Tablet.]

In order to provide a growing number of administrators with personalized seals, the stamp seal was replaced by the cylinder seal. Its larger surface increased the artistic range of the designs. Most written documents dealt with the transactions of a powerful economic administration. The complexity of those transactions is amply illustrated in the contents of the tablets: large herds of animals had to be supervised; thousands of units of barley had to be booked as either entering stores or handed over to someone. Monthly and yearly accounts were computed from daily records; there was traffic between various departments, as the brewing department had to calculate how much barley or groats it needed for so many liters of beer in order to place the proper request with the barley and groats store; and thousands of employees received daily rations of barley, using the mold-made bowls, known as beveled-rim bowls, that turn up by the thousands at every site, a usage illustrated by the pictorial sign for "allotment" composed of the bowl's image with its characteristic rim and a stylized human head.

Simpler media had prepared the way for cuneiform script, a versatile means of storing information which turns up by Uruk IVa or slightly earlier. [*See* Cuneiform.] Thus, tablets are found incised with numerical notations that record quantities only—from Chogha Mish in Khuzistan and Jebel Aruda and Habuba Kabira (South) in Syria. [*See* Habuba Kabira.] In addition to the information on numbers, the sealed clay balls yielded information on the individual responsible via the seal employed. An expanding economy needed a better means of administrative control, which made the rapid disposition of a writing system desirable. [*See* Writing and Writing Systems.]

Lists of words and signs mark the effort to order the universe. They are as much precedents of later Babylonian science as are the calculations of field sizes for later mathematics. The stratification of society in the Late Uruk period is illustrated both by a list of titles and professions arranged in ranking order and in pictorial scenes like the one on the cult vase from Uruk, now in Baghdad. Fragments of major works of art, including nearly life-sized statues of individuals, probably date to the Late Uruk period although they were found in later dumps only. In the shaping of these innovations within the 250–300 years of the Late Uruk period a considerable acceleration of a process can be seen that resulted in the expansion of Uruk to cover an area of at least 2.5 sq km (1.5 sq. mi.), making it the center of a settlement system of more than one hundred settlements in an area that previously had only eleven.

The shift to a dryer climate in the fourth millennium (see above), may have lessened the amount of the flooding of the rivers and the size of the marshes. The opening of the alluvium to large-scale settlement resulted in an unprecedented population density that accelerated the process of developing organizational means to cope with the social and economic problems that ensued. Apparently, one outcome was strict hierarchization, on the level of settlements (centers; settlement systems), of economic and political administration, or on the social level.

Local traditions had prevailed in northern Mesopotamia during the Early Uruk period, until, by Late Uruk, some settlements had adopted the Babylonian Late Uruk set of traditions, its pottery (including the ration bowls) and the use of cylinder seals. Architectural contexts are lacking because of limited excavation and insufficient evidence; yet where there has been a larger exposure at sites as in modern Syria, the architecture exactly matches Babylonian models. This adoption is part of a larger process in which Babylonian urban features spread into neighboring regions. Even Egypt produced cylinder seals and niched facades, like those found in Buto/Tell Fara'in, demonstrating a close link between Late Uruk and predynastic Egypt. Urban civilization was the culmination of a long period of development toward higher forms of social, economic and political organization. The Late Uruk period also marks the beginning of the long life of Mesopotamian civilization, characterized by splendid creations in the fields of art, literature, architecture, and the sciences.

BIBLIOGRAPHY

Adams, Robert McC. *Heartland of Cities: Surveys of Ancient Settlement and Land Use on the Central Floodplain of the Euphrates.* Chicago, 1981. Summary of archaeological surface surveys in Babylonia.

Algaze, Guillermo. *The Uruk World System.* Chicago, 1993. Deals specifically with the Uruk period of the second half of the fourth millennium.

Bernbeck, Reinhard. *Die Auflösung der häuslichen Produktionsweise.* Berlin, 1994. Discussion of the early pottery periods in Mesopotamia, with a special focus on changes in social and economic life.

The Cambridge Ancient History. Vols. 1 and 3. 3d ed. Cambridge, 1970–1976. Vols. 3.1–2. 2d ed. Cambridge, 1982–1991. Each chapter by a leading expert.

Ehrich, Robert W., ed. *Chronologies in Old World Archaeology.* 2 vols. 3d ed. Chicago, 1992. Amply documented chronological tables with pertinent archaeological evidence, carbon-14 tables, and bibliographies, from the Mediterranean to East Asia, 7000–1500 BCE.

Gebel, Hans G., and Stefan Kozlowski, eds. *Neolithic Chipped Stone Industries of the Fertile Crescent: Studies in Early Near Eastern Production, Subsistence, and Environment.* Berlin, 1994. Detailed discussion of Aceramic Neolithic evidence.

Henrickson, Elizabeth F., and Ingolf Thuesen, eds. *Upon This Foundation: The ʿUbaid Reconsidered.* Copenhagen, 1989. Most recent and comprehensive coverage of the Ubaid phenomenon.

Mellaart, James. *The Neolithic of the Near East.* London, 1975. Though in need of supplements, a still valuable account of the older evidence.

Nissen, Hans J. *The Early History of the Ancient Near East, 9000–2000 B.C.* Chicago, 1988. Covers the Neolithic period to the Third Dynasty of Ur.

Nissen, Hans J., et al. *Archaic Bookkeeping.* Chicago, 1993. Comprehensive discussion of the emergence of writing and the contents of early documents.

Nützel, Werner. "The Climate Changes of Mesopotamia and Bordering Areas." *Sumer* 32 (1976): 11–24. Summary of marine geological research in the Persian Gulf.

Oates, Joan. *Babylon.* Rev. ed. London, 1986. Well-written account of Mesopotamian history and archaeology.

Postgate, J. N. *Early Mesopotamia: Society and Economy at the Dawn of History.* London, 1994. Covers the period 3000–1500 BCE, mostly from a philogical perspective.

Redman, Charles L. *The Rise of Civilization: From Early Farmers to Urban Society in the Ancient Near East.* San Francisco, 1978. Intended as a textbook for American anthropology departments, this is a splendid account of the period from an anthropologist's point of view.

Roaf, Michael. *Cultural Atlas of Mesopotamia and the Ancient Near East.* New York, 1990. Well-written and amply illustrated coverage from the Neolithic period to Alexander.

Schmandt-Besserat, Denise. *Before Writing.* 2 vols. Austin, 1992. Documentation of the means of information storage before writing.

Tübinger Atlas des Vorderen Orients. Wiesbaden, 1977–1994. Collection of 210 physical and historical maps of the Near East and Egypt, from prehistoric to modern times.

Ucko, Peter, and G. W. Dimbleby, eds. *Domestication and Exploitation of Plants and Animals.* London, 1969.

Ucko, Peter, et al., eds. *Man, Settlement, and Urbanism.* Cambridge, Mass., 1972.

Hans J. Nissen

Ancient Mesopotamia

Shortly before 3000 BCE, the first stage of urbanization was completed with the formulation of the innovations and institutions that henceforth would characterize Mesopotamian civilization. Whereas before, Babylonia and Assyria had participated in the cultural development of the larger Near East, including notably the west Iranian (Zagros) mountains, in the Uruk period, Babylonia took a markedly different turn, eventually followed by Assyria. For some centuries to come, the pace of development accelerated in Babylonia until, in the mid-second millennium BCE, a balance of power was reached again between the various forces in the Near East. As a consequence, Babylonia relinquished its role as the driving agent. By the first millennium, empires were formed that reached even beyond the Near East proper.

While the shift to a slightly dryer climate in the fourth millennium seems to have had no consequences for northern Mesopotamia, the danger of flooding was reduced in Babylonia, in the south. In the large-scale occupation that ensued, daily life came to be described as urban. In the beginning, there was enough water alongside the fields to irrigate without canals; however, the continuing decrease in water for another millennium made it necessary to built canals to feed the areas then left dry. [*See* Irrigation.] However, because increasingly all water was used to irrigate, leaving no excess to wash away the natural salts of water and soil, irrigation had the effect increasing salinization of the soil. By the end of the third millennium, both water shortage and salinization, plus the population increase, had in created an economically tense situation. Ecological conditions seem to have ameliorated in the second millennium. The center of power shifted to northern Babylonia, accompanied by neglect of the hydraulic systems of the south. The result was a permanent loss of power in the south, except for some enclaves along the Euphrates River.

Because ethnic groups in antiquity can be identified only through their language, the bearers of early cultural development in Mesopotamia and the Near East remain anonymous. Early writing does not help identifying ethnic affiliation because texts largely employ word signs that could be read in any language. Not until either grammatical elements are written pointing to a particular language, or signs are used with their phonetical value can there be certainty about the language expressed. This stage was reached in mid-third millennium BCE texts from Babylonia. They represent a language whose main element was Sumerian with an admixture of words from other languages. [*See* Sumerian.] Texts from Ebla from the same period are the first to make full use of the potential of employing signs with their phonetic values. [*See* Ebla Texts.] From this time onward, the representation of bound language enabled the composition of texts other than economic records. [*See* Writing and Writing Systems.] Later in the third millennium speakers of Semitic languages under the various designations of Akkadian, Babylonian, Amorite, Assyrian, and Aramaic dominated the scene. Speakers of other languages, such as Kassite and Hurrian, at times played a greater role in political life, but like the Old Iranian of the Achaemenids, the languages never succeded in matching the political influence of their speakers. [*See* Akkadian; Aramaic; Hurrian.]

Jemdet Nasr/Early Dynastic (c. 3100–2350 BCE). Though additional data come from Jemdet Nasr, Nippur, and the Diyala region, Uruk remains the best source for the turn from the fourth to the third millennia. [*See* Jemdet Nasr; Nippur; Diyala.] There, a huge terrace is built to incorporate the former Anu Ziggurrat while in Eanna, instead of large buildings on ground level, a single platform, presumably surmounted by a temple, surrounded by auxiliary buildings, marks the center. [*See* Ziggurat.] This internal realignment did not affect other aspects of society, such as writing which in the style of the script and arrangement on the tablets, shows that it was responsive to the need for easier usage and fuller representation for more complex problems. [*See* Tablet.] Such tablets were also found in northern Babylonia at sites such as Jemdet Nasr and those in the Diyala region. These discoveries point, at least in this phase, to widespread economic and cultural uniformity in Babylonia.

Within at most two hundred years, by Early Dynastic I, Uruk had more than doubled its size, to cover almost 6 sq km (4 sq. mi.) within the new city-wall and beyond. In general, fewer but larger settlements housed an increased population, until by the later part of the Early Dynastic period, the number of large cities had grown at the expense of rural settlements. This population shift must have enforced pressure to enhance the existing rules of administration and conflict management in order to ensure orderly everyday life. Thus, among the texts, which subsequently were no longer confined to economic data, legal procedures are found treated in a way that presupposes a long consolidation phase. According to royal inscriptions the excessive growth of cities resulted in territorial conflicts between the various city-states ruled by local dynasties. For the first time, the representation of a bound language allows Sumerian to be identified as the language of the texts.

Fabulous wealth, including many exotic materials, is shown by the grave gifts in the royal tombs of the cemetery at Ur. [*See* Ur; Grave Goods.] Prosperity, however, was not confined to the ruling class, as indicated by the find in Eshnunna and Khafajeh of hundreds of stone statues buried alongside small neighborhood shrines, where they originally had been placed in supplication by donors. [*See* Eshnunna; Khafajeh.] Apparently, ordinary people could afford to treat themselves to statues of imported material.

Based on a number of texts, a form of government has been suggested in which the city god was the actual ruler and the king his earthly substitute. Probably, however, this was only a local form since all evidence comes from texts from a single city (Lagash), pertaining only to a limited number of years. Yet, there certainly was more variation, both contemporaneously and before. Increasingly local rulers attempt to control larger parts of Babylonia; none of these efforts, however, survived the reigns of their initiators.

First Empires (c. 2350–1900 BCE). After gaining control over all of Babylonia, Sargon, an Akkadian from preponderantly Semitic northern Babylonia, established a central state, that remained with his dynasty for several generations. Measures to enforce centrality, like monopolizing the sea trade with Oman and the Indus River valley, or keeping a standing military force at their disposal, help. Apart from being preoccupied with permanent internal rebellions, Sargon and his grandson Naram-Sin campaigned in distant lands, such as Syria and the Iranian highlands. Their fame remained vibrant into much later periods.

The art of the period reflects a profound change in concept: unlike earlier archetypal renderings of the human form, Akkadian art individualizes figures by placing them in front of a background and adding anatomical details, allowing them natural proportions. The outstanding monument in this style is a stela commemorating Naram-Sin's victory over the mountain tribe of the Lullubi (now in the Louvre, Paris).

The Semitic Akkadian begins to appear in official inscriptions, a political decision, not a reflection of a population shift. With the Akkadians stronger in the north and the Sumerians in the south, occasionally signs of both groups' self-awareness are found, but there is no indication of major tensions or even conflicts between them. However, both rebellious cities and attacks by mountain tribes (Guti) caused the Akkadian state to shrink in the end to the size of but one of several city-states, always threatened by the menace of a Gutian foothold.

Ur-Nammu, founder of the Third Dynasty of Ur, capitalizing on the prestige of his father, Utuhegal, as victor over the Gutians, was able to reunite Babylonia by 2100 BCE. Both he and his son Shulgi furthered the kind of organization necessary for a central state, such as creating districts with local civilian and military representatives. They returned to Sumerian as the official language, bringing about the so-called Neo-Sumerian period in the history of Mesopotamian literature. An encompassing reform in Shulgi's twenty-first regnal year ordering that almost all economic transactions had to be recorded, was intended to counter growing economic difficulties. Desiccation, salinization, and a growing population had combined to create serious supply problems. A remedy was sought in the tightening of controls to an extent that nothing would escape the official system of redistribution. The increased need for scribes had the side effect that Ur III became one of the most literate societies in the ancient world, as demonstrated not only by the emergence of new literary genres, but by the fact that on seals, inscriptions partly take over the function of identifying the owner.

Opposition to this omnipresent control combined with old resentments against the central state, started a rebellion in northern Babylonia. The capital was caught at its weakest point: because of its largely salinized fields, Ur depended on shiploads of grain from the north. Decisively weakened, Ur was raided by its eastern neighbor, Elam, and Ibbi-Sin, the last king, was taken prisoner. Once again, like at the end of the Akkadian period, the local element had proven strong enough to thwart a central government (Elamites).

Assyria had always been part of a larger complex with northeastern Syria and, in the first half of the third millennium, had kept its traditional pace in spite of short-term affiliations with Babylonia. This eventually changed. Statues from the late Early Dynastic Ishtar temple at Aššur show close ties with Babylonia, which remained valid through the Akkad and Ur III periods. [*See* Aššur.]

Early Second Millennium. Against measures to stop them, the Amorites had succeeded in invading Babylonia, to an extent that the spokesman of the anti-Ur III forces was the Amorite ruler of the Babylonian city of Isin. [*See* Amorites.] Isin's hope to retain central rule was soon challenged by the Amorite dynasty of Larsa, which in turn gave the Amorite dynasty of Babylon the opportunity to gain power. [*See* Larsa.] Hammurabi, the sixth ruler of the dynasty, finally succeeded in controlling all of Babylonia by starving Rim-Sin of Larsa. By intensifying irrigation schemes in northern Babylonia, and by founding many new settlements, the seat of power irrevocably shifted there. The conquest of Mari on the Euphrates, Eshnunna, and even Aššur, however, proved to be fateful: Hammurabi had destroyed the buffer zones facing the Kassites who were waiting to invade. [*See* Mari.] With the loss of these new possessions during the reigns of Hammurabi's successors in the seventeenth century BCE, Babylon became just another political entity between a dynasty of the Sealand, somewhere in southern Babylonia; Elam; the Kassite foothold-kingdom of Khana close to Mari; Aššur; and, finally, the rising power of the Hittites. [*See* Hittites.] The final blow came when the Hittite ruler Muršili, prolonging his raid on Ḫalab (Aleppo), followed the Euphrates downstream until he sacked Babylon, in 1595 BCE.

Also from this period there are many documents telling us that the despotic rule of Ur III administration had given way to a decentralized form of economic administration though from many letters it is known that politically everything was decided in Babylon; even legal cases of minor importance were brought to the attention of Hammurabi.

Though the older order of the gods still prevailed, there was a tendency to favor the sun god Shamash and to promote the city god of Babylon, Marduk, as head of the pantheon. Particular mention should be made of the many surviving mathematics texts, which show a well-advanced mastery of that field.

While a later king-list begins with "rulers living in tents," unknown otherwise, sources only testify to the existence of a local power in Aššur after the beginning of the twentieth century BCE. Shortly thereafter, Assyrian merchants made Aššur an emporium from which merchandise from several directions was forwarded to other trading partners. This information comes from thousands of tablets from Anatolia, where a network of trading colonies was established. That trade was ended by events connected with the Hittite invasion by 1700 BCE; no accounts exist from Aššur. [*See* Anatolia; *article on* Ancient Anatolia.] Better coverage is available only for the reigns of Shamshi-Adad I and his son Ishme-Dagan. Of Amorite origin, they conquered the are of Aššur and expanded their territory to include Mari and the Upper Khabur area, where they resided at Shubat Enlil, modern Tell Leilan. [*See* Khabur; Leilan, Tell.] After their expulsion, historical information is resumed only in the fifteenth century BCE. Seen in the light of political development, this is a period when, with Babylonia deposed from the first rank, new powers formed in Syria and Elam and among the Hittites. The stage was set for the next phase of rival territorial states.

Late Second Millennium. The fall of Babylon opened a period of unknown length, the so-called "dark age" for which no details are available except that a later compilation lists Kassite kings supposed to have ruled then. [*See* Kassites.] Only by the end of the fifteenth century BCE is information provided by the so-called Amarna letters found in pharaoh Akhenaten's new capital Akhetaten/Tell el-Amarna. [*See* Amarna Tablets.] A few, addressing the Kassite kings Karaindash, Kadashman-Enlil I, and Burnaburiash II, fix the regnal dates to the first half of the fourteenth century BCE.

Best known of the Kassite kings is Kurigalzu II (1345–1324 BCE) for the building of his new capital, Dur Kurigalzu/ʿAqar Quf, north of Sippar, and for his restoration of temples at the old Sumerian centers. [*See* ʿAqar Quf.] Care for tradition is also shown by the use of Sumerian in Kassite official inscriptions and by the collecting and copying of traditional literature, which survived in that canonized form into the first millennium BCE. Their own language was never written extensively and is hardly known. Kassite rule over Babylonia was never really challenged and was relatively peaceful, except for latent conflicts with Aššur. The Elamite ruler Shutruk-Nahhunte finally put an end to Kassite rule by raiding Babylonia in 1160 BCE. It is, in addition, the first certified case of looting the cultural heritage of an enemy and adorning one's own capital with the booty.

The might of Assyria reappears when the death of the Mitannian ruler Tušratta gave Ashur-Uballit (1365–1330 BCE) the chance to consolidate the independence won by his father, Eriba-Adad. Like him his successors were constantly campaigning in the regions to the east, north, and west. This certainly reflects the necessity of protecting borders, in the absence of natural boundaries, but it also shows the need to secure additional resources for an area devoid of metal or precious stones and with a limited agricultural capacity.

Under Shalmaneser I (1274–1245 BCE), Assyrian imperial ideology became apparent: the city god Ashur was converted into a god of war, who ordered the conquest of neighboring regions and was thought to march in front of the Assyrian army; this represents warfare as a divine decree, legitimizing the atrocities of war, so vividly described in Assyrian royal inscriptions and depicted in their palace reliefs.

Large-scale building activities are known, especially for the reign of Tukulti-Ninurta I (1244–1208 BCE), the first of the Assyrian rulers to build himself a new capital, Kar-Tukulti-Ninurta, opposite Aššur on the east bank of the Tigris River. [*See* Kar-Tukulti-Ninurta.] None of the various main forces of this period in the Near East—the Hittites, the Hurri-Mitanni, Aššur, Babylon, or Elam—outweighed the others. A balance of power prevailed that also prevented Assyria from becoming too powerful.

Neo-Assyrian Empire. From the end of the tenth century BCE onward, Assyria became militarily active again, following a period in which it had been barely able to defend its borders. Ashurnasirpal II (883–859 BCE) resumed campaigning in the west using improved military strategies; he even collected tribute from the Phoenician cities. [*See* Phoenicians.] At the same time, political strategy began to change: the tendency was to turn conquered areas into permanent Assyrian provinces. Assyria's main opponents were the Aramean principalities in Syria, founded there after the fall of the Hittite Empire. [*See* Arameans.] Yet, area after area was added in the west to Assyrian territory until under Sargon II (721–705 BCE) the Mediterranean was reached and part of Palestine turned into the province of Samaria. Egypt was added by Esarhaddon in 671 BCE, but it was lost by 655 BCE during the reign of Ashurbanipal. Assyria's northward expansion was obstructed by the state of Urartu, which, under the impact of constant Assyrian attacks, Sardur I was able to unite in 832 BCE. [*See* Urartu.] Urartu even expanded westward, frustrating Assyrian ambitions. Following raids by the Cimmerians, however, Sargon was able to eliminate Urartu in 714 BCE. [*See* Cimmerians.] The process of rallying took longer in the eastern mountains, however. Though the lands of Parsua and the Medes are mentioned as early as the ninth century BCE it was not until much later that Medes and Persians entered the political arena. [*See* Medes; Persians.]

Because the cultural superiority of the south was recognized, and many gods worshipped in Assyria had their cultic centers there, Assyrian relations with Babylonia were always exceptional. For a long while Babylonia was taboo for Assyrian military aspirations. However, after the Babylonian south fell to hostile Aramean and Chaldean tribes, Assyria's attitude changed, culminating in the sack of Babylon by Sennacherib in 688 BCE. [*See* Chaldeans.] The picture would, however, be incomplete without emphasizing the enormous building activities of nearly every king after Ashurnasirpal, each one erecting a splendidly decorated palace for himself. [*See* Palace.] Sargon even founded his own city, along with a palace, while Sennacherib enlarged the old city of Nineveh to cover 7 sq km (4 sq. mi.), watered by a canal that at one point needed an aqueduct to bridge a valley. [*See* Nineveh.] Apart from superb palace reliefs, certainly one of the lasting Assyrian achievements was the compilation of the library housed in the palace of Ashurbanipal in Nineveh.

Only two years after the first attacks, Aššur fell, in 614 BCE, to the Medes; then Nineveh fell in 612 BCE to a combined Median-Babylonian army. Harran was a last refuge until 609 BCE. Given the formerly unrivaled power of the Assyrian Empire, the end came quickly. The probable explanation is that by this time Assyria was finished economically. As it had been an expansionist empire, its economic balance could be secured only as long as it could tap new resources. When expansion was no longer possible, the system was bound to collapse. That is, when Assyrian expansion reached the Mediterranean coast, and the attempt to circumvent it by conquering Egypt proved to be too costly.

Chaldean Empire. Following the texts called the "Babylonian Chronicle," Kassite rule counts fifty-one kings before the Chaldean Nabopolassar became king of Babylon in 626 BCE, taking advantage of the turmoil following Ashurbanipal's death. Allying himself with Cyaxares of Media, they accomplished the final defeat of Assyria in little time, leaving Nabopolassar with large parts of the Assyrian heritage. His son, Nebuchadrezzar, consolidated Babylon's rule in the west using Assyrian strategies. He is best known for his deportation of the Jews following his conquest of Jerusalem in 597 BCE; his plans to conquer Egypt failed, however. [*See* Jerusalem.]

Immense tributes and booty from conquests enabled Nebuchadrezzar to conduct large building programs in Babylon and other centers. His works include the holy precinct of Babylon, comprising the ziggurat (Tower of Babel), the processional way and Ishtar Gate, and his palace, which was especially famous for its Hanging Gardens regarded as one of the Seven Wonders of the World. Nebuchadrezzar also built the exceptionally high and wide city wall of Babylon.

Following brief reigns by other family members, a former official, Nabonidus, was appointed king in 555 BCE. Barely enough is known to characterize this enigmatic figure who, out of his sixteen-year reign, spent ten years in the Arabian oasis Tayma', far from Babylon. [*See* Tayma'.] His favoring of the moon god Sin over Babylon's Marduk is the only piece of evidence for explaining the opposition of the priests and people of Babylon to Nabonidus. When he returned to Babylon in about 540 BCE, the Persian king Cyrus was already on his way to the city, having defeated the Medeans and the Lydians under king Croesus. [*See* Medes.] On 12 October 539 BCE Cyrus seized Babylon without resistance.

To judge from the number and size of the settlements inhabited under Chaldean rule, it had been a thriving period for all of Babylonia, as well as the highlight of Babylonian culture—in literature, religion, and the sciences. Especially noteworthy are the astronomy texts (diaries) that, in addition to plotting daily observations, give information on weather and the prices of commodities.

Achaemenids and Mesopotamia. Under the Achaemenids, Mesopotamia was only one district in a vast empire; yet, Babylon was highly respected and chosen to be one of the empire's capitals. Under Darius, a large palace was built on top of the ruins of Nebuchadrezzar's palace. Even after Xerxes responded to a rebellion in 482 BCE by destroying the city's walls and holy district, Babylon remained a main center.

Cyrus's proverbial tolerance, best known for allowing the Jews to return to Jerusalem and rebuild their temple, left life in Babylonia largely unchanged, a policy maintained by his successors. Later years, however, witnessed the large-scale decline of Babylonia, caused by paying the enormous yearly tribute demanded by the royal administration and from the resultant neglect of the irrigation systems. Following Alexander the Great's final victory over the Persian army at Gaugamela in 331 BCE, he took residence in Babylon, ordering the temple of Marduk to be rebuilt. Plans to make Babylon the capital of his empire were thwarthed as he died on 10 June 323 BCE in the palace in Babylon that Darius had errected over the ruins of the one built by Nebuchadrezzar.

BIBLIOGRAPHY

Adams, Robert McC. *Heartland of Cities: Surveys of Ancient Settlement and Land Use on the Central Floodplain of the Euphrates.* Chicago, 1981. Summary of the archaeological surface surveys in Babylonia.

Brinkman, John A. *A Political History of Post-Kassite Babylonia, 1158–722 B.C.* Rome, 1968.

Brinkman, John A. *Materials and Studies for Kassite History,* vol. 1, *A Catalogue of Cuneiform Sources Pertaining to Specific Monarchs of the Kassite Dynasty.* Chicago, 1976.

Brinkman, John A. *Prelude to Empire: Babylonian Society and Politics, 747–626 B.C.* Philadelphia, 1984. Excellent presentations of material and discussions of a neglected period.

The Cambridge Ancient History. Vols. 1 and 3. 3d ed. Cambridge, 1970–1976. Vols. 3.1–2. 2d ed. Cambridge, 1982–1991. Each chapter by a leading expert.

Cooper, Jerrold S. *Reconstructing History from Ancient Inscriptions: The Lagash-Umma Border Conflict.* Malibu, 1983. The material for, and the problems with, reconstructing late Early Dynastic history.

Ehrich, Robert W., ed. *Chronologies in Old World Archaeology.* 2 vols. 3d ed. Chicago, 1992. Amply documented chronological tables with pertinent archaeological evidence, carbon-14 tables, and bibliographies, from the Mediterranean to East Asia, 7000–1500 BCE.

Jacobsen, Thorkild. *Toward the Image of Tammuz and Other Essays on Mesopotamian History and Culture.* Edited by William L. Moran. Harvard Semitic Series, vol. 21. Cambridge, Mass., 1970. Collection of Jacobsen's writings, including his pioneering article, "Early Political Development in Mesopotamia" (1957).

Lamprichs, Roland. *Die Westexpansion des neuassyrischen Reiches.* Neukirchen-Vluyn, 1995. Excellent discussion of the Assyrian Empire as expansive system, based on written and pictorial accounts.

Larsen, Mogens T. *Old Assyrian Caravan Procedures.* Istanbul, 1967. Full discussion of the trade network of the Old Assyrian merchants.

Liverani, Mario. *Prestige and Interest: International Relations in the Near East ca. 1600–1100 B.C.* Padua, 1990. In-depth discussion of the power politics of this period.

Liverani, Mario, ed. *Akkad, the First World Empire.* Padua, 1993. The most up-to-date accounts of the various aspects of the first central state in Mesopotamia.

Nissen, Hans J. *The Early History of the Ancient Near East, 9000–2000 B.C.* Chicago, 1988. Covers the Neolithic period to the Third Dynasty of Ur.

Oates, Joan. *Babylon.* Rev. ed. London, 1986. Well-written account of Mesopotamian history and archaeology.

Oppenheim, A. Leo. *Ancient Mesopotamia: Portrait of a Dead Civiliza-*

tion. Chicago, 1964. Ingenious essays on various aspects of Mesopotamian culture.

Postgate, J. N. *Early Mesopotamia: Society and Economy at the Dawn of History*. London, 1994. Covers the period 3000–1500 BCE, mostly from a philological perspective.

Redman, Charles L. *The Rise of Civilization: From Early Farmers to Urban Society in the Ancient Near East*. San Francisco, 1978. Intended as a textbook for American anthropology departments, this is a splendid account of the period from an anthropologist's point of view.

Roaf, Michael. *Cultural Atlas of Mesopotamia and the Ancient Near East*. New York, 1990. Well-written and amply illustrated coverage from the Neolithic period to Alexander.

Tübinger Atlas des Vorderen Orients. Wiesbaden, 1977–1994. Collection of 210 physical and historical maps of the Near East and Egypt, from prehistoric to modern times.

HANS J. NISSEN

Mesopotamia from Alexander to the Rise of Islam

The death of Darius III in 330 BCE and Alexander the Great's conquest of the Achaemenid Empire mark the beginning of the so-called late periods in Mesopotamia and the Near East. The combined Seleucid, Parthian, and Sasanian periods lasted almost a millennium, until the Arab conquest in the second quarter of the seventh century CE. These late periods are characterized by the transmission and assimilation of Hellenistic and Persian ideas, fashions, arts, and crafts into flourishing local economies and, in Mesopotamia, the continuity of the long-established indigenous cuneiform recording system as late as the first century CE. [*See* Cuneiform.] The spoken languages included Greek, Latin, Aramaic, Syriac, and Mandaic—although Parthian and Middle Persian became the official languages during the Parthian and Sasanian periods. [*See* Greek; Latin; Aramaic; Syriac; Mandaic.] During these two periods, there were periodic clashes between Rome and Persia, primarily over the control of Mesopotamia and its routes and resources. There is, accordingly, a greater variety and number of historical sources relating to Mesopotamia than, for instance, to many areas of highland Iran (Frye, 1984). Mesopotamia continued to exercise a crucial role in the wider Near Eastern economy throughout these late periods, owing to its rich agricultural resources and strategic position controlling routes from Syria and the eastern Mediterranean to the Gulf and western Iran.

Alexander and the Seleucids. Following campaigns across the Iranian plateau as far east as Central Asia and the Indus River, Alexander returned with his army to Mesopotamia, where he selected Babylon as his capital. [*See* Babylon.] Alexander's earlier triumphal entry into Babylon following the battle of Gaugamela was commemorated on a cuneiform diary of astronomical and meteorological phenomena observed from 331 to 330 BCE. He ordered the restoration of the ziggurat in the central Etemenanki precinct, although this remained unfulfilled after his premature death in Babylon in June 323 BCE. [*See* Ziggurat.] A mound of brick rubble on part of the site known as Homera is thought to represent debris from this project, but only the brick core of the ziggurat itself survives. Nearby construction from this period includes a theater with a Greek dedicatory inscription recording "Dioscurides (built) the theater and a stage." [*See* Theaters.] An adjacent peristyled building may represent a gymnasium. A third-century BCE ostracon also attests a local garrison officered by men with Greek names; other Seleucid finds from the site include stamped amphorae and terracottas (Koldewey, 1914).

After Alexander's death, Seleucus Nicator (321–281 BCE) established himself as "Ruler of the East," ruling over Mesopotamia, Iran, Syria, and Anatolia. He ensured political legitimacy by minting coins at important Achaemenid centers, including Persepolis, as well as at new foundations. [*See* Persepolis.] Seleucus continued Alexander's policy of founding new cities, itself a well-developed ancient Near Eastern royal prerogative. The most important of these was Seleucia on the Tigris, situated on the eastern end of a large canal called the Nahar Malcha ("royal canal"). This canal linked the Euphrates and Tigris Rivers a short distance below the point where they enter the alluvial plains of southern Mesopotamia. [*See* Seleucia on the Tigris; Euphrates; Tigris.] Seleucia remained the eastern Seleucid capital until it was captured by the Parthians in the first century BCE. Thereafter, it continued to be occupied until the Sasanian foundation of Veh Ardashir ("New Seleucia") drew the population away.

The site of Seleucia was said to have a population of 600,000 (Pliny 6.30), appears to have been fortified, and was bisected by two major canals (initially misidentified as roads). The street plan was based on a grid, first revealed by aerial photographs. A depression at the eastern end of the city may represent a harbor, whereas a prominent mound called Tell ʿUmar, at the northern edge of the city, probably represents later Sasanian construction. The mound is located immediately north of a large three- or four-sided agoralike complex referred to by its Italian excavators as the Archives Building (Invernizzi, Negro Ponzi Mancini, and Valtz, 1985). This name reflects the discovery of a hoard of seal-impressed clay bullae; two additional hoards of bullae were recovered from University of Michigan excavations at Seleucia, mostly dealing with the administration of a local salt tax. Other identified public buildings include a theater and two temples. American excavations near the center of the city revealed an insula (a block of housing separated by streets) with remains of painted stuccoes and molded brick decoration (Hopkins, ed., 1972). [*See* Wall Paintings.] Burials were interred within intramural family-sized subterranean brick vaults, a burial method that reflects the continuation of a two-thousand-year-old mortuary tradition in Mesopotamia. [*See* Burial Sites; Burial Techniques.]

Local religious cults enjoyed royal patronage under the Seleucids, with large-scale construction and renovation in the Bit-Resh and Irigal temple complexes at Uruk (now called Orchoi). [*See* Cult; Uruk-Warka.] Despite the predominant use of parchment, clay tablets written in cuneiform continued to be used at major religious centers in southern Mesopotamia. [*See* Parchment; Tablet; Writing Materials.] The tablets provide the primary dated historical sources for Seleucid history and chronology, in addition to matters relating to temple administration, particularly at Uruk (McEwan, 1981; Sherwin-White and Kuhrt, 1993). More unusual are a small number of Late Seleucid or Early Parthian tablets, known as the Graeco-Babyloniaca series. These were inscribed with Greek transcriptions of cuneiform lexical and literary texts, including incantations and a Description of Babylon (Black and Sherwin-White, 1984).

Little is known in detail about rural settlement in Mesopotamia during this period. However, archaeological surface surveys in the northern Jezireh and excavations for the Saddam Dam Salvage Project at sites such as Tell Deir Situn (Curtis, Green, and Knight, 1987–1988) demonstrate a peak in rural settlement densities during the third–second centuries BCE, plus the appearance of new forms of bell-shaped underground silos and imported basalt grinding stones. [*See* Granaries and Silos.] The impact of Western styles of ceramics and, presumably, cuisine on Mesopotamia are reflected by the appearance of distinctive "fish plates" with overhanging rims, low ring bases, and a central interior depression that was used to contain dressing. Continuing cultural dichotomy between northern and southern Mesopotamia is demonstrated by the different methods of preferred ceramic surface treatment: whereas southern fish plates were either glazed or left plain, northern equivalents were typically decorated with reddish-brown or black slip. Moldmade ceramic lamps, sometimes with palmette handles, and classical styles of molded terra-cotta figurines also appear throughout Mesopotamia during this period, again suggesting a relatively high degree of hellenization (Oates and Oates, 1958; Hannestad, 1983).

Parthians. Seleucid control of Mesopotamia ended with the defeat and death of Antiochus VII Sidetes (138–129 BCE) and the arrival of a Parthian army commanded by Phraates II (c. 138–128 BCE). The Parthians established a garrison town and later a capital at Ctesiphon, opposite Seleucia, on the left bank of the Tigris, thus controlling a major route to western Iran via the Diyala River corridor. [*See* Ctesiphon.] Southern Babylonia broke away under Hyspaosines of Charax, who instigated direct commercial links with Palmyra via the Middle Euphrates corridor. [*See* Palmyra.] Palmyrene-style tombs on Kharg Island, in the Gulf, probably reflect these new ties. Ceramics excavated at Failaka, near the head of the Gulf, are thought to be Characenian products, although the Characenian capital of Charax Spasinu, identified with the site of Jabal Khayabir at the junction of the Karun and Tigris Rivers, remains unexcavated (Hansman, 1967). [*See* Failaka.]

Characene was reduced to vassal status by Mithradates II (c. 123–87 BCE), who also seized Adiabene and established a more secure western Parthian frontier on the Euphrates after capturing the town of Dura by 113 BCE. [*See* Dura-Europos.] This site, also known in antiquity as Europos, provides an important corpus of Parthian architectural remains, sculpture, pottery, glass, and textiles. [*See* Glass.] However, its poorly excavated stratigraphy has resulted in a mixture of Seleucid and Roman material (Hopkins, 1979). Seleucus V (125 BCE) continued to campaign in Babylonia and Media but failed to regain control of those regions. Babylonia was later lost to a usurper called Gotarzes I (c. 91–80 BCE) and the Parthian Empire fell victim to internal struggles until the accession of Vologases I (c. 51–80 CE). During this brief interregnum, the kingdom of Commagene flourished in southeast Turkey before being swallowed by Rome. Rome also attempted to play an important role in Parthian politics until the Parthian general Suren crushed a Roman army commanded by Emperor Crassus at the battle of Carrhae, in southeast Turkey, in 53 BCE.

The first century CE witnessed the emergence of a more distinctive Parthian material culture in Mesopotamia, including the replacement of Aramaic for Greek and a fire altar for the figure of an archer on the coins of Vologases I. Vologases also founded a rival city to Seleucia called Vologesocerta (Vologesias). Its location has been disputed but probably corresponds to a substantial unexcavated site called Abu Halefija, situated due southeast of Seleucia on another junction of the royal canal and the Tigris. In 115 CE, the Roman emperor Trajan succeeded in sacking Ctesiphon before reaching Charax and the head of the Gulf. However, his claims to Mesopotamia were rapidly dropped by his successor, Hadrian. Vologases and Osroes battled for control over southern Mesopotamia. A massive fortress excavated at Nippur may belong to this phase of Parthian history.

Seleucia and Ctesiphon were later captured twice by Roman armies commanded by C. Avidius Cassius in 165 CE and Septimius Severus in 197 CE—although the American excavators of Seleucia reported few traces of destruction that could be associated with these events. Septimius Severus was also responsible for extending direct Roman military control down the Euphrates corridor and establishing a network of forts commanding routes to and from the Tigris, the Jabal Sinjar, and the Khabur basin. Several of these Severan forts have been partially excavated, including ʿAin Sinu-Zagurae, Seh Qubba, Bijan, and Kifrin (Oates and Oates, 1959; Valtz, 1985). This military frontier remained substantially intact until Sasanian military advances during the mid-third century.

Archaeological excavations are providing useful groups of Parthian pottery and other finds. As in Iran, there continues to be marked regional variation in ceramic assemblages from northern, central, and southern Mesopotamia: important groups have been recovered from Dura-Europos, ʿAin Sinu, Nineveh, Seleucia, and Tell Aswad (Oates and Oates, 1959;

Debevoise, 1934). [*See* Nineveh.] Elaborate stuccoes have been recovered from Aššur, Babylon, Seleucia, and Uruk. [*See* Aššur.] Columned architecture has been excavated at Babylon (Tell Amran), Nippur, and Seleucia, but a significant innovation is the large barrel-vaulted iwan architecture found at Aššur and Hatra. [*See* Nippur; Hatra.] Babylonian-style shrines are also attested from Khiut Rabbu'a (on the outskirts of Baghdad) and Nineveh, the latter being dedicated to Hermes. Limestone and bronze statues of Herakles and figurines of Eros have been found at several other sites, including Dura, Aššur, Hatra, Seleucia and Uruk. In addition to pottery, glassware, terra-cottas, and other objects, a limestone statue of a seated Herakles, inscribed "Diogenes made (this). Sarapiodorus son of Artemidorus (dedicated this) in fulfilment of a vow" was excavated at Nineveh (Invernizzi, 1989). A stone lintel showing a pair of sinuous-bodied griffins drinking from a vase, found near the southeast corner of this mound, closely parallels contemporary Parthian temple cornices from Hatra (Curtis, 1989, p. 60).

There is widespread archaeological evidence for Parthian mortuary customs in Mesopotamia. The norm appears to have been intramural burial, the deceased being interred in a ceramic or wooden coffin placed in a vault or in a simple earth-cut shaft. Glazed ceramic "slipper coffins" were a particularly distinctive type that were popular at Babylon, Nippur, and Uruk during the first–second centuries CE (Curtis, 1979). However, large extramural cemeteries with a wide variety of types of burials are also known from Abu Skhair-Umm Kheshm (Negro Ponzi, 1972). Parthian grave goods from these and other sites included gold face masks, eye covers, mouth covers, headbands, funerary wreaths, jewelry, local and imported Roman glassware, bone "dolls," painted alabaster and ceramic statuettes, and blue-, green-, or white-glazed pottery (Curtis, 1979). [*See* Grave Goods.] The statuettes usually belong to nude or partially clothed female figures, either reclining or standing, with one hand holding a veil, or reclining male figures holding a cup in one hand (Van Ingen, 1939; Karvonen-Kannas, 1995). Finally, a rock-cut set of caves at Al-Tar, on the edge of the western Iraqi desert, appears to have been used as a burial place for nomads living on the Arabian fringe of the Parthian state; a large number of textiles are unusually preserved at this site owing to the arid local conditions (Fujii, ed., 1976).

Sasanians. The last Parthian king was Artabanus V. The end of his reign was marked by a nobles' revolt led by Ardashir I (224–240 CE), who came from the province of Fars on the Iranian plateau. In 241 Hatra was sacked and Jovian ceded five trans-Tigridian provinces under the terms of a peace treaty signed between the empires. Henceforth, northern Mesopotamia as far as the Khabur headwaters fell within the Persian Empire, the actual border running from Nisibis to Singara and Bezabde. Ardashir took the throne and adopted the Parthian capital of Ctesiphon. Zoroastrianism was adopted as the state religion, although there were other important religious communities in different parts of the empire. The Byzantine emperor Zeno's expulsion of the "Edessa school" of Christian scholars, in 489, led directly to the founding of the "Persian church" across the border, with an archbishop at Ctesiphon, to urban bishoprics and rural monasteries, and to an influential school of philosophers at Nisibis (Fiey, 1965–1969). [*See* Monasteries.] Between the third and fifth centuries, Jews living in central Mesopotamia compiled the Babylonian Talmud, a fundamental Jewish legal code and a useful historical source for reconstructing details of Sasanian agriculture (Newman, 1932; Oppenheimer, 1983). [*See* Agriculture.] Various Gnostic sects are attested, including the Mesallyene, Manichaeans, and Mandaeans. Several pagan cults are also attested from Syriac sources, who accuse them of worshiping trees and snakes (Morony, 1984).

The Sasanian Empire extended from northern Mesopotamia into the Caucasus, Central Asia, and Pakistan. Frontier zones appear to have been stiffened with Persians drawn from cities such as Isfahan and Istakhr on the Iranian plateau. [*See* Isfahan.] The desert borders were closely guarded through a combination of "long walls," forts, and regular mounted patrols. Official traffic between the Persian and Byzantine empires was restricted to a single route from Nisibis to Dara (Morony, 1984).

Heavy investment in the Mesopotamian irrigation networks was linked to large new trunk canals constructed between the Tigris and Euphrates and a massive canal network linking the Tigris and Diyala known as the Nahrawan/Katul-i Kisrawi system. [*See* Irrigation; Diyala.] Surface surveys suggest optimum exploitation of central and southern Mesopotamia during this period (Adams, 1981). Systematic settlement programs appear to have been carried out then, for which possible archaeological evidence has been detected on the Upper Tigris. Several rural settlements have been partially excavated in northern and central Mesopotamia, including Tell Abu Sarifa (Adams, 1970). At the site of Tell Abu Shi'afeh, in the Hamrin basin, a large number of sealed clay bullae were found in a storeroom inside a small administrative building; they had originally probably been attached to parchments, which usually do not survive. [*See* Hamrin Dam Salvage Project; Seals; Parchment.]

Palaces and large private houses were decorated with elaborate stuccoes, wall paintings, and occasionally mosaics; villas have been excavated at Ctesiphon and Kish (Kröger, 1982). [*See* Palace; Mosaics; Kish.] The major military and economic rival of Rome, and later of Byzantium, the Sasanian Empire had contacts with the Far East via overland trade through Central Asia. Far eastern silks and other goods were highly valued, and fine cotton cloth was produced at Merv and possibly in other Sasanian cities. Identifiable western imports are negligible, being limited to a handful of coins and some lamps from Nineveh and Veh Ardashir, thus giving the impression of a well-developed and self-sufficient

Sasanian economy. High-quality cut glassware was manufactured in Sasanian workshops, some of which was traded as far as China, Korea, and Japan. There is evidence from excavation and survey for large-scale industrial development, including glass factories, pottery workshops, and brick industries, some of which appear to have been deliberately sited on countryside canals in order to take advantage of the improved water-borne transport network (Adams, 1981).

Decorative silver vessels, often with partial gilding, were another characteristic Sasanian product, although no examples have yet been excavated in Mesopotamia. Sasanian pottery was mass produced, yet the forms occasionally copy metalwares. A distinctive range of decorative stamp-impressed jars was made and traded in central and northern Mesopotamia. The longest sequence of excavated Sasanian pottery comes from the city of Veh Ardashir/Coche, opposite Ctesiphon (Venco Ricciardi, 1984), but important groups of Early, Middle, and Late Sasanian pottery have also been recovered from Tell Mahuz, Kish, Telul Hamediyat, and Khirbet Deir Situn (Venco Ricciardi, 1970–1971; Moorey, 1978). These suggest a strong thread of cultural continuity from Late Parthian to post-Sasanian periods, with occasional new forms stimulated by developments in contemporary Sasanian metalwork.

Weakened by internal strife and additional wars with Byzantium, the Sasanian Empire finally fell to repeated Muslim Arab attacks, culminating in the Islamic conquest in the mid-seventh century. However, the Sasanian administration served as a model for the new rulers, and Sasanian art and architecture continued to have a profound effect on Early Islamic developments.

[*See also* Parthians; Sasanians; Seleucids.]

BIBLIOGRAPHY

Adams, Robert McC. "Tell Abū Sarīfa: A Sasanian-Islamic Ceramic Sequence from South Central Iraq." *Ars Orientalis* 8 (1970): 87–119.

Adams, Robert McC. *Heartland of Cities: Surveys of Ancient Settlement and Land Use on the Central Floodplain of the Euphrates*. Chicago, 1981.

Black, Jeremy A., and Susan Sherwin-White. "A Clay Tablet with Greek Letters in the Ashmolean Museum, and the 'Graeco-Babyloniaca' Texts." *Iraq* 46 (1984): 131–140, pl. 9.

Curtis, John E. "Loftus' Parthian Cemetery at Warka." *Archäologische Mitteilungen aus Iran* 6 (1979): 309–317.

Curtis, John E., et al. "Preliminary Report on Excavations at Tell Deir Situn and Grai Darki." *Sumer* 45 (1987–1988): 49–53.

Curtis, John E. *Ancient Persia*. London, 1989.

Debevoise, Neilson C. *Parthian Pottery from Seleucia on the Tigris*. Ann Arbor, Mich., 1934.

Fiey, J. M. *Assyrie chretienne*. 3 vols. Beirut, 1965–1969.

Frye, Richard N. *The History of Ancient Iran*. Munich, 1984.

Fujii, Hideo, ed. *Al-Tar I: Excavations in Iraq, 1971–1974*. Tokyo, 1976.

Hannestad, Lise. *The Hellenistic Pottery from Failaka: With a Survey of Hellenistic Pottery in the Near East*. Ikaros: The Hellenistic Settlements, vol. 2. Aarhus, 1983.

Hansman, John. "Charax and the Karkheh." *Iranica Antiqua* 7 (1967): 21–58, pls. 5–8.

Hopkins, Clark, ed. *Topography and Architecture of Seleucia on the Tigris*. Ann Arbor, Mich., 1972.

Hopkins, Clark. *The Discovery of Dura-Europos*. New Haven, 1979.

Invernizzi, Antonio, et al. "Seleucia on the Tigris." In *The Land between Two Rivers: Twenty Years of Italian Archaeology in the Middle East. The Treasures of Mesopotamia,* edited by Ezio Quarantelli, pp. 87–99. Turin, 1985.

Invernizzi, Antonio. "L'Heracles Epitrapezios de Ninive." In *Archaeologia Iranica et Orientalis: Miscellanea in honorem Louis Vanden Berghe,* edited by Léon De Meyer and E. Haerinck, vol. 2, pp. 623–636. Ghent, 1989.

Karvonen-Kannas, Kerttu. *The Seleucid and Parthian Terracotta Figurines from Babylon in the Iraq Museum, the British Museum, and the Louvre*. Florence, 1995.

Koldewey, Robert. *The Excavations at Babylon*. London, 1914.

Kröger, Jens. *Sasanidischer Stuckdekor*. Mainz am Rhein, 1982.

McEwan, G. J. P. *Priest and Temple in Hellenistic Babylonia*. Wiesbaden, 1981.

Moorey, P. R. S. *Kish Excavations, 1923–1933*. Oxford, 1978.

Morony, Michael. *Iraq after the Muslim Conquest*. Princeton, 1984.

Negro Ponzi, M. M. "Glassware from Abu Skhair (Central Iraq)." *Mesopotamia* 7 (1972): 215–237, figs. 19–22.

Newman, Julius. *The Agricultural Life of the Jews in Babylonia between the Years 200 CE and 500 CE*. Oxford, 1932.

Oates, David, and Joan Oates. "Nimrud 1957: The Hellenistic Settlement." *Iraq* 20 (1958): 114–157, pls. 16–30.

Oates, David, and Joan Oates. "Ain Sinu: A Roman Frontier Post in Northern Iraq." *Iraq* 21 (1959): 207–242, pls. 52–59.

Oppenheimer, Aharon. *Babylonia Judaica in the Talmudic Period*. Wiesbaden, 1983.

Sherwin-White, Susan, and Amélie Kuhrt. *From Samarkhand to Sardis: A New Approach to the Seleucid Empire*. Berkeley, 1993.

Valtz, Elisabetta. "Kifrin, Fortress of the Limes." In *The Land between Two Rivers: Twenty Years of Italian Archaeology in the Middle East. The Treasures of Mesopotamia,* edited by Ezio Quarantelli, pp. 111–141. Turin, 1985.

Van Ingen, Wilhelmina. *Figurines from Seleucia on the Tigris Discovered by the Expeditions Conducted by the University of Michigan with the Cooperation of the Toledo Museum of Art and the Cleveland Museum of Art, 1927–1932*. Ann Arbor, Mich., 1939.

Venco Ricciardi, Roberta. "Sasanian Pottery from Tell Mahuz (North Mesopotamia)." *Mesopotamia* 5–6 (1970–1971): 427–482, figs. 87–96.

Venco Ricciardi, Roberta. "Sasanian Pottery from Choche (Artisans' Quarter and Tell Baruda)." In *Arabie orientale: Mésopotamie et Iran méridional, de l'Âge du Fer au début de la période islamique,* edited by Rémy Boucharlat and Jean-François Salles, pp. 49–57. Paris, 1984.

ST. JOHN SIMPSON

Mesopotamia in the Islamic Period

The Sasanian hold on Mesopotamia was broken at the battle of Qadisiyha in 637 CE, a result confirmed at Nihawand in 642. From this time onward, the Arabic term *al-ʿIraq* was used to refer to Mesopotamia from the Gulf to Samarra, and *al-Jezireh* ('the island') designated the region from Samarra to Mosul and Aleppo. The Islamic armies, mainly composed of tribesmen from eastern Arabia, were settled not at the Sasanian capital of Ctesiphon, but in two new garrison cities (Ar, *misr;* pl., *amsar*), at Kufah, close to the pre-Islamic capital of the Lakhmids at al-Hira, on the desert bank of the lower Euphrates, and at Basra, at the head of the Persian Gulf. The type of settlement, with a central mosque and governor's residence surrounded by quarters allocated to each tribal unit, seems to have drawn its inspiration from Arabian multitribal settlements, such as Medina (Yathrib). The practice of founding new garrison cities, established in Iraq, was followed in all the conquered territories except Syria. At Kufah, the mosque of the Umayyad period (661–750) survives in part, and the Umayyad governor's residence *(Dar al-ʿImarah)* has been excavated (Mustafa, 1956). At Old Basra, much has been excavated, but nothing published. Iraq was administered from Kufah until the middle of the Umayyad period, when, in response to the continual rebellions there, the Iraqi army was demobilized, and a Syrian garrison installed at a third new garrison city at Wasit, south of Kut, where only the mosque has been excavated. Finally Mosul was built opposite to Nineveh on the Tigris.

These Arab-Muslim garrisons were supported by the already-existing agricultural economy of the Sasanian period, notably the well-developed irrigation network. Only a little archaeological work has been done on the Umayyad period in Iraq (e.g., Finster, 1976); not even the ceramic typology has been clearly established. What little has been accomplished tends to confirm the picture from Syria and Jordan that new development was largely on the desert edge. However, by the ʿAbbasid revolution in 750 Arab and non-Arab were increasingly integrated, partly by conversion to Islam and partly by Arab ownership of land. The rate of conversion to Islam is shown by the excavations at Ana on the Euphrates, where, in this strongly Christian town, only a small mosque was built in the Umayyad period, replaced by a large congregational mosque in the ninth century.

Real integration of the Mesopotamian state tradition and Islam was achieved by the ʿAbbasids, who settled in Iraq, notably by the second ʿAbbasid caliph, al-Mansur (754–775). A new capital was established at Baghdad in 762–766, only 30 km (18.5 mi.) from Ctesiphon, in the northern part of the alluvial plain, a region with excellent access to routes to Iran, Syria, and the Gulf. The urban type was evolved from the *amsar* with the addition of a fortified palace and administrative quarter, the Round City, with the military cantonments divided ethnically. Robert McC. Adams observes that the striking increase in the proportion of urban to cultivated area in the Diyala basin at this time may be understood as reflecting the metropolitan nature of the Baghdad area, which no longer depended solely on its hinterland (Adams, 1965, pp. 98–99). Although ʿAbbasid Baghdad has disappeared, the character of the architecture can be seen at the sole ʿAbbasid desert castle at Ukhaidir, west of Karbala, a plan based on *iwans* and apartments in the form of houses around courtyards, and more particularly at Samarra, the second ʿAbbasid capital built on steppe land 125 km (77.5 mi.) north of Baghdad by al-Muʿtasim in 836 and abandoned after 892. Here the entire range of ʿAbbasid construction has been preserved, from palaces to small houses and industrial structures, with the exception of the markets. [*See* Baghdad; Samarra, *article on* Islamic Period.]

The success of the ʿAbbasid caliphate led to a cultural dominance of the Iraqi style in the Islamic world, from the spiral minaret of the mosque of Ibn Ṭulun in Cairo, copying Samarra, to the luster tiles on the *miḥrab* (niche oriented toward Mecca) of the mosque of Kairouan (Qayrawan) in Tunisia. The islamization of the pottery typology in Syria and Jordan and possibly in Egypt, represents in fact the introduction of Iraqi types. Although glazed pottery had always been more significant in Mesopotamia, early ʿAbbasid Iraq produced first monochrome glaze over surface decorations and then the first polychrome-glazed wares about 800, stimulated probably by new types imported from China. Cobalt painting on white glaze, splash-lead glaze, and lastly luster painting were produced in southern Iraq, possibly at Basra, and spread rapidly around the Islamic world and beyond. [*See* Ceramics, *article on* Ceramics of the Islamic Period.]

Although the wealth of the ʿAbbasid state was based on the Sasanian irrigation network, the system was developed and extended; in particular two additions were made to the Nahrawan system by Harun al-Rashid (786–809) and al-Ma'mun (813–833), although there was retrenchment of the limits of cultivation, particularly in the south of Iraq, demonstrated by the surveys of Adams (1965, 1981). However, with the slowly cumulating problems of the ninth century and the complete political collapse of the second quarter of the tenth century, a widespread abandonment of the irrigation network occurred, and no new expansion occurred before modern times. Formerly the financial base of the caliphate and its wealthiest province, Iraq became a poor relation of surrounding territories. However, more accurate pottery dating shows that Adams placed this transformation too early (Adams, 1965, p. 103); *sgraffito* ware, which appears in the terminal deposits of many sites, was not introduced until the first half of the tenth century. Although the tenth and eleventh centuries were certainly periods of political instability, the essential problem may have been that the quasi-feudal medieval states, which emerged at this time, were incapable of the organizational and financial effort to maintain or replace the Sasanian canals, which may have been damaged as much by natural as by human agency. For example, movements of the beds of the Tigris and Euphrates could leave whole districts without water.

The political collapse of the ʿAbbasids installed the Iranian Shiʿi Buyids in Baghdad (945–1055) and Arab tribal principalities on the desert edge and in the Jezireh. Although little work has been done on the archaeology of this period, the regional surveys become less reliable because the areas settled are those still occupied today. The archaeological record becomes more visible again after the twelfth century. Contemporary with the medieval high culture in Syria and Iran, a fine tradition of brick architecture developed at Baghdad (al-Mustansiriyah) and Mosul. An Iraqi fine-glazed ware has been excavated at Wasit, Ana, Samarra, and elsewhere. Metalwork was made at Mosul, and miniatures painted at Baghdad and Mosul. The Mongol conquest of Iraq in 1258 marked the end of Iraqi political independence.

[*See also* ʿAbbasid Caliphate; Umayyad Caliphate.]

BIBLIOGRAPHY

Adams, Robert McC. *Land behind Baghdad: A History of Settlement on the Diyala Plains.* Chicago, 1965.

Adams, Robert McC. *Heartland of Cities: Surveys of Ancient Settlement and Land use on the Central Floodplain of the Euphrates.* Chicago, 1981.

Creswell, K. A. C. *Early Muslim Architecture,* vol. 2, *Umayyads, Early ʿAbbasids, and Tulunids.* Oxford, 1940.

Directorate-General of Antiquities. *Excavations at Samarra, 1936–1939.* 2 vols. Baghdad, 1940.

Djait, Hichem. *Al-Kufa: Naissance de la ville islamique.* Paris, 1986.

Donner, Fred McGraw. "Tribal Settlement in Basra during the First Century AH." In *Land Tenure and Social Transformation in the Middle East,* edited by Tarif Khalidi, pp. 97–120. Beirut, 1984.

Finster, Barbara. *Sasanidische und frühislamische Ruinen im Iraq.* Baghdader Mitteilungen, 8. Berlin, 1976.

Keall, E. J., and Robert B. Mason. "The ʿAbbāsid Glazed Wares of Sīrāf and the Baṣra Connection: Petrographic Analysis." *Iran* 29 (1991): 51–66.

Kennedy, Hugh. *The Early ʿAbbasid Caliphate: A Political History.* London, 1981.

Kervran, Monik. "Les niveaux islamiques du secteur oriental du tépé de l'Apadana." *Cahiers de la Délégation Archéologique Française en Iran* 7 (1977): 75–162.

Lassner, Jacob. "The Caliph's Personal Domain: The City Plan of Baghdad Reexamined." In *The Islamic City,* edited by Albert Hourani and S. M. Stern, pp. 103–118. Oxford, 1970.

Lassner, Jacob. *The Topography of Baghdad in the Early Middle Ages: Text and Studies.* Detroit, 1970.

Morony, Michael. "Continuity and Change in the Administrative Geography of Late Sasanian and Early Islamic al-ʿIrāq." *Iran* 20 (1982): 1–49.

Morony, Michael. *Iraq after the Muslim Conquest.* Princeton, 1984.

Mustafa, M. A. "Taqrīr awwalī ʿan al-tanqīb fī al-Kūfa lil-mawsim al-thālith." *Sumer* 12 (1956): 2–32 (translated by Kessler in *Sumer* 19 [1963]: 36–65).

Northedge, Alastair, et al. *Excavations at ʿAna, Qalʿa Island.* Warminster, 1988.

Northedge, Alastair. "Archaeology and New Urban Settlement in Early Islamic Syria and Iraq." In *Studies in Late Antiquity and Early Islam II: Settlement Patterns in the Byzantine and Early Islamic Near East,* edited by G. R. D. King and Averil Cameron, pp. 231–265. Princeton, 1994.

Safar, Fuad. *Wasit, the Sixth Season's Excavations* (in Arabic). Cairo, 1945.

Waines, David. "The Third-Century Internal Crisis of the ʿAbbasids." *Journal of the Economic and Social History of the Orient* 20 (1977): 282–306.

ALASTAIR NORTHEDGE